# ATHENAEUS AND HIS WORLD

## Reading Greek Culture in the Roman Empire

**David Braund** is Professor of Ancient History, University of Exeter. His books include *The Administration of the Roman Empire* (University of Exeter Press, 1988); *Georgia in Antiquity: A History of Transcaucasian Georgia, 550 BC–AD 562* (OUP, 1994); *Ruling Roman Britain: Kings, Queens, Governors and Emperors from Caesar to Agricola* (Routledge, 1996).

**John Wilkins** is Reader in Greek Literature, University of Exeter. His books include *Food in Antiquity* (University of Exeter Press, 1995), *The Boastful Chef: The Discourse of Food in Ancient Greek Comedy* (OUP, 2000), *The Rivals of Aristophanes: Studies in Athenian Old Comedy* (Duckworth and the Classical Press of Wales, 2000).

*Notes on cover illustration*

An Attic red-figure mixing-bowl (*krater*) of about 430 BC. The painter, thought to be a pupil of Polygnotus, has portrayed the later stages of a symposium. The man reclining on the left appears to have a headache, the man in the centre plays a double pipe or *aulos*, while the man reclining on the right plays the wine-flicking game, *kottabos*. Athenaeus describes these features in (among other passages) 1.34c–e, 14.626a–628f, 15.665d–669d.

    Royal Albert Museum, Exeter 28/1954.

The handle of a Greek vase in silvered copper or copper alloy, representing a partially-clad female figure. It was found in Naucratis, the home town of Athenaeus, in which, after the fashion of the day, he took inordinate pride (see chapters 1 and 5). Fine vessels of very many types are the subject of Book Eleven of the *Deipnosophistae*.

    Royal Albert Museum, Exeter, Montague collection 5/1946.

# ATHENAEUS AND HIS WORLD

## READING GREEK CULTURE
## IN THE ROMAN EMPIRE

*Edited by*

*David Braund and John Wilkins*

UNIVERSITY
*of*
EXETER
PRESS

First published in 2000 by
University of Exeter Press
Reed Hall, Streatham Drive
Exeter, Devon EX4 4QR
UK
*www.ex.ac.uk/uep/*

Reprinted 2003

**British Library Cataloguing in Publication Data**
A catalogue record of this book is available
from the British Library

ISBN 0 85989 661 7

Typeset by
Exe Valley Dataset Ltd, Exeter

Printed in Great Britain
by Antony Rowe Ltd, Chippenham

*For Professor Keith Cameron, archdeipnosophist*

# CONTENTS

## Section I

## General Introduction

## Section II

## Text, Transmission and Translation

## Section III

# Athenaeus the Reader and His World

## Section IV

## Structural Overviews

## Section V

## Key Authors

## Section VII

# The Other Athenaeus

# PLATES

*Plate 1*

Maps of the principal locations mentioned by Athenaeus.

## Plate 2

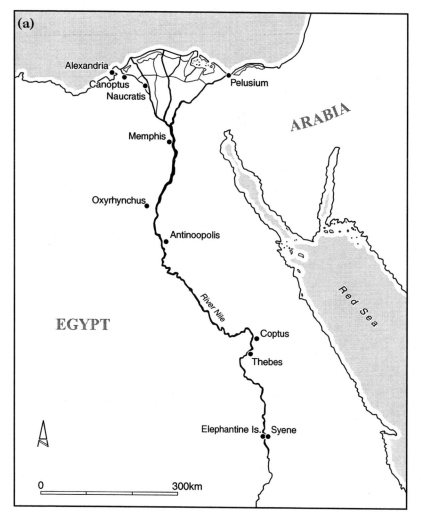

**(a)**

Alexandria
Canoptus
Naucratis
Pelusium

ARABIA

Memphis

Oxyrhynchus

Antinoopolis

River Nile

EGYPT

Red Sea

Coptus

Thebes

Elephantine Is. Syene

0       300km

**(b)**

(b) The handle of a Greek vase in silvered copper or copper alloy, representing a partially-clad female figure. It was found in Naucratis, the home town of Athenaeus, in which, after the fashion of the day, he took inordinate pride (see chapters 1 and 5). Fine vessels of very many types are the subject of Book Eleven of the *Deipnosophistae*.

(a) Egypt in the *Deipnosophistae*.

Claims for Naucratis in the *Deipnosophistae* include:

- Aristophanes the comic poet, who (says Heliodorus the Athenian) was from a Naucratite family... (6.229e)
- Apollonius of Rhodes—or of Naucratis—states in his *Foundation of Naucratis*... (7.283d)
- For some reason, as Herodotus states, Naucratis tends to have gorgeous courtesans. (13.596d)

*Plate 3*

Significant emperors (see chapter 1):

(a) Hadrian (ruled AD 117–38), the prominent philhellene much praised by Athenaeus (e.g. 8.361f).

(b) Marcus Aurelius (ruled AD 161–80), under whom Larensis held a religious post (1.2c).

(c) Commodus, Marcus' elder son (ruled AD 180–92), under whom Larensis reached high office; Athenaeus shows sympathy with Commodus' pose as Heracles (12.537f). Here Commodus' coin shows him in the guise of Heracles, wearing a lion-skin.

(d) Septimius Severus (ruled AD 193–211); the *Deipnosophistae* is set and evidently published in his reign.

## Plate 4

(a) *Iliad*: torso, with plain cuirass and remains of a sword on her right side.

(b) *Iliad*: statue base. The verses read:

"Iliad, she after Homer am I and before Homer;
Beside him, I stand, who begat me in his youth."

## Plate 5

(a) *Odyssey*: torso, decorated with images from the poem. Traces of a steering oar have been noted on her left shoulder.

These statues, of *Iliad* and *Odyssey* personified as women, had a prominent place in the great library of T. Flavius Pantaenus, which was built around AD 100 close to the Stoa of Attalus in the agora at Athens. A statue of Homer, probably enthroned between them, has not survived. Homer was thought to have written the *Iliad* before the *Odyssey*. The composition amply illustrates the prominence of Homer in the Greek culture of the Roman empire, here in a library setting (see chapters 6 and 25 in particular).

(b) *Odyssey*: torso detail, showing Scylla with her canine lower parts. Lesser figures are identified (l. to r.) as Aeolus, Sirens and Polyphemus.

# Plate 6

(a)

(a) An Attic red-figure mixing-bowl (*krater*) of about 430 BC. The painter, thought to be a pupil of Polygnotus, has portrayed the later stages of a symposium. The man reclining on the left appears to have a headache, the man in the centre plays a double pipe or *aulos*, while the man reclining on the right plays the wine-flicking game, *kottabos*. Athenaeus describes these features in (among other passages) 1.34c–e, 14.626a–628f, 15.665d–669d.

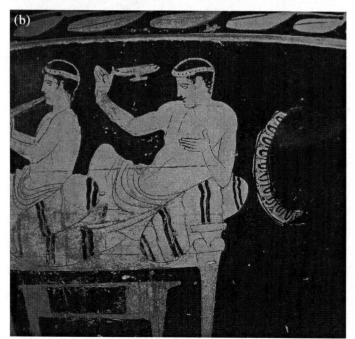

(b)

(b) Playing *kottabos*: detail.

"So, since you are unfamiliar with such a spectacle, learn from me that *kottaboi* were first introduced as a game in Sicily, the Sicels having first made this innovation, as Critias, son of Callaeschrus, says in his *Elegiacs*, as follows:

*Kottabos is from Sicel land, a splendid job,*
*which we set as a target for arrows of wine* (latagai)…

And Dicaearchus of Messene, Aristotle's pupil, says in his *On Alcaeus* that *latage* is a Sicilian term. *Latage* is the wet dregs left when a cup has been drunk down; those playing little *kottabos* used to flick out these dregs, with a twist of the wrist from on high" (15.666a–c)

# FOREWORD

*By Glen Bowersock*

A foreword to a work of the proportions of this one would seem altogether superfluous, were it not for a promise I made to the editors when I encouraged them to launch their great project on Athenaeus. So voluminous and wide-ranging an author deserves inspection from multiple perspectives, and the conference (at which many of the contributors here first appeared) represented the first comprehensive review of the *Deipnosophistae* in modern times. The work's size may be daunting, but it is thoroughly Athenaean in spirit. The eclecticism of its interpretative methods furnishes a generous sampling of most of the styles of research that are currently in (or out of) vogue in classical scholarship—from the solidly traditional to the implausibly inventive. A conscientious reader may even come across a chapter that has almost nothing to do with Athenaeus at all. But that too is a worthy homage to this delightfully chaotic writer.

It is astonishing that in none of the three epochs of concentrated attention on the Second Sophistic over the last century or so was Athenaeus ever promoted to a central place. In the days of Boulanger, von Arnim, Wilamowitz and Graindor, the garrulous deipnosophist stood in the shadows. Not even Gulick's pioneering Loeb translation helped. When Ewen Bowie and I resurrected Philostratus and his sophists to debate their role in the Graeco-Roman world they so brilliantly adorned, Athenaeus remained as neglected as before (even if a few currants were occasionally pulled out of the Christmas pudding he bequeathed to us). Pausanias managed to move into prominence alongside the sophists, but not Athenaeus. But now with a wholly new direction of research on the Second Sophistic, exploiting fresh literary and sociological approaches, Athenaeus has at last been embraced on his own. The embrace necessarily requires large and generous arms.

We have to thank David Braund and John Wilkins for conceiving the Athenaeus Project, securing funding for it and bringing this book into published form. They have magisterially convoked an assembly of deipnosophists for our time.

GLEN BOWERSOCK
*Institute for Advanced Study, Princeton*

# PREFACE

This book is the principal outcome to date of the Athenaeus Project, which was established at Exeter by the editors in 1996, with the support of colleagues in the Department of Classics and Ancient History. The Project was designed from the first to provide a stimulus and opportunity for co-operative research on an author who is important and neglected. In their different ways the editors had each been troubled by Athenaeus: while David Braund had been wrestling with him in the context of imperial Hellenism, John Wilkins had been engaged with him as a source for comedy while preparing a monograph on the discourse of Old Comedy (*The Boastful Chef*, Oxford, 2000). Meanwhile, John Wilkins had also been working with David Harvey on *The Rivals of Aristophanes* (London, 2000), whose contents will interest many readers of the present book.

However, it was clear from the first that Athenaeus needed a range of specialities such as could only be brought to bear by a team of scholars, and a large one at that. Accordingly, the editors set out to recruit the talents of the authors of the chapters gathered together in this book, as well as many others who have been involved in various ways and to various degrees. The total of those connected actively with the Project amounts to almost a hundred, with many more helping from afar, and all from an unusually wide range of countries.

The great majority of scholars involved actively in the Project met in Exeter in 1997 to share information and perspectives. The event, memorable for its camaraderie, established the intellectual framework within which the Project has worked thereafter, particularly in the creation of the present book. In this spirit of tolerance, the editors have not insisted in any very rigid manner upon their unfashionable preference for Latinized spellings in the chapters which follow, nor have they imposed party lines of any more substantial sort.

The editors would like to stress that little of this could have happened without the generous good-will of participants in the Project and the sustained academic support of their Exeter colleagues. Also vital was the thoughtful and generous support of the A. G. Leventis Foundation, both for the event of 1997 and for the production costs of this book. The editors would like to express their warmest thanks.

Finally, the editors would like also to thank those who have carried the book through to its present state. Diane Braund spent very many hours on the completion of the manuscript, while Kerensa Pearson both assisted with the manuscript and skilfully translated Chapter 19. Heather Chadwick made a valuable contribution to proof-reading; while Diane Braund and John Wilkins prepared indices of passages and subjects, respectively. On far too many occasions our colleagues in Pallas Humanities Computing were called upon to work miracles with unhappy machinery: our thanks in particular to Nac Datta and Mike Dobson. Meanwhile, the Royal Albert Memorial Museum, Exeter, provided the cover illustrations, as well as further illustrations in this book. The Ashmolean Museum provided imperial images on coins. Photographs of the statues of Iliad and Odyssey were made available by the American School of Classical Studies at Athens: Agora Excavations. To these institutions and their helpful staff we are most grateful. Maps were drawn by Seán Goddard, School of Geography and Archaeology, University of Exeter.

The University of Exeter Press is to be commended for its bravery in taking on so large a tome; Peter Wiseman is to be congratulated for his particularly valuable contributions to the design of what had threatened to be as challenging and apparently shapeless a book as the *Deipnosophistae* itself.

DAVID BRAUND
AND
JOHN WILKINS

*Note on Abbreviations*
Abbreviations follow the conventions of the *Oxford Classical Dictionary* (3rd edn) and of Liddell Scott Jones, *Greek–English Lexicon* (9th edn), with minor changes for the purposes of clarity.

# SECTION I:
## GENERAL INTRODUCTION

# INTRODUCTORY REMARKS

Few modern scholars admire Athenaeus. But then few would claim even to have read him. His principal and only extant work, the *Deipnosophistae*, is treated usually (if at all) as a quarry, from which fragments of earlier texts can be hacked out and put to use, perhaps re-arranged. After all, it has lost its beginning and some of its end. It is also very long. Moreover, the body of the work overflows with detail, often on topics usually located at the margins of modern engagements with the ancient world. Accordingly, Athenaeus himself tends to be dismissed as a dullard, worthy of consideration only because he happens to have performed the service of quotation. The purpose of this book is to take a much broader view of the author and his works, both in their own right and in the context of related current concerns, for example with the Greeks of the Roman empire or with the symposium and sympotic literature.

The forty-one chapters in this book have been arranged systematically to tackle Athenaeus and his works. First, two introductory chapters. Next, the text, transmission and translation of the *Deipnosophistae*. Third, Athenaeus as a reader in a contemporary literary and historical context, embracing both Rome and Greek Egypt. Fourth, the central issue of structure, on which a range of broad views of the *Deipnosophistae* will be offered. Fifth, Athenaeus' engagement with earlier works of key significance to him, notably the Homeric poems and the dialogues of Plato. Sixth, sympotic matters, embracing not only food and wine, but also thought, wit, music, medicine and courtesans. Finally, the other known works of Athenaeus and their relevance to the concerns of the *Deipnosophistae*.

The sheer scale of the present undertaking is indicated by the large number of essays collected here and the extensive ground which they cover in

1

their different ways. There is a considerable coincidence of view across these contributions, but the editors have not sought to remove any differences of opinion and perspective among contributors, where they exist. Indeed, we take such disagreements to be constructive dialogue, rather as among the diners of the *Deipnosophistae*. However, we have attempted to facilitate the use of this book by offering not only this General Introduction, but also a short introduction at the beginning of each of its sections, signalling, *inter alia*, disagreements as appropriate.

Our collective aim is to encourage a more sympathetic approach to Athenaeus and his works. The following chapters seek to provide a fuller understanding of what he and his works have to offer. Nevertheless, it would be absurd to pretend that these chapters cover every aspect of the *Deipnosophistae*. Of course, they do not. But they do address what seem to the editors and contributors to be the principal issues at stake.

Throughout, we talk of 'Athenaeus' as the author, for such he is, but we do not suppose that he would subscribe to all the views which he locates in the mouths of the diners. Indeed, while the humour of their exchanges makes that most unlikely, their disagreements make it impossible. Accordingly, when we consider Athenaeus' outlook, we mean the broad concerns and impact of his work taken as a whole or in large part. At the same time, however, we find it hard to imagine that the views ascribed to Larensis are anything other than those of the real patron. Often, we use the term 'dilettante' and its cognates to describe Athenaeus' outlook. The term is a little awkward, for, especially among professional scholars, it can seem to be a term of disapproval or even abuse. However, we intend no criticism in using the term. Rather, it is used here in an attempt to encapsulate the spirit of Athenaeus' work and Larensis' table. As we shall see, expertise is recognized and admired in the *Deipnosophistae*, but only in the context of the broadest cultural sophistication, wherein even experts (Galen the doctor, for example) appear also as gentlemen-amateurs, and wherein gentlemen-amateurs feel able to challenge or improve upon even acknowledged expertise. Accordingly, much of the fun at the expense of Ulpian the diner arises from his attachment to a pedantic approach which other diners find excessive and over-narrow.

In the two introductory chapters which follow, it remains to broach two large issues which echo through the book and require identification and consideration from the first: all the more so, because the editors have arrived at views which run against dominant orthodoxies. First, David Braund considers the relationship of Greek and Roman in the *Deipnosophistae*, concluding that, contrary to common opinion, the work has much of relevance for contemporary Rome, both city and empire. Second, John Wilkins addresses directly the vexed question of structure, concluding that the *Deipnosophistae* has a strong internal architecture.

# LEARNING, LUXURY AND EMPIRE
## ATHENAEUS' ROMAN PATRON

### by David Braund

Athenaeus' profound and extensive concern with the past throughout the *Deipnosophistae* can give the impression that his work has little or nothing to say about the present. Yet any such impression would be misleading for reasons both broad and specific. In broad terms Athenaeus' very concern with the past is to be recognised as a characteristic feature of his present. His antiquarian tendencies were shared by many others of his world, writing in their own particular genres. And these included not only writers of Greek, like Pausanias and Harpocration (on whom, see Chapters 10 and 13), but also writers of Latin, notably Aulus Gellius, Fronto and Apuleius (on whom, Chapter 7). The point hardly needs elaboration, for it is well enough understood.[1] However, it is perhaps worth insisting on its relevance to any appreciation of Athenaeus' writing and perspectives. Moreover, although the past predominates, the deipnosophists are seen to be admired as innovators. What they find in the old is something which is flagged as new (e.g. 6.222a–e; 14. 613c–d).

There is also Larensis. Since the beginning and end of the *Deipnosophistae* have not survived, it is possible to underestimate the prominence of Larensis in the work. It is not that he dominates the conversations in any overt way. Rather, Ulpian tends to take the initiative in raising issues and often in holding forth upon them (e.g. 14.640c). However, it is of course under the patronage of Larensis that all the proceedings take place, complete with Athenaeus himself among the guests and as the narrator of the text. And it is clear enough from the epitomized version of the beginning that we do have, that the position of Larensis was firmly and favourably asserted from the first. Larensis is not a Petronian Trimalchio. His hospitality is that of a man of high status, replete with learning and worldly sophistication. His substantial library (on which, see Chapters 6–7) is not simply for show, or an empty expression of wealth, but a demonstration of his commitment to the pursuit of learning. Nor is it complete: Larensis is still seeking to acquire further books (13.556a–b), though perhaps not all books, since some seem to him discreditable (13.567a–b with Chapter 39). However, the claimed wonders of his collection of literature surely imply that Athenaeus had access to an outstandingly wide range of original texts. Meanwhile, Larensis' own contributions to the discussions confirm that he can hold his own in this learned company. And, while Athenaeus offers his readers ample scope for (rather affectionate) humour at the expense of Ulpian and so-called Cynulcus, in particular, he pokes no fun at Larensis.

As the Epitome informs us, the *Deipnosophistae* began with a brief exchange between Athenaeus and the eager Timocrates, greedy for news of the gathering of the so-called deipnosophists, which (as Timocrates says) was the talk of the town. Athenaeus confirmed his own presence at the gathering and soon launched into a eulogy of Larensis (1.2b–d): the reported elements of that eulogy repay attention, particularly because they suggest the sort of praise that Larensis was thought to have desired. First and foremost, Larensis is praised as a patron, keen to gather numerous men of learning and to host them with words and ideas, not only with dinner and the like. Further, he is a valued participant in his own right, raising worthwhile issues and pursuing them. He does not abuse his position, but offers the fruits of real research and learning to an extent deemed admirable, if not wonderful. For all his wealth, Larensis' model is Socrates and Socratic method, for, by contrast with the false philosophers who recur through the text, Larensis is a committed scholar and thinker.

Moreover, he was as at home in Greek as he was in his native Latin, a two-sided warrior in words, like the ambidextrous Asteropaeus of Homer's *Iliad* (1.2c). Appointed by the emperor Marcus to take charge of temples and sacred rites, he participated in Greek rites no less than in those of his native Rome. And he exhibited his love of learning by his own research initiative, for he made himself expert in the religious ceremonies ordained at Rome by Romulus and Numa, as well as becoming an authority in the civil law. Athenaeus stresses that Larensis had achieved this without assistance, by his own study of ancient decrees and resolutions and by his collection of laws which had fallen into obscurity. Larensis may remind us of Fronto, with Athenaeus as a latter-day Appian, both the proud products of Greek Egypt. Champlin astutely observes the similarity in sketching what he calls 'the invasion of the West by Greek intellectuals' in the second century AD. He notes that even Fronto, the 'paragon of Latinity', not only provided patronage for Appian, the Greek historian from Alexandria, but also studied and corresponded with him intensively, not to mention the other Alexandrians in Fronto's circle.[2]

Next, Athenaeus' eulogy addresses Larensis' library. He is said to have owned more ancient Greek books than all those previously famous for their Greek libraries, from Polycrates and Peisistratus to Ptolemy Philadelphus himself. He is a true lover of the Muses. And his Mouseion, it may be inferred, is the companionable learning of his table and probably the accommodation of his home, for his invitations make Rome the homeland of all (1.3a–c with Chapter 6). Marcus Aurelius and others may have been emperors of the Roman world, but Larensis is an emperor of learning, surpassing the monarchs of the past and making Rome in the present a new Athens or Alexandria, the adopted homeland of the wise. He is an example to his contemporaries and an illustration of the general contention that the proper use of wealth is judicious euergetism (1.3d). The hyperbole is patent, but it is also subtle, achieved by the author's inference and suggestion; even when stated baldly, it is appropriate enough as eulogy of a patron.

For it is Larensis who provides the food and drink, as well as words (e.g. 8.331b). And Larensis' cook (a slave) is appropriately learned, as he shows in a *tour-de-force* disquisition of his own, complete with quotations (9.380f). In so doing, the cook also shows himself outrageously boastful on his own behalf, claiming to be the best of cooks, and on behalf of all cooks, claiming, for example, that the first Olympic victor was in fact a cook (9.382b). Boastfulness was sufficiently characteristic of cooks in Greek literature and thought, so that the bombast of Larensis' cook hardly reflects upon Larensis. The diners certainly indulge the cook, who rather ironically stresses the praiseworthiness of modesty among cooks. Moreover, Athenaeus has Larensis make a sharp distinction between his cook and apparently learned cooks elsewhere:

> So when we all had praised the cook for his ready speech and outstanding cookery, our fine host Larensis said, 'And how much better that cooks should gain a thorough learning in such matters than the state of affairs in the house of one of our fellow-citizens, who through wealth and luxury used to compel his cooks to learn the dialogues of the most excellent Plato ...'
>
> (9.382a)

The criticism is specific and cutting. Larensis proceeds to relate the hammy quotations from Plato at this other establishment and the boredom thereby inflicted upon the guests. The other host is not identified, but the criticism seems to go well beyond general characterization of the wrong sort of learned cook and the abuse and false deployment of learning. True, this false situation serves to highlight the real engagement of Larensis' dinners and, indeed, of his whole establishment. However, it seems hard to resist the impression that a real individual is under attack. He is specified as a Roman, for such must be the meaning of 'citizen' in this context, a world wherein, technically, most men within the imperial elite by now could claim to hold Roman citizenship. And he is presumably recognizable to an alert reader, especially a denizen of the city. Yet, he seems also to be dead or at least to have changed his ways, for Athenaeus has Larensis use the imperfect tense (a fact obscured by Gulick's translation): this was a practice which used to be followed, but no longer.

The passage reminds us that, well beyond the opening eulogy, a sustained function of the *Deipnosophistae* was the glorification of Larensis and his patronage. Athenaeus may be the author, but it is Larensis who gives rise to the proceedings which Athenaeus claims to report. Readers are encouraged to associate themselves with Timocrates (and the rest of Rome), whose eagerness to hear from Athenaeus of the proceedings at Larensis' table tends to confirm both the significance of the text and the significance of Larensis' learning and deployment of patronage. Meanwhile, Athenaeus seems to deploy the discourse of clientage wittily to describe not only himself but also Timocrates, grateful recipients of Larensis' generosity, directly and indirectly (e.g. 12.551a). The point cannot be pressed, for it is not entirely clear that Athenaeus is indeed referring to his own state and it is even less clear that his remarks could, even so, be taken literally. However, it is clear enough that the relationship between Athenaeus and Larensis should be understood as that between client and patron. That the relationship of patronage should be expressed overwhelmingly in the language of hospitality, friendship and commensality is entirely typical of Roman discourse on patron–client relations.[3] After all Athenaeus was a long way from his place of origin in Naucratis and, for all his patriotic attachment to that place, he claims not to have been near the Nile for many years (7.312a, evidently in his own authorial voice; see Chapter 5). We are left to wonder how many of the intervening years he had spent in the patronage of Larensis: the sheer scale and complexity of his literary offering to his patron, the *Deipnosophistae*, might indicate a long-standing relationship, for its construction must have required many years of work, as well as access to a fine library.

The need to honour his patron no doubt encouraged Athenaeus to allude to the key stages in Larensis' career. By chance we have an epitaph, which may allow us to control some of the details provided by Athenaeus.[4]

> Dis Manibus. P(ublius) Livius Larensis pontif(ex) minor hic situs est.
> Cornelia Quinta marito incomparabili fecit.

The epitaph records a religious post, but only that of a *pontifex minor*, rather less than the glorious supervision of Roman religion suggested in the eulogy. Of itself, the mismatch need not cause us to doubt the relevance of the epitaph: we may assume that Athenaeus' eulogy is inflated, for such is the tendency with eulogies. Indeed, it could be more than simple chance that Athenaeus chooses not to offer a specific title for Larensis' post under Marcus. Looking back from a time when Larensis had achieved some prominence, it was more convenient for Athenaeus to stress the personal scholarship and breadth of interest which (allegedly) informed Larensis' post. Nor is that concern limited to the eulogy: it is not far away at several points later in the work. For example, we are informed that the dinner took place at the time of the Parilia (8.361e–f), no less than the birthday of Rome. We hear of Greek and Roman celebration of Saturnalian festivals (14.639b–c). And we are told of the relevance of Janus (15.692d). Mention is also made of the contemporary temple of Hercules, said still to hold the gorgon-skin sent to Rome from Numidia by Marius (5.221f).

The forerunner of Larensis is none other than Varro, the antiquarian and philologist of the late Republic, rather as the forerunner of Cynulcus is Diogenes the Cynic himself. Larensis' notion of Varro's brand of antiquarianism, presumably with a focus on language and religion, seems to have been key to his self-image as a scholar. However, Larensis presents Varro particularly as a writer of Menippean satire and as a Roman unusually well acquainted with Greek literature (4.160d). Larensis could claim to have given rise through Athenaeus to his own Menippean work, the *Deipnosophistae* itself, and was deeply engaged with Greek texts, not to mention philology, antiquarianism and religion.

However, there is a real problem with the epitaph, which demands more attention than it has received since 1890, when Dessau authoritatively identified the P. Livius Larensis of the inscription with Larensis the patron of Athenaeus. Larensis' concern with religion might just be enough to explain his wife's decision (as it seems to be) to reduce his career to a minor priesthood. However, Athenaeus' patron was a man who had been imperial procurator of Moesia (9.398e, on which more below). It seems beyond reasonable doubt that he was also *procurator patrimonii* in the final years of Commodus, with a central role upon that emperor's demise in December AD 192, when, on the orders of Pertinax, he handed over Commodus' body for burial to the consul designate Fabius Cilo (SHA, *Commodus*, 20.1, where the MSS have Livius Laurensis).

Dessau acknowledged the problem, but only to dismiss it. He preferred to stress the undoubted honour of such a priesthood and to assert:

> The fact that on the epitaph of Larensis the titles *procurator patrimonii* and *procurator provinciae Moesiae* do not appear should not cause concern; the deceased's rank and status were signified through his lifelong priesthood as well and better than through his employment in the imperial service; it is also very possible that the role of Larensis as *procurator patrimonii* under

> Commodus entailed unpleasant memories and for that reason his epitaph
> was composed in this brief form.
>
> (Dessau 1890, 157–8)

Yet this will hardly suffice. There was no need to choose between the citation of
various offices, as Dessau tends to imply: all could be accommodated, the more
the merrier. We do not know whether or not Larensis' service under Commodus
had the associations which Dessau suggests. Certainly, in the *Deipnosophistae*
Athenaeus offers a degree of sympathy for Commodus, as we shall see: there was
no need even to mention that emperor, if that was to recall unpleasant memories.
And what of the provincial appointment? Dessau offers no particular explanation
for its omission, although it represented a further dimension to Larensis' career.
Again, Athenaeus' decision to incorporate that post in the *Deipnosophistae* (and
indeed, in the mouth of Larensis) suggests that his patron was distinctly proud of
it. In short, despite the authority of Dessau, there is surely room for doubt as to
whether the Larensis of the epitaph is really the patron of Athenaeus. We need
not be concerned that Athenaeus calls him 'Larensios'. Much more significant is
the absence of any *praenomen* from the *Deipnosophistae* and the *Historia Augusta*: the
epitaph apart, there is no reason to believe that Athenaeus' patron was a Publius.
However, for all that, Larensis is not a common *cognomen*. It remains entirely
possible that the epitaph belongs to a relation of Athenaeus' patron, perhaps his
father. Given the remarkable modesty of the epitaph, such would seem to be the
more plausible hypothesis. If that is right, Athenaeus' concern with religion may
perhaps have derived from his father.

Larensis' procuratorship in Moesia is mentioned in the *Deipnosophistae* in a
memorable vignette which serves further to illustrate Larensis' pursuit of learning
even when far from Rome. In this regard it is perhaps worth remembering that
Varro too seems to have conducted serious research far away from Rome, as in
tasting the waters of the Caspian in the entourage of Pompey (*ap.* Plin. *NH* 6. 51).
Larensis himself disingenuously raises the issue among the diners by asking,
'What do you think the *tetrax* is?' (9.398b). The unattributed response is correct,
but inadequate, 'A type of bird': apparently a form of grouse, more specifically the
Asian sandgrouse. Larensis enjoys his more precise knowledge and moves to the
next stage of his gambit by citing a mention of the *tetrax* in Aristophanes' *Birds*
(884), immediately followed by the description of a bird of that name by
Alexander of Myndus and Epicharmus' mention of it in his *Marriage of Hebe*.
Alexander of Myndus seems to have envisaged a smallish pheasant-like bird, which
fed upon fruit and which gained its name from the cackling sound it makes
(*tetrazei*) in laying its eggs. Rather by contrast, Epicharmus described the bird as a
seed-eater. The diners have nothing to say and, for once, are silent. Triumphantly

Larensis announces that he will show them the bird: it is brought into the room in
a cage while he explains how he came by the creature:

> 'As procurator of the lord emperor in Moesia and in charge of the affairs of
> the province I have seen the bird in that very land. And when I learned of
> its name among the Moesians and the Paeonians I recalled the bird from
> the lines of Aristophanes. And thinking that the creature was worth a
> mention by the most learned Aristotle in his very costly study (for the story
> goes that the Stagirite received 800 talents from Alexander for his research
> on animals), but finding nothing there on the subject, I rejoiced that I had
> the delightful Aristophanes as the most solid of witnesses.'
>
> While he was holding forth, someone brought in the *tetrax* in a cage. In
> size it was far bigger than a rooster, while in appearance it resembled a
> purple coot. It had wattles, hanging from its ears on either side, as do
> roosters. Its voice was deep. When we had admired the fine plumage of the
> bird, it was soon prepared for the table and brought in again: its flesh
> resembled that of the ostrich, which we have often eaten.
>
> (9.398e–399a)

The vignette has a light-hearted tone; Larensis enjoys his moment. For example,
he plays with the notion of Aristophanes' reliability, a notion readily defensible on
lexical grounds, but at once also absurd in the case of a comic poet. However, the
vignette encompasses two of the key ideas which recur through the work,
explicitly and implicitly.

First, competition. Larensis shows that his knowledge can be superior to
that of his learned guests. He also shows that he can fill a gap left even by the
great Aristotle, and even with regard to a bird from a land not so far from
Macedon. Indeed, at the outset Athenaeus' eulogy had listed Aristotle among
those whose libraries were excelled by that of Larensis (1.3a). Nor did Larensis
need to draw upon the massive riches of an Alexander: he could fund himself
sufficiently. There is a certain interest in expenditure of large sums on research,
whether emanating from Larensis as patron or from Athenaeus as author.[5]

Second, Larensis displays his sustained concern with learning. Even when
burdened with major responsibilities as procurator of Moesia, Larensis can brood
upon Aristophanic terminology, consider a local term of ornithology and capture a
*tetrax*. Such conduct was not immune to critical attack, but there can be no real
doubt that Athenaeus' account is intended to stress the positive side of these
concerns. The reader is surely expected to approve Larensis' commitment, not
only because he was Athenaeus' patron but also and more broadly because the
informing ideology of the whole work (for all its recurrent playfulness) is that

these were valid and admirable concerns for their own sake. Of course, more austere minds might regard Larensis' conduct as an example of the worst kind of imperialist behaviour, bringing the foods of far-off lands to corrupt Roman palates, a tendency condemned by authors from Cato to Columella and beyond. Indeed, the ownership and consumption of fancy birds had long been understood as particular marks of luxurious living, prone to attack under the Athenian democracy: Athenaeus certainly knew as much, for he evidently knew Antiphon's prosecution speech on the subject (9.397c).[6]

However, austerity is not the spirit of Athenaeus' work: rather he can combine texts and ideas on austerity with their more numerous counterparts on luxury, for each has its particular validity and context. Accordingly, for all his commitment to a form of luxury, he accepts and relates instances of Athenian democracy's critique of fine fowl, not only by Antiphon but also by the comic poets, such as Anaxilas and his *Bird-Fanciers* (14.654e–655a). In fact, he seems to share a critical perspective on the large number of peacocks kept in contemporary Rome (14.654d). In so doing, he can exploit the opportunity to connect classical Athens with Ptolemy Physcon[7] and both with contemporary Rome: the Athenian comic poets (Antiphanes, specifically) are imagined as having foreseen the plurality of peacocks at Rome, which was such that Physcon would rush to the city (14.654d–e). The tone is playful, as often, but here Athenaeus highlights a tendency that remains only implicit in most of the work, namely the interaction between texts, persons and places otherwise kept apart by centuries. He had already made a similar connection between the fishmongers of contemporary Rome and their counterparts as mocked in Athenian Comedy: again, Antiphanes is used to begin exploration of the link (6.224c). It is not only in matters of high culture but also in these baser ways that Rome has become a new Athens, with Larensis and his entourage as a new Socratic circle.

At first sight, the language of austerity might seem to threaten Larensis, but, on the contrary, Athenaeus seems to echo the views of his patron. For we have seen Larensis' active pursuit of the Roman past praised in the initial eulogy. Towards the middle of the work, Athenaeus has Larensis deliver a substantial disquisition upon earlier Roman history in the familiar discourse of morality and decline into luxury. More specifically, Scipio and Caesar (this last somewhat remarkably, and beside more obvious persons) are praised for upholding ancestral traditions and living within the *mores* of the community (6.273d). The general case runs as follows:

> For it is the mark of wise men to abide by the ancient standards by which they campaigned and overcame others, taking, together with captives, whatever they retained that was useful and fine and emulating it. And that

is what, in times long past, the Romans used to do. For at the same time they both maintained their ancestral ways and took over from the conquered any remnant of fine conduct they discovered, leaving to the conquered their bad practices, so that they would never be able to regain what they had lost. At any rate, from the Greeks they learned about machines and siege-engines [cf. 14.634a–b] and with these overcame them. And while the Phoenicians discovered seafaring, they defeated them through naval warfare. From the Etruscans, who fought in close phalanx formation, they took close-fighting tactics, while from the Samnites they took the use of the rectangular shield, and from the Iberians they took the javelin and from others they took other practices and perfected them. And in all respects they copied the constitution of the Spartans and maintained it better than the Spartans themselves. But nowadays in taking their pick of useful practices, from their enemies they also adopt pernicious standards …

(6.273d–f)

Larensis proceeds to approve Posidonius' analysis of Roman history as a decline from frugal austerity and the farmer's lifestyle into the life of luxury. Lucullus takes the blame for setting the new trend of luxury, having conquered two wealthy kings, not only Mithridates Eupator but also Tigranes the Great of Armenia, and, by implication, taking over their worse practices (6.274e–f; 12.543a; cf. Chapter 16). But Lucullus can be seen also as something of an innovator, without explicit condemnation as to the nature of his innovations (2.51a on his naming of cherries).

There can be no real doubt that the views of the character Larensis are indeed the views of the real Larensis, both here and elsewhere in the work, as when he praises married women and thereby marriage (13.555b–559e, against *hetaerae*; some may wish to recall the epitaph), or indeed when he is said to take an exceptional pleasure in the poetry of Homer (14.620b, a taste which must condition our understanding of the use of Homer through the work). His patronage demanded as much of Athenaeus, who would hardly have attributed alien views to the great man. Moreover, the prominence of religion in the speech tends to confirm that these are indeed the thoughts of Larensis, who may well have interpreted the simplicity of the performance of contemporary Roman religious rites as a relic of the actual everyday simplicity of the distant past, before Lucullus, just as his character does in the *Deipnosophistae* (6.274a–c). Moreover, Athenaeus' Larensis praises Romans who observed the sumptuary law of Fannius—characteristically enough, for we should recall the patron's exceptional concern with old laws, as noted in the initial eulogy (1.3a). He specifies the law's restrictions upon the number of guests who might be invited to dine and the cost of food purchased (6.274c–d).

At first sight, Larensis seems guilty of outrageous hypocrisy, for he holds forth in praise of sumptuary legislation while hosting numerous guests at a luxurious feast, one among a number of such feasts. Yet his position is defensible enough, for he locates himself and his feasting in a period when past limitations have fallen into complete neglect. He applies a passage of Theopompus to his own situation:

> But nowadays, as Theopompus records in the first book of his *Philippica*, there is no-one even among those of moderate prosperity who does not set out a costly table, who does not possess cooks and many other servants and who does not spend more on daily requirements than used to be spent at festivals and sacrifical rites.
>
> (6.275b)

Once again past and present are brought together. Standards have changed, it is argued, so that luxury has become the norm (cf. 15.691e). At Rome the arrival of luxury is a change ushered in by Lucullus during the late republic, while among the Greeks the quotation from Theopompus suggests a similar shift in the fourth century BC. The historicity of such claims is of marginal concern here. Far more important is that Larensis' historical outlook absolves him of any charge of hypocrisy (though the reader may choose to persist). He can look wistfully at the imagined austerity of the past, but also freely acknowledge that in his present situation the rule is a form of luxury. No doubt, luxury could be seen as a by-product of peace (cf. 1.18f). At worst, Larensis may be judged a complacent antiquarian, but even that is no doubt not the sort of judgment that Athenaeus would have his readers reach.

Rather, we may suspect that Athenaeus would have his readers view Larensis as a kind of emperor of taste, with a full awareness of earlier and morally better times. Where an emperor might take a pride in bringing new beasts to the amphitheatre (e.g. Calpurnius Siculus, *Eclogue* 7), Larensis brings a new beast to his table, the *tetrax*: as we have seen, in this company ostrich-meat is almost old hat. Further, the killing and consumption of the rare *tetrax* show the extent of his beneficence: all the diners can have a taste, it seems. Larensis is not only competitive and committed, but also generous. He has made Rome the home not only of all learned men but also of all foods, at least for the *cognoscenti* at his own table.

At the same time, Athenaeus (and no doubt Larensis) is well aware of monarchs with a strong interest in birds and their keeping and breeding. He cites the case of Ptolemy Physcon, whose keeping of the Median *tetaros* echoes Larensis' *tetrax*. Yet Ptolemy preferred to keep his birds uneaten, whereas Larensis served to his guests not only the *tetrax* but also large quantities of the birds which the king had simply hoarded (14.654b–d). We are left to wonder how long Larensis had had the *tetrax* in its cage and whether this was the only example in his possession. The portability of such birds (and of their eggs) indicates that Larensis may have had a flock of these creatures, but that is not the impression left by Athenaeus' account. Rather, the unreflecting reader might well assume that the *tetrax* is a single specimen, fresh from Larensis' period of office: much depends upon the respective dates of Larensis' procuratorship and Athenaeus' work.

It is noteworthy that Athenaeus does not name the emperor who appointed Larensis to Moesia. The most obvious explanation for that omission would be that this was the current emperor, presumably Septimius Severus, for there can no longer be serious doubt that the *Deipnosophistae* was located in the years *c.* AD 193–7. In that case, the omission of the post from the epitaph would be still harder to explain away. However, it is usual to date Larensis' procuratorship in Moesia (whether Upper or Lower is unclear) to the later years of Commodus, perhaps around AD 189.[8] For there is a good reason to deny the impression left by Athenaeus that he was appointed by Severus: in the hierarchy of procuratorial posts of the second century, procuratorships in the Moesias seem usually to have been centenary posts (with a salary of 100,000 HS) and therefore inferior to the post of *procurator patrimonii*, which usually brought a salary of twice that amount. Since Larensis had held the better post before Severus, it has reasonably been inferred that he must have held the lesser post in Moesia rather earlier, though there are no particular grounds for 189. The case is strong, though there is also some room for doubt. For in recent years it has become ever clearer that equestrian 'careers' did not follow neat courses.[9] There was a hierarchy of posts, but our evidence indicates that it was not entirely rigid. Indeed, the evidence (not least for the relationship between salaries, posts and post-holders) seems barely sufficient to permit generalizations about the usual, let alone the normal. Saller's formulation indicates the need for caution:

> the salary ... was attached to the individual, not to the office, but particular offices were regularly held by men at a particular salary level; so despite some irregularities procuratorships can be classified in a hierarchy according to salary levels (Saller 1982, 85).

As to Larensis' particular appointment in Moesia, we simply do not know the terms under which he was appointed, whatever may be thought about the norm in the Moesias.

Be that as it may, the vignette certainly brings the contemporary world and the machinery of empire within the recondite purview of the diners. Larensis' historical analysis of the decline in Roman standards during the Republic is couched in terms of the dangers of empire. It evidently owes much to Posidonius, Nicolaus of Damascus and, very probably, also to the controversial Rutilius Rufus.[10] For there is nothing very unusual in Larensis' explanation of that decline as a consequence of empire, and more specifically as the result of taking the wrong attributes from the conquered Mithridates Eupator and Tigranes. Yet in the context of the *Deipnosophistae* it has a peculiar resonance. For, with Larensis himself presiding over the luxurious proceedings, the work ranges widely across the Roman empire, east and west, and even further afield, picking out particular foods and features of interest. Larensis' importation of the *tetrax* may be seen as an example of his gathering at first hand the perquisites which he and his fellows gather to eat and discuss from all over the world, in deed and word. Evidently, Larensis and his guests consider themselves wise enough to maintain control and keep their luxury within bounds according to the norms of their luxurious society.

As for the Principate, Athenaeus shows no reluctance in including even emperors within his text and sometimes in offering judgments upon them. Augustus occurs only once and fleetingly, no doubt thanks to Nicolaus of Damascus, who is most probably the source of Athenaeus' statement that the emperor named Syrian dates after him, because Nicolaus regularly sent such dates to his imperial friend (14.652a–b). Athenaeus offers no judgment on Augustus or comment on Augustan moral legislation: the omission suggests a lack of interest, or a judgment of irrelevance. Nor was Tiberius of much interest, for all the potential of his life on Capri.[11] He served simply as a chronological marker. First, to locate the activities of Apicius, 'a very rich man of luxury' (πλουσιώτατος τρυφητής), whose antics show that he is no match for Larensis. He lacks the necessary wisdom, sailing all the way to Libya on a fool's errand in search of rumoured enormous prawns (1.7a–c); nor is he described as a host, only as a prodigious consumer. Secondly, to locate a story from Plutarch of Chaeronea on the preparation for drink favoured by a doctor in the household of Drusus, Tiberius' son (2.52d). By contrast, the emperor Gaius is of interest in his own right in that he posed as Dionysus, not only being called 'New Dionysus', but also going about and sitting in judgment while dressed as Dionysus (4.148d).[12]

Plutarch the diner (who is clearly not his homonym, the philosopher of Chaeronea) offers the only mention of Claudius, and then only through his extension to the Library at Alexandria. He indicates his contempt for the sophists of Claudius' creation. Here again, an earlier passage is brought to bear on contemporary matters, for a play of Antidotus is cited as if on these unworthy sophists (6.240b). Yet Claudius fares better than Nero, who fails to appear at all. The omission is remarkable in view of his lifestyle and his concern with the Greek world. Much less surprising is the omission of all other emperors down to Trajan, who, rather as Tiberius earlier, serves to locate an Apicius, who succeeded in sending fresh oysters to the emperor far away from the sea on campaign in Parthia (1.7d).

Hadrian is a very different matter. Athenaeus has more to say about him than about any previous emperor, and it is consistently positive. He first appears in our extant text in a speech of Magnus, who may well be a Roman, like Larensis. Magnus claims to have known a freedman of Hadrian, an Aristomenes of Athens, who was a writer and also an actor of Old Comedy. Hadrian called Aristomenes his 'Attic partridge'. More important, Athenaeus has Magnus describe Hadrian as 'the most cultured ruler' (τοῦ μουσικωτάτου βασιλέως: 3.115b). Subsequently, in the context of the Parilia, Athenaeus in his own voice describes Hadrian (founding a temple) as 'in all ways the best and most cultured emperor Hadrian' (τοῦ πάντα ἀρίστου καὶ μουσικωτάτου βασιλέως Ἀδριανοῦ: 8.361f). Towards the end of the work, Athenaeus has Myrtilus claim to have seen the monument of Alcibiades at Melissa in Asia Minor, where an ox is sacrificed annually, as ordained by 'the in all ways best Hadrian, emperor' (τοῦ πάντα ἀρίστου Ἀδριανοῦ βασιλέως), who also set up on the monument a statue of Alcibiades in Parian marble (13.574f). Finally, Athenaeus has Ulpian name Hadrian in the context of his Egyptian visit and his meeting with Pancrates, 'a poet of the people there, whom we too knew' (15.677e).[13]

Ulpian is setting forth different types of wreath. Once again, there is an element of competition here, not only among the diners, but also between the author Athenaeus and a second-century AD work on the subject, the *Wreaths* of Aelius Asclepiades. The diners' banter, explicitly eschewing this work (15.676f), serves to show the reader that the knowledge displayed by Athenaeus' Ulpian is superior: implicitly Athenaeus himself can claim to have bettered Asclepiades. The wreath linked to Hadrian is made from a lotus (properly of a rosy pink colour) named after his tragic favourite Antinous. It was Pancrates the poet who brought the flower to Hadrian's attention in Alexandria, urging that it should be named after Antinous, claiming that it sprang from the ground which received the blood of the Moorish lion which Hadrian had felled while hunting near Alexandria. Hitherto, explains Athenaeus' Ulpian, the lion had raged across Africa, making much of it uninhabitable. Hadrian was pleased by the inventiveness and novelty (καινότης) of Pancrates' conceit and bestowed upon him the right of maintenance in the Museum (15.677d–f). There is no criticism here of Hadrian's obsession with Antinous; the reader might find something reprehensible in his susceptibility to Pancrates' flattery, but the author more than balances any such reaction by recalling Hadrian's Heraclean killing of the monstrous lion in the interests of civilization and settlement.

Athenaeus' interest in Hadrian—and presumably therefore that of his patron Larensis—may be explained by several congruent considerations. First, the superlatives tell their own story: for Athenaeus (and Larensis) Hadrian is an emperor of outstanding goodness and culture. Hadrian's conception of culture gave a very large place to Greece and the Greek east, not least to Athens of course. At the same time, while Rome remained the imperial centre, his travels illustrated his broad conception of the empire and the emperor's role in it. Secondly, as the afore-mentioned instances show, there was a strong religious element in Hadrian's cultural record. Indeed, Athenaeus could have mentioned more, for example his completion of the temple of Olympian Zeus at Athens. Thirdly, the reign of Hadrian marked the beginning of the contemporary world for Athenaeus, Larensis and their circle: we have noted the claims to personal knowledge which accompany mentions of Hadrian in Athenaeus' text. And this was not simply a matter of chronology, for Athenaeus and his patron may well have taken the view that the sophistic culture of their own world at the very end of the second century AD owed a very great debt to the impetus provided by Hadrian. Hadrian himself, while emperor, was also 'most cultured', or more literally an 'outstanding votary of the Muses' (μουσικώτατος), as Athenaeus, Larensis and the other diners might hope to be.[14]

That Athenaeus' concern with Hadrian goes well beyond simple chronology is confirmed by his failure even to mention Antoninus Pius, Hadrian's successor and in that sense still more contemporary. Indeed, the emperor Marcus is mentioned only in the context of Larensis' religious appointment, while Verus is omitted entirely. However, though mentioned only once, Marcus is heartily praised as 'in all ways best', so that there is no need to surmise that Athenaeus disliked him: after all, Marcus had given a prime appointment to his patron.[15] Rather, Athenaeus simply shows no further interest in him. References to contemporary writers provided ample scope for mention of Hadrian's successors, but Athenaeus chooses not to take such opportunities. After Hadrian, the only emperor to be named in the body of the work is Commodus. His inclusion shows that Athenaeus was not afraid of controversy.

> Small wonder therefore if also in our own times Commodus the emperor had the club of Heracles lying next to him in his chariot and a lion's skin stretched out at his feet and that he wanted to be called Heracles, when Aristotle's Alexander likened himself to so many gods, and even to Artemis at that.
>
> (12.537f)

Scholars have read the passage in various ways: some see sympathy for Commodus, others only criticism or disrespect.[16] The element of criticism is evident enough:

it was outrageous for Commodus to present himself as Heracles. Earlier Athenaeus reminds us that the unstable Gaius had done something similar, as also had Antony, both mimicking Dionysus (4.148b–d). Yet Athenaeus is far from outspoken about Commodus. The opportunity for powerful denunciation is not taken. Rather, Athenaeus prefers to compare him with Alexander, a comparison which tends to mitigate Commodus' lesser claims. To that extent, sympathy. After all, Hadrian too had slain a lion, as we have seen. Under the regime of Septimius Severus, there was room for sympathy for Commodus. Severus could even present himself as Commodus' brother, another son of Marcus, and as understanding towards Commodus' more theatrical and even gladiatorial tendencies (e.g. Dio 75. 7–8). Commodus was deified. In offering a sympathetic context for Commodus' wilder tendencies Athenaeus was in tune with the wishes of Septimius Severus and no doubt also with those of his patron, Larensis, who had prospered under Commodus and remained prominent under Severus. As to Severus himself, there is no explicit mention in the *Deipnosophistae*, but Athenaeus' reference to 'the lord emperor' (9.398e) at first sight seems to concern him as ruling emperor, in no need of further identification.

Moreover, the presence of Ulpian of Tyre at Larensis' table also tends to suggest his continued favour with Severus. Ulpian's death is recorded with regret and in a spirit of warm companionship, though not all the diners were particularly fond of him (see especially 13.571a for Myrtilus' hostility and e.g. 15.697b on Cynulcus', distasteful in context; but note also 14.649e). He is second only to Larensis in the proceedings and his death is foreshadowed, suitably, as the work draws to a close: in every sense he is a dominant figure in the *Deipnosophistae* (15.686a–c). He cannot be the famous Severan jurist, but is no doubt a member of his family, very possibly his father. There are so many coincidences between the two Ulpians that the connection cannot be denied. They have the same name, come from the same city (Tyre, in which they both take a pride), are very close in time and, in their different ways, they achieve some prominence at Rome. It is principally their very different interests (Greek linguistic pedantry and Roman law respectively) and the different dates and manners of their deaths that conclusively prevents their identification.[17] Further, Masurius is praised as an outstanding jurist (14.623e): it is hard to imagine that the talents of Ulpian the jurist would have been ignored if he had been among the diners.

Larensis' association with Ulpian senior implies also a probable connection with his relation, Ulpian the jurist. The connection offers some further indication of Larensis' continued favour under Septimius Severus: there is no sign that he was an ardent supporter of Severus' enemies or had served in any discreditable fashion.[18] Indeed, it is worth remembering Larensis' keen interest in Roman law, as noted above. Therefore, Larensis and the younger Ulpian shared a major interest. Further, Larensis had the wherewithal to support the younger Ulpian's legal researches. For it has been independently observed that the jurist 'must have had a good library',[19] or, perhaps better, must have had access to a good library. Larensis' library was phenomenal and his special collection of legal materials may well have been a key resource for Ulpian the jurist. We see in the *Deipnosophistae* that Larensis makes his books available to his friends (13.556b).

It has often been suggested or implied that Athenaeus' *Deipnosophistae* has scant concern with his contemporary world and very little to tell us about it. By contrast, I have argued that the work is deeply engaged with contemporary Roman and imperial society, created for the greater glory of Larensis and his friends the diners. We have seen something of the competitive spirit that drives so much of the display of knowledge in the work. In fact, such display is central to the ideology of the work and its characters. The dinners and diners of Larensis attract widespread attention, it is claimed, because they reveal new things (καινά). It is that originality that Athenaeus claims to present. Of course, it is an idiosyncratic form of originality, achieved by the rediscovery, citation, quotation and juxtaposition of texts, largely culled from the distant past and deployed under headings or to address specific (and often very minor) issues. We have seen that Athenaeus praises his patron in the introductory eulogy for precisely that kind of textual archaeology.

In such a wide-ranging contest for originality by rediscovery there was ample scope for argument as to who was the first to rediscover a particular passage, detail or explanation. For in this sophistic milieu the traditional concern to establish 'firstness' abided powerfully. Plagiarism was therefore a very serious charge among the diners, even though the whole enterprise of the *Deipnosophistae* might be deemed plagiaristic. Near the end of the work Democritus of Nicomedia denounces the plagiaristic theft by the contemporary Hephaestion of the contents of his own work and of that of 'our noble Adrastus'. And, at the same time, Hephaestion himself is said to have accused others of plagiarism (15.673d–674a). Accordingly, those modern scholars who claim that Athenaeus himself borrowed substantially from compilations of earlier texts without acknowledgement must realize that they are also accusing him (and by extension his patron) of substantial hypocrisy. For that was plagiarism and a stinging charge. If Athenaeus had gone about his work in such a fashion, it would have been of scant interest to his patron and done little to advance Larensis' reputation. Rather the contrary. In fact, we should observe that Athenaeus (like his characters) sometimes acknowledges the use of a compilation. But there is no good reason to suppose that he otherwise used such works. After all, he had the immense library of Larensis at his disposal: the acquisition of books, especially old and obscure ones, or access to such books was the foundation of the learning of Larensis and Athenaeus, a recurrent issue in the *Deipnosophistae* (15.673e, at Rome).

Rome is the location of all this. Modern scholars have occasionally observed that Athenaeus is little concerned with Rome, but that is to underestimate the importance of the location of the *Deipnosophistae*. The opening of the work evidently made a very great deal of that location. Athenaeus says that one might even call the city of Rome 'the epitome of the world', because all the cities of the world can be seen there—golden Alexandria, fine Antioch, beautiful Nicomedia and Athens, 'the most brilliant of all the cities which Zeus created', and very many others besides. And as well as cities, in Rome there are peoples too—Cappadocians, Scythians, Pontics and others (1.20b–c). The discourse recalls the contemporary Aelius Aristides and, more broadly, the rhetor's praise for a great city. Yet it has a particular point in the *Deipnosophistae*, wherein so many cities are represented and all cities and peoples of the world are brought under discussion. Larensis, emperor of taste, presides over his own epitome of the world within the city of Rome, the self-appointed *crème de la crème*, with the support of the greatest of libraries. And Rome recurs through the work. The sounds of the Parilia intrude upon the dining, at the mid-point of the work, designedly no doubt, at the end of the eighth book (8.361e–f). And Janus himself, god of beginnings and ends, is introduced as the work comes to a close (15.692d–f). Appropriately enough, he is presented as a personage who came from the Greek world, where he figures on civic coinages, to settle in Italy on a hill beside Rome, which took from him the name Janiculum.

At the end of the second century AD, particularly for the likes of Larensis, the city of Rome is much more than Roman. Champlin is right to set the invasion of Greek scholars there beside that of Greek senators from the east.[20] Rome stands at the head of a world wherein most texts and histories of scholarly interest are Greek or in Greek. After all (and the point is too easily taken for granted) Athenaeus wrote in Greek, overtly for an eager audience located in the person of Timocrates, but more significantly for Larensis himself, for whom Greek was as natural as Latin. Larensis' speeches in the *Deipnosophistae* are of course in Greek, but they are not to be understood as Athenaeus' translations in any sense. For the contemporary Rome of Larensis, the language of cultured gentlemen was as much Greek as Latin, perhaps more so. Of course, it was possible to claim a distinct Roman and Latin identity: Athenaeus has Larensis and his guests (including Magnus, who seems also to be regarded as a Roman) explore the idea in general terms, as we have seen with the decline of Roman standards, and on very specific matters, such as Latin usage. However, nowhere in the *Deipnosophistae* is there any sign of significant conflict between Roman and Greek identities. Similarly, the jurist Ulpian (not the Ulpian of the *Deipnosophistae*) could combine his tenure of the praetorian prefecture at Rome with 'intense local patriotism' for his home city of Tyre.[21] Indeed, such conflict between patriotisms as can be found relates rather to tensions between different cities of the Greek world.

The civic patriotism of the imperial Greek world is illustrated nicely by the local commitments and passions expressed by the diners and their quotations for their various cities (e.g. 4.184b on Alexandria; 5.187d on Athens). In particular, the prominence of Naucratis in the text is only explicable in terms of Athenaeus' own love for his native city: he is quite happy to acknowledge as much, indicating that such feelings were regarded as praiseworthy or at least normal, and not in themselves reprehensible. Indeed, such attitudes were part of a broader notion that place of origin mattered greatly, even in such contexts as the source of the best bakers.[22] After all a geographical determinism, explaining differences in terms of place, was central to Greek philosophical and medical understanding (cf. 7.317f, citing Theophrastus' *On differences according to places*).

Larensis' own case shows well enough that, however fierce local patriotism might become, it was entirely possible to develop a more benign model, according to which local patriotism was not seriously at odds with other identities. As a Roman, Larensis could claim to be an Italian and by extension though myth (though he does not make the point explicitly) a Trojan or even a Greek. Contemporary Rome remained Roman, but was also much more than that: as Athenaeus observes, it might reasonably be described as an epitome of the world. The case of Antiochus IV Epiphanes of Syria tends to show how such assimilation could become inappropriate, but his supposed madness undermines any broader inferences from his behaviour (5.193c–194c). More straightforward is the case of Athenion, whose self-serving opposition to Rome is presented as integral to his multi-faceted badness as a false philosopher (Book Five, especially 211e–212f (Masurius)). He aligned himself with Mithridates, who is presented elsewhere as the source and focus of luxury and the luxurious, not only infecting Lucullus but also attracting lesser figures like Athenion and certain Lycians (12.528a). In the face of Roman power the luxurious and the austere receive their just deserts, suffering and support respectively.

It is true that the *Deipnosophistae* does show Ulpian fighting to establish and maintain a purity of Greek usage. However, it is that very tendency that is gently and affectionately mocked: he is a Syratticist, a champion of Attic usage from Tyre and as such a contradiction in terms (3.126f; cf. 9.376d, a rejection of Atticism). The occasional ferocity of Cynulcus' and Myrtilus' denunciations of Ulpian is itself so much a subject of humour that Ulpian cannot be significantly hurt by it (e.g. 3.97–8, embracing a Pompeianus also). Rather it is Ulpian's own extremism that undermines his position, as, for example, with his violent, cushion-thumping response to Cynulcus' implementation in Greek of the Latin *decocta* (3.121e–f). Cynulcus' response to this petulance is uncharacteristically measured, accepting that language changes according to place and cultural contact, so that when in Rome Greeks may reasonably adopt such terms.[23] At the same time, for all his commitment to Greek linguistic purity, there is no sign that Ulpian is hostile to Rome or, in itself, to Latin: he even credits Romans with a lively sense of humour (14.615a–e, suitably humorous, but not hostile). The impact of Roman culture upon the Greeks might be regretted and resisted without any sense of anti-Roman feeling, let alone political opposition to Roman rule. For example, Masurius quotes Aristoxenus on the Romanization of the Greek city of Posidonia (Paestum) in southern Italy as a matter for lamentation (14.632a). The barbarization of Greek culture was a particular fear for the Greeks of the second sophistic, but in this case it was the fault of the Greeks themselves, not the Romans and other non-Greeks.[24] Indeed, hellenophile Romans might themselves regret the process. It is to be noted that Masurius' name is at least of Roman origin (in fact, reminiscent of an earlier fellow-jurist of Rome). Moreover, he shows a marked concern with Janus and the Janiculum (15.692d–f). He may very well have considered himself to be a Roman.

At the same time, Roman (and Italian) elements are regularly integrated through the work, as they had been in some of its sources (e.g. Juba's *Equivalences*, 4.170e). Baiae and its undrinkable waters crop up in a list of Greek and other examples, between waters of Phrygia and Corinth (2.43b). The source cited for events at the house of Drusus at Rome is none other than the Greek Plutarch of Chaeronea (2.52d). The Latin for over-ripe olives (*druppae*) is interjected into a catalogue of details on olives (2.56a). Greek and Roman terms for cactus are casually brought together (2.70e–f). So too with breads (3.111c, Pontianus). Even sums of money can be expressed both in Greek terms and in terms of Roman denarii (4.146c–d). Roman feasts are casually set among Greek and other feasts, with citations from Greek authorities (4.153c). Paid decapitation among the Romans is cited from a Greek authority without critical comment (4.154c). Roman prodigals take their place among their Greek counterparts (4.168e). Both Greeks and Romans can suffer from hangers-on (6.252d). Sulla is listed with Greek kings (6.261c), while Romans use a Greek word for prawns (7.306d; cf. 310e on *tursio*; 330b on *rhombus*; 9.400f on *cuniculus*). The Romans call Iberia *(Hi)Spania* (8.330f), while they display an excessive desire for goose-livers (9.384c). The Roman use of the letter 'h' is integrated within a broader treatment of the letter (9.398b). A Greek author is cited on the austerity of Manius Curius (10.419a). Democritus includes Roman limitations on drinking-practice in an integrated list of controls (10.429b), while Greek forms of the Roman Saturnalia are explored (14.639b). When it comes to cakes, Roman and Greek are discussed together (14.647c–e), as also with cooks, where Roman censors sit beside Homeric sacrificers (14.660c).

Throughout the work there is a warm accommodation between Greek and Roman, as should be expected in the patronage of 'Asteropaeus'. That accommodation can cope comfortably enough with local patriotisms and rivalries, including comparisons and controversies between Greek and Roman. Larensis himself is made to complain, 'You Greeks appropriate many things, as if you yourselves had given them names or had been first to discover them' (2.50f). But there is no rancour here: it is friendly banter. Magnus, who seems to regard himself as a Roman, compares Roman figs favourably with the famous figs of the Greek world (3.75e). Similarly, Roman apples (strictly, apples brought for sale in Rome from Aquileia) are deemed superior to the apples of other lands (3.82c, perhaps Daphnus). Shortly after, Arrianus, who is described bombastically and very probably with some irony as 'the great-sophist of the Romans' (3.113d), not only speaks generically of 'the Greeks', but also, and no doubt to Ulpian's fury, transliterates the Latin *fumosus* to make a Greek word for 'smoky' (3.113d, apparently a *hapax*). It is interesting to see the 'Romans' Magnus and Arrianus combine against Greek Cynulcus, but there is no sign of an ethnic edge to their dispute, nor should we expect one. Philip V of Macedon is casually identified as 'the one defeated by the Romans' (6.251e). Contemporary Italy suffers from bandits as did Greek states (6.264f), while the Romans are praised for their expulsions of philosophers (12.547a). Indeed, in returning to praise of Roman expulsions, the Greek Myrtilus terms the Romans 'the in all ways best', the language of imperial laudation in the work, as we have seen: there is no hint of irony here (13.610f).

The Greeks are very much part of the empire. Even the most pedantic of Greeks, such as Pompeianus of Philadelphia, can of course hold forth in Greek on the excellence of the city of Rome (3.98c).[25] Moreover, Greeks can be rulers too, as we are reminded not only in terms of the past, but also in terms of the present. Democritus mentions his conversation with a fellow-citizen of Nicomedia who had been prefect of Egypt, a far more important post than Larensis' in Moesia, but one which similarly provided an opportunity for research, in this case on antidotes to the asp-venom (3.84d–e). Further, Rome itself could be stunned by Greek wisdom, whether that of an individual musical performer from Alexandria[26] or that of the Greek wisdom gathered at the table of Larensis.

# ❖ 2 ❖     DIALOGUE AND COMEDY
## THE STRUCTURE OF THE
## *DEIPNOSOPHISTAE*

by John Wilkins

The vast collection of ancient literature which makes up the bulk of the *Deipnosophistae* of Athenaeus is given some shape by a number of structural devices. The first of these is the division of the work into fifteen books, which is discussed in the chapters of Arnott, Guillén and Romeri.[1] The second device supports the first. The material is mediated to the reader through two sets of speakers, the Deipnosophists in conversation at their meal and the report of that conversation by Athenaeus to his (largely silent) interlocutor Timocrates. Almost all ends and beginnings of books are marked by exchanges between Athenaeus and Timocrates (and the exchanges between them that do not coincide with the beginnings and ends of books are few). A third shaping device is the sequence of the meal and symposium around which Athenaeus orders his material, and for which Guillén has identified firm divisions. These fall at the end of Book Five (beginning of the main courses) and in the middle of Book Ten (the end of the *deipnon* and beginning of the symposium).

The speakers who participate in the meal are numerous. Some are given much more to say than others. There are, furthermore, unnamed speakers and guests and a cook who has much to say about his comic counterparts (see below). Furthermore, the meal takes place over several days and it appears that Athenaeus reports other meetings of the Deipnosophists in addition.[2] All of these are distancing devices which indicate that Athenaeus' main aim is not to give a clear narrative of the dinner of the Deipnosophists but to use the meal for some greater purpose.

Athenaeus' meal consciously reflects the Platonic model (*Symposium* and other dialogues)[3] and reference is made to Plato on numerous occasions, to the extent of improving on Plato (5.186d–193d, 11.504c–509e). This is a fourth shaping device. Plato had set his *Symposium* within a frame of reported speech, and Athenaeus has imitated this pattern. It is also another distancing device which allows ideas to dominate over precise details of narrative. Such details can be called upon as needed. Plato's narrator cannot remember everything that was said: 'Of course, Aristodemus didn't remember all that each speaker said and I [Apollodorus] don't remember all he said. But I'll tell you the speeches of the people he remembered best and that I thought most important.' (*Symposium* 178a, trans. Gill)

So in his turn Athenaeus sometimes gives summaries of what was said (7.277b), sometimes gives interventions from unnamed speakers (7.307f, a Cynic speaks who had arrived during the evening, 6.224c, 'one of the flatterers and parasites' speaks in praise of the host) and sometimes speaks himself (in the external narrative) with little use of speakers at all (Book Twelve). This gives variety but, more importantly, enables the author to concentrate attention on the material and not the narrative. Memory is all important, not only for Plato's Apollodorus but also for Athenaeus' control of events and for Athenaeus' principal speakers, as we shall see below, page 25.

Larensis is giving a much larger dinner/symposium than Agathon had done in Plato's *Symposium*.[4] This gives Athenaeus a larger cast of speakers, both named and anonymous. Many of them are given few distinguishing characteristics, though doctor Daphnus tends to quote medical texts (2.51a, 3.79a–e, 120b–121e, 6.243d–e, 8.355a–361e), Plutarch of Alexandria to be linked with his home town (3.118f, 4.158d, 6.241f, 7.276a, 11.464b) and Plutarch, Myrtilus and Democritus to speak at greatest length (6.248c, 270a–b, 11.461f, 503f, 13.571a–610b). To some extent these imitate Plato's characters: the doctor, Eryximachus, speaking of medicine, Aristophanes speaking with comic invention, Pausanias speaking with homosexual self-interest and so on. Like Plato, Athenaeus uses his speakers to give emphasis to certain aspects of the main material. In Plato's case this was the development of the discussion of love towards the philosophical aims of Socrates and Diotima; for Athenaeus the goal is to present a detailed survey of the place of eating and drinking in the widest sense in Greek literary culture. In this wide sense, love and love affairs are included (13.555b), with the whole of Book Thirteen devoted to *hetaerae* and the male and female lovers of famous men, Plato included.

The speakers who are given most prominence are Ulpian of Tyre and Theodorus of Thessaly, a Cynic known as 'Cynulcus' or 'the Leader of the Dogs'.[5] While Larensis is host, Ulpian is the symposiarch who is in charge of proceedings.[6] Other speakers have an important part to play, not least Larensis, who intervenes often, especially on Roman matters. However, it is the sharp exchanges between Cynulcus and Ulpian which have a programmatic and methodological function throughout the *Deipnosophistae*. These we set out below. The exchanges establish the tone of what follows and the criteria adopted when searching for quotations. In this way they shape the dialogue and the material conveyed in that dialogue.

In a solo performance, Ulpian asks at 2.58b whether any guest can think of an author who cites the word *propoma* 'in the sense in which we now use it'. The task is to measure current usage against the validating test of antiquity. Everyone thinks furiously but it is Ulpian himself who cites Phylarchus as an example. Perhaps in his capacity as symposiarch he had set a difficult question to which he knew few would know the answer. He celebrates his wisdom with the request for a drink, so pleased is he with his memory that is at the ready. Programmatic elements here are:

(1) the testing of the present against the past[7];
(2) competitive testing[8] of memory as a pastime at the symposium[9];
(3) the consumption of drink or food once the verbal achievement is complete.

These elements recur in the first clash with Cynulcus (3.96e–104d). A sow's womb is brought to the table. Ulpian asks which author mentions the word *metra*, 'for we have filled our bellies sufficiently and now is the time for us to speak also'. He attacks Cynulcus and the Cynics for their excessive eating and their dog-like obsession with food and scraps.[10] Cynulcus responds with anger:

> Belly-man, belly-god man, do you know nothing of sustained discourse and can you not remember historical enquiry,[11] nor ever start off with a graceful turn of phrase but must rather waste your time on these things, seeking out whether a word is to be found or not? You ignore what is fine and seek out thorny problems.

Cynulcus focuses in particular on what he presents as Ulpian's poor understanding of Latin and the incorporation of Latin terms into Greek.[12]

Ulpian sees these witty exchanges as an exchange of blows (3.99b) and goes on to list the gluttonous associations of sow's womb, bringing in Epicurus and Archestratus to support his case.[13] The latter is mentioned first as an authority (101b–c), then as a founding father in the philosophy of pleasure (101f) and finally (104b) as the equivalent of Theognis for all gluttonous philosophers.

Additional programmatic elements here are the following:

(4) Charges of gluttony are made against each other by both Ulpian and Cynulcus.[14] While eating is the subject of the *Deipnosophistae*, gluttony, that is an excessive desire to eat, is used as a term of abuse.

(5) Ulpian specializes in thorns as opposed to 'the most pleasant flowers',[15] Cynulcus in the pleasures of eating.

(6) Ulpian is pedantic and not well-disposed to the synthesis of Greek and Roman culture, or even very good at it.[16]

(7) Exchanges may sometimes be voiced sharply or in anger but strong feeling is often mixed with jest. The banter is vigorous but not venomous among these diners.[17]

On many occasions later in the work Ulpian is anxious to continue with citations where Cynulcus is anxious to eat.[18] This is a constructive tension between them on the very subject that lies at the heart of the *Deipnosophistae*—the relationship between food, language and philosophy.

Athenaeus follows a traditional theme in building on the *problem* of food and talk: human beings have a mouth which serves two functions, to eat and to speak. These functions cannot operate at the same time and, furthermore, were not valued equally in Greek literature. In sympotic texts in the philosophical tradition in particular, speech prevailed over eating and drinking. Romeri has studied the history of the philosophical symposium, in which the problem became increasingly an issue (Romeri 1999; cf. Chapter 19).[19] Plutarch removed food as far as possible from the proceedings, while Lucian exploited the problem to underline the hypocrisy of philosophers whose claims to value talk over eating are proved false by their actions. Athenaeus composed the *Deipnosophistae* in this tradition but has a novel approach to the problem. The diners eat, drink *and* talk. Romeri claims that speech and eating and drinking are achieved simultaneously in the *Deipnosophistae* since some eat while others talk. This seems to me to go too far. Rather, it appears to be the case that for the most part one person speaks and others listen but everyone eats and drinks together (Romeri 1999; cf. Chapter 19).[20] Athenaeus presents the problem traditionally posed over eating and drinking in the banter between the diners, in the programmatic elements noted above. There are mutual accusations of gluttony and of addiction to books on luxury. Cynulcus and the philosophers are certainly picked out as susceptible to food, as hypocrites in their claims. But at the meal, this is only banter. None of the diners is interested only in food and luxury. They are all serious men who accuse each other of these susceptibilities but in fact all agree that gluttony is a bad thing. The accusations allow readers to see this true state of affairs but also (crucially) to laugh at the disputants who are sometimes put out by harsh words. This makes up the whole that is *spoudaiogeloion*, or a blend of the serious and the comic. Athenaeus alludes to just this point in his summary to Timocrates on the final page (15.702b–c).

Banter notwithstanding, the speakers/symposiasts are content to follow the lead of their symposiarch, Ulpian, who, wherever he is (1.1d–e), 'in the streets, in the philosophical walks, in the book shops, in the baths has acquired the name of Keitoukeitos.[21] This man observed a personal rule that he would not eat anything until he had asked "is it found or not found?"'[22] This procedure works well at the table and has much potential for humour, not least in the leavening of pedantic persistence with satirical comment.[23] It is particularly notable, as Romeri has shown, that these philosophers at dinner confine themselves almost entirely to words and to eating. There is no descent into komastic behaviour, sexual activity or other distraction. Food is problematized, but not in the fundamental way found among the philosophers in the works of Plutarch and Lucian.[24] We have already met charges of gluttony. Luxury will be a further problematic area: Archestratus' *Life of Luxury* has already been mentioned as a key forerunner which is torpedoed for its excesses.[25]

*     *     *     *

We pursue now some of the programmatic themes through further exchanges between the principal speakers, Ulpian and Cynulcus. To the first an anonymous speaker says in the Epitome (2.65e), 'you ask us for an account of everything and it's impossible to say anything at all that you do not test us on'. Ulpian, it seems, is the devourer of words rather than of foods,[26] the ὀνομάτων δαίδαλος[27] who contrasts with Archestratus the ὀψοδαίδαλος.[28] At the very least a word must be verified before the corresponding food may be eaten. Ulpian is often characterized as eating little; this does not prevent others from accusing him of gluttony (Cynulcus accused him above of being a 'belly-man', 3.97c, cf. n. 10) or from linking him with the excesses of Archestratus, who, according to Daphnus (3.116f), 'sailed round the civilized world for the sake of his belly and the parts below the belly'. At 3.125b, Myrtilus charges Ulpian with being a glutton, a licker of fat and fat-flatterer, while at 4.165b, Cynulcus calls him a 'well-seasoned piglet'. Despite these charges, Ulpian for the most part abstains from food in order to pursue terminology and etymology.

Cynulcus, by contrast, is often characterized as hungry and yet on a number of occasions puts words before eating.[29] His hunger is seen in Book Four where he intervenes after a long discourse (156a–b) and complains of hunger, 'I, wretch that I am', in the words of the comic poet Diphilus, 'should be a mullet because of this extreme fasting'.[30] Though hungry, he describes at length various meals enjoyed by Cynics[31] and praises lentil soup, only to find his 'erudition concerning lentil soup' laughed at (158d) and applause not forthcoming (159e). In anger he exclaims to Ulpian, 'symposiarch, these men are troubled with word-diarrhoea and are not hungry or they mock what has been said about lentil soup'. Lively exchanges follow on what might be termed Cynic literature[32] and the relationship between certain philosophical schools and food. Magnus charges 'you philosophers' (161d) with ignoring their regime, with eating surreptitiously and with admiring Archestratus' poem alone in the canon of epic (162b, 163c–d; cf 164a–b), 'for the sake of the belly'. Cynulcus produces a counter-charge that Magnus travels 'for the sake of the belly' (165a), as Archestratus had done.[33]

These charges and counter-charges serve the double purpose of adding vitality to the long quotations and maintaining the central theme of interaction between food and literature about food. Three further exchanges of this kind remain to be considered. After two long speeches by Democritus,[34] Cynulcus observes (6.270a–b), 'comrades of the mess,[35] Democritus has feasted me not unpleasantly, very hungry as I am, with his discourse on rivers of ambrosia and nectar ... but I have swallowed only words. So let's put a stop to these endless speeches ...'. Ulpian, 'who was always fighting it out with him' (*diapolemon*),[36] replies, "the agora is full of vegetables, full too with bread', but you are always hungry and do not allow us to share in good and ample discourse'. He asks a slave to feed the Cynic-dogs[37] and Cynulcus retorts (270c–d), 'if I had been invited to listen to arguments, I would have known to come when the agora is full... but if we have bathed only to dine on little bits of chatter, I am paying a great price to listen'. Cynulcus prepares to leave but is detained by the arrival of much fish and all sorts of other *opsa*, which are listed alphabetically.

Athenaeus makes use of lists as a further structural device. In Book Nine, comments by Ulpian are placed within a catalogue of animals and birds used for food. Athenaeus uses such lists from time to time, the most extensive being the list of fish in Book Seven, which is presented in the authorial voice. Such lists are often broken up by discourse, such as the speeches of comic cooks under the heading of 'conger eel' (7.288c–293f) and the similar list introduced by the Deipnosophists' cook under the heading *delphax* ('pig') in Book Nine (376c–383f). Ulpian's comments follow the latter intervention. At 9.384f–385a he is described as a censorious man who reclines alone, eating little and watching the speakers. He asks for a definition of *oxyliparon* (vinegar and oil dressing) to establish whether it corresponds with something familiar to him in his native Syria. We are reminded that Ulpian likes thorny problems as he asks 'who cites *oxalme* [oil and salt-water dressing]?'. Athenaeus continues,

> most of them told him loudly to get lost and continued with their meal, though Cynulcus shouted the lines from the *Breezes* of Metagenes, 'but my dear friend, let us dine first and then you can ask me all about it, whatever you like ...'. Then Myrtilus in a sweet sort of way signed up with Ulpian so that he might not share in any of the food but might give himself completely to chatter.'

The banter continues but our point for the present is that this exchange in terms now familiar to us takes place within the catalogue of animals used for meat. We also note that Ulpian appears to prefer to use Syria as a point of reference rather than Rome (see above).

Towards the end of the *Deipnosophistae* (15.669b) the conversation follows a review of the things performed after dinner (15.665b τῶν μετὰ τὸ δεῖπνον ἐπιτελουμένων) and a discussion about the game of *kottabos* (665d–668f). Again, Athenaeus' account confines itself to discussion, to meta-entertainment rather than *kottabos* itself. The discourse continues and there is little actual activity, in complete contrast, for example, with Trimalchio's feast in Petronius. Ulpian moves things on (668f) by capping sympotic lyrics (of Dionysius Chalcus) with some from an unknown poet, 'pour out songs like wine from left to right ...'. Cynulcus responds with bad temper:

> Cynulcus, who was for ever donning the helmet[38] against the Syrian [Ulpian] and never let up the spirited rivalry which he felt towards him, said, when uproar was beginning to take over the symposium, 'what is this chorus of caterwauling?[39] I too recall some of these verses and will recite them. This will prevent Ulpian from pluming himself on being the only one to snatch the *kottabos*-prize from the Homeridae in their words on the Mysteries.'[40]

Cynulcus diverts the conversation into garlands and love based on his 'thousand-year enquiry' into some lines of Callimachus. Proof, if it were still needed, that Cynulcus is something of a pedantic scholar himself. As with greed and luxury, the diners also practise pedantry while decrying it in all seriousness (ludicrously for the readers).

Garlands are to be the next topic for conversation, in another of Athenaeus' semi-alphabetical lists. But there is a further exchange before the list begins. Cynulcus is answered not by Ulpian but by Democritus, who, in a rare moment, uses Cynulcus' real name, Theodorus (669e).[41] Not to be deflected, Ulpian replies to Cynulcus (670b),

> with what a philosopher has the daemon lodged me! [in the words of the *Ghost* of the comic poet Theognetus] Wretch, you learnt your letters backwards and books have turned your life topsy-turvy. You have philosophized and chattered to earth and sky, both of which couldn't care less about your words. What is the origin of your chorus of caterwauling? Who worthy of note has mentioned this musical chorus?

Cynulcus replies,

> I won't tell you, sir, until I receive from you the appropriate payment. For I don't read books to select the 'thorns' from them, as you do, but for the parts that are useful and worth hearing.[42]

Cynulcus returns to the topic of garlands, to a garland from Athenaeus' own Naucratis in fact, on which Ulpian has nothing to say. Democritus takes over the catalogue of garlands. He is a contributor who has made long speeches earlier in the work.[43] The catalogue of garlands is actually recited by Ulpian, once boys have brought in the real thing (676e–f).[44] Ulpian makes to leave the symposium after this list (686c), and Athenaeus notes that he died happily (ἀπέθανεν εὐτυχῶς) a few days later, causing much grief to his companions (see below). Grief confirms the friendship between the opponents.

Cynulcus, meanwhile, has dozed off but is woken up by a guest anointing him with perfume and begins to speak instantly (686c). A list of perfumes follows, and then a list of skolia. Cynulcus returns to further abuse of Ulpian's taste in song (697b–c) and quotes literary examples of the chorus of caterwauling for the pedant (679e–f). As the symposium comes to an end, Cynulcus calls for light and 'sneaked out of the symposium, for he had become very sleepy' (701b). In this final example, many of our programmatic features return, to enliven the lists with sharp exchanges and to keep always at the forefront of our minds the problematic matters of quoting and devouring literature (is it purposeful or pedantic?) and of the links between discourse and actual consumption.

To summarize the position, the two leading speakers are presented as a lover of words and a lover of food but there is a continuing exchange between them (and others) that maintains a fluidity and an endlessly creative badinage on the joint topic of eating and talking, or, in the words of Romeri, of *mots et mets*. In the final exchanges between Cynulcus and Ulpian that we have just reviewed there are many reminiscences of Plato, with perhaps hints of the symposiarch's departure and demise reminiscent of the death of Socrates among his friends in Plato's account.[45] There is also some abuse against philosophers in these pages, but nearly always comically based, as is traditional in sympotic texts.

These methodological passages—there are many others that we might have added—highlight terms of reference and set a light, bantering tone as a context for the long series of quotations, which are quoted for their own sake. Charges and counter-charges appear exaggerated (gluttony, for example, and pedantry and ignorance) but a general disposition on the part of Ulpian to quotation and derivation over eating and other bodily needs seems clear, while Cynulcus' emphasis on bodily needs and utility and broader terms of reference is also sustained.[46] These two are part of what has been called the inner dialogue.

We turn now to the outer dialogue, the one between Athenaeus and Timocrates. The conversation between these two sets a frame similar to that used by Plato in his *Symposium* and other dialogues (1.1a, 2a).[47] As we pointed out above, most of the outer dialogue marks the ends and beginnings of books. Timocrates is directly addressed in most instances[48] but in others Athenaeus speaks for both.[49] Often these exchanges seem to be little more than opening and closing devices which divide the work into units. Sometimes, however, these exchanges in the outer dialogue serve a further, programmatic, purpose. At the end of Book Three (127d) Athenaeus proposes to move from preliminaries to the Deipnosophists' banquet, but Timocrates proposes an alternative course, to look at Macedonian banquets. Athenaeus obliges and addresses Timocrates within Book Four (130e) in order to draw out the contrast between Macedonian and Greek meals. At the beginning of Book Two (35a) Timocrates remarks on the variety (*poikilia*) that Athenaeus brings to each topic. This *poikilia* is a feature of compendious works such as this and Aelian and appears to include not only variety of topic but also variety in style. Modern readers would not allow much to be said in praise of Athenaeus' own style, but variety is provided by the mass of literary quotation, some poetic parts of which are praised for their *charis*—their wit and elegance—and so on.

A further large issue for Athenaeus is novelty. In a curious discussion with Timocrates at the beginning of Book Six, Athenaeus says that Timocrates expects certain kinds of novelty (*kaina tina*, 222a) to have been discovered by the Deipnosophists. Athenaeus quotes two comic fragments which discuss the tragic poet's use of familiar characters and mythological plots in contrast with the comic poet who must find new names, new material, new speeches and a new plot. He then claims (223d–e) that he is restoring to Timocrates the left-overs of the Deipnosophists, not giving them. This appears to mean that novelty is contained in the internal dialogue and not the finished literary work of Athenaeus. He, like a tragic poet, merely passes on what he has inherited, in his case from the speeches at the dinners. There will then be 'certain novelties' in the work, but they will all be the invention of Ulpian, Cynulcus and their companions at the table of Larensis (on whom see above).

A further address to Timocrates at 7.277a occurs not at the beginning of Book Seven but at the head of the catalogue of fish. This appears to be a device designed to give prominence to this list, the most extensive of all the lists in the *Deipnosophistae*, and situated towards its centre. It gives prominence to a compendious report of what each diner contributed from books known to them. There is only a small amount of internal dialogue in this list and the contributions made by the diners are thus not witticisms and novel inventions of their own but testaments to their novelty through vast book-learning.[50]

\*  \*  \*  \*

Comedy has contributed hugely to these exchanges. Much of the material quoted by the Deipnosophists, in the catalogue of fish and elsewhere, is drawn from comedy; some of their witty exchanges in the internal dialogue have a comic base; and the very notion of building a discourse on food and eating has a long comic history. It is to the role of comedy in the *Deipnosophistae* that we now turn.

Among the extensive comedy of the work, we may begin with a comic moment in Book Thirteen (566e–567d). Cynulcus is enraged at the words of Myrtilus on *hetaerae* (female 'companions') and prostitutes and his charges of hypocrisy among philosophers on this subject: 'you dare say these things to me though you are [not] "rosy fingered", in the words of Cratinus but rather have one leg of cow dung[51] while the shank you carry round is that of the poet your namesake who spends his time in wine shops and inns.'[52] Cynulcus adds various charges against the ethics and erudition of Myrtilus the diner, in particular,

> you, you sophist, wallow in the wine shops not with male but with female companions, keeping with you no few female pimps and forever carrying round the appropriate books, of Aristophanes [of Byzantium], Apollodorus, Ammonius and Antiphanes, together with Gorgias of Athens. All of these are authors of works on the female companions of Athens.

Comedy has supplied Cynulcus with three useful items, namely memorable phrases with which to belabour Myrtilus, a poetic namesake who may have written on this subject (linking past and present) and much reflection on the subject of prostitution (many of the quotations deployed by Myrtilus and others in Book Thirteen derive from comedy). We must consider these three items in turn.

Phrases and longer quotations from comedy make a large contribution to the internal dialogue of the *Deipnosophistae* and contribute substantially to the comic tone of the proceedings. Ulpian, Cynulcus and others often build a comic quotation into a riposte.[53]

Athenaeus does not often identify comic poets with characters in their plays, as he appears to do with Myrtilus in this instance. Cratinus appears to be treated similarly at 4.164d–f.[54] A much more common technique is to adapt a speech from comedy (without reference to the character of the author) to the requirements of the internal dialogue. Thus in the passage in Book Four just cited, Cratinus is compared with Chaerephon the parasite whose character is illustrated by two quotations from Alexis, the second of which (*Synapothneskontes* fr. 213) describes Chaerephon travelling over the sea to satisfy his appetite. A similar charge against Magnus the Deipnosophist and Archestratus the poet of parody is made in the same section of internal dialogue and was noted above. Similar comic speeches are quoted in the exchange in Book Four to illustrate the hypocrisy of certain philosophers, both Cynics and followers of Pythagoras (4.160e–162b, 163b–c). These comic attacks tend to focus on eating habits and to make general ethical points rather than detailed philosophical argument. They are thus tailor-made for the banter of Athenaeus' speakers.

Comedy's contribution to the material evidence adduced in Athenaeus' surveys of foods and banqueting is substantial. This may be seen not only in regard to prostitutes, but also, for example, in lists of vegetables, meats, parasites, cooks, gluttons, fish, cups, garlands and Athenian meals. At first sight Athenaeus gains two advantages from this exploitation of comedy. The first is the rich evidence comedy has to offer on the social and material world of the Greek city and of Athens in particular. The second is the playful tone that comedy provides, which adds a lightness of touch that is in keeping with, and suitable to, the tone of the internal dialogue.

Of course, comedy is only one of the genres to add both substance and tone to the texture of the *Deipnosophistae*. Others that are particularly important include philosophy, hexameter parody and the historians and anecdotists of the fourth century BC and later, from moralizing historians such as Theopompus to the letters of Lynceus of Samos. All of Athenaeus' sources have, in addition, passed through the filters of Hellenistic and later readings of the text, which are themselves embraced in the *Deipnosophistae*, whether it be Aristarchus on Homer or Semos of Delos on the origins of drama. Many of these genres had been harnessed in earlier forms of sympotic literature that precede the *Deipnosophists*, such as Lucian's *Lexiphanes* and *Symposium* in which philosophy and sympotic themes are put to striking satirical effect (see Romeri 1999).

Our reason for highlighting comedy is this. Comedy, whether Old, Middle or New, had singled out food and eating as its own special preserve. This area of cultural life that was central to the public and private lives of the ancients gained particular emphasis in comedy in its material and social aspects. That emphasis is not to be found in most historical and philosophical texts, even if food is a striking feature therein from time to time, as, for example, in Homeric epic. This centrality of food and the symposium is crucial for Athenaeus in the composition of his work, since the *Deipnosophistae* places food and drink centre-stage in a positive light, yet with an awareness that they can be used to highlight deviant conduct. In this respect the *Deipnosophistae* differs from its predecessors in the philosophical or literary symposium, those of Plato, Plutarch and Lucian. There food provides a distraction from philosophical discourse, as Romeri has convincingly shown (Romeri 1999; cf. Chapter 19). In Athenaeus the tension is recognized and put to comic effect, but they are allowed to co-exist. Similarly, a comic model enabled Athenaeus to concentrate on both food and drink, where other models would not: for example elegy and lyric poetry would have provided much of the sympotic drinking at the expense of eating. Sympotic poetry is extensively cited by Athenaeus, from Archilochus and Xenophanes to Dionysius Chalcus and Callimachus, but it can bear witness only to the drinking part of the institution of the *deipnon*-symposium.

Athenaeus presents the whole institution, both the *deipnon and* the symposium (as Lukinovich 1990 stresses), based largely on literary evidence. He begins with Homer and traces the literature of food from Homer to his own day. This vast survey amounts to a great scholarly task which drew heavily on Hellenistic and later readings of literature and summaries of earlier practices. It is practice which gives the framework, with Books One to Five devoted to preliminaries, the hors d'oeuvre and history of the banquet, while Books Six to Ten contain the banquet (fish and meat courses). In the middle of Book Ten hands are washed once more and the symposium begins, running through to the end of Book Fifteen. Within this framework provided by the structure of the *deipnon*-symposium Athenaeus placed both the details of the meal and drinking session and long quotations of various kinds.

The first, in Book One, is the survey of Homeric dining which appears to owe much to a fourth-century work by Dioscorides the pupil of Isocrates (see Heath 1998). This falls within the Epitome and has a number of gaps. The next is at the beginning of Book Four. This is a description of a Macedonian wedding by Hippolochus of Macedon who exchanged a series of letters with Lynceus of Samos on dazzling meals provided in Athens and Macedon at the end of the fourth century BC and beginning of the third.[55] The next major description is the well-known account of Callixenus of Rhodes on the grand procession put on in Alexandria by Ptolemy II (see Rice 1983). This is placed in Book Five where Athenaeus traces dining once again from Homeric times to Rome and the present, the latter being covered by the Roman host Larensis. Long passages on eating in the next four books, in which the main courses of the Deipnosophists' meal are served, are provided by the boastful cooks of comedy, those long accounts of food-preparation and bragadoccio which all derive from comedy. These describe in a literary form a comic version of the way in which the present meal was prepared (Athenaeus shows no desire to describe scenes in the kitchen of Larensis). As noted above, one of these lists of comic cooks is provided by Larensis' own cook who can tie in these literary extravaganzas with preparation for the actual meal of Larensis.[56] The sympotic books, ten to fifteen, offer much narrative, not least Book Twelve which has almost no internal dialogue and is given up to accounts of luxurious eating.

Athenaeus celebrates all this eating and drinking in an unusual way. As we have noted, food is not presented negatively as a distraction from philosophy as it had been by Athenaeus' distinguished predecessors Plato, Plutarch and Lucian. On the other hand, the traditional tension encourages irony. This is particularly evident in his presentation of the *Life of Luxury* of Archestratus. Athenaeus refers to this work on dozens of occasions, normally with an ironic or censorious introduction. The work was evidently important to Athenaeus, being quoted more often than Plato, his supposed model, but it is kept at an ironic distance. Desirable aspects of Archestratus are his heavy use of fish-names and descriptions of fish, together with comment on dining and sympotic practice; possibly undesirable elements are his choice of title (variations such as 'Gastronomy', 'Dinner-Lore' 'Cookery Book' are noted at 1.4e) and his quasi-comic exhortations to excess, even to crime, in order to secure good produce. Athenaeus makes heavy use of him, but also attacks him and thereby claims a moral superiority as well as a much broader perspective and content.

The comic tone allows for such ironic treatment of other elements—and that tone is continually reinforced by the internal dialogue. Thus it is that Athenaeus is able to include all kinds of comic, materialistic and corporeal detail without slipping into problematic excess. Comedy had much more to say about food, either in comic exchanges or in extended narrative, than to present in the actual form of food. Little eating or preparation of actual food takes place on the comic stage. There is also little eating in the *Deipnosophistae*, where the actual consumption of the food and drink is marginal. This also is frequently highlighted in the internal dialogue that we have reviewed. There is much more delight in the listing and description of garlands or cups or *hetaerae* than in enjoying the real thing. There is no sign of the drunkenness that Plato brings into his *Symposium* when Alcibiades arrives or of the riotous events that mark the symposium in Lucian or Petronius. For all their banter, the diners of the *Deipnosophistae* are a strikingly sober group.

\*    \*    \*    \*

The modern reader may well find the *Deipnosophistae* excessive, unwieldy and difficult to navigate, but it is not without design, structure and restraint, which would doubtless be all the more powerful if the introduction had survived *in extenso*. Impressions of excess derive from Athenaeus' attempts to include everything, as if he were compiling a glossary or encyclopaedia while maintaining a kind of narrative. We have just noted the ironic distance that the dialogue maintains towards the subject-matter, which suggests that the author is well aware of the dangers of reader fatigue in the face of his display of detailed knowledge. One thinks, for example, of the conclusion to Book Eight, where the discussion of fish is brought to a close for fear that the diners themselves become fish. This distancing effect is also achieved by the reading of much of the subject-matter through intermediate ancient scholarship. Thus the Homeric epics are read through Hellenistic filters, many anecdotes are derived from moralizing post-Aristotelian sources, and some comedy and other poetic sources are accessed through glossaries and collections of *topoi* and so on. Thus Archestratus sometimes comes direct, sometimes through a later author such as Chrysippus or Lynceus of Samos. Epicharmus sometimes comes direct, sometimes through Dorion *On Fishes*. To some extent this renders futile the modern discussion on his use of compendia.

All of this gives much scope for scholarly exploration and analysis. The *Deipnosophistae* makes little attempt to imitate the elegant narrative development of a Platonic dialogue; rather, Athenaeus revels in the excesses of the bookstack of a library. Two of our contributors, Christian Jacob and Yun Lee Too, have pursued in detail Athenaeus on books. As we have seen, it is far more important that Book Seven report to us what the Deipnosophists found in books on fish than that they themselves ate any, enjoyed that eating or got any fish bones struck in their throat. Yet, at the same time, it is also important that the reader be reminded that a meal is in progress, hence the hunger of the Cynics and the major interruptions when new courses are brought in.

Probably the most striking of these interruptions is the arrival of the cook in Book Nine. At 376c, a pig is brought in 'one half of which was carefully prepared as a dry roast, while the other was made soft, as if boiled in water'. All were amazed at the cleverness of the cook, who, we discover, is present in the room. The cook proudly shows off his handiwork: the pig has been stuffed with birds, eggs, sauces, slices of sow's womb, minced pieces of meat and pepper. For a moment we appear to find ourselves in a different work, either a narrative of a lavish dinner at a Macedonian court or a pointlessly luxurious dish out of Petronius. The guests do not know what to make of this device any more than does Encolpius at some of the more theatrical creations narrated in the *Satyrica*. However this teasing narrative moment is rapidly distanced, by *pote* (376c)—we do not know the precise moment of the narrative we are enjoying—and by the cook's nod to Ulpian with his apology for using the Latin term *isicia*. The cook is all but a diner. He rapidly proceeds to compare himself with the achievements of the great cooks of Greek comedy, and we are back in the familiar territory of quotation from ancient sources. The diners are humorously addressed at 379c as *'andres dikastai'*, as they are judges of the cook and his pig, but it is difficult not to think of them also as the judges in the comic audience listening to the actor's appeal for a vote as yet another culinary *tour de force* is quoted from the comic stage. Athenaeus' cook refuses to reveal his skills, and conversation returns to Ulpian who raises a characteristic question—where is the term 'pass round' to be found? After this exchange the cook does reveal how he has cooked the pig (381a-b), calling his audience 'talkative banqueters', which seems once again to be a comic quotation similar to *'andres dikastai'* (Aristophanes wrote a play entitled *Banqueters*). The cook even manages to find Ulpian a precedent for the term *exairesis* in the sense of 'entrails'.

The cook is applauded both for his readiness of speech and the outstanding skills of cooking on display. His learning and loquacity are music to the ears of Athenaeus' diners: his predecessors in comedy generally received a negative reception for such displays. This seems to us to be an especially playful interlude on the part of Athenaeus, who is quite capable of leaving his reader bored and in need of light relief. The interlude belongs to the comic repertory and has the lightness of tone that Athenaeus favours.

We have shown in this introduction how Athenaeus attempted to bring to the Rome of his patron Larensis a virtual library which reflected the actual library of Greek texts that Larensis had amassed. Order is imposed on the virtual library by restricting the subject matter to the *deipnon*-symposium, the occasion on which such books were often enjoyed. The guests represent areas of knowledge and expertise that were highly valued in Rome in the second and third centuries AD. They mediate their extensive reading and research to the reader by means of lively banter which draws on the types of discourse most suited to the literary symposium, that is the philosophical symposium and comedy. These two traditions allow the speakers to treat sometimes arcane topics with familiar repartee and to distance themselves ironically from gluttony and excess. Although much of the content of this virtual library concerns the Greek past, the ways in which it is mediated by the host and his guests belong very much to the imperial present.

# SECTION II:
# TEXT, TRANSMISSION AND TRANSLATION

# INTRODUCTORY REMARKS

The history of the text of the *Deipnosophistae* resembles that of many Greek texts. It is no longer possible to trace what happened to the work between the time it was first written on rolls of papyrus around AD 200 and the time it was copied by a Byzantine scribe onto the earliest surviving manuscript (probably between AD 895 and 917). Athenaeus is not often quoted in later antiquity and is unlikely to have existed in many editions on papyrus. Fragmentary versions of papyrus texts of more widely read authors have been found in abundance in Athenaeus' native Egypt, but Athenaeus' work is not among them.[1]

The text of Athenaeus that has come down to us, the Byzantine text, depends on two traditions. By far the more important is contained in a manuscript now in Venice (*Venetus Marcianus* 447); that was written by the important scribe John the Calligrapher. In Chapter 3, Geoffrey Arnott describes the character and history of this manuscript from the time of its writing in the early tenth century to its arrival in Venice (along with several hundred other Greek manuscripts) in 1423. A number of copies of the Venetian manuscript were made. The other tradition of the text of Athenaeus contains the Epitome or summarized version. This part of the tradition remains controversial but most scholars now concur with the opinion favoured by Arnott, namely that the Epitome is for the most part a shorter version of the manuscript of John the Calligrapher. Much of the 'internal dialogue' of Athenaeus' diners (which is discussed in Chapter 2) has been removed, together with many book titles of the authors cited. The Epitome remains valuable for two reasons. Some of the Venetian manuscript is missing, most notably the text of the first two and part of the third books. For these books, the text only survives in the Epitome version. Secondly, the Epitome sometimes carries readings superior to the text of the Venice manuscript. Since it is unlikely that the scribe of the Epitome corrected these errors himself, he had access either to John the Calligrapher's exemplar or to another manuscript. In the overwhelming majority of cases, however, the Venice manuscript (where it survives) has the better text. A number of copies of the Epitome survive. Arnott pursues these matters in detail.

The first printed edition of Athenaeus was published by the Aldine Press in Venice in 1514. This edition depended upon an inferior copy of the Venice manuscript. Arnott surveys the considerable scholarly interest in Athenaeus in the sixteenth century, including in his account the major commentary of Isaac Casaubon. His survey concludes with the valuable French edition of Athenaeus by Jean Schweighaeuser, which built on Casaubon's work and was published at the beginning of the nineteenth century.

Interest in the *Deipnosophistae* was not confined to scholars of ancient Greek in the sixteenth century. In addition to the scholarly concern of editing the text, translations into Latin were made which both contributed to the interpretation of the *Deipnosophistae* and disseminated the work to a wider audience. One of these was made by Natale de' Conti in 1566. This translation was published in editions in Italy, Switzerland and France. Rosemary Bancroft-Marcus examines the contribution of de' Conti. With detailed reference to Book Fourteen (on which, see Chapters 20 and 29), she both explores the concerns that Renaissance scholars had with our author and shows how de' Conti influenced later versions, such as that of Daléchamp (whose translation was later printed by Casaubon beside his commentary) and Schweighaeuser. All subsequent scholarship on Athenaeus, up to the present day, is built on Casaubon and Schweighaeuser.

# ❖ 3 ❖

# ATHENAEUS AND THE EPITOME
## TEXTS, MANUSCRIPTS AND EARLY EDITIONS

### by Geoffrey Arnott

thenaeus hailed from the Greek city of Naucratis, founded in the seventh century BC as a trading-post near the Nile delta, and visited early by Sappho's brother who brought Lesbian wine there and, as Athenaeus himself records (13.596b–c), fell in love with a local *hetaera*. Nevertheless Athenaeus' *Deipnosophistae*[1] is centred in imperial Rome, and its original framework is a Roman banquet (1.1a) that the author sets out to describe in a self-confessed imitation of Plato's *Phaedo* and *Symposium* (ζήλῳ Πλατωνικῷ, 1.1f). The imitation itself may be an artistic failure, but Athenaeus' zeal as a collector of literary excerpts has earned him the gratitude of many Hellenists. Athenaeus had two merits as an excerptor that deserve the acclamation of scholars. When he quoted an excerpt, whether of prose or of verse, he was usually precise and methodical in identifying both author and work. Secondly, he seems to have been careful in copying the words of his quotation as accurately as was possible in his time from the sources that were available to him.[2] Furthermore, his choice of excerpts has opened a window on many areas that but for him would have been totally or largely closed to the modern world. To Athenaeus we owe a high percentage of the known fragments of Middle and non-Menandrean New Comedy, and many priceless literary jewels in both verse and prose—Ibycus' ἦρι μὲν αἵ τε Κυδώνιαι μηλίδες (13.601b–c: 286 Page), some of the best pieces of Anacreon (10.427a–b, 13.599c–d, 12.533f–534b: 356, 358, 388 Page), the longer fragment of Pindar's love poem (13.564e, 601d–e: fr. 123 Snell-Maehler), the anonymous poem of spring—ἦλθ' ἦλθε χελιδών—(8.360c–d: 848 Page), the collection of *scolia* (15.694c–96a: 884–909 Page), Timaeus' vivid account of a drunken frolic in

Agrigentum (2.37b–c: *FGrH* 566 F 149), and Callixenus' account of Ptolemy Philadelphus' great Alexandrian procession (5.196a–206c; *FGrH* 627 F 2), just to cite a few examples. The *Deipnosophistae* is 'a work the loss of which would have wrought incalculable harm to our knowledge of Greek literature', as Gulick justly writes (1927, 1.xv).

And yet it was so very nearly lost, in its original, unepitomized form. One may, I think, reasonably assume that not many copies of the complete *Deipnosophistae* were made by scribes between its original composition around the turn of the second and third centuries AD,[3] and the *codex Marcianus* (A) written mainly by John the Calligrapher almost certainly between 895 and 917,[4] although some types of scribal error in the *Marcianus* (such as the repeated confusion between α and αι: see below) seem to imply that it was not the first manuscript of Athenaeus to be written in minuscule and thus copied from the uncial that minuscule replaced, but rather that it was itself copied from an existing minuscule manuscript. The *Marcianus*, however, is the one surviving ancestor, even in its present imperfect state, of all the manuscripts of an unepitomized Athenaeus, and if it had been lost, we should possess only the much inferior Epitome, which haphazardly omits, abridges and paraphrases quotations, and deliberately leaves out titles.

That an unepitomised Athenaeus by and large still survives is due primarily to the efforts of a Sicilian, more famed today as an unscrupulous intriguer and pedlar of manuscripts at the time of the Renaissance than as a classical scholar. This was Giovanni Aurispa, to whom Francesco Filelfo wrote saying *Totus es in librorum mercatura, sed in lectura mallem*.[5] Aurispa made trips to the Orient in 1405–13 and 1421–3 in order to buy Greek manuscripts and bring them to the relative safety of Italy before the last remnants of the Byzantine empire fell into non-Greek hands. One of the 238 manuscripts that he brought from Constantinople to Venice in December 1423 was the *codex Marcianus* of Athenaeus.[6] Today we shall not blame him for merchandising manuscripts rather than reading them. The *Marcianus* was then acquired by Cardinal Bessarion, and either in 1468 or on his death in 1472 it was deposited in the ducal palace and eventually transferred to its present home, the Libreria Sansoviniana, the library of St Mark's in Venice. Thus it is to Giovanni Aurispa and Cardinal Bessarion, even more than to scholars such as Musurus, Casaubon, Schweighaeuser and Kaibel, that our primary gratitude is owed when we read Athenaeus.

## 1. The codex Marcianus[7]

It is now recognized that this manuscript (A: *Venetus Marcianus* 447) is a mutilated copy of the original work, divided into fifteen books by Athenaeus himself. In the first volume of his Teubner edition of Athenaeus (1887, xxi–xxvii) Kaibel argued against this view, pointing to eleven uncial references in the margins of A to τῶν εἰς λ′ ('the divisions into thirty': 3.96d, 4.128a, 154a, 185a, 5.201b, 6.222a, 7.275b,

7.297c, 8.330c, 9.366a, 10.411a), and suggesting that Athenaeus originally wrote the *Deipnosophistae* in thirty books, which were abridged by a later scholar[8] into the fifteen books of the *Marcianus* version. Kaibel was wrong. A careful study of the *Marcianus* version, as Düring (1936) first noted, shows that although the structure of the work is rather ramshackle, it reveals at the beginning and end of virtually every one of the extant fifteen books an attempt to mark a designed quindecimal division. Thus Timocrates, to whom Athenaeus imagines that he is telling the story of the various dinner discussions at Larensis' house in Rome, is addressed regularly at the beginning (4–6, 8–15) and ending (2–4, 7–8, 11, 15) of books. Often at the end of a book a statement is made about its τέλος (3.127d, 4.185a, 8.365e), the close of a discourse (6.275b, 7.330c, 8.365e, 9.411e, 11.509e, cf. 15.702b), or a dispersal of guests as evening fell (5.222b, 10.459b, 14.644f). None of these features decorates the middle of any of the fifteen books, as one might expect if the work had originally been divided into thirty books. And at two points in the *Marcianus* there are uncial references to the quindecimal division: at the end of Books Ten and Thirteen the scribe writes τέλος Ἀθηναίου Ναυκρατίτου Δειπνοσοφιστῶν *I* and *IE* respectively. It seems clear, as Letrouit has recently suggested, that 'the version in 30' referred to a manuscript (? the one that the scribe was copying) where the fifteen books had been copied onto thirty separate rolls.[9]

The *Marcianus* suffered mutilation before it came into Aurispa's possession, almost certainly while it still remained in Constantinople. This involved the loss of the first two books and of the opening of the third (up to 3.73e in Casaubon's pagination), probably occupying between forty and fifty-five folios of the *Marcianus*, although happily the Epitome manuscripts transcribe in full Athenaeus' original opening of the work (1.1f–2b). There are gaps of a few folios after folio 214 (11.466de) and of one after folio 239 (11.502b), and the final three folios (15.699f–702c) are damaged. The surviving text occupies folios 3 to 372.

Each page has two columns, normally of forty-three lines, and each complete line of text takes fifteen to twenty-six (mainly twenty to twenty-four) letters, although gaps occupying a space of two to three letters are often inserted to mark the end of a quotation, paragraph or section. The handwriting is typical for a *codex vetustissimus* of its period, in the continuous text[10] early minuscule with large upright letters carefully and clearly written; as Kaibel notes (1887, 1. viii), the codex is 'planissima et nitidissima scriptura insignis', though less beautiful in appearance perhaps than the early Greek type used for Ximenes' complutensian polyglot New Testament or Latin italics or Arabic naskhi. It is easy to read, once the letter forms no longer used in printed texts are precisely learned: α with its long raised tail, the five letters based on similar υ shapes (β, κ, μ, ν, υ: u, ɯ, ɯ, ρ, or ɯ, υ), and the ligatures (especially ει, ετ, στ: ꙅ, ꙅ, Ꚍ). Breathings, which are angular, and accents are carefully added, although their placing does not always conform to modern practice (e.g. οὗτος, οὕτω). Their absence is sometimes a useful indication that the scribe is here copying a corrupt and meaningless sequence of letters (e.g. 12.552e = Alexis fr.148: see my commentary (1996) *ad loc.*). Word-division, when attempted, is often clumsy and inaccurate, a frequent source of corruption.

Full stops and raised points are the normal marks of punctuation, but at times the insertion of dicola (:) into quoted passages of dramatic dialogue raises a problem. Are these intended to mark sectional divisions, or are they mechanically copied from earlier manuscripts—whether complete dramatic texts or perhaps more probably collections of excerpts—in which dicola were still used to mark changes of speaker? This latter use has been noted in mediaeval manuscripts of Aristophanes,[11] and there are several passages of dialogue cited from the comic poet Alexis (e.g. frs 15.13, 129.2–20, 140.8, 177.2, 242.4, 249.3–4, with my commentary (1996) *ad loc.*) in the *Marcianus* where dicola may similarly be interpreted. Yet in other dramatic citations a dicolon sometimes marks the end of a section (e.g. Alexis frs 15.4, 47.4, 124.2 mid-sentence!, 222.9, Araros 8.2, 3, Epicharmus 35.8). Citations are often (but not consistently) marked by the sign > affixed in the left-hand margin to each relevant line; verse is always written as if it were prose, with no indication of speakers in passages of dramatic dialogue or of metrical line-ending.

Textual errors in the *Marcianus* are those normal in manuscripts of the period. It may perhaps be useful at this point to describe briefly four types of error that interest me particularly; a fuller account will be found in my forthcoming paper 'On editing fragments' and in my commentary on Alexis (1996, 879, index s.v. Textual Corruption, where the examples do not all derive from Athenaeus, however).

(a) Reference has already been made to faulty word-division in the *Marcianus*. Errors of this kind are more difficult to remove when they are compounded with different types of error. At 7.301d (Archestratus v.158 Lloyd-Jones—Parsons) A writes λαβεῖν οσχετον ἥπατον, where the absence of breathing and accent on οσχετον suggests that the scribe was at a loss; Gesner, Hemsterhuys and Valckenaer (see also section 3(d) below) corrected one ν to the similar μ and redivided: λαβέ, Μόσχε, τὸν ἥπατον. At 9.386a (Alexis fr. 177.3) A has τί λέγεις, δέσποτα· πῶς οὑτοσί; with an unallowable dactyl in the second half of an iambic metron; Dobree and V. Schmidt restored sense and metre by correcting an ω to o and dividing τί λέγεις δέ; ποταπὸς οὑτοσί;

(b) *Simplex ordo* corruption is commonly betrayed in verse texts by its non-metrical results; rarely were scribes also masters of scansion. At 8.341b

(Machon v.72 Gow) ὁρῶν αὐτὸν φερόμενον opens an iambic trimeter with a spondee in the second half of a metron, and Grotius restored scansion by transposing to φερόμενον αὐτόν. At 15.678e (Alexis fr.4.1) a sentence begins and a verse ends in the *Marcianus* with a non-metrical ὁ τρίτος δ᾽ οὗτος ἔχει, where the scribe had moved δ᾽ from its correct position after οὗτος presumably because he was ignorant of a licence that was available to writers of Middle and New Comedy to postpone particles such as δέ and γάρ to a later position in the sentence. The correction was made by Meineke.

(c) Occasionally a scribe inserts into the text his own reactions to what he is copying. This rarely causes serious textual difficulty, but it comes as an amusing reminder that scribes were human. Thus at 7.302f (Alexis fr. 159.3) A corrupts σηπίδια to σικχηπίδια (a *vox nihili*, not scanning) just because the context describes a fastidious (σικχός) buyer of σηπίδια.[12] Similarly at 6.226e (Antiphanes fr. 157.8) A corrupts τοὺς μητραγυρτοῦντας (priest of Cybele begging) to a nonsensical τοὺς μητραρπατωντασγυργοῦντας, because he was inserting his feeling that these priests were either cheats (ἀπατῶντας) or robbers (ἁρπα-) or both.[13]

(d) John the Calligrapher was a careful scribe, but perhaps without pretensions to scholarship. When at 6.224e (Amphis fr.30.12–13) we find a passage describing how a fishmonger cut off his initial syllables (συλλαβὴν ἀφελών ) and said τάρων βολῶν and κτὼ βολῶν, the scribe writes out τεττάρων, ὀκτὼ and (on one occasion) ὀβολῶν in full, affording an opportunity to Musurus, Kock and Schweighaeuser to restore what the fishmonger actually said.

Not all the errors in Athenaeus, however, are to be blamed on the *Marcianus* scribe. There seem also to be occasions when the fault lay already in the source that Athenaeus himself was using. At 9.385f and 12.516d, for example, Athenaeus appears to be making two sizable quotations from a single scene of Alexis' *Pannychis* (frs. 177, 178 Kassel–Austin). Both fragments contain lacunae (177.11, 178.3, 9, 17–18) which are most satisfactorily explained by the assumption that those lacunae already existed in Athenaeus' source manuscript.

The *Marcianus* is a unique source for the unepitomized Athenaeus. Several other manuscripts survive with this version, but all of them can be shown to be copies (or copies of copies) of the *Marcianus*, of no independent value and useful only insofar as they contain Renaissance conjectures.[14] No full list has been made of the apographs; the following manuscripts are known to me:

Ambr. = Ambrosianus 504 (Books 3–9) and 261 (Books 10–15), end of fifteenth century; Biblioteca Ambrosiana, Milan.

B = Laurentianus LX.1, written by Demetrios Damilas probably between 1476 and 1506, and supplementing (like D and P) the portions missing at the opening of the Marcianus with the corresponding portions of the Epitome; Biblioteca Laurenziana, Florence. Bandini 1768, 2.583; Dindorf 1827, 1.v; Kaibel 1887 1.xiii; Aldick 1928, 2; Desrousseaux 1956, xxxix; Hemmerdinger 1989, 117.

D = Parisinus gr. 3056 (Books 1–9 only, supplemented from the Epitome manuscripts in 1–3, like B and P), copied partly by Ermolao Barbaro in 1482; Bibliothèque Nationale, Paris. Schweighaeuser 1801, 1. lxxxv and lxxvii–viii note q; Dindorf 1827, 1. vi–vii; Sabbadini *Scoperte*, 66 n. 138, Omont 1888, 3.101; 1909, 2; Aldick 1928, 2.

Holkham = Holkham gr. 104 (formerly Holkham ms. 284), sixteenth century; now Bodleian Library, Oxford. Irigoin 1967, 424 n. 1.

M = Casaubon's Huraldinus manuscript, now BM Bibl. Regia 16.C.XXIV, sixteenth century; British Museum, London. Schweighaeuser 1801, 1. lx, Dindorf 1827, 1. vi and viii (with n.), Thompson 1889, 445; Warner–Gilson 1921, 2. 186–7; Arnott 1964, 269–70.

P = Palatinus Heidelbergensis gr. 47, written by Paolo de Canale in 1505–6, supplementing (like B and D) the portions missing at the opening of the Marcianus with the corresponding portions of the Epitome; formerly in the Vatican, then taken to Paris, now Heidelberg University Library. Dindorf 1827, 1. v–vi; Kaibel 1887, 1. xiii, Stevenson 1885, 24–5.

Q = Parisinus gr. 1833, formerly Colbertianus 1236 (Books 3–9 only), sixteenth century; Bibliothèque Nationale, Paris. Dindorf 1827, 1. vii; Omont 1888, 2. 150.

To these we need to add several manuscripts now destroyed or lost; three in particular:

(1) The copy used by Musurus for the first printed edition of Athenaeus, destroyed presumably during the printing, apart perhaps from six folios now in the University Library of Leiden (*miscellaneus codex* 32).[15]

(2) The *codex Farnesianus*, a manuscript praised by Casaubon as (*exemplum*) *longe … et emendatius et integrius* than other manuscripts of the complete Athenaeus known to him; he relied on reports of its readings made around the middle of the sixteenth century by H. Stephanus (his father-in-law) and Benedetto Egio of Spoleto. The library of Cardinal Alessandro Farnese remained in his family at Parma until 1734, when it was transferred to Naples; the Athenaeus codex no longer forms part of that library, and must be presumed destroyed.

(3) A manuscript originally in the Vatican library, mentioned in the inventory of

Pope Sixtus IV (1475) and subsequent inventories up to 1518, was probably destroyed in the sack of Rome in 1527.[16]

On some occasion in the tenth or eleventh century, after the *Marcianus* was written and before it was mutilated, an Epitome of *Deipnosophistae* was made, probably at Constantinople. Today it survives complete in four copies, and so provides a valuable but inferior substitute for the full version in those places where the *Marcianus* today is incomplete or damaged. The practice of the compiler was haphazardly to omit some of the original citations and to abridge, rearrange and paraphrase some of the citations that he retained, while removing virtually all the titles of the works that were cited; this is one of the reasons why the number of *incertarum fabularum fragmenta* is so large in the editions of dramatic fragments. The four known copies are:

## 2. The Epitome

C = *Parisinus suppl. gr.* 841, copied by Demetrios Damilas probably between 1476 and 1506; Bibliothèque Nationale, Paris. Schweighaeuser 1801; 1. lxxxv–lxxxviii; Dindorf 1827, 1. vii; Kaibel 1887, 1. xiv-xvi; Omont 1888, 3. 316 (where the contents are wrongly identified as *excerpta*); Peppink 1937, 1. xxi–xxxii; Desrousseaux 1956, xxxix; Canart 1977–9, 281–347; Hemmerdinger 1989. 117.

E = *Laurentianus* LX.2, copied by Jacob Questenberg around 1490 in Rome from a lost Vatican manuscript in Rome; Biblioteca Laurenziana, Florence. Dindorf 1827, 1. vii; Kaibel 1887, 1. xiv-xvi; Aldick 1928, 15–60; Peppink 1937, 1. xxi-xxxii; Desrousseaux 1956, xxxix; Canart 1977–9, 281–347.

Hoeschel = BM *Bibl. Regia* 16.D.X, the manuscript loaned by David Hoeschel to Casaubon but never returned (with the opening pages up to 3.82f lost), written by Michael Damaskenos (*fl.* 1525); British Museum, London. Bentley 1883, 177 = 1699, 130–1, Schweighaeuser 1801, 1. lxvi, lxxxiv; Dindorf 1827, 1. xi; Thompson 1889, 445; Warner-Gilson 1921, 2.190; Arnott 1964, 269–70; Hemmerdinger 1989, 117.

R = *Erbacensis* 4, copied by J. A. Questenberg probably from E shortly after 1490; Erbachisches Gesamtarchiv, Schloss Erbach (Odenwald). Aldick 1928, 4–14.

At least one other manuscript is known to have existed; it belonged at the end of the sixteenth century to Ioannes Levinius of Antwerp, and a few of its readings were reported by Casaubon. C and E are closely related, copied either from the same codex or from twins deriving from the one codex.[17] The Hoeschel manuscript has never been fully collated.

The textual relationship between the *Marcianus* and the Epitome has long been

## 3. The relationship between Marcianus and Epitome

controversial.[18] Cobet[19] was to my knowledge the first scholar (i) to produce an objective argument in support of the theory that the Epitome was originally compiled by a Byzantine scholar using only an undamaged *Marcianus* as his source, and (ii) on this basis to conclude that none of the Epitome manuscripts is an independent witness when their readings differ from those in the *Marcianus*. Cobet's case (a, below) has since been strengthened by three further and at first sight equally convincing arguments (b–d: below).

(a) Cobet himself noted that at 7.283a the *Marcianus* (folio 205ʳ) writes Παγκράτης δ᾽ ὁ Ἀρκάς at the beginning of a new sentence, after citing two passages from Nicander (fr. 16 Schneider, Gow) and Alexander Aetolus (fr. 2 p.122 Powell); in the *Marcianus* παγ comes at the end of line 12, κράτης at the beginning of line 13 of the first column. The Epitome manuscripts omit the fragments of Nicander and Alexander, and then proceed to write Κράτης δ᾽ ὁ Ἀρκάς. Cobet plausibly explained this error as resulting from the Epitomist's failure to note the παγ at the end of the previous line in the *Marcianus* when compiling his abridged version.[20]

(b) Maas[21] pointed out that at 13.525e the Epitome incorporates a scholion into its text: ἐν δὲ τῷ σχολίῳ τοῦ βιβλίου ὅθεν αἱ παρεκβολαὶ τάδε ἦσαν περὶ τοῦ ἄνω γεγραμμένου ῥόμβου (sc. at 525c in the citation from Democritus of Ephesus, *FGrH* 267 F 1) · ὁ ῥόμβος ἐστὶ τροχίσκος, ὃν τύπτοντες ἱμᾶσι καὶ στρέφοντες ποιοῦσι περιδινεῖσθαι καὶ ψόφον ἀποτελεῖν. ῥύμβον δὲ αὐτὸν Εὔπολις εἶπε (cf. fr. 83 Kassel–Austin) · καλεῖται δὲ καὶ βρυτήρ. This scholion occurs word for word in the *Marcianus* at 525c (folio 256ᵛ, above the second column), written in a different hand that may be dated between AD 990 and 1030. Maas believed that this clearly identified the Epitomist's source as the *Marcianus* itself, but one cannot exclude at least a possibility that the *Marcianus* was not the only early manuscript of Athenaeus to include the scholion at this point.

(c) More recently Letrouit has added two further pieces of evidence linking the *Marcianus* and the Epitome. One is that the passage 5.177a–182b in the *Marcianus* (folios 53ᵛ.2.25–56ʳ.1.41) is misplaced (it should come in 187b), and the same misplacement is repeated in the Epitome.[22]

(d) Letrouit also calls attention to a large number of errors in the Epitome manuscripts which are best explained as wild attempts to mend corruptions in the *Marcianus*.[23] Three examples will suffice here in illustration:

> 5.219a τῶν ἐν Βάκτροις καμήλων (Boissonade): τῶν ἐν βακτροις καὶ μήδων (faulty word-division: see above; confusion of Δ and Λ in uncial) A, τῶν ἐν βακτροις καὶ μήδοις CE.[24]

7.301d λαβέ (Gesner), Μόσχε, τὸν ἤπατον (Hemsterhuys, Valckenaer: see also section 1(a) above): λαβεῖν οσχετον ἤπατον (faulty word-division, confusion of μ and ν) A, λαβεῖν τὸν ἤπατον CE.

13.563d ὅστις αὐτῆς τῆς ἀκμῆς (Jacobs): ὅστις αὖ τῆς ἀκμῆς (faulty word-division, haplography) A, ὅστις αὖθις ἀκμῆς CE.

The combined weight of this evidence seems overwhelming, and Cobet's claim has accordingly convinced many scholars. Yet it faces one serious difficulty. If the *Marcianus* was the Epitomist's only exemplar, all the many readings where the Epitome is correct and the *Marcianus* corrupt, or where the Epitome provides a text significantly different from and superior to the *Marcianus*, must necessarily be interpreted as the products of Byzantine conjecture. Of course it is true that many corrections of the *Marcianus* in the Epitome manuscripts are easy and straight-forward, requiring only a basic competence in classical Greek and elementary metrics such as would have been available to Byzantine scholars, even if such corrections are no more common than occasions where attempts to heal corruption in the *Marcianus* have made the infection a good deal worse; some of these are instanced above, and Letrouit's paper includes many more.

Even so, there is still a sizable residue of passages where the Epitome's corrections seem superior to those achieved elsewhere by Byzantine scholarship, and thus are better interpreted as copied from one or more earlier manuscripts of Athenaeus totally independent from the *Marcianus*. For instance, at 3.107b–d (citing Alexis fr. 115.6–20 Kassel–Austin: see my commentary) the Epitome manuscripts are right six times where the *Marcianus* is wrong:

v. 7 of the fragment: ταῦτ᾽ οὐδὲ ἓν CE, ταὐτοῦ δὲ εν A.

10 δεῖ CE. δὴ A

14 αὐτὸ CE, αὐτὸν A.

17 πελιδνὸν ὂν CE, πελιδνὸν A.

19 νὴ Δί᾽ ἀλλ᾽ ἐγὼ CE, νὴ δία λέγω A.

19 σοφῶς CE, σαφῶς A.

Judgments based on such a passage may partly be subjective and controversial, but would Byzantine scholars have had Casaubon's flair at correcting inaccurate word-division, and would they have troubled to alter an acceptable, scanning σαφῶς here to a superior σοφῶς? There are other passages, moreover, where a correction in the Epitome manuscripts far transcends what even the best Byzantine scholar could be expected to achieve. At 8.349e (citing Machon 156 Gow) the proper name Νικοθέοντος (A) is corrected by the Epitome to Νικοκρέοντος in an anecdote where this and one other name have caused difficulties (see Gow's commentary *ad loc.*). The *Marcianus* here writes a name not found elsewhere, but not impossibly formed (Hemitheon does exist); but Nicocreon was a king in Cyprian Salamis who came to the throne in 332 BC. Would a Byzantine scholar have been aware here that Νικοθέοντος was a mistake or have known about Nicocreon?[25]

Clearly the arguments about the sole dependency of the Epitome from the *Marcianus* merit the memorable comment of the English boxer Henry Cooper: there are pros and cons for, and pros and cons against. It may accordingly be wisest to assume that the Epitome is not derived from the *Marcianus* alone, but used at least one other manuscript that was not plagued with those errors characteristic of the *Marcianus*.

## 4. Earlier editions

### (a) Editio princeps: Marcus Musurus, Aldine Press, Venice 1514[26]

Aldus Manutius considered publishing the first edition as early as 1499 or 1500, but at that time he progressed no further than printing one trial sheet of the first page of the Epitome text.[27] Musurus, who had already supervised the first Greek editions of Aristophanes (nine plays, excluding *Thesmophoriazusae, Lysistrata*, 1498) and Plato (1513) for Aldus, then produced in one *annus mirabilis* (1514) three further firsts: the lexicon of Hesychius, Athenaeus (both in the same month of August), and Alexander of Aphrodisias' commentary on Aristotle's *Topics*. There is, however, one major unsolved problem regarding Musurus' Athenaeus. Musurus had been Professor of Greek at the University of Venice since 1512, and in 1515 was asked by the Venetian Senate to be curator of the Bessarion collection of Greek manuscripts; yet his Athenaeus was printed from a corrupt apograph of the *Marcianus* (see section 1 above), which in all probability had prefixed to it (like B, D and P) those portions of the Epitome that preceded the opening page of the *Marcianus*.

But why did Musurus not use the *Marcianus* itself? One reason may well have been the general inaccessibility of the Bessarion manuscripts for half a century or more after their donor's death, hidden away in boxes behind a wooden partition in the ducal palace.[28] An alternative answer, which can be inferred from fifteenth-century records, is likely to win the sympathy of all who have suffered in modern libraries at the hands of careless cataloguers. When Aurispa brought the *Marcianus* to Venice, it had already lost its opening folios, but its colophon was and still is clearly legible: Ἀθηναίου Ναυκρατί / του Δειπνοσοθιστῶν· ιε: Aurispa here misread Ναυκρατίτου as the author's name and Ἀθηναίου as his city of origin. This is revealed in a letter that Aurispa wrote in 1424 to Ambrogio Traversari,[29] referring to 'Naucratici cujusdam Atheniensis volumen quoddam maximum'. When the *Marcianus* passed into the hands of Bessarion, this misidentification continued. A contemporary hand scribbled onto a new folio placed before the *Marcianus'* opening page Ἀθηναίου ναυκρατίτου δειπνοσοφιστῶν βιβλ(ία) λ'. . . ναυκρατίτης περὶ δείπνων. . . κτῆμα Βησσαρίωνος and when Bessarion donated the manuscript to Venice in 1468 the accompanying inventory listed the *Marcianus* as item 301, 'item Naucrates de coenis libri octo ex triginta, in pergameno'.[30] When this series of errors is added to the general inaccessibility of the Bessarion manuscripts, it is hardly surprising that Musurus failed to identify and use the *Marcianus* for his edition. Musurus' combination of extensive learning and sharp judgement made him undoubtedly the finest scholar of the Greek language in his time.[31] The claim made by him in his preface that although his apograph had unhealable wounds, he had corrected πολλὰς μυριάδας σφαλμάτων was endorsed by Aldus himself in his dedicatory preface. It is a justifiable claim, but there is a darker side to it. Despite the felicity of many of his conjectures, Musurus pardonably left a great number of corrupt passages untouched, less pardonably applied the wrong medicine to others, and made wilful interpolations to hide textual gaps.

In the sixteenth century the Alps were a severe barrier to the transmission of scholarship,[33] and Musurus' edition of Athenaeus was little known outside Italy. Bedrotus and Herlinus were two young Germans whose main aim it was to make a printed edition of Athenaeus available throughout Europe. They consulted no manuscripts, based their text on that of Musurus, but introduced many conjectures that sometimes healed corruptions in the Aldine text, sometimes made the condition of an unhealthy passage still worse.

*(b) Jacobus Bedrotus and Christianus Herlinus, published by Johannes Valderus, Basel 1535[32]*

    Between the editions of Bedrotus and Casaubon attempts to improve the text of Athenaeus and the authors he cited were made by a great number of scholars, among whom Brodaeus, the two Canter brothers,[34] Leopardus, G. Morel, Muretus, Aegius Spoletinus, H. Stephanus (Casaubon's father-in-law) and Turnebus stand out. There were also two influential translations of Athenaeus into Latin, by Natale de' Conti (Natalis de Contibus: Arivaben, Venice; Petri, Basel; also Lyon and Paris: all 1556) and the physician J. Daléchamp (Dalecampius: de Harsy, Lyon 1583),[35] the latter adding important discussions on passages of the text (*Annotationes ad Athenaeum*) which were first printed in the second edition of Casaubon's *Animadversiones* (1621); both translations, but more often Daléchamp's, imply conjectures that correct or at least improve the text of corrupt passages.

Casaubon's edition was first printed by Hieronymus Commelinus, (either Heidelberg or Geneva 1597–8[1])[36] then by Mme A. de Harsy (Lyon 1612[2]) and Huguetan-Rivaud (Lyon 1657[3]); also *Animadversiones in Athen. Deipnosophistas*, virtually a commentary, was published by de Harsy (Lyon 1600[1]), Mme de Harsy-Rivaud (Lyon 1621[2]), and Huguetan-Rivaud (Lyon 1664[3]).[37] In compiling his text, which is printed side by side with Daléchamp's Latin translation, Casaubon used the Basel edition (he had no access to the Aldine) and several manuscripts: B, M and the lost *codex Farnesianus* of the complete Athenaeus, along with the Hoeschel

*(c) Isaac Casaubon*

manuscript of the Epitome. He started work on his edition and *Animadversiones* in 1590, and often complained about the immensity and difficulty of the task; a note that he entered into his diary on 8 April 1598 will be echoed by many scholars today: 'nam finem quando videbo tam molesti laboris?' The results, however, still earn deserved praise from all scholars who consult this volume. Although Casaubon did not know the *Marcianus*, his text is far superior to that of his predecessors; many of his conjectures are palmary, and it is a pity that some of his best suggestions are relegated to his *Animadversiones*, which display remarkable and often recondite learning, fine judgement and a subtle knowledge of Greek.[38] When he undertook his edition of Athenaeus, he said in a letter to Dirk Canter[39] that 'hydram illam μυριοκέφαλον quae eum deturpavit, velim expugnare'; his wish was achieved.[40]

*(d) Jean (or Johann)[41] Schweighaeuser, Societas Bipontina, Strasbourg 1801–1807*

It is a massive edition, in fourteen volumes (five of text and Latin translation, with a long introduction in the first; eight of *Animadversiones*, a full-scale commentary; a final index volume). The introduction gives an excellent account of the manuscripts then available and a balanced critique of previous editions and translations. The text is for the first time based on the *Marcianus*, whose readings were reported to Schweighaeuser by his son Geoffroi after its theft and transfer to Paris in the Napoleonic period, while the Paris manuscript (C) is used for the Epitome. His study of the *Marcianus* led him to realize that it was the source of all the other known manuscripts of the complete Athenaeus. Schweighaeuser's commentary covers over 4,800 pages; its size is due partly to the vast range of subjects requiring consideration, partly to his full quotation of earlier discussions (particularly those of Casaubon), and partly to Schweighaeuser's own discursive style. Yet it is always a delight to read; Schweighaeuser wrote well, reported his manuscripts accurately, commanded all the relevant previous scholarship, and did not lack critical sense.[42] Some of his comments, which today might be considered inappropriate in a work of this kind, are moving as well as delightful. I well remember my own reaction when many years ago I first came across the following lines in *Animadversiones* 4.686, inserted directly after a note about a correction made by a fellow Alsatian, who was a friend and colleague at the University of Strasbourg,[43] at Athenaeus 8.365b (citing Aristophanes fr. 161 Kassel-Austin):

> Sed BRUNCKIUM, toties mihi laudatum, totiesque deinceps laudandum, BRUNCKIUM, olim ac modo etiam adhuc nostrum, nunc nominare qui possim, quin, Fuisse in his terris, fuisse nobiscum, fuisse eheu! Brunckium, imo de pectore ingemiscam!.—Posthac nonnisi Musarum in monumentis a se conditis, & in memoria hominum, Musis amicorum, vivet perennabitque praestantissimi Viri ingenium: mortales exuvias hoc ipso quo haec scribimus die alma tellus recepit.

# A DAINTY DISH TO SET BEFORE A KING

## NATALE DE' CONTI'S TRANSLATION OF ATHENAEUS' *DEIPNOSOPHISTAE*

### by Rosemary Bancroft-Marcus

Natale de' Conti's Latin translation of the *Deipnosophistae* or 'Dinner-Scholars' enjoys the distinction of being the first complete translation of Athenaeus. De' Conti[1] converted it from the original Greek into Latin, the universal language of Renaissance scholarship; versions in local vernaculars would come later. The book, entitled *Athenaei Deipnosophistarum sive Coenae sapientium Libri XV*, burst upon the world in 1556 with simultaneous printings in Venice, Basel, Paris, and Lyons.[2] In a preliminary encomium, the translator is hailed as a 'prince among men' and 'equal of the gods' for his achievement in 'leading Athenaeus from Athens to Rome', thereby making available to a grateful public 'tables laden with various feasts', a veritable cornucopia (Ἀμαλθείας κέρας) of delights. The culinary references are of course metaphorical, though inspired by part of the subject-matter. The *Deipnosophistae* was taken seriously by Renaissance readers, particularly members of literary cliques, dining-clubs, and Academies, as an important compendium of encyclopaedic information on a wide range of subjects, ranging from curious details of ancient lives and customs to serious anecdotes with significance for the modern age.

De' Conti could hardly have chosen a more influential sponsor for his translation of Athenaeus than Ferdinand, younger brother of the Holy Roman Emperor Charles V. In the dedication he styles him king of the Romans as well as of Pannonia and Bohemia; for though Ferdinand was not officially crowned Holy Roman Emperor until two years later, he had already assumed control of his ailing brother's empire. Flattery apart, de' Conti may have sincerely admired the achievements of a monarch who was distinguishing himself as a mediator and peacemaker in tricky political and religious disputes. Ferdinand was active in the negotiations which led to the Treaty of Passau (1552) and the Peace of Augsburg (1555), and maintained to the end of his life the hope that the reconvened Council of Trent might achieve union of all the Christian churches.

De' Conti singles out for special mention in the Dedication the sponsorship by Ferdinand of the first printed Syriac text of the Old and New Testaments, evidently for use by the Syrian Orthodox Church. This is a significant inclusion, for it associates de' Conti with promotion of the cause of ecumenical union. Many politicians and thinkers of the period were deeply troubled about current religious divisions, both as demoralizing to the faithful and as weakening the defences of all Christendom against the expanding Ottoman Empire.

Scholarship, religion and politics seem unlikely associates in our own age; but throughout the Renaissance period, the impetus to publish and translate ancient Greek works was closely connected with western outrage at the conquest of Byzantium in 1453. Shockwaves from this catastrophe, reinforced by the eloquence of scholarly Byzantine refugees, were still agitating intellectual circles up to a century and a half later. Some dreamers hoped for a new pan-Christian and pan-European Crusade which would recover not only Byzantium but also Athens and Jerusalem, thereby definitively clipping the Sultan's wings. Other more pragmatic Roman Catholic politicians undertook diplomatic efforts to educate and improve relations with the Orthodox believers of those eastern, Slavic, and Hellenic regions which were subject to or menaced by the expanding Ottoman Empire. Part of their motivation was a desire to persuade Greek Orthodox priests to accept the reforms proposed by the Council of Trent; a more ambitious goal was to convince the Orthodox to accept the primacy of the Pope and 'return' to Roman Catholicism (the slogan from Dante onwards was 'one shepherd, one sheepfold'). Politics and religion were thus part of the impetus behind the Renaissance activity of publishing and translating ancient Greek works, though pure intellectual curiosity also played a role. The greater accessibility of Greek works drew the attention of Western Europeans to the plight of contemporary Greeks in Ottoman-dominated territories, alerting them to the need for a concerted and generous effort to enlighten and liberate them; and Greeks themselves were made conscious of their glorious past, recovering (or acquiring) a sense of patriotic nationhood which might make them less acquiescent to Ottoman rule.

One facet of this Renaissance philhellenism is the interest taken in Greek scholarship by high-ranking Italian ecclesiastics, especially the Roman cardinals, who wanted to be able to read the Septuagint, New Testament and the Greek Fathers in the original. A few cardinals had princely wealth which they used to patronize artists and writers and to fill their palaces and villas with collections of antiquities, works of art, and Greek manuscripts. Some ecclesiastical bibliophiles employed native Greek speakers trained in classical scholarship to supplement their own linguistic deficiencies and to find, copy, and catalogue manuscripts for them. There is clear evidence, to be presented below, that this was the particular cultural environment within which Athenaeus was being studied in the first half of the sixteenth century, and for which Natale de' Conti produced his translation of the *Deipnosophistae*.

Very little is known about de' Conti; his bibliography is effectively his only biography. He was a prolific and (in his time) widely read Italian writer of scholarly compilations and translations. His name is found in several Latin variants: Natalis or Hieronymus for his Christian name, indicating a birthdate of December 25; Comes, Comitum or de Comitibus ('Count' or 'of the Counts') for his surname. The vernacular form Natale de' (='dei') Conti is an acceptable compromise, though the 1589 Italian translation of his *Histories* gives it as Natale Conti, and De Montlyard's French translation (1627) of his *Mythology* names him as Noel Le Comte. In the Graeco-Latin edition of his early poem *On the Hours*, his name appears in Greek form on the titlepage as Νατάλιος τῶν Κομίτων and in Latin form as Natalis Comitum.

He was born about 1520 in Milan, probably a member of a Venetian family which returned to Venice when he was a small child, and usually refers to himself as 'Venetus' in his compositions. Many years of his adult life were spent in Venice, and some of his work was published by the Aldine Press.

In one case, in the title-page of his account (1566) of the Siege of Malta,[3] the epithet 'Alexandrinus' replaces 'Venetus'. This is unlikely to be evidence of origin in the Egyptian city of Alexandria, but might possibly indicate a connection with the Italian town called Alessandria (della Paglia), not very far from Milan and partly founded by the Milanese. The most probable explanation is that de' Conti was identifying himself with the Hellenistic authors of Alexandria (cf. the epithet of Athenaeus, Ναυκρατίτης, 'of Naucratis' in Egypt).

Another place with which de' Conti is associated is the university city of Padua. An early Milanese biographer states that he was a 'professor of letters' in that city, but this has not been verified by any documentary evidence. Since he was certainly in contact with Paduan lawyers, classical scholars, and 'Riformatori dello Studio' (University regulatory authorities), it is not inconceivable that in his earlier years he studied or taught there on an informal basis. Some of his last years were spent in Ravenna; he died, probably in Venice or possibly in Milan, around 1582.

Before tackling his Athenaeus translation, Natale de' Conti had made himself into a competent poet in classical Greek and Latin, and a workmanlike translator. He produced the first Latin version of the works of several minor Greek rhetoricians. Among his juvenile original compositions are a poem *On the Hours* in

Greek and Latin, and some Latin love-elegies and a didactic poem on hunting. He translated into Latin Enea Vico's work[4] on coin portraits of Roman empresses, and may also have worked on its sequel, a collection of portraits of Roman emperors.

De' Conti's important study of mythology (in Latin), *Ten Books of Mythology, or Explanations of Fables* (Venice, 1567), was his next major work after Athenaeus, though he may have begun it around the time of that work's publication. It complemented and extended Giovanni Boccaccio's *Genealogies of the Gods* (1473) and Lilio Gregorio Giraldi's *On the Gentile Gods* (1548), and claimed to serve the needs of classicists, theologians and philosophers. De' Conti managed to find another royal patron for his *Mythology* in Charles IX of France (which was at that time undergoing serious public disturbances), whom he blandishes with several allusions to the respect owed to princes. He also attempts to conciliate those ecclesiastical purists (the Sorbonne?) who considered ancient myth as debauched pagan religion, by declaring his dislike of prurient stories about amorous or monstrous transformations and of far-fetched alchemical interpretations. His own approach, however, was hardly free from fanciful allegorization; he treats ancient Greek myth as parables, stories concealing and revealing moral precepts and truths from which Christians have much to learn. He was perhaps the first to draw attention to myth as a repository of traditional lore about nature and speculation about the stars and planets. Probably because of its moralizing content, de' Conti's study of mythology was the standard school text and reference work for at least two centuries.

In later life, de' Conti took to writing accounts of current affairs. One of his more stirring topics was the successfully resisted Ottoman attack on Malta in 1565; it must be observed, however, that his account of this owes much to an earlier published account attributed to Pierre Gentil de Vendôme or Marino Fracasso, even beginning with the same image of a storm at sea.

He achieved considerable popular success with the *Histories of his Time* (published in Venice 1572, often reprinted; revised and greatly augmented in 1581; and translated into the Italian vernacular). The impartiality of this interesting narrative is marred by the care he consciously took to avoid arousing the ire of public figures by criticism that was too overt.[5]

In Book XXI of the *Histories*, de' Conti gives a moving account of the Ottoman invasion of Cyprus (1569–71) and its attendant atrocities, beginning with an almost lyrical description of the island's beauties. Perhaps he had some special connection or fascination with Cyprus. The author of de' Conti's biography in the *Dizionario Biografico* suggests that his unusually detailed knowledge of behind the scenes events might be evidence of friendship with the Venetian bailo in Constantinople, Marcantonio Barbaro (1518–95).[6] De' Conti praises Barbaro's clever contrivances, even after he was imprisoned, to keep Venice informed on the progress of the war, and the discretion and secrecy with which he afterwards conducted negotiations towards an eventual peace treaty. De' Conti and Barbaro certainly shared an interest in the recording of current affairs, though the latter's *Diario* (beginning at 1537) was never published. Perhaps de' Conti had used some of Barbaro's material in his *Histories*, which began at 1545. Marcantonio Barbaro, a Venetian with a degree from the University of Padua, was a skilled diplomat, performing missions in England, France, and Constantinople. He is now best known as co-owner with his brother Daniele (editor of Vitruvius) of the Villa Maser, whose construction and decoration he supervised, and as an important patron of architects and artists.

De' Conti's multifarious interests mark him out as one of those late Renaissance humanists working to interpret ancient Greek works of which an 'established text' had already been printed. Such primordial editions were often little more than a clean copy of a single manuscript witness, either the one most accessible to the editor, or the one he found most legible.

Sometimes these printed copies were enriched (or contaminated) by glancing reference to other readings, but all too often information on the precise source of the text and variants is withheld. The printed edition was useful in providing scholars with a basic text to argue over; the margins and blank spaces of copies were often used for writing in notes, objections, emendations and variants, some of which might ultimately contribute to a new critical edition.

Once a Greek text had been printed, translation into Latin was the next step; vernacular translations rarely appeared until this preliminary work had been done, partly because Renaissance authors who chose to write in Italian or French often did so because their knowledge of Greek and Latin was for some reason substandard. A Latin translation made Greek texts accessible to a broad international intelligentsia; non-specialists used it either to acquaint themselves with the content, or as a crib, along with the Greek text, to improve their comprehension of the original. This is the market that Natale de' Conti's rendering of Athenaeus aimed to serve.

De' Conti's initial task was to establish a Greek text. In the Dedication he claims to have produced this by consulting several unspecified Greek manuscripts, where he found variants new to the extant printed editions, meaning that of Marcus Musurus (Venice, Aldus, 1514), and possibly that of J. Bedrotus and Christianus Herlinus (Basel, 1535), though de' Conti may not have had access to the latter (see Arnott, p. 51). Both are full of abbreviations, and are hard to read by modern, if not contemporary, standards. A likely surmise is that he used the Aldine edition as his basic text, perhaps writing variants into the margins as was then the custom; some of these he has transferred into the margins of his translation. He does not claim to have based his translation on any single copy, printed or unprinted. We do not know where he found his manuscript exemplars, but Rome and Venice are likely places, whether in private libraries, the Vatican, or the Biblioteca Marciana. He assures King Ferdinand, in language typical of the Renaissance textual critic, that the Greek text behind his translation has been polished and purified of many obscurities caused by the long passage of time.

The pioneering Latin translation of Natale de' Conti not only made Athenaeus' delightful and erudite work, already the object of scholarly curiosity, accessible to the Greekless general reader, but also supplied a useful benchmark to scholarly editors pondering on Greek semantics. This was the first time anyone had committed himself in print to a particular interpretation. The act of translating forces the translator to choose among the available variants in the textual tradition, and only then to render his selections in the target language. De' Conti's rendering thus opened debate both on the Greek text and the proper understanding of its component words. He divides the work into appetizing chunks with headings, deliberately presenting it in the form of a collection of essays on an assortment of topics such as those of Plutarch or the dialogues of Lucian, which Renaissance readers greatly enjoyed.

The translation of Athenaeus was Natale de' Conti's first major publication. The title-page of the 1556 edition reads roughly as follows:

> A T H E N A E I / DIPNOSOPHISTARUM / sive Coenae sapientium / Libri XV. / NATALE DE COMITIBVS VENETO NVNC / primum e Graeca in Latinam linguam vertente / COMPLVRIBVS EX MANVSCRIPTIS ANTIQVIS- / simis exemplaribus additis: quae in Graece hactenus impressis / voluminibus non reperiebantur. / Ad potentissimum Ferdinandum, Pannoniae, / Boemiae, ac Romanorum Regem. / Cum privilegio summi Pontificis Pauli .IIII. & Illustriss. / Senatus Veneti in annos XX. / [Printer's emblem showing Christ at the well talking to the Samaritan woman with her water-pot, surrounded by motto] QUI BIBERIT EX HAC AQUA NON SITIET IN AETERNVUM / Venetiis apud Andream Arrivabenum / ad signum Putei. M D LVI.

(The two lines about Ferdinand are highlighted in larger type in the text. Ligatures and font sizes are not otherwise indicated.)

Analysis of contents (numbered by folio or page):
i ͬ Titlepage
i ͮ Blank
ii ͬ Licence to bookseller for twenty years' right to reproduce, headed PAVLVS
   PAPA IIII and in Latin; followed by the Venetian licence in Italian addressed

to Principe and Signoria. From this it emerges that licence has also been granted to Arrivabene (in 1555) to print Hieronimo

Ragazoni's Italian version of Cicero's *Philippics*; Francesco Veniero's *Discorsi sopra i tre libri dell' anima di Aristotele*; the Italian translation by Fausto Longiano of all Cicero's orations; and seven sermons in Latin and Italian on the Sacrament by Vincenzo Cyconia Veronese.

ii$^v$ Encomium in six elegiac couplets headed 'BARNABAS PRAMPERGIVS / Iuriscon. ad Natalem Comitem virum doctissimum.'. (See above, first paragraph, for highlights.)

iij$^{r-v}$ DEDICATION (see Appendix 1 for Latin text)

iiij$^r$–<v$^v$> INDEX, arranged by topics, presented as chapter headings of de' Conti's own devising. Reference is to book and chapter number; in the text, chapter headings and numbers are clearly indicated by prominent type set off from the main text.

<vi$^r$> 'AD LECTOREM' (apology for inadvertent inaccuracies, excusing these as due to the difficulty of working from Greek MS exemplars, or to fatigue ('ob soporem etiam, qui solet defessis interdum subrepere'), or to the restricted time available. A short list of errata follows.

pp. 1–288 TEXT (Latin only, not bilingual)

Aa<1$^r$>—<vi $^r$> 'INDEX EORVM OMNIVM, QVAE / in toto hoc Athenaei opere observatione digna visa sunt.' This Index is quite compendious, and its headwords provide a valuable insight into what Renaissance readers found of interest in Athenaeus. It refers with reasonable accuracy to page, column, and line-number of the text.

De' Conti asserts in the Dedication (echoed in the encomium by Prampergius) that the most learned men of his day considered a translation of Athenaeus an extremely difficult undertaking. Many had begun it, but 'deterred by the difficulty of the task, they abandoned it soon after beginning, and at the very moment of setting off on their journey, laid down the burden they had taken up'. No doubt the sheer length of the work had deterred them. There is also the question of vocabulary; Athenaeus is full of unfamiliar terms relating to such items as food, drink and serving vessels. Finally, there is the problem of the text's vast literary hinterland, manifesting itself in a plethora of classical citations, fragments of unknown works, and oblique allusions to other texts. This demanded an encyclopaedic knowledge of the whole range of Greek literature which was hardly within the command of a single man.

His own success where other scholars had failed, de' Conti modestly implies, was due only to the advantage he had enjoyed of consulting experts such as the 'Cardinal Visaeus', 'Gugliemus Serletus' and 'Constantinus Rhallis' at a time when he was a frequent visitor to (or inmate of) the home of the 'Cardinal of Urbino'. Three of these advisers were Cardinals, though one had yet to be appointed; the fourth, to judge from his name, was a Greek.

To begin with the cardinals: Giulio Feltrio Della Rovere[7] (5 April 1535 to 3 or 8 September 1578), often called simply 'il cardinal d'Urbino', had been nominated to that office at the tender age of 13. Educated by humanists in Urbino, he became a politician and a patron of the arts: letters, music, theatre, and painting (he supported the artist Federico Barocci).

The 'Cardinal Visaeus', evidently a Greek scholar, must be the same man as the Cardinal Viseo mentioned (according to the *Dizionario Biografico* article) by de' Conti in the dedication of a Latin translation of Menander (1558) among several important men who had apparently honoured him with their patronage. The others named are the Cardinals Polo and Medici, the Duke of Urbino, the Doge of Venice Lorenzo Priuli, and of course the Emperor Ferdinand. De' Conti, as a prudent and ambitious Renaissance author, had clearly devoted much energy to meeting and recommending himself to eminent ecclesiastics, political figures and royalty, under whose auspices he published several notable works.

'Gugliemus Serletus' or Guillelmus Sirletus,[8] originally from Calabria, did not accede to the cardinalship until Pius IV admitted him in 1566, when he took up office as administrator of the church of St Mark (in Rome, not Venice). He is described by Ughelli as a classical polyglot: [*Italian Sacra* I. 26. 879] 'Hic ille est celebris Cardinalis Sirletus, qui Graecae, Latinae, Hebraicaeque peritissimus sui seculi doctis omnibus admirationi fuit.' He wrote commentaries on the Psalms and the Bible, speeches and letters. Among many scholars who admired him were the Venetian Paulus Manutius and the French scholar Marcantoine Muret,[9] teacher of Montaigne.

With the help of Dr David Holton of Cambridge University, I have been able to identify 'Constantinus Rhallis'[10] with one of the first pupils admitted in 1514 to the new Greek Gymnasium or College[11] at the foot of the Quirinal Hill in Rome. The school was founded at the instigation of Pope Leo X, and directed by the Greek scholar Janus Lascaris. Though it functioned for only a few years, it provided its scholars with an excellent start in life. However, the more proficient of the young Greeks, instead of returning home to educate their compatriots, stayed on in Italy, some finding posts in the households of Roman Catholic dignitaries who needed help with their Greek studies or the cataloguing of their Greek books and manuscripts.

Rhallis was quite well known. He is almost certainly the 'Constantinus Graecus' mentioned by Lilio Gregorio Giraldi in the context of a discussion of Greek poets resident in Italy. He was also one of several graduates of the Greek

College, 'condiscipuli et contubernales', who frequented the intellectual clique or *cenacolo*[12] of the Cardinal Nicolaus Rodulphus or Ridolfi[13] along with half a dozen distinguished non-Greeks named as Nicolaus Majorana, later Bishop of 'Malfecta'; Franciscus Priscianensis; Donatus Giannottus; Fr. Leonardus Malaspina; Matthaeus Herculanus; and Petrus Crassus, later Bishop of Viterbo. The other Greeks were Matthaios Devaris[14] and Nicolaos Sophianos,[15] both from Corfu, and Christophoros Condoleon,[16] known only as an epigrammatist and scholiast who commented on current religious disputes.

This information comes from Petros, nephew of Matthaios Devaris, who incorporated a short biography of his uncle into a dedication to Cardinal Alessandro Farnese introducing Matthaios's posthumously published book on the Greek particles. Matthaios was employed by Ridolfi as his permanent librarian, copyist, and Greek tutor ('in graecis ... explicandis auctoribus') and put him in charge of cataloguing his large collection of Greek manuscripts. Intellectuals of all disciplines congregated at the home or 'domicilium sapientiae' of Cardinal Ridolfi, 'apud quem per illud tempus ... multi variis disciplinarum generibus instructissimi florebant'.

Later, Devaris was involved in translating the decrees and Catechism of the Council of Trent into Greek. Like King Ferdinand's translation of the Bible into Syriac, this was an activity aimed at fostering ecumenical unity and mutual comprehension between Roman Catholics and Orthodox. This was collated with the Latin version by Cardinal Gulielmus Sirletus and Fulvius Ursinus; Petros hoped these men and Marcantoine Muret, all of whom had praised his uncle's book, might help him publish his other works. This juxtaposition of the names Sirletus and Rhallis, two of the four men mentioned by de' Conti as his consultants, confirms that de' Conti did indeed work with this group of ecumenically minded scholars around Cardinal Ridolfi to finalize an 'expurgated' (emended) Greek text of Athenaeus which he would then translate into Latin.

Sophianos worked together with Devaris on Ridolfi's library catalogue. Sometime between 1539–42 he designed a calligraphic Greek type to be used for the publication of some Greek MSS in the Vatican (the pet project of Cardinal Marcello Cervini). He seems to have left Ridolfi's employment after 1543 and moved to Venice, where he became interested in producing a series of printed vernacular translations of the ancient Greek classics (especially Plutarch and Lucian) and of theological texts which could be useful in the education of his compatriots, perhaps enabling them in time to shake off Ottoman control. He was a keen student of science, geometry and Ptolemy's geography, and published the first descriptive map of Greece (1544). He had already contributed a scene in modern Greek for Ricchi's comedy *I Tre Tiranni* (1533), and in 1545 brought out as a sample translation of a classical text Plutarch's Περὶ παιδῶν ἀγωγῆς (*De liberis educandis*, = *Moralia* 1a–14c). He does not appear to have printed any more translations, and his grammar (the first) of the Greek vernacular was not published until Legrand edited it in the nineteenth century.

As noted above, Natale de' Conti wrote a vivid and detailed account of the Ottoman invasion of Cyprus, published in the updated version of his *Histories* which appeared the year before he died. Around that time he acquired an otherwise unknown manuscript collection of Petrarchistic poems in the Cypriot dialect[17] of modern Greek, now owned by the Biblioteca Marciana of Venice. His name is inscribed both on the title-page of the outer leaves (by the librarian of the Marciana, Giacomo Morelli, 1745–1819, who had it in his private collection) and on the MS itself (f. 2$^r$) in the form *Nadal Comitis. Carmina Graeca*. The full stop after the name proves he did not compose the poems himself, but was merely its original owner. His date of death, 1582, is the collection's ultimate *terminus ante quem*. The poems themselves are dated by their editor to between 1546 and 1570. It is very likely that the collection is a copy of a manuscript owned by a refugee from the Ottoman invasion of Cyprus; many people fled the island between 1569 and 1575.

De' Conti's possession of this manuscript seems to indicate a lively interest in the language or literature of the contemporary Greek world. If so, it could be the consequence of his early friendship with Rhallis. The Rhallis family had a branch in Cyprus, one of whose members studied at Padua University early in the sixteenth century. In Venice, de' Conti must also have encountered the Cretan editors employed by the Aldine (of whom Marcus Musurus was one) and other Greek presses, and could also have met Rhallis's friend Sophianos there.

Other patrons to whom de' Conti dedicated his compositions include (in order of first attested publication):

Gabrio Panigarola, lawyer (*De Anno*, 1550)

The Cardinal Giulio Della Rovere (*De Venatione*, 1550)

King Ferdinand of Pannonia and Bohemia, Holy Roman Emperor designate (*Deipnosophistae*, 1556)

Charles IX, Valois King of France (*Mythology*, 1568; there may have been an earlier edition, now lost, *c*.1561–4)

Don Giovanni d'Austria, natural son of the Holy Roman Emperor Charles V (*Histories*, 1572, an account of current affairs from 1545 to 1556)

Francesco Contareno, Venetian Procurator of St Mark (Demetrius Phalereus' *De Elocutione*, 1577)

G.B. Bernardo, Venetian gentleman (augmented *Histories*, 1581, taking the account up to 1580)

Further, de' Conti also addressed a poetic panegyric entitled *Carmen de Alphonsi ducis ingressu in urbem Venetam* to Alfonso, Duke of Ferrara, on the occasion of his official entry to Venice in 1562.

Stylistically, de' Conti's was a 'transparent' translation, the Latin phraseology following that of the Greek almost literally and word for word. There is a lack of idiomatic rendering and of lexical variety in the Latin which makes it clear that the translation was published in some haste, before he had quite advanced beyond the stage of basic interpretation to the final polish which would have made the version read well in Latin. Some of the failures of his rendering are due to lacunae and imperfections in the Greek textual transmission. In other cases, his interpretation could have been improved by following up Athenaeus's literary allusions.

For example, in one passage early in Book Fourteen where the Greek text is admittedly faulty,[18] de' Conti misinterpreted an allusion to Agesilaus which he could have understood much better if he had looked up the passage in Xenophon: 'Existimavit Xenophon oportere Agesilaum ita ab ebrietate abstinere, atque ab insania: ita vero cibos non opportunos detestari, atque pigritiam.' This is a gross slur on the abstemious Agesilaus, who was not being urged by Xenophon to avoid strong drink, but quoted by him on the virtues of moderate consumption. In de' Conti's defence, he may not have realized that this was a literary citation; the passage begins Ξενοφῶντος δὲ τὸν Ἀγησίλαον ... (lacuna), without a verb of saying. He seems to have taken the initial genitive as a textual error for the nominative and paired it with ᾤετο; so, where Athenaeus wrote 'Xenophon said that Agesilaus thought one should abstain', he renders 'Xenophon thought that Agesilaus should abstain (from excessive drinking)'.

De' Conti also renders the sentence which follows somewhat awkwardly: 'Sed neque nos ex ijs sumus, qui plurimum bibentes ac temulenti facti ad concina ista symposia foro pleno accedamus.' The phrase 'foro pleno' is a literal rendering of πληθούσης ἀγορᾶς, literally 'the market-place being full'. De' Conti seems not to have realized that the genitive absolute is an idiom with chronological implications, and has attached the phrase to the wrong verb (it should go with 'temulenti facti'). Athenaeus meant to specify a time when drinking was inappropriate, 'at the third (or sixth) hour' or 'in the forenoon'. He leaves it ambiguous whether the riotous morning drinkers are to be identified with the symposiasts, an ambiguity preserved by de' Conti. Gulick's version, based on an οὔτε added by Casaubon, carefully separates the intemperate drunks from those worthier souls who spend their time to much better effect at learned symposia.

It cannot have been easy for Natale de' Conti to find Latin equivalents for some of the very technical vocabulary, without the lexicographical resources which became available later in the century. Casaubon, one of his first and severest critics, had very many more dictionaries and other aids to help him. Indeed, so heavy were the disadvantages under which de' Conti laboured that instead of using our privileged faculty of hindsight to castigate his deficiencies, we should more properly marvel at how much he managed to get right. In its time Natale de' Conti's translation aroused a great deal of justified favourable interest; and he still deserves credit as the pioneer who first set plough to a long stretch of virgin terrain fraught with unusual pitfalls. Later translators owe a large, though usually unacknowledged, debt to de' Conti's work. His Latin version was challenged soon after his death by the more accurate rendering of Jacques Daléchamp (Lyon, 1583), set in Loeb-like bilingual format, with a fuller index and learned marginal notes explaining names, allusions and lexical questions.

Perhaps because Italians remained capable of reading Latin long after the vernacular had become necessary in other Western European cultures, there seems to have been no early Italian translation of Athenaeus. The Italian poet Torquato Tasso wrote copious notes into one of the two Venetian folio copies of de' Conti now in the British Library. The French scholar-editor Schweighaeuser made a pastiche of both de' Conti and Daléchamp, with some improvements of his own, to accompany his nineteenth-century Latin redaction of the Greek text.

In order to show how de' Conti's groundwork was exploited and refined by subsequent translators, I have again taken as an indicative sample the same beginning of Book Fourteen, using the Loeb edition of Gulick for the Athenaeus text (exceptions are indicated). With this signalled hereafter as A, I have compared the versions of de' Conti (C), Daléchamp (D), and Schweighaeuser (S), breaking them down into rough clausal, phrasal and functional equivalents. First, a relatively straightforward prose introduction to the first section, about wine and madness. This first sentence demonstrates Schweighaeuser's mixed debt to both de' Conti and Daléchamp, with a slight bias here in favour of de' Conti:

A  Τὸν Διόνυσον ... μαινόμενον οἱ πολλοὶ λέγουσιν
C  Dionysium ... insanientem complures ... finxerunt
D  Insanum Bacchum esse ... complures aiunt
S  Bacchum ... furentem vulgo aiunt

A  ἑταῖρε Τιμόκρατες
C  amice Timocrates
D  ô amice Timocrates
S  amice Timocrates

A  ἀπὸ τοῦ (causal conjunction)
C  idcirco ... , quod
D  quod

S  eo, quod

A  τοὺς πλείονος [Musurus] ἀκράτου σπῶντας
C  ij, qui vino immoderatius utantur
D  plus iusto meri qui bibunt
S  qui multum meri hauriunt

A  θορυβώδεις γίνεσθαι.
C  fiunt tumultuosi.
D  tumultuantur.
S  tumultuosi fiunt.

      Now for a passage of verse. The verse citations in Athenaeus were a particular stumbling-block to translators, partly because of their poetic language and the unfamiliarity of many fragments, and partly because of the difficulty of rendering Greek into Latin verse without sacrificing semantic accuracy. Usually it is the metre that suffers; but we are not concerned with neo-Latin metrical (dis)abilities. In the following passage, Schweighaeuser's rendering is divided almost equally between de' Conti and Daléchamp:

A  οἶνος σε τρώει* μελιηδής, ὅς τε καὶ ἄλλους / βλάπτει
C  Sic tibi, sic alijs nocuerunt dulcia vina
D  Vinum te mellitum sauciat; vinum & alijs, / Noxium est,
S  Vinum te laedit, quod quidem & aliis / nocet,
*  De' Conti may have been aware that τρώει (epic present of τιτρώσκω) meant 'eats' in sixteenth-century vernacular Greek, and thus omitted it in translation, taking βλάπτει to cover both subjects}

A  ὃς ἄν μιν χανδὸν ἕλῃ μηδ' αἴσιμα πίνῃ.
C  Qui fusim* potare solent, nec iusta requirunt.
D  qui affatim hauriunt, & bibunt plus(.)
S  quisquis illud avidius haurit, nec modice bibit.
*  The more usual form is *fuse* ('copiously').

A  οἶνος καὶ κένταυρον ἀγακλυτὸν Εὐρυτίωνα / ὤλεσ'
C  Vinum centaurum valde* inclytum & Eurytionem / Perdidit
D  Centaurum illustres Eurytionem vinum / Perdidit
S  Vinum etiam Centaurum inclytum Eurytiona / perdidit
*  Only this adverb renders the force of the Greek prefix αγα-.

A  ἐνὶ μεγάρῳ μεγαθύμου Πειριθόοιο
C  in domibus praestantis Pirithoi

D   in atrijs magnanimi Peirithoi
S   in domo magnanimi Pirithoi

A   ἐς Λαπίθας ἐλθόνθ'.
C   qui / Venerat ad Lapithas
D   ad Lapithas profectum
S   ad Lapithas profectum

A   ὁ δ' ἐπεὶ φρένας ἄασεν οἴνῳ
C   vino saturavit ut ille / Pectora,
D   cum mentem vino ... obruit
S   hic enim postquam mentem vino corrupit

A   μαινόμενος κάκ' ἔρεξε
C   mala plurima fecit.
D   furiosus ... & quod minime iustum fuit, admisit*
S   furens mala patravit
*   D's paraphrase here is odd.

A   δόμοις ἐνὶ Πειριθόοιο.
C   Perithoi in domibus (precedes above clause)
D   in aedibus Peirithoi.
S   in aedibus Pirithoi.

It is clear from the foregoing that in spite of the scornful strictures levelled by many at de' Conti's translation, it nevertheless served its purpose as a window allowing a preliminary view, albeit slightly hazy in places, of a very complicated landscape. The sixteenth-century Latin translations of de' Conti and Daléchamp were used as the basis of two later French vernacular translations by de Marolles and Villebrune, neither of whom seems to have worked directly from the Greek. No English translation is recorded before the 'literal' version of C.D. Yonge (London, 1854).

The fact that so majestic a figure as Ferdinand, acting Holy Roman Emperor, deigned to associate himself with this project suggests that he thought it likely to redound to the credit of both author and dedicand. De' Conti's acknowledgement in the Dedication of the help he had received from cardinals and higher clerics of the Roman Catholic Church was further reassurance as to his and his text's religious credentials. Certainly there is much in the text to intrigue a wealthy Renaissance monarch. Athenaeus's accounts of the extravagant and ostentatious displays mounted by various ancient kings, highlighted in de' Conti's book by a whole series of titles and headings such as 'The dinners of King X' and 'The parade of King Y', must have been of great interest to a future emperor.

This was a time when high rank demanded an accompanying show of luxury with which to impress foreign visitors. Ferdinand would no doubt have found much to disapprove in Athenaeus, many excesses and follies to which he himself would not descend; but banquets and their accompanying entertainments were an inescapable feature of court life, and novelty to enliven them was continually being sought. Renaissance kings also prided themselves on the intellectual elevation of their courts, often inviting a few selected guests to evening parties of civilized discourse over dinner and choice wine. Athenaeus's elegant expositions of dining, drinking and curious thinking must have been wellnigh irresistible to this élite society, which included not a few ecclesiastics.

De' Conti liked Athenaeus and shows a disarming enthusiasm for the ingredients in his multifarious literary banquet. In the Dedication he whets Ferdinand's appetite with allusions to the book's contents, which he considered ideally suited for presentation to a king: in particular, the chapters recounting the delightful extravagances of kings, and the magnificent displays of previous emperors. He promises that Athenaeus will be equally informative on the customs of ancient peoples, provinces, cities, countries, and peoples (Persians, Romans, Macedonians, Egyptians, etc.). This international aspect was one which would certainly have been appreciated by a monarch whose realm extended, theoretically at least, over many countries and cultures, and whose enemies came from even more exotic lands. Athenaeus has much to teach even a king about the contrasting sorts of men, their pleasures, intemperance, frugality, tyranny, liberality, magnificence, deeds, stratagems, witty sayings, etc.

Part of the rhetoric of flattery in the Dedication rests on hints that Ferdinand himself is divine or god-like for his eminence (especially as *Holy* Roman Emperor) and personal virtues, and therefore deserves a gift suitable as an offering to a god. De' Conti's epithet of 'divine' for Athenaeus ('a divine genius of singular judgement') may thus function as an implicit compliment to his patron. The epithet also suggest a comparison with Plato, called 'divine' because many of his precepts seemed to conform with Christian teaching. Athenaeus, indeed, imitates Plato openly at the beginning of the *Deipnosophistae*. 'Divine', then could be a codeword, reinforcing the message that Athenaeus was perfectly suitable reading matter for the religious.

De' Conti professes uncertainty as to which precise category the *Deipnosophistae* belongs to—whether classical literature, history, or philosophy—for Athenaeus is equally weighty, erudite and elegant in all three fields. He suppresses all mention of (and thereby draws attention to) Athenaeus' knowledge of antiquity, his learning in poetry and music, and his curiosity in medical matters. His complacent conclusion is that he could have given his royal patron no gift more honorific, more glorious, or more … divine.

## Appendix 1: Latin text of de' Conti's dedication to the Emperor Ferdinand

SERENISSIMO AC POTENTISSIMO Principi FERDINANDO Romanorum, Pannoniae, & Booemiae Regi, Imperatori designato, Infanti Hispaniarum, Archiduci Austriae, Duci Burgundiae, &c. Comiti Tyrolis, &c. Domino clementissimo.

OPTAVI pro mea summa in te observantia, qua vel nomen ipsum Serenissimae Maiestatis tuae semper sanctissimè colui, Potentissime REX FERDINANDE, ut aliqua mihi concederetur occasio, qua possem erga Serenissimam Maiestatem tuam benevolum animum omnibus, tibique in primis patefacere. Verum cum illud vel re ipsa, vel verbis effici oportere intelligerem; quorum alterum minime pro rei dignitate poteram, alterum fucatum plerunque & fictum, in Reges praecipue, existimari consuevit, dubius animo sanè fui dudum quid mihi esset agendum. Attamen in his varijs multiplicibusque cogitationibus me lex ea gravissimi sapientissimique Lycurgi confirmavit, qua homines parva sacrificia Dijs immortalibus offerre iubebatur: tum ne gravioribus impensis deterriti ad res sacras rarius accederent: tum etiam; quòd rarius fortasse magis convenit, quia Deos ipsos non victimarum praestantiam, magnificentiámve sacrorum respicere existimabat, sed ipsos honestos, sanctos, ac pios sacrificantium animos. His ego rationibus non mediocriter commotus sum, ut te quoque, quem incredibilis humanitas, vere Regem: ingenium acutissimum, Sapientem: singularis morum praestantia, Virum bonum: eximia in Deos pietas, Admirabilem: omnia simul coniuncta, Immortalem efficiunt; non ad meorum munerum tenuitatem, sed ad integritatem animi, summumque maiestati tuae obsequendi studium respicere putaverim. Quòd si pro dignitate, amplitudineque tua tibi non planè satisfecere; non patiar tamen, ut vacuis prorsus (ut aiunt) manibus, veluti neque ad Persarum Reges licebat, accedam. Ad te igitur sapientissimum Principem, sapientissimum mitto Dipnosophistam, quem nuper non sine magno labore è tenebris, in quibus hactenus latuerat, eduxi,

Maiestatisque tuae sanctissimo nomine consecravi. Neque ullum sanè numus praestantius, honorificentius, aut magis regium à me amplitudini tuae praestari posse arbitrabar, quam illud, per quod variarum nationum mores, Regum delicias, Imperatorumque magnificentiam cognosceres: quippe cum ea omnia, quae a vobis Regibus, Regina pecunia (ut ait Satyricus) comparari possunt, elargiri sit supervacaneum omnino, & artificiosum quoddam foenerationis genus; quae neque profectò praestare possum, neque, si possem, res minus te dignas praestarem. Illa verò quae scite excogitata fuerunt, quaeque exquisito quodam studio elaborata, cum et rariora sint, et, quia divino solum ingenio comparantur, non in omnium facultate constituta; et honorificentissima esse munera, et maxime regia semper existimavi. Quare si cui dubium esset huiusmodi esse Athenaeum, qui divino ingenio praeditus plurima scite admodum excogitarit, operae precium certè foret, ut longiore uterer oratione ad illius divinissimum ingenij acumen, singulareque iudicium declarandum. Verum quia omnibus ferè viris eruditis clarum esse videtur cuiusmodi sit; hoc unum dicere ausim; nisi Plutarchus inter humaniorum literarum authores priorem locum occupasset, hunc, meo quidam iudicio, facile primum locum fuisse obtenturum. Cognosces. n. Rex Sapientissime ex huius eruditissimi hominis scriptis, quantopere differant, non modo nostrorum temporum mores ab illis antiquorum virorum: verumetiam singularum provinciarum ac civitatum homines, quod spectat [iij<sup>v</sup>] ad vivendi rationem, quantopere inter se fuerint diversi. Cognosces inquam Regum Persarum, ac omnium, qui ob res gestas celeberrimi fuerunt, Romanorum * / * [?] Macedonum, Aegyptiorum, Philosophorum, et omnium nationum, ingenium. Cognosces variorum hominum delicias, intemperantiam, frugalitatem, tyrannides, liberalitatem, magnificentiam, res gestas, stratagemata, acutè dicta, et omnia ea denique quibus ignoratis scripsit divinissimus Plato

Graecos ab Aegyptiis semper pueros fuisse iudicatos. Ita vero fit ut magnopere dubitem inter humaniorum ne literarum scriptores, an in historicorum classibus, an inter philosophorum coetum sit Athenaeus collocandus: siquidem inter hos omnium ferè gravissimus, inter illos eruditissus, inter alios elegantissimus omnium esse videtur. Verum quocumque in ordine eum collocarit, non dubito quia omnes ferè caeteros antecellet. Taceo admirabile rerum antiquarum illius studium; poeticae facultatis, ac musicae exquisitissimam doctrinam praetermitto; nihil dicam quantopere medicinae fuerit curiosus; quia in infinitum nostra protenderetur oratio. Hoc tantum dicam; nihil me potuisse honorificentius, nihil gloriosius, nihil divinius denique excogitasse, quod ad te Regem singulari ingenio praeditum mitterem. Atque res ipsa tanto mihi honorificentior est visa, quanto ab omnibus nostrae tempestatis eruditissimis hominibus difficilio fuit iudicata: nam viros complures hoc opus ipsum aggressos esse sentio, qui summam inter homines doctrinae eruditionisque opinionem consecuti fuerant, qui tamen rei ipsius difficultate deterriti, rem incoeptam reliquerunt, susceptumque onus in ipso itineris ingressu, deiecerunt. Neque ego sanè his aut audacior, aut fortior omnibus sum existimandus: sed illud non nihil mihi fuit adiumento, quod alijs fortasse non contigit, quia Reverendissimi Card. Visaei, quem dignitatis gratia nomino, cuius etiam singulare ingenium semper sum admiratus, iudicio usus sum, (dandus est. n. suus cuique honor) Gulielmique Serleti, viri ob insignem tum probitatem, tum etiam doctrinam admirabilis; atque doctissimi viri Constantini Rhalli, eo tempore, quo apud Reverendissimum Card. Urbini, quem etiam honoris causa nomino, familiariter eram. Quo etiam tempore permultis erroribus Graecum exemplar expurgavi, non sine magna antiquorum exemplarium copia. Ex quibus omnibus Serenissimae Maiestati tuae perspicuum esse arbitror, me non solum Philosophum e tenebris eductum ad te mittere, verumetiam summa diligentia expolitum, multisque sordibus, quas ex longo situ contraxerat, expurgatum. Praetermisi ego libenter cum reliquas singulares tuas virtutes, tum inauditam, nescio magnificentiam ne dicam, an literalitatem eximiam; qua, praeter caetera quotidiana in omnes beneficia, usus es; cum imperaris, summopereque curaris ut tuis sumptibus vetus, novemque Testamentum lingua Syriaca imprimeretur, omnibusque volentibus Syris largiretur: ut veram salutis ac immortalitatis inde consequerentur cognitionem; quia rei ipsius magnitudo multo aptiorem temporis opportunitatem postularet. Nam tanta est tua in omnes homines deosque pietas, ut solus et amplissimo Regis nomine, et ad quem summa totius religionis authoritatis deferatur, dignus esse videare. Unum autem illud pro singulari tua sapientia humanitateque postulo Rex omnino atque sapientissime, ut animi mei potius desiderium, summumque Serenissimae Maiestati obsequendi studium, quam rei ipsius magnitudinem spectes. Venetijs. III Cal. Feb. MDLVI.

SERENISSIMAE MAIEST. TUAE deditissimus Natalis de Comitibus.

# Appendix 2: Editions and translations of Athenaeus

*Early Renaissance editions*

1. <Aldus Pius Manutius & Marcus Musurus eds.>, Ἀθηναίου δειπνοσοφιστοῦ τὴν πολυμαθεστάτην πραγματείαν νῦν ἔξεστι σοι φιλόλογε μικροῦ πριαμένῳ πολλῶν τε καὶ μεγάλων ... καὶ ὧν ἴσως πρότερον οὐκ ᾔδεις, ἐς γνῶσιν ἐλθεῖν ... (Apud Aldum & Andream Socerum, Venice, 1514).

The Bodleian copy Auct. IR inf. 1. 1 copy of the Aldine text has marginal notes by Erasmus and Heinsius.

2. <J. Bedrotus and Chr. Herlinus eds.>, *Athenaei Dipnosophistarum, hoc est argute sciteque in convivio disserentum, lib. xv* ... (Basel, I. Valderum, 1535).

*More modern editions cited in this chapter*

Schweighaeuser, Iohannes, *Athenaei Naucratitae Deipnosophistarum libri quindecim ex optimis codicibus nunc primum collatis emendavit ac supplevit nova Latina versione et animadversionibus cum Is. Casauboni aliorumque tum suis illustravit commodisque indicibus instruxit* (Argentorati, Societas Bipontiae, 1801–7).

Gulick, C.B., *Athenaeus, The Deipnosophists* (Cambridge, Mass. and London, Harvard University Press, Loeb Classical Library, 1993).

*Natale Conti's Latin translation*

1. *Athenaei Dipnosophistarum. sive Coenae Sapientium libri xv. Natale de Comitibus veneto, nunc primum e graeca in Latinam linguam vertente: Cum pluribus ex manuscriptis antiquissimis exemplaribus additis: quae in Graece hactenus impressis voluminibus non reperiebantur: Ad potentissimum Ferdinandum, Pannoniae, Boemiae, ac Romanorum Regem* (Venice, A. Arrivabene, 1556, folio).

I consulted the Bodleian copy D. 7. 19 Art. The British Library has a copy [C. 45. g. 8] with copious notes by the Italian poet Torquato Tasso.

2. Basel, Henrichus Petrus, 1556 (octavo).

This edition includes prefatory verses by Nicolaus Stopius 'Ad politiores literaturae candidatos'. [BL 832. d. 13]

3. Paris, Franciscus Barptolomaeus Honoratus, 1556 (octavo). [Bod. Douce A. 217]

*The Latin translation of J. Daléchamp*

1. *Athenaei ... Deipnosophistarum libri quindecim ... in latinum sermonem versi a Iacobo Dalechampio* (Lyon, A. de Harsy, 1583). [Bod. 90. f. 4 (2)]

The 1597 edition [Bod. 5 D 173] announces on the title-page the inclusion of Casaubon's *Animadversiones* on Athenaeus, but the censor ordered its excision on the grounds that he was a proscribed author. It appeared separately in Lyons 1600.

*French translations*

1. M. de Marolles, *Les quinze livres des Deipnosophistes ... Ouvrage ... traduit pour la premiere fois en francois ... apres les versions latines de Natalis Comes de Padoue, & de Iacques d'Alechamp* (J. Langlois, Paris, 1680). [Bod. Douce A 549]

2. Lefebvre de Villebrune, *Banquet des savans par Athenee, traduit, tant sur les textes imprimes, que sur plusieurs manuscrits,* Paris, 1789. 5 vols. [Bod. 4 Godw. 101–5]

*English translation*

C.D. Yonge, *The Deipnosophists, or Banquet of the learned* (London, Bohn's Classical Library, 1854). 4 vols. [Bod. 29049. e. 2–4]

# SECTION III: ATHENAEUS THE READER AND HIS WORLD

# INTRODUCTORY REMARKS

Turning from the issues of text and transmission, the chapters in this section attempt to map out the social, intellectual and literary milieu within which Athenaeus lived, read and wrote. The issues raised in this section will echo through the book: the purpose here is to open pathways of approach to an author who may be characterized fairly as much used and little considered.

First, Dorothy Thompson sets Athenaeus in his background, Naucratis and Greek Egypt. This background was clearly of immense and abiding importance to Athenaeus. The world of the *Deipnosophistae* is one in which gentlemen and intellectuals are expected to take particular pride in their native towns. Nor was there anything new about that among the Greeks of the Roman empire, as Strabo amply demonstrates for his native Amaseia, for example, some two centuries earlier.[1] Thompson explores Athenaeus' concern with Naucratis and more broadly with Egypt, where Greek culture and Greekness are the dominant forces in his Egyptian landscape. No doubt Athenaeus would have been horrified to be termed an Egyptian, at least without appropriate context and qualification of the term. After all Naucratis could boast a proud history, not only of Hellenism, but also of an early panhellenism (see Hdt. 2. 178 on its Hellenion). Thompson shows how, amid the imperial vogue for panhellenic thought from the time of Hadrian in particular, Naucratis stood out as the homeland of Greek intellectuals, among whom Athenaeus was but a prominent example. At the same time, the hey-day of Greek Egypt (particularly with rose-tinted hindsight from the imperial period) was the rule of the Ptolemies. We may wonder whether Athenaeus' particular and rather unusual concern with the Hellenistic world may owe something to his affection for the Greek Egypt whence he came (further Chapter 40).

From the viewpoint of imperial *litterati* (and especially those from Naucratis, no doubt), the crowning glory of Greek culture in Egypt was the library at Alexandria. This was a material expression of Greek culture in general and of Ptolemaic commitment to that culture in particular. At the same time, the creation and maintenance of the library attested the concern of the Greek rulers of Egypt with the knowledge and wisdom that Greek thought liked to set as the proper foundation for the best manifestations of monarchy. Christian Jacob interprets Athenaeus and the *Deipnosophistae* in the context of the tradition of Hellenistic libraries and also of the Roman libraries developed in their wake. We may perhaps think of the wonderful library of the Pisones at Herculaneum, but evidently Larensis' library outshone all competition, or so Athenaeus would have it. Jacob points out that the library might incorporate a group of scholars, not only using its books, but also living and dining there. Athenaeus certainly knew as much and may well have lived such a life in the house and library of Larensis. Jacob stresses the depth and extent of his bibliographical knowledge and argues that the *Deipnosophistae* itself may be approached as a literary library.

A kindred argument is developed by Yun Lee Too, who emphasizes that, while books are texts, they are also about people. As she points out, even books are all too mortal, for they are vulnerable to neglect, abuse and accident, especially in uncultured hands. After all, the history of the Alexandrian library tends to be dominated by fire, whether fatal or not. Authors might claim the immortality of their writings, as most famously does Horace (*Odes* 3. 30), but they could only do so in a spirit of reckless optimism or denial. For where survival was maintained, writings might yet be stolen or, alternatively, falsely attributed, particularly to a respected authority. Survival was maintained through libraries which might be physical, but might also be the virtual, mental libraries of the educated intellectual's head. Accordingly, Yun Lee Too sets Athenaeus and his *Deipnosophistae* in a tradition of memory, knowledge, culture and quotation that she traces through Vitruvius on Aristophanes of Byzantium, Apuleius on himself and Eunapius on Longinus, all in a context of Roman imperial appropriation in the happier guise of Larensis' hospitality.

The next five chapters take a more detailed look at Athenaeus' process of reading and quotation from literary texts. First, Ewen Bowie considers Athenaeus' selection from early Greek elegiac and iambic poetry. Plutarch in particular offers a control for an assessment of Athenaeus' practice, wherein Bowie observes the impact of Athenaeus' dual concern with lexicography and with dining and the symposium. As Bowie shows, Plutarch and Athenaeus use a sieve designed for their own purposes, so that, for example, the martial Tyrtaeus is of interest to

Plutarch but is largely ignored by Athenaeus. Still more interesting is the comparison of their selection from the same author: for example, on the basis of their respective selections, Athenaeus' Solon is hardly recognizable as the Solon of Plutarch. It is valuable to have so clear a demonstration of the impact of authorial agendas upon the survival of earlier texts and, consequently, upon our own assessments of earlier texts and their authors as they arise from extant fragments. Bowie also broaches a question which will continue to concern us through this book, namely the extent to which Athenaeus used whole texts for his quotation, rather than compendia. Bowie cautiously shows that a strong case can be made for the former alternative, despite scholars' general tendency to prefer the latter.

Next, Keith Sidwell tackles Athenaeus' engagement with the numerous plays of comedy his relationship with with the slippery works of Lucian, who was broadly his contemporary. Like Athenaeus, Lucian had his origins in the imperial Greek east. Indeed, he came from Samosata in Commagene on the northern fringes of Syria, in which Athenaeus took some particular interest, as we shall see (Chapters 24 and 40). Sidwell explores the interest Athenaeus and Lucian shared in the texts of comedy, for all that Lucian's quotations are comparatively limited. In particular, he offers a valuable sketch of the methodology of reading and interpretation that Athenaeus and Lucian inherited from the world of Hellenistic scholarship, along with the texts themselves. In this light we can understand something of Athenaeus' approach to the comic texts which he has preserved for us. We also gain an opportunity to work back through that methodology to a rather broader appreciation of the plays themselves. Finally, in a valuable appendix, Sidwell collects the evidence for Athenaeus' and Lucian's knowledge of comedy.

Like Bowie and Sidwell, Giuseppe Zecchini also examines Athenaeus' use of texts beside the practice of one of his near-contemporaries. In this case, it is Harpocration, who may firmly be identified as a lexicographer, whereas Athenaeus remains largely a dilettante in such matters in the *Deipnosophistae*. With the help of Harpocration, Zecchini is able to develop further his earlier discussion of Athenaeus' historical sources in the standard monograph on our author (Zecchini 1989a). Rather as Sidwell and many other authorities do, Zecchini holds that we may be sure of Athenaeus' use of collections. Accordingly, he tends to minimize Athenaeus' reading of whole texts. However, it must be acknowledged that we remain a long way from certainty on this vexed question. Bowie's chapter amounts to a warning against swift judgments.

However, Frank Walbank offers a way forward in his meticulous case-study of Athenaeus' use of Polybius. Athenaeus proves to be strikingly out of sympathy with the key concerns of the text from which he quotes: Walbank finds no sign that Athenaeus was interested in Polybius' central theme, namely Rome's rapid conquest of the Mediterranean world, including the Greek east. The theme probably seemed outmoded in Athenaeus' world, and perhaps uncomfortable. Certainly, at Larensis' table the predominant mood was the co-existence of Greek and Roman cultures (see Chapter 1), not the violent creation of Roman imperial dominance. Here both Romans and Greeks might receive and offer criticisms of each other and of their fellows, but there was no threat of worse to come. Walbank suggests that Athenaeus read Polybius with an eye not to Polybius' great theme, but to his lesser concerns (notably issues of morality and the influence of courtiers), for these matched Athenaeus' own agenda.

Christopher Pelling offers a different strategy, by thinking what many scholars have assumed to be unthinkable, namely that Athenaeus has constructed the *Deipnosophistae* with an intelligent focus on his own agenda, in quotation as in much else. With his attention fixed on historiography, Pelling builds a strong case that Athenaeus may even be changing the texts which he purports to quote in order to make them suit his own ends. As Pelling stresses, it is not satisfactory to seek to explain away Athenaeus' misquotations as the consequence of his faulty memory, when his 'errors' have produced something significantly more to his taste than accurate quotations would have done. Athenaeus seems to have 'improved' his originals and to have done so with a certain care, even craft, so that his improvements can hardly be put down to his subconscious alone. Given that we rely so much upon those quotations for our knowledge of little-known authors, that is disquieting. Yet we would do well to remember, with Pelling, that the *Deipnosophistae* embraces both humour and creativity, not least in the application of old texts to new situations.

The next three chapters consider Athenaeus' engagement with the material world of art and artefacts. Yet the shift is a slight one. Instead, it is perhaps worth stressing that here too Athenaeus remains overwhelmingly concerned with literary representations of artefacts, far less with the things themselves. Accordingly, he makes very little of the mosaics which not only decorated the dining-rooms of the wealthy but even reflected his own range of concerns, for example with comedy, fish and philosophy. Moreover, while he devotes a whole book to the variety of cups (Book Eleven), he does not explore the aphorisms, banter and the like which were often to be found inscribed on tableware.[2]

In these chapters again, contemporaries are brought within the scope of the debate. First, Karim Arafat sets Athenaeus beside Pausanias, the author of another substantial text on the Greek past and present, which appeared only a decade or two before the *Deipnosophistae*. Not that we have any grounds for thinking that Athenaeus had read Pausanias' *Guide to Greece*, rather the contrary. The broad value of the comparison, which also throws up a series of more detailed points on sites and objects, is that, after the fashion of Ewen Bowie's chapter, it demonstrates again and very clearly the impact of authorial agendas upon the selection, citation and quotation of earlier texts.

John Davies is particularly concerned with Athenaeus' use of documentary sources. While we tackle elsewhere the inscriptions on *parasitoi* which Athenaeus offers in Book Six (see Chapter 22), Davies here addresses the documentary texts which appear in the rest of the *Deipnosophistae*. Here again the distinction between text and artefact proves flexible. Inscriptions are both texts *and* artefacts. Moreover, as Davies observes, many of the texts mentioned in the *Deipnosophistae* (especially the legal texts) may or may not derive from inscriptions. Accordingly, Davies restricts his discussion to overt citations of documentary texts. He concludes that Athenaeus has a very limited interest in inscriptions. His limited interest largely involves persons (especially *hetaerae*) and has a notable focus on the 320s BC. Against that background, the documentary material on *parasitoi*, though in a sense akin to that on *hetaerae*, looks all the more exceptional in the work as a whole.

Ruth Webb considers uses and functions of ekphrasis in the *Deipnosophistae*, set in the broader context of ekphrasis in the general culture of the Second Sophistic. Her concern is primarily with rhetorical ekphrasis, not with the particular application of the concept to artefacts, though, once again, in Athenaeus' work the distinction between literature and artefact is not sustainable for long. She addresses Book Five in particular, which contains, with much else, an extended account of the grand procession of Ptolemy Philadelphus, which the diner Masurius quotes from Callixenus. In so doing, she lays bare the architecture of Masurius' speech, which dominates the book, from Polybius and symposia through the topic of processions and on to palatial ships. Not only are these apparently different topics in fact coherent as remarkable facets of Hellenistic kingship, but, as Webb shows, they are all linked carefully and smoothly enough by transitional passages. Moreover, she observes a broad moral message: this was kingship to luxurious excess, bloated to the point of uselessness and exemplified by Hiero II's great ship, so enormous that it could not be put to sea. Yet her main purpose is to demonstrate that ekphrasis was understood in the culture of Athenaeus' world not as digression, but much more creatively as a means to inject vividness into a text by drawing pictures with words and so to convey the audience to the time and place of the events described and allow it to 'see' them. Masurius takes the diners (and Athenaeus thereby takes his readers) on a magical tour back to a very different past, until they and we land again in the present with a bump, brought down to earth with a smile at Ulpian's pedantry.

The two chapters which round off this section both consider key contemporary attitudes, which conditioned the authorial decisions of Athenaeus in writing the *Deipnosophistae*. First, Maria Gambato addresses the issue of luxury, raised by Ruth Webb. In particular, she explores the issues of gender and orientalism in the context of Athenaeus' survey of luxury in Book Twelve. In so doing, she valuably sets Athenaeus' work in the tradition of exemplary literature; after all, such literature often took the form of the compendia, which Athenaeus certainly knew and used to some extent, however much or little we prefer to think, for on occasion he says so (see Chapter 1). Here again, Athenaeus emerges as much more eager to illustrate and to display than to offer any hard critique or definitions of the meaning and significance of 'luxury'. And this, despite his isolation of the issue for special treatment in Book Twelve, for its own sake and no doubt also as a prelude to the discussion of love in Book Thirteen (on which, see Chapter 39). At the same time, Gambato notes Athenaeus' treatment of luxury as an eastern form of corruption, spreading west and infecting even Rome after Lucullus (see Chapter 1). Central to this notion of luxury is emasculation, not least of rulers, to the extent of their becoming feminized. There was nothing new in the stereotype. That lack of novelty and the nature of the subject itself may account for the amused detachment which Gambato finds in Athenaeus' treatment of androgynous kings of the east. The implied contrast between such rulers as these and the splendid Larensis, monarch of taste, could hardly be more stark or more amusing.

Last in this section, Keith Hopwood takes us back to the large issue which has run through these chapters and which will recur throughout this book, namely the interplay of Greek and Roman and past and present in the *Deipnosophistae* and, more generally, in the world of the Second Sophistic. Hopwood presents a case-study of one city in that world, Smyrna, whose cultural life may reasonably be claimed, for all its prominence, to echo that of many a city of the imperial Greek east. Not that the élite of Smyrna would have seen their city as anything less than outstanding and exceptional, not least as the birthplace of Homer, whatever other cities might claim. As Dorothy Thompson demonstrated for Naucratis at the beginning of this section, so Keith Hopwood here for Smyrna shows us a world of passionate local (not to say Lilliputian) civic patriotisms. He also makes the key point that such patriotisms, and Hellenic self-images more generally, could be and were accommodated beside and perhaps within a co-existing and arguably symbiotic Roman identity.

# ❖ 5 ❖ ATHENAEUS IN HIS EGYPTIAN CONTEXT

## by Dorothy Thompson

thenaeus came from Naucratis which lies some 50 miles SE of Alexandria on the left bank of the Canopic branch of the Nile in the Egyptian Delta. As a learned man Athenaeus was not alone from that city. Philostratus lists other Naucratites: earlier Theomnestus, then the lexicographer Pollux, Apollonius and Proclus, three sophists who were all of them pupils of Hadrian in Athens, where they later practised.[1] Athenaeus in contrast, escaping from the provinces, made his way to Rome.

Naucratis seems first to have been a Milesian foundation in the Nile Delta dating from the reign of Psammetichus I in the seventh century BC. Later, in the sixth century, it was refounded under Amasis with the grant of privileges and cult centres for the various groups that made it up, people from a collection of eastern Greek cities together with the island state of Aegina. Under the Ptolemies, as one of only three free Greek cities of Egypt, Naucratis continued to enjoy its special status, as it did still under the empire, when it served as a model for the emperor Hadrian's new foundation of Antinoopolis. [2]

This then was the Egypt that Athenaeus knew before he left for Rome, where he enjoyed the patronage of Larensis and his patron's excellent Greek library and composed the *Deipnosophistae* (1.3a–b). We do not know how old he was when he left his native land but it is clear from his work that Egypt still figured large in what he both read and wrote.[3] In this chapter I wish first to consider the picture of Egypt that we get from Athenaeus' work in terms of period, geography and emphasis, and then to outline just a few of the ways in which this work, which forms an unusual and sometimes valuable source for Hellenistic history, is at the same time affected by Athenaeus' particular concerns.

First, then, what does Athenaeus, who was writing in Rome in the late second or possibly early third century AD, tell us about Egypt and what, in turn, does this tell us about his concerns? With just the odd exception, Egyptian history for our author starts with the arrival of the Greeks under the pharaoh Psammetichus; Amasis is there, as in Herodotus, and also the Spartan king Agesilaus.[4] It is, however, under the Ptolemies that Egypt comes to life, and the period that gets the most Deipnosophistic coverage is without doubt the early Ptolemaic period. And for Athenaeus, history in this period is primarily the story of its rulers, of its kings and sometimes its queens. Ptolemy I Soter appears on more than one occasion as successor to Alexander (not just to Alexander's mistress Thais).[5] The long account from Callixenus in Book Five of the festival in Soter's honour set up by his son, the Ptolemaea, forms a fascinating picture of dynastic power in the making. [6] However, the outstanding figure of Egypt in Athenaeus' work is Ptolemy II Philadelphus, who reigned for almost forty years in the third century BC. Given the excesses of this ruler's life, his mistresses, the luxury of his court and the splendour of the feasts that he held, it is perhaps not surprising that in old age he suffered from gout (12.536e). Ptolemy II played an important part in the development of Alexandria's cultural life; he was a generous patron who liked to tease his retainers but might also act as a tyrant. Outspoken criticism of the king, as Sotades found to his cost, could result in a fairly nasty death by assisted drowning (14.620f–621a).[7] Of Ptolemy III Euergetes I far less is recorded;[8] of the later Ptolemies it is Ptolemy IV Philopator and his queen[9] and Ptolemy VIII Euergetes II 'Physkon'[10] who dominate Athenaeus' selection. For Philopator he had the works of Polybius and Ptolemy son of Agesarchus, for Euergetes II the *Memoirs* of the king himself. Some of the later Ptolemies also feature in his work—Ptolemy XII Auletes, who dissipated Egypt's wealth (5.206d), and Cleopatra VII, in whose reign Egypt finally fell to Rome.[11] As far as Egypt is concerned, the historical interests of Athenaeus are closely tied to Ptolemaic history.

When it comes to Roman Egypt, as usual in his work, there is little that refers to the imperial period. One contemporary Roman official (a Naucratite) is quoted as the source of the information that in Egypt criminals were fed not to the lions but to the asps; *kitrion* worked well as an antidote to their poison (3.84d–f). Sophists of the Claudian extension of the Museum in Alexandria are noted in a not altogether complimentary way—'modern professors, a disgrace even to mention' is Gulick's translation (6.240b)—and cooked meat shops (3.94c) together with Rich Man's Row, the *laura Eudaimonôn*, of that city are named (12.541a). Finally recorded is an Alexandrian wreath known as the *stephanos Antinoeios* (15.677d–e); in an Egyptian context, Hadrian's boyfriend Antinous is the closest we come to mention of a Roman emperor. And that is all there is of Roman Egypt. It is not contemporary Rome nor classical Athens but the Hellenistic period, in Egypt the era of the Ptolemies, in which this author shows the closest interest.

So much for time. What of space? The geography of Athenaeus' Egypt is very different from that of Herodotus' earlier account. It is the Greek cities of Alexandria and Naucratis, his own home town, which form the focus of Athenaeus' Egypt; Ptolemais, the third Greek city in the south, receives just one mention in his work—as the source of certain types of vessel (11.478b). And when places beyond Naucratis and Alexandria are named they tend to be those of the Delta.[12] Upstream Memphis is recognized as the earliest capital of the pharaohs (1.20c–d) and to the south, along the valley of the Nile, some other centres are briefly mentioned. Coptus occurs in several contexts; there pottery was baked with *aromata* added to the clay which improved the drinking water (11.464b) and, with the Thebaid, it was known for its somewhat thin wines (1.33f). As is clear from the map (fig. 1), Coptus lay on the Nile to the south at the end of the route across from a major Red Sea port. With the discovery of the monsoon and the opening up of the Indian trade, Coptus grew and flourished in the Roman period. The fact that Coptus is one of the few non-Greek centres of Egypt to be mentioned by Athenaeus may well reflect this importance. Generally, however, what may be described as Egypt proper—Egypt, that is, outside Alexandria—is missing from his work. It is the free Greek cities that really equal Egypt for this author from the Delta city of Naucratis.

Nevertheless there is a more general characterization of Egypt to be deduced from what Athenaeus tells and before looking in more detail at the Greek cities of Egypt it is this I want to consider. The overall picture of Egypt is one of wealth and prosperity, of fertility and plenty in this land of the Nile. The old clichés are there but when Egypt's wealth is detailed in the fine description of the Ptolemaea, with its pavilion and its rich procession, the wealth is Ptolemaic and is that displayed in Alexandria, the new capital of the country. The contrast with Herodotus and the wonders that he found could not be greater. For Athenaeus there is no discussion of the sources of the Nile, no pyramids or great Egyptian temples.[13] His Egypt is filled not with wonders but rather with interesting flora and fauna, and some of the products that led to that country's wealth. This is Egypt without the fabulous element; Athenaeus is more concerned with the here and now.[14] In Egypt pigeons have twelve not ten broods a year (9.394c); it is a land of excellent products—from vinegar to perfume, flax to flowers—and the Nile valley is good for vines. Wine[15] of course was the favoured drink of the Greeks in Egypt; the Egyptian drink was beer. The vine is even given a local origin: Dionysus, we learn early in the work, via Hellanicus, discovered the plant at Plinthine just west of Alexandria on the coast (1.34a).

The waters of the Nile play an important role in Athenaeus, both as home to many fishes (7.309a, 311f–312b, 8.356a) and as the giver of life to both man and fields (2.41f, cf. 5.203c, as Zeus). In bottling up the water of Egypt's river and sending it off to his daughter Berenice, married abroad, Ptolemy II recognized its special quality (2.45c). At an earlier date, Nile water and Egyptian salts were sent as presents to the Persian king (3.67b). Antiochus, in contrast, when sailing down the Nile, before drinking filtered the water twice over and chilled it overnight (3.124e). As drinking water, Nile water was not always safe. It had a tendency to loosen the bowels (2.41f) and when the river ran low and droughts occurred it became seriously polluted, resulting in many deaths (2.42a, 9.388a). Whether or not it is the water that was chiefly to blame, I detect a recurrent refrain of stomach problems in Athenaeus' references to Egypt. The soda that the Nile contained would also loosen the bowels (2.41f). On occasions such as these a poultice for the stomach formed of fig-mulberries, ripened local-style and mixed with attar of roses, could ease the fever of the ailing patient (2.51c). Elsewhere, and somewhat surprisingly, shell-fish or barnacles are described in favourable terms, as both diuretic and good for loosening the bowels (3.91a). What happened, one asks, when Arsinoe II came to Egypt? Earlier married to King Lysimachus, she had a tendency to throw up (14.616c). But maybe an incestuous marriage to her sister-loving brother combined with good Nile water put an end to such things.

All in all, however, the picture of Egypt to be gained from reading Athenaeus is of a remarkably fertile country where plants and wildlife flourished. The bitter native soil that prevented the successful take of cabbage transplanted from Rhodes is specified as the soil of Alexandria (9.369f). Elsewhere a wide variety of flora and fauna was found in abundance.

Before leaving the wider scene there is one subject to note in which native-born Athenaeus shows far less understanding of Egypt than did Herodotus, who was only a visitor—that is Egyptian religion. On this important aspect of Egypt Athenaeus appears to lack both understanding and sympathy for the religion of the majority of the population. But then he was a citizen of a Greek city, a *politês* (3.84d), and they were simply natives, *enchôrioi* (2.51b). Whereas this may form an interesting comment on the very Greek nature of his background, it also shows the degree to which he has come to share the Roman scorn for animal-worship. Only negative characteristics are applied to Egyptians in this context. Eels they consider as gods—which is not surprising given how much they cost, is how Antiphanes had responded (7.299e)—and Anaxandrides on the Egyptians is quoted as follows (7.299f–300a, translated Gulick):

> I couldn't bring myself to be an ally of yours, for neither our manners nor our customs agree, but stand a long distance apart from each other. You worship the cow, but I sacrifice it to the gods. You hold the eel to be a

mighty divinity, we hold it by far the mightiest of dainties. You eat no pork, but I like it very much. You worship the bitch, I beat her when I catch her eating up my best food. Here in our country, it is our custom to have our priests whole, but with you, so it appears, it is the custom to cut off their best parts. If you see a cat in any trouble, you mourn, but I am very glad to kill and skin it. The field-mouse has power with you, with me he doesn't count at all.

This is not just the Egyptians as the archetypical 'other'; this and other quotations that we find in the text add up to a critical view, to a scorn and disdain of Egyptians familiar in the Roman period. Given this attitude, it is perhaps all the more surprising that when human sacrifice is mentioned among the Egyptians it is simply the trimmings, the nesting fowl and, above all, the cakes that hold the centre of the scene for Athenaeus, who records this grisly practice from Panyassis without any further comment (4.172d).

As suggested earlier, Athenaeus' personal knowledge and real interest in Egypt seems bounded by the two Greek cities of Naucratis and Alexandria. These form the backdrop for what little he provides of historical interest, as they do for the writers and the literary culture he records. A brief consideration of his picture will make this clear.

Alexandria, of course, features as the home of Plutarchus, one of the Deipnosophists, which allows our author to include much from 'my beautiful Alexandria'. 'Beautiful Alexandria' is once termed 'the golden' and this was the city which took over as the centre of culture in the Hellenistic world. It was here and not in Athens that Machon of Sicyon (or Corinth) staged his comedies in the third century BC (14.664a), and in the great theatre of Alexandria that Hegesias, a comedian, played the works of Hesiod and Hermophantus those of Homer (14.620d). The Museum, with its garden and its books, is mentioned more than once and many of the famous literary scholars of Alexandria who flourished under Ptolemaic patronage are known from the pages of Athenaeus. Besides the theatre, the Ptolemaic palace quarter is recorded by our author, the temples of Berenice, Arsinoe II and Cronus and of course the magnificent Pharus, the site of excellent shell-fish. The city was rich and its perfume production flourished from the interest taken in it by early Ptolemaic queens. The cultural and economic importance of this city, especially under the earlier Ptolemies, cannot be overstated.[16]

Naucratis features in Athenaeus to a slightly lesser degree but, in my view, it was more important to him than has sometimes been allowed. The home to several authors, it was also noted for various of its plants (particularly the honey-lotus, 3.73a) and wildlife (such as the small fish left behind when the flood subsided, 7.301c), for its potters who gave their name to one of the city gates

(11.480d–e), for its wreaths (15.671e, 675f–676c) and above all for its famous prostitutes (13.596b–d). Sappho's brother Charaxus who came to the city on business met up here with the beautiful Doricha, the subject of one of Posidippus' many poems on local Greco-Egyptian themes. When Herodotus called her Rhodopis he simply got it wrong. It is as an Ionian city with local cults and customs that, quoting Hermeias, Athenaeus describes his city.[17] It is, as so often, the food that dominates his account and first it is special occasion dining in the prytaneum that is described (4.149d–150a), with a full account of the meal, the drink, the prayers and the special role of the priests; no woman might enter the building (flute-girls excepted), personal piss-pots were not allowed and any food left over was shared with the slaves. The quantity of food allowed to be provided was carefully controlled. On normal days those eligible to dine in the prytaneum in fact brought in their own food from home; it was only a measure of wine they received at public expense. How widely, I wonder, was public hospitality limited in this way?

In the same section of his work we meet the local τιμοῦχοι, Ionian officials otherwise known in Ptolemaic Egypt from Memphis[18] and mention of a local marriage law forbidding eggs and honey-cakes at the wedding feast (4.150a). It is, however, in the attempt to take over well-known authors that Athenaeus' Naucratite chauvinism comes through. In addition to various Naucratite writers whom he quotes, Aristophanes, the writer of comedies, is said to have hailed from the city (6.229e); Apollonius too, normally called 'of Rhodes', was yet another Naucratite and he wrote its founding story, its *Ktisis* (7.283d). Local patriotism must be the explanation here. On Egypt, therefore, in much of what we find in Athenaeus, authorial comment and interest come through; his knowledge was often local knowledge.[19] And even when the information comes at second hand, from Hermeias, Theophrastus or from many others, the selection of what features is that of Athenaeus, a citizen of Naucratis.

Finally, I want to consider here the way in which two interests of our author—dining and *tryphe*—affect the slant of information that he provides on the subject of Hellenistic kings. First, *tryphe*—luxuriousness, wantonness, luxury, extravagance. *Tryphe*, with negative connotations, is a constant concern of Athenaeus. Rulers are regularly characterized by the degree of their *tryphe*. How this affects the selection of what he records is clear in the case of the Ptolemaic royals. Ptolemy VIII Euergetes II, for instance, a much-travelled king whom the Alexandrians called Kakergetes or Malefactor, instead of Euergetes, Benefactor (4.184c), others Physkon or Fatty, has a somewhat mixed press in our author. During the visit to Alexandria of a Roman delegation, which included Scipio Aemilianus, he is described as follows (12.549e; Gulick's translation, slightly adapted):

through indulgence in luxury [*tryphe*] his body had become utterly corrupted with fat and with a belly of such size that it would have been hard to measure it with one's arms; to cover it he wore a tunic which reached to his feet and which had sleeves reaching to his wrists; but he never went abroad on foot except on Scipio's account.

This same king, as we also know from Athenaeus, wrote *Memoirs*, or *Hypomnemata*, emended the text of Homer (2.61c) and showed himself a bit of a pedant in disputing the word for pheasants (14.654b–c).

The younger son of Physkon, Ptolemy X Alexander, is described in similar terms to his father (12.550b, translated Gulick):

The master of Egypt, a man who was hated by the masses, though flattered by his courtiers, lived in great luxury [*tryphe*]; but he could not even go out to ease himself unless he had two men to lean upon as he walked. And yet when it came to the rounds of dancing at a drinking-party he would jump from a high couch barefoot as he was, and perform figures in a livelier fashion than those who had practised them.

Whereas neither of these kings was as overweight as Magas, king of Cyrene, who we are told choked to death following a fifty-year reign of over-eating and lack of exercise (12.550b–c), it is clearly Athenaeus' concern for *tryphe* that is responsible for his emphasis. Let us stop to consider. Physkon of Egypt reigned for fifty-four years, Magas of Cyrene for some fifty years and Ptolemy X for twenty-seven years before he was killed in a fight to retain the throne. How overweight really were these kings; and what do we mean by 'overweight' in this period? What Athenaeus, writing from the perspective of Rome, does not realize is that in the context of Hellenistic Egypt what he might scorn as *tryphe* was rather a desirable feature of eastern kings.[20] Coming from a Greek city in Roman Egypt and writing in Rome itself, Athenaeus either did not understand or else rejected the luxury and values of Hellenistic Egypt.

Finally, a tale of dining where Athenaeus' slant is of some historical interest. My example comes from the life of the last of the Ptolemies, Queen Cleopatra VII. The clash of the two cultures—those of Hellenistic rulers and of Rome—is the explicit context of a tale that he tells of this queen. When she realized that the Romans were getting more and more luxurious in their ways, she too decided to change. Unable to change her gold and silver dinner ware she decided just to rename it as 'regular ware' and so, I suppose, to pretend she led a simpler life (6.229c). When guests departed after dinner, the gold and silver plates she gave them to take home she called plain crocks or *keramos*. So, as the Romans adopt Hellenistic ways, Cleopatra raises the stakes. Criticism of the Romans combined with artful generosity on the part of this Hellenistic queen are both expressed in Athenaeus' account.

What I have tried to show in this chapter is Athenaeus' limited view of Egypt and its history. At times his Naucratite origin is very prominent. Throughout, his real interest in Egypt is concentrated in time on the Hellenistic period and in coverage on its Greek cities overwhelmingly Naucratic and Alexandrian. Meanwhile, for the Hellenistic period, as a source for Ptolemaic history, Athenaeus' *Deipnosophistae* is not without some value.

# ❖ 6 ❖

# ATHENAEUS THE LIBRARIAN

## by Christian Jacob

Quo innumerabiles libros et bibliothecas, quarum dominus vix tota vita indices perlegit? Onerat discentem turba, non instruit, multoque satius est paucis te auctoribus tradere quam errare per multos.

To what end books and libraries, whose owner can scarcely read the indices in the course of a whole life-time? The scholar is burdened by the mass of them, not instructed; much better to devote yourself to a few authors than to roam about through many.

(Seneca, *De Tranquillitate Animi*, 9.4)

**Introduction**

Reading the *Deipnosophistae* is comparable to entering a world of mirrors and illusions. The text relates a series of banquets and is an encyclopaedia on the subject of banquets. It belongs to the genre of sympotic literature and it is a critical discussion of that genre. It explores the cultural and culinary universe of Greek comedy, yet at the same time, the text in itself can be assimilated to a kind of comedy, with its own characters and humorous situations. Each of the characters could be interpreted as a subject in his own right, or as an incarnation of Athenaeus himself or that of his readers, even: the Deipnosophists are theatrical masks, bearing enigmatic names (that sometimes sound familiar) and displaying various intellectual skills, as well as a particular style and personality. Athenaeus' reader is permanently hesitating: from eating food and drinking wines, there is a shift towards eating words, quotations and scholarly comments about drinks and food. There is a mirror effect between the text and the symposium,[1] as well as between the dishes and drinks brought by the slaves, and the words, topics and questions that feed the learned discussion itself—the same verb, παρατίθεσθαι, refers to the exhibiting of dishes as well as to the quoting of texts.[2]

The *Deipnosophistae* can be read as a sophisticated imitation of the various learned disciplines it draws upon—etymology, lexicography, philology, ethnography, cultural history, literary studies. But where is the border between the serious and the parody, between the intellectual project and the joke?[3] Should the reader decide on the criteria of his own reading? But what was the intended readership of Athenaeus and of his epitomator?

The aim of this chapter is to comment on a specific dimension of this mirror-like construction: the quotations, the books and the library each reflect one another in a complex way. Athenaeus will be considered as a reader and as a scholar deeply concerned with the collecting, identifying and classifying of books, as well as with reading and browsing through them.

One of the most controversial questions related to Athenaeus' work is: what books did he actually read? What were his sources and to what extent did he make use of previous compilations and quote from them? Such questioning is not peculiar to Athenaeus: it is central in the tradition of Graeco-Roman scholarship that relied extensively on books as a medium to produce and to transmit knowledge, to reshape it and reorganize it, thus creating new aesthetic and intellectual effects from the various steps of compiling, summarizing and rewriting.[4] The most important thing, for Athenaeus, was to be able to quote the largest range of ancient authors, to bring together as many words, quotations and facts as possible. Personal excerpts from the original works themselves are probably mixed in an inextricable way with materials gathered from previous collections and glossaries of a similar kind. These bibliographical intermediaries, however, were not always considered as worth mentioning for themselves:[5] what mattered was the ancient author they made it possible to quote. Quoted bits of texts in the *Deipnosophistae* are in the first place data and materials of a collection, not mere bibliographical sources necessarily relying on first-hand knowledge.

Athenaeus is representative of a milieu of scholarly readers and writers who are used to buying and collecting books, to visiting libraries and to having various exchanges with other book-lovers. The *Deipnosophistae* provide us with a vivid description of such a circle, where dinners and wine-parties, loans of books and various *jeux d'esprit* were shared hobbies. Within this bookish culture, anecdotes, sayings, quotations, lexicographical entries could be transmitted through one or several intermediary written sources between the original text and Athenaeus' compilation. This compilation is at the same time the collecting pool of previous knowledge, and a starting point for multiple new traditions: the *Deipnosophistae* is a perfect case-study of devices which provide their readers with a digest of a wide range of literary and scholarly data, that could then be used and circulated for its own sake. Athenaeus' text itself provided new compilers with an ideal starting point, as the Epitome testifies. Renaissance compilers still provide us with explicit examples of recomposition of ancient sympotic encyclopaedias.[6]

Thus, we could consider Athenaeus as a librarian and his text as a library, a storage device for hundred of books that were read or browsed, summarized, paraphrased or quoted by the author or his sources. The first part of my argument will be devoted to Athenaeus' technical interest in bibliography. This concern provides a continuous thread throughout the fifteen books of the *Deipnosophistae*. In the second part, I shall consider a few general questions linked to the process of compiling and to the elaboration of a book based on excerpts drawn from previous books.

## 1. A technical interest in books: Athenaeus as a witness of Hellenistic librarianship

The abridged version of Book One sketches short portraits of the Deipnosophists. Larensis, the host of the dinner, is praised for his library.[7] This collection of ancient Greek books is integrated into the history of ancient libraries, ranging from Polycrates and Peisistratos to Euripides, Aristotle, Theophrastus and Neleus, Pergamon and Alexandria.[8] To mention such a genealogy was a significant choice. Athenaeus adapted to his own literary project a pattern of the history of ancient libraries, probably transmitted by various Hellenistic treatises and perhaps by Varro's lost treatise *De Bibliothecis* too. We should note that this historical sketch leads from Athens to Rome, through Hellenistic libraries. It also leads from city or court libraries to a Roman private library. This general pattern of the transmission of Greek literary works is historically exact and could provide us with a key for understanding the *Deipnosophistae*: Athenaeus' work is located at the crossroads and, at the same time, at the end of several traditions—Classical Greek, Hellenistic and Roman. There is a mirror effect between Larensis' library and the *Deipnosophistae*: the latter seems to rely on the former. Athenaeus' work is not the catalogue of Larensis' library, but rather its reduction, its literary and artistic embodiment.

While Larensis' book collection is defined as the temporary end of the process of development of Greek libraries, nothing is said of other Roman libraries, particularly of the development of public and imperial libraries since Asinius Pollio's foundation of a library in 39 BC.[9] Athenaeus' purpose is to stress the link between Alexandria and Pergamon, on the one hand, and Larensis' library, on the other hand. The latter appears as the heir of the two main places of Hellenistic librarian scholarship. Despite its hyperbolic evaluation, Larensis' library is typical of the private collections of books gathered by rich Romans from the second century BC, which sometimes relied on the booty taken from Greek cities and oriental kingdoms. The practice of book-collecting increased during the late Republic and the early Empire: Cicero and Atticus,[10] Petronius' Trimalchio,[11]

Pliny the Elder and Pliny the Younger[12] provide us with some well-known examples. Seneca's criticism of 'bibliomania' probably pinpointed a widespread habit among wealthy Romans of his time,[13] and Lucian wrote a suggestive portrayal of an ignorant book-collector, under the reign of Marcus Aurelius. A chapter in Vitruvius' *De Architectura* was devoted to the best location of a library within a house.[14] Private libraries could gather a large number of books. It is said, for example, that Serenus Sammonicus bequeathed his father's library, that is 62,000 papyrus rolls, to Gordian.[15] Such a figure, if credible, is superior to the collection in the library of the Alexandrian Serapeum, which amounted to 42,800 rolls, according to Tzetzes.[16] Serenus' father was a well-known scholar and physician who lived under Septimius Severus. Larensis is close to these wealthy and learned Romans who surrounded themselves with poets and writers, attracted by their private libraries as well as by their festive hospitality.[17]

Roman private libraries, like public libraries during the Empire, usually kept Greek books and Latin books in two distinct collections.[18] Larensis' library is described as a Greek library, specializing in old Greek books.[19] Larensis is also said to draw his knowledge of Roman political and religious customs from the study of archives and collections of laws.[20] Latin books in Athenaeus' text are exceptional: we find only three quotations, all of them transmitted through indirect sources.[21] Such private collections of books could be used by friends of their owner and by visiting scholars as well, to judge from Lucullus' library at Tusculum during the first century BC.[22] Lucullus was inspired by Alexandria, where the library was part of the Museum. Within the Alexandrian Museum, scholars lived together and had common meals, as Strabo testifies.[23] The excavations at Pergamon suggest that a room for symposia could have been located within the library, in the precinct of the temple of Athena Polias.[24] Larensis' dinners and symposia perhaps recall this Hellenistic model. Seneca harshly criticized the presence of large and useless libraries in Roman dining rooms.[25]

There is no evidence to suggest that Athenaeus was Larensis' librarian.[26] What we nowadays refer to as a 'librarian' had different counterparts in the ancient world. In Ptolemaic Alexandria, the scarce data available only refer to the 'Head Librarians', who were famous scholars such as, for example, Zenodotus, Eratosthenes, Aristophanes and Aristarchus.[27] We know nothing about the staff of copyists and store-keepers working within the Alexandrian Museum.[28] Callimachus provides us with a perfect example of a scholar working in the library without being the Head Librarian, at least as far as we can judge from our sources. He was charged, however, with an important cataloguing task, that is with the writing of the *Pinakes*. In the Roman world, specialized slaves or freedmen, like Tyrannio or Atticus' *glutinatores*, could repair damaged books and take care of the actual organizing of a private collection. A scholar would personally be involved in buying, cataloguing and ordering the books. Cicero's *Letters* hint at the amount of work and of personal correspondence, together with the important network of personal relationships, necessary for the development of a Greek library in Italy.[29] At the head of Roman imperial libraries, we find authentic scholars such as C. Julius Hyginus and obscure freedmen as well.

One can assume that Athenaeus, as a Greek *lettré* from Egypt, was among Larensis' advisers and that he helped in the acquisition of ancient and rare Greek books either in Italy or in the Greek world. He was also most likely one of the scholars allowed to use this collection, to read books and perhaps to borrow them. He belonged to Larensis' circle of literate and learned friends. One can be sure that, while he was in Egypt, he became well acquainted with the scholarship of the Alexandrian librarians. The book collection in the Ptolemies' Palace was not destroyed in 48 BC by Caesar, but still existed after the Alexandrian war and during the first centuries AD, as can be inferred from Strabo's *Geography* or from the scholarly activity of Didymus.[30] The Palace's library probably lost its previous prestige and prominence, but Alexandria remained a place of scholarship during the early centuries of the Empire. The Museum was most probably destroyed with the Bruchion neighbourhood, during the war between queen Zenobia and Aurelian (270–275 AD).[31] The Serapeum library as well as commercial booksellers[32] contributed too to the lasting tradition of Alexandrian librarianship. This tradition should be considered as an important background to Athenaeus' erudition.

The *Deipnosophistae* was obviously written by someone who had a deep knowledge of books, who was accustomed to searching for rare books, to checking their identification, to gathering internal and external data about them, and to browsing catalogues and various reference works. Athenaeus' work reflects his interest not only in the content of compiled books, but also in the books themselves and in the questions they were posing. Such a constant care for books differentiates Athenaeus from other compilers such as Aelian, for example. He could be compared to Aulus Gellius whose *Noctes Atticae* display the same scholarly concerns. Even if some of this bibliographical material was found in Athenaeus' sources, its repetition in the *Deipnosophistae* is relevant in itself.

Such a bibliophilic interest is shared by all the characters in the *Deipnosophistae*. Ulpian is described as a frequent visitor of bookshops, one of the places of his intellectual activity along with baths and porticoes.[33] Larensis' guests most likely had their own private libraries. The display of knowledge during the dinners relied on books, and accuracy in quoting books was or was supposed to be a key feature—whether as mere factual information or as a possible help for other book-collectors or as rhetorical markers or even just for fun. One of the rules of the cultural game they were playing was: let's link every bit of knowledge, every quoted word or sentence to a bibliographical source, to our previous reading;[34]

let's share our reading, our knowledge; let's prove that all of us share the same ideal library, that of ancient Greek literature and scholarship.[35]

We do not find a standard way of quoting books in the *Deipnosophistae*, but instead a range of formulations, from the more vague to the more precise.[36] We should however consider whether such variations are ruled by an underlying logic. For example, are more precise bibliographical references to be linked with a specific range of authors or of texts, according to their actual availability to Athenaeus as well as to the intermediary sources that provided some of his quotations? Or is there a random distribution, a given author being referred to in various ways, according to Athenaeus' sources and files? To answer these questions is beyond the scope of this chapter, but the last hypothesis is the more probable.[37] The bibliographical information is the result of several factors that should be investigated for themselves. First, there is Athenaeus' way of organizing his material, of excerpting quotations and distributing them in clusters of topics, and as a later step adding the literary frame of the dialogue between his characters. Precise references could be kept or simplified during the stages of this rewriting process. But a second factor is that Athenaeus was also relying on his sources: did previous compilations transmit the bibliographical references of the texts they quoted? Did they summarize or modify them? How were the books Athenaeus had access to entitled and edited? A third factor is: what was the purpose of giving precise and detailed bibliographical references?[38] What kind of specific knowledge was available to the reader, and to what extent was such information intended to have a practical value, that is to help the reader to refer to these sources? Last but not least, are differences to be found according to the characters who quote books, that is, do the Deipnosophists display specific skills, knowledge and ignorance when referring to the books they read and they quote from?

A large part of the ambiguity of Athenaeus' bibliographical references results from the nature of his project: he reorganizes and reshapes a huge amount of scholarly and literary material into a new book. This material comes from other books that were compiled, excerpted and summarized through several steps or at several levels, direct or indirect, some of Athenaeus' sources offering their own collection of data.[39] Books were cut into fragments, browsed through various selection principles, according to a curiosity and to interests that are Athenaeus' personal trademark. The bibliographical references lead the reader back to a step before the compilation and the deconstruction of texts, that is to the transmitted library of Greek literature, to its scholarly construction. This construction results from the work of philologists, librarians and bibliographers, who tried to establish the inventory of books from the past, to check authorship and authenticity, and sometimes to edit the texts themselves. Beyond the *Deipnosophistae*, and sometimes several steps beyond, there is the map of an ideal library, its catalogue. This πίναξ is not found in Athenaeus' text in the same way as in Book 1 of Pliny's *Natural History*: the latter's encyclopædic project and a specific method of reading and of consultation made possible a kind of table of contents as well as a systematic bibliography of the compiled sources. In the *Deipnosophistae*, libraries and their catalogues were responsible for the underlying cohesiveness of the whole project. They created an order, they allowed repetition, landmarks, classification of genres and enumeration of titles.

On a general level, one could say that the Deipnosophists are mainly concerned with quoting texts, with offering new insights on the corpus of Greek Classical and Hellenistic literature. They do so through a complex game of selection and juxtaposition of fragments, whose meaning and value are determined by their new context as well as by the specific questions to which they provide an answer or an illustration. In this respect, each of Athenaeus' characters could be considered as an abstract operator mapping out a linear path through the labyrinth, that is through the library. Their dialogue and the free association of ideas, jokes and *mots d'esprit* are the structuring factor or, at least, the *fil d'Ariane* in Athenaeus' compilation. The bibliographical references also stand as rhetorical markers—they testify to the origin, that is to the authenticity, the rarity, the interest of a fact, a word, or a quotation. The content of the conversation is a question of memory, not of fantasy. But memory has the creative power of imagination. Athenaeus' project is, to a certain extent, an exploration of the world of what was ever said or written: the space of the Greek language and of the literature that fixed it, used it and played with it.

The typology of Athenaeus' bibliographical references makes necessary a brief overview of the material status of the Greek books he used. It is well known that books, at the end of the second century AD, were still mostly papyrus rolls.[40] This was probably the only form available for old Greek books. The different 'volumes' of a single work were so many separate rolls. For example, when Athenaeus quotes Book 108 of a lexicographical collection by Dorotheos of Askalon,[41] he refers to a lexicon composed of at least 108 rolls. This was not an unusual figure for large collections of that kind. Single rolls were a usual format for a dramatic play or a short treatise. Moreover a single roll could include several shorter texts by the same writer (for example, a collection of short poems). The titles would be written at the beginning or, more often, at the end of each roll,[42] or at the beginning of a text, were several short texts to be included in the same roll. The titles of shorter poems could be written in a separate line, indented in the margin of the written column. Sometimes, too, diacritical signs marked the separation between two short untitled poems.[43] The title and the author name could also be written on an external papyrus or pergamon label (σίλλυβος, *index*, *titulus*) which was stuck to the top of the roll and was readable without unrolling it on the shelf or in the roll-box.[44] Seneca alludes to this custom when he criticizes the ignorant book-collectors who used to read only these external tags and who sometimes had so many books in their libraries that they did not manage to do this.[45]

As is well known, there was no numbering of columns allowing more precise quotation. Line numbering (stichometry) was mostly a technical indication used to calculate the copyist's fee or to check that a given text was copied without any omissions.[46] As such, the stichometric indication would be used by librarians to check the identification and the extent of a text. It also helped to determine the length of the roll needed for copying a given text as well as the approximate time required for its reading.[47] Using a stichometric indication to pinpoint the location of a precise word, sentence or development within a text, as far as we can judge, was exceptional.[48] As a matter of fact, we do not find a single stichometric location in the *Deipnosophistae*.

A basic pattern of bibliographical references is provided with a syntagm: [author's name] + [φήσι or γράφει] + [quotation]. Anonymous quotations are exceptional.[49] Sometimes, a character stresses he is unable to remember the title of the work from which he quotes a sentence: 'I know that Phylarchus wrote somewhere about large fishes ...'.[50] Neither the title nor the book's number is mentioned. This approximation, expressed by the enclitic που, is frequent in the first two abridged books of the *Deipnosophistae*[51] as well as in the whole *Epitome*: its author, obviously, did not share Athenaeus' interest in bibliography and decided to leave aside such indications.[52] Advanced bibliographical quotations add to the basic pattern the title of the work and sometimes the volume number for works composed of several book-rolls.

When quoting from large prose works, Athenaeus often mentions the book number. This is not, however, systematic.[53] Eight of the twelve quotations from Nicolaus of Damascus' *History* include the book number. Among the 144 rolls composing this large treatise, Athenaeus limits his quotations to Books 103–16. Such an objective restriction could be explained by the actual availability of the rolls in a given library. But in Nicolaus' case, however, it stresses a particular interest of the reader: Nicolaus was read as a continuation of Posidonius' *History*.[54] Focusing on a particular period, Athenaeus actually was interested in one tenth of the whole treatise. One could wonder whether such a limit reflects the actual volumes Athenaeus had access to. The nineteen quotations of Posidonius' *History* provided with a book number suggest the same selective approach to this work that encompassed fifty-two book-rolls: Books 3, 23 and 28 were quoted twice; Book 16 was quoted three times (it was devoted to king Antiochus VIII). It is indeed difficult to draw a causal relationship between the mention of a precise book number and what Athenaeus could have read personally in Posidonius' work.[55] On the other hand, there is no proof that he did not read large parts or whole books in it,[56] and smaller quotations, without book number, do not necessarily prove an indirect source, such as a lexicon.

If one considers the titles of books, Athenaeus testifies to various traditions and to successive steps of the history of books and authorship in the ancient world. Giving a book its title was not necessarily the concern of its author. Such a decision required a specific context where writers were in control of the diffusion of their works and chose to give them a precise title as well as their name when they started to circulate them through the ἔκδοσις process, either informally among a circle of friends, or commercially at a bookseller's shop.[57] After the author's death, friends and relatives, addressees of particular texts, and booksellers collected his writings and organized the corpus according to more or less defined principles. Then, Hellenistic librarians and scholars had to deal with these collections in a systematic and critical way, to fix titles and to check authenticity. Another context for the fixing of titles was linked to the rules of dramatic performances, such as in Attic festivals: the archons in charge of the contests had to register the titles of the plays at each festival. Titles were a necessary identification mark. The archons' lists were used and reorganized by Aristotle, and his work was an essential landmark in the history of ancient theatrical studies. Older texts, however, were often transmitted without specific titles. Shorter poems were not usually identifiable by title. Discourses by orators, after their public presentation, had to be entitled as written texts. Among the many heterogeneous texts that were collected in the Alexandrian library, one could imagine that some of them had lost their titles, that different copies of the same work had different titles, that there were homonymous books. It was the librarians' and literary critics' task to identify books and to organize in a systematic way the denominations of texts written by the same author, that is his bibliography.

The lexical category of the title (ἐπιγράφειν / ἐπιγράφεσθαι / ἐπιγραφή / ἐπίγραμμα) is omnipresent in the *Deipnosophistae*. Most often, Athenaeus uses a passive form: 'in [the text] that is entitled ...'.[58] This text could be a poem included within a collection, such as *Meleagros*, one of the dithyrambs of Cleomenes of Rhegium.[59] Sometimes, Athenaeus explicitly says that the author himself gave his work a precise title, as with Eupolis.[60] Sometimes too, he clearly states that the authority for a title was not the author but someone else. This is the case with Alexandrian scholars, as Lycophron on the *Gastrologia* of Archestratos,[61] Callimachus, responsible for the title of a play by Diphilos[62] or the anonymous scholars who decided to change the title of a play by Sophocles[63] and gave a comedy by Hegemon its title.[64] The ἐπιγραφή / ἐπίγραμμα was an inscription on the book-roll itself, either on its external side, or at the end of the text, as one can deduce from the quotation of Alexis' *Linus*, where Herakles is invited to take whatever book he wants and, then, to read its title.[65]

It is beyond doubt that Athenaeus had a first-hand knowledge of the main bibliographical treatises and reference books of the Hellenistic Age.[66] The best evidence is provided in the discussion about a mysterious play by Alexis, the *Asotodidaskalos*, mentioned by a Peripatetic historian of philosophy, Sotion of Alexandria.[67] Not only did this play escape as systematic a reader as Athenaeus (more exactly, Democritus, who claims to have read more than eight hundred plays of the Middle Comedy[68]), but neither was it mentioned by either Callimachus or Aristophanes,[69] or by the librarians of Pergamon. The starting point of the discussion lies in a second-hand quotation found in Sotion's text: a bibliographical *hapax*. It is striking that Democritus does not question the authenticity of this play nor Sotion's reliability, as a historian of philosophy and not of Middle Comedy. He is more excited by the rarity of the comedy and by the conviction of having discovered a bibliographical enigma that escaped even the best bibliographers in Alexandria and in Pergamon, and such an expert in comedy as Aristophanes of Byzantium. Interestingly enough, bibliographical expertise relies first on one's own personal experience of books, on the accumulation of extracts and titles gathered from on-going reading, and then on the reference works of the greatest Hellenistic libraries. The succession from Callimachus to Aristophanes (of Byzantium) and to the Pergamon librarians is significant: this was a logical sequence of reference books to be checked by anybody looking for bibliographical information.[70]

As a matter of fact, the *Pinakes* of Callimachus are quoted several times.[71] Athenaeus had referred to the sections devoted to the 'miscellaneous treatises',[72] to speeches[73] and laws.[74] He relied on the *Pinakes* for several purposes, such as finding lists of treatises about a given topic (for example authors who wrote 'dinner books' or pastry recipe books) or checking a precise book identification, its title, its first phrase, its total number of lines. Callimachus' *Pinakes* also provided biographical information, such as the name of the philosophical teacher of Lysimachos, author of a treatise *On the education of Attalus*.[75] In one case, Athenaeus gives the title of a play by Diphilos but, in quoting Callimachus, shows his knowledge that this is an alternative title to the accepted bibliography.[76] It should be stressed that Athenaeus does not explicitly use Callimachus' list of *Didaskaliai* nor its Aristotelian antecedent. The *Pinakes* were the main reference tool and they encompassed probably most of the previous material.

We also find quotations taken from the complement and correction of the *Pinakes* by Aristophanes of Byzantium, not on bibliography, but on lexicographical matters.[77] At least, Aristophanes' *addenda* to Callimachus' work was an obvious source for solving bibliographical enigmas.[78] Athenaeus used other bibliographical handbooks, such as the Βιβλίων συναγωγὴ (*Collection of Books*) by Artemon of Cassandreia, who is perhaps to be identified with Artemon of Pergamon (*c.* 100 BC), quoted in Pindar's scholia.[79] The alternate title, Βιβλίων χρῆσις (*Use of Books*), probably refers to the second volume of this treatise, which belongs to the tradition of Pergamene librarian scholarship. Artemon is quoted on the disputed authorship of a historical treatise attributed to Xanthos the Lydian. According to Artemon, the author was Dionysius Scytobrachion, but Athenaeus, relying on Ephorus, concluded that such an attribution was wrong for chronological reasons. Athenaeus, however, still quotes Artemon's typology of the skolia songs and we can suppose this handbook gave an overview of poetic genres—it is indeed relevant that Book Two was devoted to 'all the songs sung in social gatherings'.[80] In such a treatise, bibliography was closely linked to literary history and poetics. Athenaeus does not mention other similar, and more recent, handbooks, such as Herennius Philo of Byblos' pinacographical work (completed under Hadrian) or Telephus of Pergamon's treatise for book-buyers (second century AD).[81]

We could suppose, however, that the use of such reference works in the *Deipnosophistae* went far beyond their explicit mention. For example, the short bibliography of treatises on banquets, in the epitomized Book One, was probably drawn from Callimachus' *Pinakes*, precisely from the section of the 'miscellaneous treatises' that Athenaeus quotes in Book Six.[82] Here we find authors' names with their geographical origin, nicknames, short biographical data and literary genre.

Such additional details are not directly related to the topic discussed. Their purpose is to complete the identification of a given book. Among such notices, we find the total number of volumes composing a given text. In the short bibliography about banquet treatises, Athenaeus mentions 'Timachidas of Rhodes, who wrote one [treatise] in epic verse in eleven, or possibly more, books'.[83] Such an uncertainty is interesting. Did Athenaeus (or the bibliographer he relies on) deal with an incomplete copy of Timachidas' work? Why did he suspect that books could be missing? Athenaeus quotes Timachidas' work four times, but he refers to Books Four and Nine only.[84] As an introduction to a particular quotation, Athenaeus sometimes mentions the extent of the whole work, as for example: 'Nicolaus of Damascus, in his bulky (πολύβυβλος) *History* (for there are one hundred and forty-four books) says, in the one hundred and sixteenth book that ...'.[85] In such a statement, we find the location of the quotation, but also an indication about the number of rolls this work encompasses. This kind of bibliographical description is a help for the identification of the book and is probably close to what a bibliophile could find in a library's *pinakes* or in handbooks such as Artemon's treatise. It was also to be found in library catalogues such as the Rhodes inscription.[86] Diogenes Laertius also mentions frequently the total number of books of the philosophical works he lists.[87] The preserved fragments of

Callimachus' *Pinakes* do not encompass such a reference, but it is beyond doubt that the Alexandrian library registered the total number of rolls composing the books of its collection. When he gives such details, Athenaeus is concerned with a short description of the work, in a particular edition he used or referred to through an intermediary source. A mention such as 'and four books of his *Parodies* are extant'[88] clearly alludes to a bibliography where the inventory of the literary texts known from the past was checked against their actual availability in library collections.

Although not a generalized habit in the *Deipnosophistae*, mentioning the whole number of rolls of a given literary work could be considered as an aspect of a general pattern of accumulation (food, drinks, objects, words, quotations ...). In this respect, a key character is the grammarian Didymos, who 'published' so many treatises that he was unable to keep their records and was given the nickname βιβλιολάθας, 'he who forgets his books'.[89] The mention of the 3,500 writings of Didymos does not contribute at all to the topic discussed by Athenaeus: instead, it unveils in front of the reader new storage rooms and breathtaking virtual catalogues in the library the author is exploring, between Alexandria and Rome.[90] To the writer who forgot his own books one could oppose the reader who kept an infallible memory of what he had read or not, for example among the eight hundred rolls of the plays of Middle Comedy.

Another mark of the Alexandrian bibliographical tradition was identifying books through their opening words, their ἀρχή. Titles could vary. Names could be ambiguous because of homonymy. Any variant of the tradition, any mistake of the copyist or of the bibliographer, a damaged book-roll, a lost label or an unreadable title could prevent the identification of copies from a given book. The ἀρχή of a text was a more secure reference and could compensate for the uncertainties and the variations of the ἐπιγραφή. One had to unroll the text, to read its first lines and to check them against the bibliographical reference book in order to be sure of its identification.

Athenaeus reproduces a notice about Chaerephon found in Callimachus' *Pinakes*: the opening words of his dinner-book are quoted and the total amount of lines is given. There are no quotations from Chaerephon in the *Deipnosophistae*, and Athenaeus probably did not read or compile this book. But the bibliographical reference stands as a conclusion to a series of testimonies about Chaerephon who was a famous parasite, well known from comic writers:[91] any subject, any character could lead the reader towards the Alexandrian library.

Checking and comparing the ἀρχή was the best way to establish that the *Gastronomia*, the *Hedupatheia*, the *Deipnologia* and the *Opsopoiia* were a single and same text and not various poems by Archestratos.[92] The opening words were probably to be found in the pinacographic rubrics devoted to prolific authors, where authentic and spurious texts could be mixed. Such is the case with a speech ascribed to Lysias, entitled *On the Vessel-Stand* [93]. Mentioning the ἀρχή was a useful caution for prose treatises or collections of various notes and materials with generic titles, such as the Ὑπομνήματα by Hegesander of Delphi, quoted as an authority about the *kottabos* game.[94]

Athenaeus also gives the opening words of a comic play by Antiphanes, the κιθαρῳδός (singer and player of the cithara) and we can wonder whether the incipit mentioned was a means of avoiding confusion with another play by the same writer, entitled κιθαριστής (player of the cithara), also quoted by Athenaeus.[95] The first verse was a useful tool for identifying shorter poems as in the case of Pindar, Simonides of Amorgos and Alcaeus, for example.[96] Alexandrian scholarship provided such lyrical poets as Pindar and Alcaeus with editions, ordered collections of poems, commentaries—and Athenaeus obviously relied on it.

Another trademark of this bibliographical tradition is to identify the author of a book as precisely as possible. It was the only way to avoid confusion between homonymous authors, such as for example the eleven authors called 'Dionysius' who were quoted by Athenaeus. Homonymy was an immediate pitfall for ignorant book-collectors and a constant nightmare for advanced ones. It was also an exciting challenge for trained bibliographers, such as Diogenes Laertius.[97] But Diogenes most probably relied on a reference book, the treatise *On poets and homonymous writers* by Demetrius of Magnesia (first century BC),[98] a friend of Atticus. Cicero referred to him in his *Letters*.[99] Dionysius of Halicarnassus preserves a lengthy quotation from Demetrius, about the four Dinarchuses he came across.[100] Each of them received critical comments, and Dionysius disagrees with those on the orator Dinarchus, despite Demetrius' reputation as a man of great learning (πολυίστωρ). Demetrius' work probably relied on the catalogues and bibliographical tables of great Hellenistic libraries, such as Alexandria and Pergamon.

Athenaeus, indeed, knew Demetrius' treatise.[101] He used another similar reference work by Heracleides of Mopsus, where he finds a list of all the writers named Polemon.[102] And he was aware of the necessity of avoiding ambiguity when referring to writers of the past.[103] In order to do so, it was necessary to add to the author's name details that would clearly pinpoint one precise writer. Ethnic name(s), father's name, nickname, philosophical affiliation are common details in the *Deipnosophistae*. Cohesiveness was not a necessity. In order to avoid ambiguity, a range of different formulations was available for the same author. Such a famous writer as Posidonius is quoted as a Stoic,[104] as a 'philosopher',[105] as an Apamean[106] or a Rhodian,[107] as 'my Posidonius'.[108] The mention of the *History* and the frequency itself of quotations was expected to clear any ambiguity about the name 'Posidonius'.[109] There was however another Posidonius in the *Deipnosophistae*, an author from Corinth who wrote a treatise *On Fishing*.[110]

The dating of an author is less frequent. We find statements such as: 'Callias of Athens ... who flourished a little before the time of Strattis'.[111] In a few instances, Athenaeus raises a polemical debate on the relative dating of writers: for example, he demonstrates, against Hermesianax' claim, that Anacreon and Sappho did not live at the same time.[112]

Authors were identified and distributed in a general classification of literary genres. Generic labels such as 'epic writer' (ὁ ἐποποιὸς), 'comic writer' (ὁ κωμικός, κωμῳδιοποιὸς etc), 'tragic writer' (ὁ τραγικὸς), 'author of dithyrambs' (διθυραμβοποιὸς), 'author of iambic poems' (ἰαμβοποιὸς), etc., referred to categories built up by historians of literature, librarians, editors and commentators. They were indeed useful when applied to minor, or even unknown poets. Sometimes, we find a double generic definition, such as for Timocles who was a comic as well as a tragic poet and whose name was probably registered in two different lists.[113] Reminding the reader that these two Timocles were the same author was an important statement. But mentioning the literary genres could also help to distinguish between homonymous authors, such as Sotades, a writer from the Middle Comedy, who is not the same as the author of Ionic poems put to death on the order of Ptolemy II Philadelphus after he made some outrageous comments on his wedding with Arsinoe.[114] Both writers were quoted in the *Deipnosophistae*.

Athenaeus relied on Alexandrian scholarship for matters related to comedy.[115] Along with Callimachus' *Pinakes*, he used treatises such as those by Lycophron, Eratosthenes and Antiochus of Alexandria.[116] He draw from these sources information about the category a dramatic poet belonged to, namely Old Comedy,[117] Middle Comedy[118] or Italian Comedy.[119] Such labels were sometimes controversial and Athenaeus, for example, mentions that unnamed writers place Hegemon of Thasos in Old Comedy.[120] There obviously existed lists of plays from Middle Comedy that provided Athenaeus with a guideline in his extensive readings.[121]

As far as theatrical works are concerned, Athenaeus frequently makes a distinction between the first and the second, revised, edition of a play (διασκευὴ), and in a few cases, points out the fact that two works with different titles can be shown to be different editions of the same play.[122] Quite often, he provides us with double titles, for comedies: this suggests that his bibliographical sources, and perhaps the actual copies he read in the libraries he had access to, kept a record of the different editions and titles of the same play.[123]

Athenaeus' bibliographical background is especially obvious in all the cases where identifying a book or an author is shown to be problematic. Such indications could have been found in intermediary sources, glossaries or collections. But Athenaeus was interested in quoting such statements. He had to face three kinds of problems within the libraries he was working in: these were related to the titles of books, to their authors, to their authenticity. When the authenticity of a book is questioned, that is to say that one cannot be certain of its author, and one cannot propose an alternative author. Statements such as 'if it is authentic' (εἰ γνήσιον) are referred to a whole text or a part of it, a speech, or a short poem. Such warnings are not justified or explained. They express a doubt about a text that was currently included in the corpus attributed to an author. The separation of authentic works from spurious ones entailed the consideration of each text from an historical as well as a stylistic point of view. Athenaeus echoes the critical examination of some of Hypereides', Lysias' and Demosthenes' speeches. Of the latter, the speech *Against Neaera* is mentioned as spurious and is introduced as such in the *hypothesis* of the text we still read today.[124] As to Lysias' works, *On the golden tripod*,[125] *Against Lais*[126] and *Against Philonides*[127] were suspected. As to those of Hypereides, the authenticity of the speech *Against Patroclos* was also questioned.[128]

Most likely, Athenaeus or his sources relied on the critical work of Dionysius of Halicarnassus (who is not quoted in the *Deipnosophistae*) and of Caecilius of Cale Acte, whose definition of the canon of Orators, perhaps linked to Pergamene scholarship, was widely used in the *Lives of the Ten Orators* of Ps.-Plutarch.[129] Athenaeus quoted Caecilius, but not from his critical works.[130] This reorganization of the corpus of the orators reflects the previous lack of control over the circulation and attribution of their speeches and, as a consequence, the diffusion of spurious speeches under famous names, probably a common trick among Athenian booksellers.[131] The acquisition policy of the Alexandrian and Pergamon libraries was probably responsible for gathering large collections of speeches, where authentic as well as spurious texts could be found.

Attic orators' speeches, however, were not the only texts whose authenticity was suspected. Athenaeus is our source for a controversial statement regarding Theophrastus' treatise *On Kingship*.[132] According to Athenaeus' anonymous sources (πολλοί), the true author would be Sosibius, in whose honour Callimachus wrote a poem.[133] This Sosibius could be the minister of Ptolemy IV Philopator, already active in the reign of Ptolemy III Euergetes. But then, how could he have addressed his treatise to Cassander (who died in 298 or 297)? Is it a wrong identification by Athenaeus' source?[134] Or should we suppose that there were two Sosibiuses, in the same family, the grand-father and his grandson, and that the first one was the addressee of Callimachus' poem as well as the author of the treatise *On Kingship*?[135] Even if this identification is wrong, Athenaeus could be the witness to an ancient conjecture that linked two homonymous and perhaps not related characters.

Athenaeus provides us with indications about the tradition of other texts, such as Hippocrates' *On Barley Gruel*,[136] a short poem by Alexander the Aetolian, who belongs to the first generation of Alexandrian scholars,[137] the *Thessalika* by Philocrates (he quotes his Book 2),[138] Aethlius of Samos' *Chronicles of the Samians*[139] or the *Anabasis to Ammon's sanctuary* by Hellanicus.[140] The quotations from the three historians are probably drawn from lexica. However, they suggest that the Alexandrian library collected books of chronicles and local histories. Callimachus' aetiological poetry relied on such sources.

Athenaeus echoes Strabo about the acquisition, by the Alexandrian library, of a copy of Hecataeus of Miletus' *Periegesis*. Book 2 of this old geographical treatise, devoted to Asia, was registered in Callimachus' *Pinakes* with the author's name as Νησιώτης ('Islander').[141] Although Athenaeus quotes the fragment under Hecataeus' name, he was aware of the disputed authenticity of that text. We find a second warning in his Book Nine: 'Hecataeus, or whoever wrote the *Periegesis* entitled Asia ...'.[142] In a third quotation, however, Athenaeus quotes Book 2 of Hecataeus' *Periegesis* without any warning.[143] Strabo had already alluded to the bibliographical problem linked to Hecataeus' *Periegesis*.[144] What happened could be imagined in the following way: Hecataeus' geographical work entered the Alexandrian library as two separate rolls. The name Νησιώτης could have resulted from a confusion by the staff of the library: the name of the previous owner of the book (or perhaps of his geographical origin?) could have been written on the label of the roll—as Alexandrians used to do, for example, with the 'books from the boats'.[145] Or should we suspect that Callimachus or one among his collaborators, compiling the *Pinakes*, wrongly registered the name of the previous owner of the book instead of the name of the writer? The description of Europe and that of Asia were considered as two independent texts. Deeply concerned with geographical sources in the library, Eratosthenes probably solved the problem using some internal evidence and comparing the two book rolls (Europe and Asia) of Hecataeus on a material or a stylistic basis, but neither he nor Aristophanes of Byzantium corrected Callimachus' entry since Athenaeus still refers to the debate.

Athenaeus also faced problems when dealing with the attribution of old literary texts, like the *Cypria*,[146] the *Titanomachia* epic poems[147] and the *Great Eoeae*.[148] As a matter of fact, his spokesmen in the *Deipnosophistae* display their erudition through the frequent mention of the uncertain or debated authorship of the texts they quote from. This clearly alludes to a form of expert bibliophilic and philological knowledge: advanced book-collectors should know about the various attributions proposed for the same text and be familiar with the reference works that could provide them with alternative authors' names. They should even be able to choose one of them. 'Who is the author of these poems, my good Leonides, it is your task to decide, you, most famous grammarians',[149] says Dionysocles about a spurious Hesiodic quotation found in Euthydemos. In a few cases, the same book is attributed to two different authors. One can assume that Athenaeus checked that the text had the same ἀρχή. Such is the case of a treatise *On pleasure* that Athenaeus quotes under the name of Chamaeleon of Pontus, but he knows that the same book is also attributed to Theophrastus.[150]

Discussing all the statements about ambiguous authorship in the *Deipnosophistae* is beyond the frame of this chapter. I shall limit myself to some concluding remarks about Athenaeus' interest in bibliographical scholarship. He obviously witnesses the history of the transmission of Greek literature. Major landmarks in this history were Peripatetic, Alexandrian and Pergamene scholarship, and their further developments in Rome. The way he dealt with written sources stresses the many forms of confusion arising from the accidental loss of data as well as from fakes and spurious texts that were to be found in the collections of prolific and, one could guess, fashionable writers. Athenaeus is thus a major source for modern historians and philologists trying to follow the transmission of a particular author's works and the input of ancient scholars in the critical definition of his corpus.[151] My main concern, however, is to consider Athenaeus' text not as a neutral mirror of this Graeco-Roman scholarship, but as a textual construction, where erudition is part of the aesthetics of the work and of the fun of the dinners.

There was a strong collusion between Athenaeus and his ancient readers as well as between the characters of the dialogue themselves. They obviously shared the rules of their game and enjoyed themselves with this continuous flood of quotations and scholarly data. Bibliographical data, however, were too incidental to the topics discussed always to be taken seriously and too disseminated through the whole work to be used as a reference material. There was nothing like an *Index Scriptorum*, such as in Georg Kaibel's edition that changes so much our perception of the text and eventually makes its reading more easy, because more focused. Reading the *Deipnosophistae* was like entering a labyrinth, and one could wonder whether the entry point and the exit point of the reader did really matter to the understanding of the text. Bibliographical knowledge was dispersed along the infinite sequence of quotations. There were specific echoes and recurrent effects. For example, a repeated warning on the authenticity of a text, such as Hecataeus' Book 2, could be omitted in a third quotation. The reader was supposed to remember.[152] Major authors, such as Posidonius, Aristotle or Alexis were met across the whole text and extensively quoted. Minor authors produced a vertiginous diversity.

The bibliographical accumulation, however, provokes an attack of indigestion in the end. It was perhaps one of the intended effects. So many πίνακες are displayed through the text, in silver, in bronze, in wood or in papyrus. All of these trays provide the readers with so much bread and meat, so many fruits, fishes, cakes, words, texts, verses and books, incitements to pedantry and greediness! We, however, believe that the pedantic play reflected some sort of advanced bibliophilic knowledge, shared by members of literate Roman circles, who were used to visiting public libraries and bookshops, who had fun with searching for rarities, with unmasking the fakes, with cross-checking the identification of a book in various reference works.

Aulus Gellius is a valuable source for the literate society of Rome in the reigns of Hadrian and Antoninus Pius: in his *Noctes Atticae*, we meet for example a book-buyer asking a famous grammarian to check the authenticity and the editorial quality of a book, in a bookshop specializing in old texts such as Fabius' *Annals*;[153] we see true and false scholars sitting down in bookshops, reading aloud and debating about the edition and interpretation of difficult texts,[154] a literate circle in the countryside at Tibur, at the peak of a heatwave, where one could find and borrow a treatise of Aristotle from the library in the Temple of Hercules.[155] We meet Aulus Gellius and his learned friends again reading in the library Ulpiana,[156] in the library of the domus Tiberiana, reconstructed by Domitian after it was destroyed by a fire,[157] in the library of the Templum Pacis[158] or in the library of Patras, happy to find a very old copy of Livius Andronicus' *Odysseia*.[159] Bibliophily was a social hobby: talking about books, learning from others about books, playing with books, trapping friends, librarians or booksellers with books (and sometimes being trapped by them as well), exploring the world, the past, life and language from within the books, such were the innocuous games of Aulus Gellius and of Athenaeus' characters.[160]

## 2. The *Deipnosophistae* and Libraries

Considering Athenaeus as a librarian does not only imply that one investigates how he was handling books, what kind of information he believed to be important about them and how he expressed it. One should also try to define what his library or, should I say, his libraries were.

Answering such a question implies we know exactly what a library—a βιβλιοθήκη—is in the Greek world. Is it an architectural space? Or a collection of books? Is it a *'cosa mentale'*? During the Hellenistic period, the Greek word βιβλιοθήκη means 'book storage room', and perhaps even 'book storage unit'. In imperial Rome, public libraries were part of the emperors' monumental policy and were buildings in their own right, with specific characteristics. Libraries in private houses had their architectural specifications too, as Vitruvius testifies.[161] Larensis' library provides Athenaeus' project with a general frame, an abstract space where Greek literature is collected, classified and registered.

But should we not also consider Athenaeus' text itself to be a library? The *Deipnosophistae* is a collection of books that could, to a certain extent, be compared to Diodorus of Sicily's *Library of History*: a book encompassing other books, read, summarized and paraphrased. Diodorus produced a universal history in one unique treatise for his readers who without this would have had to seek out the multitude of necessary books to achieve such a global vision.[162] To spare his readers infinite navigations, from library to library, and across the rolls of papyrus, Diodorus transformed his work into a library composed of forty papyrus rolls, condensing all the previous history books.

The *Deipnosophistae* offers something similar. Athenaeus alludes to the library as a 'collection' (συναγωγὴ)[163] and he refers to his own work as a 'collection' too.[164] The symposium itself is also a συναγωγὴ[165]. The same pattern of accumulating and putting together is to be found in the library, in the written treatise and in the banquet. Athenaeus' 'books' are in some respects a storage device for hundreds of other books.[166] That is to say, the *Deipnosophistae* could be considered as a collection of books and of material excerpted from books.

In a few cases, Athenaeus summarizes or reproduces large extracts of rare texts he was lucky enough to find: for example the 'banquet letters' of Lynceus and Hippolochus:[167] 'We will give you the letters just as they are; and since that of Hippolochus is rarely encountered, I will run through its contents for your present amusement and entertainment.' Likewise, on Matro:[168] 'An Attic dinner', said Plutarch, 'is described not unwittily by Matro, the writer of parodies, and because of its rarity, I shall not hesitate, my friends, to quote it for you.' And Athenaeus quotes 122 verses. In a similar way, Athenaeus reproduces large quotations from Moschion's book about the marvellous boat of Hieron of Syracuse.[169] Callixenus' treatise *On Alexandria* is also extensively quoted.[170] Large extracts of texts and perhaps small treatises thus became integrated into Athenaeus' collection.[171]

It should be noticed that the text mirrors the exchanges between the guests of Larensis: sharing rare books each of them came across, lending books, quoting and summarizing books they have in their own private library are part of their social behaviour. The Deipnosophists came to the banquet with their bibliographical discoveries, a stock of quotations available from their recent reading and sometimes with the books themselves too. The loan of books will allow checking of the accuracy and authenticity of quotations: Cynulcus will not prevent Ulpian from reading the treatise by Clearchus, *On enigmas*, that he has acquired.[172] Larensis found Hieronymos' decree about polygamy and says: 'I will send it over to you when I have procured his book'.[173] The guests of Larensis bring nothing to the party, except their 'little speeches' (λογάρια).[174] In a similar way, while various fishes are displayed, the Deipnosophists bring contributions from their books.[175]

Compiling books within his own book, Athenaeus could be foreshadowing the ninth-century scholar Photius and his collection of reading notes and summaries, his so-called 'Library' treatise. There is however a major difference. As a general rule, Athenaeus does not preserve the textual frame of books in their entirety. We have seen that in a few instances, he reproduces very long extracts from rare books. But he is not interested in merely classifying notes and recollections from his past reading, book after book. Athenaeus' library is the result of the collecting of quotations, of words and of textual fragments, but these fragments do not follow the continuity of the texts they were extracted from. It is arranged according to thematic principles and to rules of analogy, of complementarity, of digression, of metonymy that make possible mobility within and between the topics. The collection (συναγωγὴ), whether a library, whether a treatise, or a symposium, relies on an order, a 'syntax',[176] a sequence that produces at the same time continuity and variety : the banquet, like the talks, has to keep going.

Knowledge is thus no longer produced and conveyed by books, as physical objects and intellectual entities, but by fragments of books, by short quotations, by single words highlighted within their context. Knowledge is no longer produced by writers, but by the reader who browsed their texts and gathered material from them. At first glance, we might say, the text of the *Deipnosophistae* looks like a devastated library, where books were cut up into tiny bits of texts: but 'fragmentation does not imply mere disintegration'[177] and chaos. It is a step in a process of reorganization. A word, a quotation, a factual piece of information, a paraphrase stand as autonomous objects one can extract, collect, assemble, compare with others, use as a partial piece of evidence within a sequence that will produce in the end a new kind of knowledge. In this respect, one could even minimize the question of primary and secondary sources or of direct and indirect reading. Dictionaries, previous scholarly collections, various treatises could provide Athenaeus with the data he was looking for in primary sources.[178] Each bit of information, linked to a bibliographical source, could be transmitted through various steps without losing its interest and its content, at least theoretically. In the collection, these fragments were given a new context and thus a renewed intellectual interest. Athenaeus' creative input lies in the process of selection and combination. Accordingly, the importance of books no longer lies in their intellectual or material entirety and frame, but in the way one navigates through them. Extracting material from books, repeating previously quoted passages or defining new textual units to be extracted from a work as a whole, and assembling these materials according to a principle—alphabetical order, thematic headings, analogical relationship: such is the basic writing technique of Athenaeus. The composition of his work relies on the resources of the library that forever provides new and surprising material, on the one hand, and on the ability to trace a path connecting all these quotations on the other. Like Hecataeus or Archestratus, Athenaeus is a traveller, a 'periegetes'. His work could be considered as a 'library tour': the frame of the map, however, vanished, and we are left with a labyrinthine topography of textual places, that is with a reader's itinerary, whose sequential development closely follows the steps and the rhythm of the banquet.

Putting such a strong emphasis on linking previously unrelated textual fragments together and on navigating through a wide corpus of literary materials calls for an analogy with what today we call 'hypertext':[179] reading a large and heterogeneous corpus of texts, deciding to link such and such key words or fragments, deconstructing the cohesiveness of texts in order to follow the thread of a lexical search or of a thematic investigation, define a new way of reading, but also in many respects a new form of writing. Athenaeus as an author is first and foremost a reader who appropriates other authors' texts: a compilation such as the *Deipnosophistae* reduces and perhaps cancels the gap between author and reader, in the same way as today's electronic hypertexts. Quotations, examples, comments, additional notes and variants are placed side by side, according to analogy and variations, to complementarity or presupposition. Every link proceeds from an intellectual decision, from a reading focused on specific questions, that is from a new form of authorship. Comparison, analogy, opposition, complementarity, consensus are some of the intellectual operations made possible within this artificial space of confrontation and juxtaposition. Previously unrelated authors, such as Homer, Alexis, Aristotle or Posidonius, contribute to the writing of the same book, to the conception of an encyclopædia. The information they convey is transformed into lexical entries, quotations to be discussed, compared and criticized. Athenaeus' compilation reflects a reader's point of view on the library of old Greek texts. It follows one among many possible paths, linking textual *loci* after they have been excerpted from their context. One could say that the *Deipnosophistae* is the unstable result of interlaced searches within a multi-layered database, 'a fluid network of verbal elements'[180] that was temporarily fixed in a new written form. And indeed, in his turn, it invites the readers to map out their personal and different travels in the same textual network.[181]

Until now, we have considered Athenaeus' library as a material, concrete and bibliographical way of dealing with books. This library is also the text of the *Deipnosophistae* itself, as a montage of fragments of books and a hypertext *avant la lettre*. As a conclusion to this chapter, I shall briefly discuss the relationship, that is the gap as well as the similarities, between Athenaeus as a writer and the characters who are his *porte-parole*, Larensis and his guests.

On the one hand, a learned compiler, like Pliny the Elder, Aulus Gellius, Favorinus, Diogenes Laertius or Aelian, was composing a large collection of learned materials relying on his reading. For these authors, reading was indissociable from writing.[182] We could imagine slaves or freedmen assisting them, reading books aloud and taking notes on tablets, but the basic operations were the same: annotating, extracting isolated words or sentences, small units of text from the books they were reading, copying them on papyrus rolls or on sheets of papyrus: Pliny the Elder wrote (or dictated) such *commentarii* on both sides (*opisthographi*) of 160 rolls. Did these notes follow the order of the books he had read? In that case, such a collection would be hardly more manageable for quick retrieval than the library from which it drew. Or were the extracts assembled in thematic or lexical constellations, beyond their original bibliographical origin and frame?[183] Reading these notes, finding out organizing principles, and gathering data about a given topic were parts of the rewriting process. The *Deipnosophistae* results from such an assembling of quotations: the writing process perhaps took the form of an ongoing interpolation of new extracts within thematic rubrics.[184]

On the other hand, the Deipnosophists, at least, shared a feature with Athenaeus: the wide extent of their reading. Ulpian provides us with a clear statement: 'Since you have often discussed the subject of meats and fowls, including pigeons, I too am going to tell what I have been able to discover in the course of wide reading (ἐκ πολυαναγνωσίας), over and beyond what has already been said'.[185] The Deipnosophists share also with Athenaeus a particular way of reading, relying on the selection of textual *loci* and on their archiving. When they comment upon their readings, Athenaeus' characters use various verbs. Plutarch makes a statement that he read entirely all the treatises by Hegesander (ἐξαναγνοὺς αὐτοῦ πάντα τὰ ὑπομνήματα).[186] Democritus is able to give a rough approximation of the number of plays of the Middle Comedy he has read: more than eight hundred (ἀναγνοὺς).[187] 'Running across' (ἐπιδραμοῦμαι) a text refers to the quotation and summarizing process as well as to reading.[188] Sometimes, reading is expressed as a 'meeting' (ἐνέτυχον / περιέτυχον ) with a book.[189] Reading is also located in time: it is either recent, or in the past, and as a consequence it is more or less easy for the readers to remember the content of the books.[190]

Reading, however, is only the first step. The Deipnosophists display their skill through the selecting and the excerpting of extracts (ἐκλέγειν / ἐκλογὴ). This process should be understood as a particular intellectual skill as well as a technique for organizing, archiving and retrieving the materials found across the many books read. Excerpting is a step towards organizing a collection (συναγωγὴ). What a reader selects as noteworthy unveils his personality, his curiosity and his virtuosity as well.[191] An advanced excerptor will find in famous books odd details or statements that could have escaped other readers. Cynulcus makes fun of Ulpian because of his reading method: 'I do not select thorny questions read in books, like you, but matters that are most useful and worth hearing'.[192] Ulpian answers back: 'You are one who not only picks out, but even digs up, secrets in books....'[193] These two central characters of the *Deipnosophistae* would deserve a detailed study: what did they read? what did they quote? what are they interested in?

When discussing the *Asotodidaskalos* by Alexis, Democritus alluded to the hundreds of comedies he not only read but also excerpted from:[194] καὶ τούτων ἐκλογὰς ποιησάμενος. The emphasis is not put on the process of excerpting, but on its result, that is the collection of excerpts.[195] These excerpts probably included various kinds of materials, such as literal quotations, summaries, paraphrases, single words. The Deipnosophists provide us with a huge collection of such disparate textual elements. In this respect, Athenaeus' characters consider as equivalent excerpts they made themselves and excerpts found in various intermediary sources, such as a collection of *Glosses* by Artemidorus the Aristophanean, from which a whole extract of Alexis is drawn.[196] Athenaeus' work could be considered as a collection of such extracts and even as a collection where Deipnosophists from the real world could find materials to be excerpted again and used in various banquet talks. Learned and curious readers were used to compiling their own collections of reading notes, putting together, in a condensed and carriable form, data excerpted from books. Such miscellanies could be lent or even bought between scholars.[197] They prefigure Renaissance collections of common-places, a private practice as well as an editorial phenomenon.[198]

The rule of the game was to use the fragments thus collected when one of them was relevant for the discussed topic. The same item could be used several times and about several topics. For example, the same quotation from Alexis provides evidence for two unrelated questions:[199] 'The entire passage is valuable as illustrating a number of things.'

The *Deipnosophistae*, as a collection of extracts, provides its readers with material excerpted from books, reorganized according to precise topics. Wide thematic sections offered a range of textual *loci*, of rare words, of paradoxal quotations. Their very accumulation provided the reader with a technique of *inventio*, allowing him to compose a speech according to analogical or contrastive links. The discussions of the Deipnosophists are like the user's guide to Athenaeus' text: the collection is used in context. The reader learns from them the forms, the rules and the content of sympotic conversation as well as its social ritual and its culinary programme. The Deipnosophists could be considered as Athenaeus' intended readers, putting into practice in a live performance the literate knowledge and the range of quotations they drew from his work.

Relying on their πολυαναγνωσία or on the reading of Athenaeus' collection only, the Deipnosophists had to memorize extracts, keywords, bibliographical references. Were papyrus rolls suitable for finding quickly a precise reference within a multi-volume text?[200] Hellenistic historians such as Polybius, Diodorus of Sicily or Dionysius of Halicarnassus used to open each volume of their works with a summary of the content of previous volumes and a short description of the current volume's content.[201] Pliny the Elder wrote a general table of contents of his *Naturalis Historia*, with a list of all the sources he used. The content of each volume and the specific bibliography were repeated at the beginning of every individual book. The reader was thus allowed to find in which volume and in which section a precise topic was discussed.[202] Aulus Gellius, in his *Noctes Atticae*, followed the same method: a general survey of the topics discussed in each book is given at the end of the *Praefatio*: in all the ancient manuscripts (with one exception), these lemmata are located at the beginning of each volume. Aulus Gellius explicitly defines these *capita rerum* as a help for searching and finding topics in the text.[203] Such a mechanism was only possible when the author had himself decided about the division of his work into volumes, according to a shared standard of book-production. According to the sympotic performances Athenaeus describes, memory provided the Deipnosophists with an organization, an order, a mental indexing and a 'search function' far more efficient than hundreds of book-rolls to be unrolled and run across.

From Athenaeus' perspective, memory is the key factor that helps the Deipnosophists to face reiterated challenges. Reactivating the library is a social and collective process, a game where each of Larensis' guests bring his own partial contribution. Challenging his own memory, adding new unexpected quotations to those already displayed by his fellows and eventually completing or checking them or commenting on them, answering questions proposed by others, most often by Ulpian, such are the dynamics of the conversation. In order to recall all the fragments of texts previously read, one has to dig into his own memory, to explore his own mind and to recall the memory of previous readings, ἀναπεμπάζεσθαι.[204] These readers just let the memory of words, sentences and books occur (προσπίπτειν) to their consciousness and be expressed through their discourses.[205] Is it mere rhetoric? And are the Deipnosophists a mask for the compiling process of Athenaeus, a literary embodiment of his tablets and rolls of excerpts? Or do they allude to authentic mnemotechnic performances, where one organizes knowledge excerpted from books and reactivates it?

In a famous statement, Eunapius describes the sophist Longinus as a sort of living library and walking museum (βιβλιοθήκη τις ἦν ἔμψυχος καὶ περιπατοῦν μουσεῖον).[206] Longinus was, so to speak, a human Alexandria. What could have been such a living library, that is, a library without walls, without shelves, and without material books? It was the result of the reading and browsing of hundreds of books that were cumulatively written on the wax tablets of the mind.[207] Athenaeus depicts such living libraries, whose social games recompose a whole library, as large and rich as Larensis', Pergamon's or Alexandria's libraries.

Memory (μνήμη) makes possible the literal quotations: 'Phylarchus ... says, if I have the luck to remember it ...'.[208] Sometimes, however, the character is not so lucky and is deceived by his own memory.[209] Recalling items from the mental library is a collective process: a Deipnosophist will quote the text that his fellow is unable to remember.[210] Unfortunately enough, when all of them are supposed to remember a famous text or fact, Athenaeus does not quote it: we are thus deprived of details on the development of the Alexandrian library.[211] The readers' memory aims to meet a previous and more ancient μνήμη, that of the writers themselves, who preserved information through writing a word, a name or a story.[212] The mnemonic performance aims to link a given word or object with a literary source that made mention (μνήμη) of it.[213] During the symposium, the Deipnosophists' task is to stress all that is 'worthy of memory' (τὰ μνήμης ἄξια).[214] Remembering through quotation (μνημονεύειν) is a shared process between the authors of the past, Larensis' guests who browse their mental library and Athenaeus who gives an account of the dinner and of the symposium to Timocrates. Memory is located between writing and orality, between the material archive (books and libraries) and the mental technique.

Memorizing large parts of texts or even whole texts was a common performance in the ancient world, and is attested through various school exercises or public performances.[215] A special training was provided by the arts of memory, whose tradition could be followed from Classical Greece (e.g. the sophist Hippias) to the Roman Empire and beyond.[216] The *Rhetorica ad Herennium* and Quintilian's *Institutio Oratoria* preserve the best accounts of this technique. A recurring metaphor represents the mnemonic encoding as writing on the wax tablets or on the papyrus rolls of the mind and the mnemonic retrieval as a reading of the text thus 'written'.[217] The mental tablets and the papyrus rolls stand for the *loci* of the art of memory, and one can write on them, for example, a text that is read aloud or a discourse. Such 'books of memory'[218] could fulfill the functions of Pliny's material *pugillares* and *volumina* or, at least, be complementary with them and provide the scholar with a method for indexing and retrieving data. If papyrus sheets or papyrus rolls were suitable mnemonic places, this suggests that memory could be conceived as the library of the mind.

To what extent had this metaphor an impact on Graeco-Roman scholars, on their working methods? In his catalogue of ancient mnemonists, Pliny the Elder mentions the Greek Charmadas: one could show him any book in a library, he was able to recite it by heart 'in the same way as if he read it'.[219] There was an exact correspondence between the material and the mental library. In a letter to Lucilius, Seneca comments on Calvisius Sabinus, his contemporary, who bought very expensive slaves specially trained. Each of them had memorized a different author, such as Homer, Hesiod or the lyrical poets. These 'living books' provided their master with the appropriate literary quotations during the banquet conversations.[220] They were able to browse mentally these texts and to retrieve a few verses from them. Larensis too, in the *Deipnosophistae*, remarks on cooks who had to learn by heart Plato's dialogues and to recite them while bringing dishes.[221] The Deipnosophists, however, do not need any slaves as prompters. A striking feature of such mnemonic performances is the ability to excerpt a few lines from a continuous text and even to move forward or backward in this 'book of memory', from any starting point.[222] Mary Carruthers put an excellent emphasis on this fact:[223]

> The proof of a good memory does not lie in the simple retention even of large amounts of material; rather, it is the ability to move through it instantly, directly, and securely that is admired. To produce this facility, memory must be trained as though it were a kind of calculative ability, manipulating letters, bits of text, and commonplaces in addition to numbers.

The literary games of the Deipnosophists are not very far away from these performances: for example, they allude to the citation of Homeric verses which have the same initial and final letter or whose first and last syllables compose a given word.[224]

In the *Deipnosophistae*, memory helps to recall fragments from unrelated texts. Memory allows the diners to unfold a sequence of words, of author names or quotations linked together by a key word, or a precise topic, that is by analogical links. The trigger of recollection and the principle for ordering the sequence of citations was the succession of dishes, drinks and objects displayed during the dinner and the symposium. The service provides the dialogue with its rhythm and a succession of clearly identifiable topics. The accumulation of food and objects results in the accumulation of words and of quotations.[225] It both determines and mirrors the organization of Athenaeus' text and the order of his collection of excerpts.[226] There was a dynamic shift from the material surrounding the banquet to the order of language (naming dishes and objects) and to the space and time frame of the library of ancient authors. It was not unusual to prepare oneself for a dinner with a collection of verses and proverbs ready for each of the dishes served.[227] Athenaeus' text could make the task of these performers of cultural memory easier. It was a mobile and carriable library, that offered, in a few papyrus rolls, a digest of ancient Greek literature, ready for use in banquet-talks.[228]

For modern historians and philologists, the *Deipnosophistae* is an unvaluable source for the realia and social rituals of the ancient symposium as well as about many lost books of Greek literature. As a conclusion, it should be stressed that Athenaeus is also a major actor and witness of the cultural practices and erudite techniques of the Second Sophistic, between scholarship and entertainment, between orality and writing, between the papyrus book-rolls and the library of the mind.

# ❖ 7 ❖    THE WALKING LIBRARY
## THE PERFORMANCE OF CULTURAL MEMORIES

### by Yun Lee Too

Let me introduce the theme of this chapter by citing a passage from a twentieth-century work as a retrospective comment on an ancient 'institution'—a word I use with some licence:

> 'I want you to meet Jonathan Swift, the author of that evil political book, *Gulliver's Travels!* And this other fellow is Charles Darwin, and this one is Schopenhauer, and this one is Einstein, and this one here at my elbow is Mr Albert Schweitzer, a very kind philosopher indeed. Here we all are, Montag. Aristophanes and Mahatma Gandhi and Gautama Buddha and Confucius and Thomas Love Peacock and Thomas Jefferson and Mr Lincoln, if you please. We are also Matthew, Mark, Luke, and John.'
> Everyone laughed quietly.
> 'It can't *be*,' said Montag.
> 'It *is*,' replied Granger, smiling.[1]

The passage comes from Ray Bradbury's *Fahrenheit 451*, essentially a bibliophile's horror story, and I use it to introduce the notion that texts come in very different sizes, shapes, forms, and indeed, people. The late twentieth century has worried particularly about authors, their intentions, and their deaths, and I suggest that, by notable contrast, antiquity has concerned itself particularly with the question: 'how can a text be?' I observe that literary texts can be physically located in writing, in the 'book' and in book collections, and furthermore that literary texts can be embodied by persons. If relatively recently the written text has been the privileged form of textuality, in antiquity textuality was less emphatically literary (that is, written), or at least it was literary in a far more qualified sense.

Authors such as Plato and Isocrates had characterized the written word as non-serious and defenceless offspring (cf. *Phaedrus* 274e5–275b3), or as aetiolated, because disembodied (e.g. Isocrates, *To Philip* 25–7).[2] Now I offer one of several possible sequels to this quarrel between the oral and written word. I want to tell a story about the comeback of the spoken text as one which redeems itself because it is embodied, as *logos* with voice, mind and moreover with critical facility even in the absence of its original creator. My concern is with a representation of textuality that comes largely from imperial North Africa, including Egypt, where the literary intellectual or *pepaideumenos* constructs himself and is constructed as the 'walking library', the embodied receptacle of bookish culture. The cultured man through his vast reading knowledge comes to personify the book collection, and as such he performs his own literary socializations and acculturations.

I    Antiquity's text-culture was originally a performative one. Texts were sung, as in the case of lyric poetry; spoken and recited, as in the case of epic poetry;[3] orated and delivered, as in the case of the rhetorical *logos*. Gorgias may have declared *logos* a 'powerful ruler', which by means of the smallest possible and least visible body (σμικροτάτῳ σώματι καὶ ἀφανεστάτῳ) accomplishes the most godlike deeds (θειότατα ἔργα) (*Helen* 8) but the sense was that *logos* did acquire a more substantial body along the way. It is after all the performer's body which gives the speech its mobility, its orality, its entity, and antiquity has its textual persons, individuals who lend their voices and minds to the end of embodying *logos*. Most obvious of these was the rhapsode, literally 'the stitcher of words' (cf. Pindar, *Nemean* 2.1–3), who travels throughout the Greek world performing the poetry of Homer word for word. The rhapsode is the receptacle of Homeric knowledge and culture, and in the light of Homer's emblematic status as *the* Greek author, he is thus the receptacle who reproduces Greek knowledge and culture for his audiences.

But this embodied text-culture is also originally one which is recognized as requiring careful surveillance and regulation.[4] The rhapsode, as privileged representative of oral culture, is a figure who needs to be carefully watched for the sake of textual integrity. Indeed, Xenophon depicts the rhapsode as someone who knows his epic extremely well, but is nonetheless likely to be rather stupid.[5] Plato's infamous rhapsode, Ion, may regard himself as the best general in Greece because he can recite the *Iliad*, but conversation with Socrates shows him to be lacking in understanding of what generalship is. Ion is merely the mouthpiece who speaks his texts without true understanding of them or discernment, as discussion with Socrates makes evident. He knows only Homer (536d), mistakes emotive response for interpretative response, and regards memorization as understanding.[6]

Literary representations apart, mistrust of the embodied text-culture is articulated through legislation. Precisely because the textual performer is not an author but a mediator, he can corrupt authorial intention. He may emend, elide, omit and elaborate the text; he may forget; he may introduce variations into the text.[7] This the Athenian tyrant Peisistratus recognized when he instituted the Panathenaic Rule, the law which ensured that the Homeric epics would be recited in exactly the same way and order, performance after performance (cf. *Pangegyricus* 159; [Plato] *Hipparchus* 228b; Diogenes Laertius 1.57).[8]

**II**

I want to suggest that in and *certainly* after the Hellenistic period, the status and authority of the personified text changes. At this point the embodied text implicitly becomes the authoritative and authorizing text: the previously regulated embodied 'book' becomes the regulating work with respect to the written word. What paradoxically gives rise to this situation is the establishment of a formal literary culture in the foundation of the Alexandrian library, an event which, as we shall see, reinforces Plato's double and ambivalent association of Egypt with writing as memory and as amnesia.

The libraries of Hellenistic North Africa might be regarded as declaring a very particular relation of writing to knowledge: books are to be seen as the receptacle and monument of the prior knowledges which constitute the civilized Greek world and which now stand as the basis for the Hellenistic world. There had already been public libraries or notable book collections prior to the Hellenistic period. Peisistratus' own collection of texts was supposed to have been the inspiration for Ptolemy II's Alexandrian institution (Isidore, *Etymologies* 6. 3. 3–5), and Athens had the Metroon, the building which served as the city-state's public archives. Subsequently libraries were established at Pergamum and Alexandria, as the kings of these cities struggled to set up the first such institution (Pliny, *NH* 35 10). Vitruvius claims that a jealous Ptolemy copied the Attalid king in establishing a library at Alexandria (7. praef. 4). The Alexandrian library in particular was one which attempted to contain *all* Greek culture, so that the Ptolemies could lay claim to cultural hegemony. According to Galen, Ptolemy copied all books which arrived by sea at Alexandria (Galen, *Comm. in Hipp. Epidem.* 17. 1. 606 Kühn), and both the libraries at Alexandria and Pergamum offered rewards to individuals who supplied them with volumes (cf. *Comm. in Hipp. De Nat. Homin.* 1. 44. 105).

I want to suggest that the Hellenistic library demonstrates the inadequacy of the library as a body of physical, written texts, so that the genealogy of North African text-culture founds itself (at least in subsequent representation) alongside an alternative kind of library. It emphasizes a belief, in fact a re-recognition of the

Platonic realization, that the physical text needs its human advocates. This is suggested by the textual material concerning the origins of the 'library', as an idea and as an historical institution. A story which Strabo tells about the fate of Aristotle's books, a notional precedent for the Alexandrian library, is testimony that physical texts are liable to physical abuse and neglect. The geographer relates how Aristotle passed his collection of texts to his pupil Theophrastus, who in turn taught the Egyptian kings to gather and collect books. He continues his account, telling his readers that Theophrastus then bequeathed his own and Aristotle's libraries to his pupil, the philosopher Neleus, who took them to Scepsis, where his non-intellectual descendants put the books away carelessly. A still worse desecration is to befall the texts in Strabo's narrative. Hearing that the books from their collection are being sought by the Attalid kings for the library at Pergamum, Neleus' descendants bury them in a trench and so cause their decay. A bibliophile named Apellicon subsequently restores the texts, making new copies of them and incorrectly filling the gaps. At Rome the grammarian Tyrannion and booksellers acquire and then circulate poorly edited copies of these works (13. 1.54; for Apellicon's role in acquiring Aristotle's library, see Athenaeus 5. 214e).

Strabo's narrative is a nightmare scenario of what happens when books fall into the ownership of individuals who do not understand their value. The fate of Aristotle's library warns that libraries, far from being secure or eternal monuments, are indeed vulnerable and in some sense make the existence of books more precarious. The physical library renders the whole cultural legacy (which it ideally serves to protect) liable to destruction and to irrecoverable erasure. And indeed this recognition is one that even the untrustworthy narratives concerning the burnings of the Alexandrian library by the Romans and later by the Christians and Muslims tend to confirm.

There is also a sense in which the creation of a library can paradoxically be its own worst enemy. In their eagerness to acquire volumes for the library the Ptolemies prompted the production of fake texts by offering payment for those who could bring them the writings of the Greek world. Individuals produced spurious texts in hope of a reward, and accordingly the library could never be an authoritative institution. Texts had to be authenticated, in addition to and apart from the fact that many of them, such as the Homeric epics, already had layers of editorial and rhapsodic interpolation. A narrative regarding the appointment of the first librarian at Alexandria establishes the need to supplement the textuality constituted by the conventional library. In the preface to Book 7 of *De Architectura* Vitruvius states that, after deciding to set up a rival library to Pergamum's, Ptolemy I established literary contests dedicated to the Muses and to Apollo. He sought educated judges (*iudices litterati*) to determine the victors of these contests. The king himself selected six individuals, and had Aristophanes recommended to him by the governors of the library as the seventh judge for the reason that each day he had very diligently and very carefully read in order all the books in the library (*summo studio summaque diligentia cotidie omnes libros ex ordine perlegeret*). When it came to the poetic adjudication, the first six judges agreed to give the prize to the poet who most pleased the crowd. Aristophanes alone deemed that the prize should be awarded to the individual who least gratified the audience with his composition (*De Architectura* 7 pref. 5–6). To justify his decision, Aristophanes showed that the individual he selected as winner was the only one who presented an original text, while the others had put forward plagiarized texts. He established that misappropriation had occurred by relying on his memory (*fretus memoriae*) to match the stolen works to the texts from his bookcases. The offenders were punished, and Aristophanes was made the head librarian.

The educated man after the classical period is one imbued with the *paideia* of his community, whether this is a contemporary culture, or more likely a prior one constituted by a series of authoritative and canonical texts, or both. Specifically, the learned reader becomes a textual regulator and authenticator; he is the back-up system for the physical library. And so Aristophanes is a figure who in the Vitruvian narrative comes to instantiate the textual *paideia* of Hellenistic Alexandria. He can discriminate between authentic and false texts because he has read all the works in the library, and knows them sufficiently well to be able to identify the texts of the competitors as plagiarisms. He has memorized the location of the innumerable volumes in their particular cases, for the physical structure of the library is the mnemonic aid which enables him to match the fake with its true source. Aristophanes is thus able to distinguish the copy from the original (but less than brilliant) composition in the poetic competition. He is the walking, human counterpart of the Ptolemaic library, and accordingly deserves to be its librarian.

But the Vitruvian Aristophanes is less a librarian of the Hellenistic period than one of the Roman period, as far as we can glean, and specifically of Augustus' Rome (cf. Book 1, preface 1). He is part of a fantasy, I suggest, about the potential of the library for mobility, dislocation and also for discrimination. Vitruvius frames the narrative of judgment and criticism by a set of statements which acknowledge that 'we', that is the Romans, owe our knowledge of Troy's history, of the teachings of the Greek philosophers from the pre-Socratics to Zeno of Citium, and of the accomplishments of great political leaders, to written records which memorialize them. Yet it is also the case that the Roman 'we' has to watch over the contents of its textual receptacle for cultural memory. Individuals who steal works from earlier authors and claim them for themselves must be punished, as Aristophanes' plagiarizers were (7, preface 2–3).

**III**  Subsequent authors suggest that the 'walking library' should be a notion dissociated, as seems only logical and appropriate, from the idea of the physical library.[9] In his *Lives of the Sophists* Eunapius (346–*c*.414) offers the following note on Longinus, whom he identifies as the teacher of the philosopher Porphyry (233–*c*.301) (and *not* as the author of the treatise *On the Sublime*):

> At that time Longinus was a breathing library and walking museum, and he was entrusted with the task of judging ancient [authors] just as many others before him …(456)

Longinus is compared to a 'breathing library' (βιβλιοθήκη … ἔμψυχος) and a 'walking museum' (περιπατοῦν μουσεῖον), the institutions which were active in the wholesale appropriation of Homer, archaic poetry, classical Greek literature and, in the case of the Septuagint, the Hebrew Bible at the hands of an elite Alexandrian culture and its representative agents. But whereas the original Mouseion library was constituted by a complex of buildings, by the body of professional litterati who inhabited it, and by their books, as far as Eunapius is concerned the historical individual Longinus now personifies the critical institution as a 'breathing library and walking museum'. Longinus, like the earlier library/ librarian Aristophanes, is an individual who personalizes the Hellenistic library and museum. He emblematizes the idea of textual mobility, for a 'walking library' is one that frees the institution from strict geographical location.

Eunapius' biographical sketch highlights the idea of judgement, for he adjudicates the work of prior writers and, as in the case of his predecessors, great learning validates his position as judge. The biographer goes on to declare that Longinus' literary judgement was required to legitimate the critical positions of his contemporaries: the walking library is the critics' critic.[10] The teacher of Porphyry is to be regarded as a judge *par excellence*, and as one from whom other literary experts take their advice and authority. Longinus is the keeper of a textual heritage, the individual who can discern and discriminate, and in this way he is the embodiment of library-culture as first conceived by the Ptolemies.

**IV**  Vitruvius' Aristophanes and Eunapius' Longinus are far from the only instances of the mobile, personified library in post-Hellenistic antiquity. In Apuleius' *Apology*, a text which purports to offer a defence against the charge of using magic for criminal ends, the author offers a self-portrait which articulates the idea that the educated man, the *philosophus*, is to be regarded as a polymathic walking library. The rhetorician's line of defence is that because he is a man to be associated with book-learning, eloquence and knowledge, he is also to be dissociated from evil sorcery and magic. The orator is an individual who has surrendered all physical pleasures in order to pursue *eloquentia*, such that his position as an intellectual necessarily defines him as a virtuous innocent, and thus he is the 'most skilled at speech' *(facundissimum)* and without any 'sin', *nefas (Apology 5)*

Apuleius emblematizes his identity as a learned individual in a number of ways. One of them is through his possessions, specifically the books that he carries with him wherever he goes:

> nam morem mihi habeo, quoquo eam, simulacrum alicuius dei inter libellos conditum gestare eoque diebus festis ture et mero et aliquando victima supplicare
>
> *(Apology 63.9–10, cf. 37.13–16)*

> for it is my habit to carry wherever I go an effigy of a god amongst my books and to worship it on festival days with incense, honey and a sacrifice.

The orator has a portable library, but this is merely the physical symbol of the library that he carries within his head. The *Apology* is, one notes, a carefully orchestrated performance of literary knowledge for his forensic audience, one which serves to display both his extraordinary erudition and his moral integrity. Early on in the *Apology* he declares that the 'wise man' is one who recalls learning (12.21–2; cf. *eruditionis memoriam*, 91.7). This gloss on 'philosopher' signals the performance of textual knowledge as a feat of memory. Knowledge of literature is what absolves Apuleius of the charge that he is a sorcerer *(magus)* precisely because literature has produced his identity as an intellectual. Accordingly, the oration is one in which the orator selectively recites and refers to the traditional Greek and Roman literary canon in the service of forensic defence. Thus the text of Plato *(Alcibiades I)*, together with invocations of Anaxagoras, Leucippus, Democritus, Epicurus, Epimenides, Orpheus, Pythagoras, and Ostanes, qualify the court's understanding of what a *magus* might be: Apuleius proposes a Platonic notion of *magus* as sage and philosopher-king (25–7).[11]

Apuleius presents himself as a doyen of bilingual and bicultural erudition, who operates in the midst of a generally uncomprehending and unlearned community.[12] He is as learned in Greek as in Latin *(quam Graece tam Latine ... disertissimus)* as even one of his accusers must admit (4.2–3), and as he himself readily confesses elsewhere (e.g. 19.23, 36.19, 36.38; also *Florida* 8.16, 18.91). In Chapter 25 he draws attention to his 'Hellenic eloquence' *(eloquentiam Graecam)* as one of his virtues, and at 36.19–21 the defendant announces that he will attempt to write the same things in Greek and Latin, to inquire what is missing and to make up for the deficences in all things. He virtually reiterates this thought as he describes himself as someone who will write all things which are known to the fewest people with proper and eloquent Greek and Latin words (39.23–24). In these passages the author alludes to his bilingualism in terms of Lucretian translation (cf. *De rerum natura*, 1. 136–7), which he more explicitly and verbosely details at 38.10–16:

> pauca etiam de Latinis scriptis meis ad eandem peritiam pertinentibus legi iubebo, in quibus animaduertes cum me [collegisse res] cognitu raras, tum nomina etiam Romanis inusitata et in hodiernum quod sciam infecta, ea tamen nomina labore meo et studio ita de Graecis prouenire, ut tamen Latina moneta percussa sint.

> I shall order to be read out of my Latin writings a few things pertaining to this science, in which you will notice that I have assembled both little known matters and words unaccustomed even to the Romans and, as I know, even today unformed; however, those words come from the Greek by my labour and my study in such a way that they seem to have been coined from a Latin mint.

The *Apology*'s topics and themes reinforce its identity as a Graeco-Roman text. Written in Latin, the oration's conceit of the philosopher on 'trial' for his life is a markedly Greek one.[13] The Greek text to which Apuleius' Latin oration most obviously refers and which it mirrors is Plato's *Apology* of Socrates. This text offers the model for the forensic defence as a literary construct that serves to define the identity of its dramatized speaker and/or author. Apuleius produces the defence of his life against the *crimen capitale* (4.31–32) as a latter-day Socrates going up before the jury to deliver his apologia *pro vita sua*. But the motif of the persecuted intellectual is also an Isocratean one. The Athenian rhetorician's *Antidosis* employs the fictional charges of tax-evasion and corruption of youth as a pretext for a larger defence of his educational theories and his whole life. That the Roman Apuleius is deliberately impersonating Greek Isocrates is evident from the former's emphasis on his role as teacher of youths, specifically his nephews (28.21–29), and also from his adaptation of the Isocratean encomium of *logos* (*Antidosis* 254, *Nicocles* 6–7) in Chapter 18 of the *Apology*, where now the virtue of poverty (*paupertas*), rather than *logos*, is what creates civilization and its arts.

The forensic setting of the *Apology* is poignant, for the trial serves, amongst other things, as the site of literary discrimination and judgement. The judge, according to Aristotelian rhetorical theory, is at once, in the narrow forensic sense, the authority figure who hears and deliberates the legal case, and, in the larger, metaphorical sense, the general spectator and hearer. Apuleius deliberately conflates these senses of 'judge' as far as the *Apology* is concerned.[14] The rhetorician quite deliberately installs the judge, Claudius Maximus, in the role of literary critic, when he addresses him as an individual who has spoken much and learned even more by reading (81.7; 91.8–10; cf. 95.1–2). Claudius is specifically cast as a fellow student with Apuleius of Aristotelian natural physics and science (36.11–16, 38.1–2; 41.10–11). Indeed, elsewhere Apuleius proposes that familiarity with the Platonic canon is the basis for his kinship with Maximus: both are members of the *Platonica familia* (64.8); both have identical knowledge of Platonic doctrine (51.1–2), having read the same dialogues, the *Alcibiades* (25.30), the *Timaeus* (25.25), and the *Phaedrus* (64.12–13).[15]

Apuleius also demonstrates the critical capacity which Vitruvius had attributed to Aristophanes of Byzantium and Eunapius to Longinus, the walking library. The orator becomes a latter-day Alexandrian scholar, distinguishing false from true text. He shows that an epistle in which his wife Pudentilla supposedly calls him a sorcerer *(magus)* is actually a forgery. His prosecutors have taken out of context a statement that Pudentilla is herself refuting, so that the false accusation stands unqualified (80–2). Pudentilla's words are actually part of a defence of her husband, and Apuleius asks Claudius to allow the text to assume its proper voice (83). Next the orator denies authorship of a second letter, in which he himself is supposed to have tried to charm Pudentilla into marriage (87). The forged epistle becomes evident as such, thanks to poor style, language that is not socially acceptable (87.10–1 1) and its poor calligraphy (87.5). The letter displays none of the learning which is the basis of Apuleian identity.

The crucial critical distinction in the *Apology* is between those who are educated and therefore also virtuous—as the Apuleian philosopher must be—and those who are uncultured and therefore necessarily without virtue. Accordingly, to discredit the prosecution, Apuleius emphasizes the unlearning of his opponents: they are *tam rudes, tam barbari* such that the speaker does not bother to mention the names of all the authors he has read in public libraries (91). The chief accuser Sicinius Aemilianus is ignorant about books, a rustic, boorish figure completely opposed to the urbane, learned Apuleius, who faults him for ignorance about the teachings of Archimedes on katoptrics (16.16 and 20). Aemilianus is ignorant of all literature (30), and it is because he cannot even read a Greek letter that the orator declines to cite Greek poetry to him (30). In a clearly futile attempt to educate this individual, Apuleius presents him with a reading list: Aristotle, Theophrastus, Eudemus, Lycones and other minor Platonists (36). The overall point is that this individual is ignorant of the nature of the accusations he makes (53).

So the individuals who persecute Apuleius and claim his textual culture to be sorcery are conspicuously unsocialized in bookish learning. The uneducated accusers see vice where it is absent. They see sexual *double-entendres* in the defendant's scientific writings, where such is not intended or present (34–5). Another of the prosecutors, Crassus, can only claim to have seen proof of Apuleius' magic activities because he is ignorant of Homer's *Odyssey*, (57.15–18 = *Odyssey* 1.57)). Crassus' devotion is to *studium bibendi* (57.25) rather than to the Apuleian ideal of *studium litterarum* (5.3). Rufinus maintains a household that neither speaks nor writes Greek and Latin, and the texts that he and his associates produce attest to this fact (98.26–31; also 87.10–16). By corollary, education is to be viewed as something that regulates those initiated into it, so that Apuleius becomes a defender of elite culture against all that is corrupt and foreign, whether Asian or Punic.

V In archaic Greece, knowledge of text from memory had been a requirement for entrance into the elite symposium and the later dining scene if we are to give authority to our witnesses to this culture in the archaic and classical periods. The archaic poet Xenophanes provides evidence of symposiastic recitation in fr. 1, where he steps in to regulate the sort of poetic material that may be presented if such an occasion is to be orderly and just. The participants of the drinking party are to avoid stories of giants and gods in strife and war, anticipating one of the constraints that Plato would place upon poetry in the *Republic*.[16] Later at the *Symposium* 3.5–6, Xenophon gives us Niceratus, whose father had made him learn both the *Iliad* and the *Odyssey* by heart so that he would appear to be cultured. Niceratus becomes the voice of the Homeric poems, and thus embodies these texts. The specific association of libraries and dining comes from textual material describing the Alexandrian library. The scholars of the Museum library enjoyed a common mess-hall (Strabo, *Geography* 17.1.8), while Diodorus Siculus informs us that in the ambulatory around the library were to be found depictions of all sorts of delightful foods and next to the library was an exquisite hall in which were to be found a table with couches for twenty, and statues of Zeus, Hera and the King (1.49.1–5).

It is precisely the Hellenophile community of North Africa in the Second Sophistic period which aspired to recreate, and, as I shall now suggest, to surpass this culture. In Athenaeus' *Deipnosophistae* the walking library has evolved into an enormous reference source, a collection of texts, or rather of citations from texts. The work opens with the author's observation that the subject of his work is a banquet hosted by a wealthy Roman named Larensis, who summoned to the feast men who were the most skilled in every branch of learning (τοὺς κατὰ πᾶσαν παιδείαν ἐμπειροτάτους ἐν τοῖς αὑτοῦ διατυμόνας ποιούμενος, 1.1a). Athenaeus offers a eulogy of his host, which constructs this individual as the foremost connoisseur of book culture at Rome. He gathers around himself men of learning and engages in vigorous study and research, demonstrating a critical acumen that merits the description 'Socratic' (cf. μετὰ κριτικῆς τινος καὶ Σωκρατικῆς ἐπιστήμης). He is utterly bilingual (cf. ἐπ' ἴσης ἀμφοτέρων τῶν φωνῶν προιστάμενον, 1.2b; cf. Chapter 1). Rhapsodes are present and prominent at his dinner parties, attesting to the host's extraordinary predilection for Homer (14. 620b). Larensis is also a librarian, and his book collection, in keeping with encomiastic hyperbole, is one which in size surpasses those of Polycrates of Samos, Peisistratus, Eucleides, Nicocrates of Cyprus, the kings of Pergamum, Euripides, Aristotle, Theophrastus and Neleus (1.3b). He is a latter-day Ptolemy, as Athenaeus proposes, for he has taken up the learning and writing of the ancient world and brought it to Rome. But appropriation of prior cultures is now figured as 'hospitality' (ἐπὶ τὰς ἑστιάσεις): Larensis makes his guests, wherever they come from—Elis (Leonides), Nicomedia (Pontianus and Democritus), Ptolemais (Philadelphus), Ephesus (Daphnus), Pergamum (Galen), Nicaea (Rufinus), Alexandria (Alceides) (1ld-f)—feel at home in Rome, if not actually Roman (1.3c).

The occasion of the dinner is both the context for and the enactment of the knowledge that these guests bring to it. The diverse conversation is paralleled by the numerous courses of the meal (1.1b), and it is the case that dinner protocol requires the guests to bring some contribution to the meal. Athenaeus states that many of the distinguished litterati bear *grammata* in their bedrolls; the highly educated (πεπαιδευμένος) Charmus has something to quote for each dish presented; Calliphanes had copied out the beginnings of many poems and speeches for citation during the dinner, while others had various other bits of learning to perform at the meal (1.4.c-d). The meal is—to cite a series of anachronistic analogies—a textual pot-luck, an open buffet, a smorgasbord, or in Charles Gulick's translation, a 'picnic' (1, p. 17), but it is strictly a meal by invitation only. The learned and cultured morsels are available for consumption, or perhaps more to the point, regurgitation, only to those who have already been well initiated into literary culture. The literary dinner is staged as citation, reference and name-dropping, so that familiarity with the texts as a whole is assumed and anyone without prior knowledge is excluded from enjoyment of the morsels. The walking library has now become a metaliterary institution, as the work's symposiastic context might indeed determine. More cynically, in *De Tranquillitate Animi* Seneca compares individuals who possess vast libraries but leap from passage to passage rather than reading intensively with diners who merely reach for the fine tit-bits at a dinner party and disregard its more substantial offerings (1.9.5; cf. Chapter 6).[17] Whichever interpretation we might prefer (and I am increasingly preferring the latter), the *Deipnosophistae* has become a work which classicists are unlikely to read from cover to cover; it is rather a text which they employ as a scholarly research tool, mining it for literary and biographical references.

But if these literary tit-bits—one-liners, names, and so on—are understood as a radical synecdoche for high literary culture, they also point to the pressure to which it now subjects its participants. At Larensis' dinner the privileged textual performance is the feat of memory, and literary (dis)course is most often the catalogue. Banqueters announce that they will 'recite' (καταλέξω, 573b) or that they will 'call to memory' (μνηθήσομαι, 585f) passages as prefaces to their offerings. The walking libraries are faced with a problem that the Alexandrian librarian Aristophanes did not have: no one can memorize the totality of literature any more. Even the litterati run out of memory because of the abundance of material. That Didymus the Grammarian had earned the nickname 'bookforgetter' (βιβλιολάθας) because he wrote so many volumes—3,500 treatises according to Demetrius of Troezen (4.39)—suggests that abundance of books had now become an issue for the person as literary receptacle.

The dinner, as literary metaphor, stretches Athenaeus' own powers of recollection.[18] He follows the example of Philoxenus of Cythera, who recalled from memory (μνημονεύων) many of the meats served at a grand dinner table, and himself proceeds to recall (ἀπομνημονεύσωμεν) the dishes (643a–e). A few paragraphs later Athenaeus acknowledges the limits of his memory. Because so many cakes were named (cf.καταλεξάντων) by his fellow-guests, he will mention only as many as he can remember (cf. ὅσων μέμνημαι) (643e). That is to say, this is not a complete catalogue of cakes in the ancient world. Later in Book Fifteen the author himself confesses that it is difficult to recall the things which were often uttered in banquets, because of their diversity (ποικιλία) and the similarity of novel things to one another (cf.τὴν ὁμοιότητα τῶν ἀεὶ καινῶς προσευρισκομένων) (665a).[19] The diverse nature of conversation of course mirrors the diverse nature of the banquet, which the work's length demonstrates. After all, at 411a the author cites from the satyric play *Heracles* of Astydamas a line which compares a varied banquet (ποικιλία) to a variety of literature in that neither bores its 'consumer'.

The parallelism between dinner party and literature, where the multiple courses produce equally multiple discourses, declares the materiality of the text in the Athenaean world, even in the absence of a physical library. I want to suggest that this materiality is one which symposium-culture assumes, for the languages of the drinking and dinner party are also the languages which determine the reality of the larger outside world. Historically, the symposium has protocols governing both social and literary behaviours, essentially behaviours which are one and the same (cf. Xenophanes fr. 1). The *Deipnosophistae* enacts this legacy. Portions of the dinner conversation revolve around issues of linguistic propriety: so how does one accentuate various words? (e.g. 388b; for 'hare' and its various perceived cognates, 400a–b; 490b; 484f–485a); how does one pronounce the Greek work for 'partridge', 'quail', 'quart'—with a short or a long vowel? (388f); what are the correct names for various fish (7.287a–d) and so on and on. It is no accident that Ulpian is present at the dinner, pronouncing on, amongst other issues, the correct terminology for various dishes when a ham is brought in at the beginning of Book Nine (366a–c). The discussion is not merely at the level of apparent pedantry. The virtues of moderation in early Rome, including issues of food and entertainment, are discussed (273a–f), and in Book Twelve the dinner guests reject luxurious living as the oriental other (513f, with Chapter 16). Larensis' dinner party is an occasion in which linguistic and literary regulation translate directly into social practice, as far as the symposiastic community is concerned, and in which the impact of texts on their community becomes immediately evident. The Deipnosophists are the walking receptacles of their community's texts and its knowledges, individuals who literally and metaphorically cut and chop their literary and social worlds into order.

## Conclusion

The 'walking library', I suggest, is a figure who has effaced himself in order to become a cultural medium. Textual memory re-authors the library's identity as part of a prior and geographically distant world and its texts. Note that Aristophanes of Byzantium, Apuleius and Athenaeus are all in a sense inhabitants of North Africa laying emphatic claim to Hellenic and/ or Roman identities. As Walter Benjamin notes in *The Storyteller*, the more self-forgetful the listener is, the more deeply is what he listens to impressed upon his memory.

Yet let me end on a note of cynicism. I suggest that there is also a danger that the 'walking library' in turn becomes the means of a larger cultural amnesia, for he selects, he edits, he regulates and therefore he excludes the transgressive, the variant and the fraudulent. Let me invite you to think of the library as the place where the librarian both makes available books and also tells you to be quiet: 'Shhh'—if you talk out of turn. I end by returning to *Fahrenheit 451* and the remainder of the speech of the leader of the 'books':

> *We're* book-burners, too. We read the books and burnt them, afraid they'd be found. Micro-filming didn't pay off; we were always travelling, we didn't want to bury the film and come back later. Always the chance of discovery. Better to keep it in the old heads, where no one can see it or suspect it. We are all bits and pieces of history and literature and international law, Byron, Tom Paine, Machiavelli or Christ, it's here. And the hour's late. And the war's begun. And we are out here, and the city is there, all wrapped up in its own coat of a thousand colours. What do you think, Montag?[20]

# 8

# ATHENAEUS' KNOWLEDGE OF EARLY GREEK ELEGIAC AND IAMBIC POETRY

## by Ewen Bowie

Of the four sophistic individuals other than Athenaeus from Naucratis who are known to us from the latter half of the second century AD, Apollonius, Pollux, Proclus and Ptolemy[1] it is perhaps significant that one, Pollux—C. Iulius Polydeuces—gained his literary immortality as a lexicographer.[2] Even in an age when using demonstrably good Attic Greek for certain sorts of discourse was important to the educated élite of the Greek east[3] the presence of both Pollux and Athenaeus in this group of five professional purveyors of prose might hint that Naucratis encouraged a lexicographic turn of mind. That is certainly a striking feature of Athenaeus. Put a piece of poetry in front of him that 'Longinus' might pick out for sublimity, or Plutarch for a profound moral lesson, and Athenaeus will home in unhesitatingly on the unusual word or form. This comes out very clearly in the balance of his quotations from archaic and classical iambic and elegiac poets respectively, and indeed to some extent it explains that balance.

In what follows I shall first (I) look at how Athenaus' citations are distributed between iambic and elegiac poetry, and how the distribution breaks down between individual poets within these genres; second (II) I shall offer a selective contrast with another voracious reader of a century earlier whose work is generously preserved, Plutarch; and finally (III) I shall try to assess how often Athenaeus is drawing directly from ancient texts of these poets and how often he is using an intermediary.

I     Athenaeus cites archaic and classical iambic poets slightly more often than he cites elegiac: there are some fifty-three as against forty-six citations. Lexicographical interests apart, this is not quite what one might expect either from the number of poets of whom elegiac and iambic texts respectively were available, or indeed from the relative bulk of these texts—we have much more elegy than iambus (once we put together papyrus texts, quoted fragments and pieces that have come down in a direct manuscript tradition, chiefly the *Theognidea*)—and this was almost certainly true in the second century AD too. I set out the distribution of Athenaeus' citations:

| Elegiac | | Iambic | |
|---|---|---|---|
| Anacreon | 1 | Ananius | 4 |
| Antimachus | 2 | | |
| Archilochus | 3 | Archilochus | 17 |
| Asius | 1 | Asopodorus | 3 |
| Callinus | 1 | Hermippus | 4 |
| Cleobulina | 1 | Hipponax | 15 |
| Critias | 2 | Semonides | 9 |
| Dionysius Chalcous | 6 | | |
| Euenus | 2 | | |
| Ion | 5 | | |
| Mimnermus | 3 | | |
| Periander | 1 | | |
| Simonides | 4 | | |
| Socrates | 1 | | |
| Solon | 1 | Solon | 1 |
| Sophocles | 1 | | |
| Theognis | 6 | | |
| Xenophanes | 5 | | |

It is immediately noticeable that Athenaeus' iambographic citations are drawn from only seven poets, the vast majority from Hipponax (fifteen) and Archilochus (seventeen): even Semonides of Amorgos, who comes in third with nine iambic citations, is quoted more than any elegist. Of the seventeen poets whose elegies are cited, Dionysius Chalcous and Theognis are represented by six excerpts, though those of Dionysius are concentrated in three citations; Xenophanes and Ion of Chios have five, Simonides four, Mimnermus and Archilochus only three, and the rest two or one. The difference between the iambic and elegiac profile is largely due to the much higher proportion of unusual words or forms in iambic poetry. One diagnostic point is the difference between Athenaeus and Plutarch in their citation of Archilochus: Plutarch has five citations from Archilochus' elegiacs and some eleven from his *iamboi*, Athenaeus three from his elegiacs and seventeen from his *iamboi*.

If we look more closely at Athenaeus' reasons for citation of elegiacs it seems that only two are the result of an interest in a rare word, form or grammatical feature: Asius 14W (at 3.125b–d) for the word κνισοκόλαξ, Ion 28W/von Blumenthal (at 2.68b) for ὀρίγανος as a masculine. On the other hand we should not be surprised to discover that many quotations from this most sympotic of genres illustrate sympotic practice (though so too do some iambic references, like that to Hermippus 7W—not citing any words of Hermippus—at 15.667d). Ulpian introduces one of Athenaeus' two citations of Critias (B2) in his long discussion of κότταβος at the beginning of Book Fifteen (666b); then after numerous comic citations he quotes two poems of Dionysius Chalcous (3W and 4W), the first also about κότταβος; Cynulcus caps him with some less pertinent lines of Dionysius (2W), and then Democritus cites four and a half lines on toasts (προπόσεις 1W). The nature of προπόσεις and their absence from Sparta also prompted the citation of the other piece of Critias (B6 at 10.432d), whose twenty-seven lines make it one of Athenaeus' longest elegiac citations. A wish to illustrate sympotic practice likewise elicited the twenty-four lines of Xenophanes (B1) cited near the begining of Book Eleven, at 462c, though they are offered not as an attestation of any specific phenomenon but as part of an extended comparison—offered by Plutarch—of the practice of the present symposium with that attested in the poets for the archaic and classical period. They are immediately followed by Ion 27W (463a).

Most of the remainder of Book Eleven, of course, reverts to the topic of types of drinking vessel announced by Ulpian at its beginning. That cues Athenaeus to cite (at 11.483d) one of his very few pieces of Archilochean elegy, four lines of fr. 4 on the κώθων, lines about whose context we know a little more from P.Oxy. 854.[4] His explanation of the vessel called 'Heracleion'—that it was the cup of the sun lent to Heracles to travel to the Hesperides—brings out, as well as pieces of Peisander and Stesichorus, Athenaeus' only verbatim citations of Antimachus (66W/Wyss at 11.469f) and Mimnermus (12W at 11.470a). Unlike his near-contemporary Pausanias, Athenaeus here shows only moderate interest in the mythological details in themselves. Again at 496c he cites two lines (2–3) of Ion 27W/von Blumenthal, drawn from the ten lines already cited at 463a, for the term προχύτης for a type of cup.

The sequence in Book Eleven on drinking vessels also, of course, provokes several iambic citations: Semonides 26W at 460b—documenting Semonides of Amorgos as the earliest known user of the term ποτήριον—and 27W at 480c–d for Argive cups (Ἀργεῖαι κύλικες); Hipponax for a milking pail called πέλλα at 495c (14W) and for the variant form πελλίς that he also uses (13W). The lexicographic habit that these cases exemplify is much more often the driving force in iambic citations than it is in elegiac.

This also comes out in Athenaeus' citations that attest sympotic foods, predictably more frequently from iambic poetry. Thus Ananius (3W) seems to have been cited (3.78f) for his use of σῦκα (and perhaps the esteem in which they could, in certain circumstances, be held) by Magnus in his συκολογία known to us only from the epitome of Book Three. This section also introduces Archilochus' dismissal of the fig-based diet of Paros (116W, at 76b), Hermippus' attestation of the white fig-tree, λευκερινεός (2W, at 76c), and Hipponax's description of the black fig as a sister of the vine[5] (48W, at 78b) though it must be noted that this citation also follows up a mythological point. Earlier, at 49e, Athenaeus had cited Archilochus 241W and Hipponax 60W for the word for 'plums', κοκκύμηλα: the former case was also registered by Pollux (i 232). Later, at 282a–b, in Book Seven's discussion of fish, Athenaeus cites Ananius' longest fragment, 5W, consisting of nine tetrameters and one word of a tenth, listing some foods that are best at certain seasons. The citation is a footnote to one from Epicharmus which itself quoted Ananius as saying that the fish called ἀνθίας was best in winter: the point of entry in this case is the nature and name of the fish. Compare the five lines of Hipponax cited for their use of θυννίς (26W, at 304b). A third citation of Ananius (4W) is offered to illustrate the word for cabbage, κράμβη at 9.370b. The only iambic lines from Solon—38W, five trimeters at 14.645f—are cited to attest the kind of cake called γοῦρος.

Morphology is also a prominent concern. Both Archilochus and Semonides are cited at 7.299a–c for their mention of eels, but Athenaeus' main interest is in the formation of the plural—ἐγχέλυς in Archilochus 189W (if Wilamowitz's correction is accepted), with a nominative singular ἔγχελυς and an accusative singular ἔγχελυν in Semonides 8W and 9W—not in the eel's gastronomic or nutritional claims, far less the obscene *double entendre* betrayed by the character-ization of eels as 'blind' by Archilochus in this line.[6] Again when Semonides is cited at 2.57d in the discussion of eggs it is for the spelling ὤεον (11W), and at 3.106e in the discussion of prawns for the spelling with an ω, κωρίδες (15W).

A similar focus on the history of language is found in the section on perfumes in Book Fifteen. A line of Archilochus (205W), also known to Plutarch, is cited as the earliest use of the term μύρον (688c), backed up by his use of the verb μυρίζειν in 48.5–6W.[7] Semonides 16W and Hipponax 104.21W are then cited (690b and a) to show that in them—as also, Athenaeus claims without citation, in many of the comic poets—it is called βάκκαρις.

Not all citations bearing upon food and the symposium display this linguistic dimension. Other aspects of the cultural history of symposia to elicit quotation include famous ἑταίραι (Book Thirteen, from 571e onwards), respon-sible for Athenaeus' mention of Antimachus' entitling his poem *Lyde* (t8 Wyss at 596f); and παίδων ἔρωτες (601 onwards), which allow Athenaeus to cite both an erotic pentameter of Solon (25W, at 13.602e)[8] and the story of Sophocles being teased by Euripides for being robbed of his χλανίς by an attractive boy whom he had picked up and seduced and then replying to Euripides in four witty elegiac lines (Sophocles 4W, at 604d–f).

**II**   How does this range and distribution of quotations that result from Athenaeus' blend of sympotic and lexicographic interests differ from what we find in near contemporaries? I shall look particularly at Plutarch, but sometimes other comparisons will be fruitful.

In some respects Athenaeus and Plutarch are similar. Both clearly know Archilochus quite well—indeed in a recent investigation of Plutarch's quotations[9] I concluded that, apart from the special case of Solon's political poems, Archilochus was the *only* early elegiac and iambic poet who was well known to Plutarch. In Plutarch's case this is likely to be because Archilochus was ranked high in every canon, near to Homer, to be read at school and to be quoted in philosophical or rhetorical works. The same may be true of Athenaeus. But Plutarch's purposes are different: he is usually citing Archilochus to support a moral point, and it is partly for this reason that he has a higher proportion of quotations from his elegiacs (five), though one of these (3W, about the effectiveness in close combat of the Euboean Abantes, *Theseus* 5.2–3) is to establish not a moral but a historical point. In most cases neither Plutarch nor Athenaeus seems to be much concerned with their quotation's context.

Another detail in which the two writers coincide is in almost total neglect of Callinus. Plutarch does not cite him at all. Athenaeus 12.525c claims that Callinus ἐν τοῖς ἐλεγείοις and Archilochus are evidence for the destruction of Magnesia on the Maeander as a result of its citizens' excessive self-indulgence, but cites not a word, far less a line, of the poetry. Despite the specificity of ἐν τοῖς ἐλεγείοις I doubt that Athenaeus was using a text of Callinus, whom we know otherwise only from Strabo, Pausanias, John of Stobi and Stephanus of Byzantium.

In other respects, however, the profiles of Athenaeus and Plutarch differ, and in ways that are not surprising. Plutarch twice cites an anecdote about Tyrtaeus,[10] and uses a passage of the *Eunomia* (also cited by Diodorus) in his discussion of Lycurgus' great *rhetra* (4W, at *Lycurgus* 6). He also cites one exhortatory line of Tyrtaeus (14W) at *de Stoic. rep.* 14 (*Mor.*1039e). That is not a line from the long passage cited by the Athenian orator Lycurgus (10W), nor from the sections that passed into the *Theognidea* (e.g. 12.13–16W = *Theognidea* 1003–6; 12.37–42W with changes = *Theognidea* 935–8) or into Stobaeus (11W and 12W). But at this point Plutarch is attacking Chrysippus, and it is very probable that the citation of Tyrtaeus 14W was already in his text of Chrysippus. Likewise the *Eunomia* passage (4W) had been used in earlier discussions of the *rhetra*. It is perhaps significant that, unlike Strabo (5W and 8W) and Pausanias (5–7W),

Plutarch shows no knowledge of other sections of the *Eunomia*. What we have, then, is not evidence that Plutarch made direct use of a text of Tyrtaeus. But at least he knows of elegiac poems by Tyrtaeus and, for his own reasons, cites them. Athenaeus, on the other hand, never cites Tyrtaeus, and indeed only mentions him at all in a quotation from Philochorus, the well-known passage at 14.630f about the Spartans singing Tyrtaeus' songs.[11] If Tyrtaeus had mentioned Laconian drinking vessels or Spartan broth he might have attracted the interest of Athenaeus, but exhortations to martial virtue that, being in a Ionian *Kunstsprache*, did not even admit words from the Laconian dialect, had little or nothing to offer him.

Some other poets are cited by Plutarch and not by Athenaeus for other but specific reasons. Plutarch's unusual familiarity with elegies of Melanthius and Archelaus arose from his work on fifth-century Athenian lives: he is our only source for both these groups of elegiac poems (indeed for the very existence of Melanthius), so these poets' absence from Athenaeus is unremarkable. Again Plutarch's extensive quotation of Solon arises from work on his *Life*. It is nevertheless bizarre that from Solon Athenaeus cites only one erotic elegiac couplet (25W, cf. above n. 8) and the tetrameters that attest the type of cake called γοῦρος (38W).

There are also poets who are cited—some much cited—by Athenaeus but apparently of little interest to Plutarch. Anacreon's elegiacs are passed over by Plutarch: contrast Athenaeus 11.460c, citing the three words of 4W, and 11.463a, citing the four lines of 2W (though it must be admitted that Hephaestion, 'Longinus', and the Homeric scholia are the only other sources of quotations from Anacreon's elegiacs). The philosopher Plutarch's references to Xenophanes are all to his philosophical poetry in hexameters, not to his elegiacs. Plutarch also turns only once to Ion of Chios (as against five citations in Athenaeus) for the version of Oenopion's lineage that made him a son of Theseus (*Theseus* 20.2 = 29W).

The contrast is more striking in iambic poetry. From Semonides Plutarch cites one line, and one line only (5W), no less than six times, all in his essays: ἄθηλος ἵππῳ πῶλος ὡς ἅμα τρέχει.[12] The termination of the verb is adapted to the context of citation, and since the line is taken up by the paroemiographers (*paroem. gr.* ii 541.20) and Stobaeus (4.50.19) it is virtually certain that Plutarch knew it in a gnomological context rather than directly from a text of Semonides. Contrast Athenaeus' nine citations from Semonides: whether or not Athenaeus is drawing them directly from a text of Semonides is discussed below (III).

Again in the case of Hipponax Plutarch cites a line and a half (32W) from just one poem, and that several times.[13] Plutarch's citations conflict with our other testimony, and from this and from the frequency of the citations it is probable that Plutarch knew these lines well enough to be quoting them from memory. It is also likely that Plutarch knew his line and a half from a philosophical context where they had been cited—as they are once by him at *Sto.paradox.* 6 (*Mor.* 1058D)—to illustrate the behaviour of begging philosophers. Hipponax is not an author in whom I would expect Plutarch to browse, and I believe that he never himself consulted an edition of Hipponax: by contrast I would argue (see below) that for his fifteen citations Athenaeus almost certainly did.

Athenaeus, of course, is not alone among imperial Greek authors in showing himself conversant with Hipponax. But tellingly he is in lexicographic company. Aelius Herodianus from Alexandria, whose καθολικὴ προσῳδία was dedicated to the emperor Marcus and who himself wrote a Συμπόσιον,[14] cited five words or phrases from Hipponax.[15] He was outdone by Pollux, whose *Onomasticon* has ten citations.[16] Hephaestion, who was perhaps a teacher of the emperor Verus, quotes him three times, as does the Anti-atticist;[17] the sophist and lexicographer Phrynichus cites him once,[18] as does Harpocration.[19] Earlier in the second century Hipponax had been cited twice or three times by Suetonius.[20] Interest in Hipponax does not begin in the second century, nor is it wholly restricted to grammarians and lexicographers. In the first century Erotianus, who dedicated his collection of rare words in Hippocrates to Nero's chief doctor Andromachus, cited Hipponax six times.[21] Of writers whose interests are not predominantly lexicographic Sextus, Aelian and ps-Plutarch *On Music* each cite him once, Diogenes Laertius twice, none of these for words alone.[22]

**III**    We have already touched on the issue which is the focus of the third section of my chapter: how often is Athenaeus directly using editions of the poets whom he cites? That is a question which I think must be dealt with poet by poet.

First, iambic poets. The volume of citations from Archilochus (seventeen) Semonides (nine) and Hipponax (fifteen) might seem to create a *prima facie* case for Athenaeus' direct use of these poets' texts. So too might the the fact that Archilochus' iambic poetry is also cited by a fair number of Athenaeus' rough contemporaries. His iambic trimeters are cited by Plutarch, Apollonius Dyscolus, Harpocration, Clement, Ps.-Ammonius, the Ps.-Lucianic *Amores* and Porphyry.[23] His tetrameters are cited by Dio of Prusa, Plutarch, Galen, Pausanias, Pollux and Clement.[24] Epodes of Archilochus are cited by Dio, Plutarch, Apollonius Sophista, Apollonius Dyscolus, Atticus, Aelius Aristides, Lucian, Clement, Aelian, and repeatedly, but for metre, by Hephaestion.[25] A further consideration is the way in which Athenaeus seems to know the tetrameters castigating Pericles for gate-crashing a symposium blind-drunk (124a and bW) well enough to play about with their quotation at 1.7f, though here the precise manner of their introduction is obscured by the fact that for this section we depend on the epitome.

On the other hand it must be conceded that Athenaeus only once makes reference to a specific section of an edition of Archilochus—ἐν τετραμέτροις at 10.415d (167W)—perhaps referring in fact to the poem represented by 168–71W, which was certainly metrically an epode, though perhaps it was included in some ancient editions of the tetrameter poems. I find puzzling this failure to specify the book on more than this one occasion (415d), but not puzzling enough to raise doubts about Athenaeus' having consulted texts of Archilochus.

Again in Hipponax we have a poet much consulted by some of Athenaeus' contemporaries, as we have seen above. Twice Athenaeus specifies his citation of Hipponax as ἐν τοῖς ἰάμβοις (104.47–9W at 10.370c, 166W at 7.324a); once as ἐν τοῖς ἑξαμέτροις (128W at 15.698b). On the other hand Athenaeus never gives a book number (in contrast to Erotianus' citation of 24W or to Pollux's citation of 148aW). Moreover for some of his citations Athenaeus is explicitly using an intermediary: Lysanias' book περὶ ἰαμβοποιῶν for 26W at 7.304b, Pamphilus' Γλῶσσαι for 168W at 2.69d (again the epitome), and Hermippus περὶ Ἱππώνακτος for 169W at 7.327b. From this it might be inferred that Athenaeus did not conduct a comprehensive and systematic trawl of Hipponax: perhaps he browsed, was aware that his notes were not comprehensive, and decided to supplement his primary reading by checking in handbooks. Such a procedure is not unknown in the history of scholarship. But other explanations are possible, and it certainly cannot be demonstrated beyond doubt that Athenaeus drew directly on an edition of Hipponax.

Semonides is the third of the great archaic iambic trinity. He too is familiar to Athenaeus' contemporaries, though not cited on the same scale as Archilochus or Hipponax: Plutarch cites 5W (see above), Herennius Philo 10aW, Harpocration 37W, the Anti-atticist 35W, Galen 14W and Pollux 19W. He may also be the Semonides cited by Suetonius (34*W), and he is mentioned without citation by Lucian (*Pseudologista* 2). Athenaeus identifies two of his citations as ἐν ἰάμβοις (the four words of 8W at 7.299c, the hexameter 26W at 11.460b) and the five words of 11W as ἐν δευτέρῳ ἰάμβων (2.57d, where the phrase has fortunately survived in the epitome). In his longest citation (22–23W), discussing the τυρὸς Τρομιλικός he says (14.658b):

> οὗ καὶ Σιμωνίδης μνημονεύει ἐν ἰάμβῳ οὗ ἡ ἀρχή
>     <ἦ> πολλὰ μὲν δὴ προυκπονέαι Τηλέμβοτε
> γράφων
>     ἐνταῦθα μέν τοι τυρὸς ἐξ Ἀχαίης
>     Τρομίλιος θαυμαστός ὃν κατήγαγον.

Not one of Athenaeus' citations of Semonides does he explicitly ascribe to an intermediary. Putting all these points together I conclude it is almost certain

Athenaeus consulted a text of Semonides. The argument that Athenaeus might simply have inferred the title of the section cited from the metre of his quotation is not persuasive. It fails to explain how Athenaeus could have assigned the hexameter of 26W to ἴαμβοι.

The same probably goes for Hermippus, who is known to us only though Athenaeus and some citations in scholia. Athenaeus specifies all four of his citations as either ἐν ἰάμβοις—a trimeter (2W) at 3.76c; the two-word phrase στρατιωτικὸν λυχνεῖον(8W) at 15.700d—or ἐν τοῖς ἰάμβοις—two tetrameters (4W) at 11.461e, and a reference that seems not to include a verbatim quotation (7W) at 15.700a. As in the case of Semonides, the presence of trochaic tetrameters among these citations counts against the suggestion that Athenaeus is inferring the book-title from the metre.

It is worth adding that Athenaeus' only iambic citation of Solon (38W at 645f) is described as ἐν τοῖς ἰάμβοις, but a single instance cannot count for much.

The case of Ananius is more complicated. There seems to have been disagreement on whether certain poems belonged to Hipponax or Ananius. This is shown by Aristophanes *Frogs* 659–61 (Ananius 1W) where Dionysus ascribes to Hipponax what the scholiast claims was by Ananius. Athenaeus himself at 14.625c is uncertain to which Ananius 2W belongs, and whereas he cites 3W (at 78f) as by Ananius, John of Stobi ascribes these three lines to Hipponax. Add that Athenaeus at 282b trumpets the length of his nine-line (plus one word) citation of 5W: τῶν τοῦ Ἀνανίου πλεόνων ἐμνημόνευσα, νομίζων καὶ τούτων ὑποθήκας τοῖς λάγνοις <ἡδέως> ἐκτεθήσεσθαι. Again, perhaps, these points taken together seem to me to make a case for Athenaeus' use of a text.

Next, the elegists. At least two elegists may well be known to Athenaeus only indirectly. Take first Ion of Chios. At 10.447d Athenaeus quotes just under sixteen lines of Ion's fine hymnic address to Dionysos, praising wine (26W), introducing it with the phrase φησὶν Ἴων ὁ Χῖος ἐν τοῖς ἐλεγείοις. Since he also quotes a ten-line self-referential piece at 11.463a (27W), though without saying ἐν τοῖς ἐλεγείοις, and since he makes three other references to Ion, we might be tempted to think he is likely to be using a text. But caution is in order. Lines 2–3 of 27W are also cited at 11.496c for Ion's use of the term προχύτης for a type of cup, and there this explanation of the word is credited to Simaristos ἐν τετάρτῳ Συνωνύμων: did Simaristos quote Ion too, and perhaps furnish Athenaeus with the whole fragment? We must take into account that earlier in Book Ten, in his discussion of φιλοποσία, Athenaeus (30W) had cited Baton of Sinope as saying (268 F 6) in his monograph on Ion that Ion was φιλοπότην καὶ ἐρωτικώτατον: Athenaeus continues: καὶ αὐτὸς δὲ ἐν τοῖς ἐλεγείοις ἐρᾶν μὲν ὁμολογεῖ Χρυσίλλης τῆς Κορινθίας Τελέου δὲ θυγατρός.

The phraseology seems to suggest that Athenaeus is supplementing and confirming Baton, but is it suspicious that Athenaeus does not cite a phrase of Ion, far less a line, to support his claim that Ion admitted to a passion for the Corinthian Chrysilla?

Simonides' case is not dissimilar. Of Athenaeus' four citations two are explicitly drawn from intermediaries: at 3.125c–d the six lines of 6W from Callistratus in the sixth book of his Σύμμεικτα (348 F 3), at 14.656d the single hexameter of 7W from Chamaeleon's work *On Simonides* (fr. 33 Wehrli)—both in anecdotes illustrating Simonides' capacity for poetic improvisation. Given this explicit dependence, the chances are not high that it was by reading through an edition of the elegies of Simonides that Athenaeus found the two metasympotic phrases of 4W—that wine is ἀμύντορα δυσφροσυνάων—and of 5W, the mysterious οὐ γὰρ ἀπόβλητον Διονύσιον οὐδὲ γίγαρτον.

The situation with Theognis is inevitably more complicated. At least one collection of poetry ascribed to Theognis was circulating by the early imperial period.[26] Some of the Theognidean lines cited by Athenaeus are well-known γνῶμαι: thus Theognis 215–6 at 7.317a, cf. 12.513d; *Theognidea* 457–60 at 13.560a. But that is not true of the lines cited at 7.310a as advocating ἡδυπάθεια (*Theognidea* 993–6) and pederasty (*Theognidea* 997–1002). Moreover at 10.428c Athenaeus cites as by Theognis lines 477–86 which are almost certainly by Euenus of Paros (from an apparently complete poem beginning at 467 and ending with 496), a poet whose fragment 1W (six lines) he has recently cited at 9.367d–e (and is shortly to cite line 4 once more at 10.429f). Of these six lines of Euenus the first four are also cited by John of Stobi (2.2.10). I am inclined to infer that these six lines were known to Athenaeus not from direct consultation of a text of Euenus but from an anthology; that if Athenaeus had consulted a text of Euenus he would have realized that there was a problem in citing *Theognidea* 477–86 as Theognis; and that the format of Athenaeus' Theognis was, in some respects at least, similar to ours, i.e. it had not just genuine Theognidean γνῶμαι but other pieces of early elegy like 993–6 and 997–1002, and it had the three poems by Euenus from one of which 477–86 comes.

On the other hand there are some elegists whom Athenaeus does seem to be citing directly. First Archilochus; one of Athenaeus' three citations specifies ἐν ἐλεγείοις (4W, at 11.483d); another (2W) is introduced in the epitome (1.30f) by ὃς καί πού θησιν. In none of the three citations is there a hint at an intermediary, and although 1W (cited at 14.627c) had been quoted by Plutarch in his *Phocion* (7.6), Plutarch had there changed the opening phrase from εἰμὶ δ' ἐγω to ἀμφότερον: thus Athenaeus has:

εἰμὶ δ' ἐγὼ θεράπων μὲν Ἐνυαλίοιο ἄνακτος
καὶ Μουσέων ἐρατὸν δῶρον ἐπιστάμενος

but Plutarch has:

> ἀμφότερον θεράπων μὲν Ἐνυαλίοιο ἄνακτος
> καὶ Μουσέων ἐρατὸν δῶρον ἐπιστάμενος

It seems unlikely that Athenaeus draws on Plutarch, and I am inclined to think that he did use an edition of Archilochus' elegiacs.

Xenophanes too looks a good case for autopsy. There is no clue to an intermediary in the citation of the twenty-four lines of B1 (at 11.462c) or the twenty-two lines of B2 (at 10.413f). In citing B6 (at 9.368e) for the accusative form κωλῆν as well as the form κωλῆνα the valiant sympotic fighter Leonides specifies Xenophanes ἐν τοῖς ἐλεγείοις. We cannot know just how B5 was cited, since it comes from an epitomized section (11.782a); and although Phylarchus (81 F 66) is cited at 12.526a for the Colophonians' luxury (3W), which they manifested in promenading with their hair styled with gold ornaments, the way that Athenaeus goes on ὡς καὶ Ξενοφάνης φησίν purports to offer additional information, not something that could be found in Phylarchus. Note too that Xenophanes' elegiac poetry seems to be quite neglected until the imperial period. Aristotle in the *Rhetoric* cites a tetrameter (B14) but outside Athenaeus we know his elegiacs from Clement (B14W); Diogenes Laertius (B7W, 7aW, 8W, 19W perhaps 20W); perhaps Pollux (B4W); and scholiasts and lexica. We know a trimeter from Erotianus (B45). Athenaeus may have justifiably felt that he and his contemporaries had rediscovered Xenophanes' elegiacs, and the length of two of his citations could be one consequence of this.

Critias is also a candidate for direct consultation of a text. Athenaeus cites two long pieces, B2 of fourteen lines (at 28b, i.e. the epitome) and B6 of twenty-seven lines (at 10.432d). Since the first is from the epitome we cannot be sure how it was introduced. The latter is cited as Κριτίας ἐν τοῖς ἐλεγείοις. Our other elegiac pieces of Critias are quoted by Plutarch in the *Lives* (B5 at *Alcibiades* 33.1, B8 at *Cimon* 10.5), by Hephaestion (B4) and perhaps by Diogenes Laertius (B7). A revival of interest in Critias' verse in the second half of the second century would be consonant with the known emulation of his prose by Herodes Atticus.[27]

Another possible candidate is Asius, of whom Myrtilus, pressed by Ulpian concerning his use of the word κνισοκόλαξ, cites four lines at 3.125b–d (14W). This manoeuvre of Ulpian may be designed to draw attention to Athenaeus' learning in tracking down these lines, the only elegiacs of Asius known to us.

Finally let us consider Dionysius Chalcous. Aristotle in the *Rhetoric* had criticized his metaphorical description of poetry as κραυγὴν Καλλιόπης (7W, at 1405a31). Otherwise we know him only from Athenaeus, whose characters regularly introduce their citations of Dionysius with ἐν τοῖς ἐλεγείοις (5W at

10.443c, 3W at 15.668e) or ἐκ τῶν ἐλεγείων (4W at 668f, 2W at 669e). Again, perhaps, this is a poet whom Athenaeus may feel that he has rediscovered. Hence, perhaps, his decision to pick out for the very last words of Book Fifteen some words he ascribes to Dionysius (6W): τί κάλλιον ἀρχομένοισιν ἢ καταπαυομένοις ἢ τὸ ποθεινότατον; or, as Gulick translates, 'What nobler theme for you and me, either at the beginning or at the close, than that which we desire the most ?' A fine, if enigmatic, conclusion. Let it be mine too.

# 9

# ATHENAEUS, LUCIAN AND FIFTH-CENTURY COMEDY

## by Keith Sidwell

'Whoever has business with Attic Comedy', said H. Oellacher in 1916, 'sooner or later takes Athenaeus' *Deipnosophists* in hand'.[1] My business with Attic comedy at present concerns the interpretation of fifth-century plays which can be reconstructed from the discourse about comedy contained in contemporary sources external to comedy. So it might seem at first sight that my particular interest will not be well served by examining the use of those comedies in a work of the 'Second Sophistic' which represents the philological investigations of the sort of people described scornfully by Lucian's philosopher Nigrinus as 'displaying an amazing zeal about dinners, with their complicated sauces and curious cakes' (Lucian, *Nigrinus* 33).[2] However, it happens that a study of Athenaeus allows us to view at close quarters a slice of the history of comedy's reception which can be reconstructed to help give a clearer view of what was going on in another writer of the same period, Lucian of Samosata, and to help us isolate some material which may be of crucial importance to the project I have in hand. Clearly, we cannot do anything unless we first face some questions about Athenaeus' knowledge of comedy, his sources, and his methods. So I will begin with these.

## 1. Comedy in Athenaeus

In the appendix I have laid out in section one the references to poets of the fifth century given in Athenaeus. I have reported citations as they actually are, because it is important to recognize precisely what the state of knowledge (or states of knowledge) was for Athenaeus and his epitomators. I have also listed at the end of each entry the numbers of papyrus fragments identified for the writer in question. Since Athenaeus was from Naucratis in Egypt, the spread of papyri might help with the question of first-hand knowledge. In section 2 of the appendix, I have listed from *PCG* fifth-century poets missing from his researches. This includes sixteen names of poets about whom we know little. This helps to re-emphasize the oft-stated importance of Athenaeus as a source for lost material: where the *Deipnosophistae* lets us down, we have precious little to go on.

The figure in Athenaeus for named plays by fifth-century poets (and this includes some plays we know were produced in the early fourth century) is somewhere around 260. I have restricted my enquiry to fifth-century writers. But it is worth noting that the figures for 'Middle' and 'New' Comedy are far higher. Athenaeus cites over a hundred titles for Antiphanes and 110 for Alexis (poets of 'Middle Comedy'). He knows twenty-nine titles for Diphilus, forty-seven for Menander, and twenty for Philemon (poets of 'New Comedy').

## 2. Sources

But where did Athenaeus get the material from? Did he read all the comedies himself? Did he gather the citations from earlier scholarly discussion of individual topics which occur in the work? Or was it a bit of both? Heinz-Günther Nesselrath is the most recent scholar I know of to have looked at this problem.[3] His assessment, I think, is fair: 'Jedenfalls machen die *Deipnosophistai* den Eindruck eines Werkes, das in seinem Informationsgehalt völlig ... von Vorgängern abhängig ist, die ihrerseits wieder auf frühere Gewährsleute zurückgehen' ('At any rate, the *Deipnosophistae* gives the impression of a work which in its information content completely ... relies on predecessors, who in their turn also go back to earlier guarantors'). In the appendix, in section 4, I have given a list of those authorities cited by name in the work in relation to comedy. These will merely have been the tip of the iceberg.

The evidence from papyrus finds, such as it is, tends to support Nesselrath's view.[4] Of the fragments positively ascribed to fifth-century authors, there are about forty from Aristophanes, twelve from Eupolis, eleven from Epicharmus, three each from Cratinus and Plato, two each from Diocles, Hermippus, Strattis, and Telecleides, and one each from Euthycles (?), Leucon, Lysippus and Pherecrates. Of the 155 papyrus *adespota*, only seventeen have been tentatively ascribed to fifth-century writers. Of these ascriptions, the majority are to Aristophanes (five), Cratinus (four), Eupolis (two) and Phrynichus (two). It looks as though the author most widely read was Aristophanes. He was followed most closely by Eupolis and Epicharmus. At some considerable distance come Cratinus and Plato. The rest are effectively nowhere. And the comparison between the meagre papyrus finds of Aristophanic material and the richness of those of Menander makes it abundantly clear that in Egypt it was the later comedy which was most widely read.

Lucian can help us here. He is roughly contemporary with Athenaeus.

Late in his life he seems to have lived in Egypt (*Apologia* 18). He explicitly acknowledges his debt to fifth-century comedy in the creation of his comic dialogues at *Bis Accusatus* 33.[5] As elsewhere in his oeuvre, Lucian here advertises his sources not to reveal some great secret to an unsuspecting audience, but to confirm what they already know. Hence, the audience's recognition of his cleverness in relocating and serving up as new things that are well known to his audience is all part of the literary game. This strategy he makes explicit at *VH* 1.2, in a passage which also reflects language used elsewhere about the way Old Comedy is understood.[6] Hence Lucian allows us a sort of control against which to measure the knowledge of fifth-century comedy shown in Athenaeus.

What fifth-century comedy Lucian explicitly acknowledges, I have laid out in section 3 of the appendix. It is very little indeed. And I have increased its paucity by allowing spurious works in and also citations in scholia, which only occasionally may have a bearing on the referent of the text. This is not the whole picture, however. Lucian's comic dialogues imitated plot-lines, motifs and scenes in the body of work available to him and which he could assume as a base-point for his audience. The sort of thing he did can be best seen by comparing his *Timon* with Aristophanes' *Plutus*. There is certainly a lot more of this. Some pretty well-accepted examples are these. In *Bis Accusatus*, Lucian himself is accused in court of mistreatment by Rhetoric and Dialogue. This seems to be a reworking of Cratinus' *Pytine*. In *Piscator*, the ancient philosophers beg a day off from Hades to come to the daylight and hound Lucian for his attacks on them in his dialogues. Again, the scenario appears to have been borrowed from Eupolis' *Demoi*. A couple of further possibilities are the following. His *Dearum Iudicium*, featuring the ancient beauty contest between the goddesses, may reflect a scene in Cratinus' *Dionysalexandros*. The scene in *Lexiphanes*, where a doctor makes the hyperatticist vomit up his rare vocabulary, may reflect whatever comic scene lies behind the vomiting up of five talents by Kleon in *Acharnians* 5–8.[7] The title *Zeus Elenchomenos* is very reminiscent of Plato's *Zeus Kakoumenos*.

There is much more to do here.[8] However, it is clear that Lucian's method of imitation means that my bare list of citations is not the true comparand for Athenaeus. On the other hand, I doubt whether we are talking about more than twenty or thirty plays of fifth-century comedy in all. The figure in Athenaeus for named plays is, as we have said, somewhere around 260. The figure in Lucian looks much more comparable to the evidence from papyrus finds as a reflection of normal direct acquaintance at this period than does what we read in Athenaeus.

### 3. Athenaeus' method

There is one basic point to be made about the way comedy is used in Athenaeus: it is subordinated to the search for information. The texts are the evidence used to argue points, whether of history or of linguistic usage. For example, at 1.7d a passage of Euphron provides information about Nicomedes, King of Bithynia. At 3.99f, Ulpian is made to justify current usage by reference to Cratinus, Menander and Aristophanes.[9] It is interesting to note that for these purposes the differentiation between the periods of comedy which is clearly known to Athenaeus (e.g. 7. 293a Middle Comedy; 15. 693b Old Comedy) is of no consequence, as Ulpian's use of Old and New comedy in the same breath shows. Cf. also 15. 699f. on the use of λυχνοῦχος. Occasionally, comedy is quoted simply for decoration, as at 10–11. 459. This has clear parallels in Lucian also (e.g. *Nigrinus* 7).

If we accept that the citations of comedy are second- or third-hand, an interesting conclusion follows: the way comedy is interpreted belongs to an earlier phase of the study of comedy. Nesselrath has shown convincingly that the references to Middle Comedy reflect a periodization first proposed in Alexandria.[10] There are several references to earlier scholars and their discussion of comedy which show the sort of place information was available to Athenaeus. I have listed these in the appendix, section 4. Here I want to draw attention to other tendencies in the citation of comedy which fit in with what we see in the material in Koster's *Prolegomena* and which we suspect was derived from Alexandrian or Pergamene scholarship on comedy.

(1) An interest in the biography of the poets. E.g. 1.22a: Cratinus the dancer; 10. 429, Aristophanes wrote his plays drunk.

(2) An interest in the history of comedy. E.g. the origins of comedy: 2.40a–b. The use of the *didaskaliai*: 5.216d. Periodization: see references above. Introduction of drunken characters, cooks and servants: 10.429, 14.659a–d (this last citing Aristophanes of Byzantium, *On Masks*).

(3) An interest in the persons subjected to comic treatment: 12.551b–552b (Cinesias).

(4) An awareness of disputed authorship or revision: 3.108c, 123b, 110b.

(5) Implicit aesthetic judgements: 9.398f, Aristophanes is called ὁ χαρίεις.

(6) Description of plots and characters: 3.109f (Aristophanes' *Geras*); 11.494d–e (Aristophanes' *Babylonians*); 13.561a (Aristophanes' *Gerytades*); 1.5 (Philoxenus a character in Crobylus).

Lucian's works show a similar set of connections with the remains of comic scholarship, though they do not cover the same ground. At *VH* 1.29, a joke is made out of the pretence that Aristophanes belongs to the tradition of those who tell the truth.[11] In some of the material in Koster, especially the hypotheses, we see the description of Old Comedy as having not an ἀληθὴς ὑπόθεσις ('true subject'), but a merely playful basis.[12] The passage already cited from *VH* 1.2 connects with remarks in the comic scholarship about the way in which the comedy of invective was forced to abandon openness for enigma at a certain stage.[13] Lucian is telling us here that he expects us to know who is being referred to although he has eschewed ὀνομαστὶ κωμῳδεῖν ('satirizing by name'). This in turn tells us how scholars of his generation understood the scholarship of Alexandria on this point: names were abandoned because of legislation against ὀνομαστὶ κωμῳδεῖν and instead people were referred to through enigmatic satire.

Not surprisingly, then, both Athenaeus and Lucian had available to them and used as interpretative models for comedy, the plethora of scholarship from earlier times which told them both how comedy developed and what its nature was at various times, as well as a vast number of details about the lives of its poets, their targets and their language.

## 4. The usefulness of Athenaeus and Lucian

Athenaeus is not the place to look for a true picture of fifth-century comedy. He shows no understanding of the importance of humour, for a start, which vitally affects the interpretation of any text.[14] But Lucian, though his use of comedy is to make more comedy, does not tell us anything more about it than Athenaeus. What we have opened up here, though, is a way for these authors to tell us new things about fifth-century comedy, despite themselves. Both were heirs to an established tradition of scholarship which they used as a filter for their diverse approaches to the genre.

This tradition effectively divided comedy's development up in terms of form (loss of parabasis, choral role reduced etc.), or basis of plot (fiction, or parody of myth), or invective (open, enigmatic, none at all). I have recently reexamined the evidence from fifth- and fourth-century sources and found that it was comprehensively misinterpreted by scholars after the classical period because the classical writers took for granted things which later students with only texts and scattered remarks could not be expected to read back. Aristotle shows that there were two separate traditions of comedy, one based on caricature (the iambic form, Athenian born and bred) and the other based on plot (the Sicilian brand). The history of the restriction of invective comedy was entirely separate from the development of what we call New Comedy. The restrictions in naming were centred on the focal concern of that comedy—caricature of real individuals—and not, as Lucian clearly thought, on iambic attacks by name. Alexandrian scholars did pass on information about such caricatures as they knew had been disguised: in *Knights* Paphlagon = Cleon, Slave 2 = Nicias; in *Acharnians*, Euripides' slave was Cephisophon. But their information was haphazard and they did not realize that the phenomenon was global.[15]

Let me illustrate the possibilities first from Lucian, the imitator of Old Comedy. I have already said that in *Bis Accusatus* he was using Cratinus' *Pytine*. This play was believed in antiquity to have been a self-satire by Cratinus, with himself as the drunken comic poet whose wife Comedy wishes to divorce him.[16] In that piece, as also in the *Piscator*, where he was inspired at least partly by Eupolis, Lucian presents himself under a sobriquet. In *Bis Accusatus* he is ὁ Σύρος ('the Syrian'), in *Piscator* he is Παρρησιάδης ('Freespeechson'). It seems very likely that his practice here is directly influenced by his perception of what was happening in the text. That is, the poet in Cratinus' play did not call himself Cratinus, but used a sobriquet (cf. Dikaiopolis in *Acharnians*). This in turn gives us the possibility of rejecting the ancient interpretation, which I think we must do because the discourse external to comedy shows that the comedy of invective was taken seriously. Despite appearances, it is more likely that comic poets attacked each other than that they willingly took themselves down a peg or two.

Here, then, reappraisal of the fifth- and fourth-century evidence leads to the possibility of reconstructing an aspect of the text Lucian and his audience could read and we cannot. I will give two examples from Athenaeus. They are both fragments of biography, one about Cratinus, the other about Aristophanes.

At 1.22a, Athenaeus reports that 'the old poets—Thespis, Pratinas, Cratinus, Phrynichus—were called dancers because they not only relied upon the dancing of the chorus for the interpetation of their plays, but, quite apart from their own compositions, they taught dancing to all who wanted instruction'.[17] The notion that the comic poet Cratinus was a dancer would not perhaps strike us as especially important. However, in the light of the revelation that Old Comedy was caricature-based and that certain individuals—including, as my previous example may show, comic poets—were not allowed to be represented under their own names and my recent suggestion that Philocleon in *Wasps* was meant for Cratinus, the information becomes vitally important.[18] The concatenation Cratinus, Phrynichus in Athenaeus may be fortuitous. But it is strange that in some ancient source the comic poet and the tragic poet nestled side by side, as they are shown interacting when the old poet, drunk again, is shown doing Phrynichean steps against the sons of Carcinus (*Wasps* 1482f.).

At 10.429a, Athenaeus drops the following startling piece of information: 'Alcaeus the lyric poet and Aristophanes the comic poet also were drunk when they composed their works'.[19] Now I imagine that the information about Alcaeus was gleaned from his works. But where did the tale about Aristophanes come from? After all, if you were to look for a poet of Old Comedy to categorize thus, Cratinus would be the obvious example. I do not think we can discard this statement without further ado. It probably came from one of the Alexandrian works which interested themselves in such anecdotes (though I suppose it could belong to an earlier *On Drunkenness*). Its ultimate source may have been Aristophanes himself. However, why would Aristophanes have said this about himself when it was used as a sharp criticism of Cratinus in *Knights* (533–6, cf. 400 with scholion)?

It could have come from one of his rivals: the parabasis of *Pytine*, where we know Cratinus criticized Aristophanes, is an obvious suggestion (fr. 213 *PCG*). But then, was the poet who could not write through (fictional) old age and (fictional) drunkenness not Cratinus, but Aristophanes? The evidence of Lucian and Athenaeus, filtered back through fifth-century assumptions about comedy, may well point in that direction.

## Appendix: Fifth-Century Comedy in Athenaeus and Lucian

*1. Athenaeus*

**Poets and works cited in Athenaeus** (Roman numerals followed by Arabic and letter in the form iii.107f indicate direct reference to books of Athenaeus; G followed by Arabic numerals in the form 2.7 indicate Gulick's Loeb, by volume and page numbers; the list of poets follows *PCG*; titles of fragmentary plays are given in transliterated form in *Greek* alphabetical order)

**Alcaeus**

| | |
|---|---|
| *Adelphai* | vii.316b (= G 3.421) |
| *Ganymede* | iii.110a, x.445e (= G 2.17, 4.519) |
| *Hieros Gamos* | ix.408e, x.424e (= G 4.351, 423) |
| *Callisto* | ix.399f (= G 4.309) |
| *Palaistra* | iii.107f, ix.370f, xv.691b (= G 2.7, 4.179, 293, 7. 201) |
| Untitled plays: | vii.316c (= G 3.421) |

No identified papyri.

**Amipsias**

| | |
|---|---|
| *Apokottabizontes* | xv.666a, vii.307d; x.426f; xi.473d; xv.667f (= G 7.67; 3.381; 4.433; 5.89; 7.77) |
| *Katesthion* | vii.316b (= G 3.421) |
| *Konnos* | v.218c; vii.327d; ix.368e (= G 2.489; 3.473; 4.171) |
| *Sphendone* | vi.270f; ix.400c; ix.408e; x.446d (= G 3.217; 4.313, 349, 523) |
| Untitled plays: | i.8e; ii.62f; ii.68b; xi.783e (= G 1.37, 273, 297; 5.51) |

No identified papyri.

**Apollophanes**

| | |
|---|---|
| *Kretes* | iii.75c, xi.485e (= G 1.325, 5.157) |
| *Dalis* | iii.114f, xi.467f (= G 2.39, 5.63) |

No identified papyri.

**Archippos**

| | |
|---|---|
| *Amphitryo* | iii.95e, x.426b, xi.499b (= G 1.411, 4.429, 5.229) |
| *Herakles Gamon* | vii.307d, xiv.640f, xv.678e (= G 3.381, 6.459, 7.19) |
| *Ichthyes* | iii.86c, vi.227a, vii.277f, vii.301a, vii.311e, vii.312a, vii.315b, vii.315c, vii.322a, vii.328a, vii.329b–c, viii.331c, viii. 343c, x.424b (= G 1.371, 3.23, 249, 349, 399, 401, 415, 417, 447, 477, 483, 4.5, 57, 421) |
| *Rhinon* | xv.678e (= G 7.133) |

One possibly identified papyrus (*Ichthyes?*).

**Aristagoras**

| | |
|---|---|
| *Mammakuthos* | viii.355a (?), xiii.571b (= G 4.107 with 106 n. 3, 6.85) |

No identified papyri.

**Aristomenes**

| | |
|---|---|
| *Goetes* | vii.287d, ix.384e, xiv.658a (= G 3.291, 4.239, 7.29) |
| *Dionysos* | xiv.650d, xiv.658a (= G 6.513, 7.27) |
| Untitled plays: | i.11c–d (= G 1.49) |

No identified papyri.

**Aristonymos**

*Helios Rhigon*    vii.284f, vii.285e, vii.287c, d (= G 3.279, 283, 291)

*Theseus*    iii.87a (= G 1.375)

No identified papyri.

**Aristophanes**

Came from Naucratis vi.229d–e (= G 3.33); wrote drunk x.429a (= G 4.443)

Named plays (lost):

*Aiolosikon*    iii.95e, iii.112e, vii.276d, ix.372a (second version), xv.699f (=G 1.411; 2.29; 3.243; 4.185; 7.251

*Amphiaraus*    iv.158c (= G 2.221)

*Anagyros*    iv.133b, vii.301a, ix.385f, xiv.650e (= G 2.111; 3.349; 4.245; 6.515)

*Babylonioi*    iii.86f, xi.478c, xi.494d–e (= G 1.375; 5.117, 203)

*Georgoi*    iii.75a, iii.111b, xi.460d, xiv.650e (= G 1.325; 2.23; 5.7; 6.515)

*Geras*    iii.109f, iv.133a, vii.287d (= G 2.17, 111; 3.291)

*Gerytades*    iii.95f, iii.99f, iii.112e, iv.158c, vi.261f, vii.307e, vii.321a, viii.365b, ix.367b, xi.485a, xii.551a–c, xiii.592c, xiv.650e (= G 1.411, 429; 2.29, 221; 3.177, 383, 443; 4.153, 163; 5.155, 501–3; 6.195, 515)

*Daidalos*    vii.316b, ix.367d, ix.368b, ix.374c (= G 3.421, see 453 n. f; 4.165, 169, 195)

*Daitales*    iii.119b–c, iii.127c, iv.169c, iv.183e, iv.184e, vii.299b, ix.368d–e, ix.400a, xi.484f, xii.527c, xiv.646b, xv.667f, xv.690e, xv.691c, xv.694a (= G 2.55–7, 89, 269, 311, 315; 3.341; 4.169, 311; 5.153, 379; 6.489; 7.77–9, 199, 203, 215)

*Danaides*    ii.57a, iii.114c, vii.323c, vii.324b, ix.400a, x.422e xiv.645e (= G 1.249; 2.37; 3.453, 457; 4.311, 415; 6.485)

*Delia* (?)    ix.373a (= G 4.189–91)

*Dramata (Niobos)*    vii.301b, xi.496a, xv.699f (second version) (= G 3.351; 5.211; 7.253)

*Heroes*    ix.409c (= G 4.353)

*Thesmophoriazousai*    i.29a, iii.104e, iii.117c, vii.324b, xiv.619a xv.690c–d (= G 1.127, 449; 2.49; 3.457; 6.335; 7.197)

*Kentauros* (?)    xiv.629c (= G 6.395)

*Kokalos*    iv.156b, xi.478d (= G 2.211; 5.117)

*Lemniai*    vii.299a vii.302d, vii.311d, ix.366c (= G 3.341, 357, 399; 4.161)

*Nephelai*    xi.479c (= G 5.123)

*Nesoi*    (title not mentioned: see Pollux VI 45) ii.56b (= G 1.245)

*Holkades*    iii.91b, iii.111.a, iii.118d, vii.329b (= G 1.391; 2.23, 53; 3.483)

*Pelargoi*    vi.247a, ix.368e, ix.387f (= G 3.111; 4.169, 253)

*Poleis*    (? or Philyllius or Eunicus) iii.86e, iv.140a (= G 1.373; 2.139)

*Proagon*    iii.80a, ii.95d, ix.380d, x.422e, xi.478f (= G 1.345, 411; 4.221, 413–15; 5.119–21)

*Skeuai* (? or Plato)    xiv.628e (= G 6.389–91)

*Skenas Katalambanousai*    iv.169c, vii.286f–287a (= G 2.269; 3.289)

*Tagenistai*    iii.96c, iii.110f, iv.171a–b, vi.269e, vii.285e, ix.374f, ix.410b, x.418d, x.422f, xv.677b–c (= G 1.415; 2.21, 277; 3.211, 283; 4.199, 357, 395, 415; 7.125)

*Telmesses*    ii.49c (title not given: found in Pollux x.80), vii.308f, xv.690f (= G 1.215; 3.387–9; 7.201)

*Triphales*    xii.525a (= G 5.367)

*Phoinissai*    ii.62d, iii.90a, iv.154e (= G 1.273, 385–7; 2.203)

*Horai*    ix.372b, xiv.653f (= G 4.187; 7.7)

Sixteen possible papyrus fragments identified.

Named plays (extant):

**Acharnians** (85) iv.130f–131a, (459) xi.479b, (524) xiii.570a, (606) vii.314f (a borrowing, not a citation), (616) ix.409f, (786) ix.374f, (872) iii.112f, (875) ix.388b and ix.395e, (889) vii.299a, (1092) xiv.646d (= G 2.101; 5.121; 6.79; 3.413; 4.357; 4.199; 2.29; 4.255 and 291; 3.341; 6.491)

**Birds** (67) ix.386f, (101) ix.397d, (249) ix.388b, (269) ix.397d, (304) ix.388e, (566) vii.325b, (695) ii.57d, (707) ix.388b, (761) ix.388b, (884) ix.397e, (1377) xii.551d (= G4. 249, 299; 255, 299, 257, 3.463, 1.251, 4255, 255, 301 and 303; 5.503)

**Clouds** (103) v.188c, (109) ix.387a, (122) xi.467b, (339) ii.64f, (362) v.216a, (455) iii.94f, (559) vii.299b, (665) ix.374c, (961) ix.380f (not a citation), (983) viii.345f, (1196) iv.171c (= G 2.355; 4.249; 5.59; 1.283; 2.477; 1.407; 3.341; 4.197; 4.223; 4.67 ; 2.279)

**Ecclesiazousai** (707) iii.77d; (843) iii.110a; (1117) xv.691b (= G 1.335; 2.17; 7.203)

**Frogs** (134) ii.66b, (294) xiii.566e (not a citation), (1304) xiv.636e (= G 1.287; 6.61; 6.435)

**Knights** (83) iii.122a, (92) xi.782c, (124) xi.460c, (160) iii.94d, (198) xi.460c, (300) iii.94c, (356) iii.94d, (361) vii.311c–d, (599) xi.483d, (631) ix.367a, (662) vii.328e, (864) vii.299b and c, (1094) xi.783f, (1178) iii.94d; (1289) x.446d–e (= G 2.67; 5.43; 5.5; 1.405; 5.5; 1.405; 1.407; 3.399; 5.145; 4.161–3; 3.479; 3.341, 343; 5.51; 1.407; 4.523

**Lysistrata** (203) xi.502b; (549) iii.90b (= G 5.249; 1.387)

**Peace** (27) iv.173a, (122) iii.111a, (143) xi.486e, (540) x.424b,(563) iii.119c, (788) ix.393c, (804) viii.343c, (916) xi.485a (= G 2.285; 2.23; 5.163; 4.421; 2.57; 4.279; 4.57; 5.153)

**Plutus** (179) xiii.592d, (720) ii.67c, (812) vi.229e, (1005) iv.170d, (1128) ix.368d (= G 6.195; 1.293; 3.33; 2.275; 4. 169)

**Thesmophoriazousai** (457–8) xv.680c–d (= G 7.143)

**Wasps** (330) ix.385d, (493) vii.315c, (510) vii.299b, (511) ix.396a, (855) x.424c, (884) iii.90a, (1127) vii.329b, (1208–9) v.179a–b, (1214) v.179b, (1216) xiv.641d (= G 4.243; 3.417; 3.341; 4.293; 4.421; 1.387; 3.483; 2.335; 2.337; 6.463)

Around thirty papyrus fragments identified.

Untitled plays: i.4d, i.21e–f, i.30c, ii.48c, ii.50e, ii.53a, ii.67c, iv.173d, vii.310f, x.444d, xi.485a, xi.502b, xiv.652f, xv.701b (= G 1.19, 95, 133, 211, 221, 231, 293; 2.287; 3.397; 4.513; 5.153, 249; 6.527; 7.267)

**Callias**

**Kyklopes** (or Diocles) iv.140e, vii.285e, vii.286b, vii306a–b, xi.487a, xii.524f, xv.667d (= G 2.141, 3.283, 285, 375, 5.165, 367, 7.75)

**Pedetai** iv.176f, viii.344e (= G 2.303, 4.63)[20]

Untitled plays: i.22c, ii.57a (= G 1.97, 247)

No papyrus fragments identified.

**Cantharus**

*Symmachia* (or Plato?) vii.312c, vii.314a (= G 3.403, 411)

*Tereus*      iii.81d (= G 1.351)

Untitled plays:    i.11c, ii.68b (= G 1.49, 297 [? or Plato[21]])

No papyrus fragments identified.

**Cephisodoros**

*Amazones*      xiv.629c (= G 6.393)

*Hys*      iii.119c, viii.345f, xv.701b (= G 2.57; 4.67; 7.267)

*Trophonius*      xii.553a, xv.667d, xv.689f (= G 5.511; 7.75, 193)

Untitled plays:    xi.459a (= G 5.3)

No papyrus fragments identified.

**Chionides**

*Ptochoi* (sometimes iii.119e, iv.137e, xiv.638d (= G considered spurious) 2.57: see also 2.59 n. b, 2.129, 6.447)

No papyrus fragments identified.

**Crates**

Attacked by Aristophanes in the lost *Thesmophoriazousai*: iii.117c (= G 2.49)

*Geitones*      ix.396d, x.429a, xv.690d (= G 4.295, 443; 7.199)

*Theria*      iii.119c, vi.267e (= G 2.57; 3.203)

*Lamia*      x.418c (= G 4.395)

*Paidiai*      xi.478f (= G 5.119)

*Rhetores*      ix.369c (= G 4.173)

*Samioi*      iii.117b (= G 2.47)

*Tolmai*      vi.247f, xiv.619a (= G 3.117; 6.335)

Untitled plays:    ii.47e, ii.50e (= G 1.207, 221)

No papyrus fragments identified.

**Cratinus**

Cratinus a dancer i.22a (= G 1.95); epigram on Cratinus ii.39c ( = G 1.171); Cratinus the first to use the theme of the primitive life vi.268d–e (= G 3.207)

Named plays:

*Archilochoi*      iii.86e, iii.92e, iv.164e, ix.375a, ix.410d (= G 1.373, 399; 2.247; 4.199, 359)

*Boukoloi*      xiv.638e–f (= G 6.447)

*Deliades*      ix.396a (= G 4.293)

*Dionysalexandros* iii.119b, ix.384b, xi.475a [added by Kaibel from Macrobius] (= G 2.55; 4.237; 5.99 and n. 1)

*Drapetides*      viii.344e, xi.501d–f (= G 4.63; 5.243–5)

*Euneidae*      xv.698c (= G 7.243)

*Thraittai*      xi.495a (= G 5.205)

*Kleoboulinai*      iv.171b (= G 2.277)

*Malthakoi*      iii.111e, xiv.638e, xv.681b, xv.681e, xv.685b–c, xv.685f (= G 2.25; 6.447; 7.147, 151, 169, 173)

*Nemesis*      ix.373c–e, xiv.629c, xv.666d, xv.667f (= G 4.191–3 [x 4]; 6.393; 7.69, 77)

*Nomoi*      xi.496e, xi.502b, xiv.646e (= G 5.215, 245; 6.491)

*Odysses*      ii.68c, iii.99f, vii.315b–c, ix.385c–d, x.445b, xiv.657a, xv.677f (= G 1.297–9, 429; 3.415–7; 4.243, 521; 7. 23, 129)

*Ploutoi*      iii.94e, iv.138e, vi.267e, vi.268e, vii.299b, vii.303d (= G 1.407; 2.133; 3.203, 207, 341, 363)

*Pytine*      iii.94f, x.426b, xi.494b–c (= G 1.407; 4.429; 5.201)

*Trophonios*      vii.325e (= G 3.465)

*Cheirones*      ix.392f, xii.553e (= G 4.277; 5.515)

*Horai*      ix.374d, 638f (= G 4.197; 6.449)

Untitled plays:    i.8a, i.22c, i.23b, i.29d, ii.47a, ii.49a, ii.56e, ii.62e, ii.67b, ii.68a, ii.69d, vii.305b, xi.782d, xiii.566e, xiii.596c, xiv.663a [ms.], xv.676f (= G 1.33, 97, 101, 129 (*Pytine?*), 203–5, 213, 247, 273, 293, 295–7, 303; 3.369; 5.43–5; 6.61, 215; 7.123, 7. 52, n. 3)

Three papyrus fragments identified.

**Deinolochus**
| | |
|---|---|
| *Telephos* | iii.111c (= G 2.23) |

No papyrus fragments identified.

**Demetrios I**
| | |
|---|---|
| *Sikelia* | iii.108f–109a (= G 2.13) |
| Untitled plays: | ii.56a (= G 1.243) |

One papyrus testimonium identified.

**Diocles** (or Callias)
| | |
|---|---|
| *Thalatta* | vii.307d, xiii.567c (= G 3.381, 6.65) |
| *Kyklopes* | iv.140e, vii.306a, xii.524f, xv.667d (= G 2.141; 3.375; 5.367; 7.75) |
| *Melissai* | x.426d (= G 4.431) |

Two papyrus testimonia identified.

**Ecphantides**
| | |
|---|---|
| *Satyroi* | iii.96c (= G 1.413) |

**Epicharmus**

First to bring a drunken man on stage x.429a (= G 4.443); employs parody xv.698c (= G 7.223)

Named plays:
| | |
|---|---|
| *Agrostinos* | iii.120d, xv.682b (= G 2.60; 7.153) |
| *Alkyon* | xiv.619b (= G 6.335) |
| *Atalantai* | xiv.618d (= G 6.331) |
| *Bacchae* | iii.106f (= G 2.3) |
| *Bousiris* | x.411a (= G 4.365) |
| *Ga kai Thalassa* | iii.105b, iii.106e, iii.120d, vii.313d, vii.322f, ix.370b, xiv.646f, xiv.648b (= G 1.451, 457; 2.61; 3.407, 451; 4.177; 6.487, 501) |
| *Dionysoi* | iv.158c (= G 2.221) |
| *Elpis* (or *Ploutos*) | iv.139b, vi.235e–236b (= G 2.135; 3.61–3) |
| *Heorte kai Nasoi* | iv.160d (= G 2.231 and n.d) |
| *Hebas Gamos* | iii.85c–e, iii.91c, iii.92f, iii.105a, iii.110b, vii.282a, vii.285a, vii.286b, vii.286f, vii.287b, vii.283b, vii.295b, vii.304c, vii.305c, vii.306a, vii.306c, vii.308e, vii.309d, vii.313d, vii.313e, vii.315f, vii.318e, vii.318f, vii.319c, vii.320c, vii.321a, vii.321d, vii.322f, vii.323c, vii.323f, vii.324e, vii.325f, vii.326e, vii.327c, vii.327f, vii.328c, vii.330a, ix.398d, ix.400c, xiv.646b (= G 1.367–9, 393, 399, 449; 2.19; 3.267, 279, 285, 287, 289, 295, 323, 367, 371, 373, 375, 387, 391, 407, 409, 419, 431, 433, 435, 439, 443, 445, 451, 453, 455, 459, 465, 469, 473, 475, 479, 487; 4. 303, 313; 6.489) |
| *Thearoi* | iii.107a, viii.362b, ix.408d (= G 2.3; 4.139, 349) |
| *Kyklops* | ix.366b, xi.498e (= G 4.159; 5.227) |
| *Komastai* | ix.389a (= G 4.259) |
| *Logos kai Logina* | iii.106e, viii.338d (= G 1.457; 4.35) |
| *Megaris* | vii.286c, ix.366b (= G 3.285; 4.159) |
| *Mousai* | iii.85e, iii.110b, iv.184f, vii.282d, vii.297c, vii.303d, vii.307b, vii.308e, vii.312c, vii.320e, vii.323a, vii.328b (= G 1.369; 2.19, 315; 3.269, 333, 361–3, 379, 387, 403, 441, 451, 477) |
| *Odysseus Automolos* | iii.121b, ix.374d (= G 2.63; 4.197) |
| *Odysseus Nauagos* | xiv.619b (= G 6.335) |
| *Orya* | iii.94f (= G 1.407) |
| *Periallos* | iv.139c, iv.183c (= G 2.135, 309) |
| *Pyrrha kai Promatheus* | iii.86a, x.424d (= G 1.371; 4.423) |
| *Seirenes* | vii.277f (= G 3.249) |
| *Sphinx* | iii.76c (= G 1.329) |
| *Philoktetes* | ix.371f, xiv.628b (= G 4.185; 6.387) |
| *Cheiron* | xiv.648d (= G 6.503 = xi.479b 5.121, untitled play) |

| | |
|---|---|
| Untitled plays: | i.31a, ii.36c–d, ii.49c, ii.52a, ii.56a, ii.57d, ii.58d, ii.59c, ii.60e, ii.63c, ii.64f, ii.65b, ii.68b, ii.68f, ii.70a, ii.70f, iii.119b, iii.119d, v.210b, vii.304e, vii.308c, vii.309e, vii.322b, viii.362d, viii.363e, ix.391d, xi.479b, xiv.645e (= G 1.137, 157–9, 215, 227, 243, 251, 255, 259, 265, 275, 281, 283, 297, 301, 305, 309; 2.55, 57, 449; 3.367, 385, 393, 447; 4.141, 147, 271; 5.121; 6.485) |

Around eleven papyrus fragments and two testimonia ascribed (see Austin 1973, Rodríguez-Noriega Guillén 1996).

## Epilycos

| | |
|---|---|
| *Koraliskos* | iv.133b, iv.140a, xiv.650e, xv.691c (= G 2.113, 139; 6.515–17; 7.203) |
| Untitled plays: | i.28d (= G 1.125) |

No identified papyrus fragments.

## Eunicos

| | |
|---|---|
| *Anteia* (or by Philyllios) | xiii.567c, xiii.586e (= G 6.65, 163) |
| *Poleis* (or by Philyllios or Aristophanes) | iii.86e (= G 1.373) |

No identified papyrus fragments.

## Eupolis

Named plays:

| | |
|---|---|
| *Aiges* | iii.94f, iii.106b, vii.287d, vii.301a, ix.380e, ix.409b, x.426f (= G 1.407, 455; 3.291, 349; 4.221, 353, 433) |
| *Astrateutoi* | ix.397b–c (= G 4.297–9) |
| *Autolykos* | iii.89f, v.216d, ix.368d (= G 1.385; 2.481; 4.169) |
| *Baptai* | iv.183f, ix.370b, xv.666d, (= G 2.311; 4.177; 7.69) |
| *Demoi* | iii.106b, iii.123a, vii.316c, ix.373e, |

| | |
|---|---|
| | ix.408d (= G 1.455; 2.71; 3.421; 4.193, 349) |
| *Heilotes* | iv.138e, ix.400c, xiv.638e (= G 2.133; 4.313; 6.447—the last two passages cite 'the author of *Heilotes*') |
| *Kolakes* | iii.100b, v.218b, vi.236e, vii.286b, vii.328b, vii.328e, ix.400b, xi.506f, xii.535a, xiv.630a, xiv.646f (= G 1.431; 2.489; 3.65, 285, 477, 479; 4.311; 5.277, 417; 6.399, 493) |
| *Marikas* | xv.690e, xv.691c (= G 7.199, 203) |
| *Poleis* | ix.392e, x.425a (= G 4.277, 425) |
| *Prospaltioi* | vii.326a (= G 3.465) |
| *Taxiarchoi* | iv.170d (= G 2.275) |
| *Philoi* | vi.266f (= G 3.199) |
| *Chrysoun Genos* | ix.375a, ix.406c, ix.408e, xiv.657a (= G 4.199, 339, 349; 7.23) |
| Untitled plays: | i.3a, i.17d–e, i.22f, ii.47e, ii.52d, ii.53a, ii.56a, ii.56e, ii.68a, xi.502b, xiv.623e, xiv.658d, xv.667d (= G 1.9, 77, 99, 207, 229, 231, 243, 247, 297; 5.247; 6.361; 7.31, 75) |

Twelve papyrus fragments identified.

## Euthycles

| | |
|---|---|
| *Asotoi* (or *Epistole*) | iii.124b (= G 2.77) |

One possible papyrus testimonium identified.

## Hegemon of Thasos

Nicknamed 'Lentil', placed by some among Old Comedy poets: i.5b, xv.698c–699a (= G 1.21; 7.243–7); the first parodist and some anecdotes: ix.406e–407c (= G 4.341–3)

| | |
|---|---|
| *Gigantomachia* | ix.407a (= G 4.343) |
| *Philinna* | iii.108c, xv.699a (= G 2.9; 7.247) |

No papyrus fragments identified.

## Hermippus   composed parodies xv.699a (= G 7.247)

Named plays:

| | |
|---|---|
| *Artopolides* | iii.119c (= G 2.57) |
| *Demotai* | vii.285e (= G 3.283) |
| *Theoi* | x.426f, xi.478c, xi.478f, xiv.636d (= G 4.433; 5.117, 119; 6.435) |
| *Kerkopes* | iii.123f, xi.502b, xii.551a, xiv.650e (= G 2.75; 5.245, 501; 6.515) |
| *Moirai* | viii.344c–d, x.418c–d, xi.476d, xi.486a, xi.487e, xv.668a (= G 4.61, 395; 5.107, 159, 169; 7.79) |
| *Stratiotai* | iii.77a, x.423a, xi.480e, xii.524e–526a, xiv.649c (= G 1.333; 4.415; 5.129, 367; 6.507) |
| *Phormophoroi* | xv.700d (= G 7.257–9) |
| *Iamboi* | iii.76c, xi.461e, xv.667d, xv.700d (= G 1.329; 5.13; 7.75–77, 257) |
| Untitled plays: | i.18c, i.27e–28a, i.29d–f, ii.56c, ii.59c (= G 1.81, 119, 129–31, 245, 259) |

One papyrus fragment and one testimonium identified.

### Leucon
| | |
|---|---|
| *Phrateres* | viii.343c (= G 4.57) |

One papyrus fragment identified.

### Lysippus
| | |
|---|---|
| *Bacchai* | iii.124d, viii.344e (= G 2.77; 4.63) |

One papyrus fragment identified.

### Magnes
*Dionysus I* (considered spurious) ix.367f (= G 4.167)
*Dionysus II* (considered spurious) xiv.646e (= G 6.491)
| | |
|---|---|
| *Lydoi* | xv.690c (= G 7.197) |

No papyrus fragments identified.

### Metagenes
Named plays:
| | |
|---|---|
| *Aurai* | viii.355a (or *Mammakuthos*), ix.385b–c, xiii.571b (= G 4.107, 241; 6.85) |
| *Thouriopersai* | vi.228e, vi.269e, vi.269f–270a |

| | |
|---|---|
| | (never produced), vii.327d (= G 3.29, 211, 213, 473) |
| *Philothytes* | x.459b–c, xv.700f (= G 4.583; 7.265) |
| Untitled: | vi.271a (= G 3.217) |

No papyrus fragments identified.

### Myrtilus
xiii.566e (= G 6.61 and n. h)
No identified papyrus fragments.

### Nicochares
| | |
|---|---|
| *Amymone* | x.426e–f (= G 4.433) |
| *Herakles Choregos* | xiv.619a (= G 6.335) |
| *Lakones* | xv.667e (= G 7.77) |
| *Lemniai* | vii.328e (= G 3.479) |
| Untitled plays: | i.34e, xiv.657a (= G 1.151; 7.23) |

No identified papyrus fragments.

### Nicophon
| | |
|---|---|
| *Thouriopersai* | vi.270a (never produced) (= G 3.213) |
| *Pandora* | vii.323b (= G 3.453 ) |
| *Seirenes* | iii.80b, vi.269e, ix.368b (= G 1.345; 3.211; 4.169) |
| *Cheirogastores* | iii.126e, ix.389a, xiv.645b–c, xiv.645e (= G 2.87, 4.259, 6.483, 485) |

No papyrus fragments identified.

### Pherecrates
date of production of *Agrioi* v.218d (= G 2.489–91)
Named plays:
| | |
|---|---|
| *Agathoi* (or by Strattis) | vi.248c, x.415c, xv.685b (= G 3.119; 4.381; 7.169) |
| *Agrioi* | iv.171d, v.218d (quoting Plato, *Prot.* 327d), vi.263b, vii.316e (= G 2.279, 489; 3.183, 423) |
| *Automoloi* | iii.90a, iii.119d, ix.385e, ix.396c, xiv.648c (= G 1.387; 2.57; 4.243, 293; 6.501–3) |
| *Graes* | vi.246f, ix.305b (= G 3.111, 4.289 with 288 n. 3) |

| | |
|---|---|
| *Doulodidaskalos* | iii.95b, vi.262c, vii.305f–306a, ix.396c, xi.480b, xv.699f (= G 1.413; 3.179, 373; 4.293; 5.127; 7.253) |
| *Epilesmon* (or *Thalatta*) | iii.111b, vii.308f, viii.365a (= G 2.23; 3.389; 4.153) |
| *Ipnos* (or *Pannychis*) | xii.612a (= G 6.297) |
| *Korianno* | iv.159e, x.430d, xi.479b, xi.481a, xiii.567c, xiv.653a (= G 2.227; 4.451; 5.121, 131; 6.65, 527–9) |
| *Krapatalloi* | iii.75b, iii.80a, ix.366d, xi.485d, xiv.645e, xiv.646c, xv.700c (= G 1.325, 345; 4.161; 5.157; 6.485–7, 489; 7.257) |
| *Leroi* | iii.95d, vi.228e, x.424b, xv.690d (= G 1.411; 3.29; 4.421; 7.197) |
| *Metalles* | iii.95a, vi.268e–269c, xv.685a (attributed to Pherecrates) (= G 1.413; 3.207–11; 7.169) |
| *Myrmekanthropoi* | vi.229a, vii.287a, viii.335a (= G 3.31, 289; 4.21) |
| *Persai* | iii.78d, vi.228e, vi.269d–e, xi.502a (attributed to Pherecrates), xv.685a (attributed to Pherecrates) (= G 1.339; 3.29, 211; 5.245; 7.167) |
| *Petale* | viii.343c, ix.395b–c, xv.690f (= G 4.57, 289; 7.201) |
| *Tyrannis* | xi.460c, xi.481b (= G 5.5, 133) |
| *Cheiron* | (attributed to Pherecrates) viii.364a (maybe by Nicomachus?), ix.368a, ix.388f, xiv.653e–f (= G 4.149, 167, 259; 7.7) |
| Untitled plays: | ii.55b, ii.56f, ii.67c, xi.465a, xii.535b, xiv.644f–645a (= G 1.239–41, 247, 293; 5.27, 417; 6.481) |

One identified papyrus fragment.

## Philonides
| | |
|---|---|
| *Kothornoi* | vi.228e, vi.247e, 15.701a (G 3.29–31, 115; 7.2650) |

| | |
|---|---|
| Untitled plays: | i.23e, ii.47e, ii.67d (= G 1.103, 207, 295) |

No identified papyrus fragments.

## Philyllios
Named plays:
| | |
|---|---|
| *Anteia* (or by Eunicus) | xiii.567c, xiii.586e (= G 6.65, 163) |
| *Auge* | iii.110f, ix.408e, xi.485b (2.21; 4.351; 5.155) |
| *Herakles* | iv.171d (= G 2.279) |
| *Poleis* | iii.86e (or Eunicus or Aristophanes), iii.92e (or some other author), iii.104f, iv.140a (or Aristophanes), ix.381a (or some other author) (= G 1.373, 399, 449; 2.139; 4.223) |
| *Phreorychos* | xiv.641a (= G 6.459) |

| | |
|---|---|
| Untitled plays: | i.31a, ii.52b, ii.63a (x 2), xv.700e (x 2) (= G 1.135, 227, 275; 7.261, 265) |

No identified papyrus fragments.

## Phormos (Phormis)
| | |
|---|---|
| *Atalantai* | xiv.652a (= G 6.523) |

No identified papyrus fragments.

## Phrynichus
Named plays:
| | |
|---|---|
| *Apeleutheroi* | iii.115b (= G 2.39) |
| *Ephialtes* | iv.165b, iv.184f (= G 2.251, 315) |
| *Kronos* | ix.371f (= G 4.185) |
| *Komastai* | xi.474b (= G 5.93) |
| *Monotropos* | iii.74a, vi.248c (= G 1.319; 3.119) |
| *Mousai* | vii.319a (= G 3.433) |
| *Poastriai* | iii.110e, x.424c (= G 2.21; 4.421) |
| *Satyroi* | iii.87b (= G 1.375) |
| *Tragoidoi* | vi.229a, vii.287b, ix.389a, xiv.654b (= G 3.31, 289; 4.259; 7.9) |
| Untitled plays: | ii.44d, ii.47f, ii.52c, ii.53a, ii.59c, xv.700e (= G 1.193, 207, 227, 231, 259; 7.265) |

No identified papyrus fragments.

**Plato**

Named plays:

| | |
|---|---|
| *Adonis* | x.456a (= G 4.569) |
| *Hai Aph'Hieron* | x.446e (= G 4.525) |
| *Grypes* | ix.368e (= G 4.171) |
| *Heortai* | vii.308b, ix.367c, ix.368c (= G 3.385; 4.163, 169) |
| *Europe* | vii.328f, ix.367c (= G 3.481; 4.163–5) |
| *Zeus Kakoumenos* | iii.119b, xi.478c, xv.666d–e, xv.667b, xv.677a, xv.678d (= G 2.55; 5.117; 7.69–71, 73, 125, 133) |
| *Kleophon* | iii.76f, vii.315b–c (= G 1.333; 3.415–7) |
| *Laios* | ii.68c (= G 1.299) |
| *Lakones* | ix.380e, xv.665b (= G 4.221; 7.63) |
| *Menelaos* | iii.110d, iv.170f, xiv.641b (= G 2.21, 277; 6.461) |
| *Nux Makra* | iii.110d, xv.699f, xv.700e (= G 2.19–21; 7.253, 265) |
| *Paidion* | vii.316c (= G 3.421) |
| *Peisandros* | ix.385d–e (= G 4.243) |
| *Perialges* | ix.387a (= G 4.249) |
| *Poietes* | ix.375b, xiv.644a, xiv.657a (= G 4.199; 6.475–7; 7.23) |
| *Presbeis* | vi.229f, vii.287d, x.424a (= G 3.35, 291; 4.419) |
| *Skeuai* (or Aristophanes?) | xiv.628e (= G 6.389–91) |
| *Sophistai* | vii.312b, x.422f (= G 3.403; 4.415) |
| *Symmachia* (or Cantharus) | vii.312c, vii.314a (= G 3.403, 411) |
| *Syrphax* | iii.344d–e, x.446e (= G 4.61–3, 525) |
| *Hyperbolos* | i.56f (= G 1.247) |
| *Phaon* | iv.146f, vii.425a, ix.367d, x.424a, x.441e–442a (= G 2.169; 3.461; 4.165, 419, 501–3) |

Untitled plays: i.5c–d, i.31e, ii.47d, ii.48a–b, ii.67c, ii.68b (or Cantharus?: see *Symmachia*), xi.783d–e (= G 1.21–3, 139, 205, 209, 293, 297; 5.49)

One identified papyrus fragment and two testimonia.

**Poliochos**

| | |
|---|---|
| *Korinthiastes* | vii.313c (= G 3.407) |
| Untitled plays: | ii.60b (= G 1.263) |

No identified papyrus fragments.

**Polyzelos**

| | |
|---|---|
| *Mouson Gonai* | x.370f (= G 4.179–181) |
| Untitled plays: | i.31e (= G 1.139) |

No identified papyrus fragments.

**Sannyrion**

| | |
|---|---|
| *Gelos* | vii.286c, xii.551c (= G 3.285, 5.503) |
| *Io* | vi.261f (= G 3.177) |

No identified papyrus fragments.

**Strattis** *floruit* x.453c (= G 4.555)

Named plays:

| | |
|---|---|
| *Agathoi* (or Pherecrates) | vi.248c, x.415c, xv.685b (= G 3.119; 4.381; 7.169) |
| *Anthroporestes* | iii.127c (= G 2.89) |
| *Atalante* | vii.302e, ix.399c, xiii.592d (= G 3.357; 4.307; 6.195) |
| *Kallippides* | vii.304b, xiv.656b (= G 3.365; 7.19) |
| *Kinesias* | xii.551c (= G 5.503) |
| *Lemnomeda* | vii.327e, xi.473c (= G 3.475; 5.89) |
| *Makedones* (or *Pausanias*) | vii.302e, vii.323b, ix.396a, xiii.589a, xiv.654f (= G 3.357, 453; 4.293; 6.177; 7.11) |
| *Medeia* | i.467e, xv.690f (= G 5.61; 7.201) |
| *Potamioi* | vii.299b (= G 3.341–3) |
| *Troilos* | ii.76e (= G 1.331) |
| *Philoktetes* | vii.327e (= G 3.475) |
| *Phoinissai* | iv.160b, xiv.621f, xv.699f (= G 2.229; 6.351; 7.251) |

| | |
|---|---|
| *Chrysippos* | iv.169a–b (= G 2.267) |
| *Psychastai* | iii.124c, ix.373f, xi.502e, xii.551c (= G 2.77; 4.195; 5.253, 503) |

| | |
|---|---|
| Untitled plays: | i.30f, i.32b, ii.69a (= G 1.135, 141, 301) |

Two identified papyrus fragments.

## Telecleides
Named plays:

| | |
|---|---|
| *Amphiktyones* | iii.75c, iii.82b, vi.268a–d, viii.335a, xiv.619a (= G 1.325, 353; 3.205; 4. 21; 6.335) |
| *Hesiodoi* | iii.87a, viii.344d, x.436f (= G 1.375; 4.61, 479) |
| *Prytaneis* | iv.170d, ix.370b, xi.485f, xii.553e (= G 2.275; 4.177; 5.159, 515) |
| *Sterroi* | ix.399c, xiv.639a, xiv.648e (= G 4.307; 6.449; 7.21) |

| | |
|---|---|
| Untitled plays: | ii.64f, ii.56d, xiv.644f (= G 1.245, 281 [= *Amphiktyones* : see vi.268c = G 3.206]; 6.481) |

Two papyrus fragments identified.

## Theopompos
Named plays:

| | |
|---|---|
| *Admetos* | xv.690a (= G 7.195) |
| *Althaia* | xi.501e–502a (= G 5.245) |
| *Aphrodite* | vii.324b (= G 3.457) |
| *Eirene* | ix.368c, ix.374b, xiv.652f, xv.700e (= G 4.169, 195; 6.527; 7.259 [see also 7.265]) |
| *Hedychares* | xv.690a (= G 3.383; 7.195) |
| *Theseus* | iii.82c (= G 1.355) |
| *Kallaischros* | vii.302e, ix.399d, x.422f (= G 3.357; 4.309, 415) |
| *Medos* | xi.481d, xi.485c (= G 5.135, 155–7) |
| *Nemea* | xi.470f (= G 5.77) |
| *Odysseus* | iv.165b (= G 2.249) |
| *Pamphile* | xi.485b–c, xi.485e–f (= G 5.155, 159) |

| | |
|---|---|
| *Penelope* | iv.183f, xiv.657a (= G 2.311; 7.23) |
| *Seirenes* | ix.399d (= G 4.309) |
| *Stratiotides* | xi.483e (= G 5.147) |
| *Phineus* | xiv.649b (= G 6.507) |

| | |
|---|---|
| Untitled plays: | i.23d–e, ii.50e, ii.62e, ii.68d, vi.264a, xv.700e (probably *Eirene*: see G 7.258) (= G 1.103, 221, 273, 299; 3.187; 7.265) |

## 2. Fifth-century comic poets not mentioned in Athenaeus
**Alkimenes (?)**
**Arkesilaos**
**Autokrates**
**Callistratos**
**Crates II**
**Diopeithes**
**Euphronios**
**Euxenides**
**Ion of Chios**
**Lykis**
**Menecrates**
**Myllos**
**Philonicus**
**Thugenides**
**Xenophilos**
**Xenophon**

## 3. Poets and works cited in Lucian

| | |
|---|---|
| **Adespota** | (*PCG* VIII) 457 *Hercules* 5; 458 *Iuppiter Tragoedus* 38; 459 *Muscae Encomium* 11; 460 *Nigrinus* 31; 461 *Prom. es* 2; 462 *Prom. es* 2; 463 *De Salt.* 4; 464, 465 [*Amores*] 42, 53 |
| **Aristophanes** | *Piscator* 25, *Bis Accusatus* 33, *VH.* 1.29, *Adversus Indoctum* 27; fr. 927 (loc. incert.), *Iupp. trag.* 32, *Hist. conscr.* 41 (author only known from Tzetzes) (Scholia: *Proagon* Σ*Alex.* 4; *Horai* Σ*Iupp.Tr.* 48; Σ*Anacharsis* 32 [γέρρος]) |

| Cratinus | [*Longaevi* 25] (scholia: *Archilochoi* fr. 12 and 13 Σ*Iupp. tr.* 48 and *Alex.* 4; fr. 160 *Panoptai* Σ*Alex.* 4; fr. 228 *Seriphioi* Σ*Timon* 30; fr. 283 *Horai* Σ*Timon* 30 |
|---|---|
| Epicharmus | [*Longaevi* 25]; *Hermotimus* 47 (unascribed) |
| Eupolis | *Bis Accusatus* 33, *Piscator* 25, *Adversus Indoctum* 27 (*Baptai*), fr. 102.5–8, *Demoi Demonax* 10, *Nigrinus* 7 [*Dem.enc.* 20; *Amores* 29] (Scholia Σ*Iupp.tr.* 1; fr. 45 *Astrateutoi* Σ*Alex.* 4; fr. 139 *Demoi* Σ*Alexander* 4; *Kolakes* Σ*Iupp.tr.* 48); fr.252 *Poleis* Σ*Timon* 30) |

*4. Works cited by Athenaeus with reference to comedy*

**Antiochus of Alexandria**
xi.482c (περὶ τῶν ἐν τῇ μέσῃ κωμῳδίᾳ κωμῳδουμένων Ποιητῶν 'On the poets satirized in Middle Comedy')
**Apollodorus**
xiv.648e (on ps.-Epicharmus)
**Asclepiades of Myrlea**
xi.501e (τὰ περὶ τῆς Νεστορίδος 'On Nestor's Cup': interpreting a passage of Cratinus)
**Aristophanes of Byzantium**
viii.336e; xiv.659a–b (περὶ προσώπων 'On masks': on Maison)
**Aristoxenus**
xiv.648d (on ps.-Epicharmus); xiv.621c–d (on *magodia*)
**Callimachus**
viii.336e; xi.496e–f (on Diphilos)
**Callistratus**
xi.495a (ὑπομνήματα Θρᾳττῶν Κρατίνου 'Commentary on the *Thraittai* of Cratinus')

**Chamaeleon**
ix.373f–374b (Anaxandrides), 406e–f (Hegemon of Thasos); xiv.628e (Aristophanes or Plato)
**Didymus**
xi.501e (on Cratinus)
**Dorotheus of Ascalon**
xiv.662f (Antiphanes)
**Eratosthenes**
xi.501d (περὶ κωμῳδίας bk. 11 'On comedy': attacking Lycophron)
**Herakleon of Ephesus**
xi.503a
**Herodikos**
(κωμῳδούμενοι 'Targets of satire', bk.6) xiii.586a, 591c
**Lycophron**
(περὶ κωμῳδίας 'On comedy') xi.485d (bk. 9, Pherekrates); xiii.555a (Antiphanes)
**Lynceus of Samos**
viii.344c (Alexis)
**Philochorus**
xi.464f (using Pherecrates to infer facts about practices at the Dionysia); xiv.648d (on ps.-Epicharmus)
**Semos of Delos**
xiv.622a–d (*ithyphalloi* and *phallophoroi*)
**Sosibios**
xiv.621d–e (comic pastime at Sparta)
**Theophrastus**
viii.348a (περὶ τοῦ γελοίου 'On creating laughter')
**Timarchus**
xi.501e (on Cratinus in περὶ τοῦ Ἐρατοσθένους Ἑρμοῦ 'On the Hermes of Eratosthenes' bk. 4)

# ❖ 10 ❖

# HARPOCRATION AND ATHENAEUS
## HISTORIOGRAPHICAL RELATIONSHIPS

### by Giuseppe Zecchini

In 1989 I worked out what was in Athenaeus' library,[1] in particular what histories he had read both directly and indirectly. I also compared my results with evidence from two ancient scholars contemporary with him, namely Aelian and Clement of Alexandria. My reasons for choosing these two were twofold. First, Athenaeus had much in common with them, for he wrote in the same literary genre as Aelian (the scholarly miscellany), and he shared in the same cultural environment in Egypt as Clement. Second, other modern scholars had already made such a comparison, F. Rudolph with Aelian and I. Gabrielsson with Clement.[2] In 1989, however, I did not examine Harpocration's *Lexicon of the Ten Orators*, since it is not an encyclopaedia, but is a work effectively dealing only with the history of Athens in the fourth century BC.

Yet such a comparison is useful since, as some papyrus texts published between 1938 and 1941 reveal, Harpocration and Athenaeus shared the same cultural environment at Alexandria and belonged more or less to the same generation, in the period from Antoninus Pius to Commodus.[3] Moreover, the very differences in their aims and assumptions make more meaningful their knowledge and use of the same scholarly works. Meanwhile J.J. Keaney's recent edition of Harpocration's *Lexicon*[4] constitutes an essential tool for statistical purposes, albeit marred by numerous printing mistakes in the indices. Accordingly I now propose to investigate the hitherto neglected topic of the relationship between Harpocration and Athenaeus in a historiographical context.

We may safely assume that Harpocration made extensive use of the vast collection of quotations and scholarly references by Didymus Chalcenteros (mid first century BC) in his commentary on the Attic orators. Didymus is quoted 39 times in the Lexicon, in third place after Aristotle's *Constitution of Athens* (50 times) and Philochorus (49 times). It is, however, too reductive to limit Harpocration's work to being a mere supplement to Didymus via *Atthides*, or scholarly monographs on Attica.[5] As Pamphilus for Athenaeus,[6] so Didymus for Harpocration constituted a source of reference with which to compete, not the only source of its kind. Indeed, the oldest and almost classic work on the antiquities of Attica, the περὶ τῶν Ἀττικῶν δήμων of Diodorus Periegetes (c.300 BC, quoted 28 times)[7] may perhaps have been not so much found in Didymus as added by Harpocration himself to Didymus. Certainly subsequent lexica show Harpocration's corrections of Didymus.

For example, at Π 96 s.v. προκώνια (barley cakes) Harpocration corrects Didymus and quotes a series of authors from Aristophanes of Byzantium to Atthidographers such as Autoclides, Crates and Demon; these he found in an intermediate source, probably lexicographical. Much more significant from my point of view is Λ 31 s.v. λυκιουργεῖς where Didymus' comment on the *In Timotheum* of Demosthenes is corrected on the basis of Herodotus (7.76) and Critias's *Spartan Constitution* (fr. 35 Untersteiner) (the adjective cited does not mean 'made by Lycius son of Myron', but 'made in Lycia'). In fact the same lemma is found in Athenaeus 11.486c–e, where Didymus is in his turn corrected, but, in addition to the passage from Herodotus, the same fragment of Critias is quoted more fully, and a new quotation from the *Peace* of Aristophanes (line 143) is given. It is clear, then, that Athenaeus is not copying from Harpocration, but that both are using the same post-Didymus source.

The identification of this may be hazarded. Photius in his *Bibliotheca* devotes codices 145–58 to lexica, and from this it can be seen that the longest and most important lexicon of the ten orators compiled after that of Didymus is that of Julian in the second century AD. According to Photius, Julian paid particular attention to the historical material in the orations,[8] so that that he may very well have enriched his work with quotations taken directly from historical sources. His lexicon was arranged in alphabetical order, and, according to a hypothesis on Photius now confirmed by modern scholarship,[9] from this lexicon derives the more concise lexicon of Valerius Diodorus, son of another lexicographer, Valerius Pollio. Pollio and Diodorus were both from Egypt. Moreover, their cultural relationship with Harpocration is indicated by papyri. Harpocration is quoted along with Pollio in a letter dealing with the search for texts which were rare even then (i.e. Hypsicrates and Thersagoras[10]), but not absolutely unobtainable in Egypt during the Antonine period. Diodorus abbreviated Julian, but he may also have added something of his own. Similarly, Julius Vestinus during the reign of Hadrian abbreviated the Λειμών of Pamphilus mentioned above.[11] However, it was Diodorus who established alphabetical order, and not only for the initial letter. This order had perhaps already been adopted by his father in the *Lexicon Atticum* and, on that basis, used by Harpocration.[12] In consequence, the names of the lexicographers Julian and Diodorus must be inserted between those of Didymus, and Harpocration/Athenaeus.

Such considerations suggest that the quotations from historians in Harpocration, (as in Athenaeus) could have come either indirectly from previous lexica or directly through the custom (still current in the second century AD) of commenting on lemmata of previous lexica and integrating them through personal research. That such research was possible was due to the excellent libraries in Egypt; indeed, we know that Harpocration belonged to such a circle of scholars and bibliophiles, who were capable of seeking the original text of a given author. Accordingly, the relationship between Harpocration and Greek historiography is not unambiguous, and each reference must be verified individually. Four broad observations may be made:

(1)  Harpocration knew well the three classical historians read in schools, namely Herodotus, Thucydides and Xenophon, He quotes Herodotus 20 times, Thucydides 26 and Xenophon 23. Clearly, in these cases he quotes directly. Meanwhile, the absence of quotations from these three in the surviving *Commentaries on Demosthenes* by Didymus is not sufficient evidence that Didymus did not consult them at all. It is worth observing that Harpocration quotes Xenophon's *Hellenica* 9 times, the *Anabasis* 6 and the *Cyropaedia* not at all.

(2)  Historians of the fourth century BC are represented by Ephorus, quoted 17 times, Theopompus (36 times), and Anaximenes, (10 times). Callisthenes is quoted only 4 times, and, as might be expected, the more important historians of the third century are hardly quoted at all, namely Duris twice and Phylarchus once. In my opinion, Harpocration quoted from Ephorus directly, at least from the first decade of the *Histories* (11 quotations out of a total of 17), as also from Theopompus. Some doubt remains about Anaximenes. Quotations from his works are less numerous and distributed over three works, namely the *Hellenica* and the monographs on Philip and Alexander. Jacoby believed that Didymus was the last scholar able to consult Anaximenes,[13] who seems to have been quoted in the *Commentaries on Demosthenes*,[14] but the moderate interest shown in Anaximenes by writers of the second century AD such as Clement, Athenaeus and Pausanias, and the presence of his name in successive lists of historians[15] make it difficult to

exclude the possibility that Harpocration also may have quoted from him directly.

(3) Of all the ancient works on the constitutions of the Greek πόλεις and the monographs on Attica, the most outstanding is Aristotle's *Constitution of Athens*, which is quoted most often (50 times), and, evidently, quoted directly. In addition, Harpocration also quoted 10 times from other Aristotelian constitutions (Arcadia, Cythnos, Corinth, Elis, Massilia, Opus, Pellene, Sparta—twice—and Thessaly), most probably indirectly via other lexicographers. Perhaps Harpocration got information directly also from the *Laws* of Theophrastus, since he quoted from them 15 times. Finally, the following Atthidographers are quoted frequently: Hellanicus 15 times, of which 10 are from the Ἀτθίς, Androtion 16 times, Philochorus 49 times, and Ister 11 times, of which 9 are from the Ἀτθίς. Although there may be some doubt in the case of Hellanicus, there can be none in those of Androtion and Philochorus, even though both had already been used by Didymus. Nor indeed in the case of Ister, for this is the real novelty to come out of Harpocration. Ister,[16] the pupil of Callimachus and an Alexandrian, seems to have been ignored by Didymus, and his importance in the work of Harpocration, which is on the same level as that of Hellanicus and Androtion, must depend on his provenance. In other words, Harpocration seems to pay particular attention to Ister because he is the only Atthidographer from Egypt and that in turn strongly suggests that Harpocration consulted the text of Ister directly.

(4) As a general rule, it must be assumed that all the other authors quoted by Harpocration, such as Hecataeus of Miletus and Polemon of Ilium, both quoted only 5 times, were quoted indirectly. The only exception to this could be Callixenus of Rhodes, despite the fact that his monograph περὶ Ἀλεξανδρείας is quoted only once (E3). For Callixenus was an author little known outside Egypt and hardly enters the lexicographical tradition. Indeed, it is no mere chance that Athenaeus, sharing a background in Egypt, knows his work and quotes two long fragments certainly at first hand.[17]

Of course, even among the works quoted indirectly, those concerning the antiquities of Attica predominate. The authors concerned are: Ammonius, Andron, Apollonius of Acharnae, Autoclides, Clidemus, Craterus, Demetrius of Phalerum, Demon, Dracon, Heliodorus, Phanodemus, Pherecydes, Lysimachidas, Melanthius, Meliton, Menecles/Callicrates, Nicander of Thyatira, Polemon of Ilium, who wrote the monographs *On the Sacred Way, On the Pictures in the Propylaea, On the Acropolis*, and Staphylus of Naucratis. It is noteworthy that there is only one coincidence with the *Commentaries on Demosthenes* of Didymus i.e. Demon.[18] However, with regard to the biographical tradition of the ten orators, which comes down to us in the respective pseudo-Plutarchean *Lives*,[19] the following items in Harpocration are striking. He quotes Heliodorus Periegetes four times, perhaps the original source of the *Lives*[20] and quoted always indirectly by Athenaeus as well (2.45c; 6.229d–e; 9.406d), which confirms his influence in lexicography. Also he never quotes the monograph *On the Demagogues* by Idomeneus of Lampsacus, a common source, and in all probability, the direct source of *Lives* 849d–e and of Athenaeus 13.590c-e on the loves of Hyperides.[21] Finally, Hermippus of Smyrna was the main biographer of the Athenian orators and rhetors in Hellenistic times; he was used directly by Athenaeus[22] and was an indirect but fundamental source of the *Lives*. The fact that Harpocration quotes him only twice, both times from the *On the Pupils of Isocrates*, is most surprising.

Harpocration could not devote much space to local history outside Attica. He indirectly mentions Amphiteus (on Heraclea Pontica), Archemachus (on Euboea), Aristides (on Miletus; it is to be noted, however, that his Μιλησιακά were a collection of stories, not a local history), Aristodemus of Elis (on the Olympian victors), Aristotle of Chalcis (on Euboea), Dieuchidas (on Megara), Demetrius of Chalcis (on the foundation of colonies), Philostephanus of Cyrene (on Epirus and the islands), Marsyas of Philippi (on Macedonia), Nicander of Colophon (on Colophon and Aetolia), Praxion (on Megara), Semos of Delos (on Delos), Staphylus of Naucratis (on Aetolia and Thessaly), and Xenagoras (on the islands). Otherwise he uses writers of constitutions such as Aristotle (as set out above), Critias (on Sparta) and Hellanicus (on Thessaly). On Troy, a city in a class of its own, he quotes at second hand Demetrius of Scepsis (3 times) and Palaephatus (twice). By and large, with regard to local histories, Harpocration shows a fair indirect knowledge only of those works which deal with regions bordering on Attica. To be precise, Euboea (Archemachus and Aristotle of Chalcis) and Megara ( Dieuchidas and Praxion). He reveals no knowledge of Boeotia, nor of those Aegean islands which are closely connected with the history of Athens, such as Delos and Samos.

This, then, is the panorama of historiographical knowledge which emerges from an analysis of Harpocration. Now it is appropriate to turn to the above-mentioned comparison with Athenaeus, and for this I would refer to my book on him. Six points are worth making here:

II

(1) Regarding the three main historians read in schools, Herodotus and Xenophon's *Anabasis* were read at first hand both by Harpocration and Athenaeus. However, Athenaeus, who was not particularly interested in

Athenian history, seems to have known Thucydides only indirectly. As for the other works of Xenophon, Athenaeus prefers the *Cyropaedia*, a text of prime importance for the Persian world, while Harpocration prefers the *Hellenica*.

(2) As for the historians of the fourth century, both had read Theopompus (perhaps in a large epitome) and the first decade of Ephorus. Callisthenes was lost to both of them, and I have spoken earlier of the uncertain fate of Anaximenes, but in any case Athenaeus was interested in his personality and not in his historical works, which may have been used by Harpocration.

(3) As for the Atthidographers, Athenaeus, largely unconcerned with the history of Athens, ignores completely the *Constitution of Athens* of Aristotle, which is the text most used by Harpocration. The other Aristotelian constitutions are quoted indirectly by both writers, 10 times by Harpocration, and 13 times by Athenaeus. However, only those of Massilia and Opus are common to both. Similarly, Athenaeus does not use the *Laws* of Theophrastus, nor Androtion, whom he never mentions, nor Hellanicus, nor even his fellow-countryman Ister. Only Philochorus, by far the most important Atthidographer, is used to a limited extent in the *Deipnosophists* (in the second book). It is with texts such as these that the difference between Harpocration and Athenaeus is most marked: the immediate explanation is the interest of the former in Attica and the unconcern of the latter for classical Athenian history. Yet a possible exception to that broad tendency is Phanodemus, who is quoted four times at second hand by Harpocration, but 6 times by Athenaeus. In Jacoby's opinion, the quotations at 10. 437 c-d and at 11. 465a on the Anthesteria are direct, but I believe that here too an Attic lexicon, such as those of Philemon, Crates or Dorotheus of Ascalon, was the intermediate source.[23] The fact remains, however, that Phanodemus occupies in Athenaeus a space totally disproportionate to his place in Atthidography.

(4) The list of the historians common to Athenaeus and Harpocration contains some 30 names, but that list is rather meaningless since the quotations are all at second hand and from the same lexicographical background. It is more interesting to note the presence in both authors of quotations, direct or indirect, from Egypt-orientated authors such as Callixenus (actually from Rhodes, but the author of a monograph on Alexandria), Philostephanus of Cyrene and Stephanus of Naucratis, these last two being known also to Clement of Alexandria (*Protrept.* 4.57.3; *Strom.* 1.16.77.1 and *Protrept.* 2.38.2 respectively).

(5) Of equal significance are some omissions in Harpocration of authors read and widely used by Athenaeus. These are mainly biographers, in particular Clearchus of Soli and Satyrus of Callatis, and the authors of *hypomnemata* of

varying scholarship, in particular Hieronymus of Rhodes and Hegesander of Delphi, while Carystius of Pergamum, Hermippus of Smyrna (quoted twice by Harpocration, but 19 times by Athenaeus) and Demetrius of Scepsis (quoted 3 times by Harpocration, but 16 times by Athenaeus) also fall into this category. As for authors of monographs and local historians, Athenaeus' catalogue is not confined to Attica and is much longer than Harpocration's. It is striking that the *On the Demagogues* by Idomeneus, which Athenaeus knew, is completely ignored by Harpocration, while Semos of Delos, whose work was used directly by Athenaeus, is mentioned only once by Harpocration, despite the close links between Delian and Athenian history.[24]

(6) Lastly, and briefly, must be considered the case of Polemon of Ilium. This great and prolific scholar of the second century BC has sometimes carelessly been included among the main sources of Athenaeus.[25] Instead his work was used indirectly by both Athenaeus and Harpocration, although he had written numerous monographs on Attic matters. This, in my opinion, confirms that in Egypt in the second century AD he was still known but no longer read.

**III**

To conclude then. In Egypt in the second century AD, thanks to the library at Alexandria and more generally to the circulation of rare texts among scholars and bibliophiles, as papyri attest, very many classical texts were still available, although it is difficult to establish whether the number available was closer to that in Hellenistic times, before the burning of the library during the *bellum Alexandrinum*, or to that in late antiquity, after the catastrophe of the third century AD. The number of these texts allowed a choice according to interest between a certain number of related works. Among the texts known through encyclopaedias or lexica, and thus quoted indirectly, there were those which were already lost and those which were still available but neglected. On the other hand, from those texts which were sufficiently prestigious and readily available a selection could be made of what to read and quote directly. Accordingly, in order to have an idea of what constituted the literary inheritance of the Antonine period we must consider the authors used at first hand by Alexandrian scholars in view of their tastes and needs.

The analysis of the texts used by Harpocration and the successive comparison with Athenaeus allow us to establish the following broad picture. Among the historians read were Herodotus, Thucydides, Xenophon's *Hellenica*, *Anabasis* and *Cyropaedia*. Of the historians of the fourth century Ephorus (Books 1-10) was still available as was Theopompus, and perhaps Anaximenes, but not Callisthenes. Among the Atthidographers available there were certainly Androtion, Philochorus and Ister, perhaps also Hellanicus and Phanodemus, but not of course minor authors like Demon or Melanthius. Of the Aristotelian constitutions only one still survived, namely the one we have, the *Constitution of Athens*, to which could possibly be added the *Laws* of Theophrastus.

Compared with the much larger text of the *Deipnosophists*, the *Lexicon of the Ten Orators* of Harpocration does not give any further information either on Hellenistic historians from Duris to Nicolaus of Damascus or on local historians outside Attica, or indeed on the selections of biographies and *hypomnemata* which were secondary to proper histories in the full sense of the word.

However, Harpocration's *Lexicon* does allow us to add the following authors to the list of historians read in Egypt in the Antonine period: (a) Thucydides, (b) Xenophon's *Hellenica*, (c) Anaximenes (?), (d) Hellanicus (?), (e) Androtion, (f) Ister, (g) Aristotle's *Constitution of Athens*, and (h) the *Laws* of Theophrastus. More to the point, the consideration of Harpocration's reading sheds some further light upon the Egyptian dimension of the intellectual environment of Athenaeus.

# ❖ 11 ❖    ATHENAEUS AND POLYBIUS

## by Frank Walbank

The conjunction of such dissimilar writers as Athenaeus and Polybius prompts several questions. What qualities in Polybius, the author of a history of Rome's rise to power in the second century BC, prompted Athenaeus to read and quote him? Or did the author of the *Deipnosophistae* just read anything that was available wherever he happened to be living? Why, in fact, did he read historians at all? Because he was interested in Greek history? Or was he simply looking for the kind of material he could use in his projected work? In trying to answer these and several similar questions we are fortunate to have available Giuseppe Zecchini's admirable study[1] of Athenaeus' historical sources. I shall be referring frequently to this work and I should like to begin this chapter with an acknowledgement of my great debt to it.

It is clear that we have to start from the passages which Athenaeus has taken from Polybius.[2] But we should at the outset be alert to certain possible difficulties in putting our questions. Our text of Athenaeus is not complete. For Books One and Two and part of Three we have only an epitome and there are lacunae in Book Eleven and at the end of Book Fifteen. If then we set out to assess the importance Athenaeus attached to various historians by counting the number of occasions on which he refers to them—a rough and ready, but probably valid, criterion—we must remember that our 'statistics' may to some extent be flawed or at least incomplete. Furthermore, as Zecchini points out,[3] not every reference to an author by Athenaeus necessarily indicates that he has at that point consulted him direct. Some references to an author, whom he elsewhere quotes directly, may be at second hand and taken from a list or lexicon of some kind.

I do not, however, believe that either of these difficulties is a serious one.

There is no good reason to think that, if we had Athenaeus complete, the proportion of references to the historians he quotes would be substantially different from what we find at present. And it is, in my opinion, easy to exaggerate the extent to which Athenaeus quotes his authors at second hand.

I    The latter difficulty occurs in relation to Polybius. Zecchini has argued that of the nine passages which Athenaeus quotes from Polybius' first eleven books, only four are taken directly from the historian.[4] These are (as numbered in the appendix) the death of the Illyrian king Agron (1), the use of music by the Arcadians to counter the harsh effects of their wild landscape and climate (2), the contrast between rebellious Capua and loyal Petelia (5) and the flatterer Sostratus, who corrupted the Galatian king Cavarus (8). I think we can raise this figure. One obvious passage is (7) recording Marcellus' rueful, punning remark about how Archimedes, by a variety of ingenious machines and counter-measures, had 'drummed his *sambucae* out of the party'—the *sambucae* being in fact siege-engines, which Marcellus had mounted on the Roman ships attacking Syracuse, so called from their supposed resemblance to a harp (σαμβύκη, *sambuca*). This quotation has been attributed to Biton's treatise Κατασκευαὶ πολεμικῶν ὀργάνων καὶ καταπαλτικῶν, *Constructions of war machines and artillery*, which Athenaeus has mentioned at 14.634a, only a few lines earlier.[5] This is, however, impossible for several reasons. In the first place it is likely that Biton's work, which was dedicated to an Attalus, who is probably Attalus I (not Attalus II or III, as Drachmann argued), was written about 240, well before Polybius' time.[6] But, in any case, we possess Biton's treatise[7] and it makes no reference to Polybius. Also Biton's *sambuca* is a land-machine, not one operated from ships like that of Marcellus at Syracuse (cf. Polyb. 8.4.1–11). Athenaeus cannot therefore have taken this Polybian reference from Biton. It seems altogether more likely that he had it direct from the historian himself.

The same may well be true of others of the nine passages to which reference has been made. Three of these refer to curious words, which in two cases are somewhat comically applied to natural features, namely, a place in Aetolia called 'pig's snout' (ῥύγκος) (4)—this probably comes from book eleven, not book six, as Athenaeus (or our text of Athenaeus) has it—and a river Cyathus ('wine-ladle') also in Aetolia (9). A third extract, with a reference to *passum*, the special raisin-wine drunk in place of real wine by Roman women (3), is from Book 6 of Polybius. All these three passages have been assigned to lexical lists.[8] This seems to me possible for the first two, but the passage dealing with raisin-wine is over thirteen lines long and seems therefore more likely to be taken from the original text.

Zecchini[9] also attributes passage (11)—from Book 12 of Polybius—to a lexicon. This is an extract referring to the rabbit, the *cuniculus*, found on Corsica, and occurs in Athenaeus at the end of a long list of quotations from various sources dealing with hares, a favourite culinary ingredient. It seems to me decidedly more likely that Athenaeus took this Polybian passage directly from the historian, for the point of Polybius' remark is that there were no hares on Corsica, only rabbits. The rabbit is the odd man out in this section of Athenaeus and it would seem a little unlikely that in the course of a long disquisition on hares Athenaeus would have turned to an article in a lexicon with the title '*cuniculus*', 'rabbit'; whereas he might well have recalled Polybius' comment on the absence of hares from Corsica and quoted it with the additional remark about the rabbit.

Usually, however, it will be a personal and subjective decision whether one interprets any particular quotation from Polybius by Athenaeus as direct or indirect. For a time I wondered if one might use the fact that Athenaeus nearly always mentions the number of the book from which he is quoting as an argument in favour of direct quotation. But such a criterion would be invalid, for we have no means of knowing whether the postulated lexicon or similar list would have given the number of the book or not. Athenaeus' contemporary and fellow-Naucratite, Julius Pollux, does no more than mention authors' names in his *Onomastikon*; and at a later date, while Stephanus of Byzantium mentions the number of the book in his quotations, the Suda, which takes its historians from the Constantinian excerpts, does not.

## II

To summarize what I have said so far, neither the fact that we do not possess the whole of Athenaeus nor uncertainty whether some passages are being quoted at second hand need stand in the way of our using Athenaeus' quotations from Polybius and their relative number (as compared with those from other historians) to indicate the extent of his interest in Polybius and to consider what it was in Polybius that aroused his interest.

Zecchini has shown which Hellenistic historians especially appealed to Athenaeus. That he favoured *any* Hellenistic historians is perhaps a matter for comment. The Hellenistic period is not one which had a great appeal to many writers of what is now generally referred to as the Second Sophistic. They mostly preferred classical authors together with those dealing with Alexander. And yet, when we turn to Athenaeus, the fourth-century historian Theopompus stands out among his historical sources with 70 quotations. Athenaeus is unusual in also showing a pronounced interest in the period after Alexander: we know, for example, that he wrote a history of the Syrian kings, discussed in this volume by David Braund,[10] and he draws extensively on Duris of Samos with twenty-five quotations, on Phylarchus with thirty-five, on Polybius with thirty-four (plus one probably false attribution (34)) and on Poseidonius with forty-one.

Zecchini has suggested that Duris and Phylarchus appealed to Athenaeus as 'tragic historians'. This is an appellation perhaps better avoided, for it is hard to isolate and define satisfactorily a separate, identifiable school of 'tragic historians'.[11] It is however true that these two authors went in for sensational incidents and, in many places, provided a trivial, meretricious or sentimental narrative, likely to provide suitable material for deipnosophists. That was clearly not true of Polybius; and his appeal to Athenaeus, in Zecchini's view, lay in his general merits and the content of his work. Despite his limited interest in the extravagant excesses that Athenaeus loved to pillory, he appealed to the latter, Zecchini suggests,[12] as being the first interpreter of Rome to Greece and also the first, using sources in both languages, to embark on a history, Greek in conception but Roman in inspiration, to which Athenaeus must have felt himself close. Both these remarks about Polybius seem to me to characterize fairly his historiographical achievement. But I can see little evidence that they are aspects of his work that appealed to Athenaeus.

**III**     Let us consider them in turn. As regards the first, it seems to me significant that Athenaeus quotes very few 'Roman' passages from Polybius. Of thirty-five quotations (one erroneous) only six in any way concern Rome: these are, the use of *passum* by Roman women (3), the contrast between Capua and Petelia (5), Marcellus' wry comment on his failed *sambucae* (7), a ludicrous musical performance initiated by L. Anicius, perhaps—but not necessarily—in connection with his triumph of 167 (24), Cato's remarks on the prevalence of τρυφή 'luxuriousness' in second-century Rome (27) and the abstemiousness of Scipio Aemilianus in his use of slaves (35). Of these, three, and perhaps four, reflect badly on the Romans. Marcellus appears as defeated by Archimedes (despite his eventual capture of Syracuse), L. Anicius, (by inciting two sets of musicians to play against each other, as if they were gladiators) is revealed as a barbarian at heart, and second-century Rome is, in Cato's eyes, given over to excess.

The passage dealing with Petelia (5) is rather interesting. According to the MS of Athenaeus it reads: ἕνδεκα μῆνας ὑπομείναντες τὴν πολιορκίαν οὐδενὸς βοηθοῦντος οὐδὲ συνευδοκοῦντος Ῥωμαίων παρέδοσαν ἑαυτούς: 'having endured the blockade for eleven months and receiving no help nor formal approval of their action from the Romans, they surrendered (sc. to Carthage).' This text is kept in his edition of Polybius by Hultsch and in the Loeb Athenaeus by Gulick. But Büttner-Wobst and Weil, in their Polybian editions, emend the text, in the light of Livy 23.20.4–10, who reports the Romans as saying 'We can't help: look to yourselves', which was tantamount to consenting to the Petelians' starting negotiations with the enemy. Accordingly Büttner-Wobst and Weil read: οὐδενὸς βοηθοῦντος, συνευδοκούντων Ῥωμαίων, παρέδοσαν ἑαυτούς, 'when no help

came, with the agreement of the Romans they surrendered.' Although by Book 23
Livy has not yet taken to using Polybius widely and directly, as he used him for the
fourth and fifth decades, and Polybian material in Livy is likely at this point to
have reached him via an annalist, his account here is probably a more reliable
indication of what Polybius actually wrote than our text of Athenaeus,[13] who, as we
know, often quotes historians loosely and even inaccurately. In this very passage,
for instance, he says, incorrectly, that Petelia was besieged ὑπ' Ἀννίβα. If that is
so, the interesting point in extract (5) is that Athenaeus misquotes Polybius'
account to the discredit of Rome.

Of the other two passsages dealing with Rome, that concerning *passum* is
quoted as an oddity—which does, however, contain the pejorative implication that
Roman matrons were addicted to excessive alcoholic drinking—while Scipio's
moderation in the use of slaves is something exceptional in second-century Rome.
I conclude that Athenaeus is not very interested in the Roman aspect of Polybius'
narrative and that, despite the fact that the *Deipnosophistae* is located in Rome, in
his quotations from Polybius he sometimes deliberately seizes on passages which
reflect badly on Rome or Romans. It would be interesting to see whether this
pattern is repeated in his quotations from other Greek historians who concern
themselves with Rome.

I find nothing, then, in these passages, which make up fewer than a fifth
of Athenaeus' full list of quotations from Polybius, to sustain the view that he was
interested in either Polybius' views on Rome or in Polybius' political *History*. Nor
is this surprising, for Greeks of Athenaeus' generation seem rather to have been
interested in recreating the past in a Greek image. Now it is at least possible that
Athenaeus chose to read Polybius simply because a text of that author was
available. But I think there are some themes which stand out in Polybius and
which are likely to have appealed directly to Athenaeus. I will mention two.

The first concerns flatterers, κόλακες. There are, in general, two ancient
views on the nature of personal character.[14] Some, like Tacitus, in his famous
account of Tiberius, believed that circumstances, whether these took the form of
acquiring power or being beaten down by the blows of misfortune, reveal a
person's true character. Polybius, however, took the other view. He believed that
the circumstances of life are complex and that they, along with the influence of
friends and advisers, can lead to genuine character changes. A good example of
this was Philip V of Macedonia, whose φύσις, his nature, was good, but who was
led into error by the bad advice of such men as Demetrius of Pharos and
Heracleides of Tarentum: for the latter see extract (14). Earlier Philip's behaviour
had been strongly influenced by Aratus of Sicyon for good and by the court clique
around Apelles for ill. Philip V is not an isolated case. Polybius is deeply interested
in this matter of character change and discusses the influence of flatterers and

courtiers in the Ptolemaic and Seleucid courts as well as the Antigonid. There is, incidentally, a traceable influence from Aristotle's *Nicomachean Ethics* (2.1–2, 1103 a 14–15) and also from Chrysippus (*ap.* Galen, *De placitis Hippocratis et Platonis* 5.462) in Polybius' view. However, my point here is that this theme in Polybius may well have made a direct appeal to Athenaeus, for whom κόλακες are a decided *bête noire*; see especially the long section at 6.234c–262a, not to mention references elsewhere. For three examples drawn from Polybius see passages (8), (14) and (15).

A further characteristic of Polybius that is likely to have appealed to Athenaeus is his strong moral sense. For a detailed discussion of this we must now consult Arthur Eckstein's recent book on Polybius' moral attitudes. Of particular relevance is an appendix[15] dealing with drunkenness. In this Eckstein shows that Polybius registers more negative judgments on alcoholic excess than any other extant ancient historian. Herodotus has at least 16 references to the effects of alcoholic drink, but the tone of many of these is quite neutral and objective. Polybius, in contrast, has at least thirty-seven references, almost all of them negative. I mention this as one example of Polybius' rigorous moral attitude. But this is evident in many other passages, including some quoted by Athenaeus.

**IV**    What in fact *does* Athenaeus select for quotation from Polybius? We must not expect great consistency in any answer to this question. In an interesting article on Athenaeus' historical sources, based on Herodotus, Thucydides and Xenophon,[16] Delfino Ambaglio reaches the harsh conclusion that Athenaeus' treatment of these reveals disorder, casualness and no real will to understand their meaning ('*la rinuncia a capire*'). In the case of Polybius the passages quoted (whatever their full original content and context) fall into a few groups, which represent topics common throughout the *Deipnosophistae*. I have mentioned flatterers (passages (8), (14) and (15)); while (16) also deals with court life, with its reference to courtesans in the entourage of Ptolemy IV. There is also a whole group of passages which furnish a variety of instances of excess, including drunkenness, which are exemplary of the moral attitude common to both Polybius and his excerptor. These include the drunken behaviour of the Illyrian king Agron (1) and his later successor Genthius[17] (23), and that of Polybius' erstwhile friend, the Syrian king, Demetrius I (29). Eckstein[18] draws attention to Polybius' further criticism of the deceitful behaviour of Miltiades, Demetrius' envoy to Rome, where he was prepared to counter every argument 'with an utter disregard for truth' (Polyb.32.10.7–8). Other monarchs singled out as vicious, slightly crazy or prepared to subordinate their political responsibilities to personal whims are Orophernes of Cappadocia (28), Antiochus III, who chose to get married when his whole future was at risk from the Romans (19), and Antiochus IV, with his fantastic imitation of Roman customs and his unpredictable and slightly manic behaviour generally ((21) and (22)). The important extracts dealing with Antiochus' great games at Daphne ((25) and (26)) also present Antiochus in a slightly ludicrous aspect, acting as a kind of steward supervising the procession. There are also several passages in which Polybius criticizes whole peoples and states for extravagant and irresponsible habits, namely Capua, the victim of excessive prosperity (5) (like Tarentum (Polyb.8.24.1), an example not quoted by Athenaeus), the Aetolians, overwhelmed by debt as a result not only of war, but also of their extravagant lifestyle (13), and the Boeotians, who opted for childlessness and squandering their wealth on feasting (18). This last is an ambiguous passage, which leaves uncertain whether διατίθεσθαι means 'spend on' (as Liddell and Scott take it) or 'dispose of in one's will', in which case it is the clubs to which he has left it that squander the deceased person's money on banquets after his death. Finally there is Rome itself, where the youth (apart from the slightly priggish Aemilianus) gave themselves up to excess (27).

It should be noted, however, that in several of his quotations Athenaeus seems to be singling out examples of luxury which are mentioned by Polybius without condemnation and even with admiration. For example, Polybius comments approvingly on the natural wealth and cheapness of all kinds of commodities in Lusitania (31) (perhaps a mistake for Turdetania, an error which Athenaeus seems also to have made in a passage (30) dealing with the tunny[19]); there is a parallel for this in Polybius' account of the cheapness of food in mid-second-century Cisalpine Gaul (Polyb.2.15). Similarly, Polybius comments without any suggestion of criticism on the luxury of an Iberian king's house (32), comparable, in his opinion, to the luxury of Homer's Phaeacians, except that the gold and silver vessels of the Spanish king were full of beer. Athenaeus also quotes Polybius for the fine wines of Capua (6)—though the historian may have mentioned these in the context of Capua's fatal surrender to τρυφή, 'luxuriousness'.

With one exception the remaining extracts fall into two categories. There is a handful of passages recording examples of praiseworthy behaviour: the loyalty of Petelia (5), contrasted with the luxury and treason of Capua, which we have already looked at in relation to the problem of Athenaeus' text, the modest beginnings of Perseus' reign in Macedonia (20), the use of musical festivals to counter the harsh topography and climatic conditions in Arcadia (2), the wise provisions adopted by the Romans to circumvent their womenfolk's weakness for alcohol (3) and Scipio Aemilianus' restraint in his use of slaves (35). There are several examples of odd foodstuffs or strange circumstances surrounding their provision or consumption: the famous lotus plant of North Africa (10), the rabbit in Corsica, which had no hares (11), the tunny, which fed on strange unidentifiable 'acorns' fallen from oak-trees growing, most improbably, in the shallow sea-water (some confusion here!) (30), and the underground fish of Roussillon (33). Finally, there is one bare reference (12) to Polybius' rebuttal of Timaeus' views on whether the Greeks in early times were normally served at table by purchased slaves. I believe that Athenaeus read widely in Polybius, noting such things.

V    Discussion so far has been about Athenaeus' use of Polybius, what aspects of the historian's work appealed to him and what use he made of them. But any relationship between two authors and their respective readers must to some extent be a two-way process and in conclusion I should like to add a few words on the debt of Polybius' readers to Athenaeus, who is in certain respects an important source for our text of the historian.

    Of the thirty-four passages which Athenaeus unquestionably derived from Polybius (whether directly or indirectly) twenty-five have no significant overlap with other sources for the Polybian text; but their original context can usually be established by comparison with the Polybian narrative in Diodorus or Livy. In the remaining nine passages there is a direct overlap with other more substantial sources, such as the Constantinian excerpts.[20] The great value of Athenaeus lies in the fact that he almost always indicates the book from which his Polybian extract is drawn. Out of the thirty-four clearly identified Polybian passages twenty-five give the book of Polybius correctly, in seven no book is mentioned[21] and in only three ((4), (20) and (26)) is the book quoted with less than complete precision. Quite obviously this feature in Athenaeus is of immense help in reconstructing Polybius' books and in determining how many olympiad years are covered in each. This is especially important for the later books after 18, when we no longer have the *excerpta antiqua* but are obliged to rely primarily on the surviving sections of the Constantinian excerpts—a fact which, as W.E. Thompson, following a hint from Arnaldo Momigliano, has pointed out,[22] accounts for the strange selection of passages surviving from these later books, one which often distorts the emphasis on what must have been Polybius' main concern. If, however, helped by Athenaeus, we can determine whether Polybius described one, two, three or even four olympiad years in a particular book, we can establish which events in the Mediterranean world claimed his attention as particularly important and meriting detailed treatment

VI    Summarizing, my primary aim in this chapter has been to show that Athenaeus' text furnishes no evidence that he was interested in Polybius' central theme, the conquest of the *oecumene*, including the Greek east, by Rome. Indeed, if we can judge from the thirty-four Polybian passages he quotes, he was not averse from exhibiting Rome and Romans in an unfavourable light. On the other hand,

Polybius does display certain interests—a strong moral sense and an emphasis on the historically significant role of flatterers and parasites of kings—which may have made a direct appeal to Athenaeus. I am well aware that in so a short list, especially when taken from an author like Athenaeus, chance and the whim of the moment may sometimes have counted for more than any firm pattern of interest. There is also an obvious risk in basing conclusions about Athenaeus' predilections on his choice of passages from a single one of his many historical sources. There may, however, be something to be gained from a detailed look at one author.

# Appendix

BQ = Polybian book quoted. NBQ = no book quoted.
BQI = book quoted incorrectly.

1. BQ 2.4 = Ath.10.440a: death of Agron, following drunkenness.
2. NBQ 4.20.5–21.9 = Ath.14.626a–f: use of music in Arcadia.
3. BQ 6.11a.4 = Ath.10.440e: πάσσον (= *passum*) drunk by Roman women.
4. BQI 6.59 = Ath.3.95d: location of Rhyncus = 'snout' in Aetolia; probably from book 11.
5. BQ 7.1.1–3 = Ath.12.528a–c: contrast between loyal Petelia and rebel Capua.
6. NBQ 34.11.1 = Ath.1.31d: the fine wine of Capua: may belong in book 7.
7. BQ 8.6.6 = Ath.14.634b: Marcellus' comment on his *sambucae* and Archimedes.
8. BQ 8.22 = Ath.6.252d: Cavarus and the κόλαξ Sostratus of Calchedon.
9. BQ 9.45 = Ath.10.424d: river Cyathus ('wine-ladle') in Aetolia near Arsinoe.
10. BQ 12.2 = Ath.14.651d–e: the lotus plant in north Africa.
11. BQ 12.3.10 = Ath.9.400f: presence of rabbits but no hares (in Corsica).
12. BQ 12.6.7 = Ath.6.272a, cf. 6.246c:Timaeus wrong about Greek acquisition of slaves.
13. BQ 13.1.1 = Ath.12.527b: Aetolians overwhelmed by debt (in 206/5).
14. BQ 13.4.8 = Ath.6.251e: Heracleides of Tarentum, Philip V's parasite.
15. BQ 14.11.1 = Ath.6.251e: Philon, parasite of Agathocles.
16. BQ 14.11.2 = Ath.13.576f–577a; cf.10.425e: Cleino, cup-bearer of Ptolemy II and various mimes, flute-players and courtesans at the Ptolemaic court.
17. BQ 16.24.9 = Ath.3.78e–f: Philip V's figs from Magnesia and gift to Myus.
18. BQ 20.4.1 = Ath.10.418a–b: corruption and extravagance in Boeotia.
19. BQ 20.8 = Ath.10.439e–f: Antiochus III's marriage in Euboea.
20. BQI 25.3.7 = Ath.10.445d: restraint of Perseus' early years; attributed to book 26.
21. BQ 26 1a 1–2 = Ath.10.439a: mad behaviour of Antiochus IV.
22. NBQ 26.1 = Ath.5.193d–194c: more examples of Antiochus IV's mad behaviour.
23. BQ 29.13 = Ath.10.440a: criminal drunkenness of 'Genthion' (Genthius).
24. BQ 30.22 = Ath.14.615b–c: musical performance of L. Anicius.
25. NBQ 30.25–26 = Ath.5.194c–195f: procession at Daphne. (Polybius not named.)
26. BQI 30.25–26 = Ath.10.439b–d: same procession at Daphne; book given as 31.
27. BQ 31.25.5a = Ath.6.274f–275a: Cato's remarks on τρυφή among the Roman youth.
28. BQ 32.11.10 = Ath.10.440b: Orophernes introduces debauchery into Cappadocia.
29. BQ 33.19 = Ath.10.440b: Demetrius I of Syria a drunkard.
30. BQ 34.8.1 = Ath.7.302c: the tunny feeds on 'sea-acorns'.
31. BQ 34.8.4–10 = Ath.8.330f–331b: cheapness and luxury of Lusitania (Turdetania?).
32. NBQ 34.9.14–15 = Ath.1.16c: luxury of an Iberian king's house.
33. BQ 34.10 1.4 = Ath.8.332a–b: plain of Roussillon and its underground fish.
34. NBQ Fg.73 (B-W) = Ath.2.45c: Nile water sent to Berenice: error for Phylarchus (?).
35. NBQ Fg.76 (B-W) = Ath.6.273a: Scipio Aemilianus' restraint in his use of slaves.

# ❖ 12 ❖ FUN WITH FRAGMENTS
## ATHENAEUS AND THE HISTORIANS

### by Christopher Pelling

We begin in the study of Dr Josiah Umpleby, recently murdered Head of an Oxbridge college in Michael Innes' *Death at the President's Lodging*. The detective John Appleby finds a text of Athenaeus in a book-case: Schweighaeuser's fourteen-volume edition, in fact. He immediately finds this odd, as any well-brought-up detective would. Why use Schweighaeuser when Dindorf's three volumes are so much more convenient? Then he notices Dindorf too on a neighbouring shelf—but arranged *upside down*. What academic ever keeps books upside down? And sure enough it was precisely here that the culprit (one of the four independent culprits, actually: it is one of *those* books) set up his apparatus to release a carefully timed gun-shot and give himself an alibi.[1]

This chapter too is concerned with Athenaeus and arrangement, and the clues it can give us. And if that seems an artificial and contrived transition, that is appropriate too: for artificial and contrived transitions are precisely the concern of the first part of this chapter.

Skilful transition had long been part of the stock-in-trade of many Greek genres, especially those which combined a mass of miscellaneous material. Thus, for instance, Hesiod, *Works and Days* 331–82:

> ... if you maltreat your aged parents, *Zeus* will be angry: sacrifice and pour
> libations *to the immortal gods*; call friends and especially neighbours to *feasts*
> [the things you make sacrifices and pour libations before]; get good
> measure from neighbours, treat friends well and go to those who come to

**The Art of Transition**

you, give to those who give to you, a small gift is better than nothing, small things add up, save carefully at home

then various ways of increasing one's household round off the section, for instance the warning to watch out for the sexy woman who is only after your barn.

Or consider the host of careful transitions in Herodotus Book 2, e.g. 'in *proskynesis* they drop their hands to their knees. Now on their legs they wear ...', 2.80.2–81.1; and, memorably, the transition from 'everything's full of doctors' to death-customs, 2.84–85.1. It may be that this sort of transition (what Martin West calls 'free-wheeling'[2]), often based on little more than a keyword, is especially appropriate to oral performance: certainly it suggests a conversational, almost stream-of-consciousness style. But analysis often reveals it to be extremely thoughtful and deliberate. Herodotus, for instance, holds back items from what might be their natural context and uses them later, presumably because they can offer a useful transition in the later, less obvious context. In the topsy-turvy section of Book 2, we might have expected the habit of washing clothes daily to come when clothes are first mentioned (2.36.3), the practice of circumcision for purity's sake to come where circumcision is first introduced (again 2.36.3), and for priests' shaving habits to come in under hair-customs (2.36.1). But all three items are held back to provide a neat series of transitions from 'purifying things', through 'cleaning clothes', to 'keeping clean your *aidoia*' (what you use your clothes to cover), to the priests 'not shaving to keep the body clean', to the clothes that the priests do wear (2.37.2–3)—and we have moved from cleanliness to priestliness in four easy moves. Herodotus knows what he is about: this wheeling is only apparently free.

No author can have such a mass of disparate material as Athenaeus; and this deceptively easy, conversational style of transitional organizing was thoroughly appropriate to the sympotic setting. Silence fell, then Ulpian asked if they'd all been turned into Gorgons: 'and speaking of Gorgons ...' (5.221b): surely this is Athenaeus sending himself up, rather in the style of Cynulcus' 'we want bread, ἄρτος, and I don't mean the Artos whom Thucydides talks about in Book Seven ...', 3.108f. But—just as so often in Ovid's *Metamorphoses*, or for that matter with a self-parodic Radio Four transition I once heard from dairy farming to serial murder, 'and so from milk-curdling to something a little more blood-curdling'—he can send himself up precisely because it is so conspicuous a trick of his technique.

Quotations from the historians were useful here in several ways. Most obvious, and probably most frequent, is the simple use of the historian himself as the transitional key: Theopompus says A; Theopompus also says B. We find this all over the place.[3] Perhaps the most elaborate example would be Callixenus of Rhodes at 5.203e (cf. Chapter 15): his account of the grand procession of Ptolemy

Philadelphus has ended with an account of the wealth of the kingdom, evidenced also by his number of ships—and that leads into his magnificent forty-bank ship, which Callixenus also describes. Almost as obvious is a second trick, where an extended historical quotation is introduced because it is relevant to theme A, but then happens to contain material also relevant to theme B: this is surely one reason why in some places he quotes a particular author at length, when in neighbouring pages he lists authorities much more succinctly to illustrate a point. Such choices are rarely capricious, and transitions are not the only reason[4]—but the pure transitional use is certainly frequent. Fatted geese are mentioned by Theopompus in the thirteenth book of his *Philippika* and the eleventh of his *Hellenika* ... (14.657b): the story is told at some length, and the punchline is that some visiting Thasians were told by Agesilaus to give them to the helots—and so we move on to other material on the Spartan attitude to helots. Geese to helots: that is not a transition one would have expected to be easy, but the quotation makes it possible.

Once we are this far, the surprising point is the frequency with which, at first glance, Athenaeus misses his tricks. Socrates of Rhodes comes in at 4.147e in mid-discussion of banquets, telling of Cleopatra's Egyptian banqueting (4.147e–148b; *FGrH* 192 fr. 1). This would seem to be a gift for the transition to 'Egyptian banqueting' in general: yet that only starts, rather more awkwardly, a few pages later at 4.149d. Instead we have a routine transition ('Socrates says A. He also says B') from Cleopatra's Egyptian banqueting to Antony's Dionysiac displays in Athens (4.148b–c: *FGrH* 192 fr. 2). Another example: Hegesander told of the flatterers of the short-sighted Hieron, who all pretended to reach out their hands but miss the food they had been invited to share (6.250e, *FHG* iv.415 fr. 9). Then several other Hegesander stories manage a transition to Athenian flattery, especially the remark of Athenian demagogues during the Chremonidean War that the Athenians were the only Greeks to know the High Road to Heaven (6.250f, wrongly printed in *FHG* iv.415 as still part of fr. 9); there is another Hegesander Athenian story half-a-page later at 6.251a–b (= *FHG* iv.414 fr. 7). Yet the full-scale transition to Athenian flattery only comes, again a page or so later, at 6.252f: 'Even the Athenian populace became notorious for flattery ...', and this introduces an extended section including Duris' ithyphallic song to Demetrius (*FGrH* 76 fr. 13).

Is Athenaeus just being dozy in missing these tricks? Perhaps; but symposia, especially learned classical symposia, are often rather dozy affairs, and it is better to see this sort of 'hanging transition' as a reflection of real conversational patterns, especially relaxed and sympotic ones. The delays are only for a page or so: the conversation has drifted in a particular direction, and speaker and audience have it in their mind; but there is no hurry, and the first train of thought can be finished first.

These 'hanging transitions' are relevant if we move to the next category, that of fragmentary *clusters*. Anyone working on historical fragments will have noticed how passages from particular authors tend to collect together in Athenaeus: lots of Theopompus within a few pages, or of Posidonius, or of Polybius, and so on. That is partly thematically directed, of course: if Celts are the theme, Posidonius will be the leading authority. But there is more to it than that, and a particular author can be used to provide the skeletal framework for a whole section. It expands the usual technique into a whole series of 'Posidonius says A. He also says B. He also says C....F' transitions, but leaves some of them as hanging transitions, so that different material can be interwoven into that frame. There are usually several other transitional techniques in play as well, so that keywords in one item can suggest the next point or at least the one after that; and the resulting pattern can be quite complex—so complex that there is only room to look at one case here, the Posidonian cluster in Plutarch's speech at 4.151d–154c (keywords are in italics):

(1) Phylarchus on *Celts*: ends with big roadside dinners in which even passing ξένοι benefit (*FGrH* 81 fr. 9, 4.150d–f).

(2) Xenophon on Seuthes (*Anab.* 7.3.21–31, 4.150f–51e): is the link 'generous gifts to stray ξένοι'? Also continues series of dinners distinguished by national customs, Attic/Spartan/Cretan/Persian/Egyptian/Celtic/now Thracian.

(3) Posidonius on *Celtic* dinners—how and what they eat, how they are served, what they drink (fr. 67 E-K 1–36, 4.151e–152d).

(4) Posidonius on a particular dinner of Lovernius the Celt, ending with a flattering native poet who turned up late but still had gold *tossed to him* (fr. 67 E-K 37–53, 4.152d–f).

(5) 'But in his fifth book Posidonius describes *Parthian* dinners thus ...': King's Friend, eats dog-fashion what king *tosses to him*, eventually tormented and does obeisance to tormentor as to benefactor (fr. 57 E-K, 4.152f–153a).

(6) In his sixteenth book he tells of Seleucus and his hospitality at Median court of Arsaces: 'among *Parthians*' separate table for king, laden with native dishes (fr. 64 E-K, 4.153a–b).

(7) In his thirty-fourth book he describes Heracleon of Beroea who was promoted by Antiochus Grypus and almost ejected him from his kingdom: big feast for soldiers sitting on ground, *huge loaf, meat, wine of any old sort mixed with cold water*, served in silence by *men with daggers* (fr. 75 E-K, 4.153b–c).

(8) In his second book he has Roman triumph, Heraclean banquet, *honeyed wine, large loaves, smoked meat*, large quantities. Among *Etruscans* sumptuous tables twice a day, silver cups, *handsome slaves in rich garments* (fr. 53 E-K, 4.153c–d).

(9) Timaeus has *slave-girls serving naked* until they are adult (*FGrH* 566 fr. 1), 4.153d. [Athenaeus uses the same item at 12.517d: below, p. 178].

(10) Megasthenes has separate tables among Indians, boiled rice, *lots of meats spiced with Indian condiments* (*FGrH* 715 fr. 2), 4.153d–e.

(11) But Posidonius in his thirtieth book has Germans eat *separately roasted bits of luncheon meat, washed down with milk or unmixed wine* (fr. 73 E-K, 4.153e).

(12) Some Campanians have *gladiatorial games* during dinner: Nicolaus of Damascus has Romans doing the same: custom derived from *Etruscans* (*FGrH* 90 fr. 4, 78, 4.153f–154a).

(13) Eratosthenes has *Etruscans* accompanying boxing-matches on flute (*FGrH* 241 fr. 4, 4.154a).

(14) Posidonius in his twenty-third book has Celtic *gladiatorial contests* during dinner (fr. 68 E-K, 4.154a–c).

(15) Then various snippets on entertaining deadly games go on until the end of Plutarch's speech at 4.156a.

Once again, there is clearly conscious artistry going into this, and it is not just a stream of consciousness: the Parthian material, for instance, would more naturally have come straight after the Persian kings' elaborate banquets at 4.143f–146f, but Athenaeus is holding it back to fit into the Posidonius-based strategy here. And it is telling that the most abrupt transition within the cluster is that at 4.153f, with that jump into gladiatorial games. This clutches at the hanging transition with 'Etruscan influences' a little before: but this is also the most crucial move, for it is what allows him to exit from the cluster on the theme with which he goes on to end the whole speech. He needs to manage it somehow, and this is the best he can do: but if it were a genuine stream of consciousness this would not be the most natural association to spring to mind.

So what? The most important implication for this volume is that for Athenaeus himself: he is not such a clockwork soldier as all that, not just wound up to quote at will and wholly mechanically. But there are further implications as well, for those who are as interested in the historians he quotes as in Athenaeus himself. The first of these concerns the identification of fragments.

## Identifying fragments

In the Posidonian cluster it happens to be particularly clear what is Posidonius and what is not. Elsewhere it is more difficult; and it is made more difficult still once we realize that Athenaeus can often use a dominant, named figure only as a framework and can hang independent material on that frame: he can quote Posidonius or Theopompus, drift away and drift back again, just as we have seen in our extended Posidonius instance. All too often we fall into the trap of assuming that the independent material belongs to the dominant framework-figure as well.

And it can happen to the best. Wilamowitz counted a long section at 12.534b–535b as all coming from Satyrus' life of Alcibiades:[5] on a minimum count, he therefore transferred to Satyrus one quotation from Antisthenes, one from Lysias, one from Eupolis and one from Pherecrates, all of which are presumably Athenaeus' own insertion into a Satyrus framework. (For that technique we might compare e.g. 5.213f, the introduction of Hermippus and Theopompus quotations into the long Posidonius fr. 253 E-K, acknowledged by Kidd ad loc.) Nor is it certain even that all of the initial passage at 12.534d–f is Satyrus, though it may be; no source is given by Athenaeus for the similar anecdotal material a page later at 12.535b–e, and such passages can be a catch-all medley from general knowledge. Wilamowitz also threw in 12.524f–5b and 13.574d–e, therefore giving Satyrus citations from Hermippus' *Soldiers*, Aristophanes' *Triphales*, Antiphon's *Against Alcibiades*, an unknown comic poet, and another from Lysias. Yet all these quotations are very much in Athenaeus' own manner.

The engaging character Smindyrides of Sybaris affords a further example. First 12.541b–c:

> As for Smindyrides of Sybaris and his luxury, Herodotus in Book Six observes how he sailed off to court Agariste, daughter of Cleisthenes tyrant of Sicyon, and says 'from Italy came Smindyrides of Sybaris, son of Hippocrates, the most luxurious man in history': certainly (γοῦν), one thousand cooks and fowlers attended him. Timaeus too describes him in his seventh book.

If we did not have Herodotus, the sentence about cooks and fowlers would surely have been taken as a Herodotus fragment, with a characteristic drift from direct speech to description—or perhaps it would even have been taken as part of the direct speech, with γῶν Atticised to γοῦν;[6] then the 'Timaeus *too*' would have been taken as a give-away that this is the transition to a new point. But in fact that sentence does not come from Herodotus at all: Herodotus (6.127) simply says 'from Italy came Smindyrides of Sybaris, son of Hippocrates, the most luxurious man in history (Sybaris was at its height at this time), and also Damasus of Siris …'. Whatever else we make of this case, it certainly shows Athenaeus drifting away from a quotation to incorporate extraneous material without making that transition clear.

So is that fowler-sentence by Timaeus? Jacoby thinks so, and prints it as *FGrH* 566 fr. 9. But there are other complications too. At 7.273b–c Athenaeus has already had the same item. Julius Caesar had only three slaves when he invaded Britain:

But Smindyrides of Sybaris was not like that, my Greek friends! He set off to court the daughter of Cleisthenes of Sicyon, and such was his self-indulgence and luxury that he had one thousand servants in his retinue, fishermen, fowlers, and cooks. This man wanted to make a point of how happily he lived (so Chamaeleon of Pontus says in his *On Pleasure*, though the book is also attributed to Theophrastus), and remarked that he had not seen the sun rising or setting for twenty years: he was so proud of that as an extraordinary mark of happiness. It is plain that he went to bed in the morning and got up in the evening, which was unfortunate for him in both cases ...

And so on, in familiar transitional manner, to the far more creditable Hestiaeus of Pontus who similarly never saw the sun rise or set—but because he was always in his study, unlike Smindyrides who was always in his cups. So what do we make of the fowler-sentence in this second passage? Perhaps it comes from Chamaeleon—and so Wehrli duly prints it as a Chamaeleon fragment instead (fr. 8). Just to complete the pack, we should note that the story is told by Diodorus too (8.19): so the only remarkable thing is that no-one has printed it as an Ephorus fragment as well.

Yet in neither of the Athenaeus passages is the fowler-sentence in fact *quoted*. It is an extra fact hung on the framework of quotation, either just before or just after quotations, and it can simply be a fact drawn from his general knowledge. Athenaeus is clearly interested in Smindyrides, and makes one of his characters refer to him as a model of luxury at 12.511c as well; there, as it happens, he is quoting Theophrastus, though that is likely to be the same book as he mentioned in the second passage as by either Chamaeleon or Theophrastus. Now general knowledge has to come originally from somewhere, and it *may* of course be that Timaeus originally told the story about the fowlers, and that Diodorus was using him (as Jacoby thought), and that Chamaeleon told the story too (as Wehrli thought: though note that Athenaeus is not firm evidence for the story in Chamaeleon), and that Athenaeus found it in Timaeus and/or Chamaeleon, if (that is) Chamaeleon told it at all. But all this is a hopeless mess of uncertain speculation, and I would not myself print the fowlers sentence as a fragment of anything at all. Instead I would just leave it where it belongs, as Athenaeus' text and nobody else's.

Smindyrides and his fowlers, however charming, do not matter much; other implications can be more far-reaching. Take the famous fragment of Theopompus on the sexual customs of the Etruscans (12.517d–518b, *FGrH* 115 fr. 204). I follow Jacoby's text, but have added the sentences in Athenaeus which precede (Timaeus) and which follow (Alcimus) the text he prints as Theopompus.

παρὰ δὲ Τυρρηνοῖς ἐκτόπως τρυφήσασιν ἱστορεῖ Τίμαιος [*FGrH* 566 fr. 1b; 4.153d is 1a, above p. 175] ἐν τῇ ά ὅτι αἱ θεράπαιναι γυμναὶ τοῖς ἀνδράσι διακονοῦνται. Θεόπομπος δὲ ἐν τῇ τεσσαρακοστῇ τρίτῃ τῶν Ἱστοριῶν καὶ νόμον εἶναί φησιν παρὰ τοῖς Τυρρηνοῖς κοινὰς ὑπάρχειν τὰς γυναῖκας· ταύτας δ᾽ ἐπιμελεῖσθαι σφόδρα τῶν σωμάτων καὶ γυμνάζεσθαι πολλάκις καὶ μετ᾽ ἀνδρῶν, ἐνίοτε δὲ καὶ πρὸς ἑαυτάς· οὐ γὰρ αἰσχρὸν εἶναι αὐταῖς φαίνεσθαι γυμναῖς. δειπνεῖν δὲ αὐτὰς οὐ παρὰ τοῖς ἀνδράσι τοῖς ἑαυτῶν, ἀλλὰ παρ᾽ οἷς ἂν τύχωσι τῶν παρόντων, καὶ προπίνουσιν οἷς ἂν βουληθῶσιν. εἶναι δὲ καὶ πιεῖν δεινὰς καὶ τὰς ὄψεις πάνυ καλάς. τρέφειν δὲ τοὺς Τυρρηνοὺς πάντα τὰ γινόμενα παιδία, οὐκ εἰδότας ὅτου πατρός ἐστιν ἕκαστον. ζῶσι δὲ καὶ οὗτοι τὸν αὐτὸν τρόπον τοῖς θρεψαμένοις, πότους τὰ πολλὰ ποιούμενοι καὶ πλησιάζοντες ταῖς γυναιξὶν ἁπάσαις. οὐδὲν δ᾽ αἰσχρόν ἐστι Τυρρηνοῖς οὐ μόνον αὐτοὺς ἐν τῷ μέσῳ τι ποιοῦντας, ἀλλ᾽ οὐδὲ πάσχοντας <φαίνεσθαι>. ἐπιχώριον γὰρ καὶ τοῦτο παρ᾽ αὐτοῖς ἐστι. καὶ τοσούτου δέουσιν αἰσχρὸν ὑπολαμβάνειν ὥστε καὶ λέγουσιν, ὅταν ὁ μὲν δεσπότης τῆς οἰκίας ἀφροδισιάζηται, ζητῇ δέ τις αὐτόν, ὅτι πάσχει τὸ καὶ τό, προσαγορεύοντες αἰσχρῶς τὸ πρᾶγμα.

Ἐπειδὰν δὲ συνουσιάζωσι καθ᾽ ἑταιρίας ἢ κατὰ συγγενείας, ποιοῦσιν οὕτως· πρῶτον μὲν ὅταν παύσωνται πίνοντες καὶ μέλλωσι καθεύδειν, εἰσάγουσι παρ᾽ αὐτοὺς οἱ διάκονοι τῶν λύχνων ἔτι καιομένων ὁτὲ μὲν ἑταίρας, ὁτὲ δὲ παῖδας πάνυ καλούς, ὁτὲ δὲ καὶ γυναῖκας· ὅταν δὲ τούτων ἀπολαύσωσιν, αὖθις αὐτοῖς <εἰσάγουσιν> νεανίσκους ἀκμάζοντας, οἳ πλησιάζουσιν αὐτοὶ ἐκείνοις. ἀφροδισιάζουσιν δὲ καὶ ποιοῦνται τὰς συνουσίας ὁτὲ μὲν ὁρῶντες ἀλλήλους, ὡς δὲ τὰ πολλὰ καλύβας περιβάλλοντες περὶ τὰς κλίνας, αἳ πεπλεγμέναι <μέν> εἰσιν ἐκ ῥάβδων, ἐπιβέβληται δ᾽ ἄνωθεν ἱμάτια. καὶ πλησιάζουσι μὲν σφόδρα καὶ ταῖς γυναιξί, πολὺ μέντοι γε <μᾶλλον> χαίρουσι συνόντες τοῖς παισὶ καὶ τοῖς μειρακίοις. καὶ γὰρ γίνονται παρ᾽ αὐτοῖς πάνυ καλοὶ τὰς ὄψεις, ἅτε τρυφερῶς διαιτώμενοι καὶ λεαινόμενοι τὰ σώματα. πάντες δὲ οἱ πρὸς ἑσπέραν οἰκοῦντες βάρβαροι πιττοῦνται καὶ ξυροῦνται τὰ σώματα· καὶ παρά γε τοῖς Τυρρηνοῖς ἐργαστήρια κατεσκεύασται πολλὰ καὶ τεχνῖται τούτου τοῦ πράγματός εἰσιν, ὥσπερ παρ᾽ ἡμῖν οἱ κουρεῖς. παρ᾽ οὓς ὅταν εἰσέλθωσιν, παρέχουσιν ἑαυτοὺς πάντα τρόπον, οὐθὲν αἰσχυνόμενοι τοὺς ὁρῶντας οὐδὲ τοὺς παριόντας. χρῶνται δὲ τούτῳ τῷ νόμῳ πολλοὶ καὶ τῶν Ἑλλήνων [καὶ] τῶν τὴν Ἰταλίαν οἰκούντων, μαθόντες παρὰ Σαυνιτῶν καὶ Μεσαπίων. ὑπὸ δὲ τῆς τρυφῆς οἱ Τυρρηνοί, ὡς Ἄλκιμος ἱστορεῖ [*FGrH* 560 fr.3], πρὸς αὐλὸν καὶ μάττουσιν καὶ πυκτεύουσι καὶ μαστιγοῦσιν.

As for the Etruscans and their outlandish luxury, Timaeus [*FGrH* 566 fr. 1b; 4.153d is 1a, above p. 175] observes in his first book that the men are served by naked maids. In the forty-third book of his *Histories* Theopompus says that it is also a custom among the Etruscans to possess their wives in common. These women take great care over their bodies and they often exercise naked even with men, but sometimes also with one another, since it is not shameful for them to appear naked. They do not dine next to their own husbands, but they take their seats at random and they drink to the health of whomever they wish. They are also good drinkers and very beautiful in appearance. The Etruscans rear all of the children that are born, since they do not know who the fathers are. These offspring also live in the same manner as those who reared them, often having drinking-parties and having relations with women indiscriminately. It is not shameful for the Etruscans to be seen performing sexual acts in public, not only as the active, but even as the passive partner; for this also is their native custom. And they are so far from thinking such behaviour shameful that, whenever the master of the house is having sex and someone comes looking for him, they even say that such and such a thing is happening to him, giving the act the most shameful of names.

Whenever they get together in groups of friends or kinsmen, they act in the following way. First of all, after they have finished drinking and are about to sleep, while the lamps are still burning, their servants bring in to them sometimes prostitutes, sometimes very beautiful boys, and sometimes even married women. After they have enjoyed these, their servants next bring in young men in the prime of youth, who have intercourse with the diners. On occasion they indulge their lust and have sex in full view of one another, but most often they set screens around their couches. These screens are made from interlaced rods, and cloaks are thrown over them. Although they are eager enough to have intercourse with women, they take much more delight in having sex with boys and youths. For the latter are very beautiful in appearance, since they live luxuriously and make their bodies smooth. All of the barbarians who live in the West remove their body-hair with pitch-plasters and razors. Among the Etruscans, there are many shops and craftsmen for this purpose, just as we have barbers. Whenever they visit these craftsmen, they expose every part of their bodies and they feel no shame before those who see them or those who pass by. This custom is in use even among many of the Greeks who live in Italy, who learned it from the Samnites and Messapians. And their luxury leads the Etruscans, as Alcimus observes [*FGrH* 560 fr. 3], to knead bread and box and do their flogging to the accompaniment of the flute.

(tr. M. Flower, mildly adapted)

Thus Athenaeus begins by making it clear that he is quoting, and there is a long section in indirect speech. Then, at ζῶσιν … ('these offspring also live') he switches to straight indicatives, and a lot more information is given, culminating with the notice that the same habit is in custom with Italian Greeks and with the quotation from Alcimus.

What are we to make of that drift from indirect speech into straight-forward indicatives? Jacoby magisterially decided that Athenaeus had here decided to quote verbatim, and others have naturally followed him: in his book on Theopompus—usually exemplary, I stress, in its attention to the contexts in which the later authors cite Theopompus fragments—Michael Flower seizes on this as an opportunity to grapple with Theopompus' own words and presentational strategies.[7] Yet Athenaeus need not be doing this at all. He can be using his own words here, and the quotation can end exactly where he marks it as ending, with the end of the indirect speech. A passage from Polybius (30.26) at 10.439b–d is an exact parallel: indirect speech there again drifts into indicatives, but there the indicatives clearly summarize; and in that case we can be clear that Athenaeus knew the full Polybian text, for it is he who quotes the full version in 5.195d–f. The 10.439b–d summary includes verbatim Polybian phrases, but omits much and rephrases much else.[8]

In our present case the rest of the material, or some of it, can still come from Theopompus, just as the indicative material at 10.439b–d still comes from Polybius: it suits his interests, and it meshes closely with the initial quotation (though Athenaeus would not be much of an author if he had not been able to mesh it in pretty well, and a lot of this salacious stuff is fairly commonplace). But it is not so clear where the Theopompus material stops; we already noticed, in Smindyrides' case at 12.541b–c, Athenaeus failing to mark the point where a quotation ended and extraneous material began. Here the Italian material could come from Alcimus, who clearly talked about similar things (fr. 4 = Festus p. 266 M. indicates Alcimus' interest in Etruria: he wrote a book entitled *Italike*, 10.441a = fr. 2 with Jacoby's note): his input need not be limited to the last sentence where he is quoted; and some of the earlier material could be simply Athenaeus' general knowledge (a particularly large proportion of Book Twelve is unattributed), drawing especially perhaps on his memories of Posidonius.[9]

Should this be printed at all among Theopompus' fragments? Perhaps it should, given that most fragments are not verbatim and that this material should at least be taken into account in forming a view of Theopompus' method—though on that basis we might find ourselves having to print vast chunks of Obsequens and Orosius among the fragments of Livy. But at least one should not print the present passage without a heavy health warning; and we certainly should not print it with Jacoby's wilful quotation marks to indicate verbatim citation.

There is more to classical scholarship than editing fragments, and there are other ways in which Athenaeus' transitional habits can help us. They can sometimes be a guide to how he or his speakers or his audience read the nuances of an original text, and we have come to recognize how valuable such reception-criticism can be. Take the point where he quotes Herodotus' story of Pausanias after the battle of Plataea (9.82, 4.138b–c: the speaker is Plutarch). When Pausanias saw all the luxury in Mardonius' tent and all the preparations for a sumptuous dinner, he ordered his own servants to prepare a Spartan dinner. He then laughed and sent for the Greek generals: when they arrived, he pointed the moral. (I here print both the Herodotean and the Athenaean versions: the Appendix will then discuss how close Athenaeus comes to verbatim quotation. The translation follows Herodotus, with Athenaeus' significant deviations noted in square brackets.)

## Quotation as Reception

| Athenaeus 4.138b–c | Herodotus 9.82 |
|---|---|
| ἑξῆς δὲ λεκτέον καὶ περὶ τῶν Λακωνικῶν συμποσίων. Ἡρόδοτος μὲν οὖν ἐν τῇ ἐνάτῃ τῶν ἱστοριῶν περὶ τῆς Μαρδονίου παρασκευῆς λέγων καὶ μνημονεύσας Λακωνικῶν συμποσίων φησί· | |
| | Λέγεται δὲ καὶ τάδε γενέσθαι, ὡς Ξέρξης φεύγων ἐκ τῆς |
| Ξέρξης φεύγων ἐκ τῆς Ἑλλάδος Μαρδονίῳ τὴν παρασκευὴν κατέλιπε τὴν αὐτοῦ. Παυσανίαν οὖν ἰδόντα τὴν τοῦ Μαρδονίου παρασκευὴν χρυσῷ καὶ ἀργύρῳ καὶ παραπετάσμασι ποικίλοις κατεσκευασμένην κελεῦσαι τοὺς ἀρτοποιοὺς καὶ ὀψοποιοὺς κατὰ ταὐτὰ καθὼς Μαρδονίῳ δεῖπνον παρασκευάσαι. ποιησάντων δὲ τούτων τὰ κελευσθέντα τὸν Παυσανίαν ἰδόντα κλίνας χρυσᾶς καὶ ἀργυρᾶς ἐστρωμένας καὶ τραπέζας ἀργυρᾶς καὶ παραοκευὴν μεγαλοπρεπῆ δείπνῳ, | Ἑλλάδος Μαρδονίῳ τὴν κατασκευὴν καταλίποι τὴν ἑωυτοῦ. Παυσανίην ὦν ὁρῶντα τὴν Μαρδονίου κατασκευὴν χρυσῷ τε καὶ ἀργύρῳ καὶ παραπετάσμασι ποικίλοισι κατεσκευασμένην κελεῦσαι τούς τε ἀρτοκόπους καὶ τοὺς ὀψοποιοὺς κατὰ ταὐτὰ Μαρδονίῳ δεῖπνον παρασκευάσειν. Ὡς δὲ κελεύομενοι οὗτοι ἐποίευν ταῦτα, ἐνθαῦτα τὸν Παυσανίην ἰδόντα κλίνας τε χρυσέας καὶ ἀργυρέας εὖ ἐστρωμένας καὶ τραπέζας τε χρυσέας καὶ ἀργυρέας καὶ |

ἐκπλαγέντα τὰ προκείμενα κελεῦσαι ἐπὶ γέλωτι τοῖς ἑαυτοῦ διακόνοις παρασκευάσαι Λακωνικὸν δεῖπνον. καὶ παρασκευασθέντος

γελάσας ὁ Παυσανίας μετεπέμψατο τῶν Ἑλλήνων τοὺς στρατηγοὺς καὶ ἐλθόντων ἐπιδείξας ἑκατέρου τῶν δείπνων τὴν παρασκευὴν εἶπεν· ἄνδρες Ἕλληνες, συνήγαγον ὑμᾶς βουλόμενος ἐπιδεῖξαι τοῦ Μήδων ἡγεμόνος τὴν ἀφροσύνην, ὃς τοιαύτην δίαιταν ἔχων ἦλθεν ὡς ἡμᾶς οὕτω ταλαίπωρον ἔχοντας.'

παρασκευὴν μεγαλοπρεπέα τοῦ δείπνου, ἐκπλαγέντα τὰ προκείμενα ἀγαθὰ κελεῦσαι ἐπὶ γέλωτι τοὺς ἑωυτοῦ διηκόνους παρασκευάσαι Λακωνικὸν δεῖπνον. Ὡς δὲ τῆς θοίνης ποιηθείσης ἦν πολλὸν τὸ μέσον, τὸν Παυσανίην γελάσαντα μεταπέμψασθαι τῶν Ἑλλήνων τοὺς στρατηγούς, συνελθόντων δὲ τούτων εἰπεῖν τὸν Παυσανίην, δεικνύντα ἐς ἑκατέρην τοῦ δείπνου τὴν παρασκευήν· ''Ανδρες Ἕλληνες, τῶνδε εἵνεκα ἐγὼ ὑμέας συνήγαγον, βουλόμενος ὑμῖν τοῦ Μήδων ἡγεμόνος τὴν ἀφροσύμην δεῖξαι, ὃς τοιήνδε δίαιταν ἔχων ἦλθε ἐς ἡμέας οὕτω ὀϊζυρὴν ἔχοντας ἀπαιρησόμενος.'

[Athenaeus' introduction: 'We must go on to discuss Spartan symposia. Herodotus in his ninth book tells of Mardonius' paraphernalia, and mentions Spartan symposia: his words are as follows.' Herodotus' introduction: 'This too is recounted, that …']

In fleeing from Greece, Xerxes left his paraphernalia for Mardonius [here and again below Athenaeus has κατασκευήν, Herodotus παρασκευήν] . The story goes that when Pausanias saw [Herodotus has the present tense, Athenaeus the aorist] all these things, fitted out with gold and silver and embroidered hangings, he told both the bakers and the chefs of Mardonius [Ath. has a slightly different form of co-ordination, 'Mardonius' bakers and chefs'] to prepare the kind of meal they had made for Mardonius [Ath. has a different phrase for 'just as for']. When they had done this on his orders, then [Ath. has 'after they had done this'], when he saw the gold and silver couches with their fine coverings, the gold and silver tables [Ath. has just 'silver'], and the magnificent feast [Ath. omits], he was amazed at all the good things spread there [Ath. again omits], and, for a joke, he told his own servants to prepare a typical Laconian meal. [At this

point Athenaeus moves to indicatives, Herodotus stays in indirect speech.]
When the food was ready and there was a huge difference between the two
meals [Ath. has just 'when it was prepared'], Pausanias was amused and
sent for [Ath. has just 'Pausanias sent for'] the Greek commanders. Once
they had all gathered [Ath. has 'come'] Pausanias pointed [Ath. has the
aorist of the compound verb ἐπιδείξας, Herodotus the present of the
simple verb δεικνύντα) to the two meals [Athenaeus has literally 'the
preparation of each of the two meals', Herodotus 'each of the two
preparations of the meal'] and said, 'Men of Greece, I brought you here for
this reason, that I wished [Ath. has no 'for this reason ...'] to show you [Ath.
again has the simple rather than compound verb] just how stupid the
Persian king is. He lives in the way you see [Ath. has τοιαύτην, Herodotus
τοιήνδε, for 'in this way']; yet he invaded our country to rob us of our
meagre portions [Ath. has 'came against us when our life is so miserable']!'
(tr. R. Waterfield, mildly adapted).

This is a marvellously thought-provoking passage in Herodotus.[10] The
contrast between Oriental luxury and Greek toughness has run through much of
the earlier History, though it is arguably coming to be much more complicated and
qualified, reorienting and even disorienting the reader's moral categories as the end
approaches. The contrast between luxury and minimalism has taken two basic
forms: either 'what is the point of attacking people as poor as that'—the form taken
by Sandanis at 1.71 and by others; or 'people as luxurious as the Persians are easy
meat'—the point made by Aristagoras at 5.49, for who would ever have any respect
or fear for people who wore trousers into battle? Pausanias now points 'the moral'—
but which? The passage in itself rather leads us to expect the second: no wonder
we Greeks won when they are so namby-pamby. But in fact Pausanias draws the
first: what fools they were to attack us when we live like this and they live like that.
There is another irony here, given that it is Pausanias who is speaking: he, of all
people, was not the person to think it worth invading another continent for the
dubious pleasure of eating Spartan meals.

Back to Athenaeus. Notice the transition into the passage: the speaker
Plutarch has just been talking of the austere fare of the philosophers at the
Lyceum (4.137f–138a), and quoted Plato's ironic passage in *Republic* 2. 'Won't your
citizens have relishes at dinner?' Socrates is there asked. Of course they will. Salt,
for instance; olives; cheese; and they will have lots of vegetables, and fruit, and
berries, and sip their wine in moderation; and they'll die happily and peacefully in
old age, after doing what comes naturally. That is Athenaeus' transition into the
Herodotus passage; the transition out is into the remark of the Sybarite on
Spartan dinners. It is no wonder that the Spartans are so brave: anyone in their

right mind would die ten thousand times rather than eat meals like that (4.138e; the same story is told at 12.518e).

The transition from Platonic philosophical dinners to Spartan dinners is smoothed by the Herodotus quotation: that is the technique which we saw earlier. But there is a deeper point. In Plato the ironic tone is clear, and it conveys approval and enthusiasm for the simple fare. The Sybarite's irony is clear too, but it conveys great distaste for it. Herodotus' passage is in between, and it too has its ironies, as I have suggested; but they are far harder to pin down than in either of the flanking passages. One way of putting the question is to ask whether it has more in common with the Plato passage, suggesting that the simple Spartan food was the secret of their success, or with the Sybarite, suggesting that Pausanias was a brother in Sybaritic spirit in his true feelings about Spartan fare. We need not assume that Athenaeus went through all those steps, nor that he would have made exactly these points about the Herodotus passage; but his ordering still suggests his sensitivity to the way that the passage's ironies have something in common with both the Plato and the Sybarite, that it can naturally be made to point both ways.

Herodotus affords my own Athenaeus-like transition to the final few points. (Strasburger once recommended the exercise of pretending Herodotus was known to us only through Athenaeus, and reconstructing the impression of Herodotus we would have: 'time required, two to three hours'.[11]) The comparison of those Herodotus and Athenaeus passages offers a convenient opportunity to see how closely Athenaeus keeps to the precise wording of his original, but it will be best to delay that discussion to an Appendix. First let us see some more enterprising ways in which Athenaeus remoulds, even travesties, his original. Ambaglio (1990) took a low opinion of Athenaeus' capacity to understand his originals' point; we may form a different view, and see that remouldings and travesties come not where Athenaeus had misunderstood, but where he has understood all too well where the point of an original does not serve his own argument.

## Misrepresentation and Misquotation

The first case is 6.231d, where the speaker Pontianus tells the story of Psammetichus' libation from Herodotus 2.151.1–2. In Herodotus the priest of Hephaestus had miscounted the gold goblets, and set out only eleven for the twelve kings of Egypt. Psammetichus came last, and unthinkingly used his bronze helmet to pour the libation, quite without recalling the oracle that the man who poured a libation from a bronze cup would be sole king. In Athenaeus the point of the story is lost: he has the kings drinking from silver cups, though the priests themselves used bronze; 'at any rate' (γοῦν) on one occasion they gave Psammetichus, youngest as he was, a bronze cup when they had run out of silver ones.

Brunt assumes that Athenaeus is quoting from memory, and it is a slip. Perhaps it is indeed memory: Zecchini interestingly suggests that Athenaeus the 'Egyptian' may have known Book Two of Herodotus particularly well.[12] But it is strange that Athenaeus normally gets Herodotus so right, yet here forgets in such a way as to miss the whole point of the story and *its most memorable aspect*, the helmet-part. And suspiciously strange: for Athenaeus' context is an argument that gold cups used to be extraordinarily scarce, and even the very rich used to use bronze. If the speaker Pontianus had quoted Herodotus accurately, he could not have used the story at all, for Herodotus does have his royalty using gold—indeed, no cups other than gold ones come into the story at all. It is Pontianus' inaccurate version which has no-one using gold, even the kings using silver, and the priests evidently using bronze because they can provide one of their own cups (no 'helmet') for Psammetichus. Is it not too much of a coincidence that this bizarre lapse of memory happens to provide Athenaeus, or Pontianus, with exactly what he wants for his argument?[13]

What makes it even less likely to be a coincidence is the second case, Cleomenes' self-mutilating death. At 10.436e–f Athenaeus is listing famous heavy drinkers. This time the speaker is Democritus.

> That Cleomenes of Sparta was a heavy drinker (ἀκρατοπότης) has already been stated (προείρηται); that he used a knife to slash himself to pieces through drunkenness (διὰ μέθην) Herodotus observed in his sixth book.

διὰ μέθην: either 'in a fit of intoxication' (Gulick's translation) or 'as a result of alcoholism' (Gulick's explanatory footnote, though that does not seem to mean quite the same thing). But Herodotus in fact has a much more elaborate version, with Cleomenes going mad at the end of an intricate sequence in which the gods play a big part: he adds the 'drunkenness' version only at the end, as the Spartan version (6.84), claiming that Cleomenes picked up the habit of strong drinking (ἀκρητοπότην γενέσθαι) from some Scythian ambassadors (part doubtless of the interesting Scythian–Spartan links we find several times in the *Histories*[14]):

> They say that Cleomenes kept closer company with these Scythian ambassadors when they arrived, and as a result of this unusually close company he picked up from them the habit of strong drink; that, say the Spartiates, drove him mad, and that too—so they say themselves—is the origin of the custom of saying 'Make it Scythian' (ἐπισκύθισον) whenever they want to drink it neater.

So Athenaeus is here quoting Herodotus' variant, but giving it as if Herodotus has presented it in his own authorial voice.

That is pretty small beer, one might (sympotically) think, and might again be just a faulty memory—'evidently memory' says Brunt.[15] Yet it is again exactly what suits Athenaeus' own argument, for he is here collecting various notables, especially royals, who drank like drains and often drank themselves to death.

There is a further twist. This passage is explicitly ('as has already been stated', προείρηται 10.436e) picking up on an earlier statement of Democritus at 10.427b–c. That προείρηται refers not to the slashing himself to death but to the strong drink: we see why if we compare exactly what was said at 10.427b–c.

> And the Spartans, as Herodotus says in the sixth book, say that king Cleomenes kept company with Scythians, became a strong drinker (ἀκρατοπότην), and went mad as a result of his drunkenness (ἐκ μέθης). And the Spartans themselves, whenever they want to drink a stronger mix, call it 'drinking Scythian-fashion' (ἐπισκυθίσαι). At least (γοῦν), Chamaeleon of Heraclea in his *On Drunkenness* [fr. 10 W.] writes as follows about this: '... seeing that Cleomenes of Sparta is said by the Lacedaemonians to have gone mad through keeping company with the Scythians and learning from them the habit of strong drink (ἀκρατοποτεῖν): that is the reason why, when they want to drink a stronger mix, they say 'make it Scythian!' (ἐπισκύθισον).

So first the Herodotus quotation, this time scrupulously accurate in giving it only as a Spartan variant, and not mentioning the slashing to bits (that is why the later προείρηται refers only to the drink, not the slashing): then Chamaeleon. Yet the odd thing is that the *Chamaeleon* quotation is almost word for word what *Herodotus* himself says in 6.84 (quoted above); and Athenaeus himself must have known it, given that he has just himself been quoting closely from that same passage himself. Now it may well be that Chamaeleon was quoting, or at least deriving from, Herodotus: but it is still odd that Herodotus' authority for this story is ignored, given that Athenaeus clearly knew the passage. What we should expect, in fact, is an extended Herodotean quotation, followed by a 'Chamaeleon mentions this too'.

Why does Athenaeus not do it that way? There are various possibilities. For one thing, this is rather a Chamaeleon cluster: he is also quoted at 10.429a and 10.430a. For another, our own idea of 'authority' here needs to be questioned. *We* automatically assume that Herodotus is a better authority, because earlier and presumably the 'source' for the story, but Athenaeus (or his speakers, or his audience) might attach more weight to Chamaeleon, treasure-trove as he clearly was of such hedonistic material. That was where you went for material like this. 13.560d–f gives an analogy. The speaker Leonides is there collecting material on 'wars beginning from women', and his argument overlaps closely with the beginning of Herodotus Book 3, another passage which Athenaeus of Egypt surely knew well. Herodotus there told the story of Cambyses' Egyptian concubine: he had sent to Amasis requesting a daughter for marriage; Amasis 'knew well that Cambyses intended to keep her as a concubine, not as a wife' (3.1.2), so unwisely sent him Nitetis, the daughter of his predecessor Apries, passing her off as his own. Nitetis revealed the truth, Cambyses invaded, and Egypt fell. Or (Herodotus adds) so the Persians say; there is another Egyptian version, making Apries' daughter Cambyses' mother and Cyrus' concubine, but Herodotus explains why this is deeply implausible. Athenaeus' material maps closely on to Herodotus', though he learnedly adds names to the 'Egyptian' version (Dinon [*FGrH* 690 fr. 11] and Lyceas of Naucratis [*FGrH* 613 fr. 1])—both of them fourth century or later, and therefore they cannot be the authorities Herodotus himself had in mind. However, the more striking point is that Athenaeus attributes the principal version, Nitetis as Cambyses' concubine, to Ctesias (Jacoby prints this as *FGrH* 688 fr. 13a) rather than to Herodotus. As in the Chamaeleon case, it may be that Ctesias did tell the story as well, drawing closely on Herodotus; if so he added little, only it seems the note that Cambyses wanted an Egyptian wife because he knew Egyptian women were particularly good in bed, and that Nitetis' skills did not disappoint him. Even so we would expect Herodotus to be quoted instead of, or at least as well as, Ctesias. That is what we would do ourselves. But it need not follow that Athenaeus would. Ctesias was the better source for stories like this; his was the name that added lustre and style.

Yet it is at least worth suggesting a further reason in our Chamaeleon case. Is he here covering his tracks in preparation for that misrepresentation of Herodotus a few chapters later? If so, an extended Herodotean quotation will here be precisely what Athenaeus does not want: he needs to *distract* attention from the detail of exactly what Herodotus says. Chamaeleon is the more innocuous, though also the less authoritative, figure to quote. If this last suggestion is right, it suggests the intricate care with which Athenaeus is building his web of quotations, and shows how he is already thinking some way ahead; we might have thought the gain hardly worth the trouble, but it does not follow that Athenaeus thought the same way.

Whatever the truth about that, we can certainly see that the 'quoting from faulty memory' explanation is too bland. It can hardly be coincidence that the two prize instances happen to produce exactly what Athenaeus needs for his context and his argument. And the traditional picture of Athenaeus as a plodding transcriber, faithfully preserving whatever he found, again bites the dust. We can see him taking liberties with his texts, even by our standards being a little bit naughty with them.

By our standards, perhaps, but surely not by his, nor by those of his audience or of the speakers at his symposium. For it is a poor sort of symposium that does not allow a little naughtiness from time to time, a little textual transgression. Perhaps we should indeed think of Athenaeus making these misquotations expressive, something which the informed reader will notice and admire: this is the way speakers *should* behave at this stage of the evening's experience: 'fun with fragments' is something to be had by speaker as well as reader, by internal as well as external audience. Or perhaps we should simply think of this as a licence which the author rather than the speaker allows himself, rendering his compendium of entertaining curiosities even more entertaining and curious. Either way, these are sobering instances for those who build large conclusions on the accuracy of Athenaeus' quotations in all those other, less controllable, instances.

## Appendix: Verbatim quotation?

We have just seen Athenaeus recasting his materials in substantial ways; how faithfully does he keep his sources' precise words on a smaller scale? Here we must remember that we are not always dealing with Athenaeus' original text, but sometimes only with an epitome (cf. Chapter 3).

In the standard discussion Zepernick (1921) argued that Athenaeus reproduced his originals very accurately, and his versions deserved 'die größte Glaubwürdigkeit'. He of course knew that, when we can compare Athenaeus' text with independent versions of the originals, we often find variants in detail; but he thought most of these variants similar to those which appear in any manuscript tradition—errors or alternatives caused by homoeoteleuton, haplography, confusion of visually similar letters or aurally similar words, and so on. The variants can thus (he argued) typically be explained in terms of manuscript corruption in the texts either of Athenaeus or of the originals; or of Athenaeus incorporating marginal glosses or variants into his versions; or of mistaken transcription or abbreviation by Athenaeus' epitomator.

Our earlier comparison of 4.138b–c and Hdt. 9.82 offers a convenient test case. As we saw, there are a substantial number of small variations—alterations of vocabulary or construction or word-order, small omissions, and so on—though only one or two significantly shift the original's point. They are marked in the English translation of that passage (above, p. 182–3). However, *pace* Zepernick most of the differences are *not* very similar to typical manuscript variants (though some are, for instance the variation of παρασκευήν and κατασκευήν). This example also casts doubt on the inference of Brunt (1980, 481), followed by Flower (1994, 105–6 n. 12), that Athenaeus' reliability renders him a better guide than Polybius when both quote Theopompus *FGrH* 115 fr. 225. (Athen. 6.260d–1a ~ Polybius 8.9.6–13: Jacoby prints the two versions in columns in *FGrH*, and so comparison is easy.) As far as it goes, our case would tend to support Walbank, who claims the opposite (1957–79, ii.82): Athenaeus' variations from Herodotus in 4.138b–c are quite similar to the variations which 6.260d–1a shows from the version of Theopompus preserved by Polybius.

Still, it is hard to be sure in that Theopompus instance, for Athenaeus' procedures vary a good deal from one instance to another. With Xenophon, for instance, there are several cases where quotations, especially short ones, are very close (but usually not identical) to the originals in Xenophon's own manuscript tradition: 3.121d–c ~ *Hieron* 1.22–3, 4.144b–c ~ *Ages.* 9.3, 5.188a ~ *Symp.* 1.9, 5.216e ~ *Symp.* 8.32, 9.390c–d ~ *Anab.* 1.5.3, 14.614c–d ~ *Symp.* 1.11, 15.686d–f ~ *Symp.* 2.2–4; in other cases he is clearly purporting only to paraphrase rather than quote, e.g. 4.157e ~ *Cyrop.* 1.2.11, 6.272c ~ *Poroi* 4.14 (cf. Zepernick 1921, 319). Tronson (1984, 125 n. 54) reports the result of an extended study arguing that 'out of 162 quotations of extant prose authors by Athenaeus, 90 are found to have been drastically shortened, adapted, or deliberately misquoted in accordance with the requirements of Athenaeus' contexts…'. 'Drastically' overstates it in many cases, as it would in the present example of Hdt. 9.82 ~ 4.138b–c. But it remains true that even in closely followed cases there are often adaptations of vocabulary, word-order and syntax, and whole sentences can be omitted. The omissions *could* be the work of Athenaeus' epitomator, as Zepernick suggested; but there is no reason to explain the other adaptations in that way, and in that case there seems no reason to refuse Athenaeus the licence to omit as well as adapt. Illuminating extended cases are Xen. *Anabasis* 7.3.21–31 ~ 4.150f–151e; *Cyrop.* 8.8.15–20 ~ 12.515a–d (where one of the passages omitted, §18, has already been quoted at 11.465e); Plb. 4.20.5–21.9 ~ 14.626a–f. Cases are collected by Ambaglio (1990), though he takes a very low view of Athenaeus' capacity to understand his original's point or adapt it for his own purposes.

It is interesting to wonder why these slight variations exist. There is a contrast here with, for instance, Athenaeus' verse quotations from tragedy, which seem quite accurate when we can compare them with an independent manuscript tradition of the originals (Collard (1969): cf. Villari in this volume, Chapter 33).

One would normally think of quotation from memory to explain such minor variations as we find here, and, as we shall see, a nuanced version of that view may be the right one; but it is hard to think that even Athenaeus was carrying quite so many of the texts of classical antiquity around in his head.

A possible variation would be to appeal again to the sympotic setting, and wonder whether the mild inaccuracies were intended to be noticed and expressive. Athenaeus is after all representing his *speakers* as quoting from memory, and the best of scholars might occasionally misremember Herodotus' precise words when quoting late in the evening. We might compare those passages, collected by Lukinovich (1990, 271), where Athenaeus' speakers themselves refer to the limitations of their own memories. If so, we should not regard this as a point of character-drawing, representing one speaker as knowing his texts better than another; it would rather be the sort of quotation technique thought suitable for the sympotic setting as a whole, rather as I have suggested for Athenaeus' larger-scale misquotations and misrepresentations. But this time that explanation is more far-fetched. The variations are too slight for any audience, however learned, to recognize and savour.

Yet, if Athenaeus did consult the texts and 'copied them out', would we not expect more accuracy? Perhaps we should not; it may well be that precise verbatim reproduction of prose classics, unlike verse with its metrical constraints, was not considered important, and that such minor variations do not count as inaccuracies. Bers has recently argued this position for direct quotations in classical tragedy and oratory;[16] Gourevitch argues something similar for *technical* prose texts (see Chapter 37). That is plausible, and Athenaeus may well have assumed a licence to vary wording. But we still have the difficulty of explaining why he uses that licence much more readily in some cases than in others, and why many quotations do seem verbatim, or something very close to it.

It might be helpful here to adopt a more nuanced view of his method of work, and the way in which Athenaeus might set about 'copying out'. Perhaps Athenaeus did not have all the passages before his eyes as he wrote a section—a difficult thing to do anyway, given the problem of using papyrus rolls.[17] If he looked up a group of passages before beginning on a section he could genuinely be quoting 'from memory', even if his memory had only been stocked at 9 o'clock in the morning with passages he was going to be quoting at 2 o'clock the same day. In that case, such variations in precision might not be surprising, for the memory would have been better, and more freshly, re-primed in some cases than in others.[18]

## ❖ 13 ❖ THE RECALCITRANT MASS
## ATHENAEUS AND PAUSANIAS

### by Karim Arafat

This chapter is something of a *kyathos*, dipping in where a deeper draught (in both spellings and both meanings) is needed.[1] Here I look at some of the cases where Pausanias and Athenaeus cover common ground, to consider where their accounts of the same site, building or object agree and where they differ, in the hope of shedding some light on their respective preoccupations and working methods. My title is adapted from Glen Bowersock: to quote him in full, 'some writers faced the challenge of imposing a literary character on the recalcitrant mass of facts'.[2] Bowersock rightly cites Athenaeus as one such writer; but Pausanias, too, deals with a mass of facts, and how recalcitrant some of them have proved, as have the extent and use of his sources. The 'literary character' of Athenaeus' work is explored in this book by many others in more detail than I can manage; that of Pausanias' work remains, I suggest, more shadowy.

'Literary character' encompasses several aspects, including the overt and covert use of literary sources, and of literary and rhetorical devices. It is the use of literary sources I wish to explore here, since Athenaeus refers to several which are not known from any other writer, but which we may reasonably presume to have been known to Pausanias, although he does not refer to them. Is Pausanias using such sources unacknowledged?

According to the authors of the entry for Athenaeus in *OCD*[3] he 'cites some 1,250 authors, gives the titles of more than 1,000 plays, and quotes more than 10,000 lines of verse'. I have not compiled comparable statistics for Pausanias, but the order of magnitude of difference may be gleaned from the fact that, rather than the 1,250 authors cited by Athenaeus, Pausanias, by my count, cites just over 80. Even given the discrepancy in length between the two works, this is a major difference. And there are differences also in the use of the sources, both explicit and implicit. Pausanias on occasion gives us general references to works and authors: thus, he refers to 'those who have made a special study of the history of the sculptors' (5.20.2), and says he has used at least some such works. I have explained elsewhere[3] why I think Pausanias' claims to autopsy of sites and objects are just, but there is no denying his claim to wide reading (e.g. 4.2.1). In this case, it may well be that books such as *On Sculptors* by Adaeus of Mytilene (13.606a), or Hegesander's *Statues of Men and Gods* (5.210b), proved invaluable reference works for Pausanias, although he mentions neither of them. In fact, we know of their existence only from Athenaeus.

It may, however, be possible to infer from Athenaeus one possible source used by Pausanias in his account of the fifty daughters of Thestius and their sexual liaisons with Heracles (9.27.6–7; cf. 3.19.5). Athenaeus (13.556f), citing Herodorus[4] as his source, says that Heracles slept with all fifty daughters. The accounts of Ps. Apollodorus (2.4.10) and Diodorus (4.29.3) concur, as does that given by Pausanias. However, Pausanias also gives a variant story, otherwise unattested, in which Heracles only slept with forty-nine daughters. There are other differences in these accounts: offspring are referred to only by Pausanias (who says that all the daughters bore sons, the youngest and oldest bearing twins), and Diodorus (fifty sons); and only Pausanias and Athenaeus refer to the length of time the fifty unions took (one night, and five days respectively). The latter point indicates that Pausanias and Athenaeus are not strictly following the same version of the story, but displaying a certain eclecticism. However, there is one particularly noteworthy point of similarity, namely that they both refer to 'Thestius', while the other writers refer to 'Thespius'. This is all the more striking in the case of Pausanias, since the story is told as part of the account of his visit to Thespiae, so that one might naturally expect him to use 'Thespius'. The fact that he did not may reasonably be taken to indicate adherence to a received version, perhaps that of Herodorus, named as Athenaeus' source.

Often, Pausanias gives discrepant opinions on some literary matter, although his motivation for doing so is usually not clear—perhaps through genuine uncertainty, perhaps to advertise that he knows that there are divergent views. For example, he says 'The Boeotians have a tradition that Hesiod composed nothing but the *Works* ... there is another opinion ... that Hesiod composed a great number of poems'; he then lists among them 'the poem on the soothsayer Melampus' (9.31.4–5). He does not say to which view he subscribes. The Hesiodic *Melampodia* is known from several sources,[5] and Athenaeus twice quotes it (2.40f, 11.498a–b) and cites it on a further occasion (13.609e), but he mentions no controversy over its authorship.

Many authors are mentioned by Pausanias not to show off his learning by quoting some verses or the title of a poem, play or history of a particular city, but because he has seen their tomb or statue. So, for example, Euripides' cenotaph on the Piraeus–Athens road (1.2.2) and his statue in the theatre at Athens (1.21.1), where Pausanias also saw a statue of Menander, whose grave he mentions elsewhere (1.2.2). He has nothing else to say of either author. Of Anacreon, he says only that he has seen his statue on the Acropolis (1.25.1), and that he once resided with Polycrates (1.2.3). Isocrates (1.18.8) and Arion of Methymna (9.30.2) are among writers mentioned merely for their statues. And where Pausanias does cite a poet's work or give some literary opinion, he will often mention their statue also—thus Homer (5.26.2) and Hesiod (5.26, 9.27.5, 9.30.3), Pindar (1.8.4) and Sophocles (1.21.1), among others.

There seems, therefore, to be a standardly observed rule in Pausanias' method, that the information he gives us concerning writers arises naturally from what he is writing about at the time. In other words, these authors are not mentioned or quoted simply for display, but to illuminate whatever Pausanias is detailing or discussing. While there is no contradiction in doing both, I do not think that he actually is doing both in most cases. He often acknowledges his source for a particular piece of information: added to the literary sources are the ἐξηγηταί[6] ('exegetes')and his own autopsy. Between them, they provide many detailed descriptions. On occasion, however, we have differing descriptions of the same sites, buildings or objects by other authors, including Athenaeus. It is to some of these that I turn now.

First, it must be stressed that there are many works cited by Athenaeus (and often by Athenaeus alone), usually only by title, to which Pausanias makes no reference, but to which he presumably had access and from which he may have derived information for his descriptions and discussions. I have already cited *On Sculptors* by Adaeus of Mytilene, and Hegesander's *Statues of Men and Gods*, and other examples include works on the history of Attica by Istrus (3.74e, 13.557a), Phanodemus (3.114c, 9.392d), Philochorus (6.245c, 11.495e–f, 14.637f, 15.693d), and Cleidemus (6.235a, 14.660d), although the latter is probably to be identified with the Cleitodemus named by Pausanias as 'the oldest of all the writers to have described Attica' (10.15.5).[7] Other works mentioned by Athenaeus but not by Pausanias, although of obvious relevance to his subject, include *On the city of Athens* by Telephanes (14.614e), *On the Acropolis* by Heliodorus (6.229e, 9.406c) and *On the Athenian Acropolis* by Polemo (11.472c, 11.486d, 13.587c), who was also the author of, among others, *On Painters* (11.474c).[8] Pausanias may have used Alcetas' *On the dedicatory offerings at Delphi* (13.591c) in his extensive description of the site; and when he refers to the depredations of Nero, who, he alleges, took 500 statues from Delphi (10.7.1), we may ask whether he used Theopompus' *On the funds plundered from Delphi* (12.532d, 13.604f–605a). So too, at Olympia, he may have used the *Olympic Victors* of Eratosthenes (4.154a),[9] a work to which I shall return.

It is often very hard to know whether Pausanias used a written source at all, never mind how he may have done so. Athenaeus, however, names and quotes his sources with much greater frequency, enabling us to assess more readily how he used them. It would be surprising if any two authors used the same sources in precisely the same way: in the present case, Athenaeus and Pausanias have very dissimilar agendas, and where comparison can be made, there are significant differences, as will, I hope, become apparent.

With Athenaeus, the element of display of learning seems to me much greater. But, of course, he, like Pausanias, will often just extract what he needs: for example, both Pausanias and Athenaeus refer to the iambic poet Phoenix. Pausanias tells us that he lamented in verse the capture of his home city of Colophon (1.9.7), while Athenaeus quotes him on four occasions, all to do with eating and drinking (8.359e–60a, 10.421d, 11.495d–e, 12.530e–531a). Apart from what this tells us about Pausanias' and Athenaeus' purposes, it is worth noting how very different an impression each gives of Phoenix' output and how differently we might have regarded him if we only had one of these accounts, and none of the few extant fragments.

Similarly, to return to Olympic victors, there is plenty of scope for Pausanias and Athenaeus to tell us wholly different things about individual victors. For example, Pausanias' references to Theagenes of Thasos (6.6.5, 6.11.2–9, 6.15.3) are concerned with his athletic deeds and misdemeanours, and with the story of his homicidal statue, tried for murder after falling on someone. None of this from Athenaeus, who mentions only that Theagenes 'devoured a bull all alone', quoting an epigram of Posidippus as evidence (10.412e). Prodigious eating by athletes is something of a topos, recurring, for example, in Athenaeus' account of the most 'storied' of all athletes, Milo of Croton (10.412e–413a), who is extensively treated by Pausanias (6.14.5–8), but with no reference to eating. Diodorus likewise concentrates on his strength, again making no reference to his eating (12.9.5–6).

Where Pausanias does mention the prodigious appetite of an athlete, in the case of Lepreus (5.5.4), it is in connection with Heracles, whom Lepreus challenged to an ox-eating contest; rashly one might think, but it ended in a draw. It was, however, followed by a duel and Lepreus' inevitable death. The story is also told by Aelian (*Var. Hist.* 1.24) and Athenaeus (10.412a). Neither Aelian nor Athenaeus cites a specific source for it, although Athenaeus cites the *Eulogy of Heracles* by the rhetor Matris, probably of the third century BC, for a drinking contest between Heracles and Lepreus (10.412b), and this story may also derive from it. Pausanias says no more of his source than the usual prefatory phrase 'it is said that ...'. Interestingly, where Athenaeus does give sources for stories of gluttonous athletes, they do not include Eratosthenes' *Olympic Victors*, which suggests that it is likelier to have been concerned with more serious matters, such as those Pausanias discusses in connection with the Olympic victors he cites. It is true that in the case of many of the sources cited by Athenaeus, we know nothing of whether Pausanias used them. But the very fact that we know they existed broadens the possibilities of Pausanias' use of sources in a way which would not have been possible had Athenaeus not mentioned them.

So too, with rituals, on occasion Pausanias and Athenaeus refer to the same topic but focus upon different parts. Thus the rites of consulting the oracle of Trophonius at Lebadeia in Phocis are described in more detail by Pausanias (9.39.5–14) than by any other author. Philostratus' account (*Vit. Apoll.* 8.19) is the next most detailed, perhaps drawing on Pausanias. The only reference Athenaeus makes to the rites of Trophonius is to mention that Semus, in the fifth book of his *History of Delos*, noted that he lost the ability to laugh as a result of descending into the cave of Trophonius (14.614a). This lack of interest is not in itself surprising, but it is worth setting beside the fact that Athenaeus twice quotes Dicaearchus' work *On the descent into the cave of Trophonius* (13.594e–595a, 14.641e–f). The first (and much longer) quotation concerns the route to Athens from Eleusis, and the second concerns lavish provision at dinner-parties. In other words, Athenaeus makes no reference at all to the main subject of Dicaearchus' book, nor to the details of the rites. In doing so, he uncharacteristically misses an opportunity to mention an item of food, namely the cakes which consultants of the oracle held as they descended. Lucian (*Dial. mort.* 3.2), Maximus of Tyre (14.2), and Pausanias call them barley-cakes (μάζαι), Pausanias adding that they were kneaded with honey; Aristophanes (*Clouds* 506–8)[10] and Philostratus call them honey-cakes. Philostratus adds that their purpose was to 'appease the reptiles which assail them as they descend'.[11]

The quotations in Athenaeus from Dicaearchus' *On the descent into the cave of Trophonius* constitute our only evidence for the work apart from a passing reference in Cicero (*Att.* 6.2) which gives neither its title nor its contents. The existence of Dicaearchus' work raises the possibility of Pausanias' account being derivative rather than the fruit of the autopsy he claims as one who consulted Trophonius in the manner he describes. However, for reasons explained elsewhere (see n. 3), I find it generally appropriate to believe Pausanias' claims of autopsy. In this case, he says that he knows others who have consulted the oracle, and that 'all who have gone down to Trophonius are obliged to set up a tablet containing a record of all they heard or saw'. It is by no means impossible, in fact, that Dicaearchus' account may itself derive from such tablets. Much remains speculative, but Athenaeus' references add to the range of possible sources.

Most of the works cited by Athenaeus have come down to us as titles or small fragments, but on occcasion we do have more information, enabling us to make a fuller comparison. Athenaeus is the only source for a work entitled *Customs of Phigalea* by Harmodius of Lepreum,[12] which he mentions four times, quoting the text with reference to feasting and drinking at sacrifices (4.148f–149c); to a clay bowl called a κοτταβίς (11.479c, also referred to in 4.149b); and to the inscription on the tomb of one Pytheas, noted for his acquisition of much gold and silver (11.465d). In addition, he cites Harmodius on the Phigaleans' affection for drink (10.442b). Pausanias' account of Phigalea and its vicinity is extensive. There is no trace of the points mentioned by Athenaeus, nor should we expect it: as already stated, the two authors have very different agendas. Indeed, Pausanias' visit to Phigalea was prompted primarily by a desire to see a statue of Black Demeter (8.42.11) and, if Pausanias is using the same source, it is unlikely that he would be using the same parts of it.

I turn now to some examples where Athenaeus illuminates Pausanias' descriptions of buildings or objects in differing ways. In his description of Delphi, Pausanias mentions (10.15.1) a gilded statue of Phryne by Praxiteles. Athenaeus (13.591b) refers to the statue as golden, not gilded, as do most of the writers who mention it, e.g. Aelian (*Var. Hist.* 9.32) and Dio Chrysostom (*Or.* 37.2). In Plutarch's dialogues, it is variously referred to as golden (*Mor.* 336c–d, 401d) and gilded (*Mor.* 753f).[13] While Plutarch was a priest at Delphi (*Mor.* 700e) and in a good position to describe such dedications accurately, the descriptions, attributed to Plutarch's characters rather than to himself, are not intended to be authoritative statements of the statue's technique. Pausanias' statement, on the other hand, clearly is. We may perhaps reasonably infer that Pausanias is writing from observation, while Athenaeus simply repeats the majority view. This must owe something to Pausanias' often-evident interest in technique: a gilded statue is precisely intended to look golden, and it may well have needed an enquiring mind and experienced eye to spot the difference. From an art-historical point of view, the case is interesting also for the fact that, if Athenaeus and those who concur with him are right, this would be the first-known gold statue of a mortal woman rather than a goddess.

A similar case occurs with reference to a statue of the orator Gorgias: Athenaeus (11.505d) quotes Hermippus' *On Gorgias* as referring to Gorgias dedicating a gold statue of himself at Delphi. As with the Phryne statue, Pausanias (10.18.7) calls the statue gilded rather than gold, thus placing himself at odds not only with Athenaeus but with all the other known sources, namely Cicero (*de orat.* 3.129), Valerius Maximus (8.15 ext. 2) and Pliny (*NH* 33.83), who adds in wonder at the luxury of Gorgias' statue: 'So great were the profits to be made by teaching the art of oratory!' Again, there is an art-historical point at stake here, since this would be the second-earliest occurrence of a gilded statue recorded in our sources, after several associated with Croesus.

In referring to the statues of Phryne and Gorgias, Athenaeus does not claim autopsy. Nor do the other sources, including, in fact, Pausanias in these particular instances, but his claims to autopsy are manifold and pervasive in his writings, and there is every reason to think he intended us to believe that he had seen the statue. Athenaeus' claims to autopsy are, however, many fewer. Indeed, it is in the nature of Athenaeus' approach, with so much information explicitly given at second hand through literary extracts, that there is less scope for claims of autopsy.

One exception, which brings together a variety of sources, is Athenaeus' account of the bowl of Alyattes of Lydia at Delphi. He writes as follows (5.210b–c):

> Hegesander of Delphi, in the commentary entitled *Statues of Men and of Gods*, says that the stand in Delphi made by Glaucus of Chios is a kind of vessel-stand of iron dedicated by Alyattes; it is mentioned by Herodotus [1.25], who calls it a 'bowl-stand' [ὑποκρητηρίδιον]. This, then, is what Hegesander says of it. But I too have seen it where it stands as an offering in Delphi, truly worth seeing on account of the figures of insects worked in relief upon it, as well as other tiny creatures and plants; it is capable of holding upon it mixing-bowls and other vessels besides.

In view of the last clause, it is odd that Athenaeus does not mention that Herodotus tells us that in his day, the stand did in fact have a silver bowl upon it. Pausanias also refers to the stand, as follows (10.16.1–2): 'of the offerings sent by the kings of Lydia, nothing now remains except the iron stand of Alyattes' bowl.' He goes on to mention its maker, Glaucus, and explain how it is made. Herodotus' account, in turn, refers to it as a 'great silver bowl on a stand of welded iron'. He also says it is by Glaucus, and describes it as 'worth seeing above all the votive offerings at Delphi'. The bowl, mentioned as missing by Pausanias, had disappeared by the time of Plutarch, who, acknowledging Herodotus' account, refers to 'the famous stand and base of the bowl' and notes its technique (*Mor.* 436a).

While the accounts of Plutarch, Pausanias and Athenaeus have much in common, it is interesting that it is only Pausanias who does not mention Herodotus, despite the well-established fact that there is much Herodotean in Pausanias, and that his account must surely have been written with that of Herodotus in mind. It may be that too much derives from Herodotus to be worth noting on every occasion. The passage of Athenaeus is important for his claim to autopsy, as well as for his reference to the otherwise unknown work of

Hegesander. The fact that only Athenaeus makes a specific claim (in the mouth of a diner) to autopsy of the stand implies nothing about the accounts of Plutarch and Pausanias, for reasons already given with reference to the statues of Phryne and Gorgias. Athenaeus' detailed description of the relief insects and plants may indeed be from autopsy, as he claims, or it may be a rhetorical flourish. Perhaps he mentions Hegesander's treatise in order to allow himself the opportunity to show that he is well read, but claims autopsy in order to avoid giving the impression that his account of the stand is simply derivative.

From three accounts of the same object, I turn to some items mentioned by Athenaeus but not by Pausanias. For example, Athenaeus (13.591b) cites Alcetas' *On the dedicatory offerings at Delphi* as placing the statue of Phryne at Delphi between statues of Archidamus and Philip II, while Pausanias mentions neither statue. Pausanias (10.15.1) gives the setting of the Phryne statue as being next to two statues of Apollo, but does not mention Archidamus or Philip.[14] Pausanias' apparent omission is the more curious in that elsewhere he mentions that Archidamus saved the Delphians from the Phocians (3.10.4), and that there was a statue of him at Olympia (6.4.9, 6.15.7).

Another example is the temple and statue of Artemis Corythalia in Laconia, placed by Polemo (quoted by Athenaeus, 4.139b), beside the fountain of Tiasus. Pausanias describes the general area, including the river which he calls Tiasa, but not the specific location nor the temple and statue. That is surprising, for elsewhere he mentions some sixty-five cult titles for Artemis. Polemo's writings were also available to Pausanias, but he apparently did not follow them here.[15] Pausanias may not have gone to exactly the place Polemo mentioned: if so, his omission of the temple and statue suggests that he was unwilling to include a location unless he had seen it for himself; or he may have seen it for himself but not seen what Polemo claimed was there, and did not think it worth explicitly contradicting Polemo; or he may have deliberately differed from Polemo because he followed another source, unknown to us.

Returning to Delphi, Athenaeus (13.606a) quotes 'Polemo, or whoever wrote the work entitled *Of Hellas*' when mentioning the treasury of the Spinatae. This building, which remains unidentified,[16] is not mentioned by Pausanias. However, as he mentions only five treasuries and we have foundations of twenty-three, omissions seem to be the rule rather than the exception. In fact, the building is only mentioned elsewhere by Strabo (5.1.7).[17]

Another example: Athenaeus says (11.479f–480a):

Polemo at any rate, or whoever is the author of the book entitled *Of Hellas*, when discussing the temple[18] of the Metapontines at Olympia, writes as follows: 'The temple of the Metapontines, in which are 132 silver saucers, two silver wine-jugs, a silver vessel for sacrifice, three gilded saucers. The temple of the Byzantines, in which are a Triton in cypress-wood holding a silver κρατάνιον, a silver Siren, two silver καρχήσια, a silver kylix, a golden wine-jug, two horns.

This treasure is not mentioned by Pausanias. Peter Levi's notes[19] on Pausanias' accounts of both buildings simply state that the treasuries once contained the items listed, but make no reference to Athenaeus, as if this information were gleaned from an excavation report. It may well be, as Levi's notes imply, that the treasure had disappeared between the time of Polemo, in the second century BC, and the time of Pausanias' own visit to Olympia, which he himself places in AD 173 (5.1.2). All Pausanias notes in the Metapontine treasury (6.19.11) is an ivory figure of Endymion; and of the Byzantine treasury, he gives no details (6.19.9). In part, the reason may be that gold and silver plate appears to have held no particular interest for Pausanias, whereas it was of considerable relevance to Athenaeus' purpose. However, the same points seem also to apply to the Sicyonian treasury at Delphi, which Pausanias says (10.11.1) was empty (as, in fact, he says, were all the treasuries at Delphi), whereas Plutarch (*Mor.* 675b) says that Polemo, in his *On the treasuries at Delphi*, mentioned a golden tablet dedicated in the Sicyonian treasury. The passage makes clear that the tablet was no longer there in Plutarch's day, thus lending credibility to the disappearance of treasure from the Metapontine and Byzantine treasuries at Olympia as suggested above.

Sir James Frazer notes that, while Pausanias uses θησαυρός for 'treasury', Athenaeus uses ναός, and argues that if Pausanias were following Polemo, as Athenaeus explicitly does in 11.479f–480a, he would in all probability have used the word ναός also.[20] However, Athenaeus quotes Polemo's words on the θησαυρός of Spina (13.606b), and Plutarch (*Mor.* 675b) gives the title of Polemo's work on the treasuries at Delphi as Περὶ τῶν ἐν Δελφοῖς θησαυρῶν. This suggests that Polemo himself varied in his usage, perhaps according to whether writing of Delphi or Olympia.[21] But it may be pertinent that elsewhere Athenaeus always uses ναός (as Pausanias always uses θησαυρός), while Plutarch is not consistent, referring to the treasury of Cypselus at Delphi as an οἶκος (*Mor.* 164a, 400d).[22] We may conclude from this that there was too great a flexibility in vocabulary to admit Frazer's decisiveness on the basis of a single word. It also indicates that the possibility of Pausanias' having used Polemo in this passage remains greater than Frazer allowed.

One further point of curiosity arises from this passage: Athenaeus mentions the Metapontine treasury first, then the Byzantine, while Pausanias reverses the order. All reconstructions of Olympia follow Pausanias' order and surely rightly, since he is clearly describing treasuries from west to east (the first and last, the Sicyonian and Megarian, both being identified by inscriptions[23]). The different order used by Polemo may be chance—there is no preserved context to assist us—but it is indicative of the relative standing of Pausanias and other authors (by no means only Polemo or Athenaeus) in modern perceptions, that this different order appears to receive no mention in the literature on the treasuries at Olympia, despite the tenuous nature of the identification of some of them.[24]

The passage of Athenaeus continues by turning to what he calls 'the old temple of Hera' (11.480a). Built in the early sixth century,[25] the temple of Hera must have been thought of as 'old' even by the time of Polemo; indeed, it probably was as soon as the temple of Zeus was completed in the 450s.

By Polemo's account, as Athenaeus tells us, there were in the temple of Hera 'thirty silver saucers, two silver κρατάνια, a silver pot, a gold vessel for sacrifice, a golden mixing-bowl—a votive offering of the Cyrenaeans—and a silver saucer'. Like the vessels in the treasuries of Metapontum and Byzantium, these are not mentioned by Pausanias, despite the fact that his listing of the contents of the temple of Hera (5.16.1–5.20.3) is the most detailed of all such accounts. As with the gold and silver in the treasuries, these pieces may simply have disappeared by Pausanias' day. Athenaeus does not claim autopsy, and we have no reason to think that his account does anything other than what he claims, namely repeats Polemo's statement that the gold and silver was in the temple of Hera in the second century BC. But objects did move within the temple, if we believe both Pausanias, who saw the chest of Cypselus almost certainly in the cella, and Dio Chrysostom (*Or.* 11.45) who places it in the opisthodomus.[26] There again, the gold and silver may simply have been overlooked: even in such a detailed account, Pausanias explicitly says that he is being selective, and he has a lot to describe, including at least twenty-three chryselephantine statues, the chest of Cypselus, Praxiteles' marble Hermes and Dionysus, a bronze Aphrodite and a gilded child, Hippodameia's toy couch, the discus with the Olympic rules written on it and the chryselephantine table on which the winners' wreaths were laid; and other objects besides. No shortage of material to discuss and no shortage of gold.

Indeed, Agaclytus, in his *On Olympia*,[27] noted in the temple of Hera a 'golden colossus' dedicated by Cypselus; its technique is said to be σφυρήλατος,[28] but we are not told what it represented. This is in all probability the statue meant by Plato (*Phaedr.* 236b), when he refers to a σφυρήλατος juxtaposed with a 'dedication of the Cypselids' at Olympia, implying that the Cypselid statue was also a σφυρήλατος. Plato is not specific about the location, but Strabo (8.3.30) calls the statue ὁ χρυσοῦς σφυρήλατος Ζεύς, ἀνάθημα Κυψέλου and places it in the ἱερόν at Olympia. This is most naturally understood as the Zeus temple rather than the Hera temple where Agaclytus placed it. The statue is not mentioned by Pausanias in his description of the Heraeum: while one might expect a 'colossus'[29] to have been remarked upon, one might also add that, being σφυρήλατος, a particularly fragile technique, it might not have survived to Pausanias' day, even if it had survived to Strabo's. However, Pausanias, in his general introduction to Olympia (5.2.3), refers to a story he has heard that Cypselus dedicated a golden image to Zeus at Olympia, perhaps the same piece. His failure to add any detail—including the supposed location of the statue—stems from his obvious scepticism about the story, presumably arising from his evidently not having seen the statue himself on his visit to Olympia. But if the statue did still exist in his day, and he overlooked it, whatever his personal view of its history, how much likelier he is to omit gold and silver plate. As a final point, the story suggests that Pausanias, whether or not he made any use of Agaclytus' account of the Heraeum, was at least not slavishly following him.

I have explained elsewhere why I think the temple of Hera was, by Pausanias' day at least, no longer functioning as a temple, but had become, in effect, a storeroom.[30] This conclusion, first suggested as long ago as 1894, is based on an aggregation of inferences rather than a direct statement by any ancient author, and Athenaeus' reference to so much gold and silver placed in the temple seems to me to be an important contribution to justifying the conclusion, and one which has, as far as I know, been overlooked until now.

There is nothing in all this to suggest that Athenaeus had or had not read Pausanias, although it is easier to provide indications, but probably no more, that he had not. For example, he says (14.635f) of Lycurgus the Spartan lawgiver that he 'is recorded by all, without dissent, as having arranged the first numbered establishment of the Olympic Games in conjunction with Iphitus of Elis'. Despite Athenaeus' certainty, there is in fact a dissenting view, that of Pausanias, who gives Iphitus sole credit for the establishment of the games on three occasions (5.4.6, 5.8.5, 8.26.4)—or, rather, for their revival, as he sees it and as is also implied by Athenaeus' phrase 'first *numbered* establishment'. The first of these references is the most interesting in saying that 'Iphitus ... a contemporary of Lycurgus, the Spartan lawgiver, arranged the games at Olympia'. The association of Iphitus and Lycurgus in this context is therefore common to the accounts of Athenaeus and Pausanias, even though their statements are incompatible. It is interesting that Pausanias makes no reference to what Athenaeus tells us is a universal opinion. It would be quite uncharacteristic of Pausanias not to be aware of an alternative view on such a matter, especially one supposedly held by everyone else who had written on the subject. As to Athenaeus, perhaps he had not read Pausanias. Conceivably he had done so but did not consider Pausanias' 'dissent' worth mentioning. Or perhaps he is simply confusing the roles of Iphitus and Lycurgus. Perhaps it is indeed the case, as it appears on the surface to be, that Pausanias believes something different from all other known written sources, as also in the case of the statue of Gorgias discussed above. Whether that reflects a source unknown to us and to Athenaeus, or whether it reflects the word of the 'exegetes' at Olympia, we can only speculate.

Speculate is what this chapter has been forced to do, by the nature of the two authors with which it has been concerned, and particularly by the fragmentary state of so many of the sources quoted or cited by Athenaeus. Nonetheless, I hope it has been established that Athenaeus' use of sources is much more in tune with that of his rhetorically minded contemporaries than is that of Pausanias, who repeatedly resists opportunities for such display. It is hard always to be certain of instances where Pausanias is using various literary sources without acknowledgement, although we may be sure that he often had the opportunity to do so, as the numerous works mentioned by Athenaeus indicate. But their unacknowledged use, even if it could be proved, would suggest that Pausanias is not attempting to impress his audience with his learning, but to combine his reading with his own observation, preferring autopsy and personal opinion, where possible, to a derivative account.

# ❖ 14 ❖ ATHENAEUS' USE OF PUBLIC DOCUMENTS

### by John Davies

The nature of this chapter needs some explanation. It reports on a part of the work which is being done within the framework of a long-term project which I am carrying out.* The project focuses on the study of documents (laws, decrees of state, etc.) dated ostensibly in the archaic and classical periods of Greece but preserved only in later historians, orators, antiquarians, etc. As an initial report (Davies 1996a) makes clear, that study has begun to suggest that the number of such documents which, as transmitted, have been heavily 'edited' if not wholly invented is far greater than was assumed in the initial debate of the 1960s (cf. especially Habicht 1961) sparked off by the publication of the Themistocles Decree in 1959. The aim of the project is therefore to collect all known examples of such indirectly attested documents, in order to establish the degree of authenticity and to reconstruct the historiographical and political processes involved. Attention is also being paid to the mechanics of the transmission of such material and to the functions which such documents (or 'documents') came to perform within Greek culture.

Since the process of trawling for material has to be done author by author, and since Athenaeus is so pre-eminently a source of citations, it seemed appropriate to take the opportunity of presenting a test-case. It has two focuses. One, which is especially germane to this volume, is to explore whether his interests extended beyond the literary sources which formed his main fodder to take in material which came—certainly, probably, or possibly—from epigraphic sources, and if so, whence in particular he sought and found such material. The second, which concerns more the project sketched above, is to ascertain whether he quotes any decrees or other public acts whose terms or phraseology may have undergone any of the processes of re-focusing, rephrasing, or outright invention which are perceptible elsewhere. Neither task is straightforward. It is not a matter of calibrating Athenaeus' citations against an extant historical text, as Ambaglio 1990 does with Herodotus, Thucydides, and Xenophon, nor even of assembling his citations of identifiable but largely lost historians or antiquarian writers, as Zecchini 1989a does or as Walbank does with Polybius (Chapter 11). That is because in the case of epigraphic source material there is no pre-assembled body of 'text', but rather a mass of indirectly attested potential material whose status can be determined only by working assumptions (e.g. that epigrams said to have come from statue bases were originally genuine epigraphic texts seen by one of Athenaeus' sources) or by using unreliable indicators such as the words στήλη ('inscribed pillar') or ψήφισμα ('decree'). True, some limited pre-assemblage had been done by earlier authors, notably by Craterus and Polemon, but we cannot assume that he used even those authors directly as 'texts'. What is more, and is striking, is that Athenaeus nowhere (*sauf erreur*) cites an extant inscription. We therefore have no direct means of determining whether his mode of citing such non-literary material showed the same deficiencies (hypercompression, disorder, casualness of choice, intellectual abdication) as Ambaglio (1990, 63–4) and others have detected in his use of the great historians (cf. Chapter 12 for a different perspective).

Given such handicaps, and given that the theme of the project goes against the grain of his interests and themes, it is scarcely surprising that the trawl yields limited results. Nonetheless, they are worth reporting, both for the light they throw on Athenaeus' methods and for the positive gleanings pertinent to the project. In so doing, I shall leave aside one major group of material which would otherwise come into question, that at 6.234d–248c, where he surveys Athenian *parasitoi* and most unusually supplements his more normal literary citations with extensive quotations from inscriptions. However, this material is fully discussed elsewhere[1] and is exceptional for its concentration, not (so far as I can see) for Athenaeus' methods of compilation or excerpting. The remaining relevant citations fall into two main groups:

(a) those which are more or less explicitly said to stem from inscriptions,
(b) citations from laws which may or may not derive indirectly from an inscription.

There are severe difficulties in using citations from group (b). As examples may be quoted his description of Spartan laws and customs (4.139c–143a), his description at 12.521bff. of Syracusan and Sybarite sumptuary laws, cited from Phylarchus (*FGrH* 81 F 45), and especially (as will become clear below) such citations of

Athenian laws and customs as he takes from the Atthidographers and elsewhere. The difficulties stem from three considerations. First is the near certainty, well documented in current scholarship (e.g. Nyikos 1941; Zecchini 1989a), that much of this material has been taken from literary sources (Philochorus, Phylarchus, Dosiadas, etc.), not directly from documentary sources. Second, there are clear indications that his purpose in citing laws was to illustrate customs, or even to adduce unusual words, rather than to present a code as such. Third, there must be a strong suspicion that though some citations might ultimately have had a genuinely documentary *Urtext* (e.g. the walls which carried the Athenian recodification of 410–399 BC), many if not most will have had no such tangible point of departure, and therefore cannot be safely used as case studies of transmission or of re-focusing.

It is therefore prudent to leave group (b) aside and to concentrate on the citations in group (a). In order to use the best material available for diagnosing Athenaeus' choices and methods, what follows here focuses on his profiles of citations of documents from the three richest documentary sources of Greece before his time, namely Delos, Delphi, and Athens. The initial guess that those would be the most rewarding sources is largely confirmed, as will appear, but one entertaining oddity may perhaps be quoted first:

**Text 1:** τοιοῦτος ἦν καὶ Ἀλέξαρχος ὁ Κασσάνδρου τοῦ Μακεδονίας βασιλεύσαντος ἀδελφός, ὁ τὴν Οὐρανόπολιν καλουμένην κτίσας. ἱστορεῖ δὲ περὶ αὐτοῦ Ἡρακλείδης ὁ Λέμβος ἐν τῇ τριακόστῃ ἑβδόμῃ τῶν ἱστοριῶν λέγων οὕτως· Ἀλέξαρχος ὁ τὴν Οὐρανόπολιν κτίσας διαλέκτους ἰδίας εἰσήνεγκεν, ὀρθροβόαν μὲν τὸν ἀλεκτρυόνα καλέων καὶ βροτοκέρτην τὸν κουρέα καὶ τὴν δραχμὴν ἀργυρίδα, τὴν δὲ χοίνικα ἡμεροτροφίδα καὶ τὸν κήρυκα ἀπύτην. καὶ τοῖς Κασσανδρέων δὲ ἄρχουσι τοιαῦτά ποτ' ἐπέστειλε· "Ἀλέξανδρος Ὁμαιμέων πρόμοις γαθεῖν. τοὺς ἡλιοκρεῖς οἴων οἶδα λιπουσαθεώτων ἔργων κρατίτορας μορσίμῳ τύχᾳ κεκυρωμένας θεουπογαῖς χυτλώσαντες αὐτοὺς καὶ φύλακας ὀριγενεῖς." τί δὲ ἡ ἐπιστολὴ αὕτη δηλοῖ νομίζω 'γὼ μηδὲ τὸν Πύθιον ἂν διαγνῶναι.

Such a man also was Alexarchus the brother of Cassandros the King of Macedon and founder of the city called Ouranopolis. Heraclides Lembus mentions him in Book 37 of his *Histories*, saying the following : 'Alexarchus the founder of Ouranopolis introduced peculiar expressions, calling the cock 'dawn-crier', the barber a 'mortal-shaver', the drachma a 'silveris', the *choinix* a 'day-feed', and the herald a 'loud-bawler'. Once he sent the following letter to the magistrates of Cassandreia: 'Alexarchus to the front-

205

fighters of Shared-Blood-Town, rejoice. Our sun-fleshed yeans, I wot, and dams thereof which guard the braes whereon they were born, have been visited by the fateful dome of the gods in might, fresheting them hence from the forsaken fields'. What this letter means I reckon not even the Pythian god could make out.[2]

(Heraclides Lembus, *FHG* III 169, F5 *ap.* Athen. 3. 98e–f)

The problem here is not Athenaeus' use of the *Histories* of his fellow 'Egyptian' Heraclides, for the three other known fragments also come through him, but how Heraclides knew of Alexarchus' letter. His ultimate source could have been an inscription, but the text he quotes consorts ill with the flavour of other Hellenistic royal letters, which are without exception formal and business-like. I have no solution to offer.

Less idiosyncratic is the material from Delos, whence the epigraphic harvest in Athenaeus is fairly productive. Three texts are worth quoting. One is unproblematic, viz.:

**Text 2:** Σῆμος δ' ἐν πέμπτῃ Δηλιάδος ἀνακεῖσθαί φησιν ἐν Δήλῳ χρυσῆν ἡδυποτίδα Ἐχενίκης ἐπιχωρίας γυναικός, ἥς μνημονεύει καὶ ἐν τῇ ἡ.

Semos in the fifth book of *Delias* says that there is on Delos a gold draught-sweetener dedicated by a local woman, Echenice, whom he also mentions in book 8.

(Semos of Delos, *FGrH* 396 F 9 *ap.* Athen. 11. 469c)

Since this Echenice is known from the Delos accounts as a real person, daughter of Stesileos II,[3] there is no difficulty in assuming that Semos' information came ultimately from an inventory, or even from the label attached to the object, and is reasonably reliable. However, one notes Zecchini's comment (1989a, 157–9) that though Athenaeus makes exceptionally extensive use of Semos, he may well have taken it indirectly, through a lexicon of unusual words, rather than direct from Semos. Much more problematic, but also much more informative, is a citation in Book Four:

**Text 3:** ὅθεν καὶ Πολυκράτων ὁ Κρίθωνος Ῥηναιεὺς δίκην γραφόμενος οὐ Δηλίους αὐτοὺς ὀνομάζει, ἀλλὰ τὸ κοινὸν τῶν Ἐλεοδυτῶν ἐπητιάσατο. καὶ ὁ τῶν Ἀμφικτυόνων δὲ νόμος κελεύει ὕδωρ παρέχειν ἐλεοδύτας, τοὺς τραπεζοποιοὺς καὶ τοὺς τοιούτους διακόνους σημαίνων.

Hence too, when Polycraton son of Crithon of Rhenaea brought suit against them he did not call them 'Delians', but accused the 'commonalty of table-dodgers'. And the actual law of the Amphictyones enjoins that the 'table-dodgers' are to provide water, meaning the table-layers and other such servitors.

(Athen. 4.173b).

Both sentences are part of the support cited for Apollodorus' statement (*FGrH* 244 F 151) that the Delians 'used to supply the services of cooks and table-makers to visitors arriving for the festivals' and that some had personal names derived from such functions (172f–173a). Of those personal names—Amnos, Artusileos, Artusitragos, Gongulos, Ichthubolos, Kreokoros, Kuminanthe, Magis, Sesamos, and Choirakos—two (Amnos and Artusileos) are indeed attested epigraphically on Delos in the fourth and third centuries BC, while two others (Sesame and Gongulos) are plausible formations.[4] It is therefore not impossible that epigraphically based information underlies Athenaeus' quotation, but the implausibility of the remaining names raises the suspicion that imagination—perhaps that of the writers of Middle or New Comedy—has been at work. Likewise, though an epigraphic origin for the terminology of Polycraton's lawsuit is not wholly impossible, neither his nor his father's name is known from Delos,[5] and the imputed occasion, of a collective Rhenaean action against Delians, recalls rather the mythic narrative of mutual legal hostilities between the two communities which is preserved from Hyperides' *Deliakos* by Sopater.[6] I should therefore be inclined to seek the origin of Athenaeus' material in the first part of Text 3 not in mundane epigraphy but in fourth-century comedy (for the names) and oratory (for the legal process).

However, that inclination should not be applied too readily to the second sentence of the citation. It is essential not to jump to the conclusion that in citing the 'law of the Amphictyones' Athenaeus must have been referring to the laws of the Amphictyony of Delphi–Anthela, which are preserved in part (for reasons which remain impenetrable) on an Athenian inscription of September 380 and were quoted (or misquoted) in part by Aeschines in 330.[7] The context in Athenaeus requires that the reference be rather to the *Delian* Amphictyony, known from fifth- and fourth-century epigraphic documentation as an institution under Athenian control until their loss of the island in 314.[8] The inference therefore has to be that he is quoting part of an otherwise wholly lost and unattested Law of the Delian Amphictyony. Since the archaic and classical sources for the *panegyreis* ('gatherings') on Delos conspicuously do not provide firm evidence for the hypothesis of a pre-Athenian Amphictyony,[9] it will be safer to assume that any such Law was an Athenian innovation, no doubt calqued on that of the Delphian

Amphictyony, and therefore that Athenaeus is preserving, at first or second hand, some memory of a fifth- or fourth-century document.

The third Delian example comes from the same context, wherein Athenaeus has been making his characters discuss types of cakes, and the consequential cult-names, or rude names, which were given to food-providers at the major sanctuaries of Delphi and Delos. He continues:

**Text 4:** Σῆμος δ᾽ ἐν δ᾽ Δηλιάδος "Δελφοῖς, φησί, παραγινομένοις εἰς Δῆλον παρεῖχον Δήλιοι ἅλας καὶ ὄξος καὶ ἔλαιον καὶ ξύλα καὶ στρώματα." Ἀριστοτέλης δ᾽ ἢ Θεόφραστος ἐν τοῖς ὑπομνήμασι περὶ Μαγνήτων λέγων τῶν ἐπὶ τοῦ Μαιάνδρου ποταμοῦ ὅτι Δελφῶν εἰσιν ἄποικοι τὰς αὐτὰς ἐπιτελοῦντας αὐτοὺς ποιεῖ χρείας τοῖς παραγιγνομένοις τῶν ξένων, λέγων οὕτως. "Μάγνητες οἱ ἐπὶ τῷ Μαιάνδρῳ ποταμῷ κατοικοῦντες ἱεροὶ τοῦ θεοῦ, Δελφῶν ἄποικοι, παρέχουσι τοῖς ἐπιδημοῦσι στέγην, ἅλας ἔλαιον, ὄζος ἔτι λύχνον, κλίνας, στρώματα, τραπέζας."

Semos in Book 4 of *History of Delos* says : 'To the Delphians who came to Delos the Delians provide salt and vinegar and oil and wood and bedding'. Aristotle or Theophrastus, speaking in the *Commentaries* about the Magnesians round the Maeandrus River as being colonists of Delphians, makes them fulfil the same services to foreigners present among them. He says: 'The Magnesians who dwell beside the Maeandrus River, sacred to the god, colonists of Delphians, provide to travellers a roof, salt, oil, vinegar, also lamp, beds, bedding, tables'.

(Semos of Delos, *FGrH* 396 F 7, and Aristotle,
*Hypomnemata historika* F 631 Rose, *ap.* Athen. 4.173e–f,
with Rougemont 1977a, 44)

Here, for once, as pointed out long ago by Bousquet and Amandry (see Rougemont 1977a), an extant text provides the basic explanation. This is the fourth-century agreement between Delphi and Sciathus,[10] which specifies what the Delphians were to provide for formal delegations of θεωροί ('sacred envoys') who came to Delphi: 'Δελφὸς δὲ [π]αρέχεν Σκιαθίο[ι]ς ἱστιατόρι[ο]ν, ξύλα, ὄξος, ἅλα' ('Delphians are to provide for Sciathians eating place, wood, vinegar, salt') (lines 24–7). We can safely assume that the stipulation cited by Semos was taken from a closely comparable epigraphical text which he (or, conceivably, an earlier *stelokopas* whom he was following) had seen at Delos and which specified what Delphian θεωροί visiting Delos were to be accorded as hospitality.

However, Athenaeus' second quotation here from Semos is less straightforward. Part of the problem is the need to determine, in the light of later sources, which of the various conflicting versions of the foundation myth of Magnesia on the Maeandrus was available to the author of the *Hypomnemata*.[11] More immediate, however, is the difficulty of deciding whether the author's information had a documentary basis. In respect of the list of facilities to be provided, comparison with the Delphi–Sciathus agreement strongly suggests that a similar document was available at Magnesia. However, the vagueness and limitless scope of the term τοῖς ἐπιδημοῦσιν contrasts oddly with the precision and bilaterality which normally characterize such agreements. Nor, moreover, would one expect to see in such an agreement the phraseology of the first half of the sentence quoted from the *Hypomnemata*. In fact, the citation as it stands would fit far more comfortably within a general manifesto issued by Magnesia as part of their successful efforts in the final years of the third century BC to raise the status of the festival of Artemis Leucophryene, for the citation echoes the emphasis on Apollo and on the Delphic oracles given to the colonists of Magnesia which is prominent in the monumental dossier of the festival.[12] However, on such a hypothesis either the imputed authorship of the citation would have to be abandoned, or it would have to be seen as a hybrid composed of components stemming from different chronological horizons. At present I see no means of deciding whether such a hypothesis can be sustained.

However, Text 4, for all its problems, does usefully transport us from Delos to Delphi, a sanctuary in whose monuments and documents Athenaeus shows remarkably little interest. He quotes little from the major guides and monographs devoted to the place which were in theory available to him: a single dubious citation from Anaxandridas of Delphi's *On the dedications pillaged at Delphi* (Περὶ τῶν συληθέντων ἐν Δέλφοις ἀναθημάτων),[13] one from Alcetas' *On the dedications at Delphi* (Περὶ τῶν ἐν Δέλφοις ἀναθημάτων) (Text 5 below), one from Polemon's *On the treasuries at Delphi* (Περὶ τῶν ἐν Δέλφοις θησαύρων) (Text 6 below), and none from Polemon's rejoinder to Anaxandridas or from the Δελφικά of Apollas (*FGrH* 266 F 1). To be fair, he is the only source to cite Theopompus' *On the goods pillaged at Delphi* (Περὶ τῶν ἐκ Δελφῶν συληθέντων χρημάτων),[14] and he provides one straightforward citation (from Hieronymus of Rhodes, F 48 Wehrli) of an inscription 'on a work' (ἐπί τινος ἔργου) made by Helicon of Salamis, whom Athenaeus knows as a historical person, a weaver from Cyprus (2.48b). However, the vagueness of the phrase ἐπί τινος ἔργου suggests that Athenaeus was not very interested in the actual object in its place in the sanctuary, and far more in his immediate context of beds, couches and their coverings above and below the body. It is perhaps otherwise with our next passage:

**Text 5:** αὐτῆς δὲ τῆς Φρύνης οἱ περικτίονες ἀνδριάντα ποιήσαντες

ἀνέθηκαν ἐν Δελφοῖς χρύσεον ἐπὶ κίονος Πεντελικοῦ, κατεσκεύασε δ'
αὐτὸν Πραξιτέλης· ὃν καὶ θεασάμενος Κράτης ὁ κυνικὸς ἔφη τῆς τῶν
Ἑλλήνων ἀκρασίας ἀνάθημα. ἔστηκε δὲ καὶ ἡ εἰκὼν αὕτη μέση τῆς
Ἀρχιδάμου τοῦ Λακεδαιμονίων βασιλέως καὶ τῆς Φιλίππου τοῦ
Ἀμύντου, ἔχουσα ἐπιγραφὴν 'Φρύνη Ἐπικλέους Θεσπική', ὥς φησιν
Ἀλκέτας ἐν β' Περὶ τῶν ἐν Δελφοῖς ἀναθημάτων.

Of Phryne herself the neighbouring peoples made a statue of gold and
dedicated it at Delphi on a pillar of Pentelic marble, and Praxiteles crafted
it. On seeing it Crates the Cynic called it a dedication of Greeks'
incontinence. This statue stood between that of Archidamus the king of
Sparta and that of Philip son of Amyntas, carrying the inscription 'Phryne
daughter of Epicles, of Thespiai', as Alcetas says in book 2 of his *On the
dedications at Delphi*.

(Alcetas, *FGrH* 405 F 1 *ap*. Athen. 13. 591b)

Here, exceptionally, Athenaeus does show—or reflect—an interest in the actual
object and its location. However, even so, given that this is his one quotation from
Alcetas, and given how thin his record of citation is from what was clearly an
extensive genre of writing in the later Hellenistic period, the exception has far
more to do with Phryne and with Athenaeus' obsessive interest in *hetairai* than
with Delphi itself.

His two other exhibits from Delphi show a timeless and contextless
quality. His one citation from Polemon's work on Delphi runs:

**Text 6:** Πολέμων δὲ ἢ ὁ ποιήσας τὸν ἐπιγραφόμενον Ἑλλαδικὸν 'ἐν
Δελφοῖς,' φησίν, 'ἐν τῷ Σπινατῶν θησαυρῷ παῖδές εἰσιν λίθινοι δύο, ὧν
τοῦ ἑτέρου Δελφοί φασι τῶν θεωρῶν ἐπιθυμήσαντά τινα
συγκατακλεισθῆναι καὶ τῆς ὁμιλίας μισθὸν καταλιπεῖν στέφανον.
φωραθέντος δ' αὐτοῦ τὸν θεὸν χρωμένοις τοῖς Δελφοῖς συντάξαι
ἀφεῖναι τὸν ἄνθρωπον· δεδωκέναι γὰρ αὐτὸν μισθόν.'

Polemon, or the writer of the work called *Helladikos*, says that 'At Delphi, in
the treasury of the men of Spina, there are two stone statues of boys. The
Delphians say that a sacred envoy who developed a passionate desire for
one of them was locked up together with it and left a crown as the price of
his intercourse. When he was detected and the Delphians consulted the
god, he bade them let the man go, on the ground that he had paid the
price.'

(Polemon, *FHG* III F 28 *ap*. Athen. 13.606a–b: Müller prints this as a

fragment of Polemon's *On the treasures at Delphi*, in spite of the title quoted
by Plutarch)

Not much can be got out of this story. As Athenaeus' citations in 13.605f–606b of
its congeners show, he is far more interested in its motif and its repetition than in
its setting or date. As a result, and disappointingly, he offers no help towards
identifying either the sculptor or the building, though the latter at least seems to
have been a notable affair.[15] More useful, in fact, though wholly unhistorical, is a
final Delphian citation:

**Text 7:** ἱστορεῖ δὲ τὰ αὐτὰ καὶ Φαινίας ἐν τῷ Περὶ τῶν ἐν Σικελίᾳ
τυράννων, ὡς χαλκῶν ὄντων τῶν παλαιῶν ἀναθημάτων καὶ τριπόδων
καὶ λεβήτων καὶ ἐγχειριδίων, ὧν ἐφ' ἑνὸς καὶ ἐπιγεγράφθαι φησίν·

> θάησαί μ'· ἐτεὸν γὰρ ἐν Ἰλίου εὑρέι πύργῳ
> ἦν, ὅτε καλλικόμῳ μαρνάμεθ' ἀμφ' Ἑλένῃ·
> καί μ' Ἀντηνορίδης ἐφόρει κρείων Ἑλικάων·
> νῦν δέ με Λητοΐδου θεῖον ἔχει δάπεδον.

ἐπὶ δὲ τρίποδος, ὅς ἦν εἷς τῶν ἐπὶ Πατρόκλῳ ἄθλων τεθέντων·

> χάλκεός, εἰμι τρίπους, Πυθοῖ δ' ἀνάκειμαι ἄγαλμα
> καί μ' ἐπὶ Πατρόκλῳ θῆκεν πόδας ὠκὺς Ἀχιλλεύς·
> Τυδείδης δ' ἀνέθηκε βοὴν ἀγαθὸς Διομήδης
> νικήσας ἵπποισι παρὰ πλατὺν Ἑλλήσποντον.

Phaenias records the same facts in his *Tyrants of Sicily*, viz. that the ancient
dedications and tripods and cauldrons and daggers were of bronze. On one
of them he says was inscribed :
> 'Behold me : for verily in the broad tower of Ilion / I was, when we
> fought around lovely-haired Helen :/ And Lord Helicaon son of Antenor
> carried me./ But now the sacred soil of the son of Leto holds me.'

On the tripod, which was one of the prizes offered in honour of Patroclus :
> 'I am a bronze tripod, and I am dedicated as an offering at Pytho,/ and
> swift-footed Achilleus staked me in honour of Patroclus./ Diomedes good at
> the war-cry, son of Tydeus, dedicated me,/ having won with horses by the
> broad Hellespont.'

(Phaenias of Eresos, F 11 Wehrli *ap.* Athen. 6.232cd)

In one sense, these two dedicatory inscriptions are non-problematic, for their
dramatic date during or just after the Trojan War palpably precludes any possibility
of the real transmission of a real document. However, that fact itself causes us to
ask who created them, when, and for what purpose, or why Phaenias picked them

up in the early third century BC, and why Athenaeus culled them from him. The last question is the easiest answered, since they provide ammunition for Pontianus' contention (6.231b) that gold and silver were rare in Greece until the dissemination of the Delphian treasures after the Third Sacred War. Equally, while the fact that nearly half of the known fragments of Phaenias' works (twenty-one out of forty-four) are preserved by Athenaeus might suggest some temperamental affinity between them, Phaenias' own agenda is barely discernible from the heterogeneity of his works. Beyond that we cannot safely go, for answers to the primary questions about these and other similar epigraphical inventions ostensibly referring to the Bronze Age will emerge only when the growing corpus of them can be reviewed as a group.[16]

If now we turn to Athenaeus for help with the epigraphical monuments of Athens and Attica, and if we leave aside the *parasitoi* documents, we get equally little guidance. He knows, indeed, that Heliodorus wrote fifteen books *On the Acropolis*,[17] but uses them only for the unlikely claim that Aristophanes the comic poet was from Naucratis and for a note on the words πύανος and ὀλόπυρος.[18] As for Craterus and his Ψηφισμάτων συναγωγή (*Collection of Decrees: FGrH* 342), the astounding fact is that Athenaeus displays no knowledge of his existence at all.

The Atthidographers and the Athenian law-code fare a bit better, but not much: the note of caution sounded at the start of this chapter applies. True, he does once (6.234c) refer to the Solonian *kyrbeis* (but without showing the least curiosity about them as objects), but otherwise what he quotes from such sources (mainly and very reasonably from Philochorus) is largely un-political and un-documentary. The biggest single group has to do with rituals, festivals and the mythology which underpinned Athenian religious and ritual life. The nearest we get in his citations to laws is (a) the prohibition against eating an unshorn lamb,[19] (b) the prohibition against eating oxen,[20] (c) a prohibition on the export of figs,[21] and (d) a prohibition against the sale of perfume by men.[22] Other Athenian examples (the *parasitoi* documents apart) amount to little in historical terms, though they have some documentary value. Such is our next passage:

Text 8: εὑρίσκω δὲ καὶ ψήφισμα ἐπὶ Κηφισοδώρου ἄρχοντος Ἀθήνησι γενόμενον, ἐν ᾧ ὥσπερ τι σύστημα οἱ προτένθαι εἰσί, καθάπερ καὶ οἱ παράσιτοι ὀνομαζόμενοι, ἔχον οὕτως· 'Φῶκος εἶπεν· ὅπως ἂν ἡ βουλὴ ἄγῃ τὰ Ἀπατούρια μετὰ τῶν ἄλλων Ἀθηναίων κατὰ τὰ πάτρια, ἐψηφίσθαι τῇ βουλῇ ἀφεῖσθαι τοὺς βουλευτὰς τὰς ἡμέρας ἅσπερ καὶ αἱ ἄλλαι ἀρχαὶ αἱ ἀφέται ἀπὸ τῆς ἡμέρας ἧς οἱ προτένθαι ἄγουσι πέντε ἡμέρας.'

I also find a decree passed at Athens when Cephisodorus was archon, in which the 'foretasters' are a sort of group, just like those called 'parasitoi'. It runs thus: 'Phocus proposed: in order that the Council may celebrate the Apatouria together with the other Athenians in accordance with ancestral custom, voted by the Council to release the Councillors for those days which other releasable officials (have), from the day when the foretasters celebrate for five days.'

(Athen. 4.171d, with Rhodes 1972, 30 and
Parker 1983, 157 n. 69)

Though there is uncertainty which Council (Areopagus or Council of 500) is in question, Rhodes and Parker take this decree at face value. That is probably correct, for the subject-matter is hardly such as a later generation would invent, but that is also a reason for unease, since while such one-off procedural matters as this would not normally rate perpetuation in a stone-cut inscription, it is hard to identify any other route by which the text could have been preserved to reach Athenaeus.

In contrast, the hypothesis of invention has at least to be considered in respect of the following:

**Text 9:** ἦν δ' ἡ Φρύνη ἐκ Θεσπιῶν. κρινομένη δ' ὑπὸ Εὐθίου τὴν ἐπὶ θανάτῳ ἀπέφυγεν· διόπερ ὀργισθεὶς ὁ Εὐθίας οὐκ ἔτι εἶπεν ἄλλην δίκην, ὥς φησιν Ἕρμιππος. ὁ δὲ Ὑπερείδης συναγορεύων τῇ Φρύνῃ, ὡς οὐδὲν ἤνυε λέγων ἐπίδοξοί τε ἦσαν οἱ δικασταὶ καταψηφιούμενοι, παραγαγὼν αὐτὴν εἰς τοὐμφανὲς καὶ περιρρήξας τοὺς χιτωνίσκους γυμνά τε τὰ στέρνα ποιήσας τοὺς ἐπιλογικοὺς οἴκτους ἐκ τῆς ὄψεως αὐτῆς ἐπερρητόρευσεν δεισιδαιμονῆσαί τε ἐποίησεν τοὺς δικαστὰς καὶ τὴν ὑποφῆτιν καὶ ζάκορον Ἀφροδίτης ἐλέῳ χαρισαμένους μὴ ἀποκτεῖναι. καὶ ἀφεθείσης ἐγράφη μετὰ ταῦτα ψήφισμα μήδενα οἰκτίζεσθαι τῶν λεγόντων ὑπέρ τινος μηδὲ βλεπόμενον τὸν κατηγορούμενον ἢ τὴν κατηγορουμένην κρινέσθαι.

Phryne was from Thespiae. On being prosecuted by Euthias on a capital charge she was acquitted. Euthias was so angry as a result that he never again pleaded a case, according to Hermippus. When Hyperides as advocate for Phryne was making no progress in his speech and the jurors were likely to convict her, he brought her forward into the open. Ripping away her undershifts and exposing her naked breasts he piled on the rhetorical lamentations at the sight of her and induced the jurors to feel superstitious awe, to give way to pity for the interpreter and servant of Aphrodite, and not to put her to death. After her acquittal a decree was subsequently

> passed that none of the advocates should indulge in appeals to pity and that the man or woman on trial should not be judged while in view.
>
> (Hermippus, *FHG* III F 66 and decree *ap.* Athen. 13.590d–e)

This anecdote presumably owes its preservation in Athenaeus to his concern with *hetairai*. Its credentials are highly dubious, not so much because it stems from Hermippus (though that is reason in itself),[23] or because it would not have been put on stone, as because its two clauses are an inappropriate way to try to prevent a repetition of Hyperides' melodramatic gesture: who was to decide what counted as an inappropriate degree of indulgence in appeals to pity, and how could a defendant be judged unseen when after all most of them were presumably male and conducted their own cases? My suspicion is that this decree is indeed a product of the document-manufacturing industry, perhaps coined in order to bolster the role of the γυναικονόμοι ('wardens of women') for whom Athenaeus quotes Philochorus elsewhere:[24] but if so it is a *late* product, emanating from a different horizon and betraying very different preoccupations from those which had driven the politicized reformulations of the early and mid-fourth century, i.e. the Peace of Callias, Congress Decree, etc.

One final theme needs to be explored, for no survey of Athenaeus and his use of documentary material would be complete without consideration of the ultimate *stelokopas* of antiquity, Polemon of Ilion. Polemon was the one man, in that terrifying succession of Hellenistic intellectuals, from Aristotle to Panaetius and beyond, who combined a reputation for serious and careful autopsy of inscriptions and monuments with a writing profile that made him a favourite quarry for Athenaeus. Here if anywhere we ought to be able to see the process of transmission of documents actually going on. Up to a point that is true, for no fewer than 45 of the 102 fragments collected in Müller's edition are quoted from Athenaeus. One may therefore contrast Athenaeus' extensive use of him with that made, e.g., by Plutarch (who quotes Polemon five times) or by Strabo (who quotes him twice only). Moreover, some of Athenaeus' citations look to have ultimately come from a seen physical document or monument. Eight such cases are probable:

F 1 (Athen.11.472c) (Text 10 below): dedication by Neoptolemus at Athens

F 3 (13.587c) (Text 12 below): Athenian decree

F 14 (13.577c): dedication by Lamia at Sicyon (for which see Griffin 1982, 78 and 152)

F 18 (13.574c): base of statue of courtesan Cottina at Sparta

F 20 (11.479f–480a): inventory of objects within the treasuries of Metapontum and Byzantium and the old temple of Hera at Olympia

F 44b (13.589a) (Text 11 below): grave monument of courtesan Lais in Thessaly

F 78 (6.234d–f): Athenian decree about *parasitoi* proposed by Alcibiades, *kyrbeis* about the *Deliastai*, dedication at Pallene in Attica, citation from 'laws of the (Athenian) king' (*archon*): it is not clear (see Müller ad loc.) how much of this material is from Polemon

F 79 (10.436d): funerary epigrams.

More dubious[25] are the following:

F 28 (13.606ab) (Text 6 above): possibly from a statue(-base) in the Spina treasury at Delphi

F39a (10.416b) and 39b (3.109a): notice of statues of Demeter Grain and Abundance in Sicily, perhaps ultimately drawn from the statue bases themselves

F 58 (5.210a): picture in a stoa at Phlious (but it is not clear whether Polemon is reproducing a title (or a label) or is describing what is depicted)

F 60 (11.484c): description of a statue of Dionysus Teleius (but no location stated)

F 63 (11.474c): description of a painting by Hipp(e)us at Athens of the marriage of Peirithoos

Three examples may serve to illustrate the various sub-genres represented on this list. *Dedications* form one, as instanced by F 1:

**Text 10:** Πολέμων δ' ἐν πρώτῳ περὶ τῆς Ἀθήνησιν Ἀκροπόλεως οὐδετέρως ὠνόμασεν εἰπών· τὰ χρυσᾶ θηρίκλεια ὑπόξυλα Νεοπτόλεμος ἀνέθηκεν.

Polemon in the first book of *On the Acropolis at Athens* referred to them in the neuter, saying 'The gold-plated wooden cups Neoptolemus dedicated'.
(Polemon F 1 ap. Athen. 11.472c).

This is straightforward, and is firmly datable in the 330s or the 320s if the dedicator is Neoptolemus of Melite (see *APF* 10652), as he almost certainly is. Equally straightforward are the *grave-epigrams*, among which the hetaira-theme recurs yet again, as in F 44b:

**Text 11:** Τίμαιος δ' ἐν τῇ τρισκαιδεκάτῃ τῶν Ἱστοριῶν ἐξ Ὑκκάρων· καθὰ καὶ Πολέμων εἴρηκεν ἀναιρεθῆναι φάσκων αὐτὴν ὑπό τινων γυναικῶν ἐν Θετταλίᾳ, ἐρασθεῖσάν τινος Παυσανίου Θετταλοῦ, κατὰ φθόνον καὶ δυσζηλίαν ξυλίναις χελώναις τυπτομένην ἐν Ἀφροδίτης

ἱερῷ. διὸ καὶ τὸ τέμενος κληθῆναι Ἀνοσίας Ἀφροδίτης. δείκνυσθαι δ᾽
αὐτῆς τάφον παρὰ τῷ Πηνειῷ σημεῖον ἔχοντα ὑδρίαν λιθίνην καὶ
ἐπίγραμμα τόδε·

> τῆσδέ ποθ᾽ ἡ μεγάλαυχος ἀνίκητός τε πρὸς ἀλκὴν
>  Ἑλλὰς ἐδουλώθη κάλλεος ἰσοθέου
> Λαΐδος· ἣν ἐτέκνωσεν Ἔρως, θρέψεν δὲ Κόρινθος·
>  κεῖται δ᾽ ἐν κλεινοῖς Θετταλικοῖς πεδίοις.

αὐτοσχεδιάζουσιν οὖν οἱ λέγοντες αὐτὴν ἐν Κορίνθῳ τεθάφθαι πρὸς τῷ
Κρανείῳ.

Timaeus however in the 13th book of his *Histories* (*FGrH* 566 F 24) <says
that Lais was> from Hyccara. Polemon has spoken similarly, saying that she
was murdered in Thessaly by some women after falling in love with a
Thessalian, Pausanias, being beaten to death with wooden footstools out of
envy and jealousy in a sanctuary of Aphrodite. Consequently <he says> the
sanctuary came to be called 'Of unholy Aphrodite', and that her tomb is
pointed out by the Peneius bearing as a marker a stone water-jar and the
following epigram:

> Once upon a time, proud Greece invincible in might /was enslaved by
> the god-like beauty of this woman, /Lais, whom Love engendered and
> Corinth nurtured./ She lies in the famous Thessalian plains.

So those who say she is buried in Corinth near the Craneion are
improvising.

(Polemon F 44 (b) ap. Athen. 13.589a)

Lastly, and (it has to be said) very unsatisfactorily for the project sketched at the
start of this chapter, the *decrees*. Apart from those concerned with the *parasitoi*, the
only other recognizable decree preserved through Athenaeus from Polemon is F 3:

**Text 12:** καὶ Νεμεάδος δὲ τῆς αὐλητρίδος Ὑπερείδης μνημονεύει ἐν τῷ
κατὰ Πατροκλέους. περὶ ἧς ἄξιον θαυμάζειν πῶς περιεῖδον Ἀθηναῖοι
οὕτως προσαγορευομένην τὴν πόρνην, πανηγύρεως ἐνδοξοτάτης ὀνόματι
κεχρημένην· ἐκεκώλυτο γὰρ τὰ τοιαῦτα τίθεσθαι ὀνόματα οὐ μόνον
ταῖς ἑταιρούσαις ἀλλὰ καὶ ταῖς ἄλλαις δούλαις, ὥς φησι Πολέμων ἐν
τοῖς περὶ Ἀκροπόλεως.

Hyperides mentions the flute-girl Nemeas in his *Against Patrocles* (F 142).
In her case it is right to ask in wonder how the Athenians allowed the
prostitute to be so named, bearing the name of a most famous festival, for
there had been a prohibition against giving such names not only to women

working as *hetairai* but also to other slave women, as Polemon says in his *On the Acropolis.*

(Polemon F 3 *ap.* Athen. 13.587c)

We should compare also the version preserved in Harpokration s.v. Νεμέας:

Χαράδα· Νεμέας αὐλητρίδος μνημονεύει Ὑπερείδης ἐν τῷ κατὰ Πατροκλέους, εἰ γνήσιος. ὁ δὲ Πολέμων ἐν τοῖς Περὶ Ἀκροπόλεως παρατίθεται ψήφισμα καθ᾽ ὃ ἀπείρητο Ἀθήνησιν ὄνομα πεντετηρίδος τίθεσθαι δούλῃ ἢ ἀπελευθέρᾳ ἢ πόρνῃ ἢ αὐλητρίδι. ἄξιον οὖν ἀπορῆσαι πῶς οὕτως ὠνομάζετο ἡ αὐλητρίς.

In a way, this is doubly disappointing. Not only does the concern with *hetairai* persist but also the substance of this decree is oddly parallel to that set out in Text 9 above and incurs suspicion on much the same grounds. However, that is also a considerable gain, in that the identity of provenance of the two texts, alike in Athenaeus' text and in his ultimate authority for them, allows us to begin to see them not as singletons but as (parts of?) a set, of as yet unknown origin and authorship. Such a putative set can therefore begin to be juxtaposed with the Bronze Age set, alluded to above, or with a Spartan set which is beginning to emerge from other sources, as well as with the Athenian Persian War set which is by now well identified (Habicht 1961). With luck such an approach to the material will eventually allow the various historiographical horizons to be identified more precisely.

The outcome of such a trawl through Athenaeus has therefore been helpful in a limited way. The four key points are clear enough:

(1)  He preserves only a meagre quantity of identifiable genuine epigraphic material, with little being taken even from sources such as Heliodorus or Polemon whom one might have expected him to use extensively.
(2)  The focus of what material there is (when not on words or on food) is on persons, especially *hetairai*, and concentrates interestingly on the 320s.
(3)  The material about the Athenian *parasitoi* stands out as exceptional, alike for its bulk, its concentration in one section of his text, and its likely high reliability.
(4)  There are some traces of material which may have been drawn from 'sets' of putatively manufactured decrees.

It remains to be seen whether other authors of the Early Empire, such as Plutarch or Lucian or Aelius Aristides, will show a comparable, or a very different, documentary profile of their past.

# PICTURING THE PAST
## USES OF EKPHRASIS IN THE *DEIPNOSOPHISTAE* AND OTHER WORKS OF THE SECOND SOPHISTIC

### by Ruth Webb

The descriptions of sumptuous symposia, festivals, processions and ships presented by Masurius in Book Five of the *Deipnosophistae* have received a scholarly treatment which is in many ways representative of traditional approaches to Athenaeus' work in general. Masurius' lengthy *tour de force* of recitation from Polybius and lesser known Hellenistic historians has been treated primarily as a repository of fragments to be reinserted into their Hellenistic context. Critical attention has then been focused on the distant events related in these descriptions, particularly Callixenus' accounts of Ptolemy Philadelphus' great procession in Alexandria (196a–203b) and of his magnificent ships of state (203e–206c).[1] The information is precious and the questions of the accuracy of the quotations presented by Athenaeus through the character of Masurius and of the reliability of the original passages are important ones. But in this play of mirrors the frame, Athenaeus' text, has tended to be neglected. My concern here is therefore not with the events and their Hellenistic context, known only to us at two removes, but with the possible functions of these second-hand descriptions within Athenaeus' work: how this section of Book Five fits into the dramatic situation of the *Deipnosophistae* and how such elaborate descriptive passages might have been understood by Athenaeus' audience. In order to suggest some answers to this latter question I will consider some of the uses and functions of ekphrasis in the rhetorical culture of the imperial period.

To begin with the immediate literary context, the sequence of lengthy quotations from Hellenistic sources begins abruptly as Masurius (who has been speaking since the beginning of Book Five) breaks off his monologue on feasts in Homer to quote Polybius' account of the extravagant behaviour of Antiochus IV Epiphanes which earned him the nickname 'Epimanes', 'The Mad' (193d–194c).[2] The symposia which were the occasion for Antiochus' eccentricities provide Masurius with a link between this and the previous section of Book Five. The king himself provides the link into Masurius' next quotation from Polybius, which is to be the first of the descriptive extravaganzas. Masurius begins his account of the games put on by Antiochus at Daphne in emulation of those instituted by Aemilius Paullus in Macedonia (*c*.166 BC), with the parade of magnificently-armed troops and display of wealth (194c–195f).[3] The summary account of the games which follows leads into more extravagant behaviour from Antiochus at the symposia, providing a neat closure to this Polybian section of the Book.[4]

The procession which opened Antiochus' games in turn provides the lead into the high point of Masurius' monologue: the procession arranged in Alexandria by Ptolemy Philadelphus (196a–203b), taken from Callixenus of Rhodes' work *On Alexandria*.[5] This description starts with the magnificent dining pavilion constructed for the occasion. Callixenus, as quoted by Athenaeus, then goes on to describe in detail the procession itself, the personifications, statues, women dressed as Bacchantes, a moving statue representing Nysa, fantastic wine vessels, *tableaux vivants* and a monumental golden phallus which were paraded through the city stadium.[6]

After finishing this long quotation, Masurius muses on the wealth of Egypt, enumerating the ships in Ptolemy's fleet, and it is this detail which leads to the next of his wonders, the palatial ships built by Ptolemy Philopator, which he claims to have read about in the same work by Callixenus (203e–206c). This in turn leads into an account of a ship built by Hiero II of Syracuse taken from a text by 'a certain Moschion' which Masurius claims to have read shortly before (206d–209). The account tells in detail how this feat of engineering was constructed (with the help of Archimedes), as well as describing the lavish interior.

The sequence of associations which leads Masurius from symposia to processions to ships is clearly indicated in the linking passages between the quotations. At the end of his recitation of Moschion's description Masurius himself draws attention to his digressions, acknowledging that he has allowed himself to venture on a 'catalogue of ships' of his own. The series of descriptive passages which takes up sections 194c–209e is thus clearly demarcated from the rest of Book Five by its presentation and its style. Instead of the patchwork of quotation and philological comment which is more familiar to readers of the *Deipnosophistae* we have substantial quotations evoking entertainment on an entirely different scale. These differences are enough to arouse curiosity about the function of these passages within Athenaeus' work.

However, we are given few internal indications of how to interpret them. We are told at 195f–196a that the other characters were amazed at the behaviour of Antiochus Epiphanes but no response is reported to the lavish descriptions which follow. So silent are the other characters, in fact, that when Masurius does come to the end of Moschion's account of the Syracusan ship, he is even compelled to invent a question such as Ulpian might have raised, about an obscure item of vocabulary (ἐγγυθήκη, 'vessel-stand') used by Callixenus (199c). The question reminds us that there has been an internal audience present throughout Masurius' recitation, as does an interjection by Ulpian himself (which only comes, however, as Masurius ends yet another section of his monologue, on gourmet kings and the reliability of Plato, and Xenophon's portrayals of Socrates). When Ulpian breaks in, once Masurius' flow of speech has run dry, it is to liken his fellow-diners to people drunk on words or turned to stone by the Gorgon's gaze (cf. Plato, *Symp.* 198c). The ensuing inevitable disquisition on gorgons draws the book, and this section of the proceedings, to a close. It is certainly tempting to see in this dramatic situation a case of Athenaeus poking gentle fun at the learned reciter, Masurius, but what of the other functions of the descriptions?

Some recurring themes in the *Deipnosophistae* can certainly be identified here. Athenaeus' interest in the Hellenistic period, when Greek rulers like Antiochus could rival Rome is certainly evident and, as if the verbal evocation were not enough, Masurius draws explicit attention to the wealth of the Hellenistic kings. Antiochus' 'madness' introduces a certain ambiguity, a moralizing note in line with the criticism of luxury elsewhere in Athenaeus. In this respect it is notable that Masurius mentions the end of the wealth of the Ptolemies, which was simply dissipated (206c–d). And, although no moral is explicitly drawn, one cannot help noticing that the account of Hiero's gigantic battleship ends with the observation that it was never used—it was simply too big for any harbour. Thus the celebration of abundance and power is tempered by examples of excess.[7]

However, these themes, interesting as they are, did not require the degree of detailed description which we find here. Despite the absence of internal response to these descriptions from the other diners, we can still speculate on the way in which such passages might have been received by the external audience, namely Athenaeus' readers. For the rhetorical theory of the Imperial period, with which we may assume the educated élite would have been familiar, can at least give us some idea of the function of such lavish description.

The descriptive passages from Athenaeus Book Five, starting with Antiochus' games, would certainly have been identifiable as examples of ekphrasis by any of Athenaeus' contemporaries who had received a basic rhetorical training. Ekphrasis was defined for students beginning their studies in the schools of the *rhetors* as λόγος περιηγηματικὸς ἐναργῶς ὑπ' ὄψιν ἄγων τὸ δηλούμενον, 'a descriptive speech which brings the subject matter vividly before the eyes' and it is in this sense (rather than the specialized modern sense of 'description of a work of art') that I use the term here.[8] The rhetorical handbooks which tell the student how to compose an ekphrasis are not particularly precise, but it is clear that ekphrasis was a detailed account of something, indeed anything (this is the force of the prefix 'ἐκ'—to relate thoroughly). It was the degree of detail which made an ekphrasis an ekphrasis and distinguished it from a plain narrative (Nikolaos, *Progymnasmata*, 68–9). In antiquity, ekphrasis was not restricted to any particular class of subject matter but in theory encompassed descriptions of persons, places, times and events (a list which means practically 'everything' within the conceptual frame of the rhetorician since it encompasses the four *peristaseis* or parts of narration which were susceptible to description).[9]

Masurius' passages, with their wealth of detailed information about the appearance of processions, buildings and ships would certainly fit the basic criteria for ekphrasis. Precise parallels can also be found in the rhetoricians' discussions of ekphrasis. A detailed account of the appearance of a monument, like Ptolemy's pavilion or the ships, was one type of ekphrasis represented by the model ekphrasis of the Alexandrian acropolis provided by Aphthonius in his fourth-century AD *Progymnasmata* (38–41). Events like Antiochus' games or Ptolemy Philadelphus' procession were also a canonical subject for ekphrasis in the Roman schoolroom. The earliest extant *Progymnasmata* text, that of Aelius Theon (first century AD), mentions some direct parallels from another Hellenistic source, Philistus. In discussing the use of ekphrasis in historiography, Theon mentions Philistus' accounts of Dionysius of Syracuse's funeral procession, including the decorated pyre (*FGrH* 556, F 28), and of his ship-building projects, a parallel to Moschion's account of the building of Hiero's battle-ship (Theon, *Prog.* 68.21–2). Theon's use of these examples shows both how the passages quoted by Masurius would fall within the category of ekphrasis as taught in the ancient schools and also how easily the rhetoricians assimilated the works of earlier periods into their own rhetorical categories.

The rhetoricians' remarks about ekphrasis, combined with examples of its use in the literature of the Second Sophistic, may help us to understand how Athenaeus' passages might have been received and how this type of description might have been more than a decorative interlude or a source of information and might moreover have played a special role in the depiction of the past. The distinguishing feature of ekphrasis for the ancient rhetoricians was the quality of *enargeia* ('vividness') which was said to make the audience seem to 'see' the subject matter, making them feel present at the events described.[10] Before the period termed 'Second Sophistic' by Philostratus, the ability of vivid prose to transport the listener was noted by Dionysius of Halicarnassus in his essay on Lysias.[11] For Dionysius, Lysias was a model of *enargeia*: ὁ δὴ προσέχων τὴν διάνοιαν τοῖς Λυσίου λόγοις οὐχ οὕτως ἔσται σκαιὸς ἢ δυσάρεστος ἢ βραδὺς τὸν νοῦν, ὃς οὐχ ὑπολήψεται γινόμενα τὰ δηλούμενα ὁρᾶν καὶ ὥσπερ παροῦσιν οἷς ἂν ὁ ῥήτωρ εἰσάγῃ προσώποις ὁμιλεῖν (Dion. Hal. *Lysias* 7). (No one who pays attention to the speeches of Lysias can be so inept or difficult to please or slow as not to feel that he sees the scenes taking place or that he is in the company of the characters which the rhetor introduces.)

Dionysius assumes that vivid language can make an audience feel as if the scene were being played out in front of them. One effect of *enargeia* was therefore understood to be the (illusory) abolition of temporal distance. Quintilian also refers to this time-defying quality when he uses the phrase '*tralatio temporum*' of the effect of *enargeia* ('*evidentia*' or '*sub oculos subiectio*' in Quintilian's Latin vocabulary) (*Inst. Or.* 9.2.41).

Dionysius' words are echoed by Quintilian in a better-known passage, in which he describes the reactions one should have when reading a particularly vivid part of Cicero's *Verrines* (*Inst. Or.* 8.3.64–5).[12] Here again Quintilian speaks of how the scene is brought so vividly before his mind's eye that he can see details not mentioned by Cicero. But the difference between the Latin and the Greek critic is telling: the distance in time between Dionysius and his example is far greater than that between Quintilian and Cicero. Dionysius' reader is transported from Rome to Athens, and what is more, unlike Quintilian reading Cicero, he is not just a spectator but seems to commune (ὁμιλεῖν) with Lysias' characters. Such a sense of the 'contemporaneity' of the classical past has been identified as a characteristic of the Second Sophistic which was vitally important to the Greek cities' sense of political and cultural identity.[13] The ability of *enargeia* to create the illusion that temporal distance can be abolished, making absent things seem present before the eyes of the listening audience, made it particularly suited to the methods and interests of Athenaeus and other authors of the Second Sophistic.

Nowhere is the apparent desire to commune with the past more striking than in the practice of declamation, which had its roots in the Hellenistic schools but became almost a form of popular entertainment in the Second Sophistic (at least if we are to believe Philostratus' *Lives of the Sophists*).[14] The declaimers' practice of taking on the *persona* of a character from the Golden Age of the Greek past is one way in which Greeks of the Roman period could quite literally converse with historical characters. This skill was practised in the schools through the elementary exercise of *ethopoeia*, but ekphrasis too, with its supposed ability to transport the listener to the scene described, could also contribute to this effect.

As Dionysius and the authors of *Progymnasmata* imply, readers of a vivid historian would be transported back to the events of the past. But they in turn would also be expected to be able to do the same to their own audiences in their declamations. The Greek treatise on declamation by Sopater Rhetor shows how this might work. In one example, modelled on Xenophon's account of the aftermath of the battle of Arginusae, the speaker is a general who has to defend his action in throwing the bodies of the dead overboard during a storm. The general must make his audience understand the imminent danger to the ship and the survivors. To do this the speaker must, according to Sopater, include an impressive ekphrasis of the storm. The plight of the Athenian generals at Arginusae, who found themselves accused of having abandoned shipwrecked sailors after the battle and then refused burial, is itself recorded as a theme tackled by Aelius Aristides, as both Philostratus and Hermogenes record.[15] Hermogenes cites Aristides' storm as a particularly effective example, suggesting that it made full use of rhetorical special effects to bring the urgency of the situation home to the audience.[16] Here, then, is one example of ekphrasis being used to display the events of the past to the Roman audience.

But this formulation, like the rhetoricians' claim to be able to make an audience 'see', elides many things, not least the degree of 'suspension of disbelief' and the collusion in the fiction demanded of the declaimer's audience. Most notably, the past that was evoked was a textual one, derived from the pages of the classical historians (with some imaginative rewritings of history for extra interest). In the case of Aristides' storm Xenophon lingers in the background and it is interesting to compare his treatment of the episode. Xenophon states in the briefest of terms that the generals' only defence was the magnitude of the storm which blew up after the battle, preventing them from setting out to sea again to bring help (Xen., *Hellenica* 1.7.3). From this stark statement the sophistic storms blew up. The declaimers' transposing of history was therefore just as much a rewriting of the texts of the past as it was a representation of the events.

This example of the use of ekphrasis in declamation, which it has not been possible to explore fully here, points to a complex phenomenon. The past can be made to seem present, but it is a textual past, made up (in the case of declamation) of a restricted repertoire of canonical characters and events. Another example of ekphrasis from Athenaeus' time, Philostratus' *Imagines*, shows a similar configuration of Greek past and Roman present, the former filtered through classical texts. The paintings which literally 'make present' events from the mythical past in the gallery described by Philostratus are also often based on literature, mostly poetic texts. The boy in the gallery, to whom the descriptions are addressed, is urged to act and react as if the scenes were really taking place before his eyes, and yet also to be aware of both the artist's technique and the literary background.[17] This interplay of illusion and lucidity parallels the experience of the reader who is made to 'see' the subjects of the paintings in imagination while being made aware of the sophist's verbal skill and his creative use of sources. Like the declaimers, Philostratus is engaged in retelling events recounted in a classical text in such a way as to abolish the distance and (theoretically at least) to make the new audience feel present at an event which is in fact related through a double lens of texts, namely, the classical model and the Second Sophistic reworking.

To return to Athenaeus, one effect of the borrowed ekphraseis woven into Book Five may well have been to make this past present for Masurius' audience within the text and also for the reader. In this case too an author brings before the eyes of his readers an event recorded in an earlier text, implicitly inviting them to make the events present in imagination, abolishing the distance of the levels of telling and retelling. This practice suggests that we should perhaps be careful about assuming that the only way in which Athenaeus might have altered his sources is by abbreviation. Elaboration is also a possibility. Indeed it has been suggested that in his account of Antiochus' games, the presence of gladiators might be Athenaeus' own invention, an addition which made the past event conform to the Roman present.[18] If that suggestion is correct, it is a clear example of Athenaeus making the past contemporary and a reminder of the importance of his conforming to audience expectations in the achievement of *enargeia*.[19] It also shows that in such ekphraseis it is past which is made present, rather than the opposite, and that the scene is indeed brought before the eyes of the audience.

But comparison with Philostratus and with the practice of declamation also shows up Athenaeus' peculiarities. Philostratus' mythological scenes are taken from the canonical works of Classical Greek literature: that is tragedy and Homer, as well as Pindar. These thoroughly familiar literary sources hover in the background as Philostratus reworks and recombines scenes to produce his own new distillation, just as Aristides and other sophists reworked Xenophon and other historians. Athenaeus' pictures take us into a different world: the splendour of the Hellenistic courts and the fabulous wealth of Egypt. In his appreciation of the splendid descriptions of the Hellenistic historians, Athenaeus (or his speaker Masurius) is also in keeping with his period.[20] But his choice of these and only these passages taken from obscure sources like Callixenus and Moschion is noteworthy. The choice of source alters the configuration of event, telling and retelling. Philostratus and the declaimers could expect their audiences to be familiar with the canonical versions of the scenes they evoke, but not so Athenaeus. Where the sophists and rhetors elaborate the raw material of classical text into ekphraseis, Athenaeus re-uses (as far as we can tell) an existing ekphrasis.

However, if Athenaeus cannot rely upon his readers' knowledge of the original text, nevertheless he ultimately ensures that they are made fully aware of it and that it is interposed between the new audience and the events described. As I mentioned at the beginning of this chapter, the sequence of spectacular scenes is brought to a close abruptly with a banal lexicographical comment. Having recited this catalogue of wonders—a 15-foot-high gold chest with gold vessels in it, elephants, giraffes, an image of Nysa which moved and so on—the only comment he can make is to say 'I am sure our dear Ulpian will ask us what the 'ἐγγυθήκη' mentioned by Callixenus is'. The comment adds to the gentle humour of Athenaeus' depiction of his characters: after such a verbal display of *enargeia*, the only response they can collectively summon up is a question on a point of vocabulary. But this pedantic point, which brings us back so suddenly from the sensual extravagances of a lost age to the dusty preoccupations of the sophists at dinner has other functions. It also serves to bring our attention back to the surface of the text.

As we have seen, discussions of *enargeia* in rhetorical treatises tend to focus on the imaginative and emotional impact of the mental images created by texts. The anticlimactic ending to Masurius' surfeit of *enargeia* in Book Five serves to re-establish the distance between past and present, which was temporarily abolished during his long quotations. We are reminded, brutally, that this museum, which has been established within Athenaeus' virtual library, is a museum of words. All that remains of Hiero's immense—and ultimately unusable—ship is Moschion's description and the hyperbolic epigram penned by a poet to celebrate Hiero's achievement (209c–e). The evanescent nature of the exhibits in Masurius' museum is still more clear when we remember that the spectacles described (from Antiochus' show of military strength to Ptolemy's pavilion and procession) are ephemeral, passing events, rather than enduring monuments, and they are dependent on verbal recreations.

In this chapter, I have tried to put one small element of the *Deipnosophistae* into the cultural context of Athenaeus' own period. I see the project of abolishing the distance between past and present as a characteristic feature of this context, which can be illustrated by reference to Philostratus' *Imagines* and to the practice of declamation. But the idiosyncrasy of Athenaeus also shows through, particularly the emphasis in his text on Hellenistic Egypt at the expense of Classical Athens. Even with respect to his chosen period, Athenaeus is wilfully different: just before making the transition from Ptolemy Philadelphus' procession to Philopator's ship, Masurius evokes a more mainstream achievement of the former: 'About the quantities of books and the establishment of libraries and the gathering in the

Museum what need is there to speak, these things are lodged in everyone's memories.' Athenaeus, in sharp contrast to the Philostratus of the *Imagines*, whose pictures reflect the memories of the standard classical curriculum and smack of the schoolroom,[21] is interested above all in the unusual, the uncommon example. In this he is reminiscent of the Alexandrians themselves.

❖ 16 ❖

# THE FEMALE-KINGS
## SOME ASPECTS OF THE REPRESENTATION OF EASTERN KINGS IN THE *DEIPNOSOPHISTAE*

by Maria Gambato

Athenaeus' curiosity and his passionate effort to preserve a world which had faded away caused him to explore—within the boundaries of his antiquarian and scholarly interests—some insidious and half-forgotten areas of ancient culture. In his survey of τρυφή, ('luxury', 'voluptuousness') to which the whole of Book Twelve of the *Deipnosophistae* is dedicated, Athenaeus describes a true γένος of the Antipodes, a race of 'reversed men' much like Lucian's Selenites: they are the Asian kings whom we meet at 12.528e–531a.[1] There the reader is introduced to a series of effeminate monsters as if to a sort of ethnographic curiosity. The patent oxymoron in the phrase 'female-kings' is of course a deliberate one: despite the peculiarly masculine role of kingship assigned to them,[2] these characters look nevertheless like female figures, not as a result of some freak of nature but because of their conscious drive for androgyny.[3] Indeed, Athenaeus' eastern kings embody effeminacy to the highest degree, affecting those typical womanly behaviours which are forbidden to men, and which in an orderly world mark the distinction between male and female roles.[4]

These kings lead a secluded life in their harems (Ninyas, 12.528f; Sardanapalus, 12.528f).[5] They wear women's clothes (γυναικεῖα στολή or ἐσθής: Sardanapalus, 12.529a; Androcottus, 12.530c; Annarus of Babylonia, 12.530e). They take care of their bodies in a womanly fashion (γυναικεῖος κόσμος,: Annarus, 12.539e, and see especially Sardanapalus, 12.528f). They are lustful, though sexually passive; thus Sardanapalus attempts to seduce Arbaces while playing the role of a lustful concubine (12.529a). Life among concubines means of course lasciviousness. Further, they are unfit for any sort of manly activity, as in the pathological instance of Sagaris, who takes food from the lips of his nurse (12.530c), while the royal functions are refused by Ninus (12.530e).[6] The presence of these 'kings' in Book Twelve is in my view remarkable for three principal reasons.

The first reason is of a general kind. The section dedicated to the female-kings represents both a discriminating and a clarifying feature in the seemingly shapeless sequence of *exempla* of τρυφή reviewed by Athenaeus in Book Twelve. It seems to have been the author's intention in that book to provide an exhaustive and detailed survey of τρυφή, a topic to be dealt with independently and at length within the larger framework of the meal. The intrinsic interest of the topic, and probably the novelty represented by a work entirely dedicated to its discussion,[7] prompt Athenaeus to write an unusually detailed disquisition in order to satisfy his friend Timocrates' request to learn about the most famous pleasure-loving people of the past and the sort of pleasures in which they delighted.

Athenaeus' answer comes in a rich and ambitious text opening with a sort of doctrinal introduction (12.510a–514e),[8] followed by a remarkable sequence of *exempla* arranged according to two different perspectives. The first is a general review κατὰ ἔθνη ('by peoples', 12.528e), discussing the most renowned cases of collective τρυφή. The second, κατ' ἄνδρα ('by individuals', 12.528e), is a rich collection of instances of individual τρυφή, largely drawn from the lives of famous people. Yet Athenaeus' plan fails to attain clear and original conclusions: the concept of τρυφή itself maintains its peculiar vagueness,[9] once more defying any attempt at clear-cut explanations. And the framework, based on *exempla* heavily drawn from fourth-century treatises on pleasure,[10] shows its faults, proving confused and at times contradictory. However, the female-kings, by offering a coherent idea of oriental androgynous τρυφή, help Athenaeus in his effort to define in more general terms the nature and excesses implicit in the concept of τρυφή.

The second reason concerns the arrangement of the subject matter within Book Twelve. Although Athenaeus does not openly state his purpose, a fundamental theme in his survey is the comparison of Asian τρυφή with its related historical counterparts in the western world. The issue is regarded from two different, though complementary, perspectives. On the one hand, τρυφή is imagined as a sort of epidemic disease spreading across peoples, increasingly contaminating and corrupting new regions, following in its westward movement the shifting fortunes of the powerful and prosperous ancient nations (especially in the review κατὰ ἔθνη, 'by peoples'). Eastern effeminacy first conquers the Persians, then contaminates the Lydians, the Etruscans, the Sybarites and the Ionian peoples, either because of geographical contiguity or as a result of cultural influence,[11] bringing about the decay and the destruction of empires and powerful cities.[12]

On the other hand, since the idea of τρυφή is intimately connected with that of kingship and of political power,[13] the individual *exempla* in Book Twelve provide instances of the western response to the eastern model, in patterns which reveal slight adaptations and the keeping of some distance from the original model (especially in the second part, τρυφή κατ᾽ ἄνδρα, 'luxury by individuals'). This accounts for the sequence of eastern sovereigns, illustrious Athenians, Spartans, Mede-like characters (affected with μηδισμός), Alexander the Great, Hellenistic monarchs, tyrants and so on. Since the female-kings described in the opening section represent the most oriental and ancient instances in the book, they set the pattern: western τρυφή, regarded in the context of the real lives of kings, tyrants and powerful rulers of the classical *polis* as well as of artists and philosophers, is more or less openly compared with the original model set by the androgynous kings. The oriental female-kings are a great negative paradigm which western kings have either recklessly adopted or reinterpreted according to their bent or instead resolutely rejected.

The third reason is the internal content of the section on female-kings itself. The list of *exempla* presented by Athenaeus includes Ninyas,[14] Sardanapalus,[15] the Phrygian Androcottus,[16] Sagaris the Mariandynian,[17] Annaros (ὕπαρχος (vassal) of the Persian king and sovereign of Babylonia)[18] and the Assyrian king Ninus.[19] We soon realize that only a few of them have some substance on historical grounds, whereas the majority can hardly be counted as much more than mere names, only recorded because of their power to evoke the fabulous γένος of the Antipodes. This aspect of Athenaeus' account is closely related to the original sources upon which he relied. These, in fact, did not show much concern with documentary issues and the gathering of historical evidence long before they were dissected by Athenaeus and made into isolated *exempla*. So much may be said of Ctesias' historiography, for example,[20] the markedly anti-hedonistic range of biographies—such as Clearchus' *Lives*—and the paradoxography of Mnaseas of Patara. With the exception of Sardanapalus, the female-kings become valuable instances for Athenaeus, not unlike the names of cups and of the different types of cakes. The outcome is a commonplace picture fully exploited by the author, based on the stereotype of oriental effeminacy. It is not so much the formulation of any sort of critical judgment on the issues which attracts the author's interest, as the topic of τρυφή itself, and in its most striking and self-evident aspects. Athenaeus' sylloge, in fact, reveals a circularity of reasoning typical of stereotyped thought,[21] and clearly shows how the cultural code (clearly not the author's but that of his sources, since Athenaeus always makes show of an amused detachment from his female-kings) is rooted in the misogynistic tradition, evidence of which we find in Greek culture from Hesiod and Semonides onwards. The female-kings are undoubtedly connected with the female type of the 'drone wife'[22]—a lazy, idle and lustful spendthrift, a squanderer of fortunes.

With the exception of Sardanapalus, Athenaeus' exemplary characters live secluded in a timeless dimension, in no relation at all to historical events, and are seen in their daily lives to be devoted entirely to the rites of pleasure. We may describe this typology as 'the daily life of the female-kings', as follows:

(1) The female-king spends his whole life within his palace (the royal ἄδυτον);
(2) and in the shade (σκιατροφεῖσθαι);
(3) protected by eunuch guards;
(4) among his concubines;
(5) dressed in rich, long women's clothes;
(6) shaved, depilated, his skin smoothed with pumice stone, with made-up eyes and painted face, perfumed with balms;
(7) snow-white, ἁπαλός and fat;
(8) idle or otherwise indulging in some lazy womanly activity: he languidly reclines ἀναβάδην, as he weaves and cards wool or purple cloth;
(9) has his meals to the sound of musical instruments and songs, cherished by dancers (preferably at night, by the light of oil-lamps);
(10) leads an intense erotic life with his concubines, with his eunuchs, with handsome boys (as a result of the corruption imported from Greece, as Herodotus records about Persians), and sometimes—as Theopompus reports about the Etruscans—even with his own wives.

Each of these distinctive aspects in the portrait of the female-king becomes a symptom of royal androgyny and—in the wider context of Book Twelve—a motif to be resumed, modulated and at times parodied. The resultant text testifies both to the coherence of the overall plan underlying Book Twelve (with all its ironic detachment) and to the central role in τρυφή held by the female-kings, with their distorted life-styles.

# ❖ 17 ❖

# SMYRNA
## SOPHISTS BETWEEN GREECE AND ROME

## by Keith Hopwood

Athenaeus' sophists meet in the house of Larensis, a Roman cultural dilettante.[1] Here, they display their knowledge of the Greek past and its culture for their Roman host. This cherishing of the Greek past has often been seen as an important feature of the Second Sophistic,[2] and was also part of Roman philhellenism.[3] The joint appreciation of this past was one of the ways in which Greek and Roman élite cultures could blend: to paraphrase Greg Woolf,[4] it was a way of staying Greek and staying Roman, using the shared cultural referent to experience a common sense of culture. It is worth considering the possible areas of cultural exchange available during the Second Sophistic; not for the period as a whole, since that is too vast an undertaking,[5] but to consider the phenomenon from the starting point of one city, embracing not just the high-fliers who attract the attention of Philostratus, but also the lesser sophists, *philologoi* and poetasters who provided much of the élite audience for the stars. Such a city, whose sophists are mentioned in Philostratus, and which has left copious epigraphical records, is Smyrna.

Smyrna[6] (modern İzmir) is located at the mouth of the river Hermos, at the head of an extremely large gulf, a location which prepared her for her role as a major entrepôt in antiquity and the early modern period.[7] Smyrna was not the principal seat of provincial government, which lay at Ephesus, but it was one of the centres visited by the proconsul in his assize tour.[8] It was far enough away from the capital to maintain an independent style, but still close enough for its leading citizens to have a voice there on frequent occasions.[9] It also had a suitable tradition of Hellenism, in that it had both Aeolian and Ionian credentials, and was widely believed to be the birthplace and home of Homer.[10] A local tradition closely associated him with the River Meles in particular: 'the River Meles, an excellent stream, with a cave at its sources, where, they say, Homer composed his poems.'[11] An earlier, panhellenic, tradition held that Homer was the son of the river god.[12] Aristides' citations of the River Meles flowing through earthquake-devastated Smyrna is both a literal description and a citation of the cultural heritage of this fine, now ruined city.[13] He could also cite the second founder of the city, Alexander the Great, in his letter to Marcus Aurelius and Commodus, urging them to emulate, or even surpass, their great predecessor.[14] The foundation was surrounded with its own mythic apparatus by the second century in both sophistic writers[15] and on coins,[16] dating largely to this period. Smyrna, then, was fully aware of its Greek heritage, but also existed as a city in the empire. Other studies have examined the ways in which the public face of the city responded to this dual identity.[17] In this chapter I hope to illuminate the complex management of identity undertaken by Greeks, as individuals or as groups, in Smyrna of the first and second centuries AD.

A revealing incident is related by Philostratus in his account of Apollonius of Tyana. After a prolonged absence in India, the sage stages his comeback at Smyrna.[18] His choice emphasizes Smyrna's credentials as a seat of Hellenism, and he chose his time of arrival with consummate care to emphasize both his own links to ancient Hellenic culture, and those of his prospective host city:

> When he approached Smyrna, the Ionians came out to meet him, since they were making the Panionian sacrifice at the time. He also received a decree of the Ionians in which they asked him to join their festival.[19]

Philostratus cunningly shapes the narrative to give prominence to his hero: returning to civilization, Apollonius encounters an *adventus* ceremony suitable to his intellectual and thaumaturgical stature which also, by mentioning the first-century inhabitants of Provincia Asia as 'Ionians', joins him to the revered past both of Greece and of the city he is honouring with his presence. However, it transpires that this is not an *adventus* ceremony, but the Panionian festival which was held by the major Ionian cities in turn.[20]

The position of the holy man is emphasized by the fact that this venerable, if reinvented, body should come before him as if he were an approaching dignitary. In the context of the Ionian past, we may think of Bias of Priene addressing the Panionian League concerning the Persian threat.[21] However, when Apollonius accepts the invitation of the Ionians, he also takes the opportunity to upbraid them, for, while reading the resolution, he

came across a name which was not Ionic at all, since appended to the motion was the name 'Lucullus'. So he sent a letter to the assembly criticizing them for their barbarism: he also found a 'Fabricius' and other people named in the resolution. His letter on the subject shows how severely he reproached them.[22]

Apollonius' rebuke highlights one of the tensions of the culture of the Second Sophistic: the identification of the Hellenised élite of the eastern Roman Empire with the culture of Rome herself. This problem was prominent in the late first century AD when the Greek east was adapting to turns away from philhellenism to indifference among the Roman élite. Later, in the early third century AD, this was less of a problem. An epitaph in good pseudo-Homeric verse from Colybrassus in Rough Cilicia commemorates Konon 'skilled in the Roman muse', namely law.[23] By the fourth century, such absorption of Roman culture was lamented by Libanius, as his most promising pupils in rhetoric defected to the same school in Berytus which had been Konon's *alma mater*.[24] We must not see the opposition between Greek and Roman identities as a constant in the Second Sophistic, for the developments within the period both emphasized and mitigated tensions. We cannot see how people in late first century Smyrna chose to present themselves from the epigraphic record, but an inscription of AD 124 gives us an insight into the choices of nomenclature in the early second century.[25] Here we have Claudius Bassus the agonothete, Lucius Pompeius, Claudianus the Prytane, Nymphidia the high priestess with Claudia Artemilla and Claudia Polla, Theudianos the stephanephoros (for the second time), Flavia Asklepiake, Isidore the sophist, Claudius Aristion and other such individuals. These persons were endowing a basilica, and we can see the mixture of Greek and Roman names that Apollonius had attacked only a generation earlier. There is no doubt that Smyrniotes had acquired Roman citizenship, and felt that to display their newly obtained honours was not incompatible with their Hellenic identity. The Roman identity is a complement to their local identity as Smyrniotes.

The links between panhellenic, or even Roman, culture and local identity surface in the career of the physician and sophist Hermogenes. He is almost certainly the Erasistratean physician mentioned by Galen[26] and mocked by Loukillios and Nikarchos in poems preserved in the *Palatine Anthology*.[27] Here we see the full range of interests of a Smyrniote man of letters who, with more favourable critical acclamation, might have attracted the notice of Philostratus. His local interests were represented in his works *On Homer's Wisdom, On Homer's Homeland, On Smyrna* (two books). He also wrote seventy-seven books on medical matters and other books to display his wide-ranging learning. He, like his contemporary the Elder Pliny, emphasized the breadth of his researches: *Foundations of the Cities of Asia* (two books), *Foundations of the Cities of Europe* (four books), *Foundations of the Cities in the Islands*, *Stadiasmi of Europe and Asia* (one book each), *Strategemata* (two books), and *Chronological Tables of Roman and Smyrniote Magistrates* (two books). Here was a man of prodigious learning who devoted his studies to the Graeco-Roman past. Like Plutarch, his younger contemporary, he seems to have attempted to explain Romans to Smyrniotes and Smyrniotes to Romans.[28]

Beyond the honorific, we know nothing of Hermogenes' role in Smyrna itself. In Philostratus, these years are dominated by Niketes, the first great Smyrniote sophist. He was much more the public orator who became so typical of the Second Sophistic, who 'sketched the types of the poor man and the rich, of princes and tyrants and handled arguments that are concerned with definite and special themes, for which history shows the way'.[29]

Niketes excelled in epideictic oratory and, again like many of the new sophists, eschewed performances before the general public (οὐκ ἐθάμιζεν ἐς τὸν δῆμον[30]), where his performances might be unappreciated by the uncultured.[31] Here we are introduced to the oligarchic nature of sophistic culture and performance. Learning was expensively acquired, and whether presented as the fruits of much research by Hermogenes, or as the ability to Atticize extempore by Niketes, it was clearly much more in conformity with the oligarchic political structures backed by hegemonic Rome.[32] Niketes was, however, prepared to perform in the law courts and perform those benefactions, known as *euergesiai*, which the élites of the Greek east carried out to embellish their cities and inscribe their superiority on the urban fabric.[33] The sophist was a patron of his native city, and his activities carried him beyond the province of Asia. We are told by Philostratus that Niketes had come into conflict with a consular *logistes* named Rufus over his harsh administration of Smyrna's finances,[34] which suggests that Niketes was intervening in relations between the city and the imperial government. Such a role brought prominence and danger,[35] in that the Roman official, as in the case of Rufus, might bear a grudge. The sophist, of course, by his skill and wisdom, mollified the scorned official.

He was succeeded by his pupil Skopelianos of Clazomenae who moved from his native city to Smyrna because

> the nightingale does not sing in a cage; and he regarded Smyrna, so to speak, as a grove in which he could practise his melodious voice, and thought it best worth its while to echo there. For while all Ionia is, as it were, an established seat of the Muses, Smyrna holds the most important position, like the bridge in musical instruments.[36]

The pull of Smyrna was becoming established. The history and literary precedence of the city made sure that aspiring rhetors came there. We can now perceive several generations of sophistic succession, as Smyrna enjoyed pre-eminence for over a century as the city of the sophists.

Skopelianos was descended from an extremely wealthy family whose members had been high priests of Asia[37] and were consequently accustomed to act as intermediaries between the Clazomenians and the Roman government. They also played their part in an institution of Roman foundation to harmonize relations between the provincial élites and the governor. The office entailed the presentation of games, largely Hellenic in form, but with the addition of gladiatorial games.[38] Such men already lived comfortably in the Roman administrative milieu and could combine that role with their function as arbiters of Hellenism within their own communities. This dual role was played not only by Philostratus' 'stars': an inscription from Smyrna commemorates Pomponius Cornelius Lollianus Hedianus as Ἀσιάρχην καὶ ῥήτορα at the beginning of the third century;[39] about him nothing else is known.

Skopelianos' eminence fitted him for his supreme moment when he went to Rome to plead before Domitian for the future of Asian viticulture.[40] He also took an active part in local politics, arguing cases in the council of Smyrna. His benefactions to Smyrna itself, however, were limited to the indirect ones accruing from his reputation: we are informed that Ionians, Lydians, Carians, Maeonians, Aeolians, Mysians, Phrygians, Cappadocians, Assyrians, Achaeans, Egyptians and Phoenicians attended his classes.[41]

His successor was Polemo of Laodicea, who also moved to Smyrna and established his school. In this, he resembled his predecessor Skopelianos and his successor Aristides, as well as numerous ambitious local aristocrats who moved to larger centres where their beneficence might be the more noted.[42] We are again struck by the similarity of the careers of sophists and less newsworthy councillors. Like the other sophistic luminaries of Smyrna, he found himself dealing with emperors and governors; unlike them, he carried himself with an arrogance that won him envy and admiration: 'He conversed with cities as his inferiors, emperors as not his superiors, and the gods as his equals.'[43]

His dealings with Hadrian won for Smyrna a grain market, a gymnasium, and a large temple, presumably for the imperial cult,[44] which brought for Smyrna its second neokorate. The relations between Hadrian and the city, culminating in his visit of AD 123/4, must surely have been mediated by the sophist. In return for these honours Smyrna instituted new games, the 'Olympia Hadriana', over which Polemo presided,[45] and managed the accounts. Although Smyrna does not at present figure in the list of those cities certainly participating in the 'Panhellenion',[46] Hadrian's patronage of the city and the transformation of the city's status and institutions attest to the integration of Smyrna within the emperor's scheme for the east: how could the city of Homer fail to benefit from a philhellene sovereign? Polemo's performance at the inauguration of the temple of Olympian Zeus in Athens confirms his and Smyrna's incorporation in the new order.[47]

Polemo also intervened in Smyrna's political troubles: διεστήκεσαν οἱ ἄνω πρὸς τοὺς ἐπὶ θαλάττῃ,[48] the classic problem faced by Peisistratos in archaic Athens.[49] We are not told what action Polemo took, but the problem was quickly solved. He clearly spent much time dealing with council business. His personal benefits to Smyrna lay in his attraction of students: 'He made [Smyrna] appear far more populous than before, since the youth flowed into her from both continents and the islands; nor were they a dissolute and promiscuous rabble, but select and genuinely Hellenic.'[50] Once again, a sophist who deals with Roman emperors can show that his followers are truly Greek.

But there was more to Polemo than his command of oratory: like his less famed predecessor Hermogenes, he was interested in the latest forms of knowledge, in his case physiognomics,[51] on which he left a treatise. Even when dead he benefited Smyrna, for a speech he had written was performed before Antoninus Pius at the emperor's request, and Smyrna's case prevailed.[52] His tomb, like Homer's, was never located, whether at Smyrna itself, or in his native Laodicea. The air of mystery emphasizes his status as Smyrna's second Homer.[53]

His successor was Aelius Aristides of Mysian Hadrianoutherae who also migrated to Smyrna where he achieved citizenship. Unlike the other figures we have been considering, his speeches are extant and his *Sacred Discourse* gives considerable information concerning the movements and preoccupations of a sophist. His orations for Smyrna link the city firmly into its Hellenic past which he was able to harness in his *Monody for Smyrna* and *A Letter to the Emperors concerning Smyrna* after the devastating earthquake. We have seen that he exhorted the emperors Marcus Aurelius and Commodus to emulate Alexander and become founders of Smyrna; the effect of his speeches was to ensure that among the Greek litterateurs, he held the honour of being οἰκιστής of the city.[54] His fame was entirely local: on his journey to declaim before the emperor in Rome in 143, he fell ill, and spent his time alternately convalescing near Smyrna and 'incubating' at the Asklepieion in Pergamum. His sophistic status had not been officially confirmed, so as a councillor he was deemed worthy to serve in those posts from which a certified teaching sophist was exempted. He was, consequently, several times importuned to take up various provincial and local offices. This was, of course, a gift which an ambitious man could not refuse, particularly in response to honours proposed by the local cities. In 148 he was nominated to the provincial assembly, but sent his agent Zosimos to counteract the move, and was duly returned only at third or fourth place.[55] Four years later, he was nominated ἐκλογιστής, a post charged with tax collection and, as always in antiquity, with making up any resulting shortfalls. This time the proconsul, Pollio, confirmed Aristides' election at the assizes in Philadelphia. Aristides was forced to recover the earlier verdict on his service, and hope that it would serve as an exemption. Fortunately, both the municipal authorities and the proconsul were satisfied.[56] However, the following year, his native Hadrianoutherae submitted his name on the list of men deemed worthy for service as *eirenarch*, or chief of police. He was clearly unsuited for the post because of ill health, and unwilling to disburse the necessary sums. This time, he was up against a more determined proconsul, Severus, who could trade on Aristides' honour and his own *dignitas*. After great difficulties, he secured his release, and was not further importuned.[57]

Intellectually, Aristides is more important for the *Sacred Discourse* than for his activities as a sophist and his periodic battles with Roman governors over exemption. However, as Peter Brown reminds us,[58] the sophists were leading the way in the reconceptualization of the holy that took place in the late second and early third centuries. Aristides' personal relationship with Asklepios can be viewed alongside Proteus Peregrinus' quest for the divine, or Alexander of Abonouteichos' 'invention' of the cult of Glycon. We might want to rationalize Aristides' stay at the Pergamene Asklepeion, and link with it Galen's contemporary residence there, but to do so is to lose the sense of the personal call of the god who constantly advises Aristides not only on his health and regimen, but also on how to deal with proconsuls in the cases considered above. A similar case of piety combined with sophistry is the φιλόσοφος Papinius who incubated in the shrine of Serapis, having prayed to the Nemeseis (presumably of Smyrna).[59]

Aristides' own virtues, as he believed, saved the city of Smyrna from further earthquakes:

> And on the one hand, they sent emissaries to Klaros and the Oracle was fought about, and on the other, holding olive branches, they made processions about the altars and market places and the circuit of the cities, no one daring to stay at home. And finally they gave up supplicating. In these circumstances, the god commanded me, who was then living in Smyrna, or rather in the suburbs of the city, to sacrifice publicly an ox to Zeus the saviour. ... So I boldly sacrificed. As to what happened next, who wishes to believe, let him believe, and who does not, to him I say farewell! For all those earthquakes stopped, and after that day there was no longer any trouble, through the providence and power of the gods, and by our necessary ministration.[60]

Aristides the wonder-worker foreshadows the sophists of Eunapius in his belief in the efficacy of his contact with the divine.[61] Contemporaries saw him in a broader context: an honorific from Alexandria praised him: 'ἀνδραγαθίαι καὶ λόγοις'.[62]

His successor had a more fortunate, if less distinguished, career. He was Rufinus, the grandson of Polemo. He receives only passing mention in Philostratus,[63] but is commemorated by his native city in an inscription as 'a fellow citizen of yours, who, through his vocation, in which he performed his *paideia*, spent his whole life in *logoi* as befits the sophists according to the divinely decreed exemptions from liturgies.'[64]

The commitment to the revived Greek culture was not limited to the 'stars' in Smyrna: they had a well-educated audience of potential equals, as Smyrna attracted foreign as well as home-grown talent. We have the epitaph of Agathocles, of Bithynian Nicaea, who was described as a '*philologos*' at only twenty.[65] Local talent included Daphnikos and Pistikos who also died young, but not before they had earned the title of 'sophist'.[66] All these young men would have been pupils or supporters of those whose careers are featured in Philostratus.

There were many exponents of Greek culture who eagerly proclaimed their new Roman names: Claudius Melampous was a hymnode and *theologos*, and his wife, Claudia Tryphosa, was a πομπαῖος.[67] Hymnodes also figured in the imperial cult: C. Claudius Pompeius was commemorated by his fellow hymnodes of the Divine Hadrian,[68] while a fragmentary inscription records the hymnodes of Hadrian who had performed at the inauguration of Smyrna's second neocorate on 23 September AD 124.[69] This was the occasion which Polemo's negotiation with Hadrian had brought about, a mark of particular imperial favour for the city. If Smyrna was not a member of the Panhellenion, she certainly held a place of high honour in Hadrian's eyes.

Beyond the sophists, there was a flourishing cultural life in Smyrna. We hear of a μειμολόγος, Sex. Julius Paratus,[70] and the pantomime artist Claudius Pylades.[71] The Dionysiac Artists, who were so important in Pergamene ceremonial,[72] are seen petitioning an emperor in a highly fragmentary text,[73] and using their collective resources to honour Hadrian,[74] perhaps on the occasion of his visit and the granting of the second neocorate. It may well be that their duties included some sort of show in his honour.

In the tradition recommended by Plutarch,[75] magistrates financed Greek games, and athletes were honoured. Ti. Claudius Rufus of Smyrna was honoured as victor in a local pankration,[76] while another's prowess in the same competition had won him citizenship in Smyrna, Ephesus, Cyzicus and Pergamum.[77] The most eminent athlete commemorated was M. Aurelius Antonius Lucius, a Smyrniote, who had prevailed in the Hadriana Olympia in Smyrna, the Olympia in Athens, the Aspis at Argos, the Nemean Games as both boy and man,[78] and was rewarded with bouleutic rank in Smyrna, and honorary citizenship in Athens, Ephesus, Pergamum, Cyzicus, Sardis, Miletos and Sparta. Others so honoured include the appropriately named runners Agathopous (δολιχοδρόμευς) and M. Aurelius Agathopous (the sprinter).[79] Excellence in the field of athletics was as conspicuous and well rewarded as excellence in sophistic performance.

The most prominent changes to the cultural life of the Greek city brought about by Roman influences were bath buildings and gladiatorial shows.[80] We hear of two *familiae* of gladiators available for hire in Smyrna, those of Apellikon[81] and of the Asiarch L. Timon.[82] This is a timely reminder that one of the duties of the Asiarchs, among whom several of the sophists we have been considering were numbered, was to put on these games in the Roman manner. They were at home with both the world of Greek culture and that of the Roman games. This union is epitomized by an early-third-century proconsul of Asia, L. Egnatius Victor Lollianus, 'μόνον καὶ πρῶτον τῶν ῥητόρων',[83] whose intellectual interests would have been balanced by his need to hold gladiatorial games and oversee the execution of criminals in the stadium at Smyrna.[84] We meet the man through an honorific inscription set up by his client L. Pescennius Gessius, the Asiarch, in the context of Greek-style games of the Council of Asia of which the proconsul was agonothete. Here, the worlds of Greek *agones* and Roman *munera* meet the sophistic culture.

Christians came before the governor in their interrogation and punishment. The martyrdoms of Polycarp and Pionius both illustrate the cultural life of Smyrna, as well they might, for both bishops had been educated in the same schools as the sophists and shared a common culture with them. The eirenarch, Herodes, bouleutes of Smyrna, gently chides the saint. When all else fails, the governor asks him to 'persuade the people'[85] (presumably that he should not be indicted). Polycarp was given the chance to give a speech before an audience, just like Niketes, who had pleaded with an angry governor a hundred years earlier. Like Niketes also, he refused to appear before the *demos*: 'I do not think them worthy to hear my defence.'[86] After his condemnation, the crowd demand the Asiarch Philip to throw Polycarp to the lions, but it is past the period in the assizes for these spectacles and so the saint is burned alive. Just as a century later, Lollianus the governor is associated with Gessius the Asiarch, so for the execution the anonymous governor presides with Philip the Asiarch.

Pionius' martyrdom has recently been studied in detail by R. Lane Fox,[87] so I shall concentrate on its cultural aspects. On his way to execution, Pionius is heckled by 'a certain Rufinus, one of those who had a reputation for excellence in rhetoric'.[88] The characteristically named rhetor receives in reply a suitably 'sophistic' response:

Is this your rhetoric? Are these your books? Socrates did not suffer this from the Athenians. Now each of you is an Anytos and Meletos. Were Socrates and Aristedes and Anaxarchus fools according to you because they practised philosophy, justice and endurance?

The response silences the orator. And so it should: for like all the best work of the sophists it is laconic and expressive. Delation of Christians in the Decian persecution has made informers of all those opposed to Christianity. By a deft twist, he identifies the persecuted Christians with the true philosophers and models of upright suffering bandied about the schools, indicating that the virtues for which they are so admired are now the property only of Christians, through their way of life.

Earlier, Pionius made his defence before the *demos* in the agora, beginning his speech with a proem worthy of Aelius Aristides: 'You men who boast of the beauty of Smyrna and of the River Meles, who claim to honour Homer....'[89] In this defence we find the treasuring of the past that has been seen as such a feature of the Second Sophistic, juxtaposed with the local pride in the amenities of Smyrna, provided by its élite, of whom the sophists formed so prominent but typical a part. It is this fusion of Greek past and Roman present which makes particularly poignant the meeting of Greek intellectuals as guests of a Roman aristocrat: their *euergetes*, as Pescennius Gessus honours Lollianus, governor of Asia.[90]

# SECTION IV:
# STRUCTURAL OVERVIEWS

# INTRODUCTORY REMARKS

Chapter 2 examined the structural devices which Athenaeus uses to pull the *Deipnosophistae* together, so as to make a whole out of its many parts. The two principal devices are the division into fifteen books and the 'internal dialogue' between the diners. The contributors to this section explore these and other devices which Athenaeus uses to give direction and coherence. Lucía Rodríguez-Noriega Guillén addresses squarely the division into fifteen books, arguing, in our view conclusively, that the notion of an original thirty books is a chimaera (see also Chapter 3). Guillén pays particular attention to the 'external dialogue', that is the exchanges between Athenaeus and Timocrates, as Athenaeus reports to his friend everything that was said at the feasts (the 'external' narrative reports the 'internal' dialogue). Guillén takes further recent scholarship, in particular Letrouit 1991, who shows that many of the fifteen books are framed at beginning and/or end by the 'external' dialogue.

Paola Ceccarelli also explores the internal and external dialogues of the *Deipnosophistae*. As with Chapters 4 and 29, she discusses Book Fourteen, on dancing and desserts. Ceccarelli shows that this content is subjected to a complex pattern of references which elides narrative voices and speakers. Not only is there much variety of speaker: there is also playful engagement with the time at which a narrative is set and with the process of encyclopaedic citation. Ceccarelli suggests that Athenaeus' strategy is playfully to engage both with the sources quoted and with his readers in a protean way that surprises and entertains. World-famous authorities on dance will not necessarily be quoted by Athenaeus in his main section on dance, not least because he is playing with cultural reference and meaning and not writing a straightforward work such as an encyclopaedia (cf. Chapter 27 for similar conclusions on his treatment of music).

Thereafter, Graham Anderson also explores Athenaeus' approach to his encyclopaedic material, concentrating in particular on the connection between food and drink on the one hand and poetry and wit on the other. Where Ceccarelli finds sophistication, Anderson finds excess: the temptation to include everything, he argues, was irresistible to Athenaeus. On this view, humour is ultimately sacrificed to sheer mass (on which, cf. Chapter 13).

Meanwhile, Luciana Romeri and James Davidson approach the *Deipnosophistae* from the perspective of the pleasure that is to be derived both from eating and from sympotic entertainment. Romeri builds on her study of sympotic literature (Romeri 1999), in which she showed that food (and to a lesser extent wine) were played down or problematized in the philosophical banquets of Plato, Plutarch and Lucian in order to highlight the proper philosophical pursuit of speech and thought. Athenaeus' approach, she showed, was quite different. His wise men (*sophistae*) at dinner (*deipnon*) managed to pursue orderly eating and orderly discourse at the same time. In the present volume, Romeri picks up the word *logodeipnon* ('dinner of words') which the Epitomator uses to describe Athenaeus' book (1.1b). And she shows that the internal narrative and internal dialogue are based on a tension between the pleasure of eating and the pleasure of speaking, a tension that is creative and not directed to the down-grading of eating. James Davidson takes up this theme, working from the apparent paradox that the subject-matter of the *Deipnosophistae* concerns the pleasures of eating, yet the presentation appears at first sight to be so pedantic as to make the reading of the work anything but pleasurable. He shows that the pedantry flows from the pleasure of the past remembered, that death and memory are strong themes. This is a new perspective on the uses of pedantry discussed in Chapter 2. Davidson also revisits Athenaeus' treatment of Rome, from a perspective different from that in Chapter 1, stressing both the discontinuities and the similarities between Greek and Roman culture within the *Deipnosophistae*. Tim Whitmarsh takes Athenaeus' relationship with Rome further. Focusing on the long discussion of parasites and flatterers in Book Six, Whitmarsh draws out the political and aesthetic elements of parasitism and explores how these are mapped on to the Roman setting of the meal of Larensis by the sophisticated Athenaeus. The relationship between Larensis and his guests is an ambivalent one. The guests reject parasitism and yet are guests of a very wealthy man, who offers a lavish and varied meal as a setting for their pursuit of the lavishness and variety of Greek rhetoric. Whitmarsh analyses themes of pleasure and power that Athenaeus evokes throughout the *Deipnosophistae*, and which he is at pains to offset, not least by the sharp banter between the guests, confirming the satirical tone and texture of much of this Menippean text. And all for Larensis, the new Varro (cf. Chapter 1).

The food in which guests and/or parasites took most pleasure, which most characterized a lavish banquet and which existed in the greatest variety, was fish. Antonia Marchiori explores the place of fish-consumption in the *Deipnosophistae*. There are many ramifications. Fish are the main topic of Books Six to Eight; parasites and gluttony are explored under the heading of fish-consumption; differences in fish consumption mark cultural difference, with Ulpian's Syria being the most distinctive (cf. Chapter 40); fish were a major topic of comedy (see Chapter 41). Fish were even notable in Homer—for their absence, as Malcolm Heath points out in the next section (Chapter 25). We are bound to infer that one reason at least for Athenaeus' enormous coverage of fish was its connection with good living and its almost total absence from sacrificial ritual, not to mention its rich and obscure vocabulary. This made fish a lively topic for a work concerned with luxury, gluttony, cultural identity, pedantry and ingenious banter. There is more interest in fish in the pages of Athenaeus than in those of almost any other Greek author. Marchiori pursues thoroughly this quintessentially Athenaean topic.

## ❖ 18 ❖ ARE THE FIFTEEN BOOKS OF THE *DEIPNOSOPHISTAE* AN EXCERPT?

by Lucía Rodríguez-Noriega Guillén

It is generally acknowledged that the extant version of the *Deipnosophistae* is an excerpt of a lost original, whose extent was twice the length of the present text. As is well known, this verdict is based on the existence of a series of marginal annotations in manuscript A (*Venetus Marcianus* 477), which indicate that the copied model had thirty units, usually understood to be thirty books. The annotations in question are the following:

**Book Three (96 D) fol. 14ᵛ (right margin):**
τῶν εἰς λ΄ τέλος τοῦ ε΄, ἀρχὴ τοῦ ϛ΄ (of the 30, end of the 5th one, beginning of the 6th one).

**End of Book Three, beginning of Book Four (128 A), fol. 29ᵛ (in the text, col. a):**
τῶν εἰς λ΄, ἀρχὴ τοῦ ζ΄ (of the 30, beginning of the 7th one).

**Book Four (154 A) fol. 43ʳ (central margin):**
τῶν εἰς λ΄ τέλος τοῦ ζ΄, ἀρχὴ τοῦ η΄ (of the 30, end of the 7th one, beginning of the 8th one).

**End of Book Four, beginning of Book Five (185 A), fol. 57ᵛ (in the text, col. a):**
᾽Αθηναίου Ναυκρατίτου Δειπνοσοφιστῶν τῶν εἰς λ΄ τέλος τοῦ η΄, ἀρχὴ τοῦ θ΄ (of the 30 of Athenaeus of Naucratis/ Deipnosophists, end of the 8th one, beginning of the 9th one).

**Book Five (201 B) fol. 65ᵛ (right margin):**
τῶν εἰς λ΄ τέλος τοῦ θ΄, ἀρχὴ τοῦ δεκάτου (of the 30, end of the 9th one, beginning of the 10th one).

**End of Book Five, beginning of Book Six (222 A) fol. 76ᵛ (in the text, col. b):**

τῶν εἰς λ΄, ἀρχὴ τοῦ ια΄ ς΄ (of the 30, beginning of the 11th one, 6).

**End of Book Six, beginning of Book Seven (275 B), fol. 101ᵛ (in the text, col. a):**

τῶν εἰς λ΄, ἀρχὴ τοῦ ιγ΄ ζ΄ (of the 30, beginning of the 13th one, 7).

**Book Seven (297 C) fol. 111ᵛ (right margin):**

τῶν εἰς λ΄, τέλος τοῦ ιγ΄, ἀρχὴ τοῦ ιδ΄ (of the 30, end of the 13th one, beginning of the 14th one).

**End of Book Seven, beginning of Book Eight (330 C) fol. 128ʳ (in the text, col. a):**

Ἀθηναίου Ναυκρατίτου Δειπνοσοφιστῶν τῶν εἰς λ΄, ἀρχὴ τοῦ ιε΄ η΄ (of the 30 of Athenaeus of Naucratis/ Deipnosophists, beginning of the 15th one, 8).

**End of Book Eight, beginning of Book Nine (366 A), fol. 149ʳ (in the text, col. a):**

τῶν εἰς λ΄, ἀρχὴ τοῦ ις΄ θ΄ (of the 30, beginning of the 16th one, 9).

**End of Book Nine, beginning of Book Ten (411 A) fol. 178ʳ (in the text, col. a):**

τῶν εἰς λ΄, ἀρχὴ τοῦ ιζ΄ ι΄ (of the 30, beginning of the 17th one, 10).

**End of Book Ten, beginning of Book Eleven (459 C) fol. 210ʳ (in the text, col. a–b):**

Ἀθηναίου Ναυκρατίτου Δειπνοσοφιστῶν <τέλος τοῦ> ι΄, <ἀρχὴ τοῦ> ια΄ (of Athenaeus of Naucratis' Deipnosophists, <end of Book> 10, <beginning of Book> 11).

**End of Book Eleven, beginning of Book Twelve (510 A) fol. 245ᵛ (in the text, col. a):**

Ἀθηναίου <τέλος τοῦ> ια΄, <ἀρχὴ τοῦ> ιβ΄ (of Athenaeus, <end of Book> 11, <beginning of Book> 12).

**End of Book Twelve, beginning of Book Thirteen (555 A) fol. 278ᵛ (in the text, col. a–b):**

<τέλος τοῦ> ιβ΄, <ἀρχὴ τοῦ> ιγ΄ (<end of Book> 12, <beginning of Book> 13).

**End of Book Thirteen, beginning of Book Fourteen (612 F–613 A) fol. 315ᵛ (in the text, col. b):**

Ἀθηναίου Ναυκρατίτου Δειπνοσοφιστῶν <τέλος τοῦ> ιγ΄, Περὶ Γυναικῶν, <ἀρχὴ τοῦ> ιδ΄ (Of Athenaeus of Naucratis' Deipnosophists, <end of Book> 13, Concerning women, <beginning of Book> 14).

**End of Book Fourteen, beginning of Book Fifteen (665 A), fol. 348–349 (in the text):**

<τέλος τοῦ> ιδ΄, <ἀρχὴ τοῦ> ιε΄ (<end of Book> 14, <beginning of Book> 15).

**End of Book Fifteen (702 C) fol. 372ᵛ (in the text, col. b):**
Ἀθηναίου Ναυκρατίτου Δειπνοσοφιστῶν <τέλος τοῦ> ιεʹ (Of Athenaeus of
 Naucratis' Deipnosophists, <end of Book> 15).

Starting from this premise, several other arguments have been offered in
order to corroborate the proposition that the work has not survived in a complete
form, and that, as a consequence of the work of an epitomizer, its original
structure has become blurred. The prestige of Kaibel, one of those in favour of
this thesis, has undoubtedly had much to do with the persistence of this idea,
developed in the present century, among others, by K. Mengis, in addition to A.M.
Desrousseaux, the Budé editor, contrary to the case of such as G. Wissowa and I.
Düring, who have brought weighty arguments against it.[1]

In recent years, however, voices have been raised against the *communis
opinio* that the *Deipnosophistae* consisted originally of thirty books. Thus
Hemmerdinger echoes Schweighaeuser's opinion,[2] who asserted in the introduction to his edition that the endings and beginnings of the various books confirmed
beyond all doubt that the division in fifteen books came from Athenaeus himself.
More recently Letrouit[3] has made the most telling attack on the thesis for an
abridgement; he has recalled our attention to Wissowa's and Düring's works, and
offered a new explanation for the marginal annotations of the *Marcianus*. In short,
Letrouit's theory argues that the copyist of the exemplar of A undertook the
transliteration of the work from the format of the roll to that of the codex, and
found the work contained in thirty *volumina* or rolls, numbered from one to thirty,
whose content did not coincide with the work's internal division into fifteen
books. So the marginal annotations simply refer to these thirty rolls.

Letrouit's explanation seems rather convincing, but, what of the other
arguments that have been adduced to support the abridgement theory? In my
opinion, all of them are equally refutable, as I will try to prove by examining the
most important.

Kaibel's main reason in support of the above-mentioned theory was that
Macrobius had used Athenaeus as a direct source for his *Saturnalia*, but that the
version of the work known to him was greater in extent than the present one.[4]
However, this idea has been rejected by Wissowa,[5] who has provided weighty
arguments to prove that both authors used common sources, apart from sharing
some traditional elements of sympotic literature. It must be added that Wissowa's
opinion is not even mentioned by Desrousseaux in his introduction.

Another of Kaibel's arguments rests on the fact that in Book Twelve,
which appears as a long *excursus* addressed by Athenaeus to Timocrates, the author
says in 541a: οἶδα δὲ κἀγὼ παρὰ τοῖς ἐμοῖς Ἀλεξανδρεῦσιν λαύραν τινὰ
καλουμένην μέχρι καὶ νῦν Εὐδαιμόνων ('but I also know myself of a lane in my

own Alexandria still called "Rich Man's Row" to this day').[6] Now, as Athenaeus was not a native of Alexandria, but of Naucratis, Kaibel thought that these words were originally uttered by another character, namely Plutarch of Alexandria. According to Kaibel, the man who abridged the work also altered the dialogue form of the original book or, we should say, books, to eliminate some of the interventions of the characters. Even though he did it to great perfection, and managed to make the whole of Book Twelve look like a digression of Athenaeus, this small detail remained as a trace of the original version, which was longer and in dialogic form.

However, it does not seem so strange to us that Athenaeus, who came from Egypt and very possibly lived for some time in Alexandria, considered this city as a sort of country of adoption, just as other guests at the dinner feel themselves to be Athenians, despite the fact that they are natives of other countries, as Düring pointed out.[7] Thus in 9.366a Ulpian of Tyre speaks of οἱ ἡμεδαποὶ Ἀθηναῖοι ('our native Athenians'), and in 9.406d he says Ἐλευσῖνι τῇ ἐμῇ ('in my own Eleusis'). And Myrtilus of Thessaly also refers in 13.583d to αἱ καλαὶ ἡμῶν Ἀθῆναι ('our beautiful Athens'). Therefore Kaibel's argumentation loses strength, even more if we bear in mind that, as he himself points out, Book Twelve coherently maintains the form of an *excursus* that Athenaeus addresses on his own account to Timocrates, and that, finally, the alleged original dialogue form has left no other trace, if we discard this one.

On the other hand, there are several books that, as a whole or in part, look like a lexicon or catalogue. According to Kaibel, responsibility for this format, and also for the fact that in some books the dialogue has been reduced to long interventions of just two or three characters, must be taken by the excerptor, who compressed and even suppressed dialogues, often obviating the transition from one subject to another. Nevertheless, this mistake in composition can be attributed to Athenaeus himself, who subordinated the work's formal perfection to the display of its erudite contents. So, for instance, in 7.277c Athenaeus tells Timocrates that he will arrange the fish names alphabetically, in order to help him remember what had been said without any difficulty. His words are: ἵνα δὲ εὐμνημόνευτά σοι [i.e., Timocrates] γένηται τὰ λεχθέντα, κατὰ στοιχεῖον τάξω τὰ ὀνόματα ('to make it easier for you to remember what was said, I will arrange the names alphabetically'). Something similar is also introduced in 9.368f, where the author says: ἑξῆς δὲ τούτων πολλῶν καὶ παντοδαπῶν ἐπιφερομένων ἡμεῖς ἐπισημανούμεθα τὰ μνήμης ἄξια ('although many viands of all kinds were brought in successively after those we have mentioned, we shall indicate those only which deserve record'), as well as in 14.616e, where Athenaeus explains that he will omit the speakers' names to sum up: πολλῶν οὖν πολλάκις ὄντων τῶν ἀκροαμάτων καὶ τῶν αὐτῶν οὐκ αἰεί, ἐπειδὴ πολλοὶ περὶ αὐτῶν ἐγίνοντο λόγοι, τὰ ὀνόματα τῶν εἰπόντων παραλιπὼν τῶν πραγμάτων μνησθήσομαι ('well, we often had many entertainments, not always the same, and since there was much talk about them, I will omit the speakers' names and mention what was done'). All this can sometimes be due to the fact that such material had not been thoroughly elaborated by Athenaeus, so the text retains the form and arrangement of a lexicographical source. But frequently he just seems to feel the need of not extending himself too much, and he achieves it by omitting the dialogue, so that he may concentrate on the erudite topics.

Mengis stands out among those who have claimed the existence of an original version of the *Deipnosophistae* in thirty books. He considered that the excerptor made a quite new version of the work, making one banquet out of what once were several banquets given by Larensis.[8] His theory is based on the clear references to three different days made in 10.459b, 11.459f and 14.664f, where we read:

Τοσαῦτα καὶ περὶ τῶν γρίφων εἰπόντων τῶν δειπνοσοφιστῶν, ἐπειδὴ* καὶ* ἡμᾶς ἑσπέρα καταλαμβάνει ἀναπεμπαζομένους τὰ εἰρημένα, τὸν περὶ τῶν ἐκπωμάτων λόγον εἰς αὔριον ἀναβαλώμεθα*. κατὰ γὰρ τὸν Μεταγένους Φιλοθύτην· "κατ' ἐπεισόδιον μεταβάλλω τὸν λόγον, ὡς ἂν καιναῖσι παροψίσι καὶ πολλαῖς εὐωχήσω τὸ θέατρον", περὶ τῶν ἐκπωμάτων τὸν λόγον ἑξῆς ποιούμενος.

This long discussion by the Deipnosophistae on the subject of riddles having ended, since* evening has* also* overtaken us while thinking over all that had been said, let us[9] postpone the discussion of drinking-cups until to-morrow. For, as Metagenes says in *Fond of Sacrifices*: 'I vary my talk, episode for episode, that I may delight the audience with a feast of side-dishes new and many', taking up the subject of the drinking-cups in what follows (10. 459b).

"Ἄγε δή, τίς ἀρχὴ τῶν λόγων γενήσεται," κατὰ τὸν κωμῳδιοποιὸν Κηφισόδωρον, ἑταῖρε Τιμόκρατες, συναχθέντων* γὰρ ἡμῶν καθ' ὥραν μετὰ σπουδῆς διὰ τὰ ἐκπώματα;* ὁ Οὐλπιανός, ἔτι καθημένων ἁπάντων, πρὶν καί τι διαλεχθῆναι, ἔφη ...

('Come now, what shall be the beginning of our recital', as the comic poet Cephisodorus puts it, friend Timocrates, since* we have * gathered early, spurred to eagerness for the cups?*[10] While all the guests were still seated, and before conversation had begun, Ulpian said ... etc.) (11.459f).

Τοσούτων καὶ περὶ τῆς ματτύης λεχθέντων ἔδοξεν ἀπιέναι· καὶ γὰρ ἑσπέρα ἦν ἤδη. διελύθημεν οὖν οὕτως

After all this had been said on the subject of the 'mattyê' we decided to leave; for by this time it was evening. So at this point we dissolved the meeting (14.664f).

According to Mengis, in each one of these days as many dinners were held. Furthermore, taking into account the lack of proportion in the volume of text occupied by those alleged three banquets (the first one would take place during the first ten books; the second one, over four books, from eleven to fourteen; and the third, in the space of only one book, fifteen), Mengis hints at the possibility that in the original version each of the thirty books included the narration of an independent day and banquet,[11] as in Plutarch's Συμποσιακὰ προβλήματα. Mengis sees another trace of this former frame in the fact that in 8.361e-f the banquet is said to have occurred on the Roman feast of the Parilia, in April, while in 9.372b and 9.372d the text seems to set the action in winter time, in January. Athenaeus' words are:

> Τοιούτων οὖν ἔτι πολλῶν λεγομένων τότε ἐξάκουστος ἐγένετο κατὰ πᾶσαν τὴν πόλιν αὐλῶν τε βόμβος καὶ κυμβάλων ἦχος ἔτι τε τυμπάνων κτύπος [...] ὁ οὖν Οὐλπιανὸς 'ἄνδρες' ἔφη, 'τί τοῦτο; 'εἰλάπιν' ἠὲ γάμος; ἐπεὶ οὐκ ἔρανος τάδε γ' ἐστίν'.

> While much talk of this nature was still going on, right then was heard all through the town the ringing notes of flutes, the crash of cymbals and the beating of drums, accompanied by voices in song. It so happened that it was the festival of the Parilia [...] Therefore Ulpian said: 'What is that, gentlemen? Is it a solemn banquet, or a wedding? For surely this cannot be a dinner to which all men bring their share' (8.361e–f).

> χειμῶνος δὲ ὥρᾳ ποτὲ κολοκυντῶν*[12] ἡμῖν περιενεχθεισῶν

> Once, in the season of winter, gourds* were served to us (9.372b).

> ἐθαυμάζομεν οὖν τὰς κολοκύντας* μηνὶ Ἰανουαρίῳ ἐσθίοντες

> We wondered, as I was saying, that we should be eating gourds[13] in the month of January (9.372d).

Gulick adds a third contradiction to the list, namely that in 3.99e the dinner party is set during the dog-days, in the height of summer. Athenaeus' words are:

> πρὸς ταῦτα ὁ Οὐλπιανός πως ἡδέως γελάσας "ἀλλὰ μὴ βάυζε" εἶπεν, "ὦ

ἑταῖρε, μηδὲ ἀγριαίνου <u>τὴν</u>\* κυνικὴν προβαλλόμενος λύσσαν <u>τῶν ὑπὸ κύνα οὐσῶν ἡμερῶν</u>\*, δέον αἰκάλλειν μᾶλλον καὶ προσσαίνειν τοῖς συνδείπνοις, μὴ καί τινα Κυνοφόντιν ἑορτὴν ποιησώμεθα ἀντὶ τῆς παρ᾽ Ἀργείοις ἐπιτελουμένης"

To this Ulpian, with a pleasant smile, replied: 'Nay, do not bark, comrade, nor grow savage, shooting forth the\* canine madness of \*[14] the dog-days; rather, you should fawn on and wag your tail at your fellow-guests, lest we turn our holiday into a dog-slaughter like the one celebrated at Argos').

Nevertheless, a close examination of those texts allows us to conclude that just one of the aforementioned passages, that of Book Eight indicates without doubt the date when the action of the *Deipnosophistae* takes place, the Parilia, whose main day was 21 April. On the other hand, there is no need to interpret the other two texts as unmistakably referring to the date of the banquet. In fact, what is said in 9.372b is this: 'once, in the season of winter, gourds were served to us, etc.' Judging by what is affirmed further on, the anecdote in question belongs to another occasion when (at least) part of the same group of guests assembled at Larensis' residence, but the adverb ποτέ ('once') places it in an indeterminate point of the past in relation to the 'present' dinner party. As for the mention of the dog-days in 3.99e, it is just one of the many puns and mock allusions to the Cynics made by Ulpian, and not a reference to the time of the year when the banquet is held.

With regard to the three meetings inferred from the other passages highlighted by Mengis, the key to their interpretation and to understanding the actual structure of the *Deipnosophistae* lies in the analysis of the formal procedures used by Athenaeus. Three of them have been pointed out by Düring,[15] and a fourth has been added by Letrouit.[16] They are the following:

(1) Internal dialogue, in direct speech, among the wise men who attend the banquet.
(2) Internal narration, by means of which the author sets out the content of the conversations held during the dinner, but without recording them in direct speech.
(3) External dialogue, in direct speech, between Athenaeus and Timocrates.
(4) External narration, through which the author informs the reader about the external background, that is, his meetings with Timocrates.

Bearing this in mind, the pattern of the *Deipnosophistae* can no longer be seen as an almost shapeless conglomeration of topics, full of contradictions and inconsistencies, the result of the careless work of an excerptor, as Mengis and others put it.

According to the technique of the narrative dialogue, characteristic of the sympotic genre, the work begins with the conversation between two characters, in this case Athenaeus himself and his friend Timocrates, who asks him for an account of what was said during a banquet which has been very much talked of in Rome. Timocrates seems sometimes to be accompanied by other anonymous hearers, as it can be inferred from 5.222b, where we read: ἐπὶ τούτοις τοῖς λόγοις ἀναχωροῦντες οἱ <u>πολλοὶ</u>* λεληθότως διέλυσαν τὴν συνουσίαν ('at these words most of them*[17] withdrew, and gradually dissolved the party').

This dialogue frames the central part of the work, in which Athenaeus describes the discussions of the guests at the banquet, and the banquet itself, alternating dialogue in direct speech (internal dialogue) and narration (internal narration). Then, due to the great extent of the corpus, Athenaeus has chosen to begin (and commonly also to end) each book as an external dialogue, or else as an external narration; besides, these modalities are only used at the beginning and end of the different books. The detail of this structure is shown in the following diagram:

### Outline of the structure of the Deipnosophistae
### 1st part: Introduction: Appetizers

| One | Two | Three | Four | Five |
|---|---|---|---|---|
| Extern. dial. | ? | ? | Extern. dial. | Extern. dial |
| *internal modalities* | *internal modalities* | *internal modalities* | *internal modalities* | *internal modalities* |
| ? | Extern. dial. | Extern. dial. | Extern. dial. | Extern. narrat. (A. and T. part) |

### 2nd part: Dinner (up to the middle of Book Ten)

| Six | Seven | Eight | Nine | Ten |
|---|---|---|---|---|
| Extern. dial. (new day) | *(Intern. dial.)* Extern. dial. | Extern. dial. | Extern. dial. | Extern. dial. |
| *internal modalities* | *internal modalities* | *internal modalities* | *internal modalities* | *internal modalities* |
| Extern. narrat. | Extern. dial. | Extern. dial. | Extern. narrat. | Extern. narrat. (A. and T. part) |

**3rd part: Symposion** (from the middle of Book Ten)

| Eleven | Twelve | Thirteen | Fourteen | Fifteen |
|---|---|---|---|---|
| Extern. dial. | | Extern. dial. | Extern. dial. | Extern. dial. |
| *internal modalities* | Extern. dial. | *internal modalities* | *internal modalities* | *internal modalities* |
| | | | External narrat. (A. and T. part) | |
| Extern. dial. | | | | Extern. dial. |

In general, external dialogue and external narration are quite brief, consisting frequently in just a few lines, but sometimes Athenaeus indulges in longer digressions, as happens for example at the beginning of Books Four and Six, and all through Book Twelve.

At the same time, and for the sake of verisimilitude, the author makes his long conversation with Timocrates take place in more than one day, and thus they part and meet again on several occasions. When this is stated in the modality of external dialogue, there is no ambiguity about it. But it so happens, however, that many times the author prefers the modality of external narration. And it is here where Mengis and many others with him miss the point, by taking as references to the internal dialogue data that really belong to the conversation with Timocrates. In other words, the different days pointed out by Mengis belong to the meetings of Athenaeus and Timocrates, which are at least four, and not to several meetings of Larensis' guests. In relation to this it must be pointed out that in 11.459f it is necessary to place the question mark after the name Οὐλπιανός, and not after Τιμόκρατες, since the preceding genitive absolute does not refer to the guests of the banquet, but to Athenaeus and Timocrates. The text has been quoted above according to this new punctuation.

On the other hand, on several occasions the subject of a book is announced at the end of the preceding one. So it is at the end of Books Three, Nine, Ten and Eleven. These announcements contribute to the cohesion of the work.

In short, the fifteen books of the *Deipnosophistae* appear as the account of a single banquet and what was said in it, narrated by Athenaeus to his friend Timocrates in the course of several encounters (even though there are allusions to former dinner parties at Larensis' house among the events dealt with in the work). As the author of the *Epitome* points out in 1.1b, Athenaeus has composed his work in such a way that its structure reflects the arrangement of the feast. Thus, as Martin pointed out,[18] we have a preliminary part (Books One to Five) which includes the introduction and meeting of the guests, their first conversations and the appetizers. This first section also contains several digressions of Athenaeus, always on subjects related to the banquet in general. Next comes the dinner (Books Six to mid-Ten), where many different matters are treated, though the culinary ones prevail. Finally the symposium takes place (middle of Book Ten to Fifteen), during which the guests drink, pay attention to several entertainments, and above all discuss several topics, but always related to what is happening at the feast. We can appreciate that each one of the three parts has approximately the same extent, five books. As for the beginning of the work, even though the *Epitome* has failed to preserve the introduction in its complete form, with mentions to the place, occasion, and members of the meeting, many elements taken from this lost introduction can however be traced in the excerptor's work.[19] On the other hand, it must not be forgotten that in 5.186d–e Athenaeus himself suggests that literary dialogues ought to begin with a prologue of this kind:

Ἡμεῖς δὲ νῦν περὶ τῶν Ὁμηρικῶν συμποσίων λέξομεν. ἀφορίζει γὰρ αὐτῶν ὁ ποιητὴς χρόνους, πρόσωπα, αἰτίας. τοῦτο δὲ ὀρθῶς ἀπεμάξατο ὁ Ξενοφῶν καὶ Πλάτων, οἳ κατ' ἀρχὰς τῶν ξυγγραμμάτων ἐκτίθενται τὴν αἰτίαν τοῦ συμποσίου καὶ τίνες οἱ παρόντες. Ἐπίκουρος δὲ οὐ τόπον, οὐ χρόνον ἀφορίζει, οὐ προλέγει οὐδέν. δεῖ οὖν μαντεύσασθαι πῶς ποτ' ἄνθρωπος ἐξαπίνης ἔχων κύλικα προβάλλει ζητήματα καθάπερ ἐν διατριβῇ λέγων

We will now talk about the Homeric symposia. In these, namely, the poet distinguishes times, persons, and occasions. This feature Xenophon and Plato rightly copied, for at the beginning of their treatises they explain the occasion of the symposium, and who are present. But Epicurus specifies no place, no time; he has no introduction whatever. One has to guess, therefore, how it comes about that a man with cup in hand suddenly propounds questions as though he were discoursing before a class.

The transition from the external to the internal modalities is sometimes rather careless, as can be seen for instance in 4.134d, where one of the guests, Plutarch, suddenly appears speaking, with no transition, after an *excursus* addressed by Athenaeus to Timocrates. In the inside of the different books, the modalities of internal dialogue and narration usually combine with a predominance of the former, according to the conventions of the sympotic genre. On the other hand, the conversation advances by itself, as in a real talk, and it is the development of the banquet that allows the introduction of the different topics discussed. The banquet also inspires other more speculative subjects, such as the different philosophical conceptions of pleasure. A word incidentally mentioned or a question posed by one of the guests are other of the means used by the author to introduce new topics. Though as a rule there has to be a main topic every time, it will be constantly interrupted by digressions on marginal subjects, which result in a very complicated plot.

On the other hand, the interventions of the characters are usually very long, because the author shows his erudition in each one and, besides, the association of ideas brings about a continual jump from one subject to another most of the time. As a result, in some books the dialogue is reduced to the contributions of only a few characters, a fact that does not require the intervention of an excerptor to be explained.

Also, Athenaeus frequently uses the modality of internal narration, by means of which he gives us an account of the events during the feast, and of the talk's main contents. This format implies the breaking-off of the work's dialogic form, which diminishes its formal perfection, but it has a practical reason, namely, to prevent some of the books from reaching a disproportionate extent, and to display the erudite material in a clearer way.

In short, as Letrouit argues, the fifteen books of the *Deipnosophistae* actually appear as a unitary and well-constructed work with regard to its structure and composition. The work as a whole is very suitably characterized by the use of the modalities of external dialogue and narration at the beginning and end of books, and nowhere else. Inside each book, the internal dialogue and narration develop as the feast goes on, though the action is sometimes interrupted by some digressions of the author. It is true, however, that Athenaeus is more interested in the contents of the work than in its structure, and proves sometimes to be rather careless in its composition.

Finally, I am going to analyse another argument, adduced this time by Desrousseaux,[20] in defence of the existence of an original version of the *Deipnosophistae* in thirty books. It is as follows. In δ 1152 the *Suda* quotes Athenaeus as its source on mentioning the titles of several comedies by the poet Diodorus of Sinope. The first of them, *The Flute-girl*, is said to appear in Book Ten of Athenaeus, and so it is in fact (it is mentioned in 10.431c). The other two, *The Heiress* and *Men attending a festival* are reported to be quoted in Book Twelve; this piece of information, however, does not coincide with Athenaeus' text. In fact, the latter is not in the *Deipnosophistae. The Heiress*, on the other hand, is indeed quoted, but not in Book Twelve, as the *Suda* states, but in Book Six, twice (in 235e and 239a). From this fact Desrousseaux inferred that this could be a vestige of the *Suda*'s knowledge of a former version of the *Deipnosophistae* in thirty books. According to him, the aforesaid Book Twelve is not the present one, but that of the original redaction in thirty, which in our version would correspond to Book Six, according to the equation: 12 out of 30 equals 6 out of 15. Even though in the introduction to her edition of the *Suda* A Adler[21] points out that this lexicon knew a version of the *Deipnosophistae* in fifteen books, Desrousseaux thinks it possible that a trace of the alleged division of the work in thirty books would have been preserved, due to a contamination of the sources. In fact we ought to be aware that the titles of the comedies were not taken by the *Suda* directly from Athenaeus, but from an intermediate source, probably the unabridged version of Hesychius' *Lexicon*.

Desrousseaux' idea, however, is groundless. To begin with, it would be strange that the *Suda* only showed a single trace of the alleged version of the *Deipnosophistae* in thirty books, the rest of its testimonies being unanimous in alluding to the one we know, in fifteen. But furthermore, at least another passage can be adduced where the book indicated by the *Suda* does not agree with Athenaeus' text, and where a parallel explanation to the one given by Desrousseaux for δ 1152 may be ruled out. In fact, in δ 3018 the *Suda* attributes to Athenaeus' Book Fourteen the mention of three comedies by Eriphus, *Aeolus*, *The Infantry-man*, and *Meliboea*. These works are, in fact, quoted by Athenaeus, not in Book Fourteen, but in Books Three (*Meliboea*), Four (*Aeolus*, and *The Infantry-man*), and Seven and Fifteen (*Meliboea* in both of them). In this case it cannot be supposed that the Book Fourteen mentioned is that of the alleged version in thirty, or that it has to be identified with the number seven of the present version, for Eriphus's quotations are distributed among many other books of the *Deipnosophistae*, apart from Book Seven. Nor is this the only time that the text of the *Suda* proves inaccurate in quoting Athenaeus; for example, in β 1709 it attributes to Plato the comic poet several comedies that in the *Deipnosophistae* (that is mentioned as source, this time without specification of the book) are really assigned to Bato, among them one entitled *Men attending a festival*, that, oddly enough, is not quoted by Athenaeus, as also happens in the case of the homonym comedy by Diodorus of Sinope. It is plain, therefore, that in citing Athenaeus the *Suda* frequently shows corruptions, errors or inaccuracies, and that the divergence between both works cannot be ascribed to the fact that the *Deipnosophistae* had a longer version than the one known to us. And, of course, there is no evidence at all that the *Suda* had any news of a division of the work into thirty books, contrary to Desrousseaux's opinion.

Finally, it does not really seem that there are well-founded reasons to admit that the present version of the *Deipnosophistae* is an excerpt of an original of much greater length. The combination of the work's internal analysis and of Letrouit's new explanation for the marginal annotations in manuscript A points out that, leaving aside some gaps and, of course, the lost pages of the *Marcianus*, partially reconstructed through the *Epitome*, the version of the *Deipnosophistae* we know is substantially the same that came out from Athenaeus' pen.

# 19

# THE λογόδειπνον
## ATHENAEUS BETWEEN BANQUET AND ANTI-BANQUET

### by Luciana Romeri
(translated by Kerensa Pearson)

**Viaticum**  To read Athenaeus very often means 'to use' Athenaeus, that is to say to draw on his work as the source, the sometimes irreplaceable and unique source, of a multitude of quotations of all genres (comedy, tragedy, history, philology, geography, etc.). Yet, if we all agree the *Deipnosophistae* has preserved the widest variety of texts, which would otherwise have remained unknown to us, it is also true that there is a tendency to take out of context the different quotations brought to us by Athenaeus, and to read them as they are without reference to the 'sympotic context' in which they are delivered. In this sense, Athenaeus is apt to be thought of as a compiler pure and simple. Thus his work is rarely tackled as a whole. The *Deipnosophistae* is thus destined in some ways to suffer the same fate as the texts which it has transmitted and made known: it is in its turn fragmented, or rather only transmitted (and thus known) as the fragments from which it is made up.

It must indeed be admitted that because of the length, contortion and even the pedantry which sometimes characterize the discourse of the guests, the text is not always an easy read; all the more because the uncontrolled succession of interruptions gives at times an impression of disorder and disorganization in the text. However, precisely in order to be able to follow the variety of characters and the multiplicity of speeches, it is necessary to consider the book of Athenaeus as a unitary work, complete as a whole. In other words, it is because it is about a long banquet (with the different phases that make up a banquet) that the *Deipnosophistae* is made up of long speeches and it is in reading the whole as an account of a banquet that one can follow the order of the speeches that reflect the typical disorder of a banquet. In this sense, Athenaeus himself is, in my opinion,

less a simple compiler than a true author and editor of his own text.[1] Athenaeus'
presentation of a banquet 'narrative' will be my first topic in my reading of the
*Deipnosophistae*. By following the structure of this long account of a meal of scholars
we will, I think, find a key to its reading and an unexpected perspective on the
internal cohesion of the work of Athenaeus which at first sight seems so
haphazard.

The best way to decipher this mode of presentation is to read what is said at the
beginning of Book One of the *Deipnosophistae* by the Epitomator, in his presentation of Athenaeus' book. This abridged reading of Athenaeus' text gives us the
benefit of being a kind of synopsis, an overview of the text, while allowing some
precise elements of the text to remain. These become in my view paradigmatic
(1.1a–c):[2]

## The taste for knowledge

> Athenaeus is the father of the book and addresses his discourse to
> Timocrates. The title is 'The Deipnosophist' ['Δειπνοσοφιστής'].[3] The
> subject of the discourse is the Roman Larensis, a man famous for his
> situation in life. He invites as his guests the most learned men of all, in
> every kind of education. Thanks to them, among all the finest things, there
> is nothing that Athenaeus fails to mention. In his book he brings in fish,
> their uses as well as explanations of their names [ἰχθῦς τε γὰρ τῇ βίβλῳ
> ἐνέθετο καὶ τὰς τούτων χρείας καὶ τὰς τῶν ὀνομάτων ἀναπτύξεις]—
> then every kind of vegetable and all animals [καὶ λαχάνων γένη παντοῖα
> καὶ ζῴων παντοδαπῶν], as well as men who wrote history, authors, in a
> word, wise men [καὶ ἄνδρας ἱστορίας συγγεγραφότας καὶ ποιητὰς καὶ
> ὅλως σοφούς[4]] and musical instruments, endless series of jokes,
> differences in drinking cups. He also surveyed the wealth of kings, the
> great ships and all the other things that I could not relate with ease. A day
> would not be sufficient for me to go through each kind [ἢ ἐπιλίποι με ἡ
> ἡμέρα κατ᾽ εἶδος διεξερχόμενον].[5] Further the economy of the work is
> an imitation of the opulence of the banquet and the arrangement of
> the books is an imitation of the preparation of the courses in the discourse
> [καί ἐστιν ἡ τοῦ λόγου οἰκονομία μίμημα τῆς τοῦ δείπνου πολυτελείας
> καὶ ἡ τῆς βίβλου διασκευὴ τῆς ἐν τῷ λόγῳ[6] παρασκευῆς]. The
> wonderful Athenaeus, the manager of the discourse [τοῦ λόγου οἰκονόμος]
> offers the sweetest banquet of words [ἥδιστον λογόδειπνον]. He surpasses
> himself like the orators of Athens,[7] and warming to his course, he leaps
> forward, bounding through the successive stages of the book.

There are three points in this text which attracted my attention and which will lend structure to my analysis:

(1)  the mixture of dishes and of speeches in the list;
(2)  the talk at table as a μίμημα (imitation) of the meal of Larensis, which runs parallel with Athenaeus' book as a μίμημα (imitation) of the talk at table;
(3)  The λογόδειπνον (feast of words) as a demonstration area for the δειπνοσοφισταί (Deipnosophists).

*1. The Mixture of dishes and speeches*

While the Epitomator makes a list of topics in the text of Athenaeus, the 'contents page' appears, at first sight, rather disordered. If we follow the order given by the Epitomator, the book is made up of: fish, a wide variety of vegetables and of animals of every kind, scholarly men, musical instruments, a multiplicity of jokes of every kind, drinking vessels, kings, ships.

Yet I believe that there is an explicit desire to show at one and the same time the quantity and the variety of all that can make up a sumptuous banquet which has pretensions and also the disorder which is involved in this juxtaposition of sympotic elements. But I also believe that this association is quite deliberate. The dishes of fish, of vegetables and of meat of every kind which make up the menu of Athenaeus are presented with the erudite men, whether they be compilers of history, authors or simply wise men (as ὅλως σοφούς would give one to understand).[8] That is to say, the foods served here are juxtaposed with the deipnosophists who sit at Larensis' table. In this way food and scholarship, pleasures of the table and pleasure in conversation are closely linked in the production of Athenaeus' banquet, as the Epitomator reports it (cf. Chapter 30). It will be noticed elsewhere that the verb used here to indicate the contents of the book is the verb ἐνέθετο, from ἐντίθημι which in this middle form means 'to insert', but also in a figurative sense (notably used by Aristophanes[9]), 'put into one's mouth', and thus 'eat'. This verb which can thus curiously mean *to insert* and *to eat*, is ready-made to refer to the double function of the ingredients of the banquet: they 'pass' through the mouth both because they are spoken and because they are eaten. The sphere of food and the sphere of scholarship are thus put on the same map, because all these ingredients together contribute to the particular character of Athenaeus' banquet, and more precisely to the sympotic pleasure of those who participate in it.

There is, in my opinion, a shining example of this association between culinary art and learned speeches, in the passage where fish—generally considered by the Greeks to be among the most delicious of dishes—are discussed. It is said of fish that Athenaeus has put in his book their uses, that is to say the various recipes for cooking them (καὶ τὰς τούτων χρείας), and the explanation of their names (καὶ τὰς τῶν ὀνομάτων ἀναπτύξεις). In other words, fish offers the opportunity, on the one hand, to cooks to show off their gastronomic art in preparing the fish according to the greatest variety of recipes, and, on the other hand, to deipnosophists to display their knowledge in raising typical questions at the table about the nature or the etymologies of the fish served.

Essentially most of the examples of culinary erudition about fish are to be found in Book Seven. In this book Athenaeus abandons the account of the progress of the banquet and chooses to make a long alphabetical catalogue of the various fishes served, all of which have allowed the guests to make scholarly observations (7.277a–c).

In this book Athenaeus will abandon the proper order of the banquet, in order to limit himself to giving a long series of erudite quotations. It is largely here that the great majority of recipes, of cooking advice, but also of etymological observations and anecdotes on fishes can be found. I will give one example which will illustrate the association made by the Epitomator between knowledge and cuisine. It consists of a fragment of Archestratus, a very knowledgeable cook (σοφώτατος), author of a *Gastrologia* (there are alternative titles of this work, ἡδυπάθεια, δειπνολογία and also ὀψοποιία). He expresses clearly, in his gastronomic advice, the sense in which culinary pleasure is associated with and fed by a pleasure in erudition.

> Around the sacred and broad island of Samos you will see the tuna caught with great effort, the great tuna which they call *orkys*, or sometimes *ketos*. From this fish in summer you must buy what is fitting swiftly and not <haggle> about the price. It is fine in Byzantium and in Carystus. But in the famous island of the Sicilians, the coast of Cefalù and of Tyndaris nourishes even better tuna.
>
> But if you ever go to Hipponion in holy Italy, the home of Persephone with the fine garlands, by far, really by far the best of all are there and they are the ultimate victors. On the other hand, the ones in this area have come from there after crossing the great wastes of the deep sea. We hunt them even though they are not fully grown.

In this fragment a certain pleasure in poetic language accompanies the pleasure in a good dish, and culinary advice for tuna fish accompanies comments on the geographical variability of their quality. In the mouth of Archestratus, the cook, culinary expertise is as one with his literary skill. Thus Archestratus, one of the most expert of cooks if one believes Athenaeus, becomes, in his turn, the object of a quotation in the mouth of a Deipnosophist while he is eating his dish of fish. In Athenaeus' account, the two spheres cannot be dissociated from each other. As the

Epitomator says, recipes for the kitchen and the taste of knowledge (here mythological, etymological or even geographical) are as one.

### 2. Talk at table as an imitation of the meal

This game of cross-references between the culinary moment and the erudite moment inside Athenaeus' banquet is also operated by the Epitomator himself at the end of his description of Athenaeus's text. It is the second point which interests me in his summary. The Epitomator says, in effect, that the speeches at table are an imitation of Larensis' meal (καί ἐστιν ἡ τοῦ λόγου οἰκονομία μίμημα τῆς τοῦ δείπνου πολυτελείας), and in parallel the elaboration of Athenaeus' book is, in its turn, the imitation of the speeches at table, or rather of the preparation of the dishes which follow each other in the various convivial accounts (καὶ ἡ τῆς βίβλου διασκευὴ τῆς ἐν τῷ λόγῳ παρασκευῆς). I understand here λόγος in the collective sense of dinner speeches, i.e. all arguments, discussions, quotations during the banquet. In this sense, in the interior of the *Deipnosophistae*, imitation is presented at two levels.

On the one hand, the variety of speeches made and of texts quoted by the guests echo the variety of dishes which are served to them; the magnificence and the richness of the meal are then represented (imitated) in the richness of the speeches made during the same meal. Moreover, the individual account of each guest takes shape from the dish which he has at hand and in some ways is made into a learned reproduction of that dish. An example will enable the relationship in the representation to be better understood; it is a fragment from the peripatetic Clearchus of Soli, which is one of the first quotations which the Epitomator has reported in what remains of the first book (I 4a5–b7; fr. 90 Wehrli).

Clearchus says that Charmus of Syracuse had ready short verses and proverbs for each dish served in the course of a meal. Thus for fish:
'I come, having left the salty depths of the Aegean'
For shellfish:
'Hail, whelks,[10] messengers of Zeus'
For intestines:
'Twisting and in no way healthy'
For stuffed squid:
'Wise woman, you wise woman'
For the perfect piece in a dish of boiled fish:
'Won't you scatter the crowd away from me?'
For skinned eel:
'The curls are not covering me'

Each of these sayings, here quoted by Charmus in reference to different foods, is a known quotation from tragedy or epic (respectively Euripides *Troades* 1, Homer *Iliad* 1.334, Euripides *Andromache* 448 and 245, followed by an anonymous quotation, and finally a quotation from *Phoenissae* 1485). To each dish belongs its corresponding literary offering which, ultimately, only scholarly gourmets or gourmet scholars can truly grasp. This trial of skill and of scholarship is not only exemplary of the kind of scholars gathered here, but it also illustrates this relationship of μίμημα, of imitation, which links the account, the λόγος, singular, between the guests and the preparation of the dishes which are served to them. But, the converse is true too.

The food engenders the guests' conversation. But also what they say can engender, or at least cause to appear on the table, the corresponding dishes. An enlightening example is the episode of the Asian sandgrouse (τέτραξ) in Book Nine. In a rather abrupt way, without the service requiring such a question, Larensis intervenes in order to start a new line of research (9.398b–c).

> Many other things were said during the meal concerning each of the dishes served. 'I too', said Larensis, 'in accord with our altogether noble Ulpian, propose something [προτείνω καὶ αὐτὸς ὑμῖν] because we nourish ourselves on research [ζητήσεις γὰρ σιτούμεθα]. What do you think the *tetrax* is?' Someone said, 'A sort of bird.' (Grammarians are accustomed to tell their pupils, whatever the topic may be, 'it is a sort of plant, a sort of bird, a sort of stone'.) Larensis replied, 'I also know my good friend, that the delightful Aristophanes in *Birds* referred to it in these terms: "to the purple gallinule, to the two species of pelican, to the *phlexis* and the Asian sandgrouse and the peacock" (882–4). But I want to learn from you if there is any mention of the Sandgrouse elsewhere.'

The research is proposed, brought to the front (προτείνω),[11] offered to the attention of the guests by the master of the house, as if it were a new dish to discover and taste. The research thus becomes the true *food* of the intellect of the scholars at the table, in the same way that the dishes *presented* by the cooks are for their bodies (note the curious and significant expression of Larensis, ζητήσεις γὰρ σιτούμεθα, 'we nourish ourselves on research'). The master of the house, after having clarified his question, will, himself, continue the speech by giving a string of quotations drawn from various authors who mention this bird. Following this intervention, or more precisely even while Larensis is speaking of the *tetrax*, someone (slave or cook) brings a real bird into the room (9.398f-399a).

As he was speaking, someone brought in an Asian sandgrouse in a cage. In height it was taller than the largest cock, in shape almost identical to a purple gallinule. On its ears on each side it had hanging feathers; its voice was deep. Once we had admired the beautiful colours of the bird, it was a little later prepared and served to our tables. Its flesh was similar to that of the ostrich, on which we had often dined.

The words engender the object of which they speak. Here the Asian sandgrouse, which is first of all the subject of quotations, is then admired (and appreciated) with the eyes, and finally eaten, tasted (and appreciated) by the mouth. The speech of the guests is thus a source of pleasure (for the eyes and the stomach). The pleasure of the word, of the λόγος, engenders—so to speak by a conjuring trick—the food, the τροφή and this, in its turn, gives reality to the word in making it into a real pleasure in life.

Food and erudition are, then, indissociably linked in the representation of the deipnosophists: the former engenders the latter and reciprocally the latter makes the former appear. The Deipnosophists always operate in both directions, as if their character (and their pleasure) as gourmets, were not incompatible with their character (and their pleasure) as scholars; or even better, as if their true pleasure were only in this union of understanding.

On the other hand, to continue with the Epitomator, there is also imitation at another level in the *Deipnosophistae*. Each speech of each guest, on a specific dish or on a reported banquet, is *in particular* what the book of Athenaeus as a whole (that is to say his own account to Timocrates of the individual stories) is *in general*; that is to say the representation (or even imitation) of Larensis' banquet—including all its phases (hors d'oeuvres, *deipnon*, symposion). It would seem then that, as at a banquet one speaks of food and of banquets, here too Athenaeus' account of Larensis' banquet is reproduced and repeated an infinite number of times in all the speeches on the other banquets, speeches that are made by the guests and related by Athenaeus. By a trick of mirrors, the deipnosophists are reflected in the same episodes which they tell and which reproduce them. In this sense, the text of Athenaeus operates a true '*mise en abîme*', where the convivial speeches of the scholars, which constitute Athenaeus' banquet, refer to the totality of Athenaeus' account of the same banquet.

*3. The feast of words*   It is in this sense also that we should understand the curious expression used by the Epitomator at the end of this text, to define the whole work of Athenaeus: it is about, he says, a very pleasant λογόδειπνον, an expression which I have translated here as *banquet of words*. It is exactly this expression which caught my attention and which thus constitutes the third point of interest in reading this summary.[12]

In the term λογόδειπνον, λόγος and δεῖπνον are in a relationship which exceeds simple association, inasmuch as they indicate at the same time the work of Athenaeus and the content of that work. For on the one hand the book is, just like a real banquet, the place and the opportunity for a profusion of speeches, on the other hand the banquet of Larensis is characterized by a series of speeches concerning the different elements of the meal.

Thus, if it is true that this image of a 'festival of speech' is not new and can be found, very often in Plato's dialogues, for example, to indicate the whole of the speeches made or to be made by the characters, it is also true that this expression normally only appears in contexts which are effectively sympotic, where the allusion to feast would have its literal meaning as well as a figurative one.

Thus in the *Phaedrus* we find the expression: λόγων ὑμᾶς Λυσίας εἱστία: 'Lysias offered you a banquet of speeches' (227 b7); similarly we find the expression: τοιαύτη θοίνη, 'such a banquet' (236 e8), referring to speeches heard and exchanged between Socrates and Phaedrus. Also in the *Gorgias* an 'erudite party' (ἀστεῖα ἑορτή) is mentioned in relation to the fine speeches given by Gorgias (447 a1–6). Equally, in the *Republic*, Socrates encourages the pursuit of the discussion undertaken up until then by using the image of the banquet (τὰ λοιπά μοι τῆς ἑστιάσεως ἀποπλήρωσον, 'complete for me the remains of the banquet', 1.352 b5–6). Similarly the image of the meal of words appears several times with regard even to Socrates' speeches, with the verb ἑστιάομαι (1.354 a10–b3). Finally in *Timaeus*, at the very beginning of the dialogue, one finds two allusions to two banquets, a banquet the day before and the current banquet (τῶν χθὲς μὲν δαιτυμόνων 'yesterday's guests', then ἀνταφεστιᾶν 'to invite in his turn', 17 a–b), and just before the beginning of Timaeus' speech, Socrates again makes an allusion to the banquet of words which he is about to listen to in exchange for the one which he had given the day before (ἀνταπολήψεσθαι τὴν τῶν λόγων ἑστίασιν, 'to receive a banquet of words in exchange' 27 b7–9).

Everything then happens as if, with Plato, the only possible banquet for good men was the banquet of words, in the sense that any supposed convivial meeting in his dialogues has as the only element of the banquet the λόγος, the exchange of words (cf. Chapter 26). It is particularly significant that in Plato's *Symposium* (that is to say in a work in which Plato places a dialogue in a sympotic context) there is no allusion to the slightest morsel of food partaken by the guests whatsoever. Nothing at all is said by Xenophon's guests on the meal itself and nothing memorable is spoken at the time of the meal, as if speeches and food never went together (moreover, it is certainly not by chance that Socrates' entrance is not made until the middle of the dinner, cf. 175b4–176a2). Equally, it is remarkable that the dinner of Xenophon's *Symposium* takes place in absolute silence (1.11: ἐκεῖνοι μὲν οὖν σιωπῇ ἐδείπνουν, 'thus those there ate in silence').

On the other hand, in the *Deipnosophistae*, Athenaeus, who is defined by the Epitomator as 'the admirable manager of the discourse' (ὁ θαυμαστὸς οὗτος τοῦ λόγου οἰκονόμος), presents a banquet of speeches for sure (a δεῖπνον of λόγοι, in the manner of Plato), but one which is to be found in the middle of a long account of a true banquet (a λογός of a δεῖπνον). In other words, Athenaeus is the οἰκονόμος, the true organizer, of this mimetic relationship which is established, all through the *Deipnosophistae*, between the sphere of learning and that of the kitchen: in presenting a banquet of scholars, he also presents learned speeches about food. That is why the characters of Athenaeus are *Deipnosophistai* in two senses, that is to say that they are, of course, 'scholars at table', but they are also, essentially, knowledgeable people on matters of food, scholars 'about matters of the table'.

## The recipe for pleasure

To pursue the exploration of the structure of Athenaeus' text, it is—in my opinion—important, even necessary, to sketch out the main lines of what I will call the convivial pleasure of the table companions of Larensis. The beginning of Book Seven is telling in this sense just before the arrival of the fish course.

We are here at the moment of the meal, of the *deipnon*, to speak correctly, after the hors d'oeuvres (Books One to Five). And it is here that Cynulcus when he speaks to Ulpian gives us a good example of the kind of scholarly conversation in the middle of a true meal which continues to take place during the discussion (7.275b–c):

> When the dinner was reaching its climax, the Cynics rejoiced more than the others, believing that they were celebrating the feast of the *Phagesia*. Cynulcus said, 'While we are eating, dear Ulpian, since you nourish yourself on discourse [λόγοις γὰρ ἑστιᾷ], I put this question to you [προβάλλω σοι],[13] who proclaimed the *Phagesia* and *Phagesiposia* as festivals?' Ulpian was at a loss and told the slaves to stop serving even though it was already evening. He replied, 'I have no acquaintance with that [οὐ συμπεριφέρομαι], my dear friend. So it's your chance to speak, so that you can also eat with much more pleasure.' And the other said, 'If you admit your gratitude once you have learnt the facts, I will speak.' Ulpian agreed and Cynulcus began. ...[14]

This is the beginning of Book Seven, the book on fish, which is generally recognized to be the high point of Greek banquets. As I have said, it is the book of fish in two senses: on the one hand because fish will be eaten at this precise point in the meal and on the other hand because at the same time fish will be the topic of conversation. But at the very beginning of the book, before any mention is made of fish and before even they arrive at the table, Cynulcus invites Ulpian to give an explanation of the *Phagesia* festivals (the festivals with food) and the *Phagesiposia* (the festivals with food and drink). The evidence which is used here is that of Clearchus (fr. 91a Wehrli).[15] Yet this fragment says nothing very precise about these festivals. Apart from a text of Eustathius (*Comm. ad Hom. Od.* 21.263, 1908, 43),[16] in which this kind of festival is associated with sacrificial festivals when a lot is eaten (πολυφαγεῖν), we have no other information concerning the meaning of *Phagesia* or of the *Phagesiposia* or the way they were conducted. Realistically, if these festivals did indeed exist,[17] they would have underlined the importance of food and drink at the centre of these celebrations.[18] At the heart of Larensis' meal, then, at the moment of the fish course, a conversation is introduced about festivals which celebrate food and drink as essential elements of a banquet. The banquet becomes, once again, an occasion for scholarship, and notably the study of banquets. Because the banquet is in the process of *taking place* (ἐπιτελουμένου τοῦ δείπνου) while they are preparing to serve the *pièce de résistance* (which is normally defined as the ὄψον), that the conversation turns to the knowledge and the exposition of this kind of culinary festival.

Similarly, where *trophe* is found in the middle of the banquet and of the conversation, is also to be found significant reflection on the *opsophagoi*, the people who like good food. This reflection, just by its position, is revealed as being central. A remark put forward by Myrtilus implies, in my opinion, a certain conception of culinary pleasure where thought and moderation around the table are united with good taste and good choice in food. I suspect that this mixture helps to define the pleasure of these scholarly guests. (7.276e–f).

> Since the fish that had been served and continued to be served were numerous and varied in size and species, Myrtilus said, 'It is right, dear friends that fish triumphed over all the other dishes called *opsa*, because of their excellent flesh. Fish alone is called an *opson* because of those who became mad for this kind of food. We call "gourmets" [ὀψοφάγοι ] not those who eat beef, such as Heracles who "ate fresh figs after beef" [βοείοις κρέασιν ἐπήσθιε σῦκα χλωρά ][19] (Euripides fr. 907N), nor the man who loves figs, as Plato did, as Phanocritus reports in his book *On Eudoxus* (*FHG* IV. 473). He reports too that Arcesilaus was a lover of grapes. No, it's those who drag themselves all around the fish market.

With some slight differences, the same praise of fish is found in question 4 of Book 4 of Plutarch's *Quaestiones Conviviales* (667f–668a). What is interesting, in my opinion, in this text is what is said about the *opsophagos*. This term seems, indeed, to acquire different nuances according to the context in which it appears. There is no simple or unequivocal translation. Thus, it describes sometimes simply a gourmet, a person who has good taste and enjoys a good table, sometimes a true glutton and sometimes even a debauched individual (cf. the list of *opsophagoi* in Book Seven of the *Deipnosophistae*, at 340e–346c).[20] It is then necessary, in order to explain this uncertainty, to outline the range of the term *opson* which is at the heart of the philosophical discussion.

The nub of the matter resides in the relationship between *opson* and *sitos*. Thus for example, in Xenophon, Socrates develops an analysis of the figure of the *opsophagos*, identified as a person who eats *opson* without—or with little—bread, *sitos* (*Memorabilia* 3.14. 2–4). In this sense, the *opsophagos* is not necessarily someone who eats a lot, but rather someone who only eats *opson* and purely for pleasure (ἡδονῆς ἕνεκα). In Plato *opson* is even depicted as something which threatens the peace of the city. It is exactly the element which tips over the πόλις ἀληθινή. sketched by Socrates into the πόλις τρυφῶσα hoped for by Glaucon, a city which would live in luxury. And the height of luxury are the *opsa*: to obtain this non-essential, the city would have to go to war (*Republic* 2.372a–373e).

Because it only has meaning in relation to *sitos*, and it is not consumed except in relation to *sitos*—whether it be afterwards or at the same time[21]—, *opson* is in Greek thought purely a supplement, an *extra* in relation to necessary food.[22] It can then have—in a sort of crescendo in the place and importance of *opson* in the food of the Greeks—a range of meanings which go from the pure and simple seasoning of the *sitos*, that is to say an *extra* which make the bread edible by giving it flavour (in this sense salt would be the first and most useful of the *opsa*),[23] to the finest part of the menu, the true *pièce de résistance* (often, for the Greeks, the fish course).[24] In between is the short designation of a dish, which, with the *sitos*, normally constitutes the complete Greek meal.[25] Different texts have different nuances but overall the meaning of *opson* extends over a range along the food scale, from a dietary need to the pleasure of eating.

From another perspective, the *sitos*, the basic food on every table, which might be wheat, barley or other cereals, is certainly classified as necessary, on the side of life and of survival. Thus—and at least as far as solid food is concerned— *sitos* would be enough, on its own, to guarantee subsistence of mankind.[26] By contrast *opson*, whatever it really contains, simple dishes or true delicacies, because of the fact that it accompanies bread (by being added in some way to it, is immediately placed on the side of pleasure, in that it exceeds the limits of pure need.[27] Furthermore to eat *opson* also means to eat more *sitos* for the pure pleasure of continuing to eat.[28]

If *sitos* is taken not for pleasure but only for nourishment, and if inversely it is with and for pleasure that *opson* is eaten, it is however true that without minimal *opson* (such as, for example, the salt allowed by Socrates in the *Republic* 2.372c) it would not be possible to eat at all. In other words, this *opson* which is characterized as a simple *extra* and therefore as something which could be done without, is also what allows *sitos* to be eaten.[29] It is because the *opson* makes it pleasant that at the end we are sustained by bread too. But we could then observe with Xenophon that hunger too can be an *opson* (and thus again a pleasure): 'because he [i.e. Socrates] helped himself so much to bread (*sitos*), that he ate it with relish (ἡδέως) and for this reason was so disposed that the desire for bread (ἡ ἐπιθυμία τοῦ σίτου) was for him an *opson* (*Mem.* 1.3.5).[30]

Let us get back to Athenaeus. In the *Deipnosophistae* there is no problematizing of the meaning of *opson* or of *opsophagia*. The working out of a personal *philosophy* on this question, as on any other, is not what interests Athenaeus. It is, rather, in his *mise en scène* that Athenaeus explains and *makes explicit* his thinking on this subject.

Thus, at the precise moment during the banquet when Myrtilus points out what should be understood as an *opsophagos*, it is fish that are brought to Larensis' table. They enter the scene as the epitome of *opsa*. It is in relation to the choice of this 'exquisite morsel' that a table companion will reveal himself as an *opsophagos*. For, as Myrtilus specifies, a *gourmet* is not a person who stuffs himself without really savouring his *opson*, like Hercules who could add figs to beef. Neither is it 'he who likes figs', that is someone for whom *opson* is limited to the most accessible and natural things, as a sign of moderation and temperance, 'like Plato the philosopher' or the academician Arcesilaus. Athenaeus' gourmet therefore is neither a big nor a frugal eater. He is rather someone who knows how to recognize and appreciate good things (*opson* precisely), in this case fish. In this sense, the *opsophagos* shown here is essentially one who eats for the pleasure of eating, and notably for the pleasure of eating *opson*, knowing how to prefer quality to quantity certainly but also to prefer a full measure with taste to the blandness of temperance.[31]

The distinction and the distance that Athenaeus' ὀψοφάγος shows both from the limitless greed of a Hercules and from the moderation of a Plato, reflect too a distinction and difference from the level of pleasure which Athenaeus' scholarly guests enjoy at Larensis' table. Every scholarly guest presented by Athenaeus is revealed as being a good example of the *opsophagos* described here. As it appears in the Epitomator's words, so this distance is found in the structure of Athenaus' banquet, and as much in relation to a party where pure pleasure of the stomach triumphed without any exchanges or convivial speeches as in relation to a party where pure pleasure in the conversation between guests dominated, without any culinary appreciation.

Two authors give good illustrations of these two forms of banquet and of pleasure which can be compared with the *Deipnosophistae*. Athenaeus' work might be said to be a third way, where the pleasure of the table is combined with the pleasure of knowledge.

First a passage from Lucian's *Lexiphanes*, where Lexiphanes presents to Lycinus a text which he has just written. As he says himself at the beginning it is sympotic composition which is a philosophical 'anti-banquet'. He wanted to compose 'a banquet which confronts Plato's' (the verb used is ἀντισυμποσιάζω). Thus, in the reading that Lexiphanes makes of his banquet, what is celebrated *ad nauseam* is the quantity of food and of wine served, elements which are, in fact, completely absent from Xenophon's banquet and Plato's (*Lex.* 6–8):

> Numerous and varied dishes were prepared: pig's trotters, sides of beef, tripe, the womb of a fertile sow, fried liver, pâté, spicy sauce and other similar delicacies, pancakes, savouries in fig leaves, honey cakes. Among the fish from the depths of the sea there were many cartilaginous and shelled species, and from those caught in nets slices of fish from the Black Sea and fish from Copais. There was also a domestic fowl, a cock who would crow no more and a parasite fish. There was also a whole ewe cooked in the oven and the thigh of a toothless ox. There was also good quality bread, some made during the new moon, and vegetables that grow under the earth and on the earth. The wine was not old but just out of the store. Certainly it was not yet sweet but still raw.
>
> Cups of all kinds were placed on the tables with legs in the forms of dolphins, a mixing bowl that hid diners' faces and a ladle made by Mentor with a handle easy to hold. There was a gargling bowl, a long-necked cup and many pots like those Thericles put in the oven, some vast, others with big mouths, some from Phocea, some from Cnidus. They were all as light as cloth the wind can lift up. There were also small cups, flagons and bowls with inscriptions. The cupboard was full.
>
> So we drank without ever closing our mouths and we were soon overcome. We anointed ourselves with perfume and a dancer and triangle-player moved among us.

The succession of elements in Lucian's account unfolds without order and without taste: pork with beef, tripe with liver, pâté, sauces, pancakes and honey, and then fish and shellfish, followed by chicken, mutton and then beef again; finally breads and vegetables and above all as much wine as could be drunk, with music and dancing. The disorder in the dishes and in the sequence of the banquet is total.

Food and wine, dancer and flute-player, which are marginalized in Plato's *Symposium*, are by contrast more important to Lexiphanes' banquet than any other convivial element. This is a true anti-banquet where food and wine do not draw out any shared convivial speech, unless it were purely a babble, which is a caricature of a sympotic conversation around the drinking-cup. This is how the three guests, Megalonymus, Lexiphanes and Callicles organize their *symposion*, which follows their feast (*Lex.* 14):

> 'After the drinking we chatted in our normal way, for it is certainly not out of place to chat in one's cups.'
> 'I agree', I replied, 'even more so since we represent the greatest success of the pure Attic style.'
> 'You speak well', added Callicles, 'for lively exchanges between us sharpen the tongue for talking.'

The verbs describing the conversation are here verbs typical of chatter in Lucian's dialogues: they are συννθλέω, 'to chat together', ἐρεσχηλέω 'to banter', or even ἐνοινοφλύω 'to prattle in and through wine'. The order followed is indeed that of a banquet as it ought to be: food, wine, speech. But the speech which follows the wine is a λάλη, 'chatter', and not a λόγος 'a discourse'. The λάλη, 'the chatter', is thus the term which illustrates and sums up the kind of exchange which will follow. The pleasure is above all the pleasure of the stomach, a culinary celebration which, far from inducing convivial speech-making that is useful to friendship and following the order of the banquet, generates instead noise and confusion, chatter and the mockery of an unbridled feast.

On the other hand, a text from Plutarch outlines a model of banquet where communal conversation between guests is essential as the only true pleasure of good men. The passage is from the long monologue of Solon in the *Septem Sapientium Convivium* (159d 4–9).[32]

> We, for example, just now did not look at each other or listen to each other. Each of us had his head down and was the slave of the need to eat. Now by contrast, the tables have been removed and we are free. As you see, we are garlanded and devote ourselves to conversation. We are in each other's company and we have plenty of time because we have reached the point where we are no longer hungry.

From Solon's perspective, there is no relationship between food and speech (notice that, here, it is a λόγος, a 'speech', and not a λάλη, 'chatter'). In the course of the banquet the λόγος takes place at the moment when the τροφή, the food, has fulfilled its purpose of meeting the need to eat. During the banquet, while one's head is leaning over the dish, one does not speak: food seems to isolate the guests. After the banquet, when food no longer has a place, the links between guests are recreated thanks to speech. Speech unites, and it unites in κοινωνία, 'communion', and φιλοφροσύνη, 'kindness', which are characteristic of Plutarch's banquets (cf. the dedications to Books 3, 4, and 7 of *Quaestiones conviviales*).

Food and speech are here in a relationship of reciprocal exclusion: presence of one impedes the achievement of the other. For Plutarch it is indisputable that the source of pleasure is the λόγος and not the τροφή. The pleasure of the λόγος is worthy of memory, while the pleasure of τροφή is destined to be forgotten. This is what stands out from a long passage from the dedication to Book 6 of the *Quaestiones conviviales* which, in my view, works to a paradigm different from that of the structure of Athenaeus' text (6.686b9–d9):

> But a further advantage accrues to Plato's diners, namely the close examination of what was said while they drank. The pleasures of drinking and eating procure servile and faded memories, like the smell of last night or the fumes from roasting flesh. Discussion of philosophical problems and discourse by contrast is always present and fresh and makes those who recall it very happy. It also gives them the chance to offer a banquet just as good to those who were deprived of it. They, when they hear of it, have a part in it also. Hence today all the lovers of words participate and take pleasure from the Socratic banquets, just like the people who dined at that time. Now if bodily things provided pleasure, Xenophon and Plato should have left us a text not of discourses given but of dishes, cakes and desserts served by Callias and Agathon. But things like that have never been judged worthy of discourse, even though they were in all probability the result of preparation and expense. In fact, however, in their writing they put serious philosophical questions linked to playful exchanges. They left models of how to be together, one and all, through the conversations at the symposia; and also of how to preserve the memory of the words that were said.

In this passage from Plutarch it is really an issue of ἡδονή, of pleasure. The ἡδονή of food confronts once again the ἡδονή of speech, and the first gives way to the second. Here there is no longer human isolation during the eating stage which contrasts with communion during conversation, but the nausea which follows bodily pleasures in contrast to the long-lasting freshness in philosophical pleasure. That is why the absence of memory for the dishes of a philosophical banquet, this *culinary* silence which surrounds the philosophers' banquet in Plutarch's texts, is explained by the pleasure of the λογός dominating any possible gastronomical pleasure, and not by the poverty of the food at the scholars' table. Whatever the banquet offered, Plutarch's scholarly guests seem to have no pleasure in the table, or if they do, they must not mention it. They forget it quickly.[33] The pleasure of speeches exchanged thus dominates the memories of the guests and from their memories continues to assert itself on their listeners as the only pleasure worth mentioning.

Lucian's and Plutarch's texts illustrate two opposing models of a banquet and of convivial pleasure. Pleasure of the table and pleasure in speaking characterize respectively the banquet of gluttons who hide behind an appearance of stern philosophers in Lucian and the banquet of philosophers who pass themselves off as convivial guests in Plutarch. Pleasure reveals the true nature of table companions: the false scholars unveil the nature of voracious men, giving themselves up to pure bodily pleasure; the false guests, by contrast, reveal their philosophical nature by giving themselves up to purely intellectual pleasure.

As for Athenaeus, he portrays a rich and sumptuous banquet, in the image of Lucian's, and in the style of Plutarch, he enjoys recounting all that is said by the guests during the banquet. In so doing he offers an equivalent banquet to his audience. However, if the unrestrained table companions in Lexiphanes' account eat and drink without really speaking to each other, and if Plutarch's sober table companions speak without really eating together, the Deipnosophists eat and talk together, eat to speak and speak to continue eating. Athenaeus reports the speeches made during the banquet, as Plato, Xenophon and Plutarch do, but since these speeches are born from the food and are built around the food, the pleasure of his account coincides with the pleasure which arises from what they have eaten and drunk. Thus, for the Deipnosophists (and for Athenaeus), intellectual pleasure and corporeal pleasure are one. The pleasure of the table is never disassociated from the pleasure of the word: the table is at one and the same time a source of culinary pleasure, through the variety and the richness of its courses, and the opportunity for the pleasure of erudition and knowledge, a pleasure which takes its form from the numerous speeches made by the Deipnosophists and in the account made by Athenaeus of these dinner speeches.

The scholars at Larensis' table are, then, *Deipnosophists* above all in their pleasure, which is the expression of a wise recipe consisting of bodily pleasure from their δεῖπνον (dinner) and intellectual pleasure from their σοφία (wisdom).

# 20

# DANCE AND DESSERTS
## AN ANALYSIS OF BOOK FOURTEEN

### by Paola Ceccarelli

Dance is an important part of Greek culture, and as such, it is discussed—or alluded to—in numerous passages of the *Deipnosophistae*.[1] In particular μουσική, 'music' (including obviously dance) forms one of the two principal topics discussed in the fourteenth book, the other being παρατραγήματα, 'desserts'. As the authorities on dance and music referred to in this section do not otherwise survive, the preservation of parts of their works in the *Deipnosophistae* has a considerable importance; those sources are an invaluable help for an understanding of ancient dance, and accordingly they have been extensively studied. The reasons for incorporating in the *Deipnosophistae* a section on music and dance appear also quite evident: musical entertainment had an important role in the symposion, and a discussion of this aspect fits in well with the encyclopaedic character of the work. What is however less easy to assess is the 'cultural' meaning (as distinct from the informational value), the sense of this section on music for Athenaeus himself and for his intended public.

In order to understand the way in which Athenaeus relates to this part of Greek culture, I shall proceed to an analysis of the enunciative structure of the book, and then see what the consequences of the enunciative structure are on the semantic level. This approach seems necessary because, while much work has been done—especially at the end of the nineteenth century and at the beginning of the twentieth—on the sources of Athenaeus for music and dance,[2] and while there has been much work done on specific technical problems, less attention has been devoted to understanding the semantic implications of the formal narrative structure, the way in which the structure relates to its contents.[3] It seems worthwhile to try to see if at least some of the factual difficulties presented by the contents of the section on music and dance can be explained as depending on the general project of Athenaeus, that is, if the narrative structure may help to explain the peculiarities in the content.[4] The whole of Book Fourteen, comprehending the discussion of desserts, has been taken into account, so as to cover a section of the work building on quite different kinds of sources, but also because this makes it possible to take into account an intended unit, a book.

As pointed out by Düring and then with more details by Letrouit,[5] the *Deipnosophistae* is built on the interplay between four elements:

(1) an external narration, in which Athenaeus informs the reader about his encounters with Timocrates;[6]

(2) an external dialogue, that between Athenaeus and Timocrates (either explicit, characterized by the use of the vocatives Ἀθήναιε and Τιμόκρατες, or implicit, where the pronoun σοι refers to Timocrates), including

(3) narrative sections, in which Athenaeus relates to Timocrates what happened during the symposion (and sometimes also events not directly connected with the symposion at Larensis' home[7]); and

(4) an internal dialogue, between the Deipnosophists themselves.

In what follows I shall keep to this distinction; from the point of view of enunciation, however, it must be stressed that there is no difference between the second and the third level. This means that we have to consider three levels of enunciation, corresponding to three contexts, all situated very near to each other in time, since the character Athenaeus is present in all of them; the fact that they are so very near to one another actually creates a sort of kaleidoscopic effect, for their proximity makes possible a continual shifting between their different 'times'.[8] The citations embedded in the narrative sections and in the internal dialogue form a fourth enunciative level, which, consisting of fragments of ancient authors (clearly indicated as such: παλαιοί, ἀρχαῖοι), contrasts strongly with the time distribution of the other levels; but, as I hope to show in the course of the analysis of Book Fourteen, the ancient authors, speaking as they are cited, are also taken up into the fluidity of time. This is particularly true of prose fragments: for the citations in verse are protected, as it were, from confusion by the very fact of being in verse. On the other hand, prose citations need to be very clearly delimited, or the 'text' will be indistinguishable from the 'context', and the 'I' of the authority cited (level 5) will be subsumed in the 'I' of the person citing it—one of the Deipnosophists of context 4, or the Athenaeus/character of context 2/3, or even the Athenaeus/narrator of context 1. In the following linear analysis of Book

## 1. The enunciative structure of the *Deipnosophistae*

Fourteen I shall provide evidence for such shifts between enunciative levels, and suggest that they are intentional, and done for a specific purpose.

## 2. Analysis of Book Fourteen

The external dialogue with the address to Timocrates at the beginning of Book Fourteen, 613a (Τὸν Διόνυσον, ἑταῖρε Τιμόκρατες, μαινόμενον οἱ πολλοὶ λέγουσιν, 'The majority of writers, friend Timocrates, call Dionysus mad'), coming after the rather abrupt end of Myrtilus' long speech (610d–612f) against Cynulcus, marks the beginning of the new book. The non-prepared change from internal dialogue to external dialogue functions here as a sign; the reader may retrospectively suspect that the words 'I will now bring to a close the speech here spoken against you and the other Cynic-Dogs', καταπαύσω τὸν πρὸς σὲ καὶ τοὺς ἄλλους κύνας ἐνταῦθα λόγον, with which Myrtilus had closed his speech, refer not just to the end of Myrtilus' speech but also to the end of the internal dialogue, and to the end of the book. In this case, the character Myrtilus has assumed a function reserved to the narrator, who usually announces himself the end of a book.[9]

The allusion to Dionysus 'the mad' is followed by a few citations on the topic of drunkenness, which are understood by the reader as still at the level of the external dialogue. Then, in 613c, there is a shift to the internal dialogue, prepared by the following remark of the narrator:

ἀλλ' οὐχ ἡμεῖς γε οὔτε τῶν πλεῖον πινόντων ὄντε οὔτε τῶν ἐξοίνων γινομένων πληθούσης ἀγορᾶς ἐπὶ τὰ μουσικὰ ταῦτα ἐρχόμεθα συμπόσια,

But we, at least, belonging neither to the class of those who drink too much nor to those who get drunk in the morning, resort to these erudite symposia.

Here, ἡμεῖς, 'we', refers to Athenaeus and Timocrates; at the same time, these words of the narrator 'outside' the banquet seem to direct the conversation 'inside' the banquet, as is made obvious by the following sentence, in which Ulpian asks from somebody who has repeated the words ἔξοινος οὔκ εἰμι, 'I am not drunk',[10] where the expression might be found. In fact, one of the fellow diners seems to have appropriated what the reader thought to be words of the narrator addressed to Timocrates: the external frame seems to have merged with the 'content'. Just as interesting is the fact that the word ἔξοινος has appeared already twice in the conversation of the Deipnosophists, first in 8.349a (in a citation from Machon concerning the jester Stratonicus) and then in 10.444d (in a quotation from the historian Hegesander, inserted in Pontianus' speech on the effects of wine). It is then possible to justify the repetition of the word ἔξοινος thinking of the preceding passages, which are both thematically connected with what is going on at the moment (wine and jesters are the arguments next discussed in Book Fourteen), and which pertain to the context of the banquet. The words of the narrator appear thus to introduce, in a very subtle way, a kind of cross-reference to two other sections of the work, while at the same time obscuring for a moment the distinction between the frame and the banquet.

From now on, we are in the internal dialogue, as is, however, made definitely clear only retrospectively, at 615e (ταῦτα τοῦ Οὐλπιανοῦ διεξελθόντος, 'After Ulpian had narrated these details'), when again the narrator comes to the forefront, describing the reactions of the assembled company and adding, in an aside addressed as much to Timocrates as to the reader, a cross-reference to the first book (1. 20a):

ἐγένοντό τινες λόγοι καὶ περὶ τῶν καλουμένων πλάνων· καὶ ἐζητεῖτο εἰ μνήμη τις καὶ περὶ τούτων ἐγένετο παρὰ τοῖς παλαιοτέροις· περὶ γὰρ θαυματοποιῶν ἤδη προειρήκαμεν,

certain remarks were made about the so-called *planoi*; and the question was raised whether there is any mention of these men also in more ancient writers; for on the subject of magicians we have spoken already.

The text goes then back to the internal dialogue: the narrator introduces Magnus' direct speech, in which are collected a few citations, mostly from comic poets, about the *planoi*. This time, if the beginning of the speech is clearly marked, we do not get as clear a mark for the end; the first person plural (ἡμῶν) in the sentence: 'Our dinner party did not suffer for lack of joke-lovers', Οὐκ ἠπόρει δ' ἡμῶν τὸ συμπόσιον οὐδὲ τῶν φιλοσκωπτούντων (616b), another reference to the actual banquet, together with the indication of a past tense, is the only sign that the narrator is again in charge, and that he assumes responsibility for the following anecdote, taken from the work *On Pleasure and the Good* by Chrysippus. It may be interesting to remark that the narrator, even though he is technically out of the symposion in this moment, does not give the title of Chrysippus' book, but refers to 'Chrysippus in the same book'—as the one cited immediately before by Magnus. The cross-referencing between character's discourse and narrator's discourse is a means for connecting a remark coming from the narrator, and possibly not pronounced during the symposion, to the discussions held during the symposion.

In 14.616c we have a transition to the internal dialogue: Myrtilus is overtly introduced as speaking, first in the indirect speech, depending also on the narrator, and then on his own; at the end of the anecdote (a few lines later), there is even a direct apostrophe of Myrtilus to Ulpian (σὺ δέ, ὦ Οὐλπιανέ, 'As for you, Ulpian'). One could feel that the dialogue had begun; but after a few cases of jokers punished, the narrator comes forward again, changing the subject, while Myrtilus disappears without comment.

This time, the intervention of the narrator is an important, programmatic one:

> Πολλῶν οὖν πολλάκις ὄντων τῶν ἀκροαμάτων καὶ τῶν αὐτῶν οὐκ αἰεί, ἐπειδὴ πολλοὶ περὶ αὐτῶν ἐγίνοντο λόγοι, τὰ ὀνόματα τῶν εἰπόντων παραλιπὼν τῶν πραγμάτων μνησθήσομαι,

> Well, we often had many entertainments, not always the same, and since there was much talk about them, I will omit the speakers' names and mention what was done (616e).

Its importance is underlined in different ways: from the point of view of the sonority of the language, since there is a kind of polyptoton; the wording is not so innocent either. One may think of the πραγμάτων, chosen instead of what might seem more logical, λεχθέντων, but which in its illogicality contributes to that blurring between talking and doing which is such a peculiar feature of the *Deipnosophistae*; another interesting feature of this intervention is that it takes up—in very similar words—exactly the same argument that had been used by what seemed to be the narrator but was retrospectively discovered to be Ulpian in 613d,[11] so that the narrator's discourse functions as an answer to the character's discourse.

This is a programmatic declaration, to be taken as the opening of a section in the narrative mode; instead of which, we find again a kind of indefinite internal dialogue, with pronouns such as 'one' and 'another', introducing first an indirect speech with direct citation and then a direct speech with a citation again in direct speech (περὶ μὲν γὰρ αὐλῶν ὁ μέν τις ἔφη τὸν Μελανιππίδην … εἰρηκέναι, 616e; πρὸς ὃν ἀντιλέγων ἄλλος ἔφη· 'about the *auloi* one of them said that Melanippides said …; in answer to him another said: …'). This opens the way to a long section (616e–620b) concerning the *auloi* and their evaluation (negative and positive), the terms applied to flute-playing as well as those for the varieties of songs (all this is explicitly said to come from Tryphon; other authorities are cited as well, in particular Douris, Semus of Delos, 'others', Aristoxenus and Nymphis). This section, built in the narrative mode, is in fact presented by the second interlocutor, the *allos* of 616e; it is only in 620b that the narrator breaks in (as indicated by the first person plural) and continues on his own: 'Rhapsodists were not missing from our drinking parties either. For Larensis enjoyed the poems of Homer as no one else ever has...', Οὐκ ἀπελείποντο δὲ ἡμῶν τῶν συμποσίων οὐδὲ ῥαψῳδοί. ἔχαιρε γὰρ τοῖς Ὁμήρου ὁ Λαρήνσιος ὡς ἄλλος οὐδὲ εἷς ...

The following topic, 'joy-singers', is introduced at 620d in exactly the same way, again by the narrator, using the first person plural: 'hilarodists ... continually appeared for our benefit', καὶ οἱ καλούμενοι δὲ ἱλαρῳδοί ... συνεχῶς ἡμῖν ἐπεφαίνοντο. The narration now adopts a catalogic mode; the very expression 'catalogue' appears, referring to a list of artists cited from Aristocles (καταλέγει δὲ ὁ Ἀριστοκλῆς καὶ τούσδε ἐν τῷ περὶ Μουσικῆς, 'Aristocles includes in his work *on Music* the following artists', 620e), so that the listing is cleverly attributed to an external authority and not to the narrator; and the series of local terms for the different kinds of performers goes on, building on different authorities (Aristoxenos, Alexis, Strattis, a long extract from Semus of Delos). The effect of surprise is all the bigger for the reader when, in 622d, the narrator intervenes quite heavily with an anecdote referring to the harp-singer Amoebeus. This is a case in which the wording plays a very important role. I give the relevant parts of the text, with Gulick's translation of the introductory and final parts of the story:

Ἐπεὶ δ' ἐνταῦθα τοῦ λόγου ἐσμέν, οὐκ ἄξιον ἡγοῦμαι παραλιπεῖν τὰ περὶ Ἀμοιβέως τοῦ καθ' ἡμᾶς κιθαρῳδοῦ, ἀνδρὸς τεχνίτου κατὰ νόμους τοὺς μουσικούς. οὗτός ποτε βράδιον ἥκων ἐπὶ τὸ συμπόσιον ἡμῶν ὡς ἔμαθεν παρά τινος τῶν οἰκετῶν ἀποδειπήσαντας, ἐβουλεύετο τί χρὴ ποιεῖν... κρότου δ' ἐπὶ τούτοις γενομένου καὶ πάντων ὁμοθυμαδὸν αὐτὸν καλεσάντων εἰσελθὼν καὶ πιὼν ἀναλαβών τε τὴν κιθάραν εἰς τοσοῦτον ἡμᾶς ᾖσεν ὡς πάντας θαυμάζειν τήν τε κιθάρισιν... ἐμοὶ μὲν γὰρ οὐδὲν ἐλάττων εἶναι νομίζεται τοῦ παλαιοῦ Ἀμοιβέως, ὅν φησιν ... (14. 622d–623d)

Since *we are* on the subject *I think* it not right to omit the story of Amoebeus, a harp-singer *of our time* ... He arrived (ποτε) rather late at *our* symposion, and when he learned from one of the servants that we had finished dinner', [he hesitated whether to go in or not. The cook arrives and in order to encourage him to enter the dining-room recites passages from comedy, to which Amoebeus gives an appropriate answer.] 'Loud applause followed this, and all the guests with one accord called him in; so he entered and after drinking he took up his lyre and delighted *us* to such an extent that all were amazed at his playing ... In *my* judgement, in fact, he is not a whit inferior to the Amoebeus of ancient times....

This is usually taken to mean that Amoebeus arrived late at the banquet which constitutes the occasion of Athenaeus' narration, the banquet offered by Larensis;[12] the more so, since the moment of the arrival of Amoebeus in the story, after the dinner, coincides with the 'real' situation of the Deipnosophists dining at Larensis' house. This interpretation however overlooks, so it seems to me, the indefinite ποτε; it is possible to understand here that Amoebeus 'arrived once late at our symposion', and that the narrator is relating events that happened during another banquet at which he was present, maybe one at which he was present with Timocrates, in which case the addressee of the anecdote would be the reader.[13] This would then be a 'story', marked off from the rest of the narration by the carefully underlined opening and closing statements in the first person singular. The frame for a while (from 622d to 623d) would have a different content, events relating to another symposion, told however according to exactly the same modalities as is the case for the symposion offered by Larensis, with extensive use of citations from comic poets. An examination of the very numerous deictics (pronouns, proper name, particles) shows that instead of facilitating the reference, they deliberately confuse the issue.

To begin with the proper name: this is the only appearance of Amoebeus in the *Deipnosophistae*, he does not appear in the list of the guests given at the beginning of the work, in 1.1c–f,[14] nor does he crop up again later. *Prima facie* the name Amoebeus refers, for the reader of the thirteen preceding books, to something external to the text, and there is nothing to counter the presupposition of yet another anecdote, similar to many already told. Moreover, the speaking name Amoebeus invites suspicion, since it reflects the actual situation of the harpist who plays for reward, while at the same time allowing the comparison with a player of ancient times; the final statement, according to which the performers of modern times are not inferior to the ancients, is interesting as an example of the tendency to confuse the distance between present and past. And if the first person singular pronoun may be taken as referring all along to the person of the narrator, difficulties crop up with the first person plural pronouns: the first one, ἐσμεν, probably implies, alongside the narrator, Timocrates; this means that we are in the external dialogue (level 2), or maybe in the external narration (level 1). And if καθ' ἡμᾶς may be simply taken as conveying the very general meaning 'of our time', does the following ἡμῶν still refer to the narrator and Timocrates (in which case the addressee of the whole story would be the reader), does it refer to Athenaeus, and Larensis' Deipnosophists, or to Athenaeus and some other company? The only clear signs seem to be the ποτε and the coincidence between the content of the story and the narrative situation ... and they point in opposite directions! It is possible to ascribe this confusion in the referents to negligence; but when one thinks of the very neat way in which beginning and end of the story are marked by first person statements of the narrator, one feels inclined to think that this might be another example of that indeterminacy of which we have already seen some examples.

Following this, another general consideration of the narrator enables him (in 623e) to sum up what has been going on, to make himself felt once again, and to introduce a long intervention by Masurius:

Περὶ δὲ μουσικῆς τῶν μὲν τάδε λεγόντων, ἄλλων δ' ἄλλα γ' ὁσημέραι, πάντων δ' ἐπαινούντων τὴν παιδιὰν ταύτην, Μασούριος ὁ πάντα ἄριστος καὶ σοφὸς ... ἔφη·

On the subject of music there was daily conversation, some saying things recorded here, others saying other things, but all joining in praise of this kind of amusement; and Masurius, in all things excellent and wise,..., said:

This transition formula, leading the way to the long and detailed speech by Masurius, presents three interesting features: first, the explicit admission that only a part of the things said are recorded as interesting; even if the frame and the bulk of the work might seem to allude quite heavily to an encyclopaedic project, to a will for a total recording, this is at the same time here explicitly belied by the narrator himself.[15] Secondly, the part about things said not being recorded might be read in connection with the immediately preceding story concerning Amoebeus, a story from outside the frame, something which neither did happen nor did get told at this particular banquet, but which all the same came to be recorded. Thirdly, the ὁσημέραι, 'every day', adds to the feeling of indeterminacy: all through the first part of the book, the conversation has been introduced by formulas referring to something which was happening at the very moment; this is not true anymore, nor do we know in which day the things which have been and are going to be related were said.

This formula introduces a very long and detailed speech (from 623e to 633f), in which different topics, all related to *mousike*, are touched upon. In order, Masurius cites passages from Chamæleon and Homer, to the effect that music trains and educates the character (623f–624a); Theopompus is adduced as proof of its curative virtues (624b); from here, the transition is easy to the Phrygian mode and to modes in general, for which hosts of authorities are given. The interrelationship between these authorities poses some problems, which come out quite clearly in a study of the subjects of enunciation. The first person singular, for example, appears twice in 625a ('Formerly, then, as I have said ...', πρότερον μὲν οὖν, ὡς ἔφην, and 'But I believe that', ἐμοὶ δὲ δοκεῖ), to which one may add the first person plural ('just as we say', ὡς λέγομεν). Gulick in a note to his translation tells his readers that 'the authority is still Heracleides', who had been introduced in 624c (Ἡρακλείδης δ' ὁ Ποντικὸς ... φησὶ δεῖν καλεῖσθαι ..., 'Heracleides of Pontus ... says that ...') and again parenthetically recalled in 624e (αὕτη γάρ ἐστι, φησὶν ὁ Ἡρακλείδης, ἣν ἐκάλουν Αἰολίδα, 'This, Heracleides says, is in fact the one which they called Aeolian'). But after this passage, Lasus and then Pratinas had been adduced as authorities, so that when the reader comes to the first person singular in 625a he may think of Masurius, or maybe even of Athenaeus, while feeling directly included in the first person plural 'as we say'; in any case, he is not prepared to think of Heracleides as the subject of the enunciation.

Now it is possible that Athenaeus, excerpting without thinking too much about what he was doing, may have transcribed a long piece of Heracleides, who is anyway almost certainly the source for the citations from Lasus and Pratinas, forgetting to eliminate the ἔφην and the ἐμοὶ when Heracleides came back to his own opinions; but it seems worthwhile to entertain another possibility, namely that this is being done on purpose.

For the moment, let us proceed with the analysis. In the following paragraphs, there are a number of expressions in the first person, singular and plural (Ἑξῆς ἐπισκεψώμεθα, 'Let us examine', 625b; διόπερ ὑπολαμβάνω, 'Hence I assume', and οὐχ ὁρῶ γάρ, 'Nor can I see', 625d; τρεῖς οὖν αὗται, καθάπερ ἐξ ἀρχῆς εἴπομεν εἶναι ἁρμονίας, ὅσα καὶ τὰ ἔθνη, 'These modes, then, are three, as we said of them at the beginning, as many as there are tribes of the Greeks', 625e; and an apostrophe to the hearer/reader, in 625f: ἴδοις δ' ἄν, 'You may see', concerning archaeological remains of the Lycians and Phrygians who came to Greece with Pelops. All of these are in fact probably to be referred to Heracleides and his own intended audience, but they seem here to have been appropriated by Masurius.

Then there is a rather abrupt change in the source, and Masurius makes his presence felt just for the time needed to say that Polybius is now being cited: Οὐ παραληπτέον δὲ τὴν μουσικήν, φησὶν Πολύβιος ὁ Μεγαλοπολίτης ..., 'One must not accept as a fact, says Polybius, that the music ...'. This transition marks the beginning of a long citation from Polybius[16] extending from 626a to 626f, and ending rather abruptly, since it is only the fact that another author is cited (626f: Agias, on the 'Phrygian smell' produced by the storax burnt during the festivals of the Dionysia) that enables us to understand that the extract from Polybius is finished; the reference to a 'Phrygian smell' may be constructed as echoing the remarks on the Lydians and Phrygians found at the end of Heracleides' citation, building a sort of ring around the citation from Polybius.

The following section of the text may have been taken as a whole from some ancient authority, but if this is the case, Athenaeus does not make this felt;

for all the reader knows, Masurius is himself choosing the citations with which he builds up his discourse. In any case, from 627a (τὸ δ᾽ ἀρχαῖον ἡ μουσικὴ ἐπ᾽ ἀνδρείαν προτροπὴ ἦν, 'In ancient times music was an incitement to bravery') to 628a the narrator and Masurius himself keep a low profile, and there are absolutely no references to the actual symposion. There is a καθάπερ ἐλέγομεν, 'as we were saying', at 627f, whose subject stays indeterminate; and this indeterminacy is interesting since this section is constructed on an opposition between ancient times (τὸ δ᾽ ἀρχαῖον, οἱ παλαιοί, οἱ βάρβαροι, Ὅμηρος· 'in ancient times, the ancients, the barbarians, Homer') and modern times ('we', or οἱ πολλοί, 'most people'). A continuity of sorts, instead of a contrast, is also implied by the ἡμῶν of 628a, where the uses introduced by the ancients are seen as useful for maintaining 'our' dignity (in the present).[17]

A general reflection on the fact that *mousike* exercises and sharpens the mind, and that songs and dances are the result of the soul's motions (as theorized by Damon and his school), leads to the subject of dance (628c to 631e). The discussion of dance is presented as a succession of citations from authorities; the narrator/speaker is normally absent, surfacing only from time to time for short remarks (like the οἶδα, 'I know', concerning the *maktristriai*, at 629c, possibly to be attributed to Masurius). Another first person pronoun, this time in the plural, appears in 631a, concerning the Dionysiac pyrrhic 'of our times'. Whose times are these? There is a consensus on the fact that the referent is Aristocles; this writer *On Choruses* had been cited in 630b for the *sikinnis*. After him, Aristoxenos and Scamon had been mentioned as authorities (also 630b). In 630e Aristoxenos is cited as the source for a long passage concerning the pyrrhic dance. Then comes, in 630f, a citation from Philochoros, and in 631a, that καθ᾽ ἡμᾶς, 'of our times'; after which, the next authority to be cited is once more Aristoxenos. From the practical point of view, it seems quite probable that Aristocles is the source for the whole section, comprising the citations from Aristoxenos and Philochoros. But from the point of view of the intended audience of the *Deipnosophistae*, this is not that clear, and the καθ᾽ ἡμᾶς might as well refer to the time of the narration. The more so as not long after, in 631e, there is a very clear (for once!) intervention of Masurius (who doubles here as the narrator, since the name is not explicitly given): καὶ περὶ μὲν ὀρχήσεως τοσαῦτά μοι ἐπὶ τοῦ παρόντος λέλεκται, 'So much, then, I have had to say for the present on the subject of dancing'.

Masurius then goes back to the subject of music, establishing once more an opposition between the 'olden times' (Τὸ δὲ παλαιὸν, καὶ πάλαι), full of nobility, and a decayed present (νῦν δὲ, οἱ καθ᾽ ἡμᾶς); this clear-cut contrast is followed by another contrast between past and present, contained in a passage cited from Aristoxenos, where the past is probably the same past, but the present should be the time of Aristoxenos. The clear citation-marks at the beginning (διόπερ Ἀριστόξενος... ὅμοιον, φησί, ποιοῦμεν, 'Hence Aristoxenos says, we do the same as...', 632a), in the middle (οὕτω δὴ οὖν, φησί, καὶ ἡμεῖς... καθ' αὑτοὺς γενόμενοι ὀλίγοι ἀναμιμνησκόμεθα οἵα ἦν ἡ μουσική, 'In like manner we also, says Aristoxenus, ...will get together by ourselves, few though we be, and recall what the art of music used to be', 632b) and at the end of the passage (ταῦτα μὲν ὁ Ἀριστόξενος, 'This Aristoxenos said', 632b) leave no doubt as to who is speaking.[18] At the same time, the use of the direct speech puts Aristoxenos' words on the same level as those of Masurius; Aristoxenos is in fact appropriated by Masurius as giving evidence for the Deipnosophists' own times.

After rounding off the citation (632b), Masurius goes on expressing his own opinion (Κἀμοὶ) on an altogether different subject, namely that music should be the subject of philosophic reflexion. A few examples (examples and not citations) taken from the past (Pythagoras, the men of old, Homer) are then given in support of this contention by the orator (632b–632f); Masurius continues much in this same vein, giving examples but not direct citations, or only very few and incidental ones, until the end of his speech, which he himself announces, rounding it off with one last citation from a piece of the comic poet Philetaerus (633 e–f), partly mimetic of his own words:

Ἐγὼ δὲ ἔχων ἔτι πολλὰ λέγειν περὶ μουσικῆς αὐλῶν ἀκούων βόμβου καταπαύσω τὸ πολυλογεῖν, τὰ ἐκ Φιλαύλου Φιλεταίρου ἐπειπών· ὦ Ζεῦ, καλόν γ' ἔστ' ἀποθανεῖν αὐλούμενον...

Though I might say many things more on the subject of music, I hear the loud trill of flutes, and will therefore bring my long-winded discourse to a close, after repeating the lines from *The Flute Lover* of Philetaerus: Zeus, it is indeed a fine thing to die to the music of flutes...

The following part shows once more the ability of Athenaeus in playing with the possibilities of enunciation. Masurius has stopped talking, but a ζήτησις, a question, arises, says the narrator, concerning the sambuca, and it falls again to Masurius to explain (in indirect speech: ἔφη + infinitive, so that the narrator stays marginally present) that it is a musical instrument with a high pitch. But after the end of the phrase, the discussion concerning the sambuca goes on with finite verbs, giving the impression that the narrator has resumed complete control. In fact, this part should probably be attributed to Masurius, as is shown a few lines later (634c) by an intervention in direct speech, made by one of the Deipnosophists, containing an apostrophe to Masurius (Εἰπόντος δὲ ἐπὶ τούτοις Αἰμιλιανοῦ· ἀλλὰ μήν, ὦ ἑταῖρε Μασούριε, ..., 'Upon this Aemilianus said: Look you, Masurius, friend...'. This opening is followed by an ample appendage of citations concerning the *magadis*, and rounded off in ring composition by a renewed apostrophe to the same Masurius (τὴν ἀπορίαν οὖν μοι ταύτην οὐδεὶς ἄλλος δυνήσεται ἀπολύσασθαι, καλὲ Μασύριε, ἢ σύ, 'This question, therefore, no one else will be able to solve for me, my good Masurius, but you', 634c–634e). With this, the dialogue gets restarted, and Masurius answers in direct speech (καὶ ὃς ἔφη· Δίδυμος... ἑταῖρε Αἰμιλιανέ, 'And he said, Didymus..., friend Aemilianus'). His interventions *in prima persona* are limited enough; there is an οἶδα, 'I know', at 637a; the listing of citations goes on until 639b, where an intervention by the narrator marks the end of Masurius' second speech and a change in the situation of the symposiasts, which will introduce also a change in the topics to be discussed:

> Τοσαῦτα τοῦ Μασουρίου διεξελθόντος περιηνέχθησαν ἡμῖν καὶ αἱ δεύτεραι καλούμεναι τράπεζαι, πολλάκις ἡμῖν διδομέναι,

> After Masurius had concluded this long recital, the second tables, as they are called, were brought in and set before us; they had often been served to us,

as the narrator adds, not merely during the Saturnalia, for this custom is also Greek. This introduces a discussion (by the narrator) of Saturnalia, Cronia and similar festivals, which is brought to an end in 640a by the remark in ring composition of the narrator:

> Πολλάκις οὖν, ὡς ἔφην, τῶν τοιούτων ἡμῖν παρατιθεμένων ἐπιδορπισμάτων.

> Well, as I was saying, we often had such things served to us as dessert.

This leads quite naturally to the subject of desserts, which will last until the end of the book. It is important to note here that the opening and closing remarks by the narrator imply a series of banquets, not just the one in question, and that the fact that the excursus is assumed by the narrator makes it possible to detach this, as an excursus, from the banquet of the Deipnosophists—even though the pronouns of first person plural might once more lead us in trouble.

After a few citations by the narrator, there is a transition to the internal dialogue, brought about by the reference to the actual dishes in front of the banqueters;[19] the speaker, Pontianus, goes on with his discourse on desserts, but it is not clear for how long, the end of his speech not being explicitly marked. The narrator in 643e–f is already in charge, so by then we have to assume a change, but it is difficult to know where to put it. The first deictic pronoun we find is an ἡμῖν in 641e ('Ἀριστοτέλης δ' ἐν τῷ περὶ Μέθης παραπλησίως ἡμῖν δευτέρας τραπέζας προσαγορεύει, 'Aristoteles in his treatise *On drunkenness* uses the term "second tables" much as we do in this passage'), and we cannot know whether it refers already to the narrator or still to Pontianus. The same applies to another ἡμῖν, 'to us', plus the verbal form ἀπομνημονεύσωμεν ('let us recite from memory') in 643a. The reader has to assume that either at 641e, or at 643a, or at least at 643e–f, Pontianus' speech stops and the narrator comes back, but it is impossible to pinpoint the moment in which the change takes place. Alongside this merging of subjects of enunciation, there are also traces of chronological conflations. A nice case is offered by a citation from Alexis: 'The man who first discovered desserts was smart. For he found a way to prolong the party and never have our jaw-bones idle', 642c, which in its applicability to the actual situation conflates once more the times, ancient and modern, which had been distinguished at the beginning of the speech, 641c–e; again a reference to the actual situation is in 643a (ἐπεὶ δὲ καὶ ὁ Κυθήριος Φιλόξενος ἐν τῷ Δείπνῳ δευτέρων τραπέζων <u>μνημονεύων</u> πολλὰ καὶ τῶν <u>ἡμῖν</u> παρακειμένων ὠνόμασεν, φέρε καὶ <u>τούτων</u> <u>ἀπομνημονεύσωμεν</u>, 'Inasmuch as Philoxeos of Cythera in the *Banquet mentioned* second tables and named many viands that were served to *us*, let us recite *them* from memory').

As noted above, in 643e–f the narrator is back in charge, and his intervention is a very elaborately construed one:

> Πλακούντων δὲ ὀνόματα πολλῶν καταλεξάντων, ὅσων μέμνημαι τούτων σοι καὶ μεταδώσω. οἶδα δὲ καὶ Καλλίμαχον ἐν τῷ τῶν παντοδαπῶν συγγραμμάτων Πίνακι ἀναγράψαντα πλακουντοποιικὰ συγγράμματα Αἰγιμίου καὶ Ἡγησίππου καὶ Μητροβίου, ἔτι δὲ Φαίστου. ἡμεῖς δὲ ἃ μετεγράψαμεν ὀνόματα πλακούντων τούτων σοι καὶ μεταδώσομεν, οὐχ ὡς τοῦ ὑπ' Ἀλκιβιάδου πεμφθέντος Σωκράτει· ὃν Ξανθίππης καταπατησάσης, γελάσας ὁ Σωκράτης οὐκοῦν, ἔφη, οὐδὲ σὺ μεθέξεις τούτου.

1. 'Since many of the guests enumerated names of different cakes, *I* will *share* with *you* all *I* can *remember* of them.' 2. '*I know*, too, that Callimachus in his *Pinax* of miscellaneous writings has *recorded* (in writing) writings on the making of cakes, by Aegimius, Hegesippus, Metrobius and Phaestus.' 3. '*We*, in like manner, will *share* with *you* the names of cakes which *we* have *transcribed*, not as happened to the one sent to Socrates by Alcibiades; after Xanthippe had trampled it under foot, Socrates said, with a laugh, Well, you shan't have a share of it either'.

There are a number of interesting features in this intervention, which has the function of introducing the catalogue of cakes (extending from 644a to 648c), given in the form of a catalogic narration (with each time the lemma, explanation and citations from authorities).

In the first part, the addressee (σοι) is probably Timocrates: it is difficult to think of someone else. The first person refers then to Athenaeus, and we are in the mode of the external dialogue (level 2). Athenaeus is talking to Timocrates, and says that he is going to share with him all he can remember. The rather abrupt transition to Callimachus (fr. 435 Pfeiffer) introduces the theme of writing; the speaker is still Athenaeus-the-narrator, but for the addressee we have to choose between Timocrates and an external reader, which means that we may be in the external dialogue mode (level 2) or in the external narration (level 1). The third part presents us with a first person plural, and with an explicit addressee (σοι): the (plural) speaker promises to share with the addressee the names of cakes which he has transcribed. The reader may assume that the transcribed cake-names come from the books of the authorities cited by Callimachus (the names of the cakes themselves would probably not have been given on the *pinakes*). Athenaeus would thus give to Timocrates the names of cakes mentioned by the diners, and moreover other names taken from books on cakes. The wording however does not warrant such an assumption. One possibility is to think that here the writing is badly compressed, and that the change from the first person singular to the first person plural has no meaning whatever.[20] The other possibility—but this may be over-interpreting the text—is to interpret the allusion to Callimachus as a kind of statement about literary quality:[21] if Callimachus has recorded a number of books on cakes in his *pinakes*, then books on cakes can pretend to the status of literature, and here a new one is being produced, Athenaeus' own book. The stress on terminology connected to writing is here very strong, and there are elsewhere in the *Deipnosophistae* numerous other passages in which the literary and written status of the work is underlined,[22] so that such an interpretation appears attractive. At the same time, this would have to be a gigantic—quite intelligent and amusing—joke by Athenaeus against himself: the authors here mentioned have been carefully chosen among the most forgotten of Greek literature: save for Hegesippos, who gets another mention thanks to Athenaeus (12.516d), this is their only mention in extant Greek literature; had he wanted, however, Athenaeus might have chosen authors whom he at least had cited more frequently.

All this may give a clue for the interpretation of the following first person plural. It might possibly be explained as referring to Athenaeus and his fellow guests, since in the beginning the discussion concerning the names of the cakes is attributed to many diners (πολλοί); one may compare 1.4b, where the Deipnosophists are said to be bringing as a contribution τὰ ἀπὸ τῶν στρωματοδέσμων γράμματα, 'their books tied up in rolls of bedding', or with 7.277a, where the narrator (addressing himself to Timocrates) has the diners look for names of fishes in books.[23] If the first person plural refers to Athenaeus and the Deipnosophists, the addressee might still be Timocrates, but we would have to assume, just for a moment, a conflation of frames (levels 4 + 2). The other possibility might be to think of Athenaeus (possibly with Timocrates), addressing himself to the intended audience of the *Deipnosophistae*. In a situation where the literary (written) status of the work is being heavily stressed, an address to the reader might be possible; in this case, we would be in the situation defined as external narration (level 1). The enunciative sequence of the passage would then be: Athenaeus addressing Timocrates (level 2); aside by Athenaeus (level 1), implicit addressee the reader; and Athenaeus (plus Timocrates taken almost as co-writer) addressing the external reader.[24] It may be worthwhile to point out that whereas in the cases where Athenaeus addresses Timocrates (in the external dialogue) he talks of himself using indifferently the first person singular or plural, in the cases recognized by Letrouit as external narration, when the narrator makes himself present he never uses the first person singular, and the addressee is clearly someone outside—a reader.[25]

The amusing comparison between the sharing of the name of cakes by the writer and the destruction by Xanthippe of a cake, of which no one will be able to partake (the opposition obliterating once more the distinction between what is written and the reality: sharing a cake is compared to sharing its name), provides a smooth transition to the subject of cakes. After this, the narrator surfaces twice in the beginning (644a), and then keeps in the shade, simply giving a long catalogic list (644c to 647c); this list is followed by another catalogic narration, this time taken as a whole from an authority, Chrysippus of Tyana (647c–648a). The status of this part is kept clear by the frequent use of φησί; the citation closes with an explicit: ταῦτα καὶ ὁ σοφὸς πεμματολόγος Χρύσιππος, 'All this from the wise cake-doctor Chrysippus'. The following authority (648b) is an otherwise unknown Harpocration of Mendes (in Egypt); until 648c three more examples follow, from Alcman, Epicharmus and Pherecrates, given according to the modalities of the 'narrator's catalogue'. From the point of view of enunciation the interesting feature of this catalogic section (644c to 648c) is that it is not explicitly attributed to anyone: this is interesting in view of the difficulty in determining the referent for the first person plural in 643e–f.

The speech by Ulpian in 648c begins by quickly and wittily alluding back to the question of literacy:

πόθεν ὑμῖν, ὦ πολυμαθέστατοι γραμματικοί, καὶ ἐκ ποίας βιβλιοθήκης

ἀνεφάνησαν οἱ σεμνότατοι οὗτοι συγγραφεῖς Χρύσιππος καὶ
Ἁρποκρατίων, διαβάλλοντες καλῶν ὀνόματα φιλοσόφων τῇ ὁμωνυμίᾳ;

Whence, most learned grammarians, and from what collection of books,
have popped up these very solemn writers Chrysippus and Harpocration,
who bring calumny on the names of noble philosophers by the similarity of
their own names?

This opens up an important question: the authors here mentioned are known to
us only by Athenaeus, and now he, by way of one of his characters, appears to cast
some doubt on them. Chrysippus of Tyana is mentioned here, and also cited as
authority in 3.113 a–d. There, after a catalogue of kinds of bread by Pontianus, one
of the grammarians, Arrian, never to be heard of again in all of the *Deipnosophistae*,
had made an intervention completely built on the citation of Chrysippus' *Bread-
making*. His intervention had been received with marked scorn, by the narrator as
well as by the diners, Cynulcus in particular; one of the reasons for offence had
been the fact that he (Arrian repeating Chrysippus) had used plenty of Roman
vocabulary.[26] Now it is interesting to observe that to Apollonius of Tyana (in
Philostr. *V.Ap.* V 5, and in *Ep.* 71) are attributed angry words against the habit of
the Ionians of using Roman words and even proper Roman names in Greek.
Ulpian's remarks on the calumny which these obscure authors—be they real or
invented: the second possibility would add one more interpretive level into play—
bring on the names of noble philosophers should then possibly be understood as
another *double entendre*: there is a famous Chrysippus of Soli, but the philosopher
meant here could be at the same time Apollonius of Tyana. As for the 'famous'
philosopher whose name would be defiled by Harpocration from Mendes,
'Platonicus ille videtur intelligendus, quem Caesaris familiarem fuisse Suidas
tradit': so Schweighaeuser,[27] and I do not think there is need for further comment.

This point is however not taken up by the fellow diners, so that it seems
best to take it as a way of closing, by the character, the line on literary status
opened with the Callimachean reference—itself at least partly bogus—of the
narrator; it introduces in fact the return to the dialogic mode. This time the
dialogue is quite animated, Ulpian, Larensis, Ulpian again and Democritus
intervene (648c–649c);[28] and, from 649c, there is an answering speech of Ulpian,
interrupted at the beginning by a few comments from the narrator. This speech
develops gradually into a catalogue which lasts until 653d. At this point Ulpian
asks for an explanation:

Ἐγὼ δὲ πάλιν ζητῶ τίς ἡ γενναία σταφυλὴ καὶ τίνα τὰ γενναῖα σῦκα.
ὥρα οὖν ὑμῖν ζητεῖν, ἕως ἐγὼ περὶ τῶν ἑξῆς παρακειμένων διεξέλθω.

But I again ask, What is meant by the 'choice' grapes and what are the 'choice' figs? It is high time, therefore, that you seek the answer while I discourse on the viands served in order.

Masurius answers with a speech, whose end is not clearly signalled; but in 658e we retrospectively learn that Ulpian has been talking (Τοιαῦτά τινα ἔτι τοῦ Οὐλπιανοῦ διαλεγομένου, 'While Ulpian was still discoursing in this vein'). This means that we have to locate this change in interlocutors somewhere, and the place which recommends itself is 654a:

Ἐπεὶ δὲ πολλάκις ὑμῖν εἴρηται περί τε κρεῶν καὶ ὀρνίθων καὶ περιστεριδίων, ἔρχομαι κἀγὼ λέξων ὅσα ἐκ πολυαναγνωσίας εὑρεῖν ἐδυνήθην παρὰ τὰ προειρημένα,

Since you have often discussed the subject of meat and fowls, including pigeons, I too am going to tell what I have been able to discover in the course of wide reading, over and beyond what has already been said.

Before we may put a name on this 'I' (κἀγὼ), however, we have to go through another catalogic speech, which, even though the speaker in 658d announces his will to stop ('and now, having spoken about all the dishes served to us..., I will cease my discourse', ἐπεὶ δὲ περὶ πάντων εἶπον τῶν παρακειμένων... καταπαύσω τὸν λόγον), lasts in fact a few paragraphs more, until 658e, where the narrator shows that it was Ulpian speaking.[29] Incapacity, or deliberate wish to blur distinctions? This passage presents also another inconsistency: in 654a the speaker announced, making at the same time a cross-reference to topics discussed in the ninth book (373a–406c), that he was going to add information derived from his wide reading; but in 658d, he implies that he has been talking about dishes actually served to the diners.

The arrival of a cook 'famed for learning' announcing that he has brought a '*myma*' introduces a change: the cook, seeing the surprise of the guests, begins a long speech (from 658e to 662e) on μάγειροι, 'cooks', and μαγειρική, 'cooking', stressing the erudition of cooks (he is here mimetic of his own discourse). His speech is brought to an end by a direct address to the guests, concerning the starting point of his speech, the dish called μῦμα.

In 662e the narrator comments disparagingly on this cook and describes the arrival of another cook, bringing the ματτύη; this leads to a ζήτησις, or enquiry, on the *mattye*. Two interlocutors are named, Ulpian and Aemilianus, but their intervention is simply narrated by the narrator who stays in charge. The end comes, without a proper conclusion regarding the *mattye*, at 664f:

Τοσούτων καὶ περὶ τῆς ματτύης λεχθέντων ἔδοξεν ἀπιέναι· καὶ γὰρ
ἑσπέρα ἦν ἤδη. διελύθημεν οὖν οὕτως.

After all this had been said on the subject of the *mattye* we decided to leave;
for by this time it was evening. So at this point we dissolved the meeting.

This closes the book as a unit and has to be taken, I think, as external
narration (level 1), as is the case for the ends of Books Five, Six, Nine, and Ten
according to Letrouit; the subjects are Athenaeus and Timocrates.[30] But this is
again a case of confusion in the referents, since the passage may also be
understood as referring to the end of another day of Larensis' banquet.

A fitting conclusion is offered by the beginning of Book Fifteen at 665a,
with its reference to the impossibility of recalling what was said in the banquets
(plural), not only because of the diversity, but also because of the similarity of the
novel devices brought forth from time to time.[31] Athenaeus' devices are not
inexhaustible, for we have seen all along how he has been playing with time and
reference. Here he gives up overtly the fiction of one banquet, but this had been
done already more than once.

What may be the meaning of this, what are the implications of this play on
reference for our understanding of the work?

First, the element of literary construction must not—as has so often
happened—be undervalued.[32] We may get at 'Athenaeus' by working from the
selection and the disposition of the material employed in the *Deipnosophistae*, but
the interplay between frames and content, narrator and character, and his text and
that of the authorities cited is an important factor in his work. In our case, for
example, the changes in enunciation help to underline the general structure of
Book Fourteen. An introduction in the external dialogue is followed by a dialogic
part, interspersed by remarks from the narrator. A stronger intervention by the
narrator (the one concerning Amoebeus) is followed by Masurius' two long
speeches on the subject of music. Another intervention in ring composition by the
narrator forms the centre of the book, and signals the change of topic; after this
there follows a stretch of dialogue, again interspersed by more or less heavy
interventions by the narrator. A particularly heavy intervention by the narrator
(the one about Callimachus' *pinakes*) is again followed by two long speeches in
catalogic forms; the end of the book is marked by the return to the external
dialogue.

Second, we might want to entertain the possibility of giving a different
answer from 'incapacity' to the question of Athenaeus' failure to create the illusion
of real conversations held during a real banquet. Usually this failure is explained

## 3. Semantic consequences of the enunciative play

by the difficulty of presenting in a psychologically acceptable way the enormous bulk of the material gathered.[33] As Mengis pointed out, Athenaeus does not make use of the very simple expedient of referring to the time and place of the events he is relating, in order to make it credible that he remembers them all.[34] In fact, he does not locate the distance in time between his own recital to Timocrates and the banquet(s). Could it be that for some reasons he did not want to determine and circumscribe too precisely the banquet?

The shift in the subjects of enunciation, especially when the text is built on a comparison or an opposition, whether explicit or implicit, between ancient and modern times, may assume a role in conveying particular nuances. More precisely, I would suggest that the shifts in the subjects of enunciation, when they concern not just the frames but the relationship between Athenaeus and the authorities he cites, may be viewed as a means to appropriate or subtly modify the contents of the texts cited. The lack of a strong chronological distinction between the frames themselves, and between the frames and the situation to which the text of the authorities adduced should be referred, creates a sort of vacuum, a space devoid of time in which the bits of information collected by Athenaeus find a 'textual' collocation without having any 'real' collocation. This intended decontextualization may also explain why the information provided by Athenaeus is in fact so difficult to use; the section on dance may be used to exemplify this procedure.

This section may be divided in three parts: a first general one, on the relationship between dance, war and society (14.628c–629c, drawing on different kinds of sources, mostly from literary texts); a second, catalogic one, which gives only names of dances and little more (14.629c–630a; this part finds its only parallels in *lemmata* conserved by Hesychius and Pollux); and a third part, again more general, on the pyrrhic and the sikinnis dances, for which the principal sources indicated are Aristoxenus and Aristocles (14.630b–631e). The first part gives information of a very general kind, and is paralleled in contemporary texts, so that it may be considered as echoing a general culture. The second part, however, is at the same time extremely specialized and absolutely devoid of sense, in that no context is given for those dances; for Athenaeus himself they were probably mere names. The third part, on the pyrrhic and the sikinnis, is the most interesting: for the pyrrhic was still danced in Athenaeus' time, as we know from the epigraphical evidence, and was much discussed in the contemporary scholia and metrical treatises. However, the information that Athenaeus chooses to give us presents one astonishing feature: even though he dedicates almost two pages to the pyrrhic dance and its aetiologies, he omits to mention the best-known aetiology, the one already present in Euripides' *Andromache*, the one which everybody in the imperial period knew, from Lucian to the *scholia vetera* in Pindar to the metrical treatises:[35] the aetiology connecting the dance with the son of Achilles, Pyrrhos or Neoptolemos, that is to say, the Trojan aetiology. Athenaeus certainly knew about this tradition; apparently he chooses not to discuss it.

His manipulations appear thus to have exerted themselves at many levels. From the choice of the contents, to the 'cutting' of the fragments, to the enunciative shifts—all speaks of an 'author' very present behind his work, of an author playing both with his own culture and with his reader.*

# 21

# PLEASURE AND PEDANTRY IN ATHENAEUS

## by James Davidson

The subject of my chapter can be described in terms of a paradox: the subject of the *Deipnosophistae* is pleasure and yet it is far from pleasurable to read. This relationship between a titillating subject-matter and what may be considered to be a dull, pedantic text which zooms in constantly on mere words is not, I want to argue, explicable in terms of accident or of a failure on the part of the author. It is interesting in its own right and needs to be understood as absolutely central to the whole work. However, precisely because it is so central, this paradox raises some very broad and wide-ranging questions about the *Deipnosophistae* which would require much more space than I have available to investigate properly. As a result this essay can be no more than suggestive.

To begin with (Section A) I want to ask simply 'What kind of a monument has Athenaeus constructed?' and to investigate how both pleasure and pedantry might fit into such a project. I have chosen to examine three possibilities in particular, looking at the *Deipnosophistae* as a funeral monument, a Hellenic monument and a sympotic Hall of Mirrors. These are not to be thought of as exclusive choices. In the second half (Section B), I will start at the other end of the problem, turning more directly to the difficult relationship between pleasure and scholarship in an attempt to discover what Athenaeus was trying to achieve.

## A. Athenaeus' Project

### I. The funeral monument

Nowadays it is a commonplace to see the impulse of representation in an absence, in the creation of a substitute, in a simulacrum for the lost object of love. This is a perspective which shows the influence of Lacanian psychoanalytic theory, but which also has sound Greek precedents. According to Pliny (*NH* 35.151), for instance, the terracotta portrait originated in an attempt by a modeller's daughter to preserve an image of her lover who was going abroad. She drew around the shadow cast by his face on the wall and her father filled it in with clay and baked it hard. This impulse is always most obvious perhaps in the field of the visual arts, and has been used to account for the origins of Greek sculpture as a stand-in for an absent (dead) personage, but texts too can be effigies, used to commemorate and memorialize the speaking subject.[1] Commemoration indeed is an important part of the sympotic tradition. Both Plato and Xenophon, to different extents, are commemorating Socrates, his unwritten words and a world of lost discourses in later fifth-century Athens.

We do not need to read death into the *Deipnosophistae* however. It is already clearly present. Indeed Athenaeus situates the whole work within a funerary context by opening with an adaptation of Plato's *Phaedo*, the dialogue which actually describes Socrates' death: 'Were you, Athenaeus, present in person at that fine assembly of the men called Dinnersophists, the gathering which has been so much talked of about the town? Or was the account you gave to your friends derived from someone else?' (Ath. 1.1f-2a; Plato, *Phaedo* 57a). The evocation of the *Phaedo* right at the beginning of the work immediately creates an atmosphere of loss, of nostalgia, and a slight sense of foreboding, which is only confirmed fifteen books later towards the end of the dialogue, when we hear of the death of Ulpian, one of the principal characters and perhaps the central figure in the entire work (15.686c). This is not to say that Ulpian equals Socrates and that his death is the whole point of the work, but on the other hand, these two rather startling references which almost frame the dialogue seem to be connected. If we remember, at the same time, that the Socrates of the *Phaedo* spends most of his time exalting the spiritual and denigrating 'the so-called pleasures of the body, food and drink ... and sex' (64d), we begin to see that the whole of the *Deipnosophistae* can be viewed as a kind of anti-*Phaedo*, a celebration of the sensual world to counter Socrates' contempt for it. Athenaeus was not the first to attempt this subversion of Plato.[2] Tacitus describes the death of Petronius in very similar terms. He commits a slow suicide, dying more or dying less as the mood takes him, while listening to light poetry and playful verses, and nothing philosophical, nothing on the immortality of the soul. He also reviews the scandalous life of the emperor with a catalogue of all his liaisons (*Ann.* 16.18–19).

In composing his symposium in the funerary mode, however, Athenaeus is not simply being ironic or parodic or adoxagraphic. *Bios* (life) is often treated in material, substantive terms by the Greeks as the sum of the phenomena of living, a *vivid* life, not the opposite of death, but at the opposite pole, as far as possible from the shadowy insubstantial existence of the underworld, the life of 'This is the life!', 'the good life', the life of sensation and pleasure. Of the three surviving images of *Bios* as a personification, two depict him in association with the goddess

*Truphê* (Decadent Refinement). Both, incidentally, come from Ulpian's Syria and are approximately dated to the third or fourth centuries AD.[3]

More specifically, there is a very long Greek tradition in which death and the symposium are opposed and occasional examples which extrapolate from this to present the symposium in a funereal context as an evocation of the life lost. On this subject I have little to add to Oswyn Murray's conclusion in his article on 'Death and the Symposium':

> ... there existed in the Greek world a polarity, a more or less absolute distinction between the world of the *symposion* and the world of the dead. The occasional evidences of the sympotic lifestyle in death and the occasional exceptions are to be explained not as part of a systematic vision of the afterlife, but as a pale echo of life itself, a symbol perhaps of the status of the dead man, a defiant gesture by an individual protesting against death ... Of course death, if it is to be more than the absence of life, must be a reflection of life; but for the Greeks of the classical age that reflection was no more than an *eidolon*, a ghostly shadow .... The confrontation between death and the *symposion* concerns this attempt to come to terms with mortality.[4]

This memorial perspective can be quite productive when turned on the *Deipnosophistae. Prima facie* of course it commemorates a gathering 'much talked of about the city'. After a while this single gathering turns nostalgically into a lost world with many such gatherings, a nostalgia which is especially pronounced, as Paola Ceccarelli observes, in the last few books: 'Rhapsodes were not missing from our symposia ... and those called hilarodes often performed for us' (14.620b). This is a long way from the vivid and detailed present of the earlier books and represents a kind of distancing from this world as the dialogue accelerates towards Ulpian's death, which comes to represent not merely the demise of one man, but the fact that these learned parties and this text are now over. His death is described as a falling silent (σιωπὴν 15.686c), so how appropriate to commemorate him in a discourse.[5]

I do not think it is pushing the funeral analogy too far to see the work also as a commemoration of the Life of Greece. Bios (Life) is not only conceived in material terms, it could also be generalized as the life of a nation. At the end of the fourth century BC Clearchus of Soli had compiled his *Bioi* describing the luxurious habits of various peoples and Dicaearchus of Messana wrote a *Bios Hellados*, tracing the development of victuals through history. Both are often cited by Athenaeus. Athenaeus is commemorating and celebrating three losses, then: Ulpian, the world of the *Deipnosophistae* and the Life of Greece itself.

But if death can account for the subject-matter of Athenaeus' work through a process of inversion how does the funeral analogy account for the pedantic style? It might be useful in this context to distinguish two kinds of fastidiousness. First there is the tendency not merely to allude gracefully, but to cite with references. As several contributors to this volume have noted, this is a peculiar characteristic. Many Greek writers of the Roman empire refer to classical literature, but it is an important part of the characterization of their cleverness and of the relationship with their readers that they do not spell out exactly what they are citing. In this respect they are gentlemen amateurs self-consciously carrying their knowledge lightly. They flatter and seduce the reader into a generous assumption of shared knowledge by not providing footnotes, and they preserve the mirage of dilettantism by not leadening their learning with the *banausia* of chapter and verse.[6] Why is Athenaeus so heavy-handed? Is it possible that the *Deipnosophistae* is an obituary not just for a particular group of scholarly party-guests, but reflects an anxiety for the culture of scholarship itself on the eve of the Anarchy, a memorial to conversations which could no longer be staged?[7]

The second element in Athenaeus' pedantry, his lexical correctness, can be related more easily to the funeral motif. Athenaeus is using his text to revivify dead words and lost usages. In the discussion of *opsarion*, for instance at 9.385b–386c: 'When a large fish was served once in ὀξάλμη (vinegar sauce) someone said any fish (ὀψάριον) was very nice served like this.' Ulpian immediately objects. 'ποῦ κεῖται ὀξάλμη' he demands, adding 'I know that ὀψάριον is not used by any of the living authors' (οὐδενὶ τῶν ζώντων) a rather curious way to refer to Attic usage. Ulpian who is about to die spends the symposium clinging tenaciously to the language of 'the living', deferring his demise by spinning out the symposium with long digressions.

## II. A Hellenic monument

This debate about whether it is proper to use *opson* and *opsarion* to mean 'fish' shows Athenaeus participating very directly in the Atticist debate. As I have argued elsewhere, *opson* and its derivatives were notable battlegrounds for Greek discussion of proper meaning, a debate which goes back to Xenophon and Plato and to which both Hegesander of Delphi (probably) and Plutarch had contributed. In the previous generation, Pollux of Naucratis had included *opson* in his list of words to do with fish, while Phrynichus the Arab had glossed *opsarion* as 'not fish'. Athenaeus appears here as clearly a supporter of his fellow Naucratite Pollux and the moderate Atticists.[8]

Simon Swain has argued in his recent book, *Hellenism and Empire*, that Atticism had a geo-political function in defending a Hellenic space in the Roman empire, as a kind of antidote to imperial power. From this perspective we can look at the *Deipnosophistae* as a kind of Hellenic monument, which implicitly excludes the Romans, constructing within the narrow frame of the text a world of discourse rarely contaminated by Roman references, in a language unsullied by Latin barbarisms, such as 'decocta' (3.121e–122e). Swain refers in passing to Athenaeus as a partisan of Hellenic culture, but there remains much work to be done on his attitude to Rome, especially if, as both Frank Walbank and Tim Whitmarsh tend to suggest in this volume (Chapters 11 and 22), he revealed his antipathy in a sly or covert way. Meanwhile, David Braund (Chapter 1) finds that Athenaeus and of course Asteropaean Larensis are as comfortable with Roman as with Greek culture.

So much, then, for the Atticist pedantry, but what about the pleasurable subject-matter? In fact it is not too difficult to see how Athenaeus' theme would suit such a project. Not only is there a long tradition which pits the good life of the symposium against death, but there is another well-established tradition which pits the pleasures of peace against war and private life against politics with particular emphasis on the feast. As Yvon Garlan notes:

> Contrasted to a militaristic view of Greek history, there is also the eminent place reserved for the praise of peace in both public opinion and in the works of theoreticians. Of the texts celebrating its benefits one could make an abundant, quite repetitive collection, from the writings of Homer to those at the end of the Hellenistic period. There is always the same refrain: peace was abundance, the sweetness of life, joy, the enjoyment of the simple pleasures of life.[9]

This is something I have discussed elsewhere with regard to the jokes in Attic comedy about politicians' fondness for the fish-market.[10] The classic statement of this opposition is to be found in Plato's discussion of the difference between the Athenian symposium and the Spartan *syssition* in *Laws* (639d), but it goes all the way back to the lyric poets—'How long will you stay reclining? When will you recall your strong spirits, you young men? Are you not ashamed to neglect so much the borderlands? You seem to rest in peace, but war possesses all the land.' (Callinus fr.1)—and is perhaps most vividly deployed in the plays of Aristophanes. In *Acharnians*, *Peace* and *Lysistrata* especially, the world of war and the life of peace are opposed very simplistically, with peace usually characterized in a very material way as a chance to catch up on lost pleasures of the flesh: Copaic eels, drinking and sex. The clash is most starkly illustrated in the scene from the *Acharnians* where Lamachus's preparations for fighting are contrasted and parodied in Dicaeopolis's preparations for war. The contrast is also nicely developed in Sophocles' erotic sympotic 'stratagem' which is discussed in the conclusion to this chapter.

The sympotic world of the Dinnersophists, then, can be seen as a self-conscious abdication not only from the modern world and from the Roman world, but from the world of *affaires*. As Gulick notes in his introduction (ix–x): 'only politics is touched on lightly... The *Pax Romana* still prevailed, and Athenaeus's friends were conformists in political matters.' The author has made a determined effort to edit out of his sources references to politics and war, a selective process which, again, is most clearly seen in his citations of Polybius. If Athenaeus is contesting a space to defend from Roman power, he has deliberately chosen a battleground which lies at the opposite end of the spectrum from the political and military arena.

In a positive way, however, the symposium, as an institution of Greek culture and civilization is also a very suitable place for showing off Greek learning.[11]

I am not sure how far I would like to push this anti-Roman element in Athenaeus' Hellenism, however. Certainly there is an ever-present gulf between the Roman host whose wealth and power are on every occasion providing the real food, the real entertainers etc. and the guests whose contributions (*symbolai* 1.4b etc.) are in fact *grammata* rolled up in bedding. The precision of the citations serves to remind the reader of the actuality of these books, the materiality of the dinner-guests' textual offerings.[12] In their long discourses, the Dinnersophists are singing for their supper in a very direct way. But, on the other hand, Athenaeus emphasizes the complementarity of these discursive contributions, which match precisely the material pleasures offered by their host. Throughout the *Deipnosophistae* there is a rather peculiar identification of words about food with food. There is an actual feast going on, but there is also a feasting on words, which is given much more emphasis. If a lavish *Cena Trimalchionis* is in fact taking place at Larensis' house Athenaeus does not dwell on it. In the world of the text, the host's generosity is more than matched by the lexical simulacra of goodies which are offered by the guests in return.

Moreover there are Romans also amongst the guests. The contributions of one of them, Masurius, are singled out for particular praise in the author's own voice, and exceptionally the whole of Book Five is devoted to him, 'the completely excellent Masurius' (5.185a), 'in all things excellent and wise' (14.623e). Moreover, the whole banquet is set at Rome, which is described by Athenaeus at the beginning of the work, reflecting on its cosmopolitan character, as the epitome of the civilized world (*oikoumenê*). This is a cliché of Greek encomia of the city of Rome, used by Antonius Polemo, Dio Chrysostom, Aristides and Galen.[13] Here it seems a clear reference to the Dinnersophists themselves who do indeed come from the far corners of the eastern empire, the *oikoumenê*. In fact from this perspective it would not be too difficult to see the entire dialogue as a celebration of Rome's cultural capital, as Braund argues in Chapter 1. The guests are themselves a walking talking library, a glorification of Roman power as the library of Alexandria glorified the Ptolemies (cf. Chapters 6 and 7.)

Instead of finding aggression in Athenaeus perhaps there is a more gentle assertion of the richness of a lost Greek world, *always* in implicit and sometimes explicit contrast to modern splendours. The contemporary Roman world is omitted simply because in contemporary Rome it can be taken for granted.

*III. The specular monument*

The notion of the *Deipnosophistae* as a separate world, cordoned off from death (or life), from politics, from power, is reinforced if we view it as a specular monument. This way of describing the symposium and its artefacts goes back to an article published by Luigi Rossi in 1985, which referred to the Greek symposium of the classical and archaic periods as a *spettacolo a se stesso*, drawing a contrast with the more externally oriented magnificence of the Roman convivium and the medieval banquet.

This view of sympotic representation has been usefully developed by François Lissarrague in his study of vase images which frequently reflect the drinking-party back on itself *en abîme*.[14] Again, one does not need much ingenuity to fit Athenaeus' symposium into this model of specular representation. The author is often called 'polymathic', but as many of the contributions to this volume demonstrate, his digressions are very tightly controlled and rarely stray outside his sympotic theme. In the past this has usually been seen as a feature which deserves no comment, but in fact the editing out of almost all references to the extra-sympotic stories he found in his sources, often in close proximity to the passages he cites, required an enormous amount of self-discipline. This might be seen as a deliberate and self-conscious form of gentlemanly dilettantism but I think it should be seen in a slightly more positive sense as a desire to stick to his subject. The *Deipnosophistae* indeed stands out for its single-mindedness, staying much more closely to its theme than all other examples of the polymathic genre. Even Plutarch, not to mention Plato and Xenophon, allows some of his digressions to develop into autonomous investigations, on diseases, for instance, as Rebecca Flemming observes in Chapter 36, but as soon as Athenaeus seems to be getting involved in another area he changes the subject and returns to the banquet. The *Deipnosophistae* then, is in many ways, the most perfect example of the *spettacolo a se stesso* which is ascribed by Rossi (1985) to the archaic and classical periods. Atticism and lexicographical 'pedantry' suit this kind of project very well. The normal sequence is for a sympotic event, like the arrival of an item of food, or the sitting of the guests on chairs, to provoke a metasympotic comment, a comment which becomes an event in its turn, provoking its own metadiscursive remark, the kind I have labelled 'pedantic'. This sequence may take several paragraphs to develop but can be seen in a telescoped form in the discussion of *opsarion* at 9.385b.: a fish is served, somebody says any fish is nice in *oxalmê*, Ulpian leaps on the speaker's use of the word. Pedantry serves to confine the digression, to rein in the flow of discourse. The metadiscursive commentary on words creates a reflection *en abîme* which parallels very nicely Lissarrague's mirroring images.

An examination of these three aspects of Athenaeus' project underlines his peculiarity. He has created an extraordinarily claustrophobic dialogue with a very tight economy, which simultaneously seals the participants into the symposium and the text and cuts them off from the present, from the city of Rome outside, from politics and war, from matters of importance. He has created both an echo-chamber and a time-machine, a textual ark of Life and Lives, an intellectual cocoon. He is an anthologist with a rod of iron, a heavy-handed editor of the most light-weight material.

## B. Discourse and Pleasure

I now want to investigate in more detail the difficult relationship between pleasure and scholarly discourse. This can, of course, be a very complex relationship, but I want to look at just two aspects.

(1) Learning as an antidote to pleasure. This is most apparent when people ask whether by studying a work of art we are not spoiling our enjoyment of it, and is manifest in the careful distinction between connoisseurs of wine who examine the liquid according to a set of fixed rules and who may even spit out the object of their assessment and alcoholics who are so far from appreciating what they consume that it might as well be lighter-fluid.

(2) Learning as the hand-maiden of pleasure. Quite a different relationship is suggested by our suspicions when we hear that someone has decided to undertake a scholarly study of pornography, say, or sex or drugs. Here scholarship is seen as a cover for pleasure or even as a means of extending pleasure.

The Greeks were very fond of playing with this problematic relationship between learning and pleasure. In Aristophanes' *Banqueters*, we remember, the *katapugon* son shows his *katapugosunê* by *learning* about drinking Chian wine from Spartan cups etc. In *Wasps*, the son teaches his father Philocleon how to behave at a rich man's symposium. This ironic juxtaposition serves to hint at the unnaturalness of the 'soft life'. Likewise in Xenophon's version of Prodicus' *Choice of Hercules*, Vice (*Kakia*) makes her path look like a road to the schoolroom, noting that her acolytes will not be thinking about war and public matters (again the familiar opposition), but considering (*skopoumenos*) what choice food or drink you can find ... and how you may sleep most sweetly ... and how to come by all these pleasures with the least trouble. Virtue's (*Arete's*) reply emphasizes *Kakia's* role as an educator (*paideuô*) of her friends (Xen. *Mem* 2.1.24 and 30). It might seem that pleasure-seekers are simply going with the flow and following their natural impulses, but in truth the life of pleasure is artificial.

Like Vice herself, we often find that those who choose to educate on vicious subjects are seen as themselves vicious. Philoxenus and Archestratus are themselves gluttons. Philaenis is herself lascivious.

The author of the *Deipnosophists* is very aware of this dangerous relationship between pleasure and the learned discourse of pleasure. At 10.457c–e he cites a long passage from Clearchus *On Proverbs*, which seems to describe the Deipnosophists themselves, or even Athenaeus, rather precisely:

> For in propounding riddles in their drinking-bouts, the ancients were not like the people of today who ask one another what is the most delightful form of sexual commerce or what fish has the best flavour or is at the height of excellence at that season, or what fish is to be eaten chiefly after the rising of Arcturus ... All this is precisely the mark of one who has made himself thoroughly at home in the writings of Philaenis and Archestratus ...'

The implicit attack on Athenaeus' entire project is quite clear, but elsewhere is made more direct. After the long disquisition on different kinds of fish that fills Book Seven, Democritus accuses the rest of the diners of filling the symposium with *akolasia* (8.335e), by mentioning Archestratus. To back up his argument he cites three passages in which the Stoic Chrysippus classes Archestratus with Philaenis, denouncing those who learn these authors by heart (8.335b–e). In Book Thirteen, likewise, Cynulcus makes a savage attack on Myrtilus for his attacks on philosophers and his encomium of beauty (13.567a):

> But you, my professor of wisdom, wallow in the wine-shops, not with your male friends, but with your mistresses, keeping around you not a few female pimps and always carrying around books of that sort, by Aristophanes, Apollodorus, Ammonius and Antiphanes; and further Gorgias of Athens; all of these have written treatises *On the Hetairidai of Athens. o tês kalês sou polumathias...*'

He proceeds to call him a *pornographos* like the painters Aristides, Pausias and Nicophanes. After this he launches into his own discussion of the *Hetairidai* and *Pornai*, but in antiquarian, not encomiastic vein.[15]

The other alternative is to see discourse as an antidote to pleasure. Again there are several classical examples for this attitude. Plato in *Symposium* sends away the flute-girl so the guests can have a discursive *sunousia* instead (176e). Silent drinking in the manner of the festival of *Choes* is connected with deep drinking.[16] There is plenty of evidence for the opposition between talking and eating also in Athenaeus. According to the author himself, for instance, (11.781d):

> It is even gentlemanly, Athenaeus says, to pass the time with wine, provided that one does it reasonably, not drinking too deeply and not gulping it down in a single breath Thracian fashion, but mingling discourse (*logos*) with the potation as a *pharmakon hugieias* [a health drug].

However, Athenaeus' discourse is not any old discourse, but a particularly pedantic sort which turns constantly to lexical issues. What role does this metadiscourse play in the relationship with pleasure? Let us go back once again to the discussion of *opson* at 9.385b. A fish is served, someone says all fish is nice in an *oxalmê* and Ulpian questions his terminology:

> Now most of the company told him to mind his own business and went on eating; but Cynulcus shouted the lines from the *Breezes* of Metagenes: 'Nay, my good sir, let us dine first, and after you may ask me anything you like; for just now I am hungry and somehow have an awfully poor memory.'

Myrtilus, however, decides to answer and on finishing his disquisition makes an appeal (386d): "'This being so, allow us to dine. For look! While I have been talking to you the pheasants also have sailed in alongside, looking on us with contempt because of your unseasonable loquacity (*glôssargia*).'" Ulpian, however, simply sets him another lexical puzzle, promising that if he can answer he will go to the market and buy a pheasant to eat with him. The exchange of food for discourse, we should observe, operates among the guests themselves, not just between them and their Roman host.

Talking stops eating in several other points in the *Deipnosophistae:* at 8.354d, for instance the narrator tells us: 'Because of this long discourse of words, somebody ordered the cooks to continue to see to it that the dishes they served should not get cold.' The very idea of 'cold food' leads Cynulcus into citations of Alexis and Sphaerus. Just as they are about to tuck in again Daphnus tells them to stop so he can talk on fish from a medical perspective.

## C. Conclusion

I want to conclude this essay by comparing Athenaeus' pedantic pleasure discourse with two examples from the classical period. The first is from Xenophon's *Memorabilia* 3.14. The conversation is about the names given to people according to their behaviour. Socrates notices a young man who is taking too much *opson* and asks: 'And can we say, my friends, for what kind of behaviour a man is called *opsophagos*?' There follows a discussion of how much bread or *sitos* must be consumed to avoid the designation. Towards the end the young man surreptitiously reaches for a piece of bread. Socrates asks whether he is using *opson* as *sitos* or *sitos* as *opson*. The second passage is from Ion of Chios and is quoted by Athenaeus himself at 13.603e-604d. It describes Ion's meeting with Sophocles at Chios when he was a guest of the Athenian proxenus Hermisilaus.

> A handsome wine-pourer appeared, standing by the fire, red in the face. Sophocles was stirred. He said: 'Do you want me to drink with pleasure?' And when the boy said 'Yes,' he said, 'Then do not be too rapid in handing me the cup and taking it away.' When the boy blushed still more violently he said to the man who shared his couch: 'That was a good thing Phrynichus wrote when he said: There shines upon his crimsoned cheeks the light of love'.

To this the man from Eretria (Erythrae?) who was *didaskalos grammatôn* said:

> Wise you are to be sure Sophocles, in the art of poetry; nevertheless Phrynichus did not express himself happily when he described the handsome boy's cheeks as crimsoned. For if a painter should brush a crimson colour on this boy's cheeks he would no longer look handsome. Surely one must not compare the beautiful with what is obviously not beautiful.

Laughing loudly at the Eretrian, Sophocles said:

> So, then, stranger, you do not like that line of Simonides either, though the Greeks think it very well expressed: 'From her crimsoned lips the maiden uttered speech'; nor again the poet who speaks of a 'golden-haired Apollo'; for if a painter had made the god's locks golden instead of black, the picture would not be so good. And so for the poet who said 'rosy-fingered'; for if one should dip his fingers into a rose-dye, he would produce the hands of a purple dyer and not those of a lovely woman.' There was a laugh at this, and while the Eretrian was squelched by the rebuke, Sophocles returned to his conversation with the boy.

We should notice first that in both cases, as in Athenaeus, the conversation takes off from real events in the symposium, a young man eating, a boy entering the room. In the first example, a discussion of terminology has an obvious moral and normative purpose. The pedantry is designed to define more precisely correct behaviour. In the second passage the discussion of language serves to create space and time for the contemplation of the boy. 'Take your time when approaching etc.' It extends the moment and amplifies the pleasure of looking, a savouring of the boy's complexion.

Sometimes in Athenaeus there is a normative element to the scholarly discussion, an attempt to discover the proper *taxis* for the symposium, the proper classical terms with which to discuss it. On the other hand there is nothing equivalent to Sophocles' encounter with the boy. Almost all the discussion takes off from 'real' sympotic events, but the discussion of women in Book Thirteen manifestly does not relate to any real erotic encounters with beauties of either sex. (It is significant also that Athenaeus never quotes Philaenis herself and other sex manuals, although her texts survived in his time and contained plenty of material that was not so graphic as to have put the feasters off their food.) The relationship between discourse and pleasure is symmetrical and reciprocal but it is also a question of alternatives, a relationship of substitution. From this perspective Athenaeus' banquet becomes a banquet of Tantalus, thanks to a simple rule: you cannot talk properly with your mouth full. The feast of words is a feast of not eating, an anti-feast. That frustration we often encounter in reading this scholarly text on pleasure is a frustration shared by Athenaeus' guests. It is deliberate, I suggest. It is Athenaeus' solution to the moral problem of pleasure-knowledge. The 'real' banquet, described as taking place during the conversations of the *Deipnosophistae* is evoked in the learned discussions which are provoked by it, but the author spends only the tiniest fraction of his text in describing it. Its main purpose is to protect the author from accusations of immorality. It is only referred to in order to be eclipsed by words.

Athenaeus, then, has composed a work which celebrates life and the life of Greece on a monumental scale within a text which postpones the living of it. The *Deipnosophistae* both prolongs pleasure and digresses from it indefinitely. The central paradox is not, perhaps, pleasure and pedantry, signified and signifiers, but life, death and representation.

# 22

# THE POLITICS AND POETICS OF PARASITISM
## ATHENAEUS ON PARASITES AND FLATTERERS

by Tim Whitmarsh

## 1. Introduction

That Athenaeus is an author worth reading in his own right has long been denied by fragmentarians, albeit implicitly, and (one suspects) without the effort of reading him. This chapter is premised upon the notion that the *Deipnosophistae* has a coherent literary identity, a 'poetics' both guiding the choice and presentation of subject-matter and informing the aesthetic conceptualization of the work. As this chapter sits in the midst of an enormous volume devoted to Athenaeus, I do not expect this premise to be especially controversial (at the very least, there is some safety in page numbers). My second premise, however, will be more contentious: that Athenaeus dramatizes for us a particular version of Graeco-Roman relations.[1] Of course his archaism and focus on linguistic niceties intersect with the broader cultural concerns of his period, and he is thus sometimes taken as exemplary of the supposed process whereby Greeks sought refuge from their current political subservience to Rome in the glorious classical past.[2] My thesis, however, is stronger: that Athenaeus specifically explores the structural relationship between Greek culture and Roman power in the present.

'Greek culture', 'Roman power': what do these terms mean? At a broad level, the polarity is reasonably clear: Greek writers and performers of the period generally imitate (linguistically, stylistically, thematically) their ancient heritage, notably Homer and the literature of classical Athens, constructing and inhabiting a fictive world of Greek literary and political supremacy in the days before Roman power, indeed before the Macedonian world-empire.[3] Greek culture, modelled on the past, thus constructs itself in opposition to the Roman present. It should be made absolutely clear, however, that this opposition is not so much a 'real' ethnic division of labour as a rhetorical effect generated by the Greek texts of the period. The vast majority of the Greek writers whose texts we possess were themselves Roman citizens as well as Greeks, many fully integrated into structures of Roman power (the equestrian order, the 'civil service', the Senate, even the consulate and imperial court). The figures often arrayed on the side of 'Greek culture' vs. 'Roman power' are precisely the least disempowered: the prestige garnered by literary and sophistic performance served to define them against those we might want to see as truly disenfranchised, the urban and rural poor. When we approach the polarity of 'culture' and 'power', then, we should always be aware that culture is an extremely marked and intense form of power in this period, and that any literary self-representation as the victim of power needs to be seen in the context of a larger negotiation of symbolic and economic capital.[4]

This chapter explores Athenaeus' representation of the power relationship between Greek and Roman as a literary and cultural *strategy*, not simply as an observation of an externally existing reality. It will be argued that the *Deipnosophistae* dramatizes the relationship between the sophists and their host Larensis, whom the epitomizer of the first book labels a 'wealthy Roman' (ἀνὴρ τῆι τύχηι περιφανής), as one of economic patronage, and specifically of parasitism (a phenomenon with a well-developed critical vocabulary in the literature of the principate, as we shall see).[5] The sophists' execration of flattery and parasitism (in particular, that of Democritus at 6.248d–262a) represents their humorously hackneyed and ill-conceived attempt to deflect from themselves the charge of precisely such conduct. Yet with a cunning twist, as I shall argue, Athenaeus finally re-appropriates the language which condemns flattery and parasitism to denote a positive characteristic, the playful elusiveness of his own text. The 'politics' of the *Deipnosophistae*, its representation of the relationship between Greek and Roman, are inseparable from its 'poetics,' its sense of aesthetic self-worth.

## 2. The politics of patronage

What does it mean to hold a Greek banquet in Rome? The Greek banquet, as Florence Dupont reminds us, is an overdetermined literary event, freighted with a rich cargo of allusion.[6] Behind the *Deipnosophistae* lie not only Plato's and Xenophon's *Symposia*, and all their acolytes both lost and extant (including Plutarch's *Septem sapientium convivium* and *Quaestiones conviviales*, and Lucian's *Lapithae vel convivium*), but also a tradition of sympotic poetics stretching back, through Theognis and his peers, to *Iliad* 9, and especially to the *Odyssey*. Athenaeus follows in this tradition, mixing (as his quotations alone show) comedy on the one hand, with philosophy and history on the other. Athenaeus innovates, though (as scholars note[7]) by focusing not on the drinking which comes after the meal, but on the meal itself (which Xenophon's guests sit through in silence: Xen. *Symp.* 1.11;

305

cf. Plut. *Mor.* 150c–d). This relocation of attention allows Athenaeus to explore in lavish, rich detail the interlocking aesthetics of food and textuality which underpin the *Deipnosophistae*; it does not, however, diminish the importance of convivial ethics to the society dramatized therein.

The symposium constructs an idealized society of élite males, from which women, lower classes and most foreigners are absent. Characteristic of the Greek banquet is an overriding emphasis upon *philia* ('friendship') and *isotês* ('equality'), values of sodality and solidarity.

Plutarch, writing just over a century before Athenaeus, writes of 'the table's capacity to make friendship' (τὸ φιλοποιοῦν ... τῆς τραπέζης, *Quaest. conv.* 612d; cf. *Cat. maj.* 25.4). Athenaeus himself underlines the antiquity of this tradition. An unidentifiable character in the first book derives *dais* ('feast'), with only slight etymological elasticity, from *dateisthai* ('to divide'), before quoting Zenodotus on Homer: 'an equal feast means a goodly feast' (δαῖτα ἐίσην τὴν ἀγαθήν 1.12c). The symposium creates an atmosphere within which the hierarchies of normal social life are banished in favour of relaxed camaraderie.

Yet from earliest times, Greek writers also make it clear that the ideal of élite unity anticipated in the symposium is subverted by interlopers, who out of ignorance or spite exploit the opportunity to vie for social status. To the extent that the presence of such interlopers signals the decadence of contemporary society, the rarefied community of the symposium and the exterior world interpenetrate one another: the social conflict in sixth-century BC Megara, for example, is played out in the sympotic poetry of Theognis.[8] The contrast sometimes made by modern scholars between Greek symposia and Roman convivia, that whereas the latter cement social hierarchy the former neglect it,[9] may thus oversimplify the picture. Although the rules of the symposium require equality and friendship, rules are in *practice* (I use the word in Bourdieu's sense[10]) there to be manipulated. Although constructed in terms of equality, the symposium is also a theatre of social hierarchy: offence can be caused by a slip-up in the seating-plan (see e.g. Plut. *Mor.* 148e149b), and the fragile veneer of free-speaking pleasantry[11] can be punctured by ill-judged words (e.g. Plut. *Alex.* 51).

*Philia* is one of the fundamental building-blocks of Greek society,[12] and in the literary record anyone who misuses it for private advantage is severely stigmatized. Classical Athens marks the first appearance of the language of *kolakeia* ('flattery'), in one sense a political word (denoting the practices of the demagogues),[13] but coming to refer to those who manipulate relationships of friendship for personal ends.[14] It is no surprise to discover that the latter meaning is frequently used in connection with the hierarchical relations of non- and post-democratic culture, and especially with monarchical courts. Under the Principate the problems of *kolakeia* are explored in several moral tracts, notably Plutarch's

*How to tell a flatterer from a friend*, Dio Chrysostom's third *Oration* and Maximus of Tyre's fourteenth *Oration*: two of these texts explicitly represent themselves as addressed to social superiors (Dio's to the emperor, Plutarch's to the consular and Commagenian prince Philopappus). The problem for these writers lies in how to map the language of the Greek élite tradition of *philia*, stressing equality and sodality, onto the hierarchical structure of Roman society: how can the speaker or writer, forced to confront (most obviously in Dio's case) a relationship of political and economic inferiority, present his relationship as one of equality? Self-presentation is a zero-sum game,[15] and the most powerful means of arrogating to oneself authority as a trustworthy *philos* is by impugning the *kolakeia* of others.

Whereas Plutarch, Dio and Maximus seek to establish their own credentials as *philoi* by condemning *kolakeia*, the satirist Lucian writes more knowingly about the need to indulge in it. His treatise *On hirelings* is a negative protreptic addressed to a Greek friend in whom the author claims to have detected a wish to become one of those who are tormented by friendships (*philiais*) with wealthy Romans (1). This form of friendship receives a gloss from Lucian: 'if such slavery as theirs should be called friendship' (εἰ χρὴ φιλίαν τὴν τοιαύτην αὐτῶν δουλείαν ἐπονομάζειν (1)). From the outset, Lucian establishes an uncertainty about the appropriateness of the language of *philia* to Roman hierarchical relations. The language of slavery (*douleia*) is repeatedly applied to this form of engagement (7; 8; 23; 25); the paradoxical nature of this fusion of *philia* and *douleia* is expressed through the oxymoron (borrowed, appropriately enough, from Plato's *Symposium*, 184c) *ethelodouleia*, 'willing servitude' (5). Lucian writes of the need for *kolakeia* to get by in such a situation (28; 35; 38). The fun of the piece lies in the continuously catachrestic use of the language of *philia*, to the extent that the reader is aware that any kind of dealing between Greeks and Romans in this situation presented in terms of friendship must be read ironically. Lucian's dialogue *In defence of 'Portraits'* shows an equally nuanced awareness of the politics of relationships with important Romans. In this piece, the authorial *persona*, Lycinus, hears of the reaction caused by his encomiastic dialogue *Portraits* upon its subject, namely the girlfriend of the emperor Lucius Verus: she replies that his praise is excessive, and thus constitutes *kolakeia* (2; 6). Lycinus counters that this modesty shows that his praise was too restrained (17)! He then proceeds to distinguish between flattery and praise on the basis that the latter is false and the former true (20–1). Yet this distinction is rather specious in the light of the dialogue's focus upon hyperbole: the reader is invited to question the distinction between praise and flattery, and to enjoy for their ingenious sophistry Lucian's evasions of the charge of *kolakeia*.

For Lucian, the language of *kolakeia* is an inevitable obstacle to be negotiated in hierarchical relationships, and especially those with Romans. It is crucial to bear in mind the lesson which Lucian teaches us (but which is also found at Plut. *Mor.* 53c), that denial of *kolakeia*, or the attribution of it to another, may well be a strategy of self-authorization by one who is himself vulnerable to the charge. I want to keep this point in mind as we turn to Athenaeus: the language of *kolakeia* is not simply descriptive of an anterior reality, but rhetorical, performative and dynamic, constructing and creating categories; moreover it necessarily invites the knowing reader to interrogate and challenge the status of the speaker. To condemn *kolakes* at a banquet where *philia* is the ideal is not simply to pinpoint others; it also focuses one's audience's attention upon one's own speech.

## 3. Athenaeus and the politics of parasitism

Athenaeus' section on parasites and flatterers in the sixth book (224c; 228d; 234c–262a) is introduced apparently incidentally, but (I shall argue) constitutes a passage central to an understanding of the politics and poetics of the *Deipnosophistae*. When the fish course is brought in, 'one of the parasites (*parasitoi*) and flatterers (*kolakes*)' (τις τῶν παρασίτων καὶ κολάκων, 6.224c) launches into a praise of the 'wealth and richness' of the course. Who are these hitherto unmentioned figures? Perhaps we might answer immediately, that they are clients (in Latin, *clientes*) of Larensis, the wealthy noble in whose house in Rome the *Deipnosophistae* is set. But translation inevitably raises the question of cultural difference: *kolax* means both more and less than *cliens*.[16] Specifically, *kolakeia* ('flattery') refers not to a formalized relationship, but, as we have seen, to a *style* of behaviour before a social superior which is decried by others. Whereas a Roman's *clientela* may have been (in general) readily identifiable as such, it is doubtful whether anyone outside of comedy and satire would have called himself a rich man's *kolax*. The language of *kolakeia* is manipulable for rhetorical and invective ends, and the question of who is and who is not a *kolax* is inevitably a matter of perspective.

Let us consider in greater detail the implications of the setting of the *Deipnosophistae* in the house of a 'wealthy Roman' (1.1a). Larensis is a conspicuous Hellenophile (1.2b–c), has collected an enormous library of ancient Greek books (1.3a) and himself contributes to the feast of learning. This would appear, *prima facie*, to mark him out as a 'good' Roman, such as Plutarch customarily praises for their *paideia* ('education').[17] Yet the acquisition of Greek learning (and Athenaeus' epitomizer uses of Larensis' compilation of his library the word κτῆσις, which means precisely 'acquisition') is not necessarily a positive thing. At one extreme, granted, stands Diodorus' praise of Rome for the intellectual resources it provides to the educated Greek (Diod. Sic. 1.4.2–3); at the other stands Marcellus' sack of Corinth and his expropriation of the statues, inevitably a much more morally ambiguous response to Greek culture (Plut. *Marc.* 21).[18] Rome stands for richness and luxury, but also for power and exploitation. The relationship between Greek learning and Roman power in this text is enacted through the tense, fissile language of intellectual patronage.

Athenaeus' passing reference in the sixth book to 'parasites and flatterers' reminds us, through the allusion to structures of patronage, that this feast of learning is supported by Roman finance. Although one might wish to counter that the setting of the banquet is only occasionally alluded to in the course (or courses) of the *Deipnosophistae*, the feast itself is frequently referred to in terms of 'richness' (πολυτέλεια), which serves to re-emphasize the economics of the text:[19] this is Greek *paideia* working for the Roman dollar. From this perspective we can begin to see why Ulpian, Plutarch and most of all Democritus pour out their vitriol upon flatterers and parasites: their scape-goating of such men is designed to occlude the hierarchical politics in which they are currently engaged and to proclaim the (spurious) parity of the élite feast. Athenaeus' coy satire allows his readers to see the irony of the sophists' proud words: thanks to the excess of their protest, they draw attention to their own implication in the structures of Roman patronage.

To what aspects of parasitism and flattery do the sophists object? As we shall discover, activity labelled as *kolakeia* is associated primarily with Greeks who pander to foreign despots (an association which strongly invites the reader to draw comparisons with the framing of the current banquet). For the remainder of this section (indeed, of this chapter), I wish to concentrate upon the speech of Democritus: the other major speech on parasites and flatterers, that of Plutarch (6.234c–248c), explores the archaeology of the terms and is only of marginal interest here. Democritus focuses largely upon the flattery by Greeks of tyrants: Philip of Macedon is discussed (6.248d–249a; 249c), as are Alexander (6.249d; 250f–251a), Dionysius (6.249e–250d), Hieron (6.250e), the Persian king (6.25la–c) and so forth. Here, as elsewhere (e.g. Pl. *Rep.* 575e; Max. Tyr. *Or.* 14.7), flattery and tyranny are two sides of the same coin. Democritus is contemptuous of the abasement shown by such people: 'degradation' (ἀθλιότης) is the word he uses of the *Klimakides*, the women who allow themselves to be used as ladders by Persian women (6.256d), while 'subservience' (ὑπηρεσία) is cited from Clearchus elsewhere (6.257b). Now, although such practices do go on between Greeks, there is specific criticism for Greeks who abase themselves before those from outside. Thus the Athenians come in for particular abuse for their flattering hymn to Demetrius Poliorcetes, the Macedonian puppet. They are referred to as 'flatterers *par excellence*' (οἱ τῶν κολάκων κόλακες, 6.253b); flattery is compared to a ravening beast, bringing madness into the city (6.254b). The reason for this virulence is not so much the degree of the Athenians' abasement, which hardly compares to that of (say) the Paphian aristocrats who will be mentioned soon, but in their betrayal of their proud legacy. After citing the hymn to Demetrius, Democritus proclaims haughtily:

This was the song sung by those who fought at Marathon, not merely in public, but even in their homes—those men who had put to death the man who prostrated himself before the Persian king, the heroes who had slaughtered countless myriads of barbarians!

ταῦτ᾽ ᾖδον οἱ Μαραθωνομάχαι οὐ δημοσίαι μόνον, ἀλλὰ καὶ κατ᾽ οἰκίαν, οἱ τὸν προσκυνήσαντα τὸν Περσῶν βασιλέα ἀποκτείναντες, οἱ τὰς ἀναρίθμους μυριάδας τῶν βαρβάρων φονεύσαντες. (253f)

The Athenians' acceptance of foreign domination is contrasted strongly with their proud tradition of resistance. Democritus recalls Marathon, the site of the Athenians' famous victory on behalf of Greece over the Persians, and their traditional hostility towards *proskynesis*, the prostration demanded by the Persian king which so offends Greek sensibilities so frequently in the literary tradition.[20] In the context of the *Deipnosophistae*, this stress upon the importance of cultural solidarity in the face of foreign monarchy only begs the question: does the Roman empire represent such a foreign power? Is complicity in the economic structures of Roman patronage a form of degraded parasitism? These questions are not answered as such—Romans occupy a negotiable position between the familiar and the foreign, between 'self' and 'other'[21]—but such questions *are* stimulated by the text, disquieting and disrupting the smooth, luxurious display of sophistry and power.

Modern literary criticism, especially that styled 'cultural history' or 'new historicism', rightly warns us not to neglect such indices of economic tension.[22] Issues of power—'class', but also 'race' and 'gender' (I use apostrophes because I am not sure that these terms can be transferred without nuance onto the various social structures of the Principate)—interpenetrate the literary sphere, so that not only are traces left of the means of literary production, but also the text actively engages the interpreter in the circulation of power. It is the critic's duty, I suggest, to resist the rhetoric of economic and political dominance, to read through the sheen of wealth and power for the irruptions of resistance and the hedged negotiations of complicity.

## 4. Athenaeus and the poetics of parasitism

I want to turn now to consider how Athenaeus presents flattery and parasitism, and their relationship to his overall literary strategy. It is here that my first premise comes into play, that the author is an artful organizer of his material. The remainder of this chapter will argue that this assimilation of the Deipnosophists to flatterers is a deliberate strategy on Athenaeus' part. I shall argue that Athenaeus links flattery to a kind of reckless, voluptuous literary pleasure which is best exemplified by his own text. In this way, I seek to show that the cultural–political frame is fundamentally tied to the 'poetic' frame.

The association of flattery with pleasure is first mooted in Democritus' citation of Plato's *Phaedrus*, that 'nature has added [into the flatterer] a mixture of entertainment not wholly unrefined (ἡδονήν τινα οὐκ ἄμουσον)' (6.254d = Pl. *Phaedr.* 240b). Discussions of the flatterer elsewhere emphasize his pleasurable qualities (e.g. Plut. *Mor.* 55a). This tradition of the welcome parasite is an important one, stretching from Philippus in Xenophon's *Symposium* (who turns up uninvited, but amuses all with his jokes) down to the παράσιτος Gnathon in Longus' *Daphnis and Chloe* (who is clearly in the favour of his master). Pleasure is the currency of the banquet, and we might thus detect here a more positive evaluation of the sympotic role of the flatterer. Plutarch, in his speech, records a number of witty sayings by parasites (6.242b–c; 245d–247e). Notable too in this connection are the *geloiastai* ('laughter-mongers') assembled by Ptolemy Philopator (6.246c–d), who recall the role of Xenophon's Philippus as *gelotopoios* ('laughter-maker', *Symp.* 1.11). Democritus' speech, too, emphasizes the relationship between flattery and laughter, relating a number of instances of joke-lovers (6.26lc–e), culminating with the story derived from Theophrastus' *On Comedy* of the attempt of the people of Tiryns to cure themselves of laughter-loving. Flattery is also associated with erotic pleasure: the lover (ἐραστής) is a flatterer, according to Clearchus (6.255c, following Pl. *Phaedr.* 240b). The association of flattery with fun and desire suggests the pleasures of the symposium, and links flattery to the aesthetics of the banquet.

What, then, is wrong with the pleasure produced by flatterers? Is it not precisely in keeping with the spirit of the occasion? It transpires from Democritus' speech that the problem is one of *excess*: the banquet requires 'proper order' (ὁ πρέπων κόσμος, as Plutarch puts it, *Mor.* 147f) as well as pleasure. Within the tradition of literary symposia, the serious and the playful interact.[23] Wine and the ideal of moderate drinking invite the participant to negotiate for himself the correct balance between playful liberation (of language and desire) and self-control. Flattery, on the other hand, gives nothing but pleasure. For example, Democritus, explaining why Amasis, king of Egypt, hosted parasites, quotes Herodotus' comment that he was a 'joke-loving man, not serious' (φιλοσκώμμων καὶ οὐ κατεσπουδασμένος ἀνήρ, 6.261c = Hdt. 2.174). Amasis loves his fun, but fails to combine this with the requisite earnestness. Flattering pleasure can go beyond the bounds of sympotic pleasure, to eastern decadence. Emblematic of this is the story of the Paphian prince, cited from Clearchus, who indulged in 'excessive luxury' (ὑπερβάλλουσαν τρυφὴν, 6.255e), whilst lying on 'expensive' (πολυτελῶν) carpets from Sardis, as his 'aristocratic flatterers' (εὐγενῶν κολάκων) attended to him. His main flatterer is referred to as a 'soft-flattering flatterer' (κόλαξ μαλακοκόλαξ, 6.258a).

Flattery provides pleasure untempered by seriousness. As an extension, it is also presented as a form of seductive falsity, or pleasure without *truth*. Flattery, Democritus tells us (following Theopompus), brought into Athens 'false witnesses' (ψευδομάρτυρες), 'lying accusers' (συκοφανταί) and 'false summoners' (ψευδοκλήτηρες, 6.254c). This partially explains the association of parasitism with Odysseus, the archetypal liar (6.251d).[24] Flatterers, moreover, are connected with acting. The sobriquet 'Flatterers-of-Dionysus' (Διονυσοκόλακες, 6.249f; 254b), usually applied (since Aristotle, *Rhet.* 1405a) to actors, is here used of the courtiers of the tyrant Dionysius; the theatrical association is mobilized, though, when Democritus tells us that these men 'used to pretend' (προσεποιοῦντο, 6.249f; προποιήματος is also used at 6.255c) to be short-sighted, since Dionysius was (6.249f); when Dionysius spat, they would present their faces/masks (πρόσωπα means either) to be spat upon; this process has already been referred to as 'acting with' (συνυποκρίνεσθαι) someone (6.249a; cf. 6.237c). Later, the flattery of the Paphian prince is said to have a 'lead actor' (πρωταγωνιστής 6.257b).

There is, however, a problem here. I argued earlier that, for all that the deipnosophists condemn those who pander to foreign rulers, they are condemned by the very framing of the text to reproduce that subservience. Similarly, with pleasure: although Democritus and, to a lesser extent, Plutarch condemn the excessive, luxuriant, false pleasure provided by flatterers, Athenaeus presents the banquet as a display of precisely these qualities: a surfeit of mimetic language, pandering to the reader's sensual pleasure.[25] The aesthetics of the *Deipnosophistae* are characterized by excess, multiplicity and openness. The text repeatedly slips metaphorically between food and words: the organization of the dialogue, the epitomator tells us, is an 'imitation' (μίμημα) of the feast (1.1b), for which he coins the term 'word-feast' (λογόδειπνον 1.1b). The sophists' words are described by the narrator as 'titbits' (λείψανα, 6.223d; see also e.g. 6.222a). This blurring of the boundaries between signifier and signified (is this text a meal about scholarship or scholarship about a meal?) encourages what others might see as an irresponsible pleasure in the consumption of words for their own sake.[26]

Alessandra Lukinovich has shown that the *Deipnosophistae* presents itself under the signs of *poikilia* ('variety') and *poluteleia* ('richness').[27] Words denoting multiplicity recur time and again at crucial junctures. The adjective *pantodapos* ('multiple'), for example, a word which will become important for us below, arises sixty times in the course of the text, often referring to textual surrogates such as food (παντοδαπῶν 3.109b) and wreaths (στέφανοι ... πολλοὶ παντοδαπῶν ἀνθέων 4.128e). This multiplicity denotes, as well as the variety, the *dialogic openness* of this text, which operates at several levels.[28] First, at the level of narrative, the text resists 'closure'. This complex word is used with many different senses, but here I mean something quite simple: Athenaeus conspicuously resists drawing his text to a close, as is evidenced most clearly by the enormous volume of it. This resistance is signalled by the author's comments at the ends of several books, as he draws matters to a conclusion by apologizing for the 'length' (μῆκος: 3.127d; 6.275b; 7.330c; 8.365e; 11.509e.[29]

At the level of articulation, too, the text is open and multiple. Much of the text is made up of passages cited by characters within the dialogue, cited again by 'Athenaeus' the character within the text who interacts with the character Timocrates stage-managed by 'Athenaeus' the authorial *persona*. That makes for four levels of citation. Formally, too, the *Deipnosophistae* is a composite work, a prosimetric, polyphonic revel[30] which—like Lucian's work (e.g. *Zeux.* 1)—celebrates explicitly its own novelty (καινότης, 6.222a). It is a work of extraordinary scholarship, but it is also a work *against* scholarship, satirizing the pretensions of professors, pitting one dogmatist against another for the sake not of establishing a hierarchy of truthfulness but of counteracting the absolutist tendencies of scholarship. Openness and plurality are its key features.

The luxurious, irresponsible, mimetic pleasures of the flatterer, then, seem appropriate to the poetics of the *Deipnosophistae* itself. In a key passage, Democritus characterizes the flatterer using terms which are exactly appropriate to Athenaeus' text:

> For in addition to playing the flatterer as described, he obsequiously imitates (*apoplattetai*) the posture (*skhêma*) of those whom he flatters, now crossing his arms, now wrapping himself closely in his ragged cloak. Whence some call him 'armcrosser,' others 'shape-shifter' (*skhêmatothêkên*). In fact, the flatterer is the very image of Proteus. At any rate, he becomes multiple (*pantodapos*) not only in shape but also in words, so variable-voiced (*poikilophônos*) is he.

> πρὸς γὰρ τῶι τοιούτωι κολακεύειν καὶ τὸ σχῆμα τῶν κολακευομένων ἐπακολουθῶν ἀποπλάττεται παραγκωνίζων καὶ σπαργανῶν ἑαυτὸν τοῖς τριβωναρίοις. ὅθεν αὐτὸν οἱ μὲν παραγκωνιστήν, οἱ δὲ σχηματοθήκην καλοῦσι. κατ' ἀλήθειαν γὰρ ὁ κόλαξ ἔοικεν εἶναι τῶι Πρωτεῖ ὁ αὐτός. γίγνεται γοῦν παντοδαπὸς οὐ μόνον κατὰ τὴν μορφήν, ἀλλὰ καὶ κατὰ τοὺς λόγους· οὕτω ποικιλόφωνός τις ἐστίν.

> (6.258a)

The 'variability' (*poikilia*) of the flatterer is found elsewhere, as is the notion that he 'imitates' his victim (notably, earlier in Democritus' speech: 6.248f–249a).[31] This passage, however, is extremely suggestive in terms of the links drawn between flattery and textuality. The word *skhêma* is commonly used of gesture and posture, which is the primary meaning here, but equally frequently of rhetorical 'figures', especially those which conceal the speaker's purpose.[32] The figure of Proteus, here linked with flattery, was typically associated in antiquity with sophistry since Plato's famous words at *Euthydemus* 288b (where he asks his interlocutor not to 'imitate', μιμεῖσθον, the Egyptian sophist Proteus by beguiling him).[33] Most suggestive of all, however, is Democritus' use of two key terms in Athenaeus' own poetics, *pantodapos* (also used of Proteus by Plato Ion 6.54le) and *poikilophônos* ('variable-voiced'). The polyvocal, polymorphous, Protean qualities of the flatterer are precisely those of the *Deipnosophistae* itself.

The conceit underlying this association of flattery with the sophistic text is a literary allusion to a famous passage in Plato's Gorgias (462b–463c).[34] There Socrates argues that, unlike philosophy, rhetoric is not a *tekhnê* ('art'), but an 'experience in producing gratification and pleasure' ([sc. ἐμπειρία] χάριτος καὶ ἡδονῆς ἀπεργασίας): in this respect, he subsumes it under the broad rubric of *kolakeia*. Athenaeus is clearly alluding to and building on the Platonic model for the association of sophistry with *kolakeia* (although he does not need to signal explicitly the allusion, such a central author is Plato to the culture of Roman Greece). It is worth noting in passing that Athenaeus is not the only writer to invert the terms of this Platonic passage. Lucian is a writer whom we have already noted as a sensitive and canny satirist of the ruses of flattery: his dialogue *The parasite* presents an argument to the effect that the *tekhnê* of parasitism is superior to not only philosophy but even rhetoric! Lucian's satire on Plato not only arrogates to parasitism the right (specifically denied to it in the Gorgias) to be called a *tekhnê*, but also places it above philosophy and rhetoric. Athenaeus, however, goes one better than Lucian. The passage from Plato's Gorgias not only makes rhetoric a branch of flattery, but also compares it to cooking![35] Like his Platonic model, Athenaeus deftly conflates the pleasures of food, sophistry and flattery; yet he also turns on its head Plato's anti-sophistic discourse, so that the ability of language to produce pleasure and gratification is prized over the philosophical ambition to tell the truth. By allying his text with the comestible pleasures of Gorgianic rhetoric, Athenaeus also allies it with parasitic pleasure: *le plaisir* without *la loi*, the Symposium without the restrictions of philosophical dogma.

## 5. Conclusion: the politics and poetics of parasitism

This chapter has proceeded from two premises: firstly, that the *Deipnosophistae* is a text with a coherent and identifiable poetics; secondly, that its interpretation requires it to be sited within the context of Graeco-Roman relations. It can now be seen that the 'poetics' and the 'politics' of the text, at least as they relate to the theme of parasitism and flattery, are not readily distinguishable. In order to understand Athenaeus' presentation of Graeco-Roman relations, we need to be sensitive to the satires, ironies and self-subversions of the text; and, conversely, in order to appreciate the subtleties of the author's literary play we need to be aware of the embattled terrain of Roman patronal power. The cultural politics of the text cannot be read in isolation from its literary ambitions, and vice versa.

What is at stake for Athenaeus in all this? I want to suggest in conclusion that the *Deipnosophistae*, while it mimics the patterns of authority, also represents itself as a subversive text, flouting the regulations of social order, using its polytropic dialogism to contest social hierarchy. The whole point of siting the banquet within a Roman patronal context is to explore the politics and hidden agendas of friendship. Unlike Dio and Plutarch, who attempt to brush over the realities of social and political hierarchies by representing their relationships with their superiors in terms of *philia*, Athenaeus (like Lucian in *The parasite* and Alciphron in the *Letters of the parasites*) self consciously re-appropriates the role of the underling. To be a parasite or a flatterer is to be deceptive, playful, luxury-loving and sensual: but these are no longer to be regarded simply as negative qualities disdained by an austere philosophical tradition, but as 'poetic' traits to be celebrated by a joyous sophistry.

This is not, however, to argue that the *Deipnosophistae* dramatizes the victory of 'poetics' over 'politics', of aesthetic form over socio-economic hierarchy. On the contrary, Athenaeus' *contestation* of social order also involves the *construction* of a social élitism: from a different perspective (say, that of an urban or rural worker), the Greek sophists in this text are thoroughly complicit with, indeed they are vehicles of, Roman power. The *Deipnosophistae* might be (and, indeed, often is[36]) taken as a monument to the cultural achievements and economic hegemony of the Graeco-Roman élite. Viewed in this context, the sophistication and sophistry of the *Deipnosophistae* mark it not as a subversive text but as a testimony to the subsumption of Greek *paideia* into the imperialist project. Power is a complex phenomenon: multiform, diffuse and at times difficult to observe, it is nevertheless never absent from cultural production.[37] The point, as I see it, is that 'politics' and 'poetics' are in a state of constant and dynamic interaction. Consequently, Greek 'culture' should not be opposed to Roman 'power'; or, at any rate, it should be acknowledged that to articulate such an opposition is to present only a partial (and, inevitably, a *strategically* partial) account of the relationship between Greek literature of the Principate and the socio-economic background against which it emerged.[38]

# THE BANQUET OF BELLES-LETTRES
## ATHENAEUS AND THE COMIC SYMPOSIUM

### by Graham Anderson

There is a brief anecdote in Philostratus' *Lives of the Sophists* which can take us a long way towards the atmosphere of Athenaeus' *Deipnosophistae*:

> σοφιστῇ δὲ ἐντυχὼν ἀλλᾶντας ὠνουμένῳ καὶ μαινίδας καὶ τὰ εὐτελῆ ὄψα 'ὠ̂ λῷστε', εἶπεν 'οὐκ ἔστι τὸ Δαρείου καὶ Ξέρξου φρόνημα καλῶς ὑποκρίνασθαι ταῦτα σιτουμένῳ'.

> When Polemo of Laodicea ran into a sophist buying sausages and sprats and cheap delicacies he said 'I say, sir! It is not possible to give a fine performance of the thoughts of Darius and Xerxes by feeding on foods like these!' (*VS* 541).

For Philostratus this is an instance of the comic wit and wisdom of Polemo, one of a number of witticisms attributed to this overbearing prima donna. But it would certainly not look out of place in the sophistic banter supplied by Athenaeus. Indeed the latter has provided us with a more developed form of the same witticism: Antigonus Gonatas rebuked the epic poet Antagoras for cooking a dish of conger-eels in the camp in the dress of a cook. Asked if he thought Homer had recorded Agamemnon's exploits when cooking eels, Antagoras asked whether Agamemnon had performed his exploits while investigating who was cooking a conger-eel in his camp (*Deipnosophistae* 8.340f). We have here in rhetorical terms a double *chreia*: a mock epic *bon mot* by a ruler, typically capped by an equally erudite rejoinder on the part of the poet. Part of the fun of this kind of 'adoxography' is that the *pepaideumenos* tends to get his own back on the ruler.

Both these passages seem to me to be rich and suggestive for the overall characterization of Athenaeus: they evoke trivial situations in a heroic past: for Philostratus that past is in the Golden Age of Athens; for Athenaeus it is perhaps the *Diadochenzeit* and the Homeric world, rather than the Athenian fifth century. And the trivialization is extreme. Eating ordinary food a fixed number of times a day, not to say cooking it oneself, is likely to be no one's finest hour: we might think of Philostratus' other anecdote about how the wit Lucius caught out the sophist Herodes Atticus for eating 'white radishes in a black house' while mourning his wife Regilla (*VS* 557). One thinks too of the great anticlimax pointed out by Longinus in a passage of Theopompus, where the enormous quantity of salt meats specified at the end of a long passage on luxurious gifts offered to the king of Persia in Egypt detracts from the majesty of the rest of the description (*Subl.* 43.2). And yet that is the aspect of antiquity that the Deipnosophists must highlight as a matter of course: this is the text where Agamemnon is more likely to be burning the cakes than directing the battle.

And so to the theme of this chapter: why and how are symposia such fun, and why is Athenaeus in a class by himself, and not just in length: someone who does not quite fit our expectations, whatever they may be? In the first place dinners are major social events in antiquity: a natural place for human interaction and the observation of people.[1] They are also a major opportunity for relaxation, and hence for scoptic situations.[2] These are already provided for in the institution of the Greek parasite and *gelotopoios* as well as the Latin *scurra*: whatever the level of the feast, the joker is an institution.

Secondly, by Athenaeus' age and well before, symposia have been long established in the repertoire of literary classics: not just in Plato's *Symposium*, which is extensively quoted not to say plundered, while Plato's own trivia are scoffed at, as in the reference to hiccups and its cure (*Deipn.* 5.187c; Plato *Symp.* 185d–e). Moreover Athenaeus traces a sympotic tradition stretching back to Homer, with his lively exchanges between Odysseus and Alcinous, and the after-dinner story of the adultery of Aphrodite. From the succeeding repertoire there is little as far as we know to which Athenaeus, the prince of erudite quotation, could not have gained access and quoted had he so chosen. Not all of that tradition would have been comical or witty; and not all the comedy and wit that is quoted is necessarily reproduced for its comic content (as opposed to items of philological or antiquarian interest). Yet the natural inference would be that the diners and the author do indeed wallow in the ludicrous content of so much Old and Middle Comic deipnosophistry, as well as in the improbable virtuosity with which it is quoted, sometimes even by cooks themselves. Many of the now lost works known to Athenaeus are also cited either for facetious material or in a facetious context: we hear (4.162b–e) of *sympotikoi dialogoi* by the Hellenistic general Persaeus, allegedly popular with philosophers for questions such as how the toasts should be ordered and when the beautiful boys and girls should be brought in. And Athenaeus supplies tantalizing glimpses of a largely lost Cynic symposium tradition,[3] including brief allusion to the *Symposium* of Menippus (14.629f).[4] Some areas are, however, cordoned off by the peculiar selectivity of Late Greek aesthetic proprieties: there is the usual distancing from the classics of Roman satire, though the Roman host Larensis is naturally allowed to cite Varro, claimed as an actual ancestor (4.160c);[5] and while the cut-off point is unusually late in allowing much Hellenistic material especially from Ptolemaic courts, the materials in the novel or in near-contemporary sophistic symposiac literature are avoided. As we shall see, Athenaeus' vast work naturally overlaps in subject-matter and to a lesser extent in outlook and nuance with a predictably wide range of the symposium tradition: but often the places where he seems not to overlap are as illuminating as those where he does.

## The Repertoire of Sympotic Humour

What jokes can one make at symposia, short of dancing on the tables and saying that Hippocleides doesn't care?[6] The symposium is an ideal setting for comic action because such a wide variety of incidents and situations can be allowed to take place naturally and spontaneously. Absurd behaviour can be covered and up to a point excused by drunkenness; amusing social gaffs can readily be contrived; and anything that is impossible can still be brought in by report: Plutarch's *Banquet of the Seven Sages* even puts Arion's miraculous delivery by the dolphin into a messenger speech (*Mor.* 160e-162b).

We might attempt to divide sympotic humour into broad and sometimes overlapping categories:

(a) Social gaffes by those who do not know how to behave at symposia, with *nouveaux riches* as the perpetually obvious targets: this is perhaps the preoccupation of satirical scenes in Roman satire, for obvious enough social reasons, but there is a plentiful supply in Greek as well, for example in Theophrastus' *Characters*.[7] The fact that dinners automatically entail problems of etiquette gives rise to such a joke as *Philogelos* 20, where two *scholastici* escort each other home so that neither can get any sleep.[8]

(b) Universal slapstick, especially that related to drunkenness or sex,[9] but other varieties are possible, as when Aesop's Samian master invites his friends to an impromptu meal, and asks Aesop to prepare bean soup, which he does, with one bean (*Vita Aesopi* 39–41).

(c) Literary and cultural entertainment, not least that which draws on the now long-established repertoire of previous sympotic literary situations.

(d) We might also try to separate a long tradition of *spoudogeloion*, reaching at least as far back as Plato, as well as the the roots of the *Seven Sages* tradition: this is a category as elastic as it is indefinable.[10]

Perhaps the most distinctive feature of Athenaeus as we have him is the relative absence of the first two types in their own right. Even in a most conspicuous case where he does mention a tasteless host in Rome, the latter's crime is of a typically literary kind, consisting of training his slaves to cite quantities of Plato (*Deipn.* 9.381f-382a). Athenaeus' symposium is not really the place to come looking for overdone thrushes, clodhopping waiters, tasteless hosts, or awnings falling down, the natural fallback in Horace or Petronius. There are no drunken Alcibiades' speeches to speak of either,[11] and even the banter may be considered relatively minimal, though in fact the narrative has its facetious moments, as when we are told that Ulpian was on the brink of *aperantologia* when the food was brought in (6.262). The focus is on food and its discourse, and if overall there is a pervasive or controlling humour, it is the emphasis on just this, and at such length, that seems new and extraordinary. So often the mainline symposium tradition seems to be trying to escape or minimize the details of the courses and dishes (unless to show up the host's pretentions or garrulity).

Correspondingly, there is a great deal of the third category, literary and cultural entertainment, at least some of which approaches comic effect. Perhaps the most literal illustration would be such a passage as Lynceus' Letter of Poseidippus (14.652d): 'in the matter of tragic suffering Euripides is not superior to Sophocles; but in the matter of figs, Attic ones are far better than all others.' In the eyes of the deipnosophists and their authorities, figs are as legitimate and extensive a subject as Attic Tragedy! Central to this cultural humour we should suggest the recurrent series of paradoxes on the idea that philosophers are cooks or gluttons,[12] and that cooks for their part are really philosophers. Ulpian puns almost inevitably on the appropriateness of Cynics gnawing jaw and head-bones, as appropriate for dogs (3.96f); Baton parades Stoics as gluttons at dinner (3.103d–e), and Epicrates has the philosophers attempting to classify a pumpkin (2.59 d–f). There is a corresponding facetiousness about promoting cooks or master-chefs to the status of philosophers: Archestratus[13] is said to anticipate Epicurus in his doctrine of pleasure; and he gives us advice in wise sayings after the manner of the poet of Ascra, telling us not to follow certain persons but rather to heed only himself. Cooks for their part need to be conversant with all manner of *naturales quaestiones* (3.102a); Chrysippus is cited for the remark that the centre of Epicurean philosophy is the *gastrologia* of Archestratus,[14] claimed as the Theognis of the *gastrimargoi*, the Moses of the munchers (3.104b).[15] A subtle inversion is contained in the notion of the meal of meagre philosophic doctrine from Theognetus' *Phasma* (3.104b): τῶν γὰρ ἐκ τῆς ποικίλης στοᾶς λογαρίων ἀναπεπλησμένος νοσεῖς ('For you are ill with stuffing yourself with the tiny titbits of terms from the Painted Porch'). And a cook is brought on in person to deliver a massive fragment of Sosipater on the skills and strategies necessary to the cook as sophist (9.376c, 377f).

A further category of humour built into the *Deipnosophistae* lies in the prominence afforded to whole banks of information on the lighter side of sympotic entertainments outside the actual business of dining itself: hence a collection of sympotic jokes (14.614), or extensive treatments of such professions as parasites and flatterers (especially 6.234c–262a) and courtesans (much of Book Thirteen). While accumulations of jokes seldom make for the enhancement of humorous effect, there can nevertheless be a certain facetiousness in the sheer tour de force of assembling so many: devotion of the whole of Book Thirteen to women (and in practice to *erotica*) in itself underlines this impression.

We should note also the frequency and cleverness with which culinary parody can transform its context: the *Iliad* cannot be quite the same again after δεῖπνα μοι ἔννεπε, Μοῦσα, πολύτροφα καὶ μάλα πολλά (4.134d, from the parodist Matron); or Timon is quoted in parody of *Il.* 1.225 (δειπνομανές, νεβροῦ ὄμματ' ἔχων, κραδίην δ' ἀκύλιστον) (4.162f); while the fragment quoted from Xenophanes' didactic poem on banqueting is serious (11.462c–463a), Homeric parody is set in a symposiac context in a fragment from the Parodies (2.54e). Much work remains to be done on the sense of incongruity between the gravity of cited authorities and what exactly they are cited for, as when Plato is cited on healthy food (*Deipn.* 4.138a, *Rep.* 372c), on drunkenness (*Deipn.* 10.431f, *Laws* 775b), or even on luxurious bedding (*Deipn.* 2.48a, *Politicus* 280b). And the learned might have been relied upon to remember that when Athenaeus quotes Homer for a fragrance spreading to earth and heaven, he is in effect comparing the rose dish to the toiletries of Hera (*Deipn.* 9.406b, *Il.* 14.173).

There are other recurrent but less easily classifiable traits in the literary texture: a good deal of humour attaches to the pretentious titles accorded to the chefs in particular, with of course Archestratus as *opsodaidalos* (3.105e), or Cynulcus addressed as *grammatikotate* (5.184b), or the cook addressing the company as ἄνδρες δαιταλεῖς (9.404e) ('Gentlemen of Dinnerville', Gulick). The Deipnosophists also tend to exaggerate their bibliophile reactions: 'If Juba recounts anything of the sort (about the citron, 3.83c), then you are to renounce both his *Libyan History* and his *Wanderings of Hanno* as well.' An extreme instance is Cynulcus' wish that the previous speaker on slaughter at dinner had met the same fate as Thracians who hanged themselves at banquets (4.156a). But the most distinctive brand of humour—if that is the right word for it—is in excursions over the border from pedantry into humour. The subject of food lends itself peculiarly well to this, in a way and to an extent that a book on medicine or music might not: there is a whole pseudo-history of dining-habits of the great and the famous; or we find courtesans (13.568e–569b) in the line of battle, or Sybarites with yellow tunics over their breastplates (12.519c); or Olympias writing to Alexander urging him to purchase a cook (14.659f).

The bulk of Athenaeus should not blind us to the fact that he has established an arresting interplay between at least some of the combatants at the dinner: Ulpian as a pedant and Cynulcus as a *scurra*, with more occasional forays by Myrtilus and others. As with the accumulation of citations themselves, there is a degree of wit in sheer excess once the *odium philologicum* really comes into its own: for example Ulpian plies Cynulcus at 3.99e–100b with a mixture of clever if banal banter on the canine aspects of Cynics, interspersed with asides in a way calculated to inflame his opponent with facile philology:

> In reply Ulpian remarked with a pleasant smile: 'but you must not bark, my friend, or snarl, launching your mad-dog act during the dog-days; instead, you should fawn and wag your tail for your fellow-guests, or we'll turn our holiday into a dog-massacre like the one they celebrate at Argos. 'Foddered', my very good sir, is a word used in the sense I used by Cratinus in the *Odysseis* [six further examples follow in close order]. These instances, then, I can cite off the cuff for you, Cynulcus, but tomorrow, or 'on the morrow's morrow', as Hesiod speaks of the day after tomorrow, I'll fodder you with blows if you can't tell me where the word 'gutgod' is found'.

Cynulcus is routed and promised a beating, whereupon the company are delighted ἐπὶ τοῖς πεπαιγμένοις. Ulpian has not taken the slightest notice of Cynulcus' criticisms of his pedantry, but goads him with a kind of two-pronged philological thrust, with the Hesiod tossed in almost as a free footnote. After much more of the same the narrator slips in a witticism of his own, when crayfish are brought in 'larger than the orator Callimedon', so nicknamed for his fondness for the delicacy. Most striking among the minor parts is perhaps the cook who gives the account of a *myma* in a massive monologue (14.658e-662e), 'crushing not only the previously mentioned ingredients but ourselves as well').

It is useful in this connexion to look sideways and slightly backwards at other early imperial sympotic texts. Plutarch's *Quaestiones Conviviates* from around a century earlier invites comparison, as an example of sympotic treatment from outside a seriously sophistic milieu. Here the emphasis of the enquiries assigned to a much greater range of occasions is rather less one-dimensional than in Athenaeus. Instead of the impression of almost a cento of ancient authors, we have a genuine attempt at a texture of philosophical argument, as opposed to bare assemblage of proof-texts in the manner of grammarians. It would be difficult to imagine a more extreme contrast than that between the risqué and occasionally salacious contents of Athenaeus on courtesans (Book Thirteen) in contrast to the staid, urbane and slightly inhibited discussion on the right time for sex in Plutarch *Quaest. Conv.* 3.6, itself looking back to Xenophon's touch of sending men back after the drinking-party for sex with their wives (Xen. *Symp.* 9.7), and centring on the propriety of Epicurus' inclusion of such a topic in his own symposium. Plutarch's whole discussion is obviously conceived as primarily instructive and useful: one has to know when intercourse is likely to be harmful as well as indecent. Athenaeus' purpose lies almost in a sort of skilfully scholarly perversity: not just 'what-the-actress-said-to-the-bishop' jokes, of which there are plenty, but the more or less clear subtext that courtesans follow a profession superior to that of their overbearing clients, whoever these may be. There is the facetious undertone that the girls are yet another delicacy in the dinner itself.[16] Or again, even when Plutarch sets the occasion as the victory of Strato the comic playwright, and the discussion ensues in the house of an Epicurean, the question revolves round a serious discussion of mimesis of emotions only modulating into a light-hearted ending with the funny story of Parmeno's proverbial pig (5.1, *Mor.* 673c–674c).

But in Plutarch too there is conscious sympotic wit: he is able to exploit the familiar Platonic topos that only an expert can be considered competent to judge in this specialist field: (*Mor.* 668c): as the skilled doctor is the best judge of medicines and the most intense lover of music *philomousotatos* is the best judge of the quality of melodic lines, so the greatest gourmet is the best judge of the excellence of delicacies: hence Plutarch's Polycrates is able to set aside the views of Pythagoras or Xenocrates. Instead one must rely on such connoisseurs as the painter Androcydes, said to have such a taste for fish that he rendered the fish in a picture of Scylla with particular empathy in a most lifelike manner. Of a similar order is the *adoxon* at *Sept. Sap.* 158c–f: do away with tables, and altars and civilization will collapse. This assertion is soon refuted by Solon; in Athenaeus it might well have gone unchallenged, or rather would have been reinforced by the monologues of several chefs from comedy each claiming to be the architect of civilization.

It is when one contrasts Athenaeus with several of Alciphron's *Letters of Parasites* that one is most acutely aware of the difference of focus between Athenaeus' work and more obviously sophistic materials. Alciphron has a brief point of contact with Athenaeus over the hypocrisy and gluttony of philosophers at banquets. In overall ethos too the pair stand close together: both are concerned with mosaics of courtesans and parasites, and the exhibition of comic poets and their Attic vocabulary is as characteristic a part of Alciphron's *raison d'être* as it is of Athenaeus'. Where they differ abruptly is that Athenaeus stacks this material in a card-index manner. Alciphron's *Symposium* contents itself with Themistagoras the Peripatetic seeing happiness not just in terms of body and soul, but also of external goods, so that he asks for more cakes and a variety of meats (*Ep.* 3.19.7). Athenaeus' reflex is to produce a whole swathe of examples of gourmet philosophers: two quotations from Alexis present Chaerephon as a parasite (4.164f.); and we have the priceless story that when Heracles chose a book from Linus' library it was a cookery book, from which he is inferred to be a philosopher as a matter of course (4.164b–c).

It is naturally to Lucian that one looks for determinedly comic use of the sympotic tradition. Lucian's own *Symposium*, like Alciphron's, deals with the hypocrisy of philosophers, thus corresponding with the kind of accusations aired at *Deipn.* 4.160d–165a and elsewhere. This piece has another and perhaps unexpected light to throw on Athenaeus. The latter develops at some length the philological problem concerning why Menelaus arrives at Agamemnon's feast uninvited (*Il.* 2.408, *Deipn.* 5.177c–178e). The detail is developed as a sympotic question in its own right. For Lucian its incorporation is much more facile and concise: it is the defence the Cynic Alcidamas uses to gate-crash the banquet, and it is dismissed as no more than a commonplace (*Conv.* 12), readily countered by the no less Homerically equipped among the invited guests. The outlook of the two authors could scarcely be more effectively contrasted. Again, we have telling vignettes in *Historia Conscribenda*, where Lucian is parodying historians who deviate from the grand theme of the Parthian Wars to talk about Mausacas buying wrasses cheap in Caesarea, or to incorporate reminiscences of dinners and toasts in Afranius Silo's funeral speech for Severianus, said to have cut his throat with expensive crystal (28; 26). The incongruity of these titbits in narrative historiography underlines the incongruity of the Deipnosophists and their culinary pedantry in so many historical contexts.

Lucian also provides a useful corroboration and development of the phenomenon of hyperatticism. In Athenaeus this can only take the form of a check-list of ludicrous affectations used by Ulpian and Pompeianus and their circle according to Cynulcus (3.97c–99e). It is characteristic of Lucian's outlook that we have so to speak a horizontal realization of the material for which Athenaeus provides the vertical: a hyperattic narrative pastiche including the description of a dinner in this outlandishly pretentious and solecising idiom (*Lexiphanes* 13):

Let us be drinking, then, quoth Megalonymus, for I am come bringing you this senile flagon, green cheese, windfallen olives—I keep them under

> wormscriven seals—and other olives, soused, and these earthen cups of cockle-shell, stanchly bottomed, for us to drink out of, and a cake of chitterlings braided like a topknot. My lad, pour in more of the water for me, that I may not begin to have a head and then call your keeper to come for you. You know that I have my pains and keep my head invested ... (tr. A.M. Harmon)

Lucian's *de mercede conductis* is important for its overlap with the themes and preoccupations of Roman satire: it is here that one looks for convergence with the fixations of Juvenal and Roman satirists in general with the absurdities of the client-patron relationship. But this is conspicuously *not* the world of Athenaeus: miseries of the client are easily illustrated from comic poets on parasites, and the fictitious Roman host of Lucian has nothing in common with Livius Larensis. Indeed the level of learning presented by Lucian here is no more than suits the ambience of Petronius' relatively unlearned company: asked by the pretentious host 'Who was the king of the Achaeans?' the terrified *graeculus esuriens* answers: 'They had a thousand ships' (11). He would not have found a place in Athenaeus, except conceivably in a random digression on 'gaffs of the great'.

Perhaps the closest coincidence in material is over the subject of parasites, and as ever Athenaeus opts for the inventory and the anecdotal approach: learned facts about the historical situations of famous parasites, and in a separate context, allusion to the famous passage of the *Gorgias* on philosophy and cookery. Lucian is able to combine the two themes with brilliant effect: his parasite is a latter-day Archestratus in his manipulation of the pseudo-philosophy of cookery, effortlessly overturning the Platonic orthodoxies on expertise on their head by exalting *parasitikê* as a *technê* (*Paras.* 1f.). This is a creative humour which Athenaeus seems incapable of attaining: one suspects that his approach would have been to cite such a work from a Hellenistic cultural context had he known it. Similarly in the case of the courtesans so readily associated with ancient dining: Athenaeus is adept in the *chreia* tradition and able to produce an impressive anthology of *bons mots* of ancient courtesans; Lucian in the *Dialogi Meretricum* creates a squad of considerably less gnomic but more human and delightful ladies from the same New Comic milieu, to entirely different effect.

It is perhaps noteworthy that Athenaeus contains less of the material of fantastic symposia than one might have expected: whereas Lucian constructs a very concise banquet of heroes and sages in the Islands of the Blest in his lying travelogue in *Verae Historiae* (2.14–19); and even the rather more serious Dio assigns a smartly allegorical banquet of life to the dying Charidemus (*Or.* 30.29–44). Rather more understandable is the absence of the kind of parade of popular superstitions that characterize the raconteurs of novellae in Petronius and

Apuleius (Niceros and Trimalchio, *Sat.* 61–63, Thelyphron at Byrrhaena's banquet in Apuleius, *Met.* 2.21–30): the ultra-sophisticates and their creator tend to regard the very popular with no literary associations as beneath their notice. One might note too the relegation of sympotic riddles to a mere digression in contrast to their dramatic prominence in Plutarch (*Sept. Sap.*, *Mor.* 151b–154c) or even Petronius: again the closer the material to the popular end of symposium tradition, the less interested Athenaeus is likely to be, unless there is respectable literary authority (as Old Comedy was considered to be).

It is almost sacrilegious to set Athenaeus side by side with Petronius: only the latter has succeeded in his sympotic technique in interweaving the twin themes of food and taste into a truly effective dramatic ensemble, where cumulative excess is used to devastating literary effect as the comic protagonists become bored and frustrated but are unable to escape. Relihan does attempt comparison, but points of contact tend to be more significant for the differences than for the similarities: when the cook in Petronius produces the pig stuffed full of delicacies, the whole business is presented as a clever but tasteless party-trick in which Encolpius as so often is genuinely and naively caught out (*Sat.* 49.3–10). In Athenaeus' case we have a significantly different variety of amusement, with the picture of the cook taking on even Ulpian himself (with apologies for not speaking Attic), and engaging in a vast *tour de force* of sophistic display if only in quoting sophist-like cooks, (9.376c–380c). There is plenty of learned extravagance, but the sense of a cleverly contrived joke against the narrator is absent.

On the other hand Athenaeus attains his usual high value as a source for miscellaneous information which serves students of the *Satyrica* no less well in matters of minute detail, in some cases correcting our view of aspects of the comic symposium tradition through the sheer range and bulk of his information. The normal assumption is that much of Trimalchio's banquet is typically Roman rather than Greek, but a patient exploration of Athenaeus underlines how much of the material is likely to have belonged already to the Greek world in the broadest sense. For example, Trimalchio embarrassingly draws attention to the availablity of relief (*Sat.* 47.5); Athenaeus quotes the comic poet Eubulus to the effect that there are lavatories at hand (10.417d). Slaves let loose around the table may be a topical subject for Trimalchio's own time;[17] but Archytas (*Deipn.* 12.519b) establishes the licence for Greek symposia. The funeral aspects are not novel either: the description of the *bon viveur* Trimalchio's tomb has its counterpart in that of Sardanapalus (*Sat.* 71; *Deipn.* 12.529f–530c); a trumpet is used to end a banquet at *Deipn.* 4.130b as well as by the well-intentioned brass-players who bring out the fire-brigade at the end of Trimalchio's feast; the whole funeral ensemble at a banquet is cited by Athenaeus from Alexis (*Deipn.* 3.124a–b).

## A Special Case: Athenaeus and the *Cena Trimalchionis*

Trimalchio has a cook called Daedalus, again a title of Archytas of Tarentum (*opsodaidalos* 3.110a, *Sat.* 70.2); Trimalchio's servants create a hunting-scene (*Sat.* 40), while Athenaeus discusses the use of gladiators at dinners outside a Roman context (4.154a). The preference for home-grown food seems a natural pre-occupation of the *nouveaux riches*, but was already a preoccupation of Xerxes (*Sat.* 38; *Deipn.* 14.652b). The arresting remark that if bears eat men, men should eat bears (66.6) is at least hinted at in *Deipn.* 4.163d, where only the faint-hearted and vegetarian are to abstain from eating the flesh of the man-eating shark.

So much, then, for samplings and soundings. I hesitate to reach conclusions on so open-ended a subject: Athenaeus comes towards the end of a long line of sympotic literature in which comic diversions play a part. As with so many other aspects of this vast author, closer inspection tends to suggest an odd sort of selectivity. And the use of comedy in an encyclopaedic way creates an artistic problem not fully solved by the author, though one might say that as with Favorinus on the Winds in Aulus Gellius, there is a vitality in sheer sophistic excess. But in almost every case where a worthwhile parallel can be adduced from comic sympotic details in other authors, Athenaeus' inclusive tendency seems always in the way. In some respects I should be tempted to look further to the point in Late Antiquity where once more inventory threatens to offset a splendid comic ideal, as happens a little later in Julian's *Caesars*.

But there is a wider issue than the effectiveness and selective nature of Athenaeus' humour: the question of humour has also a bearing on genre itself. One could say that this is a one-off work like Ovid's *Metamorphoses* or Rabelais or *Tristram Shandy*: one could see the work as the ultimate embodiment of a library genre, or as a monster miscellany. But we should also be tempted to see the Deipnosophists as epic warriors wielding the weapons of philology: dinners are Homeric battle grounds at *Deipn.* 10.420f, where *Il.* 2.420 is actually cited: 'Now go to dinner, so that we may join battle' is hilariously misapplied. After all, Larensis is Asteroparus (see Chapter 1). But I let Lucian have the last word on the cast list of his *Symposium*: three words to sum up the whole of Athenaeus: *mouseion to symposion*, and we might interpret them how we will. But Athenaeus as usual can furnish a parallel of his own: Alexis is quoted (6.242d) for a list of parasites with food names (Gudgeon, Mackerel and the like): the list is greeted with ἀγοράσματ', οὐ συμπόσιον εἴρηκας—'you speak of a supermarket, not a symposium'. To the historian of culture, humour, or both, this tag might be applied to Athenaeus' work itself.

# ❖ 24 ❖

# BETWEEN ICHTHYOPHAGISTS AND SYRIANS
## FEATURES OF FISH-EATING IN ATHENAEUS' *DEIPNOSOPHISTAE* BOOKS SEVEN AND EIGHT

### by Antonia Marchiori

In Athenaeus' rich and valuable work, great attention is paid to the culinary use of fish, whether salted, boiled, roasted or fried, and to its dietetic properties.[1] A great deal of information is also given about the most fishy areas, as if to create a sort of fish-map of the Mediterranean, the Black Sea and the Nile. Moreover, Athenaeus also talks about fish-eaters, drawing from his countless sources various types of consumers or abstainers. All these pieces of information can be found throughout Athenaeus' work, but they are concentrated in Books Seven and Eight especially. My aim here is to analyse all the types of fish-eaters presented by Athenaeus, to organize the data as a coherent and organic whole, and to consider, as far as possible, different linguistic, historical and ethnological levels.

**1. Παῖδες ἰχθυοφάγοι**

At 8.345e Athenaeus recalls the παῖδες ἰχθυοφάγοι, literally ("boy fish-eaters') mentioned by the peripatetic Clearchus (98 Wehrli):[2]

I am not ignorant, either, of the παῖδες ἰχθυοφάγοι whom Clearchus mentions in his work *On Sandy Deserts*. He alleges that Psammetichus, the king of Egypt, kept παῖδες ἰχθυοφάγοι because he wished to discover the sources of the Nile.'

This is a peculiar piece of news, and needs some explanation, because it is not reported elsewhere. Through a series of amusing anecdotes Athenaeus is reviewing some more or less famous characters of the past well known for their gluttony, the ὀψοφάγοι ('gluttons'). In this section Athenaeus includes two curious notes: one, taken from Clearchus, refers to the παῖδες ἰχθυοφάγοι, the other mentions the oxen of Mossynum, in Thrace, fed on fish. The *fil rouge* connecting the theme of the gluttons to these two episodes is a fish-based diet, while the common element shared by the two episodes is their anomalous fish-consumption. Fish used as the only food in human diet and as food for cattle are sufficiently idiosyncratic to attract the Deipnosophists' attention.

Who are the παῖδες ἰχθυοφάγοι? The discrepancies in modern translations indicate scholars' uneasiness, mainly owing to the brevity of the quotation. Gulick translates 'fish-eating slaves'; Wehrli interprets as 'Knaben'.[3]

After referring to the παῖδες ἰχθυοφάγοι, Clearchus goes on to describe how Psammetichus taught others (sc. παῖδες) to endure thirst, in order to explore the sandy deserts of Libya. According to Wehrli, the passage from Clearchus belonged to a work on a biological subject dealing with human survival under particular environmental conditions, in which diet played a relevant role. Psammetichus, king of Egypt, brought up some παῖδες on a diet strictly based on fish, so that they could survive in extreme conditions, where raw fish was supposed to provide both food and liquids. We know from Herodotus that Psammetichus was no stranger to 'pseudo-scientific' experiments on children. He also relates Psammetichus' use of new-born children of common people to find out the most ancient language (2.2).[4] So the παῖδες from Clearchus' passage are not necessarily slaves, as suggested by Gulick's translation.[5] Herodotus also narrates Psammetichus' expedition in search of the sources of the Nile, but he does not mention the παῖδες ἰχθυοφάγοι.

We might suppose a relationship between Clearchus' παῖδες ἰχθυοφάγοι and a nomad population of Fish-eaters living at Elephantine, who are mentioned in the third book of Herodotus' *Histories* in the context of Cambyses' explorations a century later (3.19–25). What we learn from Herodotus is:

1. Psammetichus is looking for the sources of the Nile, that is to say the first cataract, located between Syene and Elephantine (2.28);
2. Psammetichus sets up a garrison of soldiers in Elephantine (2.30);
3. Fish-eating nomads are found in the city of Elephantine in Cambyses' times, that is about a century later than Psammetichus.

If there were a relationship between the παῖδες ἰχθυοφάγοι and Herodotus' Fish-eaters, Clearchus' passage would be the first and the only one to attest a contact between king Psammetichus and the tribes of Fish-eaters living between the Nile and the African coast of the Red Sea. The possibility of such a relationship is attractive, but is not well grounded from a linguistic point of view. First of all, the term ἰχθυοφάγος in Clearchus' passage is used as an adjective, not as a noun; in the second place, the term ἰχθυοφάγος is found two more times in Athenaeus (8.344a, 355c), as a synonym of φίλιχθυς ('fond of fish') or of ὀψοφάγος ('gluttonous epicure', but also 'fish-lover'). Athenaeus never uses the word to refer to a people.

The wholly fish diet of Psammetichus' παῖδες is perceived as uncultured and primitive, like that of the Fish-eaters mentioned by Herodotus in Book Three and described later by Agatharchides of Cnidus,[6] but it is also felt to be unnatural, because it is forced. A similarly primitive and unnatural situation is the one reported of the cattle of Mossynum fed on fish. Fish is food for man, not for animals; it is a part of human nutrition, but not the only one. Psammetichus and the Thracians both share an incorrect use of fish.

The word ἰχθυοφάγος is found in two more passages from *Deipnosophistae* Book Eight. Hegesander (*FHG* IV. 417 *ap. Deipn.* 8.344a) mentions a Phoryscus ἰχθυοφάγος who devoured a whole fish while declaiming a line from Sophocles' *Antigone* (714); another ἰχθυοφάγος, called Euphranor, is said by Aristodemus (*FHG* III. 310 *ap. Deipn.* 8.345b) to have died after swallowing an exceedingly hot slice of fish. For Athenaeus, then, an ἰχθυοφάγος is a man who is greedy for fish, but who cannot even appreciate it, because he eats it too quickly. This feature of the ἰχθυοφάγος makes him similar to the φίλιχθυς with whom he shares the same negative connotation.[7]

**2. Ἰχθυοφάγος, φίλιχθυς, ὀψοφάγος**

At the international conference *Food in Antiquity* held in 1992, Dwora Gilula wrote on gluttony in Athenian comedy and James Davidson analysed the political meaning attributed to ὀψοφαγία ('gluttony,' but also 'love of fish') in Athens.[8] In the light of these contributions I would like briefly to outline the lifestyle of the φίλιχθυς / ὀψοφάγος.

The φίλιχθυς:

1. buys up fish up in the market-place (like the Athenian rich men, Phayllus and Callimedon, in Alexis);[9]
2. eats any sort of fish (like the diviner Lampon in Cratin. iun., 62 K-A *ap. Deipn.* 8.344e);
3. eats with excessive gluttony (like the music-master Dorion in Mnesimachus, 10 K-A *ap. Deipn.* 8.338b);

4. paints Scylla's fish (like the painter Androcydes of Cyzicus in Polemo Hist., 66 Preller, *ap. Deipn.* 8.341a).[10]

The figure of the ὀψοφάγος is presented in even more detail. Athenaeus dedicates a substantial section of Book Eight (340e-45a) to a catalogue of fish-lovers.[11]
    The ὀψοφάγος:

1. is a spendthrift;[12]
2. roves the fish-market;[13]
3. buys up fish, adding to the wealth of fishmongers and leaving the market in a state of 'fishlessness';[14]
4. in the market-place devours large slices of salt fish;[15]
5. allows nobody, not even his slave, to touch his fish;[16]
6. snatches food from other people;[17]
7. shows his tongue and licks his lips;[18]
8. swallows whole fish;[19]
9. eats hot fish;[20]
10. if female, displays a voracity that is both astonishing and disgusting;[21]
11. does not give up gluttony even at a funeral banquet, or sacrifices fish for funerals;[22]
12. plays dice;[23]
13. associates with prostitutes;[24]
14. has tyrannical manners;[25]
15. dies from gluttony.[26]

References to the ὀψοφάγος mainly come from Comedy as well as from the orators (Aeschines and Demosthenes) and historians (Hegesander, Polemo and Ister). All these sources condemn ὀψοφαγία. In the comic poets and orators criticism is directed against the *truphe* of the upper classes, as highlighted by James Davidson. In the other sources, historians and biographers, criticism generally is against the whimsical personalities of artists and thinkers.[27] Their ὀψοφαγία, undoubtedly related to their wandering lives (as poets, actors, musicians, painters and philosophers), is ridiculed and morally condemned. This happens particularly with philosophers. Among the ὀψοφάγοι are mentioned Zeno and Bion, about whom the same anecdote is reported,[28] and Diogenes, who is punished for his gluttony and dies suffocated by the octopus he has swallowed.[29] Aristippus and Aristotle are mentioned as well.[30] Satire against banqueting philosophers is a cliché in an antiphilosophic tradition from comedy to Lucian's *Symposium*.[31] These wandering ὀψοφάγοι mingle with the crowd of parasites at the rich people's banquets, but they are secondary characters and have a negative connotation.[32] Further, ὀψοφαγία cost the lives of Diogenes, the poet Philoxenus of Cythera, and Queen Atargatis, with her pointedly named son, Ichthus. Finally, Melanthius, a character from Archippus' *Fishes*, is charged with ὀψοφαγία in a trial and given over to the Fishes to be devoured, in a sort of retaliation.[33]

Athenaeus draws the condemnation for ὀψοφαγία from his sources, but, unlike the comic poets and the orators, whose condemnation of gluttony has a strong political aspect, his concern is convivial decorum. Athenaeus detaches the ὀψοφάγοι from their historical context and sets them as examples of bad manners. The ὀψοφάγος is reproachable as he is the victim of an irrational and uncontrollable desire: he is mad for it, ὀψομανής, as Chrysippus says in *Deipn.* 11.464e.[34] But the ὀψοφάγος does not face blame if he retains a refined and well-drilled taste.

To return to the framework of the *Deipnosophistae*. Athenaeus enthusiastically describes a rich banquet, with a great variety of fish.[35] This gives him the opportunity to display his erudition about fish, ranging through science, mythology, medicine and gastronomy. This also provides an appropriate context for making fun of the Cynic philosophers who hasten learned debates to the end so as to rush on to food:[36] they are termed the true ὀψοφάγοι at Athenaeus' banquet, the γαστρὶ χαριζόμενοι ('those indulging their belly'). While pretending they are eating moderately, κοσμίως (*Deipn.* 4.16l d), they eat up everything and only appreciate among epic poems Archestratus' *Gastrologia* (*Deipn.* 4.162b). There is a great difference between their ὀψοφαγία and that of Archestratus, who is not simply a glutton but a gourmet and keen on good cooking. In 7.278d Athenaeus describes him as a peculiar type of researcher who carefully tests and accurately expounds the delights of the table, particularly of fish dishes. In other passages Athenaeus calls him an ὀψοδαίδαλος ('tit-bit artist'), σοφός ('wise').[37] Athenaeus himself is an ὀψολόγος ('tit-bit authority') who, in his show of gastronomic erudition, admits his bent for fish.[38] Fish is a component of the varied and complex diet of the rich and magnificent society of which he is part, of civilization *tout court*.

## 3. The ancient Egyptians

In three passages from Antiphanes, Anaxandrides and Timocles, Athenaeus reminds us that ancient Egyptians did not eat eels, because they were sacred fish.[39] This is the context. After listing the dietetic properties of the eel, Athenaeus makes a few linguistic remarks, suggesting a number of uses of the word ἔγχελυς ('eel') in its various terminations. Then, going back to the great importance which the Greeks ascribe to the eel, Athenaeus quotes Antiphanes 145.1–3 K-A (*Deipn.* 7.299e):[40] 'They say that Egyptians are clever in other ways too, but especially in recognizing the eel as equal to the gods. In fact she is much higher priced than the gods.'[41] It takes twelve drachmae to smell an eel,

Antiphanes explains, while the admittance to the gods is free. The quotation from Antiphanes is the starting point for a digression about the customs of the ancient Egyptians. Athenaeus does not give his opinion on the subject, but lets his sources talk, that is the poets of comedy. A similar reference to the Egyptians is made by Anaxandrides (40.5–6 K-A *ap. Deipn.* 7.299f), who shows the same irreverence regarding the cult of the eel: 'You hold the eel to be a mighty divinity, we hold it by far the mightiest of dainties.'

The opinion about the Egyptians' dissimilar customs is expressed facetiously through the quotation from Timocles (1.2–3 K-A *ap. Deipn.* 7.300b): 'When people who sin against those gods whom all confess don't pay the penalty straightway ...'

Behind the jokes of comedy may be seen political opposition in Athens to the Egyptian policies promoted by Chabrias,[42] and the prospect of an alliance with the Egyptians in a possible war against the Persians; but as usual Athenaeus deprives the passages of their original message, and uses them for his own purposes.

With the pride of a Naucratite, Athenaeus emphasizes the fishiness of the Nile.[43] At 7.311f-312b he makes a list of about twenty kinds of fishes of the Nile.

## 4. The agroikoi

Again from Antiphanes, fr. 127.1–6 K-A, quoted in *Deipn.* 7.303f, we learn of an ἄγροικος ('rustic') who rejects some kinds of fish:[44]

> A. This fellow here, reared in the country, eats nothing out of the sea, except what comes close to shore, a conger-eel, maybe, or an electric eel, or the ground parts of the tunny.
> B. What do you mean by that?
> A. The lower parts, I say.
> B. You would eat such things as those?
> C. Why, yes; for I account all other fish as cannibals.

Athenaeus includes this passage from Antiphanes' *The Hairdresser* because it contains an allusion to the use of the tail-cut of the tunny. The joke, of course, is that the tunny lives mostly in the deep sea, and in ancient times it was considered a flesh-eating fish.[45] The butt of the comic poet is once again the Boeotian ἄγροικος, who pretends and fails to understand what is said. The ἄγροικος, as Theophrastus (*Char.* 4.14) says, is satisfied with salt fish—the kind of fish poor people eat. A hint of this aversion can also be found in Archestratus (*SH* 154), in relation to dog-fish flesh:[46]

> Nay, not many mortals know of this heavenly viand, or consent to eat it—

all those mortals, that is, who possess the puny soul of the booby-bird, and are smitten with palsy because, as they say, the creature is a man-eater.

The abstinence from 'anthropophagous' fish is considered coarse by Antiphanes and stupid by Archestratus, because: 'Every fish loves human flesh, if it can but get it.' Archestratus invites the people who tell such stories to devote themselves to vegetables, *lachana*, traditional vegetarian food, and to 'pythagorize' in a sober form of life, following the precepts of the philosopher Diodorus of Aspendus. But maybe the reason for this strange deviation is to be sought elsewhere. Antiphanes says in his *Agroikos* or *Butalion* (fr.69.11–13 K-A *ap. Deipn.* 7.313b), distinguishing big fish from small ones, among which are the sprats:

A. I hold that all these large fishes are man-eaters.
B. How's that, dear friend? Man-eaters! What do you mean?
C. He means, of course, what a man would eat.

The dialogue is based on a double misunderstanding: by saying ἀνθρωποφάγοι the first character, Philoumenos, means that those fish can consume a man's estate by their high cost; the second character, the countryman, interprets the word as meaning 'man-eaters'; finally, the third character, Pistos, probably a household slave,[47] understands it as meaning 'man-eaten' fish, that is edible fish. Eustathius explains more clearly, in his *Commentary on the Odyssey*, 1630.11,[48] that 'anthropophagous fish' are the most expensive, and are so called because they consume rich men's estates. The rejection of 'anthropophagous fish' suggests on the one hand, ἀγροικία (and with it the unjustified refusal of the big sea fish) and on the other hand the impossibility here of spending the large sums of money needed to buy the sea fish used for rich people's banquets. Those who abstain from 'anthropophagous fish' in comedy do not conform to the rules of ἀστειότης ('politeness'), and are strangers to the cultural world of Archestratus. As a consequence, they become a part of Athenaeus' *kosmos* that is marginal and strange.

## 5. The Pythagoreans

The link which Archestratus establishes between the rejection of 'anthropophagous fish' and the Pythagoreans' alimentary taboos is probably ironic, but it is not a casual one. The people who do not eat big fish reject a κάλλιστον βρῶμα ('delicacy') and keep a temperate, but also miserable, diet. It was the Pythagoreans, as Archestratus seems to say in the passage quoted above, who spread the 'barbaric' custom of abstinence from fish in the Greek world.[49] A 'barbaric' custom, because it is so alien to the Greeks over many centuries[50] as still in Athenaeus' day. In

7.308c, Ulpian, discussing the etymology of the Homeric epithet ἔλλοψ ('dumb?' 'scaly?'), says:

> I will also explain, even if the question has not been asked, why the Pythagoreans who eat moderately of other live animals, some of which they even sacrifice, nevertheless utterly refuse to touch fish alone. Is it because of their silence? They regard silence, in fact, as divine.

To explain the Pythagorean alimentary taboo, Ulpian refers to an *aition* in pseudo-syllogistic form: the Pythagoreans consider silence sacred;[51] fish are silent: so the Pythagoreans consider fish sacred, and they do not eat them. A large number of references to the alimentary habits of the Pythagoreans can be found in Athenaeus' work. They are mostly taken from comedy and are concentrated in one section of Book Four (160f-2b).[52] From these fragments collected by Athenaeus we can infer some features of the supposed diet of the Pythagoreans which do not perfectly match with the data provided in Book Seven. Comedy attacks Pythagorean abstinence from all the living animals, not only from fish. In Book Seven however, Athenaeus tells us that Pythagoreans eat moderately of other living animals, some of which they even sacrifice, but refuse to touch fish.

Athenaeus is one of the many victims of the ambivalent Pythagorean tradition, which sets the absolute prohibition on eating animals against a partial prohibition regarding only some animals or some sacrificial practices.[53] His contradictions on Pythagorean matters, therefore, depend on his heterogeneous sources. The nearest source to the passage in Book Seven is possibly Plutarch. In his *Quaestiones Conviviales*, 8.8, a whole *question* is devoted to the Pythagoreans' refusal of fish: it contains the same information given by Athenaeus, that is the cause of the total abstinence from fish[54]. This passage from Plutarch may not be Athenaeus'source, but the two authors seem at least to have had the same source. In principle, we might identify in Athenaeus an explicit reference to Plutarch's passage in the clause λέξω καὶ μὴ προβληθέντος ('I will also explain, even if the question has not been asked')—which is a technical formulation in the *Quaestiones*. In Plutarch, however, the details of the subject are much more closely examined. There, the learned Empedocles, who expounds the theme, distinguishes the ancient Pythagorean from the disciples of the neopythagorean Alexicrates' contemporaries (8.8,1). There is no trace in Athenaeus of the part of Plutarch's dialogue, where the Pythagoreans' taboo is related to the customs of the Egyptian priests (8.8,2),[55] and by analogy to the moderate diet of the Syrians and of the Homeric heroes (8.8,3).[56]

Athenaeus does not distinguish ancient Pythagoreans from neo-Pythagoreans and seems to confuse the various degrees of abstinence.[57] His knowledge of Pythagorean cooking, and in particular of the use of fish, seems to come from late and generic interpretations. On the whole, he points out the frugality of these wise men and sets it against the gluttony of the Cynics at the Deipnosophists' banquet,[58] but he disregards the gist of the Pythagorean doctrine, that is the exhortation to live in purity and to set up the way of life that Plato called 'Pythagorean' (*Rep.* 10. 600a). Therefore, Athenaeus deals with a subject which was fashionable both in contemporary society, because of the diffusion of neo-pythagorean sects,[59] and in late Hellenistic literary production; but he maintains a rather superficial attitude, mildly ironic towards a kind of diet alien to his way of life, or better, to the way of life pictured in the *Deipnosophistae*. He is closer, in the way he describes the Pythagoreans, to the spirit of the comic poets whom he quotes than to the intellectuals of his time.[60]

## 6. The Syrians

With the same attitude Athenaeus deals with another perverse use of fish, that of the Syrians.[61] In 8.346d the Deipnosophist Democritus protests because the Syrian Ulpian, to be faithful to the traditions of his native land, has taken fish away from his table-companions, and keeps suggesting new subjects for discussion. Earlier, at the beginning of Book Seven, at 275c, Ulpian orders slaves to stop passing the food, because he wants to continue the debate about the Eating-festival. Then comes the account of fishes extending throughout Book Seven and a section of the following book. In this context, Democritus' humorous protest provides the opportunity to deal with the Syrians' abstinence from fish.[62] First of all the *aition* of abstinence is presented, taken from Antipater of Tarsus (64, *SVF* 3. 257):

> And yet the Stoic Antipater of Tarsus says in the fourth book of his work *On Superstition* that it is asserted on the part of some authorities that Queen Gatis of Syria was such a fish lover that she published an edict forbidding anyone to eat fish apart from Gatis. Not understanding this phrase, the masses call her Atargatis, and abstain from fish.

The passage is taken from *On Superstition*, and contains, with the origins of the Syrians' custom—the edict[63] of the ὀψοφάγος queen—the etymology of Atargatis (ἄτερ Γάτιδος = 'apart from Gatis'), based on the obviously wrong assumption that the name was Greek.[64] Plutarch dealt with the same subject in his *On Superstition*, Chapter 10.[65]

Then Athenaeus reports a passage of the historian Mnaseas of Patara (*FHG* III 155), who relates the same *aition* in his second book *On Asia*, adding more noteworthy data:

In my opinion Atargatis was a cruel queen and ruled the peoples harshly, even to the extent of forbidding them by law to eat fish; on the contrary, they must bring them to her because of her fondness for that food. For this reason the custom still holds that whenever they pray to the goddess, they bring her offerings of fish made of silver or gold; but the priests bring to the goddess, every day, real fish which they have fancily dressed and served on the table. They are boiled or baked, and priests of the goddess, of course, consume the fish themselves.

Finally, Democritus tells us about Atargatis' end, quoting Xanthus of Lydia, a historian of the fifth century BC (*FGrH* 765 F 17):

Atargatis was captured by Mopsus the Lydian[66] and with her son Ichthus was immersed in the lake of Ascalon because of her outrageous conduct, and eaten up by the fish.

The pieces of information which Athenaeus draws from three different sources are not perfectly coherent. On the one hand we have the legend of the cruel and tyrannical ὀψοφάγος queen, who publishes an edict forbidding all her subjects to eat fish. In the end she is punished for her *hybris* and she is thrown, together with her son Ichthus, into the lake of Ascalon, where she is devoured by the fish in a sort of retaliation. On the other hand we have the reference to a cult practice still existing in Athenaeus' time: the tyrant's 'opsophagy' continues in the ritual priests' ὀψοφαγία. The Syrians' abstinence from fish was a literary *topos*, as is shown by the numerous references in Greek and Latin authors throughout ten centuries at least, from Xanthus to Porphyry, *Abst.* 4.15.[67]

There were many legends on the origins of the taboo regarding fish. One is in Eratosthenes, *Cat.* 38, and is ascribed to Ctesias: Derketo, Aphrodite's daughter, having fallen into the lake near Bambyke (Hierapolis), was saved by a fish. The goddess then turned into a fish: her rescuer generated two sons, who, as a reward, became the constellation of Pisces; since then the Syrians have abstained from fish to honour the goddess.[68]

According to Diognetus Erythraeus (*FGrH* 120 F 2), quoted by Hyginus, *Astr.* 2.30, the goddess, called Venus, drowned herself with her son Cupid in the river Euphrates, to avoid the passion of Typhon.[69] Then she turned into a fish; since then the Syrians have abstained from fish, in order to avoid eating the two divinities, or the fish that rescued them.

There is another story in Ctesias reported by Diodorus, 2.4. 2,[70] which has some similarities with the aforementioned version by Xanthus. Derketo fell in love with a young man and had a daughter, Semiramis. Then, ashamed of herself, she jumped into the lake of Ascalon with her daughter and she turned into a fish; since then the Syrians have abstained from fish and considered them sacred.

Athenaeus relates the prohibition on fish to a cult practice, for a goddess who was in origin an ὀψοφάγος queen. If we suppose that Athenaeus knew more versions of the legend (cf. Chapter 40), we may conclude that he has chosen the most popular and irreverent one. For while, according to Athenaeus, the origin of the Syrians' abstinence from fish was an act of *hybris*, a tyrannical manifestation of ὀψοφαγία, the other versions of the legend have in common the connection between the metamorphosis of the deity and the cult of fish. The abstinence from fish was due to the fact that it was considered the incarnation of the deity. In the same way the priests' fish-eating can be explained. The priests have the double function of *mageiroi* and sacrificers; they eat fish to take the god into themselves[71]. But Athenaeus shows little knowledge of these rites. He concludes that among the Syrians fish is food for gods, not for human beings. The taboo of the Syrians seems to be the opposite of the Greek ideal of banqueting.[72]

In Books Seven and Eight there is no mention of the Homeric heroes, Greeks whose diet excluded fish (*Deipn.* 1.9d–13d).[73] It is strange that Athenaeus does not hint at this fact in his catalogue of fish. One might think that he does not deal with this subject here simply because he has already expounded it elsewhere. However, I would give another reason.

Athenaeus looks at the Homeric world, and particularly at its convivial code, as an unparalled *exemplum* of temperance and virtue. But all this is far from his taste as far as food is concerned. The Homeric heroes' ἐγκράτεια ('temperance') belongs to a remote past.[74] The exclusion of fish from the Homeric banquet cannot be taken as a model. It is almost embarrassing in a context in which fish-eating has become a sign of civilization. Hence Athenaeus' silence.

## Conclusion

Although this chapter may seem to bring together heterogeneous data, I believe that all the cases I have described share one common feature: the interest in an anomaly, that is, in eccentric aspects of (non-) fish-eating.

Of course, we can find elsewhere in Athenaeus too an ethnographic concern, an interest in the marginal and paradoxical, which is an interest he shared with various contemporary and slightly earlier writers (Plutarch, Lucian and Gellius). But there is more than this.

According to Athenaeus, there is a strong connection between gastronomy and the community which practises it.[75] The παῖδες ἰχθυοφάγοι, used like animals for biological experimentation, are totally alien to his cultural world. Ὀψοφαγία may be a manifestation of upper-class intemperance in the past (especially that past expressed in comedy) as well as in the present, but Athenaeus does not condemn it without appeal: there is no reproach for refined eating as such, provided that it was kept within the bounds of social and philosophical decorum.

As far as the Pythagoreans are concerned, Athenaeus displays a sort of ironic detachment, extended also to the people who illogically abstain from some sorts of fish. Meanwhile he sympathizes with the poor Syrians, who are forbidden to eat fish by a cruel law.

All these interesting cases contrast with the gastronomy of the Greek élite of the Roman empire as they appear in the *Deipnosophistae*. A century later, the neoplatonic Porphyry and Iamblichus, and still later Julian, consider the rejection of fish to be ascetic, for the very reason that it signifies giving up the pleasures of the table and luxury. But at the Deipnosophists' banquet there is an extraordinary variety of fish, as Athenaeus says at the beginning of his work. On the other hand, excesses in fish-eating are not allowed: the Deipnosophist Zoilus claims he is not ὀψοφαγίστατος ('I am not much of a fish-eater myself,' *Deipn.* 7.277d); Democritus protests that he has come to the banquet οὐκ ὀψοφαγήσων ('not to play the fish-eater,' *Deipn.* 8.346c); Athenaeus himself admits he is not as φίλιχθυς ('fond of fish') as the character described in Antiphanes' *Boutalion* (*Deipn.* 8.358d).

On this view, fish must be carefully chosen for its dietetic properties, cooked and eaten with gastronomic wisdom, and exalted by the flavours of Mediterranean cooking. To that extent, Athenaeus is the keeper of a refined, developed gastronomic heritage, in which fish is used with intelligence and taste. This heritage was destined to be challenged by the Christians, who raised fish to the level of a symbol of their faith,[76] a sign of penitence and abstinence from flesh, by contrast with the flesh-eating barbarians.[77]

# SECTION V:
# KEY AUTHORS

# INTRODUCTORY
# REMARKS

The *Deipnosophistae* is built on the works of earlier authors. Christian Jacob has described how the work is a literary version of a library. This book would be far longer than it is if it analysed all the texts which Athenaeus had taken down from the shelf and quoted in his book. The authors discussed in this section exemplify some of the choices of text that Athenaeus made, and something of the overall direction that he gained from those choices (and vice versa). These exemplary authors are Homer, Plato, Lynceus of Samos and Crates of Mallus.

Homer was the corner-stone of Greek literature and an inevitable subject for Hellenistic scholarship. Athenaeus both cited Homer extensively and concerned himself with later commentaries and readings of Homer. Malcolm Heath examines precisely how Athenaeus used Homeric scholarship, to inform debate in the 'internal dialogue' at crucial points in the *Deipnosophistae*, in Books One and Five, where parameters are set for the discussion throughout the whole work. The Epitome has obscured some of the argument in Book One, on luxury and on the status of certain foods and drinks at the symposium (though not disastrously), while in Book Five Homer is declared to have defined the true symposium in a way that Plato was unable to do.

This brings us to Michael Trapp's chapter. Plato had written the definitive literary symposium in his dialogue of that name. He is evoked at the beginning and end of the *Deipnosophistae* and at many points in between. A number of studies of the literary symposium have charted developments after Plato, for example Martin (1931), Relihan (1993a) and Romeri (1999). In many ways Athenaeus' version is the most radical since it restored to the literary symposium the food and drink that had been down-played since Plato. Athenaeus takes issue with Plato on several occasions. There is, however, more at stake than Plato's model for the literary symposium. Trapp's chapter explores Athenaeus' treatment of Plato's work as a whole, both his Platonic citations and his commentary on Plato as a philosophical writer. We might bear in mind the unflattering portraits of philosophers that recur in the *Deipnosophistae*, to which reference has been made in Chapters 1 and 2.

Our third key author is Crates of Mallus. Maria Broggiato is concerned to identify what is likely to be his work in Athenaeus and what should be attributed rather to his namesake Crates of Athens. Crates of Mallus was an important scholar of the first century BC who was embroiled in the scholarly disputes of the period and appears to have acted as librarian at the great library of Pergamum. He took an interest in questions of language and classification, with special reference to the poems of Homer, for which he offered allegorical readings. In a number of ways Crates shares the interests of Athenaeus and the diners: he was a Greek who visited Rome (as Athenaeus evidently did, himself a Greek of the Roman imperial east); he was interested in libraries and he engaged in scholarly dispute. To a considerable extent, Athenaeus' interests, as expressed in the *Deipnosophistae*, are as grammatical and lexicographical as they are literary and historical. Very often his diners cite an earlier authority for the use of a word or for an inflected form of the word or for its meaning rather than for its literary or social context. Crates of Mallus is one of many scholarly predecessors who shaped Athenaeus' approach to the past, and not least to the poems of Homer which in Books One and Five are read through strong scholarly filters.

Lynceus of Samos did not bequeath to posterity a body of work that was cherished. It is symptomatic that he is not given an entry in the third edition of the *Oxford Classical Dictionary*. Apparently the brother of the influential historian Duris of Samos, Lynceus wrote in the late fourth or early third century BC in a range of genres. He wrote a comedy, letters and even a treatise on a subject more to be expected of the twenty-first century AD—shopping. Andrew Dalby has collected the fragments of Lynceus, and offers a review of his output. Lynceus exemplifies four aspects of much broader importance in the *Deipnosophistae*. First, no author was too obscure for consideration (if anything, rather the contrary): Athenaeus quotes Matro's poem *The Attic Dinner* precisely for its rarity (4.134). Second, Lynceus' generic range appealed. The scholar in Athenaeus looked for range as well as specialization, for the minor as well as the principal works. Third, the content of Lynceus' work tended to focus on the good life, not to say extravagance. This was grist to the mill that opposed luxury at the symposium. Finally, and most important, Lynceus employed the exemplary anecdote, the well-told incident which made a telling point. Anecdotes abound in Athenaeus' authors, in prose and verse, whether it be a historian of the fourth century BC (such as Phaenias of Ephesus or Timaeus of Tauromenium) or a lewd story of a courtesan in a comic text or in the *Chreiae* of Machon. Anecdotes were ideal for the literary symposium, as we see early on in Aristophanes' *Wasps*, in Plato's *Symposium* or in Xenophon's *Symposium*. The short illustrative tale fitted perfectly, where extended narrative or analysis did not.

# DO HEROES EAT FISH?
## ATHENAEUS ON THE HOMERIC LIFESTYLE

### by Malcolm Heath

## 1. Background

Eating is a serious business and raises moral issues—eating fish, especially, for fish is a luxury food: 'gastronomy grew in Greek cities as the fresh fish market grew.'[1] Hence Plato, outlining the simple regime that is to keep the guardians of his *Republic* in peak condition (*Rep.* 4, 404bc), notes that Homer's heroes on campaign do not eat fish, despite being encamped by the Hellespont, but only beef; moreover, they eat their beef roast, not boiled (since soldiers should not encumber themselves with cooking-pots); and, of course, they do not eat delicacies at all, in keeping with the general practice of those who want to keep themselves in good physical condition. These observations are unlikely to have been original with Plato, since there are parallels in fourth-century comedy (Eubulus fr. 118.1–3; Antiphanes fr. 248). But the origins and earlier history of discussion of the Homeric diet cannot now be recovered.[2] Its subsequent development, however, is better attested, and will lead in due course to Athenaeus' first book, which repeatedly turns its attention to these and related topics.

Plato speaks specifically of the heroes on campaign (ἐπὶ στρατιᾶς). The qualification is important, for while it is true that the heroes do not eat fish in the *Iliad*, fish are eaten in the *Odyssey* by the companions of Menelaus (*Od.* 4.368) and of Odysseus (*Od.* 12.331). The Separatists (χωρίζοντες), the small minority of ancient grammarians who held that the two poems were by different poets, used this apparent discrepancy as one piece of evidence in favour of their position (ΣA Il. 16.747a).[3] Ancient scholars responded to this argument in a variety of ways. Some argued that the companions of Menelaus and Odysseus were in desperate straits, and that actions taken under extreme conditions should not be used as evidence for the Homeric diet in general. A number of scholia emphasize this point: the heroes do not eat fish, except when starvation compels them to do so (ΣA *Il.* 16.407c; ΣB *Od.* 4.368). A second line of response examined the implications of the Odyssean episodes. The heroes involved in them either have fishing-tackle with them, or else know how to improvise it; and they know to use it. So these incidents provide indirect evidence that the heroes were familiar with fishing; it must have been part of their culture. This observation appears in Athenaeus, in a context (1.2a–b) to be discussed below. Thirdly, it could be argued that there is evidence of familiarity with fishing even in the *Iliad*. The appearance of a fisherman in a simile (*Il.* 16.406–9) is not decisive, since the question is not whether the poet was familiar with fishing and fish-eating, but whether his heroes were. But when a simile drawn from oyster-fishing is put into the mouth of Patroclus (*Il.* 16.746–8), it is clear that the poet assumes a familiarity with fishing on the part of his heroes as well. Aristarchus made this point in his reply to the Separatists (ΣA *Il.* 16.747a); and the same conclusion could be drawn (although without implications for the Separatist question) from Odysseus' narrative at Odyssey 10.124 (ΣT *Od.* 10.124).

A later commentator, whose views on Patroclus' reference to oyster-diving are recorded in the exegetical scholia (ΣbT *Il.* 16.747b), was still worried about the apparent discrepancy between this passage and Homer's portrayal of the heroic diet elsewhere: after all, not even the Phaeacians (despite their soft lifestyle) or the suitors are portrayed eating fish. Perhaps, then, this anomalous reference to fishing should be explained in the same way as the two episodes in the *Odyssey*. Patroclus speaks of someone diving for oysters *from a ship*; so it is possible that he has in mind someone eating fish out of necessity in the course of a long voyage, rather than the inclusion of fish as part of the normal heroic diet. This commentator adds that in general the poet restricts his heroes' diet to roast beef because they prepare their food themselves, and it would be demeaning to show the son of Thetis gutting a fish or making a stew.

In this last point, at least, the exegetical commentator concurs with Aristarchus' view that the poet avoided the portrayal of fish-eating because of its 'triviality' (τὸ μικροπρεπές, ΣA *Il.* 16.747a). But it seems that Aristarchus would not have accepted the claim that the heroes ate other kinds of food than roast meat only in exceptional circumstances. In his discussion of Patroclus' reference to oyster-fishing Aristarchus goes on to point out the evidence that the heroes cultivated vegetables (ΣA *Il.* 16.747a, citing *Od.* 17.299); this proves that vegetables were eaten in the heroic world, even though the eating of vegetables is never directly portrayed in the poems. The same reasoning applies, by implication, to the eating of fish. Therefore, although Aristarchus and the exegetical commentator both say that the poet does not portray the heroes eating fish, they say it with significantly different emphases. For the exegetical commentator, the poet does not portray the heroes *eating* fish: that is, he portrays them as familiar with the practice, but not as indulging in it themselves (except in extreme circumstances). For Aristarchus, the poet does not *portray* the heroes eating fish: that is, it is tacitly assumed that they do eat fish, but for aesthetic reasons the poet has chosen not to show it happening.

What of the preparation of the meat? Aristarchus inferred from the simile of the boiling cauldron at *Iliad* 21.362–5 that the poet was familiar with boiled meat, even though he does not portray the heroes eating it (ΣA *Il.* 21.362a). But another commentator draws our attention to the ox-foot thrown at Odysseus (*Od.* 20.299): ox-feet are not roasted, so boiled meat was consumed as well (ΣbT Il. 21.362b). We know that this observation goes back to Crates (Eustathius ad loc.). This acute observation on the significance of the ox-foot neatly illustrates with what careful attention, even to seemingly incidental details, Hellenistic scholars studied the poems in order to establish an account of heroic society and culture.[4] The conclusions they reached were sometimes (as we have seen) distinguished by quite subtle nuances of emphasis; we in turn need to pay equally careful attention to detail when we read reports of their views.

## 2. Athenaeus on the heroic lifestyle: introduction

Questions concerning the heroic lifestyle are considered repeatedly and at length by Athenaeus in the first book of the *Deipnosophists*. In what follows I shall try to elucidate his use of this material in the light of the background of ancient Homeric scholarship summarized above. Although (predictably) it is the question of Athenaeus' sources that has tended to preoccupy modern scholars, that is not my primary concern. My aim is instead to clarify the issues that arise, and the logic of the positions adopted, in the course of the Deipnosophists' discussion. These points are often, at first sight, unclear.

Book One survives only in epitome, and the pervasive lack of clarity is likely to be, at least in part, a result of the epitomization. Our discussion will therefore inevitably involve some attempt at reconstructing Athenaeus' original text. This in turn must lead to a consideration of its literary form. Athenaeus wrote a dialogue; but the epitomator, having no interest in this aspect of the work he was condensing, has generally eliminated traces of the dialogical framework. It is an open question how far that poses a significant problem for our understanding of Athenaeus, and how far we can hope to address the problem by recovering the structure of the original dialogue. As we shall see, some traces of the dialogue form have been preserved in the epitome; in the sections relevant to our present concerns there are a number of tags and boundary markers which the epitomator retained, not because he was interested in the dialogue whose structure they marked, but because they involved an interesting turn of phrase. These traces allow us to get an initial grip on the problem. But it would be surprising if the epitomator had retained evidence for all the framework sections, so some more speculative work will also be required.

The first challenge is to locate changes of speaker. Changes in subject provide one possible indicator; but the fact that in the full text we find rambling speeches which touch on many topics shows that this is not a sufficient criterion. We may also look for shifts in the view being taken of a single topic. But here, too, caution is needed: speakers may contradict themselves, and may quote divergent opinions from different sources without being committed to any of them; indications that an opinion is quoted (not asserted) by the speaker may have been elided in the epitome. Conversely, different speakers may have similar or over-lapping positions; so the fact that the same thing is said is not enough to prove that the same speaker is saying it. The uncertainty is even greater when we try to move beyond locating changes of speaker and seek to identify the particular speakers involved; this question requires us to make debatable assumptions about (*inter alia*) the extent to which Athenaeus aimed at, and achieved, consistency of characterization. The difficulties in the kind of reconstruction envisaged are therefore formidable; but the experiment may still be worth making.

In what follows, I first use the overt traces of the dialogue framework preserved by the epitomator to map out the general structure of the Deipnosophists' discussion of the Homeric lifestyle. I shall then attempt a more detailed (and more speculative) analysis of the dialogue on the basis of implicit evidence.

## 3. Athenaeus' dialogue: general structure

At 1.11b we read: 'thus spoke the Thessalian sophism, i.e. the sophist from Thessaly: Athenaeus is perhaps making a jocular allusion to the proverb' (ταῦτ' εἶπε τὸ Θετταλὸν σόφισμα ἤτοι ὁ ἐκ Θετταλίας σοφιστής· παίζει δ' ἴσως πρὸς τὴν παροιμίαν ὁ Ἀθήναιος). Here, clearly, the epitomator has preserved a trace of the dialogue framework because of the interesting turn of phrase it used. Decoded, the comment indicates that the speaker in the section that has just ended was the Thessalian sophist Myrtilus. That section, which began at 8e, was the first devoted to the Homeric lifestyle. There is further material on the Homeric lifestyle after the tag that concludes Myrtilus' speech; we may provisionally infer that a different speaker takes up the subject at 11b, and I shall argue below that this inference is confirmed by a significant change in characterization.

Where does the second Homeric discourse, beginning at 11b, end? Discussion of Homer continues to 19a, where it is neatly rounded off by a quotation from Pindar that sums up the martial spirit of the *Iliad*: 'Hear me, Battle Cry, daughter of War, prelude to spears' (fr. 78: κλῦθ' Ἀλαλά, Πολέμου θύγατερ, ἐγχέων προοίμιον).[5] But it is difficult to be confident that this whole stretch comprises a single speech; the more detailed analysis to be offered below will suggest that it does not. For the present it is sufficient to note that in identifying Homeric 'discourses' at this stage of the investigation I am not committing myself to a single speaker; I mean merely stretches of Homeric material bounded by preserved traces of the dialogue framework.

What follows the Pindaric quotation in 19a is not concerned with Homer, although it does pick up some of the topics that were touched on in the second Homeric discourse (especially dancing, at 21f–22c). The next clear pointer to the dramatic structure occurs at 22e, where we find a reference to 'verbal diarrhoea' (λογοδιάρροια). This word occurs elsewhere only at 159e, where the speaker is the cynic Cynulcus; it reflects his characteristic impatience with learned discussion, his eagerness to get down to the eating and drinking, and his crudity of expression. Probably the reference to Timon's satire on the Alexandrian Museum at 22d marks the beginning of Cynulcus' sarcastic intervention. This interlude ends with wine being served at 23a, where we may note the *hapax* 'dog-discoursing' (κυνολογήσασιν); the Dog-star has just been mentioned (22e–f), so the coinage is parallel to Athenaeus' other compounds expressing the subject-matter of a discussion (e.g. συκολογεῖν, ἰχθυολογεῖν, οἰνολογεῖν), but combines with that an allusion to the cynic's contribution to the dialogue and a pun on 'discuss' (κοινολογεῖν).[6]

The interlude is followed by a lexical section (23a–24b); there is no way of telling whether this was originally in the voice of the narrator, or in a character's voice. Then the subject of Homer recurs. This third Homeric discourse is preceded by another fragment of Pindar, 'glued together, like wood to wood' (fr. 241: ποτίκολλον ἅτε ξύλον παρὰ ξύλῳ); the same fragment is quoted again at 6.248c, where a new speaker uses it to introduce his turn. Here too, therefore, the epitomator has retained a trace of the dialogue framework because of his interest in the way it is expressed. I suspect that this third Homeric discourse continues to 25e, where a further quotation from Pindar, 'wine that is old, but the bloom of songs more recent' (*Ol.* 9.48–9: παλαιὸν μὲν οἶνον, ἄνθεα δ᾽ ὕμνων νεωτέρων), looks like a way of introducing a new subject, wine. But there is an element of continuity in the treatment of this new subject-matter, since there are allusions to Homer in 26a–b. The beginning of Galen's discourse on Italian wine at 26c marks the definitive end of the discussion of Homer.

## 4. Athenaeus' dialogue: detailed analysis

We have identified three discourses concerned (mainly) with Homer, to which at least three speakers contribute. In Athenaeus' original text this series of Homeric discourses was set in a context that provided a degree of variety by interspersing discourse on other topics. We shall now consider how far variety was also achieved by the contrasting characteristics of different speakers on Homer.

The first speaker, positively identified as Myrtilus, takes an emphatically and exclusively moralizing approach. On his view, Homer aimed to encourage moderation and self-control (σωφροσύνη) by giving the heroes a simple, self-sufficient way of life. In particular, he gave them a simple diet—all of them, irrespective of status. It is true that Priam's good-for-nothing sons eat lambs and kids; but their father regards this departure from the customary diet as a matter for rebuke (9d, quoting *Il.* 24.262). Even the luxurious Phaeacians and suitors conform to usual diet (compare the exegetical scholion, ΣbT *Il.* 16.747b, discussed above). The heroes eat roast meat, mainly beef; Homer does not 'place before them' (παρατίθησι) fish, birds, cakes or fruit, and he does not put into his poetry (ποιεῖ) the heroes eating fish or wearing garlands and using perfume or incense. Not only do they have a simple diet, but they are moderate in their indulgence of it. This moderation has a healthy effect on their constitution; hence, for example, male visitors can be bathed by young women without sexual impropriety. The reference here (10de) is to passages such as *Odyssey* 3.464–5, where Nestor's daughter Polycaste bathes Telemachus; this practice caused some concern to ancient scholars. Aristarchus simply noted it as an archaic custom (ΣA *Il.* 9.905a), though some preferred to believe that Polycaste did no more than arrange for Telemachus to be given a bath (ΣT *Il.* 9.905b; ΣHMQ *Od.* 3.464).[7]

In Book Eight (363d–364a) Myrtilus discusses (with references to Homer) how the ancients arranged religious celebrations in such a way as to accustom people to indulging in pleasures 'in a well-disciplined and orderly manner' (εὐτάκτως καὶ κοσμίως), since the presence of gods encouraged them to conduct themselves 'in an orderly and self-controlled manner' (κοσμίως καὶ σωφρόνως). Hence they ate seated, not reclining, and drank in moderation, unlike people today. The moralizing tone of this later passage is exactly the same as that of Myrtilus' speech in Book One. Ulpian offers a different perspective on Myrtilus' moralizing when he attacks him as rich and fond of delicacies but too mean to pay for them (3.108d–e); this invective is relevant to an aspect of Athenaeus' literary technique that will be mentioned in the conclusion.

*4.1 First Homeric discourse: 8e–11b (Myrtilus)*

Right from the start the second discourse on Homer in Book One has a different tone. The speaker's approach is less moralistic and more antiquarian. There is an interest in 'factual' details about heroic eating: how many meals did the heroes eat?[8] Were tables cleared between courses? What happened to the left-overs? And so on. The speaker cites earlier scholars more often, and is willing to engage in debate with them (he criticizes Philemon and Zenodotus). He is less focused, allowing himself to digress from Homer in order to include interesting information on the history of ball-games and on dancing (14d–16a). Unlike Myrtilus, he recognizes that Homer does put into his poetry people eating fish and birds,

*4.2 Second Homeric discourse: 11b–19a (Masurius? unattributed, Myrtilus?)*

although he chooses not to mention such food in connection with the heroes' regular meals (δεῖπνα) for reasons of heroic dignity (13a–d). It is this passage which is the source of the observation mentioned earlier, that the fishing episodes in the *Odyssey* imply that the heroes had fishing-tackle and knew how to use it; this is a good example of the speaker's attention to factual detail.

Can this second speaker be identified? The question of the number of meals recurs in Book Five (193a), where Masurius is the speaker. The verb which Masurius uses to refer back to the earlier discussion, 'we have said before' (προειρήκαμεν), may imply that he was the speaker there as well; alternatively, it may simply mean more generally that the topic 'came up in our discussion before'. Masurius does share some characteristics with our second speaker: the reappearance of the question of the number of heroic meals reflects a shared interest in antiquarian details (192e on sitting at dinner; 192f on equal portions; 192f–193a on cups and 'pledging', πρόποσις; 193a on the number of meals). Masurius asserts Homer's superiority to later writers of symposiastic literature (177b), just as the second speaker asserts his superiority to later literature on fishing (13b–c). Both are interested in the history of dance (181c); and Masurius, an expert on music, also refers to Homer in a technical discussion of song and dance in Book Fourteen (627e–f). Moreover, the second speaker's tendency to digress is paralleled in the rambling structure of Masurius' contribution to Book Five, a huge speech which starts from Homer's superiority to Plato, Xenophon and Epicurus as a writer on symposia, and eventually works its way back to criticism of the philosophers, but which takes in a profusion of other topics on the way. There is one discrepancy: the second speaker in Book One accepts without question (14a) the presence of acrobats in Menelaus' palace in *Odyssey* 4, whereas in Book Five Masurius argues (180d) that Aristarchus interpolated them from *Iliad* 18.604, a view attested also in the scholia (ΣMT *Od.* 4.17). But this perhaps is a minor detail, and one which Athenaeus could easily have overlooked. It is possible, therefore, but not certain, that the speaker in the first part of the second discourse (let us call him speaker 2A) is Masurius.

In adding fish and birds to the Homeric diet speaker 2A has taken a step away from Myrtilus' emphasis on the complete simplicity of the Homeric diet. The statement at 16c that Homer is familiar with 'varied foods' (ποικίλαι ἐδωδαί) and every kind of modern extravagance seems to mark a more radical departure from Myrtilus' position. It is tempting, therefore, to postulate a new speaker (speaker 2B) at this point, even though the epitome preserves no explicit marker of the change. By contrast with speaker 2A (tentatively identified as Masurius), speaker 2B is alert to signs of a still more lavish lifestyle. But he retains an interest in the moral implications of Homer's portrayal of the heroes' way of life, and insists that, unlike later writers who also introduce such extravagance into the heroic world, he keeps things decent and orderly; even the suitors do not indulge in the kind of impropriety dramatized by Aeschylus and Sophocles (17c–f).

Further evidence for a multiplicity of speakers within the second discourse is found in 17f–18a, where it is remarked that the heroes sit to eat, rather than reclining. Speaker 2A had already made this in passing at 11f, and there is no obvious reason why he should come back to it here; moreover, the moralizing slant given to the observation in 18b, where the Homeric custom is contrasted with the degenerate modern practice, is foreign to the more antiquarian approach of speaker 2A. There seems also to be a difference of emphasis between 17b, where speaker 2B asserts the potency of perfumes in Homer as part of his argument for the presence of luxury in Homer, and 18e, which insists that Paris is the only hero to use them. The two passages are not perhaps in any strict sense contradictory, but the fact that the same topic is revisited with a significantly more restrictive emphasis may point to a different speaker (speaker 2C). This inference is supported by the way in which the whole section from 17f to 19a represents a reaction against the progressive abandonment of Myrtilus' interpretation of the Homeric lifestyle: by contrast with speakers 2A and 2B, speaker 2C reasserts the meat-based diet, stresses the simplicity of the lifestyle (the heroes are not ashamed to prepare and serve food themselves), and strongly contrasts this with modern decadence (18a–b). In fact, speaker 2C might actually be Myrtilus restating his position: Myrtilus (9c) and speaker 2C (18b) both cite Chrysippus, and Myrtilus' speech in Book Eight likewise gives a moral slant to the fact that the heroes sat rather than reclining, making the same contrast with modern decadence (363f). If speaker 2C is Myrtilus, then the concluding contrast (18f–19a) between the *Odyssey* and *Iliad* could be read as his way of taking on board and explaining the evidence of a more lavish lifestyle drawn from the Odyssey by speaker 2B.

We have begun to see, therefore, a genuine debate emerging, although the details are admittedly conjectural. The speaker in the third Homeric discourse fits well into this pattern.[9] He begins by taking up and modifying or supplementing points made by speaker 2A: he starts (24b) with Seleucus' critique of and alternative to the interpretation of the word δαίς ('feast') accepted at 12c, and then proceeds to make further comments on ball-games (24bc, cf. 14b–15c), and (picking up from speaker 2C at 18bc) on baths (24c–e). But his main function is to reassert and elaborate on the diversity of the Homeric diet (24e–25e): Homer sets before his heroes (and at regular meals, δεῖπνα, contrary to what speaker 2A had said at 13c) not just roast meat but vegetables, onions, fruit, fish and birds—that is, although he passes over in silence (παρέλιπε) foods which he thought beneath heroic dignity (25d), he provides indirect evidence that these things were eaten;

*4.3 Third Homeric discourse: 24b–25f (unattributed)*

similarly he 'hints at' (ἐμφανίζει) the use of boiled meat (25d–e). So far from the heroic diet being completely plain, therefore, there is a variety of foods and a variety of ways in which food is prepared (25e); Homer thus points the way to the luxury cuisine of later times. The concluding reference (25f) to the fact that old men, not just young, go to bed with women in Homer is perhaps a counter to Myrtilus' stress on the sexual self-control that came from the simple heroic diet (10d–e); on the contrary, the heroes had a varied diet, and they were highly sexed.

## 5. Conclusions

It is particularly regrettable that the full text of Book One has been lost. The reader fresh to Athenaeus who begins at the beginning will soon be tempted to give up in perplexity and disgust, revisiting Athenaeus (if at all) only to extract snippets of information without regard to their context. But the perplexity which this material prompts is a response to the epitomator, not to Athenaeus; when we look behind the epitome, we find an author with more literary skill than is often suspected. If one approaches the Homeric material in Book One remembering that Athenaeus was writing a dialogue, and with an awareness of its scholarly background, a genuine dialogue comes to light—a debate in which a variety of approaches and views are pitted against each other and interact.

This discovery has a number of implications. It has a bearing, for example, on the question of Athenaeus' sources. The *Suda*'s article on Homer (O251) includes an extract made from the full text of Book One (8e–9c), introduced by the words 'Dioscorides says in *Customs in Homer*...' (ὅτι Διοσκορίδης ἐν τοῖς παρ' Ὁμήρῳ νόμοις φησίν...). In 1888 Robert Weber published a collection of what he believed were fragments of this work (he refers to its author as Dioscurides) preserved in various contexts of Athenaeus and in other authors, together with an attempted reconstruction. Weber's conclusions have had distinguished advocates: Jacoby accepted them, as did (in broad outline) Martin Schmidt in a valuable monograph on the exegetical scholia to the *Iliad*.[10] But Weber's hypothesis, never well founded, now proves to be unsustainable. If the attribution in the *Suda* has any real basis,[11] it is probable that the speaker in this section (Myrtilus) explicitly cited Dioscorides, and that this indication of his source has been eliminated by the epitomator. But that does not prove that the quotation from Dioscorides extends beyond the section preserved in the *Suda* to include everything said by Myrtilus; still less is it legitimate to assume that Dioscorides was the source of what is said by other speakers.[12] In fact, the hypothesis that Athenaeus was drawing his material from any single main source seems to be excluded by the discovery that multiple and conflicting viewpoints are represented in the sequence of Homeric discourses.

The failure of this exercise in *Quellenforschung* does not mean that we have to abandon the enterprise of reconstructing lost texts; but before we enquire into

Athenaeus' sources we need a proper understanding of his text, which in the sections preserved only in epitome means that the *Deipnosophists* itself is the first lost text in need of reconstruction. Indeed, even if we are not interested in Athenaeus' sources, there is good reason to try to reconstruct the original text. For if the argument of this chapter is right the material Athenaeus uses is too deeply embedded in its context to be extracted safely without regard for that context; to understand it, we need to know how Athenaeus was shaping and using it—and that is not evident from the epitome alone.

Unfortunately, it is by no means clear that such a reconstruction is possible elsewhere in Athenaeus. A number of circumstances have worked in our favour in this investigation. My impression is that tags and markers of the dialogue structure are more often preserved in the sections of the epitome with which we have been concerned than they are in later sections; since epitomization is usually less radical near the beginning of a text, the first part of Book One is in principle the most promising place to attempt a reconstruction. Moreover, the discussion of the Homeric lifestyle goes repeatedly over the same ground, making it possible to diagnose subtle shifts of position. The fact that this subject had engaged the close attention of ancient scholars, and that we have comparatively rich evidence for the background to Athenaeus' treatment of it, also helped in giving us a purchase on his manipulation of the material. To assess the prospects for further reconstruction it would be necessary to undertake a detailed study of Athenaeus' dialogue technique, and also to make a systematic comparison of the epitome with the full text where both are preserved, so as to achieve a better understanding of the epitomator's practice. It may well be that the scope for further reconstruction would prove to be limited; if so, we should at least be aware of the implications for our use of material preserved in the epitome alone.

I end with three further observations about Athenaeus. First, it is clear that he has a good grasp of the issues that had been raised in connection with the Homeric lifestyle; this contrasts strikingly with the limited and superficial understanding which Athenaeus displays of many of the technical subjects covered in his work.[13] This difference is perhaps to be expected, since the interpretation of Homer falls within the professional expertise of a *grammatikos*. Secondly, it can be argued that Athenaeus is less concerned to establish a view of Homer and his heroes than to record what has been said on those topics by earlier writers. Since Athenaeus is writing a dialogue it would in any case be wrong to attribute any of the varied and contradictory opinions voiced by his characters to Athenaeus himself; but even the narrator's voice happily refrains from reaching a conclusion. For example, although the discussion of pleasure in Book Twelve starts with a seemingly firm assertion of personal opinion (510c) supported by references to Homer (511a–c), it soon settles down to report different (and conflicting) readings of the poet in a wholly non-committal manner (512d–3e). For Athenaeus, to study Homer is perhaps primarily to become a participant in a tradition of discourse about Homer.

But that is not to say that Athenaeus' devotion to this tradition is uncritical. For we may note, finally, how the material considered here reflects Athenaeus' playfulness and his sense of irony. The hyperbolically lavish banquet that he describes is introduced by a heavily moralizing speech that extols the simplicity of the Homeric lifestyle and diet, and the discussion moves on to condemn modern luxury by contrast; this, surely, is in line with the often satirical stance which Athenaeus takes towards his characters—a feature which Barry Baldwin has emphasized.[14] But it is perhaps not only towards his characters that Athenaean irony is directed. The other major concentration of Homeric material is in Masurius' speech in Book Five. Masurius assesses Homer as a writer of symposiastic literature, to the disadvantage of authors such as Plato, Xenophon and Epicurus. When authors other than Homer are criticized for the unbecoming quarrelsomeness of the participants in their symposia (186a), the creator of the often fractious Deipnosophists is surely making fun of himself as well.

## ❖ 26 ❖

# PLATO IN THE
# *DEIPNOSOPHISTAE*

## by Michael Trapp

Αὐτός, ὦ ᾿Αθήναιε, μετειληφὼς τῆς καλῆς ἐκείνης συνουσίας
τῶν νῦν ἐπικληθέντων δειπνοσοφιστῶν, ἥτις ἀνὰ τὴν πόλιν
πολυθρύλητος ἐγένετο, ἢ παρ᾽ ἄλλου μαθὼν τοῖς ἑταίροις
διεξήεις; "αὐτός, ὦ Τιμόκρατης, μετασχών." ἀρ᾽ οὖν
ἐθελήσεις καὶ ἡμῖν τῶν καλῶν ἐπικυλικίων λόγων μεταδοῦναι—τρὶς δ᾽
ἀπομαξαμένοισι θεοὶ διδόασιν ἄμεινον, ὥς πού φησιν ὁ Κυρηναῖος
ποιητής—ἢ παρ᾽ ἄλλου τινὸς ἡμᾶς ἀναπυνθάνεσθαι δεῖ;

'Athenaeus, were you yourself a participant in that splendid gathering of the
people now known as Deipnosophists, which became the talk of the town?
Or was the account you gave of it to your friends derived from someone
else?' 'I was there in person, Timocrates.' 'Will you please then let us too
share in the splendid discussions you had over your drinks—"the gods grant
better fortune to those who take three impressions," as I believe the poet
of Cyrene says—or must we ask someone else to inform us?'

So begins the *Deipnosophistae*. The Epitomator, to whom we owe the quotation,
draws attention to its Platonic flavour, δραματουργεῖ δὲ τὸν διάλογον ὁ
᾿Αθήναιος ζήλῳ Πλατωνικῷ, ('Athenaeus imitates Plato in the composition of his
dialogue': 1f) and commentators have hastened to specify the two objects of
imitation more precisely. The very first words, αὐτός, ὦ ᾿Αθήναιε, followed by the
answering , αὐτός, ὦ Τιμόκρατες, echo the *Phaedo*, while the subject specified (a
dinner-party, referred to as a συνουσία ('gathering'), which has become famous,
and about which the story has already been told to others) recalls the *Symposium*.[1]

And in addition to these specific echoes, Athenaeus' opening paragraph is rich in generally Platonic vocabulary: πολυθρύλητος ('talk of the town'),[2] ἆρ' οὖν ἐθελήσεις ('will you please then'),[3] λόγων μεταδοῦναι ('let [us] too share in the … discussions'),[4] and perhaps also ἀναπυνθάνεσθαι ('ask to inform').[5] Athenaeus has fitted his two Platonic texts together with ostentatious cleverness in this opening adaptation.

The cleverness resides, first, in having seen that *Symposium* and *Phaedo* can be spliced together in a single imitation, because they sketch similar scenes. In both of them Plato constructed a framing dialogue in which an enquirer asks a potential informant whether he can report on one of Socrates's conversations from first-hand experience. Echecrates questions Phaedo in the *Phaedo*, while the unnamed Companion and Glaucon both question Apollodorus in the more complicated set-up in the *Symposium*. But in addition, and with rather more ingenuity, Athenaeus has also seen (and wants it to be seen that he has seen) that there is a further situational link between the two dialogues, and one that is very much to his present purposes. In both of them the event that is being inquired about in the opening exchange is a discussion within a closed social circle that took place 'over a drink'.[6] The resulting blend of Platonic models is presented with an element of slyness, and a challenge to the reader's ability to keep up with this author's ingenuity. Athenaeus leads off in his first few words with evocation of the *Phaedo*, the dialogue apparently further away in its subject-matter from his own concerns. He then glides into the more obviously appropriate territory of the *Symposium*, challenging the reader (or listener) both to realize that he is weaving together separate models, and to appreciate that the two models in question— once they have been juxtaposed—turn out to go together better than one might at first think.

Evocation of Plato's *Symposium* at the beginning of the *Deipnosophistae* is obviously very much to the point. For it acknowledges straight away that Athenaeus is working with a literary form of which Plato is, if not the founder, by a long way the most distinguished classical practitioner. It also alerts the reader to be on the lookout for similarities in episode and subject-matter in the work to follow. Like Plato's *Symposium*, Athenaeus' *Deipnosophistae* is going to survey a broad range of privileged forms of knowledge and cultivated discourse (including, prominently, comic and tragic drama, medicine, oratory and philosophy); there is going to be a lot of Aristophanes, a lot of Socrates, some Alcibiades and some Gorgias in it. Whether one can see the same kind of point in the evocation of the *Phaedo*, I am less sure. There will be a certain amount about hemlock, and other drugs, and one of the leading characters will exit to his death, but that is not so very much by way of resemblance or coincidence of themes.[7] The opening reference to the *Phaedo* is better taken instead, I think, as contributing to a game of literary one-upmanship on Athenaeus' part. As I have already suggested, the combined evocation of the *Symposium* and *Phaedo* establishes our author as one who knows his Plato, and can play clever imitative/innovative games with his text. But perhaps there is a further element, turning on the question of the authority and immediacy with which Athenaeus presents himself as speaking.

Phaedo in the *Phaedo*, when asked if he can report the Last Conversation of Socrates from first-hand knowledge, is made by Plato to reply (like Athenaeus) in the affirmative (*Phaedo* 57a); Apollodorus in the *Symposium*, by contrast, is made to insist that his knowledge of the talk at Agathon's victory party is both second-hand and incomplete (*Symp.* 172b–173b). By evoking both of the Platonic texts together at the beginning of his own venture, Athenaeus cheekily highlights this discrepancy to his own advantage. In constructing his own neo-*Symposium*, he is not going to present its contents as several times mediated, and thus perhaps to some degree garbled and unreliable. He is instead going to opt for a greater directness, one that is still Platonic, but for some reason not used by Plato in the most nearly parallel case. As it were: 'here is *my Symposium*, and it comes to you from the horse's mouth, without all the Chinese whispers that Plato saw fit to encumber *his* with.' However this little dig does not amount to a rejection of the Platonic *Symposium* as a worthy model. So much is underlined by the quotation from Eratosthenes (the 'poet of Cyrene') that follows immediately in Athenaeus' text.[8] Rather than reinforcing the sense of a difference between Athenaeus in the *Deipnosophistae* and Apollodorus in the *Symposium*, the idea that taking repeated impressions from a given model is a profitable activity points instead to an important similarity: namely the fact that both of them are at the time of speaking giving a repeat performance, having previously told the story of the party and its discussions to another audience.

Athenaeus, it would seem, wants to have his cake and eat it . He is as keen to align himself with Plato and his narrator (claiming Platonic precedent for his own literary procedures), as he is to suggest that his own symposium-narrator has an edge over his Platonic forebear. Nor is this the only place in the *Deipnosophistae* where Platonic reminiscence is used to prompt tongue-in-cheek comparisons: the same game seems to be played at the very end of the work, with Athenaeus' final half-quotation from *Epistle* 2. 314c, which playfully contrasts the 'serious' matter of the *Deipnosophistae* with Plato's characterization of his own dialogues as 'the jesting of the young and beautiful Socrates'. The *Deipnosophistae* begins and ends, there-fore, with an elegant and skilful acknowledgement of Plato as the great, standard-setting predecessor in the literary game of recording a party for the sake of its erudite and cultivated conversation, combined with a gentle (and urbanely ironic) sense of rivalry.

But Plato cannot remain the formal model for long. Loss of the full version of the first two-and-a-bit books of Athenaeus' work prevents us from discovering just how much more imitation of Plato he employed in in his scene-setting pages. But however much (or little) there was, it must have given out as the discussion proper got under way. Both the immensely greater scale of the work, and its concentration on food-and-party-centred antiquarian (dis)play rather than philosophical debate, militate against any use of the *Symposium* (or any other Platonic dialogue) as a sustained or recurring point of reference in the construction of Athenaeus' own dinner-party narrative. When the full text becomes available, from the middle of Book Three onwards, we look in vain for any such traces.[9] What we find instead, and in abundance, is Plato and Plato's writings as matter for discussion. He is a topic, not a model. This is, of course, anything but surprising. The *Deipnosophistae* is an exercise—perhaps the most elaborate and sustained of all such exercises—in educated play with the classical literary-cultural heritage, and Plato is an unavoidable element in that heritage (even when, as in the present case, it is being viewed principally from the vantage-point of the dining-table). It is worth exploring this in more detail, by means of the different sub-headings under which Plato claims Athenaeus' learned attention. He is, first, a great individual, with a character and a career that demand commemoration and comment. Thus we hear, for instance, of his relations with the other Socratics, above all Xenophon, Aeschines and Antisthenes;[10] of his invention of a night-clock;[11] of his love for figs;[12] of his habits as a host;[13] of his journeys to Sicily;[14] and of his girl-friend Archeanassa.[15]

Next, Plato is the great literary figure, to be acknowledged and used both as a stylist (an authority on good Hellenic usage) and as the author of a specific set of classic, canonical works. Thus, to take the stylistic point first, he is quoted at least ten times for individual items of vocabulary,[16] and in one (albeit fleeting) reference, the dominant feature of his style is identified as χάρις ('grace').[17] As for Plato as author of classic works, almost every dialogue is mentioned at some stage in the course of the *Deipnosophistae*, if only in the form of a reference to one of its principal characters. Leaving some of the minor *Spuria* out of account, it seems that only the *Euthyphro*, *Theages*, *Lysis*, *Clitopho* and *Sophist* pass entirely without mention. In terms of frequency of reference, the *Symposium* is in a class of its own; then come the *Republic* and *Laws*; then (some way behind) the *Phaedrus*, *Gorgias*, *Timaeus*, *Phaedo* and *Protagoras*; the *Apology*, *Meno* and *Philebus* all achieve slightly more than minimum visibility; the real bit-part players are *Alcibiades I*, *Charmides*, *Crito*, *Epistles*, *Euthydemus*, *Laches*, *Parmenides*, *Politicus* and *Theaetetus*; as also *Alcibiades II*, *Cratylus*, *Critias*, *Epinomis*, *Hippias Maior* and *Minor*, *Ion* and *Menexenus*.[18] Finally, of course, Plato earns his place as the intellectual authority, a great thinker whose views demand to be known and discussed. Characteristically, he is most frequently consulted on points of symposium procedure, and the social proprieties of eating, drinking and partying—topics on which not only the *Symposium*, but also the *Republic*, *Laws* and *Protagoras* turn out to have a good deal to say. So, to give just the first couple of examples in order, Plato is cited at 1.4e for his view of the proper number of participants at a well-organized dinner (?*Laws* 762c), and in 1.21b for the genteel way to wear a cloak (*Tht.* 175e). But he can also be appealed to for points of doctrine and information in the fields of anatomy, politics, psychology, and the theory of pleasure.[19]

The simple quantity of references to Plato and Platonic texts, combined with the variety of roles in which Plato appears, would seem on the face of it to indicate a considerable respect. The impression can, moreover, easily be strengthened. The only two philosophers whose words are more frequently quoted by Athenaeus are Aristotle and Theophrastus (who have between them so much to say about the edible portions of the natural world); the only other 'thinker' quoted anything like a comparable number of times is Clearchus of Soli (with his moralizing interest in luxury, parasites and flatterers). In terms of numbers of named references (admittedly a crude measure), Aristotle's name comes up about 170 times, Plato's about 140, Theophrastus's about 110, Clearchus' and Socrates' around 80, Posidonius' about 40, Epicurus' about 35, and Speusippus' and Aristoxenus' about 30 apiece. It is also noteworthy that, when an epithet is attached to Plato's name in the attribute position, it is almost always commendatory. Discounting three instances of ὁ φιλόσοφος ('the philosopher', in contradistinction to ὁ κωμῳδοποιός, 'the comic poet'), there are a dozen cases: θεῖος, θειότατος ('divine', 'most divine') five times, θαυμασιώτατος ('most admirable') and καλός ('noble') twice each, λαμπρότατος ('most illustrious'), ἱερώτατος ('most holy') and σοφός ('wise') once each. In only two of these twelve cases is there an immediate suspicion of irony. But this initial impression of deference and respect is only part of the story about Athenaeus' references to and uses of Plato. For in a substantial number of cases when Plato's name and works come up in the *Deipnosophistae* it is in fact for criticism rather than for praise.

Plato is indeed acknowledged throughout as a great figure, in the sense of an unavoidable topic for discussion, but he is far from being presented in a uniformly adulatory light. Thus, many of the biographical references are coolly detached or satirical in tone, as is only to be expected, when comedy is such a significant source for this kind of information about him, and indeed when such tones are so characteristic of ancient literary-biographical tradition in general.[20] But, more significantly still, the *Deipnosophistae* boasts no fewer than three major set-piece discussions in which Plato is either the joint or the sole object of attention, and in which he is treated with disapproval or with downright scorn. These are: Masurius' twin discussions of symposia and their literary presentation and of the implausibilities and inconsistencies in Plato's portrayal of Socrates in

Book Five (at the two ends of a single long speech); and Pontianus's dissection of Plato's moral and intellectual flaws in Book Eleven.[21]

The first of these set-pieces begins in 186d and takes the form of a systematic, point-by-point analysis of Homeric symposia. Its aim is to demonstrate their superiority both as exercises in literary presentation and as instructive models of proper conduct. Woven into this, among other things, is some strongly worded anti-Aristarchan polemic.[22] More to the point is the fact that the shining excellence of Homer as both describer of symposia and preceptor of sympotic manners is brought out by repeated comparisons with the *Symposia* of Xenophon, Epicurus and Plato. The latter are very occasionally commended for following Homer's lead, but far more often condemned for deserting it. And of the three, it is Plato who receives the most sustained criticism. He may have learned from Homer how to set his scene, introduce his characters, construct an interestingly varied cast-list (186e)[23] and ensure that the gods receive their due libations (179d), but he got practically everything else terribly wrong. For the sake of a silly joke, he misunderstood or twisted what Homer said about Menelaus in *Iliad* 2. 408;[24] properly understood, the scene in fact teaches a useful lesson about the etiquette of invitation (177c–178e). He allows his symposiasts—above all Alcibiades—to drink to unseemly excess, in stark contrast to the moderation Homer teaches (179e–180b). He lets them jeer and mock at each other, and ridicules them himself as author (182a–187f);[25] contrast again the mutual mannerliness of Homer's diners. And, finally, Plato lets his party drag on until day is breaking and all but one of the guests have gone to sleep, instead of bringing it to a seemly close at a decent hour (191d–192b).

The second of the three set-pieces follows towards the end of Book Five, where Masurius turns to Plato's presentation of Socrates under arms. It is all, he claims, the most outrageous fiction;[26] the role Plato assigns Socrates on the three campaigns to Potidaea, Delium and Amphipolis[27] simply does not square with reputable historical sources, above all Thucydides (215d–216c)—or, come to that, with what Plato himself makes Socrates say elsewhere.[28] The particular case paves the way for a more general diatribe on the lies philosophers tell when pretending to give historical accounts, with special reference to their many and manifest anachronisms (216c–218e). Masurius begins with Xenophon's *Symposium*,[29] but quickly rounds on Plato's, which in its turn is declared to be 'total nonsense' (ὅλως ... λῆρος), on the grounds that Plato was only fourteen when Agathon's party took place. From here, Masurius moves on to the chronological implausibilities of the *Gorgias* and the *Protagoras*.[30] At this point, the chronological thread is dropped, and we return to the question of Plato's fictionalizing: first the ridiculous story about Chaerephon and the Delphic Oracle (218e–219a); then the suspicious mismatch between what Plato tells us about Socrates's family and love-life (particularly as regards Alcibiades), and what we find in the comic poets—if what Plato says were true, we would surely find them going to town over it too. At 200a Masurius finally leaves Plato and turns instead to the abusiveness of his fellow Socratics, Aeschines and Antisthenes.[31]

In both these two set-pieces in Book Five, Plato has not been the sole target of obloquy, but has shared his pillory with Xenophon, Epicurus, Aeschines and Antisthenes. Further, attention has been directed more to his works than to the man himself. However, in the third and last set-piece, at the beginning of Book Eleven, he is much more like the sole target, and it is his character quite as much as his works that is under fire.

This time the starting-point is the mutual rivalry between Xenophon and Plato, seen not only in the way they disagree with each other in the details of their respective *Symposia*, but in many other snubs and contradictions besides (11.504e-505b).[32] In 505b Plato takes centre stage, to be taken to task successively for hypocrisy, plagiarism and lack of originality, spiteful invention, ill will, vanity, fatuousness, contempt for his readers, and the corruption of his pupils. Here is the man who banished the mimetic poets, yet himself wrote mimetic dialogues, for which he took the idea from someone else (505b); who invented discreditable facts about his philosophical adversaries, and discreditable lines for them to speak, as can be seen with special clarity in the cases of Gorgias and Parmenides (505d); whose spiteful insults to all and sundry can be traced through the *Ion*, *Meno*, *Euthydemus*, *Laches*, *Symposium*, *Alcibiades I* and *II*, *Gorgias*, *Crito*, *Republic*, *Protagoras* and *Menexenus* (506a); who had bad relations even with his fellow Socratics and with Socrates himself (507a); whose vanity and ambition emerge clearly from his desire to found a whole state (507d); whose principal doctrines (on the soul and on politics) are either plagiarized, or of no practical use, or both (507e); who insults his readers by serving them up with symposia and encomia of Eros when what they really want is useful doctrines about Man (508d); and who transmitted this contemptuous attitude to his pupils, turning them into tyrants and slanderers (508d).

These three set-pieces, though located in two different speeches, by Masurius and by Pontianus, share a good deal of common ground, both in topic and in wording. The question of Plato's malice towards his contemporaries and rivals crops up in the first set-piece as well as the third, while that of inconsistencies between his various dialogues occurs in both the first and the second;[33] his chronological imprecisions are picked up both in the second and in the third.[34] A hostile quotation from the orator Demochares is used in two different adaptations in 187d and in 215c. Plato's own quotation of the first line of Stesichorus' *Palinode* is turned against him in both 216b and 505b. Aeschines' obscene nickname for Plato, Satho, is gleefully paraded in 220de and 507a, in almost exactly the same words. And there is the same aposiopesis of what Plato said about Alcibiades in 182a and 506c.

Given that just about everything in Athenaeus is under suspicion of being taken over from some earlier writer, these overlaps and repetitions point strongly towards a common source, not just for the particular repetitions, but for the bulk of the three set-piece discussions. This common source is convincingly identified as the writings of the second-century grammarian Herodicus of Babylon (Herodicus the Cratetean), whose name can indeed be found in 192b, 215f and 219c, characteristically credited with just three isolated items rather than the larger disquisitions in which they are embedded.[35] On the classic analysis given by Ingmar Düring in his *Herodicus the Cratetean. A study in anti-Platonic tradition* of 1941, *Deipnosophistae 5.* 215c ff. and 11.505b ff. draw on the treatise *Against the Socrates-lover*, while 5.186d ff. draws on the *On Symposia*. According to Düring, however, Athenaeus did not derive his Herodican material directly from the original treatises, but quarried it from an intermediary source—Düring's favoured candidate being Favorinus' Παντοδαπὴ Ἱστορία (*Historical Miscellany*).[36] On this view, Athenaeus was thus taking already excerpted and contaminated material and reorganizing it once again to make the speeches of Masurius and Pontianus, in what Düring represents as a clumsy, mechanical process of cutting and pasting.[37]

Now, I am not myself wholly convinced by every detail of Düring's analysis; there is surely room to argue that Athenaeus has done a better and less mechanical job with his Herodican material than he suggests. For instance, it seems to me that Masurius' discussion of Homeric and other symposia in 5.186d–193 has a clear structure and agenda, and maintains both a coherent sequence of thought and a uniform tone and style throughout. There is indeed something of a tension between the basic structure and agenda (praise of Homer's moral and literary virtues at the expense of all possible competitors) and the urge to follow up every scholarly talking point that arises, with full documentation. But this is surely part of the fun, a controlled and intended part of the kind of work Athenaeus is trying to construct, and of the *ethos* he wishes to evoke, not the accidental consequence of literary incompetence. However, the important point is that, even on Düring's story, Athenaeus is not *just* transcribing straight from his copy of Favorinus, or Herodicus or whoever; he has at the very least reorganized the material taken over, and to that extent made it part of his own creative venture. In virtue of this selection and reorganization, it is just as much his as the more sporadic Platonic references and quotations outside the three set-pieces surveyed in the first half of this chapter.

We are therefore justified in asking what role the set-pieces might be thought to play in some grander scheme of Platonizing in the *Deipnosophistae* And the fairly obvious reply is that what we see is an effort on Athenaeus' part to incorporate two views (or perhaps better, a spectrum of views) of Plato into his work: to demonstrate to his audience an awareness on his part not only of Plato's claims to greatness, but also of the way those claims have not, historically, always been very warmly received; and to exploit and enjoy the possibilities for entertaining polemic and informed insolence that this mixed heritage of critical appreciation makes available. Mastery of the heritage for a cultivated author can mean knowing (and displaying, and playing with) the critical tradition as well as the classic works themselves—for Plato quite as much as for, say, Homer. Moreover, the dialogue form in which Athenaeus is writing is particularly well suited to this state of affairs. Its built-in plurality of voices and its dynamics of debate and display allow the divergence of critical perceptions to be preserved even when brought together in a single text, while at the same time enabling the author to avoid having to declare directly for one rather than another.

But perhaps there is a further element besides. Looking at the three 'anti-Platonic' set-pieces, it is particularly striking how regularly they recur to one central Platonic text—the *Symposium*. It is of course the central focus in the first set-piece, but it is prominent also in the other two.[38] It would, I think, be very boring indeed to take this as mere coincidence, the accidental product of mechanical excerption. I would much prefer to see it as deliberate and purposeful, and to connect it with the fact that Athenaeus is himself engaged in the compilation of a new *Symposium*, surveying the whole field of literate knowledge, as Plato had once surveyed the range of his own era's resources for dealing with the topic of *eros*. For this would in turn allow us to make a link with that double strategy of both bowing to and ironically vying with the great model that I suggested we can see in the very opening words of the *Deipnosophistae* and in its conclusion. Just as, in his introduction, Athenaeus can be seen juxtaposing two Platonic dialogues in such a way as to insinuate the thought that his own imitation can claim an edge, so in the body of his giant *Symposium* he not only sets in motion two views of Plato, the adulatory and the critical, but also, within the critical portions, takes care to highlight the very text to which he himself is most indebted.

*　*　*

I have been arguing that Athenaeus' co-option of Plato into the world of the dining sophists needs to be understood in terms both of form and of content. Both because of Plato's general status as a monument of Greek culture, and because of his role as one of the founding fathers of sympotic literature, it is of the greatest importance to Athenaeus' project to demonstrate not only familiarity with Plato's major works, and the characters, issues and episodes they embrace, but also acquaintance with and appreciation of his literary procedures. At the same time, he needs also to demonstrate acquaintance with traditions of Platonic scholarship:

both Plato's biography, and the main lines of critical reception. In the process (as so often elsewhere in *Deipnosophistae* with other authors and topics), he preserves a number of quotations and near-quotations from a writer, Herodicus, whose work is otherwise almost entirely lost. A 'traditional' approach to Athenaeus—such as is represented in this area most prominently by Düring—would concentrate attention on these quotations, treating the bulk of Athenaeus' text as a base medium from which the precious fragments of the earlier (and better) writer's work were to be extracted without delay. I hope that it is clear—both from my own chapter and (*mutatis mutandis*) from others in this volume—how limited an approach this is, and how adherence to it impoverishes our understanding both of Athenaeus and of the reception and exploitation of Plato's writing in later Greek culture.

For attentive examination of Athenaeus' 'Platonism' can significantly enhance our appreciation of a number of important general features of the *Deipnosophistae* as a whole. I have stressed the care Athenaeus has taken to include not only quotation and summary of Plato's own works, but also elements from subsequent scholarly and critical debate over them, and how in the process he has displayed both positive and negative evaluations of this classic *oeuvre*. In this specific case, as in others elsewhere in the *Deipnosophistae*, we see that the relationship Athenaeus seeks to construct with Hellenic tradition and the classics of the Hellenic literary heritage is not one of either straightforward idolization or outright criticism, but something that permits a dialectical oscillation between the two. The net effect is indeed to affirm the canon, and the canonical status of the authors (and/or the topics) involved, but in a way that allows some independence and some critical elbow-room to its modern adherents and perpetuators. At the same time, attention to the nature of the debates into which Athenaeus' speakers enter over Plato, and to the kind of material from the dialogues most frequently evoked, confirms the sense we gain from other parts of the work of the particular vantage-point from which Athenaeus has chosen to view the whole field of Greek culture. As Graham Anderson in particular has emphasized in Chapter 23, the lens through which Athenaeus regards his authors and their material, the filter through which he passes them on the way into his text, is overwhelmingly that of the *grammatikos*, the student and devotee of literature and verbal presentation, rather than that of a specialist in any of the particular fields in which they work. So it is too with his Plato: this is the Plato of the literary scholar, rather than that of the committed philosophical amateur (Plutarch's *Quaestiones Conviviales* and *Platonicae* make a telling contrast),[39] still less that of the Platonic commentator. This observation in turn reminds us of important truths about the standing of Plato in Imperial Period Greek culture. The evidence of Athenaeus stands together with that of, say, Dio Chrysostom, Plutarch, Favorinus and Maximus of Tyre to establish the (fairly obvious) point that Plato remains a central point of reference as much for his literary as for his philosophical qualities in this period.[40] But, more subtly, this comparison of 'Platonist' authors also brings home the lively variety of *different* appropriations, and different *modes* of Platonizing, that could be practised even within the category of 'literary' composition. Athenaeus' embedding of debates over Plato's quality and value within a Platonic literary frame, which itself both defers to and challenges the master's authority, is a unique and intriguing feature in this larger landscape. And it is this enrichment of our broader view of imperial period culture as much as our sense of the nature and quality of the *Deipnosophistae* that we stand to forego if we persist in looking through Athenaeus to the predecessors he reworks, rather than reading him as a creative composer in his own right.

# 27

# ATHENAEUS, CRATES AND ATTIC GLOSSES
## A PROBLEM OF ATTRIBUTION

### by Maria Broggiato

The problem concerns two authors and a work. The first author is the somewhat obscure Crates of Athens, author of a work *On Sacrifices at Athens*, of which three fragments are extant, and who must have lived between the time of Demetrius Poliorcetes and Didymus.[1] The second Crates is the much better-known Crates of Mallus, the noted grammarian who was active in Pergamum in the first half of the second century BC.[2] Our sources agree in considering him among the most influential representatives of ancient philology and grammar; in particular, Sextus Empiricus[3] ascribes the perfection of grammar, between the second half of the third and the first half of the second century BC, to Crates, Aristophanes of Byzantium and Aristarchus. Crates was best known in antiquity for his work on the text and interpretation of Homer, of which about eighty fragments remain; in addition to these, a handful of fragments discussing Hesiod, lyric poets and Euripides have come down to us,[4] to which must be added the famous fragments in Varro's *de lingua Latina*, discussing the problem of grammatical analogy. Furthermore, Crates was interested in poetics as well, and precisely of evaluation of poetry, according to the testimony of the Epicurean philosopher Philodemus in his treatise *On Poems*.[5]

The work variously attributed to these two authors is a learned collection of Attic glosses in at least five books, the Περὶ τῆς ᾽Αττικῆς διαλέκτου. It must have been written between the time of the comic poet Philippides (fourth century BC) and that of the grammarian Seleucus (first century AD).[6] It was probably arranged according to subjects, given that all the fragments from its second book are connected with religion and cult.

The *On Attic dialect* is quoted seven times in Athenaeus. The problem is further complicated by the fact that other sources, above all the scholia to Aristophanes, preserve a small number of fragments with explanations of Attic words from a 'Crates', unspecified, without mentioning the title of the work.[7] Do they all go back to the glossographical work, or did Crates of Mallus write a commentary on Aristophanes? In this second case, a further problem would arise, namely the distribution of the fragments between the two works.

Editors of Crates of Mallus and editors of Crates of Athens have always assigned our work to their own author—Wachsmuth 1860 and Mette 1952 to Crates of Mallus, Müller[8] and Jacoby (*FGrH* 362)[9] to Crates of Athens. Moreover, Mette, in his book *Parateresis*, makes extensive use of material from this work in his controversial reconstruction of Crates of Mallus' theories on language: the anomalist and anti-Atticist attitude evident from the fragments of the work on the Ἀττικὴ διάλεκτος is in his opinion to be connected with an empirical methodology, based on observation (παρατήρησις) of current use of language (συνήθεια) for the determination of ἑλληνισμός, correct Greek.[10]

The attribution to Crates of Athens, however, has to be taken very seriously for a number of reasons, which Jacoby discusses at length in his commentary to the fragments (*FGrH* 3b. 121–2; 406–7). I will try briefly to summarize his argument.

1. The only other occurrence of a reference to a 'Crates' in Athenaeus is at 11.490e; in this case, however, Athenaeus specifies that he is referring to the grammarian of Pergamum by adding the epithet ὁ κριτικός, which Crates preferred to γραμματικός and by which he was widely known in antiquity.

2. An interest in both ancient cults and dialect glosses is not uncommon in other authors of the first century BC. Crates of Athens, who wrote on sacrifices at Athens, could well have written also on Attic dialect, and be dated to the first century BC.[11]

3. Some of the fragments of our work polemicize against those who took too narrow a view of what Attic usage was: these fragments show that words considered of Asiatic origin (Crates, or perhaps our source, uses the terms Ἀσιανός and Ἀσιαγενής)[12] were in fact to be found in Aristophanes' plays and in what he calls 'ancient hymns'. Could Atticism be so far developed in the time of Crates of Mallus that he felt the need to reject its more extreme positions?

Latte's answer[13] to that last question is negative, encouraging the attribution of our collection of Attic glosses to the later author, Crates of Athens. I am convinced of the contrary, and I shall try to prove that Crates of Mallus has as many, if not more, claims to the authorship of *On Attic dialect* than the Athenian antiquarian.

* * *

Let us have a closer look at each of these points, starting from the last and most important one. It is true, as far as I know, that this work is the earliest to show a polemical attitude towards an excessively narrow concept of the Attic dialect. On the other hand, dialect and Attic glosses had begun to be collected well before the rise of the Atticist movement; these collections were later to be the source of the Atticistic lexica of the imperial age.[14] Some of the material I am going to present in what follows has already been used in the discussion of the question of the origin and dating of rhetorical Atticism; other evidence I hope will be new. What I would like to emphasize, however, is that a dialectological discussion of whether a certain word belonged to the Attic dialect or not is not necessarily to be connected with the polemic against Asianist rhetoricians and could well antedate it. If we want to try to make an outline of the Greeks' interest in Attic glosses, a piece of firm ground in this field is of course the Λέξεις of Aristophanes of Byzantium, who lived a generation before Crates of Mallus; a section of this work was the Ἀττικαὶ λέξεις (frr. 337–47 Slater).[15] Another work (frr. 1–36 Slater) was significantly dedicated to the words supposed to be unknown to the ancients (Περὶ τῶν ὑποπτευομένων μὴ εἰρῆσθαι τοῖς παλαιοῖς). It has often been suggested that it could have discussed rare words that were supposed to be non-Attic.[16] We could interpret in this sense F 34 in Slater's collection, where two medical terms are said not to be ἀνάττικα.[17] This does not mean necessarily that Aristophanes was rebutting an opponent's views, but I think it is significant that at his time words could be discussed from the point of view of their belonging or not to the Attic dialect. Aristophanes' treatise also was used as a source by the so-called Antiatticist, an anonymous lexicon written in opposition to the excesses of later Atticism; more than one word in three of those discussed by Aristophanes is to be found in the Antiatticist as well.[18]

If we want to go back before Aristophanes' time, however, we find many traces of an early interest in Attic rare words. A certain Philemon of Athens, contemporary of Callimachus, wrote a collection of this kind, which is quoted several times by Athenaeus. He is possibly to be identified with a grammarian who worked on Homer's text, cited in the Homeric scholia.[19] Other authors of similar works are Hister of Paphus ὁ Καλλιμάχειος, of the end of the third century BC (*FGrH* 334), and Nicander of Thyateira in Lydia, *FGrH* 343 (Jacoby dates him between 200 BC and Didymus), author of a learned collection of Attic glosses, in at least eighteen books, which is often quoted in Athenaeus.

Furthermore, we have relevant evidence from some recently discovered papyri. The Oxyrhynchus papyrus 2744, published in 1968 by Lobel, containing a commentary on an unknown text, preserves a fragment from the third-century BC glossographer Amerias the Macedonian that proves without doubt that Amerias was interested in Attic glosses.[20] Amerias is known to us largely from Athenaeus and Hesychius, and we already knew that he collected Homeric as well as ethnic glosses. In our papyrus he quotes the gloss βολεών, 'dung-heap', a word that occurs in later collections of Attic words (Nicander of Thyateira, Harpocration).

Another Oxyrhynchus papyrus, no. 3710, published by Haslam in 1986, preserves in the context of a commentary on *Odyssey* 20 a fragment of the glossographer Parmeno of Byzantium, identified by Haslam with the third-century BC iambographer:[21] according to him the verb κορεῖν was used by the Athenians for καλλύνειν, 'to sweep'. The word κορεῖν is found in the Atticistic lexicon of Phrynichus (second century AD).

At this point we should make a distinction between this interest of early Hellenistic grammarians in the Attic dialect on one side, and Atticism in a rhetorical sense on the other, that is, the tendency to consider the language written in Athens in the fifth and fourth centuries BC the only possible model for spoken and written Greek. The material I have presented does not necessarily have a bearing on the controversial question of the origins and dating of rhetorical Atticism: its rise has been dated from as early as the second century BC[22] to as late as around 60 BC. The secondary literature on this issue has been rightly described as resembling a jungle by Jacob Wisse, who conveniently summarizes it in a recent article.[23]

It is only natural, however, that grammarians at Alexandria and Pergamum, who worked on Athenian authors of the fifth and fourth century, would have a close interest in classical Attic forms. A generation before Crates of Mallus, in the second half of the third century BC, the Alexandrian poet, scientist and grammarian Eratosthenes of Cyrene in his work *On Old Comedy* (fr. 149 Strecker = sch. Ar. *Frogs* 1263) seems to have discussed Attic forms in connection with the identification of spurious plays: he speaks of ψευδαττικοί who supposedly interpolated into Aristophanes' text non-Attic forms in order to prove the authorship of inauthentic plays.

A possible clue pointing to an early contrast between Attic on one side and common Greek usage on the other has been noted also, even if not in a grammatical context, in a fragment of the comic poet Posidippus, a younger contemporary of Menander (fr. 30 K.-A.): here a Thessalian, accused of not speaking in the Attic dialect (ἀττικίζειν), defends the right of people from other Greek cities to speak Greek (ἑλληνίζειν).[24]

All these elements could lead us to think that very subtle distinctions between Attic and non-Attic usage could have been made already in Crates of Mallus' time, and could justify a polemical attitude towards excesses of this kind.

But let us go back to the first and second arguments Jacoby thinks are in favour of a later composition of the work. As for the first, as Mette rightly noticed (1952, 49), the reference to Crates of Mallus at Athenaeus 11.490e is actually an extract from the treatise *On Nestor's Cup* by Asclepiades of Myrlea. It is in fact Asclepiades, and not Athenaeus, who uses the epithet of κριτικός to refer to Crates. Lastly, Jacoby also argues that an interest in ancient cult and in local glosses seem to go together in other authors of the first century BC, which would point in the direction of Crates of Athens as the author of our glossographical work. Obviously an interest in dialect glosses would be perfectly appropriate for a grammarian of the second century BC as well.[25]

So far, I have tried to show that it would not have been impossible for Crates of Mallus to write a collection of Attic glosses where he took up a position against the excesses of those who had too narrow a view of what Attic usage was. This does not prove however that he was the author of our work. Some evidence in this sense can be found, I think, in his other fragments: I would like to point out a series of clues that could point in that direction.

First, our grammarian was interested in ethnic and non-Greek glosses. He uses them to explain the meaning of difficult words in Homer, such as βηλός in *Iliad* 15.23, the threshold of the house of Zeus on Olympus; he connects it with a Chaldaic word—in all probability, the name of the god Bel, in order to prove that Olympus in Homer was to be identified with the sky.[26] Similarly he derives the name of the island of Cos from the Carian word for 'cattle'.[27]

Secondly, take the discussion of a variant (or conjecture?) in *Iliad* 21.282, where Achilles complains to Zeus that his fate is to die ignobly trapped (ἐρχθέντ'), like a young swineherd who is swept away by a torrent (*Il.* 21.281–3). Crates derives his reading εἰλθέντ' from εἴλλω ('to shut in'), and quotes as a parallel a legal term (ἐξουλῆς) used by Solon in his laws, written on the Ἄξονες, which he quotes word for word: 'If someone forcibly keeps (someone else) from taking possession of a property, in consequence of a judgement in court, he will be liable to pay the value of the property to the state and to the private citizen, in equal parts.' And then he cites also a line from Sophocles in the *Daedalus*.[28] The quotation from the Ἄξονες may seem significant if we compare it with the references to Attic documents and other archaic texts in the Ἀττικὴ διάλεκτος (the 'king's law', 'ancient hymns'). The author of this work was clearly well read, and that might also point rather in the direction of Crates of Mallus, who had access to the large book-collection of the Attalids in Pergamum and who in other fragments seems also to have a tendency to quote less than well-known authors.[29]

Decisions on the attribution of the work on Attic dialect have to be based on the little evidence we possess, but I see no serious obstacle to its assignation to Crates of Mallus.

However, an associated issue arises. Do the fragments of a Crates in the Aristophanic scholia belong to this same work? Most of them are short explanations of single words that could well fit into a collection like the Ἀττικὴ διάλεκτος, and at least some of them certainly did, like the scholion on Aristophanes' *Peace* 269, on the Greek words for 'pestle' and 'leather-tanner', where the problem discussed is certainly lexicographical and not exegetical.[30] But two fragments could seriously claim to derive from a commentary, one from the scholia to the *Frogs* and the other from an ancient introduction to the *Peace*.

In the scholion to Aristophanes *Frogs* 294 Crates is concerned with Empusa, a monster that could change her shape at will. Dionysus does not dare to look and asks Xanthias about her appearance: one of her legs is made of bronze, and the other is said to be made 'of cow's dung', βολίτινον. Crates' annotation apparently had an exegetical content, describing the appearance of the monster, which could change its shape at will.[31] The word βολίτινος, however, was certainly discussed in relation to its belonging to the Attic dialect: compare our scholion with an entry in the lexicon of the Antiatticist, where the word βολίτινος is said to be Attic, given that Aristophanes uses it in our passage.[32]

The other fragment that could not easily fit into a glossographical work is Crates' reference to another version of the *Peace* in one of the introductions to the play.[33] 'The records of productions report that Aristophanes likewise produced the *Peace*. Eratosthenes says that it is not clear whether he restaged the same play or produced another which is not preserved. Crates, however, is acquainted with two plays, for he writes: 'at any rate in the *Acharnians*, or in the *Babylonians*, or in one or in the other *Peace*'; and from time to time he cites lines that are not found in the surviving play.[34] Is the author of this introduction referring to a commentary or to a glossographical work? This is a difficult question to answer, if we keep in mind that it was not uncommon in antiquity to extract material from one to use it again in the other.[35] This fragment however is interesting because it is certainly a verbal quotation from Crates—the sentence does not fit into the context as it stands.

A neat solution might be that the particles ἀλλ' οὖν γε were Crates' own lemma from Aristophanes' text, as Alan Griffiths has suggested to me. However, while ἀλλ' οὖν is certainly an Aristophanic idiom, we do not find ἀλλ' οὖν γε in the extant plays: in fact, γε is not usually immediately juxtaposed with οὖν in classical Greek.[36] If this is a lemma, Crates could be discussing whether the locution was Attic or not. Even if it is not, it remains likely that the writing referred to was a collection of glosses. On the whole, I think it is not unreasonable to assign these fragments also to the Ἀττικὴ διάλεκτος.[37]

What the meaning of this is for the reconstruction of Crates' theories on language is a question that remains open. One of our fragments from the Ἀττικὴ διάλεκτος might however be of interest in this sense (*FGrH* 362 F 11 = *Deipn.* 9.366d): Crates, Athenaeus writes, quoted a line from the *Knights* (631) with the variant reading σίναπυ instead of νᾶπυ 'mustard'; Athenaeus quotes as his source for Crates the monograph Περὶ Ἑλληνισμοῦ of Seleucus, a grammarian of the time of Augustus and Tiberius.[38] An interest in correct Greek, and in dialects as well, is already evident a century earlier in the work of the grammarian Philoxenus.[39] It is well known that one of the issues of Hellenistic grammar was that of *hellenismos* or 'correct Greek'; in the Stoic grammatical system it was one of the ἀρεταὶ λόγου, 'virtues of speech', to be free from such vices as barbarism and solecism.[40] The evidence in this field is so lacunose that the context of our fragments makes a big difference to their interpretation. None the less, there abides the possibility that the polemical attitude of the Ἀττικὴ διάλεκτος towards too narrow a view of what Attic usage was, may be seen in the broader context of Hellenistic discussions about what 'correct Greek' was.[41]

# Appendix: The Fragments of Crates, On the Attic Dialect

| Source | Reference to the book | Comments |
|---|---|---|
| *Deipn.* 3.114a: θάργελον (a type of bread) | ἐν β΄ Ἀττικῆς διαλέκτου | — |
| *Deipn.* 6.235b–d: παράσιτος (parasite) | ἐν δευτέρῳ Ἀττικῆς διαλέκτου | C. quotes Attic law (ὁ τοῦ βασιλέως νόμος); 'the same is attested by Philochorus' |
| *Deipn.* 11.495a–c: πελίκη (a cup) | ἐν δευτέρῳ Ἀττικῆς διαλέκτου | C. quotes Ion of Chios fr. 10 N²; the gramm. Callistratus is quoted imm. before Crates |
| *Deipn.* 11.497f: σαννάκια (Persian cup) | ἐν πέμπτῳ Ἀττικῆς διαλέκτου | C. quotes Philemon fr. 90 K.-A. |
| *Deipn.* 14.653b: σταφυλή (bunch of grapes) | ἐν δευτέρῳ Ἀττικῆς διαλέκτου | the word is not Ἀσιαγενές, because Crates cites it; he says it is found ἐν τοῖς ὕμνοις τοῖς ἀρχαίοις |
| *Deipn.* 9.366d: in Ar. *Kn.* 631 Crates read κἄβλεπε σίναπυ (κἄβλεψε νᾶπυ Ar.) | ἐν τοῖς Περὶ τῆς Ἀττικῆς λέξεως | Crates is quoted by Seleucus, Περὶ Ἑλληνισμοῦ |
| *Deipn.* 14.640c–d: list of sweetmeats | no work title | C. quotes Philippides fr. 20 K.-A. |
| Sch. on Ar. *Wasps* 884: ἀκαλήφη (stinging-nettle) | no work title | — |
| Argum. Ar. *Peace* A 2 Holwerda | no work title | Crates quoted lines from the other version of the *Peace* |
| Sch. on Ar. *Peace* 269: ἀλετρίβανος (pestle), βυρσοδέψης (leather-tanner, *Kn.* 44) | no work title | C. (or our source) uses the word Ἀσιανός |
| Sch. on Ar. *Fr.* 294 : βολίτινος (of cow-dung) | no work title | C. discusses the appearance of Empusa |
| Sch. on Ar. *Kn.* 793: γυπάριον (cranny) | no work title | Κράτης Su.codd.: Κρατῖνος cett. |
| Sch. on Ar. *Kn.* 963: μολγός (wretched) | no work title | Σωκράτης codd.: Κράτης sch. Triclinii, Valckenaer |
| Sch. on Ar. *Wasp* 352: σέρφος (ant) | no work title | Κράτης dobree: Κρατῖνος codd. (Cratin. com. fr. dubium 511 K.-A.) |
| Harpocr., Phot.: προκώνια (of unroasted barley) | no work title | Ar. Byz. (fr. 343 S.) is mentioned imm. before Crates |
| Phot.: βλιτάδες | no work title | new fr. (first published in Phot. *lex.* Ed. Theodoridis) |
| Hsch.: ἡμεροῦν (to cultivate the land) | no work title | Crates com. fr. dubium 58 K.-A. |
| Phot.: ῥῆσις (decree) | no work title | Crates com. fr. dubium 59 K.-A. |
| Harpocr.: Ὁμηρίδαι (descendants of Homer) | ἐν ταῖς Ἱεροποιίαις (?) | Crates is quoted by Seleucus (?) Περὶ βίων |
| C. P. G. 1.416.3 Leutsch-Schneid.: ἦ δ᾽ ὅς (said he) | no work title | Crates did not write ὅς with a rough breathing |

# 28

# LYNCEUS AND THE ANECDOTISTS

## by Andrew Dalby

Lynceus of Samos, brother of Duris, pupil of Theophrastus, was on any estimate a minor author. He serves here as a touchstone for some important changes in Greek literature of around 300 BC—changes that reflect the political upheavals of that remarkable period. He also helps us to trace the origin of a literary genre that has implications for our reading of historical sources. For this reason if for no other, it needs to be recognized for what it is.

A chapter on the early anecdotists is appropriate to a book on Athenaeus because it is largely through his *Deipnosophistae*, with its rich fund of quotations from Lynceus and contemporaries, that we can begin to map this literary period. Lynceus himself would be practically unknown if it were not for Athenaeus. Of the thirty-six surviving fragments of his writings, and three additional mentions in Greek literature, a total of thirty-six are embedded in the *Deipnosophistae*. Plutarch, Harpocration and the Suda offer one item each.

**1. Lynceus:**
*Centaur*

Lynceus wrote in at least three genres. To scholars of Athenian comedy, however, he is the author of one surviving fragment of one known comedy: 'Lynceus 1' in the collections of Kock and Kassel and Austin. Since those scholars are compiling comedy fragments, this is the only fragment of Lynceus' work that they print.

Lynceus in *Centaur*, making fun of Attic dinners, says:

'Now, cook, your patron and my host is a Rhodian: I his guest am Perinthian. Neither of us likes Attic dinners. There is a sort of foreign unpleasantness about them. They serve you a big dish with five little dishes on it: one with garlic, one with two sea urchins, one with a sweet bird-pastry, one with ten shellfish, one with a bit of sturgeon. While I eat this, he's finished that; while he's still on that, I've finished this. I want some of this and some of that, my dear fellow, but I want what can't be had ... So what have you got? Oysters?'

'Lots.'

'Then serve them on a dish by itself, a big one. Have you sea urchins?'

'That can be another dish. I bought it myself: eight obols' worth.'

'Then it is the only side dish you need serve. So everyone will have the same, not one thing for me and another for him.'[1]

This is surely the beginning of the play. There is no other good reason for the guest to identify everyone, addressing the cook as 'cook' and carefully giving an ethnic to his host and to himself. It is an unlikely conversational gambit, but it will pass if the audience is now carried forward to something more memorable.

In this case, however, we are not carried into a comedy plot, or even into a prologue that might give the story so far and the personal relations among the characters. We are taken straight into a discussion of a dinner menu. If this is a full-scale play, the dinner menu can be no more than a digression. It seems equally possible that what we have here is no full-scale play at all, but a playlet, for private reading or performance.[2]

Another feature of this passage is to be noted: the near-silence of the cook, compared with the cooks in other Middle and New Comedies excerpted by Athenaeus. In most of those, the cook is heard lecturing about food, more or less tediously, until his interlocutor—usually his employer—cuts in, more or less rudely. In others, the cook is explaining how the food is to be prepared, or is giving or taking instructions about the organization of the dinner.[3] In practically all cases, the cook's interlocutor is either his employer or a slave of the household in which he is to work. The present passage is, in its small way, unique among the surviving fragments of Athenian comedy: the cook is being told by a third party how to dish up the food.

It is not difficult to propose a reason. The Perinthian guest begins the dialogue as he does, with his revisionist and slightly anti-Athenian gastronomic opinions, because he represents the author. This author is a gourmet who happens to be writing a dramatic piece, rather than a playwright who happens to be a gourmet. Before looking further at questions of genre, it is after all necessary to tease out the aims and interests of Lynceus as an author.

He wrote other plays, according to the Suda,[4] but we know nothing of them. Why is this piece called *Centaur?* Was the dinner to be broken up violently?

## 2. Lynceus: the Letters

The second genre in which Lynceus wrote was that of the literary letter. In the history of Greek literature down to about 300 BC this is a chapter of which all too little is known. There are several collections of letters attributed to very well-known figures, including Hippocrates, Socrates, Plato, Isocrates and Demosthenes, but most of them, possibly all of them, are forgeries.[5]

The opening pages of Book Four of the *Deipnosophistae* are, in these circumstances, very valuable. Combined with a brief aside by Plutarch[6] they suggest to us a coterie of men who wrote letters to one another, letters which circulated among others and which continued to circulate long enough for Plutarch and then Athenaeus to refer to them, five centuries later. These are letters that it would have been worth nobody's while to forge: nobody in later centuries had any interest in their authors.

Athenaeus gives us the topic of the exchange of letters between Lynceus and Hippolochus. They described dinners:

> [Hippolochus] had given a promise—so one may learn from his letters—to tell Lynceus about any very sumptuous dinner he might attend, Lynceus having made him a similar pledge in return. And in fact letters about dinners by both of them survive: Lynceus describes the dinner that Lamia, the Attic flute-girl, gave at Athens for King Demetrius called Poliorcetes (Demetrius was Lamia's lover) while Hippolochus describes the wedding of Caranus the Macedonian. We have come across other letters of Lynceus to this Hippolochus, too, telling him about King Antigonus's dinner at Athens to celebrate the Aphrodisia, and about King Ptolemy's.

Athenaeus then gives most of the text of Hippolochus' letter on the wedding of Caranus.[7] As for Lynceus' letters to Hippolochus, we have only the most minute possible fragments of them. Their significance for social history would have been far from negligible. Three Hellenistic kings successively visited the venerable epicentre of the Greek culture of the time before their own, and, while there, they dined in such style as only Hellenistic monarchs knew how to dine. Lynceus described Ptolemy's dinner,[8] he described Antigonus' dinner and he described the dinner that the ageing flute-girl Lamia gave for Demetrius Poliorcetes.[9] What a dinner this was! In terms of Athenian tradition, a *hetaera* was entertaining one of her admirers to supper. But those suppers, part of the old Athenian way of life, were paid for by the lady's admirers. For *this* supper the city was taxed so heavily that Lamia herself was awarded the nickname *helepolis*, 'city-capturer' by one of the comic poets.[10] We are speaking of a cultural crossroads at which supper in a brothel is being transmuted into a municipal welcome for a foreign king (Athens was, after all, the first state that gave Demetrius the title 'king') and an act of worship to a god (Athens had called him 'saviour-god'). It is a pity that the letter is lost.

In his other letters, to Poseidippus, Apollodorus[11] and Diagoras, Lynceus stuck to the subject of food, or so it seems: but then the fragments survive in Athenaeus, and Athenaeus was interested in food. It is difficult to escape the conclusion that the letter to Diagoras, at any rate, consisted of a sustained comparison between the gastronomic delights of Athens and of Rhodes.

> When you lived in Samos, Diagoras, I know you were often at the drinking-parties at my house, at which a flask beside every man used to be poured out to give each a cupful at pleasure:[12]

We may conclude that this is the beginning of the letter, naming the recipient and setting the convivial theme from which the real topic will develop. In classical Athens, one of the duties of the host or symposiarch was to decide the ruling strength of the wine–water mixture; in other words, to supervise the inebriation of the participants and to make sure that they did not get too drunk too soon. To drink was more or less compulsory. A wine-waiter, *oinokhóos*, kept each participant's cup filled.[13] Lynceus talks of his own more individualistic practice—a more civilized practice, he may well have thought—of allowing his guests to regulate their own alcohol intake.

In spite of the brevity of the remaining fragments we can see something of the structure of the letter to Diagoras. Lynceus sustains the use of 'she' for Rhodes and of 'they' for the Athenians,[14] no doubt avoiding repetition of the names, a stylistic exigence that he will have learnt from Theophrastus just as Theophrastus learnt it from Aristotle.

These are 'letters' in a very literary sense. Yes, certainly, Lynceus' letters were written by Lynceus and Hippolochus' letter by Hippolochus:[15] there was a long way to go before entirely fictional exchanges, like Alciphron's, would be written. But the aim of writing such letters as those of Lynceus was only partly to convey information from the writer to the named recipient. The convenience of addressing a single named person, a format very widely adopted in classical literature, was this: the author did not have to consider whether his subject and treatment were of sufficient public importance, or seriousness, or respectability, to interest an ideal fellow citizen.[16] He built on the fact—or created the fiction—that there was *one* other person ready to be interested in his topic, and addressed that one person, writing, as personally as he liked, about as minute a subject as he chose.

One more letter known from Athenaeus, though not linked with Lynceus and his correspondents, emerges from precisely the same milieu (for Lynceus and Hippolochus were both students of the Lyceum, as was Hieronymus).

Hieronymus [of Rhodes], in his *Letters*, quotes Theophrastus as saying that Alexander was not particularly potent sexually. Olympias was aware of this, as was Philip; they were worried that he might be effeminate. She sent the Thessalian *hetaera* Callixeina, who was stunningly beautiful, to bed with him, and frequently urged him to make love to her.[17]

The same personal address format gives Athenaeus himself, in the *Deipnosophistae*, the excuse to be as contentious and as non-serious as he chooses.

### 3. Lynceus: *Shopping for Food*

Lynceus' *Shopping for Food*[18] is described as having been 'addressed to one of his friends who found shopping difficult'. In this literary sense it counts with the letters, and it shows the playfulness, even irresponsibility, typical of their personal style:

> To quell [the fishmongers'] steely gaze and unwavering prices it is not ineffective to stand over the fish and criticize it, recalling Archestratus who wrote the *Life of Pleasure* or another such poet, and quoting the line
> 'The inshore morme, a poor fish, never worthy';
> and if it's spring,
> 'Bonito: buy in autumn ...'
> and if it's summer,
> 'Grey mullet's wonderful when winter comes!'
> There are many possibilities. You will frighten off most of the shoppers and bystanders, and so the man will have to settle at the price you choose.

It is a sign of this playfulness that the three passages of apparent verse quotation are plucked out of the air. The judgment on the μόρμυρος, morme or striped bream, avers that this fish is 'never worthy', οὐδέ ποτ᾽ ἐσθλός. The phrase is out of Hesiod, but Hesiod did not say it of a fish; he said it of his home town, Ascra, in a famous line, Ἄσκρῃ, χεῖμα κακῇ, θέρει ἀργαλέῃ, οὐδέ ποτ᾽ ἐσθλῇ ('Ascra, bad in winter, hard in summer, never worthy').[19] The opinion on the ἀμία, 'Bonito: buy in autumn', may sound like Archestratus; but Archestratus, as it happens, issued an instruction to *cook* bonito in autumn, and not in the words given here.[20] The line on the κεστρεύς, grey mullet, is no more likely to be a straight quotation of existing poetry. Archestratus, for example, wrote something quite different on grey mullet.[21]

### 4. Lynceus: the *Anecdotes*

Now to the genre that is the focus of this chapter. An immediate necessity is an overview of Lynceus' subject matter, and that is easily given. All the anecdotes have as backdrop the social life of Athens of the fourth and early third centuries

BC: a special subculture, of course, that of the celebrities—playwrights, professional comics, intelligent and independent women, prostitutes, even a few political figures, foreign royalty.[22] This is equally the backdrop to a rich, varied and profound literature. Some of Lynceus' anecdotes concern people of no individual historical importance. Others, however, touch on people of great significance— their presence in Athens, their behaviour or reputed behaviour in intimate company.

We soon realize that Lynceus is not the only source for anecdotes of this kind at this precise period. One tale is shared between Lynceus and Chares of Mitylene:

> The sophist Callisthenes—so Lynceus of Samos says in his *Apomnemoneumata*, also Aristobulus and Chares in their *Histories*—at Alexander's drinking party, pushed away the cup of neat wine as it came to him.
> 'Why aren't you drinking?' someone asked him.
> 'I don't want to swallow Alexander's potion and end up needing Asclepius's.'[23]

This is an important little story, a well-known stage on the road to Callisthenes' downfall. If we like to look for literary sources, we can suppose that Lynceus and Chares both got this story by reading Aristobulus. Aristobulus was the only one of the three who went on Alexander's expedition and so might conceivably have been there to hear Callisthenes make this dangerous remark. But even Aristobulus was not one of the boon companions of Alexander, as Callisthenes was. The more likely conclusion is that all three authors, all contemporaries, heard the story and wrote it down. Such stories come from oral tradition.

Looking further at Lynceus and his subject-matter we stumble on the drinking parties of Philip and the flatterers who attended them. Here Lynceus is in company with Satyrus, a later student of the Lyceum, whose *Life of Philip* appears to have contained plenty of stories of the kind. Hegesander of Delphi was to draw on the same fund.[24] Lynceus and Satyrus are both cited in Athenaeus' introduction to three tales of Cleisophus and Philip, though only Lynceus is credited with the stories:

> Cleisophus, for example, is described by all as the 'flatterer' of King Philip of Macedon: he was Athenian in origin, according to Satyrus the Peripatetic in the *Life of Philip*. Lynceus the Samian, in his *Anecdotes*, calls him a 'parasite', writing as follows:
> 'Cleisophus, Philip's parasite, was told off by Philip because he was always asking for things'.

'It means you don't forget me,' said Cleisophus ...'[25]

Another public incident, full of scandal and recrimination, slips into Lynceus' *Anecdotes:* Harpalus and his bribes and the fate of Demosthenes:

> At the time when Demosthenes had got the goblet from Harpalus, Lark said: 'He called others wineskins, but he's grabbed the big one himself.'

Elsewhere in this same fragment Ptolemy reappears. He was the host at one of these dinners, and a typical Athenian parasite, Eucrates 'the Lark', was fetched in to entertain the king:

> At Ptolemy's a stew was going round but never seemed to get to him.
> 'Is it that I'm drunk, Ptolemy?' said Lark. 'Or can you see things going round and round me as well?'[26]

We know a little more of the banter that went to and fro at Ptolemy's entertainment in Athens, even though Lynceus' letter on the subject is lost. Beside his own anecdote there are some tales by Machon: 'One of his companions once asked Eucrates the "Lark" how Ptolemy was treating him. "I'm not too sure yet," he said: "he's given me what I need to drink, like a good doctor, but he hasn't yet prescribed a solid diet."'[27]

## 5. Other anecdotists

These cross-references encourage us to look further at the authors who were working the same vein, and I think we may say writing in the same genre, as Lynceus. It is sensible to begin with the shelf-load of gossip and reminiscence of Alexander's court. Some of it is in Athenaeus; some of it surfaces, unattributed, in Plutarch, in Quintus Curtius and even in Arrian. A mass of it is lost, clearly. What survives is, superficially, better authenticated than most of what we think we know about Alexander's great deeds, for it comes labelled with the authorship of writers who were themselves contemporaries of these astonishing events.

In talking of Alexander, Lynceus is in company once more with Satyrus, whose Lives told of Anaxarchus, the philosopher of eudaemonism and 'one of Alexander's flatterers' who, when they were travelling and suddenly heard a tremendous clap of thunder, famously said, 'Can it be that you, Alexander son of Zeus, did that?'.[28] The story is repeated, not attributed to Satyrus, by Plutarch. Immediately before it, Plutarch tells a story of when Alexander was wounded by an arrow, and said, 'What you see flowing, my friends, is blood, and not "Ichor such as flows in the blessed gods".' It was admirably cool of Alexander to quote Homer when critically wounded in the assault on the township of the Malli—the only recorded incident to which the story could relate. Can we be sure he did, though? Because the quote is used in another source too. Athenaeus, just after giving the story of the thunderclap, adds,

> Aristobulus of Cassandreia says that Dioxippus, the Athenian pancratiast, when on some occasion Alexander was wounded and the blood was flowing, said: 'Ichor such as flows in the blessed gods'.[29]

So whose line was it?

None of this is surprising. Once again we are reading material that was written down from oral tradition, both by Aristobulus and by Plutarch's unnamed source. They were contemporaries of the events (at any rate Aristobulus was) but their information was still second-hand.

Among the anecdotists who probably wrote soon after Alexander's death were 'Nicobule (or whoever ascribed those writings to her)',[30] a source on how Alexander overdid it when drinking with Medeius; Ephippus, *On the tomb of Alexander and Hephaestion*, who tells another of the stories of how Alexander came to drink himself to death, and tells plenty about the feasts at Alexander's court;[31] and of course 'Chares the royal usher',[32] so variously rated as a historian (Tarn: 'a trifler, immersed in court ceremonies and dinners, the minutiae of his office'; Schachermeyr: 'one of the three great works [the others are Ptolemy and Aristobulus] of the Alexander period'). On Chares, whatever our estimate of him, we rely for some fairly important historical material.[33]

A further group of anecdotists can be identified as having dealt with the successors of Alexander, or rather with their flatterers and parasites. Stories just like those of Lynceus are quoted by Athenaeus from the *Geloia apomnemoneumata* of Aristodemus.[34] 'Aristodemus in *Humorous Anecdotes II* lists parasites: Sostratus of King Antiochus, Euagoras the Hunchback of Demetrius Poliorcetes, Phormio of Seleucus', Athenaeus says elsewhere.[35] Antiphanes' *On the hetaerae of Athens* must have been a not dissimilar work.[36] Hieronymus of Rhodes, whose *Letters* have been quoted above, also wrote *Notes*: these are the source for mocking exchanges between Euripides and Sophocles, notably Sophocles' remark that Euripides was a woman-hater in his tragedies but a woman-lover in bed.[37] These writers are all approximate contemporaries of Lynceus, it would seem.

Not long afterwards come the iambic anecdotes of Machon that are called *Khreiai*, overlapping with the tales of others and differing only in the fact that they are in verse:

Machon the Sicyonian, too, is one of the comic poets who were contemporaries of Apollodorus of Carystus. He presented his comedies not in Athens but in Alexandria. He was as good a poet as any, next to the Seven: hence Aristophanes the grammarian was eager to study with him as a young man.[38]

Machon, like Lynceus, Aristodemus and Antiphanes, seems to have no special interest in monarchs. Beside his mention of Ptolemy, however, he does tell three rude stories about Demetrius (Poliorcetes) and the whores Lamia, Leaena and Mania. It is interesting to find a story about Stratocles, who organized the dinners in Athens for Demetrius and also figures in Plutarch's *Demetrius* and in Matron's epic parody of an Attic dinner. Machon shares the story that Lynceus tells about Phryne and Gnathaena, 'What if you had the stone ...?'—but Machon tells it about Mania and Gnathaena.[39] Certain other fourth-century figures continued to attract jokes and anecdotes: Machon has stories of Stratonicus and of Philoxenus the dithyrambist and fish-lover.[40]

Satyrus, already mentioned, is apparently an early second-century writer, younger than Machon, older than Hegesander. Satyrus had a close contemporary in Cato the Elder, whose collection of anecdotes in Latin was among the earliest pieces of prose literature in the language.[41]

The adventures of Stratonicus, of Dorion the flautist, and others were in due course to be rehearsed once more in what must surely have been a bumper fun book, the *Notes* of Hegesander of Delphi. This was a work of the mid second century BC, a good deal later than Lynceus and the early anecdotists. It is relevant here only as probably dependent on the earlier texts; as an additional source for Alexander material;[42] and as one of the sources for a historical landmark to which we will return:

> Hegesander of Delphi adds this story about Philip. He used to send a supply of cash to those who gathered at the Diomean Heracles at Athens and told jokes; he would arrange for some of them to write down what was said and send it to him.[43]

Finally, having traced a line of transmission from Chares via Lynceus to Hegesander, it is necessary to go back in time and mention two authors of anecdote collections who are certainly older than any others now known. Both, again, are students of the Lyceum—students of Aristotle himself. One, easily datable by his fall from grace and early death, is Callisthenes, historian, philosopher and flatterer, subject of at least one anecdote as we have seen, but also author of *Anecdotes of Stratonicus*.[44] The other, longer-lived and more prolific, is Clearchus of Soli. From his *On Friendship* Athenaeus quotes an anecdote of

Stratonicus, not really funny, but indistinguishable in style from those of others mentioned in this section:

> The harpist Stratonicus, going to bed, always used to tell the slave to bring him a drink. 'Not because I'm thirsty,' he explained; 'so that I won't be thirsty.'[45]

We have not enough of Clearchus *On Friendship* to judge whether it was all like this; Callisthenes' *Stratonicus* book, on the other hand, was clearly a string of short anecdotes, and is the oldest identifiable text of this kind in Greek literature.

It may be surprising that this chapter is the first study, and certainly the first collected text, of the surviving fragments and testimonia of Lynceus. The reason is that anecdote collections, as such, fall between the stools of modern scholarship. Authors of anecdotes have sometimes been counted as historians, especially if their other works can be comfortably classed as history. This applies to Callisthenes, whose book about Alexander is counted as history. They have sometimes been classed as philosophers: this applies to Clearchus. Their anecdotal works, if focusing on well-known figures, have sometimes been generously adjudged to be history: this applies to Chares and Hegesander. None of this is true of Aristodemus, of Machon or of Lynceus.

The question matters not merely because of the relative accessibility of the fragments, but also because of the relative seriousness with which historians tend to treat them. Chares is classed as an Alexander historian; basing themselves on what does not survive, some have argued (as we have seen above) that Chares is one of the major contemporary historians of Alexander's expedition. His work and that of Hegesander are certainly potential sources for some of the later Alexander authors whose sources everybody worries about. From the historical standpoint I am hinting that the genre of 'anecdote' must be recognized, even when dressed and labelled as historical writing, and its relation with possible real events must be evaluated warily.

## 6. A literary context

The political and cultural landscape of Greece was utterly different at the time of Lynceus' birth and at his death: we can say this with confidence though we know no precise dates. Greece had been a country of independent, or at least autonomous, city states, albeit overshadowed by Persia and Macedon. Now Macedonian warlords, successors to Alexander, competed for control of his empire, and of the city states themselves.

For Greeks, the source of power and wealth was little different. Beyond one's own city one looked, as before, to the governors and kings to the east. But the opportunities were now greater and more enticing: armies to command as well as to fight in; booty to be brought home; cities to govern as well as to settle in; royal courts whose whole personnel, from top to bottom, was suddenly Greek-speaking. Equally surely, the cultural focus was shifting east. Artists, writers, philosophers and other flatterers go where the money is. Suddenly there were courts and capitals in the east, Antioch, Alexandria and soon Pergamum, where money flowed like water and where Greeks were welcome as exponents not only of medicine and military arts but also of art and literature.

Two literary shifts emerge from this political maelstrom. The first is the codification of existing Greek culture: the making of classics and cultural heroes. This grew out of the need for maintaining, even asserting, Greekness in those vast eastern realms with their largely new, largely Greek, wholly Greek-speaking élites; in spite of migration Greeks were spread thin, at first, till gradually more people began to become Greek. Hellenism had to be held on to. The second is that at this period some more genres turn from being purely oral in their manifestation to forming the basis of literary texts. To us this means that they appear to be 'new genres' because ancient Greek oral literature is, except in some sidelong way, unknowable to us.

But although these processes are evidently typical of early Hellenistic Greek literature, and easily explainable in that context, they can in fact be seen beginning earlier, in the fourth century, when Macedonia was in the process of becoming Greek. The Hellenization of Macedonia was led from above, with royal patronage.

Three of these 'new genres' are particularly relevant to Lynceus and his milieu. One is the literary letter. It is not the focus here and requires exploration far beyond the material provided by Athenaeus. In fact Athenaeus comments on the genuineness of the apparently older fifth- and fourth-century letters only in that he scarcely acknowledges any of them.[46] Another is the philosophical or scientific lecture. Here Aristotle marks the point at which the genre turns from being purely oral to being written down and to circulating in writing.[47] The only visible influence here, on Lynceus and others (many were, like him, students of the Lyceum) is a stylistic one. As Aristotle's intentionally difficult style, very specific to this genre, influenced Theophrastus and was developed by him, so Lynceus in turn was influenced, and in his letters we see the euphony and the avoidance of repetition that we know so well from Theophrastus' *History of Plants*.[48]

A third 'new genre' is the anecdote. There are, of course, anecdotes, joky and serious, in earlier literature: Herodotus told many stories that could be classed as such, and so did Ion of Chios in his *Visits*.[49] The anecdote collection, as such, now emerges as a written genre for the first time. Lynceus and his contemporaries are early exponents. Callisthenes must be allowed to defeat Clearchus for the honour of being the earliest author of an anecdote collection of which fragments survive.

Slightly earlier than Callisthenes' fleeting *floruit*, however, is the true historical turning point. The beginning of the anecdote collection as a written genre and the name of its inventor, its *protos heuron*, are both on record. One version of the event has been quoted above, and here is the other:

> They met in the Diomean temple of Heracles, 60 in number, and that is what they were called in town: 'the 60 said so-and-so,' 'I've been with the 60.' Among them were Callimedon 'Crayfish' and Deinias, and again Mnasigeiton and Menaechmus, according to Telephanes in his *On the City*. Their wit was so famous that Philip the Macedonian, when he heard of them, sent a talent to have their jokes written up and sent to him.[50]

This is a fine example of the way in which a literary genre may shift from oral to written and of the reasons for it. Philip had Athenian symposia, Athenian flute-players and Athenian *hetaerae*. Athenian anecdotes were a part of this scene and he needed them too. Since he was not in Athens he had to get them in writing. As Greek culture spread beyond its old boundaries, and beyond the reach of word of mouth, there was a need for codification.

Although its written history begins with a joke collection, the genre I am discussing is by no means wholly humorous.[51] The variously told anecdote of the Chaldaeans' warning to Alexander is not at all funny: its true punch-line is not Alexander's iambic trimeter reply, but the fact (which our sources have no need to drive home) that the prediction of his death in Babylon would prove true.[52] We are talking of a form of wisdom literature, wise enough, pointed enough, useful enough to be taken seriously by authors as different as Callisthenes and the elder Cato.

We have some great works of literature from 300 BC, and we have the political history. But for a good deal of the cultural background Athenaeus, almost overwhelmingly, is the provider of our textual source material. The rewarding feature is his astonishing richness of reference, leading us to such minor, forgotten figures as Lynceus of Samos. The risk we must take is that of playing Athenaeus' game: we are seeing Greek social history through his eyes.

# Appendix: The fragments of Lynceus

1. Λυγκεὺς δ᾽ ἐν Κενταύρῳ διαπαίζων τὰ᾽ Αττικὰ δεῖπνά φησι·

  μάγειρ᾽, ὁ θύων ἐστὶ δειπνίζων τ᾽ ἐμὲ

  ῾Ρόδιος, ἐγὼ δ᾽ ὁ κεκλημένος Περίνθιος.

  οὐδέτερος ἡμῶν ἥδεται τοῖς᾽ Αττικοῖς

  δείπνοις. ἀηδία γάρ ἐστιν᾽ Αττικὴ

  ὥσπερ ξενική· παρέθηκε πίνακα γὰρ μέγαν

  ἔχοντα μικροὺς πέντε πινακίσκους ἄνω·

  τούτων ὁ μὲν ἔχει σκόροδον, ὁ δ᾽ ἐχίνους δύο,

  ὁ δὲ θρυμματίδα γλυκεῖαν, ὁ δὲ κόγχας δέκα,

  ὁ δ᾽ ἀντακαίου μικρόν. ἐν ὅσῳ δ᾽ ἐσθίω,

  ἕτερος ἐκεῖν᾽, ἐν ὅσῳ δ᾽ ἐκεῖνος, τοῦτ᾽ ἐγὼ

  ἠφάνισα. βούλομαι δέ γ᾽, ὦ βέλτιστε σύ,

  κἀκεῖνο καὶ τοῦτ᾽, ἀλλ᾽ ἀδύνατα βούλομαι·

  οὔτε στόματα γὰρ οὔτε χεῖρας πέντ᾽ ἔχω.

  ὄψιν μὲν οὖν ἔχει τὰ τοιαῦτα ποικίλην,

  ἀλλ᾽ οὐθέν ἐστι τοῦτο πρὸς τὴν γαστέρα·

  κατέπασα γὰρ τὸ χεῖλος, οὐκ ἐνέπλησα δέ.

  τί οὖν ἔχεις; – ὄστρεια πολλά. – πίνακά μοι

  τούτων παραθήσεις αὐτὸν ἐφ᾽ ἑαυτοῦ μέγαν.

  ἔχεις ἐχίνους; – ἕτερος ἔσται σοι πίναξ·

  αὐτὸς γὰρ αὐτὸν ἐπριάμην ὀκτὼ ὀβολῶν.

  – ὀψάριον αὐτὸ τοῦτο παραθήσεις μόνον,

  ἵνα ταὐτὰ πάντες, μὴ τὸ μὲν ἐγώ, τὸ δ᾽ ἕτερος.

Athenaeus 131f.

2. ῾Ιππόλοχος ὁ Μακεδών, ἑταῖρε Τιμόκρατες, τοῖς χρόνοις μὲν γέγονε κατὰ Λυγκέα καὶ Δοῦριν τοὺς Σαμίους, Θεοφράστου δὲ τοῦ ᾽Ερεσίου μαθητής, συνθήκας δ᾽ εἶχε ταύτας πρὸς τὸν Λυγκέα, ὡς ἐκ τῶν αὐτοῦ μαθεῖν ἐστιν ἐπιστολῶν, πάντως αὐτῷ δηλοῦν εἴ τινι συμπεριενεχθείη

δείπνῳ πολυτελεῖ, τὰ ὅμοια κἀκείνου ἀντιπροπίνοντος αὐτῷ. ἑκατέρων οὖν σῴζονται δειπνητικαί τινες ἐπιστολαί, Λυγκέως μὲν τὸ Λαμίας τῆς Ἀττικῆς αὐλητρίδος ἐμφανίζοντος δεῖπνον Ἀθήνησι γενόμενον Δημητρίῳ τῷ βασιλεῖ, ἐπίκλην δὲ Πολιορκητῇ ('ἐρωμένη δ' ἦν ἡ Λάμια τοῦ Δημητρίου) τοῦ δ' Ἱππολόχου τοὺς Καράνου τοῦ Μακεδόνος ἐμφανίζοντος γάμους. καὶ ἄλλαις δὲ περιετύχομεν τοῦ Λυγκέως ἐπιστολαῖς πρὸς τὸν αὐτὸν γεγραμμέναις Ἱππόλοχον, δηλούσαις τό τε Ἀντιγόνου τοῦ βασιλέως δεῖπνον Ἀφροδίσια ἐπιτελοῦντος Ἀθήνησι καὶ τὸ Πτολεμαίου τοῦ βασιλέως.

Athenaeus 4.128a.

3. χωρὶς δὲ τούτων αὐτὴ καθ' ἑαυτὴν ἡ Λάμια τῷ βασιλεῖ παρασκευάζουσα δεῖπνον ἠργυρολόγησε πολλούς, καὶ τὸ δεῖπνον οὕτως ἤνθησε τῇ δόξῃ διὰ τὴν πολυτέλειαν, ὥσθ' ὑπὸ Λυγκέως τοῦ Σαμίου συγγεγράφθαι.

Plutarch, *Demetrius* 27.3.

4. Λυγκεὺς δὲ διαγράφων τὸ Λαμίας τῆς αὐλητρίδος δεῖπνον, ὅτε ὑπεδέχετο Δημήτριον τὸν Πολιορκητήν, εὐθέως τοὺς εἰσελθόντας ἐπὶ τὸ δεῖπνον ἐσθίοντας ποιεῖ ἰχθῦς παντοίους καὶ κρέα. ὁμοίως καὶ τὸ Ἀντιγόνου τοῦ βασιλέως δεῖπνον διατιθεὶς ἐπιτελοῦντος Ἀφροδίσια καὶ τὸ Πτολεμαίου τοῦ βασιλέως ἰχθῦς πρῶτον παρατίθησι καὶ κρέα.

Athenaeus 3.101e.

5. Λυγκεὺς δ' ὁ Σάμιος ὁ Θεοφράστου γνώριμος καὶ τὴν σὺν ὀπῷ χρῆσιν αὐτῆς οἶδεν. ἀναγράφων γοῦν τὸ Πτολεμαίου συμπόσιόν φησιν οὕτως· μήτρας τινὸς περιφερομένης ἐν ὄξει καὶ ὀπῷ.

Athenaeus 3.100e.

6. Λυγκεὺς δ' ὁ Σάμιος ἐν τῇ πρὸς Διαγόραν ἐπιστολῇ γράφει· καθ' ὃν χρόνον ἐπεδήμησας Σάμῳ, Διαγόρα, πολλάκις οἶδά σε παραγινόμενον εἰς τοὺς παρ' ἐμοὶ πότους, ἐν οἷς λάγυνος κατ' ἄνδρα κείμενος ᾠνοχοεῖτο, πρὸς ἡδονὴν διδοὺς ἑκάστῳ ποτήριον.

Athenaeus 11.499c.

7. Λυγκεὺς δ᾽ ἐν τῇ πρὸς   Διαγόραν ἐπιστολῇ ἐπαινῶν τὸν κατὰ τὴν ᾽Αττικὴν γινόμενον    Νικοστράτιον βότρυν καὶ ἀντιτιθεὶς αὐτῷ τοὺς ῾Ροδιακούς φησιν· τῷ δ᾽ ἐκεῖ καλουμένῳ βότρυι  Νικοστρατίῳ τὸν ῾Ιππώνιον ἀντεκτρέφουσι βότρυν, ὃς ἀπὸ ῾Εκατομβαιῶνος μηνὸς ὥσπερ ἀγαθὸς οἰκέτης διαμένει τὴν αὐτὴν ἔχων εὔνοιαν.

Athenaeus 14.654a.

8. Λυγκεὺς δ᾽ ὁ  Σάμιος ἐν τῇ πρὸς   Διαγόραν ἐπιστολῇ ἐπαινῶν τὰς ῾Ροδιακὰς ἀφύας καὶ ἀντιτιθεὶς πολλὰ τῶν ᾽Αθήνησι γινομένων πρὸς τὰ ἐν τῇ ῾Ρόδῳ φησί· ταῖς μὲν  Φαληρικαῖς ἀφύαις τὰς  Αἰνάτιδας καλουμένας ἀφύας, τῷ δὲ γλ<α>υκίσκῳ τὸν ἔλοπα καὶ τὸν ὄρφον ἀντιπαρατιθεῖσα, πρὸς δὲ τὰς ᾽Ελευσινιακὰς ψήττας καὶ σκόμβρους καὶ εἴ τις ἄλλος παρ᾽ αὐτοῖς ἰχθὺς ἐπάνω τῇ δόξῃ τοῦ  Κέκροπος γέγονεν ἀντιγεννήσασα τὸν ἀλώπεκα καλούμενον. <ὃν> ὁ τὴν  ῾Ηδυπάθειαν γράψας παρακελεύεται τῷ μὴ δυναμένῳ τιμῇ κατεργάσασθαι τὴν ἐπιθυμίαν ἀδικίᾳ κτήσασθαι.

Athenaeus 285e.

9. ἀλλ᾽ ὅ γε ᾽Αρχέστρατος περὶ τοῦ ῾Ροδιακοῦ γαλεοῦ λέγων τοῖς ἑταίροις πατρικῶς πως συμβουλεύων φησίν·

> ἐν δὲ ῾Ρόδῳ γαλεὸν τὸν ἀλώπεκα· κἂν ἀποθνήσκειν
> μέλλης, ἂν μή σοι πωλεῖν [ἐ]θέλῃ, ἅρπασον αὐτόν·
> ὃν καλέουσι  Συρακόσιοι κύνα πίονα· κᾆτα
> ὕστερον ἤδη πάσχ᾽ ὅτι σοι πεπρωμένον ἐστίν.

τούτων τῶν ἐπῶν μνησθεὶς καὶ  Λυγκεὺς ὁ  Σάμιος ἐν τῇ πρὸς  Διαγόραν ἐπιστολῇ φησιν καὶ δικαίως παρακελεύεσθαι τὸν ποιητὴν τῷ μὴ δυναμένῳ τιμὴν ἀριθμῆσαι ἀδικίᾳ κτήσασθαι τὴν ἐπιθυμίαν. καὶ γὰρ τὸν  Θησέα, φησί, γεγονότα καλὸν ὑπολαμβάνω τοῦ  Τληπολέμου τὸν ἰχθὺν τοῦτον αὐτῷ παρασχόντος παρεσχηκέναι.

Athenaeus 7.294f, cf. 286a.

10. Λυγκεὺς δ' ὁ Σάμιος ἐν ἐπιστολαῖς τὰς καλλίστας γίνεσθαί φησι ψήττας περὶ Ἐλευσῖνα τῆς Ἀττικῆς.

Athenaeus 7.330a.

11. ...Ῥόδου, ἣν εὔιχθυν εἶναί φησιν ὁ ἥδιστος Λυγκεύς.

Athenaeus 8.360d.

12. Τῶν δὲ ἐν Ῥόδῳ γινομένων σύκων μνημονεύει Λυγκεὺς ἐν ἐπιστολαῖς σύγκρισιν ποιούμενος τῶν Ἀθήνησι γινομένων καλλίστων πρὸς τὰ Ῥοδιακά. γράφει δὲ οὕτως· τὰ δὲ ἐρινεὰ τοῖς Λακωνικοῖς ὥστε συκάμινα σύκοις δοκεῖν ἐρίζειν. καὶ ταῦτ' οὐκ ἀπὸ δείπνου καθάπερ ἐκεῖ διεστραμμένης ἤδη διὰ τὴν πλησμονὴν τῆς γεύσεως, ἀλλ' ἀθίκτου τῆς ἐπιθυμίας οὔσης πρὸ δείπνου παρατέθεικα.

Athenaeus 3.75e.

13. κἀν τῇ πρὸς Διαγόραν δὲ ἐπιστολῇ γράφει οὕτως· ἡ δὲ γῆ ταῖς μὲν χελιδονίοις ἰσχάσιν ἀντιπαρατιθεῖσα τὰς Βριγινδαρίδας καλουμένας, τῷ μὲν ὀνόματι βαρβαριζούσας, ταῖς δὲ ἡδοναῖς οὐδὲν ἧττον ἐκείνων ἀττικιζούσας.

Athenaeus 14.652d.

14. Λυγκεὺς δ' ὁ Σάμιος ἐν τῇ πρὸς Διαγόραν ἐπιστολῇ συγκρίνων τὰ Ἀθήνησι γινόμενα τῶν ἐδωδίμων πρὸς τὰ ἐν Ῥόδῳ φησίν· ἔτι δὲ σεμνυνομένων παρ' ἐκείνοις τῶν ἀγοραίων ἄρτων, ἀρχομένου μὲν τοῦ δείπνου καὶ μεσοῦντος οὐθὲν λειπομένους ἐπιφέρουσιν· ἀπειρηκότων δὲ καὶ πεπληρωμένων ἡδίστην ἐπεισάγουσι διατριβὴν τὸν διάχριστον ἐσχαρίτην καλούμενον, ὃς οὕτω κέκραται τοῖς μειλίγμασι καὶ τῇ μαλακότητι καὶ τοιαύτην ἐνθρυπτόμενος ἔχει πρὸς τὸν γλυκὺν συναυλίαν ὥστε προσβιαζόμενος θαυμαστόν τι συντελεῖ· καθάπερ γὰρ ἀνανήφειν πολλάκις γίνεται τὸν μεθύοντα, τὸν αὐτὸν τρόπον ὑπὸ τῆς ἡδονῆς ἀναπεινῆν γίνεται τὸν ἐσθίοντα.

Athenaeus 3.109d.

15. ΕΧΙΝΟΣ. Λυγκεὺς ὁ Σάμιος ἐν τῇ πρὸς Διαγόραν ἐπιστολῇ ἐκ παραλλήλου τιθεὶς τὰ κατὰ τὴν Ἀττικὴν ἐξαιρέτως γινόμενα τοῖς ἐν τῇ Ῥόδῳ γράφει οὕτως· τῇ δὲ περὶ τὸν ἄμητα δόξῃ τὸν καινὸν ἀνταγωνιστὴν ἐπὶ τῆς δευτέρας εἰσάγουσα τραπέζης ἐχῖνον. ὑπὲρ οὗ νῦν μὲν ἐπὶ κεφαλαίου· παραγενομένου δὲ σοῦ καὶ συντεθέντος κατὰ τοὺς ἐν Ῥόδῳ νόμους ἅμα μασησαμένου πειράσομαι πλείω περιθεῖναι λόγον.

Athenaeus 14.647a.

16a. ΗΔΥΠΟΤΙΔΕΣ. ταύτας φησὶν ὁ Σάμιος Λυγκεὺς Ῥοδίους ἀντιδημιουργήσασθαι πρὸς τὰς Ἀθήνησι θηρικλείους, Ἀθηναίων μὲν αὐτὰς τοῖς πλουσίοις διὰ τὰ βάρη χαλκευσαμένων τὸν ῥυθμὸν τοῦτον, Ῥοδίων δὲ διὰ τὴν ἐλαφρότητα τῶν ποτηρίων καὶ τοῖς πένησι τοῦ καλλωπισμοῦ τούτου μεταδιδόντων.

Athenaeus 11.469b.

16b. ΡΟΔΙΑΣ. ... μνημονεύει αὐτῶν ... Λυγκεύς τε ὁ Σάμιος ἐν ταῖς ἐπιστολαῖς.

Athenaeus 496f.

17. Λυγκεὺς δὲ ἐν τῇ πρὸς τὸν κωμικὸν Ποσείδιππον ἐπιστολῇ, ἐν τοῖς τραγικοῖς, φησίν, πάθεσιν Εὐριπίδην νομίζω Σοφοκλέους οὐδὲν διαφέρειν· ἐν δὲ ταῖς ἰσχάσι τὰς Ἀττικὰς τῶν ἄλλων πολὺ προέχειν.

Athenaeus 11.652c.

18. Λυγκεὺς δ᾽ ὁ Σάμιος ἐν τῇ πρὸς Ἀπολλόδωρον ἐπιστολῇ γράφει οὕτως· ἵνα τὰ μὲν αἴγεια τοῖς παισί, τὰ δὲ συάγρεια μετὰ τῶν φίλων αὐτὸς ἔχῃς.

Athenaeus 9.401f.

19. Λυγκεὺς δ᾽ ὁ Σάμιος καὶ τέχνην ὀψωνητικὴν συνέγραψε πρός τινα δυσώνην, διδάσκων αὐτὸν τίνα δεῖ λέγοντα πρὸς τοὺς ἀνδροφόνους ἰχθυοπώλας λυσιτελῶς, ἔτι δὲ ἀλύπως ὠνεῖσθαι ἃ βούλεται.

Athenaeus 6.228c.

20. Λυγκεὺς δ' ὁ  Σάμιος ἐν τῇ ὀψωνητικῇ τέχνῃ, ἣν προσεφώνησέ τινι τῶν ἑταίρων δυσώνῃ, φησίν· οὐκ ἄχρηστον δὲ πρὸς τοὺς ἀτενίζοντας καὶ μὴ συγκαθιέντας τῇ τιμῇ καὶ τὸ κακῶς λέγειν παρεστηκότα[ς] τοὺς ἰχθύας, ἐπαγόμενον ᾿ Αρχέστρατον τὸν γράψαντα τὴν ῾ Ηδυπάθειαν ἢ τῶν ἄλλων τινὰ ποιητῶν καὶ λέγοντα τὸ μέτρον "μόρμυρος αἰγιαλεὺς κακὸς ἰχθὺς οὐδέ ποτ' ἐσθλός," καὶ "τὴν ἀμίαν ὠνοῦ φθινοπώρου," νῦν δ' ἐστὶν ἔαρ, καὶ "κεστρέα τὸν θαυμαστόν, ὅταν χειμὼν ἀφίκηται," νῦν δ' ἐστὶ θέρος, καὶ πολλὰ τῶν τοιούτων. ἀποσοβήσεις γὰρ πολλοὺς τῶν ὠνουμένων καὶ προσεστηκότων· τοῦτο δὲ ποιῶν ἀναγκάσεις τὸ σοὶ δοκοῦν λαβεῖν αὐτόν.

Athenaeus 7.313f.

21a. ὅτι ᾿ Αρχέστρατος ὁ  Συρακούσιος ἢ  Γελῷος ἐν τῇ ὡς  Χρύσιππος ἐπιγράφει Γαστρονομίᾳ, ὡς δὲ  Λυγκεὺς καὶ  Καλλίμαχος ῾ Ηδυπαθείᾳ, ὡς δὲ  Κλέαρχος Δειπνολογίᾳ, ὡς δ' ἄλλοι ᾿ Οψοποιίᾳ ...

*Epitome of Athenaeus* 1.4d.

21b. Κλέαρχος δὲ ὁ  Σολεὺς Δειπνολογίαν καλεῖ τὸ ποίημα, ἄλλοι ᾿ Οψολογίαν,  Χρύσιππος Γαστρονομίαν, ἄλλοι ῾ Ηδυπάθειαν.

*Suda* s.vv. 'Athenaios', 'Charmos'.

22. Λυγκεὺς ὁ  Σάμιός φησιν· ἀκαλήφην ἡ θάλασσ' ἀνίησιν, ἡ δὲ γῆ ὕδνα.

*Epitome of Athenaeus* 2.62c.

23. τῆς δὲ Γναθαίνης ἤρα δεινῶς, ὡς καὶ πρότερον εἴρηται, Δίφιλος ὁ κωμῳδιοποιός, ὡς καὶ  Λυγκεὺς ὁ  Σάμιος ἐν τοῖς ἀπομνημονεύμασιν ἱστορεῖ. ἐν ἀγῶνι οὖν ποτε αὐτὸν ἀσχημονήσαντα σφόδρα ἀρθῆναι ἐκ τοῦ θεάτρου συνέβη καὶ οὐδὲν ἧττον ἐλθεῖν πρὸς τὴν  Γνάθαιναν. κελεύοντος οὖν τοῦ Διφίλου ὑπονίψαι τοὺς πόδας αὐτοῦ τὴν Γνάθαιναν, ἡ δὲ "τί γάρ, εἶπεν, οὐκ ἠρμένος ἥκεις;"

Athenaeus 13.583f.

24–25. Γναθαίνης δὲ πολλὰς ἀποκρίσεις ἀνέγραψεν ὁ  Λυγκεύς. παρασίτου γάρ τινος ὑπὸ γραὸς τρεφομένου καὶ τὸ σῶμα εὖ ἔχοντος, "χαριέντως᾿ γ᾿, ἔφη, ὦ νεανίσκε, τὸ σωμάτιον διάκεισαι." "τί οὖν οἴει, εἰ μὴ ἐδευτεροκοίτουν;" "τῷ λιμῷ ἄν, ἔφη, ἀπέθανες." Παυσανίου δὲ τοῦ Λάκκου ὀρχουμένου καὶ εἰς κάδον τινὰ ἐμπεσόντος, "ὁ λάκκος, ἔφη, εἰς τὸν κάδον ἐμπέπτωκεν." ἐπιδόντος δέ τινος οἶνον ἐν ψυκτηριδίῳ μικρὸν καὶ εἰπόντος ὅτι ἐκκαιδεκαέτης, "μικρός γε, ἔφη, ὡς τοσούτων ἐτῶν." νεανίσκων δέ τινων παρὰ πότον ὑπὲρ αὐτῆς τυπτόντων ἑαυτοὺς ἔφη πρὸς τὸν ἡττώμενον "θάρρει, παιδίον· οὐ γὰρ στεφανίτης ὁ ἀγών ἐστιν, ἀλλ᾿ ἀργυρίτης." ὡς δ᾿ ὁ τὴν μνᾶν τῇ θυγατρὶ δοὺς αὐτῆς οὐδὲν ἔτι ἔφερεν, ἀλλ᾿ ἐφοίτα μόνον, "παιδίον, ἔφη, ὥσπερ πρὸς Ἱππόμαχον τὸν παιδοτρίβην μνᾶν δοὺς οἴει ἀεὶ φοιτήσειν;" Φρύνης δὲ πικρότερον εἰπούσης αὐτῇ "εἰ δὲ λίθον, ἔφη, εἶχες;" "ἀποψήσασθαι ἄν σοι ἔδωκα." ἐτύγχανεν δὲ ἡ μὲν αἰτίαν ἔχουσα λιθιᾶν, ἡ δὲ κοιλίαν προπετεστέραν ἔχειν. τῶν δὲ πινόντων παρ᾿ αὐτῇ συμβαλλομένων εἰς βολβοφακὴν καὶ τῆς παιδίσκης ἐν τῷ καθαίρειν εἰς τὸν κόλπον ἐμβαλλομένης τῶν φακῶν, ἡ Γνάθαινα ἔφη "κολποφακὴν διανοεῖται ποιεῖν." Ἀνδρονίκου δὲ τοῦ τραγῳδοῦ ἀπ᾿ ἀγῶνός τινος, ἐν ᾧ τοὺς Ἐπιγόνους εὐημερήκει, πίνειν μέλλοντος παρ᾿ αὐτῇ καὶ τοῦ παιδὸς κελεύοντος τὴν Γνάθαιναν προαναλῶσαι, "ὀλόμενε παίδων, ἔφη, ποῖον εἴρηκας λόγον." πρὸς δὲ ἀδολέσχην τινὰ διηγούμενον ὅτι παραγέγονεν ἀφ᾿ Ἑλλησπόντου, "πῶς οὖν, φησίν, εἰς τὴν πρώτην πόλιν οὐχ ἧκες τῶν ἐκεῖ;" τοῦ δ᾿ εἰπόντος "εἰς ποίαν;" "εἰς Σίγειον," εἶπεν. εἰσελθόντος δέ τινος ὡς αὐτὴν καὶ ἰδόντος ἐπί τινος ἀγγείου ᾠὰ εἰπόντος τε "ὠμὰ ταῦτα, Γνάθαινα, ἢ ἑφθά;" "ἔγχαλκα, ἔφη, παιδίον." Χαιρεφῶντος δ᾿ ἀκλήτου ἐπὶ δεῖπνον ἐλθόντος, προπιοῦσα ποτήριον αὐτῷ ἡ Γνάθαινα "λαβέ, ἔφησεν, ὑπερήφανε." καὶ ὃς "ἐγὼ ὑπερήφανος;" "τίς δὲ μᾶλλον, εἶπεν ἡ Γνάθαινα, ὃς οὐδὲ καλούμενος ἔρχῃ;"

Νικὼ δὲ ἡ Αἲξ ἐπικαλουμένη, φησὶν ὁ Λυγκεύς, παρασίτου τινὸς ἀπαντήσαντος λεπτοῦ ἐξ ἀρρωστίας, "ὡς ἰσχνός," ἔφη. "τί γὰρ οἴει με ἐν τρισὶν ἡμέραις καταβεβρωκέναι;" "ἤτοι τὴν λήκυθον, ἔφη, ἢ τὰ ὑπο<δή>ματα."

Athenaeus 13.584b.

26–27. Λυγκεὺς δ᾽ ὁ Σάμιος ἐν τοῖς ἀποφθέγμασι, Σιλανός, φησίν, ὁ Ἀθηναῖος Γρυλλίωνος παρασιτοῦντος Μενάνδρῳ τῷ σατράπῃ, [παρ᾽] εὐπαρύφου δὲ καὶ μετὰ θεραπείας περιπατοῦντος ἐρωτηθεὶς, "τίς ἐστιν οὗτος;" "Μενάνδρου, ἔφησεν, ἀξία γνάθος."

Χαιρεφῶν δέ, φησίν, ὁ παράσιτος εἰς γάμον ἄκλητος εἰσελθὼν καὶ κατακλιθεὶς ἔσχατος καὶ τῶν γυναικονόμων ἀριθμούντων τοὺς κεκλημένους καὶ κελευόντων αὐτὸν ἀποτρέχειν ὡς παρὰ τὸν νόμον ἐπὶ τοῖς τριάκοντα ἐπόντος, "ἀριθμεῖτε δή, ἔφη, πάλιν ἀπ᾽ ἐμοῦ ἀρξάμενοι."

Athenaeus 6.245a.

28. ἀναγράφει δὲ αὐτοῦ τὰ ἀπομνημονεύματα Λυγκεὺς ὁ Σάμιος Εὐκράτην αὐτὸν καλεῖσθαι κυρίως φάσκων. γράφει δ᾽ οὕτως· Εὐκράτης ὁ Κόρυδος πίνων παρά τινι σαπρᾶς οὔσης τῆς οἰκίας, "ἐνταῦθα, φησίν, δειπνεῖν δεῖ ὑποστήσαντα τὴν ἀριστερὰν χεῖρα ὥσπερ αἱ Καρυάτιδες." Φιλόξενος δ᾽ ἡ Πτερνοκοπὶς ἐμπεσόντος λόγου ὅτι αἱ κίχλαι τίμιαί εἰσι καὶ τοῦ Κορύδου παρόντος, ὃς ἐδόκει πεπορνεῦσθαι, "ἀλλ᾽ ἐγώ, ἔφη, μνημονεύω ὅτε ὁ κόρυδος ὀβολοῦ ἦν."

Athenaeus 6.241d.

29–30. τοῦ δὲ Κορύδου ἀποφθέγματα τάδε ἀναγράφει ὁ Λυγκεύς· Κορύδῳ συμπινούσης τινὸς ἑταίρας, ᾗ ὄνομα ἦν Γνώμη, καὶ τοῦ οἰναρίου ἐπιλιπόντος εἰσφέρειν ἐκέλευσεν ἕκαστον δύο ὀβολούς, Γνώμην δὲ συμβάλλεσθαι ὅ τι δοκεῖ τῷ δήμῳ. Πολύκτορος δὲ τοῦ κιθαρῳδοῦ φακῆν ῥοφοῦντος καὶ λίθον μασησαμένου "ὦ ταλαίπωρε, ἔφη, καὶ ἡ φακῆ σε βάλλει." ... λέγοντος δέ τινος τῷ Κορύδῳ ὡς τῆς αὐτοῦ γυναικὸς ἐνίοτε καὶ <τὸν> τράχηλον καὶ τοὺς τιτθοὺς καὶ τὸν ὀμφαλὸν φιλεῖ "πονηρόν, ἔφη, τοῦτ᾽ ἤδη· καὶ γὰρ ὁ Ἡρακλῆς ἀπὸ τῆς Ὀμφάλης ἐπὶ τὴν Ἥβην μεταβέβηκε." Φυρομάχου δ᾽ ἐμβαψαμένου εἰς φακῆν καὶ τὸ τρύβλιον ἀνατρέψαντος "ζημιωθῆναι αὐτόν, ἔφη, δίκαιον, ὅτι οὐκ ἐπιστάμενος δειπνεῖν ἀπεγράψατο." παρὰ Πτολεμαίῳ δὲ ματτύης περιφερομένης καὶ κατ᾽ ἐκεῖνον ἀεὶ λειπούσης, "Πτολεμαῖε, ἔφη, πότερον ἐγὼ μεθύω ἢ δοκεῖ μοι ταῦτα περιφέρεσθαι;" Χαιρεφῶντος δὲ τοῦ παρασίτου φήσαντος οὐ δύνασθαι τὸν οἶνον φέρειν "οὐδὲ γὰρ τὸ εἰς τὸν οἶνον," ἔφη. τοῦ δὲ Χαιρεφῶντος γυμνοῦ ἔν τινι δείπνῳ διαναστάντος "Χαιρεφῶν, εἶπεν, ὥσπερ τὰς ληκύθους ὁρῶ σε μέχρι πόσου μεστὸς εἶ." καθ᾽ ὃν δὲ καιρὸν Δημοσθένης παρ᾽ Ἁρπάλου τὴν κύλικα εἰλήφει "οὗτος, ἔφη, τοὺς ἄλλους ἀκρατοκώθωνας καλῶν αὐτὸς τὴν μεγάλην ἔσπακεν." εἰωθότος δ᾽ αὐτοῦ ῥυπαροὺς ἄρτους ἐπὶ τὰ δεῖπνα φέρεσθαι, ἐνεγκαμένου τινὸς ἔτι μελαντέρους, οὐκ ἄρτους ἔφη αὐτὸν ἐνηνοχέναι, ἀλλὰ τῶν ἄρτων σκιάς.

Φιλόξενος δὲ ὁ παράσιτος, Πτερνοκοπὶς δ᾽ ἐπίκλην, παρὰ Πύθωνι ἀριστῶν παρακειμένων ἐλαῶν καὶ μετὰ μικρὸν προσενεχθείσης λοπάδος ἰχθύων πατάξας τὸ τρύβλιον ἔφη "μάστιξεν δ᾽ ἐλάαν." ἐν δείπνῳ δὲ τοῦ καλέσαντος αὐτὸν μέλανας ἄρτους παρατιθέντος "μὴ πολλούς, εἶπε, παρατίθει, μὴ σκότος ποιήσῃς." τὸν ὑπὸ τῆς γραὸς τρεφόμενον παράσιτον Παυσίμαχος ἔλεγεν τοὐναντίον πάσχειν τῇ γραίᾳ συνόντα· αὐτὸν γὰρ ἐν γαστρὶ λαμβάνειν ἀεί.

Athenaeus 6.245d.

31. Λυγκεὺς ὁ Σάμιος ἐν τοῖς ἀπομνημονεύμασι παράσιτον ὀνομάζει λέγων οὕτως· "Κλείσοφος ὁ Φιλίππου παράσιτος ἐπιτιμῶντος αὐτῷ τοῦ Φιλίππου διότι ἀεὶ αἰτεῖ, 'ἵν᾽, ἔφη, μὴ ἐπιλανθάνωμαι." τοῦ δὲ Φιλίππου δόντος αὐτῷ ἵππον τραυματίαν ἀπέδοτο. καὶ μετὰ χρόνον ἐπερωτηθεὶς ὑπὸ τοῦ βασιλέως ποῦ ἐστιν, "ἐκ τοῦ τραύματος, ἔφη, κεῖνου πέπραται." σκώπτοντος δ᾽ αὐτὸν τοῦ Φιλίππου καὶ εὐημεροῦντος "εἶτ᾽ οὐκ ἐγὼ σέ, ἔφη, θρέψω;"

Athenaeus 6.248d.

32. Λυγκεὺς δ᾽ ὁ Σάμιος, ὁ Θεοφράστου μὲν μαθητής, Δούριδος δὲ ἀδελφὸς τοῦ τὰς ἱστορίας γράψαντος καὶ τυραννήσαντος τῆς πατρίδος, ἐν

τοῖς ἀποφθέγμασιν· Δωρίωνι τῷ αὐλητῇ φάσκοντός τινος ἀγαθὸν ἰχθὺν εἶναι βατίδα, "ὥσπερ ἂν εἴ τις, ἔφη, ἐφθὸν τρίβωνα ἐσθίοι." ἐπαινοῦντος δ' ἄλλου τὰ τῶν θύννων ὑπογάστρια "καὶ μάλα, ἔφη, δεῖ μέντοι γε ἐσθίειν αὐτὰ ὥσπερ ἐγὼ ἐσθίω." εἰπόντος δὲ "πῶς;" "ἡδέως," ἔφη. τοὺς δὲ καράβους ἔφη τρία ἔχειν, διατριβὴν καὶ εὐωχίαν καὶ θεωρίαν. ἐν Κύπρῳ δὲ παρὰ Νικοκρέοντι δειπνῶν ἐπήνεσε ποτήριόν τι. καὶ ὁ Νικοκρέων ἔφη· "ἐὰν βούλῃ, ὁ αὐτὸς τεχνίτης ποιήσει σοι ἕτερον." "σοί γε, ἔφη, ἐμοὶ δὲ τοῦτο δός," οὐκ ἀνοήτως γε τοῦτο φήσας ὁ αὐλητής· λόγος γὰρ παλαιὸς ὡς ὅτι

ἀνδρὶ μὲν αὐλητῆρι θεοὶ νόον οὐκ ἐνέφυσαν,

ἀλλ᾽ ἅμα τῷ φυσῆν χὠ νόος ἐκπέταται.

Athenaeus 8.337d.

33. καὶ Ἄλεξις δ᾽ ὁ ποιητὴς ἦν ὀψοφάγος, ὡς ὁ Σάμιός φησι Λυγκεύς· καὶ σκωπτόμενος ὑπό τινων σπερμολόγων εἰς ὀψοφαγίαν ἐρομένων τε ἐκείνων τί ἂν ἥδιστα φάγοι, ὁ Ἄλεξις "σπερμολόγους, ἔφη, πεφρυγμένους."

Athenaeus 8.344c.

34. Καλλισθένης δὲ ὁ σοφιστής, ὡς Λυγκεὺς ὁ Σάμιός φησιν ἐν τοῖς ἀπομνημονεύμασι καὶ Ἀριστόβουλος καὶ Χάρης ἐν ταῖς ἱστορίαις, ἐν τῷ συμποσίῳ τοῦ Ἀλεξάνδρου τῆς τοῦ ἀκράτου κύλικος εἰς αὐτὸν ἐλθούσης ὡς διωθεῖτο, εἰπόντος τέ τινος αὐτῷ, "διὰ τί οὐ πίνεις;" "οὐδὲν δέομαι, ἔφη, Ἀλεξάνδρου πιὼν τοῦ Ἀσκληπιοῦ δεῖσθαι".

Athenaeus 10.434d.

35. Λυγκεὺς δὲ ἐν δευτέρῳ περὶ Μενάνδρου, ἐπὶ γελοίοις, φησί, δόξαν εἰληφότες <Εὐκλείδης> ὁ Σμικρίνου καὶ Φιλόξενος ἡ Πτερνοκοπίς· ὧν ὁ μὲν Εὐκλείδης ἀποφθεγγόμενος οὐκ ἀνάξια βιβλίου καὶ μνήμης ἐν τοῖς ἄλλοις ἦν ἀηδὴς καὶ ψυχρός, ὁ δὲ Φιλόξενος οὐδὲν ἐπὶ κεφαλαίου περιττὸν λέγων ὅτε λαλήσειεν, εἰ πικρανθείη πρός τινα τῶν συζώντων καὶ διηγήσαιτο, πᾶν ἐπαφροδισίας καὶ χάριτος ἦν μεστόν. καίτοι γε συνέβη τὸν μὲν Εὐκλείδην κατὰ τὸν βίον ...., τὸν δὲ Φιλόξενον ὑπὸ πάντων φιλεῖσθαι καὶ τιμᾶσθαι.

Athenaeus 6.242b.

36. ΙΘΥΦΑΛΛΟΙ. Ὑπερείδης ἐν τῷ κατ' Ἀρχεστρατίδου· οἱ τοὺς ἰθυφάλλους ἐν τῇ ὀρχήστρᾳ ὀρχούμενοι. – ποιήματα τινα οὕτως ἐλέγετο τὰ ἐπὶ τῷ φαλλῷ ᾀδόμενα, ὡς Λυγκεὺς ἐν ταῖς ἐπιστολαῖς φησίν.

Harpocration 160.


**Testimonia**

37. ... πλακοῦντες ἕκαστα γένη, Κρητικῶν καὶ τῶν σῶν, ἑταῖρε Λυγκεῦ, Σαμιακῶν καὶ Ἀττικῶν ...

Hippolochus, *Letter to Lynceus* [Athenaeus 4.130c].

38. σὺ δὲ μόνον ἐν Ἀθήναις μένων εὐδαιμονίζεις τὰς Θεοφράστου θέσεις ἀκούων, θύμα καὶ εὔζωμα καὶ τοὺς καλοὺς ἐσθίων στρεπτούς, Λήναια καὶ Χύτρους θεωρῶν· ἡμεῖς δ' ἐκ τοῦ Καράνου δείπνου πλοῦτον ἀντὶ μερίδων εὐωχηθέντες νῦν ζητοῦμεν οἱ μὲν οἰκίας, οἱ δὲ ἀγρούς, οἱ δὲ ἀνδράποδ' ὠνήσασθαι.

Hippolochus, *Letter to Lynceus* [Athenaeus 4.130d].

39. ΛΥΓΚΕΥΣ Σάμιος, γραμματικός, Θεοφράστου γνώριμος, ἀδελφὸς Δούριδος τοῦ ἱστοριογράφου, τοῦ καὶ τυραννήσαντος Σάμου. σύγχρονος δὲ γέγονεν ὁ Λυγκεὺς Μενάνδρου τοῦ κωμικοῦ καὶ ἀντεπεδείξατο κωμῳδίας καὶ ἐνίκησε.

*Suda* s.v. 'Lynkeus'.

# SECTION VI:
# SYMPOTICA

# INTRODUCTORY
# REMARKS

The chapters in this section combine to explore Athenaeus' engagement in the *Deipnosophistae* with food, drink and their various accompaniments at the table of Larensis, especially humour, philosophizing, music and love. Of course, since these matters stand at the very heart of Athenaeus' work, the chapters in this section often echo issues and discussions elsewhere in this book.

First, Milanezi considers the place of laughter and laughter-making in the *Deipnosophistae*, with particular reference to Book Fourteen. As later chapters in this section will also show, humour is a key feature of the work. Yet the aim is humour of a measured sort. As Milanezi stresses, humour here is not presented as antagonistic to serious discussion. Rather the humour of Book Fourteen in particular ensures that the proceedings end in a suitably convivial spirit, whatever conflicts have arisen hitherto and may continue to rumble on. In that sense, humour is presented as constructive in enabling disagreements without excess of rancour, not a destructive force inimical to serious discussion (note the closing sentiments at 15.702b–c).

Stoneman recalls particularly the earlier discussions of Trapp on Plato and Romeri on the anti-banquet by stressing the role of food as a philosophical issue, both in the *Deipnosophistae* and more broadly in the philosophical world within which Athenaeus himself thought and wrote. For Stoneman, the Cynic at the feast fulfils a key function in maintaining attention upon that issue. His observation helps to account for recurrent reference to the philosopher through the text under the sobriquet Cynulcus, an appellation which sets his philosophical allegiance permanently in the foreground. A philosopher, and above all perhaps a Cynic philsopher, famously austere and principled, risked charges of hypocrisy by enjoying the fine hospitality of a Larensis. We should recall the tendency through the text to denounce certain philosophers as frauds and hypocrites. It is also worth remembering Tacitus' cutting remarks against the philosophers whom Nero brought to perform after his dinners:

> Nero used even to give time to teachers of wisdom after dinners, so that he might enjoy their discord as they asserted contrary cases. And there were men who desired to be seen with glum faces and expressions amidst regal splendours.
>
> (Tac. *Ann.* 14.16)

Yet, by contrast, Athenaeus treats Cynulcus lightly enough: he is among friends and such criticism as he receives is convivial banter, a part of the humour of the work and by no means the denunciation of a Tacitus.

The potential for humour in Athenaeus' work is often neglected; few have seen that it can be funny and perhaps satirical. Indeed, the *Deipnosophistae* seems more often to have inspired irritation among its modern readers. However, such reactions seem excessively unsympathetic. Quite apart from banter surrounding Cynulcus, there is humour through most of the work, except where Athenaeus chooses to offer synthesized catalogues. So much so, indeed, that Athenaeus felt the need to assert finally, at the close of Book Fifteen, that there was a serious substance to the reported conviviality. Gilula discusses a comic figure to whom the diners choose to refer, the famously funny Stratonicus. He fits well enough in a work which contains so much from comedy and other more real jokers, notably the witty *hetaerae* of Book Thirteen. As she shows, the historical Stratonicus is elusive, but as a figure of legend he has a lot in common with the diners. He shares their cosmopolitan outlook, particularly through travelling. And that outlook in his case is accompanied by an almost malevolent distaste for locations which he considers to be marginal or in some other way insignificant, through smallness of size for example. One may wonder whether the cosmpolitanism of Athenaeus, Larensis and the other diners is similarly encumbered. Certainly, they share Stratonicus' fondness for humour, for word-play, for quotation and for the appropriate adaptation of texts of the past to conditions of the present.

It is perhaps easy to lose sight of Stratonicus' musical talents amidst his wealth of witticisms. Yet he was also at home in the talk of the diners by virtue of his musicianship, for music is important in the work, a prominent feature of convivial society. Barker demonstrates that Athenaeus is not concerned to approach the topic of music after the fashion of those who wrote what may be termed technical treatises about it. Rather, in the field of music as in so much else, Athenaeus is a determined dilettante. For Athenaeus, it seems, music is fine, while witty musicians are even better; one might argue amusingly about the origins of instruments, the more recondite the better perhaps. Musicology, by contrast, is eschewed, no doubt a vulgarity. Crucially, Villari shows that the rejection of technical musicology was not the fruit of simple ignorance. It was a deliberate choice. For Athenaeus not only read Aristoxenus, but provides us with approximately one fifth of Aristoxenus' extant fragments.

Musicology is not alone in being shunned. Athenaeus displays a similar indifference, at best, towards oenology. Brock and Wirtjes show that there is scant concern with the science of wine as such in the *Deipnosophistae*. Rather, the substantial concern there is with the impact of wine upon character, behaviour and artistic creativity, as well as lexicography. Accordingly, and to an extent that is perhaps surprising, wine and local varieties of wine occur largely in passing. In particular, there is no catalogue of wines, such as that devoted to fish, for example, in Book Seven. The omission is pointed all the more by the inclusion of the catalogue of cups and containers in Book Eleven. Subsequently, Niafas offers a case-study of Athenaeus' interest in wine as a historical and cultural phenomenon rather than for its own sake. He develops that argument powerfully to suggest that the Athenian cult of Dionysus Orthos was a counterpart to the more familiar cult of Artemis Orthia at Sparta, which happens to have enjoyed a particular vogue in Athenaeus' day.

The relationship between consumption and health recurs through the *Deipnosophistae*, as the discussions of Stoneman, Brock and Wirtjes and Niafas aptly demonstrate. The three papers of Flemming, Gourevitch and Corvisier offer a range of perspectives on Athenaeus' engagement in the work with doctors and medicine. Here again, as with music and wine, Athenaeus appears as well read and well informed, but with the outlook and agenda of a determined dilettante.

Flemming observes the prominence of doctors and of medical matters in the *Deipnosophistae*. She also points out that medicine had an established place in sympotic discourse long before Athenaeus. The doctors among the diners can therefore be allowed to display their special knowledge, but their display is largely focused upon the food and drink on the table or at least arises from that. Medical discourse is thereby incorporated within the broader discourse of the diners, while the doctors show that they are more than their profession: they too share the broader cultural knowledge and values of their fellows, with their own quotations at hand from non-medical texts and plays. Indeed, as Flemming valuably observes, those diners who could not claim to be doctors are nevertheless permitted to hold forth on medical matters from time to time. Evidently, the special knowledge of doctors is acknowledged, but, like many another speciality (such as law, for example), medicine is neither exclusive to doctors nor exclusive of others in the culture of the *Deipnosophistae*. These dilettanti dabble in medicine, while in their company even doctors take on the manners of dilettanti. Meanwhile, Athenaeus, the architect of all this, once more shows that he has read not only the standard medical works (or possibly standard medical collections), but also works rather off the beaten track.

While Villari can find Aristoxenus, Gourevitch shows that Athenaeus has had access to a medical writer as obscure as Hicesius, so that he constitutes a significant source for Hicesius' writings, which she presents and discusses at length. No doubt, obscurity made Hicesius all the more attractive to Athenaeus. Galen himself was among the diners, surely the great doctor, but there was little to be gained from quoting from his voluminous works. He was by no means obscure. It was enough to have him in the company. Thereafter, Corvisier sets about establishing the depth and breadth of Athenaeus' concern with medicine. Here the limitations of Athenaeus' interest are particularly striking. We should probably expect him to be concerned with little more than dietetics, but Corvisier shows that even in this field his concerns are decidedly that of the well-read generalist. Corvisier thereby offers a valuable caution to those who would exploit the *Deipnosophistae* as the mine of medical information which, nevertheless, it also remains.

Finally, in this section, Henry takes us to *hetaerae*, who are the key women of the text, though a few other women (queens and female authors in particular) are mentioned from time to time. Athenaeus, Larensis and all the other diners are of course men, discussing the women in question. Henry reflects upon her earlier treatment of Athenaeus as the first writer known to have used the term 'pornographer'. She explores the stark limitations of what seem to be his views and assumptions about *hetaerae*. Not that Book Thirteen is simply about *hetaerae*, of course. For Athenaeus introduces the book as a study of love and matters pertaining to love (13.555b), which leads eventually, notably through a treatment of homosexuality, to a sustained treatment of *hetaerae*. He has Larensis introduce the discussion with praise of married women, a speech which Larensis ends with the summative declaration that 'there is not one of the wild beasts that is more fatal than the *hetaera*' (13.558e). In principle, there was nothing very innovative in debates on the relative merits of marriage and other forms of relationship.[1] It would seem that this was a matter upon which Larensis had strong views, for it is hard to imagine Athenaeus according him such a speech otherwise and in so prominent a position at the outset of the book.

Here too there is plenty of humour. Yet Henry must be right to detect not only humour, but also a certain dubious relish in Book Thirteen of the *Deipnosophistae*. At the same time, here too—as with wine, medicine and song—Athenaeus' perspective is that of a dilettante and, as ever, his focus is upon words far more than upon the matters they signify. Henry stresses that Athenaeus' *hetaerae* form an ahistorical stereotype: he shows no concern to offer distinctions between individuals. And with *hetaerae* his emphasis is again very much upon language, particularly verbal wit. He shows rather little interest in the physical appearance of his individual subjects, though there are passing references to physical attributes and there is a general concern with the issue of real vs. false or deceptive beauty (e.g. 13.568d) and the power of *hetaerae*, not least through their physical charms (e.g. 589d). For Athenaeus—or at least for his Cynulcus—the term 'pornographer' is an insult, applicable especially to painters of the physical and corporeal (13.567b) and only by extension to painters in words. We have seen that Athenaeus is very much a man of words, with *hetaerae* as with all else. Accordingly, if we consider Athenaeus himself to be a pornographer, his must be a pornography in words, not in pictures. After all, his is a text which can embrace the notion that people can even fall in love with each other simply through hearing words about the objects of their desire (13.575a).

# 29

# LAUGHTER AS DESSERT
## ON ATHENAEUS' BOOK FOURTEEN, 613–616

### by Silvia Milanezi

Larensis' hospitality offers sociability, cultural research, *euphrosyne, hesychia, charis* and harmony.[1] At the beginning of Book Fourteen Athenaeus invites Timocrates to choose a Dionysus *metrios* (*measured*), as opposed to a Dionysus *mainomenos* (*mad*), a condition *sine qua non* of a *mousikon symposion* (613a–c). In consuming wine, the banqueters consume the god himself; and such experience of the divine manifests itself in discussions, games, joy and laughter.[2] In a sense, laughter is a Dionysiac manifestation that rolls through the hall of the banquet, strengthening the links of friendship—*philia*—and increasing the pleasure of the banqueters from the first (e.g. Diphilus, fr. 86 = *Deipn.* 2.35d). Here we have a picture of an ideal *symposion* in which 'measure' rules. And measure depends largely on the right mixture of wine and its proper consumption. But *hybris* can transform the *symposion* into a battle-field, where bad words and laughter in the form of mockery and sarcasm are dangerous weapons which generate disorder (as in Epicharmus, fr. 148 Kaibel = 175 Olivieri = *Deipn.* 2.36c–d). While there is no *symposion* without laughter (burial banquets excepted),[3] it is very important to control all its manifestations which might trouble the *philia* of the occasion, the friendship among the participants. To maintain such control, the Greeks often chose a *symposiarchos* (Plut. *Moralia*, 620a–622b), giving him the role of a 'censor'. He must prevent bad jokes and mockery—for example, making a bald man comb his hair or a disabled man jump (Plut. *Moralia*, 621d).[4] For besides the laughter deriving from language and word-play between participants, *symposia* generated another kind of laughter, namely that which derived from shows (*acroamata*),[5] particularly from performances by the professionals of laughter (the *gelotopoioi*) who were hired by the host for his guests' pleasure. Therefore, in what follows I have chosen to examine Athenaeus' fourteenth book, in which the author (for the greatest pleasure of Timocrates, his public, and ourselves, his readers) treats the entertainments suitable for *symposia*, ending with a catalogue of desserts—*epidorpismata, tragemata, deuterai trapezai*. At the same time, behind the discourse about entertainments meant for laughter and dessert, we can also consider the ethics of the *symposia*, coloured by the philosophical legacy, to which Athenaeus adds his own reflections. This is often difficult for us, because it is based on sustained quotation from ancient authors. In the hope of greater clarity I shall focus upon 14.613–16. I shall consider, first of all, the *gelotopoioi*. Next, I shall focus upon Athenaeus' discourse about the reception of such shows, which is also evidently a study of laughter. Finally, I shall conclude with a brief note on laughter and dessert. I hope this antipasto will not be indigestible.

In his *Deipnosophistae*, Athenaeus has a well-defined programme: to imitate a *mousikon symposion*, that is to say, a show of *logoi*. As Lukinovich has pointed out, the sophistic discussion goes along with every stage of the *symposion*: in the *Deipnosophistae*, the banquet is the context for *logoi* and *logoi* concern the banquet.[6] In this sense we can safely say that the *Deipnosophistae* is a *meta-symposion*. Book Fourteen can be read from very much that kind of perspective: its purpose is to reconstruct the last part of a banquet, and more precisely, its drinking stage, where both shows and desserts are presented. Accordingly we may hope to find here *meta-acroamata*.

After an appeal for measure, addressed to Timocrates (613a–c), Athenaeus returns to the narrative mode in order to make way for the *sympotikos logos*, the discussion that goes on between guests. He gives the role of symposiarch to Ulpian, who parodies Socrates in Xenophon's *Symposion* (2.2), and praises the excellence of Larensis' hospitality. He stresses his careful way of introducing different kinds of *acroamata* in his banquets (613c–d). This praise at the same time serves to introduce the new topic for discussion : the *gelotopoioi*:

Ἐπεὶ δὲ ἑκάστης ἡμέρας μετὰ τοὺς παρ' ἡμῶν καινοὺς αἰεὶ λεγομένους λόγους καὶ ἀκροάματα ἑκάστοτε διάφορα ἐπεισάγει ὁ λαμπρὸς ἡμῶν ἑστιάτωρ Λαρήνσιος ἔτι τε καὶ γελωτοποιούς, φέρε λέγωμέν τι καὶ ἡμεῖς περὶ τούτων.

Since our illustrious host Larensis, following our discussion of novel topics brought up continually every day, introduces for our entertainment various diversions on all occasions, and notably brings on the scene buffoons, come, let us talk a while on that subject.

Ulpian's proposition is exciting mainly because we know very little about the so-called *gelotopoioi*. Literally this word means 'those who produce laughter' or 'those who make us laugh'.[7] Hence we translate it as 'buffoon','jester' or 'clown'. Although its adjectival form occurs in Aeschylus (fr. 180. 2 N.) meaning 'ridiculous', nevertheless as a noun indicating a profession, *gelotopoios* appears first only in the fourth century BC (Xen. *Symp*, 1.11, *An.* 7. 3, 33; Pl. *R.* 620c). The lateness of its appearance as such might be explained, conceivably, by the loss of a great number of Greek texts or by authorial preferences: Aristotle, for example, seems to use *bomolochos* or *alazon* (as in *Rh.* 3. 1419b, 2–9) for *gelotopoios*, in contexts where no allusion is made to the characters of ancient comedy.[8]

But who are those whose profession is to produce laughter, if they are not comic poets or comic types? And have they a *techne* ? Xenophon who presents in his *Symposion* a *gelotopoios*, Philip,[9] Plato who criticizes this sort of entertainer (*Rep.* 606; 620b) and in particular Athenaeus who gives a list of *gelotopoioi* (*Deipn.* 1.19a–20b),[10] are our best guides to their buffoonery. In fact, arriving at Callias' home, Philip, the *gelotopoios*, announces that he has come with everything necessary to dine at other people's expense (συνεσκευασμένος δὲ ἔφη παρεῖναι πάντα τἀπιτήδεια ὥστε δειπνεῖν τἀλλότρια, Xen. *Symp.* 1.11 = *Deipn.* 14.614c). *Epitedeia*, in this precise context, means effort, the ability to make people laugh and the tricks, the *techné*, to obtain laughter.[11]

*Gelotopoioi* were famous for their wit, their jests and their puns (Xen. *Symp*, 2. 27). Philip of Macedon, hearing about the jests of the so-called Sixty at Athens paid a great amount of money in order to have them copied for his own use (*Deipn.* 14.614d, see also 6.260b = Hegesander of Delphi, *FHG*, IV. 413). They were also very good at imitations of all kinds: men, women, professionals, animals, animal voices, different noises.[12] They could also sing, dance, recite and parody every sort of art, and do a series of tricks as acrobats, jugglers and illusionists. They were 'one-man shows', as was Philip the *gelotopoios*, who could parody comic and tragic scenes, dancers and acrobats, and also was very good at mimicking people, *eikasmos* (Xen. *Symp*. 6.8–9 and 7 1; see also Lucian, *Symp*. 18).

It is hard to know when they first appeared, though Anaxandrides comically states in his *Gerontomania* (fr. 10) that Palamedes and Rhadamanthys were the first to create *geloia* (Ἀναξανδρίδης δ᾽ ἐν Γεροντομανίᾳ καὶ εὑρετὰς τῶν γελοίων φησὶ γενέσθαι Ῥαδάμανθυν καὶ Παλαμήδην: *Deipn.* 14.614c). Placing the beginnings of the profession in mythical time, in a mythical sphere, he gives it a respectable appearance that is at the same time mocking. *Geloia*, like numbers and other inventions created by Palamedes[13] for the benefit of mankind, were thought of as a *symbolon* (contribution) that permits participation in banquets for those who are otherwise *asymboloi*:[14]

κaίτoι πoλλoί γε πoνoῦμεν.
τὸ δ᾽ ἀσύμβoλoν εὗρε γελoῖα λέγειν Ῥαδάμανθυς καὶ Παλαμήδης.

And yet, many of us suffer indeed. For Rhadamanthys and Palamedes invented the custom of letting the gentry that pay no scot utter jests.

Therefore it is not surprising that some scholars have found in ancient authors links between *gelotopoioi* and the *akletoi*, beggars, flatterers and parasites, who ate at other people's expense.[15] This problem of identification is a difficult one and must be studied at length. We may hypothesize that at first they did make people laugh in order to pay for their food—even if their performance did not take place at the *deipnon* stage[16]—but that what began as improvisation, for the sake of the stomach, gradually became a *techne*, and a well-remunerated one at that.[17] The *gelotopoios* Philip represents the last stage in the transition of this tradition of barter into a recognized profession. The so called *akletoi* (or, at least, some of them) transformed themselves into an ornament for a house or a royal court: they were hired by the wealthy hosts for the guests' pleasure. They somehow demonstrated the refinement and wealth of the ancient host.[18]

Autonomous entertainers at first (such as Philip, Eudicus, Cephisodorus), they joined others to form associations or 'troupes' (such as the troupe at Callias' banquet or the Sixty of Athens). If we believe Athenaeus, we must consider that some entertainers may have formed schools, whose pupils' success could surpass that of their teachers, such as Xenophon, the *thaumatopoios,* and his pupil Cratisthenes of Phlius. It is not very difficult to suppose that teacher and pupils performed together. We might also find families of *gelotopoioi,* like those of the fifth-century Athenian tragic and comic poets or actors.[19] Athenaeus observes that Mandrogenes was related to Straton of Athens, performing in a Macedonian circle with his wife, who was more than 80 years old (Hippolochos, *Letter to Lynceus = Deipn.* 4.128a–b and 130c).

If we consider the way Athenaeus refers to the *gelotopoioi*, we can say that the term can cover a wide range of practices. Sometimes Athenaeus presents *thaumatopoioi* (or *thaumatourgoi*) 'wonder-workers' or 'acrobats', and *planoi* 'vagabonds' or 'impostors' as *gelotopoioi*,[20] because their tricks produce laughter. Nevertheless we can say that they are related to the genres of drama and particularly to comedy. On the other hand, Attic comedy is full of their tricks,[21] and if we consider the phlyax vases as theatrical evidence, we must accept that their shows were also included in comedy.[22] If they were associated with *planoi*, the acrobats and illusionists, they may have belonged to the troupes evoked by Aristotle in his *Poetics*, whose business is Attic comedy (1448a 37–8).[23] At the same time, they could be linked to genres related to comedy, such as the mime, because all their work is imitation, *mimesis*; or to pantomime which found a wide public not only in classical Athens, in the Hellenistic world, and also in imperial Rome. At first entertainers at private dinners, they also showed their art in the agora and played an important role at public displays, probably during festivals.[24]

However it is important to note that the antiquarian Athenaeus, in Ulpian's speech (and Magnus', which completes Ulpian's), does not cite any *gelotopoioi* of his own time, only those from the past, and particularly from the fourth and third centuries BC, in Athens or in the Macedonian spheres of influence. He gives a list of such entertainers, but he does not describe their shows. So our idea of the *meta-symposion* or of *meta-acroamata* might appear to be compromised. But we must remember that Athenaeus uses the past as a mirror of his present. The very mention of the names of the *gelotopoioi* indicates that they had not disappeared. The ancient texts that attest to them are kept alive in the *Deipnosophistae*. Moreover, Athenaeus does tell us that Larensis hired a lot of entertainers to amuse his guests and himself (14.613c–d). Whether fiction or reality, Larensis' symposia, as Athenaeus describes or narrates them, must be understood as great masterpieces of cooking and the arts. And Athenaeus' genius lies precisely in the fact that by suggestion and allusion he awakes in his public too all the possibilities of the shows of the *gelotopoioi*. In so doing he draws his readers away from a passive role and gives them a creative one. Thus it is clear that Athenaeus' programme of creativity (as proposed by Ulpian and Larensis) cannot be confined to a simple list of names. It extends further to the *meta-acroamata*. His programme consists, in my opinion, in both the study of the reception of the shows of the *gelotopoioi* and, at the same time, in the reaction to laughter and its use.

In fact, Ulpian opens his speech on *gelotopoioi* with a reflexion on the reception of such shows, or to be clearer, on the power of *mimesis* on banqueters. At first sight, their reaction appears to be highly negative. Ulpian remembers that the Scythian prince, Anacharsis,[25] who was famous for his wisdom, did not appreciate the performance of *gelotopoioi* at banquets (ἐν συμποσίῳ γελωτοποιῶν εἰσαχθέντων ἀγέλαστον διαμείναντα), but he would laugh at the representation of a monkey because it was funny by nature (πιθήκου δ' ἐπεισαχθέντος γελάσαντα φάναι (ὡς οὗτος μὲν φύσει γελοῖός ἐστιν)—*Deipn.* 14.613d). Inspired by Anacharsis, Ulpian introduces in this section the broad question of *mimesis*, of its perception or appreciation. But in what way is a monkey's *physis* funny? Isn't it because monkeys are the most mimetic of animals?[26] Isn't it because monkeys' attitudes resemble those of men?[27] Anacharsis despised the professional entertainer's *techne* perhaps because it implied that men transform themselves into monkeys, or perhaps because the *gelotopoioi* are compelled to do their tricks in order to flatter those who pay their wages; or more simply because they must imitate what in a man is the most worthy of blame, since comic *mimesis* is based, as Aristotle puts it, on 'errors', on the vilest aspects of human nature (*Poet.*, 1449a; 1448b). And even if man is mimetic by nature (Arist., *Poet.*, 1448b), he is not supposed to be *geloios*, 'ridiculous' or a 'buffoon' by nature. Thus

Anacharsis did not laugh at the distorted representation of a man by another man, but at his reflection in an animal which is the most akin to man. He did not laugh at a man in particular but at a version of human nature that is deprived of all that hides its true ego.

If Anacharsis did not appreciate *gelotopoioi*, Euripides or, more precisely, one of the characters of *Melanippe Bound* (and perhaps Melanippe herself) also condemned those who used *kertomoi*, mocking jests or insults, in order to be funny. This is mainly because *kertomoi* are dangerous weapons in the unbridled mouths of outcasts and threaten the men of rank:

> ἀνδρῶν δὲ πολλοὶ τοῦ γέλωτος εἴνεκα
> ἀσκοῦσι χάριτας κερτόμους. ἐγὼ δέ πως
> μισῶ γελοίους, οἵτινες τήτῃ σοφῶν
> ἀχάλιν' ἔχουσι στόματα· κὰς ἀνδρῶν μὲν οὐ
> τελοῦσιν ἀριθμόν, ἐν γέλωτι δ' εὐπρεπεῖς...

(fr. 492 Nauck = Deipn.14.613d–614a).

> Many men there be who to make fun practise mocking jests. But I somehow detest these funny men, who when wise thoughts fail them keep their lips unbridled; and though they have no rating in the ranks of true men, they put on a specious front of laughter.

Interestingly such verses do not apply precisely to *gelotopoioi* as professional entertainers, unless we consider that *geloios* is a synonym for *gelotopoios* in Euripides. Some scholars believe that Euripides' *geloioi* can be understood as the comic poets and particularly as Aristophanes: on such a view, the tragic poet is here returning the abuse they used to fling at him. This interpretation is founded perhaps on pseudo-Xenophon's ideological remarks on the use of insults in Attic Comedy: he stresses that comic poets attack the *kalokagathoi* for the sake and pleasure of the democratic *demos* (*Const. Ath.*, 2. 18). So Ulpian perhaps quotes these lines as relevant to the *gelotopoioi* in order to move on the discussion to a moral perspective. However, at this point, we must consider the development of his speech: in evoking Anacharsis, Ulpian seems to emphasize his interest in non-verbal jesting based on gesture and silent *mimesis*.[28] By manipulating these Euripidean lines, Ulpian stresses the danger of shows in which laughter provoked by verbal violence is φθόνος, 'ill will', 'envy'. In fact, *kertomein/kertomoi* are used from Homer onwards to indicate verbal violence. These terms evoke particularly the attacks of Thersites against Agamemnon (*Il.* 2.256),[29] where in a parody of a heroic *aristeia*, he is a *gelotopoios* whose life is true excess. But words evolve and are replaced; they change meaning. In classical prose and in comic poetry *loidoria* and *skomma* replace *kertomoi* (which in the fifth century appears mostly in tragic poetry).[30] However, *kertomoi, loidoria* or *skomma* are precisely the trumps of the entertainer's art. And Athenaeus makes this clear in the case of Nymphodorus, the *thaumatopoios*, who 'taking offence at the people of Rhegium, as Duris tells us, was the first to ridicule them for their cowardice' (1.19f). So too Plato, when he presents, in the last myth of his *Republic* (10.590b), Thersites as a *gelotopoios* choosing for his reincarnation the soul of a monkey. Neverthless, by evoking Anacharsis and Euripides, Ulpian does not eliminate *gelotopoioi* from banquets: he stresses the different performances that they can offer, and commends, as Plato, Aristotle and Plutarch do, those that are suitable for a *mousikon symposion* in which laughter—like the guests—must be *eutrapelos* and *epidexios* (Arist., *EN*, 1128a 10 and 17).[31]

But even if Anacharsis and Euripides would rather eliminate *gelotopoioi* from their acquaintance, nevertheless people cannot live without laughing. The story of Parmeniscus of Metapontum is clear enough. Once again, apparently there is no direct link in this anecdote with *gelotopoioi*. Parmeniscus, a Pythagorean, loses the gift of laughter after consulting the oracle of Trophonius (Παρμενίσκος δὲ ὁ Μεταποντῖνος, ὡς φησιν Σῆμος ἐν ε΄ Δηλιάδος, καὶ γένει καὶ πλούτῳ πρωτεύων εἰς Τροφωνίου καταβὰς καὶ ἀνελθὼν οὐκ ἔτι γελᾶν ἐδύνατο—*Deipn.* 14.614b = Semus, *FGrH* 396, F10).[32] Even though Pausanias explains his very experience of the consultation—*katabasis* into the grove of Trophonius, *incubatio* and *anabasis* (9. 39, 14)—stressing that those who submit to it would not be able to laugh immediately afterwards, we are not told what could cause such a loss.[33] Pausanias seems to explain this phenomenon as a psychoanalytical problem, which raises many questions, mainly because it is also a religious problem. But what is the meaning of this loss ? An initiatory or transitory state, a ritual or a death ? The case of Parmeniscus is very disturbing: he is unable to come out from his ritual journey, he cannot laugh any more. Returning home, he does not recover the gift of laughter as expected, even though the Delphic oracle had predicted that he would find it again when meeting his mother (εἴρη μ᾽ ἀμφὶ γέλωτος, ἀμείλιχε, μειλιχίοιο· δώσει σοι μήτηρ οἴκοι· τὴν ἔξοχα τῖε: *Deipn.* 14.614a–b). In the meantime he goes on living *ameilichos*, 'unrelenting', and his life is incomplete without such *charis*. One day visiting the Delian temple, as a tourist, he decides to see Leto's statue. Observing the *xoanon* of the goddess, he laughs (ἰδὼν δ᾽ αὐτὸ ξύλον ὂν ἄμορφον παραδόξως ἐγέλασεν: *Deipn.* 14.614b). He laughs at something *amorphos*, a bad or an ugly *mimesis* of the deity. Parmeniscus laughs at a surprising spectacle, in which the representation of the deity functions as a *gelotopoios*. Now, to laugh at gods was usually thought to be an act of impiety. But, unlike the mythical Ascalabus (Ant. Lib., *Tr.*, 24; Ov., *Met.*, 5. 446) or Cambyses (Hdt., 3.37), Parmeniscus is not condemned for laughing. Leto becomes for him a spring of life, a new mother, and his sonorous laughter, as a spell-breaker, awakens him and drags him away from Trophonius' cave, from the depth of his *ameilichos* mind.

In spite of Anacharsis' prejudice and Euripides' dislike for laughter, which is stressed even in his biography (*Vita* 1. 65 Méridier),[34] laughter is a very important part of human life—an indispensable one in fact. And Ulpian demonstrates as much by recounting Parmeniscus' experience. Laughter is *charis*, a divine *charis*, and thus a serious matter. Provoked by human, animal, natural or divine *mimesis*, laughter is a means to katharsis, which is, simply, life in its plenitude. So in broad terms we may say that laughter is the best medicine for the soul. But this text goes further: it also demonstrates that laughter is a matter of intelligence and depends not only on a simple imitation, but also on the mental representations that we form of objects, events, gods and men. What Bergson might call inadequacy and surprise[35] is for me a shock between mental representation and mimesis: laughter is the external explosion of this established conflict. To laugh is to be complete, perfect in a sense, laughter being a pledge of harmony both for individuals and for their communities. So, thanks to Parmeniscus, *gelotopoioi*, comic mimesis and laughter obtain a place at Larensis' *mousikon symposion*.

After these considerations, Ulpian evokes another type of reaction to laughter by turning to the *philogelotes*. This epithet (meaning literally ' friend or lover of laughter', 'those who make laughter their own') is applied to men such as Philip II of Macedon (14.614e), Demetrius Poliorcetes (*Deipn.* 14.614e), Sulla and Lucius Anicius (*Deipn.* 14.615a). These men not only love laughing and their relationship with *gelotopoioi*, but they may even transform themselves sometimes into *gelotopoioi*. So Philip II, king of Macedon paid a great amount of money in order to have the jokes of the Sixty of Athens copied (*Deipn.* 14.614e, 6.260b).[36] But his love for laughing goes farther: in his court he gathered a colourful crowd, wherein *mimoi* or *gelotopoioi* were placed first. Moreover, at his banquets and especially at *symposia*, he was himself a show, playing dice, getting drunk and mixing with the professionals of laughter and the riotous (Dem. *Olynth.* 2. 19). On that tradition, he transformed himself into a jester or a buffoon (*Deipn.* 6.248e, 260c; 10.435c).

Demetrius' way of life, it was said, did not differ a great deal from Philip's: clever, strong on the battle-field, and addicted to debauchery in peace-time (Plut. *Dem.* 19, 3–6).[37] From Antigonus his father he had learned not only how to fight but also, if we believe Plutarch, the art of teasing and perhaps the ability to be laughed at (D.S. 22, 9) and to mock in turn (*Dem.* 19, 3–6). But his love of laughing is mostly linked in our sources with political abuse, as it was used in ancient comedy. Unlike Philip, he did not collect anecdotes about laughter or puns: he created them. In fact, after 306 BC, when Alexander's successors begun to call themselves kings, Demetrius, considering that only his father and himself deserved this title as the true heirs of the Macedonian, incited his companions or his flatterers to pledge 'Demetrius as King, but Seleucus as Master of the Elephants, Ptolemy as Admiral, Lysimachus as Treasurer, and Agathocles of Sicily as Lord of the Isles' (Phylarchus, *FHG.* I. 339 and 341; Plut. *Dem.* 15,3; *Deipn.* 6.261b). We can take for granted that the aim of this joke was the debasing of his enemies. But his particular whipping-boy was Lysimachus, against whom he fought for Macedonia. He got all the more pleasure out of mocking Lysimachus since this king was a sour man (Plut. *Dem.* 25. 6; *Deipn.* 14. 614f-15a; 616c). He delighted in repeating over and over again that 'the court of Lysimachus differed in no respect from a scene of comedy' (Phylarchus, *FHG* I. 335, 165 = *Deipn.* 14.614d–f). This jibe, based on the two-syllable names of comic characters (such as Chremes or Pheidon in Aristophanes or Antiphanes), was meant to hurt Lysimachus through his companions (or his flatterers) Bithys and Paris, by transforming him into a comic protagonist—clearly an unsuitable role for a king. This mischievous jibe is the corollary to the case of Demetrius. It seeks to demonstrate that Lysimachus was ridiculous precisely because he was an impostor, an *alazon*, playing the king's role. Similarly, Demetrius' laughter is an extension of his battles, of his (real or imagined) victories over those he considered (or would like to consider) as insignificant enemies. But even if his laughter is a weapon against his enemies, a means to spread his political propaganda, Demetrios is himself a *gelotopoios* acting as the 'metteur en scène' of Greek politics.[38]

But Philip and Demetrius are not the only *philogelotes* evoked by Athenaeus.[39] Their passion is shared by a great number of kings, public men or individuals in Hellenistic and imperial times among whom we find also Sulla, the Roman *dictator*. Sulla's life was imagined as an eternal feast. His love for *gelotopoioi*, *mimoi*, theatre, wine, jokes, laughing and debauchery is stressed by Plutarch, Sallust[40] and other historians, who knew Sulla's *Commentarii*. Athenaeus also studied all these sources but he prefers to quote Nicolaus of Damascus' *Histories*, in which Sulla appears not only as a lover of laughter, but also as a producer of laughter. Indeed, he is said to have written satirical comedies (*FHG* III. 416 = *Deipn.* 6.261c).[41] Specialists in Roman literature question the authenticity of this information: the fact that *atellanae*, 'satirical comedies', became a literary form precisely in Sulla's years does not imply that the Roman dictator was an author, competing with Novius and Pomponius, the greatest exponents of the genre. But we cannot deny that his relationship with the theatre and theatre-people goes beyond his love for debauchery, as emphasized by ancient authors and particularly by Plutarch. Indeed, in citing his feasts in the company of the *lusiodos* Metrobius (*Sulla*, 2, 6; 36, 2), of the *komikos* Roscius (36, 2), of the *archimimos* Sorix (36, 2), of *mimoi* women, citharists and *histriones*, Plutarch tries to present Sulla as an outcast. The words in which Plutarch chooses to express himself—ἐπὶ στιβάδων ἀφ' ἡμέρας συμπίνων—imply Sulla's membership of a Dionysiac *thiasos*[42] and perhaps his literary activity as a comic writer. However, Athenaeus, embracing the political abuse with which Sulla's contemporaries attacked him, demonstrates once again how the love for laughter pushes distinguished men to transform themselves into *gelotopoioi*.

Philip collected Attic jokes, Demetrius distilled puns, Sulla wrote *atellanae* and Lucius Anicius Gallus made a fool of himself by transforming his one triumph over the Illyrian king into a pantomime (*Deipn.* 14.615a–e).[43]

It is clear that the criticisms of Philip scattered about by Demosthenes (*Olynth.* 2. 19) and repeated first by Theopompus (*ap.* Polybius, 8. 9–13) were driven in great part by the political problems that touched Athens in the fourth century BC. It is a fact that Demosthenes fought against Philip for the preservation of Athens and its *hegemonia*. In his attacks, Philip, who is said to have loved debauchery, appears as a barbarian by nature, because he does not respect the severe conception that the Greeks had of political leaders. How can a man who finds pleasure mainly in laughter and in acquaintance with low and outcast men, claim to manage the politics of Greece? Thus, Demosthenes and Theompompus, in order to defend Athenian and Greek cities, transformed Philip into a character of comedy, into a man incapable of making good and serious decisions, and so into a *gelotopoios*. On the other hand, even if we agree with Plutarch that Demetrius was a bad and unsuitable example of human behaviour (*Dem.* 1. 5–7), we must bear in mind also that he used Phylarchus as a source, as did Athenaeus. Now, it is very likely that his moralizing discourse on Demetrius borrowed many of its ideas from Philippides, the comic poet and great friend of Lysimachus.[44] As for Sulla, we need only consider the second book of Lucan's *Pharsalia* to suspect that Plutarch's or Athenaeus' sources for his debauchery derive from Marius' household. In repeating these ancient negative paradigms, Athenaeus criticizes *mimeseis* that provoke laughter which is not expected or not suitable—as those provoked by the true *gelotopoios* must be, for his task is to make people laugh and not necessarily to be ridiculed.

But if *philogelotes* demonstrate a lack of control, *philoskoptontes*, who love mockery, sarcasm and insult, go further. Their wit (a dangerous one, as Athenaeus points out in Myrtilus' speech) can provoke not only laughter, but also the rupture of alliances and even condemnation to death. For instance, a disgusting joke made by the Egyptian king Tachôs caused the rupture of an alliance with the Spartan king, Agesilaus (*Deipn.* 14.616c). Worse is the case of Lysimachus' officer, Telesphorus, who was condemned to death for a pun which touched the honour of the king's wife (*Deipn.* 14.616 b–c). Put in a cage, Telesphoros died of starvation.[45]

But why were these jokes so disturbing, so out of place? Let us consider Telesphorus. In a banquet he said:

κακῶν κατάρχεις τήνδ' ἐμοῦσαν εἰσάγων

You are starting trouble by bringing in this vomiting woman

This pun was based on Euripides' *Antiope* (fr. *adesp.* 395+184, Nauck):

κακῶν κατάρχεις τήνδε μοῦσαν εἰσάγων
ἀργόν, φίλοινον, χρημάτων ἀτημελῆ.

You are starting trouble by bringing in this Muse, idle, lover of wine, careless of money.

It arose from a discussion between the brothers Zethus and Amphion in which the latter is mocked because of his love for music.[46] By parodying the first line and changing the pronunciation of two words (turning τήνδε μοῦσαν into τήνδ' ἐμοῦσαν), Telesphorus changed completely the meaning of this verse in order to mock Arsinoe, Lysimachus' wife. The fact that Arsinoe was subject to vomiting became by his pun a matter of public knowledge; we can understand why Arsinoe and Lysimachus were displeased. But Telesphorus' pun went further, because his parody presupposed also the knowledge of the second line of this fragment by which he implied perhaps that Arsinoe's sickness was provoked by wine. If historians are right, and if Arsinoe was Lysimachus' *éminence grise*, both his lover and also his political Muse, Telesphorus' insult was a very inconvenient one: Lysimachus was transformed into a marionette in the hands of a dangerous woman, a king that was unable to rule his state. Those who love insulting jokes are dangerous perhaps because they often unveil truths that must be keep covered for the sake of kings, rulers, politicians and rich individuals. Moreover, they are to be censured because they do not unveil truths in order to transform a bad man into a good one; they poke fun for their own pleasure. While they pretend to be advisers, they are only impostors, *alazones*.

Nevertheless, once a *philoskopton*, always a *philoskopton*. Such is the meaning of the first example presented by Athenaeus in this section: a man condemned to death, when offered a last wish, claimed he only wanted to make jokes:

ἔτι ἕν τι ἔφη θέλειν ὥσπερ τὸ κύκνειον ᾄσας ἀποθανεῖν. ἐπιτρέψαντος δ' ἐκείνου ἔσκωψεν

(*Deipn.* 14. 616b–c)

when he said that he was willing to die after he had said one more thing in the way of a swan song. On the executioner giving him permission, he made jokes.

A *philoskopton* cannot stop laughing or mocking even if this 'penchant' invites trouble:[47] he is the worst *gelotopoios* in the world, he is the man through whom scandal arrives. He is the incarnation of disorder.

Thus, in Athenaeus' text we can find a progression in laughter or, more precisely, in the love of laughter, from its right measure to the loss of all restraint. Citing the *philogelotes* and the *philoskoptontes* Athenaeus criticizes shows of the amateur *gelotopoioi*, which should be left to professionals. The man who shows himself off at banquets, and leaves his place as a spectator, breaks the equilibrium of this institution. He transforms the other guests into actors, into characters of a bad tragedy, a bad comedy, a perverse *agon* in which rupture will fatally be produced. In a sense he who provokes such rupture gives up the necessary *katharsis* in which harmony is founded. He leaves or is expelled from his community and is transformed into an animal. For if there is no *philia*, there is no community.

But Athenaeus demonstrates also that in a *mousikon symposion* there is always a place for a *philogelos* or for a *philoskopton*. In fact he stresses that these men were also among Larensis' guests (14.616b); and the best example of them all is Ulpian himself. He is often quarrelling with Cynulcus. They often attack each other for the sake of giving pleasure to the other guests. But their literary quarrels end up in a joyful and convivial laughter, because their jests or puns are *asteioi*. In this section in Book Fourteen Ulpian plays the *asteios gelotopoios* by his discourse, which is also at the same time an *akroama*—so we find here *meta-acroamata* in a *meta-symposion*—and a serious reflection on laughter. Narrating the story of Lucius Anicius, the last topic of his exposition, Ulpian provokes laughter which brightens all Larensis' hall, just as the laughter of the gods in the first book of the *Iliad* makes the immortal house of Zeus shine.

Nevertheless Athenaeus does not proceed like Plutarch (*Moralia*, 710c) who eliminates or criticizes many spectacles at the banquet. For, when discussing entertainments at the *symposion*, Plutarch recalls Xenophon and his *Symposion*, which shows that such an author is not ashamed to bring before Socrates, Antisthenes and other guests, a man like Philip the *gelotopoios*, rather as an onion is brought to be eaten with the wine.[48] If we set aside what could be taken as criticism, we can see that laughter and dessert—onion is a dessert dish in ancient Greece—are closely linked and are both presented at banquets in order to give pleasure to the guests. It is not surprising that philosophers (particularly Plato) condemn laughter and to a lesser degree dessert, stressing that they may produce decadence and disorder.[49] However, as Plutarch and Athenaeus were aware, laughter as dessert may actually help to preserve due measure. For dessert neutralizes the power of wine, preventing headaches[50] and drunkenness, as do laughter and humorous spectacles, which brighten the spirits. They appeal to the intelligence, which struggles with the fumes of wine, and dominates it. The power of laughter and the power of the entertainer is proved by Plato in his *Symposion*. For in that dialogue, Aristophanes the comic poet—who could be taken to be a *gelotopoios*—is the only guest able to argue with Socrates at the end of this famous *symposion*. From this point of view we can say that laughter and dessert are the antidotes of excess. So Athenaeus in Book Fourteen demonstrates that he does not believe in banishing shows of laughter from the *symposia*, because he believes them to constitute a necessary *charis* for human life. At the same time, Athenaeus presents laughter as a remedy. And, satiated by laughter at the entertainment, the guests set aside insults and the *hybris* that could intervene. For this reason, Athenaeus urges all guests to come to the right measure in the consumption of laughter, the sweetest of desserts.

## ❖ 30 ❖     YOU ARE WHAT YOU EAT
### DIET AND PHILOSOPHICAL *DIAITA* IN ATHENAEUS' *DEIPNOSOPHISTAE*

#### by Richard Stoneman

Is food a suitable topic of discussion for a dinner-party, particularly a party of wise and learned men? There is a prevailing attitude among ancient Greek philosophers, from Socrates onwards (and perhaps even earlier) that food is a necessity not worthy of attention beyond that required to stay alive and cultivate the higher part of man (cf. Chapter 19). Chrysippus is quoted by Athenaeus (8.335d) as classing the *Gastronomy of* Archestratus with the books on sexual pleasure by Philaenis: he says 'It would not be advisable to study the writings of Philaenis or the *Gastronomy* of Archestratus as tending to make a person live better.' One is hard put to it to find in the writings of the Second Sophistic, particularly among Greek writers, anything which suggests that the discussion of food is a serious activity. The nearest approach is in Plutarch's *Banquet of the Seven Sages* (*Mor.* l58cf): Solon has just stated: 'It is plain that the next best thing to the greatest and highest of all good is to require the minimum amount of food; or is it not the general opinion that the greatest good is to require no food at all?' Cleodorus responds to this statement of the traditional view with an encomium of food and of agriculture: 'When the table is done away with, there go with it all these other things: the altar fire on the hearth, and the hearth itself, wine-bowls, all entertainment and hospitality—the most humane and the first acts of communion between man and man.' This amounts, indeed, to a defence of food as something worth paying attention to, but scarcely as something worth a philosopher's detailed discussion.

The corollary question, whether philosophers are suitable people to have as guests at dinner at all, is also raised. Plutarch remarks on one advantage, at *Banquet of the Seven Sages* 150c:

as I noticed that the dinner was plainer than usual, there came the thought that the entertainment and invitation of wise and good men involves no expense, but rather curtails expense, since it does away with over-elaborate viands and imported perfumes and sweetmeats and the serving of costly wines, all of which were in fairly free use every day with Periander in his royal position and wealth and circumstance.'

But Plutarch also has more positive reasons for the encouragement of philosophical discussion at the dinner-table. First is the fact that conversation is part of the friend-making character of the dinner-party, and that the great philosophers have all recorded discussions over dinner. He cites Plato, Xenophon, Aristotle, Speusippus, Epicurus, Prytanis, Hieronymus and Dio of the Academy (*Qu. Conv.* 1.612e): one wonders if he is being slightly tongue-in-cheek here, since the discussions in the *Quaestiones Conviviales* are mainly not of a philosophic kind, but rather antiquarian. He insists, however, that conversation is to be properly directed: 'for no drink or food is so disagreeable or unwholesome, for lack of the right treatment, as is conversation that drifts about randomly and foolishly at a party' (*Qu. Conv* 8.716e). In fact philosophers may be the worst in this regard: at another point in the *Quaestiones Conviviales* (692b) Plutarch mentions a man called Niger who had

> 'returned from a brief course of instruction under a noted philosopher. The time had been long enough ... for students, though they might not take hold of the man's teaching, to catch some of his annoying habits .... When we were entertained at dinner by Aristion, Niger began to find everything too costly and elaborate. Specifically, he told us that wine ought not to be filtered, but ought to be drunk straight from the wine-jar'

—and so the discussion goes on.

The rule of etiquette which Plutarch is illustrating is precisely the one enunciated by Oliver Wendell Holmes in *The Autocrat of the Breakfast Table:*[1]

> All generous minds have a horror of what are commonly called 'facts'. They are the brute beasts of the intellectual domain. Who does not know fellows that always have an ill-conditioned fact or two which they lead after them into decent company like so many bull-dogs, ready to let them slip at every ingenious suggestion, or convenient generalization, or pleasant fancy? I allow no 'facts' at this table. What! Because bread is good and wholesome, and necessary and nourishing, shall you thrust a crumb into my windpipe while I am talking? Do not these muscles of mine represent a hundred

loaves of bread? and is not my thought the abstract of ten thousand of these crumbs of truth with which you would choke off my speech?

Perhaps it is this capacity of philosophers to be pedantic and annoying at dinner that led to the Epicurean ban on serious discussions at mealtimes.

> On the one hand [writes Plutarch, *non posse suaviter vivi secundum Epicurum* 1095c], Epicurus says in the *Disputed Questions* that the sage is a lover of spectacles and yields to none in the enjoyment of theatrical recitals and shows; but on the other he allows no place, even over the wine, for questions about music and the enquiries of critics and scholars and actually advises a cultivated monarch to put up with recitals of stratagems and with vulgar buffooneries at his drinking parties sooner than with the discussion of problems in music and poetry.[2]

Epicurus is also supposed to have devoted a good part of his *Symposium* to a discussion about the proper time for sexual intercourse: the speakers in a passage of Plutarch's *Quaestiones Conviviales* (3.653c) argue that 'for an older man to talk about sex in the presence of youths at a dinner-party and weigh the pros and cons of whether one should make love before dinner or after dinner was ... the height of indecency'.

From all this there emerges some kind of received view as to the appropriate topics for discussion at dinner. Philosophy, antiquarian topics, perhaps even the benefits of agriculture; but not sex and not food or wine. The former are the topics to which Plutarch's dinner-table conversations limit themselves (with some limited discussion of wine) in his adherence to antiquarian and grammatical topics (an exception is a short paragraph on Romulus' views on sobriety at 11.14). Unfortunately we are deprived of many of the *Symposia* of contemporary philosophers, except that we do learn something about the discussions of the Epicureans. Epicurus, in fact, emerges very often as the villain of the piece, the opposite of everything that a philosopher ought to be.

If we turn to the pages of Athenaeus himself, we find that, despite the almost exclusive concentration of his book on food, the Epicureans are still treated as objects of scorn precisely for their interest in luxury and the pleasures of the table and the flesh. The one thing that everybody knows and knew about the Epicureans is that they enjoyed food: Epicurus is quoted *(Deipno.* 12.67, 546d–f) as saying 'The origin and root of all good is the pleasure of the stomach; and all excessive efforts of wisdom (τὰ σοφὰ καὶ τὰ περιττά) have reference to the stomach'.[3] (In actuality Epicurus was as austere as the next philosopher, ready always to praise the pleasures of bread and water;[4] but he did say 'even frugality has a limit'.[5]) At *Deipno.* 7.278d–f Chrysippus is quoted as calling Archestratus (the gastronomic writer) 'the teacher of Epicurus and of all those who follow his rules, in everything which belongs to pleasure, which is the ruin of everything'. Yet these references to Epicurus, and to the other sects which favoured pleasure, such as the Cyrenaics (12.544a–f and 13.564e; 7.279a–f), the followers of Mnesistratus, and even Speusippus (7.279e-f) are always couched in a tone of opprobrium. In fact Athenaeus' speakers frequently speak with disfavour of luxurious behaviour, irrespective of any connection with Epicurus. At 8.345b–c a story is told of an epicure who died of over-indulgence. At 4.148d–f the gluttony of the Thebans is explicitly denounced, in a story about one Attaginus who gave an enormous feast to Mardonious and fifty other Persians: 'I think they would never have escaped, and that there would have been no necessity for the Greeks being marshalled against them at Plataea, as they would certainly have been killed by such food as that.'

One of the most striking things about Athenaeus' book is the amount of space devoted to discussion of philosophers and their ideas. Geoffrey Arnott has remarked[6] that most named persons in Athenaeus are *parasitoi or hetaerae:* I would suggest, rather, that a great many of them are also philosophers. (Sometimes, as we shall see, there may be little difference between a parasite and a philosopher.) There are many discussions of philosophical attitudes, and of the views of individual philosophers and schools on particular points, usually but not always related to food. And yet it is very striking that the main participants in Athenaeus' dinner are *not* philosophers—with the one exception of the Cynic Cynulcus. It is a commonplace to observe that Cynulcus is introduced as a kind of foil to the other participants. One of his early interventions into the discussion at 4.156a is to close a long disquisition on the banquets of the ancients by a simple statement that he is hungry and would like to get on with the eating. He goes on to describe a Cynic banquet, which was delayed in its beginning while the six guests had an argument about the best kinds of water. When this was over, the lentils were served. Cynulcus quotes Theopompus (4. 157d–e): 'for to eat much, and to eat meat, takes away the reasoning powers, and makes the intellect slower, and fills a man with anger, and harshness, and all sorts of folly'; then he mentions Xenophon's praise of austerity, and Socrates' habit of walking up and down to make himself sufficiently hungry to enjoy the simple meal (presumably of bread) that he was about to have.

Cynulcus' intervention in the discussion is not greeted very politely. The character Plutarch bursts into a fit of mocking laughter. Shortly afterwards the host, Larensis, caps Cynulcus' learning about lentils with some rather pointless anecdotes including an obscure proverb 'Perfume thrown on lentils', attributed to the Roman writer Varro, whom he describes as his forefather (4.160c–d). Then the

diner Magnus takes up the discussion with a long attack on Cynulcus, suggesting
that if he wishes to go in for austerity he might as well go to the extremes
represented by Pythagoras and his followers. He accuses Cynulcus of greed
(4.161d) and of boorishness, as a 'Cynic who never sacrificed to the Graces, nor
even to the Muses' (4.163a). His attack culminates at 4.164a in this outburst:

> If you in reality, O philosophers, do admire contentment and moderation in
> your feasts, why is it that you have come here without being invited? Did
> you come as to a house of intemperance, in order to learn to make a
> catalogue of a cook's instruments?... according to the *Cedalion* of Sophocles[7]
> ... you philosophers always have your minds set upon banquets; and you
> think it constantly necessary to ask for something to eat or to devour some
> Cynic food.

One begins to wonder why Cynulcus does not simply get up and leave this dinner
where he is to be the subject of such abuse; however, he delivers an attack on
Magnus as being quite as much of a parasite as himself; and Ulpian then changes
the subject.

It comes as no surprise, however, when a book later (at 5.211a) Masurius[8]
launches into an attack on philosophers in general (not just Cynics this time; cf.
Chapter 40). The attack begins with a story about the Epicurean philosopher
Diogenes of Babylon being humiliated by Alexander Balas the king of Syria
(161–146 BC). Masurius goes on to tell stories of some philosophers who made
themselves tyrants in their cities: the first is Athenion of Athens, who, among his
other vices, as a Peripatetic had formed a mistaken idea of the amount of food the
human frame requires, and did not even feed his people adequately (5.214e-f).
The story is taken from Posidonius, which indicates that Masurius is supposed to
have devoted some time to reading the works of a Stoic philosopher, if only to
attack philosophy itself. He also has a briefer story about one Lysias of Tarsus, an
Epicurean philosopher who likewise made himself a tyrant. Also attacked are
Pythagoras (213e-f), Antisthenes (216b) and Plato: he describes the latter's
*Symposium* as 'nonsense' (217a–d ), and likewise the *Symposium* of Epicurus. 'In
every respect the philosophers tell lies' (216c). 'Most philosophers are of such a
disposition that they are more inclined to evil speaking than the Comic writers'
(220a).

At the end of this tirade Ulpian once again turns the subject, and from
there on the discussion settles into topics specifically related to eating, drinking
and the serving of food. I think it would not be an exaggeration to see these first
five books as intended, at least in part, to deflect the criticism that food is an
unworthy subject for discussion at a dinner, by ridiculing or abusing the

philosophers who, as a class, were regarded as being most opposed to the paying of undue attention to such bodily matters.

The context is a very Roman one. Aulus Gellius is another author who is impatient with philosophy: as Holford-Strevens writes,[9]

> 'Again and again Gellius dismisses all philosophy not directed to improving human life as a waste of time, at best to be dabbled in, not dwelt on, and inveighs against philosophers whose beards and cloaks and moral saws are belied by their behaviour, or who use philosophy as a pretext for their vanity and vices.'

This description of Gellius' attitude might have been written about Masurius! Gellius finds sufficient wisdom and guidance in Cato and Aesop; and alongside his suspicion of philosophy he also purveys the traditional attitude of admiration for frugality and contempt for ostentation which characterized Cato. There may seem to be some inconsistency here, in both condemning philosophers and inveighing against luxury, which is something that philosophers also do. However, for philosophers luxury is bad only for your soul, whereas the vice of luxury was regularly regarded by Roman writers as a cause of moral and even political decline. We may think equally of Sallust or of Seneca.[10] Practice did not always match theory. Holford-Strevens points out that rich Romans of the Antonine period were not about to curtail the pleasures of their table; but they enjoyed listening to the reading of the praises of frugality 'as they munched their thrushes and their truffles' (188–9). Miriam Griffin puts it more kindly (311): 'In his insistence on frugality, Seneca puts into philosophical form the attraction asceticism had for the high-living'. Athenaeus' diners seem to be men of this stamp rather than of the Greek philosophical schools; the praises they utter of frugality, and their attacks on luxury, serve as a distraction from their attention to the details of luxury they discuss at length; and any awareness they feel of their own bad faith is deflected by attacks on the philosophers for their hypocrisy in eating at all.

The whole of the twelfth book of the *Deipnosophistae* is a discourse, in the author's own person, to his addressee Timocrates, on luxury and those who have been notorious for it in history. It begins with what looks as if it may become a philosophic defence of pleasure, for it suggests that Timocrates is an adherent of the Cyreneic school, and cites such admirable authors as Sophocles for their enjoyment of pleasures. By 546e Athenaeus is quoting the main points of Epicurus' defence of pleasure. But then , at 547a, he goes on

> 'Well then did the Romans, who are in every respect the most admirable of men, banish Alcius and Philiscus the Epicureans out of their city, when

Lucius Postumius was consul, on account of the pleasures which they sought to introduce into the city.'

And at 551a Athenaeus says 'How much better, then, is it, my good friend Timocrates, to be poor and thinner than even those men whom Hermippus mentions in his *Cercopes,* than to be enormously rich'—and goes on to list a number of famous thin people. The conclusion at this point seems to be that the Romans are right in their disapproval of luxury, as well as their dismissal of philosophers.

In Book Thirteen, however, a discourse by Myrtilus (587f-588f), which is part of a long discussion on courtesans, seems to present a favourable view of Epicurus, calling him a 'devoted lover of truth', and quoting him as praising a young man who has come over to the study of philosophy 'unimbued with any system'. He goes on (588c) to discuss the liaisons of Aristippus, the noted hedonistic philosopher, and Diogenes the Cynic, with Lais the courtesan.[11] At 607a all philosophers are described as more amorous than elephants, but at 610f we are back with the story about the Romans banishing the philosophers as corrupters of the young. This time the philosophers are characterized as Cynics:

> While the dog is a also a snarling and greedy animal, and also hard in his way of living, and naked; these habits of his you practise, being abusive and gluttonous, and besides all this, living without home or hearth. The result of all which circumstances is that you are destitute of virtue, and quite unserviceable for any useful purpose in life. For there is nothing less philosophical than those persons who are called philosophers.

At this point I want to digress a little to consider the various discussions of the luxury of Alexander the Great in Athenaeus. The discussion will serve to deepen the presentation of the Cynic approach to luxury. Alexander is treated by many Roman writers as exhibiting two vices characteristic of the tyrant: the first is pride and vanity, τῦφος, and the second is luxury and self-indulgence, including lust. Lucan, for example, treats Alexander as the quintessential tyrant, puffed up with luxury and vanity.[12] Rufus Fears[13] shows that this line on Alexander is predominantly followed by Roman Stoic writers, not by Greek ones. Its roots, however, are in Cynic responses to Alexander. The favourable presentation of Alexander by his historian, Onesicritus,[14] a Cynic, is not typical of his school and was regarded by W.W. Tarn[15] as perverse if not actually hypocritical (perhaps he was one of those parasite philosophers!). Other Cynics, such as Teles and Crates,[16] attacked Alexander for his desire for deification, and one of the pseudonymous *Letters of Diogenes* (no. 24) described him as having been 'conquered by

Hephaestion's thighs'. Dicaearchus and Theophrastus also attacked Alexander's lust.[17]

The defining moment of the traditional Cynic view is the story of the encounter of Alexander with Diogenes, when Alexander offered the philosopher a gift, and Diogenes asked him to stop blocking the sunshine.[18] Seneca was thinking of this story when he wrote 'far more powerful, far richer was he than Alexander, who then was master of the whole world; for what Diogenes refused to receive was even more than Alexander was able to give' (*de ben* 5.4). The contrast is often developed in ways that are in part favourable to Alexander, especially in the writers of the later imperial period such as Dio Chrysostom (Or. 4) who used Alexander as a representative of the Cynic–Stoic idea of the philosopher as the true king. (The idea is mocked, by implication, in Masurius' diatribe about philosophers who made themselves tyrants.)

The view of Alexander as a tyrant became less dominant from the reign of Trajan, though it had been the keynote under the early Empire and especially in the time of the 'philosophic opposition' to Nero. It stems ultimately from the fate of the philosopher Callisthenes who objected to Alexander's adoption of Persian ways and Persian luxury: he fell from favour, was implicated in the Conspiracy of the Pages, and ended his days in a filthy cage, dying of some nameless disease. Tarn[19] argued that there was a philosophic opposition to Alexander of specifically Peripatetic character, because Callisthenes was a nephew of Aristotle and therefore Aristotle's followers supported his cause. Tarn's view was demolished by Badian,[20] and it is better to term the attitude more simply 'philosophical'—there is a continuum of generic philosophical attitudes to Alexander across Stoics, Cynics, Peripatetics and even Platonists (though Plutarch, who admired Alexander, is a big exception).

Not all writers saw the main cause of Callisthenes' disgust with the king as philosophical. According to Plutarch *(Qu. Conv.* 1.6, 623d–e):

> Callisthenes incurred the enmity of Alexander because, so the story goes, he could not endure to dine with the king on account of the strong drink. Indeed, even the great loving-cup of Alexander's, when once it was passed to him, he thrust aside with the remark that he did not wish to drink from Alexander's cup and so stand in need of Asclepius'.' (623f–624a).

This view is in contrast to the account, in Arrian (*Anab.* 4.12.3–5) and elsewhere, that has Callisthenes refuse the act of *proskynesis*—as a sign of Persian obeisance— rather than the cup.[21] This sympotic interpretation of Callisthenes' behaviour may or may not be true, but it chimes at least with the personal dynamics of Alexander's court. Callisthenes' great rival at the court, Anaxarchus, is described by Athenaeus (12.548b) as a eudaemonist; and Eugene Borza in his elegant discussion of this man's career[22] has shown how his acquiescence in Alexander's self-indulgence set him at odds with the austere Callisthenes.

Athenaeus' discussion of Alexander treats him as an exemplar of luxury in general (12. 537d–540a)—gold bedsteads and so on—and the anecdotes in 10. 434a–437b treat him as an example of drunkenness rather than anything of more philosophical or political import.[23] The treatment of this figure, who occupied such an important place in philosophical and rhetorical discussions of the nature of kingship, and indeed of virtue and vice in general, indicates that Athenaeus is keeping his discussion very firmly at the level of sympotic anecdotes. He does not wish to engage in wider philosophical discourse; he seems, like the Epicureans, to regard such serious discussion as inappropriate to the dinner-party context.

It is difficult to see the anecdotes about Alexander's luxury as either approving or disapproving: they have simply become exemplars, brought forth in the rhetorical manner, but without any obvious rhetorical purpose besides cumulation. In this respect they are unlike the anecdotes deployed by Valerius Maximus, for example, which invariably show the protagonist in an action of moral significance, one which involves the king's relations with other people. Athenaeus draws no moral conclusions. Even Aulus Gellius[24] claims that his anecdotes about Alexander are examples of good parenthood, or wit, or brevity, or something— though one suspects the stated point is simply the excuse for telling the story. What Athenaeus has to say about Alexander emphasizes his lack of interest in philosophical debate on one of the most morally debated figures of antiquity. Like Gellius, he is assembling antiquarian data rather than anything more profound.

But is there not a sense in which an interest in food defines you as in some sense a philosopher anyway? After all, the book is called *Deipnosophistae*, and the -sophist part of that must be meant to mean something. Ancient writers were aware that eating habits were an important part of your definition as an insider or an outsider to a particular group.[25] The Pythagoreans, for example, were united by particular food taboos—though the sources differ in part as to what they were: for example, did they abstain only from beans, and if so on what grounds; or were beans Pythagoras' favourite food?[26] or were they vegetarians; or did some Pythagoreans even eat meat, like Milo of Croton, the athlete? Closer to Athenaeus' own period, Bardaisan of Edessa in his *Book of the Laws of Countries* expressed his awareness of the relativeness of national customs largely in terms of diet (though marriage customs were also critical).[27] Jews were often seen as philosophers simply because of their dietary and purity rules.[28] The splinter group of the Essenes was defined not least by their participation in a communal meal.[29] Philo's presentation of Jewish habits is made in terms of praise of philosophical austerity rather than of food taboos or the demands of the Lord.[30] Diet could even be regarded as an important part of philosophy: the Brahmans whom Alexander encounters, in the rather numerous works written in antiquity about this encounter,[31] define their virtue not least by their abstinence from any meat or anything cooked; they live simply on fruit.

Athenaeus' diners do evince an awareness that the ingestion of food is not value-free. You are what you eat; that is, you define yourself as a certain kind of person by whether you eat or not, by whether you talk about it or not, and by what you eat. The Philosophers *at* Dinner are also the Philosophers *of* Dinner.

Furthermore, rejection of prevailing eating practices, such as Diogenes' attempt to prove a point about the natural life by eating a raw octopus (it was the last thing he did, for it killed him)[32] is tantamount, at least in Greek circles, to a rejection of the *polis* and its social dimension.[33] It is the function of the Cynic in this gathering to make the other participants think, and show that they are thinking, about the process of eating and talking about food. Cynics were often regarded as a kind of leaven in the body politic: Epictetus at one point calls Cynics Messengers of God,[34] and also stated that the Cynic would be unnecessary in a city of wise men (σοφοί (*Disc.* 3.22.67)): his purpose was precisely to catalyse unspoken assumptions and force reflection on them. To that extent the Cynic was living a natural life, one that questioned the life ruled by *nomos*, convention.[35]

There is nothing frivolous about Athenaeus' claims for his book, and for the pursuits of the diners whom Cynulcus constantly undermines. 'These things', he writes in his final sentence, 'my good Timocrates, are not, as Plato says, the sportive conversations of Socrates in his youth and beauty, but the serious discussions of the Deipnosophists.' Athenaeus has, to his own satisfaction, defined and produced a new kind of philosophy—a kind which his Roman contemporaries could enjoy. It would massage their prejudices about luxury and about the uselessness of philosophers as well as their fondness for historical examples and their intense, but not, of course, Epicurean, interest in food.

# 31

# STRATONICUS, THE WITTY HARPIST

by Dwora Gilula

*For Shalom Perlman*

Athenaeus is our main source for almost all that is known about the harpist Stratonicus, whose claims to fame are innovations in music and a sharp tongue ... A large collection of witticisms attributed to Stratonicus and some testimonia (8.347d–352d), collected from several sources, are inserted into a lengthy discussion on fish and delivered by Cynulcus as part of his contribution to the conversation (8.347d–8.354d).[1] His speech sheds some light on the frame of the work and on the strategies of its composition. It is not that Athenaeus' work lacks structure, just that the structure is not always easily detected.[2]

The subject of fish is introduced into the discussion as early as 3.104c. In 8.331c Cynulcus is already tired of it and is about to interfere and steer the discussion to another topic when Democritus, guessing his mood, usurps his turn (αὐτὸν προφθάσας ἔφη) and plunges into a profusion of fish. His long discourse finally ends with a question directed at Ulpian (8.331c–347c). This time it is Cynulcus who, by shouting, appropriates the right to speak. Instead of allowing Ulpian to answer he makes fun of his tendency to carry constant inquiries into minutiae (8.347d). This tendency is set out in the frame of the dialogue as a characterization of Ulpian: his investigations, albeit of intricate problems, are of details, of the spines or backbones of small fish, while he passes over the big fish (1.1d–e; 6.228e). The metaphor serves as an immediate link with the Stratonicus collection, for Stratonicus' first quoted saying is a riddle with which Cynulcus challenges Ulpian (8.347f). It fits the sympotic frame very well, since riddles were a regular form of amusement at symposia. The riddle speaks of big fish (οὐδεὶς κακὸς μέγας ἰχθύς); how then, asks Cynulcus, can Ulpian understand and explain anything that has to do with big fish when he concerns himself only with the small ones?

Cynulcus offers three solutions to the riddle, the third one from Aristotle's *Constitution of Naxos*; then the grounds for the insertion of further material of Stratonicus are overtly stated: 'But I do not think it untimely, now that I have mentioned the harp-player Stratonicus, to add something myself to what has been said about his cleverness in repartee' (8.348d).[3] After the Stratonicus detour Cynulcus again discusses Aristotle, thus framing the Stratonicus collection.

Another aspect which highlights Athenaeus' strategies of structuring materials is the anticipation of the Stratonicus collection by three shorter collections of jokes and anecdotes also woven into the discussion on fish (those of Philoxenus of Cythera (8.341a–e), Dorion (8.337b–338b) and Lasus of Hermione (8.338b–d)).

The collection of Stratonicus' sayings, and of the testimonia appended to it, is drawn from several sources: Clearchus, Theophrastus, Aristotle, Machon, Hegesander, Charicles, Capito, Callisthenes, Ephorus and Phainias. As might be expected, they are not arranged chronologically nor according to genre, and should be disentangled, for chronological sequence reveals, with some certainty, the time of Stratonicus' activity and how his image, or his persona, has developed.

## 1. Testimonia

The earliest of the three testimonia at the end of the collection, pertaining to Stratonicus' life and activities, is by the historian Ephorus (*c.*405–330 BC), the second by Phainias and the third anonymous. However, the earliest source mentioning Stratonicus, the Middle Comedy poet Philetaerus, is not cited by Athenaeus. In a fragment of his comedy *Oinopion* (14 K A) Philetaerus, son of Aristophanes, active in the first quarter of the fourth century BC,[4] refers to Stratonicus as a successful teacher with many students. Ephorus, in his book *On Inventions*, among other firsts, apparently attributed to Simonides of Ceos the invention of sharp aphorisms and mentioned Stratonicus and Philoxenus of Cythera as his followers and emulators (*FGrH* 70.2 = *Deipn.* 8.352c). On the basis of this passage it is assumed that there was in existence a collection of Simonides' sayings, as well as those of Stratonicus and Philoxenus, which Ephorus saw. Hence, in the time of Ephorus' activity—the second third of the fourth century BC—Stratonicus was already known as a brilliant wit worthy of comparison with Simonides and considered his follower.[5]

In the second volume of his book *On Poets*, the Peripatetic Phainias from Eresos in Lesbos, a contemporary of Theophrastus, confirms the evidence of Philetaerus and Ephorus that Stratonicus was a music teacher and a wit, and also adds some new information. Only from Phainias do we learn that Stratonicus was an Athenian, and that he was an innovator in music, especially instrumental music, in particular unaccompanied cithara-playing (8.352c).[6]

Immediately following the quotation from Phainias, Athenaeus brings the collection to its end with anonymous testimony pertaining to Stratonicus' death, according to which he was executed by Nicocles, the king of Cyprus, because of his disregard for the conventions of polite behaviour or because of outspoken jesting (παρρησία): 'he was compelled to drink poison for poking fun at the king's sons' (8.352d). This Nicocles became king of Salamis in Cyprus in 373/2 BC and was assassinated some time before 354/3 BC.[7] If there is any truth in the story, for such anecdotes are also told about others, especially about philosophers who practised *parrhesia* (cf. Chapter 40), Stratonicus' death must have preceded that of Nicocles while his activities belong to the first half of the fourth century.[8]

## 2. Witticisms

The most ancient witticisms quoted by Athenaeus are from a collection of sayings and anecdotes attributed by a scholiast to the historian Callisthenes of Olynthus (*FGrH* 124 F 5 = *Deipn.* 8.350d–352c).[9] What characterizes the collection is the large number of names of places (fourteen) and people (ten) mentioned in it. Stratonicus travels, meets different people and talks with them. He converses with the father of the piper Chrysogonus, with the shoemaker Mynnacus, the harper Zethus, the piper Telephanes, the innovative dithyrambic poet Polyidus, the harpist Areius; he mentions the piper Phaon, the sophist Satyrus, the tragedian Carcinus the younger, and the dithyrambic poet Timotheus, the principal representative of the younger school of dithyrambic poets. Five of them—Mynnacus, Zethus, Areius, Phaon and Satyrus—apparently well known in their time are unknown today, a fact which points to the early date of the sayings in which they are mentioned. The others—Chrysogonus, Telephanes, Polyidus, Carcinus and Timotheus—were active at the end of the fifth century and the beginning of fourth and have to do in one way or another with music.[10] The shoemaker Mynnacus discussed music with Stratonicus, and the sophist Satyrus took part in a festival at Troy in which there were obviously contests of rhetors, and perhaps also musical contests. Two other anecdotes in which names of persons are not mentioned deal with music or with music instruction. Anecdotes and sayings on other subjects—medicine, lazy slaves, a tanner—are perhaps earlier and were associated with Stratonicus before his persona, his typical image, was formed.

Stratonicus is presented as a professional musician who travels from place to place and makes a living from his profession:

> When somebody asked him why he roamed all over Greece, instead of stay-
> ing continuously in one city, he answered that he had received all Greeks as

toll from the Muses, and he exacted pay from them for their ignorance. (8.350e)

His travels are an essential part of his persona. He is said to have visited Teichiusa near Miletus, Heracleia (apparently Pontica), the Crimean Bosporus, Maroneia on the Thracian coast, Cardia in the Thracian Chersonesus, Sicyon, Phaselis in Pamphylia and Pella in Macedonia. Other sayings that do not overtly mention that Stratonicus visited the places named in them nevertheless create the impression that what Stratonicus said—witty, playful or biting—was said on the basis of personal knowledge, such as for example the climate in Aenus on the Thracian coast 'freezing for eight months of the year and winter during the other four', or his remarks on the behaviour and character of the people of Rhodes, Byzantium, Leucas and Ambracia. It is the experience of a traveller that we find in the anecdotes about peculiar locations of buildings in a town, undrinkable water, multiplicity of wine shops or of whore-houses, and observations on the smallness of a town which can hardly be called a town, or another one that is unable to fill its stocks with criminals. Three anecdotes pertain to public bath-houses, an institution much needed by a traveller. If Stratonicus actually visited all the places mentioned above, his travels by land and sea took him to the west coast of Greece, to Macedonia, Thrace, the Black Sea, Asia Minor and Rhodes, in addition to the Greek mainland. Be that as it may, Stratonicus acquired a reputation as one who travelled to the north and east of the Greek world, encountered other people and had a taste of their culture and customs.

The following anecdote combines several traits of Stratonicus' persona: a traveller to exotic places, in need of their facilities, knowledgeable on their laws and customs and a wit able to articulate his sense of superiority over the 'natives':

> In Phaselis, the bath-tender got into quarrel with Stratonicus' slave over the fee, it being the custom to charge foreigners a higher price for a bath. He [Stratonicus] said, 'You foul slave, you have nearly made me into a Phaselite by the turn of a paltry farthing.' (8.351f-352a)

Another example of this type is the often-cited anecdote telling of Stratonicus' visit to Teichiusa, a town where a mixed population lived:

> When he observed that all the tombs belonged to foreigners he said: 'Let's get out of here, slave. For it appears that foreigners in this place die, but not a single citizen.' (8.351a–b)

The humour of the sayings consists mostly of puns: πόλις–μόλις; Ambrakia– Membrakia (the exact meaning not clear); κακόδαιμον–νακόδαιμον; double meanings: to carry—to bear; Carcinus—a name of an animal and of a person; *nomos*—a law and a type of a musical composition; Harmonia—harmony and also the wife of Cadmus; 'to be held' (which also has a sexual connotation); or quotations, proverbs and idioms, used unconventionally, playfully changed or twisted and adapted to new circumstances. Witticisms not based on language are less prominent and gain their pungency from satirical references to specifics of towns and places, such as the anecdotes quoted above: only foreigners die in Teichiusa; the climate in Aenus; or: public baths too close to a temple; undrinkable water in Pella.

Sayings which are not accompanied by descriptions of situations, all of them pertaining to travel, are probably the most ancient part of the collection. Descriptions of situations, narrative frames or other explanations in which the sayings are embedded, seem to be a later addition, perhaps built around the witticism by the collector .

Athenaeus quotes three sources on the enigmatic, nonsensical riddle mentioned above, οὐδεὶς κακὸς μέγας ἰχθύς (*a poor nobody makes a large fish*, 8.347f, tr. Gulick) and its versions. The earliest is a passage from Aristotle's *The Constitution of Naxos* (fr. 510R = *Deipn.* 8.348a–c), unfortunately cut off by a lacuna before the saying, at the end of its prolonged explanation, is quoted. Theophrastus, in his book *On the Ridiculous*, attributes the saying to Stratonicus. According to him it is a distortion of the proverb μέγας οὐδεὶς σαπρὸς ἰχθύς (*a poor nobody makes a rotten fish*, 130W = 8.348a) directed by Stratonicus at the third-rate tragic actor Simycas called 'the roarer', active in the sixties of the fourth century BC,[11] whereas Clearchus of Soli, a pupil of Aristotle, who quotes the version οὐδεὶς κακὸς μέγας ἰχθύς in his book *On Proverbs* (8.347f), considers Stratonicus its author. He relates that Stratonicus directed it at the harpist-singer Propis of Rhodes, otherwise unknown, with the intention of criticizing the low quality of his voice. Clearchus offers an explanation, a sort of solution to the riddle: Propis 'was first of all a nobody, then poor, and moreover, though large, he was a fish in his lack of voice'.

Athenaeus quotes another anecdote of Clearchus from the second volume of his book *On Friendship* which illustrates the unusual hours Stratonicus kept and his excessive drinking:

> The harp-player Stratonicus, whenever he started for bed, would tell his slaves to bring him a drink, 'Not so much because I am thirsty,' he said, 'as because I don't want to be thirsty.' (8.349f)[12]

Athenaeus took a series of nine anecdotes (8.348e-349f) from the *Chreiae* of Machon, a book of anecdotes written in iambic trimeter (8.348e-349f).[13] Machon, a New Comedy poet (fl. 260–250 BC), based his work on literary sources which he worked over and adapted to his artistic purposes, literary and prosodic. The source for at least two anecdotes of Machon is, so it seems, the collection of Callisthenes. But the other anecdotes are also clearly an adaptation of earlier literary sources.

A comparison of Callisthenes' anecdotes with the elaboration of Machon shows that Machon uses Callisthenes as a point of departure for a new and different work. From the anecdote on Pella (8.352a) he borrows the basic notion that the water in the town is undrinkable and develops it into an entirely different story. Callisthenes describes a meeting near a well between Stratonicus and the town inhabitants. Machon transfers the encounter to a bath-house. The description preceding Stratonicus' witticism is long and detailed, as are his words. Stratonicus saw that the young men in the bath-house were healthy with well-formed bodies, yet the door-keeper had an enlarged spleen. He remarked that it seemed to him that people deposit their spleen with the door-keeper before entering the bath-house so as not to be crowded inside (8.348e-f). Machon took much greater liberty with the following anecdote of Callisthenes: 'He said that he was particularly surprised at the mother of the sophist Satyrus because she had carried for ten months one whom no city could bear for ten days' (8.350f). Machon puts the saying—changing the version—into the mouth of an old woman from Corinth and applies them to Stratonicus himself. He fashions a small dramatic situation: the woman stares at Stratonicus for some time in the way one stares at a marvel and when he demands an explanation she answers 'I wondered that your mother could carry you for ten months and hold you in within her womb, when our city smarts with the pain of keeping you a single day' (10. 449d–e). By contrast with all the other anecdotes, Stratonicus is the butt of the witticism and not the one who voices it.

The story about Stratonicus' death also exhibits the liberty with which Machon treats his sources. He preserves the core of the story as cited by Phainias (see above): Stratonicus met his death in Cyprus by a king's order because of *parrhesia*. All the other elements are changed: he makes fun of the king's wife, not of his sons, he does not drink hemlock but is drowned in the sea, and the name of the king is not Nicocles but Nicocreon (8.349e).

All in all the image of Stratonicus that emerges from the *Chreiae* of Machon is not much different from that of the earlier sources: a well-known and witty harpist who travels from place to place voicing his biting opinions. Machon brings Stratonicus to Pella, Abdera, Pontus, Corinth, Cyprus and Ephesus, concluding each anecdote with a witticism supposedly delivered on the described occasion. The majority of the sayings are known quotes, proverbs or idioms, including a quotation from Homer, humorously adapted to present circumstances. In addition to the king of Cyprus and his wife, Paerisades and a musician Cleon are also named.

Three anecdotes quoted by Athenaeus from a collection of Hegesander of Delphi (second century BC), have the form 'when asked by somebody... he answered'[14] characteristic of *chreiae*:

> When he was asked by someone who were the most god-forsaken people, he said that of the Pamphylians, the Phaselites were the most so, but of the inhabited world, the people of Side were the most god-forsaken. (8.350a)

> When he was asked whether the Boeotians were perhaps more uncivilized than the Thessalians he replied, 'the Eleans'. (8.350b)

This form creates a narrative structure for the witty saying. The name of the person who asks the question and the place where the conversation is held are immaterial and therefore not mentioned, thus focusing attention on the answer and the answerer. Both anecdotes assume that the person asked for his opinion is able to answer the question from personal experience, a primary source of evidence. Stratonicus, who is a traveller whom earlier anecdotes brought to Phaselis in Pamphylia (8.351f-352e), perhaps also visited Side, an Aeolian colony not far away from Phaselis, whose inhabitants had forgotten the Greek language and spoke in a barbaric patois. The second anecdote quoted from Hegesander has the same form, but now Greeks who acquired a reputation for being uncivilized are its butt. The humour is based on the comic surprise of passing over the Thessalians and the Boeotians and choosing the Eleans.

This form of the *chreia* easily permits elaboration, changes, additions and deductions, chiefly changing the person to whom the saying is attributed, the places and the circumstances, and sometimes even giving an identity to the person who asks the question, granting that the attribution of the aphorism to the person asked is plausible and in harmony with his image. Thus a person who travels a lot must be an expert on types of ships:

> Asked by someone which boats were safer, the fast galleys or the round-bottomed merchantmen, he answered, 'those which are safely moored'. (8.350b)

This witticism suits Stratonicus very well; it is, however, also attributed to another character with the reputation of a traveller, Anacharsis.[15]

The aforementioned anecdotes, which bear a clear formal and literary similarity, share the common structure of a question of either-or, to which the witty saying is an answer which completely ignores the alternatives offered in the question and surprisingly comes up with a third possibility which is immediately perceived as an apt and appropriate choice. Surprise and the recognition that the answer is right are the anecdote's comic elements.

Among these anecdotes is one of a different type which disturbs the sequence:

> And once he set up a trophy in his school-room with the inscription, 'In protest against all bad harpists'. (8.350b)

This anecdote is a variation of an anecdote from Callisthenes' collection, according to which Stratonicus participated in a musical contest in Sicyon, apparently in honour of Asclepius (whose temple there is described by Pausanias (2.10.2–3)), and celebrated his victory by dedicating a trophy in the god's temple:

> Victorious over his competitors in Sicyon, he dedicated in the temple of Asclepius a trophy with the inscription: 'Dedicated by Stratonicus from the spoils of bad harp-players. (8.351e–f)[16]

In Hegesander's anecdote, the moving of the trophy from the temple of Asclepius to Stratonicus' school-room strips the anecdote of actual realities of place and situation, and with it the reason for erecting a trophy in a public space. A school-room is not a place where trophies are habitually erected. The trophy according to Stratonicus in public space as a mark of his victory in a musical contest over bad harpists is changed into a private joke, and the dedicatory inscription supposedly inscribed on the trophy (as erected from fees paid by his bad harp students,) is changed accordingly.

The last anecdote from Hegesander's collection, a story about the lack of appreciation of the people of Rhodes, again describes Stratonicus as a travelling professional; it may be added to other stories about uncivilized audiences not able to appreciate fine art:

> Giving a recital in Rhodes and receiving no applause, he left the theatre remarking, 'If you won't give that which costs you nothing, how can I expect to receive any contribution from you?'. (8.350b)

When the anecdotes of Hegesander are compared to the anecdotes in the collection of Callisthenes, what immediately stands out is their literary character and their lack of specificity, the absence of actual circumstances and actual people. Whereas in Callisthenes' anecdotes Stratonicus visits certain places, reacts to actual situations and converses with people identifiable from other sources, in the

Hegesander anecdotes names of places are not mentioned and there is no specific situation. Somebody nameless asks Stratonicus' opinion on people he met in past travels, or on a subject pertaining to them. The anecdotes are not descriptive of countries and people, but are rather ethnic jokes attached to Stratonicus as an apt persona for their utterance.

The following anecdote, quoted from the first volume of Charicles' book *On the City Contest*, is the only surviving fragment of Charicles, a writer whose work and time are otherwise unknown:

> He used to say: 'Let Eleans manage athletic contests, Corinthians musical contests, and Athenians dramatic contests. If, however, any of them makes a mistake, let the Lacedaemonians be flogged for it.' (*FGrH* 367 F 1 = 8.350b–c)

Stratonicus' aim, Charicles explains, was to satirize the flagellations held in Sparta.

Athenaeus cites four stories from a late work by the epic poet Q. Pompeius Capito, the fourth book of his *Notes Addressed to Philopappus* (cos. AD 109). In the first of them Stratonicus meets Ptolemy, king of Egypt:

> When King Ptolemy was discussing with him, rather too contentiously, the art of harp-playing, he said, 'O King, a sceptre is one thing, [a plectrum is another.]' (8.350c)

The anecdote is clearly apocryphal. If Stratonicus was put to death by Nicocles before 354/3 BC, he could not have been still alive and travelling when the first Ptolemy became the king of Egypt in 305.[17]

From the collection of Capito, Athenaeus took also the following two anecdotes. First:

> And having been invited on one occasion to hear a harp-singer, after the recital he quoted: 'And the father granted one part to him, but denied him the other.' When someone asked 'Which part?' he answered: 'He granted him the power to play badly, but denied him the power to sing beautifully.' (8.350d)

Stratonicus is presented here as a connoisseur called upon to express a professional evaluation. The focus is on Stratonicus and his wit; the harpist-singer himself is unimportant and therefore nameless. The form is again that of a *chreia*. The humour is based on the adaptation to new circumstances, in a surprising way, of a passage from Homer (*Il.* 16.250).

The second anecdote attributes to Stratonicus a certain degree of unconventional thinking, its humour again based on punning:

> And once a beam (δοκός) collapsed and killed a bad man. He said: 'Gentlemen, meseems (δοκῶ) there are gods; if not, there are beams (δοκοί).' (8.350d)

Some of the anecdotes that Athenaeus cites are anonymous. The following anecdote, in the form of a *chreia*, is based on the witty use of an idiom:

> Being a teacher of harp-players, he had in his studio nine statues of the Muses, one of Apollo, and just two pupils; and when somebody asked him how many pupils he had, he replied, 'With the assistance of the gods, a round dozen.' (8.348d)

The anecdote is ascribed to Stratonicus because of his reputation as a music teacher. The Muses in his schoolroom are patrons of education, Apollo is there as a patron of cithara-playing. But since Stratonicus was held to be a successful teacher with many pupils (see Philetaerus, fr. 14 K-A above), the situation on which the repartee is based, the small number of students, does not suit his image. It suits much better Diogenes the Cynic to whom it is attributed elsewhere (*Diog. Laert.* 6.2.69)—a fine example of the ease with which a witticism could be transferred from one person to another, and of the tendency of characters to attract to themselves anecdotes and sayings that fit a certain aspect of their established persona, even when it negates other aspects known from other sources.

This tendency is especially apparent in apocryphal anecdotes which are composed on the basis of the image of Stratonicus that became fixed and crystallized with time. Two anecdotes found in Strabo are based on two traits which characterize Stratonicus' persona: travelling in Asia Minor and wittily using verses of poets by adapting them to new situations. In one anecdote Strabo brings Stratonicus to Caunus in Caria (14.2.3), the other to Assus on the south shore of the Troad (13.1.57). In the latter he is made to quote a line of Homer (*Il.* 6.143), in the former a line from an unknown poet is assigned to him. A fine example of the way a character attracts sayings and anecdotes which suit his image is the following anecdote found in Plutarch (*Mor.* 602a):

> Stratonicus asked his host in Seriphus what crime was punished there with banishment; when told that persons guilty of fraud were expelled, he said: 'Then why not commit fraud and escape from confinement?' (trans. De Lacy and Einarson)

The island Seriphus was already a symbol of smallness in earlier times, but at the time of the Roman empire, owing to its small size and the poverty of its inhabitants, it became a place of punishment to which persons were exiled from Rome.

To sum up: What emerges from the anecdotes and the pointed sayings attributed to Stratonicus is not necessarily the historical Stratonicus but his literary image, based on some traits that may have had a historical basis, an image which attracts certain types of stories. This fictitious character is a travelling harpist, no longer a member of any community but living off all, a music expert whose opinion is valued; he is a traveller with a keen eye and a sharp tongue, quick in repartee and daring, a man with a rather 'cynical' cosmopolitan spirit. To this we may add what Stratonicus is not: he is not an ambassador of a polis, does not reveal interest in politics nor is his advice sought by politicians or kings. He is not asked questions about religion or ethics. What he is asked about pertains to his professional expertise, to places he saw in his travels and the local characteristics of people he met. He is not an original, creative poet. The sayings attributed to him are not linguistically striking nor are they mimetic representations of reality. Their humour derives from puns, some of the basic variety, or from idioms or quotes from known poets or writers, adapted to new circumstances. Since the sayings attributed to him contain a large number of idioms, proverbs and literary quotations, it is easy to create apocryphal anecdotes, which relate what he supposedly said in places and situations that are of interest to later narrators, and attribute them to him.

# 32

# ATHENAEUS ON MUSIC

## by Andrew Barker

Most readers of Athenaeus use the *Deipnosophistae* merely as a collection of odds and ends from earlier sources, to be raided piecemeal for whatever scraps they can find to feed their own special scholarly appetites. Perhaps those readers are wise. If we take away the embedded fragments of other people's writings there may seem rather little left to attract our attention. Reflection on the fragments that interest me, however—that is, primarily, the ones connected in some way with music—has convinced me that there is something rather remarkable about them when they are taken as a collection, not merely one by one. That conviction has led me to raise questions about the nature of the author's own interest in the topics which he makes his cultured conversationalists discuss—or at any rate about his interest in the broader subject, music.

Of course any attempt to excavate authorial intentions from a text is going to be both theoretically suspect and bristling with practical difficulties, all the more so when the author has a façade of fictional dialogue to hide behind. We can eliminate reference to the author if we like. Nevertheless some version of that question remains. Music is a large subject, and earlier Greek writers had a great deal to say about it. So why does the *Deipnosophistae* assemble just *these* quotations, snipped from their contexts at just *these* points and grouped together in just *these* combinations? What are the issues on the text's musical agenda?

We might try to answer these questions in either or both of two ways. One would be to assume that the issues on which the bundles of quotations are intended to bear are simply the ones which the persons of the dialogue explicitly use to introduce them. That would be convenient, and the approach can indeed take us some distance. But we shall find, perhaps unsurprisingly, that it runs into serious difficulties, and these are not only of a theoretical sort. There appears to be at best an obtrusively awkward fit between the declared aims of the discussions and the quoted fragments which give them their content. I shall return to this point in due course. Alternatively, we may set the learned diners and their explicitly stated intentions aside, and regard the incorporated babble of quotations as a construction in its own right, as something like a second layer of fictional dialogue superimposed on the first and relatively independent of it; and we may try to abstract from the conjunction of its miscellaneous voices themselves some sense of the ideas which they are jointly called upon to convey, the problems they are summoned to address and the interests for whose sake they have been commandeered. It is important to stress the admittedly obvious point that the second-level dialogue between these ancient voices is as fictional as the first, an original and artificial construct of the *Deipnosophistae* itself. Even in the unlikely event that every passage is accurately quoted and correctly attributed (so that in a certain sense the individual utterances are 'real'), a scenario in which a third-century technical writer is answered by a sixth-century lyric poet and a couple of characters from fourth-century comedy is evidently fictitious to the point of fantasy. It is also in the highest degree improbable that all the quotations in any given group were directed, in their original settings, to the same concerns that bring them together here. Indeed the concerns of the *Deipnosophistae*, whatever they are, may be alien to all of them. If we look, then, beyond the individual quotations and ask what it is that is constructed by their conjunction, we have a line of enquiry that might plausibly be thought capable of leading us towards the agenda of Athenaeus' work itself.

It is in the spirit of this second suggestion, at any rate, that I have attempted to gain some sense of the *Deipnosophistae*'s concern with the subject of music. Yet the first result of this approach is largely negative. There seems to be no recognizable facet of the subject which any of Athenaeus' groups of quotations could plausibly be construed as addressing, let alone illuminating in any significant way. One can produce a rather impressive list of musical topics with which Greek writers regularly concern themselves, and in which this text appears to have no interest at all. Thus, for example:

(1) No conjunction of his quotations is assembled so as to shed light on musical history. He shows no interest in chronology, absolute or relative, and no sense of music's past as development or process, or as a series of identifiable phases.
(2) Though he draws freely on Aristoxenus and mentions Pythagoras in a musical context, he engages with no issues in theoretical or scientific musical analysis, of the sorts with which those names were, in his time, most famously associated.

(3) Despite his many references to individual musicians, sometimes amounting to quite lengthy reports, the passages he collects, from a musical point of view, are uniformly trivial. They tell us almost nothing of these people's musical achievements, what they did, in their role as musicians, to deserve their lasting reputations.

(4) Unlike so many writers of the period, he shows no sign of being interested in philosophical speculations on the aesthetic, ethical, social and psychological dimensions of music. One longish quotation from Heraclides[1] has a tangential bearing on such matters, but it is not set in a context of other contributions to these debates, and the major players in this game (Plato, Aristotle, Stoics and Neopythagoreans) are all conspicuously absent.

(5) Two very substantial passages, in Books Four and Fourteen, are devoted to discussion about instruments. Yet I think it unlikely that readers will come away from them with the conviction that they are noticeably better informed about the character, the structure, the properties or the uses of these instruments than they were when they began. I shall examine one of these passages in more detail at a later stage.

(6) Many poetic references to music get their energy from myth. But though scraps of musical mythology inevitably crop up in Athenaeus from time to time, there is no attempt to shed light on the topic of musical myth as such, or on any of the individual legends. There is nothing here about the patrons and paradigms of music, no Apollo, no Orpheus, no Olympos, no Muses.

(7) Again, despite his copious quotations from early lyric poetry, Athenaeus' arrangement of his material does nothing to exploit, underline or illuminate its most pervasive musical themes, that is, its evocations of music's delightfulness and its mysterious power. Here as elsewhere he differs very markedly from the general run of writers in the imperial period, for whom this was a *topos* that was virtually bound to be developed in the course of any extended disquisition on the subject.

(8) Finally, there is no sustained attempt to assemble quotations which would jointly convey the character or purposes of music in the context of the symposium. Given the overall setting and subject-matter of the work, this is a particularly noteworthy omission. Relevant comments are of course made from time to time as the discussions proceed, but there is no passage of which we can confidently say that this is its primary concern.[2]

The list is so substantial that one may reasonably wonder what themes or issues can possibly be left to provide the motivation behind this text's selection and arrangement of its material.

It seems to me, however, that there is a more positive conclusion to which all this negative evidence persuasively points. Whatever else it is, the musical contents of the *Deipnosophistae* cannot be *just* a miscellaneous jumble, guided by nothing more than the accident of what Athenaeus stumbled on in his reading. If that were all, mere chance would have ensured that at least some of the topics I have mentioned would have surfaced from time to time, since between them they include virtually all the major themes that Greek musical writers traditionally addressed. It seems that the available material has been passed, whether deliberately or subconsciously, through a distinctly curious process of filtration, which has systematically sieved out everything that had ever been of interest to genuine students and connoisseurs of music. It seems an extraordinary procedure; but I can find no other hypothesis that fits the facts.

To proceed beyond (perhaps alarming) generalized discussion, I shall devote the rest of this chapter to a review of one stretch of the text itself, namely 4.174a—185a. This passage is a little unusual, in that Athenaeus has contrived for once to give it at least the semblance of an argumentative structure, at the level of the primary dialogue between the guests themselves; and it is on that first level of dialogue that I shall concentrate most (though not all) of my attention. However, we must also consider whether this overt argumentative form has any real connection with the rationale behind the selection of the material that gives it its content, the material provided by the ghostly voices of the participants in the second dialogic stratum.

The passage begins as the sound of a *hydraulis* (an organ whose air-pressure was hydrostatically regulated) is heard from next door. Everyone present admires it; and the Tyrian Ulpian takes the opportunity to tease his fellow-guest, the Alexandrian *mousikos* Alkeides, about the dismal musical tastes of the Alexandrians. 'Do you hear that fine and beautiful sound, you most musical of men? he asked. '... It's not like the *monaulos* so pervasive among you Alexandrians, which gives its hearers pain rather than any musical delight.' (174b)

Alkeides rises to the bait; and the rest of our passage is cast as his defence of the Alexandrians against this charge of unmusicality, mainly through a review of the very many types of instrument with which (so Alkeides asserts) they are in fact familiar. Despite the length and characteristic ramblings of the discourse, Athenaeus reminds us of this dramatic motive for the monologue often enough along the way, maintaining a coherent conversational thread. But we must suspect from the start that the real thrust of the argument is rather different. The accusation which Alkeides sets out to rebut is transparently trumped up; other sources, (Dio Chrysostom, for example[3]) make it clear that music was in fact the great love of the Alexandrians' life. If this material is put together for any real purpose, it is probably not quite the one that Athenaeus explicitly uses to glue the passage together.

Alkeides' speech can be broken down into six parts. I shall briefly sketch the gist of each of them before tackling the issues they raise.

(1) In the first (174b–f) he picks up Ulpian's reference to the *hydraulis*, and claims it as an Alexandrian invention, quoting sources to support the thesis. As it happens, the claim is perfectly accurate.

(2) Next (174f-175d), he mentions two rather obscure instruments, the *gingras* and the *nablas*. He finds quotations that seem to connect them with the Phoenicians—we must of course remember that Ulpian is a Phoenician , from Tyre—and he compares them unfavourably with the Alexandrian *hydraulis*.

(3) His third move (175e-176e) focuses on the *monaulos*, which according to Ulpian takes up all the air-time in Alexandria. The collection of literary references Alkeides assembles, however, does not make it altogether clear what line of argument he is trying to take about this instrument; he seems to vacillate between at least two which fit together only rather uncomfortably.

(4) The next passage (176e-182e) presents a medley of allusions to different sorts of wind instrument, sixteen of them in all. Here the point is to display the Alexandrians as a highly musical people, on the grounds that they are familiar with wind instruments of all these various kinds.

(5) The fifth section (182e-184a) pursues the same strategy for stringed instruments, again putting together literary references to some fifteen or sixteen supposedly distinct types.

(6) The sixth and final episode (184a–f) serves as a broader and more compendious justification for his championship of the Alexandrians' musicality. It has some genuine interest; but I shall postpone an account of it until we have looked more closely at the earlier parts of the speech.

Now if we summarize Alkeides' discourse in the way I have done, it appears to have a tolerably coherent strategy. The admired *hydraulis* is Alexandrian; the despicable *gingras* and *nablas* are characteristic of the Phoenicians. Here he has quite effectively turned Ulpian's mode of criticism back on its author. Evidence about the *monaulos* is then deployed in a manner which is apparently calculated to take the sting out of Ulpian's opening innuendo; and the musical credentials of the Alexandrians are further underlined by the catalogue of over thirty different varieties of instrument with which they are said to be familiar. Even if we leave the final section out of account, Alkeides seems to have put up quite a persuasive case.

But when we begin to examine the details, the appearance of cogent argument dissolves. To begin with, there is nothing whatever in the passage to show that Alkeides or any other Alexandrian is personally acquainted with instruments of any sort. All he has demonstrated is his ability to quote various authors who mention them; and very few of these authors have any link with Alexandria.

Secondly, despite his barrage of quotations, he establishes almost nothing about any of these instruments—what they are like, how they are used, and so on. We can glean a scrap or two of information about a handful of them, but no more; there is certainly no attempt to build up a dossier confirming the contention that the Alexandrians know all about them, or even that the authors quoted do so. Even in the case of the *hydraulis*, where he at least quotes a description given by the scholar Aristokles at moderate length, the account he has chosen turns out to be largely empty and in so far as it says anything it is wholly misleading. No instrument could possibly work in the way that Aristokles sketches.[4] This is all the odder since Athenaeus also makes him mention, without quoting it, another description of the *hydraulis* by the engineer Ktesibios, who was probably in fact its inventor; and since he is named as a *mechanikos*, his account might have been expected to be technically informative and accurate. But Alkeides mentions the description only on the strength of a reference to Ktesibios in yet another author, Tryphon, and he neither quotes it nor summarizes the information it gives. It appears that Athenaeus has either not taken the trouble to track down Ktesibios' description, perhaps because Aristokles' fantastical account was sufficient for his purposes, or else he has examined it and chosen to suppress it. In either case he shows no sign of interest in the pursuit and transmission of reliable information for its own sake.

Thirdly, there is something almost perverse in the selection of quotations that Alkeides sets out in support of his line of argument. I have already suggested that they do nothing to confirm the familiarity with instruments that he claims; and the strategy seems even less comprehensible in the sections on the *nablas* and *gingras*, and on the *monaulos*.

Let us take the *monaulos* first. 'Since you criticize the Alexandrians for being unmusical', he says to Ulpian, 'and you are constantly mentioning the *monaulos* as endemic among us, listen to what I can tell you about it right now, off the cuff' (175e). What he can tell comes, of course, in the form of quotations. The first is from Juba, the king of Mauretania under Augustus who was also a notable scholar. Alkeides cites Juba's *History of Theatre* for the statement that according to the Egyptians, the *monaulos* is an invention of Osiris. That claim would seem to connect the instrument solidly with Egypt, if not with Alexandria, and it gives it august religious credentials. The instrument has a divine ambience and origin, and we might suppose that Alkeides is planning to work up a defence of its status in Alexandria as a musical instrument; and this would seem a reasonable enough line of argument for him to adopt.

But the next batch of quotations, from Sophocles, Araros, Anaxandrides, Sopatros, Protagorides, Posidonius and others, does not seem to fit into that argumentative pattern at all. One of them, from Protagorides' work on the festivals at Daphne, does speak of someone 'humming the loveliest melodies on the lovely *monaulos*'; and in an epigram of Hedylus a player of the instrument is described as a 'sweet piper', *glukus auletes*; but none of the others say or imply anything at all about its musical qualities. Nor do they link it with Egypt; among its contexts are the legend of Thamyras the Thracian, the birth of the god Pan, some bits of domestic Attic comedy, and an account of a war between Apamea and Larisa. Alkeides draws no conclusion from his sundry collection of references. We might offer him the inference that Ulpian was wrong to twit the Alexandrians in particular for their devotion to the *monaulos*, since it is obviously well known elsewhere and is mentioned in sources going back long before Alexandria was founded. But he makes no such assertion himself; and it would have been perverse to set off on that track with a quotation placing the instrument explicitly in Egypt. The quotations are also uniformly uninformative about what sort of device the *monaulos* was. The snippets from Araros and Anaxandrides, both comic poets of the fourth century, will give the flavour: 'He snatched up the *monaulos* at once and leaped, as lightly as you can imagine'; and: 'He picked up a *monaulos* and played the wedding tune'. There is really not much to be gleaned from remarks of that sort.

The passage on the *gingras* and the *nablas* (174f–175d) is at first sight more promising. These are the instruments which Alkeides wishes to link with the Phoenicians, and to portray as musically useless. He finds several sources to make the Phoenician connection, Xenophon and Democlides, together with a neat bit of historical linguistics involving Corinna and Bacchylides for the *gingras*, Sopatros the parodist for the *nablas*. He also has a pair of fragments which purport to cast doubt on their musical virtues. A character in a comedy by Axionikos says that lovers of Euripides' music are so besotted with it that everything else strikes them as '*gingras* melodies, dreadful stuff'; and Sopatros says of the *nablas* that 'no one ever woke up with a cry of joy at *its* melodious cry of pleasure'. These passages offer precisely the kind of innuendo that Alkeides seems to require. But then, we may reasonably ask, why does he immediately undermine his case by quoting *in extenso* two further passages, again from comedy, which take exactly the opposite position? According to a character in the *Dithyrambos* of Amphis, the *gingras* is an absolutely marvellous novelty, all the rage at Athenian symposia, and is bound to make a stunning impression when it is performed publicly in the theatre; and someone in Philemon's play *The Adulterer* tells a character who has never heard of the *nablas* that in that case he must be ignorant of all the best things: 'Don't you even know what a harp-girl is?', he asks, presumably with a salacious nudge. If we suppose that Athenaeus is trying to give Alkeides a consistent line of argument, we must also suppose that he has no real idea of what consistent reasoning is.

While Alkeides' speech, as I commented earlier, does at least convey the impression of developing a definite line of thought, I have tried to show that in fact it does no such thing, and that the chauvinistic posturings of Ulpian and Alkeides lack serious engagement with their subject. I chose this passage because it seemed to promise some identifiable focus on its musical topic—others lack even that much co-ordination—but on inspection it dissolves into nothing.

We must therefore ask whether there is anything else in the passage which might give a more substantial clue to its overall meaning. I think we might find just a hint of one in the closing section, about which I have so far said nothing.

Here Alkeides looks back with some satisfaction at the display of erudition he has given. 'All that,' he says to Ulpian with more than a trace of sarcasm, 'you get from us Alexandrians, the people obsessed with the *monaulos*. What you don't realize,' he goes on, citing a couple of historical authorities en route, 'is that the Alexandrians were the educators of all the Greeks, and of the barbarians too' (184a–b). He explains that he is referring to the time when the time-honoured scheme of rounded liberal education had broken down in the turbulent period following the death of Alexander. What sparked off an educational renaissance in Greek life was the act of the seventh Ptolemy, in expelling the scholars from Alexandria. A whole flood of grammarians, philosophers, geometers, *mousikoi*, painters, athletic trainers, doctors and other experts was released into the wider world; and since they had no other means of support, they set themselves up as teachers, and taught many distinguished men (184c).

The whole focus of this punchy little paragraph is on education. Alkeides is plainly identifying his own parade of knowledge with the content of the education that these earlier experts had given, in so far as it was related to music. He goes on to connect it, further, with the style of education that was normal in the great days of Greece, back in the fourth and fifth centuries, quoting a string of respectable authorities to show that everyone of any significance, in that noblest phase of Greek culture, was skilled in music and learned, in particular, to play musical instruments (184d–e). It was the ideal embodied in that enlightened form of education, so Alkeides implies, that was revived as the result of the scholarly exodus from Alexandria.

What Alkeides seems not to notice is that the thesis implicit in this chain of connections is thoroughly bogus. Alkeides portrays himself as a latter-day representative of a movement that renewed throughout Greece the admired educational system of classical times; he is Renaissance Man. But by his own evidence, the two schemes of education were utterly different. The classical curriculum was a practical, hands-on business; the people he mentions are described, with emphasis, as having learned to play instruments, especially the pipes. What his own style of learning provides is simply the ability to *mention* instruments, and specifically to do so in quotations from the literature of the past. I should emphasize once again that this book-learning is apparently not acquired even with a view to gaining scholarly knowledge *about* musical instruments. In these few pages of Athenaeus, some seventy passages are cited from earlier writings; yet the amount of real organological information they convey could be jotted comfortably on a postcard. It seems hard to resist the conclusion I suggested earlier, that as much of that 'hard' information as possible has been systematically screened out.

One of the main purposes of the older sort of musical education was straightforwardly social. To be able to take one's place in civic choruses, and to sing and play at symposia, were proper accomplishments for a gentleman; without them one was inadequately equipped to play an appropriate part in the life of the city. By the late fourth century the focus of education in its musical aspect was already shifting. Performance, even choral performance, was becoming the exclusive preserve of professionals; and though boys still learned to play and sing, the way in which adults now displayed their musical sophistication was mainly through talk. In this department, as in others, education was moving decisively towards a focus on knowledge as it exists in words, and on the ability to express one's knowledge in suitable language. The activities made possible by expert knowledge, and specifically the practical performance of music, were no longer the main point. The accomplishment of an educated man lay simply in his ability to speak, and the acquisition of practical skills was beneath the dignity of a leisured free citizen, alien to his social image.[5]

It seems clear, however, from writings of the fourth century and the third, that the talk engaged in by these cultivated upper-class men was often genuinely well informed, and indeed that they were expected to be abreast of the latest scholarship emerging from places like the Lyceum on musical theory, history, ethics and the rest.[6] A similar attitude, though with an antiquarian slant, is still detectable in writers contemporary with Athenaeus.[7] But Athenaeus seems to have taken the process a step further. In his conception of the musical learning that a man may properly and proudly display in company, actual knowledge of facts and theories about music is no longer included. Perhaps this is because it would betray evidence of hardworking intellectual study and application, which would be as inappropriate to the social image these people were striving for as was evidence of genuine practical skill in the time of Aristotle. The social demands placed on a liberal education will now allow it to contain no more than the literary trimmings; and hence everything but these have been excluded from the discourses of the *Deipnosophistae*. The allegedly musical erudition of Alkeides and his fellow guests is as trivial as the ability to quote one line from Christopher Smart and one from Robbie Burns when somebody mentions mice.

This dreary diagnosis seems to be confirmed by Athenaeus' treatment of musicians themselves. A good many famous composers and performers of the past are mentioned—though there are also some notable omissions—and a few of them are discussed (or rather, made the subject of collections of quotations) at considerable length. We might have expected that at least some of this voluminous material would have a substantial musical focus.

The remarkable fact is that it does not. Here too Athenaeus seems to have worked on a principle of selection that reduced to the barest minimum its musical interest, whether practical, theoretical, philosophical, historical or anything else. He has two passages, for instance, one of them quite long, on Dorion of Delphi, a fourth-century pipe-player with a significant place in the history of the art, as we know from elsewhere.[8] There is no trace of the fact in Athenaeus. All we learn from the sources he quotes is that Dorion was at Philip's celebratory banquet after the battle of Chaeronea, that he had a line in witty repartee, and that he liked fish (337b ff, 435b). He recites material about the great fourth-century kitharist and singer Stratonikos of Athens at even greater length, stringing quotations together for page after page (347f–352d, with brief allusions also at 163f, 169e). Hidden away in a couple of lines is one tiny nugget of precious musicological information.[9] All the rest is a string of anecdotes, designed to put on record Stratonikos' quick-witted capacity for clever one-liners, sardonic comments on places he had visited and catty remarks about his fellow musicians. One or two of them are faintly amusing; *en masse* they make grim reading, and further comment on them would in any case be otiose here (see further Gilula, in this volume).

A final example will help to show how rigorously selective Athenaeus can be, even when he is choosing between items of which none has any serious musical content. There was a singer to the kithara during the later fourth century called Aristonikos of Olynthos, who is rated by some of our authorities as the most famous *kitharodos* of his day. He had an exciting life in political and military contexts, quite apart from his musical activities; he was a sort of fifth-columnist in the Bosporos region in 353 BC; later he went with Alexander on campaign, and died fighting bravely with Alexander's troops, 'showing a noble courage uncharacteristic of a kitharode'. It is quite an epitaph. Alexander is said to have commanded that a statue of him be set up at Delphi, with a kithara in one hand and a spear in the other. Regardless of their historical reliability, these stories kept the name of Aristonikos alive and his reputation high in later times.

But all this information comes from other sources, Polyaenus, Arrian and Plutarch.[10] Though Aristonikos puts in an appearance in Athenaeus, we hear not one word of the exploits on which his fame had been built. All we are offered is the information that he was there, along with the witty Dorion, at Philip's convivial festivities after Chaeronea. It looks as if he is being mentioned in the one kind of setting in which musicians, as Athenaeus conceives them, are properly at home. Stories in which a musician appears as an active adventurer, a spy or a soldier, have no more place in his picture than do accounts of his technical achievements or his exhibitions of professional skill. All such matters are discreetly overlooked.

From these passages and others I am forced to conclude that the main use Athenaeus has for the figure of the 'great musician' has little or nothing to do with music itself, and nothing to do with a life of action and stirring deeds. His role is that of an entertaining and superficially sophisticated talker, welcome for that reason—much less for his musical talents—at the courts of kings and other notables. What the work succeds in doing, through its citations of ancient literature and especially through what it omits, is to present the musician in the guise of an ideal guest at Athenaeus' own style of trivially erudite dinner party. He is conceived precisely in the image of the musically 'educated' dilettante that was conjured up in the speech of Alkeides. And a refined dinner-guest's talk *about* musicians, like the reported talk of musicians themselves, must be literate, witty, and at all costs devoid of significant musicological content.

# ARISTOXENUS IN ATHENAEUS

## by Elisabetta Villari

This chapter constitutes preliminary work for an edition of and commentary on the fragments of Aristoxenus of Tarentum.[1] As such, it does not pretend to consider, let alone exhaust, all the many problems (be they philological, historical, exegetical or, above all, musicological in nature) which are posed by the twenty-seven fragments of Aristoxenus contained in the fifteen books of Athenaeus' *Deipnosophistae*.[2] Rather, I have the following four objectives:

(1) To emphasize the importance of Athenaeus for the indirect transmission of fragments of Aristoxenus, particularly those of a historical or biographical nature;

(2) To emphasize the importance of Aristoxenus as a source for Athenaeus;

(3) To evaluate the possibility of the presence of Aristoxenus in Athenaeus in the form of paraphrases or unmarked quotations, be they direct or indirect, by undertaking an analysis of the manner in which quotations are employed in the *Deipnosophistae* as compared with the Epitome.

(4) To demonstrate the need for a new edition of the fragments of Aristoxenus with an accompanying commentary that would take account of the last thirty years of research.

The *Deipnosophistae* has historically been the '*grande bouffe*' of classical studies. Since any attempt to consider the work in its entirety requires a profound and wide-ranging erudition, more often than not it has been the *disiecta membra* of this corpus of information that have nourished the diverse branches of our knowledge of antiquity, rather than any comprehensive study. The difficulties posed by any attempt to consider the book as a whole, as well as the work's interest, were apparently equally obvious in late antiquity, as the *Deipnosophistae* underwent a process of abridgement.

Athenaeus' omnivorous and gluttonous erudition, the plenitude and finesse of his work, and his taste for information on the past, combined with the precision of his citations and the exactitude of his documentation, make the *Deipnosophistae* an almost unending source of precious information. It is well known that Athenaeus, that supreme polymath, transmitted an enormous quantity of information on ancient music and that much of this material was taken from Aristoxenus. In the first, fourth, and fourteenth books of the *Deipnosophistae* is to be found a great deal of invaluable information on music in antiquity:[3] in particular, in the fourth book he considers musical instruments, and in the fourteenth dance, different types of songs, musical genres and kinds of harmony. The musicological issues are all raised by three participants in the symposium: two experts on music, Masurius and Alceides of Alexandria, who are joined by Amoebeus in the fourteenth book. Alceides of Alexandria and Amoebeus, harp-player and singer, are musicians.[4] Of the twenty-seven fragments of Aristoxenus transmitted by Athenaeus, the majority (eighteen fragments + one not considered by Wehrli) are drawn from writings on music and on dance, and of these sixteen are contained in Book Fourteen. Eight fragments in all are taken from works of a biographical nature.

Given that there are no exhaustive studies of Athenaeus and that the most important work on the musical sources of Athenaeus remains that of C.A. Bapp (1885, 87–160), we must also recognize that, in the thirty years since Wehrli augmented and refined his 1945 edition of the fragments of Aristoxenus in 1967–8, fundamental contributions have been made to the study of the fragments of Aristoxenus.[5]

As I have already remarked, Athenaeus is an extremely important source for the tradition of the works of Aristoxenus which related to the history of music and to biography. There are two attestations to Aristoxenus' fame as an author of biographies in antiquity. We know from Hieronymus,[6] who cites Suetonius, that among the writers of *Lives* in Greek, '*omnium longe doctissimus Aristoxenus musicus*', and from Plutarch that Aristoxenus wrote biographies.[7] One of the characteristic elements of Aristoxenus' biographical endeavours was considered to be the clearly polemical nature of his judgments. As a result, Aristoxenus used his biographies as a means better to express his own likes and dislikes: for example, he showed sympathy towards Pythagoras and Archytas and to their doctrine, while he had a clear distaste for Socrates[8] and Plato.[9] His malevolence towards Plato is documented in and explained by his opinions on music.[10]

In view of these factors, Arrighetti considers it unlikely that one might find set out in the *Lives* of Aristoxenus the events of an individual's life; he suggests rather that Aristoxenus considered only what needed to be interpreted for his polemical purposes.[11] The *Life* of Telestes, a dithyrambic poet of the end of the fifth century BC, even if it has reached us only in fragments, can be explained in the light of Aristoxenus' immediate interests, which led him to debate the most recent theoreticians of musical instruction, among whom figured prominently Telestes.[12]

Zecchini's analysis of Athenaeus' biographical sources demonstrates that a limited number of biographers are cited in the *Deipnosophistae*, including Clearchus and Hermippus, as well as Chamaeleon, Phaenias (on the Sicilian tyrants), Satyrus (on Alcibiades), Antigonus of Carystus (on Zeno), perhaps Eratosthenes (on Arsinoe) and Apollodorus.[13] However the oldest biography cited explicitly by Athenaeus is the *Life of Archytas* by Aristoxenus, in a single but lengthy quotation in Book Twelve. This would be 'the richest of historiographic materials received in the original words'. This fragment considers Polyarchus' diplomatic mission to Tarentum for Dionysius II and his praise of his τρυφή.[14]

In Book Thirteen (13.555d–556) reference is made to another biography, this time of Socrates; but, as we shall see, this citation is in all probability second-hand, since Aristoxenus is contained in a list of authors cited by Panaetius of Rhodes on the question of the philosopher's bigamy. Athenaeus values Aristoxenus as a historian, a biographer and a theoretician of music. First of all, for most of the twenty-six plus one fragmentary texts of Aristoxenus preserved for us by Athenaeus (out of the 139 contained in the second edition of Wehrli's collection of the fragments), he is the only authority. Furthermore, Athenaeus, in his *Deipnosophistae*, preserves more fragments of Aristoxenus than any other author. A simple comparison with Plutarch, who had good reason to cite Aristoxenus, is telling. Plutarch, writer of the *Lives*, the author to whom we attribute a *De musica*, cites Aristoxenus only sixteen times in the entire corpus of his works (works which reach us in their entirety), as opposed to the twenty-six plus one citations found in the incomplete *Deipnosophistae*.

Secondly, Aristoxenus had an importance for Athenaeus that is not limited to works of a specifically musical nature. We must not underestimate the fact that Aristoxenus, in his capacity as author of a symposium entitled *Summikta Sympotika*, is numbered among the most ancient precursors of Athenaeus. Athenaeus knew this work and cited a long and important fragment (14.632 a = F 124 Wehrli), which is among the most important for the history of the people of Poseidonia who 'once were Greeks and now have become Etruscans'.[15]

The *Summikta Sympotika* is among the oldest examples of the genre of the symposium which we find within Athenaeus' encyclopaedic work. Other important predecessors in the genre are: the *Symposium* of Heraclides of Tarentum, the *Symposium* of Herodian, the *Leschai* of Heraclides Ponticus the Younger, the

*Quaestiones conviviales* and the *Septem sapientium convivium* of Plutarch, and the *Symposiaka summikta* of Didymus.

Before undertaking a survey of how Aristoxenus is quoted by Athenaeus, it is important to recognize that the current state of our knowledge of the majority of fragments of Aristoxenus found in Athenaeus does not enable us to distinguish between direct and indirect citation, but require us rather to suspend our judgment and operate with working hypotheses. One interesting example of a probable second-hand citation is provided by fragment 57 Wehrli (= Athen. *Deipn.* 13.555d). This is the only case in the *Deipnosophistae* where Aristoxenus is quoted in a list with other authors, in the context of a discussion of the life of Socrates and his bigamy:

ἐκ τούτων οὖν τις ὁρμώμενος μέμψαιτ' ἂν τοὺς περιτιθέντας Σωκράτει δύο γαμετὰς γυναῖκας, Ξανθίππην καὶ τὴν Ἀριστείδου Μυρτώ, οὐ τοῦ δικαίου καλουμένου (οἱ χρόνοι γὰρ οὐ συγχωροῦσιν) ἀλλὰ τοῦ τρίτου ἀπ' ἐκείνου. εἰσὶ δὲ Καλλισθένης, Δημήτριος ὁ Φαληρεύς, Σάτυρος ὁ περιπατητικός, Ἀριστόξενος, οἷς τὸ ἐνδόσιμον Ἀριστοτέλης ἔδωκεν ἱστορῶν τοῦτο ἐν τῷ περὶ Εὐγενείας (fr. 75 R.)· εἰ μὴ ἄρα συγκεχωρημένον κατὰ ψήφισμα τοῦτο ἐγένετο τότε διὰ σπάνιν ἀνθρώπων, ὥστ' ἐξεῖναι καὶ δύο ἔχειν γυναῖκας τὸν βουλόμενον, ὅθεν καὶ τοὺς τῆς κωμῳδίας ποιητὰς ἀποσιωπῆσαι τοῦτο, πολλάκις τοῦ Σωκράτους μνημονεύοντας. παρέθετο δὲ περὶ τῶν γυναικῶν ψήφισμα Ἱερώνυμος ὁ Ῥόδιος (fr. 26 Hi.), ὅπερ σοι διαπέμψομαι εὐπορήσας τοῦ βιβλίου. ἀντεῖπε δὲ τοῖς λέγουσι περὶ τῶν Σωκράτους γυναικῶν Παναίτιος ὁ Ῥόδιος.

Proceeding, then, from this fact, one may find fault with those writers who ascribe to Socrates two wedded wives, Xanthippê and Myrtô, daughter of Aristides; not the one who was called the Just (since chronology is against that), but the third in descent from him. These writers are Callisthenes Demetrius of Phalerum, Satyrus the Peripatetic, and Arixtoxenus, and it was Aristotle who gave them the keynote by telling this story in his treatise *On Noble Birth*; a story we may doubt unless, to be sure, this bigamy was made allowable by special decree at that time because of scarcity of people, so that any one who so desired was permitted to have two wives; this would explain why the comic poets passed it over in silence, although they often mention Socrates. Hieronymus of Rhodes has quoted a decree pertaining to women which I will send over to you when I have procured his book. But Panaetius of Rhodes has given the lie to those who talk about the wives of Socrates.

(F. 57 Wehrli: The *Life* of Socrates = Athen. *Deipn.* 13.555d)

The citation of Aristoxenus appears in the midst of a list of authors (Demetrius of Phalerum, Callisthenes and Satyrus, then Aristoxenus, followed by Hieronymus of Rhodes); the idea originated with the *Peri Eugeneias*, attributed to Aristotle. A similar list is also attested in Plutarch. Plutarch's list (*Aristides*, 27) does not include Callisthenes and Satyrus:

καὶ τὰς μὲν θυγατέρας ἱστοροῦσιν ἐκ τοῦ πρυτανείου τοῖς νυμφίοις ἐκδοθῆναι δημοσίᾳ, πόλεως τὸν γάμον ἐγγυώσης καὶ προῖκα τρισχιλίας δραχμὰς ἑκατέρᾳ ψηφισαμένης, Λυσιμάχῳ δὲ τῷ υἱῷ μνᾶς μὲν ἑκατὸν ἀργυρίου καὶ γῆς τοσαῦτα πλέθρα πεφυτευμένης ἔδωκεν ὁ δῆμος, καὶ ἄλλας δραχμὰς τέσσαρας εἰς ἡμέραν ἑκάστην ἀπέταξαν, Ἀλκιβιάδου τὸ ψήφισμα γράψαντος. ἔτι δὲ Λυσιμάχου θυγατέρα Πολυκρίτην ἀπολιπόντος, ὡς Καλλισθένης (*FGrH* 124 F 48) φησί, καὶ ταύτῃ σίτησιν ὅσην τοῖς Ὀλυμπιονίκαις ὁ δῆμος ἐψηφίσατο. Δημήτριος δ' ὁ Φαληρεὺς (*FGrH* 228 F 45) καὶ Ἱερώνυμος ὁ Ῥόδιος καὶ Ἀριστόξενος ὁ μουσικὸς (F 58 W) καὶ Ἀριστοτέλης (F 84R) - εἴγε δὴ τὸ περὶ εὐγενείας βιβλίον ἐν τοῖς γνησίοις Ἀριστοτέλους θετέον - ἱστοροῦσι Μυρτὼ θυγατριδῆν Ἀριστείδου Σωκράτει τῷ σοφῷ συνοικῆσαι, γυναῖκα μὲν ἑτέραν ἔχοντι, ταύτην δ' ἀναλαβόντι, χηρεύουσαν διὰ πενίαν καὶ τῶν ἀναγκαίων.

And it is stated that his two daughters were publicly married out of the prytaneum, or state-house, by the city, which decreed each of them three thousand drachmas for her portion; and that upon his son Lysimachus the people bestowed a hundred minas of money, and as many acres of planted land, and ordered him besides, upon the motion of Alcibiades, four drachmas a day. Furthermore, Lysimachus leaving a daughter, named Polycrite, as Callisthenes says, the people voted her, also, the same allowance for food with those that obtained the victory in the Olympic Games. But Demetrius the Phalerian, Hieronymus the Rhodian, Aristoxenus the musician, and Aristotle (if the *Treatise of Nobility* is to be reckoned among the genuine pieces of Aristotle) say that Myrto, Aristides's granddaughter, lived with Socrates the philosopher, who indeed had another wife, but took her into his house, being a widow, by reason of her indigence and want of the necessaries of life.

(Plutarch, *Aristides* 27; tr. John Dryden)

Here, with all probability, one can speak of second-hand citation.[16] It has also been suggested that the passage cited by Athenaeus was taken from Panaetius (Fr. 133 van Straaten), who is quoted by both Athenaeus and Plutarch at the end of a section refuting the claims regarding Socrates' polygamy. But if we take into account the results of the work of Collard on the fragments of the tragedians in the *Deipnosophistae* and in its Epitome, it is clear that Athenaeus sometimes cites directly, giving the author's or the work's name, or indirectly, naming the author from whom the citation was taken, but often paraphrasing the passage.[17] The research of Collard shows 'the quality of the indirect transmission in Athenaeus of fragments' and demonstrates the precision and fidelity of Athenaeus' citations. From Collard's results we know that Athenaeus 'quotes a text identical (apart from very small errors) with that of the author's main tradition' and furthermore that 'there are about 40 allusions to or paraphrases of tragic texts or vocabulary'. The research of Collard remains a point of reference of great importance, even if it is obvious that in the case of fragments from the tragedians the issues to be resolved are quite different. First of all, he is considering poetry and not prose, and thus text much more easily cited from memory and presumably more widely diffused and better known than the tracts of Aristoxenus (cf. Chapter 12). Furthermore, in many cases, we are able to evaluate the fidelity of Athenaeus' citations of the tragedians by comparing them with the original text.

We can begin with a simple consideration: Athenaeus cites Aristoxenus twenty-six plus one times in the *Deipnosophistae*, and ten times in the Epitome. For these ten fragments, at least, it is thus possible to consider what kinds of modifications the text of the Epitome presents:

| | | |
|---|---|---|
| F 95 Wehrli | = *Deipn.* 4.174e | = Epitome, vol. 2.1, p. 58, l. 22 |
| F 97 Wehrli | = *Deipn.* 4.182f | = Epitome, vol. 2.1, p. 62, l. 6 |
| F 96 Wehrli | = *Deipn.* 4.184d | = Epitome, vol. 2.1, p. 63, l. 1 |
| F 28 Wehrli | = *Deipn.* 10.418f | = Epitome, vol. 2.2, p. 27, l. 18 |
| F 87 Wehrli | = *Deipn.* 11.467a | = Epitome, vol. 2.2, p. 54, l. 30 |
| F 89 Wehrli | = *Deipn.* 14.619d | = Epitome, vol. 2.2, p. 127, l. 20 |
| F 111 Wehrli | = *Deipn.* 14.620e | = Epitome, vol. 2.2, p. 128, l. 3 |
| F 110 Wehrli | = *Deipn.* 14.621e | = Epitome, vol. 2.2, p. 128, l. 27 |
| F 103 Wehrli | = *Deipn.* 14.630e | = Epitome, vol. 2.2, p. 134, l. 22 |
| F 98 Wehrli | = *Deipn.* 14.635e | = Epitome, vol. 2.2, p. 136, l. 32 |

It is clear that the techniques of citation are varied in the *Deipnosophistae*. Aristoxenus is cited with indication of the work and the book; with indication only of the work; and with such expressions as, 'A. says', 'A. says that', 'A. believes'… . In the case of one fragment (F 87 Wehrli) we find the expression 'A. πολλάκις', that is, 'A. often says', evidently alluding to different passages in the same work or in other works. There is also only one fragment (F 57 Wehrli), already discussed, where the name of Aristoxenus is found in a list of names of other authors. Citations frequently occur in the context of polemics with other authors (Plato,

Pythagoras, Aristarchus, Didymus, etc.) as well as in the negative ('Aristoxenus doesn't think this').

We can list the degree of precision of the citations in the following manner:

In four fragments, Athenaeus cites the author and the title of the work, specifying the number of the book. These all appear in Book Fourteen (F 45, F 101, F 109, F 89) which we will recall contains fully sixteen citations (of which a total of seven contain at least the title of the book):

F 45 ὥς φησὶν Ἀριστόξενος ἐν ὀγδόῳ Πολιτικῶν Νόμων (*FHG* II 289)

F 101 οὗ μνημονεύειν Ἀριστόξενον ἐν πρώτῳ περὶ Αὐλῶν Τρήσεως (FHG II 286)

F 109 ὡς ἱστορεῖ Ἀριστόξενος ἐν πρώτῳ Συγκρίσεων (*FHG* II 284)

F 89 Ἀριστόξενος δὲ ἐν τετάρτῳ περὶ Μουσικῆς (*FHG* II 287)

In four fragments, Athenaeus cites both the author and the title of the work, omitting the number of the volume (F 100, F 124, F 129, F 50). Fragment 50 Wehrli appears in Book Twelve; all the others are contained in Book Fourteen.

F 100 Ἀριστοξένου τοῦτ' εἰπόντος ἐν τοῖς περὶ Αὐλητῶν ἢ ἐν τοῖς περὶ Αὐλῶν καὶ Ὀργάνων

F 124 διόπερ Ἀριστόξενος ἐν τοῖς Συμμίκτοις Συμποτικοῖς (*FHG* II 291)

F 129 ἐν δὲ τοῖς κατὰ βραχὺ Ὑπομνήμασιν ὁ Ἀριστόξενος

F 50 Ἀριστόξενος δ' ὁ μουσικὸς ἐν τῷ Ἀρχύτα Βίῳ (*FHG* II 276)

In the remaining nineteen fragments, Athenaeus mentions only the name of Aristoxenus, omitting both the title of the work and the volume number. In total, the titles of works by Aristoxenus cited in the *Deipnosophistae* are as follows:

F 45 Πολιτικοὶ Νόμοι (*FHG* II 289)

F 101 περὶ Αὐλῶν Τρήσεως (*FHG* II 286)

F 109 Συγκρίσεις (*FHG* II 284)

F 89 περὶ Μουσικῆς (*FHG* II 287)

F 100 περὶ Αὐλητῶν περὶ Αὐλῶν καὶ περὶ Ὀργάνων

F 124 Σύμμικτοι Συμποτικοί (*FHG* II 291)

F 129 Ὑπομνήματα

F 50 Ἀρχύτα Βίος (*FHG* II 276)

But if we undertake a comparison of the text of the *Deipnosophistae* (as we have received it) with its epitome, using only fragment F 89 Wehrli, with which it is possible to undertake such a comparison (because the complete title and the book number is present), we find that the title and the book number have been eliminated from the text of the epitome: Ἀριστόξενος (δὲ ἐν τετάρτῳ περὶ Μουσικῆς). Juxtaposition of the two versions demonstrates the point:

1. *Deipn.* 14.619d (= F 89 Wehrli)

> Ἀριστόξενος δὲ ἐν τετάρτῳ περὶ Μουσικῆς (FHG II 287) 'ᾖδον', φησίν, 'αἱ ἀρχαῖαι γυναῖκες Καλύκην τινὰ ᾠδήν. Στησιχόρου δ' ἦν ποίημα (fr. 43), ἐν ᾧ Καλύκη τις ὄνομα...'.

> Aristoxenus, in the fourth book of his work *On Music*, says, 'The women of old sang a song called Calyce. It was composed by Stesichorus, and in it a maiden named Calyce...'

2. Epitome, vol. 2. 2, p. 127, l. 20

> Ἀριστόξενος δέ φησίν· 'ᾖδον αἱ ἀρχαῖαι καλύκην τινὰ ᾠδήν. Στησιχόρου δ' ἦν ποίημα, ἐν ᾧ Καλύκη...'.

> Aristoxenus says, 'The women of old sang a song called Calyce. It was composed by Stesichorus, and in it Calyce...'

As already mentioned, at 11.467a in the *Deipnosophistae* we find the word πολλάκις ('often'), which appears in a variety of contexts where the citation was originally given. If we compare this passage with the version in the Epitome, we find that the adverb πολλάκις ('often') has been eliminated.[18]

These examples suggest that where the edition reaching us is exclusively that of the Epitome (particularly in the case of Books One and Two), the text is missing many of the references which most likely were present in the original version, and further that in the case of the fragments we miss the information about the title of work or number of book. This is how they could become *adespota*.[19]

# Appendix: Fragments of Aristoxenus in Athenaeus

*I. Synoptic table of fragments of Aristoxenus in Athenaeus ordered by book number*

| | | | |
|---|---|---|---|
| F 135 | Wehrli | 1.19f | =Book 1, Kaibel paragraph 35, line 21 |
| F 112 | Wehrli | 1.22b | =Book 1, Kaibel paragraph 40, line 3 |
| F 27 | Wehrli | 2.47a | =Book 2, Kaibel paragraph 26, line 20 |
| F ? | | 4.174c | =Book 4, Kaibel paragraph 75, line 17 |
| F 95 | Wehrli | 4.174e | =Book 4, Kaibel paragraph 75, line 36 = (Epitome), Vol. 2,1, page 58, line 22 |
| F 97 | Wehrli | 4.182f | =Book 4, Kaibel paragraph 80, line 30 = (Epitome), Vol. 2,1, page 62, line 6 |
| F 96 | Wehrli | 4.184d | =Book 4, Kaibel paragraph 84, line 11 = (Epitome), Vol. 2,1, page 63, line 1 |
| F 28 | Wehrli | 10.418f | =Book 10, Kaibel paragraph 13, line 8 = (Epitome), Vol. 2,2, page 27, line 18 |
| F 87 | Wehrli | 11.467a | =Book 11, Kaibel paragraph 30, line 29 =(Epitome),Vol.2,2, page 54, line 30 |
| F 50 | Wehrli | 12.545a | =Book 12, Kaibel paragraph 64, line 1 |
| F 57 | Wehrli | 13.555d | =Book 13, Kaibel paragraph 2, line 23 |
| F 89 | Wehrli | 14.619d | =Book 14, Kaibel paragraph 11, line 14 = (Epitome), Vol. 2,2, page 127, line 20 |
| F 129 | Wehrli | 14. | =Book 14, Kaibel paragraph 11, line 25 |
| F 111 | Wehrli | 14.620e | =Book 14, Kaibel paragraph 13, line 7 = (Epitome) Vol.2,2, page 128. line 3 |
| F 110 | Wehrli | 14.621e | =Book 14, Kaibel paragraph 14, line 1) =(Epitome), Vol. 2,2, page 128, line 27 |
| F 78 | Wehrli | 14.624b | =Book 14, Kaibel paragraph 18, line 39 |
| F 107 | Wehrli | 14.630b | =(Book 14, Kaibel paragraph 28, line 6 |
| F 103 | Wehrli | 14.630e | =(Book 14, Kaibel paragraph 29, line 2) = (Epitome), Vol. 2,2, page 134, line 22 |
| F 108 | Wehrli | 14.631b | =Book 14, Kaibel paragraph 30, line 9 |
| F 109 | Wehrli | 14.631d | =Book 14, Kaibel paragraph 30, line 30 |
| F 124 | Wehrli | 14.632a | =Book 14, Kaibel paragraph 31, line 16 |
| F 100 | Wehrli | 14.634d–c | =Book 14, Kaibel paragraph 35, line 15 |
| F 101 | Wehrli | 14.634e | =Book 14, Kaibel paragraph 36, line 4 |
| F 99 | Wehrli | 14.635b | =Book 14, Kaibel paragraph 36, line 28 |
| F 98 | Wehrli | 14.635e | =Book 14, Kaibel paragraph 37, line 19 =(Epitome),Vol. 2,2, page 136, line 32 |
| F 136 | Wehrli | 14.638b | =Book 14, Kaibel paragraph 42, line 22 |
| F 45 | Wehrli | 14.648d | =Book 14, Kaibel paragraph 59, line 14 |

*II. Synoptic table of fragments of Aristoxenus in Athenaeus, divided and numbered according to the sections of Aristoxenus' work in the order of Wehrli's edition of Aristoxenus.*

*Pythagorean Maxims*

F 27 =Athen. *Deipn.*2.47a=Book 2, Kaibel paragraph 26, line 20

F 28 Wehrli =Athen. *Deipn.* 10.418f=Book 10, Kaibel paragraph 13, line; (Epitome), Vol. 2,2, page 27, line 18

*Political Laws*

F 45 Wehrli =Athen. *Deipn.* 14.648d=Book 14, Kaibel paragraph 59, line 14

*The life of Archytas*

F 50 Wehrli =Athen. *Deipn.* 12.545a=Book 12, Kaibel paragraph 64, line 1

*The life of Socrates*

F 57 Wehrli =Athen. *Deipn.* 13.555d=Book 13, Kaibel paragraph 2, line 23

*On Music*

F 78 Wehrli =Athen. *Deipn.* 14.624b=Book 14, Kaibel paragraph 18, line 39

F 87 Wehrli =Athen. *Deipn.* 11.467a=Book 11, Kaibel paragraph 30, line 29; (Epitome), Vol. 2.2, page 54, line 30

F 89 Wehrli =Athen. *Deipn.* 14.619d=Book 14, Kaibel paragraph 11, line 14 ; (Epitome), Vol. 2.2, page 127, line 20

*On Auloi and Musical Instruments , On the Boring of Auloi , On Auloi-Players*

F 95 Wehrli =Athen. *Deipn.* 4.174e=Book 4, Kaibel paragraph 75, line 36; (Epitome), Vol. 2,1, page 58, line 22

F 96 Wehrli =Athen. *Deipn.* 4.184d=Book 4, Kaibel paragraph 84, line 11; (Epitome), Vol. 2,1, page 63, line 1

F 97 Wehrli =Athen. *Deipn.* 4.182f=Book 4, Kaibel paragraph 80, line 30; (Epitome), Vol. 2,1, page 62, line 6

F 98 Wehrli =Athen. *Deipn.* 14.635e=Book 14, Kaibel paragraph 37, line 19; (Epitome), Vol. 2,2, page 136, line 32

F 99 Wehrli =Athen. *Deipn.* 14.635b=Book 14, Kaibel paragraph 36, line 28

F 100 Wehrli =Athen. *Deipn.* 14.634d–e=Book 14, Kaibel paragraph 35, line 15

F 101 Wehrli =Athen. *Deipn.* 14.634e=Book 14, Kaibel paragraph 36, line 4

*On the Chorus, On dancing in Tragedy, Comparisons*

F 103 Wehrli =Athen. *Deipn.* 14.630e=Book 14, Kaibel paragraph 29, line 2; (Epitome), Vol. 2,2, page 134, line 22

F 107 Wehrli =Athen. *Deipn.* 14.630b=Book 14, Kaibel paragraph 28, line 6

F 108 Wehrli =Athen. *Deipn.* 14.631b=Book 14, Kaibel paragraph 30, line 9

F 109 Wehrli =Athen. *Deipn.* 14.631d=Book 14, Kaibel paragraph 30, line 30

F 110 Wehrli =Athen. *Deipn.* 14.621e=Book 14, Kaibel paragraph 14, line 1 ; (Epitome), Vol. 2,2, page 128, line 27

F 111 Wehrli =Athen. *Deipn.* 14.620e=Book 14, Kaibel paragraph 13, line 7; (Epitome) vol. 2,2, page 128. line 3

F 112 Wehrli =Athen. *Deipn.* 1.22b=Book 1, Kaibel paragraph 40, line 3

*Table Talk*

F 124 Wehrli =Athen.*Deipn.* 14. 632a =Book 14, Kaibel paragraph 31, line 16

*Shorts notes, Notes*

F 129 Wehrli =Athen. *Deipn.* 14 =Book 14, Kaibel paragraph 11, line 25

F 135 Wehrli =Athen. *Deipn.* 1.19f =Book 1, Kaibel paragraph 35, line 21

F 136 Wehrli =Athen. *Deipn.* 14.638b=Book 14, Kaibel paragraph 42, line 22

# 34

# ATHENAEUS ON GREEK WINE

## by Roger Brock and Hanneke Wirtjes

Athenaeus is an essential source for anyone who wishes to investigate Greek wine, providing an invaluable repository of information and testimonia on its varieties and their reputations and characteristics. It comes as something of a surprise, therefore, to discover, when one looks closely at his treatment of wine, that there is very little in it which we today would consider 'wine appreciation' and that he himself reveals little interest in wine of the sort which we might expect.

His own sources of information are largely obscure, the problem being exacerbated by the fact that his discussion of wine, which he places in a leading position, preceded only by Homer, survives only in the Epitome, with almost all the dramatic framework pared away. One hint at his working methods is the appearance of a similar listing of wines in Pollux (6.15–18) which, like Athenaeus, includes an account of the etymology of the Sicilian wine called Pollian. In 1.31b Athenaeus offers an explanation which derives the name from Pollis of Argos, ruler of Syracuse, citing Hippys of Rhegium, in order to identify Pollian as Bibline and so connect it to his discussion of that problematic *cru*. Pollux gives much the same etymology but distinguishes the Argive from the Sicilian Pollis and does not mention Hippys, citing Aristotle instead. It therefore appears plausible that both are using a glossary of unknown authorship and either making different selections in the light of different concerns or adding different supplementary material. Athenaeus also draws on Theophrastus (*HP* 9.18.10–11) for some snippets of curious wine lore which appear without attribution in the Elder Pliny (*Nat.* 14.116 cf. Aelian *VH* 13.6, who omits the example from Troezen) but he does not seem to make any real use of technical writings: he says nothing about viticulture as such, despite having consulted Theophrastus, nor does he mention writers of treatises on oenology such as those referred to by Pliny (Euphronius, Aristomachus, Commiades, Hicesius; *Nat.* 14.120). Thirdly, there are the medical writers, reflected both in the famous passage attributed to Galen on the wines of Italy (1.26c–27d) and in a later section on the medical characteristics of wine (1.32c–33c). The latter is without attribution: André Tchernia (1986, 203–5) places the period in which doctors had an influence on fashion in wine in the first century AD, and it is tempting therefore to assign the passage in Athenaeus, which concentrates on Greek wine but is aware of Falernian and Alban, to Rufus of Ephesus, a Hippocratic of the later first century AD who is cited by Galen and the only attested author of a treatise *On Wine*.[1] The Galen passage would seem to be straightforward enough, but is, if anything, more problematic. The name Galen suggests that we are about to read a discussion of Italian wines of the second half of the second century AD Περὶ Ἰταλικῶν οἴνων φησὶν ὁ παρὰ τούτῳ τῷ σοφιστῇ Γαληνός, 'Galen, who is in the presence of this learned author, speaks on the subject of Italian wines', is how the Epitomator introduces the character of Galen, but his function in the drama is lost to us: we are not told to whom he is responding or how his speech is received. Also, neither the Epitomator's introduction nor Galen's own words betray any awareness of chronology. Galen is said to have died in 199: if he was still alive when Athenaeus completed his work, which is entirely possible, he would have been an old man.[2] Given his wide experience and extensive knowledge, he would have been able to speak with great authority. The words that are put into Galen's mouth are just a series of bald statements, however. No comparisons are made between the wines of Galen's mature years and those of Galen's youth or between those of Galen's own time and the preceding half-century, despite the fact that 'Galen' here says that the Sorrentine needs twenty-five years to mature. Historical perspective is limited to optimum drinking dates; otherwise, Athenaeus lives in a perpetual oenological present.

The list of Italian wines is also quite without the precision and critical acumen that characterize Galen's writing on wine. Galen himself lays down five categories that should be used in the description of a wine: χρόα, 'colour', γεῦσις, 'taste', σύστασις, 'consistency', ὀσμή, 'smell', and δύναμις, 'strength' (15.627). Assuming that σύστασις is what we would now call 'weight' or 'body', these are exactly the criteria that form the basis of a modern tasting-note—the professional tasting-note, that is, and not the impressionistic and often hyperbolic variety that turns up in much of today's popular journalism. Galen outlined his criteria in a commentary on Hippocrates, when he felt the need to augment and correct Hippocrates' own perception that there were four kinds of wine: sweet, strong, white and black. Galen knew an incomplete and unsystematic list when he saw one.

Let us then compare the vocabulary used in Athenaeus' 'Galen' passage with Galen's own descriptive terms.[3] The first thing that strikes us is the paucity of the descriptions given in the Athenaeus passage: none of them adds up to a proper tasting-note. To be fair, Galen himself does not give full tasting-notes either, but when he lists wines he does so in order to compare them for a specific, generally medical, purpose, using a particular and relevant criterion: for example, that Sabine should be given for fevers because it is ἄτονος, 'low in alcohol' (15.648). Although the Athenaeus passage sometimes mentions the medical effects of the wines it discusses, it does not do so consistently. The passage is a list without any organizing principle and without an introduction or conclusion.

If we group the descriptive terms used in the passage under Galen's five headings, we find that the organoleptic vocabulary used by Athenaeus does not always correspond to Galen's own. The words used for colours of wine can be traced in Galen: μέλας, 'dark', and its comparative μελάντερος, used of the Erbulan and of the sweeter Falernian respectively; κίρρος, 'yellow', applied to the drier variety of Falernian; χρυσίζει, 'is golden', said of the Spoletine, and λευκός, 'white', said of the Erbulan after a few years. How does the Erbulan change from dark to white? Why should the sweeter version of Falernian be darker than the drier? Athenaeus' Galen does not bother to tell us and does not seem at all curious about the chemical process that must be involved. Modern red wines do become lighter in colour with age but not white, so what is going on here is certainly without a modern parallel. Where a dry and a sweet style are made of the same wine, as with modern Soave, the sweet style can be a little darker, but μελάντερος would seem to be an overstatement. All we get is a quick statement of fact—or perhaps factoid—instead of an explanation.

Athenaeus' 'Galen' has nothing to say about the second, and to us most important, item in a tasting-note, the smell, or as we would say 'nose', of a wine. Galen himself has only three descriptive terms: εὐώδεις, 'having a pleasant smell', οὐκ εὐώδεις, its opposite, and ἄοδμος, 'without any smell' (15. 627). This is a world away from the modern taster's 'almonds with cherry stones' or 'minty blackcurrants'. εὐώδεις and οὐκ εὐώδεις are vague terms of approval and disapproval, but ἄοδμος is curious. Were there wines in Galen's day that smelt of absolutely nothing? Or was it that the practice of coating the inside of a wine jar with resin to make it impermeable took away the wine's own aroma? And did all Galen's tasting samples come ready-diluted, obscuring the nose of the wine? Whatever the explanation, Athenaeus' Galen cannot be expected to give us descriptions of bouquet if Galen himself did not do so.

The Athenaeus passage has a little to say about what the Italian wines tasted like, but it does not go into much detail: as in Galen's own writings, the terms used tend to be variations on 'sweet' and 'bitter'. For 'sweet' it has γλυκάζων, of the sweeter styles of Falernian and Alban, and ἡδύς, applied to the Labican and the Spoletine, which is described as πινόμενος ἡδύς, 'sweet when it is drunk', where the participle merely states the obvious. Presumably γλυκάζων is less sweet than ἡδύς. Its opposite is αὐστηρός, 'dry', which denotes a wine with little or no residual sugar: it is applied to the style of Falernian that is not γλυκάζων, and the Massic is described as πάνυ αὐστηρός, 'very dry'. The adjective ὀμφακίας is used in opposition to γλυκάζων in order to describe the drier Alban: given its etymology, it ought to mean 'acidic, unpleasantly dry', but in this context it appears to convey no suggestion of its earlier and more usual meaning, 'made from unripe grapes'. However, ὀμφακίας does not appear as a synonym for αὐστηρός in Galen's own works. There are two further epithets that may refer to the taste of particular wines, but it is hard to determine what their exact, or even approximate, meanings are. The adjective σαρκώδης literally means 'meaty' or 'fleshy', and describes the wine of Massilia, which is otherwise said to be καλός, 'good', but rare and παχύς, 'weighty, full-bodied'. It is possible that σαρκώδης is just a synonym for παχύς, describing body, not flavour, but certain modern full-bodied wines could be described as tasting 'meaty'.[4] It is impossible to tell which is right, but either way the wines of Massilia must have improved a great deal since Martial's day, when they were cheap and nasty (10.36). Or is Athenaeus misinformed? Another puzzling term is γεωδέστερος: the Trifolian is 'more earthy' than the Sorrentine. Again, this is not a term that is attested in Galen's writings, and what does it mean? As well as being 'more earthy', the Trifolian βράδιον ... ἀκμάζει, 'reaches its high point of maturity more slowly', so are we dealing with a heavy red wine, something like a modern Salice Salentino, which could well be called 'earthy'? Or do we have to say that the Greeks and the Romans treated their wines so differently from the way that we treat ours that such comparisons are pointless?

The next category, σύστασις, 'body' or 'weight', is less elusive than 'taste'. It is not the same as 'alcoholic strength', which Galen himself rightly regards as a separate category, because alcoholic content is only a component, though a major one, of 'weight': others are, in order of importance, the level of dissolved solids and the level of glycerol. Some wines are light: the Tiburtine is λεπτός, 'thin', and evaporates easily (εὐδιάπνευστος); the Nomentan is οὔτε λίαν ἡδὺς οὔτε λεπτός, 'neither too sweet nor too thin'. The Privernian is λεπτομερέστερος, 'thinner', than the Rhegian, and ἥκιστά τε καθαπτόμενος κεφαλῆς, 'not in the least likely to go to one's head', a combination of attributes which shows that 'body' and 'alcoholic strength' are closely related. Similarly, the Erbulan is τρυφερός, 'light', as well as κοῦφος, 'low in alcohol'. The Sorrentine is ψαφαρός, 'light, watery', as well as ἀλιπής, literally 'lacking in oil', i.e. 'not fat, lacking in glycerol'. Glycerol is a by-product of fermentation, which makes a wine taste faintly sweet. As a dry wine matures, the tannins cease to obscure the glycerol, so that the fruit is more easily perceived on the palate (as Galen knew: 11. 656). This is what happens as claret matures; interestingly, our author adds that Sorrentine takes long to reach maturity, which could imply that this wine appears to be short on glycerol in its youth. The adjective λιπαρός, 'fat, high in glycerol', is applied to the Anconitan. The Labican is said to be ἡδύς, 'sweet', as well as λιπαρός, which would support the sense of 'high in glycerol' for λιπαρός. The Formian, too, is fat—or, rather, fatter than the Rhegian, and it matures more quickly, which again lends support to the conjectured sense of λιπαρός. The Gauran is παχύς, literally 'thick', but, since it is also εὔτονος, 'strong', we cannot say whether παχύς is a synonym for λιπαρός or for εὔτονος. The Fundan is πολύτροφος, which could mean 'full-bodied' or could refer to its high alcoholic content: it is also, like the Gauran, εὔτονος—so much so that it attacks the head and the stomach and is therefore not often drunk at symposia: one does not want to get drunk too quickly, after all.

Alcoholic strength is clearly not easy to distinguish from 'weight'. The words that are used for 'low in alcohol' and 'high in alcohol' are κοῦφος and εὔτονος respectively: we have already encountered them. The Venafran is κοῦφος and also εὐστόμαχος, 'good for the stomach'. The Calenian, too is κοῦφος, and εὐστομαχώτερος, 'better for the stomach' than the Falernian. The Caecuban, on the other hand, is εὔτονος, 'strong', and πληκτικός, literally, 'likely to hit you'. The Tarentine wines are οὐ πλῆξιν, οὐ τόνον ἔχοντες, ἡδεῖς, εὐστόμαχοι: 'they don't hit you, because they have no strength, they are sweet and good for the stomach.' Wholesomeness is equated with low alcoholic content; strong wines are bad for you.

What this passage has to say about the effects of wine on one's health is simplistic and certainly not what one would expect from the foremost medical authority in antiquity. The contrast with the other medical survey in 1.32–33 is marked: the latter is clearly organized, properly focused on medical issues and specific in its statements and terminology. Other observations arouse suspicion, too: the strange transformation of Erbulan from dark to light, and the equally odd habit that Falernian is said to show of becoming sweetish and dark when wind blows from the south as the vintage approaches. These are just assertions, never explained and without parallel in other writers on wine: would Galen not have checked his facts and tried to come up with explanations for these phenomena?

Also, this passage uses descriptive terms not found in Galen: σαρκώδης, γεωδέστερος, τρυφερός, ὀμφακίας. ὀμφακίας is particularly suspect because it is used without pejorative connotations, as a synonym of αὐστηρός: surely Galen would not have used such imprecise language. His own terms for 'dry in an unpleasant sense' are πικρός and δριμύς (11. 656), which are absent from this text. Galen uses στρυφνός to denote a wine that is astringent in its youth, which is another precise descriptive term that does not occur in this text. σαρκώδης and γεωδέστερος, too, are uncharacteristically vague for Galen. This list of Italian wines, which is passed off as Galen's own, bears a very faint resemblance to Galen 14. 15–16, so it is understandable that it should have been attributed to Galen. However, bearing in mind that Galen himself was sufficiently concerned about false attributions to draw up and publish a list of his genuine writings, we would suggest that these pages from Athenaeus are not by Galen.[5] It is difficult, then, to say much with confidence about Athenaeus' sources in this field, other than that he seems to have a fairly eclectic approach. The dominance of comic poets might tempt one to speculate on the existence of a lost treatise on wines mentioned in comedy; certainly, the character and dating of the sources cited for the leading Greek wines is very striking (see Appendix). Pramnian covers the widest range, from Homer to Semus and Didymus in the second and first centuries BC and Alciphron, perhaps in the second century AD, but is perhaps a special case, since it came to be a widely distributed wine style, and its origins were a matter of controversy.[6] Otherwise, testimonia for Mendean extend from Hermippus and Cratinus in the later fifth century to Menander in the late fourth[7] and for Thasian from Hermippus and Aristophanes to Epinicus in the second century BC. Chian goes from Hermippus and Aristophanes to Hedylus and an anecdote of the younger Demetrius in the third century—473a and 167e respectively, so both outside the main discussion in Books One and Two, where the latest citation would be Eubulus, Epilycus or Theopompus. Finally, testimonia for Lesbian run from Antiphanes and other comic poets of the early fourth century to Baton in the third. To these earlier sources must be added our anonymous medical writer (who does not mention Mendean or Thasian). We have already noted that the great majority of the authors cited are comic poets, dating very largely from the fifth and fourth centuries,[8] and the same is true for citations of lesser Greek wines. The only authors who do not conform to the pattern (our medical writer apart) are Homer, Archilochus and Alcman, Archestratus, Menippus and Timachidas of Rhodes. In the case of non-Greek wines, we *do* encounter a scattering of later sources, including Polybius, Posidonius and Agatharchides. The most noteworthy feature of the discussion of wine types, however, is that Athenaeus seems to draw no distinction between different periods. This impression is doubtless exacerbated by the Epitomator, but it can hardly be entirely his fault that there is no indication anywhere in the main discussion of wine (or, apparently, elsewhere) of the huge changes in trade and taste in wine, Greek wine included, which had taken place over the six or seven centuries between the classical period and Athenaeus' own time.

Some sense of these changes may be gained from a comparison with Pliny,

*Natural History* 14, a book whose evidence can be supported by reference to modern discussions, particularly those based on amphora studies. Maronean and Pramnian continued in Pliny's time, at least as wine styles (14. 53), both benefiting from Homeric associations, to which he alludes, but when he returns to foreign wines at 14. 73, he speaks of Thasian and Chian in the past tense (*fuere*), although the vines were still grown (14. 25, 74; cf. Verg. *G.* 2.91), and at 14. 95–7 he mentions evidence for Roman use of Thasian and, down to the time of Julius Caesar, Chian and Lesbian, while the naturally salty taste of Lesbian is mentioned in the present tense in 14. 74 (note Verg. *G.* 2.90 and, two centuries later, Longus 2.1, 4.10.3). Conversely, Varro mentions Chian but not Lesbian (*R.* 2.3, *Men.* 104, *L.* 9.67). There are also a number of references to Lesbian and Chian in Augustan poetry, though we should bear in mind the possibility that these might owe more to literary convention than personal experience. Thasian seems to have disappeared by about the end of the second century BC, and Mendean perhaps a little earlier.[9] By the early Hellenistic period, the wines of north-west Greece, together with Peparethian, seem to have been in vogue, or at least medically approved (Plin. *NH.* 14.76);[10] the former appear in Athenaeus only in the anonymous medical writer (1.33b) and one mention in Eubulus (1.29a), while the latter is only represented by two citations from fifth-century comedy, and one of those is disparaging.

The most striking development of all, however, was the increasing dominance of Greek wines treated with sea-water. The most celebrated variety of this type was Coan, which had always been made in this way, hence Cato's provision of a recipe for counterfeiting it (*Agr.* 112–13), but it was joined in due course by Rhodian, Clazomenean—the most popular in Pliny's day (14.73)—and others from the south-east Aegean. Myndian and Halicarnassan are mentioned in Athenaeus' medical passage, together with Rhodian and Coan, but none of these immensely popular wines makes an appearance anywhere else in his work, apart from a citation of Timachidas of Rhodes (late second century BC) for a Rhodian wine called ὑπόχυτος ('adulterated'; 1.31de) which presumably was of the same style. Coan was certainly popular at Pompeii, to judge from inscriptions painted on amphorae found there; even more so were sweet *passito* wines from Crete, a variety whose export trade only began in the first century BC and enjoyed a boom under the Roman empire.[11] This is mentioned only once by Athenaeus, as a point of comparison for the sweetness of the *passum* which the Romans allowed women to drink (10.440f). Outside Greece, there are even more conspicuous lacunae: Pliny lists a number of highly regarded wines from the Levant (14.74), an area which in Athenaeus' discussion appears only in a fragment of Archestratus (1.29b) at all. Equally, apart from two allusions to the wine of Massilia, one in 'Galen' and one in Posidonius (1.27c, 4.152c), there is no mention of any wine from the western

Mediterranean, even though Spanish and Gallic wines became increasingly important under the empire.[12]

Athenaeus' reflection of developments in fashion, taste and trade in wine is thus limited and, one rather suspects, inadvertent to the extent that it exists. A range of factors seems to be at work here. One is the particular mix of interests in wine which Athenaeus has. Some of these, notably its impact on behaviour and character, and its value as a stimulus to artistic creativity, do not require any interest in wine as such: it is simply the one culturally acceptable source of alcohol as the active element which produces these effects. There is also a marked enthusiasm for list-making, etymology, aetiology and curious lore, a tendency clearly revealed in another seam of wine references, the long list of types of cups and containers in Book Eleven, and likely to lead to a concentration on what are to us peripheral attributes of individual wines such as their names. It will also tend to direct the curiosity of the author or his sources back into the past and towards the conspicuous or the curious. Certainly, the wines which his classical sources single out are the *grands crus* of antiquity rather than the cheaper and more mundane wines which were drunk every day: even Rhodian and Cretan, though just as much imports to the Rome of Athenaeus' day, had much less cachet than Coan or Chian. A focus on the remote past inevitably places much of one's subject matter beyond recovery to any real degree. By Athenaeus' time, Mendean and Thasian were long gone and Lesbian and Chian clearly little seen. Athenaeus' citations are like the nineteenth-century silver decanter labels which one encounters for 'Bucellas' and 'Carcavelhos' and which reflect a vogue created by officers returning from Portugal after the Peninsular War for wines rarely encountered today, if they survive at all. He is unlikely to have had either the opportunity or the means to experience for himself the majority of the wines to which he alludes.

A further element in Athenaeus' treatment of wine is the medical approach. Hippocratic attention to the characteristics and potential benefits of wine was already well established in the classical period,[13] but, as we have already noted, the influence of doctors on choice of wine seems to have increased in the late Republic and, given Athenaeus' decision to include Galen among his *dramatis personae*, one would expect the medical viewpoint to be to the fore.[14] Even if we have seen reason to doubt its authenticity, the catalogue of Italian wines is programmatically placed almost at the beginning of the section and given a medical colouring, just as the treatment of old wine which opens the section is mainly devoted to an exposition of its medical benefits and concludes with a couple of lines on the digestibility of white wines (1.26a–c; cf. 2.45d–f). The inevitable result is a temporal disjunction between the discussion in contemporary terms of the medical aspects of wine and the antiquarian colour of many of the other themes which we have noted. This disjunction is only slightly mitigated by quotation of medical authors of the fourth and third centuries BC, in our anonymous medical author at 1.32c–33c.

There is one striking exception to the apparent absence of interest in wine as such, and it comes in the discussion of Egyptian wine at 1.33c–f. In the Epitome, this brief discussion is highlighted by quotations: it is introduced by a fragment of Sophocles (757 K–Sn.) on breaking silence and a (presumably unconnected) line 'I shall be my own Iolaus and Heracles too', while the closing frame is a line from Philemon: 'you praise yourself like Astydamas, woman' (fr. 160 K–A). We may infer that in the full original version one of the participants took on the task of lauding the wines of his native land in mock-heroic style and was mocked for it in turn. While there are other characters of Egyptian origin in the dialogue, it is extremely tempting to assign this section either to Plutarch of Alexandria or to Athenaeus himself: wine production prospered in Egypt in the imperial period and the wines were widely exported, reaching Rome among many other markets,[15] so our author would have been able to maintain his enthusiasm for the products of his native province. Here, we may suggest, he can be glimpsed for a moment as a wine-lover in the modern sense, raising his glass from behind his piles of antiquarian tomes.

# Appendix: Athenaeus' sources for Greek wines

Authors are listed for each wine in order of first appearance in the text; for wines discussed at length, a century (Roman numeral) or half-century (Roman numeral with superscript) *floruit* is given for each author where possible (BC unless noted otherwise). The anonymous medical author of 1.32c–33c is cited as [Rufus] for convenience. A few purely historical references are omitted. References are to Book One unless otherwise stated.

### *Pramnian*
Homer (10b) VIII?
Ephippus (28f) IV[1]
Aristophanes (29a, 30c) V[2]
Eparchides (30c)?
Semus (30c) II[1]
Didymus (30d) I
Alciphron (31d) II AD?

### *Mendean*
Cratinus (29d) V[2]
Hermippus (29e) V[2]
Phaenias of Eresus (29f) IV[2]
Philyllius (31a) IV[1]
Hippolochus (4.129d) IV[2]
Menander (4.146e = 8.364d) IV[2]

### *Lesbian*
Clearchus (28e) IV[2]
Alexis (28e) IV[2]
Ephippus (28f) IV[1]
Eubulus (28f) IV
Archestratus (29b–c) IV
Philyllius (31a) IV[1]
[Rufus] (32f)
Hippolochus (4.129d) IV[2]
Matron (4.137a) IV[2]
Baton (7.279c) III
Antiphanes (11.471c) IV[1]
Menander (4.146e = 8.364d) IV[2]

### *Thasian*
Epilycus (28d)?
Antidotus (28e) IV
Alexis (28e, 2.47d, 10.431b) IV[2]
Antiphanes (28f, 14.641f) IV[1]
Eubulus (28f) IV
Aristophanes (29a, 11.478d) V[2]
Archestratus (29c) IV
Hermippus (29e) V[2]
Philyllius (31a) IV[1]
[Theophrastus (31f-2a) IV[2]]
Hippolochus (4.129d,f) IV[2]
Epinicus (10.432c) II
anecdote *re* courtesans (13.579e) IV[2]

### *Peparethian*
Aristophanes (29a) V[2]
Hermippus (29f) V[2]

### *Chian*
Theopompus (26b) IV
Epilycus (28d)?
Eubulus (28f) IV
Aristophanes (29a, 11.484f = 12.527c) V[2]
Hermippus (29e) V[2]
Philyllius (31a) IV[1]
[Rufus] (32f, 33c)
anecdote *re* younger Demetrius (4.167e) III
anecdote *re* courtesans (13.579e) IV[2]
Hedylos (11.473a) III
Anaxilas (12.548c) IV

### *Bybline*
Archestratus (29b) IV
Achaeus (31a) V?
Philyllius (31a) IV[1]

### *Rhodian*
Timachidas (31e) II-I

[Rufus] (32e)

*Coan*
[Rufus] (32e, 33b)

*Other Greek wines*
Achaea: Theophrastus (31e)
Akanthos: Amphis (30e)
Arcadia: Theophrastus (31e)
Ariusian: [Rufus] (32f)
Cnidian: [Rufus] (32e, 33b)
Corcyra: [Rufus] (33b)
Corinthian: Alexis (30f)
Erythraean: Theophrastus (32b)
Euboean: Alexis (30f)
Halicarnassian: [Rufus] (33b), Menippus (*ib.*)
Heraclean: Theophrastus (32b)
Ikarian: Amphis (30b)
Ismarian: Archilochus (30f)
Lemnos: Homer (31b)

Leucadian: Eubulus (29a), [Rufus] (33b)
Magnesian: Hermippus (29e)
Myndian: [Rufus] (32e, 33b)
Phliasian: Antiphanes (27d)
Psithian: Eubulus (28f), Anaxandrides (*ib.*)
Samagorean: Aristotle (10.429f)
Skiathos: Strattis (30f)
Spartan: Alcman (31cd)
Thrace: Anaxandrides (131f)
Troezen: Aristotle (31bc), Theophrastus (31f)
Zacynthian: [Rufus] (33b)

*Non-Greek wines*
Beneventan: Plato Com. (31e, cp.(for 'smoky' wine) 4.131f, 6.269d)
Capuan: Polybius (31d)
Chalybonian: Posidonius (28d)
Issan: Agatharchides (28d)
Massilian: 'Galen' (27c), Posidonius (4.152c)
Tuscan: Sopater (15.702b)

# 35

# ATHENAEUS AND THE CULT OF DIONYSUS ORTHOS

## by Konstantinos Niafas

The *Deipnosophistae* displays Athenaeus' interest in wine, which embraces not only its physical aspects, its properties and varieties, but also its place in his contemporary culture, its history and origins. His antiquarian curiosity finds ample scope in the discussion of various sympotic customs. On the origins of wine-mixing, a custom basic for the drinking culture of the Greeks, he quotes numerous authorities, among them the following passage from Philochorus:

> Φιλόχορος δέ φησιν ᾽Αμφικτύονα τὸν ᾽Αθηναίων βασιλέα μαθόντα παρὰ Διονύσου τὴν τοῦ οἴνου κρᾶσιν πρῶτον κεράσαι. διὸ καὶ ὀρθοὺς γενέσθαι τοὺς ἀνθρώπους οὕτω πίνοντας, πρότερον ὑπὸ τοῦ ἀκράτου καμπτομένους, καὶ διὰ τοῦτο ἰδρύσασθαι βωμὸν ᾽Ορθοῦ Διονύσου ἐν τῷ τῶν ῾Ωρῶν ἱερῷ· αὗται γὰρ καὶ τὸν τῆς ἀμπέλου καρπὸν ἐκτρέφουσι. πλησίον δ᾽ αὐτοῦ καὶ ταῖς Νύμφαις βωμὸν ἔδειμεν, ὑπόμνημα τοῖς χρωμένοις τῆς κράσεως ποιούμενος· καὶ γὰρ Διονύσου τροφοὶ αἱ Νύμφαι λέγονται. καὶ θέσμιον ἔθετο προσφέρεσθαι μετὰ τὰ σιτία πᾶσιν ἄκρατον μόνον ὅσον γεύσασθαι, δεῖγμα τῆς δυνάμεως τοῦ ᾽Αγαθοῦ Θεοῦ, τὸ δὲ λοιπὸν ἤδη κεκραμένον, ὁπόσον ἕκαστος βούλεται· προσεπιλέγειν δὲ τούτῳ τὸ τοῦ Διὸς Σωτῆρος ὄνομα διδαχῆς καὶ μνήμης ἕνεκα τῶν πινόντων, ὅτι οὕτω πίνοντες ἀσφαλῶς σωθήσονται. (cf. *Deipn.* 15.693d–f)

Philochorus has this: 'Amphictyon, king of Athens, learned from Dionysus the art of mixing wine, and was the first to mix it. So it was that men came to stand upright, drinking wine mixed, whereas before they were bent double by the use of unmixed. Hence he founded an altar of the 'upright' Dionysus in the shrine of the Seasons; for these make ripe the fruit of the vine. Near it he also built an altar to the Nymphs to remind devotees of the mixing; for the Nymphs are said to be the nurses of Dionysus. He also instituted the custom of taking just a sip of unmixed wine after meat, as a proof of the power of the good god, but after that they might drink mixed wine, as much as each man chose. They were also to repeat over this cup the name of Zeus the Saviour as a warning and reminder to drinkers that only when they drank in this fashion would they surely be safe.'

(*Deipn.* 2. 38c–d = Philochorus *FGrH* 328 F5b; trans. Gulick)

Philochorus comes at the end of a long tradition of Atthidographers, starting probably with Hellanicus, who had been using the story of Amphictyon, son of Deucalion, taking refuge in Athens to reinforce Athenian claims to autochthony.[1] Again, in *Deipn.* 5.179e, Amphictyon is said to have established a *sanctuary* of Dionysus Orthos (ἱερὸν Διονύσου ὀρθοῦ—a case of Athenaeus misquoting himself) and to have taught Athenians how to mix their wine. For the common Greek mindset every new social or technological development ought to have had its start at a particular point in time, often due to the action of a particular 'inventor' or culture-hero.[2] Amphictyon is here presented as a typical culture-hero in that he introduces a new practice and also establishes a cult to sanctify it. The account of Philochorus is rationalistic: wine must be mixed, because, when drunk mixed and with moderation, it is ὀρθός (right, safe), not σφαλερός (slippery, perilous).

Other sources in Athenaeus explain the invention of wine-mixing and the concomitant sympotic customs differently.[3] According to the physician Philonides (*Deipn.* 15.675b–c), it all happened by chance, as symposiasts on a beach (ἀκτή) were dispersed by a sudden storm. The rain filled up a crater still holding some wine. On their return, they were delighted to discover the new mixture. So, Philonides continues, when unmixed wine is served during the meal, the Greeks invoke Ἀγαθὸς Δαίμων, who is the same as Dionysus.[4] After the meal, when the mixed wine is brought in, they appropriately invoke Zeus Soter, as god of the rain.[5]

The proliferation of similar stories shows that the explanation of the custom in Philochorus is contentious. The purpose of this chapter is to suggest possible contexts for a cult of Dionysus Orthos in Athens. In the absence of epigraphic evidence or any certain material remains, the existence of such a cult is far from definite. The above passage is the only direct reference to it. All the same, while the dedication of an altar by Amphictyon could be dismissed as an invention, whose main object is to provide an origin for a widespread sympotic ritual (θέσμιον),[6] the adjective *orthos* is an intriguing detail which may need some further explanation. I am going to consider three possibilities for its use as a cultic adjective.

I  The word ὀρθός has a range of meanings and different associations. In this particular context an obvious interpretation would be the one offered by Philochorus himself, who associates it with moderation in the drinking of wine, and wine-mixing in particular, and understands it as meaning 'sober, safe'. Athenaeus not only often makes mention of the medicinal qualities of wine, but also preserves sources which attribute healing powers to Dionysus.[7]

For the Greeks, correct mixing was conducive to harmless pleasure and polite company and a hallmark of civilized behaviour in the symposium.[8] On the other hand, excessive drunkenness, which was caused by the unguarded consumption of neat wine, was commonly regarded as disastrous. In a fragment of Eubulus (93 K–A, in *Deipn.* 2.36c) Dionysus, the speaker, runs through the climax of effects from one to ten bowls of wine. The final stage brings extreme inebriation and is described as follows:

δέκατος δὲ μανίας, ὥστε καὶ βάλλειν ποιεῖ.
πολὺς γὰρ εἰς ἓν μικρὸν ἀγγεῖον χυθεὶς
ὑποσκελίζει ῥᾷστα τοὺς πεπωκότας.

The tenth bowl belongs to madness, who also causes people to fall down; because much wine poured into one little vessel trips up very easily those who have drunk it.

The verb ὑποσκελίζει shares some shades of meaning with σφαλερός and καμπτόμενος ("on one's knees'), as used by Philochorus. In such contexts the physical postures of standing up and lying down acquire an almost moral symbolism. The same idea is well illustrated in the story of Icarius and Erigone.

According to one version of the myth, having received the gift of wine from Dionysus, Icarius loads his ox-cart with wine skins and goes about Attica, offering people the new drink to taste.[9] Some cowherds, unaccustomed to drinking strong neat wine, fall to the ground,[10] making incomprehensible utterances, and fall into deep sleep.[11] Their comrades, thinking that they have been poisoned, kill Icarius and bury him under a tree.

Icarius' killing and the suicide of his daughter Erigone, who hanged herself from the tree over her father's grave, brought ritual impurity to the land. Madness was visited upon the women of Athens, who started committing suicide in a similar fashion, until they expiated themselves for her death with the institution of the festival of the *aiora*. Callimachus assigns to her memory the second day of the Anthesteria, the day of the Choes or wine-mixing.[12]

Icarius' entertainment of Dionysus is commonly paralleled by Celeus' hospitality towards Demeter; as a culture-hero he is paired with Triptolemus. Their stories were part of the early history of Attica.[13] It is easy to see how the myth of Icarius, through its connection with the primary wine-festival in Athens, could be used as a cautionary tale, promoting ritual purity in the symposium and in particular the proper consumption of wine.

If *orthos* was used as a cultic epithet for Dionysus in Athens, it is likely that it was used during proceedings on the second day of the Anthesteria, which took place in the sanctuary *en Limnais*. It is not unreasonable to relate Orthos as a cultic title to the cult of Dionysus *en Limnais*. Another historian of Athens, Phanodemus, explicitly connects the latter location with the invention of wine-mixing:

> Φανόδημος δὲ πρὸς τὸ ἱερόν φησι τοῦ ἐν Λίμναις Διονύσου τὸ γλεῦκος φέροντας τοὺς Ἀθηναίους ἐκ τῶν πίθων τῷ θεῷ κιρνάναι, εἶτ᾽ αὐτοὺς προσφέρεσθαι· ὅθεν καὶ Λιμναῖον κληθῆναι τὸν Διόνυσον, ὅτι μιχθὲν τὸ γλεῦκος τῷ ὕδατι τότε πρῶτον ἐπόθη κεκραμένον· διόπερ ὀνομασθῆναι τὰς [πηγὰς] Νύμφας καὶ τιθήνας τοῦ Διονύσου, ὅτι τὸν οἶνον αὐξάνει τὸ ὕδωρ κιρνάμενον. ἡσθέντες οὖν τῇ κράσει ἐν ᾠδαῖς ἔμελπον τὸν Διόνυσον, χορεύοντες καὶ ἀνακαλοῦντες Εὐάνθη καὶ Διθύραμβον καὶ Βακχευτὰν καὶ Βρόμιον.

> Phanodemus says that at the temple of Dionysus in the Marshes the Athenians mix the must which they bring from their casks in honour of the god, and then drink it themselves; hence Dionysus was called god of the marsh, because the must was mixed and drunk with water on that occasion for the first time. Hence, too, the Nymphs were called nurses of Dionysus, because water increases the wine when mixed with it. Delighted, then, with the mixture, men celebrated Dionysus in song, dancing, and calling upon him with the names Flowery, Dithyrambus, Reveller, and Bromius.
> (*Deipn.* 11, 465a = Phanodemus *FGrH* 325 F12: trans. Gulick)

The information we get from Phanodemus touches on a number of subjects shared with the passage of Philochorus. Both are interested in the origins of the mixing habit. According to Philochorus, Amphictyon was the first to mix wine (πρῶτον κεράσαι) and dedicated a sanctuary or altar to Dionysus Ὀρθός. According to Phanodemus, young wine (γλεῦκος) was drunk mixed for the first time in the sanctuary ἐν λίμναις (τότε πρῶτον ἐπόθη κεκραμένον). Phanodemus, like Philochorus, mentions the nymphs (but not the Horai) in the same context. He further remarks that the Athenians, happy with the benefits of the mixing, sang in honour of Dionysus (ἡσθέντες οὖν τῆι κράσει ἐν ὠιδαῖς ἔμελπον τὸν Διόνυσον).

As the Phanodemus passage suggests, Dionysus ἐν λίμναις was the god of the Anthesteria.[14] A much later source, Philostratus (*VA* 4.21), mentions certain dances during the festival where the participants were dressed up as Horai, Nymphs and Bacchae (τὰ μὲν ὡς Ὧραι, τὰ δὲ ὡς Νύμφαι, τὰ δὲ ὡς Βάκχαι πράττουσιν). The juxtaposition of the three fits well the establishment of the sanctuary of Dionysus Ὀρθός as known from Philochorus.

The connection with the Anthesteria is even more interesting, in view of the claim of Theopompus, preserved in the Aristophanic scholia, that the ritual of the Chytroi, third day of the celebration, in which a πανσπερμία (a ritual offering of mixed seeds and fruit) was boiled in a pot and offered to Hermes, was made in commemoration of the people who had drowned in the Deluge.[15] This points us back to the stories about Amphictyon, son of Deucalion.

**II**    The word ὀρθός is also attested in contexts where it means 'ithyphallic'. Ithyphallic processions were an important part of the Rural Dionysia.[16] A well-known passage from the *Acharnians* provides a vivid illustration of the ritual (241–79). There the adjective ὀρθός is used twice for the phallus (243, 259).[17]

The Aristophanic scholia on the *Acharnians* (243) relate a tradition according to which the Athenians did not accept with appropriate honour the statue of the god which Pegasus brought from Eleutherae. In retribution the god sent them some sort of venereal disease (νόσος κατέσκηψεν εἰς τὰ αἰδοῖα τῶν ἀνδρῶν). An embassy (θεωροί) was sent to the oracle,[18] which returned with the answer that the city ought to make a formal procession in honour of the god (διὰ τιμῆς ἁπάσης ἄγοιεν τὸν θεόν). The Athenians responded to that by preparing *phalloi*, in private and in public (ἰδίαι τε καὶ δημοσίαι), and with these they honoured the god (ἐγέραιρον), as a reminder of their misfortune.[19] To this antiquarian lore the scholiast adds a rationalistic explanation for the link of Dionysus with the phallus, namely that the consumption of wine induces sexual desire.[20] Servius (*ad G.* 2.389) claims that phalloi were hung from trees during the *aiora*.[21]

Ithyphallic processions were associated with drunkenness. The excesses of the drinking club of the *ithyphalloi* are related in the speech of Demosthenes *Against Conon* (54.14, 16, 17, 20). Semos of Delos in his work on the Paeans mentions that the *ithyphalloi* used to wear the masks of drunken characters and to enter the orchestra in silence, then, reaching the middle, turn to the audience and sing (*Deipn.* 14.622a–d):

ἀνάγετ᾽, ἀνάγετ᾽, / εὐρυχωρίαν ποιεῖτε / τῶι θεῶι· θέλει γὰρ ὁ θεὸς / ὀρθὸς ἐσφυδωμένος / διὰ μέσου βαδίζειν.

Bring up and make space for the god; for the god wants to pass through the middle, upright and throbbing.

It is unclear where this particular procession took place or during which festival.[22] What is certain is that excessive consumption of wine is implied by our sources dealing with the ithyphallic cult of Dionysus.

The building complex discussed by Pausanias in the following passage is presumed to have been somewhere along the Sacred Way from the Dipylon Gate through the Cerameicus (which, he claims, was named after the hero Ceramus, son of Dionysus and Ariadne). In his age it took in the house of Pulytion, who was involved in the affair of the parody of the Mysteries in 415. Pausanias does not mention the sanctuary ἐν Λίμναις nor that of Dionysus Ὀρθός, because he ignores them or they did not exist in his times.[23] In fact, we do not know how old the sanctuary he describes actually is. Pausanias states:

ἡ δὲ ἑτέρα τῶν στοῶν ἔχει μὲν ἱερὰ θεῶν, ἔχει δὲ γυμνάσιον Ἑρμοῦ καλούμενον· ἔστι δὲ ἐν αὐτῇ Πουλυτίωνος οἰκία, καθ᾽ ἣν παρὰ τὴν ἐν Ἐλευσῖνι δρᾶσαι τελετὴν Ἀθηναίων φασὶν οὐ τοὺς ἀφανεστάτους· ἐπ᾽ ἐμοῦ δὲ ἀνεῖτο Διονύσῳ. Διόνυσον δὲ τοῦτον καλοῦσι Μελπόμενον ἐπὶ λόγῳ τοιῷδε ἐφ᾽ ὁποίῳ περ Ἀπόλλωνα Μουσηγέτην. ἐνταῦθά ἐστιν Ἀθηνᾶς ἄγαλμα Παιωνίας καὶ Διὸς καὶ Μνημοσύνης καὶ Μουσῶν, Ἀπόλλων τε ἀνάθημα καὶ ἔργον Εὐβουλίδου, καὶ δαίμων τῶν ἀμφὶ Διόνυσον Ἄκρατος· πρόσωπόν ἐστίν οἱ μόνον ἐνῳκοδομημένον τοίχῳ. μετὰ δὲ τὸ τοῦ Διονύσου τέμενός ἐστιν οἴκημα ἀγάλματα ἔχον ἐκ πηλοῦ, βασιλεὺς Ἀθηναίων Ἀμφικτύων ἄλλους τε θεοὺς ἑστιῶν καὶ Διόνυσον. ἐνταῦθα καὶ Πήγασός ἐστιν Ἐλευθερεύς, ὃς Ἀθηναίοις τὸν θεὸν ἐσήγαγε· συνεπελάβετο δέ οἱ τὸ ἐν Δελφοῖς μαντεῖον ἀναμνῆσαν τὴν ἐπὶ Ἰκαρίου ἐπιδημίαν τοῦ θεοῦ.

One of the porticoes contains shrines of gods, and a gymnasium called that of Hermes. In it is the house of Pulytion, at which it is said that a mystic rite was performed by the most notable Athenians, parodying the Eleusinian mysteries. But in my time it was devoted to the worship of Dionysus. This Dionysus they call Melpomenus (*Minstrel*), on the same principle as they call Apollo Musegetes (*Leader of the Muses*). Here there are images of Athena Paeonia (*Healer*), of Zeus, of Mnemosyne (*Memory*) and of the Muses, an Apollo, the votive offering and work of Eubulides, and

Acratus, a daemon attendant upon Dionysus; it is only a face of him worked into the wall. After the precinct of Apollo is a building that contains earthenware images, Amphictyon, king of Athens, feasting Dionysus and other gods. Here also is Pegasus of Eleutherae, who introduced the god to the Athenians. Herein he was helped by the oracle at Delphi, which called to mind that the god once dwelt in Athens in the days of Icarius.

(Paus. 1.2.5; trans. W.H.S. Jones)

All the important figures for the introduction of Dionysiac cult in Athens are here: Icarius, Amphictyon, Eleuthereus. As in the story of the Aristophanic scholia, there is a pronounced link with Delphi. Pausanias says Μελπόμενος is equivalent to Μουσηγέτης, a well-known epithet of Apollo. Within the sanctuary there were statues of Athena, Zeus, Mnemosyne and the Muses, and Apollo. Indeed, the role of the Delphic oracle is pronounced clearly: συνεπελάβετο δέ οἱ (sc. Πηγάσωι) τὸ ἐν Δελφοῖς μαντεῖον ἀναμνῆσαν τὴν ἐπὶ Ἰκαρίου ποτὲ ἐπιδημίαν τοῦ θεοῦ.

While the scholiast of Aristophanes claims that the proper re-introduction of Dionysus Eleuthereus in Athens was a result of oracular consultation in the face of an unaccountable venereal disease, Pausanias represents the Delphic oracle reminding the Athenians of the previous stay of the god in Athens, during the time of Icarius. Having shown disrespect to the god during his first visit, they needed to reintroduce him properly. Offence is offered to the divinity, in Pegasus' case by indifference, in Icarius' case by ignorance.

For Pausanias the oldest sanctuary of Dionysus in Athens is the one of Dionysus Eleuthereus by the theatre (1.20.3).[24] It is not improbable that as a result he mixes two different local traditions about two different instances for the introduction of the god in Athens, one in the time of Amphictyon and another in the time of Pegasus of Eleutherae.

A remarkable feature of the sanctuary of Dionysus Μελπόμενος was a wall mask of a daemon, follower of Dionysus, by the name of Acratus, i.e. 'Unmixed Wine' (cf. *Deipn.* 15.675b). This may have been an edifying allusion to the myth of Icarius, whose image, unlike Amphictyon's, is absent from the complex.

Two details in Pausanias' description may allow the hypothesis that this sanctuary may be related to the cult of Dionysus Orthos, as it is presented in the passage of Philochorus: the complex of Amphictyon and the wall-mask of Acratus. As we have seen, Philochorus claimed that Amphictyon was the first to teach the mixing of wine (πρῶτον κεράσαι), so that people could at last stand on their feet (ὀρθοὺς γενέσθαι), while they were previously falling down by drinking unmixed wine to excess (πρότερον ὑπὸ τοῦ ἀκράτου καμπτομένους). This corresponds exactly to the experience of the first wine-drinkers as presented in the myth of Icarius and the mosaic of Paphos. The difficulty of this attribution is that

Pausanias does not mention any sanctuary of the Horae or altar of the Nymphs in the precinct; they might be hidden behind the general reference to ἄλλους τε θεούς, who enjoy Amphictyon's hospitality.

Erwin Rohde believed that the Ἀγαθὸς Δαίμων is the closest Greek equivalent to the *Lar familiaris* of the Romans.[25] But the Greeks soon forgot its original meaning of the soul of a forefather who becomes the good spirit of his house. The deity, like so many chthonic powers, had the outward appearance of a snake. If the association of a cult of Dionysus Orthos with the Anthesteria carries any weight, it is well to remember that the third day of the celebration (Chytroi) is thought to have been dedicated to the dead.[26] A third meaning for the adjective ὀρθός, less often encountered, may be 'infernal, rising up from the Underworld'. This is difficult to prove conclusively, but there is some evidence to make it plausible.

Orthos, as a name, is associated with stagnant water and the Underworld. In Hesiod, Echidna mates with Typhon and bears Orthos, a dog for Geryon, Cerberus, a dog for Hades, and Hydra, a lake creature (*Th.* 304–18). All three creatures were defeated by Hercules.[27] Ortho is the name of a daemon of the Underworld in a third-fourth century AD magical text (*SEG* 38. 1837.7, 46).

Furthermore, the adjective ὀρθός is often connected with excessive mourning or madness (P. Ross. Georg. I.11, vv. 39–40: οὐ γὰρ δὴν πάλι Λύσσα κελεύοντος Διονύσου| ὀρθῆισ[ιν μ]αν[ίηι]σιν ἀνήγειρεν Λυκόοργον [was it not Lyssa again who, obeying Dionysus, stirred Lycurgus with infernal madness?], cf. Theocritus 11: ὀρθαῖς μανίαις), and also with the Erinyes.[28]

In Apollodorus 3.15.8 the daughters of Hyacinthus are named as Antheis (cf. Anthesteria, Dionysus Antheus), Aigleis (Aigle is the name of a bacchant in Nonn. 14.221), Lytaia (cf. Dionysus Lysios), and Orthaia; they were sacrificed at the tomb of the Cyclops Geraistos.

Artemis Orthia, who had a sanctuary in Cerameicus, was also known as Orthia or Λιμνᾶτις in Sparta, where her sanctuary was situated in a place called Λιμναῖον.[29] She was also called Λυγοδέσμα (cf. Dionysus Κισσός (*and* Μελπόμενος) in Acharnai). According to Hesychius (s.v. Λόμβαι), women sacrificed to Artemis Orthia in Sparta. Female sacrifice is an unusual occurrence, but one that is paralleled by the similar practice of female sacrifice by the γέραιραι at the Anthesteria. Their name is derived from the phallic accessories of their ritual dress:

αἱ τῆι Ἀρτέμιδι θυσιῶν ἄρχουσαι, ἀπὸ τῆς κατὰ τὴν παιδιὰν σκευῆς. οἱ γὰρ φάλητες οὕτω καλοῦνται.

Those who make sacrifices to Artemis, from their jesting equipment. For this is what the phalluses are called.

There is archaeological evidence for the use of masks in the cult of Artemis Orthia.[30] The sanctuary is said to have contained the *xoanon* of the Taurian Artemis brought by Orestes and Iphigeneia. Pausanias presents the counter-claims of other temples to possess that original, but suggests that the bloodthirsty custom of whipping the ephebes in the sanctuary proves the barbaric origin of the Spartan statue.[31]

I suggest that there is an evident structural parallel between the cult of Artemis Orthia and certain aspects of the cult of Dionysus in Athens: a sanctuary in the vicinity of water, female sacrifice, use of masks, use of phallic imagery, initiation rites,[32] cultic statue in the form of a *xoanon*, origins of the cult in the myth of Orestes and Iphigeneia. Both divinities were believed to be ruthless in their revenge, exemplified in myth in their actions against Actaeon and Pentheus.[33]

This leads us to the final passage which may be thought to provide evidence, if not for a cult of Dionysus Orthos in Athens, at least for the use of the adjective as a ritual epithet of Dionysus in certain contexts, namely Euripides' *Bacchae*:

> ὡς κλῶν' ὄρειον ὁ ξένος χεροῖν ἄγων
> ἔκαμπτεν ἐς γῆν, ἔργματ' οὐχὶ θνητὰ δρῶν.
> Πενθέα δ' ἱδρύσας ἐλατίνων ὄζων ἔπι,
> ὀρθὸν μεθίει διὰ χερῶν βλάστημ' ἄνω
> ἀτρέμα, φυλάσσων μὴ ἀναχαιτίσειέ νιν,
> ὀρθὴ δ' ἐς ὀρθὸν αἰθέρ' ἐστηρίζετο,
> ἔχουσα νώτοις δεσπότην ἐφήμενον·
> ὤφθη δὲ μᾶλλον ἢ κατεῖδε μαινάδας.

In this way the stranger pulling with his hands the mountain branch bent it to the earth, performing deeds not mortal. And having sat Pentheus on the fir branches he began to let the shoot go upright, passing it through his hands without it shaking, taking care that it should not toss him off, and it began to tower upright into the upright air of heaven with my master sitting on its back. But rather than seeing the maenads he was seen by them.

(Euripides *Bacchae* 1068–75; trans. Seaford)

The glen where the action happens is described as well watered and full of pine-trees: ἦν δ' ἄγκος ἀμφίκρημνον, ὕδασι διάβροχον,/ πεύκαισι συσκιάζον ... (1051–2).[34] There are references to the cult of Dionysus δενδρίτης in Plutarch (*Mor.* 675f) and of ἔνδενδρος in Hesychius (s.v.).

It has been thought that many details of the action in the *Bacchae* are meant to represent Dionysiac initiatory ritual. The emphatic repetition of the word ὀρθός in this passage may actually echo a ritual invocation. A remarkable link with Philochorus is his use of the verb κάμπτειν in common with Euripides. Of course, not every detail of the myth should be expected to represent ritual practice. Yet a passage in Tacitus shows that the scene of Pentheus climbing up the tree was probably re-enacted at Messalina's bacchanal during her parody of a sacred marriage with Silius. Imitation of the *Bacchae* is possible, but all the same this was a ritual, not theatrical performance.[35]

I believe that all three possible interpretations of ὀρθός may correspond to different cultic functions of the adjective, all relevant to the consecration and consumption of wine. The Greeks themselves believed that the Dionysiac cult had undergone historically a process of rationalization. There is, for example, a pronounced difference between the reality of maenadic cult in historical times and its projection in myth. It seems that for Philochorus, and even more for Athenaeus, Dionysus has shed the vestiges of chthonic, agricultural cult to preside over the civil banquet.

# 36

# THE PHYSICIANS AT THE FEAST

## THE PLACE OF MEDICAL KNOWLEDGE AT ATHENAEUS' DINNER-TABLE

### by Rebecca Flemming

Physicians make a significant contribution to Athenaeus' literary feast. Before reaching the first course (1.1e–f), the audience is introduced to Daphnus of Ephesus (pure in both his art and his attitude), to Galen of Pergamum (who has surpassed his predecessors in the volume of his publications on matters medical and philosophical, and equalled them in the skill of his exposition) and to Rufinus of Nicaea (who comes without attributes and never reappears in the text as it survives, seemingly replaced by one Dionysocles), for these men are among the deipnosophists. Before the banquet ends we have met over a dozen more doctors, summoned to participate in the discourse if not the dining itself.

It is worth dwelling for a moment on these figures, as present in life or only in learning, and their various interrelationships. Galen of Pergamum is the only recognisable name amongst those actually in attendance, though Ephesus certainly, and Nicaea to a lesser extent, are recognisably good names of places for physicians to come from.[1] Galen was an older contemporary of Athenaeus; but, though Athenaeus' judgement on the volume of Galen's literary output is correct, none of this abundant material appears at the dinner party itself. The words Galen speaks to the other guests and wider audience are not his own, and no reference to any of his works is made elsewhere. Rather, Athenaeus draws on a group of medical writers from a much earlier period, extending only up to the first century BC. That Athenaeus' medical sources do extend this far towards his own time, however, does indicate that he was using something other than a standard work of medical doxography, which tend to close with Erasistratus in the Hellenistic period.[2] The particular authors and texts he cites also confirm his place outside the medical mainstream.

Going back to Hippocrates, the father-figure for the Greek literary medical tradition, was, of course, obligatory, and Athenaeus uses the works ascribed to him as a lexicographical (2.57c and 9.399b) as well as medical (2.45e–f and 2.46b–c) resource; demonstrating, as he does so, his awareness of the problems of authorship and title that attend them. Philistion of Locri, Diocles of Carystus, Mnesitheus the Athenian, and Dieuches are all names that often accompany that of Hippocrates in ancient lists of key figures in the history of medicine; and all appear in the *Deipnosophistae*.[3] Philistion, a contemporary of and perhaps influence on Plato, is mentioned only briefly, and Dieuches features only as the teacher of Numenius of Heracleia, the author of a treatise on banquets; but the other two later figures from the fourth century BC are called upon more frequently and fully.[4] For Diocles authored a major treatise *On Health* and Mnesitheus one *On Victuals*, both replete with advice on food and drink.

In some senses, Athenaeus' coverage gets more patchy, and his priorities more obvious, as he moves further into the Hellenistic era. Praxagoras of Cos, a key figure in the development of rationalist medicine who lived and worked towards the end of the fourth century BC, appears on a handful of occasions. His pupil Phylotimus, the author of a work *On Nourishment* in at least ten books, is more frequently and substantially cited, and his pupil Plistonicus is mentioned once.[5] However, Praxagoras' most famous pupil, the great anatomist, and founder of his own medical lineage, Herophilus, is not referred to at all; though two Herophileans are mentioned, namely, Andreas, the physician to Ptolemy IV Philopator, and Apollonius Mys, who flourished in the late first century BC.[6] Andreas, however, is better known for his contributions to pharmacology and his instrument for reducing dislocations than for the treatises Athenaeus attaches to his name—*On Poisonous Animals* (7.312d) and *On False Beliefs* (3.115e–f). And it is similarly only Athenaeus who provides testimony to Apollonius' authorship of a work *On Perfumes* (quoted extensively at 15.688e-689b) to be placed alongside his better known tracts, such as those *On the Sect of Herophilus* and *On Common Remedies*.

Herophilus' contemporary and fellow anatomist, Erasistratus of Iulis on Cos, makes a few fleeting appearances in the *Deipnosophistae*, together with his treatises *On the Art of Cooking* and *On General Practice* (2.46c, 7.324a, 12.516c and 15.666a); but he too is eclipsed by his followers. Or rather, by one follower in particular, that is Hicesius, the founder of an Erasistratean medical school in Smyrna in the first century BC and author of a work *On Materials* (on whom, see Chapter 37), who is a most favoured authority; while the otherwise-unknown Erasistratean Menodorus merits only the most passing of references (2.59a). The medical writer most often cited by Athenaeus, however, is Diphilus of Siphnos, a physician who flourished at the time of the Successor Lysimachus and composed a work *On Provisions for the Diseased and the Healthy*.[7] Neither the man nor the text are mentioned anywhere else in the surviving literature.

Finally, Heraclides of Tarentum, writing during the first century BC, was one of the leading adherents of the Empiric Sect; that he composed a *Symposium*, as well as numerous pharmacological texts and works of Hippocratic exegesis, is not widely publicised outside the *Deipnosophistae*.[8] And, if Athenaeus' Philonides, the physician and author of *On Perfumes and Wreaths* (15.675a, 15.676c and 15.691f–692b), is from Sicily then he was not only a near contemporary of Heraclides, but also shared his interests in Hippocrates and, most probably, drugs (though with less impact).[9]

Thus Athenaeus draws on the canonical, classical, core of the Greek literary medical tradition, but then diversifies, in respect to both authors and texts, through the Hellenistic period, before coming to a complete halt. Whether, however, this earlier, core, material came to him in a mediated form, in a compilation (or compilations) of some sort which he then unravelled, while the later material was taken direct from the treatises themselves, is difficult to say. For, though the indications within the extant medical tradition would support such a suggestion, *if* the *Deipnosophistae* were itself a part of that tradition, of course it is not; and enquiries of this kind are harder to make among the rather less substantial remains of sympotic literature.

That medicine was an integral element of sympotic discourse is attested by Plutarch's *Symposiakoi* and Macrobius' *Saturnalia*, not to mention Plato's *Symposium*; but all these are literary projects of a rather different kind from Athenaeus'.[10] In particular, they are more synthetic, even creative, and polished affairs than Athenaeus' assemblage of authorities and quotations. So, though Plutarch is more narrowly medically mainstream than Athenaeus, with only Erasistratus (*Mor.* 663c, 698d, 699a), Philistion of Locri (699c), Hippocrates and his pupil Dioxippus/Dexippus (699c) and Asclepiades (731a) referred to at his parties, without the specific citation of works, and only Hippocrates (*Sat.* 7.5.19) and Erasistratus (7.15.3 and 8) make it as far as Macrobius, this does not mean that other sympotic texts, now lost, did not more closely resemble the *Deipnosophistae* in appearance.[11] Athenaeus might, therefore, have made use of medical resources already collected around the materials and manners of a certain form of dining. Indeed, such a situation would explain why, though Athenaeus knows Galen's name and achievements, he does not employ his works; the first comes directly from the world around him, while the latter are taken from a literary tradition that seems to have substantially closed (as did many others) around the time of Augustus.[12] Whatever their precise route into Athenaeus' text, however, the range of names and works that do make it is an impressive indication of the real profusion of classical medical writing.

Further comparison with Plutarch and his sympotic pieces is also useful in drawing out the particularities of the ways in which Athenaeus makes use of his medical resources, their topical configuration within the *Deipnosophistae*. For, while the display of medical knowledge clearly constitutes one of the manners of the literary banquet, it may take one of (at least) two forms. Athenaeus essentially presents medical knowledge about what is going on there and then at the feast. Plutarch (and after him Macrobius), on the other hand, demonstrates medical knowledge that is about itself, directed not inwards towards the events of which it is a part, but outwards towards a topic of discussion that may arise from, but extends well beyond, feasting. Thus, while the former's deipnosophists marshal medical material on food and drink, eating and drinking, perfumes and garlands, material which comes both from the core and the periphery of the medical tradition, the latter's symposiasts bring medical thinking to bear on such general questions as why women are least, and old men most, liable to become drunk, and thence to the even broader issues of whether women have a hotter or colder constitutional mixture than men, and whether wine has a cooling faculty; they are even happy to tackle entirely autonomous medical matters, such as whether it is possible for new diseases to come into existence and what might cause them (*Mor.* 650a–3b and 731a–4c).[13] Since these are debates conducted in terms of basic physiological and pathological concepts and principles (at least within rationalist medicine), there is no need to reach outside the centre of medical learning, or even to cite names and texts for dealings in such common currency.

Plutarch, like Athenaeus, Macrobius and also Plato, numbers physicians among the guests; and, in all these writers, medical men are the main, but by no means only, founts of medical knowledge in the discussions. The fragmentary survival of parts of the *Deipnosophistae* makes precise analysis problematic, but it is clear that the majority of the conversational contributions made by the doctors present are primarily of a medical character, though a couple of their comments have nothing about them that betrays their profession at all. Both Galen and Daphnus announce themselves as representatives of their art, an art that has its proper role to play in the business of discursive dining. Relatively early on in proceedings, as the bread is brought in, Galen asserts that:

> We shall not dine until you have heard from us also what the sons of the Asclepiadae have to say about bread, cake and meal.
>
> (3.115c)

Later on (8.355a), Daphnus similarly criticises the discussion thus far on fish for its omission of what the medical authorities have said, an omission he too goes on to rectify at some length.

The disquisitions that follow, and that appear elsewhere, are mainly composed of citations from medical authors and works, more or less clearly arranged and attributed. They usually cover the basic points of the relationship between the relevant food or drink or style of eating, drinking or whatever, and health, expressed in very general terms. Galen's discourse on breads, for instance (3.115c–16a), reports the verdicts of Diphilus, Philistion and Mnesitheus on the relative merits of breads baked in different styles, from different flours, and eaten fresh or dry. These merits are broadly judged in terms of flavour or succulence, nourishment, and the ease or difficulty with which the body processes them, with some reference to their effects on its workings, particularly excretion. More specific properties are rarely mentioned, nor is much attention paid to particular conditions or diseases: unground or uncooked breads produce wind, torpor, cramps and headache, while there is (according to Andreas) a Syrian mulberry bread that causes hair-loss. Little explanation or justification is offered for these judgements, though there is an implicit physiological framework in place, based fundamentally on the qualitative continuity between food and body, and in which the qualitative interaction between the two produces both benefits and risks.

Physicians also say things that come from many other, non-medical, kinds of sources. Having exhausted Phylotimus, Mnesitheus and Diphilus on fish, for instance (8.358c–359e), Daphnus moves on to the comic poets Antiphanes and Ephippus, though they have nothing much to contribute on matters of health. Somewhat more integrated into another of Daphnus' predominantly medical narratives, this time on the proper balance between eating and drinking when dining, and the foods best placed in the intervals between drinks (3.120b–1e), are the historian Ephippus of Olynthus' comments on excessive Macedonian drinking habits and the descriptive remarks of the geographer Strabo and the lexicographer Pamphilus on different kinds of fish which may or may not be pickled to eat after, and as a counterweight to, drinking. Such non-medical authorities may also, however, address themselves to distinctly medical matters. In the same discourse, Daphnus also cites the 'most accomplished' Xenophon, (or Simonides in conversation with Hieron as reported by Xenophon) as completely condemning sharp, acrid, and harsh foods, against, or at least in contradistinction to, the view of Mnesitheus on their utility (3.121d–e). Similarly, Plutarch deploys some poetic lines of Eupolis and Euripides to contradict Erasistratus in defence of Plato's view that liquid drunk passes through the lungs (*Mor.* 699a); lines repeated by Macrobius in his version of this debate (*Sat.* 7.15.23; cf. Aulus Gellius *NA* 17.11).

Medical knowledge also appears in the various catalogues of fish and vegetables that Athenaeus incorporates in his literary feast. Though here there is no named speaker, these passages share some similarities with the interventions of the physicians. Most such entries contain some comment about the nutritional, or more generally somatic, effects of the item in question taken from a medical writer, comments that intermingle with a range of other definitional, dramatic, lexicographical and historical excerpts. Often, indeed, medical authors provide this kind of information too, or even solely. The line from Diocles' *On Health* included in the section on the fishes called 'thrushes and blackbirds' (7.305a–d) makes a point of classification, placing these creatures in the broader category of rock fish; a category characterised by soft-flesh but without further dietetic qualification. Nor does any other authority fill the hygienic gap in a passage almost entirely devoted to matters of spelling, terminology and description. This is, however, simply a more extreme example of the general principle of the commensurability of literary resources as organised by Athenaeus.

Lastly, medical knowledge may be deployed by non-physicians in the discussions. Masurius, the jurist and polymath, speaks, in the course of the conversation on perfumes and wreaths at the end of the work, of their healthful qualities (15.687d–688c). He repeats the poet Alexis' line about a large part of health being the provision of suitable smells for the brain; and justifies Alcaeus' and Anacreon's poetic recommendations of pouring perfumes over the chest by citing Praxagoras, Phylotimus, Homer, Sophocles and Plato as holding that the seat of the soul is in the heart, and thus beneficially affected by these applications. This juxtaposition, on seemingly equal terms, of physicians such as Praxagoras and poets such as Homer is, moreover, reminiscent of the arguments for placing the seat of the soul in the heart attributed to the Stoic Chrysippus by a hostile Galen in his work *On the Doctrines of Plato and Hippocrates*. Indeed, this intertwining of medical and non-medical authorities and materials is sometimes taken a step further. Daphnus, for instance, quotes Diphilus quoting the poet Alexis on the aphrodisiac properties of the octopus (8.356e); and, in turn, Alexis is quoted as having a character in one of his plays cite Mnesitheus' maxim that one should avoid excess in everything (10.419b–c).

The physicians are, then, at Athenaeus' feast primarily in order to make it a healthy feast. This alignment of the banquet with the goal of health, and the importance of that goal, is, moreover, made more or less explicit in the final sections of the *Deipnosophistae*. The last, and perennially popular, scolion sung towards the end of the feast ranks being healthy above all the other fortunate situations of mortal man (15.694e); and the point is underlined by Ariphron's famous hymn to Hygieia—divinely personified health—with which Athenaeus' host almost brings proceedings to a close (15.702a–b). Health is here praised as the fundamental precondition for, the necessary divine companion to, all human happiness and achievement. This is not to be forgotten while feasting; indeed such convivial occasions are to be positively organised towards health. For the banquet is a place where many of the key themes of healthy living are enacted and articulated; it is a forum for dietetic practice and discussion, recognised as such by doctors and lay-men alike. To write works on the symposium, on cooking or perfumes, was as proper to the medical profession as it was for littérateurs such as Athenaeus, Plutarch and Macrobius to write the medical profession and medical knowledge into their literary productions.

Athenaeus, his physicians and his medical knowledge, work towards the goal of health, however, in a rather relaxed and roundabout fashion. There may not be a surfeit of food and drink at this feast, but there certainly seems to be a surfeit of talk; completeness has the upper hand over clarity, cultural accomplishment over programmatic precision. Athenaeus does impose a certain order on proceedings: in the distribution of his discourse he allocates most (but not all) of its medical portions to the doctors present, but on the same terms as everybody else. Their contributions are just as untidy and rambling, similarly composed of a mix of materials, variously joined and juxtaposed, dominated in this case by medical writings, but also articulating Athenaeus' other ongoing concerns, his larger patterns of cultural display; just as speakers who specialise in other areas of convivial conversation may have issues of health caught up in their reflections. The authority of these physicians, and of those cited, derives, moreover, precisely from this concentration, the repetition of this discursive distribution, rather than any kind of deeper epistemological privilege. On any given point of medical import, what Xenophon or Euripides has to say, for example, is as valid (if not more so) than what any doctor, such as Mnesitheus or Erasistratus, says; but these latter have systematically addressed themselves to the goal of health in a way that the former have not. The leading position of the doctor in such matters is only thus assured.

In all this, therefore, Athenaeus illustrates the manifold richness and cultural integrity of classical medicine. The physicians at his feast are somewhat un-canonical in their reading, as are the opinions they offer, for they are caught up in someone else's literary project; but they readily participate in such a project (on the same terms as everybody else). They are an intrinsic part of the cultural monument that Athenaeus erects.

# 37

# HICESIUS' FISH AND CHIPS

## A PLEA FOR AN EDITION OF THE FRAGMENTS AND TESTIMONIES OF THE περὶ ὕλης

### by Danielle Gourevitch

Athenaeus 'has contrived to bring into his book an account of fishes, their uses and names with their derivations; also vegetables of all sorts and animals of every description' (*Deipn.* 1.1a). For the rest of the work, Athenaeus quotes endlessly from famous and less famous writers (cf. Chapter 36), among them Hicesius the doctor who concerns me here.

At the beginning of the first century AD, Hicesius was a disciple of Erasistratus (*Deipn.* 3.87b, ὁ Ἐρασιστράτειος). He founded a medical school in Smyrna which followed the teaching of his own indirect master. It does not seem to have lasted long:

**1. Hicesius, the doctor**

> Between Laodicea and Carura is a temple of Men Carus, as it is called, which is held in remarkable veneration. In my own time, 'a great Herophilean school of medicine has been established by Zeuxis, and afterwards carried on by Alexander Philalethes, just as in the time of our fathers the Erasistratean school[1] was established in Smyrna by Hicesius, although at the present time the case is not at all the same as it used to be.[2]

According to Diogenes Laertius (5.94), Hicesius had at least one known disciple or successor: under the name of Heracleides, number eight in the list is ἰατρὸς τῶν ἀπὸ Ἱκεσίου (while number nine is another doctor, from Tarentum, who belonged to the empirical sect, ἐμπειρικός). Metrodorus, another disciple of Erasistratus, was a friend of his (φίλος, *Deipn.* 2.59 a);[3] this Metrodorus was also interested in food, especially vegetables, according to Athenaeus. According to Regnault, Hicesius had a grandson, Artemon, who was himself a doctor and had a stele erected in his honour in Smyrna.[4]

His name appears among the *auctoritates* of Pliny's Books 14–15 and 20–7, which appears to indicate that he had himself written about the subjects there treated, that is to say: Book 14, fruit trees, wines; 15, olives, olive oil, fruit trees; 20, remedies from garden plants; 21, flowers and wreaths; 22, plants for wreaths; 23, cultivated trees; 24, wild trees, forest trees; 25, self-grown plants; 26, other remedies; 27, other plants. He is also quoted by Pliny elsewhere several times. For example at 27. 31, according to which Hicesius was a real authority on certain medical matters: *non parvae auctoritatis medicum*. As a surgeon he was not forgotten by Tertullian,[5] who had a low opinion of him, since he was not against embryotomy, for *iam natis animam superducens ex aeris frigidi pulsu* (*De anima* 25. 6 ed. Waszink, p. 25), therefore *et naturae et artis praevaricator* (ibid. 2). He was a famous pharmacologist and invented a famous recipe, the black remedy, later used by Heracleides of Tarentum among others according to Galen, and Paul of Aegina still lists it (3. 64 and 7. 17).

## 2. Hicesius, the author of a treatise περὶ ὕλης

Athenaeus is a particularly important source for fragments of the περὶ ὕλης which concern food. But are his quotations of it reliable?

According to Zepernick 1921, Athenaeus is fairly reliable. Good readings in fact have sometimes been preserved by him, when the text had been distorted elsewhere. Zepernick's study covers the whole *Deipnosophistae*, but he chose very famous literary authors, for whom there was a strong tradition. He did not check scientific writers. How accurately did Athenaeus quote them?

Let us consult the excellent article by Sharples and Minter (1983). At *Deipn.* 2. 61–2, that is to say in chapters of the *Epitome* (on whose possible impact, see Chapter 33), Athenaeus attributes to Theophrastus five passages concerning fungi. Two of them are not in the transmitted text of *Historia Plantarum*: does that mean that they come from another work by Theophrastus? Either way no comparison is possible, which is exactly the case for all our passages attributed to Hicesius.

What about the other three passages for which a comparison can be drawn with the *Historia Plantarum*? The answer, as we shall see, is that, whether personally or through another writer, Athenaeus quotes with inaccuracies and alterations.

The first of these three passages (2.61e-f) is introduced by the formula, φησὶ δὲ [ὁ Θεόφραστος] καὶ ὅτι, which makes things grammatically straightforward, no grammatical change being necessary inside the quotation. Yet this quotation is not correct, Athenaeus (or his predecessor?) misplaces a detail about the Pillars of Heracles (which came earlier in Theophrastus) and thus the whole passage is falsified; two separate details have been put together, either because the writer did not care, because he did not know what he was speaking about, or for the sake of prettiness to keep a picturesque geographical detail.

The second passage (2.61f) is a list of fungi, or more precisely of smooth-skinned plants, according to Athenaeus, who says he is quoting Theophrastus: ὕδνον, μύκης, πέζις, γερανεῖον, while the list in Theophrastus himself is one of plants with no roots, which is not exactly the same: ὕδνον, μύκης, πύξος, κράνιον. In Theophrastus there was actually a list of smooth-skinned plants, but it was different and it came earlier. In such conditions the identification of those fungi is almost impossible. This error may be due to over-hasty compression or to ignorance.

The third passage (also a list) gives evidence again of confusion, careless quotations, over-compression, special choices owing to the particular interests of the author: the quotations from Theophrastus by Athenaeus are not reliable.

After such a survey, we cannot be very optimistic about reconstructing Hicesius' thought and writings, but not too pessimistic either: Athenaeus, I am sure, did not read his scientific sources carefully and did not try very hard to understand and evaluate them. But, since Hicesius is quite 'matter of fact' most of the time, Athenaeus can quote him without much hesitation; he interferes little. Therefore I believe an edition of Hicesius' fragments should be attempted, Athenaeus being a fairly accurate reporter in his case.

Why should such an undertaking be embarked upon? First, in an excellent article dealing with the problem of 'fragmentation and the Greek medical writers', Ann Ellis Hanson regrets that 'no magisterial and wide-ranging collection of testimonia and fragments, analogous to Felix Jacoby's *Die Fragmente der griechischen Historiker* or Hermann Diels' *Die Fragmente der Vorsokratiker* has yet been compiled for the medical writers whose works do not survive in extant manuscript copies from the Byzantine period'.[6] Second, there is nowadays a new interest in *realia* in antiquity. Third, the Loeb collection has never been interested in tiny realistic details, while the Collection des Universités de France (the Budé text) never went further than the second book .[7] Fourth, Hippocrates and Galen have been so much scrutinized these last twenty years that many of us medical historians are now keen to move on to something else. Fifth, a new approach to ancient medical thought might be attempted through the study of minor writers.

If we cannot compare various versions of our medical writer, we can at least try to understand how Athenaeus quotes Hicesius. How are the words and opinions of Hicesius introduced into Athenaeus' text? I shall look at every quotation from Hicesius, a study which seems not to have been made hitherto.

\* \* \*

The classic formula, according to our grammar-books, is φησίν, followed by a propositional infinitive. In fact, that is what we find in 3.87b; 7.312c, 313 a, 313d, 314b, 315e, 321a, 323a, 328b; 15.681c. The inconvenience is that the required propositional infinitive does not allow a real quotation, because the form of the verbs and the case of the subjects (with their adjectives and so on) are necessarily modified. The situation is the same with ἱστορεῖ, which needs the same construction (3.116e). Meanwhile, in 7.282d, there is a propositional infinitive without any verb, just because a few lines before appears the verb μνημονεύει, with another subject. Sometimes too, there is the indirect construction without any φησί at all, because φησί is still implied: 7.278a and 7.315d, a propositional infinitive without an introductory verb.

To keep the real words and style of the source, φησί + ὅτι or ὡς proves more convenient: 7.298b. And still easier φησί, followed by a direct quotation 7.285b, 306d, 328c; 15.689c; or the same, after an understated φησί which appeared in a previous sentence (7.278a, because just before there is Ἀριστοτέλης φησί with a propositional infinitive). In 7.308d there is direct quotation, with φησί inside, as a parenthetical clause. Or instead of φησί alone, ὥς φησί, 7.309b, 313e, 321a.

Grammatically speaking, direct quotation or quotation after ὅτι or ὡς are easier, when Athenaeus does not want to interfere. This type of quotation must be closer to the primary text. Therefore, if the secondary writer wants in some way to distort or to modify the source, the change due to the propositional infinitive will make easier other changes in the words and ideas, and will make these changes less apparent (cf. Chapter 12). But as far as Hicesius is concerned the situation seems to be not too bad after all.

## 3. Hicesius' treatise περὶ ὕλης: a semantic study[8]

### (a) A hierarchy among foods

A hierarchy among different sea-foods and fish dishes can be traced—first, of course, according to the very meaning of the words with which they are described. But also a rank is given them, through verbs, adjectives and their degrees, and verbal oppositions with opposing prefixes.

The important verb in this case is διαφέρειν, 7.285b, 298b, 309b (διαλλάσσειν 315e). But note also its contrary (λείπεσθαι, 313a), or its participle, when comparing mussels from Ephesus to cockles (the former being inferior to the latter, λειπόμενοι, 3.87c). At 3.87b the noun διαφορά is also used, about cockles which can be extremely different according to their size: κατὰ τὰ μεγέθη καὶ τὰς διαφορὰς εἶναι κρατίστας. The adjectives are: πρῶτος 7.310f and δεύτερος 306e; βελτίων, 3.87c, 7.294c and ἄριστος 7.306e, 328b; ἥσσων 310f and μέσος 308d, 323a. Καταδεέστερος 306e, 313d. See also μᾶλλον and various compound words with εὐ-, κακο-, ὀλιγο-, πολυ and ἀ-.

There is a vocabulary of taste and nutrition for sea-food and fish used by Hicesius which can be compared with that of other medical writers on the same topics.

*(b) Vocabulary of consumption and excretion*

First, vocabulary of pleasure in general: ἀπολαυστικός 3. 87e, 'producing enjoyment': more enjoyable than the rest of them are the 'livers' of the purple-shells (87e,-τεραι).

Next, that of taste. In general: γεῦσις. So, 7.306e ἄριστοι πρὸς τὴν γεῦσιν, 'best as regards taste', are the 'cephalos' mullets; 320e the deep-water scorpion fish is superior in taste, διαφέρει τῇ γεύσει; and 323a 'uninviting to the taste are the hammer-fishes', ἀπειθεῖς δὲ τὴν γεῦσιν. A positive adjective on taste/texture is ἁπαλός, tender: 7.294c ἁπαλωτέρος, one sort of dog-fish is 'more tender' than the other. A positive noun is γλυκύτης, 'sweetness of taste': 7.328b the gilt-head are superior in sweetness (γλυκύτητι) and flavour generally

Negative terms are ἀπειθής, 'uninviting to the taste', a rather unusual meaning, one which seems to be peculiar to Hicesius. Some mussels (3.87c) and (7.323a) hammer-fishes: ἀπειθεῖς τὴν γεῦσιν καὶ ἀστόμους (verb ἀπειθέω, 'to be disobedient', 'to refuse compliance').

Feel in the mouth entails εὐστομία, pleasantness to the mouth, goodness of taste, flavour: 7.309b, εὐστομία διαφέροντες the gobies are excellent in flavour; 310f the sea-bass are rated first in goodness of taste, εὐστομία πρῶτοι κρίνονται; 315e the belly-pieces of the horse-mackerel are superior in flavour to the other parts, τῇ εὐστομία πολὺ διαλλάσσειν τῶν ἄλλων μερῶν.

328b the gilt-head are superior in sweetness and flavour generally, καὶ τῇ ἄλλῃ εὐστομία). Accordingly, the adjective εὔστομος, 'pleasant to the mouth, palatable':

315e shoulder-bones of horse-mackerel (a sort of tunny) are more palatable than the belly-pieces, εὐστομώτερα (cf. Theoph. *HP* 2. 6. 10). Its negative counterpart is ἄστομος, 'unpalatable': 323a hammer-fishes: ἀπειθεῖς τὴν γεῦσιν καὶ ἀστόμους (cf. Diosc. 1, 110).

Next, nourishment. As far as τὸ τρόφιμον is concerned: 7.320 e: διαφέρει δὲ τῇ γεύσει καὶ τῷ τροφίμῳ ὁ πελάγιος, 'the deep-water scorpion fish is superior in taste and nourishment'. Adjectives are τρόφιμος and its cognates: 7.312c: eels are τροφίμους, 'nourishing'. Its comparative, τροφιμώτερος, 'more nourishing' is found at 3.87c; scallops are more nourishing. At 7.309b τροφιμώτεροι, 'more nourishing' are the yellow gobies and 323a, hammer-fishes; and its superlative, τροφιμώτατος, 'extremely nourishing' applies to (7.313e) sea-bream and (328b) gilt-head.

πολύτροφος, 'nutritious': 7.298b eels are nutritious; 320e scorpion fish are nutritious. This adjective can be used with οὐ (not): οὐ πολύτροφοι, to describe a type of mullet called *chellones* (306e) and the sea-bass (310f). Negative counterparts are: ὀλιγότροφος, 'which gives little nourishment' and ἄτροφος, 'not nourishing at all'.

Thus, ὀλιγότροφος: 7.308d ὀλιγοτρόφοι are the meagres, and cockles (3.87b); 7.309b gobies too. And ἄτροφος: 314b the electric ray is especially not nutritious, ἀτροφωτέραν. Oysters are less nourishing than other shellfish (ἀτροφωτερά, 3.87c) and some mussels are less nourishing than others, and the periwinkle less than the mussels (87d; cf. Diphilus at 2.54a, Dios. 2.79). Note also πλήσμιος, which gives the impression of satiety, filling, but which is not nourishing *ipso facto*: such are oysters (3.87c) and eels (7.298b). See also 2.32f.

Next, digestion and juice (χυλός and χυμός which are virtual synonyms). Thus, εὐχυλία, 'good quality of juice': 3.87c, mussels from Ephesus are good, τῇ εὐχυλίᾳ, and 7.306e, ἄριστα πρὸς τὴν εὐχυλίαν, the *cephali* are the best as regards juices; 308d, εὐχυλίᾳ μέσον, the meagres are of mean quality as regards juices. Accordingly, εὔχυλος, 'which produces good juice', and πολύχυλος, 'which produces much juice'.

εὔχυλος: 7.282d the fish called 'wolf' or 'beauteous-of-name' produces good juices; 310f the sea-bass produces good juices. Instead of the superlative, a phrase with σφόδρα is used at 7.306e, σφόδρα εὔχυλοι are the mullets called 'bacchi', which produce perfectly good juices. And the comparative is found at 298b, εὐχυλότεροι: eels produce better juices than any other fish. At 313a sprats are εὐχυλότεραι than gobies.

πολύχυλος: 7.309b, πολύχυλοι fish are gobies and (320e) scorpion fish.

A negative counterpart is ἄχυλος, 'which produces no juice' (rather than 'not tasty, insipid, without flavour', as Gulick writes): so at 7.314b the electric ray is rather lacking in juices (ἀχυλοτέραν). Also, κακόχυλος: cockles, 3.87b, and scallops, 87c, are κακόχυλος. These produce bad juices. As to χυμός, one negative adjective is used, κακόχυμος, 'which produces bad juices' (and therefore is not nourishing), 7.309b: gobies are of little nourishment and produce bad juices, ὀλιγότροφοι καὶ κακόχυμοι (for the superlative see 1.24f, κακοχυμότατος, and Sextus 13. 29, Galen 2. 179).

Next, the stomach. The juices so produced go through the stomach and may be good for it: εὐστόμαχος, εὐστομαχία, two words the meaning of which actually is not very clear, probably 'wholesome' and 'wholesomeness'. Note 7.298b on eels: εὐστομαχίᾳ διαφέρουσι τῶν πλείστων, 'in wholesomeness they excel most'; 3.87d the necks of the periwinkle are 'wholesome'. At 7.314b Hicesius says the electric ray is 'very wholesome', εὐστόμαχον πάνυ, but at 282d the wolf or beauteous-of-name is said to be οὐκ εὐστόμαχον.

Next, excretion, ἔκκρισις. At 7.310f sea-bass are said to 'be inferior as far as excretion is concerned' (πρὸς τὴν ἔκκρισιν ἥσσονες), while at 278a the fish called amia (bonitos?) are 'rather mediocre as far as excrement is concerned' (πρὸς τὰς ἐκκρίσεις μέσας). According to 313a sprats are inferior to gobies ... in assisting elimination from the digestive tract: λείπεσθαι ... τῷ πρὸς τὴν ἔκκρισιν τῆς κοιλίας συνεργεῖν, while oysters are rather easy to eliminate, εὐεκκριτώτερα (3.87c)

The adjective εὐέκκριτος is used for foods which are easily excreted, or eliminated, after digestion.[9] Cockles are easy to pass (3.87b) and limpets are still more easy to excrete, λεπάδας ... εὐεκκρίτους (87c), and so are oysters (87c εὐεκκριτώτερα). The fish called 'wolf' is easily eliminated (εὐέκκριτον, 7.282d); so are *chellones* (306e), the meagres (308d), gobies (309b) and scorpion fish (320e).

Sometimes, the adjective is used together with a complement (κοιλίας), as for instance in 3.116e on young tunnies, which are not easy to eliminate from the bowels, οὐκ εὐεκκρίτους κοιλίας (116e). Conversely, the negative adjective δυσέκκριτος is also available: for instance scallops are especially difficult to pass, δυσεκκριτώτεροι (3.87c).

Next, medical properties, which are sometimes noted but are evidently not very important to Athenaeus. On this issue he certainly obscured Hicesius' thought: this is quite clear if we examine whether these notions are present in direct or indirect passages.

In all the passages in indirect speech only two specifically medical properties are listed: the purgative and the astringent. As to σμηκτικός, 'purgative', note 7.320e: scorpion fish are purgative (cf. 2.55b, 64b and Diosc. 2, 4);. Also παραστύφειν, 'to be slightly astringent' (different from στύφειν): one of the sea breams is slightly astringent and is nourishing: ... μικρῶς παραστύφειν καὶ;... (cf. 7.313d; cf. 3.73a (Diphilos)).

The situation is very different in 3.87b–f., a paragraph which is very nicely built. It starts rather emphatically with Ἰκέσιος ὁ Ἐρασιστράτειος φησι, a sentence which insists on the authoritative importance of our author. Here propositional infinitives follow φησι. In 87c Ἰκέσιος is named again, but with no verb; only further propositional infinitives. But what follows (almost a whole page in the Loeb edition) is a direct quotation, without any introductory verb. It may be thought that this page was really written by Hicesius. It is much more medical than all the rest which have survived, and from it we might be able to understand what his book was like. Let us content ourselves with the medical details for the moment. Solid excrement has been discussed through ἔκκρισις and its cognates, as we has seen. Here a more descriptive phrase is chosen, ἐπὶ τὴν κοιλίαν φερόμενοι, and the way liquid excrement is produced is compared with the way the solids are: οὐρητικώτεροι μᾶλλον ἢ ἐπὶ τὴν κοιλίαν φερόμενοι.

With σκιλλώδης there is a new type of problem (87d and e); the adjective, built on the name of the squill (*Urginea maritima*), is used to qualify some type of mussels and purple-shells. One needs to know that this squill is a big onion which grows by the sea, develops a beautiful show of white flowers, and was used especially to treat dropsy. I think, therefore, the comparison cannot be between the appearance of the shells and that of the onions but between the effects of the sea-food and of the medical plant, not mildly diuretic, but drastically so, and helpful in case of severe dropsy. Hicesius' statements are: (87c) 'Among them some have the same effect as squills, produce bad juices and are uninviting to the taste'; (87d) 'are more diuretic, produce better juices than those which have the same effect as squill'; (87e) '... except for the fact they have the same effect as squill'. Cf. 3.21a, on mackerel: according to Diphilos, 'the mackerel has rather the same effect as squill and produces rather poor juices, but is nourishing' (ὁ κολίας δὲ σκιλλωδέστερος καὶ κακοχυλότερος, τρόφιμος).

In that paragraph the author develops a consistent dietetic view: the right choice of the right food can keep you in good health even if your predisposition is not so good. An example is the following (87d): 'For persons with weak stomachs, who do not easily work off their food into the abdominal tract, [the "necks" of the periwinkle] are useful'. Why? There comes an elaborate theory about what is good for the stomach: the 'neck' of the periwinkle in fact 'is not easily broken down'. Generally speaking, 'this is because foods admittedly easy to digest are, by a reverse process, alien to a morbid constitution of this kind (= with a weak stomach), since their tenderness and solubility make their breaking-down easy'.

Hicesius returns to the precise case: 'hence the "livers" of these are not good in a case of good tension of the stomach but are beneficial for weakness of the bowels.' What is the 'tension' of the stomach? The nervous strength necessary to do what has to be done. The meaning of διαθέσις is clearer in the plural (end of 87e): when they are cooked, the 'necks' of purple-shells are good 'for states of morbid predisposition of the stomach', that is to say when the stomach is too weak but not actually sick. Were it really weak, then a disease would occur.

Something similar is found in 15.689c–d, another rather long direct passage, which uses a specifically medical adjective, πεπτικός, helpful to digestion: gillyflowers are extremely helpful to digestion (σφόδρα πεπτικός).

## 4. What was the plan of περὶ ὕλης?

The title is not very specific: 'On matter'. Gulick, in his note to 681c, writes as follows: 'on materials for food, from the point of view of a physician writing on diet as well as materia medica'. Ὕλη is attested as materia medica, for instance in 3.118 b, sometimes with an adjective, as for instance in the title of Dioscorides' book: ὕλη ἰατρική. We should remember also that ὕλη is sometimes a part or a stage of a diet (for instance Soranos 2.46; 2.15. Ὕλη τροφιμωτέρα also, 1.36, 1.95 etc.). But these are not the uses that Hicesius has in mind. Therefore, I suggest,

'On materials for health' since the author is interested in food itself, in food as a remedy and also in a few remedies *stricto sensu*.

The work had several parts since it is described with a plural: Ἱκεσίος ἐν τοῖς περὶ ὕλης (7.282d, 294c, 298b); at least two, since 15.681c has ἐν δευτέρῳ περὶ ὕλης and 689c ἐν β΄ περὶ ὕλης. This second book is quoted for flowers and perfumes, but fish is also mentioned at 3.118a–b. Thus we can guess the first was about meat (which is never quoted by Athenaeus nor by any other), sea-food and fish (which is quoted).

Let us be more precise about the second book. Note that 15.681c praises τὸ λευκόιον, the gillyflower, and τὸ μέλαν, the violet, for their nice fragrance. Their medical use was probably as a decoction. But perfumes were also used to prevent drunkenness, and flowers make wreaths for the symposium. Then there might come a few chapters about wine: *de conditura vini*, as Pliny himself writes, quite fit to be inserted in this plan. In fact wine is at once a food, a remedy, and a poison (against the abuse of which the doctor must do something). Probably this second book ended with compound remedies, and the choicest one was the Ἱκέσιος or Ἱκεσίου.

There is a proposal to publish περὶ ὕλης, with an English translation, using the fragments in Athenaeus and other ancient writers, both in Greek and Latin. That might be the first part of a book on all the medical writers in Athenaeus not otherwise published.

## ❖ 38 ❖ ATHENAEUS, MEDICINE AND DEMOGRAPHY

### by Jean-Nicolas Corvisier

**Introduction**

Scholarly study of the valuable contents of the *Deipnosophistae* has for the most part been confined to questions of language, drinking vessels, food in a cultural context and nutritional selection. Meanwhile, Wilkins and Hill have recently exploited the text of Athenaeus to restore to us the work of Archestratus.[1] As far as the study of demography is concerned, there has been much interest in the famous census of Demetrius of Phaleron, but no one has asked whether Athenaeus himself was really interested in details about population. As for medicine in Athenaeus, there is, as far as I know, no specific study, even though, as is well known, there are frequent quotations from medical authors in the *Deipnosophistae*. Hence the need for the present study, which however does not claim to exhaust the subject. Others have addressed medical topics in this volume (especially Chapters 36 and 37), but my purpose is both broader and more modest. Some years ago, I wrote a work on Plutarch and medicine, the aim of which, among others, was to ascertain why the philosopher of Chaeronea, while no doctor, nevertheless possesses a solid knowledge of medicine. The same questions can be asked of Athenaeus. I have thus set myself the task of determining whether his knowledge of physiology and therapy is correct, when compared with other surviving medical authors. I also hope to establish the scope of this knowledge. Equally I shall seek to establish whether Athenaeus can really be counted as a source of medical knowledge. Once I have some answers to these questions I will be able to return to the demographic data in order to establish from a medical perspective their value and credibility.

First, I must set out the size of the task with a global estimate. In the *Deipnosophistae*, I have found 105 passages of shorter or greater length which have a medical interest. Their distribution may be set out in a table:

| Book | 1 | 2 | 3 | 4 | 5 | 6 | 7 | 8 |
|---|---|---|---|---|---|---|---|---|
| Number of references | 20 | 30 | 17 | 1 | 0 | 0 | 2 | 8 |

| Book | 9 | 10 | 11 | 12 | 13 | 14 | 15 |
|---|---|---|---|---|---|---|---|
| Number of references | 6 | 9 | 3 | 6 | 3 | 3 | 7 |

Such a distribution is revealing. The most numerous references are to be found in the first three books whose main focus is food (Book One: Homeric heroes, wine; Book Two: wine and vegetables; Book Three: vegetables and meat). In the three following books, references are few because of their content (Book Four: the greater or lesser frugality of various peoples; Book Five: meals in history, ships and philosophers; Book Six: parasites). It is surprising to see so few in Book Seven, which is devoted to fish. Books Eight and Nine, which are devoted respectively to fish and meat, and especially to birds, contain more, as does Ten, which addresses drunkenness. Book Eleven is concerned with drinking vessels: no surprise, then, that there are only three medical references. Book Twelve is on pleasure and love: with six references, medical data are clearly not absent. Books Thirteen and Fourteen concern beauty, particularly feminine beauty, for the first and music for the second. Neither is particularly suitable for medical references. Finally, Book Fifteen is devoted to games, to verse and also to perfumes, which explains the number of passages referring to medicine.

This long but necessary list already allows us to understand the medical orientation of Athenaeus, namely towards diet and nutrition. Statistics on the content of the references reinforce this:

|  | References/times mentioned[2] |
|---|---|
| Nutritional recommendations | 55 |
| Non-nutritional recommendations | 6 |
| Diseases cited | 41 |
| Treatments cited | 23 |
| Doctors cited by name | 73 |
| Doctors practising their art | 7 |
| Physiology | 17 |
| Passages on health | 4 |
| Drunkenness | 20 |
| Reproduction | 18 |

A statistical table of this kind reveals the interests of Athenaeus; it can also serve as an approach to reading Athenaeus.

*(a) Nutritional recommendations*

It is clear that the foods that provide material for medical comment do not constitute all those that were consumed by the ancient Greeks. If some vegetables are found (pumpkin, mushroom, truffle, asparagus, onion, lettuce, broad bean, palm fruit, cucumber, turnip, beet, leeks, chick peas), others are not mentioned. Cress, lentils and celery, for example, are missing. The carrot is only mentioned for its effect in reproduction (9.371b). It is more surprising still that the cabbage is found only on this same occasion (9.370c: cabbage is given to women in childbirth) and incidentally in the discussion of wine at 1.34c–e. It is well known that in the Roman world at least this vegetable was considered to be one of the key elements in the pharmacopaea, as Pliny the Elder makes clear. Athenaeus, who was writing at the end of the second century AD, cannot have been unaware of this. As far as fruits are concerned, if cherries, mulberries, chestnuts, walnuts, melons, figs, apples, citrons and quinces are present, there is a notable absence of grapes, plums, pomegranates, dates, almonds, peaches and apricots. Now, Athenaeus knew of them since they appear elsewhere in his work. Are we to believe that they have no medical applications? Comparison with the Hippocratic corpus, *Regimen* for example, and with Galen proves the reverse. A further absence is seen in meat, which is minutely described by the two great ancient doctors and also by Plutarch in his *Precepts on Health* and *Table-Talk*. They are known to Athenaeus, who cites them elsewhere. Should we put this omission down to the problems of textual transmission? I do not propose to take sides in the debate over the integrity or otherwise of the text of Athenaeus, but it is quite certain that a number of different meats were known to Athenaeus. So is it perhaps his medical data which are at the bottom of this? I shall return to this point.

On the other hand, as far as concerns an interest in medicine, the information brought by Athenaeus seems to be relatively secure, if partial. In more than 20% of cases, an equivalent of a food found in Athenaeus is not found in Hippocrates and Galen. Finally, in more than 15% of cases, those two authorities seem to contradict Athenaeus.

I note, lastly, that the medical data offered by Athenaeus—or his sources— is far from absurd, when judged by modern comparisons. I have studied only the vegetable data in the light of the work of Dr J. Valnet. In 80% of cases the information provided by Athenaeus corresponds to modern findings.

*(b) Non-nutritional recommendations*

The importance of this area is much reduced in Athenaeus. There are only six references. Baths are barely mentioned: public baths were only recently introduced into towns (1.18b–c), which is understandable since they soften up the body, especially when they are hot. The pouring of water over the head is particularly recommended because this reduces fatigues and reduces sweating, a fact already noted by Homer and Aristotle (1.24d–e). As for exercise, it is found only as practised by Theophrastus (1.21a), at Pella (8.348d–e) and on the occasion of ball-games and dancing (1.13d–16a). It is little, in comparison with the Hippocratic *Regimen* or the *Precepts on Health* of Galen or of Plutarch. Athenaeus seems not to have been interested in them, neither as preventative nor as curative medicine.

Disease appears most often in the *Deipnosophistae* in incidental fashion. That is true for lice, which are only mentioned because the Greek term is accented on the final syllable, and for gout, which is mentioned in relation to mulberries. According to Hegesander, in his time the mulberry trees bore no fruit and there was an epidemic of gout (2.52a). Similarly for fever, which can be mentioned only in a quotation from drama (3.75b, 80b). In other cases it is a fruit or a vegetable that gives protection from a disease. But beyond these associations of ideas, there are some interesting pieces of information. Bile and shivering are caused by figs (3.80b) and cucumbers (3.74b–c), while asparagus is bad for the bladder and kidneys (2.62f). The connection between drunkenness and damage to the sight is established with reference to Dionysius the Younger, tyrant of Sicily (10.435d), and between drunkenness and pleurisy with reference to Agron, king of Illyria (10.439f-440a), a fact that Athenaeus derived from Polybius but which is also mentioned by Plutarch and corresponds with ancient thought. Other facts known from elsewhere also occur, such as the breast tumour of Atossa which was cured by Democedes of Croton (12.522a–b), a detail evidently borrowed from Herodotus. But the interest in these diseases that are mentioned goes far beyond the mere collection of examples drawn from ancient authors. The vocabulary itself deserves examination. Thus we might note the use of the term *lethargos*, which in the Hippocratic corpus designates a particular type of fever which is pseudo-continuous, with sleepiness, delirium and sometimes abundant expectoration (*Diseases* 2.67). Fever is, furthermore, described not only by the term *puretos*, which is in current usage, but also with violent spasms, the author saying of the disease that it *sphakelize* (3.75b), a most Hippocratic term. Headaches are cited with the technical term *cephalalgia* (1.26c). The consequences of drunkenness, when Bacchus has brought in the vine, are described with very precise medical vocabulary (15.675b–c): 'some, like maniacs, did not know what they were saying, while others fell as if dead (*nekrois*), because of the drowsiness that it produced (*apo tes karoseos*)'. The term for nausea is described by the word *nautia*, which first occurs in this sense in Plutarch but is also current in Galen. It would be pointless

*(c) Diseases mentioned*

495

to rehearse all the examples of this kind. It is clear that Athenaeus has the medical vocabulary at his disposal, at least at a minimal level. The only question that remains is whether the use of the terms is original to him or to his sources.

Finally, in this section, diseases may be considered from a statistical perspective. Their distribution, irrespective of what the source of the citation might be, is as follows:

| | |
|---|---|
| Fevers | 8 |
| Bronchial and lung disorders | 1 |
| Intestinal disorders | 7 |
| Sight disorders | 2 |
| Obesity | 1 |
| Gout | 1 |
| Renal disorders (including lithiasis) | 4 |
| Lice | 1 |
| Epilepsy | 1 |
| Trauma | 5 |
| Nervous diseases | 4 |
| Heart disease | 1 |
| Lameness | 2 |
| Others | 4 |

In all we reach a total of forty-two references to diseases, thirty-eight of which we can do something with. There are thirty-seven if we exclude wounds and trauma. We might ask whether the frequency of citation is random or whether it corresponds to any reality. It might be interesting to compare it with the references we find in a number of earlier authors. These are given in the following table:

| | Plut. *Lives* | Hipp. *Epid.* | Plut. *Mor.* | Hipp. *Aph.* | Lucian Refs | Athenaeus Refs |
|---|---|---|---|---|---|---|
| Fevers | 16.6% | 17.8% | 16.6% | 22.4% | 15.0% | 21.6% |
| Broncho-pulm. | 9.2% | 15.8% | 12.8% | 15.6% | 19.4% | 2.7% |
| Intestines | 9.2% | 11.0% | 12.8% | 13.9% | 7.5% | 18.9% |
| Sight | 3.7% | 0.4% | 7.7% | 2.0% | 11.9% | 5.4% |
| Obesity | 9.2% | — | 7.7% | — | — | 2.7% |
| Trauma | 11.1% | 4.0% | 7.0% | 1.3% | — | 13.5% |
| Gout | 5.5% | — | 3.8% | 2.4% | 5.9% | 2.7% |
| Hydropsy | 5.5% | 0.8% | 3.8% | 3.0% | — | — |
| Lice | 5.5% | — | 3.8% | — | — | 2.7% |
| Epilepsy | 3.7% | 0.4% | 2.6% | 2.0% | — | 2.7% |

It is quite clear that any attempt at interpretation can only be made with caution, given that the samples are not directly comparable: there are fifty-four cases that we can use of diseases described in Plutarch's *Lives*, compared with about 300 in the Hippocratic *Epidemics*, seventy-nine useable cases in the references made in the *Moralia* of Plutarch compared with 298 references in the Hippocratic *Aphorisms*, and finally fifty-seven cases in Lucian. Nevertheless, the data has been set out by identical criteria, and that allows us to venture certain conclusions. We can see a certain convergence on the high numbers for fevers and intestinal disorders and on the low but real numbers for epilepsy, sight disorders or lice (we should note that the ancients believed that an abundance of lice led to stomach ulcers, a disorder that killed Sulla, it was said). The variation in figures for trauma can be put down to the varying nature of our sources. Thus it appears logical to conclude that the significant frequency of fevers and of intestinal disorders found in Athenaeus corresponds well with reality. On the other hand, the low figure in Athenaeus for pulmonary disorders, which were widespread in ancient Greece, escapes all logical explanation. No doubt the character of the source is responsible for this. Athenaeus' main interest is food and nutrition and the link between these two was hardly made at all by ancient doctors.

In the *Deipnosophistae* a certain number of treatments are mentioned in passing. Some of them are linked to wine which eases digestion and makes the blood better able to flow (1.26a–b), which is good for those with ulcers (2.36a–b), according to Mnesitheus, the medical author. Plato also says wine is good for the health (2.38d).[3] Water is used for pouring over the head and in order to arrest haemorrhage, while hot water has a sedative effect, a property that Athenaeus derives from Homer but that Hippocrates would not have disputed (*Aphorisms* 5.23 and elsewhere). Various vegetables are also useful: beet or carrot as a destroyer of worms (9.371a), a property for which I have found no evidence elsewhere; the cabbage as a specific against drunkenness (1.34c), a property well known among the ancients, but which is not in accord with its qualities as they are now understood (for it is an excellent cleanser of the blood). On the other hand, the fact that marjoram plays a similar role is barely attested, even by Hippocrates (VIII, 271 and 295 L.). For the treatment of renal or bladder disorders, together with those of the trachea, mallow is recommended by Diphilus (2.58e), a use that is partially confirmed by Hippocrates, who describes it as a vegetable that washes the stomach and facilitates evacuation but does not give it the importance claimed by Diphilus. However, according to contemporary medicine, mallow is diuretic and can ease respiration when applied to the chest. Also cited are notable uses for perfumes that are rubbed on or poured on (Hicesius at 15.689c–d; cf. 688e–f), salves for black eyes (3.97f)—nothing surprising in that—or cupping glasses for a black eye (10.424b).

*(d) Treatments mentioned*

    In two cases, a longer course of treatment is described. The first is the use of garlands to bind the temples in cases of headaches with tension in the veins that are caused by drunkenness. Here Athenaeus draws on Aristotle and Ariston the Peripatetic (15.674b). He makes no reference to Plutarch, who, in one of his *Table Talks*, addressed the same question. Still more curious is the medical use of fine needles to wake up an obese patient who is somnolent. The patient is pierced through the fat until the flesh is reached, and this wakes him (12.549a–b). I have found no trace of this treatment elsewhere.

*(e) Athenaeus'*
*physiological knowledge*

As one reads the *Deipnosophistae* it is possible to pick out certain passages in which some physiological or medical knowledge is discernible. Traces of the system of humours appear with at least a mention of phlegm (1.10a) or of the pituitary gland (4.132e), but it is not described in more detail. Such is also the case with the theory of satiety and evacuation (1.9f). Athenaeus is more interested in digestion, which, after the Hippocratic doctors, is seen as a series of coctions, which come about through a kind of putrefaction (7.276d–e): there Athenaeus' text gives entirely technical language. Similar are numerous quotations on the digestion of drinks which should not be drunk in quantity before the meal and which must be taken in proportion to the foods consumed (2.45d, which draws in part on Hippocrates (II.332 L.)). In another passage, which quotes Alcaeus, we find the belief that liquids pass into the lungs.[4] What is striking is that Athenaeus has not indicated that this way of looking at drinking was no longer recognized by doctors—which proves that physiology was not central to his purpose. The same can perhaps be said when he cites the *Timaeus* almost literally by saying that 'the creator of the universe placed the lungs near the heart, making it soft and deprived of blood and then pierced with cavities like a sponge, so that the heart when it beats rapidly in fear of all danger should only strike this soft part, which can yield to it and then return to its place' (15.688b). Still with digestion, he asks the question already raised by Aristotle and Plutarch, namely to find out whether old men get drunk more quickly than younger counterparts, and he draws on Aristotle to confirm that the former have little internal heat and the latter a great deal—a view confirmed by Plutarch (*Table Talk* 1.625a–c and 3.650) and Hippocrates. In another class of ideas, he comes to the terminology for the human body. Thus, in a context of butchery, he notes that Hippocrates uses the term *psyai* to describe the loin muscles, as does Clearchus in his second book *On the Skeleton* (9.399b). At 11.479b, in the context of the drinking cup of the same name, the *kotule* is the term for the cavity in the hip joint, the *koilotes*.

It is clear that the physiological knowledge of Athenaeus is limited and out of date. He does know and quote some medical authors. But how far does he take them and in what regard does he hold the doctors?

It commonly happens that Athenaeus quotes the doctors to support his statements. While it is not my purpose to study them systematically, certain indications can at least be made. A number of doctors are quoted in the *Deipnosophistae.* If we exclude those who are imagined to participate in the meal, he mentions Diocles of Carystus, Mnesitheus, Hicesius, a member of the school of Erasistratus (3.87b), Diphilus who lived at the time of Lysimachus (2.51a–b), Herophilus, Phylotimus, Heraclides of Tarentum, Praxagoras of Cos and Hippocrates of course. For medical material he also draws on Homer, Plato, Aristotle, Theophrastus, Timaeus, Alexis and Plutarch, who were not doctors. He makes no great distinction between them and gives no greater credence to the former than the latter. Better still, if in matters of nutrition he draws essentially on Diocles, Mnesitheus and Diphilus, he does not use Hippocrates in this area but often bases himself on *The History of Plants* of Theophrastus or his lost *Treatise on Waters.* In matters of physiology, one recalls that, apart from Hippocrates, he uses only non-medical writers. Finally, he seems to know neither Galen's work nor Rufus of Ephesus. His information is thus far from orthodox.

Besides, when he turns to medical practice, the picture he paints of doctors is far from flattering. He retains the characters of Democedes of Croton, whose considered opinions on political matters were well known (12.521f-522b); Menecrates, the absurd doctor who took himself for Zeus and believed that he was so much master of his patients that he made them his slaves (7.289a–e); an unknown and nameless doctor who sends his patients to Hades the day that he sees them (8.351a); a doctor full of boasting (9.377f); a doctor whose language pretends to knowledge (14.621d–e). The picture, as we see, is indeed black. We are bound to ask whether it has influenced the way in which Athenaeus views medicine.

We should nevertheless modify this rather sombre judgement. It remains true that Athenaeus has transmitted to us certain information on the work of these doctors that passes totally unnoticed in our other sources, even including Galen. He gives us titles of works, outlines and even fragments. The celebrity of Hippocrates is also noted by Athenaeus, who calls him 'most sacred' (*hierotatos)* (9.399b) and shows that the titles of his works could vary. This could have affected the transmission of the text of, for example, *Regimen,* which some entitle *Acute Diseases,* others *On Barley Gruel,* others again *Refutation of Cnidian Principles* (2.45e–f). He gives an indirect tradition for what we know as *Regimen in Acute Diseases.*

All in all, then, even if the medical interests of the *Deipnosophistae* are far from being as important as we might wish, they are far from being negligible. Athenaeus, though, does not have a scientific mind. In his work there is no trace of the Hippocratic triangle, and he is not really interested in the patient. As regards medicine, he knew only dietetics and ignores exercise and preventative measures. Nor does he seek to trace effects back to causes. At least that is not one of his priorities. His mental processes are not based on logical reasoning but on reasoning by analogy and by the association of ideas. He is not a philosopher either. The rarity of medical metaphors and of the abstract notion of good health, when Athenaeus is compared with Plutarch, makes this clear.

**Athenaeus and reproduction**

I have found eighteen passages in the *Deipnosophistae* which concern reproduction. They are distributed as follows.

(1) References to alimentary products which are considered aphrodisiacs and promote fertility, or alternatively lead men to impotence and women to infertility. Aphrodisiacs are thus carrots (9.371b), fish (notably cephalopods) (8.356c–d) and tassel hyacinths (1.5c). Some of these beliefs were shared by the ancient doctors. Carrots are approved by Galen (11.862 K), as were cephalopods (11.777 K). Other foods are approved by modern doctors, though on carrots they are silent. Perhaps we should detect there some trace of sympathetic magic based on the shape of the vegetable. Antaphrodisiacs are lettuce (2.69e–f) and cucumber, despite its shape, (3.74b–c)—notions confirmed by Galen (11.777 K) but not by modern authorities. Sleeping on sponges could excite men to amorous pleasures (1.18d–e). Temperature can make men very fertile, as is the case in Spain (8.330f-331a). The water of the Nile, Athenaeus tells us, increases fertility (2.41e–f); that is a conviction shared by many ancient authors. As for wines, some stimulate men and make women fertile—for example those of Arcadia—while in Achaea, Troezen and Thasos the effect is the reverse, so much so that Achaean wine induces abortions in women (1.31e–f, on the authority of Theophrastus). Similarly, at Massilia and Miletus it is forbidden for women to drink wine, while at Rome wine was denied to free women, adolescents of less than 30 years and slaves. It is also wine that made Alexander impotent (10.434d–f): that is explained by the fact that, according to Aristotle, the sperm of those who give themselves excessively to drink becomes watery (cf. *Problems* 3.10).

(2) There are some references which concern the mechanisms of reproduction with more or less directness. Thus, after Theophrastus (*History of Plants* 9.18.9, cited at 1.18d–e), we find that some men have the ability to copulate seventy times, an ability which leads in the end to the ejaculation of blood. We learn of the enervation of one, Deinias, who, according to Heraclides Ponticus (cited by Athenaeus at 12.552f–553a), became impotent and castrated himself. As for women, it is said that the red mullet was a fish that brought on periods (8.355e–f), a notion that is scarcely confirmed by ancient

authors and even less by modern authorities. Its red colour appears to be the only explanation. We may note also that Athenaeus is aware of the suppression of periods (3.99d–e), of making women into eunuchs, which was attributed to the Lydians (12.515d: γυναῖκας εὐνουχίσαι; sterilization or circumcision?), and of the giving of cabbage to women in childbirth in Athens as a nutritional antidote (*antipharmakos*, 9.370c). This property of cabbage is otherwise unknown, but might be linked with the ability of cabbage to heal scars when applied externally.

Overall, then, the list is deceptive. We find the classic ancient restrictions on wine as an abortifacient, the normal alimentary prescriptions for aphrodisiacs, but there is little on the mechanisms of reproduction. This topic (medical texts aside) preoccupied as great an author as Aristotle, whose work was well known to Athenaeus. We must infer that the latter was not really interested in it. That conclusion is not without significance for the following survey of Athenaeus as a demographic source.

Demographic references are few and far between in the *Deipnosophistae*. They can be classified into four groups:

(1) References to sexuality. Further to the discussion above, we may note that to have an active sexual life is normal not only for the young but also for old men (1.25f). The existence of the age of puberty for girls was also known to him (6.269b).
(2) References to the desirable number of children. There is only one such reference. According to the poet Phoenix of Colophon, all that one can wish for a perfect girl is to find a rich and famous husband, and to put into the arms of her father in his old age a son and in the lap of her mother a daughter. She will raise this daughter as a future wife for one of her kinsmen (8.359d–e).
(3) References to the myth of sharing women in common. It is said to have existed among the Etruscans (12.517d) and among the Athenians before the time of Cecrops (13.555d), until Solon, who created the system of courtesans in order to protect marriage (13.569d–e).
(4) Numerical references. The cavalry of the Sybarites came to more than 5,000 men, so it was said (12.519c). Similarly, according to Theopompus, the Ardians had in their service 300,000 *prospelatai*, whose status was similar to that of helots (10.443b).

This very small number of references (in particular, references to figures) gives us little. It allows us, though, to situate the famous passage in Book Six on the census

**Athenaeus and demography**

of Demetrius of Phaleron. When it is taken in context, we see that it follows a long study of slaves and of dependants somewhere between the status of slave and free man. Having described, among others, *penestai* and helots, Athenaeus adds that, according to Theopompus in his thirty-second book, on the Messenian wars, it became necessary to substitute helots for dead citizens. Theopompus also asserts, among other details, in book two of his *History of Philip*, that the Ardians have in their service 300,000 *prospelatai* (6.271c–e). This passage is followed by a passage on the helots and on the error of Timaeus who claimed that the Greeks did not use slaves, even though he says elsewhere that the Corinthians had 460,000 slaves (6.272a–c). Then Ctesicles reports that at the census of Demetrius of Phaleron the figures for Attica were 21,000 Athenians, 10,000 resident aliens and 400,000 slaves (6.272b–c). We find in the *Ways and Means* of Xenophon that Nicias had a thousand slaves and rented them out for work in the mines. Finally, Aristotle reports in the *Constitution of Aegina* that there were 470,000 slaves. The man who provides all these details is Masurius, who quotes from Philip of Theangela. Larensis interrupts, to affirm that the Romans had an infinite number of slaves (272d) and that the numerous Athenian slaves only worked in the mines. These Athenian slaves, according to Posidonius, rebelled and captured the fortress of Sounion at the time of the second slave revolt in Sicily, after which more than a million slaves perished (272e–f).

We may conclude that the only thing that interested Athenaeus here was the number of slaves and that his goal was to show that the number of slaves owned by Greeks was no less than those owned by Romans. Since the number of the latter had been set at a million, the barrier to cross was high. There is thus no point in doubting the transmission of the text and in postulating, as did Beloch, that instead of 400,000 slaves one should read 40,000. In fact, it is all the numbers for slaves that should be treated with caution. On Aegina, there is no room for 470,000 slaves, unless there was a population density of 10,000 to the square kilometre. It is also difficult to see, given the limited territory of Corinth, where all the slaves lived. It is clear that these figures are of no value, except as a statement of excess. We have seen that Athenaeus had no interest in quantifying things for its own sake, and equally that his system of logic is not ours. If this is true of medicine, it is even more true of demography.

At the end of this short survey of the world of Athenaeus, it is worth underlining what we do owe to him. He remains a source of great value, a mine of detailed information, even on medicine, but in a strictly defined area only. It is important not to take him into areas which are not his own.

## ❖ 39 ❖          ATHENAEUS THE UR-PORNOGRAPHER

by Madeleine Henry

In this chapter I consider the impact of Athenaeus' pornography upon the European and British pornographic traditions. That impact is probably greater than we are commonly aware; owing to the subject-matter and treatment, it has been insufficiently acknowledged. I believe that the *Deipnosophistae* is a pornographic work, and that we can thank Athenaeus for some concepts of pornography that remain operant today: he is the *Ur*-pornographer.[1]

In my earlier work on Athenaeus, I made some observations regarding scholarly treatments of Athenaeus that are also made in the present volume, namely: the near-universal neglect of Athenaeus' thought, or perhaps the assumption that Athenaeus' work lacks conceptual thought, or any notion of form and arrangement; the modern scholar's tendency to mine Athenaeus only for the precious vein: e.g. Satyrus, Alexis, Semonides, or references to Egypt. I also argued that the concept of the pornographic which runs through the *Deipnosophistae* is perfectly congruent with certain feminist definitions of the pornographic and of pornography. This might prove useful as a way of seeing some unity of thought in Athenaeus, or at least as a way to examine some 'habits of mind' that he displays. I also hoped to encourage those historians of ideas who habitually locate the birth of pornography somewhere around the time of Sade to be less presentist in their investigations.

The main point of my earlier work, however, was to consider what Athenaeus meant when he used the word *pornographos*. Matters of arrangement and transition seemed less important than finding the germs of a representational ideology. We can apply to the Naucratite Kappeler's remarks that 'pornography is not a special case of sexuality; it is a form of representation'[2] and her additional observation that the gaze is male, a gaze that its eroticized object does not return. To Athenaeus we can also apply Daly's observation that woman is the mute, and touchable, caste.[3] The only women who speak in Athenaeus' vast work confirm and validate their own subordination. In Kappeler's words: 'It is indeed one of the well-tried pornographic devices to fake the female's, the victim's, point of view ... The so-called female point of view is a male construction ... .'[4] For example, the courtesans praised by Myrtilus in Book Thirteen speak only as the self-defined objects of men's sexual pleasure. They speak of their own bodies as if they do not live in them, and their remarks are confined to sexual and monetary allusions and puns. The self that their reported speech creates is a wholly sexualized self. Lastly, I found that Athenaeus creates, through his superb ahistoricism, the illusion of a seamless sameness of outlook. That ahistoricism may well have been part of the Naucratite's plan to construct the perfect (because timeless) sympotic world, as other chapters in this volume show. The symposiasts quote their *chreiae* as if all were cards from the same deck. Woman is but one of the categories of objects to be enjoyed at the symposium, and women are discussed in much the same way as are types of food and utensils. We can extract analogous prescriptions for the use of women and food: it is important that men be able to obtain both food and women and to enjoy them masterfully but temperately. Other chapters in this volume discuss Athenaean dietetics and the relationship between gastronomy and community. Moderate communal consumption is mandated and exemplified (though only verbally) by the dialogue itself, which effectively creates a group identity. Men must also be able to detect disguise in the preparation of food and the use of cosmetics by women, but at the same time they must not pay attention to the cultivation of the foodstuffs they eat and the physical realities of the lives of the women they discuss.

The remark of an anonymous diner encapsulates the ideas put forth above, namely that for Athenaeus food and women are to be used and consumed by men in analogous ways:

> When an eel was served, a follower of Epicurus who was among the diners said, 'The Helen of dinners is here; and so I shall be Paris'. And before anybody had yet stretched out his hands for the eel, he fell upon it and stripped off the sides, reducing it to just its backbone. (7.298d5–e1)

However, Book Thirteen provides the most concentrated presentation of the pornographic sensibility seen elsewhere in the work, with a telling invocation of the Muse Erato. Furthermore, it provides us with the first attested use of the word *pornographos*, 'pornographer'. In Book Thirteen several diners debate the respective merits of sexual relations with (different types of) women. While

Myrtilus advocates the cultured enjoyment of elegant foods and kindly *hetaerae*, Larensis decries the bestial destructiveness of harlots. Leonidas finds *hetaerae* a solution to the problem of nagging wives—a *hetaera* is forced to be nice, because the law is not on her side. But Cynulcus brings the argument down to earth and the earthy. He advocates cheap brothels: in an amazing patchwork of comedic quotes, he sets forth why the brothel is the best:

> On this account I advise you... to cleave only to the women in brothels and not consume unprofitably the wealth of your sons... Or... to quote Eubulus' <comedy> *The Vigil*, 'Decoy-birds, Aphrodite's trained fillies, naked and arrayed in battle-line, stand in finely woven scarves... Safely and securely, you cheaply buy your pleasure from them.' Again, in *Nannion*, Eubulus says, 'Isn't he who mates stealthily and in the dark the wretchedest of all men? For he can in broad daylight gaze at naked girls... he can cheaply buy his pleasure, and not pursue a clandestine lust.'... Zenarchus also, in *The Pentathlon*, censures those who live as you do and who are eager for highly paid *hetaerae* and freeborn married women '... for there are very pretty girls in the brothels here, whom youths can see basking in the sun, bare-breasted and arrayed in battle-line; of these one may choose the one that pleases him, thin, fat, rounded, lanky, shrivelled, young, old, middle-aged, overripe ... for the women themselves use force and drag the men in, calling the older ones "Daddy" and the younger "Dearie". And you can see any one of them easily, cheaply, by day, at evening, and in any way you want.' ... And Philemon, too, in *The Brothers*, tells that Solon, on account of the turning point which comes to young men, bought and situated females in brothels...: 'You, Solon, bought and stationed women in various neighbourhoods, ready and available for all. They stand naked, lest you be deceived; look at everything. Perhaps you're not feeling quite yourself; perhaps you're worried about something. The door is open; the price, one obol! Jump right in and there isn't any dissembling or nonsense. She doesn't snatch herself away; but straightaway, <take her> as you wish and in whatever way you wish. You exit, and you can tell her to go to hell. She's a stranger to you.' (13.568d–569f)

I locate the climax of Cynulcus' harangue in his quotation of a comic fragment from Philemon's *Brothers* (3 K–A). In this fragment a character credits the sage Solon with having established state brothels to relieve the sexual tensions of the youth without endangering their patrimony or subjecting the lads to the reputational or financial dangers of adultery.

That comic fragment, though it is very much later than Solon's day and is attested only here, is the only evidence of any kind that Solon established state brothels. For no sound reason this factoid has found its way into various histories of sexuality in classical antiquity.

Furthermore, Cynulcus follows this statement with the Aristophanic claims that Aspasia kept a brothel and was in part responsible for the outbreak of the Peloponnesian War (13.569d–570b). What better way to justify prostitution than to ascribe its origin to one of the Seven Sages and to identify as a madam and procuress the consort of the great Pericles?

Yet Cynulcus, who had just legitimated his own advice by reference to literary works, does not allow Myrtilus to do the same when the latter praises erotic beauty in a return volley of citations from philosophers and poets. In disapproval of Myrtilus' habit of wasting time by hanging about wineshops with prostitutes and pimps, he thunders:

> So you're no different from Amasis of Elis. Theophrastus says in his treatise *On Erotic Love* that Amasis was skilled in love affairs. Nor would one be wrong to call you a *pornographos* also, like the painters Aristides, Pausias, and also Nicophanes. (13.567b)

It is important to note that Cynulcus does not object to hiring prostitutes but rather to consorting with expensive ones publicly and to representing this activity in words or in art.

It is not clear why Cynulcus mentioned these three artists, information about whom he gleans from Polemon's work *On the Painted Tablets in Sicyon,* which was probably written in the late third or early second century BC. Polemon wrote numerous treatises on art and sculpture. Aristides, a fourth-century figure and probably the grandson of the homonymous student of Polyclitus, was from Thebes. He was noted for conveying character and emotion. Paintings of the courtesans Leontion and Byblis were attributed to him by Pliny (*N.H.* 35.98–100) as well as emotionally affecting genre scenes. About the Sicyonian Pausias more is known (Pliny *NH* 35. 123–7, 128, 137). A famous painter of the mid fourth century, he wrought miniatures, children and genre scenes. When the city was in debt, it sold most of his paintings and Pliny notes that a copy of one fetched an enormous price in Rome. The style of his student Nicophanes is described by Pliny (*NH* 35.111) as *elegans* and exhibiting *diligentia*.[5]

It is quite possible that the word *pornographos* appeared as early as Polemon. His *floruit* (190 BC) is somewhat later than what has been called the 'golden age of the *hetaera*', both in Greek society and on the comic stage, that is the fourth century BC. But the *locus classicus* for the word *pornographos*, as far as we know, are these words of Cynulcus in Athenaeus. In an earlier study, I concluded that a *pornographos*, to Cynulcus, is one who represents prostitutes in speech, in writing, or in pictorial form, one who publicly admits knowledge of prostitutes and shares this knowledge. Thus for Cynulcus, pictorial and verbal representation are analogous, and he wishes not to censor pornographers and pornography but instead to contain their venues. The beauty of the encomium to Solon is that Philemon's Solon created the paradigm: an enclosed space, sanctioned and supported by the *polis*, wherein the youth of the city could relieve themselves of sexual tension in a literal outlet. The encomiast's naming of young men's sexual urges as producing a *krisis* is telling, for it is a medical term. The ideology of the prostitute as a less-than-human receptacle necessary to the health of the male body politic, and situated at strategic points in the city, will surface again in eighteenth-century French discourse on prostitution.

In recent years classicists have had little to say about pornography as ideology. This is regrettable, given how well the volume *Pornography and Representation in Greece and Rome* had framed the questions and suggested some methodologies. [6] As a group we have retreated to the safer, rhetorically complex and politically unconfused realms of 'cultural studies' and 'gender studies'. The postmodern collection *Before Sexuality: the Construction of Erotic Experience in the Ancient Greek World* describes in its introduction the one radical feminist essay in the book as coming from an 'untraditional but very poetic perspective".[7] Von Reden's *Exchange in Ancient Greece* gives short shrift to the places occupied by women in the exchange system.[8] Kampen's collection *Sexuality in Ancient Art* makes greater strides. Kurke's essay on 'inventing the *hetaera*' studies the cultural rhetoric that created a concept of *hetaera* out of that of the *porne*. But that study ignores the materiality of the *porne*, the 'buyable woman' who was the substrate, and concentrates only on the poetics of the use of the *hetaera* in sympotic poetry and anecdote.[9]

Classicists interested in pornography, however, were not out of step with other members of the academy. Radical feminism's credibility was brought down by its uneasy alliance with right-wing Christian opponents of pornography. Meanwhile, liberal feminist objections to censorship were vindicated: censors began to block the publication and shipment of various forms of erotica, in a manner that was predictably prejudiced against homoerotic material. We now hear that pornography is liberating. We have not moved far from the points articulated by Myrtilus, Leonidas, Cynulcus and Larensis. Thus, the 'pornography wars' of cultural studies in Europe and North America burned themselves out, and within classical studies —as in other disciplines—politically engaged and philologically astute approaches to sexuality studies have been replaced with ludic, i.e. postmodern, approaches.

But while all this was transpiring, *in Arcadia ego*. While investigating the biographical tradition of Aspasia, I continued to find evidence for the evolution of pornography. As much as Athenaeus helped me when I was searching for the discourse I came to call 'protopornography', he did not much help me in my investigation of Aspasia's life, and I, too, am guilty of having relegated him to footnotes. But a discovery of sorts had been made.

One can discern the beginning in certain discourses of the Hellenistic and imperial worlds which can be called 'protoprosopography', 'protopornography', 'subhistory' and 'subbiography'.[10] Nearly all the fragments, and definitely the relevant fragments of every author one might detect and persuasively identify as a contributor to these forms (e.g. Matro, Machon, Lynceus of Samos), are preserved in Athenaeus. Much of the time they are preserved only in Athenaeus. Moreover, most of the more sexually explicit fragments of the comic poets are preserved in Athenaeus and nowhere else. We can ask to what extent Athenaeus has skewed our perception of a great deal of Greek literature.

Athenaeus' role in helping to establish the western pornographic sensibility is threefold. First, he provides us with a word and a concept, *pornographos*, that lets us see that pornography is not a natural kind of sexuality but a species of representation. The term is not found in the abstract as *pornographia*. Pornography is what someone does or what someone represents. Moreover, that constructed representation can be written or visual; Cynulcus uses it to refer to the lover of literary and painted representations of the material in question.

Secondly, for Athenaeus, women and food are analogous and women are as much the instruments of dietetics as of erotics. This fusion of the erotic with the dietetic sets us on our way to binding up the subject-matter of pornography— *pornai* or buyable women—with the hygiene of the body politic, with the medicalization of prostitutes, and with utopian and libertine views, that would surface in late eighteenth-century France, in the idea of the brothel as a temple of health.

Thirdly, because of the manner in which the *Deipnosophistae* has come down to us, Athenaeus has unwittingly bestowed on us the concept of pornography as that which is found in the curio cabinet. Pornography must needs be something secret, preserved from near-loss, requiring effort, expense and erudition.

Kendrick's recent work *The Secret Museum: Pornography in Modern Culture* understands Athenaeus as the author who gave us a word for the concept, and understands the preciosity of Athenaean pornography as constructed by inheritors of the classical tradition. Even though Kendrick knows that the first appearance of the word *pornography* in English was in a medical dictionary and the word was defined as 'a description of prostitutes or of prostitution, as a matter of public hygiene', he does not see that this usage could not have come from Athenaeus. To have observed that Athenaeus gives us the *locus classicus* was enough.

Kendrick periodizes his study of the concept and practice of pornography by postulating a 'pre-pornographic' era. That era roughly ended with the discovery and publication of the sexually explicit representations at Pompeii.[11] The publication of this material as something élitist and secret allows Kendrick to emphasize, in Foucauldian terms, 'the accelerating incitement to control all things, especially the forbidden, by making them subjects of discourse'.[12] Other scholars of the recent past also miss the point; they identify the beginnings of a western pornographic sensibility with Sade.[13] Yet all around is evidence that earlier readers of Athenaeus, particularly the French litterati, had noticed more than Kendrick.

Rabelais (1490–1553) must have known Athenaeus very well, very possibly from the Aldine edition of 1514. In *Gargantua and Pantagruel* he mentions Athenaeus respectfully as an antiquarian of note, no fewer than seven times. Was it Casaubon's great edition that Voltaire (1694–1778) requested by letter in 1765?[14] The 'Athenaean sensibility' was also appreciated by a person less well-remembered than Voltaire, and the influence of Athenaeus' work may have had much to do with the emergence of a modern notion of the pornographic text. It is not possible to claim precise influences of Athenaeus on Restif de la Bretonne (1734–1806) or of Restif on others, but a correspondence of ideological viewpoint is clear. In his utopian works, Restif institutionalizes the brothel; a new Solon, he provides buyable women to be sexually available. In that way, he is the same kind of pornographer as Cynulcus (on Myrtilus' view). Since so much of his work is prescriptive, imaginative and impracticable, he is a representationist rather than an activist.

Born of peasant stock in rural Burgundy, Restif was sent by his father to the nearby town of Auxerre in 1751 at the age of 16 to learn a trade. He was a printer by day, and read voraciously by night. It is not known whether he knew Latin or Greek. Athenaeus had appeared in French translation in 1583 and 1690, so that Restif may have read him in the vernacular. After moving to Paris and replicating this lifestyle, Restif published his own first book, a forgettable novel, in 1767. He worked and played hard in Paris for the rest of his life.[15] His utopianism was a crude, sentimental fusion of Epicurus and Rousseau. Fully accepting 'man's sentient capacity',[16] Restif set about theorizing various types of utopias which would allow for simultaneous fulfilment and regulation of the passions, the most important of which was Love. Beginning in 1769, he published prolifically.[17]

The gendered aspects of Restif's social programmes are interesting though hardly surprising. He is a biological essentialist, who believes that it is the female's duty to please the male. No other education was necessary for woman. At the same time, he is aware of the dangers of libertinism as a source for the oppression of women. He loathed his slight acquaintance the Marquis de Sade, who, he felt, was aggressive and criminally harmful to women. The influences of Plutarch's *Life of Lycurgus* are evident in most of Restif's utopian works, but there is much that also resonates with the Naucratite's thirteenth book.

By writing about the need to regulate prostitution so that all might be gratified, Restif's notion that civic health was bound up with the health of the male citizen body is certainly in line with Philemon's Solon, and anticipates the medicalization of prostitution we see in Victorian England and in France and the United States in the nineteenth century.[18]

Restif's vision was also in harmony with that of other utopianists of the time, for example that of the architect Claude-Nicolas Ledoux (1736–1806), who is said to have drawn 'buildings for which there was no hope of realization.'[19] One of Ledoux's most ambitious projects was for a state brothel, which he called an *oikema*, and whose phallic architecture is based on a Roman model: the Forum of Augustus. (Like Sade, Ledoux called for brothels to service women as well as men.) But the idea that the state should provide for the sexual gratification of citizens, at a reasonable cost, is an idea as old as Philemon's Solon, the Solon of Athenaeus' Cynulcus. It cannot be proved that Restif knew Athenaeus, but the fact that his first published utopian work was '*Le Pornographe*', and that this word is Athenaean, is very telling. Also telling is the fact that the Germans found Restif's book worthy of translation, and that through German scholarship the word found its way into the English language.

Thus, Athenaeus can be called the West's *Ur*-pornographer. He has given us the word which describes the activity, however contested the concepts of pornography and the pornographer may be. The autonomous individual of the Enlightenment, and that individual's monstrous child the libertine shortly thereafter, have come to delight in the work of the pornographer. Since pornography is a species of representation rather than of sexuality, the generic qualities of pornography are one of its most easily grasped aspects. 'Writing about prostitutes' remains a crucial part of pornography today. Hearty supporters of pornography often cite its value in breaking down sexual inhibitions, sometimes by giving inhibited individuals a new set of scripts. At the same time, the concept of the curio cabinet and the forbidden are a part of pornography, into which Athenaeus plays as an author who could be received as a 'forbidden' author.

While treatments of the pornographic by scholars of the modern period may frustrate classicists looking for a fuller understanding of the classical tradition, the best outcome of that frustration would be to motivate someone to map the influence of Athenaeus, the whole influence, on more recent concepts of the pornographic.

# SECTION VII:
# THE OTHER ATHENAEUS

# INTRODUCTORY REMARKS

The foregoing chapters have been concerned variously to contextualize Athenaeus and the *Deipnosophistae* in order to offer new interpretations and a better understanding of them. In this final section we consider a different kind of context. For the following pair of short chapters address in turn the other known works of Athenaeus, besides the *Deipnosophistae*, namely his study of Archippus' *Fishes* and his broadly historical treatment of the kings of Syria. Of course, it is entirely understandable that these two works have been so overshadowed by the huge *Deipnosophistae*, for we can know next to nothing about them until perhaps a lucky papyrus comes to light. Indeed, we owe our knowledge of their very existence to passing mentions of them in the *Deipnosophistae* itself.

The primary purpose of the following chapters is not to speculate about the actual contents of these works in any detail, though some broad observations may be worthwhile. Rather, these chapters seek primarily to explore the relevance of the two works to Athenaeus' concerns as evidenced in the *Deipnosophistae*. In this way a limited form of hermeneutic dialogue may be attempted, with the major work and the minor works offering insights about each other and their shared author. In particular, we must at least consider the very fact of the mention of the minor works in the *Deipnosophistae*. Why did Athenaeus make the authorial decision to mention these two works at all?

It would be helpful to know whether these were his only other works. The voluminous nature of the *Deipnosophistae* may give the impression that Athenaeus wrote very freely, but we cannot be sure about that. If these were only two of many works, then why are they included and the others not, at least in our extant text? One may wonder about Larensis in this context: had these two works also been composed under his patronage, and these alone until the *Deipnosophistae*? If so, that might help to account for their inclusion. It would also colour the conclusions of the following two chapters, according to which the minor works address topics which are central to the *Deipnosophistae*. It may well be that these topics were matters of prime interest to Larensis, possibly forerunners to the completed *Deipnosophistae*. It is worth considering such questions as these, but we should not expect to find immediate answers.

Certainly, the manner of their mention in the *Deipnosophistae* is remarkable for its studied casualness. Each of the minor works seems to be dropped into the huge text: there is no great fanfare and no particular pause for thought or appreciation of the author. This is especially the case at 5.211a, where Masurius mentions *On the Kings of Syria* and proceeds to quote from it. It is true that 7.329c on Archippus is a rather noisier mention, but even this is buried towards the end of an exhaustive catalogue of fish, which itself has no clear speaker. The effect is rather quietly to confirm the status of Athenaeus himself as one worthy to be among the diners. His writing is mentioned with approval among the diners, with the result that Athenaeus' readers are encouraged to see him not merely as a reporter of events at Larensis' table but also as a full member of that renowned (as Athenaeus would have it) society of intellectuals. He not only writes about the dinners, but also participates in them both in person and through mention of his own writings there. That is a powerful strategy, which requires understatement, a studied casualness and minimal fuss. Athenaeus seeks to persuade his readers that there was nothing remarkable in the diners' reference to his minor works. Indeed, it is remarkable that Athenaeus sees fit to have his own works mentioned and quoted, when the voluminous Galen is never accorded that privilege in the *Deipnosophistae*. If we may rely on the Epitome, there is no more than a broad statement that Galen is an author.[1]

David Braund is largely concerned to explore ways in which Syria might have mattered to Athenaeus and his patron. The issue has already been broached in this book from a rather different perspective in the two earlier chapters of Gambato and Marchiori (chs. 16 and 24). In what follows, Braund stresses that the kings of Syria constituted a very large part of a Hellenistic world in which Athenaeus seems to have been rather more interested than many of his contemporaries. Accordingly, Syria gave rise to much of the best of Hellenistic culture, in which context Poseidonius of Apamea stands out. And its kings offered fine and familiar enough examples of the use and abuse of monarchy, not to mention the rapprochement of the Hellenistic Greek world and the expanding Roman empire. These are themes central to the *Deipnosophistae*, and indeed to any intelligent debate in Athenaeus' day. However, it would be a mistake to imagine that we really know anything much about the contents of Athenaeus' *On the Kings of Syria*. Even to call it a work of history in a modern sense is to beg the question.

By contrast, John Wilkins can bring to bear the known fragments of Archippus' *Fishes* to sketch, as far as possible, the nature of the play. That in turn allows him to explore the large issues raised through the play, which are shared also through the *Deipnosophistae* and can be imagined confidently enough as prominent in Athenaeus' special treatise on the play. In particular, Wilkins draws out the theme of fish which has recurred through the present book (notably in the chapters of Heath and Marchiori, chs. 24–5). Indeed, the first topic mentioned by the Epitome in its list of contents is fish. For Athenaeus displays a massive interest in the natures, purchase and consumption of fish and other marine life. The relationship between the world of fish and the human world, between land and sea, occupies not only Archippus' *Fishes* but also the central books (6–8) of the *Deipnosophistae*. At the same time, it is at least an interesting coincidence that the two minor works named in the *Deipnosophistae* may be taken themselves to bear on related issues, for while Syria was renowned for its kings, it was renowned also for its idiosyncratic attitudes towards the consumption of fish. Athenaeus wrote about both: he gave a prominence to both in the *Deipnosophistae* and dedicated a treatise to each of these twin concerns.

# ATHENAEUS, *ON THE KINGS OF SYRIA*

## by David Braund

The key problem for any consideration of Athenaeus' work *On the Kings of Syria* is that we know almost nothing about it. The only definite allusion to it appears in the *Deipnosophistae* itself, where, fleetingly, Athenaeus is both author and subject.[1] He makes the diner Masurius mention the work, as follows:

Ἐπαινῶ δ᾽ ἐγώ, ἄνδρες φίλοι, τὸ γενόμενον παρ᾽ Ἀλεξάνδρῳ τῷ βασιλεῖ τῆς Συρίας συμπόσιον. ὁ δ᾽ Ἀλέξανδρος οὗτος ὢν Ἀντιόχου τοῦ Ἐπιφανοῦς υἱὸς ὑποβληθείς, ... διὸ εἶχον μῖσος πάντες ἄνθρωποι εἰς Δημήτριον· περὶ οὗ ἱστόρησεν ὁ ἑταῖρος ἡμῶν Ἀθήναιος ἐν τοῖς περὶ τῶν ἐν Συρίᾳ βασιλευσάντων. τὸ οὖν συμπόσιον τοῦτο τοιόνδε τι ἐγένετο. Διογένης ὁ Ἐπικούρειος, ἕξιν ἔχων ἱκανὴν ἐν οἷς μετεχειρίζετο λόγοις, τὸ μὲν γένος ἦν ἐκ Σελευκείας τῆς ἐν Βαβυλωνίᾳ, ἀποδοχῆς δ᾽ ἐτύγχανε παρὰ τῷ βασιλεῖ καίτοι τοῖς ἀπὸ τῆς στοᾶς λόγοις χαίροντι. ἐπολυώρει οὖν αὐτὸν ὁ Ἀλέξανδρος καίπερ ὄντα τῷ βίῳ φαῦλον, ἔτι δὲ βλάσφημον καὶ βάσκανον ἕνεκά τε τοῦ γελοίου μηδὲ τῶν βασιλέων ἀπεχόμενον. καὶ αἰτησαμένῳ αὐτῷ φιλοσοφίας ἀλλοτρίαν αἴτησιν, ὅπως πορφυροῦν τε χιτωνίσκον φορήσει καὶ χρυσοῦν στέφανον ἔχοντα πρόσωπον Ἀρετῆς κατὰ μέσον, ἧς ἱερεὺς ἠξίου προσαγορεύεσθαι, συνεχώρησε καὶ τὸν στέφανον προσχαρισάμενος. ἅπερ ὁ Διογένης ἐρασθείς τινος λυσιῳδοῦ γυναικὸς ἐχαρίσατο αὐτῇ. ἀκούσας δ᾽ ὁ Ἀλέξανδρος καὶ συνάγων φιλοσόφων καὶ ἐπισήμων ἀνδρῶν συμπόσιον ἐκάλεσε καὶ τὸν Διογένη· καὶ παραγενόμενον ἠξίου κατακλίνεσθαι ἔχοντα τὸν στέφανον καὶ τὴν ἐσθῆτα. ἄκαιρον δ᾽ εἶναι εἰπόντος νεύσας ἐσαγαγεῖν ἐκέλευσε τὰ ἀκούσματα, ἐν οἷς καὶ ἡ λυσιῳδὸς εἰσῆλθεν ἐστεφανωμένη τὸν τῆς

Ἀρετῆς στέφανον, ἐνδῦσα καὶ τὴν πορφυρᾶν ἐσθῆτα. γέλωτος οὖν πολλοῦ καταρραγέντος ἔμενεν ὁ φιλόσοφος καὶ τὴν λυσιῳδὸν ἐπαινῶν οὐκ ἐπαύσατο. τοῦτον τὸν Διογένη ὁ μεταλαβὼν τὴν βασιλείαν Ἀντίοχος, οὐκ ἐνέγκας αὐτοῦ τὴν κακολογίαν, ἀποσφαγῆναι ἐκέλευσεν. ὁ δ' Ἀλέξανδρος προσηνὴς ἦν ἐν πᾶσι καὶ φιλόλογος ἐν ταῖς ὁμιλίαις καὶ οὐχ ὅμοιος Ἀθηνίωνι τῷ περιπατητικῷ φιλοσόφῳ, τῷ καὶ διατριβῆς προστάντι φιλοσόφου Ἀθήνησί τε καὶ ἐν Μεσσήνῃ, ἔτι δὲ καὶ ἐν Λαρίσῃ τῆς Θετταλίας, καὶ μετὰ ταῦτα τῆς Ἀθηναίων πόλεως τυραννήσαντι. περὶ οὗ καθ' ἕκαστα ἱστορεῖ Ποσειδώνιος ὁ Ἀπαμεύς, ἅπερ εἰ καὶ μακρότερά ἐστιν ἐκθήσομαι, ἵν' ἐπιμελῶς πάντας ἐξετάζωμεν τοὺς φάσκοντας εἶναι φιλοσόφους καὶ μὴ τοῖς τριβωνίοις καὶ τοῖς ἀκάρτοις πώγωσι πιστεύωμεν. κατὰ γὰρ τὸν Ἀγάθωνα

εἰ μὲν φράσω τ'ἀληθές, οὐχί σ' εὐφρανῶ.
εἰ δ' εὐφρανῶ τί σ', οὐχὶ τ'ἀληθὲς φράσω.

ἀλλὰ φίλη γάρ, φασίν, ἡ ἀλήθεια, ἐκθήσομαι τὰ περὶ τὸν ἄνδρα ὡς ἐγένετο.

I commend, dear friends, the symposium which took place at the court of Alexander the king of Syria. This Alexander, being the suppositious son of Antiochus Epiphanes … on account of which all mankind harboured a hatred for Demetrius. On that subject[2] our comrade Athenaeus has provided a historical study in his books on those who ruled in Syria. So this symposium took place in the following manner. Diogenes the Epicurean, whose capacity was appropriate to the arguments in which he dealt, was by birth from Seleucia in Babylonia; he was received at the court of the king, for all the king's attachment to the arguments of the Stoa. So Alexander made much of him, despite Diogenes' vile lifestyle and slanderous, vicious ways, a man who for the sake of humour did not even spare royalty. And Diogenes made a request alien to philosophy, namely that he might wear a short purple tunic and a gold crown which had the face of Virtue in the middle. He considered that he should be addressed as her priest. Alexander gave his assent and even presented Diogenes with the crown. However, when Diogenes conceived a passion for a woman who was a Lysis-singer,[3] he presented her with his paraphernalia. When Alexander had heard of this and was gathering a symposium of philosophers and distinguished men, he extended an invitation also to Diogenes. And he asked Diogenes to take his place on a couch dressed in his crown and tunic. When Diogenes responded that it was not convenient, Alexander gave a nod to bring on the entertainment, among which the Lysis-singer entered, wearing the crown of Virtue and dressed in the purple tunic. A gale of laughter broke out, but the philosopher held his ground and praised the Lysis-singer to the skies.

When Antiochus took over the throne he could not endure Diogenes' foul mouth, and ordered that he be killed. But Alexander was tolerant in all matters and scholarly in his dealings with others; he was not like Athenion the Peripatetic philosopher, who was head of schools of philosophy at Athens and also at Messene, not to mention Larisa in Thessaly, and who later was tyrant at Athens. On this subject Posidonius of Apamea provides a detailed historical study, which I shall set out for all its relative length, so that we may closely examine all those who claim to be philosophers and not put our faith in their ragged coats and unkempt beards. For, as Agathon has it:

If I speak the truth, I shall give you no pleasure;

If I give you some pleasure, I shall not speak the truth.

However, the truth is dear, they say. I shall set out the story of the man Athenion, as it happened.

(5.211a–e)

The lacuna at the head of the passage is particularly unwelcome. The lack of a main verb confirms that something has fallen out of Athenaeus' text. But probably not very much, only a few words on Demetrius, if even that much.[4] For there was no point (even by Athenaeus' standards) in introducing Alexander (that is, Alexander Balas) and thereafter his dealings with a hypocritical philosopher only to interject something substantial on another ruler. We may reasonably speculate that Athenaeus' Masurius, having mentioned Alexander's beginnings as the 'son' of Antiochus IV Epiphanes, added a few words also on his end, ousted by Demetrius (II). While Alexander Balas is presented here as a benign ruler, Demetrius is universally hated, not least perhaps for removing Balas. Gulick assumes that Athenaeus presented the cause of Demetrius' unpopularity in the same fashion as Josephus, who attributes it to his seclusion, laziness and negligence, but we cannot be sure that there was only one view on the king. Indeed, Demetrius II may even be seen in a positive light.[5] Kaibel seems closer to the mark in making Alexander (and his removal, no doubt) the reason for Demetrius' unpopularity as stated in the *Deipnosophistae*.[6]

The lacuna notwithstanding, scholars have taken Athenaeus' Masurius to be quoting the story of Alexander and Diogenes from *On the Kings of Syria* (literally, *On those who ruled in Syria*), so that Athenaeus is here quoting himself.[7] For it is in the manner of our author to cite an authority in this way, amongst others; he does the same towards the end of the quoted passage, when citing Posidonius as his authority on Athenion, the Peripatetic and tyrant. Accordingly, I follow the orthodoxy in taking the *Deipnosophistae* here to include a fragment of the *On the Kings of Syria*, perhaps in summarized form, although one might wish for a clearer attribution in the extant text.

Therefore, the *Deipnosophistae* provides a taste of the Syrian work, while it also permits further inferences. The title of the work (like the fragment) demands that the Seleucids be treated at length, probably including not only male but also female royalty. We are left to wonder whether earlier rulers of Syria were also included, particularly Sardanapalus and Semiramis. Certainly in the *Deipnosophistae* Athenaeus explicitly presents the former as ruler of Syria (12.530a, quoting Clitarchus). The concept of Syria was also flexible enough to include, for example, Tigranes the Great of Armenia, who held much of northern Syria in the first century BC, or the rulers of Commagene, which could be taken to be part of Syria. Accordingly, Lucian of Samosata in Commagene could be not only a Syrian, but even an Assyrian.[8] The *Deipnosophistae* demonstrates Athenaeus' interest in Tigranes (e.g. 6.274f), Sardanapalus (e.g. 8.335f) and the royalty of Commagene (8.350c, Capito's work for Philopappus). Meanwhile, Athenaeus' Masurius seems to refer to books *On the Kings of Syria*, in the plural. We may feel confident that this was a smaller work than the *Deipnosophistae*, though we do not have any real grounds for such a feeling.

We must also consider the very fact that the Syrian work is mentioned at all. Since Larensis is so major a presence in the *Deipnosophistae* (see Chapter 1), and since Athenaeus evidently depended upon Larensis' patronage in writing that work, it may reasonably be inferred that Larensis was at least comfortable with the Syrian work. Otherwise, it would not have been mentioned. Indeed, it is entirely possible that Athenaeus had written the Syrian work too for Larensis. At any rate, the issue of kingship was germane to the process of patronage (cf. Chapter 22); it must have bulked large in *On the Kings of Syria*, as the fragment tends to confirm. Therein Alexander Balas is presented as the most tolerant of monarchs through his attachment to learning, almost to a fault in the face of bad behaviour. An alert Larensis can only have compared himself and his own 'court'.

In this context, we must beware of the magnetism of Julia Domna and her much-vaunted circle, into which Athenaeus has been drawn in the imagination of some modern scholars. She was herself from Syria (Emesa) and from AD 187 she was the wife of Septimius Severus, soon to be emperor. However, as Syme wisely observes of Domna's (and other) circles, 'when subjected to scrutiny, membership tends to disperse'.[9] Moreover, Domna came a little too late. The Syrian work must predate the *Deipnosophistae*, whose dramatic date is *c.*193–7 and whose date of composition seems to be not much later (though there remains room for argument on the latter point). Further, the scale and complexity of the *Deipnosophistae* would tend to suggest a substantial gap between the works, unless we imagine synchronous composition. The *Deipnosophistae* will certainly have taken a long time to compose, even with the aid of Larensis' great library. By contrast, Domna's circle, whose scope is best understated, seems not to have flourished until the late 190s, that is more probably after the completion of the *Deipnosophistae*, not some years before it.[10] Accordingly, Julia Domna is absent from the work, as also no doubt from the *On the Kings of Syria*. As Dessau understood more than a century ago, it was the circle of Larensis that mattered to Athenaeus.[11]

There is much to be said for Desrousseaux's focus on the prominence of Ulpian in the *Deipnosophistae* as a possible mark, or even a cause, of Larensis' Syrian interests.[12] After all, Ulpian is the head of the proceedings at table, for all that Larensis is host and patron. Appropriately, Ulpian's death ushers in the end of the *Deipnosophistae*, not only as a text but also as a society of companions: without the idiosyncratic Ulpian, the group will never be the same again (cf. Chapter 21). And Ulpian's Syrian origins are repeatedly brought to the fore among the diners, not least because there is something incongruous in the fact that so determined an Atticist came not from Athens and Attica but from Tyre and Syria, a 'Syratticist' (3.126f).[13] It is perhaps worth observing that, taken together, the three key figures in the *Deipnosophistae* (Larensis, Athenaeus and Ulpian) are a formidable trio who may be taken to represent Rome, Egypt and Syria respectively, though imperial Greeks could also see the Seleucids, Ptolemies and others as all of a piece, as 'Macedonians'.[14]

Syria was well suited to attract the attention of the patron of the *Deipnosophistae*. The interaction of kingship and patron here has already been noted. Further, the issue of luxury was readily explored in the context of wealthy Syria (cf. Chapter 16). Athenaeus affords Larensis himself a speech on Rome's decline into luxury which gives a prominent place to Lucullus' dealings with not only Mithridates but also Tigranes I, whose realm then included much of Syria. As has been argued (Chapter 1), it is hard to imagine that Athenaeus would have attributed alien notions to his patron: Larensis may well have placed the blame for Roman moral decline into luxury substantially at the door of Syria, as well as the rather more familiar province of Asia. Meanwhile, the key issue of fish and fish-consumption had a particular significance in Syria, where fish were even more an issue than in Greece and Rome (see Chapters 2 and 24). In Syria, it could even rain fish (8.333b–c, on Tryphon, ruler of Syria). The fact that the *Deipnosophistae* mentions a third work of Athenaeus, on the *Fishes* of the comic playwright Archippus, tends to confirm the possible importance of fish for Athenaeus' (and perhaps Larensis') interest in Syria.

The power of the literary tradition is also to be recognised. Quite apart from early and marginal Syrian rulers, the wealth of the Seleucids had been accorded a place in comedy, as early as Antiphanes on Seleucus I, as it seems (4.156d; cf. 9.405e–f). The impact of comedy on the *Deipnosophistae* is palpable: its impact on the Syrian work can hardly be excluded, whether direct or indirect. After all, the comic stage treated not only Seleucids but also broader Syrian attitudes to fish-consumption, as Athenaeus knew (8.341f on Timocles). Rather later, Libanius shows the existence in his own day of a range of apparently long-standing Syrian traditions, history and quasi-history.[15] Some were no doubt conveyed by obscure local historians, two of whom Athenaeus seems to name, evidently drawn to do so by their exoticism (3.126a). Quite how much was known to Athenaeus, or was in texts owned by Larensis, is beyond our knowledge. But both would surely have relished the challenge of a rich and complex tradition. Athenaeus certainly knew something of Mnesiptolemus of Cyme, court historian of Antiochus III (15.697d). He reports that Mnesiptolemus' work contained trivial detail on the drinking-habits of Seleucus I, indeed to a comically inappropriate degree (10.432b). Drink was a recurrent problem for several of the Seleucids, as told by Phylarchus and others.[16] There were further historical sources, which Athenaeus shows no sign of knowing (though he may have done): for example, in the *Deipnosophistae* we hear nothing of Timochares' work *On Antiochus*.[17] Yet Athenaeus did have a wealth of stories and details about the Seleucids, as the *Deipnosophistae* amply testifies.[18]

Meanwhile, the broader histories of Timagenes and Pompeius Trogus were also part of the many-sided tradition on the Seleucids and other Hellenistic rulers. For the later Seleucids, in particular, the *Histories* of Posidonius were clearly of the first importance. After all, Posidonius was himself from Syrian Apamea. Athenaeus evidently knew his work well and valued it highly (e.g. 15.692c; cf. 687d). No doubt, the problem for Athenaeus was how to respond to it in his own work on Syria. A recent commentator on Posidonius is less than complimentary in denouncing Athenaeus' 'magpie methods', by which he is said to have created 'a jumble of miscellaneous pickings'.[19] The virtues of polymathy, variety and vignette were more apparent among imperial Greeks, not only Athenaeus of course, but also Aelian, Polyaenus and others besides.[20] Yet we must also acknowledge Athenaeus' real difficulty in accommodating the towering presence of Posidonius' legacy and going beyond it. It is perhaps worth observing that even where Athenaeus quotes himself in the passage of the *Deipnosophistae* set out above, the excerpt is framed by two more from the inescapable Posidonius.

There was also the abiding issue, so prominent in the *Deipnosophistae*, of Rome's relations with the Greek east (cf. Chapter 1). Athenaeus shows himself aware of the key role of Syria therein, particularly through Polybius' writing on

Antiochus III (Rome's humbled opponent), on Antiochus IV (Rome's energetic emulator) and on Demetrius I (Rome's defiant one-time 'hostage'; cf. Chapter 11). Of course, Appian's treatment of Seleucid history, completed *c*.AD 150, was very much couched in terms of morality, luxury, decline and Roman imperialism, such as Athenaeus would have found familiar.[21] Yet, perhaps not wholly congenial, or so some would have it. Appian's treatment of the Seleucids and their conquest by the Romans has been taken by some readers to exhibit significantly anti-Roman attitudes. So much so that hostility to Rome has been used as a principal clue to his sources on the Seleucids. It is primarily for that reason that Marasco argues for his dependence upon the work of Timagenes: there is little otherwise to support such a view.[22]

However, to say the least, it remains to be established that Appian was indeed anti-Roman.[23] Rather, his commitment to Rome seems very strong: after all, he was close to Fronto and gained the rank of procurator under Antoninus Pius.[24] While Appian was a proud son of Alexandria, and had substantial reservations about the Roman republic as a political system and about some particular instances of Roman behaviour, he was also a pronounced adherent of monarchy and enthusiastically comfortable with the Antonines (App. *BC* 4. 16). For him the Roman emperors were certainly kings, whatever else they might be called (App. *Praef.* 6). The key point in all this must be that, occasional criticisms notwithstanding, his political attitudes do not make him anti-Roman, still less the unthinking purveyor of the anti-Romanness of his source(s). On the contrary, Appian would have been at home among the deipnosophists with their passionate civic attachments and their bantering comparisons of Greek and Roman. At the same time, he could have enjoyed debate with Larensis, whose attachment to the imagined standards of the Roman republic before Lucullus may be inferred from Athenaeus' attribution of such views to his patron (e.g. 6.273–4). There too we may be sure that Ulpian would have had strong words with him about the quality of his Greek.[25]

However, Appian died in the 160s, at about which time Larensis had his religious post under Marcus. It seems that Appian was born too early to join in at Larensis' table. Yet Athenaeus can hardly have ignored his substantial treatment of the Seleucids in preparing his own work on kings of Syria a few years later. The fact that Appian came from Alexandria made him still harder for the Naucratite to ignore. Appian offered a major challenge to Athenaeus; in a sense even more so than Posidonius. However, in the *Deipnosophistae*, where Posidonius is quoted very often, Appian does not occur at all. We may suspect that the Syrian work treated the two authors in that same fashion. For while Posidonius was an esteemed part of the hallowed past, Appian was too close, too much like a rival and (if only by virtue of his very contemporaneity) less interesting for Athenaeus and his patron, except as competition. Such, at least, is the outlook of the *Deipnosophistae*, from which contemporary works are all but absent (see Chapter 1). The nature of Athenaeus' response to Appian is hard to gauge, but we do seem to have a fragment of *On the Kings of Syria*, so that we can hope to taste the flavour of that work.

What sort of work, then, was Athenaeus' *On the Kings of Syria* ? The title does not tell us much; its form was not unusual.[26] The fragment shows a much lighter touch than is usual for Appian. In the fragment the tone is humorous, but with point. Diogenes is shown up as a fraud, and a shameless fraud at that. His misuse of the privileges which Alexander had granted him may recall Herodotus' account of similar events at the Persian court (Hdt. 9.108–13). And of course Herodotus was well-established in the canon, very familiar to Athenaeus (e.g. 10.438b). However, whereas Herodotus' story is fraught with deadly intrigue, Athenaeus prefers gentle mockery. The vainglorious 'philosopher' Diogenes had shown his fraudulence by his initial request; in any case, it was already indicated by his brand of philosophy (cf. 2.101f; 12.546e; Chapter 30). Alexander had no difficulty in granting privileges which were by nature so absurd and so revelatory of Diogenes' fatuousness, for it was the realization of a metaphor (cf. 7.281d). By simply making the grant, Stoic Alexander had shown the moral superiority of his philosophy over that of Epicurean Diogenes. Then Diogenes compounded his lack of perception by giving over the symbols of his (lack of) moral worth to a woman of dubious morality; indeed, he had deserved them about as much as she did. Worse still, he was driven to do so not by any rational process, but by the exigencies of an uncultured passion. Alexander has his final victory in revealing Diogenes' conduct (and its implied lack of real philosophy) with consummate elegance. A Lysis-singer was a female who played a male role, dressed as a man. In this instance Alexander had the singer dressed in the very specific role of Diogenes himself, before having her brought forth to entertain at his symposium. In the process the king shows that he is in control not only of the Lysis-singer, whose appearance and dress he commands, but of philosophy and therefore of himself. He can tolerate even Diogenes, whose only defence is his shamelessness. Faced with the nonsense of his lowly girl-friend dressed in his particular attire and therefore appearing as himself, Diogenes applauds the performance, perhaps straightforwardly, for he is in love not so much with the girl as with himself. Diogenes' brand of philosophy is demonstrably not a threat but an affirmation of Alexander's much-loved Stoicism.

Was Athenaeus' *On the Kings of Syria* all like this? So much might be suspected from the author of the *Deipnosophistae* and a work on Archippus' *Fishes*. Of course, we rely upon inference. Yet it is hard to see how the fragment could have fitted into a work such as that of Appian, for example. Athenaeus' historical work was not, it seems, that kind of history. The fragment shows a set of concerns similar to that of the *Deipnosophistae*: there we have philosophies in conflict, bantering japes, a banquet setting, a Lysis-singer, and love of sorts—all set in an atmosphere of humorous sophistication and luxury at a royal court. Conceivably, the fragment was an isolated and exceptional vignette, chosen as such for the more suitable context of the *Deipnosophistae*. But, although no certainty can be claimed, it seems much easier to believe that the fragment was also at home in the texture of *On the Kings of Syria*. As we have seen (and the likes of Sardanapalus apart), the Seleucids offered ample opportunities for such treatment, from comedy and Nicator onwards to the *Deipnosophistae* itself.

There was something a little unusual in Athenaeus' concern with the Hellenistic world. Pausanias famously bemoans the lack of accounts of Hellenistic history (1.6.1). Athenaeus' *On the Kings of Syria* is regularly cited as an exception to that tendency to neglect Hellenistic subjects, beside Arrian and Dexippus on the Diadochi, the hellenistic *Lives* of Plutarch and of course Appian.[27] It might be argued that Athenaeus' decision (or that of his patron) to write the Syrian work was driven by the perception of such a gap, though hardly by Pausanias himself (see Chapter 13). However, if the foregoing collation of inferences has any substance, Athenaeus' *On the Kings of Syria* is probably better seen not so much as the kind of narrative history which Pausanias might have found useful for his purposes, nor as an ethically orientated disquisition in the manner of an Appian, but as a treatise with an approach and agenda akin to that of the *Deipnosophistae*, where the Hellenistic world also bulks very large. We should think perhaps not so much of Appian as of the *Comic Histories* of Protagorides or the writings of Phylarchus, who each had a certain penchant for Seleucid themes.[28] The writing of history was evidently in vogue; perhaps almost too much for the taste of Athenaeus and Larensis. Moreover, the Parthian War of Lucius Verus (AD 162–6) had made the east a particular focus of that vogue. Athenaeus' *On the Kings of Syria* is not to be imagined as among the historical works criticized by Lucian in his *How to Write History*,[29] but even so we may wonder what Lucian (from Syrian Commagene and author of *On the Syrian Goddess*) might have made of it.

# ATHENAEUS AND THE *FISHES* OF ARCHIPPUS

by John Wilkins

One of the lost works of Athenaeus is his monograph on the *Fishes* of Archippus, a comedy that was written in Athens in about 400 BC, as far as we can tell. He refers to this work at 7.329c. While the contents of this book are largely inaccessible to us, its very composition enables us to include Athenaeus among the commentators on comedy. The book may have resembled Callistratus' work on the *Thracian Women* of Cratinus (cf. Chapter 27). Athenaeus clearly knew the *Fishes* of Archippus. He had read a text of the play. Keith Sidwell suggests that the number of comedies read by Athenaeus and his friends was comparatively few, and that much quotation from comedy was drawn from earlier compendia and commentaries (Chapter 9). Sidwell may be right, though we should note that one of the diners in the *Deipnosophistae*, Democritus, claims to have read eight hundred plays of Middle Comedy (8.336d). No one could seriously deny that many quotations of comedy do derive from earlier collections, but Athenaeus' knowledge of this play of Archippus indicates at the very least that his reading of the texts of comedy extended beyond the plays of Aristophanes, Cratinus and Eupolis.[1] Comic discourse is also the bedrock of the lively exchanges between the fictional diners created by Athenaeus.

This chapter is divided into two sections: (I) Athenaeus' adaptation of comic discourse into those lively exchanges and (II) his approach to the *Fishes* of Archippus.

I

After a lengthy attack on the Cynics and other philosophers by Larensis and Magnus, Cynulcus the Cynic retaliates at 4.164e–165b. He cites three lines from the *Archilochi* of Cratinus (fr. 6 K—A):

Did you see that Thasian salt-sauce—the things that he barked out!
Good and speedy was his revenge—instant in fact.
Of course the blind man does not seem to chatter as far as the deaf man is concerned.[2]

Cynulcus continues,

[Magnus] takes no notice of the lawcourts in which he makes his displays of beautiful iambics. Under the influence of his gluttony (*gastrimargia*) and sweet discourse (*hedulogia*) he recites Thracian dances and 'songs that are played strangely on the pipes and cymbals that are struck off the beat'.[3] And after these fine lapses in taste (*amousologiai*) he goes round people's houses seeking out those in which dazzling dinners are being prepared, going even beyond that famous Athenian Chaerephon of whom Alexis in the *Fugitive* says [fr. 259 K—A is quoted] ... Nothing restrains this man [Chaerephon], just like our fine Magnus here, from making cross-border journeys for the sake of his belly,[4] as the same Alexis has said in *Dying Together* [fr. 213 is quoted, along with Theopompus fr. 35 on the parasite Euripides] ...' Everybody laughed at this and then Ulpian said in response, 'From where did those pleasure-loving solecists derive the term *hedulogia*?' Cynulcus replied, 'well, you well-seasoned piglet, Phrynichus the comic poet ....

And so it goes on.

This exchange, which is typical of Athenaeus' diners, brings together citations of plays, the characters satirized in the plays and the deipnosophists into a homogenized discourse of comic consumption—humans who both consume (as parasites) and are consumable (as pigs). Cynulcus begins his attack, as do the deipnosophists on many occasions, with some lines from comedy. The aggressive tone is reinforced by the choice of comedy to be quoted, the *Archilochi* of Cratinus. It is presumably the poetry of Archilochus that is described as *halme*, salty seasoning for food and salty seasoning for speech.[5] Magnus, claims Cynulcus, is influenced by his insatiable belly and his love of sweet words (we might say that he consumes tasty food and quotes tasty verse). All is excess; there are charges of uncontrolled desire and of a use of words that lacks elegance and true meaning. The deipnosophists revel in the raillery of Archilochus and the parasitical behaviour of Chaerephon as made available to them by the verses of Cratinus and Alexis. Terms suitable for foods can be extended to discourses of words, and similar restraints can be expected. All of this has been inherited by Athenaeus from comic and sub-comic discourses in which invective, consumption and poetic rivalry are combined. The deipnosophists attack each others' appetite and grasp of words just as comic poets attacked their victims, who were often other poets. We recall the attacks of Aristophanes on supposedly gluttonous tragic poets such as Melanthius at *Peace* 804 and on the supposedly drunk Cratinus in the parabasis of *Knights*, the comments of Cratinus himself on his own supposed drinking in *The Wine Flask*, and of the poets of Middle and New Comedy on such poets as Archestratus of Gela, and of Machon on Diphilus.

The significant difference between those comic versions and the *Deipnosophistae* is that the characters of Athenaeus are speaking their sweet[6] and clever words in a sympotic context rather than in the theatre where the audience feast on words alone.[7] The deipnosophists enjoy another course before moving on to further discourse, whereas in the theatre the audience are offered verbal nourishment only—a share in the sacrifice of the sheep and in the victory meal after the play in *Peace*, for example. That distinction noted, there is much common ground between comic and sympotic texts since the symposium is so extensively incorporated into comedy. The drinking of wine, the games, the *hetaerae* and the foods are all present in comedy in such profusion that when Athenaeus wished to illustrate an aspect of sympotic culture such as wine cups, the game of *kottabos* or the proportions in which wine and water were mixed in the krater, it was to comedy that he first turned.[8]

The *Deipnosophistae* is above all a representation of the symposium whose material reality had been transformed into poetic discourse by comedy centuries earlier. Comedy had wrought a similar transformation on many other aspects of the material world such as fruits, vegetables, meat and fish. Thus when Athenaeus chose to illustrate a particular fish, he might turn to a zoological account from Aristotle's *History of Animals* or a medical account from Hicesius *On Materials*, but he was rather more likely to prefer Attic and Sicilian comedy, drawing in particular on the *Marriage of Hebe* or *The Muses* of Epicharmus.

Such texts, but above all Attic comedy, provided in addition those two touchstones of the period in which Athenaeus was writing, antiquity and pure Attic diction. For Athenaeus, Epicharmus guaranteed great antiquity while Pherecrates, for example, was both *attikotatos* (6.268e) and of good antiquity. Naturally, comedy was not the only playful adaptor of the material world. There were other sympotic genres that linked scholarship and wit.

The author of the first book of the *Deipnosophistae* in its current excerpted form introduces the reader to the content, characters and format of the work before proceeding to germane matters of literature on the subject. The content, we are told, is drawn from the material world, with emphasis on variety and plenty. The first category is fish (which has to wait until Books Three, Six, Seven and Eight for full attention). The characters of the work are wordsmiths, Larensis a polymath and iambic poet second only to Archilochus; the *grammatikoi* are full of *charis*, the philosophers polymaths; Philadelphus, intriguingly, is tried not only in philosophy but in life; Cynulcus the Cynic is dog-like, while Ulpian of Tyre is the linchpin of the whole gathering in his relentless pursuit of precedents in literature to lend literary support to the food before it is eaten and to unusual words before they are accepted into the discourse. He represents before all others the intense desire to validate the present in the past, that is the past as demonstrated in a text—hence his nickname Keitoukeitos, *'Found-not-found'* (1.1e). Athenaeus and other deipnosophists share the focus on the past in frequent appeals to the practice of the ancients.[9] These characters bring literary and philosophical approaches to bear on the foods and drinks that are the raw materials of the work. The format within which they speak is based on Plato's *Symposium* (1.1d), and that format later appears to be taken by Athenaeus to comprise the use of dialogue and argument by semi-fictionalized characters on sympotic themes (elements contained within Plato's dialogue after all, and very prominent at times), together with two prominent features fed through the Platonic tradition, a moral system based on restraint of bodily pleasure and an interest in definition, albeit hardly definition as prescribed by Socrates.

Much of the *Deipnosophistae* is a gathering of materials—often listed in such categories as vegetables, fruits, fish, wine-cups and cakes—and verbal elaboration either on that category or on some aspect contained within it, especially sympotic forms of dithyramb, parody, skolia, riddles and so on. The excerptor of Athenaeus brings such verbal elaboration to bear almost from the outset. He surveys the qualities of the host—which conform with the correct conduct of rich men and kings in giving dinners—and his all-important library of 'ancient Greek books' (1.2d) and then diverts to the otherwise unknown Charmus of Syracuse. He it was who could convert verses and proverbs into tags for any food: tragedy or epic could be applied in this way. He was the kind of person who would come to a rich man's feast and in order not to appear a parasite singing for his supper would bring 'contributions as it were of learned material tied up like bed rolls'.[10] Here we have a model for the characters sharing Athenaeus' learned banquet (at which the author himself was present). Cleanthes of Tarentum was another who thought up verse tags for dishes, together with Pamphilus the Sicilian.

The tone is set: the earliest material that Athenaeus (excerpted) has brought to bear is clever versification by ludic authors, all of them drawn from Clearchus of Soli, the peripatetic writer. Clearchus is an important source for Athenaeus, on anecdotal lives of poets and parodists such as Archestratus, on sympotic riddles and on proverbs. Athenaeus' interest in unusual authors continues with Archestratus of Syracuse or Gela, introduced in such a way that he too may be thought a parasite (1.4e–f; cf. 1.4a). Attention turns to writers of treatises on banquets, and then to Plato the comic poet's parody of a 'cookery book of Philoxenus' (Plato com. fr. 189), which introduces anecdotes on various parasitic and gluttonous Philoxeni (the most important of whom is the dithyrambic poet Philoxenus of Cythera) and on Apicius. These extraordinary authors eventually give place to substantial authors, that is comic poets, their early progenitor, Archilochus, and Homer. It is to comedy that I now return.

Athenaeus mentions his monograph on the *Fishes* of Archippus at 7.329c,[11] in the **II** context of the identity of the Thraittai or *'Thracian Women'*, a species of small seafish.[12] Zoology is just one of his interests. Athenaeus writes:

> Archippus composed the following in the written treaty between the fish and the Athenians. 'We will hand over each other's property that we control: we will surrender the *Thracian Women* and Atherine[13] the pipe-girl and Cuttlefish wife of Thursus and the *Trigliai* and Eucleides the archon and the Meagre from Anagyrus, the son of Goby from Salamis and Monkfish the *paredros* from Oreos.' In this connection, if someone should ask what these *Thracian Women* in the keeping of the fish happened to be, which they contract to hand back to men, I will now set forth the chief points since I have written specifically about it.

These chief points are three:

(1) Mnesimachus—identified as a writer of Middle Comedy—mentions the fish in his *Hippotrophos*;
(2) Dorotheus of Ascalon in his *Lexeis* (Book 108) ruled that the Attic orthography requires *thetta* not *thraitta* (either because he had a faulty text of the play or because he corrected it himself), but he is ignorant of Attic usage.
(3) The fish is small, as indicated by a passage from the *Lycurgus* of Anaxandrides and the *Etruscan* of Antiphanes.

Athenaeus, then, picks up identification of the fish, proper grammatical form, and size. To this we can add a fourth element, the interchange between the world of fish and the world of humans, which is effected through the various senses of *'Thracian Women'*.[14]

Did Athenaeus in fact have any interest in zoology? A certain contribution, at least as regards fish suitable for eating, is manifest in Book Seven of the *Deipnosophistae*, for in addition to citations from Aristotle and Dorion he adds what appears to be his own observation: 'in my own city of Naucratis they call *hepsetoi* (boiled fish) those little fish left behind in the canals when the Nile comes to the end of its flood' (7.301c). He tries to remember the *Fishes* of the Nile after a long absence at 7.312a–b. (For contributions based on his own experience we might compare his note on the 'boiled-meat shops' of Alexandria in the introduction to the category of meats boiled in water at 3.94c, all of which examples are then taken from comedy, and the inclusion of the prytaneion of Naucratis in his survey of meals served by various Greek poleis (4.149d–150b: no great number of examples is listed)). It is not clear whether there was any discussion in the monograph on *Fishes* on the identification of species. It remains a possibility, and indeed may explain Athenaeus' choice of that particular play over other plays of Archippus or of other authors. The identification of species is certainly an interest in the *Deipnosophistae*.

In his monograph Athenaeus is writing within the tradition of Lycophron and the Hellenistic editors of comedy who saw the need to provide glosses and other lexical aids for readers of that very versatile genre. Thus many of his citations on fish focus not on zoology or eating quality but where they are cited in the dative case, for example, or in a particular inflected or dialect form.[15]

It is not the aim of this chapter to divine the contents of the monograph of Athenaeus beyond the interests identified above;[16] rather, to investigate the contribution Athenaeus makes to our knowledge of the *Fishes* of Archippus in the *Deipnosophistae*, since his testimony to the play in the large work resembles the little we know of the monograph and is characteristic of his work on comedy in general. Many works of Greek literature survive only in citations from Athenaeus, among them many comedies. The complaint is often made that Athenaeus has failed to record what we want to know, and has instead concentrated only on aspects of eating and drinking when comedy happens to have mentioned them. Such a criticism begs the question of what we need to know about comedies, implying that eating, drinking and sympotic features are not of much interest when set beside such elements as plots and characterization. It is also worth asking whether a 'better' author than Athenaeus writing at a time closer to the time of composition of most of the plays—say Lycophron in the early third century BC— would necessarily have commented differently.

What picture, then, of the *Fishes* do we gain from Athenaeus in the *Deipnosophistae*? Twenty one fragments are listed by Kassel and Austin, of which eight are not from Athenaeus. Of his fragments,

24   and 26 list fish;[17]
16   playfully personifies fish, while 17 and 18 cite priest-fish;[18]
23   attacks a fish-monger;[19]
28   attacks the tragic poet Melanthius, alleging gluttony;[20]

30  introduces a speech with the phrase 'gentlemen fish';[21]
27  cites the part of the peace treaty quoted above.

Other fragments: a periphrasis for the herald-shell (25);[22] one fish eats another (19);[23] 20 mentions the *amia* (one of the tunas);[24] 21 concerns a ladle.[25]

The fragments cited by others are: Harpocration on 'caught-twice', a term applicable to magistrates and fish (14),[26] Stephanus of Byzantium on seer-fish (fr. 15), Pollux on the terms *mulekoron* (22), *nakotiltoun* (33), *pantopoleion* (34);[27] Photius on a rare term (32),[28] *Prov. cod. Par.* on the proverb 'the buttocks of the land' (29),[29] a Platonic scholion on Anytus the prosecutor of Socrates who was satirized in the *Fishes* (31).

The play probably resembled the *Birds* of Aristophanes:[30]

(1)  the *agon* appears to have rested on conflict between humans and fish and to have been resolved in a fantastic treaty. Certain humans were particularly reprehensible, notably merchants and gluttons (frr. 23, 27, 28);
(2)  there was some assimilation of the world of fish and humans (fr. 16); and
(3)  fish were endowed with human forms of rhetoric (30);
(4)  There was perhaps some challenge to religious categories (17, 18).[31]

Fragments in which Athenaeus has more than a passing interest are 30, 28, 27, 23 (mentioned twice), 17 for the acute accent and 16 for the masculine noun *salpes*.

The fishmonger and the glutton are of enormous interest to comedy, more so to Middle and New Comedy than Old, as far as we know. These exemplify comic features which Athenaeus has found eminently suitable for his own work. Thus at 6.224b–c he writes:

> then slaves came among us carrying a huge quantity of fish from both sea and lake on silver plates. We marvelled at the wealth and luxury of it all. ... And one of the parasites and flatterers said that Poseidon had sent them to our Nittunius [Neptune], though not through the fish-merchants of Rome who charge so much; he provided them from Antium, others from Tarracina and the Pontian islands opposite, others from Pyrgi, which is an Etruscan city. The fish-merchants of Rome in no way fall short of those in Attica who were once attacked in comedy. On them, Antiphanes says ...

—and he continues at length with comic examples. The deipnosophists are equipped with those standbys of comedy, fish-merchants and parasites; their patronage by Poseidon resembles that god's arrival with fish in the *Marriage of Hebe* or *The Muses* of Epicharmus, fr. 54 Kaibel. The poet as glutton is very much grist to

Athenaeus' mill, as noted above, an important inheritance from playful comic and sympotic poetry, which Athenaeus transfers to his own work. His own characters take on the qualities of what they eat and what they are obsessed by.

Fragment 30 of *Fishes* (`Gentlemen Fish') introduces a playful and imaginative leap at 8.331c. In Book Eight, the survey of fish continues in a different mode from that seen so far, with the gazetteer or list of Book Seven abandoned in favour of the theme of over-indulgence. At the end of Book Six, the utopian passages cited from various plays are said by Cynulcus to have been a not unpleasant feast but to have left him quite famished because 'I have gulped down nothing but words' (6.270b).[32] Just in time, 'a multitude of fish and *opsa* of all kinds rolled in' to save the day (270e)—apparently not unlike the fish and their consumers presented in extracts from the comedies of Ameipsias and Heniochus, *Sphendone* and *Polypragmon*, the first on the rich host, who may act as a role-model for Larensis, the second on multitudes of fish 'playing' in the sea. Book Six ends on a note of luxury, linking the two themes of slaves and fish in the new imports into Republican Rome in texts such as Cato's polemic against imports of salt fish and pretty boys. The fish served by Larensis were huge and varied (exactly as we find in the verse of Matro and Epicharmus) and seasonal (as we find in the verse of Archestratus and again of Epicharmus). The long list of fish in Book Seven proves boring to Cynulcus (8.331c) but the discussion continues with more inspiration from Archippus: 'But no, Gentlemen Fish, (to quote Archippus)' and follows the theme of luxurious eating. 'And there we have it in that form, Gentlemen Fish. For in gathering all that material together, you have thrown us as food for the fish, not the *Fishes* for us, talking at such length as not even Icthyas the Megarian philosopher or Ichthon achieved' (8.334f-335a). Cynulcus eventually manages to move the conversation away from fish (8.347d) by introducing an alternative wordsmith, Stratonicus (Chapter 31). But this is only after exhaustive coverage that has included nutrition and non-Greek forms of fish-eating, focusing among other things on fish in Syria, Ulpian's cultural background.

Comedy has contributed much to this exhaustive treatment of fish, providing material both on the consumption of fish and on varieties. Comedy in the gazetteer was often preferred to Aristotle and others as a validating text. It is no surprise that Athenaeus used Archippus, since his comedy probably drew the human and piscine world closer together than any other. But many other plays presented the plethora of fish, the gourmandise and the particular attraction of this form of expensive foodstuff. Wherever fish was to be found on the menu, luxury could not be far behind, with the allied phenomena of buying in the commercial markets, spending ancestral inheritances and consumption and failure to control appetite.[33] Books Six to Eight are a splendid complement to the surveys of luxury which fill Books Four and Twelve. In the combining of human and fish in

Archippus' play, Athenaeus also draws near to those passages which link women in particular with fish for consumption (Book Thirteen above all):[34] when men are not spending money on fish they are chasing expensive women. In these books Athenaeus is thus able to deploy much material (he has more on fish than other foods)[35] and at the same time to tie it into that sub-Platonic discourse against luxury. This enables him to maintain a strand of dialogue at odds with all this wonderful profusion, a satirical note of censure that is often uttered either by Ulpian or the Cynic.[36] Athenaeus allows his material to run away with him, but excess is not entirely out of place—even Plato hints at excessive behaviour in the *Symposium*, as does Xenophon in his version. The excess sweetness and fat is, as it were, cut by the satirical mustard. The author uses various devices to control the work, many might say with little success. At 7.277b–c he writes, 'I shall record for you what the deipnosophists said about each fish, for they all brought to each other their contributions from books whose names I shall omit because of their multitude'.

We find something similar in Athenaeus' presentation of one of his favourite sources, the 'parodic' *Life of Luxury* of Archestratus. This work, written in hexameters in the fourth century, is related to comedy[37] and draws on both Epicharmus and earlier comedy, while later comedy in turn quotes from it. Like his fellow-parodist Matro, Archestratus also has a ludic relationship with Homer and Hesiod—putting fish into the fish-starved verses of epic. He advises elegance and diligent searching for the best fish, but at the same time he is as good as his title, searching at the expense of self-control, paying anything, even advocating theft to get the desired fish, one of which even takes on this very quality of unrestrained indulgence.[38] Many of Athenaeus' introductions to quotations of this author share the sarcasm of some deipnosophists for each other: there is, we might say, a creative tension between the enormous interest generated by the material foods and some notion of restraint.

A further feature of Archestratus which makes him invaluable for Athenaeus' catalogue of fish in Book Seven is the provision of variant names of fish presented as if glosses for the reader. So, for example, at fr. 21 he writes:

> In Rhodes the *alopex* is the *galeos*. And even if you risk your life, if they refuse to sell it to you, seize it. This is the fish they call fat dog in Syracuse. Afterwards put up with whatever is fated for you.

Such glosses in the sub-comic text of Archestratus are mirrored to a much lesser extent in earlier comedy (Epicharmus fr. 42–3.11, a special case, Aristophanes *Banqueters* fr. 233 and possibly *Wasps* 1137). (Archestratus' reference to the Syracusan term 'fat dog' may in fact refer to fr. 68 of Epicharmus.) Fish particularly lend themselves to the work of the glossator since in their multiplicity they raise problems of identification. Archestratus' comments on the *alopex* are clear antecedents for Athenaeus' work on the *Thracian Women*.

Archestratus was one of those rare authors introduced at the beginning of the *Deipnosophistae*, and he is cited more than sixty times by Athenaeus. Significant though Archestratus is for the *Deipnosophistae*, he pales beside the comic poets. Drama with its focus on the material, its abundance, its need for scholarly exegesis and its embracing the sympotic is Athenaeus' premier literary resource. Comedy also serves other functions. Timocrates is addressed at the beginning of Book Six: 'since you frequently ask when we meet, friend Timocrates, what was said by the deipnosophists, thinking that we were inventing some new creations, we will remind you of what is said in the *Poetry* of Antiphanes'. In a famous fragment (189), a comic poet, or one purporting to be one, sets out how much more difficult is the writing of comedy than tragedy since tragedy always uses the same material while comedy must find something new, new names, new events, new words. Athenaeus aims at both the wit and the novelty of comedy, the overpowering *inventiveness* of the genre.

Wit, novelty, sympotic *logoi*—all are brought to bear on the material world. Archippus had endowed his fish with human discourse in giving them one or more speeches beginning with the address 'Gentlemen Fish'. Like all the other comic poets he had presented an intensely materialist world of utensils and foodstuffs, perhaps in this case more fish than meat or plants, but other comedies put the balance elsewhere. Many comedies present foods in various forms of discourse, in lists, in sympotic and myriad other settings; they present foods on stage in material form—the sheep for sacrifice in *Peace*, for example. All are transformed into comic discourse, seen for example in the contrast between the festive Dicaeopolis and the warrior Lamachus at the end of *Acharnians*. Foods are by no means the only material objects in comedy—far from it—but they are a prominent part of the material world as far as comedy is concerned. Comedy provides the discourse of the material world, transformed by an infusion of cultural significance comparable to sympotic poetry in which wine is surrounded by ritual, games and *logoi* in poetic forms analogous to the sophisticated vase paintings analysed by Lissarrague (1990).

Now a symposium such as Plato's excludes the material world for much of its length—wine is not wanted, nor is the pipe-girl, and eating is rapidly over and done with. Sympotic and material elements are limited until the arrival of Alcibiades when wine and *hetaerae* are restored. Then there is scope, even in Plato's symposium, for the transformation of the material world in the eulogy of Socrates. How different is the symposium of Athenaeus! The material world is restored in a form that far exceeds even comedy.[39] Diners are served with appetizers, fish and cakes and so on, and comedy is used to integrate these materials into the sympotic. Where is radish mentioned in literature? Where sea-bass?

It is in many ways surprising, then, that Athenaeus offers as much of the plot of the *Fishes* of Archippus as he does. In order to see the converse, the ways in which Athenaeus will exploit parts of comedies for his own purposes, it is worth examining Athenaeus' contribution to our knowledge of a further comedy, the *Mandragorazomene* of Alexis, a play I have chosen not quite at random since it benefits from the recent commentary of Geoffrey Arnott. This time Athenaeus has no interest in the plot, though some reconstruction can be attempted: Arnott (1996) reviews the possibilities. This is one of the comedies for which Athenaeus is the sole witness to the text. There are five fragments in all.

Fr. 145 is a general reflection on the perversity of human nature in its desire for the contradictory: it is cited by Athenaeus in a discussion of the use of snow and cold drinks at symposia (lines 10–13):

> We contrive to drink snow,
> But if the *opson* is not hot we launch into abuse.
> And we spit out wine that is vinegary
> But go into Bacchic ecstasy over sharp sauces.[40]

The material food and drink in Alexis illustrate a feature of social psychology but are put to use by Athenaeus ostensibly for a material point, the consumption of ice and snow in drinks. At the same time, alert as ever to the broader picture, Athenaeus in the same passage[41] cites fr. 184 of the *Parasite* of Alexis which compares cool water from a well with the frigid poetry of Araros—presumably the son of Aristophanes and a comic poet in his own right.[42] Fragments which follow on the theme also have a twist, the place of snow in the life of luxury. In all four cases Athenaeus ventures well beyond his material topic.

Fr. 146 is cited by Athenaeus as an illustration of that comic character, the foreign doctor. He quotes Sosibius in an important passage on primitive forms of comedy found in Sparta and elsewhere.[43] It is difficult to tell whether Athenaeus, Sosibius or another is responsible for the insertion of Alexis' Doric-speaking doctor.[44] Dialectal differences in this passage centre on barley gruel, measuring-cups and beet. The material world here serves two purposes, identification of the outsider and linguistic comment, both of them of great importance for Athenaeus, for whom Alexis has paved the way. Fr. 147 resembles fr. 146 in identifying regional variation:

A:   I will come then, bringing *sumbolai* with me.

B:   How do you mean *sumbolai*?

A:   The people of Chalcis call ribbons and *alabastoi sumbolai*, old lady.

Athenaeus (8.365d) cites the fragment to illustrate the meaning of *sumbolai* as contributions to a communal feast, though the context here appears to be funerary.[45] This is not the only place in the *Deipnosophistae* where Athenaeus' judgement or interpretation might be called into question. Fr. 148:[46]

A:   You're in a bad way. By Zeus, you're a virtual sparrow-chick!
     You've been Philippidized!

B:   Don't chatter new-fangled stuff at me.
     I'm close to death. A: Poor you! How you've suffered!

Alexis focuses on the emaciated body in a characteristic comic interest with fat and thin people, and develops the idea with a new coinage. This combination of the physical and linguistically inventive, so characteristic of comedy, is also the kind of discourse to be taken into the text of Athenaeus, who has other variations of verbal dexterity applied to the emaciated at 12.550f–552f. Most of his examples are comic, which is not the case for the vast majority of the citations in the discussion of luxury which is the topic of Book Twelve. Fr. 149 illustrates Athenaeus' use of comedy best of all:

If there are any strangers that I love more than you,
     may I become an eel, so that Callimedon the Crayfish may buy me!

The speaker, perhaps a parasite, wishes on himself, if he is not true to his word, the worst fate, to become an eel, whose main predator is the rapacious politician with an appetite out of control and a consumption of fish such that he is imagined to have metamorphosed into a crayfish.[47] Athenaeus has much to say on this topic in Books Six and Eight,[48] much of it deriving from comedy. We cannot say whether Callimedon ever ate an eel in his life or whether he was addicted to the consumption of fish, nor is the question of much interest. Much more important for both comedy and its verbose descendant Athenaeus is that the material eel and crayfish have been transformed in ludic discourse into terms that signify something quite different: in the discourse of luxury a crayfish consuming an eel has little to do with a marine contest to the death[49] and everything to do with the all-consuming politician exercising his purchasing power to placate his insatiable appetite which extends far beyond a tasty dish of eels.

So it is that we come to the speeches of boastful chefs[50] which Athenaeus inserts into his book at strategic points: into discussion of the highly prized conger in Seven, briefly in Fourteen on the status of cooks, and in Nine where they are twice introduced by the deipnosophists' cook who claims training and novelty to match any comic chef and indeed mocks his predecessors, all of whom prove to be from comedy (9.376c–383f, 403e). The comic chef, for all his usefulness in explaining how to cook an eel in a pot with herbs and seasonings, serves the much larger purpose of the comic poet which is to extend the range of the material and the processor of material to the metaphorical and the abstract: the chef becomes a stock character, a philosopher, a social organizer, a bore or whatever. The material world remains ever important, but the verbal extension of its significance and its transformation into verbal word-play is a major objective of both comedy and Athenaeus.

At the end of three long books on the cultural significance of fish, Athenaeus declares to Timocrates[51] that it is fitting now to bring to an end the logos on fish 'lest someone may think that, like Empedocles, we were once incarnated as fish'. Fish, which of all the creatures eaten by humans are the most alien—because they inhabit the dense medium of water—have become, through the transforming discourse of comedy and Athenaeus, the major raw material for the whole work, challenged for supremacy only by wine. Athenaeus could draw on hundreds of comedies for references to fish which would support his interest in their identification and their place in banqueting and feasting. Where the *Fishes* of Archippus differs from the *Mandragorazomene* of Alexis, and as far as I know from all other ancient comedies, is in giving the fish a voice. They complain of their treatment by human beings, fishmongers in particular. And they address human beings and each other in comic speeches. Of all ancient animals, fish were the most silent. Aristotle in the *History of Animals* (535b13–536a4) notes the absence of voice in fish, though certain species utter squeaking or croaking noises. Archippus' fishes thus achieve more on the stage than Aristophanes' birds or Eupolis' goats, whose song and bleating were familiar to all human ears. This play, in which fish speak, appealed to Athenaeus and he developed the idea in his eighth book. His loquacious diners, who are so addicted to speech that they neglect the food served to them, have discussed fish to such an extent[52] that they are in danger of becoming fish themselves. If that were to happen they would lose their powers of speech and their identity as deipnosophists—unless they were fish in the play of Archippus.

# EPILOGUE

Collectively, the foregoing chapters have attempted to set our understanding of Athenaeus on a new footing. In the face of their reasoned barrage it will surely be much more difficult to ignore or dismiss the author. Again and again, from a range of perspectives, Athenaeus has emerged as a writer worthy of consideration in his own right, not as a mere compiler, but as a creative force with an agenda of his own. The sheer scale, range and density of the *Deipnosophistae* make it a difficult text on any account, while the need to rely on the Epitome for so much at its beginning further compounds that difficulty. It has also to be acknowledged that the whole enterprise of the *Deipnosophistae* does not make a strong appeal to modern tastes: pedantic lexicography, a focus on minutiae of the past and the self-congratulatory approach of our author may well deter potential readers. However, it may reasonably be hoped that the arguments presented by the many contributors to this volume have combined to show that Athenaeus repays the effort of engagement with his text.

We have seen that the *Deipnosophistae* may profitably be read as a way into questions of literary patronage. For there is no room for doubt that Larensis is its sponsor, as well as the host and a major participant in the proceedings which the work purports to relate. Further, the *Deipnosophistae* may be read as a fundamental text on the symbiosis of Greek and Roman in the Second Sophistic. It shows how strong commitment to traditional Hellenism, local patriotism and even to the purest Atticism could be accommodated comfortably enough at Rome and might even flourish there. As befits Asteropaean Larensis its patron, the world of the *Deipnosophistae* recognizes a distinction between Greek and Roman, but only to savour it. In this company, at least, the distinction is not corrosive of social and intellectual relationships, but part of their dynamic.

Throughout, we have seen humour. Athenaeus deserves a prominent place in any discussion of humorous writing, and indeed of satire, in the Greek culture of the Second Sophistic and in the imperial literature of Rome. Further, there is a strong feeling of human warmth at the learned table of Larensis, for all the banter, principled disagreement and occasional niggles. The diners enjoy themselves, while the reader is invited to share in that enjoyment. At the same time, at another level of engagement, the reader may feel privileged to share in the personal report of proceedings which Athenaeus conveys to his friend Timocrates, when all Rome was bursting to have such a share. Athenaeus offers his readers privilege and pleasure, but of a higher sort. Through the *Deipnosophistae* the company of gentlemen sets about an evolving programme of discussion which, for all its fun, claims seriously to tackle large issues of language, culture, history and philosophy. The sustained concern with Plato, in the form and the content of the work, gives some substance to that claim. Of course, the *Deipnosophistae* has much to offer on food, which may seem banal, but such material is integral to the larger programme, not an end in itself.

The *Deipnosophistae* will always be hacked about as a mine of fragments. Insofar as it is constructed as a library, so much may be thought a key purpose of its author. Scholars who would extract fragments from the work have a certain interest in imagining its author as an anal dunderhead, for as such he offers no obstacle to good access to his sources. Certainty is seldom attainable in such matters, but many of the chapters in this book have given powerful reasons to reject the notion of Athenaeus as a diligent bore. The balance of probability must now be that Athenaeus was diligent, certainly, but also creative and intelligent. That is why Larensis offered him patronage and no doubt access to his outstanding library. We have seen that there is a great deal of structure in the *Deipnosophistae*, both as a whole and in particular books. We have also seen that Athenaeus has selected and connected quotations not only according to his own agenda, but even with an artfulness that complicates the use of his work. Moreover, while we will never be in a position adequately to reconstruct Athenaeus' reading habits, good reasons have been offered for the hitherto unpopular view that he drew many and perhaps most of his quotations from whole texts, which were available in Larensis' library, not merely from earlier compendia. Indeed, there is a stress on novelty and the *ben trovato* throughout the *Deipnosophistae*: that is why, as we are told, all Rome is so eager to hear of the discussions at Larensis' table.

We have seen that Athenaeus had vital access to a wealth of texts in the library of Larensis. Indeed, a further function of the work is the display and advertisement of that wealth and Larensis' achievement in collecting it. In that context it seems almost perverse of so much modern scholarship to insist that Athenaeus was forced to rely heavily on quotations made by intermediary writers. All the more so when we have seen that Athenaeus often had a strong reason to address a text in the context of such an intermediary (notably, Heath in Chapter 25). Homer offers a clear case-study. For we can be completely sure that Athenaeus had full texts of Homer, yet we can also see that he seeks to discuss them not only in their own right but also in the context of intermediary scholarship. To that extent his practice is akin to the modern scholar's norm of discussing not only an ancient text but also the previous scholarship on that text. Therefore, to insist that Athenaeus depended upon intermediaries for his very knowledge of many texts is not only to deny the much-vaunted worth of Larensis' library, but also to misapprehend the scope of Athenaeus' outlook, which takes in not only original texts but also the works of his scholarly predecessors.

The present book is very large. However, Athenaeus and the *Deipnosophistae* remain an enormous scholarly opportunity. Here we have attempted to examine old assumptions and to offer new directions for future work, beyond the more particular arguments from chapter to chapter. And yet, such is the vastness of the work, the multiplicity of its issues and (it must be said) the substantial neglect in modern scholarship that this book cannot claim to offer the last word on anything. We hope, however, that we have succeeded in showing that Athenaeus and his work have much more to offer than those who pick up our book and thumb through its chapters may at first have supposed.

# NOTES AND REFERENCES

## Section I: General Introduction

### 1 Learning, Luxury and Empire: Athenaeus' Roman Patron

1. The now classic paper is Bowie 1970. Cf. for example, Bowersock 1990; Swain 1996.
2. Champlin 1980, 58–9. On Appian, Swain 1996, 248–53.
3. See especially Saller 1982.
4. *CIL* VI 2126 = *ILS* 2932; Dessau 1890.
5. Cf. 3.85a on the amount spent by Theopompus of Chios; 4.168b on expenditure to enable writing by Democritus of Abdera.
6. Cartledge 1990.
7. Thereby bringing his own Greek Egypt into play; Swain 1996, 251 observes that for Appian the Alexandrian at least the Ptolemies were 'my kings'.
8. Pflaum 1960, 531–2 (no. 194); 1068.
9. Demougin 1993, 243 (with bibliography).
10. 6.274c; cf. 4.168e, observing that this Roman wrote in Greek; 12.543a–b.
11. Syme 1989.
12. It is worth noting that Athenaeus or his speaker feels the need to explain the name Caligula here, whether for the benefit of the imagined company or for his readers. On Dionysus, see especially Chapters 29, 34 and 35.
13. On Hadrian and the Parilia, Birley 1997, 111. On Pancrates, Birley 1997, 244–5.
14. Cf. also 15.669d, where Cynulcus addresses Democritus with the term, albeit ironically.
15. For the opposite view, see Zecchini 1989a, 20.
16. Baldwin 1976 finds sympathy; Zecchini 1989a, the opposite; Honoré 1982, 12 finds disrespect.
17. Honoré 1982, 12–15; Athenaeus' Ulpian died before Galen, who is alive in the *Deipnosophistae* and died *c*.AD 199–216; Ulpian the jurist died in AD 223, with a violence quite unlike the death indicated for Athenaeus' Ulpian; cf. Zecchini 1989a, 11–13.
18. *PIR²* L297 is overly speculative on Dio, 73.1–2.
19. Honoré 1982, 225.
20. Champlin 1980, 58–9.
21. Honoré 1982, 12.
22. Cappadocia, even better than Lydia and Phoenicia: 3. 112b–113c. On local patriotisms, see further Chapters 5 (Naucratis) and 17 (Smyrna).
23. 3.121f–122e, citing Greek precedents; cf. 15.671c on Cynulcus' claim to utility against Ulpian's extreme bookishness.
24. Braund 1997 collects some instances.
25. Of course, Aelius Aristides had done still more: Swain 1996, 254–97.
26. 4.183e, with Chapter 32; cf. 10.425a on Roman debts to Aeolian practice.

### 2 Dialogue and Comedy: The Structure of the Deipnosophistae

1. For the case against thirty books see Chapters 3 and 18; cf. Letrouit 1991 and Hemmerdinger 1989.

2. We are often told something happened 'once' (ποτέ). Unity of time is not an objective of Athenaeus.

3. See Chapters 19 and 26.

4. Agathon, after all, is entertaining friends privately the day after the main festivities to celebrate his dramatic victory.

5. Theodorus is reticent about his name and is generally known as Cynulcus. See below.

6. 2.58b ὁ τῶν δείπνων ταμίας, 4.159e. Ulpian initiates the symposium after the feast at 10.422e–426a.

7. Compare 3.126e. At 3.126b Aemilianus remarks on Ulpian's admiration for Nicander as a polymath and lover of the past.

8. That testing is often aggressive. The verb ἀντικορύσσεσθαι, 'to don the helmet in opposition to', 'to take up arms against', is used of lively exchanges at 3.108f, 15.669b and 701b. Ulpian's memory is challenged by Myrtilus at 3.107b and by Aemilianus at 3.126b. Ulpian sometimes rejects competitive citation by others (3.127a).

9. There are no games in Athenaeus to resemble those at Trimalchio's feast or at Greek and Macedonian symposia. There do not even appear to be flute-girls or *hetaerae* present. Cf. Chapter 29 on entertainments.

10. He quotes against the Cynics Plato *Protagoras* 347c on men who through lack of education prefer pipe-girls, harp-girls and dancing-girls hired in the market place to talking and listening even when drunk. The Cynics are like these girls who get in the way of conversation and live (as Plato says in *Philebus*) a sub-human, mollusc-like life. Jokes on dogs at the Cynics' expense pepper the *Deipnosophistae*.

11. Myrtilus also charges Ulpian with ignorance of history at 3.125b.

12. He charges Ulpian with misunderstanding Latin *strena* ('a new year's present'); he got the gender of *phainoles* wrong when translating *paenula* ('a woollen outer garment') into Greek; Ulpian resembles other pedants who misunderstand words. His Greek term for *miliarion* ('in baths, a tall and narrow vessel for drawing and warming water') is laughable. Ulpian (and his followers) stand charged with an inability to match Roman cultural and linguistic practice against Greek equivalents. This is a theme for the whole work which places itself in the Greco-Roman synthesis of the Second Sophistic: cf. Chapter 1.

13. Archestratus is later said to be an author favoured by Ulpian (3.119a) and by Cynulcus (4.162b, 163c–d). Archestratus is a touchstone for luxury in the *Deipnosophistae*, batted back and forth not only among the diners but also when cited as an authority. He is used both as an ancient author whose testimony to eating is valuable and as an immoral guide, according to context. See further n. 10 and Chapter 39.

14. Myrtilus charges Ulpian with gluttony at 3.125b and 9.386c.

15. Ulpian's gathering of 'thorns' or spiky problems are referred to at 6.228c, 8.347d–e (with a pun on the small bones of the fish known as the *hepsetos* or 'boiler'), 385a–b.

16. Ulpian identifies *decocta* as a barbarism (3.121e–123e) but Cynulcus defends foreign words in Greek in general and defends his use of the term by pointing out that he lives in imperial Rome. The cook claims that Ulpian likes *isicia* (rissoles) even though he does not approve of the Latin term.

17. See, for example 3.108d–f where Ulpian is first vexed and then jests.

18. Bread (3.108f), fish (6.270a–e).

19. She considers in particular Plato, *Symposium*, Plutarch, *Banquet of the Seven Sages, Table Talk*, Lucian, *Lexiphanes, Symposium* and Athenaeus.

20. 3.120b A desire to drink follows the course of shell-fish but Daphnus delays drinking for all by citing medical texts on the subject.

21. 'Mr Found-not-found'. Nicknames are important in Athenaeus. They indicate the fame of the diner who is renowned in Rome. Ulpian is a star, if an imperfect one. We shall see below that Cynulcus, 'Leader of the Hounds', much prefers this name to his given name, Theodorus of Thessaly.

22. See, for example 9.380d, 'Ulpian said: "By those who faced peril at Artemisium, no one will taste anything until I am told where the term 'to pass round' is found. For I am the sole authority on snacks (*geumata*)."'

23. Pedantry is frequently challenged in the *Deipnosophistae* but not deprecated as a school for sophists and aggressive questioning. Contrast Plutarch's comments in *Table-Talk* (e.g. 712a).

24. In Plutarch (*Banquet of the Seven Sages, Table-Talk*) through debate, in Lucian (*Lexiphanes, Symposium*) through narrative.

25. The book is singled out for early mention in the *Deipnosophistae* (1.4e).

26. At 9.401d–e Democritus observes, 'You are ever accustomed, Ulpian, to take your share in none of the dishes until you have learnt whether the use of the term is ancient. You run the risk in these concerns of resembling Philetas of Cos who sought the so-called false account of words. Like him you may wither away.'

27. 9.396a. The phrase occurs in a discussion of 'choked' or stewed meat, on which Ulpian declares: 'I shall choke myself to death if you won't tell me where indeed you found such bits of meat. I shall never use the term until I have learnt about it.'

28. 3.105e. At 7.301a–b Athenaeus cites Alexis fr. 17 on small fish that were called *daidaleioi*, adding, 'all beautiful works they call works of Daedalus'.

29. Compare John Moles' assessment of Cynics (OCD³, 418), 'to maximize their audience the Cynics (despite avowed rejection of literature) wrote more voluminously and variously than any ancient philosophical school: relatively formal philosophical treatises, dialogues, tragedies, historiography, letters, diatribes, various kinds of poetry and of literary parody, prose-poetry hybrids' (for the last he compares Menippus). Many of these genres are prominent in the *Deipnosophistae*—Cynulcus quotes, for example, a list of literary parodies at 15.698a–699c. Athenaeus' treatment of Cynics, though, is ambiguous, for as philosophers they are often selected for criticism (in particular in Book Four).

30. On the *kestreus* or 'faster'-mullet with its apparently empty intestine see Athenaeus 7.307c–308b, a further passage where a Cynic makes a link with this fish. Food and eater in this example are once again assimilated.

31. His source is the otherwise unknown Parmeniscus. One Cynic meal is hosted by Carneius of Megara, identified as a *kunoulkos* or leader of dogs, our speaker's own nickname.

32. The host Larensis adds a contribution from 'Varro the Menippean' and notes Cynulcus' delight in his nickname at the expense of his real name (160b–d).

33. The cook claims at 9.383 that many cooks include journeys round Asia and Europe in their CVs.

34. In the middle of which (262b) he had stopped for a drink and would have been delayed by endless speeches from Ulpian had not more food arrived and given Democritus the chance to continue. It is not clear why the arrival of food silences Ulpian but not Democritus.

35. ἄνδρες σύσσιτοι.

36. The verb contributes to Ulpian's claim to austerity: he is a fighting man and not a luxurious Sybarite.

37. Speakers in the *Deipnosophistae* often make jokes on the supposed canine behaviour of the Cynics or Dog-philosophers.

38. Compare n. 8.

39. The translation of Gulick. The phrase 'συρβηνέων χόρος' appears to be taken from the *Thracian Women* of Cratinus, fr. 89.

40. Quoted from Plato, *Phaedrus* 252b.

41. At 692b he is addressed as Cynulcus Theodorus.

42. Cynulcus is accused by Democritus of practices similar to Ulpian (678f): 'You not only select secret things in books but even dig them out.'

43. He enters into polemic against other book lovers who have stolen his ideas or ideas found in books and present them as their own (673d–674a).

44. During the recitation he accuses Cynulcus of stuffing his belly (685a); cf. above.

45. See Romeri 1999; cf. Chapter 19.

46. Athenaeus' Cynics to a limited extent share characteristics with Lucian's philosophers in his *Lexiphanes* and *Symposium*: see Romeri 1999.

47. On the use of Plato see in particular Romeri 1999; Chapter 26.

48. 1.1a, 2.35a, 2.71e, 3.127d, 4.128a, 4.185a, 5.185a, 6.222a, 8.330f, 8.365e, 9.366a, 10.411a, 11.459f, 11.509e, 12.510a, 13.555a, 14.613a, 15.665a, 15.702b–c.

49. Chapter 18 sets out the details of where the outer dialogue is present and not present.

50. One further address to Timocrates which does not frame a book occurs at 12.550f–551a.

51. Adapted from Aristophanes, *Frogs* 295.

52. A poet of Old Comedy. Kaibel suggests the charge is based on one of the plays of Myrtilus.

53. Compare Metagenes, *Breezes* and Theognetus, *Ghost* cited above, together with Archippus, *Fishes* fr. 30, with Chapter 41.

54. Other poets are treated in this way, in particular Archestratus of Gela (on whom see below) and Philoxenus of Cythera (or another Philoxenus). For the details see Wilkins, forthcoming.

55. On Lynceus see Chapter 28. This period was probably important in the history of eating in Greece as in many others, as the Greek states moved from their own styles of eating to those based on the courts of kings and tyrants.

56. Similarly, Larensis' staff are not described at market. Rather, we are given accounts taken from comedy of the fishmongers of ancient Athens who are said to be no more rapacious than their Roman counterparts in the time of Larensis; cf. Chapter 1.

## Section II: Text, Transmission and Translation

### Introductory Remarks

1. For a general history of Greek texts on papyrus and their copying on to codices, see Turner 1987; cf. Reynolds and Wilson 1991. Note also the excellent summary in *OCD*,³ 249–52 (Maehler).

### 3 Athenaeus and the Epitome: Texts, Manuscripts and Early Editions

1. The plural title is correct, despite the statement at the beginning of the Epitome (1.1a) claiming that Δειπνοσοφιστὴς δὲ ταύτῃ [τῇ βίβλῳ] τὸ ὄνομα.

2. See especially Zepernick 1921, Brunt 1980 and Ambaglio 1990. Accusations of carelessness, omissions and paraphrase have sometimes been made—e.g. by Sharples and Minter 1983, Tronson 1984—but more often than not the alleged faults are the work of the Epitomist, not Athenaeus himself. Compare Chapters 33 and 37.

3. On the date of composition see my commentary on Alexis (1996, 34 n.1, with bibliography).

4. He himself wrote all but the last twenty-four folios of the codex. Cf. Wilson 1962, 147–8, arguing convincingly that this manuscript was not commissioned by Arethas, unlike other manuscripts (the Clarke Plato, two of Aristides) written by John the Calligrapher.

5. See Bigi 1962, 594. Filelfo also wrote 'Es tu sane librorum officina; sed ex ista tua taberna libreria nullus unquam prodit codex nisi cum quaestu'.

6. Aurispa wrote in 1424 to Ambrogio Traversari (Traversari 1759, 1027, letter xxiv, 53): 'gentilium auctorum volumina Venetiis habeo ducenta triginta octo, ex quibus aliqua tibi, quae rarissimo inveniri solent, nominatin dicam … Naucratici cujusdam Atheniensis [*sic*: an error which had momentous consequences: see below] volumen quoddam maximum, ne adhuc finitum [presumably an inaccurate reference to the missing folios at the beginning], de coenis: nihil usquam facetum dictum est, quin ibi non inveniatur.' Cf. Bolte 1886, 314, Sabbadini 1891, Bigi 1962, 593–5 and Hemmerdinger 1989, 114. On Renaissance pedlars and collectors of books see Reynolds–Wilson 1991, 146–54.

7. See especially Schweighaeuser's edition of Athenaeus 1801, 1. lxxxviii-cvii; Dindorf 1827, I.iii-v and 1870, 73–115; Cobet (works cited in n. 19); Kaibel 1887, 1. vii-xiii; Imhof 1961, 302–3; Desrousseaux 1956, xxxii-xliii; Hemmerdinger 1989, 113–14.

8. Cf. Schweighaeuser's edition 1801, 1. xiv-xvi, suggesting that Athenaeus himself condensed an original work in thirty books to one in fifteen.

9. See particularly Düring 1936, 226–70 and Letrouit 1991, 33–40; cf. Hemmerdinger 1989, 113–14.

10. Uncial is used, however, for notes written in the margin (normally subject headings) or at the end of books.

11. See Andrieu 1954, 210, Lowe 1962, 27–42.

12. Cf. Fraenkel 1950, 655 n. 1, 683 n. 3, and Arnott 1957, 194 and 1996, commentary on Alexis fr. 159.3.

13. Cf. also Kaibel 1883a, 4–5 and Kassel–Austin (vol. 2, 1991) ad loc., for different views.

14. Schweighaeuser's edition 1801, I.ci, Schöll 1869, 160–7, Dindorf 1870, 73–115, Kaibel 1883a.

15. See de Meyier 1955, 273, Irigoin 1967, 418–24.

16. Devreesse 1965, 54, 108, 143, 221, Irigoin 1967, 420 n. 2.

17. Aldick 1928, 16–31, Canart 1977–9, 281–347.

18. Those who argue for the Epitomist's sole dependence on the *Marcianus* are Cobet (works cited in n. 19); Dindorf 1860, 1. xiii, and 1870, 73–115; Maas 1928, 570–1; 1934, 165; 1935, 299–305; 1936, 30; 1937, 185–6; 1938, 201–2; 1948, 6; 1952, 1–3 = 1973, 521–2; 1957, 32; Erbse 1957, 291–92 and in Maas 1953, 441 n.1, Hemmerdinger 1989, 108, and Letrouit 1991, 33–7. Those who oppose this interpretation are Schöll 1870, 160 n.1; Kaibel 1883a, 4; 1883b, 5; 1887, 1. xix; Aldick 1928, 3, 16; Peppink 1936, 5, 10, 12–16, and 1937–9, 1. ix, 2. x; Vollgraff 1940, 172–96; Pappenhoff 1954; Erbse 1950, 75–92; Desrousseaux 1956, xxxiii, xxxix, xli; Collard 1969, 157–79.

19. Cobet in his *epistula* (published in Hemmerdinger 1989, 108), as well as 1847, 104–9; 1858, 12, 130; 1873, 127; 1891, 315, 354–5, 531–2, 538–46, 549, 556, 560, 575–7. Cf. Letrouit 1991, 37, noting that in manuscript E of the Epitome (folio 182ʳ) a second hand has added the missing παγ in the text and margin.

20. See Peppink 1936, 19; cf. also Maas 1937, 186; Hemmerdinger 1989, 116; Letrouit 1991, 37.

21. Maas 1948, 6, 1952, 1–3 = 1973, 521–2; cf. 1958, 51–2. Cf. Letrouit 1991, 34.

22. Letrouit 1991, 34. Cf. Casaubon's *Animadversiones* (1620, 198, 201); Schweighaeuser, *Animadversiones* (1802, 2.661–6; 3.13–14).

23. Letrouit 1991, 34–7.

24. Cf. Schweighaeuser, *Animadversiones* (1804, 5.605).

25. See especially Casaubon's commentary ad loc. (*Animadversiones*, 1620, 607), and Wilson 1983, 202–3. Here Maas 1935, 300–1 arbitrarily dismisses the Epitome correction Νικοκρέοντος as a 'lucky hit' (*Zufallstreffer*), and σοφῶς as 'fine, but not too far' from the ductus.

26. The best account of Musurus is given by Geanakoplos 1962, 111–66; cf. 1966, 126–30; see also Legrand 1885, 1. cviii-cxxiv; Menge 1868, 5.1–57; Sandys 1908, 2. 79. On his edition of Athenaeus, see also Casaubon's *ad lectorem* preface to his *Animadversiones* of 1620; Schweighaeuser's edition of 1801, 1. xxiv-xxix; Dindorf 1827, 1. xiii-xiv; Irigoin 1967, 418–24; Reynolds–Wilson 1991, 154–8; Lugato 1994, 245–6 (no. 145, with photograph p. 195).

27. See Schweighaeuser's edition of 1801 (1.xxv–xxvii n. t); Bühler 1955, 104–6, reporting the existence of a copy of this sheet in the Pierpont Morgan Library (MA 1346–230).

28. See especially Labowsky 1979, 57–63, Lowry 1979, 229–33, 242 .

29. See n. 6.

30. Bessarion's *acte de donation* and inventory are printed fully in Omont 1894, 129–87 and Labowsky 1979, 147–89; the *Marcianus* appears as item 301 (Omont 1894, 160; Labowsky 1979, 169). The error was corrected in the 1524 inventory (item 216; Labowsky 1979, 256).

31. Erasmus, who had been a pupil of Musurus, described him as 'gente etiam graecus ... eruditione graecissimus' (1642, col. 629); cf. e.g. Schweighaeuser's edition of 1801 (1. xxviii n. a); Kaibel 1887, 1. xiii–xiv; Reynolds–Wilson 1991, 158. On his command of metre see Fraenkel 1962, 94 n. 2.

32. See Casaubon's *ad lectorem* preface to his *Animadversiones* 1620; Schweighaeuser's edition of 1801 (1. xxix-xxxii); Dindorf 1827, 1. xiv-xv.

33. Cf. Pfeiffer 1976, 88.

34. On these two brothers see especially Mund-Dopchie 1975, 232–45 and 1984, 239–61 (on Willem); Collard 1995, 243–51 (on Dirk = Theodorus).

35. See Schweighaeuser's edition of 1801 (1. xxxiv–xxxv, xxxix–xliii). The name is spelled Dalechamps by d'Amat 1961, 1518 and in Catalogue of the Bibliothèque Nationale 35 (1929, 225–6), but more correctly Daléchamp by Desrousseaux (1956, xlvi).

36. The title page gives no place of publication, and existing copies are printed sometimes with MDXCVII as the date, sometimes with MDXCVIII.

37. Daléchamp's *Annotationes* are printed at the end of the 1612 and 1657 editions of Casaubon's. The latter's diary (1850) for the second half of 1598 is full of accusations gainst Mme de Harsy and her husband; she is labelled 'insigniter impudens et ἀναίσχυντος' (VI Kal. Aug.), 'dolis consuta ... huic perfidae et scelestae ... ὀλοαῖς μανίαις insanit' (V Kal. Aug.), 'monstrum ... scelus scelestae istius' (X Kal. Sept.) and her husband is accused of 'fraudes, scelera, impiamque mentem' (V. Kal. Sept.). The entry for IV Kal. Sept clarifies the situation: the scholar had been outmanoeuvred by a pair of unscrupulous publishers, 'ille enim impius simplicitatem meam quaestui, imo praedae, habuit'. Cf. Pattison 1892, 127–8.

38. Cf. Elmsley's praise of the commentary (1803, 184–5), 'We know of no work of this kind, except perhaps Bentl<e>ys dissertation on Phalaris, in which the reader is presented with such a mass of pertinent information ... the erudition of the critic, although ample, is displayed without ostentation.'

39. Letter xxxvi (in the collection edited by ab Almeloveen, 1709).

40. Thus Wilamowitz refers to his marvellous learning 1982, 54–5, and most other scholars have been equally enthusiastic: e.g. Schweighaeuser's edition of 1801 (1. liii–lvi); Dindorf 1827, 1. viii; Pattison 1892, 50, 108–28; Sandys 1908, 2. 204; Desrousseaux 1956, xlvii–xlviii; Reynolds–Wilson 1991, 176–7. Pfeiffer 1976, 120–2 is remarkably less enthusiastic.

41. In Germany Schweighaeuser is considered to be German (e.g. Wilamowitz, 1982, 104), in France French (e.g. *Nouvelle biographie generale*, 1864, 609–11*)*. He was an Alsatian of German ancestry who was born (1742) and educated in Strasbourg, where he lived most of his adult life and died 1830. Alsace was part of France from 1648 until 1871. From the middle of the eighteenth century French was the preferred language of the Strasbourg bourgeoisie, and Schweighaeuser used French in letters to his family and his diary. See especially Pfister 1926, 175–85, 223–30, 272 = 1927, 5–22, 24: the *separatum* is accompanied by engravings of both Jean and his son Geoffroi.

42. See especially Elmsley 1803, 181–94 (reviewing the first two volumes of text and the first two of commentary with criticism of Schweighaeuser's metrical inadequacies), and Grotefand 1806, 121–56; also Dindorf 1827, 1. xvi–xvii; Sandys 1908, 2. 396; Wilamowitz 1982.

43. Philippe Brunck died from 'apoplexy' on 12 June 1803. His family came originally from Sweden, emigrating to Alsace at the end of the fourteenth century.

## 4 A Dainty Dish to Set Before a King: Natale de' Conti's Translation of Athenaeus' Deipnosophistae

1. On de' Conti's biography and bibliography, see Ricciardi's article in the *Dizionario Biografico degli Italiani* (Rome, Enciclopedia Italiana, 1960– ), 28. 455/1–57/1; also Cestaro's article with bibliography in the *Enciclopedia Italiana di scienze, lettere, ed arti* (Rome, Istituto Giovanni Treccani, 1931– ), 11 (1949), 234, col. 2; cf. Kristeller and Cranz 1971, 2. 31, cols. 1–2.

2. Details of Renaissance translations and editions of Athenaeus are given in Appendix 2.

3. Balbi 1932.

4. Vico 1558: Natale de' Conti's contribution is acknowledged in the Dedication.

5. His fears were not without foundation; cf. the publication

*Difesa del cardinale Cristoforo Madriccio, contro Natale de' Conti* (Madriccio was offended by something he read in the *Histories*).

6. On Marcantonio Barbaro, see Logan 1972, 173–4, 187, 191–2, 299; and *Dizionario Biografico*, vol. 6, 110/1–113/1.

7. On Giulio Feltrio Della Rovere, see Ferdinando Ughelli, *Italia Sacra*, in the ten-volume augmented edition of N. Coleti (Venice, S. Coleti, 1717–22), 2. col. 799, item 43; and *Dizionario Biografico*, 37. 356/1–357/2.

8. On Sirletus, see Ughelli (above, note 7), vol. I, col. 879, item 26.

9. Muret came to Italy in 1552 to escape accusations of immorality, and made a name for himself there as a classical scholar; see *Grand Larousse Encyclopédique* (Paris, Librairie Larousse, 1963), 7. 598/2.

10. On Rhallis, see Legrand 1885, 1. cxcv; Giraldi 1551, 64; also Layton 1994, 460. This admirable book contains a mass of information about Greek scholarship in the Renaissance.

11. On the Greek College of Rome, see Legrand 1885, 1. cl-clii. There may have been an offshoot of the Greek College in Milan c.1518–21, and plans were made for one in Paris.

12. The word *cenacolo* means literally refectory or dining-hall, but was used metaphorically of a literary coterie. See Logan 1972, 71; cf. the conversational dining-clubs of Oxbridge colleges.

13. On Ridolfi, see Ughelli, vol. I, col. 1477–8, item 59; and Legrand 1885, 2. 53.

14. On Devaris, see Layton 1994, 460–4. Petros's dedication appears in Devarius 1588 and is reproduced in Legrand 1885, 2. 52–9; see also item 179 for Matthaios's book on the Greek particles.

15. See Legrand 1885, 1. clxxxvii–cxciv on Nicolas Sophianos, one of the first pupils at the Greek college in Rome; also Layton 1994, 461–72 (and Index). His grammar of modern Greek was recently edited (Papadopoulos 1977).

16. On Condoleon, see Legrand 1885, 1. cli, n. 2; Layton 1994, 337, n. 3, 460.

17. On the Cypriot love-poems, see Siapkaras-Pitsillides 1975, especially 3–5 on de' Conti's signature.

18. *Deipnosophistae* 14. 613b–c; p. 251/1 in de' Conti.

## Section III: Athenaeus the Reader and His World

### Introductory Remarks

1. For example, *Geog.* 12.3.39, with the discussion of Clarke 1997, 99.

2. On mosaics, see Westgate 1997/8 and 1999. Elsner 1998, 102–3 observes the spirit of Athenaeus in surviving inscriptions on tableware.

### 5 Athenaeus in His Egyptian Context

1. Philostratus, *V S* 1.6 (486), Theomnestus; 2.12 (592–3), Pollux; 2.19 (599–600), Apollonius; 2.21 (602–4), Proclus. For a Naucratite 'quasi-Mafia', see Baldwin 1976, 40; Zecchini 1989a, 17; cf. Dittenberger 1903, 26–8.

2. Naucratis: Herodotus 2.178–9; Strabo 17.1.18 and 23; see *OCD,*[3] s.v., for further details.

3. On his sources, see Zecchini 1989a and 1989b.

4. Psammetichus I: 6.231d, his bronze-cups (from Herodotus but in a different version: See Chapter 12); 8.345e, his fish-eating slaves (from Clearchus). Amasis: 6.261c, fond of drink and jokes (from Herodotus); cf. 10.438b–c; 13.560d–f, slights Cambyses; 15.680b–c, his gift of a wreath makes him king; for far earlier pharaohs: 15.680a, Babys/Typhon; 10.438b, Mycerinus fond of drink. Agesilaus: 4.144b–c, 12.511c, 14.613c, his tough and abstemious life-style (from Xenophon); 12.550e, despises Asiatic softness; 9.384a, receives Egyptian gifts of geese and calves (from Theopompus); 13.609b, defeats Lysandridas in Sparta; 14.616d, his small stature derided by Tachôs.

5. 5.196a–203b, 11.472a, Ptolemaea in honour of Ptolemy I; 11.497c, Soteria; 15.696f, paean sung in his honour on Rhodes; 13. 576e, Thais; 4.171c, appointed taster for Alexander; 6.244b, return from Attica (parasite Archephon).

6. See further, Thompson, forthcoming.

7. 1.3b, his library; 13.576e–f, his mistresses; 13.583a–b, Hippe mistress of Theodotus drank with the king; 10.425e–f, Cleino, his wine-pourer, celebrated with statues (cf. 11.497b–c, Arsinoe with rhyton; perhaps a false identification); 12.536e, cultural concerns, immortality and gout; 11.502b, celebrated together with Arsinoe II; 3.100e–f, 4.128b, 5.196a–203b, as a host. His officials: 8.334a, 14.621a, Patroclus; 4.183f, 14.634a, Pythagoras; 13.583a, Theodotus in charge of fodder; 11.493f, Sosibius (teased); 11.497d, Ctesibius. Arsinoe II Philadelphus: 15.689a, her interest in perfumes; 7.318c–d, 11.497d, the subject of poetry.

8. 6.251d, his respect for Greek culture exploited by his parasite Callicrates; 12.552c, his companion Panaretus receives 12 talents per annum.

9. 5.203e–206c, his ships; 6.246c, his fellow-drinkers; 8.354e, wax chickens on his table (Sphaerus); 6.251e, Philon, his

friend (parasite of Agathocles); 7.276b, concern for Dionysus; 7.276a–c, *Lagynophoria* festival (and wife's disapproval); 13.577a, overthrown by *hetaira* Agathocleia; 6.246c, 10.425e–f, 13.577f–578a, Ptolemaeus son of Agesarchus his historian.

10. 6.252e, Hierax of Antioch, flute-player for women in drag, an influential *kolax* of the king; *Memoirs*: 9.375d, given pig in Assus; 2.43d–e, spring near Corinth; 2.71b–c, fish and artichokes in Cyrene; 12.549e–f, his priesthood of Apollo and generosity as host in Cyrene; 6.229d, 12.518f–519a, on Masinissa of Libya; 10.438d–f, on revelry of Antiochus Epiphanes in Rome; 9.387e, 14.654b–d, the palace zoo and pheasants; 2.71b–c, a pupil of the *grammatikos* Aristarchus; 12.549d–e, visit of Roman embassy; 4.184b–c, on death of brother expels intellectuals and others from Alexandria, so spreading *paideia* to both Greeks and barbarians throughout the Mediterranean.

11. 4.147e–148b, she entertains Antony; 6.229c, precious table-ware renamed crockery; see below.

12. The Mendesian nome in the Delta was renowned for its fish (3.118f) and its perfume (15.688f).

13. *Pyramides* in Athenaeus are a type of cake, 14.642f, 647c; the source of the Nile gets a mention as the reason Psammetichus kept fish-eating slaves, 8.345e; the stone temple at Tindium is home to acacias, 15.679f, cf. those near Abydus, 15.680a.

14. Egypt characterized: 15.689a Alexandria's wealth; 2.39f, 5.203c, Egyptian wealth; 5.206d, squandered by Ptolemy Auletes; 1.27f, sails and papyrus; 10.451d–e, its flax; 2.67c, best vinegar; 2.66c, 3.124b, 12.553d–e, 14.642e, 15.688f–690a, perfume.

15. Wines: 1.33d–f, Mareotic (white and diuretic), Taeneotic (pale, oily and aromatic), Nile valley (various), Antylla (the best), Thebaid and Coptus (thin and easily digested; good for fever); 1.34c–e, boiled cabbage the best cure for a hangover. Beer: 10.418e, 447c–d.

16. 1.3b, 4.158d, 10.420e, 14.650b, 15.677f, 'beautiful'; 1.20b, 'golden'; 6.242a, 'city of Cecrops by the Nile' (Machon); 4.184b–c, 6.251d, centre of culture; 5.203e, the Museum and books; 6.242a, its garden; 6.240b, its Claudian wing; 12.536e, palace overlooking the sea shore; 14.654c, the palace zoo; 5.203e–206c, 208f, 209b, harbour and ships; 5.202d, Berenice shrine; 11.497d, Arsinoe Zephyritis temple; 3.110b, temple of Cronus; 13.576f, monument at Eleusis to Stratonice; 3.90c, Canopus (for cockles); 3.87f, Pharus (for mussels); 15.689a, Arsinoe, Berenice and the perfume industry; 3.94c, cooked meat shops; 3.118f, 121b, 7.326a, 8.356a, Alexandrian fish; 3.72b, 3.109b, 110b, 111b, 4.158d, 14.648b, food; 1.33d, edible grapes; 2.51b–d,

14.650b, fruit; 14.649e, trees; 6.242a, vegetation; 15.677d, 679e, wreaths; 9.390d, bustard catching; 4.174b, 175e, 176e–f, 183d, 184a–c, music; 1.20d, tragic dancing; 11.471c, 472a, 478b, 497d, cups and vessels; 8.364f, dinners by contribution. Alexandrian authors: Agatharchides (of Cnidus), Amarantus, Andron, Antiochus, Capito, Hegesianax, Pamphilus, Sotion, Tryphon. Poets writing in Alexandria: Posidippus, Hedylus, Callimachus, Machon, Theocles and many others.

17. 4.149d–150a, Hestia Prytanitis, Dionysus, Apollo Comaeus, and Apollo Pythius; 15.676a–c, Aphrodite.

18. 4.149f, cf. Herodotus 2.178; *UPZ* I 149.16, 37 (220–210BC)

19. Some further examples: 2.51b–c, sycamore fig ripens in three days, cf. Theophrastus, *Hist. pl.* 4.2.1, takes four days; 3.87f, flange-mussels from Pharus are larger but less easily digested; 4.149e, prytanic clothes still so called in Naucratis; 2.42b, Egyptian climate; 3.84d–f, asps (information second-hand); 3.110b, 111b, different breads of Alexandria (perhaps from written source); 4.158d, predominance of lentils in Alexandria; 3.118f, 121b, 7.326a, 8.356a, fish of Alexandria, sometimes with personal comment; 4.174b–184c, Alexandrian music (in part at least from Juba); 5.210c, Alexandrian terminology; 8.331b, an Alexandrian price; 9.388a, local mythology on the francolin; 10.450a, Egyptian ichneumon; 11.477f, drinking cups compared to Egyptian lotus.

20. See Heinen 1983, perhaps further connected with Dionysus (and so Alexander). A similar case of misunderstanding is recorded in Plutarch, *Life of Lucullus* 2.5–3.1.

## 6 Athenaeus the Librarian

1. The epitomized prologue stresses the theme of the μίμημα between the text and the dinner: 1.1b. On symposium as the frame of Athenaeus' text, see Lukinovich 1990, 264–9. See also Relihan 1993, 233 who stresses 'an odd and often ridiculous aping effect'.

2. Relihan 1993, 234. See also Lukinovich 1990, 267 commenting on the richness and variety (ποικιλία) as a shared feature of the banquet and of the guests' conversation. Quoting: 2.60d–e; 3.76a; 3.84c; 3.127b; 4.170e; 6.269e; 7.304b; 7.317a; 9.387d; 10.423f; 10.442e; 11.467d; 11.472e; 11.479c; 11.485 d–f; 11.501e; 12.525e; 14.629a; 15.676d; 15.679b; 15.692f. Exhibiting of dishes: 1.7d; 1.8f; 1.9a; 2.59f; 2.69c; 2.70f; 3.90b; 3.100d etc.

3. Similar questions in Anderson 1997, 2183: 'We are in a world of grammarians' fancy and flamboyance.'

4. Useful comparisons can be made with authors such as

Clement of Alexandria or Plutarch: see Van Den Hoek 1996; Helmbold and O'Neil 1959. An excellent discussion of the question of sources in Diogenes Laertius' and Aulus Gellius' compilations is to be found in Goulet 1997, who draws a distinction between sources and authorities.

5. The key question is whether Athenaeus' use of authors such as Didymos, Tryphon, Pamphilos of Alexandria is restricted to their explicit quotations or goes far beyond them.

6. See Jeanneret 1987, 68–70, who comments on J. Stuckius, J.C. Bulengerus, P. Ciacconius, E. Puteanus.

7. 1.3a–b. Larensis' identity was much discussed. The identification with Herodes Atticus (F. Rudolph) is today dismissed. There is a funerary inscription with the name *P. Livius Larensis pontif. minor* (CIL VI 2126): see Chapter 1.

8. Such a history of libraries in Greece relies on confused foundations. Other versions are found in Aulus Gellius, *Noctes Atticae*, 7.17.1–2; Isidore, *Etymologies* 6.3.3–5; Tertullian, *Apologeticus* 18.5. On this tradition, see Canfora 1986, 139–44, with Chapter 7. The mention of the foundation of a 'public library' (Aulus Gellius) by Peisistratos is anachronistic. Peisistratos is believed to have fixed the Homeric epic in a written form (see Cicero, *De orat.* 3.34; Pausanias, 7.26.6; Aelian, *Varia Historia*, 13.14) and these were probably the only 'books' available at his time. In the historiographical tradition, there is an assimilation between the foundation of the Alexandrian library (and the Pentateuch translation, as developed in the *Letter of Aristeas* and its tradition) and the constitution of the Homeric text that would be linked to the founding of the Athenian library: see Canfora 1996, 28–31, 109. We know nothing about Polycrates' library. Literary sponsorship was a policy shared by a number of tyrants. Eucleides is probably the Athenian archon who officially introduced the Ionian alphabet in Athens (403 or 402 BC). From Aristotle onwards, however, this outline of the history of libraries is more firmly grounded. Athenaeus' account of the transmission of Aristotle's books in 1.3b could be compatible with his mention of Apellicon's library in 5.214d–215a and Strabo's version (*Geography*, 13.1.54), followed by Plutarch, *Sulla*, 26.3, if one considers that Neleus sold to the Ptolemies books previously owned by Aristotle and Theophrastus, not their original treatises: see Canfora 1986, 38–9, and 1999. See also recent discussions in *DphA*, I, s.v. Aristote de Stagire, pp. 434–5 (Goulet); Lindsay 1997. The emphasis on Ptolemy Philadelphus as a founder of the Alexandrian library is a common-place of the tradition. The role played by Demetrius of Phalerum, however, clearly shows that this foundation took place under the reign of Ptolemy Lagus: see Fraser 1972, 1. 314–15, 321; 2a, 475, nn. 112–13); Canfora 1986, 25–8 and 113–14.

9. We do not find either any alllusion to the great private libraries in Italy. In his account of the acquisition of Aristotle's library by Apellicon of Teos, Athenaeus does not mention it was taken to Rome by Sulla as a part of his booty (5.214d–215a). Lucullus is mentioned in the *Deipnosophistae* (2.50f–51b) because he brought to Italy the first cherry tree, not because he brought to Rome a large collection of Greek books (see Plutarch, *Lucullus*, 42). On the development of libraries in Rome, see Langie 1908; Wendel 1955; Marshall 1976; Fehrle 1986; Fedeli 1988; Blanck 1992, 152–78; Pesando 1994.

10. See Cicero, *Ad Atticum*, 1.7; I.10.4; 1.20.7; 2.6.1; 4.4.4a.1; 4.5.4; 4.8.2; *Tuscul.* 2,9; 3, 7; *Ad Fam.* 16,20.

11. Petronius, *Satirica*, 48.4.

12. Pliny the Younger, *Epist.* 1.8 ; 2.17.

13. Seneca, *dial.*, 9.9.4.

14. Vitruvius, *De Architectura*, 6.7.

15. SHA, *Gord.* 18.2. See RE, I A2, 2129–31. According to the *Suda*, s.v. Ἐπαφρόδιτος, Epaphroditus, Nero's powerful freedman, had 30,000 books in his private library. He was the master of Epictetus. See also Isidore, *Etymologiae*, 6.6: Pamphilius the martyr had nearly 30,000 volumes in his personal library (third century AD).

16. *Prolegomena de comoedia*, p. 32 (Koster).

17. See Martial, *Epigrammata*, 7.17 ; 9 *proem.* (on Iulius Martialis and Stertinius Avitus); Pliny the Younger, *Epistulae*, 4.28.1 (on Herennius Severus). See Wendel 1955, 117.

18. In the Villa dei Papiri the Greek library was separated from the Latin texts. On separate collections in private libraries, see Cicero, *ad Quintum fratrem*, 3, 4, 5; Petronius, *Satiricon*, 48.4; Sidonius Apollinaris, *Epistulae*, 4.11.6, on Claudianus Mamertus' *Romana*, *Attica* and *Christiana* library. The separation of Greek and Latin collections in Roman public libraries appears with Julius Caesar's and Varro's project (Suetonius, *Caesar*, 44) and its achievement by Asinius Pollio (Isidore, *Etymologiae*, 6.5.2). See Fedeli 1988, 41; Settis 1988, 61 ; Blanck 1992, 157, 162, 164, 166.

19. 1.3a. One should not exclude the possibility that this specialization results from Athenaeus' literary project and interest: no allusion is made to the Latin part of the library because the Deipnosophists were not interested in it.

20. 1.2d–3a. See Aulus Gellius, *Noctes Atticae*, 11.17.1–2: the

author and his friends incidentally found old praetors' edicts in the library of the Temple of Trajan. Cf. Settis 1988, 63, who comments on the testimonies of the *Historia Augusta*.

21. 4.160c: Varro and Roman grammarians; 4.168e: P. Rutilius Rufus' *History of Rome* (but he wrote in Greek); 6.273b: Cotta's treatise on the *Roman Constitution*; see Zecchini 1989a, 236–9, who stresses the lack of interest of Athenaeus in Latin literature and his use of Greek sources to comment on Roman matters. See also Anderson 1997, 2180 on the treatment of Roman matters: 'Rome remains characteristically at the margin of a sophists's world', and, for a different view, see Chapter 1.

22. Plutarch, *Lucullus*, 42. See also Cicero, *De finibus*, 3.7–8.

23. Strabo, *Geography*, 17.1.8.

24. Callmer 1944, 151.

25. Seneca, *De Tranquillitate Animi*, 9.5.

26. Desrousseaux, however, wrote (1956, xiii): 'Que [Larensis] soit le protecteur de notre Graeculus, cela semble évident. Il devait non seulement faire de lui son bibliothécaire, mais encore enrichir ses propres collections de livres (manuscrits, s'entend), grâce aux recherches et trouvailles du fureteur à la piste d'auteurs moins copiés que les plus lus ou célèbres … . Qui payait? Le patron, sans doute, pour sa bibliothèque.' See also Hemmerdinger 1989, 113: 'Etant le bibliothécaire et le complaisant de Larensis, Athénée est daté par là. Il florissait en 180–192.'

27. See *P Oxy.* 1241, col. II; Tzetzes, *De comoedia*, p. 43 (Koster).

28. In this respect, the sources for the Alexandrian library are far more scarce and elliptical than the sources on the history of imperial Chinese or medieval Arabic libraries: the latter help us to imagine the various specialities involved in the daily management of a State collection of manuscript books. For a general discussion of the materials, see Drège 1991 and Eche 1967. One should also stress that nothing is said about the material organization and staff of Larensis' library—probably slaves and freedmen.

29. For a good synthesizing discussion, see Fedeli 1988, 34–8.

30. For an in-depth discussion of the tradition on the destruction of the library by Caesar, see Canfora 1986, 79–84, 116–17, 145–58, who concludes that the fire destroyed a storehouse in the harbour, with blank papyrus book-rolls probably intended for export. In describing the museum of Alexandria, Strabo does not allude to the library nor to its destruction. This silence can be explained if the library was not a building but the collection of books belonging to the Mouseion itself, and if this collection still existed during his visit in Egypt (between 27 and 20 BC). See Canfora 1986: 145–58. Strabo's *Geography* relies extensively on Alexandrian science and literary scholarship.

31. Ammianus Marcellinus, 22, 16, 15.

32. Strabo, *Geography* 13.1.54. Strabo refers to Roman book-sellers as well.

33. 1.1d.

34. A perfect example is found in 13.610d: Cynulcus says that, according to Phylarchus, there are neither courtesans nor pipe-players in the cities of the Ceians. 'Where did Phylarchus say such a thing? I read his whole *History*', says Myrtilus. 'In book twenty three' answered Cynulcus.

35. See 14.648c: 'Whence, most learned grammarians, and from what collection of books, have popped up these very solemn writers Chrysippus and Harpocration …' (πόθεν ὑμῖν, ὦ πολυμαθέστατοι γραμματικοί, καὶ ἐκ ποίας βιβλιοθήκης ἀνεφάνησαν οἱ σεμνότατοι οὗτοι συγγραφεῖς Χρύσιππος καὶ Ἁρποκρατίων...).

36. The quoting of books introduces the quoting or the paraphrasing of texts. Athenaeus' 'high standards of care and accuracy … in the transcription of citations' are a trademark stressed by Arnott 1996, 53; cf. 34–5, after Zepernick 1921 and Collard 1969.

37. Goulet 1997, 151 reaches the same conclusion about the link between quotation and direct use of the source in Diogenes Laertius.

38. See a suggestive discussion in Delattre 1997, 122–5 on the purpose of precise bibliographical quotations in Philodemus' treatises.

39. Among many examples, see 9.375d–f: three citations of Aeschylus (without the title of the plays) quoted from Chameleon's treatise *On Aeschylus*.

40. For a general survey of the material presentation of ancient book-rolls, see Birt 1882; Turner 1987; and a synthesizing discussion in Blanck 1992, 75–86.

41. 7.329d.

42. See however Delattre 1997, 113, who stresses the fact that we have no actual example of a papyrus book-roll from Egypt or Herculaneum with a title at its beginning: most often, the beginning of the roll was not preserved.

43. On titles in ancient books, see Nachmanson 1941; Oliver 1951; Delattre 1997; Irigoin 1997.

44. Dorandi 1984. Delattre 1997, 113 rightly stresses that these labels allowed the identification of the content of the book on a shelf or within a box.

45. Seneca, *De Tranquillitate Animi*, 9.4 and 6. See also Lucian, *Ind.*, 18.

46. Ohly 1928; Birt 1882, 162–77.
47. See Delattre 1997, 112.
48. See the discussion in Birt 1882 175–6. Diogenes Laertius (7.33) refers to a passage in Zeno's *Republic* and (7.187) to a passage in the Περὶ τῶν ἀρχαίων φυσιολόγων by Chrysippus. See also 7.188 on Chrysippus' *On Justice*. It is noteworthy that these references occur in a critical discussion of the conceptions of these Stoic philosophers. Athenodorus the Stoic, who was in charge of the Pergamene library, is said to have expunged from these works unorthodox passages (Diogenes Laertius, 7.34). Zeno's and Chrysippus' stichometric locations should probably be considered more as markers in an editorial process than as a normal way to quote precise *loci* in a text.
49. See 12.546b: two quotations of Euripides and Sophocles (fr. 486 Nauck² and *TrGF*, 4, 133) are attributed to the same (unnamed) poet (καί πού τις καὶ ποιητὴς ἐφθέγξατο).
50. 8.334a; see also 3.99b.
51. Respectively fourteen occurrences and nine occurrences.
52. Arnott 1996, 37: 'The practice of its compiler was to omit some citations haphazardly and all titles of cited works (hence the number of *incertarum fabularum fragmenta* for Alexis and other dramatists), and to cut out or paraphrase sections of frs.'
53. Delattre 1997, 118, in his discussion of the quotation of titles in Philodemus' papyri, observes that ἐν τοῖς περί refers to works composed of at least two books, while ἐν τῷ περί refers to books composed of one book only. Athenaeus does not use these expressions in a consistent way: see for example 3.88a (Ἀριστοτέλης δ' ἐν τῷ περὶ ζῴων) and 7.286b (Ἀριστοτέλης ἐν τοῖς περὶ ζῴων).
54. See Zecchini 1989a, 117–20.
55. See Zecchini's cautious position (1989a, 106 and 114).
56. See 15.692c: 'As I read book twenty eight of Posidonius' *Histories* ... .'
57. van Groningen 1964.
58. See the relevant comments made by Arnott 1996, 228–9 n.1, on the different grammatical constructions introducing the citation of titles.
59. 9.402a.
60. 6.236e.
61. 7.278a–b.
62. 11.496e–f.
63. 8.365b.
64. 15.699a.
65. 4.164b–d. See Arnott 1996, 408.
66. It should be stressed, however, that the various titles of a given text could also be recorded in the *subscriptio* of a papyrus book-roll. See Delattre 1997, 106 n. 4 on a treatise by Polystratos in Philodemus' library at Herculaneum (*Pherc* 1150).
67. 8.336d. On this fragment and its spurious authenticity, see Arnott 1996, 819–22.
68. While Athenaeus attributes extensive reading to Democritus, this is a likely description also of his own method of work.
69. Fr. 439 (Pfeiffer); fr. 402 (Slater).
70. See also Dionysius of Halicarnassus, *De Dinarcho*, 1 (Fr. 447 Pfeiffer). Athenaeus does not rely explicitly on Roman adaptation of Alexandrian and Pergamene librarian scholarship. Marcus Terentius Varro (116–27 BC) was certainly a key actor in this process. He was asked by Caesar to prepare the foundations for a large public library in Rome (Suetonius, *Caesar*, 44.2) and wrote a treatise in three books *De bibliothecis*. Caesar's assassination put an end to his dream, but in 39 BC the first public library was founded in Rome, after Asinius Pollio's Dalmatian campaigns. Varro was probably consulted and read by Pollio and, although still alive, his was one of the many busts of Greek and Latin authors who decorated the library: Pliny the Elder, *Naturalis Historia*, 7.115. See Blum 1991, 187, following Schmidt, on the Callimachean influence in a bibliography in *Res Rusticae*, I.1.8sq. We find only one quotation of Varro in Athenaeus: 4.160c. One should also remember that Athenodorus of Tarsus, a Stoic philosopher and a librarian at Pergamon, was taken to Rome by Cato the Younger: Plutarch, *Cato minor*, 10.1–3, 763e–f.
71. Anderson 1997, 2176 stresses the prominent presence of Alexandrian literature and of Callimachus in Athenaeus, compared to other sophistic writers. On the *Pinakes*: see Schmidt 1922; Blum 1991. On Callimachus' method as a bibliographer, see Dover 1968b, 23–5 .
72. 6.244a (fr. 434 Pfeiffer); 14.643e (fr. 435 Pfeiffer).
73. 15.669 d–e (fr. 430 Pfeiffer).
74. 13.585b (fr. 433 Pfeiffer): Athenaeus quotes the third roll of the Laws section.
75. 6.252c (fr. 438 Pfeiffer; *FGrH* 170 T 1).
76. 11.496e–f (fr . 440 Pfeiffer). See *IG* II² 2363, 34–6: a Peiraeus inscription.
77. 9.408f; 410b–c.
78. 8.336d.
79. 12.515d–e and 15.694a. See *FHG*, IV 342; *FGrH* 32 T 6 and Kommentar, p. 510; *RE* II.2, 1446–7 (Wentzel); R. Goulet, s.v. Artémon, in *DphA*, I, 434, pp. 615–16.
80. 15.694a.
81. On Herennius Philo, Περὶ κτήσεως καὶ ἐκλογῆς βιβλίων βιβλία ιβ', see *RE* 15, 653–4 (Gudeman); on Telephus of

Pergamon, Βιβλιακῆς ἐμπειρίας βιβλία γ΄, ἐν οἷς διδάσκει τὰ κτήσεως ἄξια βιβλία, see *RE* 19. 369–71 (Wendel).

82. 1.5a–b. See 6.244a (fr. 434 Pfeiffer). In 12.516f, a list of writers of *Opsartutika*. See also 13.567c–d: a list of comedies whose titles are names of *hetaerae*.

83. 1.5a–b (trans. Gulick).

84. Respectively 3.82d; 15.684f; and 7.283c

85. 6.249a–b. Other occurrences of the number of books: 2.60d–e (Cephisodorus, *Animadversions in Aristotle*, four books); 6.229e (Heliodorus of Athens, *On the Acropolis*, fifteen books); 7.312e (Sostratos, *On animals*, two books); 13.597a (Hermesianax of Colophon, three books of Elegiacs); 15.673e (Adrastus, five books *On Questions of History and Style in the Morals of Theophrastus*; a sixth book *On the Nicomachean Ethics of Aristotle*).

86. Blum 1991, 185.

87. See Goulet 1997, 165, who suggests that bibliographical details such as stichometrical figures and the total number of books could help in identifying lists of various origins used by Diogenes Laertius.

88. 15.698b (transl. Gulick), on Euboios of Paros. See also 4.128a.

89. 4.139c–d.

90. We could also mention the 6,000 books of Origen read by Hieronymus: see Isidore, *Etymologiae*, 6.7.

91. 6.242f–244a. Another quotation of an incipit and of line numbers from Callimachus' *Pinakes* is found at 13.585b: *Rule for dining in company* by Gnathaena.

92. 1.4d–e.

93. 5.209f. See also 13.611e: a long quotation of the beginning of Lysias' *Against Aeschines the Socratic*. Athenaeus is a valuable witness to the uncertainties related to the corpus of Lysias' speeches. According to the *Lives of the Ten Orators* (Ps.-Plutarch), 836a, 425 speeches were attributed to Lysias, but Dionysius and Caecilius considered only 230 were genuine. See Dionysius of Halicarnassus, *The ancient Orators*, 2.17.7 (200 forensic speeches). Dionysius wrote lost critical treatises where he checked the authenticity of Lysias' corpus, as well as of other orators, such as Demosthenes. We can suppose it was a critical revision of Callimachus' *Pinakes*. See Dover 1968b, 15–22.

94. 11.479d (*FHG* IV 419).

95. 15.681c. There is another ἀρχή (two words) of a dramatic text: the *Semele* of Carcinus, 13.559f.

96. Respectively: 13.573f–574a; 14.658c; 3.85e–f (the source is Callias of Mitylene who also quoted the end of an Alcaeus poem and wrote a commentary on Sappho and Alcaeus, according to Strabo. On his relationship to Aristophanes of Byzantium's edition of Alcaeus, see Gudeman, *RE* X. 2, coll. 1629–30). See also 1.6a–b: first line of a wedding song by Philoxenos, quoted by Clearchus (*FHG* II.309); 10.455c–d: opening verse of a *Hymn to Demeter* by Lasos, quoted by Heraclides Ponticus; 14.636c–d: four opening verses of a song to Artemis quoted by Dicaearchus.

97. See Blum 1991, 8, who refers to Diogenes Laertius' lists of homonymous writers or other famous persons at the end of some of his *Lives of philosophers*: see for example Theodorus (2.103–4); Demetrius (5.83–5); Heraclides (5.93–4); Diogenes (6.81); Heraclitus (9.17); Democritus (9.49) etc.

98. My interest in this author arises from Blum 1991, 193. We find many references to Demetrius in Diogenes Laertius: see 1.38, 79, 112, 114; 2.52, 56, 57; 5.3, 75, 89; 6.79, 84, 88; 7. 31, 169, 185; 8. 85; 9. 15, 27, 35–6, 40; 10.13. It should be stressed that Diogenes Laertius does not include Demetrius of Magnesia in his list of the writers named 'Demetrius' (5.83–5). Demetrius of Magnesia also wrote a treatise *On homonymous cities*. See *RE* IV/2, 2814–17 (Schwartz); *FHG* IV.382.

99. Cicero, *ad Atticum*, 4.11.1–2; 8.11.7; 8.12.6; 9.9.2.

100. Dionysius of Halicarnassus, *De Dinarcho*, 1.

101. 13.611b.

102. 6.234c–d.

103. See 14.648c: Ulpian makes the precise point that Chrysippus and Harpocration are homonymous with famous writers and asks his fellows in what library they found these authors.

104. ὁ ἀπὸ τῆς στοᾶς: 4.151e; 6.263c; 8.333b; 9.369c; 14.649d; ὁ ἀπὸ τῆς στοᾶς φιλόσοφος: 4.176b; ὁ στωικός: 6.266e; 12.549d.

105. 6.272e; 9.401a; 11.494f.

106. 5.211d; 6.246c; 6.252e; 10.439e.

107. 6.252e.

108. 6.233d

109. 6.272e.

110. 1.13b.

111. 10.453c. See also 4.128a (Hippolochos of Macedonia was a contemporary of Lynceus and Duris) and 2.51a; 2.71a–b; 4.183e; 5.218b–c; 11.470f; 15.698a.

112. 13.599c. See also 12.515d–e: a criticism of Artemon of Cassandreia about the date of Dionysius Scytobrachion.

113. 9.407d.

114. 7.293a. See 14.620e–f, where Athenaeus quotes the treatise of Carystius of Pergamon on Sotades as well as the treatise written on Sotades by his son Apollonius.

115. Although not exclusively. We find also quotations from the peripatetic tradition: Theophrastus, *On Comedy*, 6.261d–e; Chamaeleon of Heraclea, *On Old Comedy*, 9.374a and 406e–407c: Chamaeleon registered various identifying data, such as nickname, ethnic name, main literary field, quotations (see *RE* III. 2, coll. 2103–4). In 9.374a, Chamaeleon is quoted as a source on the comic writer Anaxandrides who used to crush his papyrus roll in order to make incense from it when his play did not win at the festival. Athenaeus wonders how the *Tereus* and other plays were preserved.

116. Lycophron: 4.140a; 7.278a–b; 11.485d; 11.501d–e; 13.555a; Eratosthenes: 2.41d; 4.140a; 11.499e; 11.501d; Antiochus of Alexandria: 11.482c.

117. 3.126e; 6.267e; 15.693b; 15.698c; 15.699a.

118. 7.293a; 7.329d; 9.387a; 10.422f; 13.587d.

119. 9.402b.

120. 1.5b. See also 15.699a: Hegemon wrote a comedy in the old style.

121. 8.336d.

122. 3.110b; 6.247c; 8.358d; 10.429e; 11.496f. See also 9.373f–374e: Athenaeus (or his source) refers to a πίναξ of dramatic representations, when he stresses that Anaxandrides' comedies were preserved although they did not win the prize.

123. See for example a comedy by Alexis, *Demetrius or Philetaerus*, quoted either with the double title (6.241b) or with *Demetrius* alone : 3.108a, 7.314d, 8.338d, 14.663c, this last quotation suggesting that *Demetrius* could be the title of a second production, perhaps the text read by Athenaeus: see Arnott 1996, 155–6.

124. 13.573b and 586e. Athenaeus mentions that the speech was delivered by Apollodorus, a friend of Demosthenes. He was perhaps the actual author of this text. See Dionysius of Halicarnassus, *De Demosthene*, 57.

125. 6.231b. On the history of the *Corpus Lysiacum*, see Dover 1968b. On the role of booksellers during the fourth century BC, see Dover 1968b, 25–6.

126. 13.586e and 592e.

127. 13.586e–f and 592c.

128. 13.566f.

129. See Dover 1968b, 14–22.

130. 6.272f; 11.466a.

131. See Dover 1968b, 25–6, 152–3; Canfora 1994, 440–4.

132. 4.144e. Diogenes Laertius quotes this treatise in his bibliography of Theophrastus: 5.47 and 49; *P Oxy.* vol. 13, p. 133 (Grenfell and Hunt): 1611, fr. 1, col. 2.38–3.54. See Theophrastus, frr. 600–9 (Fortenbaugh et al.).

133. Fr. 384 and 384a (Pfeiffer).

134. Fraser 1972, 2b, 1004–5, n. 1, concludes that Callimachus' mention in Athenaeus would be a later addition by a scribe or a commentator.

135. Pfeiffer, n. 1 ad fr. 384, p. 311.

136. 2.57c: half of the treatise is a fake, or, according to some, the whole of it. 2.45e–f: various titles of *On Diet* according to Athenaeus' sources: *On Barley Gruel, Refutation of Cnidian Principles*. Galen of Pergamon would have been a perfect *porte-parole* for such philological indications since, in his *Commentary on the treatise on Diet*, he refers to the debate about the various titles of this text (Helmreich, 133. 23 sq). See also *On Dogmas of Hippocrates and Plato*, 9. 6 (Kühn, 5. 762 = Lacy 572 f.). According to Galen, the correct title was *On Diet* (περὶ διαίτης ὀξέων). The variant περὶ πτισάνης is first attested by Erotian (first century AD). See Jouanna 1997, 63–4, 73, who does not quote Athenaeus among the witnesses of the bibliographical tradition of this treatise.

137. 7.283a. See also 10.455c: about a song by Lasus of Hermione.

138. 6.264a (*FHG*, IV, 477).

139. 14.653f (*FHG*, IV, 287).

140. 14.652a (*FGrH* 4 F 56).

141. 2.70a. See *FGrH* 1 T 15 (*Kommentar*, p. 318).

142. 9.410d–e.

143. 10.447c–d.

144. Strabo, *Geography*, 1.1.11.

145. Galen, *In Hippocratis librum III epidemiarum commentarii*, III (Kühn, 17, p. 606).

146. 8.334b–c; 15.682d–e. The attribution of the *Cypria* was controversial at least from the time of Herodotus (*Histories*, 2.117).

147. 7.277c.

148. 8.364c.

149. 3.116a–d.

150. 6.273c.

151. See Düring 1950, 40–57 on Athenaeus as a witness to the transmission of Aristotle's zoological writings.

152. Such 'cross-references' perhaps could explain some inconsistencies of Athenaeus when citing titles. See the examples of abbrevations provided by Arnott (1996: 198, n. 1): the title in full appears first, the abbreviated title comes later.

153. *Noctes Atticae*, 5.41.

154. *Noctes Atticae*, 13.31; 18.4.

155. *Noctes Atticae*, 19.5. See also 9.14.3 (Tibur's library).

156. *Noctes Atticae*, 11.17.1–4.

157. *Noctes Atticae*, 13.20.

158. *Noctes Atticae*, 16.82. See *DphA*, I, 509, s.v. Aulu Gelle, p. 685 (Goulet).
159. *Noctes Atticae*, 18.9.5–6.
160. See also the funny description of an ignorant book-collector in search of rare books and autograph editions, in Lucian, *Ind.*, especially 1–2, 4.
161. Vitruvius, *De Architectura*, 6.5.1.
162. Diodorus of Sicily, *Library of History*, 1.3.4–8. The authenticity of Diodorus' title is testified by Pliny the Elder, *Naturalis Historia, Praefatio*, 25.
163. 1.3a; 5.203e. See also the title of Artemon's treatise, 12.515e.
164. 2.71e; 11.509e. Other books quoted as a συναγωγή in the *Deipnosophistae*: 7.321f (Mnaseas, author of a collection of παίγνια); 7.329d (Dorotheos of Ascalon, author of a collection of λέξεις); 9.390b (Menecles); 13.609a (Hippias the Sophist).
165. 5.192b. See also 8.365b–c: some dinners were called συναγώγιμα by Alexis and by Ephippos. Athenaeus adds: ἔλεγον δὲ συνάγειν καὶ τὸ μετ' ἀλλήλων πίνειν καὶ συναγώγιον τὸ συμπόσιον.
166. See Bolter 1991, 88: 'A library amasses books; an encyclopædia condenses them. Both seek to organize and control books in order to make them available to the reader.' See also p. 99: 'What the reader does metaphorically in the encyclopædia, he or she can do literally in the library—move into and through a textual space.'
167. 4.128a–c (transl. Gulick). Athenaeus is speaking to Timocrates.
168. 4.134d. See *RE* XIV.2, 2298–300 (Diehl).
169. 5.206d–209e.
170. 5.196a–203b, 203e–206c;
171. But see 7.314c: unable to recall a long quotation of Clearchus, the speaker leads the listeners back to the written treatise: ὑμᾶς δὲ ἐπὶ τὸ σύγγραμμα ἀναπέμπω.
172. 7.126a.
173. 13.556b (transl. Gulick).
174. 8.331b–c. See also 6.270d.
175. 7.277b–c. See also 1.4b: ὥσπερ συμβολὰς κομίζοντας τὰ ἀπὸ τῶν στρωματοδέσμων γράμματα. This suggests that Larensis' guests brought material books as well as their stock of citations.
176. 5.186c (rules of a symposium); 7.321f (the collection of παίγνια by Mnaseas); 13.585b (collection of sympotic laws).
177. Bolter 1991, 9.
178. Aristotle's zoological quotations in the *Deipnosophistae* are drawn mainly from Pamphilus and Alexander of Myndus, who were themselves middlemen transmitting Hellenistic materials. See Düring 1950, 41: 'as to Athenaeus I am sure that he never himself unrolled an original work of Aristotle.'
179. For a stimulating discussion of this concept, see Bolter 1991.
180. Bolter 1991, 5, on the electronic book.
181. That is to make their own collection of extracts and to reorganize it according to their own criteria and, eventually, to produce an *Epitome*. In such a way of transmitting knowledge, any new step in the compiling process is narrowing and deconstructing the literary and semantic field and makes more difficult, and sometimes impossible, any return towards the original works. This compiling process is condensing a whole library within the extent of a book.
182. The best description of an ancient compiler's method is found in Pliny the Younger, *Letters*, 3.5. For a broader picture of the ancient technique of excerpting, see Skydsgaard 1968 on Varro; Mejer 1978, 16–29 and Goulet 1997 on Diogenes Laertius. See also Small 1997, 188–9.
183. One could imagine that Athenaeus started to organize his reading notes and collection of extracts in categories such as 'wine', 'cups', 'fishes', 'courtesans', 'water', 'parasites' etc.
184. See for example Arnott 1996, 664, who, following Meineke (1.519ff), comments on the confusion in Athenaeus 13.562d–e: two quotations of Alexis have been separated by the later addition of a reference to Theophrastus who himself paraphrased Chaeremon and quoted Euripides.
185. 14.654a (transl. Gulick).
186. 3.83a–c.
187. 8.336d.
188. 4.128c. See also Lucian, *Ind.*, 2 : the emphasis is put on the speed of reading, on the visual process itself.
189. 1.13c; 3.113a; 5.206d; 5.216f; 14.650b; 15.672a; 15.675f; περιέτυχον: 4.128b; 7.329d; 8.336d, with the additional mention: ἐγὼ γὰρ οὐκ ἀπήντησα τῷ δράματι. See Arnott 1996, 406, n. 1. Chantraine 1950, 122–5 offers a full discussion of the meaning of this verb in the Hellenistic and imperial periods. In 15.668f, ἐπιλέγων refers to quoting from memory rather than to reading an actual book, as one can deduce from Cynulcus' words in 669b.
190. 5.206d; 6.263a–b; 9.402a; 15.675f.
191. See for example 15.692c (pinpointed by Anderson 1997, 2178): 'As I was reading the twenty-eighth book of Posidonius' *Histories*, I noticed a very nice remark about perfumes, which is not alien to our symposium.'

192. 15.671c (transl. Gulick). See also 3.97d; 6.228c; 8.347d; 9.385d.

193. 15.678f (transl. Gulick).

194. 8.336d.

195. See also 1.4c: Calliphanes 'had copied out the beginnings of numerous poems and speeches, and could repeat as many as three or four lines, thus seeking to win repute for wide learning' (transl. Gulick).

196. 14.663c: ἔχει δ᾽ <οὕτως> ἡ σύμπασα ἐκλογὴ οὖσα ἐκ τοῦ διεσκευασμένου δράματος ὃ ἐπιγράφεται Δημήτριος.

197. Aulus Gellius, *Noctes Atticae*, 14.6. See also Pliny the Younger, *Epist.*, 3.5.17: Pliny the Elder could have sold his *commentaria* for the price of 400,000 sesterces. See the relevant comments of Goulet 1997, 153 on Aulus Gellius and Pamphile's *Hypomnemata*.

198. See Blair 1992; Moss 1996.

199. 3.95a and 3.107a–b (transl. Gulick): it should be noticed that the two *loci* (within the same book-roll and not too distant) are 'cross-referenced' by Athenaeus: he reproduces the quotation in the second of them only. In 11.496a Athenaeus alludes to the previous quotation of an Alexis text (actually in 3.125f, but ancient readers did not get this precise location!). See also 9.402a–b (to 4.128a); 10.453c–e (to 7.276a); 14.615a (to 6.261c). Similar anaphorical references, but in close context: 1.4c (to 4a); 3.95d; 3.107a (to 95a); 4.183f (to 182e); 6.241e (to 239f); 6.244a (to 242d); 6.247e (to 246f); 7.300d (to 282d); 7.315c (to 315b); 7.319c (to 319b); 9.373d (to 373c); 9.397e (to 397c); 10.436e (to 427b);11.496b (to 784b); 11.496d (to 475f); 11.497c (to 467d); 11.497f (to 783e); 11.500f (to 497b); 11.505f (to 505d); 13.586e (to 567c); 13.591d (to 567e); 14.646f (to 642f); 15.684e (to 681b); 15.691d (to 691c). Cataphorical references: 3.95a–107b.

200. On the historical circumstances of the development of 'research tools' helping to 'use' and not only to ' read ' manuscript books, see Rouse and Rouse 1991.

201. See Irigoin 1997, 130–1.

202. See Small 1997, 17–18; Irigoin 1997, 130 raises the question whether Pliny's text subdivisions were already numbered.

203. Aulus Gellius, *Noctes Atticae, praef.* 25. See Small 1997, 19, who compares these *lemmata* with 'abstracts of papers'.

204. 6.263a–b. See also 8.362d, where the retrieval process is stressed; in 10.459b and 15.665a, the verb applies to Athenaeus himself, trying to recall the conversations of the Deipnosophists for Timocrates.

205. 3.74c–d. See also 3.97d.

206. Eunapius, *Vitae sophist.*, 4.1.3.

207. On the importance of mnemotechnics in ancient literary culture, see Small 1997 who collects most of the ancient and secondary sources and discusses them in the light of modern cognitive studies.

208. 2.58c (transl. Gulick). See also 8.332b–c; 8.334b–c; see 13.555a–b: Athenaeus invokes the Muse at the beginning of his catalogue of love stories.

209. 3.115a.

210. 3.107a–b: ἐπεὶ τὰ νῦν διὰ μνήμης οὐ κρατεῖς, αὐτὸς ἐγὼ διεξελεύσομαι. See also 7.314c ; 8.359d–e ; 9.402a: Democritus is able to remember the author, but not the citation, 'for it is a long time since I have happened to read the dithyrambs of Cleomenes of Rhegium'. He leaves it up to Ulpian. See Lukinovich 1990, 271 and n. 48: '[the Deipnosophists] submit to the evidence that books are superior to their own memories as a means of storing words and information: they arrive at, or are brought to, the conclusion that their memory is faulty, and hence that the oral tradition has its limits.'

211. 5.203e.

212. 3.83a. See also 2.52b; 3.85c; 3.116d; 4.160d; 4.164d; 9.398e; 10.442a–b; 15.677b; see also 6.242b: ... ὁ μὲν Εὐκλείδης ἀποφθεγγόμενος οὐκ ἀνάξια βιβλίου καὶ μνήμης ...

213. 9.371e: τοῦτο δὲ τὸ ὄνομα μνήμης εὑρίσκω τετυχηκὸς παρὰ μὲν Εὐβούλῳ ...; 9.384b: ποῦ μνήμης ἠξίωται παρὰ τοῖς ἀρχαίοις ...; 9.398c; 14.615e: καὶ ἐζητεῖτο εἰ μνήμη τις καὶ περὶ τούτων ἐγένετο παρὰ τοῖς παλαιοτέροις.

214. 9.368f.

215. On school exercises, see for example Plato, *Protagoras*, 325a. Xenophon, *Symposium*, 3.6: Niceratus was able to recite the *Iliad* and *Odyssey* from memory. See also the various Hellenistic inscriptions about contests of recitation collected by Hadot 1984, 27–8 nn. 7–8.

216. See Yates 1966. On antiquity, see Blum 1969.

217. *Rhetorica ad Herennium*, 3.19.32.

218. See the full treatment of this tradition in Carruthers 1990.

219. Pliny the Elder, *Naturalis Historia*, 7.24. See also Vitruvius, *De Architectura*, 7. *praef.* 4.

220. Seneca, *Ad Lucilium*, 3.27.5.

221. 9.381f–382a.

222. See also Seneca the Elder, *Controversiae*, 1, *praef.* 2; Augustine, *De natura et origine animae*, 4.7.9.

223. Carruthers 1990, 19.

224. 10.458a–f.

225. See Lukinovich 1990, 267.

226. See 15.665b: the *taxis* of the dinner-courses was a frequent topic of the discussion.

227. Such as Charmus the Syracusan, according to Clearchus: 1.4a–c.
228. It should be stressed however that, in its actual form, Athenaeus' text does not include an initial table of contents or *capita rerum* at the beginning of each volume that could help the reader in consulting this huge library of quotations. See 1.1a–b for an announcement of the content in the epitomized Book one.

## 7 *The Walking Library: The Performance of Cultural Memories*

1. Bradbury 1950, 135.
2. See Too 1995, 119ff.
3. See Nagy 1989, 7.
4. E.g. Hermeias expresses his doubts about the authorship of the *Eroticus* at 12.26, ὁ Λυσίας, ἤτοι ὁ λόγος αὐτοῦ, but insists that it comes from the pen of Lysias at 35.19ff; cf. D.L. 3.25; Helmbold and Holther (1952, 14.9, 412f.) think the speech is by neither Lysias nor Plato; Richards thinks the idea belongs to Lysias, but that the words are supplied by Plato (Richards 1900).
5. *Memorabilia* 4.2.10; cf. Nagy 1989, 8.
6. As the philosopher declares, the rhapsode is either a cheat, deceiving his audience about his knowledge, or else a 'divine'; Ion unsurprisingly opts for the latter description of himself (542bl–2). As far as Plato is concerned, memorization is an irresponsible mode of textual transmission, for it does not constitute true learning or understanding. In the *Phaedrus* Phaedrus is taken to task as the unthinking mouthpiece of an unthinking speech: Socrates' interloctuor has paid insufficient attention to the content of the speech and failed to recognize its inadequacies.
7. See Nagy 1996, 78.
8. See Davison 1955, 1–22; Too 1995, 37 and 143–4.
9. Note that the Alexandrian library was supposedly burnt down, all or in part, as a result of the siege by Julius Caesar in 47 BC, and was destroyed by Christians in AD 391 and Muslims in AD 642. In the last two instances, pagan literature was perceived as a danger to biblical literature, or to the Qur'an. The accounts of the burning are inaccurate.
10. ἦν γὰρ ὁ Λογγῖνος μακρῷ τῶν τότε ἀνδρῶν τὰ πάντα ἄριστος, καὶ τῶν βιβλίων τε αὐτοῦ πολὺ πλῆθος φέρεται, καὶ τὸ φερόμενον θαυμάζεται καὶ εἴ τις κατέγνω τινὸς τῶν παλαιῶν, οὐ τὸ δοξασθὲν ἐκράτει πρότερον, ἀλλ' ἡ Λογγίνου πάντως ἐκράτει κρίσις. (*VS* 456)
11. Literature is Apuleius' witness on other points. The discussion of the defendant's use of mirrors involves numerous literary and historical *exempla*: Agesilaus refusing to allow himself to be sculpted (15), Socrates and Demosthenes using mirrors in the service of self-knowlege (15), Epicurus on images (15) and Archytas on katoptrics (16), while Plato features prominently again in the discussion of the orator's statue of Mercury (64–5). To establish scientific research as merely curious activity, the orator cites Vergil (19–20 = *Eclogue* 8.64ff.) and Naevius (30.35–40 = Baehrens, p. 292) on vegetation, while he signals his familiarity with the Greek poetic corpus by declaring that he might have recalled (*memorassem*) in his defence portions of Theocritus, Homer, Orpheus, and much more from the Greek comedians, tragedians and historians ('memorassem tibi etiam Theocriti paria et alia Homeri et Orphei plurima, et ex comoediis et tragoediis Graecis et ex historiis multa repetissem', 30.29–30; cf. 30.30; 31.7 = *Iliad* 12.741; 31.9–10 = *Odyssey* 4.455ff, 12.25ff; 31.13 = *Odyssey* 11.91ff, 234ff., 31.14 = *Iliad* 23.214).
12. On the autonomy of textual identity in Apuleius, see Harrison 1990.
13. More or less contemporary with Apuleius' speech are the apologies of Lucian and Dio of Prusa, and Philostratus' *Life* of Apollonius of Tyana.
14. In Chapter 37 of the oration he recalls how Sophocles read his *Oedipus at Colonus* before judges (*iudicibus* 37.6, 9), so that they could determine whether or not he was mad. The play is forced to function both as a literary text and as a forensic apologia, not unlike Apuleius' own: hence, the *iudices* of this work become at once the audience of a dramatic and a legal *agôn*.
15. The *Apology* provides a second judge-figure, Lollianus Avitus, who is no less learned than Maximus. With the latter, he shares a literary style, which speaks to their textual kinship, on the assumption that similar ways of writing and speaking attest to similar characters (94.16–18; 95.18–20; cf. Seneca *Ep*.114).
16. On the symposium as emblematic of order and civilisation, see Booth 1991.
17. '*Sicut plerisque ignaris etiam puerilium litterarum libri non studiorum instrumenta sed cenationum ornamenta sunt.*' The philosopher criticizes the 'innumerable books and libraries' which no one person can thoroughly read, advocating knowledge of a few texts instead.
18. At the beginning of Book Thirteen, which concerns itself with women and love, Athenaeus invokes the Muse Erato to come to the aid of his memory (cf. εἰς μνήμην) before he embarks on his 'erotic catalogue' (τὸν ἐρωτικὸν ἐκεῖνον κατάλογον) (555a).

19. Daléchamp suggests the reading ἀνομοιότητα, 'dissimilarity'; see Gulick ad loc.
20. Bradbury 1950, 135.

## 8 *Athenaeus' Knowledge of Early Greek Elegiac and Iambic Poetry*

1. Philostratus *VS* 2.12, 15, 19 and 21.
2. The *Onomasticon* was most recently edited by E. Bethe in 1937 as Volume 9 of *Lexicographi graeci*. For the chronology of its publication late in the 170s and early in the 180s, see Avotins 1975, 320–1; Swain 1990, 214–6.
3. For analyses and explanations of this phenomenon, see Swain 1996, esp. 17–64; Schmitz 1997, esp. 67–110.
4. For a rereading of the papyrus (and the observation that it is in the same hand and probably from the same roll as Ad.El. 61W = P.Oxy.2507, thus making it almost certain that these too are elegies of Archilochus) see *ZPE* 121 (1998), 94.
5. συκῆν μέλαιναν, ἀμπέλου κασιγνήτην.
6. πολλὰς δὲ τυφλὰς ἐγχέλυς ἐδέξω.
7. τῷ δὲ τοῦ μύρου ὀνόματι πρῶτος Ἀρχίλοχος κέχρηται λέγων 'οὐκ ἂν μύροισι γραῦς ἐοῦσ ἠλείφε το' (the same trimeter in Plutarch *Per.* 28.7) καὶ ἀλλαχοῦ δ' ἔφη ἐσμυριχμένας κόμην καὶ στῆθος, ὡς ἂν καὶ γέρων ἠράσσατο.
8. ἐσθ' ἥβης ἐρατοῖσιν ἐπ' ἄνθεσι παιδοφιλήσῃ. μηρῶν ἱμείρων καὶ γλυκεροῦ στόματος.
   The pentameter is also cited by Apuleius *Apol.* 9, and the whole couplet by Plutarch *Amat.* 751b.
9. Bowie 1997.
10. *Agis* 23.4, *de soll. anim.* 1 (*Mor.* 959e); the anecdote also appears in the Ps.-Plutarchan *Apophth. Lac.* (*Mor.* 235e cf. 230d).
11. Philochorus 328 F 216. On the interpretation of this passage, see Bowie 1990, 221–9.
12. The places are: *de prof. virt.* 14 (*Mor.* 84f–d), *de tuenda san.* 24 (*Mor.* 136a), *de virt. moral.* 7 (*Mor.* 446d–e), *an seni gerenda resp.* 12 (*Mor.* 790e), *de esu carn.* 2.2 (*Mor.* 997d) and fr. 210 Sandbach.
13. At *de cupid. div.* 2 (*Mor.* 523e), *Sto. paradox.* 6 (*Mor.* 1058d) and *de comm. notit.* 20 (*Mor.* 1068b). For a more detailed discussion see Bowie 1997, 106.
14. Steph. Byz. p. 230.20M. For a good brief account of Herodianus, son of Apollonius Dyscolus, see *PIR²* A 189, *Kleine Pauly*, Herodianus (1).
15. 16W, 19W, 155W, 155aW, 155bW (these last three together).
16. 56, 57, 58, 118a, 148a, 150, 162, 163, 171, 173 in West's numeration.

17. Hephaestion's *Encheiridion* on metre cites 119W, 122W and 175W. On Hephaestion, and his possible identity with the *grammaticus* who taught Verus (SHA *Verus* 2.5), see *Kleine Pauly*, Hephaestion (2). For the Anti-atticist, who cites 136W, 140W and 142W, see Swain 1996, 53.
18. Phrynichus (for whom see Swain 1996, 53) cites 138W in his *praep. soph.* for the gender of ἄσβολος.
19. Harpocration's Λέξεις τῶν ἱ ῥητόρων cites 51W for the word μάλθη (also in Demosthenes 46.11): for Harpocration, who may also have been a teacher of Verus, SHA *Verus* 2.5, see *Kleine Pauly*, Harpokration (2).
20. In περὶ παιδιῶν Suetonius cites 129aW. In *de blasph.* he cites 114cW and 147*W: the latter is generally taken to be a misquotation since the phrase has also turned up in Herodas 5.74, but quotation of Hipponax by Herodas might also be considered.
21. 24W, 59W, 78aW, 114aW, 121W, 151bW. For Erotianus, see *Kleine Pauly* under that name.
22. Sextus cites 124W (quoting an anecdote about *grammatici*), Aelian 114bW (almost certainly drawing on Aristophanes of Byzantium), ps.-Plutarch *On Music* 153W (for Hipponax's attribution of the νόμος Κραδίας to Mimnermus), and Diogenes Laertius 63W (for mention of Myson) and 143W (for a sculptor Bion).
23. Plutarch 19W, 21W, Apollonius Dyscolus 34W, Harpocration 36W, Clement 20W, Ps.-Ammonius 30W, the Ps.-Lucianic *Amores* 33W, Porphyry 37W.
24. Dio 114W, Plutarch 101W, 107W, 108W, 118W, 122W, Galen 114W, Pausanias 93bW, Pollux 114W and 126W, Clement 110W, 111W, 127W.
25. Dio 185W, Plutarch 181W, 184W, 185W, Apollonius Sophista 212W, Apollonius Dyscolus 174W, Atticus 176W, Aelius Aristides 183W, 185W, Lucian 178W, Clement 177W, Aelian 185W, Hephaestion 168–172W, 182W, 188W, 190W, 195–7W.
26. For a guide to the voluminous recent bibliography on Theognis and the *Theognidea* (1921–89) see Gerber 1991, 186–214; for some further reflections Bowie 1996.
27. Philostratus *VS* 2.1.564.

## 9 *Athenaeus, Lucian and Fifth-Century Comedy*

1. 'Zur chronologie der altattischen Komödie', *Wiener Studien* 38 (1916) 81–57, cited in Nesselrath 1990, 65.
2. Lucian, *Nigrinus* 33: καὶ μὴν κἀκείνους διεγέλα τοὺς θαυμάσιόν τινα τὴν σπουδὴν περὶ τὰ δεῖπνα ποιουμένους χυμῶν τε ποικιλίαις καὶ πεμμάτων περιεργίαις.
3. Nesselrath 1990, 68.

4. The figures are compiled from *PCG*.
5. Lucian, *Bis Accusatus* 33: εἶτά μοι εἰς τὸ αὐτὸ φέρων συγκαθεῖρξεν τὸ σκῶμμα καὶ τὸν ἴαμβον καὶ κυνισμὸν καὶ τὸν Εὔπολιν καὶ τὸν Ἀριστοφάνη, δεινοὺς ἄνδρας ἐπικερτομῆσαι τὰ σεμνὰ καὶ χλευάσαι τὰ ὀρθῶς ἔχοντα. 'And then he brought me to the same place and shut me up with jokes, iambics, cynics, Eupolis and Aristophanes, men well-versed in criticising serious institutions and pouring scorn on what is right.'
6. καὶ τῶν ἱστοπουμένων ἕκαστον οὐκ ἀκωμῳδήτως ᾔνικται πρός τινας τῶν παλαῖν ποιητῶν τε καὶ συγγραφέων καὶ φιλοσόφων πολλὰ τεράστια καὶ μυθώδη σγγεγραφότων, οὕς καὶ ὀνομαστὶ ἂν ἔγραφον, εἰ μὴ καὶ αὐτῷ σοι ἐκ τῆς ἀναγνώσεως φανεῖσθαι ἔμελλον. 'And each part of the events has been aimed enigmatically in a manner not a million miles away from comedy at some of the ancient poets, historians and philosophers, who have written many amazing and mythical things. I would even have written down their names, if it were not going to be perfectly obvious from your reading even to you who they are.'
7. Malcolm Heath suggested this to me. I have elsewhere suggested that the play referred to was by Eupolis (Sidwell 1993, 379–80).
8. See Ledergerber 1905.
9. One is reminded of the example of Eupolis fr. 332 which must be in the back of Lucian's mind as justification for his description of the addressee of *Pseudologistes* as ἀποφράς ('ill-omened'). I owe this observation to Malcolm Heath.
10. Nesselrath 1990, 186–7.
11. Lucian passes Nephelokokkygia on his way back to earth from the moon: καὶ ἐγὼ ἐμνήσθην Ἀριστοφάνους τοῦ ποιητοῦ, ἀνδρὸς σοφοῦ καὶ ἀληθοῦς καὶ μάτην ἐφ' οἷς ἔγραφεν ἀπιστουμένου. 'And I remembered Aristophanes the poet, a wise and truthful man, whose account is wrongly disbelieved.'
12. E.g. Koster 1975, 7, lines 9–10: οἱ μὲν οὖν τῆς ἀρχαίας κωμῳδίας ποιηταὶ οὐχ ὑμοθέσεως ἀληθοῦς, ἀλλὰ παιδιᾶς εὐτραπέλου γενόμενοι ζηλωταὶ τοὺς ἀγῶνας ἐποίουν. 'The poets of Old Comedy entered the contests as zealots not of truth, but of wit.'
13. Above n. 6. E.g. Koster 1975, 27: ἀλλὰ ψήφισμα θέντος Ἀλκιβιάδου κωμῳδεῖν ἐσχηματισμένως καὶ μὴ προδήλως αὐτός τε ὁ Εὔπολις Κρατῖνός τε τὰ συμβολικὰ μετεχειρίσαντο σκώμματα. 'But when Alcibiades proposed a decree that people should satirize covertly and not openly, Eupolis himself and Cratinus used symbolic jokes.' (id.: 71: οἱ ἄρχοντες Ἀθήνησιν ἤρξαντο κωλύειν τοὺς κωμικοὺς τοῦ φανερῶς οὕτω καὶ ὀνομαστὶ ἐλέγχειν τοὺς ἀδικοῦντας ... ὅθεν ὥσπερ αἰνιγματωδῶς καὶ οὐ φανερῶς ἠλέγχοντο ὑπὸ τῶν κωμικῶν. 'The rulers at Athens began to prevent the comic poets from attacking wrongdoers so openly and by name ... and hence they began to be attacked as it were enigmatically and not openly by the comic poets.'
14. For that sort of discussion, we can now look to that Deipnosophist's delight, James Davidson 1997.
15. For these arguments, see Sidwell 2000 (forthcoming).
16. Scholion on Aristophanes *Knights* 400a (= *PCG* vol. IV, p. 219, *Pytine* Tii).
17. οἱ ἀρχαῖοι ποιηταί, Θέσπις, Πρατίνας, Κρατῖνος, Φρύνιχος ὀρχησταὶ ἐκαλοῦντο διὰ τὸ μὴ μόνον τὰ ἑαυτῶν δράματα ἀναφέρειν εἰς ὄρχησιν τοῦ χοροῦ, ἀλλὰ καὶ ἔξω τῶν ἰδίων ποιημάτων διδάσκειν τοὺς βουλομένους ὀρχεῖσθαι.
18. See Sidwell 1995.
19. καὶ Ἀλκαῖος δὲ ὁ μελοποιὸς καὶ Ἀριστοφάνης ὁ κωμῳδοποιὸς μεθύοντες ἔγραφον τὰ ποιήματα.
20. xiii.577b–c (= G 6.117) mentions a comic poet called Kalliades, but Meineke altered the text to read Kallias. However, there is a fourth-century poet of this name (see *PCG* IV) and he is mentioned by Athenaeus at ix.401a (= G 4.315).
21. This will probably be *Symmachia*, disputed between Cantharus and Plato (see references ad loc.).
23. This will probably be *Symmachia*, disputed between Cantharus and Plato (see references ad loc.).

## 10 *Harpocration and Athenaeus: Historiographical Relationships*

1. Zecchini 1989a.
2. Rudolph 1884 and 1891; Gabrielsson 1906–9.
3. Chronology of Athenaeus: Zecchini 1989a, 11–14; chronology of Harpocration: not clear from Suda A4014 Adler; now reconstructed on the basis of *P Ryl.* 532 and *P Oxy.* 2192 and *P Merton* 30.
4. Keaney 1991.
5. Thus Gärtner Kl. Pauly, 2.944.
6. Thus Wentzel RE 2.2026–33 followed in part by Zecchini 1989a, 234 and 255.
7. On whom see Schwartz RE 5.662. Diodorus Periegetes is quoted by Athenaeus just once at 13.591e.
8. Phot. Biblioth. cod.150: τοῦτο τὸ βιβλίον ... ἑρμηνεύον ... καὶ εἴ τι καθ' ἱστορίαν ἰδιάζουσαν αὐτοῖς οἱ ῥήτορες παρειλήφασιν ἢ κατά τι πάτριον ἔθος ἀπεχρήσαντο ('this book ... explaining ... what orators drew from the local history of their town or from ancestral customs').

9. Gudeman RE 10.9–10.
10. *P Oxy.* 2192, col. II, ll. 28–38. Cf. Turner 1952, 91–2.
11. On Julius Vestinus and on these lexicographers in general cf. Tolkiehn RE 12.2. 2448–9.
12. Keaney 1973.
13. Jacoby 1926, 106.
14. Pearson and Stephens 1983, 22, 29, 34, 35 and 39.
15. Zecchini 1989a, 44–5 and Rabe 1910.
16. On Ister, cf. *FGrH* IIIb Suppl. 618–27 and Pearson 1942, 136–44.
17. Athen. 5.196a–203e and 203e–206c, on which see Zecchini 1989a, 191–2.
18. Pearson and Stephens 1983, 42.
19. Cuvigny 1981.
20. Thus Keil 1895.
21. Cuvigny 1981, 25 and Zecchini 1989a, 134–5 and 211.
22. Cuvigny 1981, 25 and Zecchini 1989a, 208–10.
23. Jacoby 1954, 185; Zecchini 1989a, 133.
24. Semos in Athenaeus: Zecchini 1989a, 157–9; quoted by Harpocration: E 14; on Semos in general cf. Lanzillotta 1996.
25. On the relationship between Polemon and Athenaeus, cf. Zecchini 1989a, 227–31.

## 11 Athenaeus and Polybius

1. Zecchini 1989a.
2. They are listed below in the appendix to this chapter.
3. 1989a, 7.
4. 1989a, 86–92.
5. Zecchini 1989a, 87.
6. See Marsden 1971, 5–6; Drachmann 1963, 11.
7. Published in Marsden 1971, 61–103.
8. Zecchini 1989a, 87.
9. 1989a, 88.
10. See Chapter 40.
11. On 'tragic history' see Walbank 1955 and 1960 (= 1985, 224–41); Zegers 1959; Meister 1990, 95–102 (with bibliography) and 222 n. 22; Hornblower 1994, 44–5, 52 n. 134; Marincola 1997, 23–4.
12. 1989a, 86.
13. On Polybius as Livy's source at this point see De Sanctis 1917, 285–9.
14. See Bruns 1898, v–viii, Walbank 1972, 92–6.
15. Eckstein 1995, 285–9.
16. Ambaglio 1990.
17. MS A reads τενθίωνα, corrected by Casaubon to Γενθίον; Kaibel read Γενθίωνα.
18. Eckstein 1995, 25 n. 105.

19. Walbank 1979, 599–601.
20. These are (1), (2), (7), (11), (13), (14), (18), (20) and (27).
21. In (25) the Polybian origin is clearly indicated from (26) but the historian is not named.
22. Thompson 1985, 119–39.

## 12 Fun with Fragments: Athenaeus and the Historians

1. Innes 1936, 33.
2. West 1978, 45.
3. From a host of examples cf. Clearchus at 8.332b, Mnaseas at 8.346e, Theopompus and then Phylarchus at 12.536c ff., Posidonius at 12.540a–c, Clearchus at 12.548b–c, etc.
4. For instance, the extensive Posidonius story of Athenion at 5.211d–215b (fr. 253e–K) contains incidental material which picks up many of the themes of Masurius' long speech and the book as each approaches its conclusion, not merely philosophers and kings and philosophers at symposia (the springboard for its inclusion) but also elaborate processions, sumptuously decorated houses and costumes, artists of Dionysus, and so on.
5. von Wilamowitz-Moellendorf 1880, 74.
6. As seems, for instance, to have happened in Athenaeus' Atticized rendering of a famous fragment of Alcaeus (fr. 249V.): Gentili 1988, 57, 230. Zepernick 1921, 338–40 gives further examples, noting that Herodotus' dialect-forms are altered 'very often'. The example taken below, 4.138b–c ~ Hdt. 9.82, includes several instances, including an οὖν for an ὦν.
7. Flower 1994, 190–2; it is one of the few fragments he prints in an appendix, 219–20.
8. On Polybius, see Walbank in this Section, Chapter 11. Cf. e.g. 8.338b–c for less spectacular drift from indirect speech into (presumably) summarizing; 1.15e–16a, 9.374a–b for similar drifts from direct speech into summary; and, to confuse matters still further, 4.138b–c (quoted below) for a case where half-way through a quotation he replaces the indirect speech of the Herodotean original with his own indicatives (but still the whole passage should count as 'direct quotation', even if inexact: see Appendix below). For a case of drift from indirect to direct quotation, cf. Aristoxenus at 12.545f, but that is much clearer (he is *resuming* direct quotation from 12.545a–e). For similar doubtful cases, 8.330f–331c = Plb. 34.8.4–10 on Lusitania, where the second half (ῥόδα μὲν γὰρ αὐτόθι...) is marked as direct quotation by Kaibel, Gulick, and Büttner-Wobst, but not by Schweighaeuser (who knew his Athenaeus) or Paton. At 9.400d–e a citation of Hegesander of Delphi is

marked by Kaibel and Gulick as verbatim (both the indirect and the direct parts): but is it really quotation, or rather summary? Müller, *FHG* iv.421 fr. 42 does not mark it as a quotation.

9. Cf. fr. 53b E-K = 4.153c–d, above p. 191, with Diod. 5.40.3 and Flower 1994, 191 for Posidonius' interest in Etruria; also fr. 237 E-K.

10. I discuss it in Pelling 1997, where the viewpoint sketched in this paragraph is argued more fully.

11. Strasburger 1977, 22.

12. Brunt 1980, 480–1; Zecchini 1989a, 27 and 31.

13. Compare Walbank's point (p. 180) about the quotation of Plb. 7.1.1–3 at Athen. 12.528a–c, the Carthaginian siege of Petelia. Livy 23.30.1 makes it clear that the attacking Carthaginian commander was not Hannibal himself, as Athenaeus has it (ὑπ' Ἀννίβα), but Himilco. We must assume that Polybius would have got this detail right, whether or not he was here Livy's source. Athenaeus' adjustment gives a neater contrast with the immediately preceding item, the behaviour of Capua: Capua called in Hannibal and was chastised by the Romans, Petelia resisted Hannibal and was let down by the Romans. It may also be that Athenaeus here overstates the Roman faithlessness. If we read οὐδὲ συνευδοκοῦντος with Kaibel, Gulick, and Athenaeus MSS at 12.528c, that makes the Petelians surrender 'without any Roman giving assent', and obscures the more magnanimous Roman invitation 'to do whatever they thought in their own best interests' (*consulere sibimet ipsos in reliquum <pro> praesenti fortuna*, Livy 23.20.6). Editors of Polybius generously emend the text to συνευδοκούντων 'Ρωμαίων, 'with Roman approval'; Schweighaeuser notes that this brings Polybius into line with Livy and with App. *Hann.* 29. But it is just as likely that Athenaeus is again misquoting his Polybian original, either to present Rome in a more negative light or simply to sharpen the contrast with Capua.

14. On this see esp. Cartledge 1993, 80–2 and more fully 1990b.

15. Brunt 1980, 481.

16. Bers 1997.

17. This builds on the more general picture of historians' and biographers' methods developed in Pelling 1979, where I argued that Plutarch, like other authors, would naturally have only one text open before his eyes as he composed, but could supplement this from memory, often a memory re-primed by recent reading.

18. A less likely alternative might be to reconstruct the working methods of Athenaeus' epitomator in this way: in that case it would be he who would be working from a recently re-stocked memory rather than from a text in front of his eyes. But the procedure makes less sense for an epitomator, working in a linear fashion through a text, than for an Athenaeus who is making his own artistic selection and combination from a number of texts.

This paper was given at the University of Southern California in March 1998 as well as in Exeter: my thanks to the participants on both occasions, especially the editors, David Harvey, Tim Whitmarsh, Ruth Webb, John Marr, Carolyn Dewald, Peter O'Neill, and Vincent Farenga; to Judith Mossman for reading an early draft and for the timely gift of Michael Innes' novel; and especially to Michael Flower for his magnanimous and learned assistance with a study devoted, in part, to dissent from his own position.

## 13 *The Recalcitrant Mass: Athenaeus and Pausanias*

1. Translations from Athenaeus are those of Gulick; translations from Pausanias are from Frazer 1898.

2. Bowersock 1985, 682.

3. Arafat 1996, 17–19.

4. This passage of Herodorus is known only from Athenaeus : *FHG* ii.31.

5. Merkelbach and West 1967, 133–8.

6. On the meanings covered by the word, Arafat 1996, 9 and n. 18.

7. On Cleidemus/Cleitodemus, *FHG* i.359–65; also Gulick, ad 9.409f, 10.425e, 13.609c, 14.660a.

8. For Polemo, *FHG* v.108–48. See also pp. 215 below.

9. *FGrH* 241 F4–8. On the relationship of Eratosthenes' work to the victor lists of Hippias, Aristotle and Timaeus, Pfeiffer 1968, 163–4.

10. Dover 1968a, 163.

11. On the cult of Trophonius, Schachter 1994, 66–89, listing (81 n. 2) sources for the use of honey-cakes. Also, Frazer 1898, 5.200.

12. *FHG* iv.411–2, *FGrH* F 319.

13. The word used for 'gilded' by Plutarch (*Mor.* 753F) is κατάχρυσος, while Pausanias uses ἐπίχρυσος, as does Polemo (*Deipn.* 11.479f).

14. Neither Aelian (*Var. Hist.* 32) nor Dio Chrysostom (*Or.* 37.28) mention statues neighbouring that of Phryne.

15. On the possible use of Polemo by Pausanias, Frazer 1898, l, 83–90.

16. E.g. Dinsmoor 1912, 400 and n. 1, 480.

17. I disagree with Dinsmoor 1912, 400, that Pliny (*NH* 3.120, not 3.129 as Dinsmoor) writes of a treasury rather than of treasure. Nor, *pace* Alfieri and Gentili 1976, do Dion. Hal.

*Ant. Rom* 1.18.4 (not 1.18.5) and Strabo 9.3.8 refer to a treasury.

18. The Greek is ναός. As often, 'temple' embraces the concept of 'treasury'.

19. Levi 1971, 2.340 n. 159, 2.341 n. 163.

20. Frazer 1898, 4.57.

21. Dyer 1905, 301, 311–12.

22. The nature of the building is clear from Herodotus' (1.14) reference to it as a θησαυρός. Dyer 1905, 301, 305 notes that οἶκος is a sacred term used in inscriptions from Delphi and Delos.

23. W. Dörpfeld in Curtius and Adler 1892, 40, 45 (Sicyonian), 51 (Megarian).

24. Notably W. Dörpfeld in Curtius and Adler 1892, 44–56.

25. Dinsmoor 1950, 53.

26. Arafat 1995, 465.

27. *FHG* iv.288.

28. That is 'wrought' as opposed to 'cast'. On the sources for, and technique of, the Cypselid dedication at Olympia, Dickie 1996, 247, and Papadopoulos 1980, 86–7. On the technique itself (standardly applied to bronze rather than gold), Arafat 1996, 71–2 and n. 68.

29. On the meaning of 'colossus', and the techniques of manufacture in the Hellenistic period, Dickie 1996.

30. Arafat 1995.

## 14 Athenaeus' Use of Public Documents

\* The project forms part of the portfolio of research work currently supported by the terms of my Leverhulme Trust Professorship. I gratefully acknowledge the support for such scholarship which the Trust is providing. I am also glad to acknowledge the help provided by my part-time research assistant Matthew Lockey in carrying out the initial trawl through the text of Athenaeus.

1. Schmitt-Pantel 1992, 101–4; Parker 1996, 250 n. 109 and 331; Davies 1996b, 634–7; Chapter 22.

2. Provisionally, and gratefully, I take over Gulick's heroic attempt at translation, with a couple of 'improvements' : more can probably be extracted from Weinreich 1933, 108–10. Müller disappointingly threw in the towel ('Epistolam vertere ausi sunt Villebrunius et Dalecampius; quorum hariolationes mittendas esse duxi'). For Cassandreia, see now Cohen 1995, 95–9 (but he adds nothing to the point for Athenaeus). For Alexarchus' foundation of Ouranopolis on the Athos peninsula see Strabo 7. fr. 35, Ernst Wüst, *RE* 9A (1961) 965–6 s.v. Uranopolis (1), and Cohen 1995, 105–6.

3. Ἐχενίκη (2) in *LGPN* I, following Vial 1984, 75, stemma XI, who cites other of her donations *c.*250 (a golden kylix, a phiale, a perfume vase) from the Delos accounts.

4. 'Gongulos' is well attested at Eretria, and 'Sesame' at Delos itself. See *LGPN* I s.vv.

5. But 'Crithon' is known from Athens, Eretria and Telos (see *LGPN* I and II s.v.).

6. Hyperides F 70.

7. *CID* I 10 : Aisch. 2.115 and 3.107–11.

8. Documentation in *IG* XI, 2 and in *I. de Délos* 89–104/33. Brief sketches of the Athenian amphictyony in Laidlaw 1933, 57–93 and Reger 1994, 160–2 and 215–17. More generally for Atheno-Delian relations Habicht 1997, 246–63.

9. *H.H.Apollo* 56–8 and 147–64 and Thuc. 3.104 ; for the hypothesis, Gallet de Santerre 1958, 296. The term περικτίονες in Thuc. 3.104.3 cannot be pressed too far in a formal direction.

10. *CID* I, 13, superseding previous publications (*F de D.* III 4, 371; Sokolowski 1962, no. 41; Bengtson 1962, no. 295). Rougemont ad loc. suggests a date in the second quarter of the fourth century, with all appropriate caution.

11. See Prinz 1979, 111–37, with in particular Strabo 14.1.11 and 40 and Plut. *Mor.* 402a (but the latter text should not be taken, as by Prinz 1979, 119, as evidence that the Magnetes sent an ἀνθρώπων ἀπαρχὴ ('tithe-offering of men') to Delphi during the Third Sacred War).

12. Cf. especially the link with Delphi reflected in the oracle of 221/20 (Kern, *I. von Magnesia* 16) and the mythic narrative of *ib.* 17. Further discussion in Chaniotis 1988, 34–40 and Zecchini 1989a, 170–1.

13. *FGrH* 404 F 6 *ap.* Athen. 11.105, p. 108, 2 K.

14. *FGrH* 115 F 247 (Athen. 13.604f–605a), 248 (13.605a–d), and 249 (12.532d–e), agreed by Jacoby ad loc. (p. 389), Zecchini 1989a, 58–9, and Flower 1994, 36–7 to have been a separate book, not part of the *Philippica*.

15. Dion. Hal. *Ant. Rom.* 1.18.4 ; Strabo 5.1.7 and 9.3.8. For the tentative identification of the building as feature 342 on the 1975 *Atlas* of the site see Bommelaer 1991, 231–2, with references.

16. Wehrli 1969, 30 cites the Lindian Temple Chronicle (*FGrH* 532) and Charon, *FGrH* 262 F 2, but there is much more material. For Phaenias see also Zecchini 1989a, 200–2.

17. *FGrH* 373 T1 (6.229e) and F 4 (6.229e).

18. F 4 (6.229e); F 3 (9.406c–d). There is also F 8 (2.45c), about Antiochus IV and the city of Antioch, which might conceivably come from a note by Heliodorus on Antiochus' dedications above the theatre (Paus. 5.12.4) (thus Jacoby *ad* F 8), but it is a long shot.

19. Quoted at 1.9cd from Philochorus (328 F 169(a)) and at 9.375b from Androtion (324 F 55) : but even here Jacoby (Commentary on Androtion F 55, followed by Harding 1994, 182) reckoned that the quotation came not directly from the Atthidographers but indirectly via Aristophanes of Byzantium.
20. Quoted at 9.375bc from Philochorus (328 F 169 (b)) (unless there is an underlying confusion with 169 (a)).
21. Quoted from Istrus, *FGrH* 334 F 12 : an interesting variant, not echoed elsewhere and presumably due to confusion, on the well-attested prohibition on the export of olives or olive oil.
22. 13.612a and 15.687a, quoted directly from Solon's laws in both contexts.
23. See *Kl. Pauly*, Hermippus (2), with references.
24. *FGrH* 328 F 65 *ap.* Athen. 6.245c.
25. With much reluctance I leave out of even the 'dubious' list F 36 (9.372a), where Polemon is quoted for the custom that whoever offers the largest spring onion (γηθυλλίς) to Leto at the Theoxenia in Delphi gets a portion from the table, on the ground that Leto when pregnant had a craving for them. His authority might ultimately have been a Delphian *lex sacra*, but why that should be quoted from his book *On Samothrace* I cannot imagine. All the same, the notion of the Theoxenia (for which in general see Jameson 1994) functioning as the town's fruit and vegetable show, presumably in Theoxenios (approximately April), is too engaging to pass over.

## 15 *Picturing the Past: Uses of Ekphrasis in the* Deipnosophistae *and Other Works of the Second Sophistic*

1. E.g. Studniczka 1914; Rice 1983 with further discussion; Foertmeyer 1988.
2. Polybius, 26.1. See Walbank 1957–1979, 284. Another version, which differs slightly in wording, is given by Diodorus, 29.32.
3. The source is Polybius 30.25–6. See Walbank 1957–1979, 448 and Zecchini, 1989, 88. A shorter version of part of the passage is repeated in Book Ten of the *Deipnosophistae* (439).
4. On Polybius in the *Deipnosophistae* see Chapter 11.
5. On Callixenus see Rice 1983, 134–79.
6. For the procession in its Hellenistic context see Rice 1983.
7. On the theme of luxury see Zecchini 1989a *passim*. It is interesting to note that the final section of Masurius' monologue also contains the cautionary tale of Athenion, a philosopher-king turned tyrant.

8. For the definition see Theon, *Progymnasmata*, 118.7.
9. The other two *peristaseis* were the cause (αἰτία) and the manner (τρόπος). Athenaeus makes use of these categories in his criticism of Epicurus when he praises Homer for defining the times, places and occasions of his feasts (186d).
10. Graf 1995; Webb 1997b.
11. Zanker 1981.
12. On this passage of Quintilian, see Nisbet 1992 and Webb 1997a.
13. Desideri 1992. I am grateful to Larry Kim for drawing my attention to this article.
14. Russell 1983 106–28; Desideri 1992.
15. Philostratus *Lives*, 584; Hermogenes, *Peri ideon*, 244–5; Desideri 1992, 60.
16. Aristides' speech was evidently presented in the persona of a third party. See Philostratus, *Lives*, 584.
17. Elsner 1995, 33–4.
18. Guenther 1989.
19. Webb 1997a and b.
20. Zecchini 1989, 68–9a.
21. Pernot 1998 points out that the restriction of subject matter to the classical period and classical models is typical of pedagogical works and therefore not necessarily representative of the rhetorical production of the Second Sophistic as a whole.

## 16 *The Female-Kings: Some Aspects of the Representation of Eastern Kings in the* Deipnosophistae

1. The section is marked by a clear beginning (cf. the opening lemma at *Deipn.* 12.528e: Κτησίας ἐν τρίτῃ Περσικῶν καὶ πάντας μέν φησι τοὺς βασιλεύσαντας τῆς Ἀσίας περὶ τρυφὴν σπουδάσαι ('Ctesias in the third book of his *Persika* says that those who reigned in Asia indulged in luxury'), and by an end consisting of the so-called epitaph of king Ninus (Phoen. 1 Powell; *Deipn.* 12.530e–531a). The quotation from Ctesias can surely be considered a lemma, or even a 'thema', like the opening statement about the Persians (*Deipn.* 12.513e–f); the final quotation is an epitaph, just symbolizing the *de profundis* for the whole world of the fabulous Asian kings. The following instances (Straton of Sidon and Nicocles, king of Salamis on Cyprus, *Deipn.* 12.531a–e; the Thracian king Cotys, *Deipn.* 12.531e–532a) constitute a new section, without lemma but clearly defined, including kings who are both on margins of the Asian world and strictly connected with Greece, so that they are a sort of link between Asian and Greek τρυφή; then there is the section on eminent

Athenians (*Deipn.* 12.532a–535e). Every personage included in the section on female-kings must be considered a 'king', even if lacking any sure historical identity.

2. Apart from Semiramis, who is notably omitted from the section, kingship is of course *naturaliter* a male affair: in Book Twelve we have an *e contrario* demonstration, provided by Clearchus' account about Omphale and her gynaecocratic dominion over the Lydians, which is the most remarkable instance of perverted and corrupted society in the book (43a Wehrli; *Deipn.* 12.515e–516c); the phantom of gynaecocracy hovers about Theopompus' description of Etruscan society and customs (*FGrH* 115 F 204; *Deipn.* 12.517d–e).

3. Effeminacy is meant here, and not a kind of sacred hermaphroditism, which can perhaps be found in the origins of the effeminate Midas in Clearchus' account about Lydian τρυφή (51a Wehrli; *Deipn.* 12.516b); also the king of frankincense country (the Persian king? or rather the king of Sabaeans? cf. Strabo 16.4.19) is suspected of a sexual ambiguity deriving perhaps from ancient religious customs (Heraclid. Cum. *FGrH* 689 F 4; *Deipn.* 12.517bc); bisexuality of a religious kind is not relevant in this section, which is rather the result of a literary *topos*, with only the exception of Sagaris (see below, n. 17); on Dionysos–Sardanapalus, Sabatius–Sardanapalus and effeminate buffoons, see Weissbach *RE* Sardanapal, 2473–5; on hermaphroditism in Greek religion, see Delcourt 1958, 28–50.

4. Effeminate kingship is a particular case in the general *topos* of Asiatic effeminacy, and it is a case deserving of specific attention: Herodotus, who knows and uses the general *topos* to explain great events (see the account concerning Lydian effeminacy, 1.155, where he provides an aetiology of the *topos* itself; see also the famous conclusion of Book 9: φιλέειν γὰρ ἐκ τῶν μαλακῶν χώρων μαλακοὺς ἄνδρας γίνεσθαι, 'it is natural that soft men arise from a soft soil', 9.122) seems to be unacquainted with effeminate kingship; the same can be said about Xenophon, who subscribes to the commonplace of Asian softness (cf. *Ages.* 1.28), but says nothing of effeminate kings (neither Astyages nor Cyaxares in *Cyropaedia* can be so defined); effeminacy plays an important role in Plato's *Leg.* 3.694d–695e, and also in Xen. *Cyr.* 8.8.15–19, where Persian decadence is discussed, but effeminacy is not yet something morbid; the invention of female-kings can probably be ascribed to Ctesias, and could be connected with Ctesias' arrangement of the so-called *translatio imperii*: Assyrian kings' effeminacy is clearly functional to the general outline of Asiatic empires' alternation, and the effeminate king embodies not only the imagined military ineptitude of the whole nation, but also its turning into a ready-to-conquer prey; on Ctesias and *translatio imperii* see Zecchini 1988, 364.

5. On the motif of secluded life see also Midas (Clearch. 51a Wehrli; *Deipn.* 12.516b); the king of frankincense country (Heraclid.Cum. *FGrH* 689 F 4; *Deipn.* 12.517bc); Ninyas (Ctes. *FGrH* 688 F 1.21); Sardanapalus (Ctes. *FGrH* 688 F 1.23); the Parsondes' story (Nic.Dam. *FGrH* 90 F 4, an interesting variation: Nanarus king of Babylonia turns a man into a woman by secluding him); see also Justin, 1.2.11, where we find another metamorphosis from male to female: away from men's eyes, Ninyas changes his sex with his mother's.

6. Laziness and programmatic refusal of royal and manly activities are the main features of Ninyas in the diodorean Ctesias (*FGrH* 688 F 1.21), and the king justifies it with a bogus philosophical argument: τρυφή and ῥαθυμία ('luxury and indolence') only cause εὐδαιμονία ('happiness'), and this is the τέλος ('aim') of royal power.

7. No previous works of the same kind are recorded to our knowledge, except the problematic Alciphron's Περὶ παλαιᾶς τρυφῆς (*On ancient luxury*), on which see Zecchini 1989a, 178, and despite Wentzel *RE* 'Athenaios', 2033 suggesting that Athenaeus might have relied upon an anonymous (and to us unknown) Περὶ τρυφῆς (*On luxury*). On the sources for Book Twelve, see Zecchini 1989a, 5.

8. Athenaeus fails to define the concept of τρυφή. He introduces some remains of the fourth-century debate on pleasure, including unfavourable opinions (*Deipn.* 12.510b–511c), the assertion that ἡδονή ('pleasure') and δόξα ('glory') are incompatible (Thphr. 84 Wimmer, *Deipn.* 12.511cd), a quotation from Plato's *Republic* (9.559b), demonstrating that only the excesses of pleasure are rejectable, not pleasure at all, and making Plato a forerunner of Epicurus (*Deipn.* 12.511e–512a), and finally an apologia of pleasure (Heraclid.Pont. 55 Wehrli; *Deipn.* 12.512ae) followed by the peripatetic Magaclides' commendation of Heracles' luxury, and Odysseus' defence from the charge of hedonism (Megaclides, *FHG* 4.443, *Deipn.* 12.512e–513e).

9. It is often hard to specify the exact meaning of the word: vagueness begins indeed from the etymology and the primary meaning of τρυφή, on which see Nenci 1983, 1021, proposing something like 'fastidiousness', that is Milesian rich people's fastidious food consumption by cutting food into little pieces, while the poor consume their food with rough voracity; I am not acquainted with semantic researches about τρυφή: I simply observe that one peculiar

feature is its frequent use in hendiadys (not less than twenty cases in the *Deipnosophistae*), such as χλιδή καὶ τρυφή, 6.273c. It is associated with πλοῦτος ('wealth') 9.382a; μαλακία, ('softness') 10.429b, 11.496e, 12.523c; λαγνεία ('lasciviousness') 12.513e; ἀνανδρία 12.516b ('emasculation'); ῥαθυμία ('indolence') 12.517b; ἡδονή ('pleasure') 12.523f; ἡδυπάθεια ('life of pleasure') 12.531a; ἀσέλγεια ('debauchery') 12.531e; ὑπερηφανία ('insolence') 12.536b; ἀπόλαυσις ('enjoyment')12.541f; πολυτέλεια ('expense, profusion') 12.543c, 12.544b, 14.663a; περίστασις ('pomp') 12.547f; ἀδηφαγία ('gluttony') 12.549ab and so on.

10. On fourth-century treatises Περὶ τρυφῆς and Περὶ δικαιοσύνης (*On Luxury, On Justice*), their structure and polemical aims, see Bignone 1936, 1. 276–86.

11. Τρυφή can be reached through μάθησις, ζῆλος, μίμησις ('learning', 'envy', 'imitation'), for luxury is the moralistic transcription of an acculturation process: see Nenci 1983, 1027–9.

12. On the moralistic perspective implying τρυφή as an historiographical category see Passerini 1934; Cozzoli 1980; Bonamente 1980. On τρυφή in fourth-century historiography, see Connor 1968; Ferretto 1984; and Musti 1987.

13. See Heraclid.Pont. 55 Wehrli = *Deipn.* 12.512a; Aristox. 50 Wehrli = *Deipn.* 12.545c. Athenaeus clearly distinguishes τρυφή, which is a typical affection of power and wealth, from its bourgeois version, ἀσωτία ('debauchery'; cf. *Deipn.* 4.165d–169b).

14. Ctes. *FGrH* 688 F 1n. Son of Ninus and Semiramis (cf. *FGrH* 688 F 1.21), Ninyas is also known with the name Ninus (cf. Justin 1.2.11); no sure identification can be proposed for him; his name recalls Nineveh, the Assyrian capital city: see Weidner Ninyas *RE* 643–4.

15. Ctes. *FGrH* 688 F 1p. Greek name of Ashurbanipal, the last great Assyrian king (668–626 BC), who has no connection with the effeminate figure of Greek accounts; Ctesias' Sardanapalus is more probably to be connected with Shamash-shum-ukin, brother of Ashurbanipal: cf. Macginnis 1988, 37. Other sources: Hdt. 2.150; Hellan. *FGrH* 4 F 63; Ctes. *FGrH* 688 F 1.23–28; the *topos* of Sardanapalus' luxury is found first in Ar. *Birds.* 1021, where the king's name means perhaps κόμπος ('ostentation', 'parade'): cf. Dunbar 1995, 563–4.

16. Mnaseas, *FHG* 3. 152, 530c. Schweighaeuser (6.422–3) suggests an identification with Sandrocottus, who is yet king of Indians (cf. Arr. *Anab.* 5.6.2; Plut. *Alex* 62; Strabo 15.9; *Deipn.* 1.18d), putting forward the interesting hypothesis that it could have been a confusion between the (mysterious) Paphlagonian ruler Cottas, to whom

Sardanapalus sends his children, (cf. Ctes. *FGrH* 688 F 1.26.8; Jacoby suggests *dubitanter* to read Corylas, cf. Xen. *Anab.* 5.5.12) and an unknown Phrygian king.

17. Clearch. 53 Wehrli = *Deipn.* 12.530c. Name of a Phrygian river *ap.* Ps.-Plut. *Fluv.* 12: Sagaris, son of the Phrygian king Mygdon, threw himself into a river, called previously Xenobates, because of the madness caused in him by the Great Mother; according to other traditions, son of Midas (*EM* 707.18); founder of Sybaris (Solin. 2.10); Clearchus' anecdote seems to depend from the Homeric similitude in which Agamemnon is compared with the bird's young nourished through their mother's beak (*Iliad* 9.324).

18. Ctes. *FGrH* 688 F 6 = *Deipn.* 12.530d. Annarus is perhaps to be identified with Nanarus, satrap of Artaius, sixth king of the Median dynasty (cf. D. S. 2.33.1; Nic Dam. *FGrH* 90 F 4; Plut. *Mor.* 1095d).

19. Phoen. 1 Powell = *Deipn.* 12.530e–531a. This Ninus cannot be identified with Semiramis' husband; the name is perhaps an equivalent of Ninyas (Justin also confuses the names, cf. 1.2.11); it is also possible that we have here a fictitious bourgeois character without any historical consistency (so Kaibel, who defines him as a glutton, distinguished from 'king Ninus' of Phoen. 3 Powell = *Deipn.* 10.421d), but it is more probable that Phoenix's Ninus is a free elaboration of the Assyrian king-type; see Barigazzi 1981, 34–5.

20. On the dubious concept of 'tragic historiography' see Marasco 1988; cf. the greater nuance of Chapter 11.

21. The commonplace (Asian effeminacy) proceeds indeed by assuming as an argument what might be demonstrated, with statements like: 'the Lydians are feminized, indeed they live in the shade': cf. Clearch. 51a Wehrli, *Deipn.* 12.516b: Λυδοί, φησί, διὰ τρυφὴν παραδείσους κατασκευασάμενοι καὶ κηπαίους αὐτοὺς ποιήσαντες ἐσκιατροφοῦντο, τρυφερώτερον ἡγησάμενοι τὸ μηδ' ὅλως αὐτοῖς ἐπιπίπτειν τὰς τοῦ ἡλίου αὐγάς, 'The Lydians in their luxury laid out parks, making them like gardens, and so lived in the shade, because they thought it more luxurious not to have the rays of the sun fall upon them at all' (trans. Gulick), so that the different aspects which define the female-king are related to each other (e.g. the whiteness refers to the secluded life, the secluded life to laziness, laziness to lust or passivity and so on); the dependence upon the commonplace belongs largely to the sources, firstly to Ctesias, and after him to many writers, most of all to Clearchus; but more generally the dependence is found even in Aristotle, whose ethnographic thought proceeds sometimes by circular commonplaces

too: on Aristotle's statements about Asiatic softness see Bottin 1985, 34–5.

22. Cf. Hes. *Th.* 590–602; *Op.* 302–6, 702–5.

## 17 *Smyrna: Sophists between Greece and Rome*

1. On Larensis, see Chapter 1. Cf. Fronto (Champlin1980), Aulus Gellius (Holford-Strevens 1988) and, of course, Apuleius (cf. Chapter 7) as figures equally comfortable in Greek and Roman letters.
2. See Bowie 1970, Swain 1996, Ch.3.
3. The Romans often contrasted the Greeks of the past with the current, decadent, people who annoyed proconsuls and other administrators and were therefore only suitable to be governed (Wardman 1976, Ch. 4; Woolf 1994, 118–25).
4. Woolf 1994.
5. On this see now Bowersock 1969, Anderson 1993, Swain 1996.
6. For an exhaustive, if somewhat dated, treatment, see Cadoux 1938.
7. In the medieval period, Smyrna was largely a backwater as Levantine trade moved along the Arab-held coasts: Goffman 1990, Ch.1.
8. Assize tour: Habicht 1975, Lane Fox 1986, 484–6.
9. On the location of Oxford and Cambridge, see Robbins 1992, 5.
10. On belief in Smyrna as Homer's birthplace, see Aristides *Or.* 17, 15; Paus. 7, 5, 12 in our period. Pindar, of course, also hailed Homer as both Smyrniote and Chiot (fr. In Ps.-Plut. *Vit. Hom.* 2.2.
11. Paus., cited n. 10.
12. Ephorus FHG 1. 277 (164), and Ps.-Plut. cited n. 10 above.
13. Aristides *Or.* 18, 9; 20, 21.
14. 19.4.
15. Aristides *Or.* 20, 7; Paus. 7, 5, 1–3 for the fully embellished account.
16. BMC 14, 279, 346.
17. On Ephesus, see Dörner 1935, Rogers 1991. On baths as the most visible architectural representation of the adoption of Roman lifestyle, see Woolf 1994, 126–7. No bath building has yet been located at Smyrna, although Aristides (17, 11) remarks that 'there are so many baths, you would not know where to bathe'. These may, as with other bathing establishments in Asia Minor, have been associated with gymnasia (see Smith 1979), one of which Hadrian endowed massively at Polemo's request (Philostr. *VS* I, 25). Smaller endowments were associated with such establishments (IGRR 4. 1431, line 16).

18. Dated by Cadoux (1938, 244), to *c.* AD 64. By the time of the consulship of C. Lucceius Telesinus (AD 66), he was in Rome.
19. *Vit. Ap.* 4. 5.
20. Caspari 1915.
21. Hdt. 1. 170.
22. *Vit. Ap.* 4. 5.
23. Bean and Mitford 1970, no. 49, line 3.
24. Discussion by Liebeschuetz 1972, 243–4, with refs at 243, n. 10.
25. IK Smyrna 697.
26. 11.432, Kuhn.
27. 11, 114; 131; 237.
28. IK Smyrna 536 (= IGRR 4. 1445).
29. *VS* 1, 481.
30. *VS* 2, 511.
31. On the sophistic insistence of Atticism as the essential criterion for membership of an élite, see Swain 1996, Ch. 1.
32. de Ste Croix 1981, App. IV.
33. Niketas' *euergesiai*: Philostr., *VS* 1. 511. On euergetism in general, see Veyne 1976.
34. Philostr., *VS* 1. 512, and Cadoux 1938, 252–3.
35. Prominence: Bean 1965, 127 (Side); Bean and Mitford 1970, 13 (Kotenna).
36. Philostr., *VS* 1. 516.
37. Philostr., *VS* 1. 515. On the office of High Priest see Price 1984, 122.
38. Robert 1940, 269–75. For Smyrna, see IK Smyrna 637 (with discussion in Robert, *Hellenica* V, 81–2) for an Asiarch honoured for his provision of a five-day show.
39. IGRR 4. 1424.
40. Philostr., *VS* 1. 520.
41. Philostr., *VS* 1. 518.
42. For Southern Asia Minor alone, see M. Aurelius Obrimianus Konon of Kasai, who moved to Side (Bean and Mitford 1970, no. 21), and the family of Hermogenes of Kagrai, who became involved in politics in Selge (Bean and Mitford 1970, nos 5–11).
43. Philostr., *VS* 1. 535.
44. Philostr., *VS* 1. 531.
45. Philostr., *VS* 1. 530.
46. Spawforth and Walker 1985, 80.
47. Philostr., *VS* 1. 530: sadly, this was a brief renaissance for Smyrna, for all these buildings were swept away in the earthquake under Antoninus Pius. It is futile to speculate on our understanding of the archaeological record had the earthquake not occurred.
48. Philostr., *VS* 1. 531.
49. Arist., *Ath. Pol.* 13. 4.

50. Philostr., *VS* 1. 531.
51. Physiognomics: Anderson 1994a, 100ff; Barton 1994, Ch. 2.
52. Philostr., *VS* 1. 540.
53. Philostr., *VS* 1. 543.
54. Philostr., *VS* 2. 582.
55. *Sacred Discourse*, 4, 103–4.
56. *Sacred Discourse*, 4, 96–9.
57. *Sacred Discourse*, 4, 72–94. See now Lendon 1997, 203–14.
58. 1978, 41–5.
59. IGRR 4. 1403; Cadoux 1938, 220–3, on the Smyrniote Nemeseis.
60. *Sacred Discourse*, 3, 38–40, trans. Behr (adapted).
61. On Eunapius' sophists, see now Penella 1990, s.v. Theurgy.
62. IK Smyrna 901.
63. *VS* 2. 608.
64. IGRR 4. 1402 (= IK Smyrna 602).
65. IGRR 4. 1446 (= IK Smyrna 439; republished also by Robert, OMS III, 1588, and Hellenica XIII, 48).
66. Daphnikos; IK Smyrna 538: Pistikos; IK Smyrna 550.
67. IK Smyrna 500 (= CIG 3348).
68. IGRR 4. 1436 (= IK Smyrna 595).
69. IGRR 4. 1398 (= IK Smyrna 594).
70. IGRR 4. 1446 (= IK Smyrna 468), discussed by Robert, OMS I, 675. On mimes see now Leppin 1992.
71. IK Smyrna 658, cf. Robert, OMS I, 222.
72. On their role, see Allen 1993.
73. IGRR 4. 1430 (= IK Smyrna 598).
74. IK Smyrna 622.
75. *Praec. Reip. Gerendae*, 818C.
76. IK Smyrna 657.
77. IK Smyrna 660.
78. IK Smyrna 661.
79. IK Smyrna 662 and 663.
80. Woolf 1994: on baths, see n. 17 above.
81. IGRR 4. 1453.
82. IGRR 4. 1454.
83. IK Smyrna 635.
84. Executions in the stadium: *Martyrdom of Polycarp*, 8 and 9; *Martyrdom of Pionius*, 21.
85. *Martyrdom of Polycarp*, 10.
86. *Martyrdom of Polycarp*, 10.
87. 1986, 462–90.
88. *Martyrdom of Pionius*, 17.
89. *Martyrdom of Pionius*, 4.
90. IK Smyrna 635, line 17.

## 18 Are the Fifteen Books of the Deipnosophistae *an Excerpt?*

1. Cf. Kaibel 1887–90; Mengis 1920; Desrousseaux 1956; Wissowa 1913; Düring 1936.
2. Cf. Hemmerdinger 1989; Schweighaeuser 1801–7.
3. Cf. Letrouit 1991.
4. Cf. Kaibel 1887, xxxi–xxxvii.
5. Cf. Wissowa 1913.
6. Here and in the following pages I quote Gulick's translation, but in certain points, marked with an asterisk (*), the translation is mine.
7. Cf. Düring 1936, 238–9.
8. Mengis 1920, 22.
9. 'Evening overtook us while we were thinking over all that had been said; so let us …', Gulick.
10. "… friend Timocrates? For we had gathered early, spurred to eagerness for the cups; and while all the guests …', Gulick.
11. Cf. Mengis 1920, 4–5.
12. 'Cucumbers', Gulick.
13. 'Cucumbers', Gulick.
14. 'Canine madness during the dog-days', Gulick.
15. Düring 1936, 231.
16. Letrouit 1991, 38.
17. "Most of the guests", Gulick.
18. Martin 1931, 274–5.
19. Cf. Düring 1936, 229.
20. Desrousseaux 1956, xxii.
21. Adler 1928, xxi.

## 19 The λογόδειπνον: *Athenaeus between Banquet and Anti-Banquet*

1. I do not intend here to go into philological discussion on whether the original work consisted of thirty or fifteen books, because—even if we only possess a summary—I believe nonetheless that we can assume that the structure of the work of Athenaeus would not be different. And it is this structure and its interior functioning that is essentially of interest to me here. It is for this reason that when I refer to the work of Athenaeus I am referring to the work which has come down to us, that is a text of fifteen books. Moreover the most recent studies consider the fifteen current books to be the whole work: see Letrouit 1991, as well as Chapters 3 and 18.
2. For the Greek text of the *Deipnosophistae* I will follow the edition established by A.M. Desrousseaux (1956), for Books One and Two (i.e. for most of the *Epitome*) and for

the other books I will use Gulick's edition (1951–61). For quotations of fragments I will also give the number and the reference of the standard edition followed. Lastly, the translations of the various passages quoted from Athenaeus, as well as all the fragments, will always be mine.

3. Here we find the title of the work oddly in the singular. If it is true that 'the age of summaries can only 'personalize', and thus unify, that which was collective' (cf. Desrousseaux 1956, 1, n. 2), it is tempting to see here—like the title of a true comic play—the designation of precise character, that of the scholar at table, and thus to read this singular as the indication of a universal comic type. This would, at the beginning of the work, cast a comic light over Athenaeus' text, a light which would offer the opportunity to deploy an infinity of other comedies.

4. In place of ὅλως σοφούς Gulick here gives φιλοσόφους, following Kaibel, who, in his commentary indicates that this comes from a correction made by Wilamowitz-Moellendorf (cf. Kaibel 1887: 1); ὅλως σοφούς is E's reading and ὅλους σοφούς is C's reading. I am inclined to follow E's reading, chosen by Desrousseaux, where ὅλως has a generalizing meaning at the end of the sentence. Cf. n. 8. Thus also Schweighaeuser, Dindorf, Meineke.

5. Exactly the same expression can be found in a passage of Demosthenes: cf. *On the Crown* 296 (ἐπιλείψει με λέγονθ' ἡ ἡμέρα ..., 'the day would not be long enough for me to say ...'). It could be said that the Epitomator himself in his summary follows the rules of rhetoric so as better to seduce and convince the audience, that is to say, to attract the audience by this idea of the breadth of the work to reading Athenaeus. But the fact that Larensis' account of the banquet cannot be contained in a single day is effectively confirmed by Athenaeus' scene-setting, which develops its own account to Timocrates over several days. On this cf. Chapter 18.

6. Gulick here gives δείπνῳ instead of λόγῳ, here again following Kaibel's correction. This is in no way justified since both C and E give λόγῳ. Schweighaeuser, Dindorf, Meineke keep λόγῳ too.

7. Again an allusion to rhetoricians: it appears that, through his reading, the Epitomator gives an important place to the rhetorical form which will characterize the text and which will thus mark the importance of the spoken word in the setting of Athenaeus' banquet.

8. This series of ἄνδρες, men, must, in effect, be composed of a set of different examples which are identified as a unity in the definition of 'generally wise' (καὶ ὅλως σοφούς). They are really all of a piece. That is to say all the scholars (of all forms of παιδεία) who are present at Larensis' table, whether as guests or as scholars 'from the past', are quoted by the scholars present in flesh and blood. For this usage of ὅλως which generalizes and at the same time summarizes that which has gone before, cf. Plato *Cratylus* 406a; *Republic* 4.437b; and also Aristotle's *De Anima* 403a7.

9. *Knights* 51 where this verb is associated with two other verbs from the culinary sphere, ῥοφέω, 'to gulp down', and ἐντρώγω, 'to swallow'. The context is one of demagogy brought about by the Paphlagonian which operates by means of culinary terms associated with the art of flattering speeches, (48–9:ἤκαλλ' ἐθώπευ' ἐκολάκευ' ἐξηπάτα κοσκυλματίοις ἄκροισι, 'he wheedled, he fawned, he flattered, he deceived with fine strips of leather').

10. In Greek there is a perfect homonym (κήρυξ is a messenger, but also a kind of shell-fish) which is entirely lost in its translation into English.

11. For the use of this verb see n. 13. Cf. Chapter 1 for a different angle on the same passage.

12. In the *Thesaurus Linguae Graecae*, s.v. τὸ λογόδειπνον, the only example of this term given is that of Athenaeus; we read (vol. 5, 359): 'q.d. coena sermocinatrix, Athen. in praefatione suorum librorum quos Δειπνοσοφιστῶν inscripsit' [p. 1 B].

13. This verb προβάλλω ('throw forward', 'propose') can designate the attitude of someone who 'proposes' a subject of research to someone else; moreover this verb (or the same verb βάλλω with other suffixes like ἐν or κατά) is often used in the *Quaestiones Conviviales* of Plutarch to indicate the subjects of discussion proposed by guests. In Plutarch's text, one sees that questions which are 'thrown' are simply forms of exercise, without a link with the banquet itself, 'thrown into the middle of the guests' solely in order to draw them into the discussion. I give three examples: 3.646a 7–9: 'but I, knowing well that Ammonius had thrown his speech into the middle [of us] to draw out our spirit of research ...' (γυμνασίας ἕνεκα καὶ ζητήσεως καταβέβληκεν ἐν μέσῳ τὸν λόγον); 3.650a5–6: 'then [Florus] threw into the middle of those present this test' (προύβαλεν ἐν μέσῳ σκοπεῖν) , and finally, 3. 651a2: 'Avitus ... after having thrown an argument in the spirit of research' (ἐμβαλών τινα τῇ ζητήσει διατριβήν). It should be noticed, in fact, that from the verb προβάλλω, as well as from the verb προτείνω, mentioned earlier, are derived the two quasi-technical terms for dialectical confrontation in Aristotelian analysis, that is πρόβλημα and πρότασις (cf. *Topica* 1.4, 101 b16–29; 10, 104 a3 to 11, 104 b19). In Aristotle too πρόβλημα and πρότασις are found associated

with exercise and research (cf. ibid. 1.2, 101a 27–28, 2.104 b17, 2.105a9; 7.5, 159 a25–26). See also Brunschwig 1967, xxv–ix.

14. This kind of final exchange is reminiscent of Plato *Republic* 1.338b.

15. Cynulcus' speech continues (275c–276a): 'Clearchus of Soli, disciple of Aristotle, in his first book *On Riddles* (I am master of the term because these matters are very dear to me) said something like this: "*Phagesia*, others call the festival *Phagesiposia*. It has fallen into disuse, just like the rhapsodes who celebrated it ... and the festival of Dionysus. In it the rhapsodes came forward and put on their song in honour of the god". That is what Clearchus said. If you don't believe it, my friend, I own the book and will not begrudge it to you. From it after learning various things you will have plenty of propositions to make. In fact, he reports that Callias of Athens composed *The Grammatical Tragedy* from which Euripides made the songs and plots of *Medea* and Sophocles of *Oedipus*'. All admired the erudition of Cynulcus, and Plutarch said, 'in similar fashion a festival was held in my town of Alexandria, the *Lagynophoria*, to which Eratosthenes refers in his book entitled *Arsinoë*'.

16. Eustathius states: 'Here he observed that those who care not for the gods necessarily arrive at the sacrificial banquet and make quite sure that they eat during the sacrifice. Thus was defined a festival of eating, of the kind Clearchus the pupil of Aristotle describes. He observes that the Athenians have a festival of food (*phagesia*) which others call "food and drink" (*phagesiposia*). In fact, he says he is master of the expression because Clearchus is very dear to me.'

17. Wehrli comments (1948, 77, ad loc.): 'In den φαγήσια oder φαγησιπόσια scheint M. Nilsson, *Griechische Feste* p. 469, eine scherzhafte Erfindung Klearchos's zu sehen. Irgend einen historischen Anhalt möchte ich annehmen schon wegen der zusammen mit diesem Fest genannten ῥαψῳδῶν ἑορτή, die in keiner Weise verdächtig ist. Wie von dieser hat Klearchos außerdem wohl auch von den φαγήσια den Ort der Begehung angegeben; Anlaß der Erwähnung müssen griphosartige Veranstaltungen gewesen sein. Gegen pure Erfindung spricht schließlich, daß Athenaeus 276a unter Berufung auf Eratosthenes die alexandrinischen Lagynophoria zum Vergleich heranziehen konnte.'

18. In the *Thesaurus Linguae Graecae* we find (s.v. φαγήσια, φαγησιπόσια): 'Festa quaedam in quibus cibo potuque ad satietatem usque exhilarbantur, ut ex Athen. 7 init. [p. 275] discimus [...] Ibid. locum quendam ex Clearcho citat, ubi dicit hoc festum exolevisse' ('festivals during which

there were celebrations with food and drink until satiety, as we learn from Athenaeus 7 beginning on page 275 [...] In the same place, a passage from Clearchus is quoted where he says that this festival has disappeared.'

19. It is evidently a question of 'madness' in the sense of an excessive gastronomic passion for fish as a food. On the expression here used by Athenaeus, cf. Eustathius, *Comm. ad Hom. Il.* Λ 629, 868, 15–19. Elsewhere we find in Plutarch a reference to fish, as an animal, to describe people without intelligence: 'but, when we want to annoy or to mock, we call ignorant and stupid people "fish"' [ἰχθῦς δὲ τοὺς ἀμαθεῖς καὶ ἀνοήτους λοιδοροῦντες ἢ σκώπτοντες ὀνομάζομεν ] (Plut. *Moralia*, 975b). On the association between philosophers and fish, a hypothesis has been made that in the *Silloi* of Timon of Phlius a fishing scene took place where the fishes represented the various philosophers of the period (fragments 30, 31, 32, 38, 52, 63, 64 Di Marco were read in this sense); cf. for example Diels 1901 and Helm 1906, 303–5. Against this interpretation cf. Di Marco 1989, 27–9, 194–8. On the other hand for a true catch of philosopher-fish, cf. Lucian *Piscator*, 47–51.

20. In his commentary on the *Categories* of Aristotle, Simplicius suggests an interesting distinction between φίλοψος and ὀψοφάγος. He reports a criticism by some Stoics of the Aristotelian definition according to which quality (ποιότης) is that according to which certain things are qualified (ποιοί)—which implies a connection between the qualified and the quality which qualifies (*In Arist. Cat.* 212, 12–33; cf. Aristotle *Cat.* 8b 25). Some Stoics would have opposed to that idea a distinction between three senses of the qualified. cf. Brunschwig 1988, 113–15.

21. Cf. *Thesaurus Linguae Graecae* 's.v. ὄψον: opsonium, omne id quo praeter panem vescimur sive quod una cum pane comedimus.'

22. Compare Davidson 1995, 205–6, who, however, does not dwell on the problem of the traditional relationship between these two solid elements of the meal, but rather on the ambivalence of the ὄψον category at the centre of the Greek diet, a true supplement, at one and the same time non-essential and also complementary to bread.

23. It is significant that it is salt (ἅλας) which constitutes the first element of minimal ὄψον conceded by Plato's Socrates to the men of the true city, ἀληθινὴ πόλις, in the *Republic* (cf. 2.372a–374a). In this long passage, Socrates, who is forced to allow ὄψον into his city, will conceive of an ὄψον as it were without danger, without luxury, an ὄψον made up of salt, olives, cheese, tassel hyacinths and vegetables, to which were added some cakes (τραγήματα) made with figs, chick peas and beans. It is also interesting

to read a veritable eulogy of salt made by Plutarch who underlines the importance and even the necessity of this ὄψον, the only one of them all which cannot be overlooked, ἀπαραίτητον (cf. *Moralia*, 4.668d–669c and 684e–685f). This is problematic since ὄψον is generally considered to be what is non-essential.

24. Cf. Davidson 1993. I am convinced by his idea of a close link between fish and luxury, power, pleasure and even danger. But Davidson makes too close an analogy between ὄψον and fish, depriving the former of any other possible culinary interpretation in a wider sense. Thus, in Aeschines' speech against Timarchus, where τοὔψον (1.65) is mentioned, which Davidson understands as 'fish-stall', there is no justification for interpreting this ὄψον as the place where fish is sold, despite Davidson 1993: 62, n. 74. Even if the phrase εἰς τοὔψον is found in Aristophanes fr. 258 associated with seafood (cf. also Pollux 2.76), this does not prevent the reference here being also to a place for other delicacies. Paradoxically Davidson insists on 'explicit evidence' on the part of those who support a more general sense for ὄψον, while it is he himself who should bring decisive evidence which would allow him to identify—as he does—this location as a place specifically given over to the sale of fish. There is nothing to prevent the scholiast of Aeschines being completely right when he understood τοὔψον as: 'the place in the market place where the ὄψα were sold: because from the products sold in one place the Athenians also named the place'. Cf. also Pollux 10.19 and 9.47. Also in Aristophanes fr. 557 ἐπὶ τοὔψον has no specific meaning. The expression is interpreted by Kock generically as *ad opsonium emendum*. There is an analogous scene in Plautus' *Menaechmi* (219–20), which is the more interesting because one can see what will comprise a meal prepared with *obsonia* bought at the market (208–11): 'Order them then to prepare a meal at your house for us three/ and to buy something delicious in the market/ pig meat, gammon/ or even a half head of pig or something of that kind'. No fish is mentioned by Plautus among the delicacies (*obsonia*) from the market. And because indisputably *obsonia* (or *opsonia*) is the corresponding Latin term for *opsa*, one can realistically deduce that a general sense of 'place of delicacies' is always possible *a fortiori* in the ὄψα of Greek markets. Nothing justifies reading τοὔψον as 'fish-stall', except *LSJ* which is quoted by Davidson—which does not constitute evidence.

25. The σῖτος and ὄψον, the solid elements of the meal, are accompanied by a third component, the liquid element (οἶνος or simply ποτόν). Thus, for example, in the *Gorgias* (518b8–c1) Plato distinguishes between bread, ἄρτος,

dainties, ὄψον, and wine, οἶνος (cf. Plutarch *Moralia*, 706a3–4). For this distinction which is generally valid for the classical Greek menu cf. Davidson 1995, 205; and Dalby 1996, 22–4.

26. In Homer the σῖτος can mean generically *food*—without being in relation to ὄψον and, when mentioned with wine, it simply designates solid food which, without having a particular specification, nourishes and satisfies mankind: cf. *Odyssey* 9.87; cf. *Iliad* 10.706, where Diomedes invites his companions to satisfy their hearts with σῖτος and οἶνος, which give strength and courage to the warrior. Σῖτος can also mean the basic food of a banquet which the householder gives to nourish and welcome his guests. Cf. *Odyssey* 4.60, where Menelaus invites Telemachus and Pisistratus to devote themselves to the enjoyment of the σῖτος before speaking. He in fact offers them a real banquet of beef (65–7): (cf. 9.9 where Odysseus, speaking to Alcinous who has welcomed him, makes reference to σῖτος, to meats (κρέα) and to wine (μέθυ) to describe the joy which is born from a convivial party (2–11). Cf. also 12.19 where Circe offers Odysseus and his companions a banquet composed of σῖτος, meats (κρέα) and wine (οἶνος).

27. In the *Odyssey* (3.479), Telemachus leaves to look for his father carrying with him bread, wine and dainties (ὄψα). Ὄψον is generally associated with σῖτος and it covers everything which goes with bread, (πᾶν τὸ συνάμα σιτίοις ἐσθιόμενον) (cf. Eustathius *Comm. ad Hom. Il.* Λ 638, 867, 48). However already in Homer ὄψον can be found on its own to indicate like σῖτος—'food' generically: but in this case, in a different way from simple σῖτος, which is there to nourish, an ὄψον makes a reference, it seems to me, to the flavour and the taste which characterize it. In this sense it is more than *simply food*, and it has a connotation of agreeable, savoury food, which additionally is also always accompanied by wine. Cf. *Odyssey* 5.265–7 where Calypso sends Odysseus away after giving him wine, water, provisions and plenty of tasty ὄψα; also 6.76–6 where Nausicaa is on her way to the river where she will meet Odysseus, bringing in her basket every kind of delicious food, ὄψα and wine.

28. It is in terms of this function of ὄψον, as a stimulant of the appetite, that I understand the Homeric expression according to which the onion is the ὄψον of drink (*Iliad* 9. 629): the onion is an ὄψον because it encourages drinking. This was, if one believes Eustathius, a strategy to continue to drink until the heat made it difficult to drink any more. Cf. Eustathius *Comm. ad Hom. Il.* Λ 629, 867 33–5: 'he says that the onion is an ὄψον for the drink because it makes those who eat it thirsty, as do small cakes, while its heat

makes it uncomfortable to drink too much.' Cf. also the text of Eustathius which follows where the different nuances in the meanings of ὄψον are discussed as well as its compound ὀψοφάγος.

29. If it is true that the term ὀψοφάγος can sometimes imply disorder and instability, it seems to me nevertheless that Davidson's interpretation (1995) of ὀψοφαγία could be nuanced. I think he is a victim of the moralizing character of the texts he uses. When he has just illustrated the ambiguity of the role of ὄψον in Plato's *Republic* and Xenophon's *Memorabilia* (1995, 206–8), Davidson then goes on to read the attitude of the ὀψοφάγος as essentially 'a radical subversion of the normal order' by linking the ὀψοφάγος to corruption, indeed to revolution, as do certain comic texts (1995, 210–12). See also Davidson 1993.

30. Xenophon pursues a similar idea in the *Cyropaedia* (1.5.12) where Cyrus says, speaking of his soldiers, that they 'help themselves to hunger (λιμός) exactly as though it were ὄψον'. These same soldiers were used from childhood to eat very simply, bringing plain bread as σῖτος and some watercress as the only ὄψον (cf. 1.2.8).

31. Conversely we have already seen Socrates' criticism of the character of the ὀψοφάγος in Xenophon, *Mem.* 3.14.2–4. He accuses his neighbour at table of not respecting the relationship between bread and ὄψον but of giving himself up to the pleasure of ὄψον.

32. For a more detailed analysis of this same passage from Plutarch, which also relates it to Plato's *Timaeus* (75d–e), see Romeri 1997.

33. Socrates was going 'almost to forget' ὄψον for the men of his πόλις ἀληθινή (Plato *R.* 2.372c4: 'I had forgotten that they will have ὄψον as well'). But the ὄψον finally allowed by Socrates was not really appetizing and therefore did not show itself as a true ὄψον, as it would be understood at least by people today (that, at least, is what Glaucon thinks, 373e1: the ὄψα 'exactly like those which people have today').

## 20 Dance and Desserts: An Analysis of Book Fourteen

1. 1.14d–e, 15c–16b, 21c–22d; 2.37a–b (dance and wine); 3.97a–c, 114f, 4.129d, 130a, 134a–c, 155a–c (dance in armour at the court of Antiochus), 177a (discussing *auloi*); 5.179e–182a; 8.361f–362d; 10.424e–f; 12.520c–f (horses dancing); 13.605c, 578a, 607c–d; 14.615a–e, 616e–623d, 623e–632e.

2. See in particular the dissertations by Bapp 1885 and Latte 1913.

3. A notable exception for music being Restani 1988.

4. For other work going in this same direction see Lukinovich 1990, who underlines the fact that the *Deipnosophistae* as a literary work is construed on the interplay between the two levels of content (sympotic) and narrative context (a banquet). A detailed analysis of Book Eleven (on vases) has been proposed by Gulletta 1991; for Book Four, cf. Bruit and Schmitt-Pantel 1986, building on the thematic sequencing of the citations.

5. Düring (1936, 231) proposed a distinction between *dialogus exterior*, *dialogus interior*, and *partes enarrantes*; I follow here the more detailed subdivision proposed by Letrouit 1991, 38.

6. According to Letrouit 1991, this external narration has the function of marking the end of Books Five, Six, Nine, Ten and Fourteen, by referring to the temporary interruption of the conversation between Athenaeus and Timocrates (so already Mengis 1920, 4; see discussion below); it is this conversation which lasts over three days. Those caesurae do not refer to the end of one day's banqueting. Letrouit's arguments seem to me convincing. The very fact, however, that the interpreters dissent on the interpretation of these passages (Gulick 1927–41, I (*Introduction*), X–XI for example thinks of a banquet going on for three days, and this opinion is widespread) is interesting, for this might be used to show that the distinction between the frames is expressly blurred by Athenaeus.

7. Like the insert on Caranos' banquet according to Hippolochos, in 4.128a–130e: this is something which was *not* told during the banquet at Larensis' house. I should add that strictly speaking, from the point of view of enunciation, the interlocutors are in both cases Athenaeus and Timocrates.

8. As Lyons 1977, II puts it, 'The canonical situation of utterance is egocentric: the spatio-temporal zero-point (the here and now) is determined by the place of the speaker at the moment of the utterance, and it is this which controls tense'. Here the speaker in the two first levels is Athenaeus, supplemented in the specific level of the symposion by the Deipnosophists, but the referential context keeps changing.

9. And in very similar terms in 6.275b: ἐπεὶ δὲ εἰς ἱκανὸν μῆκος προὔβη τὰ τῶν ἀπομνημονευθέντων, αὐτοῦ καταπαύσωμεν τὸν λόγον, 'Since the matters here recorded have reached a sufficient length, let us stop our discourse at this point', directed to Timocrates, and 8.365e, see below n. 22. Here and in the following I shall be using, with some modifications, Gulick's 1927–41 translation.

10. καὶ γὰρ ὁ φιλεπιτιμητὴς Οὐλπιανὸς πάλιν τινὸς ἐπείληπτο εἰπόντος "ἔξοινος οὔκ εἰμι", λέγων "ὁ δ' ἔξοινος ποῦ", καὶ ὃς "παρ' Ἀλέξιδι ..." ἔφη, 'Yes, when one repeated the word saying "I am not drunk"', Ulpian, who is given to criticism, caught him up by saying: "where does *exoinos* occur?", to which the other replied "In Alexis ...", 14.613c. The *ordo verborum* here leaves it unclear whether it is Ulpian who once more (πάλιν) intervenes, or whether the πάλιν refers to the repetition of the word. Schweighaeuser 1805, 329 feels the difficulty of the connection formed by the καὶ γάρ introducing Ulpian's question, and explains the καὶ γάρ as prolectic of the words of the character which the narrator is going to relate ('Quod vero adiicitur, καὶ γάρ... , mira videri poterat huius ῥήσεως cum superioribus connexio per coniunctionem καὶ γάρ, etenim. Sed, nisi librariorum culpa aliquid hic peccatum est, hoc dixisse videtur Athenaeus: 'consulto dico non esse nos τῶν ἐξοίνων: nam eodem vocabulo usus est aliquis convivarum, dicens, ἔξοινος οὔκ εἰμι''').

11. Ἐπεὶ δὲ ἑκάστης ἡμέρας μετὰ τοὺς παρ' ἡμῶν καινοὺς αἰεὶ λεγομένους λόγους καὶ ἀκροάματα ἑκάστοτε διάφορα ἐπεισάγει ὁ λαμπρὸς ἡμῶν ἑστιάτωρ Λαρήνσιος ἔτι τε καὶ γελωτοποιούς, φέρε λέγωμέν τι καὶ ἡμεῖς περὶ τούτων, 'Since our illustrious host Larensis, following our discussion of novel topics brought up continually every day, introduces for our entertainment various diversions on all occasions, and notably brings on the scene buffoons, come, let us talk a while on that subject'.

12. Gulick 1927–41 I (*Introduction*) XXII inserts Amoebeus in the list of the participants to Larensis' banquet; the same is stated for example in Restani 1988 and Baldwin 1977, 41. The late arrival at the banquet of an uninvited guest (an ἄκλητος) is, starting with Alcibiades in Plato's *Symposion*, a *topos* of the literary symposion (cf. Mengis 1920, 19–20). This theme had already been touched upon, albeit slightly, in 7.307f (where a cynic ἑσπέριος ἐλθών, 'arriving in the evening', is introduced to speak).

13. Throughout the work there is an indefiniteness about the 'banquet': is there just one banquet at Larensis', are there many banquets? See for example the passage cited earlier, 14.616e; 14.623e; 15.665a (see below, n. 31) and Mengis 1920, 3. For another ποτέ at 9.372b that, once taken into account, allows us to solve one of the big structural problems of the *Deipnosophistae*, see Chapter 18.

14. It is true that this part has come to us only via the epitome, and that, apart from Amoebeus, six other characters, not mentioned expressly as guests in the introduction, are introduced as speaking in the course of the work; moreover, other guests are presupposed by the expression ῥητόρων τε

ἦν ἄγυρις τῶν κυνικῶν κατ' οὐδὲν ἀπολειπομένη, 'Of orators there was a company as numerous as that of the Cynics', (1.1d), even if no names are given for those rhetoricians. In the case of musicians, however, there is the specific mention of just one (2.1f: μουσικὸς δὲ παρῆν Ἀλκείδης ὁ Ἀλεξανδρεύς, 'And a musician was there, Alceides of Alexandria').

15. This accords with the point made by Barker in Chapter 32, on music in Athenaeus: there is practically no overlap between the information one can gather from Plutarch or Lucian, and what we find in the *Deipnosophistae*. There has been a careful choice, and the statement here might then be taken as a kind of acknowledgement by the author of this aspect of his work.

16. Long and quite correct, since in this case it is possible to check: cf. Polyb. 4.20.5–21.9.

17. ἀλλὰ μὴν οἱ ἀρχαῖοι καὶ περιέλαβον ἔθεσι καὶ νόμοις τοὺς τῶν θεῶν ὕμνους ᾄδειν ἅπαντας ἐν ταῖς ἑστιάσεσιν, ὅπως καὶ διὰ τούτων τηρῆται τὸ καλὸν καὶ σωφρονικὸν ἡμῶν, 'But the ancients included also in their customs and laws the singing of praises to the gods by all who attended feasts, in order that our dignity and sobriety might be retained with their help'.

18. This suggests strongly that many of the cases which from the point of view of the definition of the subject of the enunciation appear rather puzzling are so on purpose and not because of inadvertent cutting of sources. Cf. Chapter 12; it may well be that also in the section on music and dance too much has been attributed to authorities and too little to Athenaeus' own ingenuity.

19. 14.640c: μέλλοντος οὖν τοῦ Ποντιανοῦ λέγειν περὶ ἑκάστου τῶν παρακειμένων..., 'As Pontianus, therefore, was on the point of talking about the dishes served to us, ...'

20. In order to save Athenaeus from the charge of incapacity one might want to attribute this and other incoherences to the work of the phantom epitomator who supposedly reduced the *Deipnosophistae* from thirty to fifteen volumes ... if such an edition existed. See however Letrouit 1991, and Chapters 3 and 18.

21. Callimachus' *pinakes* are alluded to in two other passages of the *Deipnosophistae*, 6.244a (referring to this same miscellaneous *pinax*, à propos of writers of *deipna*); and 13.585b (referring to the third *pinax* of *Nomoi*; but the rules here recorded are those fixed by the courtesan Gnathaena for her guests). In both cases, the allusion to Callimachus may have the intention of underlining the literary status of texts which might have difficulties in pretending to such a status.

22. For stress on the status of the *Deipnosophistae* as a book cf. 3.127d: Ἐχέτω τέλος καὶ ἥδε ἡ βίβλος ἐπὶ τοῖς λόγοις τοῖς περὶ τῶν ἐδεσμάτων ἔχουσα καταστροφήν, 'So let this book come to an end, concluding with this discourse on "dishes"', and 4.185a: Ἐπὶ τούτοις τέλος ἐχέτω καὶ ἥδε ἡ βίβλος, ἑταῖρε Τιμόκρατες, ἱκανὸν εἰληφυῖα μῆκος, 'Upon this, let the present book come to its close, friend Timocrates, since it has taken on sufficient length'. Cf. also 8.365e: οὐκ ἀνάρμοστον δὲ καὶ τούτου τοῦ συγγράμματος τέλος εἰληφότος, ἑταῖρε Τιμόκρατες, αὐτοῦ καταπαύσω τὸν λόγον, 'Since this book has also reached an end [taken a toll] not inappropriate, friend Timocrates, I will bring the discourse to a close here', which has, as it were, Timocrates present during the writing. On this Mengis, 1920, 51 comments: 'Hier zeigt sich die Konfusion des Schriftstellers in besonders grellem Licht. Offenbar denkt sich Athenaios seinen Freund, dem er die Erzählung gibt, anwesend, er ist sogar im Dialog mit ihm begriffen (1.2a–b, 3.127d–e). Andererseits lassen gewisse Wendungen an ein vom Schriftsteller verfaßtes Buch deuten, dessen Teile er einen Abschluß geben will (3.127; 4.185a; 6.275b; 8.365c; 11.509e)'.

23. A passage raising many questions: do the 'proper seasons' imply many banquets? The deipnosophists are here represented by their books; however, the stress is on memory, of the narrator and of Timocrates, who is supposed to remember (this justifies the alphabetic order of the list of fishes). 7.277a: πολλῶν οὖν ὄντων τῶν ἰχθύων, οὓς κατὰ τὰς ἑκάστας ὥρας ἐδαινύμεθα, ὦ θαυμασιώτατε Τιμόκρατες, ... ἀπομνημονεύσω δέ σοι ἃ περὶ ἑκάστου ἔλεξαν οἱ δειπνοσοφισταί. πάντες γὰρ συνεισήνεγκαν εἰς αὐτοὺς τὰς ἐκ βιβλίων συμβολάς, ὧν τὰ ὀνόματα διὰ τὸ πλῆθος παραλείψω ... ἵνα δὲ εὐμνημόνευτά σοι γένηται τὰ λεχθέντα, κατὰ στοιχεῖον τάξω τὰ ὀνόματα. 'The fishes, then, were numerous, and we feasted on them in their proper seasons, most admirable Timocrates ... I shall, then, quote for you what the Deipnosophists said about each one. For they all brought to the company their contributions from the books, the names of which I will omit because of their number. [citation from Amphis] To make it easier for you to remember what was said, I will arrange the names alphabetically'.

24. It is a pity that the beginning of the *Deipnosophistae* (from Book One to the beginning of Book Three) is known to us only through the *Epitome*, for it might have given more detailed indications on the relationship between Timocrates and Athenaeus, as well as on the context of their encounters. As it is, we may only guess.

25. So in 6.275b: Ἐπεὶ δὲ εἰς ἱκανὸν μῆκος προὔβη τὰ τῶν ἀπομνημονευθέντων, αὐτοῦ καταπαύσωμεν τὸν λόγον, 'Since the matters here recorded have reached a sufficient length, let us stop our discourse at this point' (the subjunctive points, however, to an exhortation, and it seems easier to understand it as addressed to Timocrates rather than to the reader; this has to be taken as something between external dialogue, level 2, and external narration, level 1); in 9.411a: Ἡμεῖς δ' ἐνταῦθα καταπαύσαντες τὸν λόγον ἀρχὴν ποιησόμεθα τῶν ἑξῆς ἀπὸ τῆς τοῦ Ἡρακλέους ἀδηφαγίας, 'As for us, we will bring our account to a close here, and will resume what is to follow with the story of Heracles' gluttony' (the next book begins with an address to Timocrates); 10.459b: Τοσαῦτα καὶ περὶ τῶν γρίφων εἰπόντων τῶν δειποσοφιστῶν ἐπειδὴ καὶ ἡμᾶς ἑσπέρα καταλαμβάνει ἀναπεμπαζομένους τὰ εἰρημένα, τὸν περὶ τῶν ἐκπωμάτων λόγον εἰς αὔριον ἀναβαλώμεθα, 'The Deipnosophists having said all that on the subject of riddles, since the evening overtakes us while thinking over all that had been said, let us postpone the discussion of drinking cups until tomorrow'; 14.664f: Τοσούτων καὶ περὶ τῆς ματτύης λεχθέντων ἔδοξεν ἀπιέναι· καὶ γὰρ ἑσπέρα ἦν ἤδη. διελύθημεν οὖν οὕτως, 'After all this had been said on the subject of the *mattye*, we decided to leave; for by this time it was evening. So at this point we dissolved the meeting' (there follows, at the beginning of Book Fifteen, an address to Timocrates).

26. For example twice ματερία, 'substance', 3.113b and 113c, cf. Schweighauser 1802, 290; and for the scornful reception, cf. 3.113 d–e: Ταῦτ' ἐκθεμένου τἀριστάρχεια δόγματα τοῦ Ῥωμαίων μεγαλοσοφιστοῦ ὁ Κύνουλκος ἔφη Δάματερ σοφίας· οὐκ ἐτὸς ἄρα ψαμμακοσίους ἔχει μαθητὰς ὁ θαυμάσιος Βλεψίας καὶ πλοῦτον ἀπηνέγκατο τοσοῦτον ἐκ τῆς καλῆς ταύτης σοφίας ὑπὲρ Γοργίαν καὶ Πρωταγόραν, 'When the great Roman scholar had expounded his lore, worthy of Aristarchus, Cynulcus said: "In the name of Demeter, what learning! It's no wonder our admirable Bright-eyes has disciples by the hundreds, and has won so much wealth by this splendid erudition, surpassing Gorgias and Protagoras ..."'. For Roman words in this passage, cf. e.g. 14.647e: κάτιλλος δὲ ὀρνάτος παρὰ Ῥωμαίοις ..., 'The *catillus ornatus*, as the Romans call it, ...'. Schweighaeuser 1805, 556 suggests however that this Chrysippus might be the one mentioned by Diog. Laert. 7. 186, as having Γεωργικὰ γεγραφώς.

27. Schweighaeuser 1805, 573. It must be said, however, that it is quite appropriate to have a Harpocration of Mendes (in Egypt) speaking of the παγκαρπία in Alexandria. On how Athenaeus 'invents' the names of his diners cf. Mengis

1920, 40–3: the example given concerns the doctors Daphnus of Ephesus and Rufinus of Nicaea: clearly built on the real and well-known doctor Rufus of Ephesus. In the case of Daphnus (as, I would suggest, for Chrysippus of Tyana) the origin is crucial for the trick.

28. This part is problematic, insofar as two subjects already discussed, the *hemina* (a cup) and the *amylon* (a cake of the finest meal), are taken up by Ulpian as new, and then discussed by Larensis, without any mention being made of the preceding discussion; a fragment of Epicharmus already cited earlier on the *hemina* is cited again (14.648d = 11.479b); see Schweighaeuser 1805, 574–75 for a possible explanation (the difference between the use in the neuter and in the masculine; this does however not seem sufficient). For the explanation of the joke in 14.649a–b (a passage interpreted by others as incoherent) cf. Mengis 1920, 92.

29. Lukinovich 1990, 270 recognizes the change in speaker (she uses it to develop her argument that Ulpian's 'supplementary speech' imitates on the level of discourse the character of the 'second tables' brought in at the banquet a little before); but Gulick ad loc. does not signal it, nor do Casaubon and Schweighaeuser 1805, 616; what is astonishing is that they do not seem to have perceived the resulting incoherence. Even if we did not have to look for a change in speaker, the κἀγὼ would seem to point to such a change.

30. Cf. above n. 25, Letrouit 1991, and Chapter 18. I must admit that I am perplexed in some of the cases; the beginning of Book Nine in particular seems difficult to accommodate. One wonders how much one is prepared to accept in order to explain away structural difficulties.

31. 'If some god should give me the sweet-tongued melodiousness of Nestor or Phrygian Antenor, as the all-wise Euripides says, O friend Timocrates, I should be quite unable further to recall for you the things that were said so often in these banquets of ours, because of the diversity, but also of the similarity of the novel devices brought forth from time to time', Εἴ μοι τὸ Νεστόρειον εὔγλωσσον μέλος / Ἀντήνορός τε τοῦ Φρυγὸς δοίη θεός, κατὰ τὸν πάνσοφον Εὐριπίδην, ἑταῖρε Τιμόκρατες, οὐκ ἂν δυναίμην ἀπομνημονεύειν ἔτι σοι τῶν πολλάκις λεχθέντων ἐν τοῖς περισπουδάστοις τούτοις συμποσίοις διά τε τὴν ποικιλίαν καὶ τὴν ὁμοιότητα τῶν ἀεὶ καινῶς προσευρισκομένων.

32. The only detailed study of Athenaeus' literary technique is still Mengis 1920, who, however, uses his observations to sustain the thesis of the existence of an original edition in thirty volumes; to this study may be added Lukinovich 1990.

33. Cf. Mengis 1920, 47: 'Die diegematische Form nun, die an sich schon bedeutend schwieriger ist als die rein dramatische Form, stellte den Schriftsteller vor eine Ausgabe, bei der sein geringes künstlerisches Vermögen versagen mußte.'

34. Mengis 1920: 47, pointing to Plato's habit of inserting at particular significant points a χθές, an expedient imitated by Cicero's *nuper* and Putarch's ἔναγχος.

35. Eur. *Andr.* 1129–36; Luc. *Salt.* 9; schol. Pind. *Pyth.* 2. 127 (citing Aristotle, fr. 543, 1 Gigon = 519 Rose); schol. B Heph. 299 Consbr.; Hes. π 4464 πυρριχίζειν, and other texts.

\* My warmest thanks to Giovan Battista D'Alessio, Annette Loeffler and Pierre Voelke for reading and discussing this paper with me.

## 21 *Pleasure and Pedantry in Athenaeus*

1. Stewart 1997, 43, 63–5.
2. For Athenaeus' subversion of Plato cf. Anderson 1993, 173, 178.
3. *LIMC* s.v. *Bios*, Leipen 1969, 231 on Royal Ontario Museum Accession No. 967.132 from Homs.
4. Murray 1988, 4–5, Grottanelli 1995, 62–89, who discusses some Roman examples including Petronius and Martial.
5. I do not intend to go into the question of Ulpian's identity here. It seems to me very likely that the Syrian Ulpian of the *Deipnosophistae* is indeed supposed to represent the famous jurist from Tyre, for whom see now the entry in *OCD*³ s.v. *Domitius Ulpianus*. The main problem with this identification concerns his death. He was appointed praetorian prefect by Severus Alexander but was murdered by his troops in 223. Athenaeus does indeed describe his own Ulpian's death as sudden, coming a few days after his departure from the banquet and allowing 'no opportunity for illness' to afflict him. He also describes his death as 'fortunate' (εὐτυχῶς), however, although causing much grief to his companions. Some have thought this description impossible to reconcile with murder. However, Athenaeus explains the use of the word 'fortunate' with reference only to the absence of illness. We might also note the lengths to which Athenaeus goes to exclude politics and violence from his dialogue. A reference to Ulpian as praetorian prefect here would be jarring. But see Chapter 1. Finally, the parallels with Socrates' death in Plato's *Phaedo* are easy to draw. Both are intellectual martyrs, victims of the violent and disorderly state. Yet Plato's entire dialogue is designed to demonstrate that Socrates' judicial murder is an occasion for happiness rather than

despair. At the end the philosopher prays for a happy
(εὐτυχῆ) removal to the other side, a removal which, like
Ulpian's, is marked, finally, by silence in response to a
question. Phaedo notes that he was mourning not Socrates
but his own misfortune in being deprived of such a
'companion' (117c–18a).

6. Sophists occasionally resorted to citations in order to
confute an upstart opponent. Herodes Atticus, for
instance, was supposed to have performed a *tour de force* of
learning by citing Epictetus chapter and verse, a feat more
notable, perhaps, because it was unusual.

7. This sense of loss for an entire intellectual world underlies
Plato's dialogues too of course. The force of this
interpretation depends on a late date for Athenaeus. If he
is writing after the death of Ulpian of Tyre, he would be
close to what Graham Anderson has identified as an
apparent hiatus in the world of letters, as in much else
(Anderson 1993, 39–41). In this respect the
Dinnersophists might be close to Philostratus' *Lives of the
Sophists*, a résumé of a group whose *Blütezeit* might seem to
be passing. It remains, however, completely circumstantial,
the coincidence of a text clinging unusually strongly to
older texts at a time of increasing chaos. There are,
moreover, other, perhaps more plausible, ways of
accounting for Athenaeus' peculiar fondness for citation,
notably the arcane nature of his material and the bitterly
argumentative nature of the discussion.

8. Davidson 1997, Ch. 1, cf. Anderson 1993, 93–4.
9. Garlan 1995, 55.
10. Davidson 1997, 264–5 cf. Anderson 1993, 180–5.
11. Cf. Murray 1983, esp. 270–1.
12. Ephebes were required to submit 100 rolls to the
Ptolemaion at Athens on graduation. The tradition of
books as gifts was well established. Rare books were
particularly valuable, a value which is underlined
perhaps by the esoteric nature of the Dinnersophists'
contributions.
13. Swain 1996, 364 (with notes 19 and 20).
14. Lissarrague 1990, esp. Ch. 5.
15. Cf. Anderson 1993, Ch. 9.
16. Davidson 1997, 51–2.

## 22 *The Politics and Poetics of Parasitism: Athenaeus on Parasites and Flatterers*

1. *Contra* e.g. Swain 1996, 11–12, claiming that Athenaeus
does 'not have much to say about the relationship *between*
Greece and Rome' (his emphasis).
2. Implicit at Bowie 1974, 180; explicit at Swain 1996, 49–51.

Athenaeus does not, however, entirely ignore the Roman
present: see Baldwin 1976, 22–3 and Chapter 1.
3. Bowie 1974 is still fundamental; see also Bowie 1982.
4. The terms 'symbolic' and 'economic capital' derive from
the trenchant analysis of Bourdieu 1977. For a successful
application of Bourdieu's ideas to the culture of Roman
Greece, see Gleason 1994, xx–xxvi.
5. For a discussion of the relationship between the terms
παράσιτος and κόλαξ, see Nesselrath 1985, 88–121. The
two terms, however, overlap to a great degree in the Roman
world (Damon 1997, 14–15), and I have not drawn an
overly firm distinction between them. Damon 1997
usefully discusses the relationship between the literary
sources on parasitism and Roman society more generally;
the book, however, appeared at a late stage during the
composition of this chapter and it has not been possible to
integrate its findings more thoroughly into the discussion
here.
6. Dupont 1977, 9–16.
7. Dupont 1977, 46–7.
8. Donlan 1985.
9. 'Unlike the practice at the early Greek sympotic gatherings
… Roman convivial equality can never have been other
than a very fragile kind' (D'Arms 1990, 318). D'Arms is
right to contrast the aristocratic nature of Greek banquets
with the more demotic flavour of *convivia*, but the
implication that early Greek feasts were free of social
hierarchy is misleading.
10. Bourdieu 1977 argues against attempts to understand
societies in terms of rules and regulations; social life, he
argues, fundamentally depends not only upon the
proclamation of rules, but also upon their manipulation and
infringement. See further Bourdieu 1990.
11. Plut. *Mor.* 152d; Jeanneret 1991, 98.
12. Konstan 1996 is the most thorough survey, but his polemic
against cultural relativism (3–6; 14–18) is to my mind
misplaced. See also Nagy 1979, 103–8; Taillardat 1982;
Herman 1987.
13. Classical Athens associates κολακεία with demagoguery:
see Eupol. frr. 156–90 Kassel-Austin, *Grg.* 463b and ff.
*passim*, esp. 503a (κολακεία … καὶ αἰσχρὰ δημηγορία);
Ar. *Wasps.* 45; 418–9. κολακεία does not appear before the
fifth century: the Asius fragment (= Athen. *Deipn.* 125d)
employs the word κνισοκόλαξ, but is of doubtful date; nor
can the passages in the *Apophthegmata septem sapientium* (fr.
4.4) and Aesop (*Fab.* 93 [3], 10; 126[2], 11; 151a[l], 5;
163[2] 7; 163[3], 6; 222[1], 7; 166[a l.], 17; 224[a I.], 10;
*Prov.* 135.1; (3) be dated securely before the fifth century.
14. Xen. *Mem.* 2.9; Pl. *Resp.* 575e; Ar. *Eth.* Nic. 1159a14–15; see

also 1127a7; 1124b30–1125a2, with Millett 1989, 32. See further Konstan 1996, 93–8.

15. The idea of a 'zero-sum game' is that '[t]he cultural understanding of competition was not simply that winners gained rewards and honor, but that losers were stigmatized with shame and penalties in proportionate amounts, or, to put it another way, winners won at the direct expense of losers' (Winkler 1990, 47).

16. Roman systems of patronage have evoked much interest in recent years: see esp. Saller 1982 and the essays in Gold 1982 and Wallace-Hadrill 1989a, esp. Braund 1989, Rich 1989, Wallace-Hadrill 1989b.

17. Swain 1990.

18. Pelling 1989, 203.

19. On Athenaeus' use of the language of πολυτέλεια, see Lukinovich 1990, 267.

20. See e.g. Plut. *Alex.* 74.2–3; Philostr. *VA* 1.27–8; Hld. *Aeth.* 7.19.1–3

21. Greeks traditionally defined themselves exclusively, in opposition to non-Greek 'barbarians': after Roman conquest, the question of what to do with the Romans became an urgent and knotty one. In the best-known solution, addressed to (or purporting to be addressed to) the city of Rome, Aelius Aristides asserts that the Romans have replaced the Greek/barbarian distinction with a Roman/non-Roman division (*Ad Rom.* 63).

22. For an introduction to the issues, see esp. Montrose 1989; Gallagher 1989.

23. Xenophon writes of the need for a σπουδή as παιδιά (*Symp.*1.1; see also 4.28; Plut. *Mor.* 147f; Ath. *Deipn.* 15.702c) See further Dupont 1977, 45–6.

24. Odysseus' fondness for his belly and his behaviour at the suitors' table make him an ideal parasite *avant la lettre;* see Luc. *Parasit.* 10; 11; 49.

25. Lukinovich 1990, 269–71; Jeanneret 1991, 67–70

26. See Jeanneret 1991, 112–39 on this process.

27. Lukinovich 1990, 267–8. Athenaeus' language of ποικιλία also marks him as a miscellanist, comparable to Aelian of the ποικίλη ἱστορία (Anderson 1997, 2182–3).

28. Bakhtin from whom the critical study of narrative 'dialogism' claims descent, singles out Athenaeus for providing especially interesting evidence for ancient precursors of the novelistic *'polyglossia'* which he sees as culminating with Dostoyevsky: see Bakhtin 1981, 53.

29. The apology for length is a standard epideictic trick: see Dem. 60.6; *Hyper.* fr. 4.2 Blass, and further Philostr. *VA* 4.34; 6.35; 7.2.

30. Relihan 1993, 5, 18 opposes Frye by excluding the *Deipnosophistae* from the genre of Menippean satire. This is

a shame, as his arguments could be extended interestingly to cover Athenaeus.

31. See esp. Plut. *Mor.* 51b–c; 53b–54f on the mimetic qualities of the flatterer; see *Mor.* 52b for the description παντοδαπός ... καὶ ποικίλος.

32. Ahl 1984, 177, 185–92; Hesk, forthcoming.

33. Cf. *Euthryphr.* 15d and esp. *Ion* 54le; cf. also Hld. *Aeth.* 2.24.4. Proteus' *poikilia* is evoked as an aesthetic by Nonnus (*Dion.* 1.14).

34. On the importance of this passage for later writers, see Jeanneret 1991, 79–82.

35. Plutarch also compares flattery with cooking (*Mor.* 51c).

36. Baldwin 1976, 22–3.

37. I do not wish to affirm without reservations a Foucaultian theory of power, but I too see 'the space of language, culture and society as an open, mobile and dynamic 'field' of interrelations, in which power is everywhere and comes from everywhere' (Bannet 1989, 168).

38. This chapter has benefited greatly from responses to it as a result of the Athenaeus Project excellently organized by David Braund and John Wilkins. In addition, I should like to thank Jon Hesk for his helpful comments. All unattributed references are to Athenaeus' *Deipnosophistae*, cited from the edition of G. Kaibel (Leipzig, 1887–90).

## 23 *The Banquet of Belles-Lettres: Athenaeus and the Comic Symposium*

1. See now in general Murray 1990; Slater 1991.

2. It is no surprise that the first example in Bremmer's new treatment of jokes and joke-books in antiquity (Bremmer 1997) should be from Xenophon's *Symposium* (11).

3. Athenaeus mentions a Cynic symposium by Parmeniscus (156c). Helm 1906 remains a valuable collection of material on Cynic tradition, though the general argument is dangerously speculative (on Lucian's *Symposium*, Helm 1906, 254–74).

4. For a brief overview of the sympotic tradition relative to Lucian, see Bompaire 1958, 314–20. As far as Menippus is concerned, Relihan (1993, 228f.) seems as sure as Helm did long ago as to the character of Menippean satire: but the alleged survivals are very varied

5. For the gastronomic tradition in Horace, see Rudd 1966, 202–23.

6. Cf. *Deipn.* 14.628c–d, alluding to the story told by Herodotus 6.129; Lucian uses it typically as a proverbial tag, *Apol.* 15.

7. For possible echoes in Petronius, see Walsh 1970, 133f.

8. In fact the proportion of jokes on food or sympotic activity

in the *Philogelos* is surprisingly small, considering the focus on the world of the everyday which such a collection of *facetiae* naturally reflects. This may underline the fact that symposia at least in a Greek context are associated with culture and refinement.

9. Note that in Plutarch, *Quaest. Conv.* 3.6 (Mor. 653e) it is felt that Zeno should have sited his discussion on the right time for sex ἐν συμποσίῳ τινὶ καὶ παιδειᾷ rather than a treatise on government.

10. For an attempt to survey the Menippean tradition associated with it, see Relihan 1993b.

11. The speech may be briefly referred to at 5.186a, if we accept the plausible emendation proposed in Gulick's note ad loc. It is characteristic of Athenaeus' tastes that the longest catena of passages about Alcibiades concerns his luxurious habits (12.534b–5e).

12. For this 'adoxographic' outlook on culture as a whole in the sophistic outlook, see Anderson 1993, 171–99 (on Athenaeus, 176–85, *passim*).

13. For his role in the tradition, see now Wilkins and Hill 1994, 9–19.

14. Brief commentary in Wilkins and Hill 1994.

15. I am less sure than Relihan (1993a, 234) about making Athenaeus himself a cook of the work: one might play with words ad infinitum and style the work a confection. But there is no getting away from the fact that cookery is the ultimate kind of anti-Platonism, and that the author is well aware of this.

16. Cf. Henry 1992: we have of course to bear in mind that love in general is susceptible to treatment as a food metaphor ('If music be the food of love....'), and that Athenaeus is inclined to exploit a wide range of metaphors between all sorts of subjects and food.

17. Cf. Sullivan 1968, 134f., quoting Seneca *EP.* 47.

## 24 *Between Ichthyophagists and Syrians: Features of Fish-eating in Athenaeus'* Deipnosophistae *Books Seven and Eight*

1. I refer first of all to the large quotation from Diphilus of Siphnos, in *Deipn.* 8.355a–7a, and then to the great number of references from Diocles of Carystus, Hicesius and Lynceus of Samos in Book 7.

   My best thanks are due to Stefania Dai Prà for helping me to translate this paper from Italian; I have to thank also D. Asheri, O. Longo and E Avezzù for reading my work; very special thanks to K. Sidwell for correcting my English.

2. The English translations of Athenaeus quoted below are those of Gulick.

3. Those who translated into Latin did not have the same difficulties, because the Latin term they used, *pueri*, means either children or slaves. Daléchamp translated, for instance, *pueri ab incunabulis piscibus nutriti*; Schweighaeuser, *piscibus vescentes pueri*.

4. Cf. Sulek 1983, 75–85.

5. The verb τρέφω, however, often refers to slaves, cf. *LSJ*, s.v. τρέφω, II 2.

6. See on this subject Longo 1987, 9–53. Agatharchides' work, *De mari Erythraeo*, is lost, but we find large excerpts of it in Photius (*Bibl.* 7.30–49) and Diodorus (3.15–21); they are collected in a synoptic edition in *GGM* I 129–41: see also Burstein's translation (Burstein 1989). Fish-eating tribes lived on the coasts of north-east Africa, in the Arabian peninsula and in modern Baluchistan (between Iran and Pakistan). Agatharchides speaks essentially about Fish-eaters of Africa and the Arabian peninsula. Another source, Nearchus' *Periplus*, quoted by Arrian, *Ind.* 22–31, refers to Gedrosian Fish-eaters. A third fragmentary source, the anonymous *Periplus maris Rubri*, mentions some fish-eating tribes living on the Arabian coast of the Red Sea and on the South Yemen coast. Also Porphyr., *Abst.* 4.21 refers to the borderline case of Nomads, Troglodytes and Fish-eaters, to whom all abstinence was foreign.

7. We can see it both in Athenian comedy (Alexis, Timocles, Antiphanes) and in the historians (Polemo Periegetes, Clearchus). The term φίλιχθυς is applied in *Deipn.* 1.5e to the musician Philoxenus; in *Deipn.* 3.104d and 8.338f it refers to Callimedon; in 8.337e it is used about Dorion; in 338d about Phayllus, in 341a about Androcydes of Cyzicus; in 344c about the auletes Technon; in 358d it refers to a certain Philoumenos, a character of Antiphanes' *Agroikos* or *Butalion*.

8. Gilula 1995, 386–99; Davidson 1993, 53–66; Davidson 1995, 204–13 and 1997, 2–22; 26–35 and 144–7. I fully agree with Davidson that ὄψον, ὀψοφάγος, ὀψοφαγεῖν concern fish, not food in general.

9. In Alex., 47 K-A *ap. Deipn.* 8.338d, Phayllus, like a hurricane, takes with him the whole fish catch; in Alex., 249 K-A *ap. Deipn.* 8.340b, Callimedon manifests a tyrannical behaviour at the fish-market; see also Antiph., 188 K-A *ap. Deipn.* 8.343a.

10. Plutarch, *Quaest. Conv.* 4.2, 3 adds that Androcydes painted Scylla's fish out of passion rather than for art's sake.

11. Most of the ὀψοφάγοι (Hypereides, Timarchus, Aristonicus, Callias, Callimedon, Callisthenes, Misgolas) are well-known names in fourth-century Athens. Phayllus might be the son of Pheidippus and related to a wealthy Athenian family; in epigraphic documents his name is

related to the expenses of the trierarchy; cf. Davies 1971, 533. Taureas, mentioned with Phoinicides, might be identified with a well-known Athenian citizen, contemporary with Demosthenes and also involved in the Harpalus affair (cf. Kassel-Austin, *ad* Antiph., 188).

12. From comedy: Alex., 76.7–8 K-A *ap. Deipn.* 6.226f; Antiph., 27.10–11 K-A *ap. Deipn.* 8.338f. As for the orators, Aeschin., 1.95 censures Timarchus and his friend Hegesander because they ruined themselves with ὀψοφαγία. Dem., 19.229, charges Philocrates with ὀψοφαγία, corruption and connivance with the enemy Philip. As for historians: the ὀψοφάγος Diocles is censured by Theocritus of Chios, *FHG* II. 87 *ap. Deipn.* 8.344b; the tragic poet Choerilus spends on ὀψοφαγία the four minae a day he receives from Archelaus in Ister, *FGrH* 334 F 61 *ap. Deipn.* 8.345d.

13. It is one of the most typical traits of the ὀψοφάγος, according to *Deipn.* 7.276f; Hermippus (Hist., 68a II Wehrli *ap. Deipn.* 8.342c) says that Hypereides used to take walks in the fish-market early in the morning.

14. Callimedon in Alex., 249 K-A *ap. Deipn.* 8.340b , Maton and Diogeiton in Antiph., 188.16–18 K-A *ap. Deipn.* 343a; Hypereides in Timocl., 4 K-A *ap. Deipn.* 341f; 17 K-A *ap. Deipn.* 342a.

15. Phoenicides and Taureas in Antiph., 188.4 K-A *ap. Deipn.* 8. 342f.

16. The poet Antagoras, in Hegesand., *FHG* IV. 416 *ap. Deipn.* 8. 340f; cf. Plut. *Quaest. Conv.*, 4.4.2.

17. The sophist Maton in Antiph., 117 K-A *ap. Deipn.* 8.342d and in Anaxil., 20 K-A *ap. Deipn.* 8.342d. The parasite Telephus, in 5.186d snatches the upper parts of the fish from Zeno (from Bion, in *Deipn.* 8.344a).

18. Theophrastus used to do it, in order to imitate the glutton's typical gestures (Hermippus Hist., 51 Wehrli *ap. Deipn.* 1.21 a–b). Cf. Fortenbaugh-Huby-Long 1985, 274). No wonder Theophrastus, who composed *Characters* and a work Περὶ ὑποκρίσεως *On playing a part*, according to D.L. 5.48, was concerned with the typical traits of the ὀψοφάγος.

19. Phoryscus in Hegesand., *FHG* IV 417; Zeno eats up a whole octopus (290, *SVF* I 66 = Antig., p. 119 Wilamowitz).

20. Callimedon in Eub., 8 K-A *ap. Deipn.* 8.340d; Phoenicides, in Euphanes, 1 K-A *ap. Deipn.* 8.343b; the ὀψοφάγος Diocles in *Deipn.* 8.344b; Pythillus used to wear a kind of glove to put hot foods into his mouth in Clearch., 54 Wehrli *ap. Deipn.* I 6d. *Suda*, s.v. ὀψοφάγος mentions a certain Philoxenus of Leucas, bearing the same name of Philoxenus of Cythera. He accustomed his hands and his mouth to hot water, in order to swallow hot fish; cf. *Suda*, s.v. Τιμαχίδας.

21. Hedylus, epigr. 9 Gow-Page *ap. Deipn.*, 8.345b. The table-companions beg Cleio to eat by herself: a real sign of wildness. In Ael. *VH* 2.41, among the lovers of wine (φιλοπόται), we can find a woman, Cleo, who might be identified with the Cleio from Hedylus. During the symposia Cleo used to compete with men in drinking wine, and she often won 'shameful victories'.

22. Diocles in Theocritus of Chios, *FHG* II. 87 *ap. Deipn.* 344b; the piper Technon in Clearchus, 58 Wehrli *ap. Deipn.* 8.344c.

23. Hypereides in Philet., 2 K-A; Callias in Axionic., 4 K-A.

24. Philocrates in Dem. 19. 229, Timarchus in Aeschin., 1.42.

25. Atargatis in *Deipn.* 8.346d–f, Nisaeus, the elder of the two sons of Dionysius, in Theopomp., *FGrH* 115 F 187 *ap. Deipn.*, 10.436a–b. Nisaeus is mentioned among the lovers of wine in Ael. *VH* 2.41; on the tyrannical ὀψοφάγος at the fish-market, see above n. 9.

26. Philoxenus of Cythera, in Machon, 9 Gow *ap. Deipn.* 8.341a–d, dies from an attack of indigestion; Diogenes dies from cholera, because he has eaten a raw octopus (cf. D.L., 6.2). Julian, in *Adv. cyn. ign.* 12.16–18, offers an ascetic view of this anecdote: he suggests that Diogenes had eaten a raw octopus in order to defeat gluttony and attain *apatheia*.

27. In Book 8: the piper Dorion (8. 337c–8b); the poet Antagoras (340f-1a); the painter Androcydes of Cyzicus (341a); Philoxenus of Cythera (341b–e); the politicians Hypereides and Callias (341e–2c); the philosopher Aristotle (342c); the sophist Maton (342d); the tragic poet Melanthius (343c); Aristippus the Socratic (343c–d); the Argive tragedian Leontheus (343e–f); the cynic Bion (344a); the piper Technon (*Deipn.* 344c); the comedy writer Alexis (344c); the tragic poet Nothippus (344c–d); the tragic actor Mynniscus (344d–e); the *mantis* Lampon (344e–f); Zeno of Citium (*Deipn.* 345d); the poet Choerilus (*Deipn.* 345d), and others. Antagoras, Philoxenus and Androcydes are mentioned as gluttons in Plut. *Quaest. conv.* 4.4,2 too. Dorion used to be a guest at Nicocreon's banquets, according to Lynceus of Samos, and a guest of Philip II of Macedon, according to Theopomp., *FGrH* 115 F 236; Antagoras lived for some time at Antigonus Gonatas' court, as Hegesander says *(FHG* IV 416); Choerilus lived at Archelaus' court, as Ister says *(FGrH* 334 F 61).

28. *Deipn.* 8.344b. The philosopher Bion eats up greedily the upper parts of the fish snatched from his companion, quoting Eur. *Bacch.* 1229: he would be Ino, while the fish would be Pentheus. The story is linked with Zeno in *Deipn.* 5.186d (291, *SVF* I.291) and in D.L. 7.19, where it is said that the Stoic philosopher simulated gluttony to teach a lesson to a greedy fellow.

29. *Deipn.* 8.341e = D.L., 6.77.
30. Timae., *FGrH* 556 F 156, and *Suda*, s.v. Ἀριστοτέλης. On Aristotle's gluttony see also an epigram of Theocritus of Chios, 738 Lloyd-Jones Parsons. Other opponents condemned Aristotle's luxury: the Pythagorean Lycon of Iasos and Isocrates' disciple Cephisodorus: cf. Düring 1957, 377–8.
31. Luc. *Symp.* 11, 42–43; *Herm.*, 11; Alciphr. 3.19.
32. On the parasite's role at the banquet, see Longo and Avezzù 1992, 14–22; cf. Chapter 22.
33. Archipp., 28 K-A *ap. Deipn.* 7 343c; cf. Eust. 1201.3. See further Chapter 41.
34. The word ὀψομανής is used by Chrysippus, *SVF* 3. 167, to indicate a slave to the passion for *opson*; the 'mad for dainties' is compared to the οἰνομανής ('mad for wine') and the γυναικομανής ('mad for women'). The charge of gluttony has a revival in the Neoplatonic philosophers (e.g. Porph. *Abs.* 1.2. 3) and in Christian writers (e.g. Clem. Al., *Protr.* 2.38. 4 Mondrésert).
35. *Deipn.* 7.276e.
36. 'The Cynics, thinking that the Eating-festival was to be celebrated, cheered up more than anyone else.' (*Deipn.* 7.275c); 'The long discussion on the subject of fish was evidently irksome to Cynulcus.' (*Deipn.* 8.331c).
37. On Athenaeus' views of Archestratus, see Chapter 2. Another refined figure is that of the master cook mentioned in Machon, 2 K-A *ap. Deipn.*, 8.346a–b): 'I am a gourmand [...] He who would not spoil the materials entrusted to him must have a passionate love of them.'
38. So Eustathius, 1720.59, can say: 'The same orator (sc. Athenaeus') appreciates fish which—he says—not even the blessed gods despise.' He refers to 7.302e, where Athenaeus quotes from Eriphus, 3.4 K-A.
39. Athenaeus does not say, but surely knew, that in Egypt there was a large number of sacred fish. We draw this datum from other sources: Herodotus, 2.72, mentions, among the sacred fishes of the Nile, the λεπιδωτός, perhaps the *Perca nilotica* (which Athenaeus puts in his list of Egyptian fishes in 7.312b); Plutarch, *Is. et Os.* 18, mentions also ὀξύρυγχος, λάτος, and φάγρος as fishes venerated in Egypt: but every place had its own sacred fish. On this subject, Thompson 1947; Hopfner 1913; Cumont 1914. There may be a connection between the cult of the eel and the Egyptian god Atum: cf. Daressy 1904; Hopfner 1913, 55 associates the eel with the Nile.
40. Cf. Gilula 1995, 391.
41. Eustathius, 1720, 53 explains that the most precious fish, like *anthias* (cf. Thompson 1947, 14–16), and *labrax*, the bass, and others used to be called 'gods'. The glutton

Callisthenes calls the eel θεά in Antiph., 27.10–11 K-A. Cf. Eubul., 64.3 K-A. Hegesander (*FHG* IV. 416 *ap. Deipn.*, 8.338a), remembers that ὀρφώς (perhaps stone bass), γλαύκισκος (impossible to identify) and γόγγρος (conger) were gods' names for the ὀψοφάγος Dorion.
42. Cf. D.S., 15.92, 3, C. Nep. *Chabr.* 2. 2–3, Plut., *Ages.* 37.
43. Cf. Boulenger 1907, 402–5. On fish-eating in ancient and Hellenistic Egypt, see Stöckle R.E. 4. 459–60.
44. Cf. Gilula 1995, 391.
45. According to Arist. *HA* 591b 10–13, θυννίς, like the other species of tunny, belongs to an intermediate class of fishes, which is between the herbivorous (e.g. rock-fishes) and flesh-eating fishes (dolphin, dentex, gilthead, selacians and cephalopoda); cf. *HA* 591b 17. Also Renna 1995, 111–26.
46. Athenaeus quotes lines 1–17 in 7.310 a–e; lines 13–20 in 4.163c.
47. See Kassel-Austin ad loc.
48. See also Eust. 1720.52.
49. It is noticeable that Athenaeus does not mention the various rules forbidding fish-consumption which were in use in ancient Greece. We know them from other sources, Plutarch and Aelian especially. According to Ael., *NA* 9.51, the initiates to the Eleusinian mysteries were forbidden to eat the red mullet, as were Hera's priests at Argos (*NA* 9.65). In Plut., *Quaest. conv.* 8.8, 4 the same prohibition concerns Poseidon's priests at Leptis. In 8.355b, quoting from Semus of Delos, Athenaeus recalls that the Delian women sacrifice to Brizo all types of flesh except fish. But he does not relate this sacrifice to any alimentary taboo; cf. also Porph., *Abst* 4.16, Paus. 1.38, 1; see Bodson 1975, 47–51.
50. Eust. 1720.23 points out that in *Erechtheus* [sic], Aristophanes used the word ἄπιχθυς 'one who has not tasted fish' referring to the 'barbarian' Syrians.
51. Cf. Porph. *Abst.* 2.34, 2.
52. Cf. Burkert 1962, 194.
53. Cf. D.L. 8.37–38; cf. Delatte 1915, 289–91.
54. Plutarch adds the quotation of the Pythagorean dogma στεγάσαι φρενὸς ἔλλοπος εἴσω (*VS* 31 B 5).
55. Cf. Hopfner 1921, 243.
56. Eust., 1720. 30–2, resolutely objects that there was no connection between Pythagoreans' abstinence and the heroic age.
57. Plutarch distinguishes ancient Pythagoreans from Alexicrates' disciples (*Quaest. conv.* 8.8,1). The distinction between *Pythagorikoi* (Pythagoras' disciples), *Pythagoreioi* (the second generation of disciples) and *Pythagoristai* (later imitators), mentioned in *Schol. Theocr.* 14, 5a and in *Suda*, s.v. *Pythagorikoi*, is not prominent in comedy or in Athenaeus.

58. Silence is the only Pythagorean rule the Cynics observe (Cynulcus notwithstanding) at the Deipnosophists' banquet, according to Magnus in *Deipn.* 4.162b; and this is due only to their incapacity for discourse. Cf. *Deipn.* 7.308d.
59. See Donini 1982; Dodds 1970, 30–1.
60. With the exception of Aelian, whose anecdotes on Pythagoras and his disciples are similar in spirit to those of Athenaeus.
61. 'Das Fisch-Tabu der Syrer fiel den Griechen immer wieder auf,' Burkert 1972, 228. On the Syrian custom Burkert 1972, 227–31.
62. Another reference to this custom is taken from Timocles, 4.9 K-A *ap. Deipn.*, 8.342a; Meleager of Gadara, in his *Charites* (= Ath, 4.157b), asserts that Homer was Syrian by birth, because he excluded fish from the Achaeans' banquets.
63. Cf. Luc., *Syr. D.* 45; an inscription from Smyrna of the first century BC attests a sacred law protecting the Syrian Goddess' fish. See Sokolowski 1955, 17.
64. Athenaeus' Greek etymology, Simplicius' and other Semitic etymologies are analyzed by Oden 1977, 60–73.
65. Menander, 745 Koerte-Thierfelder (in Porphyr. *Abst.* 4.15, 5) remembers the corporal punishment of those Syrians who broke the taboo on sacred fish. According to Sandbach 1973, 720–1, Menander's fragment comes from the *Deisidaimon*; on the Syrian Goddess' punishments, see also Mart. *Epigr.* 4.43, 7 'iuro per Syrios tibi tumores;' Pers. 5.187.
66. As far as Mopsus is concerned, we do not know whether he was a Lydian by birth or Lydos' son. Kruse R.E. 16.1, 242–3, associates him with Mopsus' image on a post-Trajanic coin found in Hierapolis of Phrygia.
67. The texts are analysed and compared by Van Berg 1972; see also Cumont 1914 , 843–5
68. Cf. Eratosth. *Cat.* 38, p. 180 Roberts; Schol. Arat. 386, p. 85, 27–8.; *Schol. German.* 176, 17 Breysig; Hygin. *Astr.* 2.30; *Fab.* 197.
69. Cf. Ovid, *Fast.* 2.460.
70. Cf. Ovid, *Met.* 4. 46, 5.331.
71. See Cumont 1929, 184.
72. Cumont 1914, 847: 'Im allgemeinen darf man sagen, dass im Gegensatz zu den Syrern, die den Fisch opferten, aber nicht aßen, die Griechen ihn überall aßen, aber nicht opferten.' Durand 1979, 9–10, 178–9, remarks that fish is not usually related to sacrificial practices in ancient Greece, with a few exceptions (e.g. the tunny).
73. This is a common topic in Greek literature, from comedy (Eub., 118 K-A *ap. Deipn.* 1.25b) and Plato (*Rep.* 3.404b–c) to Plutarch, *Quaest. Conv.* 8.8, 14; *Is. et Os.* 7.

74. As does the age of Kronos, whose ἐγκράτεια Porphyry, *Abst.* 4.2, remembers with fond regret.
75. See Murray 1990.
76. See Cumont 1914, 847–50; Doelger 1922.
77. See Montanari 1988.

## 25 Do Heroes Eat Fish? Athenaeus on the Homeric Lifestyle

1. Dalby 1996, 28. Cf. Purcell 1995; Davidson 1997.
2. For an overview of Homeric studies down to the fourth century see Richardson 1993, 25–35. More detailed discussions can be found in Apfel 1938; Richardson 1975, 1981.
3. This is fr. 7 in Kohl 1917. Montanari 1976 has suggested that Plato and Eubulus are evidence that the separatist inference had already been drawn in the fourth century; but this and the other instances he cites show only that problems of consistency that could lead to a separatist conclusion had been identified, not that this conclusion had in fact been reached.
4. A good account is given in Schmidt 1976.
5. On Athenaeus' use of quotations as a transitional device see Mengis 1920, 75; more examples will be mentioned below.
6. Thus Casaubon 1621: see Schweighaeuser 1801, 180, 183.
7. The same function is performed by free women and goddesses at Od. 4.252 (Helen), 5.264 (Calypso), 10.361, 450 (Circe), *Il.* 5.905 (Hebe), as well as by assorted female slaves (*Od.* 4.49, 8.454, 17.88, 19.317, 23.154, 24.366). For the ancient discussion see Schmidt 1976: 173–80.
8. On this question and the intepretation of 11b–f, see Heath 1998.
9. The speaker who uses Pindar fr. 241 to introduce a new section at 248c is Democritus; but I have not found any grounds for arguing that he is the speaker here too, nor evidence to support any other attribution of this speech.
10. Weber 1888. Cf. *FGrH* 594 F8; Schmidt revises Weber in detail with regard to the assignment of material to Dioscurides and other sources (Schmidt 1976, 17–18; cf. 163–4, 175–6, 180 n. 30, 195 n. 25).
11. Schwartz (*RE* s.v. Dioskurides (7)) takes the view that the *Suda*'s attribution arose from a misunderstanding of the reference to 'Dioscurides the pupil of Isocrates' at 11a–b; for reasons explained in the following note, this seems to me unnecessary.
12. This point has implications for the identification of Dioscorides/Dioscurides. There seem to be three possible inferences from the reference to 'Dioscurides the pupil of

Isocrates' near the end of Myrtilus' speech (11a–b): (i) that the Dioscorides quoted by Myrtilus in turn cited this Dioscurides; (ii) that Myrtilus cited two authors named Dioscorides or Dioscurides; (iii) that Myrtilus cited one Dioscurides (the pupil of Isocrates) at the beginning and at the end of his speech. This last possibility is usually discounted on the grounds that Athenaeus' source must be post-Aristarchean; but that argument depends on the assumption that Athenaeus is using the same source beyond Myrtilus' speech, for nothing that Myrtilus himself says (so far as I can see) depends on Aristarchus. It therefore seems to me quite possible that Myrtilus' speech is based on a late fourth-century source, named at the beginning and end of the speech.

13. See e.g. Chapter 32.
14. Baldwin 1976, 38, 41–2.

## 26 *Plato in the* Deipnosophistae

1. *Phd.* 57a; *Symp.* 172b (συνδείπνῳ), 172c and 173a (συνουσία(v)), and 172ab (Apollodorus has already told the story before).
2. *Phd.* 100b; *Rep.* 566b.
3. E.g. *Lys.* 206c, *Euthyd.* 295a, *Grg.* 449b.
4. *Lys.* 204a, 211c, *Rep.* 539d.
5. Common also in Herodotus, Aristophanes and Xenophon, but coming at the end of such a thoroughly Platonic passage, it too can perhaps be felt *pro tem.* as Platonic (cf. e.g. *Soph.* 243d, *Hipp. Min.* 363b).
6. I.e. both *Symp.* and *Phd.* recorded ἐπικυλίκιοι λόγοι ('discussions over a drink') even if the cup in question in the latter was not entirely of the conventional kind. This way of understanding the events recorded in *Phd.* is not a mere idiosyncratic quirk of Athenaeus': note that Socrates in *Phd.* assimilates the cup of hemlock to a wine-cup when he asks if he can pour a libation from it (*Phd.* 117b), and that other later authors besides Athenaeus could see an interesting juxtaposition between Socrates' cup in the *Phd.* and Alcibiades' *psykter* (wine-cooler) in *Symp.* (Max. Tyr. 25.7).
7. Ulpian, 686c. Compare and contrast however James Davidson's suggestion (Chapter 21) that the *Deipnosophistae* can be read as a funerary or commemorative text, mourning Ulpian, and pointedly reversing *Phaedo*'s insistence on the worthlessness of the body and bodily pleasure. To my mind, this would need an ampler evocation of *Phaedo* at the outset, and a more overtly funerary character to the *Deipnosophistae* than I think we find.

8. The quotation (known only from this passage) is Eratosthenes fr. 37 Hiller = 30 Powell.
9. Compare and contrast Davidson (n. 7) again.
10. 343cd; 504e–505b; 507a–d.
11. 174c.
12. 276f.
13. 419d.
14. 527cd.
15. 589cd; cf. Diog. Laert. 3. 31, Asclepiades (*sic*) *Anth. Pal.* 7. 217.
16. 23c, 35b, 92f, 99bc, 237a, 247a, 247c, 365b, 424d, 640e, 653c.
17. 187b; for this view of Socratic writing, compare for example Dio Chrysostom 18. 13ff., Demetrius *Eloc.* 27 and 181 (with Trapp 1990, 145, 155 and forthcoming. It is interesting to note in passing how very brief and isolated Athenaeus's reference to the general character of Plato's style is. Like that of his character Ulpian (Κειτούκειτος), his stylistic interest is much more in ἐκλογὴ ὀνομάτων ('selection of vocabulary') than in σύνθεσις ('composition'): contrast the discussions of Plato's style in Dion. Hal. *Demosth.* 5–7, 23–30 and *Ep. Pomp.* 1–2, and [Longin.] *Sublim.* 12.3–13.4.
18. Approximate figures: *Rep.* c. 19 references; *Leg.* 15; *Phaedr.* 7; *Grg.* and *Tim.* 6; *Phd.* and *Prot.* 5; *Ap.*, *Meno* and *Phileb.* 3; *Alc. I* to *Tht.* 2; remainder 1 each.
19. 94e, 123c, 314a, 381f, 433f, 443f, 444a, 511d–f, 527cd, 679ab, 688b.
20. See e.g. 59d, 66d, 276f, 354d; on reductive tendencies in ancient biography, Lefkowitz 1981, *passim* and 136–8, Riginos 1976, 199–200.
21. 5.186d–193, 215c–220a; 11.540e–509e. Notice how these Platonic set-pieces are positioned at the end of Part I and the beginning of Part III of the *Deipnosophistae* on the 'three act' analysis proposed by Lucía Rodríguez-Noriega Guillén in Chapter 18.
22. 180c–182a, 188f–190a, contesting Aristarchus' readings at *Od.* 4. 15–19 and 74.
23. Ruth Webb points out to me that what Homer is here said to teach (and Plato to have learned from him) is standard rhetorical procedure for *ekphrasis* (cf. Chapter 15).
24. *Symp.* 174bc: the complaint is that Plato is irresponsible in suggesting that when Homer presented Menelaus going uninvited to Agamemnon's feast in *Il* 2. 408, he was offending against the proverbial principle that 'good men go uninvited to the feasts of good men'.
25. Making Aristophanes hiccough and Alcibiades disgrace himself, and passing disparaging comments on Agathon's prose-style—just as, elsewhere in his dialogues, he gets at

Charmides and Euthydemus, and the city of Athens itself. This passage extends over only two Loeb pages; the numbering suggests more because of Kaibel's transpositions.

26. τερατολογία ('portentous nonsense'), πεπλασμένη ἀνδραγαθία ('fabricated heroism').
27. *Ap.* 28e, cf. *Lach.* 181b, *Symp.* 220e.
28. That he had never been abroad except to the Isthmus, *Crito* 52b.
29. Pointing out that, on grounds of age, Xenophon could not have been present at a party given in the year when Autolycus won his victory; and (more dubiously and contortedly) that comparison with Plato's *Symposium* shows that Pausanias could not already have said what Xenophon's Socrates claims he had.
30. The references to Archelaus and to Arginusae do not square with the statement that Pericles is only recently dead; if Protagoras is on his second visit, Hippias cannot be there as well, because in that year there was no truce between Athens and Elis.
31. Flitting briefly back to Plato in 220f for a concluding quotation of *Phdr.* 229d.
32. Cf. Gellius 14.3 and Diog. Laert. 3.34, with Holford-Strevens 1988, 198–9; also Dion. Hal. *Ep. Pomp.* 1.
33. Malice: 187cd, 505d ff.; inconsistency: 187ef, 216b.
34. 505ef, as well as 216c ff.
35. Herodicus seems also to be behind a couple of anti-Platonic paragraphs in Aelius Aristides' *In Defence of the Four*: Aristides 3. 577–8 and 579–82.
36. On Düring's account Favorinus is responsible, among other things, for the infusion of anti-Aristarchan material found in the discussion of symposia (drawn from the first-century AD grammarian Seleucus, named in 188f), and the intrusive apologia for Socrates in 217f–18a. But may not this weaving together of strands be Athenaeus' own work instead?
37. Düring has a deliciously low opinion of Athenaeus' intelligence and literary skill, briefly set out in *Herodicus* and more fully articulated in his earlier work on Athenaeus (1936, 226–70): see for instance Düring 1941, 57, 87 and 95.
38. At 216a, 216c, 216f–217c and 219b in set-piece number two, and at 504e, 506c and 508d in the third.
39. Note particularly *Symposiaca* 7. 1–2, 8. 2 and 9.5 (any of which could as well have been included in the *Platonicae Quaestiones*).
40. See (e.g.) Jones 1916, Dillon 1977,184–230, Holford-Strevens 1988, 72–92, Moreschini 1994, Trapp 1990, 1997, xxii–xxxii, xxxv–xxxvi and forthcoming.

### 27 *Athenaeus, Crates and Attic Glosses: A Problem of Attribution*

1. The fragments of Crates of Athens have been collected by Jacoby (*FGrH* 362). Demetrius is cited in one of them (*FGrH* 362 F 2 = Phot. lex. 1.358.11 and Suda κ 2706), while Didymus is *terminus ante quem* for the Sophoclean scholia, source of another (*FGrH* 362 F 4 = sch. Soph. Oed. Col. 100). Another, but less certain, *terminus post quem* is that a Crates of Athens is not mentioned in the list of writers called Crates in Diog. Laert. 4.23, a list that should go back to the work of Demetrius Magnes (first century BC) (see Jacoby's notes on *FGrH* 362, 3b.122).
2. The only available collection of his fragments was published in 1860 by K. Wachsmuth and is now outdated (Wachsmuth 1860) by papyrus findings; for partial collections, see Helck 1905 and 1913–14; Mette 1936 and 1952.
3. *Adv. math.* 1.44.
4. Hesiod: see Wachsmuth 1860: 55–6 (= Mette, fr. 47 and 48); another fr. is in a *Life of Dionysius Periegetes*, 72.56 (Kassel 1985). Lyric poets: p. 53 Wachsmuth (= fr. 27 Mette); pp. 63, 69–70 Wachsmuth. Attic theatre: pp. 56–59 Wachsmuth (= frr. 49–51 Mette).
5. Fr. 20 Mette (Romeo 1993 provides a new edition of these papyri); fr. 86 Mette (cf. Mangoni 1993, coll. 24–29). On Crates in Philodemus *On Poems*, see now Janko 1995a and 1995b.
6. Philippides is mentioned in *FGrH* 362 F 12 = *Deipn.* 14.640c–d (Athenaeus does not mention the book title here, but the fragment is in all probability to be assigned to our work); Seleucus quotes our work (*FGrH* 362 F 11 = *Deipn.* 9.366d).
7. See the table in the Appendix.
8. FHG iv.369–70.
9. Krates von Athen, *FGrH* 362 F 1–13; Jacoby earlier defended this view in the *RE* entry on Crates of Athens: cf. Krates 12), *RE* 11. 2, 1633–4.
10. Mette 1952: 48 ff. Mette sees in the term παρατηρεῖν a key word of Crates' methodology in the study of language; it is wrong, however, to use it for the attribution of fragments, as he does, in view of the fact that it is a common term in later grammatical literature; cf. Schroeter 1955.
11. Jacoby (*FGrH* 362, 3b.121, with n. 10) quotes the cases of Theodorus ὁ Παναγής (*FGrH* 346) and of Lysimachides (*FGrH* 366).
12. Searches in the TLG for Ἀσιανός and Ἀσιαγενής failed to bring to light any significant parallel of Crates' usage before the Roman period—however, this is a common and often

insoluble problem when working on Hellenistic grammarians: when do our later sources preserve the original wording of the earlier scholars they quote and when are they using their own later terminology? See Montanari 1997, 285–7; on this particular case see Dihle 1977: 177 n. 56: the terms Ἀσιανός and Ἀσιαγενής often appear in later grammatical literature, but it is difficult to assign them to a specific Hellenistic source.

13. Latte 1915: 386 ff.; the argument is accepted by Jacoby on *FGrH* 362, 122.

14. On the interest of Greek grammarians in local dialects see Cassio 1993.

15. Slater 1986.

16. See for example von Wilamowitz-Möllendorff 1900: 42: Aristophanes *'muß puristische Überstreibungen kennen'*; Dihle 1977: 167–8.

17. Eust. 1599.14 (on Od. 8.311): Ἐπικύλλωμα ἢ κατακύλλωμα. ὧν ἀμφοτέρων μνησθεὶς Ἀριστοφάνης ὁ γραμματικὸς οὐδέτερον αὐτῶν ἀνάττικον εἶναι φησιν. The two words are unknown: 'crookedness, crooked swelling' is the translation offered by Slater. Then: 'Aristophanes the grammarian makes mention of both these words and says that they are both used in Attic.' Slater in his notes interprets the fragment in the sense that it is Eustathius, and not Ar. Byz. who is discussing whether these glosses belong to the Attic dialect or not.

18. Slater 1986, xvi.

19. See Wendel, *RE* 19.2, 'Philemon (12) and (13)', 2150–51: both lived between the third and the second century BC. See Degani 1995, 510–11.

20. Emanuele Dettori first called my attention to this papyrus. Amerias' other fragments are in Hoffmann 1906, who dates him to the third century BC, and certainly before Aristarchus, who polemicizes against him in sch. A ad L 754 a (cf. Hoffmann: 3).

21. *P.Oxy.* 3710; on his interest in Attic glosses see Dyck 1987, 121 n. 8.

22. See Norden 1915–18, 1.149–50, and the new appendix in the Italian translation of Norden's work (Calboli 1986, 1050–73).

23. Wisse 1995; see also Nicolai 1992, 77 n. 79 and 201–2, on rhetorical Atticism and grammatical analogy.

24. David Blank called my attention to this passage. On this fragment see Latte 1915, 386.

25. Moreover, two other interests, glossography and poetics, seem to go together in Crates of Mallus' lifetime and earlier. Take the example of Andromenides, an obscure author who was interested, like Crates, in problems connected with the evaluation of poetry, and whose work Crates knew, according to Philodemus' *On Poems*. The only other fragment of Andromenides known to us, outside the Herculaneum papyri, is a gloss in Hesychius (ε 3231: Ἐνοδία). A much better-known author interested in poetics (another of Philodemus' adversaries in the *On Poems*), Neoptolemus of Parium, who lived before Aristophanes of Byzantium (who quotes him), wrote collections of Homeric and of Phrygian glosses. See Mette 1980 for his fragments.

26. See sch. T on *Il.* 15.23 b[1]; sch. *B on *Il.* 1.591; Eust. on *Il.* 15.23 (1003.38); they are fr. 22 Mette 1936 = 1 Helck 1915 = p. 44 Wachsmuth).

27. See EM p. 145.53 (Et. Gen. p. 45.4 Miller) = fr. 53 Mette 1952.

28. Sch. Ge ad F 282e Erbse: < ἐρχθέντ᾽ ἐν μεγάλῳ·> ... Κράτης· εἰλθέντ᾽ ἐν μεγάλῳ· εἴλλειν γάρ φησιν εἶναι τὸ εἴργειν, ὥστε τὴν τῆς κωλύσεως δίκην ἐξουλῆς καλεῖσθαι, καὶ παρατίθεται Σόλωνος ἐν πέμπτῳ ἄξονι (fr. 569a Martina) "ἐξουλῆς· ἐάν τις ἐξίλλῃ ὧν ἄν τι <ς> δίκην νικήσῃ, ὁπόσου ἂν ἄξιον ᾖ, εἰς δημόσιον ὀφλανεῖ καὶ τῷ ἰδιώτῃ, ἑκατέρῳ ἴσον. Ὁ Σοφοκλῆς ἐν Δαιδάλῳ ρ. (fr. 158 R.): ἐλλημενήσω τόνδ᾽ ἀχαλκεύτῳ πέδῃ'. *Similiter P. Oxy.* 221, col. xiv (Pap. XII Erbse, pp. 105–6 = Pack² 1205).

29. See sch. Ge on F 195b , where he quotes the presocratic philosopher Hippon (fr. 38 B 1 D.-K.).

30. So already Latte 1915: 386.

31. Sch. RVQ ad Ar. *Frogs* 294: καὶ σκέλος χαλκοῦν ἔχει; .. τὸ δὲ ὅλον, φησὶ Κράτης, ἔοικέ τι εἶναι φάντασμα παντοδαπὸν γινόμενον.

32. Antiatt. p. 86.8 Bekker: βο<λί>τινον [*correxi*] Ἀριστοφάνης Βατράχοις.

33. It is not necessary to suppose that the Crates mentioned here could still read a copy of the other version of the *Peace*, already lost for the Alexandrians: there is the possibility that he quoted the passages from an earlier collection of glosses: so Boudreaux 1919, 79–80.

34. Argum. RVGLh Ar. *Peace* A 2 Holw. (sch. vet., Tr.): φέρεται ἐν ταῖς διδασκαλίαις δεδιδαχὼς Εἰρήνην ὁμοίως ὁ Ἀριστοφάνης. ἄδηλον οὖν, φησὶν Ἐρατοσθένης, πότερον τὴν αὐτὴν ἀνεδίδαξεν ἢ ἑτέραν καθῆκεν, ἥτις οὐ σῴζεται. Κράτης μέντοι δύο οἶδε δράματα γράφων οὕτως· "ἀλλ᾽ οὖν γε ἐν τοῖς Ἀχαρνεῦσιν ἢ Βαβυλωνίοις, ἢ ἐν τῇ ἑτέρᾳ Εἰρήνῃ" καὶ σποράδην διὰ (<ἴ>δια Janko, fort. delendum Holwerda) τινα ποιήματα παρατίθεται, ἅπερ ἐν τῇ νῦν φερομένῃ οὐκ ἔστιν. The translation is based on Sommerstein 1985, xix.

35. See the cases discussed in Arrighetti 1977 (glosses from commentaries on Homer and Demosthenes). On the

36. Denniston 1950, 441–2.

37. A small element in favour of this solution is that, as Kaibel noticed, with one exception all our quotations from the second *Peace* come from Atticist sources, possibly the collection of Crates himself (Kaibel 1889, 43 n. 2).

38. Our fragment is fr. 69 in Müller 1891.

39. He wrote a treatise Περὶ Ἑλληνισμοῦ as well as works *On the Dialect of Syracuse, On the Laconian Dialect, On Ionic Dialect, On Roman Dialect*: see the fragments in Theodoridis 1976 (SGLG 2), and his introduction, 10–12.

40. Cf. Diog. Laert. 7.59, where it is one of the ἀρεταὶ λόγου, virtues of speech, in the Stoic grammatical system; on the Stoic *technai* on sound see e.g. Schenkeveld 1990. On the importance of *hellenismos* in Crates' work see Janko 1995b: 232–3.

41. I wish to thank those who met in Exeter in September 1997, as well as A.C. Cassio, E. Dettori and R. Janko, for their useful comments on earlier drafts of this paper; and R. Nicolai for discussing with me some of the issues presented here.

## 28 Lynceus and the Anecdotists

1. See Appendix, Text 1.

2. As suggested to me orally by Geoffrey Arnott. One recalls the classic distinction in modern European literature between novel (French and German *Roman*) and novella (*Novelle*): in the latter, background histories and even full names can be dispensed with.

3. E.g. Menander, *Dyskolos*.

4. Text 39. Further, according to the *Suda*, he defeated Menander. But it is a commonplace that Menander lost contests unfairly. We may suspect that the *Suda*'s entry is constructed out of Athenaeus and guesswork.

5. The texts are conveniently collected in Hercher 1873.

6. Text 2 (translated in part below) and 3.

7. For comments on Hippolochus' letter, itself highly informative on the developing synthesis of Greek, Macedonian and Persian styles of dining and entertainment, see Dalby 1996.

8. As observed orally by Dorothy Thompson, we may presume that this was Ptolemy II's visit to Athens, since no visit by Ptolemy I is recorded.

9. Texts 2–5.

10. So Plutarch, *Demetrius* 27. If Plutarch actually saw Lynceus'

letter—he does not say so explicitly—it may have been the source for his own description of the dinner.

11. Texts 17, 18.

12. Text 6. The fragments explicitly assigned to this letter by Athenaeus are 6–9, 13–15. Texts 10–11 and 16 also fit its theme.

13. Plato, *Symp.* 176 and *passim*; Athenaeus, *Deipn.* 10.426b–431f; Plutarch, *Quaestiones conviviales* 1.4.

14. Text 8, in particular, makes it clear that Athens is 'they' and Rhodes is 'she'. In text 9 Tlepolemus, as mythical founder of Rhodes, makes an appropriate boy-friend for Theseus in a seduction scene helped along by fish.

15. Martin 1931 suggested that Hippolochus' letter was written by Lynceus. He must have had cloth ears. Lynceus writes well and stylishly; Hippolochus writes badly, and there are grammatical and logical faults in his letter which neither Lynceus nor Athenaeus would have committed.

16. See Text 17. Here, no one would argue that the comparison being made is of appropriate seriousness.

17. Hieronymus of Rhodes quoted by Athenaeus, 10.435a. Hieronymus studied under Lykon, after Theophrastus' death (Diogenes Laertius 5.68), so is presumably reporting Theophrastus' table talk at second hand.

18. Texts 19–21.

19. Hesiod, *Works and Days* 640.

20. He wrote τὴν δ' ἁμίαν φθινοπώρου, ὅταν πλειὰς καταδύνῃ, /πάντα τρόπον σκεύαζε. τί σοι τάδε μυθολογεύω; (Archestratus 35.1 Brandt).

21. Editors of Archestratus take Lynceus' throwaway line as a new fragment of their poet, fragment 44 Brandt, no. 175 Lloyd-Jones and Parsons.

22. An analogous subculture is the one that most interests writers and readers of some modern journalism.

23. Text 34. The three authorities are nowhere quoted verbatim, so we do not know to what extent their versions coincided.

24. As a fine specimen of this oral tradition and its nature we may quote a Philip story from Hegesander (the source is Athenaeus 6.248e):

> Hegesander the Delphian retails the following of Cleisophus in his *Notes*:
> King Philip said that a letter had arrived for him from Cotys, King of Thrace. Cleisophus, who was present, said: 'By the gods, excellent!' 'What do you know of what's in the letter?' said Philip …

What was the reply? Was it 'By Zeus the Greatest, you have criticized me rightly' as Athenaeus tells it? A reply that is scarcely punchy. Was it rather '… Excellent criticism!', with a pretence of completing the sentence that Cleisophus had already begun? *That* exchange, with *that* punchline, is related of Dionysius of Syracuse and his flatterer Democles by the historian Timaeus, quoted by Athenaeus 6.250d. Between which monarch and which flatterer, if any, did the exchange actually take place? The seriousness of Satyrus matters not least because he is the source for the statement that Philip took a new wife on each campaign, a practice finally resulting in a deadly insult to Alexander (Athenaeus 13.557b).

25. Text 31.
26. Both quotations from Text 29.
27. Athenaeus 6.242a; also 13.583b and 6.244b, but the last is set in Egypt after Ptolemy's return.
28. Satyrus quoted by Athenaeus 6.250f; Plutarch, *Alexander* 28.
29. Aristobulus quoted by Athenaeus 6.251a.
30. Athenaeus 10.434c; see also 12.537d. Pliny cites Nicobule, *Natural History* 1.12–13.
31. *FGrH* 126. Athenaeus 10.434a, 12. 537d, *Epitome of Athenaeus* 1.20a.
32. Plutarch, *Alexander* 46.
33. *FGrH* 125. Notable fragments are from Athenaeus 12.538b on the mass wedding, 13.575a the Oriental love story that is a version of the tale of Nala in the *Mahabharata*, 10.437a on the drinking contest held by Alexander to commemorate the Indian philosopher Calanus. Chares is also cited by Plutarch, Pliny, Arrian and Aulus Gellius.
34. Athenaeus 13.585a–f. Aristodemus qualifies for vol. 3 of Müller's *Fragmenta historicorum graecorum*.
35. Athenaeus 6.244f, cf. 8.338a on the flautist Dorion.
36. Athenaeus 13.567a, 13.586b.
37. Athenaeus 13.557e, cf. 13.604d.
38. Athenaeus 14.664a. Machon is quoted at unusual length by Athenaeus: see the edition by Gow.
39. Athenaeus 13.577d, 577e, 579a, 580d, 578e. On Ptolemy: n. 27 above. For the mention of Stratocles by Matron see Athenaeus 4.137c.
40. Athenaeus 8.348e, 341a.
41. Astin 1978, 186–8. The one fragment explicitly attributed to this collection is in Cicero's *De Oratore* 2.271.
42. Hegesander (quoted by Athenaeus 6.249b) tells of the parasite who said to Alexander, 'Those mosquitoes are so much happier than all other mosquitoes, for they have tasted the blood of Alexander!' Müller and others assert that this was a parasite of Alexander of Epirus, but for no good reason. Hegesander on Stratonicus: Athenaeus 8.350b.
43. Athenaeus 6.260a.
44. A collection of jokes featuring Stratonicus, Athenaeus

8.350d–352c, is probably to be attributed (in spite of a slight textual difficulty) to this work by Callisthenes. See Chapter 31.
45. Fragment 18 Wehrli, quoted by Athenaeus 8.349f. Clearchus's *Gergithius* was a study of flatterers and parasites: to judge from the two known fragments (19–20, Athenaeus 6.255c, 258a) it was, like his other works, a good deal more sententious and orotund than the books of anecdotes.
46. Though he does refer to Plato's terse description of life in Sicily, 'a life of stuffing yourself twice a day and never sleeping alone at night' (*Letter* 7.326b).
47. Though Aristotle's scientific lectures or treatises were not circulated outside his school in his time.
48. And see Dalby 1996, 157–62, for the parallel between the local scientific and political studies of Aristotle and Theophrastus and the developing interest in regional cuisine shown by their less intellectual students.
49. See Athenaeus 13.603e–604d.
50. Athenaeus 14.614d.
51. I am grateful to Bernard Besnier for showing me that the genre is best treated as that of the anecdote, though its early manifestations are predominantly in the form of jokes.
52. The story was told in some form by Aristobulus, and variously by others: see Arrian, *Alexander* 7.17; Diodorus of Sicily 17.112. From this point onwards 'Chaldees' as magicians or astrologers begin to multiply in the sources: *Daniel* 1.4 and elsewhere; Eupolemus quoted by Eusebius, *Praeparatio Evangelica* 9.17; *Magic* attributed to Aristotle, fr. 35 Rose; Cato, *On Farming* 5.

## Section VI: Sympotica

### Introductory Remarks

1. Cf. in Latin, the sixth satire of Juvenal, written about a century earlier; Hawley 1993 sketches the Greek literary background to such debates in a useful treatment of Book Thirteen, which shows an unusual and welcome sympathy for Athenaeus as a writer.

### 29 Laughter as Dessert: On Athenaeus' Book Fourteen, 613–616

1. On this topic, see Schmitt-Pantel 1990, 14–33 and particularly 23; Vetta 1983, xiii–lx, particularly xxxvi; Slater

1981, 205–14 and particularly 207. For the use of laughter in Greek culture, see Halliwell 1991, 279–96.

2. On this point, cf. Bielohnlawek 1983, 95–116.

3. As Philip, a *gelotopoios*, states in Xenophon's *Symposion*, 4.50: ὅταν δέ τι κακὸν λάβωσι, φεύγουσιν ἀμεταστρεπτί, φοβούμενοι μὴ καὶ ἄκοντες γελάσωσι.

4. On the role of the *symposiarchos*, cf. von der Mühl 1983, 3–28 and particularly 17–18.

5. For Athenaeus the term *acroamata* means the shows that are seen or heard. The same meaning is found in Hellenistic and imperial inscriptions. On the other hand, and as Robert 1936, 236 pointed out ' an *acroama* is an artist, singer, musician, actor or dancer'.

6. Cf. Lukinovich 1990, 263–71, esp. 266.

7. Cf. *GEL*, s.v. γελωτοποιέω and γελωτοποιός.

8. The comic hero in ancient comedy is sometimes an *alazon*, 'impostor' or 'boaster' (linked also to *eiron* 'ironic man') or a *bomolochos* 'buffoon'. Aristotle (*EN* 4.8) seems to recognize *alazon* and *eiron* as comic types, like the *bomolochos* or the *agroikos*: see Cornford 1968, 119–21, Whitman 1971, 21–58; Ussher 1977, 75–9; Janko 1984, 216–18 and Hubbard 1991, 1–15. Other Greek words for *gelotopoios* are *geloios* or *geloiastes*. Cf. Suidas, s.v. γέλοιος· ὁ καταγελαστότατος, προπαροξυτόνως. Γελοῖος δὲ ὁ γελωτοποιός; Photius, s.v. γελοιος· ὁ καταγελαστότατος, προπερισπωμένως. ὀξυτόνως δὲ ὁ γελωτοποιός. Hesychius, s.v. Γελοῖος ἱλαρός. γελοιαστὴς καὶ ὁ καταγέλαστος ἄνθρωπος καὶ λοίδορος.

9. We cannot identify this character, as some other guests of Callias. Xenophon does not give details of his deme nor his family name. And we do not find another *gelotopoios* in writers of this period. Studying Xenophon's *Symposion* as an answer to Plato's *Symposion*, Segoloni 1994, 34 states that Lycon stands for Aristophanes. I think that Philip would make a good literary counterpart for the comic poet.

10. List of professional entertainers: *gelotopoios*: Eudicus, Cephisodorus, Pantaleon and Philip; *thaumatourgos*: Diopeithes from Locri; *thaumatopoioi*: Xenophon and Caristhenes from Phlius, Nymphodorus, Scymnus from Taras, Philistides from Syracuse, Heraclitos from Mitylene; *ethologos*: Noemon; *planos*: Matreas from Alexandria; *parodos*: Oenomas, a Greek from Italy. Plutarch evokes Philip in *Mor.* 629c, 709 e–f, 710c. On these professional entertainers, see: Στέφανες 1988, who quotes also Plutarch, *Mor.* 1095d and adds to our collection of *gelotopoioi* Agrian, Thrasyleon, Callias and Cardax.

11. Philip imitates a scene of mourning (1. 14) and a dance (2. 21–23); he shows his ability to criticize politics (2. 13); to produce wit (2. 27) and please the other guests with his

penchant for εἰκάζειν (6. 8–9; 7. 1). Plato gives us a list of imitations forbidden for guardians and *kaloikagathoi* in *Republic* 395c, imitations in which probably the *gelotopoioi* were very expert. See also *Deipn.* 1.19–20; Lucian, *Symposion*, 18.

12. Cf. Plato, *R.* 395 c.

13. On Palamedes and his creations, see Platthy 1968, particularly 6–22; on Anaxandrides and Palamedes, Phillips 1957, 267–8.

14. It is not clear what *symbolon* the guests of a private banquet were supposed to pay. We may suppose that in this case the *do ut des* rule applied: an invitation for the banquet is repaid by a return invitation. But *gelotopoioi* are not necessarily penniless professionals, unable to return an invitation. They share their lot with philosophers. The latter pay their *symbolon* by philosophizing, the former by producing laughter. It is interesting to remark that some parasites were invited to attend a banquet precisely because they were able to make the guests laugh, as Athenaeus puts it in 4.162f-163a.

15. On *akletoi*, see Fehr 1990, 185–95; on parasites, Ziehen *RE* 18, 1377–81 and Bruit Zaidman 1995, 196–203. See also, Brown 1992, 91–107 and Avezzù 1989, 235–40.

16. Philip was not allowed to produce laughter at the *deipnon*-stage of Callias's banquet (1. 14). The first laughter provoked by Philip stresses the frontier between the *deipnon* and the *symposion*, and is obtained by mimicking (most probably a parody of a tragic character or more precisely of the Aeschylean Niobe, mourning for herself, 1. 14–15). After this liberating laughter, Philip maintains his success till the end of this banquet.

17. Philip in Xenophon's *Symposion* states that he is proud of his profession centred in *gelotopoiia* (3. 11), as Nikeratos is of his Homeric knowledge (3. 5) and Socrates of his *mastropeia* (3. 10).

18. Cf. Caranus' wedding feast, *Deipn.* 4.128a–131f; Trimalchio's feast in Petronius, *Satyrika*, 59, see also 52, 53, 56, Pliny, *Ep.* 1.15, 2; 9.17.

19. On families of actors see Sutton 1987.

20. Cephisodoros and Pantaleon are presented by Athenaeus as *planoi* (14.615e–f = Dionysius of Sinope, *Namesakes*, fr. 4; Nicostratus, *The Syrian*, fr. 25; Theognetus, *He liked his Master*, fr. 2 and Chrysippus, *SVF*, 3. 199, but at *Deipn.* 1.20b as *gelotopoioi*. Manetho seems to establish the same link between *planoi* and *gelotopoioi* in *FHG* iv.382 and iv.445–9: see Robert 1929, 427–38.

21. Examples : the onomatopoiea of the song of frogs, Ar. *Fr.* 209, etc.; of the rope, Ar. *Fr.* 1286, 1288, 1290; the song of the birds, Ar. *Birds*, 738, etc. See also Ar. *Kn.* 10 and *Th.*, 231.

22. See Trendall and Webster 1971, 128, 129, 137; Taplin 1993, plates 10.2, 15.13, 16.16.

23. Their *techné* seems very close to that of the *deikelistai* and that of the *autokabdeloi*: see Pickard-Cambridge 1968, 270–2.

24. Athenaeus surveys the entertainers of the fourth and third centuries BC (1.19e), noting in a critical tone that 'the Athenians yielded to Potheinus the marionette-artist the very stage on which Euripides and his contemporaries performed in the inspired plays. They even set up a statue of Eurycleides in the theatre along with those of Aeschylus and his rivals.' This is confirmed by later inscriptions where *thaumatopoioi*, *ethologoi* and other entertainers who were victorious in public *agones* were honoured by different cities in the Greco-Roman world mostly in the second and third century of our era. Cf. for example, Robert 1929, 227–438; Robert 1936, 235–54; Jones 1991, 185–98, esp. 185 for the formula.

25. The source of Anacharsis' discourse is not found in Herodotus, 4. 46, 4. 76–7; Plato, *Republic* 600a; Aristotle *An. Post.* 1. 78b30; Strabo, 7. 303; Diogenes Laertius 2. 9; Plutarch *Solon*, 5; Lucian *Anacharsis* 6 and *Scythian or The Proxenos* 3. 9, 10, where famous sayings of Anacharsis are collected. We must conclude that the source of this text is lost or that Athenaeus-Ulpian recreate the past for the sake of this discourse.

26. Cf. Gal., *De usu partium* (*UP*), 1. 80 Kuhn.; Aesop., *Fables*, 25; Ael., *NA*, 7. 21; D.S. 17. 90–2–3. For other texts on this point and commentaries on the nature of monkeys, see Demont 1997, 457–79 and Lissarrague 1997, 455–72.

27. On monkeys and man, see Aristotle *HA*, 502 a 17b, 24 and *PA*, 683b 23. Also the *Tract on Physiognomy*, 124 of the Anonymus Latinus, who states that the monkey is *malignum, ridiculum, turpe* and men who resemble them are *imitatores ingeniorum alienorum, ipsi imperfectum ingenium habentes*. See also Taillardat 1965, 10 and 406.

28. Reekmans' study (1996, 227–41) of non-verbal jesting in Plutarch gives us a further insight into Anacharsis' attitude towards laughter .

29. See also 5. 419–26, 20. 200 and *Odyssey*, 20. 117 and *Homeric Hymn to Hermes*, 1. 55–6. On this verb, see Arnould 1990, 115.

30. Cf. Degani 1993, 2–36.

31. Cf. Degani 1993, 2–5.

32. Athenaeus knew also the περὶ τῆς εἰς Τροφωνίου καταβάσεως of Dicaearchus, cf. 13.594e and 14. 641e = *FHG* II. 266. On Parmeniscus, see also Iamb. *VP* 267 and *IG* XI. 161b. 49–54 (Parmeniscus had dedicated in the temple of Delian Artemis a mixing-bowl; cf. *BCH* 14. 403;

15. 127–128). It is interesting to note that Eubulus wrote a comedy on Parmeniscus (see fr. 83). Our Pythagorean from Metapontum could be a fifth-century man (Iamb. *VP* 267), or a tradesman (whose citizenship is unknown) accused by Darius in the fourth century BC (Demosthenes, *Against Dionysodoros*, 5, 7, 9, 10). The adventure of Parmeniscus from Metapontum would make a good plot for a comedy. However, his adventure seems more funny when we consider the relationship between Pythagoras and laughter (Iamb. *VP* 10 and 71).

33. Cf. also Plutarch, *De genio Socratis*, 589f–592e. On the terrors of this katabasis, cf. Aristophanes, *Clouds*, 506–8 (εἰς τὼ χεῖρέ νυν, δός μοι μελιτοῦτταν πρότερον· ὡς δέδοικ' ἐγὼ εἴσω καταβαίνων ὥσπερ εἰς Τροφωνίου) and scholia. On oracles, consultation and revelation, Clark 1968, 63–75; Schachter 1984, 258–67, on the origin of Trophonius' oracle, Simoneta 1994, 17–32.

34. Cf. also Alexander Aetolus 7 Powell. Cf. Lefkowitz 1981, 166–7.

35. Cf. Bergson 1900. See also on the theories of laughter, Morreall 1983.

36. For other anthologies of funny histories, cf. on Protagorides, *Deipn.* 3.124d; on Aristodemus's *Funny Memoirs*, *Deipn.* 6. 244f–245a.

37. Cf. *Deipn.* 13.577c–d; 578 f; 592a.

38. In comparing his own court at Athens to a tragedy, he seems to echo the literary discussions that went on about the dramatic genres in the fourth century.

39. See also, for example, Antiochus, 5. 194b–5f; 10. 438e–9f; Philopator, 6. 246c; Dionysius 10. 440c; Antony 4. 148b–c; Agron, an Illyrian king, 10. 439f-40a; Genthion, an Illyrian king, 10. 440a; Agathocles, D.S., 20. 63.

40. See also Plut. *Sull.* 2 and 36; Sallust, *Cat.* 11; *BJ*, 95–6.

41. On his literary activity and on the theatre, cf. Pascucci 1975, 283–96 and Garton 1964, 137–56.

42. On the *stibas*, see Philostratus, *VS*, II, 3. Cf. also Dunbabin 1991.

43. On his triumph at the *Quirinalia* of 167 or 166, see Livy, 43. 14; Velleius Paterculus, 1. 9. 5; Appian, *Ill.* 9. For the last topic of Ulpian's speech is the mention of a real action by Lucius Anicius Gallus. Praetor in 169 BC, Anicius obtained a victory over Genthion, the Illyrian king, Perseus' ally, in a campaign that lasted only thirty days. His victory in 168 BC eased matters for Aemilius Paullus who in the same year would conclude the Macedonian war. But his triumph and particularly his *ludi* in the Circus Maximus, for the sake of laughter, had broken all the rules of Roman *decorum*. He invited hired artists, great musicians, members of Dionysiac Guilds (*technitai*) to mime on stage his battles

against the Illyrians, transforming their show into a pantomime. Expecting to give pleasure to the Roman public he transformed himself into a *gelotopoios* and his victory into a cheap farce.

44. On Philippides, see Kassel–Austin vii.333–52, and *IG* II², 2323a. 41; 2325. 164.
45. Telesphorus was perhaps the commander of the infantry of Antigonus in 303 BC (D.S. 19. 74). Plutarch (*Mor.* 606b) mentions the torture of Telesphorus but does not give the reason. Lysimachus had him put in a cage and showed him as a warning to Theodorus of Cyrene : 'his eyes gouged out, his nose and ears lopped of, his tongue cut out, and said : 'To this plight I bring those who injure me". Plutarch (*Mor.* 634f) quotes the same joke, attributing it to Timagenes, without any reference to Lysimachus. For other outrageous jokes, cf. *Deipn.* 6.237a; 6.241; 8.352c–d.
46. Cf. Jouan and Van Looy 1998, 230.
47. Cf. also the tendency of the people of Tiryns and the Cretans to laugh, *Deipn.* 6.261d–e.
48. Plutarch (*Mor.* 710c) notes Xenophon's *Symposion*. The comparison is based on *Iliad* 11. 630.
49. *Republic*, 372c7. Cf. also 372d7–e1 (for the introduction of couches and tables); 372e and 374a (for the consequences of this type of banquet). A good analysis of this topic can be found in Tecusan 1990, 238–60.
50. Von der Mühl 1983, 16.

## 30 You Are What You Eat: Diet and Philosophical diaita in Athenaeus' Deipnosophistae

1. Holmes 1857–8, 20.
2. Perhaps this may be connected with Andrew Barker's observation (Chapter 32) that what Athenaeus has to tell us about music is quite banal.
3. Cf. 7.279e.
4. Fr. 37 Bailey; see Gaskin 1995, 59. Cf. *Vatican Sayings* 59 and 69.
5. *Vatican Sayings* 63.
6. In a paper forthcoming in D. Harvey and J. Wilkins, *The Rivals of Aristophanes* (London).
7. Soph. fr. 329 Lloyd-Jones; 'Villains, robbers, eaters of other men's food.'
8. His name may be borrowed from a Roman jurist called Masurius Sabinus who lived in the first half of the first century AD: he became an *eques* under Tiberius and his works were the subject of a commentary by Ulpian. See *RE* s.v.
9. Holford-Strevens 1988, 192.
10. Griffin 1976, 295 nn. 8–9.

11. Cf. Diog. Laert. 2.75.
12. Lucan *Phars.* 10.20–46.
13. Fears 1974, and bibliography.
14. Brown 1949; cf. Pearson 1960, 83–111.
15. Tarn 1939; cf. Tarn 1948, 404–5.
16. Teles *ap.* Stob. *Ecl.* 97.31; Crates: Diog. Laert. 6.3.23.
17. *Deipn.* 13.603a, 10.435a.
18. Plut. *Alexander* 14, with Hamilton's notes ad loc.
19. See n. 15.
20. Badian 1958, 156; Seibert 1972, 24–5, with bibliography. Luisa Prandi's argument (Prandi 1985, 113–26) that reference to Callisthenes as *sophistes* represents the anti-Callisthenean tradition, while reference to him as *philosophos* represents the Peripatetic tradition, cannot in my opinion be sustained.
21. The literature on this episode is considerable. See Bosworth 1988, 285–6; Seibert 1972, 202–4.
22. Borza 1981.
23. Chapter 11 discusses the importance of drunkenness as a category of historical interpretation in Polybius. Perhaps it assumed a similar role in the Alexander historians.
24. 9.3.4; Holford-Strevens 1988, 30.
25. Cf. Douglas 1970, 64.
26. Burkert 1962, 96, etc; Iamblichus, *On the Pythagorean Life.* 106–9.
27. Drijvers 1966.
28. Aristobulus 12.8 called Judaism ἡ καθ ἡμᾶς αἵρεσις,: see especially Schäfer 1997, 35, 39; also the puzzling passage of Epictetus, *Discourses* 2.9.19–22.
29. Jos. *BJ* 2.130–3.
30. E.g. *de mutatione nominum* 245–7.
31. Stoneman 1994a, xx–xxi.
32. Diog. Laert. 6.76; cf. 6.34; *Deipn.* 8.341e et al.; Sayre 1938, 88–9.
33. Detienne 1994, 44–5.
34. *Disc.* 3.22.23, 4.80.30–31; Dudley 1937, 181; Downing 1992, 42–4, 133.
35. As a modern day Cynic, Oleg Kulik, has observed (while living naked except for a collar and chain in a New York art gallery): 'The evolution of cognition involves a process of experimentation which allows observation from the point of view of the object.' There was an entertaining account (with photograph) of this piece of performance art in the *Sunday Telegraph* for 1 June 1997.

## 31 Stratonicus, The Witty Harpist

1. In addition to Athenaeus see Str. 13.1.57; 14.2.3; Plut. *Mor.* 525b; 602a; Artem. *Oneirocrit.* 4. 31; *Gnom. Vat.* 519–32; see

also Osborne and Byrne 1994, 406. If the passage from Plaut. *Rud.* 930–6, which describes Stratonicus as living a life of pleasure, travelling by sea from town to town, was in the Greek original of the *Rudens* by Diphilus, it seems that Stratonicus' image was well established in the third century BC, and that Plautus was not afraid that his Roman audience would not understand the reference to Stratonicus; see Marx 1959, 172–3; Anderson's claim 1986, 560–3 that the historical Stratonicus travelled only by land seems to be erroneous; Athenaeus refers to Stratonicus once again, when he quotes a passage from Timaeus (*FGrH* 566F 16 = 4.163e–f) in which Stratonicus is said to have sent a letter by a messenger to Diodorus of Aspendus, a Pythagorean who lived in the manner of Cynics. The content of the letter is not quoted, but how Stratonicus described Diodorus to his messenger: 'that henchman of Pythagoras who keeps the Porch crowded with people marvelling at his beast-robbed madness and insolence.' Aspendus was a Greek town in Pamphylia not far from Phaselis, thus also Timaeus brings Stratonicus to Asia Minor, but this is the only anecdote about Stratonicus that mentions letter writing; on Diodorus see Burkert 1972, 202–3. All the translations of Athenaeus' quotations are from Gulick's Loeb edition.

2. On the literary form of the *Deipnosophistae*, see Lukinovich 1990, 263–71. On structure, see Chapter 2; cf., on transitions, Chapter 12

3. Thus Cynulcus. The two sayings are Athenaeus' way of inserting anonymous material. Then the rest follows with no pretext, just as a matter-of-fact continuation of the subject, characteristic of Athenaeus.

4. Philetaerus was victorious at the Lenaea of *c.*370 BC (*IG* II² 2325,143), Pickard-Cambridge 1968, 114; Webster 1952, 17.

5. See Barber 1935; Bell 1978, 64 n.141; Molyneux 1992, 6–23; Gow and Page 1965, 2, 516; on Philoxenus see Barker 1984, 94–5.

6. See Wehrli 1969; on his musical innovations, see Winnington-Ingram quoted by Gow 1965, 81.

7. Gow 1965, 90–1 attributes also this anonymous testimony to Phainias; so already Casaubon; cf. Schweighäuser 1803 *ad loc.*

8. Machon has a different account of Stratonicus' death (8.349e), see Gow 1965, 90–1; also Hill 1949, 145 n. 5; Maas, 'Stratonicus' (2) *RE* 4 A1. 326. Maas assumes that Stratonicus was born in 410 BC; Webster 1952, 17, that he was born in 390 BC and lived at least until 323 BC.

9. He died in 327 BC. According to Jacoby, Callisthenes collected sayings only of his contemporaries. Jacoby, who asserts the authenticity of the collection, has divided it into 31 paragraphs, or items. However, item 31 (8.352c) is different from the rest, for it is not a saying or an anecdote but an explanation of item 13 (8.351c). Athenaeus may have found the entire collection in a book of the epic poet Capito (see below) and seems not to have used the work of Callisthenes himself.

10. On Timotheus of Miletus see Pickard-Cambridge 1962, 48–51; 1988, 261; Hall 1993, 44–80; Anderson 1994, 132–4; the tragedy writer Carcinus competed at the Lenaea *c.*376 BC and won the first of his victories at the Dionysia shortly before 372 BC, Pickard-Cambridge 1988, 112; he was the grandson of the tragic poet Carcinus who won a victory at the Dionysia in 446 BC *ibid.* 1988, 114; Chrysogonus was a Pythian victor, who played for Alcibiades' rowers when he returned to Athens in 408 or 407 BC (Plut *Alc.* 32. 2); there was another piper of that name, active in 355 BC, whose father's name was Stesichorus the second (Didymus *in Dem.* 12, 61–2; *Marmor Parium* A73); Webster 1952, 17 who thinks that it is this Chrysogonus who is meant here, places the first victory of Polyidus in Athens between 399 and 380 BC; Telephanes is perhaps the piper who assisted Demosthenes (21.17), and the one whose tomb Pausanias (1.44.6) saw on the road from Megara to Corinth; for his epitaph see *AP* 7.159, Gow and Page 1965, 2. 427–8; he was from Samos; there was, however, another Telephanes, of Megara, mentioned by Plutarch, *On Music*, 1138a, as inimical to the syrinx; see Howard 1893, 32–4; see also Sutton 1989: Timotheus no. 33; Philoxenus no. 34; Polyidus no. 37.

11. Theophrastus is a relatively early source, as he was active approximately at the time of Callisthenes. Only this passage from *On the Ridiculous* has survived. It is clear that Athenaeus does not quote it in its entirety. Apparently Theophrastus quoted both the original proverb—the one which Athenaeus quotes from Clearchus—and its distorted version by Stratonicus. Since Athenaeus does not quote an explanation of the proverb by Theophrastus, it may be assumed that the proverb was well known in his time and he did not find it necessary to explain it in the way Clearchus did, or—less likely—that the explanation quoted from Clearchus was actually Theophrastus' explanation, which Clearchus copied; Simycas is mentioned by Demosthenes (18.262); see also Pickard-Cambridge 1988, 134,169.

12. On Clearchus (*c.*340–250 BC) see Wehrli 1948; see also Robert 1968, 416–57.

13. Gow 1965, 21

14. They are apparently quoted from the *Commentaries* of

Hegesander mentioned earlier (4.162a). The form is named by Theon '*eidos apokritikon*', see Hock and O'Neil 1986, 29–30; there is only one such anecdote in the collection of Callisthenes (8.350e)

15. *Diog. Laert.* 1.104; Anacharsis is said to have come to Athens, see Hartog 1996, 118–27; cf. Baldwin 1983, 101.

16. See Griffin 1982, 19–20, 158–64; Skalet 1928, 167–8, 176–9; Edelstein and Edelstein 1945, 2,190 n. 26.

17. Webster, who attempts to save the historicity of this late anecdote by claiming that it relates to the time when Ptolemy became the satrap of Egypt in 323 BC (1952, 17), rejects the testimony that Stratonicus was put to death by Nicocles (8.352d); moreover, 'sceptre' is a symbol of kingship and Ptolemy is addressed as 'King'; ἕτερον δὲ πλῆκτρον, is an addition of Musurus.

## 32 Athenaeus on Music

1. The passage begins at 624c and ends at 626a, but is probably not Heraclidean throughout. Athenaeus seems to have inserted excerpts from other authors at various points along the way.

2. Comparisons can most usefully be made with the pseudo-Plutarchan treatise *De Musica*, which is probably quite close to Athenaeus in date. This dialogue, like that of Athenaeus, is in large part a farrago of extracts and paraphrases from earlier writers, and it is not a work of great intellectual distinction. But for its attention to major musicological issues and for the amount of substantial information it conveys, it is in an altogether different league from the *Deipnosophistae*.

3. See particularly Dio Chrysostom *Or.* 32.20–24, 54–70.

4. Aristokles seems to believe that the pipes of the instrument actually stand with their ends in the water; and having observed, one supposes, the action of the 'boy' who supplied air by working the handle of a pump, he imagines that his task is to 'stir up the water vigorously' (174d), as though this could conceivably produce the desired result. For a more intelligent discussion of the instrument's operation see Vitruvius 10.8.

5. Compare for instance Aristotle, *Pol.* 1339a, 1341a.

6. Even writers for the comic stage could presuppose in their audience a knowledge of musical theory, or at least the terminology of the subject, sufficient to enable them to appreciate allusions to the esoteric discourses of Aristoxenus and his like. See for instance Damoxenus fr. 2 (Kassel–Austin), especially lines 47–62.

7. The point can be made by reference to the many learned musicological allusions in Plutarch, and especially to his trenchant remarks at *non posse suaviter* 1095e.

8. See ps.-Plut. *De Mus.* 1138b.

9. It is incorporated in a remark quoted from the Peripatetic Phaenias (fr. 32 Wehrli) at 352c–d.

10. The sources are Polyaenus *Strateg.* V.44.1, Arrian *Anabasis* IV.16.6–7, Plutarch *de Alexandri magni fortuna* 334f.

## 33 Aristoxenus in Athenaeus

1. Aristoxenus of Tarentum (FF 1–9 Wehrli), the famous scholar of music in antiquity (FF10 a–b Wehrli), was the son of a musician and seems to have used music for therapy (F 6 Wehrli). He lived in the fourth century BC, a contemporary of Theophrastus and of Alexander the Great (Suda s.v. Ἀριστόξενος). Aristoxenus is an author in whom biographical, critical and musicological interests converge. Cicero speaks of his relationship with Dicaearchus (Dicaearchus FF 70, 4.62 Wehrli). The Suda enumerates as teachers his father Spintharos, Lampros of Eretria, the Pythagorean Xenophilos (F 25 Wehrli) and finally Aristotle. Of his travels we know that he went first to Mantinea and then sojourned in Athens, where he became the disciple of Xenophilus and Aristotle; he left the Peripatetic School when Theophrastus succeeded Aristotle as its head (Suda s.v. Ἀριστόξενος). We have however no indication of a possible return to Italy, nor any notice of the date of his death. Aristoxenus led an extremely productive literary life; the lexicon Suda (s.v.) attributes 453 books to him. Although, as in the case of Aristotle, we are left with the difficulty of determining which works are properly his own (many of them are without a doubt summaries produced by students, apocryphal works, and sections of larger works with their own separate titles), the number offered by the Suda can serve as a guide to Aristoxenus' productivity in general, and specifically in relationship to that of his teacher.

   On Aristoxenus and music, see Laloy 1904; Winnington-Ingram 1968, 10–17, 48–55, 71–88; Levin 1972, 211–34; Pintauda 1978, 12–14; Brancacci 1984, 151–85; Bélis 1986; Barker 1978, 9–16; 1984, 23–64; 1996, 169–70; Najock 1996, 59–76.

   On his activites as a biographer, see Leo 1901, 102; Täger 1923; Arrighetti 1964, 12–13; Momigliano 1974, 79–80; Villari 1996, 696–706; Zaminer 1996, 1152–4.

2. These fragments—twenty-six listed by Wehrli plus one he does not consider—constitute approximately one fifth of the fragments contained in Wehrli's edition of Aristoxenus.

3. See Restani 1988, 26–34.

4. A new commentary on the fragments of Aristoxenus will no longer be able to avoid taking into account how the fragments are distributed in the course of the dialogue, in what context they are cited, and by which personage. Citations from Aristoxenus are often used in arguments with the opinions of other authors or musicians. See Baldwin 1977; Restani 1988.

5. On the musicological problems posed by Book Fourteen, I note here only a few of the indispensable contributions made since Wehrli's edition: Bélis 1986; Barker 1989 (which contains a selection of ancient writings with commentary); Restani 1988, with the other papers in the volume in which it occurs.

6. Hieronymus, *De viribus illustribus, praef.* (cf. Suetonius fr. 1 Reifersc.): 'hortaris me, Dexter, ut Tranquillum sequens ecclesiasticos scriptores in ordinem digeram et, quod ille in enumerandis gentilium literarum viris fecit illustribus, ego in nostris faciam etc. ... fecerunt hoc idem apud Graecos Hermippus Peripateticus, Antigonus Carystius, Satyrus doctus vir, et omnium longe doctissimus Aristoxenus musicus.'

7. Plutarch, 'Non posse suaviter vivi secundum Epicurum', 1086c: TLG 1093, section C, line 3, Βίους ἀνδρῶν Ἀριστόξενος (fr.10a W.) ἔγραψεν.

8. See Cox 1983, 10–13.

9. See Leo 1901, 102; Wehrli on FF 47, 50–60, 61–8; cf. Wehrli 10.118f.

10. Cardini has also remarked on anti-Platonic polemic in Aristoxenus' biographical works: see *I Pitagorici. Testimonianze e frammenti*, esp. fasc. II, 85 and n. 4; fasc. III, 272 ff.

11. Arrighetti 1964, 12.

12. Cf. P. Maas, *RE* V A I, 391 n. 6; Wehrli ad loc.

13. See Zecchini 1989a.

14. A complete consideration of the problems associated with this fragment is found in Zecchini 1988, 362–71.

15. Of the vast and recent bibliography on this fragment, Fraschetti's contribution (1981, 97–115) remains fundamental.

16. The genesis of this discussion about the bigamy of Socrates is considered in Prandi 1985, 62–6.

17. 1969, 157–79; cf. Chapter 6.

18. Fr. 87 Wehrli = *Deipn*. 11.467a: καθάπερ πολλάκις Ἀριστόξενός φησι. Contrast Epitome, vol. 2.2, p. 54, l. 30: ὡς Ἀριστόξενός φησι.

19. These findings further support the hypothesis presented in a recent article (Villari 1996) on the possibility of attributing to Aristoxenus a sourceless fragment contained in the first book and repeated with surprising lexical

analogies in the anonymous *Life* of Sophocles. The correspondence found between the narration of Athenaeus (1.20 e) and the information contained in the anonymous *Life* (3, 5, 32) suggests that there may have been a common source, perhaps biographical or scholarly in nature, for these two texts. The article reconsiders the similarity between the text of Athenaeus and that of the *Vita Sophoclis*, using criteria other than those used by Leo. The common information provided by both Athenaeus and the *Life* contain the following elements: an early education related to dance, received by the young Sophocles; the name of his music teacher, Lampros; his role in the chorus which intoned the *epinikion* on victory at Salamis; and the performance of the poet dressed in the clothes of the Thracian singer Thamyris. There are many sources used by Athenaeus and cited in the anonymous *Life*: Istros (1, 3, 6, 14, 17), Straton (1), Satyrus (6, 13, 14), Aristoxenus (1, 23), Hieronymos (12) and Aristophanes the comic poet (22). It must be noted that Aristoxenus, an author known to the compiler of the biography, must have been a particularly important source for the biography of Sophocles, because he is cited twice in twenty-three extremely brief paragraphs. One citation occurs in a passage considering the profession of the father of Sophocles (1), evoked in a polemical manner with respect to other authors. The second occurs in a more technical passage, which is nonetheless of great importance from a musical history perspective, namely the adaptation of the Phrygian *melopoiea* (typical of the dithyramb) by Sophocles for tragedy (23). Villari 1996 argues that the text of Athenaeus and that of the *Vita Sophoclis* depend on the same source and that the most likely candidate is Aristoxenus.

## 34 Athenaeus on Greek Wine

1. On this treatise see now Sideras 1994, 1094 and 1187–8; Ullmann 1994, 1318–19, with references to earlier literature. It is a potential objection to the attribution that the authorities cited in our passage all go back to the later fourth or early third centuries BC, though the dietetic approach is in line with Rufus' known interests.

2. This is the conventional date, which derives from the biography in the Suda. Recently, it has been argued that the Arabic sources, which report that Galen died in his eighties, are to be preferred; since the year of his birth is fairly firmly established in 129, this would give a death-date after 210, perhaps 216 (Nutton 1973, 159–61; 1984, 320–4); conveniently reprinted together as Chapters 2 and

3 of Nutton 1988). This would not affect the argument here, however, except to make Galen a very grand old man and increase the probability that he was alive when *Deipnosophistae* was published.

3. On this topic in general, see Breitschädel 1986. Classical Greek perception of wine seems to focus more on aroma, a tendency reflected in the passages cited by Athenaeus: Brock 1994, 466–7.

4. The term is, with one exception (368e = Xen. *Cyn.* 5.30) also used figuratively in its other appearances in Athenaeus (all citations) with reference to the texture of a fish's flesh: 106d, 121c, 355d (Diphilus of Siphnos); 327d (Hicesius; on whom, see Chapter 37).

5. A similarly sceptical view is expressed more briefly on general grounds by Scarborough 1981, 19–21.

6. See Brock 1994, 466, for a brief account of the problems of Pramnian and Bibline.

7. Mendean does not appear in ms. A in 4.146e (fr. 224.5 of Menander's play *Methe* or *Drunkenness*), but does so at 8.364d, whence it was restored (with a change of word-order) in the earlier passage by Porson (Professor Arnott kindly confirmed the manuscript readings).

8. On wine in Athenian comedy see also Dalby 2000.

9. Salviat 1986; 1990.

10. Strictly speaking, Apollodorus' pamphlet was presumably a prescription and, while he praised Peparethian above all other wines, he noted that it was less celebrated ('minoris famae') because it took six years to reach maturity.

11. Marangou 1993; Marangou-Lerat 1995.

12. On Roman imports see esp. Tchernia 1986, 100–7, 153–7, 240–9, 358; cf. Paterson 1982; Purcell 1986.

13. Jouanna 1996.

14. See further Chapters 36–8, for the importance of dietetics in contemporary medicine and in Athenaeus' medical interests.

15. Empereur 1993.

## 35 Athenaeus and the Cult of Dionysos Orthos

1. Cf. Harding 1994, 185. Wagner (*RE* 2.1904) distinguishes Amphictyon the king from the son of Deucalion, not taking into account Apollod. 1.7.2, who is elsewhere (3.14.6) uncertain.

2. Cf. Nestle 1936, 155; Jacoby 1949, 133–4.

3. So Plato in *Philebus* (*Deipn.* 10.423a–b) attributes the mixing of wine to Dionysus or Hephaestus or some other deity. Athenaeus on wine-mixing and libations: 2.37e–38f, 5.179e, 11.464f-465c, 14.628a–b, 15.675b–c, 15.693d–f and *passim*.

4. Cf. the name *Agathodaimonistai* for a drinking club in Athens: Parker 1996, 335.

5. Cf. *Deipn.* 1.26b: ἡδὺν γὰρ εἶναι τὸν οἶνον παρεγχεομένης θαλάσσης. Note that Akte or Aktaia were known as an early name for Attica (Eur. *Hel.* 1673; Strabo 8. pp. 391, 397; Paus. 1.2.6; Hesych. s.v.). The anecdote of Philonides might be an allegorizing variant of the myth of Amphictyon, son of Deucalion, introducing mixed wine to Attica after the Deluge.

6. This is consistent with the general antiquarian interests of Philochorus; cf. Jacoby 1949, 108, 117, 121–2. Athenaeus duplicates the description of the sympotic custom in 15.693d–e, which too suggests that this is the important part of the more extended quotation in Book Two.

7. Cf. Dionysus ἰατρός, the Doctor, and ὑγιάτης, the Health-giver, in *Deipn.* 1.22e, and 2.36b; Asclepius was known as ὄρθιος (*RE* 2.1677).

8. Anacr. *Fr.* 300 Page, Euenus *AP* 11.49, Ar. *Poet.* 25.1461a14–6.

9. Hyg. *Astr.* 2.4, *Fab.* 130.3–4, Schol. Germ. BP p. 66, 6, Ampel. 2.6, Ael. *VH* 7.28, Nonn. 47.34–264; Eratosthenes *Erigone*: καὶ βαθὺν ἀκρήτωι πνεύμονα τεγγόμενος (*CA* 25 Powell).

10. *Conciderunt*, Hyg. *Fab.* 130.2.

11. The scene is depicted in a mosaic in the 'House of Dionysus' in Paphos: Icarius with his cart and two other prostrate and inebriated figures (οἱ πρῶτοι οἶνον πιόντες); cf. *LIMC* s.v. Dionysos/Bacchus 257.

12. Call. *Fr.* 178.3–4: Ἰκαρίου καὶ παιδὸς ἄγων ἐπέτειον ἀγιστύν,/ ᾿Ατθίσιν οἰκτίστη, σὸν φάος, Ἠριγόνη.

13. Apollod. 3.14.7, Luc. *Salt.* 39–40.

14. Cf. Burkert 1985, 237–42.

15. Schol. Ar. *Ach.* 1076, *Ran.* 218; Robertson 1993, 201 may be wrong in his claim that 'the flood story has no connexion anywhere with the worship of Dionysus, no connexion either with any of the mythical figures who are avowedly responsible for the ritual of the Anthesteria: Orestes, Erigone and Icarius.'

16. Plut. *Mor.* 527d: 'the phallos signalled the end of the procession of the Country Dionysia at Athens'. Cf. Pickard-Cambridge 1988, 43; Burkert 1985, 163.

17. In *Ach.* 259–60 ὦ Ξανθία, σφῶιν δ᾿ ἐστὶν ὀρθὸς ἑκτέος / ὁ φαλλὸς ἐξόπισθε τῆς κανηφόρου, Dicaeopolis celebrates a Dionysiac phallic procession (cf. 243: ὁ Ξανθίας τὸν φαλλὸν ὀρθὸν στησάτω). As he finishes singing a hymn to Φαλῆς (263 ff.: Φαλῆς, ἑταῖρε Βακχίου...), he is interrupted by the chorus who pelt him with stones (280 ff.: οὗτος αὐτός ἐστιν, οὗτος. / βάλλε, βάλλε, βάλλε, βάλλε, / παῖε πᾶς τὸν μιαρόν. / οὐ βαλεῖς; οὐ βαλεῖς;).

Cf. also *Thesm.* 643–4: <u>Κλεισθ</u>. ἀνίστασ' ὀρθός.—ποῖ τὸ πέος ὠθεῖς κάτω; / <u>Μίκκα</u> τοδὶ διέκυψε καὶ μάλ' εὔχρων. ὦ τάλαν.; *Lys.* 995 ὀρσὰ Λακεδαίμων πᾶα καὶ τοὶ σύμμαχοι. ibid. 833–4: ὦ πότνια Κύπρου καὶ Κυθήρου καὶ Πάφου / μεδέουσ'. ἴθ' ὀρθὴν ἥνπερ ἔρχει τὴν ὁδόν. In these passages the adjective ὀρθός carries sexual connotations.

18. Relevant oracular responses from Delphi and Dodona are preserved in D. 21.51–3.

19. Cf. Faraone 1992, 105 and n. 69.

20. So Laius, for example, forgot the injunction against having children when he got drunk (E. *Ph.* 21 f.). Cf. Ar. *Prob.* 953b30.

21. Based on Orphic sources (*RE* 17.974)?

22. Cf. Pickard-Cambridge 1962, 140. Parker 1996, 162, n. 32 has a number of references to other phallic gods celebrated in Athens, among whom there was a certain *Orthannes* (also a title of a play by Eubulus).

23. Pickard-Cambridge 1946, 4.

24. Cf. Hooker 1960, 116.

25. Rohde 1898, 254.

26. Cf. Burkert 1985, 238. Robertson 1993, 203–5 refutes this.

27. Hooker 1960, 117 interestingly suggests that the way to the Underworld which Heracles took to fetch Cerberus was situated in the sanctuary *en Limnais*.

28. Cf. A. *Pers.* 687, *Ch.* 496, *Eum.* 318, 963; Maniae are the same as Erinyes: Paus. 8.34.1.

29. Paus. 3.16.7: τὸ δὲ χωρίον τὸ ἐπονομαζόμενον Λιμναῖον Ὀρθίας ἱερόν ἐστιν Ἀρτέμιδος. Gruppe 1906, 742–4 claims that the epithet Orthia is also a local title and traces it in the Carian city of Orthosia, which also had a flourishing Dionysiac cult (*contra* Ruge, *RE* 36.1493).

30. Cf. Vernant and Frontisi-Ducroux 1983, 32ff. Cf. also Paus. 8.39.5–6 (Phigalia in Arcadia): ἔστι δὲ Σωτείρας τε ἱερὸν ἐνταῦθα Ἀρτέμιδος καὶ ἄγαλμα ὀρθὸν λίθου· ἐκ δὲ τοῦ ἱεροῦ καὶ τὰς πομπάς σφισι πέμπειν κατέστη. [...] πεποίηται δὲ καὶ Διονύσου ναός· ἐπίκλησις μέν ἐστιν αὐτῶι παρὰ τῶν ἐπιχωρίων Ἀκρατοφόρος, τὰ κάτω δὲ οὐκ ἔστι σύνοπτα τοῦ ἀγάλματος ὑπὸ δάφνης τε φύλλων καὶ κισσῶν. ὁπόσον δὲ αὐτοῦ καθορᾶν ἔστιν, ἐπαλήλιπται *** κιννάβαρι ἐκλάμπειν. (Here there is a sanctuary of Artemis Saviour with a standing image of stone. From this sanctuary it is their custom to start their processions. [...] A temple also of Dionysus is here, who by the inhabitants is surnamed Acratophorus, but the lower part of the image cannot be seen for laurel-leaves and ivy. As much of it as can be seen is painted...with cinnabar to shine.)

31. Ibid.3.16. 9: μαρτύρια δέ μοι καὶ τάδε, τὴν ἐν Λακεδαίμονι Ὀρθίαν τὸ ἐκ τῶν βαρβάρων εἶναι ξόανον [...]; 11· οὕτω τῶι ἀγάλματι ἀπὸ τῶν ἐν τῆι Ταυρικῆι θυσιῶν ἐμμεμένηκεν ἀνθρώπων αἵματι ἥδεσθαι· καλοῦσι δὲ οὐκ Ὀρθίαν μόνον ἀλλὰ καὶ Λυγοδέσμαν τὴν αὐτήν, ὅτι ἐν θάμνωι λύγων εὑρέθη, περιειληθεῖσα δὲ ἡ λύγος ἐποίησε τὸ ἄγαλμα ὀρθόν.

32. Cf. D. 54.17.

33. Pentheus, Agave and Actaeon appear symmetrically opposite Dionysus and his followers, maenads and a satyr, in an Apulian Underworld funerary crater. Dionysus is clasping the hand of Hades. This is a gesture which reveals the god's special relationship with the Underworld and alludes to specific, Orphic, soteriological beliefs; cf. Johnston and McNiven (1996). See also *TrGF* II.630, fr. a, and Bierl 1991, 247.

34. The description of the miraculous action of Dionysus is reminiscent of the way the robber Sinis is depicted in Attic vase-painting as bending down a tree and challenging Theseus; in some depictions of the story the roles are reversed and Theseus restrains the terrified villain with the one hand, while with the other he prepares for him the same gruesome death he meted out to his victims. In *Table Talk* Plutarch discusses the association of the pine with Dionysus and Poseidon (675dff.).

35. *Annales* 11.31: At Messalina non alias solutior luxu, adulto autumno simulacrum vindemiae per domum celebrabat. Urgeri prela, fluere lacus; et feminae pellibus accinctae adsultabant ut sacrificantes vel insanientes Bacchae; ipsa crine fluxo thyrsum quatiens, iuxtaque Silius hedera vinctus, gerere cothurnos, iacere caput, strepente circum procaci choro. Ferunt Vettium Valentem lascivia in praealtam arborem conisum, interrogantibus quid aspiceret, respondisse tempestatem ab Ostia atrocem, sive coeperat ea species, seu forte lapsa vox in praesagium vertit. (But Messalina had never given voluptuousness a freer rein. Autumn was at the full, and she was celebrating a mimic vintage through the grounds of the house. Presses were being trodden, vats flowed; while, beside them, skin-girt women were bounding like Bacchanals excited by sacrifice or delirium. She herself was there with dishevelled tresses and waving thyrsus; at her side, Silius with an ivy crown, wearing the buskins and tossing his head, while around him rose the din of a wanton chorus. The tale runs that Vettius Valens, in some freak of humour, clambered into a tall tree, and to the question, 'What did he spy?' answered: 'A frightful storm over Ostia'—whether something of the kind was actually taking shape, or a chance-dropped word developed into a prophecy. (tr. Jackson). Cf. Plutarch's *Crassus* 33.2–4 for another re-enactment of the *Bacchae*.

## 36 The Physicians at the Feast: The Place of Medical Knowledge at Athenaeus' Dinner-Table

1. Notable Ephesian physicians of the imperial period include both Rufus and Soranus; and a Paul of Nicaea appears in the Byzantine period.
2. As, shown, for example, in the *De Morbis Acutis et Chroniis* of Anonymus Parisinus, an imperial text that nonetheless includes no post-Hellenistic doxographical material.
3. Testimonies to, and fragments of, the former pair are collected in Wellman 1901; for the latter pair they are collected in Bertier 1972.
4. Philistion: 3.115d and 12.516c; Dieuches 1.5b; Diocles: 2.46d, 2.53d–e, 2.55b, 2.57b, 2.59b, 2.61c, 2.68d–e–f, 3.86b–c, 3.110b, 3.116b, 3.120d, 7.301c, 7.305b, 7.316c, 7.320d, 7.324f, 7.326a, 9.371d and 12.516c; Mnesitheus: 1.5a, 1.32d, 2.22e, 2.36a, 2.54b, 2.57b, 2.59b, 3.80c–e, 3.92b, 3.96d, 3.106b, 3.115f, 3.121d, 8.355a, 8.357a, 10.419b–c and 11.483f.
5. Praxagoras: 1.32c, 1.41a, 1.46d and 15.687e; Phylotimus: 2.53f, 3.79a, 3.81a, 3.82f, 7.308e and 8.355a; Plistonicus: 2.45d. Complete collections of testimonies and fragments are contained in Steckerl 1958.
6. For Herophilus and the Herophileans, see von Staden 1989.
7. 2.50b, 2.51a–b, 2.51f, 2.53f–54b, 2.54c–d, 2.55b and f, 2.57c, 2.58e, 2.59b, 2.61c–e, 2.62c–f, 2.64b, 2.69e, 2.71e; 3.73a, 3.74c, 3.80b–c, 3.80e, 3.82f, 3.90a and b–e, 3.91e–92a, 3.106c–d, 3.115c, 3.120e–121a, 3.121b–d; 8.355a–357a, 8.369d, e–f, 8.371a, b, d, e; 14.650b.
8. 2.53c, 2.64a, e, 2.74b, 2.76d–e, 3.79e and 3.120b; for the rest of Heraclides' works see Deichgräber, 1930, 172–202.
9. Philonides of Sicily appears in Erotian's Hippocratic lexicon of the first century AD (36. 8–9 and 84. 19–21 Nachmanson) and Galen *Diff. Puls.* (8. 748 K). Andromachus the Younger, also in the first century AD, includes a recipe of Philonides among his drugs appropriated by Galen (13. 978 K).
10. Some of the medical material in Book 7 of Macrobius' *Saturnalia* comes more or less direct from Plutarch, but it is also accompanied by material drawn from the more anonymous (or pseudonymous) traditions of medical and natural questions or problems.
11. On Asclepiades, see Vallance 1990. His omission by Athenaeus is also noteworthy in that it indicates that he was not reliant on the standard philosophical–doxographical tradition (in which Asclepiades regularly appears) either.
12. Of course, reputations may also travel faster, and further, than texts: see Nutton 1984.

13. Macrobius' discussants cover the first three topics (*Sat.* 7.6–7) but not the last; though they do treat subjects as distant from the dinner-table as why spinning round and round causes dizziness and why hair goes grey (7.6.9–10). The conventions of convivial conversation that Macrobius articulates, however, pertain to both tone and subject-matter, striving for some continuity between dining and discussion on both fronts (1.1 and 7.11.1); see Bertier 1972.

## 37 Hicesius' Fish and Chips

1. For Hellenistic medicine and for the medical schools of the Roman period, see the papers collected in Grmek 1995. For the fragments, von Staden 1989; Garofalo 1988.
2. The end of this sentence is not very clear. Corais tried to emend it, as did Meineke after him.
3. For another possible member of this school, cf. Wellmann 1892.
4. Regnault 1900; I could not find this inscription in the *IKA*.
5. But we do not know how Tertullian knew about him.
6. Hanson 1997, 289.
7. I am told that Books 3 and 4 are in preparation.
8. Cf. Bertier 1972 and Dumont 1988.
9. See Gourevitch 1984.

## 38 Athenaeus Medicine and Demography

1. Wilkins and Hill 1994. See also Olson and Sens, 2000.
2. The total exceeds 105 because there are multiple references in some cases.
3. Note that Athenaeus does not restrict himself to medical authors, citing Plato from *Laws* 674b.
4. Compare Plutarch *Table Talk* 7.1. 698, on Plato *Timaeus* 70d.

## 39 Athenaeus the Ur-Pornographer

1. Cf. Henry 1985, 1991, 1995.
2. Kappeler 1987, 2.
3. Daly 1984, 232.
4. Kappeler 1987, 90–1.
5. See Pollitt 1990 ad loc.
6. Richlin 1991.
7. Halperin, Winkler and Zeitlin 1990, 19.
8. von Reden 1995.
9. Kurke 1997.
10. Henry 1995, 57ff..
11. Kendrick 1987, 1996, 42.
12. Kendrick 1987, 1996, 33.

13. E.g. Griffin 1981.
14. *Letters* vol. 8 no. 8984. A few years later, Voltaire remarked, in a brief essay on the novel, upon some charming narrative byways to be found in Athenaeus (*Letters* vol. 12, no. 14239).
15. See Poster 1971.
16. Poster 1971, 6.
17. 1769: *Le Pornographe*; 1770: *Le Mimographe*; 1777: *Les Gynographes*; 1782: *L'Andrographe*; 1789: *Le Thesmographe*; 1796–7: *Le Glossographe* (in *Monsieur Nicolas*). Though Poster concentrates on *Les Gynographes*, *L'Andrographe* and *Le Thesmographe* and skilfully contextualizes them, he says very little about the first in the series, *Le Pornographe*, which is the only one to have enjoyed much popularity. Indeed, it was translated into German and Italian; in discussing Restif's influence on German thought, Poster neglects to mention *Le Pornographe*, the first and arguably most influential of Restif's works.
18. Walkowitz 1980, Bernheimer 1989, and Kendrick 1987.
19. Marder 1979, 174.

# Section VII: The Other Athenaeus

## Introductory Remarks

1. *Deipn* 1.1e, with Nutton 1995; Dalby 1996, 260n.15; cf. 1.1c on Masurius.

## 40 Athenaeus, On the Kings of Syria

1. *FHG* III. 656–7 offers the interesting observation that the *Suda's* mention of a Syrian work in three books by a Timaeus could be the consequence of ancient misattribution of Athenaeus' *On the Kings of Syria* to Timaeus. If that were so, it would follow that Athenaeus' work was in three books (unless that too was muddled, together with authorship). Athenaeus' work certainly entailed at least two books (see further below).

However, for all its interest, the observation lacks support in the evidence: we might do better to wonder whether a Timaeus (indeed, Timaeus of Tauromenium himself) did write a Syrian work, an *On the Kings of Syria*. If so, that work should be included among the forerunners of Athenaeus' own treatment. We may be sure that we have lost not only a vast number of ancient texts, but also a great deal even of titles and the names of authors. Why should we doubt the *Suda's* evidence that a Timaeus (or *the* Timaeus) did indeed write a work on Syria?

2. But on which subject precisely? There is a problem in the Greek here, perhaps connected with the foregoing lacuna; the general sense seems to be that Athenaeus wrote not about Demetrius, but about Alexander and his symposium, on which more below.
3. This was a form named after a certain Lysis, who seems to have flourished *c.*300 BC. The key point for this anecdote is that the form entailed females taking male roles, dressed as men. The singer shortly appears in the role of Diogenes himself, dressed accordingly.
4. Kaibel's neat emendation (ad loc.) requires the addition of no more than a single letter, making διό into δι'ὅν. Yet, as Gulick notes ad loc., the hanging nominatives still need a verb.
5. Gulick ad loc., with Jos. AJ 13. 36; for a more positive assessment, see Marasco 1982, 173 n. 26.
6. That is the result of his emendation: see n. 4
7. Much depends on the interpretation of περὶ οὗ, which could in principle refer to Alexander, his symposium or Demetrius, though the sense seems to require the first of these, namely Alexander.
8. Jones 1986, 6–7. Note also that Lucian wrote *On the Syrian Goddess*.
9. Syme 1980, 101, also supporting the identification of Athenaeus' Ulpian as the father of the jurist, no doubt correctly: see Chapter 1.
10. Bowersock 1969, 101–9 is judicious.
11. Dessau 1890.
12. Desrousseaux 1956, xv.
13. E.g. 8.346c; 12.571a; 14.649c; alias his Phoenician origins, e.g. 4.175a; 15.697a.
14. See Edson 1958, with the critique of Marasco 1982, 172 n. 21, and the literature there cited; cf. also Swain 1996, 252.
15. Downey 1963, 45–72 collects some examples. I am grateful to Michel Austin for bringing Libanius' possible relevance to my attention.
16. 10.438c–440b; a Seleucus (Nicator?) was among the kings after whom a cup was named, 11.487f.
17. *FGrH* 165.
18. Notably, 1.18e, aphrodisiacs from India; 2.45e, water; 2.73b, Nature and Syria; 4.155a–b. Antiochus III, dancing and a historian in a sympotic context; 4.193d, Antiochus IV's banquet; 4.194c, his Roman-style parade at Daphne; 6.244f (cf. 7.290a), a Seleucid parasite; 6.245f-5a, (Athenian) Lemnos honours Seleucids; 12.540a–c, Daphne; 13.593e, a mistress; 14.652f, an Indian king; cf. 4.153a–b; 12.578a.
19. Kidd 1988, 913–14; cf. 11–12.
20. E.g. Rutherford 1989, 87–8.

21. Marasco 1982; Swain 1996, 249.

22. Marasco 1982, 74–5 with the literature he cites. Even the careful study of Zecchini 1990 (esp. 230–2) gives credence to the notion, though valuably he notes that Athenaeus shows no sign of having read Timagenes, whose work the author is likely to have known, but not approved. Those searching for the sources of Appian's Syrian work have looked rather towards Polybius (Brodersen 1993, 357), whom Athenaeus certainly knew and used for the *Deipnosophistae* (Chapter 11). Can we really suppose that Polybius had no impact on Athenaeus' Syrian work also?

23. Recent discussions (notably Brodersen 1993, 355–60; Swain 1996, 248–53) show the limitations of the notion.

24. See Swain 1996, 249 n. 36.

25. Swain 1996, 253 is judicious on what may be Appian's inadequate attempts at Atticism.

26. Zecchini 1990, 222 offers predecessors: did Athenaeus also write an *On the Kings of Egypt*? If so, we must explain his failure to mention it, at least in his extant text.

27. E.g. Ameling 1996, 120–1; Bowie 1974, 180; Bowie 1996, 211–12.

28. *FHG* IV. 485; note *Deipn.* 3.124d for Protagorides' treatment of Antiochus' journey on the Nile; 4.150c shows Athenaeus' awareness also of Protagorides' *Games at Daphne*; cf. 13.593e on Phylarchus, with Marasco 1982, 145–7 and the works there cited.

29. For a survey, see Georgiadou and Larmour 1994.

## 41 Athenaeus and the Fishes of Archippus

1. See further Chapter 9.

2. εἶδες τὴν Θασίαν ἅλμην οἷ' ἄττα βαύζει,
   ὡς εὖ καὶ ταχέως ἀπετείσατο καὶ παραχρῆμα.
   οὐ μέντοι παρὰ κωφὸν ὁ τυφλὸς ἔοικε λαλῆσαι.

3. An iambic line either from comedy (Adesp. fr. 1254 K) or satyr (Adesp. fr. 93 Nauck²). It is not included in Kassel and Austin's edition of the comic fragments.

4. Cynulcus is responding to charges that he and other philosophers hypocritically admired Archestratus of Gela whose *Hedupatheia* had shown readers how to traverse the Mediterranean to satisfy the belly.

5. Compare Aristophanes, *Merchant Ships* fr. 426 ὦ κακοδαίμων ὅστις ἐν ἅλμι πρῶτον τριχίδων ἀπεβάφθη (presumably a human being and not a fish is addressed).

6. Note that in Greek ἡδύς may include savoury as well as sweet flavours.

7. Unless we believe Philochorus in an ambiguous fragment at 11.464f.

8. Those who believe the symposium was the preserve of the rich reckon without comedy, which represents sympotic themes as part of itself in the popular theatre. See Wilkins, forthcoming.

9. οἱ ἀρχαῖοι. Reference to the past is a major theme. One of the most remarkable statements in Athenaeus (and there are many to choose from) is οὐκ ἐμέθυον οἱ πάλαι (the ancients did not get drunk), at 10.427e.

10. For the image editors compare the *Stromateis* of Clement of Alexandria.

11. For a different approach to the place of Archippus in comic criticism, see Kaibel 1889.

12. A member of the sardine family: Thompson 1947, 77–8. Wellmann contends (1888, 179) that here Athenaeus, in his zeal for his own work, has omitted other regular sources used in Book Seven, such as Archestratus, Diocles and Dorion. He may be right, but *thraittai* are not the only item in the catalogue of fish to depend on comedy alone.

13. The fish is the sand-smelt according to Thompson 1947, 3–4.

14. Athenaeus might well have commented on the *komoidoumenoi* given the names of fish, but does not do so.

15. On the Hellenistic editors of comedy see Pfeiffer 1968, 119–20, 159–62, 224, 249. An early example of a commentary on a single comedy was by Euphonius on the *Plutus* of Aristophanes.

16. He shows no interest in the choreography or significance of the chorus, on which see Lawler 1941, who has interesting material also on fish, the sacred (see below) and fertility ritual.

17. 24 (= 3.86c):λεπάσιν, ἐχίνοις, ἐσχάραις, βαλάνοις τε τοῖς κτεσίν τε.
    26 (= 7.312a): τοὺς μαιώτας καὶ σαπέρδας καὶ γλάνιδας.

18. 16 (= 7.322a):ἐκήρυξεν βόαξ, σάλπης δ' ἐσάλπιγξ' ἔπτ' ὀβολοὺς μισθὸν φέρων.
    17 (= 7.315b):ἱερεὺς γὰρ ἦλθ' αὐτοῖσιν ὀρφώς του θεῶν.
    18 (= 7.328b):ἱερεὺς Ἀφροδίτης χρύσοφρυς Κυθηρίας.

19. = 6.227a Αἰγύπτιος μιαρώτατος τῶν ἰχθύων κάπηλος, Ἕρμαιος, ὃς βίαι δέρων ῥίνας γαλεούς τε πωλεῖ καὶ τοὺς λάβρακας ἐντερεύων, ὡς λέγουσιν ἡμῖν.

20. = 8.343c. Athenaeus lists comic poets who attacked Melanthius.

21. (= 8.331c) ἄνδρες ἰχθύες: neither play nor the exact formula is certain.

22. (= 3.86c) κῆρυξ θαλάσσης τρόφιμος, υἱὸς πορφύρας.

23. (= 7.301a) καὶ τὴν μὲν ἀφύην καταπέπωκεν + ἑψητὸς ἐντυχών.

24. 7.277f.

25. (= 10.424a–b) κύαθον ἐπιάμην παρὰ Δαισίου.

26. παλιναιρέτους.
27. 22 τὴν ἀγορὰν μυληκόρωι, 33 νακοτιλτοῦτα.
28. ἀπαγκωνισάμενος.
29. ἀγροῦ πυγή.
30. See e.g. Meineke 1839–57, 205–8.
31. Athenaeus elsewhere explores the few cases he could find of fish belonging to the sacred in Greek culture: see 7.282e–284d, 296a–297c, 297e–298a, Lawler 1941, Detienne and Vernant 1989, 221.
32. Compare 9.402d: 'The dinners spoken of by the comic poets provide the sweetest sounds for the ear rather than sweetness for the throat.'
33. On this aspect of fish see Davidson 1997.
34. On the 'edible woman' see Henry 1992; cf. Chapter 39.
35. Note that more species of fish exist than any other human foodstuff: Davidson 1999.
36. For example, on authors of books on cakes, Ulpian observes (14.648c), 'Grammarians of great learning, from where and from what collection of books (*bibliotheke*) have these most revered writers Chrysippus and Harpocration made their epiphany? They slander the names of those noble philosophers [Chrysippus of Soli and Harpocration—the Platonist?] by sharing their names.'
37. As Lycophron and Polemon made clear: see Athenaeus 7.278a, 15.698b–699c.
38. Fr. 31: the kitharos 'takes pleasure in big spenders and is unchecked in extravagance'.

39. Jeanneret 1991 has valuable comments on Athenaeus as a materialist, and on the reception of Athenaeus and the less materially based Plutarch as authoritative texts in the Renaissance.
40. ἐπὶ ταῖς ἀβυτάκαισι δ' ἐκβακχεύομεν.
41. 3.123e–124c.
42. For similar comparison between cold water or snow and frigid poetry see 13.579e–580a, a citation of Machon (258–84 Gow) on observations of the *hetaira* Gnathaina on the poetry of her lover Diphilus the comic poet.
43. 14.621d–622d. Sosibius on the *deikelistai* and *phlyakes*, Semus of Delos on the *ithyphalloi* and the *phallophoroi*.
44. Passages from Middle Comedy relating to Thebes are liberally inserted into the text of Athenaeus from 14.621d to 623c.
45. See Kock, Arnott 1996, 435.
46. 12.552e–f.
47. The crayfish is both a predator of other fish and a favoured food for humans: Callimedon is theoretically both a consumer and consumable.
48. Fr. 149 is cited at 8.340c.
49. On the *karabos* and the consumption of congers and squid see Thompson 1947, 102–3.
50. See Giannini 1960, Dohm 1964, Berthiaume 1982.
51. 8.365e.
52. They even coin the verb ἰχθυολογεῖν, 'fish-speaking' or 'fish-collecting' at 8.360d.

# BIBLIOGRAPHY

Adler, A. 1928 *Lexicographi Graeei: Suidae Lexicon* (Stuttgart).

Ahl, F. 1984 'The art of safe criticism in Greece and Rome', *American Journal of Philology* 105. 174–208.

Aldick, C. 1928 *De Athenaei Dipnosophistarum epitomae codicibus Erbacensi Laurentiano Parisino* (diss. Münster).

Allen, R.E. 1993 *The Attalid Kingdom: A Constitutional History* (Oxford).

Ambaglio, D. 1990 'I *Deipnosofisti* di Ateneo e la tradizione storica frammentaria', *Athenaeum* 78. 51–64.

Ameling, W. 1996 'Pausanias und die hellenistische Geschichte', in Bingen, J. (ed.), *Pausanias–Historien* (Entretiens Fondation Hardt 41, Geneva), 207–30.

Anderson, G. 1993 *The Second Sophistic: A Cultural Phenomenon in the Roman Empire* (London).

Anderson, G. 1994a *Sage, Saint and Sophist: Holy Men and their Associates in the Early Roman Empire* (London).

Anderson, G. 1994b 'Aulus Gellius: A Miscellanist and his World', in *Aufstieg und Niedergang der römischen Welt* II.34.2. 1834–62.

Anderson, G. 1997 'Athenaeus: the sophistic environment', *Aufstieg und Niedergang der römischen Welt* II.34.3. 2173–85.

Anderson, W.D. 1994 *Music and Musicians in Ancient Greece* (Ithaca and London).

Anderson, W.S. 1986 'Gripus and Stratonicus: Plautus' *Rudens*, 930–36', *American Journal of Philology* 107. 560–3.

André, J. 1960 'Notes sur une édition récente d'Athénée', *Revue de Philologie* 34. 51–7.

Andrieu, J. 1954 *Le Dialogue antique, structure et presentation* (Paris).

Apfel, H.V. 1938 'Homeric criticism in the fourth century BC', *Transactions of the American Philological Association* 69. 245–58

Arafat, K.W. 1995 'Pausanias and the temple of Hera at Olympia', *Annual of the British School at Athens* 90. 461–73.

Arafat, K.W. 1996 *Pausanias' Greece. Ancient Artists and Roman Rulers* (Cambridge).

Arnott, W.G. 1957 'Split anapaests, with reference to some passages in Alexis', *Classical Quarterly* 7. 188–98.

Arnott, W.G. 1964 'A note on the two manuscripts of Athenaeus' *Deipnosophistae* in the British Museum', *Scriptorium* 18. 269–70.

Arnott, W.G. 1996 *Alexis: The Fragments. A commentary* (Cambridge).

Arnott, W.G. (forthcoming), 'On editing fragments', in Wilkins J. and Harvey D. (eds), *The Rivals of Aristophanes* (London).

Arnould, D. 1990 *Le Rire et les larmes dans la littérature grecque d'Homère à Platon* (Paris).

Arrighetti, G. 1964 *Satiro, Vita di Euripide* (Pisa).

Arrighetti, G. 1977 'Hypomnemata et Scholia: Alcuni problemi', *Museum Philologum Londiniense* 2. 49–67

Arrighetti, G. 1987 *Poeti eruditi e biografi, momenti della riflessione dei Greci sulla letteratura* (Pisa).

Astin, A.E. 1978 *Cato the Censor* (Oxford).

Austin, C. 1973 *Comicorum Graecorum Fragmenta in Papyris Reperta* (Berlin).

Autori vari, Ministero per i beni culturali 1987 *L'alimentazione nel mondo antico* (Rome).

Avezzù, E. 1989 'Il ventre del parassita: identità, spazio e tempio discontinuo', in Longo, O and Scarpi, P. (eds) *Homo Edens* (Verona), 235–40.

Avotins, I. 1975 'The holders of the chairs of rhetoric at Athens', *Harvard Studies in Classical Philology* 79. 320–1.

Badian, E. 1958 'The Eunuch Bagoas', *Classical Quarterly* 8. 144–57.

Bailey, C. 1926 *Epicurus: The Extant Remains* (Oxford).

Bakhtin, M. 1981 *The Dialogic Imagination: Four Essays* (C. Emerson and M. Holquist trans.; Austin).

Balbi, H. A. 1932 *Some Bibliographical Notes on the First Book Printed on the Siege of Malta, 1565—followed by a Bibliographical Notice of Natali Conte and his History of the Siege of Malta* (Malta).

Baldwin, B. 1976 'Athenaeus and his work', *Acta Classica* 19. 21–42.

Baldwin, B. 1977 'The minor characters in Athenaeus', *Acta Classica* 20. 37–48.

Baldwin, B. 1983 *The Philogelos or Laughter–lover* (Amsterdam).

Baldwin, B. 1985 *Studies in Greek and Roman History and Literature* (Amsterdam).

Bandini, A. M. 1768 *Catalogus codicum manuscriptorum Bibliothecae Mediceae Laurentianae* II (Florence).

Bannet, E.T. 1989 *Structuralism and the Logic of Dissent: Barthes, Derrida, Foucault, Lacan* (London).

Bapp, C.A. 1885 'De fontibus quibus Athenaeus in rebus musicis lyricisque enarrandis usus sit', *Leipziger Studien zur Klassischen Philologie* 8. 85–160.

Barber, G.L. 1935 *The Historian Ephorus* (Cambridge).

Barigazzi, A. 1981 'Fenice di Colofone e il giambo di Nino', *Prometheus* 7. 22–34.

Barker, A. 1978 'Music and perception: a study in Aristoxenus', *Journal of Hellenic Studies* 98. 9–16.

Barker, A. 1984 'Aristoxenus' theorems and the foundation of harmonic science', *Ancient Philology* 4. 23–64.

Barker, A. 1984 *Greek Musical Writing*, Vol. I: *The Musician and his Art* (Cambridge).

Barker, A. 1989 *Greek Musical Writings* (Cambridge).

Barker, A. 1996 'Aristoxenus', in Hornblower, S. and Spawforth, A. (eds) *The Oxford Classical Dictionary* (3rd edn, Oxford and New York), 169–70.

Barton, T. 1994 *Power and Knowledge: Astrology, Physiognomics and Medicine under the Roman Empire* (Ann Arbor, Mich.).

Bean, G.E. 1965 *The Inscriptions of Side* (Ankara).

Bean, G.E. and Mitford, T.B. 1970 *Journeys in Rough Cilicia 1964–1968* (Vienna).

Becker, C. 1996 'Nourriture, cuillères, ornements. Les témoignages d'une exploitation variée des mollusques marins à Ayos Mamas (Chalcidique, Grèce)', *Anthropozoologica* 24. 3–17.

Bélis, A. 1985, 'La théorie de l'âme chez Aristoxène de Tarente', *Revue de Philologie de la littérature et d'histoire anciennes* 59. 240–46.

Bélis, A. 1986 *Aristoxène de Tarente et Aristote: Le traité d'harmonique* (Paris).

Bell, J.M. 1978 'Simonides in the Anecdotal Tradition', *Quaderni Urbinati di Cultura Classica* 28. 29–86.

Bengtson, H. 1962 *Einführung in die alte Geschichte* (4th edn revised, Munich).

Bentley, R. 1883 *Dissertations upon the Epistles of Phalaris* (London).

Benveniste, E. 1969 *Le vocabulaire des institutions Indo-européennes, Vol. I* (Paris).

Bergson, H. 1900 *Le Rire. Essai sur la signification du comique* (Paris).

Bernheimer, C. 1989 *Figures of Ill Repute: Representing Prostitution in Nineteenth–Century France* (Cambridge, Mass.).

Bers, V.A. 1997 *Speech in Speech: Studies in Incorporated Oratio Recta in Attic Drama and Oratory* (Lanham).

Berthiaume G. 1982 *Les Rôles du Mágeiros* (Leiden).

Bertier, J. 1972 *Mnésithée et Dieuchès* (Leiden).

Bertier, J. 1988 'Les animaux dans la diététique hippocratique', in Bodson, L. (ed.) *L'animal dans l'alimentation humaine* (Paris), 83–90.

Bielohnlawek, K, 1983 'Precettistica conviviale e simposiale nei poeti greci (da Omero fino alle silloge Teognidea e a Crizia)', in Vetta, M. (ed.) *Poesia e simposio nella Grecia Antica* (Roma and Bari), 95–116.

Bierl, A.F.H. 1991 *Dionysos und die griechische Tragödie* (Tübingen).

Bigi, E. 1962, in Pavan M. and others (edd.) *Dizionario biografico degli Italiani 4* (Rome), 593–95.

Bignone, E. 1936 *L'Aristotele perduto* (Florence).

Birley, A. 1997 *Hadrian: The Restless Emperor* (London).

Birt, T. 1882 *Das antike Buchwesen* (Berlin).

Blair, A. 1992 'Humanist Methods in Natural Philosophy: the Commonplace Book', *Journal of the History of Ideas*, 43.4. 541–51.

Blanck, H. 1992 *Das Buch in der Antike* (Munich).

Blum, H. 1969 *Die antike Mnemotechnik* (Hildesheim and New York).

Blum, R. 1991 *Kallimachos. The Alexandrian Library and the Origins of Bibliography* (trans.; Madison).

Bodson, L. 1975 *Hiera Zoa, Contribution à l'étude de la place de l'animal dans la religion grecque antique* (Brussels).

Bodson, L. (ed.) 1988 *L'animal dans l'alimentation humaine* (Paris).

Bolgar, R.R. 1963 *The Classical Heritage and its Beneficiaries* (Cambridge).

Bolte, J. 1886 'Eine Humanistenkomödie', *Hermes* 21. 313–18.

Bolter, J.D. 1991 *Writing Space. The Computer, Hypertext and the History of Writing* (Hillsdale NJ and London).

Bommelaer, J.F. 1991 *Guide de Delphes: le site* (Paris).

Bompaire, J. 1958 *Lucien écrivain* (Paris).

Bonamente, G. 1980 'Criteri moralistici nella storiografia del iv secolo' in *Tra Grecia e Roma, temi antichi e metodologie moderne* (Rome), 147–54.

Booth, A. 1991 'The Age for Reclining and its Attendant Perils', in Slater, W.J. (ed) *Dining in a Classical Context*, 105–20.

Borthwick, E. 1991 Review of Pearson: *Aristoxenus, Elementa Rhythmica* (1990), *Classical Review.* 41.2. 474.

Borza E.N. 1981 'Anaxarchus and Callisthenes: academic intrigue at Alexander's court', in H. Dell (ed.), *Ancient Macedonian Studies in Honor of Charles F. Edson* (Thessaloniki).

Bosworth, A.B. 1988 *Conquest and Empire: The Reign of Alexander the Great* (Cambridge).

Bottin, L. 1986 'Introduzione', in Ippocrate, *Arie acque luoghi* (Venice).

Boulenger, G. 1907 *Zoology of Egypt. The Fishes of the Nile* (London).

Bourdieu, P. 1977 *Outline of a theory of practice*, trans. R. Nice (Cambridge).

Bourdieu, P. 1990 *The logic of practice*, trans. R. Nice (Cambridge).

Bowersock, G.W. 1969 *Greek Sophists in the Roman Empire* (Oxford).

Bowersock, G.W. 1985 'Athenaeus', in Easterling, P.E. and Knox, B.M.W. (eds), *The Cambridge History of Classical Literature* I (Cambridge), 682–3.

Bowersock, G.W. 1990 *Hellenism in Late Antiquity* (Cambridge).

Bowie, E.L. 1970 'The Greeks and their Past in the Second Sophistic', *Past and Present* 46. 3–41, repr. with revisions in M.I. Finley (ed) *Studies in Ancient Society* (London and Boston, 1974) 166–209.

Bowie, E.L. 1982 'The importance of sophists', *Yale Classical Studies* 27. 29–59.

Bowie, E.L. 1990 '*Miles ludens?* The problem of martial exhortation in early Greek elegy', in Murray, O. (ed.), *Sympotica: A Symposium on the Symposion* (Oxford), 221–9.

Bowie, E.L. 1996 'The *Theognidea*: a step towards a collection of fragments?', in G.W. Most (ed.), *Aporemata* 1. 53–66.

Bowie, E.L. 1997 'Plutarch's citations of early elegiac and iambic poetry', in Schrader, C, Rámon, V., Vela, I. (edd.), *Plutarco y la Historia–Actas del V Simposio Español sobre Plutarco* (Zaragoza).

Bradbury, R. 1950 *Fahrenheit 451* (New York).

Brancacci, A. 1984 'Aristosseno e lo statuto epistemologico della scienza armonica', in Giannantoni, G. and Vegetti, M. (edd.), *La scienza ellenistica. Atti delle tre giornate di studio tenutesi a Pavia dal 14 al 16 aprile 1982* (Naples), 151–85.

Brancacci, A. 1993 'Diogene di Babilonia e Aristosseno nel De Musica di Filodemo', in *Epicureismo greco e romano* (Naples), 573–83

Brandt, P. (ed.) 1888 *Corpusculum poesis epicae Graecae ludibundae*, Vol. I. *Parodorum epicorum Graecorum et Archestrati reliquiae* (Leipzig).

Braund, D. 1989 'Function and dysfunction: personal patronage in Roman imperialism', in Wallace–Hadrill, A.F. (ed.), *Patronage in Ancient Society* (London), 137–52.

Braund, D. 1994 'The Luxuries of Athenian Democracy', *Greece and Rome* 41. 41–8.

Braund, D. 1997 'Greeks and barbarians: the Black Sea region and hellenism under the early empire', in Alcock, S. (ed.), *The Roman Empire in the East* (Oxford), 121–36.

Breitschädel, W. 1986 *Die romanische Terminologie der Weinbeurteilung* (diss. Cologne).

Bremmer, J. 1997 'Jokes, Jokers and Jokebooks in Ancient Greek Culture', in Bremmer, J. and Roodenburg, H. (edd.), *A Cultural History of Humour* (Oxford), 11–28.

Brienne–Poitevin, F. 1996 'Consommation de coquillages marins en Provence à l'époque romaine', *Revue archéologique de la Narbonnaise* 26. 313–20.

Brock, R. 1994 'Greece: ancient Greece', in Robinson, J. (ed.), *The Oxford Companion to Wine* (Oxford).

Brodersen, K. 1993 'Appian und sein Werk', *Aufstieg und Niedergang der römischen Welt* II. 34.1. 339–63.

Brown, P.G. McC. 1992 'Menander's fragments 745 and 746 K–T, Menander's *Kolax*, and parasites and flatterers in Greek Comedy', *Zeitschrift für Papyrologie und Epigraphik* 92. 91–107.

Brown, P.R.L. 1978 *The Making of Late Antiquity* (Cambridge, Mass.).

Brown, T.S. 1949 *Onesicritus: a study in hellenistic historiography* (Berkeley).

Bruit, L. and Schmitt–Pantel, P. 1986 'Citer, classer, penser. A propos des repas des Grecs et des repas des autres dans le livre IV des *Deipnosophistes* d'Athénée', *AION: archeologia e storia antica* 8. 203–21.

Bruit–Zaidman, L. 1995 'Ritual Eating in Archaic Greece', in Wilkins, J, Harvey, D. and Dobson, M. (edd.), *Food in Antiquity* (Exeter), 196–203.

Bruns, I. 1898 *Die Persönlichkeit in der Geschichtsschreibung der Alten* (Berlin).

Brunschwig, J. (ed.) 1967 *Aristote. Topiques*, livres I–IV (Paris).

Brunschwig, J. 1988 'La théorie stoïcienne du genre suprême et l'ontologie platonicienne', in Barnes, J. and Mignucci, M.(edd.) *Matter and Metaphysics* (Naples), 19–127.

Brunt, P.A. 1980 'On historical fragments and epitomes', *Classical Quarterly* 30. 477–94.

Bühler, C.F. 1955 *Gutenberg Jahrbuch* 30. 104–6.

Burkert, W. 1962 *Weisheit und Wissenschaft: Studien zu Pythagoras, Philolaos und Platon* (Nüremberg).

Burkert, W. 1972 *Homo necans* (Berlin and New York).

Burkert, W. 1972a *Lore and Science in Ancient Pythagoreanism*, trans. E.L. Minat (Harvard).

Burkert, W. 1985 *Greek Religion* (Oxford).

Burstein, S.M. 1989 *Agatharchides: On the Erythraean Sea* (London).

Byl, S. 1993 'Les aliments dans le corpus hippocratique', in Jansen–Sieben, R. and Daelemans, F. (edd.), *Alimentation et médecine* (Archives et bibliothèques de Belgique; Brussels), 29–39.

Byl, S. 1993 'Le vin selon les âges et les sexes dans le monde gréco–romain', in Jansen–Sieben, R. and Daelemans, F. (eds), *Alimentation et médecine* (Archives et bibliothèques de Belgique; Brussels), 41–47.

Cadoux, C.J. 1938 *Ancient Smyrna: A History of the City from the Earliest Times to 324 AD* (Oxford).

Callmer, C. 1944 'Antike Bibliotheken', *Opuscula Archeologica* (Skifter Utgivna av. Svenzka Institutet 1. Rom X) 3. 145–93.

Canart, P. 1977–79 'Démétrius Damilas, *alias "librarius florentinus"*', *Rivista di studi bizantini* e *neoellenici* 14–16. 281–347.

Canfora, L. 1982 'Origine della "stemmatica" di Paul Maas', *Rivista di Filologia e d'Istruzione Classica* 110. 362–79.

Canfora, L. 1986 *La véritable histoire de la Bibliothèque d'Alexandrie* (Paris).

Canfora, L. 1992 *Histoire de la littérature grecque d'Homère à Aristote* (Paris).

Canfora, L. 1994 *La Bibliothèque d'Alexandrie et l'histoire des textes* (Liège).

Canfora, L. 1996 *Il Viaggio di Aristea* (Bari).

Canfora, L. 1999 'Aristotele "fondatore" della Bibliotheca di Alessandria', in *Scritti in Onore di Italo Gallo* (Rome).

Carlier, P. (ed.) 1996 *Le IVe siècle av. J.–C. Approches historiographiques* (Paris).

Carruthers, M. 1990 *The Book of Memory* (Cambridge).

Cartledge, P. 1990a 'Fowl play: a curious lawsuit in classical Athens', in Cartledge, P., Millett, P. and Todd, S. (edd.), *Nomos: Essays in Athenian Law, Politics and Society* (Cambridge), 41–62.

Cartledge, P. 1990b 'Herodotus and "The Other": a Meditation on Empire', *Echos du monde classique* 9. 27–40.

Cartledge, P. 1993 *The Greeks* (Oxford).

Casaubon, I. 1621 *Animadversiones in Athenaei Deipnosophistas* (Lyons).

Casaubon, I. 1709 *Epistolae* (ed. D. Janson ab Almeloveen, Rotterdam).

Casaubon, I. 1850 *Ephemerides*, (ed. J. Russell, Oxford).

Caspari, M.O.B. 1915 'The Ionian Confederacy', *Journal of Hellenic Studies* 35. 173–88.

Cassio, A. 1997 'Iperdorismi callimachei e testo antico dei lirici' in Pretagostini, R. (ed.), *Tradizione e innovazione nella cultura greca da Omero all' età ellenistica* (Rome).

Champlin, E. 1980 *Fronto and Antonine Rome* (Cambridge, Mass.).

Chaniotis, A. 1988 *Historie und Historiker in den griechischen Inschriften. Epigraphische Beiträge zur griechischen Historiographie* (Stuttgart).

Chantraine, P. 1950 'Les verbes grecs signifiant "lire" ', in *Mélanges H. Grégoire*, 2 (Brussels), 115–26.

Chrimes, K.M.T. 1949 *Ancient Sparta. A Re–examination of the Evidence* (Manchester).

Clark, R.J. 1968 'Trophonios: The Manner of his Revelation', *Transactions of the American Philological Association* 99. 63–75.

Clarke, K. 1997 'In search of the author of Strabo's *Geography*', *Journal of Roman Studies* 87. 92–110.

Cobet, C.G. 1845 'Epistula ad Gaisfordium de edendo Athenaeo', in Hemmerdinger 1989.

Cobet, C.G. 1847 *Oratio de arte interpretandi grammatices et critices fundamentis innixa* (Leiden).

Cobet, C.G. 1854, 1873 *Variae lectiones* (Leiden).

Cobet, C.G. 1858 *Novae lectiones* (Leiden).

Cobet, C.G. 1891 *Brieven van Cobet* (ed. R. Fruin and H. W. van der Mey, Leiden).

Cohen, G.M. 1995 *The Hellenistic Settlements in Europe, the Islands, and Asia Minor* (Berkeley).

Collard, C. 1969 'Athenaeus, the Epitome, Eustathius and quotations from tragedy', *Rivista di Filologia e d'Istruzione Classica*, 97. 157–79.

Collard, C. 1995 'Two early collectors of Euripidean fragments: Dirk Canter and Joshua Barnes', *Antiquité Classique* 64. 243–51.

Comotti, G. 1989 *Music in Greek and Roman Culture* (Baltimore).

Connor, W.R. 1968 *Theopompos and Fifth–Century Athens* (Cambridge, Mass.).

Cornford, F.M. 1968 *The Origin of Attic Comedy* (2nd edn, Gloucester).

Cox P. 1983 *Biography in Late Antiquity, A Quest for the Holy Man* (London).

Cozzoli, U. 1980 'La τρυφή nella interpretazione delle crisi politiche' in *Tra Grecia e Rome, temi antichi e metodologie moderne* (Rome), 133–46.

Cumont, F. 1914 *Ichthys*, *RE* IX 1 coll. 843–5.

Cumont, F. 1929 *Les religions orientales dans le paganisme romain* (Paris).

Curtius, E. and Adler, F. (edd.) 1892 *Olympia* II (Berlin).

Cuvigny, M. 1981 *Plutarque. Oeuvres morales XII–1* (Paris).

Dalby, A. 1996 *Siren Feasts: A History of Food and Gastronomy in Greece* (London).

Dalby, A. (forthcoming) 'τοπικὸς οἶνος', in Harvey, F.D. and Wilkins, J.M. (edd.), *The Rivals of Aristophanes* (London).

Daléchamp, J. 1583 Latin translation of Athenaeus (Lyons).

Daléchamp, J. 1621 and 1657 *Annotationes* at the end of the Casaubon 1621 and 1657 editions of the text.

Daly, M. 1984 *Pure Lust: Elemental Feminist Philosophy* (Boston).

d'Amat, R. 1961 "Dalechamps (*sic*)", in *Dictionnaire de biographie française* (Paris) 9, 1518.

Damon, C. 1997 *The Mask of the Parasite: A Pathology of Roman Patronage* (Ann Arbor, Mich.).

D'Arcy Thompson. *See* Thompson, D'Arcy W.

Daressy, G. 1904 'L'anguille consacrée à 'Itm', *Recueil de travaux* 26. 133–7.

D'Arms, J. 1990 'The Roman *convivium* and the idea of equality', in Murray, O. (ed.) *Sympotica: a Symposium on the Symposion* (Oxford), 308–20.

Davidson, A., 1981 *Mediterranean seafood* (2nd ed., London).

Davidson, A. 1999 *The Oxford Companion to Food* (Oxford)

Davidson, J. 1993 'Fish, Sex and Revolution in Athens', *Classical Quarterly* 43. 53–66.

Davidson, J. 1995 '*Opsophagia*: revolutionary eating at Athens', in Wilkins, J., Harvey, D. and Dobson, M. (edd.), *Food in Antiquity* (Exeter), 204–13.

Davidson, J. 1997 *Courtesans and Fishcakes: The Consuming Passions of Classical Athens* (London).

Davies, J.K. 1971 *Athenian Propertied Families, 600–300 BC* (Oxford).

Davies, J.K. 1996a 'Documents and "documents" in fourth–century historiography', in Carlier, P. (ed.) 1996, *Le IVe siècle av. J.–C. Approches historiographiques* (Paris), 29–39.

Davies, J.K. 1996b 'Strutture e suddivisioni delle "*poleis*" arcaiche. Le ripartizioni minori', in Settis, S. (ed.), *I Greci. Storia, Cultura, Arte, Società. 2.1: Una storia greca—formazione* (Turin), 599–652.

Davison, J.A. 1955 'Peisistratus and Homer', *Transactions of the American Philological Association* 86.1–21.

de Meyier, K.A. 1955 *Codices Vossiani graeci et miscellanei* (*Codices manuscripti* vol. 6) (Leiden), 273.

de Sanctis, G. 1917 *Storia dei Romani* (Turin).

de Ste Croix, G.E.M. 1981 *The Class Struggle in the Ancient Greek World* (London).

de Vries, G.J. 1968 'Aristoxenos über *Peri tagathou*' *Hermes* 96. 124–26.

de' Conti, N. 1556 Latin translation of Athenaeus (Venice, Basel, Lyons and Paris).

Degani, E. 1993 'Aristofane e la tradizione dell' invettiva personale in Grecia', in Degani, E. (ed.) *Aristofane: sept exposés suivis de discussion* (Vandoeuvres/Geneva) 1–49.

Degani, C. 1995 'La lessicografia', in Cambiano, G., Canfora, L., and Lanza, D. (edd.), *Lo spazio letterario della Grecia antica II* (Rome), 505–27.

Deichgräber, K. 1930 *Die griechische Empirikerschule* (Berlin).

Delatte, A. 1915 *Études sur la littérature pythagoricienne* (Paris).

Delattre, D. 1997 'Les titres des oeuvres philosophiques de l'épicurien Philodème de Gadara et les ouvrages qu'il cite', in Fredouille, J.–C., Goulet–Cazé, M.–O. *et al.* (edd.), *Titres et articulations du texte dans les oeuvres antiques. Actes du colloque international de Chantilly 13–15 décembre 1994* (Paris) 105–26.

Delcourt, M. 1958 *Hermaphrodite. Mythes et rites de la bisexualité dans l'Antiquité classique* (Paris).

Demont, P. 1997 'Aristophane, le citoyen tranquille et les singeries', in Thiercy, O. and Menu, M. (edd.), *Aristophane: la langue, la scène, la cité. Actes du colloque de Toulouse, 17–19 mars 1994* (Bari), 457–79.

Demougin, S. 1993 'Appartenir à l'ordre équestre au IIe siècle', in Eck, W. (ed.), *Prosopographie und Sozialgeschichte* (Cologne), 233–50.

Denniston, J.D. 1950 *The Greek Particles* (Oxford).

Desideri, P. 1992 'Filostrato: la contemporaneità del passato greco', in Gascó, F. and Falque, E. (edd.), *Pasado renacido: uso y abuso de la tradición clásica* (Seville), 55–70.

Desrousseaux, A.M. 1942 *Observations critiques sur les livres III et IV d'Athénée* (Paris).

Desrousseaux, A.M. 1956 *Athénée de Naucratis. Les Deipnosophistes. Livres I et II* (Paris).

Dessau, H. 1890 'Zu Athenaeus', *Hermes* 25. 156–8.

Detienne, M. 1994 *The Gardens of Adonis: Spices in Greek Mythology* (Princeton).

Detienne, M. and Vernant, J.–P. 1989 *The Cuisine of Sacrifice among the Greeks* (Chicago).

Devarius, M. 1588 *Liber de Graecae linguae particulis* (Rome).

Devréesse, R. 1965 *Le Fonds grec de la Bibliothèque Vaticane des origines à Paul V* (Vatican City).

Dickie, M.W. 1996 'What is a *Kolossos* and how were *Kolossoi* made in the Hellenistic period?', *Greek, Roman and Byzantine Studies* 37. 237–57.

Diels, H. (ed.) 1901 *Poetarum Philosophorum Fragmenta* (Berlin).

Dihle, A. 1977 'Der Beginn der Attizismus', *Antike und Abendland* 23. 162–77.

Dillon, J. 1977 *The Middle Platonists* (London).

Di Marco, M. (ed.) 1989 *Timone di Fliunte. Silli* (Rome).

Dindorf, W. (ed.) 1827 *Athenaeus* (Leipzig).

Dindorf, W. 1860 *Sophocles* (3rd edn, Oxford).

Dindorf, W. 1870 'Über die venetianische Handschrift des Athenaeus und deren Abschriften', *Philologus* 30. 73–115.

Dinsmoor, W.B. 1912. 'Studies of the Delphian treasuries', *Bulletin de Correspondence Hellénique* 36. 439–93.

Dinsmoor, W.B. 1950. *The Architecture of Ancient Greece* (London).

Dittenberger, W. 1903 'Athenäus und sein Werk', *Apophoreton* (Berlin), 1–28.

Dodds, E.R. 1965, *Pagans and Christians in an Age of Anxiety* (Cambridge) (Italian translation 1970).

Doelger, F. J 1922 *ICHTHUS. Das Fisch–Symbol in frühchristlicher Zeit* (Münster).

Dohm, H. 1964 *Mageiros* (Munich).

Donini, P. 1982 *Le scuole, l'anima, l'impero: la filosofia antica da Antioco a Plotino* (Turin).

Donlan, W. 1985 'Philos, pistos hetairos', in Figueira, T.J. and Nagy, G. (edd.) *Theognis of Megara: poetry and the polis* (Baltimore).

Dorandi, T. 1984 'Sillyboi', *Scrittura e Civiltà* 8. 185–99.

Dörner, F.K. 1935 *Der Erlass des Statthalters von Asia Paullus Fabius Persicus* (Berlin).

Douglas, M. 1970 *Natural Symbols* (Harmondsworth).

Dover, K.J. (ed.) 1968a *Aristophanes: Clouds* (Oxford).

Dover, K.J. 1968b *Lysias and the Corpus Lysiacum* (Berkeley).

Downey, G. 1963 *Ancient Antioch* (Princeton).

Downing, F.G. 1992 *Cynics and Christian Origins* (Edinburgh).

Drachmann, A.G. 1963 *The Mechanical Technology of Greek and Roman Antiquity* (Copenhagen).

Drège, J.–P. 1991 *Les Bibliothèques en Chine au temps des manuscrits (jusqu'au Xe siècle)* (Paris).

Drijvers, H. 1966 *Bardaisan of Edessa* (Assen).

Dudley, D.R. 1937 *History of Cynicism* (London).

Dumont, J. 1988 'Les critères culturels du choix des poissons dans l'alimentation grecque antique: le cas d'Athénée de Naucratis', *Anthropozoologica*, 2. 99–113.

Dunbabin, K.M.D. 1991 'Triclinium and Stibadium', in Slater, W.J. (ed.), *Dining in a Classical Context* (Ann Arbor), 121–48.

Dunbar, N. (ed.) 1995 *Aristophanes: Birds* (Oxford).

Dupont, F. 1977 *Le plaisir et la loi: du 'Banquet' de Platon au 'Satiricon'* (Paris).

Durand, J.–L. 1979 'Bêtes grecques. Propositions pour une topologie des corps à manger', in Detienne, M., and Vernant, J.–P. (edd.) *La cuisine du sacrifice en pays grec* (Paris), 133–66.

Düring, I. 1936 'De Athenaei Dipnosophistarum indole atque dispositione', in *Apophoreta Gotoburgensia Vilelmo Lundström oblata* (Göteborg), 226–70.

Düring, I. 1941 *Herodicus the Cratetean. A study in anti–Platonic tradition* (Stockholm).

Düring, I. 1950 'Notes on the History of the Transmission of Aristotle's Writings', *Symbolae Philologicae Gotoburgenses*, 3. 37–70.

Düring, I. 1956 'Review of Da Rios (Hrsg.): *Aristoxeni Elementa harmonica* (1954)', *Gnomon* 28. 278–82.

Düring, I. 1957 *Aristotle in the Ancient Biographical Tradition* (Göteborg).

Durling, R.J. 1993 *A Dictionary of Medical Terms in Galen* (Leiden).

Dyck, A.R. 1987 'The Glossographor', *Harvard Studies in Classical Philology* 91:119–60.

Dyer, L. 1905. 'Olympian treasuries and treasuries in general', *Journal of Hellenic Studies* 25. 294–319.

Easterling, P.E. 1957 'Sophocles' *Ajax*: collations of the manuscripts G, R and Q', *Classical Quarterly* 17. 52–79.

Ebert, T. 1996 *Ludic Feminism and After: Postmodernism, Desire, and Labor in Late Capitalism* (Ann Arbor, Mich.).

Eche, Y. 1967 *Les Bibliothèques Arabes publiques et semi–publiques en Mésopotamie, en Syrie et en Egypte au Moyen Age* (Damascus).

Eckstein, A.M. 1995 *Moral Vision in the Histories of Polybius* (Berkeley).

Edelstein, E.J. and Edelstein, L. 1945 *Asclepius* (Baltimore).

Edelstein, L. and Kidd, I.G. 1988–9 *Posidonius: the Fragments,* i²–ii (Cambridge).

Edson, C. 1958 '*Imperium Macedonicum*: the Seleucid empire and the literary evidence', *Classical Philology* 53. 153–70.

Elfieri, N. and Gentili, G.G. 1976 'Spina', in Stillwell, R. (ed.) *The Princeton Encyclopedia of Classical Sites* (Princeton), 857.

Elmsley, P. 1803 'Review of Schweighaeuser', *Edinburgh Review* 3. 181–94.

Elsner, J. 1995 *Art and the Roman Viewer: the Transformation of Art from the Pagan World to Christianity* (Cambridge).

Elsner, J. 1998. *Imperial Rome and the Christian triumph* (Oxford).

Empereur, Y.–E. 1993 'La production viticole dans l'Égypte Ptolémaïque et Romaine', *Bulletin de Correspondence Hellénique, Supplément* XXVI. 39–47.

Erasmus 1642 *Epistolarum D. Erasmi libri xxxi et P. Melancthonis libri iv* (London).

Erbse, H. 1950 *Untersuchungen zu den attizistischen Lexica* (Berlin), 75–92.

Erbse, H. 1957 'Review of Desrousseaux', *Gnomon* 29. 290–96.

Faraone, C.A. 1992 *Talismans and Trojan Horses. Guardian Statues in Ancient Greek Myth and Ritual* (Oxford).

Fears, J.R. 1974 'The Stoic View of the Career and Character of Alexander the Great', *Philologus* 118. 113–30.

Fedeli, P. 1988 'Biblioteche private et pubbliche a Roma nel mondo Romano', in Cavallo, G. (ed.), *Le biblioteche nel mondo antico e medievale* (Bari).

Fehr, B. 1990 'Entertainers at the Symposion: The *Akletoi* in the Archaic Period', in Murray, O. (ed.), *Sympotica. A Symposium on the Symposion* (Oxford), 185–95.

Fehrle, R. 1986 *Das Bibliothekswesen im alten Rom* (Wiesbaden).

Ferretto, C. 1984 *La città dissipatrice. Studi sull'excursus del libro decimo dei Philippika di Teopompo* (Genoa).

Finley, M.I. (ed.) 1974 *Studies in Ancient Society* (London).

Flower, M.A. 1994 *Theopompus of Chios. History and Rhetoric in the Fourth Century B.C.* (Oxford).

Foertmeyer, V. 1988 'The Dating of the Pompe of Ptolemy II Philadelphus', *Historia* 37. 90–104.

Fornara, C.W. 1983 *The Nature of History in Ancient Greece and Rome* (Berkeley).

Fortenbaugh, W.W., Huby, A. and Long, A. 1985 *Theophrastus of Eresos. On his Life and World* (New Brunswick and Oxford).

Fraenkel, E. (ed.) 1950 Aeschylus, *Agamemnon* (Oxford).

Fraenkel, E. 1962 *Beobachtungen zu Aristophanes* (Rome).

Fraschetti, A. 1981 'Aristosseno, i Romani e la "barbarizzazione" di Posidonia', *AION* 3. 97–115.

Fraser, P.M. 1972 *Ptolemaic Alexandria*, 3 vols (Oxford).

Frazer, J.G. 1898 *Pausanias's Description of Greece* I–VI (London).

Gabrielsson, I. 1906–1909 *Über die Quellen des Clemens Alexandrinus I–II* (Uppsala and Leipzig).

Gallagher, C. 1989 'Marxism and the new historicism', in Veeser, fl.A. (ed.) *The New Historicism* (New York and London).

Gallet de Santerre, H. 1958, *Délos primitive et archaïque* (Paris).

Garlan, Y. 1995 'War and Peace', in J–P. Vernant (ed.), *The Greeks* (Chicago), 53–85.

Garton, T. 1964 'Sulla and the Theatre', *Phoenix* 18:137–56.

Garofalo, I. 1988 *Erasistrati fragmenta* (Pisa).

Gaskin, J. 1995 *The Epicurean Philosophers* (London).

Geanakoplos, D.J. 1962 *Greek scholars in Venice* (Cambridge, Mass.).

Geanakoplos, D.J. 1966 *Byzantine East and Latin West* (Oxford).

Gentili, B. 1988 *Poetry and its Public in Ancient Greece* (Baltimore and London).

Georgiadou, A. and Larmour, D.H.J. 1994 'Lucian and historiography: *De Historia Conscribenda* and *Verae Historiae*', *Aufstieg und Niedergang der römischen Welt* II. 34.2. 1448–1509.

Gerber, D.E. 1991 *Lustrum* 33:186–214.

Giannini, A. (1960) 'La figura del cuoco nella commedia greca', *Acme* 13. 135–216.

Gilula, D.1995 'Comic Food and Food for Comedy', in Wilkins, J., Harvey, D., and Dobson, M., (edd.), *Food in Antiquity* (Exeter), 386–99.

Giraldi, L. 1551 *Dialogi duo de poetis* (Florence).

Gleason, M. 1995 *Making Men: Sophists and Self–presentation in Ancient Rome* (Princeton).

Gold, B. (ed.) 1982 *Literary and Artistic Patronage in Ancient Rome* (Austin).

Goffman, D. 1990 *Izmir and the Levantine World 1550–1650* (Seattle).

Goulet, R. 1997 'Les références chez Diogène Laërce: sources ou autorités?', in Fredouille, J.–C., Goulet–Cazé, M.–O., *et al.* (edd.), *Titres et articulations du texte dans les oeuvres antiques. Actes du colloque international de Chantilly 13–15 décembre 1994* (Paris), 149–66.

Gourevitch, D. 1995 'L'alimentation animale de la femme enceinte, de la nourrice et du bébé sevré', *Caesarodunum*, no. sp., *Homme et animal dans l'Antiquité romaine*, 283–93.

Gow, A.S.F. (ed.) 1965 *Machon: The Fragments* (Cambridge).

Gow, A.S.F. and Page, D.L. 1965 *The Greek Anthology, Hellenistic Epigrams* (Cambridge).

Gowers, E. 1993 *The Loaded Table: Representations of Food in Roman Literature* (Oxford).

Graf, F. 1995 'Ekphrasis: Die Entstehung der Gattung in der Antike', in Boehm, G., and Pfotenhauer, H. (edd.), *Beschreibungskunst–Kunstbeschreibung: Ekphrasis von der Antike bis zur Gegenwart* (Munich), 143–55.

Griffin, A. 1982 *Sikyon* (Oxford).

Griffin, M. 1976 *Seneca: A Philosopher in Politics* (Oxford).

Griffin, S. 1981 *Pornography and Silence: Culture's Revenge Against Nature* (New York).

Grmek, M.D. (ed.) 1995 *Histoire de la pensée médicale en occident 1* (Paris).

Grotefand, F. 1806 *Jenaîsche Allgemeine Literaturzeitung* 4. 121–56.

Grottanelli, C. 1995 'Wine and Death—East and West', in Murray, O. and Tecuşan, M. (edd.), *In Vino Veritas* (British School at Rome), 62–89.

Gruppe, O. 1906 *Griechische Mythologie und Religionsgeschichte* (Munich).

Guenther, L.–M. 1989 'Gladiatoren beim Fest Antiochos' IV zu Daphne', *Hermes* 117. 250–2.

Gulick, C.B. 1927–1941 *Athenaeus. The Deipnosophists*, 7 vols (London).

Gulletta, M.I. 1991 'Il lessico dei vasi in Ateneo: macro e micro struttura del libro XI dei Deipnosophistai', *Giornale italiano di filologia* 43. 299–310.

Habicht, C. 1961 'Falsche Urkunden zur Geschichte Athens im Zeitalter der Perserkriege', *Hermes* 89. 1–35.

Habicht, C. 1975 'New Evidence on the Province of Asia', *Journal of Roman Studies* 65. 64–91.

Habicht, C. 1997 *Athens from Alexander to Antony* (Cambridge, Mass. and London).

Hadot, I. 1984 *Arts libéraux et Philosophie dans la pensée antique* (Paris).

Hägg, R. (ed.) 1994, *Ancient Greek Cult Practice from the Epigraphical Evidence* (Stockholm).

Hall, E. 1993 'Drowning by Nomes: The Greeks, Swimming and Timotheus', in H.A. Khan, (ed.), *The Birth of the European Identity; Nottingham Classical Literature Studies 2.* (Nottingham), 44–80 .

Halliwell, S. 1991 'The use of laughter in Greek culture', *Classical Quarterly* 41. 279–96.

Halperin, D., Winkler, J. and Zeitlin F. (edd.) 1990 *Before Sexuality: the Construction of Erotic Experience in the Ancient Greek World* (Princeton).

Hamilton, W. 1947 'Review of Fritz Wehrli: *Die Schule des Aristoteles. Texte und Kommentar. Heft I: Dikaiarchos. Heft II: Aristoxenos*', (Basel 1944, 1945), *Classical Review* 61. 97–8.

Hani, P. 1976 *La religion égyptienne dans la pensée de Plutarque* (Paris).

Harding, P. 1994 *Androtion and the Atthis* (Oxford).

Harrison, S.J. 1990 'The Speaking Book: The Prologue to Apuleius' *Metamorphoses*', *Classical Quarterly* 40. 507–13.

Hartog, F. 1996 *Mémoire d'Ulysse* (Paris).

Hawley, R. 1993 'Pretty, witty and wise: courtesans in Athenaeus's *Deipnosophistae* Book 13', *International Journal of Moral and Social Studies* 8. 73–91.

Heath, M. 1998 'Athenaeus 1. 11b–f: heroic meal–times', *Eikasmos* 9. 216–18.

Heiberg, I.L. 1921 *Paulus Ægineta, CMG* (Leipzig and Berlin).

Heinen, H. 1983 'Die Tryphè des Ptolemaios VIII. Euergetes II. Beobachtungen zum ptolemäischen Herrscherideal und zu einer römischen Gesandschaft in Ägypten (140–39 v.Chr.)', in *Althistorische Studien Hermann Bengtson zum 70. Geburtstag dargebracht.* Historia Einzelschriften 40 (Wiesbaden), 116–30.

Helck, J. 1905 *De Cratetis Mallotae studiis criticis quae ad Iliadem spectant* (Leipzig).

Helck, J. 1913–14 *De Cratetis Mallotae studiis criticis quae ad Odysseam spectant*, Beigabe zum Jahresbericht des Gymnasiums zum heiligen Kreuz in Dresden (Dresden).

Helm, R. 1906 *Lukian und Menipp* (Leipzig and Berlin).

Helmbold, W.C. and Holther, W.B. 1992 *The Unity of the Phaedrus* (Berkeley).

Helmbold, W.C. and O'Neil, E.N. 1959 *Plutarch's Quotations* (Philological Monographs XIX, APA).

Hemmerdinger, B. 1959 'Deux notes papyrologiques, note II 'Les papyrus et la datation d'Harpocration', *Revue des études grecques* 72. 107–9.

Hemmerdinger, B. 1989 'L'Art d'éditer Athénée', *Bolletino dei Classici* 10. 106–17.

Henry, M. 1985 *Menander's Courtesans and the Greek Comic Tradition* (Frankfurt and New York).

Henry, M. 1990 'Ancient Prostitution: Evidence and Approaches', unpublished paper, CAMWS.

Henry, M. 1992 'The Edible Woman: Athenaeus's Concept of the Pornographic', in Richlin, A.S. (ed.), *Pornography and Representation in Greece and Rome.* (Oxford and New York), 250–68.

Henry, M. 1995 *Prisoner of History: Aspasia of Miletus and her Biographical Tradition* (New York).

Henry, W.B. 1998 'An Archilochus papyrus?', *Zeitschrift für Papyrologia und Epigraphik* 121. 94.

Herman, G. 1987 *Ritualised Friendship and the Greek City* (Cambridge).

Hercher, R. (ed.) 1873 *Epistolographi Graeci* (Paris).

Hesk, J. forthcoming 'The rhetoric of anti–rhetoric in Athenian oratory', in Goldhill, S. and Osborne, R. (eds) *Performance and Democracy in Athenian Culture* (Cambridge).

Hill, G.F. 1949 *The History of Cyprus* (Cambridge).

Hirzel, R. 1895 *Der Dialog, ein literarhistorischer Versuch* (Leipzig).

Hock, R.F. and O'Neil, E.N. 1986 *The Chreia in Ancient Rhetoric: The Progymnasmata* (Atlanta).

Hoffmann, O. 1906 *Die Makedonen, ihr Sprache und ihr Volkstum* (Göttingen).

Holford–Strevens, L. 1988 *Aulus Gellius* (London).

Holmes, O.W. 1858 *The Autocrat of the Breakfast Table* (New York).

Honoré, T. 1982 *Ulpian* (Oxford).

Hooker, G.T.W. 1960 'The topography of the *Frogs*', *Journal of Hellenic Studies* 80. 112–17.

Hopfner, T. 1913 *Der Tierkult der alten Ägypten nach den griech. und lat. Berichten und den wichtigsten Denkmälern* (Wien).

Hopfner, T. 1921 *Griechisch–Ägyptischer Offenbarungszauber* (Leipzig).

Hornblower, S. 1994 *Greek Historiography* (Oxford).

Howard, A.A. 1893 'The Αὐλος or Tibia', *Harvard Studies in Classical Philology* 4. 1–60.

Hubbard, T.K. 1991 *The Mask of Comedy. Aristophanes and the Intertextual Parabasis* (Ithaca and London).

Hudson, R. 1989 'Food in Roman Satire', in Braund, S.H. (ed.), *Satire and Society in Ancient Rome* (Exeter), 69–87.

Hummel, P. 1997 *Philologica lyrica. La poésie lyrique grecque au miroir de l'érudition philologique de l'antiquité à la Renaissance* (Paris).

Hutchinson, G.O. 1988 *Hellenistic Poetry* (Oxford).

Imhof, M. 1961, 'Zur Überlieferungsgeschichte der nichtchristlichen griechischen Literatur der römischen Kaiserzeit', in Hunger, H. (ed.), *Geschichte der Textüberlieferung der antiken und mittelalterlichen Literatur* I (Zurich), 285–307.

Innes, M. 1936 *Death at the President's Lodging* (Harmondsworth).

Irigoin, J. 1967 'L'édition princeps d'Athénée et ses sources', *Revue des Études Grecques* 80. 418–24.

Irigoin, J. 1997 'Titres, sou–titres et sommaires dans les oeuvres des historiens grecs du Ier siècle avant J.–C. au Ve siècle après J.–C.', in Fredouille, J.–C., Goulet–Cazé, M.–O., *et al.* (edd.), *Titres et articulations du texte dans les oeuvres antiques. Actes du colloque international de Chantilly 13–15 décembre 1994* (Paris), 127–34.

Jacoby, F. 1926 *Die Fragmente der griechischen Historiker* (Berlin).

Jacoby, F. 1949 *Atthis* (Oxford).

Jameson, M.H. 1994, 'Theoxenia', in Hägg, R. (ed.), *Ancient Greek Cult Practice from the Epigraphical Evidence* (Stockholm), 35–57.

Janko, R. 1984 *Aristotle on Comedy: Towards a Reconstruction of Poetics II* (Berkeley).

Janko, R. 1995a 'Reconstructing Philodemus' On Poems', in Obbink, D. (ed.), *Philodemus and Poetry. Poetic Theory and Practice in Lucretius, Philodemus, and Horace* (Oxford), 69–96.

Janko, R. 1995b 'Crates of Mallos, Dionysius Thrax and the Tradition of Stoic Grammatical Theory', in Ayres, L. (ed.), *The Passionate Intellect. Essay on the Transformation of Classical Traditions presented to Professor I.G. Kidd* (New Brunswick), 213–33.

Jansen–Sieben, R. and Daelemans, F. 1993 (edd.), *Alimentation et médecine* (Brussels).

Jeanneret, M. 1987 *Des Mets et des Mots. Banquets et propos de table à la Renaissance* (Paris).

Jeanneret, M. 1991 *A Feast of Words: Banquets and Table–talk in the Renaissance*, trans. J. Whiteley and E. Hughes (Cambridge).

Johnston, S.I. and McNiven, T.J. 1996 'Dionysos and the Underworld in Toledo', *Museum Helveticum* 53. 25–36.

Jones, C.P. 1986 *Culture and Society in Lucian* (Cambridge, Mass.).

Jones, C.P. 1991 'Dinner Theater', in Slater, W.J. (ed.), *Dining in a Classical Context* (Ann Arbor), 185–98.

Jones, R.M. 1916 *The Platonism of Plutarch* (Menasha, Wisc.).

Jouan, F. and Van Looy, H. (edd.) 1998 *Euripides. Fragments. Aigeus–Autolikos* (Paris).

Jouanna, J. 1996 'Le vin et la médecine dans la Grèce ancienne', *Revue des Études Grecques* 109. 410–34.

Jouanna, J. 1997 'Remarques sur les titres dans la collection hippocratique', in Fredouille, J.–C., Goulet–Cazé, M.–O., *et al.* (edd.), *Titres et articulations du texte dans les oeuvres antiques. Actes du colloque international de Chantilly 13–15 décembre 1994* (Paris), 55–73.

Kaibel, G. 1883a *Observationes criticae in Athenaeum* (Rostock).

Kaibel, G. 1883b *De Athenaei Epitome* (Rostock).

Kaibel, G. 1896 'Archippos', *RE* 2. 542–3.

Kaibel, G. 1887–1890 *Athenaei Naucratitae Dipnosophistarum libri XV* (Leipzig).

Kaibel, G. 1889 'Zur attischen Komödie', *Hermes* 24. 42–66.

Kampen, N. (ed.) 1996 *Sexuality in Ancient Art* (Cambridge).

Kappeler, S. 1987 *The Pornography of Representation* (Minneapolis).

Kassel, R. 1985 'Antimachos in der Vita Chisiana des Dionysius Periegetes', in Schaeublin, C. (ed.), *Catalepton, Festschrift für B. Wyss* (Basel).

Kassel, R. and Austin, C. 1983– *Poetae Comici Graeci* (Berlin/New York).

Keaney, J.J. 1973 'Alphabetization in Harpocration's Lexicon', *Greek, Roman and Byzantine Studies* 14. 415–23.

Keaney, J.J.1991 *Harpocration. Lexeis of the ten Orators* (Amsterdam).

Keil, B. 1895 'Der Perieget Heliodorus von Athen', *Hermes* 30. 199–240.

Kendrick, W. 1996 *The Secret Museum: Pornography in Modern Culture* (2nd edn., Berkeley).

Kerényi, K. 1960 'Parva realia', *Symbolae Osloenses* 36. 5–16.

Kidd, I.G. (ed.) 1988 *Posidonius, II: The Commentary* (Cambridge).

Kohl, J.G. 1917 *De Chorizontibus* (Darmstadt).

Konstan, D. 1996 *Friendship in the Classical World* (Cambridge).

Koroneos, J. 1979 *Les mollusques de Grèce* (Athens).

Koster, W.J.W. 1975 *Scholia in Aristophanem. Pars I, Fasc. 1A. Prolegomena de Comoedia* (Groningen).

Kristeller, P.O. and Cranz, F.E. (1971) *Catalogus Translationum et Commentariorum: Medieval and Renaissance Latin Translations and Commentaries* (Washington, D.C.).

Kurke, L. 1997 'Inventing the Hetaira: Sex, Politics and Discursive Conflict in Ancient Greece', *Classical Antiquity* 16. 106–50.

Labowsky, L. 1979 'Bessarion's Library and the Biblioteca Marciana', *Sussidi Eruditi* 31 (Rome).

Laidlaw, W.A. 1933 *A History of Delos* (Oxford).

Laloy, L. 1904 *Aristoxène de Tarente et la musique de l'antiquité* (Paris).

Landels, J.G. 1998 *Music in Ancient Greece and Rome* (London).

Lane Fox, R. 1986 *Pagans and Christians* (London).

Langie, A. 1908 *Les Bibliothèques publiques dans l'ancienne Rome et dans l'Empire romain* (Fribourg).

Lanzillotta, E. 1996 'Semo di Delos', in *Le Cicladi e il mondo egeo*: (Rome), 287–326.

Latte, K. 1913 *De Saltationibus Graecorum capita quinque* (Gießen).

Latte, K. 1915 'Zur Zeitbestimmung des Antiatticista', *Hermes* 50. 373–94.

Lawler, L.B. 1941 'Ichthues Choreutae', *Classical Philology* 36. 142–55.

Layton, E. 1994 *The Sixteenth Century Greek Book in Italy: Printers and Publishers for the Greek World* (Venice).

Ledergerber, P. 1905 *Lukian und die altattische Komödie* (Ph.D. diss., Freiburg in der Schweiz).

Lefkowitz, M.R. 1981 *The Lives of the Greek Poets* (London).

Legrand, E. 1885 *Bibliographie hellénique, ou description raisonnée des ouvrages publiés en grec par les Grecs aux XVe et XVIe siècles* (Paris).

Leipen, N. 1969 'A New Mosaic in the Royal Ontario Museum', *Archaeology* 22. 231.

Lendon, J.F. 1997 *Empire of Honour: The Art of Government in the Roman World* (Oxford).

Leppin, H. 1992 *Histrionen: Untersuchungen zur sozialen Stellung von Bühnenkünstlern im Westen des Römischen Reiches zur Zeit der Republik und des Prinzipats* (Bonn).

Letrouit, J. 1989 'Passages parallèles chez Athénée et Harpocration', *Maia* 41. 123.

Letrouit, J. 1991 'A propos de la tradition manuscrite d'Athénée: une mise au point', *Maia* 43. 33–40.

Levi, P. 1971 *Pausanias. Guide to Greece* 1–2 (London).

Levin, F.R. 1972 'Synesis in Aristoxenian Theory', *Transactions American Philological Association*. 103. 211–34.

Liebeschuetz, J.H.W.G. 1972 *Antioch: City and Imperial Administration in the Later Roman Empire* (Oxford).

Lindsay, H. 1997 'Strabo on Apellicon's Library', *Rheinisches Museum* 140.3–4. 290–98.

Lissarrague, F. 1990 *The Aesthetics of the Greek Banquet* (Princeton).

Lissarrague, F. 1997 'L'homme, le singe et le satyre', in Cassin, B. and Labarrière, J.-L. (edd.), *L'animal dans l'antiquité* (Paris), 455–72.

Lloyd-Jones, H. and Parsons, P. 1983 *Supplementum Hellenisticum* (Berlin/New York).

Logan, O. 1972 *Culture and society in Venice 1470–1970* (London).

Longo, O. 1987 'I mangiatori di pesci: regime alimentare e quadro culturale', *Materiali e discussioni per l'analisi dei testi classici* 18. 9–53.

Longo, O. and Avezzù, E. 1992 *Alcifrone. Lettere di parassiti e di cortigiane* (Venice).

Longo, O. and Scarpi, P. (edd.) 1989, *Homo edens. Regimi, miti e pratiche dell'alimentazione nelle civiltà del Mediterraneo* (Verona).

Lowe, J.C.B. 1962 'The manuscript evidence for change of speaker in Aristophanes', *Bulletin of the Institute of Classical Studies* 9. 27–42.

Lowry, M. 1979 *The World of Aldus Manutius* (Oxford).

Lugato, E. 1994 'Catalogo', in Marconi S. and Zorzi, M. (edd.), *Aldo Manuzio e l'ambiente Veneziano 1494–1515* (Venice).

Lukinovich, A. 1990 'The play of reflections between literary form and the sympotic theme in the *Deipnosophistae* of Athenaeus', in Murray, O. (ed.), *Sympotica. A Symposium on the Symposion* (Oxford), 263–71.

Maas, P. 1928 'Review of Aldick 1928', *Gnomon* 4. 570–71.

Maas, P. 1934 'Review of vol. III of *Suidae Lexicon* ed. A. Adler', *Byzantinische Zeitschrift* 34. 164–65.

Maas, P. 1935–36 'Eustathios als Konjekuralkritiker', *Byzantinische Zeitschrift* 35. 299–307 and 36. 27–31.

Maas, P. 1937 'Review of Peppink 1936', *Byzantinische Zeitschrift* 37. 185–6.

Maas, P. 1938 'Review of vol. I of Peppink 1937', *Byzantinische Zeitschrift* 38. 201–2.

Maas, P. 1948 'Greek literature', *The Year's Work in Classical Studies* (*1939–45*) 33. 1–8.

Maas, P. 1952 'Verschiedenes zu Eustathios', *Byzantinische Zeitschrift* 45. 1–3.

Maas, P. 1953 'Review of A. Turyn, *Studies in the Manuscript Tradition of Sophocles*', *Gnomon* 25. 441–2.

Maas, P. 1957 *Textkritik*[3] (Leipzig).

Maas, P. 1958 *Textual Criticism* (Oxford).

Maas, P. 1973 *Kleine Schriften* (Munich).

Macginnis, J.D.A. 1988 'Ctesias and the Fall of Nineveh' *Illinois Classical Studies* 13. 36–42.

Mangoni, C. 1993 *Filodemo, il quinto libro della poetica* (Naples).

Marangou, A. 1993 'Le vin de Crète de l'époque classique à l'époque impériale: un premier bilan', *Bulletin de Correspondence Hellénique, Supplément* XXVI. 177–82.

Marangou–Lerat, A. 1995 *Le vin et les amphores de Crète de l'époque classique à l'époque impériale* (Athens and Paris).

Marasco, G. 1982 *Appiano e la storia dei Seleucidi fino all'ascesa al trono di Antioco III* (Florence).

Marasco, G. 1988 'Ctesia, Dinone ed Eraclide di Cuma e le origini della storiografia "tragica" ', *Studi Italiani di Filologia Classica* 81.6. 48–67.

Marder, T. 1979 'Context for Claude–Nicolas Ledoux' OIKEMA', *Arts* 54. 174–6.

Marincola, J. 1997 *Authority and Tradition in Ancient Historiography* (Cambridge).

Marsden, E.W. 1971 *Greek and Roman Artillery: Technical Treatises* (Oxford).

Marshall, A.J. 1976 'Library resources and creative writing at Rome', *Phoenix* 30. 252–64.

Martin, J. 1931 *Symposion. Die Geschichte einer literarischen Form* (Paderborn).

Marx, F. (ed.) 1959 *Plautus: Rudens* (Amsterdam).

Mathiesen, T.J. 1974 *A Bibliography of Sources for the Study of Ancient Greek Music* (New York).

Mathiesen, T.J. 1981 'New fragments of ancient Greek music', *Acta musicologica* 53. 14–32.

Mathiesen, T.J. 1988 *Ancient Greek Music Theory: A Catalogue Raisonné of Manuscripts* (Munich).

Mazzini, I. 1986 'Alimentazione e salute secondo i medici del mondo antico: teoria e realtà', in Longo, O. and Scarpi, P. (edd.) *Homo Edens* (Verona), 257–64.

Meineke, A. 1839–57 *Fragmenta Comicorum Graecorum* (Berlin).

Meister, K. 1990 *Die griechische Geschichtsschreibung von den Anfängen bis zum Ende des Hellenismus* (Stuttgart).

Mejer, J. 1978 *Diogenes Laertius and his Hellenistic Background* (Wiesbaden).

Mele, A. 1981 'I pitagorici e Archita', in *Storia della società italiana*, I (Milan), 271–9.

Menge, R. 1868, in Schmidt, M. (ed) *Hesychius* (Jena) 5. 1–57.

Mengis, K.1920 *Die Schriftstellerische Technik im Sophistenmahl des Athenaios* (Paderborn).

Merkelbach, R. and West, M.L. (edd.) 1967 *Fragmenta Hesiodea* (Oxford).

Mette, H.J. 1936 *Sphairopoiia. Untersuchungen zur Kosmologie des Krates von Pergamon* (Munich).

Mette, H.J. 1952 *Parateresis. Untersuchungen zur Sprachtheorie des Krates von Pergamon* (Halle).

Mette, H.J. 1980 'Neoptolemus von Parion', *Rheinisches Museum* 123. 1–24.

Mewaldt, J. 1904 *De Aristoxeni Pythagoricis Sententiis et Vita Pythagorica* (Diss. Berlin).

Michaelidis, S. 1978 *The Music of Ancient Greece, an Encyclopaedia* (London).

Millett, P. 1989 'Patronage and its avoidance in classical Athens', in Wallace–Hadrill, A.F. (ed.), *Patronage in ancient society* (London), 15–48.

Mitchell, S. 1974 'The Plancii in Asia Minor', *Journal of Roman Studies* 64. 27–39.

Molyneux, H. 1992 *Simonides: A Historical Study* (Wauconda).

Montanari, F. 1976 'Omero, Eubulo, i pesci e i Chorizontes', *Studi Classici e Orientali* 25. 325–31.

Montanari, F. 1997 'The Fragments of Hellenistic Scholarship', in Most, G. (ed.), *Collecting Fragments* (Göttingen).

Montanari, M. 1988 *Alimentazione e cultura nel Medioevo* (Roma and Bari).

Montrose, L.A. 1989 'The poetics and politics of culture', in Veeser, H.A. (ed.), *The new historicism* (New York and London).

Morelli G. 1963 'Aristofonte in Eustazio e in Ateneo,' *Rivista di Filologia e d'Istruzione Classica* 91. 340–7.

Moreschini, C. 1994 'Aspetti della cultura filosofica negli ambienti della Seconda Sofistica', *Aufstieg und Niedergang der römischen Welt* II. 37. 6 (Berlin and New York).

Morreall, J. 1983 *Taking Laughter Seriously* (Albany).

Moss, A. 1996 *Printed Commonplace–Books and the Structuring of Renaissance Thought* (Oxford).

Mossman, J. 1997 'Plutarch's Dinner of the Seven Wise Men and its place in symposion literature', in Mossman J. (ed.), *Plutarch and his Intellectual World* (London).

Müller, C. 1851 *Fragmenta historicorum graecorum* (Paris).

Mund–Dopchie, M. 1975, in *Album offert à Charles Verlinden* (Ghent), 232–45.

Mund–Dopchie, M. 1984 *La Survie d'Éschyle à la Renaissance* (Louvain), 239–61.

Murray, O. 1983, 'The Greek Symposion in History', in Gabba, E. (ed.), *Tria Corda: Scritti in onore di Arnaldo Momigliano* (Como), 257–72.

Murray, O. 1988 'Death and the Symposium', *AION* 10. 239–57.

Murray, O. 1990 'Sympotic History', in Murray, O. (ed.), *Sympotica. A Symposium on the Symposion* (Oxford), 3–13.

Musti, D. 1987 'Protagonismo e forma politica nella città greca', in *Il protagonismo nella storiografia classica* (Genoa), 9–36.

Musurus, M. 1514 *Athenaeus: editio princeps* (Venice).

Nachmanson, E. 1941 *Der griechische Buchtitel. Einige Beobachtungen* (Göteborg and Darmstadt).

Nagy, G. 1979 *The best of the Achaeans* (Baltimore).

Nagy, G. 1989 'Early Views of Poets and Poetry', in Kennedy, G. (ed) *The Cambridge History of Literary Criticism* (Cambridge).

Najock, D. 1996 'Aristoxenos und die Auloi', in Faber, R. and Seidensticker, B. (edd.), *Wörte, Bilder, Töne. Studien zur Antike und Antikerezeption. Bernhard Kytzler zu ehren* (Würzburg), 59–76.

Nenci, G. 1983 'Tryphé e colonizzazione', in Nenci, G. (ed.), *Forme di contatto e processi di trasformazione nelle società antiche*, Atti del convegno di Cortona, 24–30 maggio 1981 (Pisa and Rome), 1019–31.

Nesselrath, H.–G. 1985 *Lukians Parasitendialog: Untersuchungen und Kommentar* (Berlin).

Nesselrath, H.–G. 1990 *Die attische Mittlere Komödie*, (Berlin and New York).

Nestle, W. 1936 'Die Horen des Prodikos', *Hermes* 71. 151–70.

Nicolai, R. 1992 *La storiografia nell'educazione antica* (Pisa).

Nisbet, R.G.M. 1992 'The Orator and the Reader: Manipulation and Response in Cicero's fifth *Verrine*', in Woodman, T. and Powell, J. (edd.), *Author and Audience in Latin Literature* (Cambridge), 1–17.

Norden, E. 1915–18 Die antike Kunstprosa VI Jhdt v. Chr bis in die Zeit der Renaissance (3rd edn, Leipzig, Italian edition 1986, with a note by G. Calboli).

Nuebecker A. 1992 Altgriechische musik 1958–1986, *Lustrum* 32. 99–176.

Nutton, V. 1973 'The chronology of Galen's early career', *Classical Quarterly* 23. 158–71.

Nutton, V. 1984 'Galen in the eyes of his contemporaries', *Bulletin of the History of Medicine* 58. 315–24.

Nutton, V. 1988 *From Democedes to Harvey: Studies in the History of Medicine* (London).

Nutton, V. 1995 'Galen and the traveller's fare', in Wilkins, J., Harvey, D. and Dobson, M. (edd.), *Food in Antiquity* (Exeter), 359–70.

Nyikos, L. 1941 *Athenaeus quo consilio quibusque usus subsidiis Dipnosophistarum libros composuerit* (diss. Basel).

Oden, R.A. Jr. 1977 *Studies in Lucian's De Syria Dea* (Missula, Montana).

Ohly, K. 1928 *Stichometrische Untersuchungen* (Leipzig).

Oliver, R.P. 1951 'The first Medicean MS of Tacitus and the titulature of ancient books', *Transactions of the American Philological Association* 82. 232–61.

Olson, S.D. and Sens, A. 2000 *Archestratos of Gela* (Oxford).

Omont, H. 1888 *Inventaire sommaire des manuscrits grecs de la Bibliothèque Nationale*, II and III (Paris).

Omont, H. 1894 'Inventaire des manuscrits grecs et latins donnés à Saint–Marc de Venise par le cardinal Bessarion', *Revue des Bibliothèques* 4. 129–87.

Omont, H. 1909 *Anciens Inventaires et Catalogues de la Bibliothèque Nationale* (Paris).

Osborne, M.J. and Byrne, S.G. 1994 *A Lexicon of Greek Personal Names: Attica* (Oxford).

Papadopoulos, J. 1980 *Xoana e sphyrelata. Testimonia delle fonti scritti* (Rome).

Papadopoulos, Th. Ch. 1977 Γραμματικὴ τῆς κοινῆς τῶν Ἑλλήνων γλώσσης (Athens).

Pappenhoff, H. 1954 *Zum Problem der Abhängigkeit der Epitome von der venezianischen Handschrift des Athenaios* (diss. Gottingen).

Parker, R. 1983 *Miasma* (Oxford).

Parker, R. 1996 *Athenian Religion: A History* (Oxford).

Pascucci, G. 1975 'I commentarii di Sulla', *Stuli Urbinati* 49: 283–96.

Passerini, A. 1934 'La τρυφή nella storiografia ellenistica', *Studi Italiani di Filologia Classica* 11. 35–6.

Paterson, J. 1982 ' "Salvation from the sea": amphorae and trade in the Roman west', *Journal of Roman Studies* 72. 147–57.

Pattison, M. 1892 *Isaac Casaubon 1559–1614* (2nd edn., Oxford).

Pearson, L. (ed.) 1990 *Elementa rhythmica. The Fragment of Book II and the Additional Evidence for Aristoxenean Rhythmic Theory* (Oxford).

Pearson, L.A. 1942 *The Local Historians of Attica* (Philadelphia).

Pearson, L.A. 1960 *The Lost Historians of Alexander the Great* (Chico).

Pearson, L.A. and Stephens, S. (eds) 1983 *Didymi in Demosthenem Commenta* (Stuttgart).

Pelling, C.B.R. 1979 'Plutarch's method of work in the Roman Lives', *Journal of Hellenic Studies* 99. 74–96 (repr. with a 1994 Postscript in B. Scardigli (edd.), *Essays in Plutarch's Lives* (Oxford, 1995), 265–318).

Pelling, C.B.R. 1989 'Plutarch: Roman heroes and Greek culture', in Griffin, M. and Barnes, J. (edd.), *Philosophia Togata: Essays on Philosophy and Roman Society* (Oxford).

Pelling, C.B.R. 1997 'East is East and West is West—or are they? National stereotypes in Herodotus', *Histos* 1 (Durham University Electronic Journal) March 1997.

Pellizer, E. 1983 'Della zuffa simpotica', in Vetta, M. (ed.), *Poesia e simposio nella Grecia Antica* (Roma and Bari), 29–41, 137–9.

Pellizer, E. 1990 'Outlines of Sympotic Entertainment', in Murray, O. (ed.), *Sympotica. A Symposion on the Symposion* (Oxford), 177–84.

Penella, S.J. 1990 *Greek Philosophers and Sophists in the Fourth Century AD: Studies in Eunapius of Sardis* (Leeds).

Peppink, S.P. (ed.) 1936–39 *Observationes in Athenaei Deipnosophistas* (Leiden).

Peppink, S.P. (ed.) 1937–39 *Epitome of Athenaeus* (Leiden).

Pernot, L. 1998 'La rhétorique de l'Empire ou comment la rhétorique grecque a inventé l'Empire', *Rhetorica* 16. 131–48.

Pesando, F. 1994 *Libri et biblioteche* (Rome).

Pfeiffer, R. 1968 *History of Classical Scholarship from 1300 to 1850* (Oxford).

Pfeiffer, R. 1976 *History of Classical Scholarship* (Oxford).

Pfister, C. 1926–7 'La Chaire de littérature grecque', *Bulletin de la Faculté de Lettres de l'Université de Strasbourg*, 4. 175–85, 223–30, 271–80, and 5. 1–9, (Paris).

Pflaum, H.–G. 1950 *Les procurateurs équestres sous le haut empire Romain* (Paris).

Pflaum, H.–G. 1960 *Les carrières procuratoriennes équestres sous le haut empire Romain* (Paris).

Phillipps, E.D. 1957 'A suggestion about Palamedes', *American Journal of Philology* 78. 267–8.

Pickard–Cambridge, A.W. 1946 *The Theatre of Dionysus in Athens* (Oxford).

Pickard–Cambridge, A.W. 1962 *Dithyramb, Tragedy and Comedy* (2nd edn, Oxford).

Pickard–Cambridge, A.W. 1988 *The Dramatic Festivals of Athens* (2nd rev. edn, Oxford).

Pintauda, M. 1978 *La musica nella tragedia greca* (Cefalù).

Platthy, J. 1968 *Sources of the Earliest Greek Libraries* (Amsterdam).

Pollitt, J.J. 1990 *The Art of Ancient Greece: Sources and Documents* (2nd edn, Cambridge).

Poster, M. 1971 *The Utopian Thought of Restif de la Bretonne.* (New York).

Prandi, L. 1985 *Callistene: uno storico tra Alessandro e i Macedoni* (Milan).

Price, S.R.F. 1984 *Ritual and Power: The Roman Imperial Cult in Asia Minor* (Cambridge).

Prinz, F. 1979, *Gründungsmythen und Sagenchronologie* (Munich).

Purcell, N. 1986 'Wine and wealth in ancient Italy', *Journal of Roman Studies* 76. 1–19.

Purcell, N. 1995 'Eating fish: the paradoxes of seafood', in Wilkins, J., Harvey, D. and Dobson, M. (edd.), *Food in Antiquity* (Exeter), 132–49.

Rabe, H. 1910 'Die Listen der griechischen Profanschriftsteller', *Rheinisches Museum* 65. 339–44.

Reekmans, T. 1996 'Non–Verbal Jesting in Plutarch's Lives', in Van der Stockt, L. (ed.), *Plutarchea Lovaniensia. Miscellany of Essays on Plutarch* (Louvain), 227–41.

Reger, G. 1994 *Regionalism and change in the economy of independent Delos* (Berkeley).

Relihan, J.C. 1993 'Rethinking the History of the Literary Symposium', *Illinois Classical Studies* 17.2. 213–44.

Relihan, J.C. 1993b *Ancient Menippean Satire* (Baltimore).

Renna, E. 1995 'Il tonno e la quercia', in Longo, O., Ghiretti, F. and Renna, E. (edd.), *Aquatilia. Animali di ambiente acquatico nella storia della scienza* (Naples), 111–26.

Restani, D. 1983 'Il Chirone di Ferecrate e la 'nuova' musica greca', *Rivista italiana di Musicologia* 17. 139–92.

Restani, D. 1988 'Problemi musicali nel 14 libro dei *Deipnosophistai* di Ateneo: una proposta di lettura', in Gentili, B. and Pretagostini, R. (edd.), *La musica in Grecia* (Rome and Bari), 26–34.

Restif de la Bretonne, N.E. 1769 *Le Pornographe, ou Idées d'un Honnête–homme sur un Projet de Reglement pour les Prostitutés* (London and Paris).

Reynolds, L.D. and Wilson, N.G. 1991 *Scribes and scholars* (3rd edn., Oxford).

Rhodes, P.J. 1972 *The Athenian Boule* (Oxford).

Rice, E.E. 1983 *The Grand Procession of Ptolemy Philadephus* (Oxford).

Rich, J. 1989 'Patronage and international relations in the Roman republic', in Wallace–Hadrill, A.F. (ed.) *Patronage in ancient society* (London), 117–36.

Richards, H. 1900 'The Platonic Letters—II' *Classical Review* 14. 342–4.

Richardson, N.J. 1975 'Homeric professors in the age of the sophists', *Proceedings of the Cambridge Philological Society* 21. 65–81.

Richardson, N.J. 1981 'The contest of Homer and Hesiod and Alkidamas' Mouseion', *Classical Quarterly* 31. 1–10.

Richardson, N.J. 1993 *The Iliad: a Commentary*, Vol. 6 (Cambridge).

Richlin, A.S. (ed.) 1991 *Pornography and Representation in Greece and Rome* (Oxford).

Riginos, A.S. 1976 *Platonica* (Leiden).

Robert, L. 1929 'Epigraphica VIII. Au théâtre de Delphes', *Revue des Études Grecques*, 427–38.

Robert, L. 1936 ΑΡΧΑΙΟΛΟΓΟΣ, *Revue des Études Grecques*, 235–54.

Robert, L. 1940 *Les Gladiateurs dans l'Orient Grec* (Paris).

Robert, L. 1968 'De Delphes à l'Oxus', *Comptes rendus de l'Académie des Inscriptions et Belles–lettres*, 416–57.

Robertson, N. 1993 'Athens' Festival of the New Wine', *Harvard Studies in Classical Philology* 95. 197–250.

Rodríguez–Noriega Guillén, L. (ed.) 1996 *Epicarmo de Siracusa: Testimonios y fragmentos* (Oviedo).

Rogers, M. 1991 *The Sacred Identity of Ephesos: Foundation Myths of a Roman City* (London).

Rohde, E. 1898 *Psyche* (Leipzig and Tübingen).

Romeri, L. 1997 'La parole est servie', *Revue de Philosophie Ancienne* 15. 1. 65–93.

Romeri, L. 1999 *Philosophes entre mots et mets: Plutarque, Lucien et Athénée autour de la table* (diss. EHESS, Paris).

Romeo, C. 1993 'Ancora un contributo alla ricostruzione di un rotolo della Poetica di Filodemo', *Cronache Ercolanese* 23. 99–105.

Rossi, L. 1985 'Il simposio greco arcaico e classico come spettacolo a se stesso', in *Atti del VII Convegno di Studio: 'Spettacoli conviviali dall'antichità classica alle corti italiane del '400' (Viterbo, May 1983)*, 41–50.

Rougemont, G. 1977a 'Les théores d'Andros à Delphes', *Études Delphiques* (*Bulletin de Correspondence Hellénique, Supplément* IV), 37–47.

Rougemont, G. 1977b *Corpus des Inscriptions de Delphes*, I (Paris).

Rouse, M.A. 1991 'The Development of Research Tools in the Thirteenth Century', in Rouse, M.A. and Rouse, R.H. (edd.), *Authentic Witnesses: Approaches to Medieval Texts and Manuscripts* (Notre Dame).

Rudd, N. 1966 *The Satires of Horace* (Cambridge).

Rudolph, F. 1884 'De fontibus quibus Aelianus in VH componenda usus sit', *Studien zur Klassischen Philologie* 7. 1–138.

Rudolph, F. 1891 'Die Quellen und die Schriftstellerei des Athenaios', *Philologus, Suppl.* 6. 109–62.

Russell, D.A. 1983 *Greek Declamation* (Cambridge).

Rutherford, R. 1989 *The Meditations of Marcus Aurelius: A Study* (Oxford).

Sabbadini, R. 1890–91 *Biografia documentata di Giovanni Aurisp* (Noto).

Sabbadini, R. 1905–14 *Le Scoperte dei codici latini e greci ne' secoli XIV e XV* (Florence).

Sadie, S. 1980 *The New Grove Dictionary of Music and Musicians* (London).

Saller, R.P. 1982, *Personal patronage under the Early Empire* (Cambridge).

Salviat, F. 1986 'Le vin de Thasos: amphores, vin et sources écrites', *Bulletin de Correspondence Hellénique, Supplément* XIII, 145–96.

Salviat, F. 1990 'Vignes et vins anciens de Maronée à Mendé' in Μνημη Δ. Λαζαριδη, (Kavala and Athens) 457–76.

Sandbach, F.H. 1973 *Menander. A Commentary* (Oxford).

Sandys, J.E. 1903–1908 *A History of Classical Scholarship* (Cambridge).

Sayre, F. 1938 *Diogenes of Sinope* (Baltimore).

Scarborough, J. 1981 'The Galenic Question', *Sudhoffs Archiv* 65. 1–31.

Schachter, A. 1984 'A Consultation of Trophonios (IG 7, 4136)', *American Journal of Philology* 105. 258–67.

Schachter, A. 1994 *Cults of Boiotia* III (London).

Schäfer, P. 1997 *Judeophobia: Attitudes towards the Jews in the ancient world* (Cambridge, Mass.).

Schenkeveld, G. 1990 'Studies in the History of Ancient Linguistics', *Mnemosyne* 43: 86–108.

Schlesinger, K. 1970 *The Greek aulos* (Groningen).

Schmidt, F. 1922 *Die Pinakes des Kallimachos* (Berlin).

Schmidt, M. 1976 *Die Erklärungen zum Weltbild Homers und zur Kultur der Heroenzeit in der bT–Scholien zur Ilias* (Munich).

Schmitt-Pantel, P. 1990 'Sacrificial Meal and Symposion', in Murray 1990, 14–33.

Schmitt–Pantel, P. 1992 *La cité au Banquet. Histoire des repas publics dans les cités grecques* (Rome).

Schmitz, T. 1997 *Bildung und Macht* (Munich).

Schöll, R. 1869 'Zu Athenaeus', *Hermes* 4. 160–73.

Schroeter, R.S. 1955 'Review of Mette 1952' *Gnomon* 27. 326–31.

Schweighæuser, J. 1801 *Animadversiones in Athenaei Deipnosophistas* (Argentorati).

Schweighæuser, J. (ed.) 1801–1807 *Athenaei Deipnosophistarum libri XV* (Strasbourg).

Segoloni, L.M. 1994 *Socrate a banchetto: il simposio di Platone e i Banchettanti de Aristofane* (Rome).

Seibert, J. 1972 *Alexander der Grosse: Erträge der Forschung* (Darmstadt).

Settis, S. 1988 'La Colonna', in Settis, S., La Regina, A., Agosti, G., Farinella, V. (edd.) *La Colonna Traiana* (Turin).

Settis, S. (ed.) 1996 *I Greci. Storia, cultura, arte, società*, 2,1: *Una storia greca–formazione* (Turin).

Sharples, R.W. and Minter, D.W. 1983 'Theophrastus on fungi: inaccurate citations in Athenaeus', *Journal of Hellenic Studies* 103. 154–6.

Siapkaras–Pitsillides, Th. 1975 *Le Petrarquisme en Chypre: Poèmes d'Amour en dialecte chypriote d'après un manuscrit du XVIème siècle* (2nd edn., Paris and Athens).

Sideras, A.1994 'Rufinus von Ephesos und sein Werk im Rahmen der antiken Medizin', *Aufstieg und Niedergang der römischen Welt* II.37.2. 1077–253.

Sidwell, K. 1993 'Authorial Collaboration? Aristophanes' *Knights* and Eupolis', *Greek, Roman and Byzantine Studies* 34. 365–89.

Sidwell, K. 1994 'Aristophanes' *Acharnians* and Eupolis', *Classica et Mediaevalia* 45. 71–115

Sidwell, K. 1995 'Poetic rivalry and the caricature of comic poets', in *Stage Directions: Essays in Honour of E.W. Handley* (*Bulletin of the Institute of Classical Studies* Supplement 66) (London), 56–80.

Sidwell, K. 2000 'From Old to Middle to New? Aristotle's *Poetics* and the History of Athenian Comedy', in Harvey, D. and Wilkins, J. (edd.) *The Rivals of Aristophanes* (London) forthcoming.

Simoneta, R. 1994 'La nascita dell'oracolo di Trofonio', *Aevum* 68. 27–32.

Sisti, Fr. 1980 'Ateneo III 119d–f', *Bollettino dei Classici* 3a s., 1. 131–3.

Skalet, Ch. H. 1928 *Ancient Sicyon with a Prosopographia Sicyonia* (Baltimore).

Skydsgaard, J.E. 1968 *Varro the Scholar. Studies in the First Book of Varro's de Re Rustica* (Copenhagen).

Slater, W.J. 1986 *Aristophanis Byzantini Fragmenta* (Berlin).

Slater, W.J. (ed.) 1991 *Dining in a Classical Context* (Ann Arbor).

Slater, W.J. 1981 'Peace, the Symposion and the Poet', *Illinois Classical Studies* 205–14.

Small, J.P. 1997 *Wax Tablets of the Mind. Cognitive Studies of Memory and Literacy in Classical Antiquity* (London and New York).

Smith, A.C.G. 1979 'The Gymnasium at Alexandria Troas: Evidence for an outline Reconstruction', *Anatolian Studies* 29. 23–50.

Sokolowski, F. 1955 *Lois sacrés de l'Asie mineure* (Paris).

Sokolowski, F. 1962 *Lois sacrées des cités grecques: supplément* (Paris).

Sommerstein, A. (ed.) 1985 *Aristophanes: Peace* (1985).

Spawforth, A.J. and Walker, S. 1985 'The World of the Panhellenion I: Athens and Eleusis', *Journal of Roman Studies* 75. 78–104.

Stannard, J. 1974 'Squill in the ancient and medieval materia medica with special reference to its employment for dropsy', *Bulletin of the New York Academy of Medicine* 50, 2nd ser., 285–318.

Steckerl, F. 1958 *The Fragments of Praxagoras of Cos and his School* (Leiden).

Stephanes, I.E., 1988 Διονυσιακοι Τεχνιται (Heracleon).

Stevenson, H. 1885 *Codices manuscripti palatini graeci Bibliothecae Vaticanae* (Rome).

Stewart, A. 1997 *Art, Desire and the Body in Ancient Greece* (Cambridge).

Stoneman, R. 1994a *Legends of Alexander the Great* (London).

Stoneman, R. 1994b 'Who are the Brahmans: Indian Lore and Cynic Doctrine in Palladius' *De Bragmanibus* and its models', *Classical Quarterly* 44. 500–10.

Strasburger, H. 1977 'Umblick im Trümmerfeld der griechische Geschichtsschreibung', in *Historiographia Antiqua: Commentationes Lovanienses in honorem W. Peremans septuagenarii editae* (Louvain), 3–52.

Studniczka, F. 1914 *Das Symposion Ptolemaios' II nach der Beschreibung des Kallixeinos wiederhergestellt* (Leipzig).

Sulek, A. 1983 'Quomodo rex Psammeticus in pueris expertus sit', *Meander* 3. 75–85.

Sullivan J.P. 1968 *Petronius' Satyricon, A Literary Study* (London).

Sutton, D.F. 1987 'The Theatrical Families of Athens', *American Journal of Philology* 108. 9–26.

Sutton, D.F. (ed.) 1989 *Dithyrambographi Graeci* (Hildesheim).

Swain, S. 1990 'Plutarch's Lives of Cicero, Cato and Brutus', *Hermes* 118. 192–203.

Swain, S. 1996 *Hellenism and Empire: Language, Classicism and Power in the Greek World 50–250 AD* (Oxford).

Syme, R. 1980 'Fiction about Roman jurists', *Zeitschrift der Savigny–Stiftung für Rechtsgeschichte* (Rom. Abt.) 97. 78–104 (= *Roman Papers* 3. 1393–1414).

Syme, R. 1989 'Diet on Capri', *Athenaeum* 77. 261–72 (= *Roman Papers* 6. 409–20).

Täger, H. 1923 *De Aristoxeni libro Pythagorico* (diss. Göttingen).

Taillardat, G. 1982 'ΦΙΛΟΤΗΣ, ΠΙΣΤΙΣ et *foedus*', *Revue des Études Grecques* 95. 1–14.

Taillardat, J. 1965 *Les images d'Aristophane. Études de langue et de style* (Paris).

Taplin, O. 1993 *Comic Angels and Other Approaches to Greek Drama through Vase–Paintings* (Oxford).

Tarn, W.W. 1939 'Alexander, Cynics and Stoics', *American Journal of Philology* 60. 41–70.

Tarn, W.W. 1948 *Alexander the Great* (Cambridge).

Tchernia, A. 1986 *Le Vin d'Italie Romaine* (Rome).

Tecuşan, M. 1990 '*Logos Sympotikos* : Patterns of the Irrational in Philosophical Drinking : Plato Outside the Symposion', in Murray, O. (ed.) *Sympotica. A Symposium on the Symposion* (Oxford), 238–60.

Theodoridis, C. (ed.) 1976 *Die Fragmente des Grammatikers Philoxenos* (Berlin and New York).

Thompson, D.J. (forthcoming) 'Philadelphus' procession: dynastic power in a Mediterranean context', in *Proceedings of Bertinoro conference.* Studia Hellenistica 38 (Louvain).

Thompson, D'Arcy W. 1947 *A Glossary of Greek Fishes* (London).

Thompson, E.M. 1889 'Classical Manuscripts in the British Museum', *Classical Review* 3. 440–5.

Thompson, W.E. 1985 'Fragments of the preserved historians, especially Polybius', in Jameson, M.H. (ed.), *Literature and History: Papers Presented to A. E. Raubitschek* (Saratoga), 119–39.

Thornton, B. 1997 *Eros: The Myth of Ancient Greek Sexuality* (Boulder).

Too, Y.L. 1995 *The Rhetoric of Identity in Isocrates* (Cambridge).

Trapp, M.B. 1990 'Plato's *Phaedrus* in second–century Greek literature', in Russell, D.A. (ed.), *Antonine Literature* (Oxford).

Trapp, M.B. 1997 *Maximus of Tyre. The Philosophical Orations* (Oxford).

Trapp, M.B. (forthcoming) 'Plato in Dio', in Swain, S.C.R. (ed.), *Dio Chrysostom* (Oxford).

Traversari, A. 1759 *Ambrosii Traversarii latinae epistolae* (Florence).

Trendall, A.D. and Webster, T.B.L. 1971 *Illustrations of Greek Drama* (Edinburgh).

Tronson, A. 1984 'Satyrus the Peripatetic and the marriages of Philip II', *Journal of Hellenic Studies* 104. 116–26.

Turcan, R. 1996 *The Cults of the Roman Empire* (Cambridge, Mass.).

Turner, E.G. 1952 'Roman Oxyrhynchus', *Journal of Egyptian Archaeology* 39. 78–93.

Turner, E.G. 1987 *Greek Manuscripts of the Ancient World*, 2nd edn, Institute of Classical Studies, Bulletin Suppl. 46 (London).

Ullmann, M. 1994 'Die arabische Überlieferung der Schriften des Rufinus von Ephesos', *Aufstieg und Niedergang der römischen Welt* II.37.2. 1293–349.

Ussher, R.G. 1977. 'Old Comedy and "Character": Some Comments', *Greece and Rome* 24. 71–9.

Vallance, J.T. 1990 *The Lost Theory of Asclepiades of Bithynia* (Oxford).

Van Berg, P.L. 1972 *Corpus cultus Deae Syriae*, 1, *Répertoire des sources grecques et latines*; 2. *Étude critique des sources mythographiques grecques et latines* (Leiden).

Van Bremen, H. 1996 *The Limits of Participation: Women and Civic Life in the Greek East in the Hellenistic and Roman Periods* (Amsterdam).

Van den Hoek, A. 1996 'Techniques of quotation in Clement of Alexandria. A view of ancient literary working methods', *Vigiliae Christianae* 50. 223–43.

Van der Valk, M. 1971 *Eustathii commentarii ad Homeri Iliadem pertinentes* (Leiden).

Van der Valk, M. 1986 'Eustathius and the Epitome of Athenaeus', *Mnemosyne* 39. 400.

Van Groningen, B.A. 1964 'Ekdosis', *Mnemosyne* 16. 1–17.

Veeser, H.A. (ed.) 1989 *The New Historicism* (New York and London).

Vernant, J.–P. and Frontisi–Ducroux, F. 1986 'Figures du masque en Grèce ancienne', in Vernant, J.–P. and Vidal–Naquet, P. (edd.), *Mythe et tragédie en Grèce ancienne*, Vol. II.

Vetta, M. (ed.) 1983 *Poesia e simposio nella Grecia Antica* (Rome and Bari).

Veyne, P. 1976 *Le Pain et le Cirque: sociologie historique d'un pluralisme politique* (Paris).

Vial, C. 1984, *Délos indépendante. Étude d'une communauté civique et de ses institutions* (Bulletin de Correspondence Hellénique, Suppl. X) (Paris).

Vico, E. 1558 *Delle immagini delle Donne Auguste* (Rome).

Villari, E. 1996 'Une hypothèse sur les sources d'Athénée (Deipn. I 20e–f) et de la Vita Sophoclis (§§ 3–5):

Aristoxène, musicien et biographe', *Revue des Études Grecques* 109. 696–706.

Visser, M. 1991 *The Rituals of Dinner: The Origins, Evolution, Eccentricities and Meaning of Table Manners* (New York).

Vollgraff W. 1940 'Observations sur le texte d'Athénée à propos d'une édition récente', *Revue des Études Grecques* 53. 172–96.

Von der Mühl, P. 1983 'Il simposio greco', in Vetta, M. (ed.), *Poesia e simposio nella Grecia Antica* (Roma and Bari), 3–28.

Von Reden, S. 1995 *Exchange in Ancient Greece* (London).

Von Staden, H. 1989 *Herophilus: The Art of Medicine in Early Alexandria* (Cambridge).

Von Wilamowitz–Möllendorff. *See* Wilamowitz–Möllendorff.

Wachsmuth, K.1860 *De Cratete Mallota disputavit adiectis eius reliquiis* (Leipzig).

Walbank, F.W. 1955 'Tragic history: a reconsideration', *Bulletin of the Institute of Classical Studies* 2. 4–14.

Walbank, F.W. 1957–79 *A Historical Commentary on Polybius* i–iii (Oxford).

Walbank, F.W. 1960 'History and tragedy', *Historia* 9. 216–34.

Walbank, F.W. 1972 *Polybius* (Berkeley).

Walbank, F.W. 1985 *Selected Papers: Studies in Greek and Roman History and Historiography* (Cambridge).

Walkowitz, J. 1980 *Prostitution in Victorian Society: Women, Class, and the State* (New York).

Wallace–Hadrill A. (ed.) 1989a *Patronage in Ancient Society* (London and New York).

Wallace–Hadrill, A. 1989b 'Patronage in Roman society, from republic to empire', in Wallace–Hadrill, A. (ed.) 1989 *Patronage in Ancient Society* (London), 1–14.

Walsh, P.G. 1970 *The Roman Novel* (Cambridge).

Wardman, A. 1976 *Rome's Debt to Greece* (London).

Warner, G.F. and Gilson, J.P. 1921 *Catalogue of Western Manuscripts in the Old Royal and King's Collections in the British Museum* II (London).

Webb, R. 1997a 'Imagination and the Arousal of the Emotions in Greco–Roman Rhetoric', in Morton, S. and Gill, C. (edd.), *The Passions in Roman Thought and Literature* (Cambridge), 112–27.

Webb, R. 1997b 'Mémoire et imagination: les limites de l'enargeia', in Lévy, C. and Pernot, L. (edd.), *Dire l'évidence* (Paris), 229–48.

Weber, R. 1888 '*De Dioscuridis* περὶ τῶν παρ' Ὁμήρῳ νόμων *libello*', *Leipziger Studien zur klassischen Philologie* 11. 87–197.

Webster, T.B.L. 1952 'Chronological Notes on Middle Comedy', *Classical Quarterly* 2. 17.

Wehrli, F. 1948 *Die Schule des Aristoteles. Klearchos* (Basel).

Wehrli, F. 1969 *Die Schule des Aristoteles: Phainias von Eresos, Chamaileon, Praxiphanes* (Basel and Stuttgart).

Weinreich, O. 1933 *Menekrates Zeus und Salmoneus* (Stuttgart).

Wellmann, M. 1888a 'Diphilos und Hikesios', *Neue Jahrbücher für Philologie und Pädagogik*, 137. 364–8.

Wellmann, M. 1888b 'Dorion', *Hermes* 23. 179–93.

Wellmann, M. 1888c 'Zur Geschichte der Medizin im Alterthume. II', *Hermes* 23. 556–66.

Wellmann, M. 1889 'Sextius Niger. Eine Quellenuntersuchung zu Dioscorides, *Hermes* 24. 530–69.

Wellmann, M. 1892 in Franz Susemihl, *Geschichte der Griechischen Literatur in der Alexandriner Zeit*, II, 418.

Wellmann, M. 1900 'Zur Geschichte der Medicin im Altertum. V', *Hermes* 35. 349–67.

Wellmann, M. 1901 *Die Fragmente der Sikelischen Ärzte Akron, Philistion und des Diokles von Karystos* (Berlin).

Wendel, C. 1955 'Das Griechische–Römische Altertum', in Milkau, F. and Leyh, G. (edd.) *Handbuch der Bibliothekswissenschaft* 3.1² (Wiesbaden).

Wentzel, G. 1896 'Athenaios', *RE* 2. 2026–33.

West, M.L. (ed.) 1978 *Hesiod: Works and Days* (Oxford).

West, M.L. 1992 *Ancient Greek Music* (Oxford).

Westgate, R.C. 1997/8 'Greek mosaics in their architectural and social context', *Bulletin of the Institute of Classical Studies* 42. 93–115.

Westgate, R.C. 1999 'Genre and originality in Hellenistic mosaics', *Mosaic* 26. 16–25.

Whitman, C.H. 1971 *Aristophanes and the Comic Hero* (Cambridge, Mass.).

Wilamowitz–Möllendorf, U. 1880 *Aus Kydathen* (*Philologische Untersuchungen* 1).

Wilamowitz–Möllendorff, U. 1900 'Asianismus und Atticismus', *Hermes* 35. 1–52.

Wilamowitz–Möllendorff, U. 1982 *History of Classical Scholarship* (London).

Wilkins, J. 2000 *The Boastful Chef: the Discourse of Food in Ancient Greek Comedy* (Oxford).

Wilkins, J. and Hill, S. 1993 'Fishheads of ancient Greece', in Walker, H. (ed.), *Look and Feel: Studies in Texture, Appearance and Incidental Characteristics of Food. Proceedings of the Oxford Symposium on Food and Cookery* (Totnes), 241–4.

Wilkins, J. and Hill, S. 1994 *Archestratus: The Life of Luxury* (Totnes).

Wilkins, J., Harvey, D. and Dobson, M. (edd.) 1995 *Food in Antiquity* (Exeter).

Wilson, N.G. 1962 'Did Arethas read Athenaeus?', *Journal of Hellenic Studies* 82. 147–8.

Wilson, N.G. 1983 *Scholars of Byzantium* (London).

Winkler, J.J. 1990 *The Constraints of Desire: The Anthropology of Sex and Gender in Ancient Greece* (New York and London).

Winnington–Ingram, R.P. 1958 'Ancient Greek music 1932–1957', *Lustrum* 3. 5–157.

Winnington–Ingram, R.P. 1968 *Mode in Ancient Greek Music*, (2nd edn, Oxford).

Wisse, J. 1995 'Greeks, Romans, and the Rise of Atticism', in Abbenes, G. J., Slings, S. R., Sluiter, I. (edd.), *Greek Literary Theory after Aristotle. A Collection of Papers in Honour of D. M. Schenkeveld* (Amsterdam), 65–82.

Wissowa, G. 1884 'De Athenaei Epitome observationes', in *Commentationes philologae in honorem Augusti Reifferscheidii* (Breslau), 22–8.

Wissowa, G. 1913 'Athenaeus und Macrobius', *Nachrichten von der königlichen Gesellschaft der Wissenschaften zu Göttingen, philologisch–historische Klasse*, Heft 3. 325–37.

Woolf, G. 1994 'Becoming Roman, Staying Greek: Culture Identity and the Civilizing Process in the Greek East', *Proceedings of the Cambridge Philological Society* 40. 116–43.

Yates, F. 1966 *The Art of Memory* (Chicago).

Yonge, C.D. 1854 *The Deipnosophists or Banquet of the Learned of Athenaeus. Literally Translated* (London).

Zaminer, F. 1996 'Aristoxenus von Tarent', in *Der Neue Pauly. Enzyklopädie der Antike*, 1152–4.

Zanker, G. 1981 'Enargeia in the Ancient Criticism of Poetry', *Rheinisches Museum* 124. 297–311.

Zecchini, G. 1988 'Una nuova testimonianza sulla translatio imperii (Aristosseno, Vita di Archita, fr. 50 Wehrli )', *Klio* 70. 362–71.

Zecchini, G. 1989a *La cultura storica di Ateneo* (Milan).

Zecchini, G. 1989b 'Linee di Egittografia antica', in Criscuolo, L. and Geraci, G. (edd.), *Egitto e storia antica dall' ellenismo all' età araba: bilancio di un confronto* (Bologna), 703–13.

Zecchini, G. 1990 'La storiografia lagide', in Verdin, H., Schepens, G., and De Keyser, E. (edd.), *Purposes of History: Studies in Greek Historiography from the 4th to the 2nd Centuries BC. Proceedings of the International Colloquium, Leuven, May 1988* (Louvain), 213–32.

Zegers, N. 1959 *Wesen und Ursprung der tragischen Geschichtsschreibung* (diss. Cologne).

Zepernick, K. 1921 'Die Exzerpte des Athenaeus in den Deipnosophisten und ihre Glaubwürdigkeit', *Philologus* 77. 311–63.

# SUBJECT INDEX

| *Deipnosophistae* | *page* | *Deipnosophistae* | *page* | *Deipnosophistae* | *page* |
|---|---|---|---|---|---|
| 7.313d | 489 | 8.342a | 576n.62 | 8.355b | 575n.49 |
| 7.313e | 487 | 8.344a | 329 | 8.355c | 329 |
| 7.313f | 389 | 8.344b | 574nn.12 and 28 | 8.355e–f | 500 |
| 7.314b | 488 | 8.344c | 393 | 8.356a | 80 |
| 7.314c | 551n.171, 552n.210 | 8.344e | 329 | 8.356c–d | 500 |
| 7.315e | 487 | 8.345b | 329 | 8.356e | 481 |
| 7.317a | 133 | 8.345b–c | 416 | 8.358c–359e | 480 |
| 7.317f | 20 | 8.345d | 574n.12 | 8.358d | 338, 573n.7 |
| 7.318c–d | 544n.7 | 8.345e | 327, 544n.4, 545n.13 | 8.359d–e | 501, 552n.210 |
| 7.320e | 487, 489 | 8.346c | 338, 591n.13 | 8.359e–360a | 194 |
| 7.323a | 487 | 8.346d | 335 | 8.360c–d | 41 |
| 7.324a | 131, 477 | 8.347d | 423, 530 | 8.360d | 387, 593n.52 |
| 7.327b | 131 | 8.347d–e | 540n.15 | 8.361e–f | 7, 19, 249 |
| 7.328b | 487 | 8.347d–352d | 423 | 8.361f | 15 |
| 7.329c | 512, 523, 527 | 8.347d–354d | 423 | 8.362d | 552n.204 |
| 7.330a | 387 | 8.347f | 423, 427 | 8.363d–364a | 347 |
| 7.330b | 21 | 8.347f–352d | 443 | 8.363f | 349 |
| 7.330c | 43, 313 | 8.348a | 427 | 8.364d | 588n.7 |
| 8.330f | 21 | 8.348a–c | 427 | 8.365b–c | 551n.165 |
| 8.330f–331a | 500 | 8.348d | 424, 432 | 8.365d | 534 |
| 8.331b | 5 | 8.348d–e | 495 | 8.365e | 43, 313, 567n.9, |
| 8.331c | 423, 530 | 8.348e–f | 428 | | 569n.22, 593n.51 |
| 8.331c–347c | 423 | 8.348e–349f | 427 | 9.366a | 247 |
| 8.333b–c | 518 | 8.349a | 274 | 9.366a–c | 123 |
| 8.334a | 544n.7 | 8.349e | 428 | 9.366d | 370, 371 |
| 8.334b–c | 550n.146 | 8.349f | 427, 581n.45 | 9.367d–e | 133 |
| 8.334f–335a | 530 | 8.350b | 429, 430 | 9.368e | 588n.4 |
| 8.335b–e | 300 | 8.350b–c | 431 | 9.369f | 80 |
| 8.335d | 413 | 8.350c | 431, 517 | 9.370a | 131 |
| 8.335e | 300 | 8.350d | 431, 432 | 9.370b | 127 |
| 8.335f | 517 | 8.350d–352c | 425, 581n.44 | 9.370c | 494, 501 |
| 8.336d | 523, 548n.67 | 8.350e | 426, 586n.14 | 9.371a | 497 |
| 8.337b | 443 | 8.350f | 428 | 9.371b | 494, 500 |
| 8.337b–338b | 424 | 8.351a | 499 | 9.372a | 559n.25 |
| 8.337d | 393 | 8.351a–b | 426 | 9.372b | 249, 250, 568n.13 |
| 8.338b | 329 | 8.351c–352c | 585n.9 | 9.372d | 249 |
| 8.338b–d | 424 | 8.351e–f | 430 | 9.373a–406c | 288 |
| 8.338d | 573n.9 | 8.351f–352a | 426, 429 | 9.373f–374e | 550n.122 |
| 8.340b | 573n.9 | 8.352a | 428 | 9.374a | 550n.115 |
| 8.340c | 593n.48 | 8.352c | 425 | 9.375b | 559n.19 |
| 8.340e–345a | 330 | 8.352c–d | 586n.9 | 9.375d | 545n.10 |
| 8.340f | 316 | 8.352d | 425, 586n.17 | 9.375d–f | 547n.39 |
| 8.341a | 330 | 8.354d | 301 | 9.376c | 36, 320 |
| 8.341a–d | 574n.26 | 8.354e | 544n.9 | 9.376c–380c | 325 |
| 8.341a–e | 424 | 8.355a | 479 | 9.376c–383f | 535 |
| 8.341e | 584n.32 | 8.355a–357a | 573n.1 | 9.376d | 20 |
| 8.341f | 519 | 8.355a–361e | 24 | 9.377f | 320, 499 |